www.hsh.com/pamphlets
www.ibcdata.com
www.ici.org
www.ici.org/aboutfunds
www.ifebp.org
www.iiin.com/iiincompanies.html
www.IMF.org
www.imf.org/external
www.imuni.com
www.instruct.westvalley.edu/barnikel
www.insurance.state.pa.us
www.interestratecalculator.com
www.intermoney.com
www.investing.com
www.investing.wsj.com
www.investinginbonds.com
www.investment-banking-resources.com
www.investorhome.com
www.ire-net.com/pubs
www.jsc.nasa.gov
www.kc.frb.org
www.lexis-nexis.com/universe
www.library.wwu.edu/ref
www.liffe.com
www.lombard-st.co.uk
www.luc.com
www.marketclues.net
www.marketplacedata.com
www.mastercard.com
www.mathematical-finance.com
www.mfea.com
www.mhhe.com/economics/mcconnell
www.missouri.edu
www.mizuho-sc.com
www.mizuho-sc.com/english
www.money.cnn.com
www.moneycentral.msn.com
www.mortgagesincanada.com
www.namic.org
www.nasdaq.com
www.ncua.gov
www.nd.edu
www.newsmax.com
www.ny.frb.org
www.nyscul.org
www.oanda.com
www.occ.treas.gov
www.opengroup.com
www.ots.treas.gov
www.palgrave.com
www.pensionsurveys.com
www.pionline.com
www.piperinfo.com
www.planetx.bloomu.edu

www.plunkettresear...
www.preview.mcgraw-hill.com
www.proposedmerger.com
www.publicdebt.treas.gov
www.publicdebt.treas.gov/sec/secfaq.htm
www.pueblo.gsa.gov
www.pvlinton.com/securiti.htm
www.qualisteam.com/eng/conf.html
www.quote.yahoo.com
www.rate.net
www.rbnz.govt.nz/banking
www.riskandinsurance.com
www.riskbooks.com
www.savingsbond.com
www.sec.gov
www.sec.gov/consumer/imperf.htm
www.sec.gov/invkhome.htm
www.securities.com
www.sfe.com
www.smart.net
www.smartcrd.com
www.smartmoney.com
www.speculativebubble.com
www.state.ct.us
www.state.nh.us/nhdoj
www.stats.bls.gov
www.stern.nyu.edu
www.stls.frb.org
www.stockpickcentral.com
www.stomaster.com
www.straightdope.com
www.streetwatch.com
www.sysmod.com/eurofaq.htm
www.taxes.about.com/library
www.taxplanet.com/prez
www.thestreet.com
www.toerien.com
www.topics.newsedge.com/topic.nst
www.toron.com
www.treas.gov
www.trinity.edu/dwalz
www.wabash.edu/depart/economic
www.wdfa.org
www.wdfi.org
www.wholesaleaccess.com
www.woccu.org
www.woodrow.mpls.frb.fed.us/research
www.worldbank.org
www.worldbank.org/finance
www.worldbank.org/html
www.wright.edu
www.wsj.com
www.wwquote.com

Money and Capital Markets

Financial Institutions and Instruments in a Global Marketplace

The McGraw-Hill/Irwin Series in Finance, Insurance and Real Estate

Stephen A. Ross
Franco Modigliani Professor of Finance
and Economics
Sloan School of Management
Massachusetts Institute of Technology
Consulting Editor

FINANCIAL MANAGEMENT

Benninga and Sarig
Corporate Finance: A Valuation Approach

Block and Hirt
Foundations of Financial Management
Tenth Edition

Brealey and Myers
Principles of Corporate Finance
Seventh Edition

Brealey, Myers and Marcus
Fundamentals of Corporate Finance
Third Edition

Brooks
FinGame Online 3.0

Bruner
Case Studies in Finance: Managing for Corporate Value Creation
Fourth Edition

Chew
The New Corporate Finance: Where Theory Meets Practice
Third Edition

DeMello
Cases in Finance

Grinblatt and Titman
Financial Markets and Corporate Strategy
Second Edition

Helfert
Techniques of Financial Analysis: A Guide to Value Creation
Eleventh Edition

Higgins
Analysis for Financial Management
Seventh Edition

Kester, Fruhan, Piper and Ruback
Case Problems in Finance
Eleventh Edition

Nunnally and Plath
Cases in Finance
Second Edition

Ross, Westerfield and Jaffe
Corporate Finance
Sixth Edition

Ross, Westerfield and Jordan
Essentials of Corporate Finance
Third Edition

Ross, Westerfield and Jordan
Fundamentals of Corporate Finance
Sixth Edition

Smith
The Modern Theory of Corporate Finance
Second Edition

White
Financial Analysis with an Electronic Calculator
Fourth Edition

INVESTMENTS

Bodie, Kane and Marcus
Essentials of Investments
Fourth Edition

Bodie, Kane and Marcus
Investments
Fifth Edition

Cohen, Zinbarg and Zeikel
Investment Analysis and Portfolio Management
Fifth Edition

Corrado and Jordan
Fundamentals of Investments: Valuation and Management
Second Edition

Farrell
Portfolio Management: Theory and Applications
Second Edition

Hirt and Block
Fundamentals of Investment Management
Seventh Edition

FINANCIAL INSTITUTIONS AND MARKETS

Cornett and Saunders
Fundamentals of Financial Institutions Management

Rose
Commercial Bank Management
Fifth Edition

Rose
Money and Capital Markets: Financial Institutions and Instruments in a Global Marketplace
Eighth Edition

Santomero and Babbel
Financial Markets, Instruments, and Institutions
Second Edition

Saunders and Cornett
Financial Institutions Management: A Risk Management Approach
Fourth Edition

Saunders and Cornett
Financial Markets and Institutions: A Modern Perspective

INTERNATIONAL FINANCE

Beim and Calomiris
Emerging Financial Markets

Eun and Resnick
International Financial Management
Second Edition

Levich
International Financial Markets: Prices and Policies
Second Edition

REAL ESTATE

Brueggeman and Fisher
Real Estate Finance and Investments
Eleventh Edition

Corgel, Ling and Smith
Real Estate Perspectives: An Introduction to Real Estate
Fourth Edition

FINANCIAL PLANNING AND INSURANCE

Allen, Melone, Rosenbloom and Mahoney
Pension Planning: Pension, Profit-Sharing, and Other Deferred Compensation Plans
Ninth Edition

Crawford
Life and Health Insurance Law
Eighth Edition (LOMA)

Harrington and Niehaus
Risk Management and Insurance

Hirsch
Casualty Claim Practice
Sixth Edition

Kapoor, Dlabay and Hughes
Personal Finance
Sixth Edition

Skipper
International Risk and Insurance: An Environmental-Managerial Approach

Williams, Smith and Young
Risk Management and Insurance
Eighth Edition

Money and Capital Markets

Financial Institutions and Instruments in a Global Marketplace

Eighth Edition

Peter S. Rose
Texas A&M University

Boston   Burr Ridge, IL   Dubuque, IA   Madison, WI   New York   San Francisco   St. Louis
Bangkok   Bogotá   Caracas   Kuala Lumpur   Lisbon   London   Madrid   Mexico City
Milan   Montreal   New Delhi   Santiago   Seoul   Singapore   Sydney   Taipei   Toronto

McGraw-Hill Higher Education

A Division of The McGraw-Hill Companies

MONEY AND CAPITAL MARKETS:
Financial Institutions and Instruments in a Global Marketplace

Published by McGraw-Hill/Irwin, a business unit of The McGraw-Hill Companies, Inc., 1221 Avenue of the Americas, New York, NY, 10020. Copyright © 2003, 2000, 1997, 1994, 1992, 1989, 1986, 1983 by The McGraw-Hill Companies, Inc. All rights reserved. No part of this publication may be reproduced or distributed in any form or by any means, or stored in a database or retrieval system, without the prior written consent of The McGraw-Hill Companies, Inc., including, but not limited to, in any network or other electronic storage or transmission, or broadcast for distance learning.

Some ancillaries, including electronic and print components, may not be available to customers outside the United States.

This book is printed on acid-free paper.

domestic   2 3 4 5 6 7 8 9 0 CCW/CCW 0 9 8 7 6 5 4 3
international   2 3 4 5 6 7 8 9 0 CCW/CCW 0 9 8 7 6 5 4 3

ISBN 0-07-248676-7

Publisher: *Stephen M. Patterson*
Developmental editor: *Jennifer Rizzi*
Executive marketing manager: *Rhonda Seelinger*
Producer, Media technology: *Melissa Kansa*
Senior project manager: *Jean Lou Hess*
Production supervisor: *Gina Hangos*
Director of design BR: *Keith J. McPherson*
Supplement producer: *Matthew Perry*
Senior digital content specialist: *Brian Nacik*
Cover illustrator: *Tom Nemoda, Asylum Studios*
Cover design: *Trudi Gershenov*
Typeface: *10/12 Times Roman*
Compositor: *GAC Indianapolis*
Printer: *Courier Westford*

Library of Congress Cataloging-in-Publication Data

Rose, Peter S.
    Money and capital markets : financial institutions and instruments in a global marketplace / Peter S. Rose — 8th ed.
        p. cm.— (The McGraw-Hill/Irwin series in finance, insurance, and real estate)
    Includes bibliographical references and index.
    ISBN 0-07-248676-7 (alk. paper) — ISBN 0-07-119880-6 (international : alk. paper)
    1. Finance—United States.   2. Money market—United States. 3. Capital market—United States.   I. Title. II. Series.
HG181 .R66 2003   2002069217

INTERNATIONAL EDITION   ISBN 0-07-119880-6

Copyright © 2003. Exclusive rights by The McGraw-Hill Companies, Inc. for manufacture and export. This book cannot be re-exported from the country to which it is consigned by McGraw-Hill. The International Edition is not available in North America.

www.mhhe.com

To My Family

Preface

The global tragedy in terror that rocketed into the headlines in September of 2001 has served as a reminder to us of how fragile our lives are on this planet and how all of our institutions can be significantly impacted by shocking, unexpected events. Anything that happens to us as individuals or to our key institutions, including sudden changes in the economy and the financial system, can profoundly change how we look at life and how we prepare for the future.

However hard as it is to believe, there is often a small glimmer of light behind such tragedies. We begin to appreciate, more than ever before, our loved ones and our institutions and take positive steps to protect them and keep our lives moving forward.

One of the consequences of the September 2001 tragedy in terror was a clear demonstration of how important the financial system of money and capital markets that girdles the globe is to our economic and personal well-being. The terror attacks on New York City damaged or put out of commission the offices of several leading banking and securities houses in this world financial center. Frightened investors in stocks and bonds suddenly lost contact with many members of the financial-services community and feared for the fate of their savings and their investments. Payments that needed to be made to security traders and those repaying old loans or seeking new loans were suddenly shut down or delayed. The U.S. economy—strongest in the world—slowed and then tipped into a recession with rising unemployment and business bankruptcies. Yet, the financial system of money and capital markets soon righted itself; financial-service businesses that suffered huge losses of talented people and funds fought their way back to full service to the public with amazing speed and determination.

Recent tragedy, then, has demonstrated how resilient is the institution we are about to study—the money and capital markets that make up the heart of our global financial system. Recent events have also shown the many important ways the money and capital markets and the financial system—when operating at full speed and efficiency and when dealing with crisis—impact every household (individual or family) and every business and governmental institution around the globe. More than ever before, we recognize how much we rely upon the vital services that our financial markets and institutions readily provide us every day.

Today more than ever we recognize the money and capital markets as that important institution in our society that *supplies credit* to those in need of borrowing funds; *encourages saving* for the future on the part of millions of businesses and individuals; *allocates whatever savings are available into investments* in new plant and equipment and stocks of goods so that businesses may grow and provide more jobs; provides a channel through which trillions of currency units pass daily to *carry out payments* so that spendable funds flow from buyers to sellers; supplies *a method for liquidating our assets* to provide ready cash (liquidity) for spending that must be done; offers *risk protection* in the form of insurance policies, derivatives, and other financial products; and serves as a *policy channel* by which governments work to regulate their economies and achieve each nation's economic goals, including full employment, avoidance of inflation, and sustainable economic growth.

What an incredible array of jobs for one of society's great institutions! How lucky we are to have the money and capital markets and the surrounding financial system! Moreover, as recent global tragedies illustrate, how different our lives become when it is significantly damaged or can no longer perform as efficiently as we might wish!

WAYS THIS BOOK CAN BE USED

As *Money and Capital Markets* enters its eighth edition, the book, though somewhat shorter with 26 chapters instead of the original 30 chapters, continues to be one of the most comprehensive texts in its field. So comprehensive, in fact, that it offers professors, instructors, and other users not one approach to the field, but several alternative routes through the vast playing field represented by the money and capital markets and the financial system. Every reader and every teacher can self-select the type of course they would like to offer dealing with the financial system.

- *A Security Markets–Oriented Course.* For example, users of this text who would like to focus upon security markets and security trading would be more likely to read or assign to those they work with parts One (Chapters 1–4), Two (Chapters 5–9), Three (Chapters 10–14), Six (especially Chapters 21 and 22), and Seven (particularly Chapter 25).

- *A Financial Institutions–Related Course.* In contrast, those who want to know as much as possible about financial-service firms, including the great financial institutions represented by banks, insurance companies, mutual funds, pension funds, finance companies, and security dealers, would find it most helpful to center their course around Part One (Chapters 1–4) and Chapters 5–7 and 11–14 as well as Part Four (Chapters 15–18), and Chapters 21, 22, and 26.

- *A Policy and Regulations–Oriented Course.* For our readers and instructors who have the greatest interest in public policy and government regulation within the financial system, key chapters to assign would include Part One (Chapters 1–4), Chapters 5 and 6, Chapters 11–14, Chapters 18–20, and Chapters 23–24.

- *An Internationally Focused Course.* The increasing globalization of our financial system has aroused great interest in a global view of the money and capital markets and financial-service firms. While internationally focused material appears throughout this text, certain sections and chapters do have a heavier emphasis on the international finance field. A strongly internationally focused course would want to emphasize such portions of the text as Part One (Chapters 1–4), Chapters 5, 7, and 9, Part Three (Chapters 10–14), Chapters 15 and 18, Chapters 21 and 22, and Part Seven (Chapters 25 and 26).

- *A Financial Theory–Oriented Course.* For readers and teachers most interested in the basic theoretical concepts of Finance there are several chapters that deserve special note. These include Part One (especially Chapters 1 and 2), Part Two (especially Chapters 5, 7, 8, and 9), Part Three (especially Chapters 10 and 13), Chapter 19, and Chapters 21 and 22.

KEY FEATURES OF THIS BOOK

As in the earlier editions, *Money and Capital Markets* in its eighth edition pursues its key goals by employing a variety of helpful learning aids for the user. For example:

- Each chapter begins with a statement of that chapter's *learning objectives* (now expanded from earlier editions)—what do we hope the reader will learn in that chapter and the key issues each chapter addresses.

- Following the learning objectives is a *topical outline* of the key concepts and issues to be presented in each chapter.

- Numerous graphs, tables, and examples appear in the text's pages in order to make key points more vivid and memorable.

- Numerous *boxes* reporting special events and key facts within the financial system appear throughout the text. These boxes, which heighten the reader's interest in the subject, carry such labels as *Management Insights, International Focus,* and *Financial Developments.* These boxes of pertinent information have been expanded and updated and represent one of the key highlights of this new eighth edition.

- Nearly all the end-of-chapter problems from the previous edition have been retained and at least one new problem added to each chapter in the new edition.

- Especially important in this new eighth edition are the greatly expanded references to Internet Web sites dealing with money and capital markets issues. Each chapter contains a box near the front, listing key Web sites dealing with the topics presented in the particular chapter. Then, scattered liberally throughout the book in the text margins are additional URLs for readers who prefer to make extensive use of the Web to learn as much as possible about the financial system.

- *Questions to Help You Study* are placed at strategic points within each chapter to aid the reader in making sure he or she has understood key points just made.

- *Key Terms* are listed at the end of each chapter, along with their page numbers to help the reader find them again. Moreover, a *Money and Capital Markets Dictionary* at the end of the book allows the reader to double-check his or her understanding of each key term.

- In this new eighth edition a *Chapter Summary,* with key points bulleted, appears at the close of every chapter in the text. This feature makes it so much easier for users of the text to make sure they have mastered the most important points in any reading assignment.

- New to this edition, Standard & Poor's Market Insight problems will be available on the Rose, *Money and Capital Markets,* eighth edition Web site, www.mhhe.com/business/finance/rose8e, for both students and faculty. Some chapters ask for problem solutions that could benefit from the use of the Educational version of *Market Insight,* a Standard and Poor's Compustat® database. See how easily this Web asset, unique to McGraw-Hill/Irwin, can add value to your entire teaching and learning experience. Over 300 companies and key financial data will be available as a problem-solving resource, of which over 40 are financial-service institutions.

Many *new topics* appear in this latest edition, including such key items as:

- The debate over *personal financial privacy*—protecting the consumer's private information from unwanted viewing, solicitation, identity theft and fraud.

- The *restructuring of banks and financial holding companies* in the wake of the Gramm-Leach-Bliley (GLB) Financial Services Modernization Act and the rise of *universal banking* in the United States.

- The continuing *integration of Europe's money and financial system* and the struggle of the Euro to become a key vehicle currency and assert leadership around the globe.

- The rising concern over *terrorism* and its implications for the stability of the economy and financial system as well as the health and welfare of law-abiding citizens.

- The *changing focus of financial institutions' regulation,* relying more heavily today upon the private marketplace (i.e., market discipline), rather than rigid government-imposed rules, to govern how financial institutions operate and perform for the public.

- The rising fear in selected nations (such as Japan), not about inflation, but about *deflation* as a weakening economy leads to falling prices for goods and services and lower interest rates.

- *Tax reform* and the new U.S. Economic Growth and Tax Relief Reconciliation Act and its implications for saving, investment, and the financial marketplace.

- The great debate over the "good" and "evil" of *subprime and predatory lending to lower income individuals and families* and its implications for consumers and financial institutions.

- The financial disaster represented by the *collapse of Enron Corporation*—the seventh largest U.S. company—and its consequences for businesses, employees, pension funds, and regulators.

- Whether *bankruptcy reform* is really needed to stem the rising tide of bankrupt businesses and households or if tougher bankruptcy laws might do more harm than good.

There are so many *new* topics and issues in the eighth edition that the list above seems just to scratch the surface!

SUPPLEMENTARY MATERIALS

Important supplements strengthen the usefulness and teaching impact of this new edition. Among the key supplements instructors may wish to draw upon is:

- **Instructor's Resource CD ROM** (ISBN 0072486791)—This contains:

  Instructor's Manual and Test Bank   This important supporting material outlines each chapter and contains hundreds of questions and problems available for testing or for use in classroom presentations.

  Power Point Presentation System   It is a recent addition to *Money and Capital Markets* and contains clear and concise slides that provide the instructor and his or her class with sharply focused ideas and illustrations. There are numerous graphs, charts, and examples as well as frequent listings of key points to be retained. The user can easily edit or rearrange each slide set to meet his or her unique style.

ACKNOWLEDGMENT OF THE MANY PROFESSIONALS WHO HAVE HELPED MAKE THIS BOOK BETTER OVER TIME

As this book has worked its way through eight editions, it has benefited beyond measure from the criticisms and helpful suggestions of numerous professionals. These are people who care about the quality of classroom instruction and about their students achieving a richer understanding of the financial world and our place within it. There have been so many great contributors to this book over the years that the author is always hesitant to start a list for fear of omitting at least some worthwhile contributions and the names of several deserving professional educators.

However, among the most significant contributors through the editions have been James C. Baker of Kent State University, Ivan T. Call of Brigham Young University, Eugene F. Drzycimski of the University of Wisconsin System, Mona J. Gardiner of Illinois Wesleyan University, Timothy Koch of the University of South Carolina, David Mills of Illinois State University, John P. Olienyk of Colorado State University, Colleen C. Pantalone of Northeastern University, Richard Rivard of the University of South Florida, Paul Bolster of Northeastern University, Robert M. Crowe, formerly of the American College at Bryn Mawr, Joseph P. Ogden of SUNY–Buffalo, Donald A. Smith of Pierce College, Oliver G. Wood, Jr., of the University of South Carolina, Larry Lang of the University of Wisconsin–Oshkosh, Jeffrey A. Clark of Florida State University, James F. Gatti of the University of Vermont, Gioia P. Bales of Hofstra University, Ahmed Sohrabian of California State Polytechnic University at Pomona, Thomas A. Fetherston of the University of Alabama at Birmingham, Mary Piortrowski of Northern Arizona University, Rick Swasey of Northeastern University, Owen K. Gregory of the University of Illinois at Chicago, Thomas Dziadosz of the American College, and Tom Potter of the University of North Dakota.

The author adds a special note of gratitude to those who helped with their comments and suggestions in the construction of this eighth edition: Lester Hadsell of State University of New York–Albany, John Hysom of George Mason University, Frank Ohara of the University of San Francisco, Robert Schweitzer of the University of Delaware, and Donald J. Smith of Boston University.

In addition, the author expresses deep appreciation to the staff of professionals at McGraw-Hill, particularly Steve Patterson, Jennifer Rizzi, and Jean Lou Hess, whose guidance, suggestions, and kindnesses throughout the revision and production process were truly invaluable.

A special thank you also goes to Professor Yee-Tien (Ted) Fu, Visiting Scholar at Stanford University, for his work on creating the Instructor's Manual, Test Bank, and PowerPoint presentations. In addition to these outstanding contributors are many associations and institutions that have contributed to the content of this text in a wide variety of ways over the years. These important institutions and associations include the American Council of Life Insurance, the *Canadian Banker* (official publication of the Canadian Bankers Association), the Chicago Board of Trade, the Credit Union National Association, the Insurance Information Institute, Moody's Investors Service, and Standard and Poors' Corporation.

The author also gratefully acknowledges the support and patience of the members of his family, who made the completion of this new edition possible. Any shortcomings that remain belong to the author, who nevertheless, strives to make the text better with each successive edition.

A NOTE TO THE STUDENT AND OTHER READERS OF THIS TEXT

The money and capital markets, along with the financial system that supports them, are an exciting area for study. What goes on daily in these markets and within the financial system as a whole has a powerful impact upon our daily lives. Indeed, our ability to function as human beings and as professionals in our chosen careers is shaped, in so many ways, by the functionings of the financial system. Moreover, the money and capital markets and the financial system in which they do their work are constantly in a state of flux. Broad changes are forever remaking the financial marketplace as new institutions, new methods, new problems, and new services continually appear.

The rapidity of change that characterizes the financial system means that we have no choice but to try to keep up with our unfolding financial world. Indeed, so rapid and sweeping are the changes going on in the money and capital markets today that no book, no matter how many times it is revised, can serve as more than an *introduction*—indeed an invitation—to learn about the goings-on within the financial marketplace.

Without question you need to read this book and understand what it is trying to say. But reading this book cannot be the end of the road. You cannot stop here. A great American poet, Robert Frost, admonished each of us that we "cannot stop here" for we have "promises to keep" and "miles to go before we sleep." For the sake of your own future success, personally and professionally, plan to enjoy what you discover in the pages that follow, but view this book as only the first step in what must, of necessity, be a lifetime journey of learning about the financial system and its effects on our everyday existence. Truly, each one of us has promises to keep to ourselves and others and miles to go before we can be satisfied at what we have accomplished.

As you begin each new chapter in this book set your sights on true *mastery* of the subject. Make the most of the time you spend with this text. Plan for success and hit the target dead center through your determination and well-organized study.

But how can you do that? How can you learn what you need to know in today's complex financial world?

First, begin with the *Learning Objectives* and the *Key Topics Outline* that open each chapter. These are really road signs, alerting you to the key questions and issues each chapter will address. They tell you what you should *expect to learn* in the pages that follow. It is a useful idea to review the list of learning objectives and the Key Topics Outline as you sit down to tackle each new chapter and then to review them when you are finished reading. Have you touched base with each learning objective and each key topic as you read the material? If you are not sure of one or more of the learning objectives or key topics, please go back and review the relevant portions of the chapter that apply to that particular topic or objective. Ask yourself if the learning objective or key topic you are focusing upon makes sense to you and if you now feel better informed about it than you did before.

Next, examine the list of *Key Terms* at the close of each chapter. There are page numbers telling you where each key term is defined and discussed. Return to the pages where any key terms appear that still seem to be a mystery to you. Let me suggest that you make a list of these key terms in your personal computer or in a notebook and accumulate them as the assigned chapters roll by. This is much more than an act of memorizing terms; rather, this is reaching out to learn the "language" of the financial marketplace.

You want to make the language of the money and capital markets second nature to you so that everything you subsequently read and hear about the financial system you will understand and be able to make it work for you. You may even want to write out or type into the computer a definition of each key term and then double-check that definition against the meaning that appears in the *Money and Capital Markets Dictionary* that appears at the end of this book.

In each chapter, at selected points, appear *Questions to Help You Study*. These questions appear at key places so you can pause after reading several pages and ask yourself: Do I really understand what I just read? Try to answer each of these study questions, either verbally or, better still if you have time, by writing out a brief answer and then double-checking its accuracy by referring back to the relevant portion of the chapter you are working on. You may want to store the answers you develop in your personal computer or in a paper file for future reference, particularly just before exams come along.

In each chapter of this new eighth edition several useful *Web sites* are given. First, there is a box near each chapter's opening that gives key Web site addresses for the topics in the chapter you are reading. Then, scattered in the margins throughout the text are additional URLs to let you enter the World Wide Web and learn more. Check out these Web sites, pursuing especially those that interest you or seem the most challenging. This is a way to repeat key text ideas through a new format. As always, *repetition* is a key to learning.

At the end of each chapter are *Problems* to work through, many requiring numerical calculations. This is another important dimension of our subject for you to tackle. Finance is about problem solving and the better a problem solver you can become in this field, the greater your chances for success. As you work through each problem save the solutions for future reference, either in your computer, in a notebook, or in a paper file.

Finance in general and the money and capital markets in particular are moderately difficult disciplines to master. Finance does have its challenges. Group study sessions are often helpful in tackling its hardest issues and problems. See if you can form a study group that periodically gets together and goes over some of the hardest concepts and problems. Be a contributor to these sessions, take the lead in explaining and helping others. *Teaching others* is one of the best ways to learn a new subject for yourself.

Try to keep in mind that this book has two fundamental purposes: (1) to give you an arsenal of *analytical tools* that you can apply to any financial problem so as to make better financial decisions; and (2) to make you feel comfortable with the *language of the financial marketplace* so you can learn to speak that language fluently with comfort and with maximum understanding. A truly successful course of study will develop in you both the tools and the language of the financial system and get you started along the road to mastery and personal success.

This course is a foundation-stone for many promising future careers. Perhaps you've considered becoming the financial manager or CEO of a large corporation, the head of the financial division of an important unit of government, possibly a member of a legislature or of the Congress, a trader (dealer or broker) in securities or derivative contracts, a consultant or adviser to those who must enter the global financial marketplace, or an active investor in your own right, striving to build up your personal wealth and prepare for a rewarding life style. Wherever your career path leads you, superior knowledge and understanding of the financial marketplace will be an absolutely essential companion on your journey.

But you already know from prior experience with other challenging fields of study that to make the money and capital markets and the financial system your faithful servant, mastery of them will *not* be easy. Your future success in moving forward, in the words of the poet, to keep the "promises" you have made and to travel successfully the many "miles to go" before you "sleep," will depend crucially upon the energy and enthusiasm, the commitment to excellence, and the hard work that you bring to this subject. By any measure, it is a challenge worthy of your best efforts. Good luck on your journey!

Peter S. Rose

Brief Contents

Table of Contents

Part **One**

The Global Financial System in Perspective

Part One of *Money and Capital Markets* focuses on the different roles, functions, and services performed and provided by the global financial system. It discusses the vital roles and missions that the financial system of markets performs in encouraging saving, supplying capital for investments, and creating money and other financial assets. This initial part of the text also explores the different sources of information about the operation of the financial marketplace and the services it provides. It closes with a glimpse at the future of the financial system and of the financial institutions within it, examining how changes going on in the economy, the population, and society are likely to impact the money and capital markets in the years ahead.

Part One of the book helps us to understand why we should *care* about the money and capital markets and how well they are functioning to serve us. It emphasizes the many dimensions through which the financial system affects our daily lives, including building up our savings and the accumulation of wealth to meet our future financial needs, supplying our requirements for instant spending power (liquidity) when that power is needed, making payments to purchase the goods and services we wish to buy, insuring access to credit to supplement our current incomes so that we can achieve the standard of living all of us wish to enjoy, offering us risk protection to help protect our lives, health, property, and incomes, and serving as a critically important channel for government economic policy to do its work so that the nation can achieve its key goals, such as full employment for all who wish to work, the avoidance of serious inflation that could erode our savings and accumulated wealth, and achieving sustainable economic growth to steadily increase our living standard over time.

Chapter **One**

Functions and Roles of the Financial System in the Global Economy

Learning Objectives in This Chapter

- You will understand the functions performed and the roles played by the system of financial markets and financial institutions in the global economy and in our daily lives.

- You will explore several key terms and concepts about the money and capital markets that you will need repeatedly as we work our way through this course of study.

- You will discover how important the money and capital markets and the whole financial system are to increasing our standing of living, generating new jobs, and building our savings to meet tomorrow's financial needs.

What's in This Chapter? Key Topics Outline

How the Financial System Interfaces with the Economy

The Importance of Savings and Investment

The Nature of Financial Claims and Financial Markets

Functions of the Money and Capital Markets: Savings, Wealth, Liquidity, Credit, Payments, Risk Protection, Setting Public Policy

Money Markets versus Capital Markets

Perfect and Efficient Markets

The Dynamic Financial System: Key Trends Under Way

INTRODUCTION

This book is devoted to the study of the **financial system**—the collection of markets, institutions, laws, regulations, and techniques through which bonds, stocks, and other securities are traded, interest rates are determined, and financial services are produced and

One of the most widely published areas on the World Wide Web focuses on the financial system and the money and capital markets. This is largely because this critical segment of our economy produces and distributes financial services and stimulates saving and investment which help the economy to grow and create new jobs. Not surprisingly, many of the Web sites have to do with savings and investment and how individuals can benefit from knowledge of the money and capital markets in order to be more effective as savers and investors.

One of the best examples here is the Web site of the U.S. Securities and Exchange Commission (the SEC) which can be reached at the general URL of *www.sec.gov.* Not long ago the SEC set up an Office of Investor Education and Assistance which helps people trying to make plans to save and make decisions on what might be the best investments for them. A good way to approach these saver/investor issues is to dial up *http://www.sec.gov/consumer.*

delivered around the world. The financial system is one of the most important inventions of modern society. *Its primary task is to move scarce loanable funds from those who save to those who borrow to buy goods and services and to make investments in new equipment and facilities so that the global economy can grow and increase the standard of living enjoyed by its citizens.* Without the global financial system and the loanable funds it supplies, each of us would lead a much less enjoyable existence.

The financial system determines both the cost of credit and how much credit will be available to pay for the thousands of different goods and services we purchase daily. Equally important, what happens in this system has a powerful impact upon the health of the global economy. When credit becomes more costly and less available, total spending for goods and services falls. As a result, unemployment rises and the economy's growth slows down as businesses cut back their production and lay off workers. In contrast, when the cost of credit declines and loanable funds become more readily available, total spending in the economy often increases, more jobs are created, and the economy's growth accelerates. In truth, the global financial system is an integral part of the global economic system. We cannot really understand one system without understanding the other.

THE GLOBAL ECONOMY AND THE FINANCIAL SYSTEM

Flows within the Global Economic System

To better understand the role played by the financial system in our daily lives, we begin by examining its position within the global economy.

The basic function of the economic system is to allocate scarce resources—land, labor, management skill, and capital—to produce the goods and services needed by society. The high standard of living most of us enjoy today depends on the ability of the global economy to turn out each day an enormous volume of food, shelter, and other essentials of modern living. This is an exceedingly complex task because scarce resources must be procured in just the right amounts to provide the raw materials of production and combined at just the right time with labor, management, and capital to generate the products and services demanded by consumers. In short, any economic system must combine inputs—land and other natural resources, labor and management skill, and capital equipment—to produce output—goods and services. The global economy generates a flow of production in return for a flow of payments (see Exhibit 1–1).

EXHIBIT 1–1
The Global Economic System

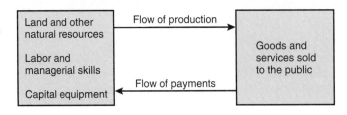

We may also depict the flows of payments and production within the global economic system as a *circular flow* between producing units (mainly businesses and governments) and consuming units (principally households). (See Exhibit 1–2.) In the modern economy, households provide labor, management skill, and natural resources to business firms and governments in return for income in the form of wages and other payments. Most of the income received by households is spent to purchase goods and services from businesses and governments. In 2001, for example, about 99 percent of the nearly $9 trillion in total personal income received by individuals and families in the United States was spent on the consumption of goods and services or paid out in taxes to purchase government services. The remainder of personal income—about 1 percent—was set aside as *savings*. The result of this spending is a flow of funds back to producing units as income, which stimulates them to produce more goods and services in the future. The circular flow of production and income is interdependent and never ending.

The Role of Markets in the Global Economic System

In most economies around the world, *markets* are used to carry out this complex task of allocating resources and producing goods and services (though in a so-called "command economy" such as in China and the former Soviet Union, governments also allocate resources and produce goods and services). What is a **market?** It is an institution set up by society to allocate resources that are scarce relative to the demand for them. Markets are the channel through which buyers and sellers meet to exchange goods, services, and productive resources.

The marketplace determines what goods and services will be produced and in what quantity. This is accomplished through changes in the *prices* of goods and services offered in the market. If the price of an item rises, for example, this stimulates business firms to produce and supply more of it to consumers. In the long run, new firms may enter the market to produce those goods and services experiencing increased demand and rising prices. A decline in price, on the other hand, usually leads to reduced production of a good or service, and in the long run some suppliers may leave the marketplace.

Markets also distribute *income*. In a pure market system, the income of an individual or business firm is determined solely by the contributions each makes to producing goods and services demanded by the marketplace. Markets reward superior productivity and sensitivity to consumer demands with increased profits, higher wages, and other economic benefits. Of course, in economic systems where governments play major roles, government policies also affect the distribution of income and other benefits.

Types of Markets

There are essentially three *types of markets* at work within the global economic system: (1) factor markets, (2) product markets, and (3) financial markets (see Exhibit 1–3). In factor markets, consuming units sell their labor and other resources to those producing units offering the highest prices. The *factor markets* allocate factors of production—land, labor, managerial skills, and capital—and distribute income—wages, rental payments, and so on—to the owners of productive resources.

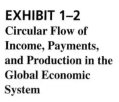

EXHIBIT 1–2
Circular Flow of Income, Payments, and Production in the Global Economic System

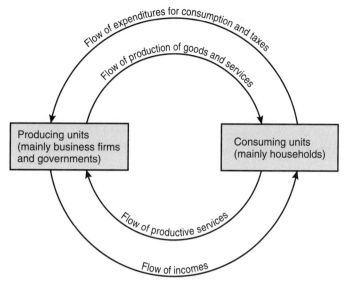

EXHIBIT 1–3 **Three Types of Markets in the Global Economic System**

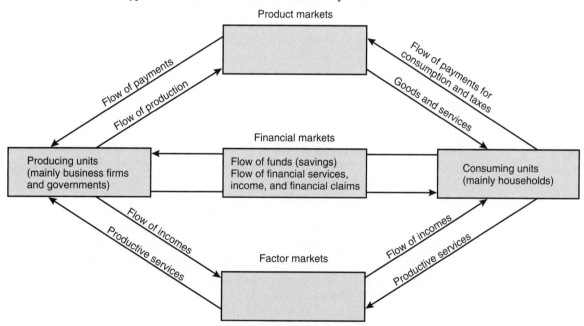

Consuming units use most of their income from factor markets to purchase goods and services in *product markets*. Food, shelter, automobiles, theater tickets, and clothing are among the many goods and services sold in product markets.

The Financial Markets and the Financial System: Channel for Savings and Investment

Of course, not all factor income is consumed. A proportion of after-tax income received by households each year—about $120 billion in 2001—is earmarked for *personal saving*. In addition, business firms save billions of dollars each year to build up their reserves for future contingencies and for long-term investment. For example, in 2001 U.S. corporations earned nearly $750 billion in profits, of which almost $80 billion was set aside (undistributed) for possible future needs as *business savings.* It is here that the third kind of market, the **financial market,** performs a vital function within the global economic system. The financial markets channel savings to those individuals and institutions needing more funds for spending than are provided by their current incomes. The financial markets are the heart of the global financial system, attracting and allocating savings and setting interest rates and the prices of financial assets (stocks, bonds, etc.).

Nature of Savings

As we will see more fully in Chapter 5, the definition of **savings** differs depending on what type of unit in the economy is doing the saving. For households, savings are what is left from current income after current consumption expenditures and tax payments are made. In the business sector, savings include current earnings retained inside business firms after payment of taxes, stockholder dividends, and other cash expenses. Government savings arise when there is a surplus of current revenues over current expenditures in a government's budget.

Nature of Investment

To learn more about savings and investment see Bankrate.com at www.bankrate.com/brm

Most of the funds set aside as savings flow through the global financial markets to support **investment** by business firms, governments, and households. Investment generally refers to the acquisition of capital goods, such as buildings and equipment, and the purchase of inventories of raw materials and goods to sell. The makeup of investment varies with the particular unit doing the investing. For a business firm, expenditures on *capital goods* (fixed assets, such as buildings and equipment) and *inventories* (consisting of raw materials and goods offered for sale) are investment expenditures. Households invest (that is, make expenditures on capital account) when they buy a new home or purchase furniture, automobiles, and other durable goods; in contrast, their purchases of food, clothing, and fuel are considered to be consumption spending (i.e., expenditures on current account), not investment. Government spending to build and maintain public facilities (such as buildings, monuments, and highways) is another form of investment.

Modern economies require enormous amounts of investment to produce the goods and services demanded by consumers. Investment increases the productivity of labor and leads to a higher standard of living. However, investment often requires huge amounts of funds, far beyond the resources available to a single firm or government. By selling financial claims (such as stocks and bonds) in the financial markets, large amounts of funds can be raised quickly from the pool of savings accumulated by households, businesses, and governments. The business firm or government carrying out the investment then hopes to repay its loans from the financial marketplace by drawing on future income. Indeed, the money and capital markets operating within the financial system make possible the *exchange of current income for future income* and the *transformation of savings into investment* so that production, employment, income, and living standards can grow.

Those who supply funds to the financial markets receive only *promises* in return for the loan of their money. These promises are packaged in the form of attractive financial claims and financial services, such as stocks, bonds, deposits, and insurance policies (see Exhibit 1–4). *Financial claims* promise the supplier of funds a future flow of income in the form of dividends, interest, or other returns. But there is no guarantee that the expected income will ever materialize. However, suppliers of funds to the financial system expect not only to recover their original funds but also to earn additional income as a reward for waiting and for assuming risk.

EXHIBIT 1–4
The Global Financial System

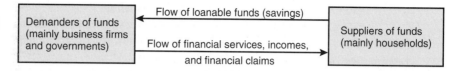

The role of the financial markets in channeling savings into investment is absolutely essential to the health and vitality of the economy. For example, if households set aside savings and those funds are not returned to the spending stream through investment by businesses and governments, the economy will begin to contract. The amount of income paid out by business firms and governments will *not* be matched by funds paid back to those same sectors by households. As a result, future income payments will decline, leading, in turn, to reduced consumption spending. The public's standard of living will fall. Moreover, with less spending going on, the need for labor will be curtailed, resulting in fewer jobs and rising unemployment.

Questions *to Help You Study*

1. Why is it important for us to understand how the global financial system works?

2. What are the principal links between the financial system and the economy? Why is each important to the other?

3. What are the principal functions or roles of the global financial system of money and capital markets? How, in general, do the money and capital markets and financial system fulfill those roles or functions?

4. What exactly is *savings? Investment?* Are these terms often misused by people on the street? Why do you think this happens?

5. How and why are saving and investment important determinants of economic growth? Do they impact our standard of living? How?

FUNCTIONS PERFORMED BY THE GLOBAL FINANCIAL SYSTEM AND THE FINANCIAL MARKETS

The great importance of the financial system in our daily lives can be illustrated by reviewing its different functions. The global financial system has seven basic functions.

Savings Function

As we noted earlier, the global system of financial markets and institutions provides a *conduit for the public's savings.* Bonds, stocks, and other financial claims sold in the money and capital markets provide a profitable, relatively low-risk outlet for the public's savings, which flow through the financial markets into investment so that more goods and services can be produced (i.e., productivity will rise), increasing the world's standard of living. When savings flows decline, investment and living standards begin to fall in those nations where savings are in short supply.

Wealth Function

For those businesses and individuals choosing to save, the financial instruments sold in the money and capital markets provide an excellent way to *store wealth* (i.e., preserve the value of assets we hold) until funds are needed for spending. Although we might choose to store our wealth in "things" (e.g., automobiles), such items are subject to depreciation and often carry great risk of loss. However, bonds, stocks, and other financial instruments do *not* wear out over time and usually generate income; moreover, their risk of loss often is much less than for many other forms of stored wealth.

Incidentally, what is **wealth?** For any individual, business firm, or government, wealth (W) is the sum (Σ) of the values of all individual assets (A_i) held. That is,

$$W_t = \Sigma_i A_{it} \qquad \textbf{(1–1)}$$

Wealth is built up over time by a combination of current savings plus income earned on previously accumulated wealth. In symbols,

$$\Delta W_t = S_t + r_t \cdot W_{t-1} \qquad \textbf{(1–2)}$$

where ΔW_t represents the change in wealth in the current period, S_t is the volume of current savings, r_t is the current average rate of return on accumulated assets, and W_{t-1} is the initial value of all accumulated wealth (assets) held.

The portion of wealth held by society in the form of stocks, bonds, deposits, and other financial assets (i.e., in financial wealth) is substantial. For example, in 2001 about $70 trillion in securities, deposits, and other financial assets were held by domestic businesses, households, and governments in the United States, while foreign investors held almost $8 trillion in financial instruments that were issued inside the United States. Individuals and families (households) alone held more than $30 trillion in stocks, bonds, and other financial assets. These forms of *financial wealth* broke down as follows for the various segments making up the U.S. economy in 2001:

Holders of Financial Assets	U.S. Financial Wealth Holdings (Financial Assets) in 2001 ($ Billions)*
Individuals and families (households)	$30,404
Nonfinancial business firms	9,596
Banks and other financial institutions	28,833
Federal, state, and local governments	1,924
Foreign businesses, individuals, and governments active in U.S. financial markets	7,812
Total wealth holdings in financial assets in the United States	$78,569

Source: Board of Governors of the Federal Reserve System.

*Data annualized as of the third quarter of 2001.

If we subtract total debts owed by the above U.S. businesses, households, and governments, which amounted to about $19 trillion in 2001, we obtain what is called **net wealth.** The total *net* financial wealth (financial assets − debts) held by U.S. individuals and institutions was nearly $60 trillion. Wealth holdings represent *stored purchasing power* that will be used in future periods as income to finance purchases of goods and services and to increase society's standard of living. Therefore, as Equation 1–3 below reminds us, income emerges from the wealth function of the global financial system. Income (Y_t) is created by the rate of return (r_t) that current wealth holdings (W_t) generate for their owners. Or,

$$Y_t = W_t \cdot r_t \qquad \textbf{(1–3)}$$

In turn, that wealth-created income leads to *both* increased consumption spending (C_t) and to new saving (S_t):

$$Y_t = C_t + S_t \qquad\qquad (1\text{--}4)$$

resulting in a higher standard of living for those who hold wealth in income-generating forms.

Liquidity Function

For wealth stored in financial instruments, the global financial marketplace provides a means of converting those instruments into cash with little risk of loss. Thus, the world's financial markets provide **liquidity** (immediately spendable cash) for savers who hold financial instruments but are in need of money. In modern societies, *money* consists mainly of deposits held in banks and is the only financial instrument possessing perfect liquidity. Money can be spent as it is without the necessity of converting it into some other form. However, money generally earns the lowest rate of return of all assets traded in the financial system, and its purchasing power is seriously eroded by inflation. That is why savers generally minimize their holdings of money and hold other, higher-yielding financial instruments until they really need spendable funds. Of course, money is not the only means of making purchases of goods and services. In many lesser-developed economies around the world simple bartering—exchanging one good or service for another—performs many of the same services that money provides in a developed economy.

Credit Function

In addition to providing liquidity and facilitating the flow of savings into investment to build wealth, the global financial markets furnish **credit** to finance consumption and investment spending. Credit consists of a loan of funds in return for a promise of future payment. Consumers need credit to purchase a home, buy groceries, repair the family automobile, and retire outstanding debts. Businesses draw on their lines of credit to stock their shelves, construct new buildings, meet payrolls, and grant dividends to their stockholders. State, local, and federal governments borrow to construct buildings and other public facilities and to cover daily cash expenses until tax revenues flow in.

The volume of credit extended by the money and capital markets today is huge and growing. In the United States alone, as shown in Exhibit 1–5, total net credit funds raised in U.S. financial markets in 2001 (including issues of corporate stock) amounted to more than $2.3 trillion, compared to less than a third of that figure only a decade before. Growth of the economy, inflation, and the tax deductibility of some interest payments all appear to have fueled this rapid growth in credit usage by businesses, households, and governments.

Payments Function

The global financial system also provides a *mechanism for making payments for goods and services.* Certain financial assets, including checking accounts and negotiable order of withdrawal (NOW) accounts, serve as a medium of exchange in making payments. Plastic credit cards issued by banks, credit unions, and retail stores give the customer instant access to short-term credit but are also widely accepted as a convenient means of payment. Plastic cards and electronic means of payment, including computer terminals in homes, offices, and stores and digital cash, will eventually displace checks and other pieces of paper as the principal means of payment in the future. Indeed, electronic means of payment are in widespread use today and are growing rapidly.

EXHIBIT 1–5

Net Funds Raised in
U.S. Financial Mar-
kets by Major Sector,
2001*

Sector and Funding Source		Amount of Funds Raised ($ Billions)	Percentage of Total Net Funds Raised (%)
Net borrowing by sector:			
Households (individuals and families)		$ 616.2	26.5%
Nonfinancial business firms:			
Farms	$ 3.1		
Nonfinancial corporations	248.9		
Other business firms	108.6		
Total for all business firms		360.6	15.5
Private financial institutions		265.7	11.4
Governments:			
U.S. government and federally sponsored agencies	1,076.3		
State and local govts.	43.0		
Total for all governments		1,119.3	48.2
Foreign borrowers in the U.S., net		−126.8	−5.5
Total net borrowings		$2,235.0	96.2%
Net funds raised by issuing new corporate stock (equities)**		88.9	3.8
Total net borrowings and equity funds raised in U.S. financial markets		$2,323.9	100.0%

*Figures are for third quarter of 2001.

**Totals for private financial institutions exclude mutual funds shares issued that are included in new corporate stock (equities) issues in the next to last line of the exhibit.

Source: Board of Governors of the Federal Reserve System.

Risk Protection Function

The financial markets around the world offer businesses, consumers, and governments *protection against life, health, property, and income risks.* This is accomplished, first of all, by the sale of insurance policies. Policies marketed by life insurance companies indemnify a family against possible loss of income following the death of a loved one. Property-casualty insurers protect their policyholders against an incredibly wide array of personal and property risks, ranging from ill health, crime, and storm damage to negligence on the highways. In addition to making possible the sale of insurance policies, the money and capital markets have been used by businesses and consumers to "self-insure" against risk; that is, holdings of wealth are built up as protection against future losses.

Policy Function

Finally, in recent decades, the financial markets have been *the principal channel through which government has carried out its policy of attempting to stabilize the economy and avoid inflation.* By manipulating interest rates and the availability of credit, government can affect the borrowing and spending plans of the public, which, in turn, influence the growth of jobs, production, and prices. As we will see later on, this task of economic stabilization has been given largely to central banks, such as the Federal Reserve System in the United States, the Bank of England, and the new European Central Bank (the ECB).

Financial Developments Assault on the Financial System—Terror and Its Aftermath

On September 11th, 2001, the United States experienced one of the most devastating tragedies in its history when hijackers took control of four crowded commercial airliners and crashed two of the four into the World Trade Center in New York City and one into the Pentagon in Washington, D.C. More than 3,000 people lost their lives or remain missing.

The assault on the World Trade Center was more than just an attack on two large buildings in downtown New York City. It was also an attack on a key global trading center within the financial system—a place where several major dealers in securities, large banks, and other major financial-service institutions served clients around the globe. When the trade center structures collapsed, several financial firms officed there faced severe disruption, losing their communications links and suffering death or serious injury to their employees.

Still the flexibility and resilience of the money and capital markets in adjusting to this terrible tragedy proved to be remarkable. Within a handful of days the New York Stock Exchange was reopened and major security, banking, and insurance firms found new space from which to continue to serve their customers.

Of course, even with the remarkable "bounce back," of the financial system to terror and tragedy, significant damages to the economy and financial system were felt. The World Trade Center attacks appeared to further slow the U.S. and the other global economies. Layoffs of workers, slowing retail sales and production, reluctance to travel by both businesses and consumers, as well as many other negative effects, began to surface right away.

The external shock represented by the terrorist bombings also impacted the global money and capital markets from many different directions. Lenders and investors became instantly more concerned about *risk*. Stock prices around the globe fell for a time as investors sold riskier securities and fled into government bonds and insured bank deposits. Insurance companies braced for an unprecedented volume of financial claims related to deaths and the destruction of property.

These tragic events remind us of several key points. First, the economy and the financial system of money and capital markets are intimately connected to each other—a tragedy or other external shock that affects one instantaneously affects the other. Second, though a great institution, the financial system and its money and capital markets are fragile and need the support of governments and the confidence of the public to operate efficiently and perform their many essential functions. Third, the financial marketplace is now unquestionably global rather than belonging to a single nation—significant events in almost any nation, either good or bad, quickly spread around the world and affect all markets in roughly the same way.

Questions *to Help You Study*

6. According to this textbook what seven vital *functions* does the financial system of money and capital markets perform?

7. Why is each function of the financial system important to households (individuals and families), businesses, and governments? What kinds of lives would we be living today if there were no financial system or no financial markets?

8. What exactly do we mean by the term *wealth?* Why is it important?

9. What is *net wealth?* What does it reveal to each of us?

10. Can you explain what factors determine the volume of wealth and of net wealth each of us has?

TYPES OF FINANCIAL MARKETS WITHIN THE GLOBAL FINANCIAL SYSTEM

Charged with many different functions, the global financial system fulfills its various roles mainly through *markets* where financial claims and financial services are traded (though in some lesser-developed economies government dictation and even barter are used). These markets may be viewed as *channels* through which moves a vast flow of loanable funds that is continually being drawn upon by demanders of funds and continually being replenished by suppliers of funds.

The Money Market versus the Capital Market

The flow of funds through financial markets around the world may be divided into different segments, depending on the characteristics of financial claims being traded and the needs of different investors. One of the most important divisions in the financial system is between the *money market* and the *capital market*.

The **money market** is designed for the making of short-term loans. It is the institution through which individuals and institutions with *temporary* surpluses of funds meet the needs of borrowers who have *temporary* funds shortages (deficits). Thus, the money market enables economic units to manage their liquidity positions. By convention, a security or loan maturing within one year or less is considered to be a money market instrument. One of the principal functions of the money market is to finance the working capital needs of corporations and to provide governments with short-term funds in lieu of tax collections. The money market also supplies funds for speculative buying of securities and commodities.

In contrast, the **capital market** is designed to finance long-term investments by businesses, governments, and households. Trading of funds in the capital market makes possible the construction of factories, highways, schools, and homes. Financial instruments in the capital market have original maturities of *more than one year* and range in size from small loans to multimillion dollar credits.

Who are the principal suppliers and demanders of funds in the money market and the capital market? In the money market, commercial banks are the most important institutional supplier of funds (lender) to both business firms and governments. Nonfinancial business corporations with temporary cash surpluses also provide substantial short-term funds to the money market. On the demand-for-funds side, the largest borrower in the U.S. money market is the Treasury Department, which borrows billions of dollars weekly. Other governments around the world are very often among the leading borrowers in their own domestic money markets. The largest and best-known corporations and securities dealers are also active borrowers in money markets around the world. Due to the large size and strong financial standing of these well-known money market borrowers and lenders, money market instruments are considered to be high-quality, "near money" IOUs.

In contrast, the principal suppliers and demanders of funds in the capital market are more varied than in the money market. Families and individuals, for example, tap the capital market when they borrow to finance a new home. Governments rely on the capital market for funds to build schools and highways and provide essential services to the public. The most important borrowers in the capital market are businesses of all sizes that issue long-term IOUs to cover the purchase of equipment and the construction of new facilities. Ranged against these many borrowers in the capital market are financial institutions, such as insurance companies, mutual funds, security dealers, and pension funds, that supply the bulk of capital market funds.

Divisions of the Money and Capital Markets

The money market and the capital market may be further subdivided into smaller markets, each important to selected groups of demanders and suppliers of funds. Within the money market, for example, is the huge *Treasury bill* market. Treasury bills—short-term IOUs issued by many governments around the world—are a safe and popular investment medium for financial institutions, corporations of all sizes, and wealthy individuals.

Somewhat larger in volume is the market for *certificates of deposit* (CDs) issued by the best-known banks and other depository institutions to raise funds in order to carry on their lending activities. Two other important money market instruments that arise from large corporations borrowing money are *bankers' acceptances* and *commercial paper.* In another corner of the money market, *federal funds*—the reserve balances of banks plus other immediately transferable monies—are traded daily in huge volume. Another segment of the money market reaches around the globe to encompass suppliers and demanders of short-term funds in Europe, Asia, and the Middle East. This is the vast, largely unregulated *Eurocurrency market,* in which bank deposits denominated in the world's major trading currencies—for example, the dollar, the pound, and the Euro—are loaned to corporations and governments around the globe.

The capital market, too, is divided into several sectors, each having special characteristics. For example, one of the largest segments of the capital market is devoted to residential and commercial *mortgage loans* to support the building of homes and business structures, such as factories and shopping centers. In the United States, state and local governments sell their *tax-exempt (municipal) bonds* in another sector of the capital market. Households (individuals and families around the world) borrow in yet another segment, using *consumer loans* to make purchases ranging from automobiles to home appliances. There is also an international capital market for borrowing by large corporations represented by *Eurobonds* and *Euronotes.*

Probably the best-known segment of the capital market is the market for *corporate stock* represented by the major exchanges, such as the New York Stock Exchange (NYSE) and the Tokyo Exchange, and a vast over-the-counter (OTC) market, including electronic stock trading over the Internet. No matter where it is sold, however, each share of stock (equity) represents a certificate of ownership in a corporation, entitling the holder to receive any dividends paid out of current earnings. Corporations also sell a huge quantity of *corporate*

EXHIBIT 1–6

Principal Financial Instruments Traded in the U.S. Money and Capital Markets by Domestic and Foreign Investors, 2001* ($ Billions)

Financial Instruments	Amount Outstanding	Percent of Totals
Principal money market instruments:		
U.S. Treasury bills	$ 620.1	4.5%
Bank and thrift large certificates of deposit ($100,000+)	802.0	5.9
Small time and savings deposits at banks and thrifts	3,144.3	23.0
Securities of federal and federally sponsored agencies	4,823.7	35.3
Federal funds sold and repurchase agreements	1,287.8	9.4
Eurodollar deposits at U.S. banks	1,518.8	11.1
Commercial paper	1,453.8	10.6
Bankers' dollar acceptances	9.9	0.1
Total for the Money Market	$13,660.4	100.0%
Principal capital market instruments:		
Mortgage loans	$ 7,016.5	22.3%
Corporate stocks	13,625.2	43.3
Corporate and foreign bonds	5,528.1	17.6
Marketable U.S. Treasury bonds and notes	2,057.9	6.5
State and local government (municipal) securities	1,635.3	5.2
Consumer nonresidential loans	1,622.8	5.2
Total for the Capital Market	$31,485.8	100.0%

Source: Board of Governors of the Federal Reserve System.
*Figures for the third quarter or third quarter months.

notes and *bonds* in the capital market each year to raise long-term funds. These securities, unlike shares of stock, are pure IOUs, evidencing a debt owed by the issuing company. (A list of the principal financial instruments traded in the U.S. money and capital markets is shown in Exhibit 1–6.)

Open versus Negotiated Markets

Another distinction between markets in the global financial system that is often useful focuses on **open markets** versus **negotiated markets.** For example, some corporate bonds are sold in the open market to the highest bidder and are bought and sold any number of times before they mature and are paid off. In contrast, in the negotiated market for corporate bonds, securities generally are sold to one or a few buyers under private contract.

An individual who goes to his or her local banker to secure a loan for a new car enters the negotiated market for auto loans. In the market for corporate stocks there are the major stock exchanges, which represent the open market. Operating at the same time, however, is the negotiated market for stock, in which a corporation may sell its entire stock issue to one or a handful of buyers.

Primary versus Secondary Markets

The global financial markets may also be divided into **primary markets** and **secondary markets.** The primary market is for the trading of *new* securities never before issued. Its principal function is raising financial capital to support new investment in buildings, equipment, and inventories. You engage in a primary-market transaction when you purchase shares of stock just issued by a company or borrow money through a new mortgage to purchase a home.

In contrast, the secondary market deals in securities previously issued. Its chief function is to provide *liquidity* to security investors—that is, provide an avenue for converting

Financial Developments
The Low Savings Rate in the U.S. Economy

As we have seen earlier in this chapter, *saving* is vital to support the growth of *investment* in new capital equipment and new technologies so that economies can grow and increase the standard of living of their citizens. Although the national savings rate of the United States—its gross savings, including business depreciation reserves, as a percent of the U.S. gross domestic product—has remained fairly stable for most of the nation's history, the United States today posts one of the lowest savings rates in the world, with a savings-to-gross domestic product ratio well below that of Japan and Germany, for example.

One reason for declining savings rates may simply be changing public attitudes toward saving itself. Older generations remember the Great Depression of the 1930s, with millions of people out of work. Younger savers, however, are more likely to have experienced periods of prosperity and low unemployment and see less need for savings protection.

Moreover, the U.S. government's Social Security and Medicare systems promise most workers at least a minimal level of retirement income, reducing the apparent need for maximizing personal savings due to the presence of forced government saving, at least in the minds of many savers. Thus, many younger individuals see less reason to make strenuous efforts to save based on their own life experiences and the availability of publicly supported pensions. Moreover, when inflation rises, many consumers prefer to buy now rather than add to their savings. The consequences of a low rate of savings in the United States include higher interest rates, which make it more expensive for business firms to invest and result in fewer new jobs being created.

The currently low U.S. savings rate may well come back to haunt Americans in the future. For example, a relatively low savings rate coupled with a relatively low investment rate make the economy more prone to inflation because, with less investment in new equipment, fewer goods and services can be produced as demands for goods and services increase. Living standards of individuals and families are likely to grow more slowly in the future. However, some economists believe that the U.S. personal savings rate will begin to rise in the future as the population ages because there will be more Americans concerned about building their savings for retirement. Let's hope they are right!

For further discussion of the importance of savings see *www.bankrate.com/brm*

financial instruments into ready cash. If you sell shares of stock or bonds you have been holding for some time to a friend or call a broker to place an order for shares currently being traded on the American, London, or Tokyo stock exchanges, you are participating in a secondary-market transaction.

The volume of trading in the secondary market is far larger than trading in the primary market. However, the secondary market does *not* support new investment. Nevertheless, the primary and secondary markets are closely intertwined. For example, a rise in security prices in the secondary market usually leads to a similar rise in prices on primary-market securities, and vice versa. This happens because some investors will switch from one market to another in response to differences in price or yield.

Spot versus Futures, Forward, and Option Markets

We may also distinguish between *spot markets, futures* or *forward markets,* and *option markets.* A spot market is one in which assets or financial services are traded for immediate delivery (usually within one or two business days). If you pick up the telephone and instruct your broker to purchase Telecon Corporation shares at today's price, this is a spot market transaction. You expect to acquire ownership of Telecon shares within a matter of minutes.

A *futures or forward market,* on the other hand, is designed to trade contracts calling for the *future delivery* of financial instruments. For example, you may call your broker and ask to purchase a contract from another investor calling for delivery to you of $1 million in government bonds six months from today. The purpose of such a contract would be to reduce risk by agreeing on a price today rather than waiting six months, when government bond prices might have risen.

Finally, *options markets* also offer investors in the money and capital markets an opportunity to reduce risk. These markets make possible the trading of options on selected stocks and bonds, which are agreements (contracts) that give an investor the right to either buy from or sell designated securities to the writer of the option at a guaranteed price at any time during the life of the contract. We will see more clearly how and why such transactions take place when we explore the financial futures and options markets in Chapter 9 and the forward markets for foreign currencies in Chapter 25.

Factors Tying All Financial Markets Together

Each corner of the global financial system represents a market segment with its own special characteristics. Each segment is insulated from the others to some degree by investor preferences and by rules and regulations. Yet when interest rates and security prices change in one corner of the financial system, *all* of the financial markets likely will be affected eventually. This implies that, even though the global financial system is split up into many different markets, there must be forces at work to tie all financial markets together.

Credit, the Common Commodity

One unifying factor is the fact that the basic commodity being traded in most financial markets is *credit.* Borrowers can switch from one market to another, seeking the most favorable credit terms wherever they can be found. It is not uncommon, for example, for an oil company to finance the construction of a drilling rig through short-term loans from the money market, because interest rates in the capital market today are unusually high, but to seek long-term financing of the project later on when capital market conditions are more favorable. The shifting of borrowers between markets helps to weld the parts of the global financial system together and to bring credit costs in different markets into balance with one another.

Speculation and Arbitrage

Another unifying element is profit seeking by demanders and suppliers of funds. *Speculators* in securities are continually on the lookout for opportunities to profit from their forecasts of future market developments. The speculator in the financial marketplace gambles that security prices or interest rates will move in a direction that will result in quick gains due to his or her ability to outguess the market's collective judgment. Many speculators are *risk seekers,* willing to gamble their funds even when the probability of success is low. Speculators perform an important function in the financial markets by leveling out the prices of securities, buying those they believe are underpriced and selling securities thought to be overpriced.

For an overview of the concept of arbitrage see especially http://www.finpipe.com/derivglossary.htm

Still another unifying force in the financial markets comes from investors who watch for profitable opportunities to **arbitrage** funds—transferring funds from one market to another whenever the prices of securities in different markets appear to be out of line with each other. *Arbitrageurs* help to maintain *consistent prices between markets,* aiding other security buyers in finding the best prices with minimal effort.

Perfect and Efficient Markets

There is some research evidence today suggesting that all financial markets are closely tied to one another due to their near perfection and efficiency. What is a **perfect market?** It is one in which the cost of carrying out transactions is zero or nearly so and all market participants are *price takers* (rather than being able to dictate prices to the market). In such a market, there are no significant government restrictions on trading and the movement of funds; rather, competition among buyers and sellers sets the terms of trade. No financial market today is perfect, but several seem to come quite close to being so.

Some financial markets may also have another desirable characteristic: *The prices of financial instruments may accurately reflect their inherent value and fully reflect all available information.* Moreover, any new information supplied to the market may quickly be impounded in a new set of prices. A market in which prices fully reflect the latest available information is an **efficient market.** In an efficient market, no information that might affect security prices or interest rates is wasted. Thus, no buyer or seller can expect to reap excess profits from collecting information that is readily available in the marketplace and then trading on the basis of that information. As we will see in Chapters 3 and 22, numerous studies of the financial markets spanning decades suggest that they approach fairly closely the ideal of a perfect and an efficient marketplace.

For a discussion of the efficient markets concept see *www.investorhome.com*

Financial Markets in the Real World: Imperfection and Asymmetry

Unfortunately, as we will see in subsequent chapters, as nearly perfect and efficient as many financial markets are, there is still a great deal that is *imperfect* in our financial system. Not all financial-service markets are fully competitive, and collusion to fix prices and interest rates does occur. Recent scandals involving the trading of new U.S. government securities in which a handful of traders attempted to control that market, the funding of criminal activities worldwide through the ill-fated Bank of Credit and Commerce International (BCCI), and the financing of the international terrorist network more recently remind us that the functioning and regulation of our financial marketplace still leaves substantial room for improvement.

Moreover, we now realize that not all the information needed by purchasers of financial services is readily or cheaply available all over the world. Increasingly, we are coming to an awareness of the importance of **asymmetric information** in our global financial system—that is, different participants in the financial markets often operate with different sets of information, some possessing special or inside information that others do not possess. The result is that some market players may be able to earn excess profits by taking advantage of the special information they possess. Moreover, as we will see in Chapter 3, high-quality financial assets and services may be driven from the market when the asymmetrical distribution of information in the marketplace is particularly severe.

The Dynamic Financial System

There is an old saying: "You cannot step into the same river twice, for rivers are ever flowing onward." That statement can be applied with equal force to the global financial system—it is rapidly changing into a *new* financial system. Powerful trends are under way to convert even smaller national financial systems into an integrated global system, at work 24 hours a day to attract savings, extend credit, and fulfill other vital roles. Satellites, computers, and other automated systems now tie together financial-service businesses and trading centers as widely dispersed as London, New York, Tokyo, Singapore, Hong Kong, and Sydney. This process of integrating financial systems globally has been aided by gradual deregulation of financial institutions and services on the part of leading industrialized nations (such as Australia, the United States, Japan, Canada, and members of the European Economic Community). Many of these countries have also begun to "harmonize" their regulations so that financial-service firms operate under similar rules no matter where they are located. The results have been increasingly intense competition for customers, the development of many new financial services, increased risk to financial-service firms and their customers, and a wave of mergers and failures among financial institutions. One of the purposes of this book is to help us understand why these global trends are occurring and what they are likely to mean for all of us in the future.

Questions *to Help You Study*

11. Can you distinguish between the following institutions?

    money market versus *capital market*

    open market versus *negotiated market*

    primary market versus *secondary market*

    spot market versus *forward or futures market*

12. If we follow the money and capital markets around the world each day it soon becomes apparent that interest rates and security prices in different markets tend to move together, albeit with some leads and lags. Why do you think this is so?

13. What forces appear to bind the various components of the global financial system together?

14. Can you explain what is meant by the term *perfect market*? What about an *efficient market*? What real-world elements might limit the perfection and efficiency of money and capital markets?

15. What is meant by the term *asymmetric information*? Why do you think this concept might be important to you and to other participants in the financial system?

THE PLAN OF THIS BOOK

This text is divided into seven parts, each devoted to a particular segment of the financial system. Part One provides an overview of the global financial system—its role in the world's economy and its basic characteristics. The vital processes of saving and investing, lending and borrowing, and creating and destroying financial assets are described. Part One surveys the principal sources of information available today on the workings of the worldwide financial marketplace and presents an overview of the financial system of the future.

Part Two examines the forces that shape interest rates and the prices of financial instruments. Because the rate of interest is the key price in the financial system, this section begins in Chapter 5, which presents a variety of views about how interest rates are determined. Subsequent chapters address such important topics as the measurement of interest rates and security prices, yield curves, duration, inflation, the risk of default, and taxes. Part Two concludes with a review of methods for forecasting and hedging against interest rate and asset price changes, including swaps, futures, and options.

Part Three draws our attention to the money market and its principal institutions and instruments and to a government institution that often dominates the tone of the money market—the central bank. Chapters in this section examine the characteristics of Treasury bills, federal funds, repurchase agreements, bank certificates of deposit, commercial paper, federal agency securities, bankers' acceptances, and Eurocurrency deposits. Part Three also presents a thorough examination of the many roles and functions of the central bank within the financial system. It contains an in-depth look at the history, organizational structure, and policy tools of the Federal Reserve System as well as the policy tools used by other central banks around the world. Part Three concludes with a review of the goals and targets for implementing central bank monetary policy.

In Part Four, the spotlight turns to private financial institutions—commercial banks, credit unions, savings and loan associations, money market funds, insurance companies, pension funds, mutual funds, and other financial-service firms. The reader is presented with an overview of their financial characteristics, regulation, current problems, and management tools designed to deal with many of those problems.

Part Five turns to the role of governments—federal, state, and local—within the global financial system. The opening chapter explores the fiscal policy and debt management policy activities of the U.S. government. This chapter explains how Treasury financing operations impact the economy, interest rates, and the supply of credit, and looks at the pros and cons of having government debt. This part concludes with an overview of state and local government financial activities, including state and local government borrowing, spending, and taxation.

Part Six focuses our attention on the financial activities of nonfinancial business firms and consumers. Chapter 21 explores business borrowing, especially the pricing and marketing of corporate bonds, and Chapter 22 looks at recent developments in the stock market and the growing volume of research on the efficiency of trading in equities. The financial characteristics of consumers, both families and individuals, are also considered in Part Six. Chapter 23 examines the types of consumer debt and savings instruments available today and reviews current laws that affect the consumer of financial services. Chapter 24 takes a detailed look at one of the largest of all consumer debt markets—residential mortgages—in which recent innovations have created many new options for financing home purchases.

Finally, Part Seven is devoted heavily to the international financial system and future trends in global finance. Topics covered include international trade and the balance of payments, the markets for foreign currencies, hedging against currency risk, and international banking.

Throughout this text, there is a strong emphasis on the innovative character of modern financial systems and institutions. A veritable explosion of new instruments and trading techniques has occurred within the global financial system in recent years. Moreover, the pace of innovation in financial services appears to be accelerating under the combined pressure of increased competition, rising costs, and growing risks. As we will see in the pages that follow, these forces of innovation, competition, rising costs, and growing risk are profoundly reshaping the structure and operations of our whole financial system today.

Summary of the Chapter

The opening chapter of *Money and Capital Markets* presents us with an introduction to the global financial system in which the money and capital markets play central roles. It also highlights the principal institutions that shape the character and functioning of the world's financial marketplace. The chapter's clear emphasis is on the roles and functions performed by the financial system to make our daily lives better, more enjoyable, and more personally and professionally rewarding.

- The *financial system* produces and distributes financial services to the public. Among its most important services is a supply of *credit* which allows businesses, households, and governments to invest and acquire assets they need for daily economic activity. The financial system of money and capital markets determines both the amount and cost of credit available. In turn, the supply and cost of credit affect the health and growth of the global economy and our own economic welfare.

- Credit and other financial services are offered for sale in the institution we call a *market.* Markets allocate financial and physical resources that are always scarce relative to the demand for them.

- Another key role played by markets operating within the financial system is to stimulate an adequate volume of *savings* by the public and to transform those savings into an adequate volume of *investment.* In turn, investment generates new products and services, creates new jobs and new businesses, resulting in faster economic growth and a higher standard of living. By determining interest rates within the financial system the money and capital markets bring the volume of savings generated by the public into balance with the volume of investment in new plant and equipment and in inventories of goods and resources available for sale.

- One important way to view the financial system of money and capital markets is by examining its seven key functions or roles, which include generating savings, stimulating the accumulation of wealth, providing liquidity for spending, providing a mechanism for making payments, supplying credit to aid in the purchase of goods and services, providing risk protection services, and supplying a channel for government policy in helping to achieve each of the nation's economic goals (including full employment, low inflation, and sustainable economic growth).

- The markets that serve the financial system may be classified in several different ways, including *money markets,* supplying short-term loans (credit) of less than a year, and *capital markets,* supplying long-term loans (credit), lasting longer than one year. There are also *open markets* where anyone may participate as buyer or seller versus *negotiated markets* where only a few bidders seek to reach agreement on a financial transaction. There are *primary* versus *secondary* markets; in the former, *new* financial instruments are traded in contrast to the latter where existing, rather than new, instruments are exchanged. Additional types of financial markets that make up the global financial system include those markets that deal in the immediate purchase or sale of goods or services, called *spot markets,* and those that promise future sale and delivery, known as *futures, forward,* or *option markets.*

- While there are many different segments that make up the money and capital markets around the globe, all of these markets share the common purpose of supplying credit to answer global demands for borrowed funds and all encourage saving to make investment (and therefore, economic growth) possible. Funds flow easily and, for the most part, smoothly from one segment of the financial marketplace to another, spurred by such forces as *arbitrage* and *speculation.* For example, *arbitrage* causes credit, savings, and investment to flow toward those areas or market segments that offer the most favorable returns, helping different markets to price resources more consistently and to rapidly eliminate price disparities for the same goods and services. Prices are also brought into better balance from market to market by the force of *speculation,* which seeks out underpriced and overpriced services and goods.

- Finally, the money and capital markets have revealed themselves to be highly *efficient* institutions, gathering and quickly using all relevant information to price credit and other financial services. Some are nearly *perfect* markets where competition sets prices and allocates resources. However, imperfections do exist within the financial system where competition is sometimes restricted and excess profits are sometimes earned by those who stifle competition and gain access to inside information not freely available to all due to *asymmetries* within the financial marketplace.

Key Terms

Financial system, *2*	Liquidity, *9*	Secondary markets, *14*
Market, *4*	Credit, *9*	Arbitrage, *16*
Financial market, *6*	Money market, *12*	Perfect market, *16*
Savings, *6*	Capital market, *12*	Efficient market, *17*
Investment, *6*	Open markets, *14*	Asymmetric information, *17*
Wealth, *8*	Negotiated markets, *14*	
Net wealth, *8*	Primary markets, *14*	

Problems

1. Please *classify* the following financial transactions as to whether they fit in (a) the money market or the capital market, (b) the primary or the secondary market, (c) the open or negotiated market, and (d) the spot or futures/forward market. (*Note:* The transactions below may fit in more than one of the above categories of markets. Be sure to include all of the appropriate types of markets that each transaction fits.)

   Financial transactions to classify:

   a. You visit a local bank today and secure a three-year loan to finance the purchase of a new car and some furniture.

   b. You purchase a new U.S. Treasury bill for $9,800 through the Federal Reserve bank in a neighboring city for delivery today.

   c. Responding to a rise in the price of Texaco common stock, you have just purchased 100 shares of that company's stock through a phone call to your broker, who is linked to a major stock exchange.

   d. Concerned about recent trends in the price of the Mexican peso, you contact a large money center bank in the region and purchase 10,000 pesos at today's dollar/peso exchange rate for delivery in six months, when you plan to fly to Mexico City.

   e. Receiving an unexpected windfall, you contact a local savings and loan association and purchase a $15,000 two-year CD bearing an interest rate on which you and the association's officer have agreed.

   f. The corporation you represent needs to raise $25 million immediately to purchase raw materials. You contact a securities dealer who agrees to advertise the sale of $25 million in commercial paper, maturing in 90 days, this afternoon. The dealer expects to sell all the notes within 24 hours.

2. What *functions of the financial system* do the following transactions illustrate or represent? (*Note:* Some transactions may involve more than one function. Be sure to identify *all* of the financial system functions involved in each transaction.)

   a. James Rhodes purchases health and accident insurance policies through the company where he works.

   b. Sharon MacArthur uses her credit card to purchase wallpaper for a home remodeling project.

   c. Fearing a slowdown in the rate of economic growth and increasing joblessness, the Federal Reserve System and the Bank of England move to lower interest rates.

   d. Dynamic Corporation places some of its current earnings in a bank CD, anticipating a need for funds in about a year to build a new warehouse.

   e. The Italian government sells new bonds in the open market to cover a large budget deficit.

   f. Cal and Jane Lewis hope to put their three young children through college someday. Accordingly, they begin buying U.S. savings bonds.

   g. Needing immediate spending power, Hillcrest Corporation sells its holdings of Denton County bonds through a security broker.

3. From the information presented below on the U.S. economy, please calculate (a) the volume of current savings for all U.S. households, business firms, and governments and (b) the volume of current investment for households and businesses. (*Hint:* Not all of the information below needs to be used to answer this question; decide what is and is not needed.)

Total personal income . . . . .$4,677.7 billion	Undistributed business profits . .42.1 billion
Personal tax and nontax payments . . . . .709.0 billion	U.S. government budget outlays . . . . .424.5 billion
Personal consumption expenditures . . . . .3,697.6 billion	State and local government budget outlays . . . . .677.3 billion
Change in business inventories . .9.6 billion	U.S. government budget surplus (or deficit) . . . . −143.0 billion
Expenditures on nonresidential plant and equipment . . . . .532.4 billion	State and local governments' budget surplus . . . . .39.2 billion
Residential construction . . . . .218.2 billion	
Capital consumption on business plant and equipment . . . . .500.0 billion	Purchases of durable goods . . .481.9 billion

4. In a recent year, the following amounts of money market and capital market instruments—loans and securities—were issued and outstanding in the United States:

Business inventory loans . . . . . .$185 billion	Residential mortgages to support the construction of homes and apartments . . . . . .3,137 billion
Treasury notes and bonds . . . . .1,650 billion	
Commercial mortgages for the construction of factories and equipment . . . . .740 billion	Treasury bills . . . . .540 billion
	Eurodollar deposits . . . . .390 billion
Foreign bonds . . . . .295 billion	School and highway construction bonds . . . . .75 billion
Bank certificates of deposit . . . . .442 billion	
Corporate stock (equities) . . . .4,158 billion	State and local government (municipal) notes and bonds . . . .601 billion
Federal funds and repurchase agreements . . . . .187 billion	Commercial paper . . . . .545 billion
Corporate notes and bonds . . .1,491 billion	Federal agency securities . . . . . . .398 billion
4-year and 5-year automobile loans to consumers . . . . .285 billion	Farm mortgages . . . . .80 billion
	Bankers' acceptances . . . . .41 billion
Loans to security dealers . . . . . . .87 billion	Eurobonds . . . . .137 billion

Based on the discussion in this chapter, *classify* each of the above instruments as to whether they usually qualify as (a) a money market instrument or (b) a capital market instrument. If the above instruments represent all U.S. money and capital market instruments outstanding, what was the total dollar size of the U.S. money market? the total size of the U.S. capital market?

5. The household sector (individuals and families) recorded current income of approximately $3.35 trillion in a recent year and total consumption expenditures (including taxes) of $2.89 trillion in that same year. The household sector held about $24.36 trillion in the total value of its wealth (including stocks, bonds, bank deposits, accumulated retirement savings, houses, etc.) at the beginning of the year and earned an average rate of return of 4.5 percent on its wealth holdings during the year. Calculate the change (growth) in wealth for the household sector that occurred during the year.

6. The Wilkins family held total assets, including a home, stocks, bonds, and other accumulated assets, of $175,000 at the beginning of the year. If the family's accumulated wealth increased by $4,400 this year and its income and consumption spending amounted to $36,000 and $34,800, respectively, what was the average rate of return on the family's accumulated wealth during the year?

7. Suppose that banks held total financial assets (loans, securities, and other financial instruments) of $3,786 billion, while the banking sector's total liabilities amounted to

$3,631 billion. What is the banking system's *net* financial wealth? If the banking system began the year with total financial assets of $3,639 billion and saved $53 billion during the year, how much income was earned on previously accumulated assets? What was the banking system's *net* financial wealth at year-end?

8. What *roles* or *functions* of the global financial system are being described in the items listed below?
   a. Exxon Corporation issues new shares of stock to finance its expansion into foreign markets.
   b. The Williams family withdraws its bank deposit in order to purchase new furniture for their home.
   c. Robert Enlow plans to purchase a new home in three years, but in the interim, he makes a loan to a friend who needs ready cash for a down payment on an automobile.
   d. Deutsche Bank develops and offers to its customers a new savings plan that combines traditional bank deposits with the availability of shares in a growth-oriented mutual fund.
   e. Randy Bose plans to retire in 18 months but elects to loan a portion of his long-term savings to his son Robert, who is starting a new business and has recently married.
   f. The Greater Asia Insurance Corporation has managed to attract $100 million in annuity investments from savers over the past six months and plans to make a loan to Eastman Hotel Corporation, which is beginning construction on a series of luxury resorts in Honolulu and Singapore.

9. What concept, institution, or instrument is described by each of the phrases or sentences listed below:
   a. All market participants are price takers.
   b. No information that might affect financial asset prices or interest rates is wasted.
   c. Different participants in the financial markets often operate with different sets of information.
   d. Transferring funds from one market to another due to differences in price.
   e. Risk seekers.
   f. Trading of loans and securities in which any individual or institution can participate.
   g. Mechanisms set up by society to trade newly issued loans and securities.
   h. Set up to channel temporary cash surpluses into temporary loans.
   i. Immediately spendable cash.
   j. Assets minus liabilities held by an economic unit.
   k. Expenditures on capital goods or raw materials.
   l. Current earnings retained in a business.
   m. Funds left over out of current income after deducting current consumption expenditures.
   n. An institutional mechanism for trading goods and services.
   o. Collection of markets, individuals, institutions, laws, and regulations through which financial services are produced and delivered.

Questions about the Web and the Money and Capital Markets

1. Why are the acts of savings and investment such an important facet of the operations of our financial system and the money and capital markets? To find out more about savings and investment activity where on the Web could you look?

2. For new savers and investors who want to become active in the financial system where are some of the key places on the Web that they can go to get help?

Selected References

Duca, John V. "The Democratization of America's Capital Markets." *Economic and Financial Review,* Federal Reserve Bank of Dallas, Second Quarter 2001, pp. 10–19.

Parkin, Michael. *Macroeconomics,* 2nd ed. New York: Addison-Wesley, 1993.

Parry, Robert T. "Financial Services in the New Century." *Economic Letter,* no. 98-15. Federal Reserve Bank of San Francisco, May 8, 1998, pp. 1–3.

Peach, Richard, and Charles Steindel." A Nation of Spendthrifts? An Analysis of Trends in Personal and Gross Savings." *Current Issues in Economics and Finance,* Federal Reserve Bank of New York, September 2000.

Sundaresan, Suresh M. *Fixed Income Markets and Their Derivatives.* Cincinnati: South-Western, 1996.

Chapter Two

Financial Assets, Money, Financial Transactions, and Financial Institutions

Learning Objectives in This Chapter

- You will see the most important channels through which funds flow from lenders to borrowers and back again within the global financial system of money and capital markets.

- You will discover the nature and characteristics of *financial assets*—how they are created and destroyed by decision makers within the financial system.

- You will explore the critical roles played by *money* within the financial system and the linkages between the volume and growth of money and inflation in the prices of goods and services.

- You will examine the important jobs carried out by financial intermediaries and other financial institutions in lending and borrowing funds and in creating and destroying financial assets within the global system of markets.

What's in This Chapter? Key Topics Outline

Financial Assets: What Are They? What Are Their Features?

Creating and Destroying Financial Assets

Financial Identities: Assets, Liabilities, Net Worth

Deficit and Surplus Budget Units

Money: What Is It? What Are Its Principal Functions?

Inflation, Deflation, and Money: Thinking in Real Terms

Types of Financial Transactions

Financial Intermediation and Types of Financial Institutions

Disintermediation

INTRODUCTION

The financial system is the mechanism through which loanable funds reach borrowers. Through the operation of the financial markets, money is exchanged for financial claims in the form of stocks, bonds, and other securities. And through the exchange of money for financial claims, the economy's capacity to produce goods and services is increased. This happens because the global money and capital markets provide the financial resources needed for real investment. Although it is true that the financial markets deal mainly in the exchange of paper claims and computer entries evidencing the transfer of funds, these markets provide an indispensable conduit for the transformation of savings into real investment, accelerating the economy's growth and developing new businesses and new jobs.

This chapter looks closely at the essential role played by the global financial markets in converting savings into investment and how that role has changed over time. We begin by observing that nearly all financial transactions between buyers and sellers involve the creation or destruction of a special kind of asset: a *financial asset.* Moreover, financial assets possess a number of characteristics that make them unique among all assets held by individuals and institutions. In the next section, we consider the nature of financial assets and how they are created and destroyed through the workings of the global financial system.

THE CREATION OF FINANCIAL ASSETS

What is a **financial asset?** It is a *claim* against the income or wealth of a business firm, household, or unit of government, represented usually by a certificate, receipt, computer record file, or other legal document, and usually created by or related to the lending of money. Familiar examples include stocks, bonds, insurance policies, futures contracts, and deposits held in a bank or credit union.

CHARACTERISTICS OF FINANCIAL ASSETS

Financial assets do *not* provide a continuing stream of services to their owners as a home, an automobile, or a washing machine would do. These assets are sought after because they promise *future* returns to their owners and serve as a *store of value* (purchasing power). Their value rests on *faith* that their issuer will honor his or her contractual promise to pay.

A number of other features make financial assets unique. They *cannot be depreciated* because they do not wear out like physical goods. Moreover, their physical condition or form usually is *not* relevant in determining their market value (price). A stock certificate is not more or less valuable, for example, because of the size or quality of paper it may be printed on, because it may be frayed around the edges, or because of the type and format of the computer file in which it may appear.

Because financial assets are generally represented by a piece of paper (certificate or contract) or by information stored in a computer, they have little or no value as a commodity and their cost of transportation and storage is low. Indeed, the cost of the storage and transfer of funds and other bits of financial information declined sharply in the 1990s and into the twenty-first century due to rapid advances in computer and electronic technology, causing financial assets to grow faster than world trade and faster than the growth of the economic system as a whole. Finally, financial assets are *fungible*—they can easily be changed in form and substituted for other assets. Thus, a bond or share of stock often can be quickly converted into any other asset the holder desires.

The financial markets perform an indispensable function for every one of us, not only in encouraging us to save and invest for the future, but also in helping us manage our money—the short-term liquid balances we hold for immediate spending power. One of the critical jobs of the financial marketplace is money management and the World Wide Web has created numerous Web sites to aid in that important function.

One of the most popular is *Money Magazine*'s money.com, which helps individuals track the assets they already hold or might wish to hold. Examples include stocks, mutual funds, residential real estate values, insurance, and other portfolio items. This site enables users to stay abreast of what their money is doing and offers new investment ideas when the Web site visitor decides to take a new tack in his or her investment strategy.

The Web also has numerous articles concerning the impact of inflation on the value of money and other financial assets that you and I hold. There are key sites that carefully define the meaning of "inflation"—for example, Encyclopedia.com as well as such detailed sites as *www.westegg.com* that allow us to determine how much things are worth after the effects of inflation and to work our way back into the past to see how the purchasing power of our money has changed over time—a handy tool for market investors.

Different Kinds of Financial Assets

Although there are thousands of different financial assets, they generally fall into four categories: money, equities, debt securities, and derivatives.

Any financial asset that is generally accepted in payment for purchases of goods and services is **money.** Thus, checking accounts and currency are financial assets serving as payment media and, therefore, are forms of money. In the modern world money—even the forms of money issued by the government—depends for its value only upon the issuer's pledge to pay as promised. **Equities** (more commonly known as *stock*) represent ownership shares in a business firm and, as such, are claims against the firm's profits and against proceeds from the sale of its assets. We usually further subdivide equities into *common stock,* which entitles its holder to vote for the members of a firm's board of directors and, therefore, determine company policy, and *preferred stock,* which normally carries no voting privileges but does entitle its holder to a fixed share of the firm's net earnings ahead of its common stockholders.

Debt securities include such familiar instruments as *bonds, notes, accounts payable,* and *savings deposits.* Legally, these financial assets entitle their holders to a priority claim over the holders of equities to the assets and income of an individual, business firm, or unit of government. Usually, that claim is fixed in amount and time (maturity) and, depending on the terms of the *indenture* (contract) that accompanies most debt securities, may be backed up by the pledge of specific assets as collateral. Financial analysts usually divide debt securities into two broad classes: (1) *negotiable,* which can easily be transferred from holder to holder as a marketable security, and (2) *nonnegotiable,* which cannot legally be transferred to another party. Passbook savings accounts and U.S. savings bonds are good examples of nonnegotiable debt securities. In this book, our primary but not exclusive focus is on negotiable (marketable) debt instruments such as Treasury bonds and corporate notes and bonds.

Finally, **derivatives** are among the newest kinds of financial instruments that are closely linked to financial assets. These unique financial claims have a market value that is tied to or influenced by the value or return on a financial asset, such as stocks (equities) and bonds, notes, and other loans (debt securities). Examples include futures contracts, options, and swaps. As we will see in future chapters, these particular financial instruments are often employed to manage risk in the assets to which they are tied or related.

The Creation Process for Financial Assets

How are financial assets created? We may illustrate this process using a rudimentary financial system in which there are only two economic units: a household and a business firm.

Assume that this financial system is *closed,* so no external transactions with other units are possible. Each unit holds certain assets accumulated over the years as a result of its saving out of current income. The household, for example, may have accumulated furniture, an automobile, clothes, and other items needed to provide entertainment, food, shelter, and transportation. The business firm holds inventories of goods to be sold, raw materials, machinery and equipment, and other assets required to produce its product and sell it to the public.

The financial position of these two economic units is presented in the form of balance sheets, shown in Exhibit 2–1. A balance sheet, of course, is a financial statement prepared as of a certain date, showing a particular unit's assets, liabilities, and net worth. *Assets* represent *accumulated uses of funds* made by an economic unit; *liabilities* and *net worth* represent the *accumulated sources of funds* that an economic unit has drawn upon to acquire the assets it now holds. The net worth (equity) account reflects total savings accumulated over time by each economic unit. A balance sheet must always balance; total assets (accumulated uses of funds) must equal total liabilities plus net worth (accumulated sources of funds).

EXHIBIT 2–1
Balance Sheets of Units in a Simple Financial System

HOUSEHOLD
Balance Sheet

Assets		Liabilities and Net Worth	
Accumulated uses of funds:		Accumulated sources of funds:	
Cash	$13,000	Net worth (accumulated savings)	$20,000
Furniture	1,000		
Clothes	1,500		
Automobile	4,000		
Other assets	500		
Total assets	$20,000	Total liabilities and net worth	$20,000

BUSINESS FIRM
Balance Sheet

Assets		Liabilities and Net Worth	
Accumulated uses of funds:		Accumulated sources of funds:	
Inventories of goods	$ 10,000	Net worth (accumulated savings)	$100,000
Machinery and equipment	25,000		
Building	60,000		
Other assets	5,000		
Total assets	$100,000	Total liabilities and net worth	$100,000

The household in our example holds total assets valued at $20,000, including an automobile, clothes, furniture, and cash. Because the household's financial statement must balance, total liabilities and net worth also add up to $20,000, all of which in this instance happens to come from net worth (accumulated savings). The business firm holds total assets amounting to $100,000, including a building housing the firm's offices, equipment, and inventory. The firm's only source of funds currently is net worth (accumulated savings), also valued at $100,000.

By today's standards, the two balance sheets shown in Exhibit 2–1 look very strange. Neither the household nor the business firm has any outstanding debt (liabilities). Each unit is entirely self-financed, because each has acquired its assets by saving and by spending within its current income, not by borrowing. In the terminology of finance, both the household and the business firm have engaged in **internal financing:** the use of current income and accumulated savings to acquire assets. In the case of the household, savings have been accumulated by taking some portion of each period's income and setting money aside rather than spending all income on current consumption. The business firm has abstained from paying out all of its current revenues in the form of expenses (including stockholder dividends), retaining some of its current earnings in its net worth account.

For most businesses and households, internally generated funds are still the most important resources for acquiring assets. For example, in the U.S. economy, well over half of all investment in plant, equipment, and inventories carried out by business firms each year is financed internally rather than by borrowing. Households as a group save substantially more than they borrow each year, with the savings flowing into purchases of real assets (such as homes and automobiles) and into sizable purchases of stocks, bonds, and other financial assets.

Suppose that the business firm in our rudimentary financial system wishes to purchase new equipment in the form of a drill press. Due to inflation and shortages of key raw materials, however, the cost of the new drill press has been increasing rapidly. Internal sources of funds are not sufficient to cover the equipment's full cost. What can be done? There are four likely alternatives: (1) postpone the purchase of the new equipment until sufficient savings can be accumulated, (2) sell off some existing assets to raise the necessary funds, (3) borrow all or a portion of the needed funds, or (4) issue new stock (equity).

Time is frequently a determining factor here. Postponement of the equipment purchase probably will result in lost sales and lost profits. A competing company may rush ahead to expand its operations and capture some share of this firm's market. Moreover, in an environment of inflation, the new drill press surely will cost even more in the future than it does now. Selling some existing assets to raise the necessary funds is a distinct possibility, but this may take time, and there is risk of substantial loss, especially if fixed assets must be sold. The third alternative—borrowing—has the advantage of raising funds quickly, and the interest cost on the loan is tax deductible.[1] The firm could sell additional stock if it hesitated to take on debt, but equity financing is usually more expensive than borrowing and requires more time to arrange.

If the business firm decides to borrow, who will lend the funds it needs? Obviously, in this two-unit financial system, the household must provide the needed funds. The firm must engage in *external financing* by issuing to the household securities evidencing a loan of

---

[1]An added advantage associated with issuing debt is the *leverage effect.* If the firm can earn more from purchasing and using the new equipment than the cost of borrowing funds, the surplus return will flow to the firm's owners in the form of increased earnings, increasing the value of the company's stock. The result is positive financial leverage. Unfortunately, leverage is a two-edged sword. If the firm earns less than the cost of borrowed funds, the owners' losses will be magnified as a result of unfavorable (negative) financial leverage.

money. In general, if any economic unit wishes to add to its holdings of assets but lacks the necessary resources to do so, it can raise additional funds by issuing financial liabilities (borrowing)—provided that a buyer of those IOUs can be found. The buyer will regard the IOUs as an asset—a financial asset—that may earn income unless the borrower goes out of business and defaults on the loan.

Suppose that the business firm decides to borrow by issuing a liability (debt security) in the amount of $10,000 to pay for its new drill press. Because the firm is promising an attractive interest rate on the new IOU, the household willingly acquires it as a financial asset. This asset is *intangible:* a mere promise to pay $10,000 at maturity plus a promised stream of interest payments over time. The borrowing and creation of this financial asset will impact the balance sheets of these two economic units. As shown in Exhibit 2–2, the household has purchased the firm's IOU by using up some of its accumulated cash. Its total assets are unchanged. Instead of holding $13,000 in non-interest-bearing cash, the household now holds an interest-bearing financial asset in the form of a $10,000 security. The firm's total assets and total liabilities *increase* due to the combined effect of borrowing (*external finance*) and the acquisition of a productive real asset.

What would happen to the balance sheets shown in Exhibit 2–2 if a business firm decided to issue stock (equities), rather than debt, to finance the purchase of its equipment? In this case, the household would show its acquisition of the firm's stock in the amount of $10,000 as a financial asset. However, on the business firm's balance sheet, net worth would rise to $110,000 (because the issuance of new stock adds to a business's net worth) and there would be no liability account because the household would be a part owner (stockholder) in the business firm rather than merely a creditor.

EXHIBIT 2–2
Unit Balance Sheets Following the Purchase of Equipment and the Issuance of a Financial Asset

HOUSEHOLD
Balance Sheet

Assets		Liabilities and Net Worth	
Cash	$ 3,000	Net worth (accumulated savings)	$20,000
Financial asset	10,000		
Furniture	1,000		
Clothes	1,500		
Automobile	4,000		
Other assets	500		
Total assets	$20,000	Total liabilities and net worth	$20,000

BUSINESS FIRM
Balance Sheet

Assets		Liabilities and Net Worth	
Inventories of goods	$ 10,000	Liabilities	$ 10,000
Machinery and equipment	35,000	Net worth	100,000
Building	60,000		
Other assets	5,000		
Total assets	$110,000	Total liabilities and net worth	$110,000

FINANCIAL ASSETS AND THE FINANCIAL SYSTEM

This simple example illustrates several important points concerning the operation and role of the financial system in the economy. First, the act of borrowing or of issuing new stock simultaneously gives rise to the creation of an equal volume of financial assets. In the foregoing example, the $10,000 financial asset held by the household lending money is exactly matched by the $10,000 liability of the business firm borrowing money. This suggests another way of defining a financial asset: *Any asset held by a business firm, government, or household that is also recorded as a liability or claim on some other economic unit's balance sheet is a financial asset.* As we have seen, many different kinds of assets satisfy this definition, including stocks, bonds, bank loans, and deposits held with a financial institution.

For the entire global financial system, the sum of all financial assets held must equal the total of all financial liabilities (claims) outstanding. In contrast, real assets, such as automobiles and buildings, are not necessarily matched by liabilities (claims) somewhere in the financial system.

This distinction between *financial assets* and *liabilities,* on the one hand, and *real assets,* on the other, is worth pursuing with an example. Suppose that you borrow $4,000 from the bank to purchase an automobile. Your balance sheet will now contain a liability in the amount of $4,000. The bank from which you borrowed the funds will record the transaction as a loan—an interest-bearing financial asset—appearing on the asset side of its balance sheet in the like amount of $4,000. On the asset side of your balance sheet appears the market value of the automobile—a real asset. The value of the real asset probably exceeds $4,000, since most banks expect a borrower to supply some of his or her own funds rather than borrowing the full purchase price. Let's say the automobile was sold to you for $5,000, with $1,000 of the cost coming out of your savings account and $4,000 from the bank loan. Then, your balance sheet will contain a new real asset (automobile) valued at $5,000, a liability (bank loan) of $4,000, and your savings account (a financial asset) will decline by $1,000.

Clearly, there are two equalities that hold not only for this transaction but whenever funds are loaned and borrowed in the financial system. First,

$$\begin{array}{lcl} \text{Volume of financial} & & \\ \text{assets created for} & = & \text{Volume of liabilities} \\ \text{lenders} & & \text{issued by borrowers} \end{array}$$

$$\begin{array}{lcl} \text{In this case, a bank} & = & \text{A borrower's IOU of} \\ \text{loan of \$4,000} & & \$4,000 \end{array} \tag{2-1}$$

Second,

$$\text{Total uses of funds} = \text{Total source of funds}$$

$$\begin{array}{lcl} & & \text{Issuance of a \$4,000} \\ \text{Purchase of \$5,000} & = & \text{borrower IOU} + \$1,000 \\ \text{automobile} & & \text{drawn from a savings} \\ & & \text{account} \end{array} \tag{2-2}$$

Every financial asset in existence represents the lending or investing of funds transferred from one economic unit to another.

Because the sum of all financial assets created must always equal the amount of all liabilities (claims) outstanding, the amount of lending in the financial system must always equal the amount of borrowing going on. In effect, *financial assets and liabilities (claims) cancel each other out across the whole financial system.* We can illustrate this fact by reference to the balance sheet of any unit in the economy—business firm, household, or government. The following must be true for *all* balance sheets:

$$\text{Total assets} = \text{Total liabilities} + \text{Net worth} \qquad \textbf{(2–3)}$$

Then, because all assets may be classified as either real assets or financial assets, it follows that

$$\text{Real assets} + \text{Financial assets} = \text{Total liabilities} + \text{Net worth} \quad \textbf{(2–4)}$$

Because the volume of financial assets outstanding must always equal the volume of liabilities (claims) in existence, it follows that the aggregate volume of real assets held in the economy must equal the total amount of net worth. Therefore, for the economy and financial system *as a whole:*

$$\text{Total financial assets} = \text{Total liabilities} \qquad \textbf{(2–5)}$$

$$\text{Total real assets} = \text{Net worth (i.e., accumulated savings)} \qquad \textbf{(2–6)}$$

This means that the value of all buildings, machinery, and other real assets in existence matches the total amount of *savings* carried out by all businesses, households, and units of government. We *are not* made better off in real terms by the mere creation of financial assets and liabilities. These are only pieces of paper or blips on a computer screen evidencing a loan or the investment of funds. Rather, society increases its wealth only by saving and increasing the quantity of its real assets, for these assets enable the economy to produce more goods and services in the future.

Does this suggest that the creation of financial assets and liabilities—one of the basic functions of the global financial system—is a useless exercise? Not at all. The mere act of saving by one economic unit does not guarantee that those savings will be used to build or purchase real assets that add to society's stock of wealth. In modern economies, saving and investment usually are carried out by different groups of people. For example, most saving is usually carried out by households (individuals and families), and business firms account for the majority of investments in productive real assets. Some mechanism is needed to ensure that savings flow from those who save to those who wish to invest in real assets, and the financial system of money and capital markets is that mechanism.

The *financial system* provides the essential channel necessary for the creation and exchange of financial assets between savers and borrowers so that real assets can be acquired. Without that channel for savings, the total volume of investment in the economy surely would be reduced. All investment by individual economic units would have to depend on the ability of those same units to save (i.e., engage in internal financing). Many promising investment opportunities would have to be forgone or postponed due to insufficient savings. Society's scarce resources would be allocated less efficiently than is possible with a system of financial markets. Growth in society's income, employment, and standard of living would be seriously impaired without a vibrant global financial system at work.

Questions *to Help You Study*

1. Exactly what do we mean by the term *financial asset*?
2. How do financial assets come about within the functioning of the financial system?
3. Carefully explain why it is that the volume of financial assets outstanding must always equal the volume of liabilities outstanding?
4. What is the difference between *internal finance* and *external finance?*

5. When a business, household, or unit of government is in need of additional funding, what are its principal alternatives? What factors should these different economic units consider when they have to choose among the different possible sources of funds?

6. What exactly is the relationship between the process of creating financial assets and liabilities and the acts of saving and investment? Why is that relationship important to your financial and economic well-being?

LENDING AND BORROWING IN THE FINANCIAL SYSTEM

Business firms, households, and governments play a wide variety of roles in modern financial systems. It is quite common for an individual or institution to be a lender of funds in one period and a borrower in the next, or to do both simultaneously. Indeed, financial intermediaries, such as banks and insurance companies, operate on both sides of the financial markets, borrowing funds from customers by issuing attractive financial claims and simultaneously making loans available to other customers. Virtually all of us at one point or another in our lifetimes will be involved in the financial system as both a borrower and a lender of funds.

A number of years ago, economists John Gurley and Edward Shaw (1960) pointed out that each business firm, household, or unit of government active in the financial system must conform to the following identity:

$$R - E = \Delta FA - \Delta D$$

$$
\begin{array}{l}
\text{Current income receipts} \\
- \text{ Expenditures out of} \\
\text{current income}
\end{array}
=
\begin{array}{l}
\text{Change in holdings of} \\
\text{financial assets } - \\
\text{Change in debt and} \\
\text{equity outstanding}
\end{array}
\qquad \textbf{(2–7)}
$$

If our current expenditures (E) exceed our current income receipts (R), we usually make up the difference by (1) reducing our holdings of financial assets ($-\Delta FA$), for example, by drawing money out of a savings account; (2) issuing debt or stock ($+\Delta D$); or (3) using some combination of both. On the other hand, if our receipts (R) in the current period are larger than our current expenditures (E), we can (1) build up our holdings of financial assets ($+\Delta FA$), for example, by placing money in a savings account or buying a few shares of stock; (2) pay off some outstanding debt or retire stock previously issued by our business firm ($-\Delta D$); or (3) do some combination of both of these steps.

It follows that for any given period of time (e.g., day, week, month, or year), the individual economic unit must fall into one of three groups:

Deficit-budget unit (DBU): $E > R$; and so $\Delta D > \Delta FA$
(net borrower of funds)

Surplus-budget unit (SBU): $R > E$; and thus $\Delta FA > \Delta D$
(net lender of funds)

Balanced-budget unit (BBU): $R = E$; and, therefore, $\Delta D = \Delta FA$
(neither net lender nor
net borrower)

A *net lender of funds (SBU) is really a net supplier of funds to the financial system.* He or she accomplishes this function by purchasing financial assets, paying off debt, or retiring equity (stock). In contrast, a *net borrower of funds (DBU) is a net demander of funds from the financial system,* selling financial assets, issuing new debt, or selling new stock. The business and government sectors of the economy tend to be net borrowers (demanders) of funds (DBUs) in most periods; the household sector, composed of all families and individuals, tends to be a net lender (supplier) of funds (SBU) in most (though not all) years.

Net lending and borrowing sectors in the U.S. economy in 2001 reflected the foregoing patterns. For example, as shown in Exhibit 2–3 households during 2001 were net lenders of funds, though by a relatively small margin of $4.7 billion. This slim margin of household sector net lending activity was not nearly enough to fully accommodate the principal net borrowers in the American economy—nonfinancial businesses and governments (federal, state, and local). Businesses demanded $31.2 billion more in borrowed funds than they contributed to the financial system through their net acquisition of financial assets. Likewise, federal, state and local governments combined were net borrowers to the tune of just over $112 billion in total.

In short, businesses and governments had combined net borrowings of slightly more than $140 billion in 2001, but households, acting as net lenders, contributed less than $5 billion of this total. Then where did the extra needed funds come from? As Exhibit 2–3 clearly shows, it was *foreign investors* who more than made up the difference with a net lending total of more than $376 billion. Foreign participants in U.S. financial markets sought out dollar-denominated assets inside the United States, including corporate stock, government bonds, and thousands of other American financial instruments. Many of these overseas investors (net lenders) saw the United States as a relatively safe haven for their funds in contrast to the struggle and turmoil that characterized many foreign markets.

Of course, over any given period of time, any one household, business firm, or unit of government may be a deficit-, surplus-, or balanced-budget unit. In fact, from day to day and week to week, many households, businesses, and governments fluctuate from being deficit-budget units (DBUs) to surplus-budget units (SBUs) and back again. Consider a large corporation such as Ford or Exxon. Such a firm may be a net lender one week, supplying monies to deficit-budget units in the financial system for short periods of time through purchases of Treasury bills, bank Euro-deposits and CDs, and other financial assets. The following week, a dividend payment may be due company stockholders, bonds must be refunded, or purchases must be made to increase inventories and expand plant and equipment. At this point, the firm may become a net borrower of funds, drawing down its holdings of financial assets, securing loans by issuing financial liabilities, or selling equity (stock). Most of the large institutions that interact in the global financial marketplace continually fluctuate from one side of the market to the other. This is also true of most households today. *One of the most important contributions of the global financial system to our*

EXHIBIT 2–3 **Net Acquisitions of Financial Assets and Liabilities by Major Sectors of the U.S. Economy, 2001[*]**
($ Billions)

Major Sectors of the Economy	Net Acquisitions of Financial Assets during the Year	Net Increase in Liabilities during the Year	Net Lender (+) or Net Borrower (−) of Funds
Households	$857.8	$853.1	$ +4.7
Nonfinancial business firms	216.0	247.2	−31.2
State and local governments	29.2	68.6	−39.4
Federal government	179.5	252.2	−72.7
International sector:			
Foreign investors and borrowers	435.4	58.6	+376.8

[*]All figures shown are for the third quarter of 2001, annualized. Figures do not add exactly due to omitted groups and statistical discrepancies.

Source: Board of Governors of the Federal Reserve System, *Flow of Funds Accounts.*

*daily lives is in permitting businesses, households, and governments to adjust their finan-
cial position from that of net borrower (DBU) to net lender (SBU) and back again,
smoothly and efficiently.*

MONEY AS A FINANCIAL ASSET

What Is Money?

The most important financial asset in the economy is *money*—one of the oldest and most
useful inventions in the history of the world. Metallic coins served as money for many centuries until paper notes (currency) first appeared in China during the Tang Dynasty over a
thousand years ago (618–907 C.E.) and in Sweden in 1661. The Federal Government of the
United States did not issue paper money until 1861 in the form of notes known as "green-
backs" because of the green ink showing on the back of each note. Many other assets besides currency and coin have served as money in earlier periods, including beads, seashells,
salt, cigarettes, and even playing cards.

All financial assets are valued in terms of money, and flows of funds between lenders
and borrowers occur through the medium of money. Money itself is a true financial asset,
because all forms of money in use today are claims against some institution, public or private. For example, one of the largest components of the money supply today is the checking account, which is the debt of a bank or other depository institution. Another important
component of the money supply is currency and coin—the pocket money held by the public. The bulk of currency in use today in the United States, for example, consists of Federal
Reserve notes, representing debt obligations of the 12 Federal Reserve banks. In fact, if the
Federal Reserve ever closed its doors (a highly unlikely event!), Federal Reserve notes held
by the public would be a first claim against the assets of the Federal Reserve banks. Other
forms of money gaining in popularity include credit and debit cards to allow instant borrowing or the withdrawal of funds from a bank deposit; stored-value ("smart") cards that
are encoded via computer with a fixed amount of money available for spending; and digital cash available through the Internet computer network from a variety of financial service
providers.

As we will see in the accompanying box on alternative definitions of the money supply,
some concepts of what money is today include savings accounts at banks, credit unions,
and money market funds—all forms of debt, giving rise to financial assets.

One of the most important developments in the monetary field as the twenty-first century began was the creation of an entirely new monetary unit, the *Euro,* to serve the transactions needs of citizens and businesses trading across national borders within the newly
formed European Community (EC). Euros should rise to play a significantly more important role in the global currency markets than any of the traditional European currencies,
such as the franc, the lira, and the mark. The Euro should greatly simplify commerce and
trade in Europe because buyers and sellers will have to pay less attention to currency exchange rates in pricing goods and services and will face less currency risk when conducting business inside the EC. But switching to a new form of money isn't easy or cheap; it
has cost billions of dollars for European businesses and financial systems to change their
accounting, billing, and marketing systems to the Euro.

The Functions of Money

Money performs a wide variety of important services. It serves as a *standard of value* (or
unit of account) for all the goods and services we might wish to trade. Without money, the
price of every good or service would have to be expressed in terms of exchange ratios with

As discussed in this chapter, money performs several important functions in the financial system, serving as a medium of exchange, a store of value (purchasing power), a standard for valuing goods and services (unit of account), and a source of liquidity (spending power). These different functions of money in the financial system have given rise to a variety of different definitions of the actual money supply available to the public, with each definition reflecting a different role or function that money performs for those who hold it. For example, in the United States the principal definitions of money in use today are:

M1 = The sum of all U.S. currency and coin held by the public (outside the cash in the vaults of the U.S. Treasury, the Federal Reserve banks, and depository institutions), traveler's checks issued by nonbank financial institutions, and checking accounts (demand deposits), NOW accounts, and Automatic Transfer Services at all commercial banks, credit unions, and thrift institutions (except for interbank, U.S. government, and foreign bank deposits and Federal Reserve float). (In 2002 M1 totaled just over $1 trillion.)

M2 = The sum of M1 plus small savings and time deposits (under $100,000 each in amount), balances held in general-purpose and broker-dealer money market fund accounts, short-term repurchase agreements (bearing overnight maturities and continuing contracts that can be canceled with 24-hours notice) issued by depository institutions, and overnight foreign U.S. dollar deposits (Eurodollars) issued to U.S. residents by foreign branches of U.S. banks worldwide. (In 2002 M2 amounted to more than $5 trillion.)

M3 = The sum of M2 plus large time deposits (each over $100,000 in amount) and longer-term repurchase agreements issued by all depository institutions, longer-term foreign U.S. dollar deposits (Eurodollars) held by U.S. residents at foreign branches of U.S. banks worldwide and at all banking offices in the United Kingdom and Canada, and balances in institution-only money market funds. (In 2002 M3 was just over $8 trillion.)

Note that M1, the narrowest definition of the supply of money or money stock, focuses mainly upon immediately spendable money (such as pocket change and checking accounts) and, therefore, views money primarily as a *medium of exchange*. In contrast, M2 and M3 reflect mainly money's *store of value* role as captured by savings accounts, money market fund shares, and short-term borrowing in the money market by depository institutions. No single definition of money is necessarily "right" or "wrong." Each reflects a different dimension of money's function as an important financial asset in the economy.

Want to know more about the money supply and what makes it up? See especially *www.frbatlanta.org/publica*

all other goods and services—an enormous information burden for both buyers and sellers. We would need to know, for example, how many loaves of bread would be required to purchase a quart of milk, or what quantity of firewood might exchange for a suit of clothes. To trade just 12 different goods and services, we would have to remember 66 different exchange ratios! In contrast, the existence of money as a common standard of value permits us to express the prices of all goods and services in terms of only one good—the *monetary unit*. In the United States and Canada that unit is the dollar; in Britain, the pound; in Japan, the yen. But whatever the monetary unit is called, it always has a constant price in terms of itself (e.g., a dollar always exchanges for a dollar). The prices of all other goods and services are expressed in multiples of the monetary unit.

The importance of money within the financial system is discussed further in *http://encarta.msn.com*

Money also serves as a *medium of exchange*. It is usually the only financial asset that virtually every business, household, and unit of government will accept in payment for goods and services. By itself, money typically has little or no use as a commodity (except when gold or silver, for example, is used as the medium of exchange). People accept money only because they know they can exchange it at a later date for goods and services. This is why modern governments have been able to separate the monetary unit from precious metals such as gold and silver bullion and successfully issue *fiat money* (i.e., pieces of paper or data stored in a computer file or on a plastic card) not tied to any particular commodity. Money's service as a medium of exchange frees us from the terrible constraints of barter, allowing us to separate the act of selling goods and services from the act of buying goods and services. With a medium of exchange, buyers and sellers no longer need to have an exact coincidence of wants in terms of quality, quantity, time, and location.

Money serves also as a *store of value*—a reserve of future purchasing power. Purchasing power can be stored in currency, in a checking account, or in a computer file until the time is right to buy. Of course, money is not always a good store of value. The value of money, measured by its purchasing power, can experience marked fluctuations. For example, the prices of consumer goods represented in the U.S. cost-of-living index roughly quadrupled between 1960 and 2000. If individuals or families had purchased in each of these years the identical market basket of goods and services represented in the cost-of-living index, they would have found that the purchasing power of each unit of their money had decreased by more than two-thirds during this period.

Money functions as the *only perfectly liquid asset* in the financial system. An asset is liquid if it can be converted into cash quickly with little or no loss in value. A liquid asset possesses three essential characteristics: *price stability, ready marketability,* and *reversibility.* An asset must be considered *liquid* if its price tends to be reasonably stable over time, if it has an active resale market, and if it is reversible so that investors can recover their original investment without loss.

All assets—real and financial—differ in their *degrees of liquidity.* Generally, financial assets, especially bank deposits and stocks and bonds issued by major corporations, tend to be highly liquid; on the other hand, real assets, such as a home or an automobile, may be extremely difficult to sell in a hurry without taking a substantial loss. *Money is the most liquid of all assets because it need not be converted into any other form to be spent.* Unfortunately, the most liquid assets, including money, tend to carry the lowest rates of return. One measure of the "cost" of holding money is the income forgone by the owner who fails to convert his or her money balances into more profitable investments in real or financial assets. The *rate of interest* determined by the financial system is a measure of the penalty suffered by an investor for not converting money into income-earning assets.

THE VALUE OF MONEY AND OTHER FINANCIAL ASSETS AND INFLATION

The value of money—its *purchasing power*—changes due to **inflation,** defined as a rise in the average price level of all goods and services. Inflation lowers the value or purchasing power of money and is a special problem in the financial markets because it can damage the value of financial contracts (such as a bond or a deposit). Financial loss due to inflation is particularly likely where the amount of price inflation has not been fully anticipated or if the people and institutions who agreed to a financial contract were simply not able to fully adjust to the inflation that subsequently occurred.

The opposite of inflation is **deflation,** where the average level of prices for goods and services actually declines. Far less common than inflation, deflation benefits those whose income doesn't also decline with prices and, therefore, can buy more goods and services than they could in the past. Unfortunately, deflation is often accompanied by a troubled economy so that even though living costs are less, many people may still find themselves with sharply reduced income (purchasing power).

Today most economists and financial analysts measure inflation using popular **price indices,** such as the Consumer Price Index (CPI), the Producer Price Index (PPI), or the Gross Domestic Product (GDP) Deflator Index. The CPI or Cost of Living Index measures the cost of a market basket of goods and services normally purchased by an urban family of four people. To determine this measure of the cost of living the prices of designated consumer items are collected from thousands of stores in several cities across the United States each month, averaged, and combined into one index number. A number of other nations, particularly in Europe, have begun in recent years to compile their own CPIs in order to monitor and compare their cost of living and the effects of inflation.

While the CPI or Cost of Living Index is probably the best known inflation measure, the prices faced by businesses are reflected most accurately in the Producer Price Index (PPI), collected monthly for nearly 3,000 types of business raw materials, intermediate products, and finished products in the United States. The combination of *both* consumer and business prices can be found in a third well-known price index, the GDP deflator series, which captures the average price of all newly produced final goods and services produced within a nation's geographic boundaries within a given year. Calculated quarterly, the GDP deflator is generally considered the best overall measure of price changes (and inflation) in the economy.

To learn more about U.S. inflation and how to adjust costs for inflation's effects see *http://stats.bls.gov*

We can use any of the foregoing indices to measure percentage changes in price levels (and inflation) relative to some base year using the following relationship:

$$\Delta P = \frac{(PI_t - PI_{t-1})}{PI_{t-1}} \times 100$$

where ΔP is the percentage change in prices or in the price index we are following between two time periods (t and $t-1$), PI_t is the price or price index in period t, and PI_{t-1} is the price index in some previous time period ($t-1$).

For example, suppose the U.S. CPI rises from 100 to 125 over a five-year period. We know that this cost-of-living index has climbed

$$\frac{(125 - 100)}{100} = 0.25 \text{ or } 25 \text{ percent}$$

over the five-year period we are studying. Unless the value of our incomes and our investments in financial assets and other forms of wealth has also gone up at least 25 percent during the same time period, we would have suffered a decline in purchasing power and in the true value of our wealth in terms of the goods and services we can now buy.

What else can a price index tell us? In 2000 the U.S. Consumer Price Index (CPI) averaged about 175. This index value was based on the base period 1982–84 when the CPI was set at 100. This means that between 1982–84 and 2000 consumer prices in U.S. urban communities climbed an average of about 75 percent (that is, $(175-100) \div 100$). We can use numbers such as these to help figure out what has happened recently to the purchasing power of the basic monetary unit in the country that we live in.

For example, suppose we wish to know what has happened to the purchasing power of the U.S. dollar recently. We could use this relationship:

$$\text{Purchasing power of the U.S. dollar} = \frac{1}{\begin{array}{c}\text{Cost of Living Index} \\ \text{where goods and services} \\ \text{are sold in dollars}\end{array}} \times 100$$

As an illustration, if the American CPI stood at 175 in the year 2000 and was equal to 100 in 1982–84, the U.S. dollar's relative purchasing power would have fallen to

$$\frac{1}{175} \times 100 = 0.57$$

between 1982–84 and 2000. In other words, the purchasing power of the average U.S. dollar in 2000 was just 57 percent of its purchasing power roughly two decades earlier (1982–84). On average, one dollar at the end of the twentieth century bought only about 57 percent of what it would have purchased in 1982–84.

These dramatic changes in the purchasing power of money, even in the United States where inflation is relatively modest, give us a very stern warning. We should get into the habit of thinking in terms of **real** or "purchasing power adjusted" values of things—incomes, goods, services, financial assets such as bonds, stocks, bank deposits, and so on— rather than only in terms of their **nominal** (or face) values, which can be highly misleading in periods of significant inflation or deflation.

Questions *to Help You Study*

7. What do the following terms mean?

    deficit-budget unit (DBU)

    surplus-budget unit (SBU)

    balanced-budget unit (BBU)

    Why are the above concepts important?

8. Which were you last year—a deficit-, surplus-, or balanced-budget unit? Why is it important to know?

9. Explain what *money* is. What are its principal functions or roles within the system of money and capital markets? within the economy?

10. Does money have any serious limitations as a financial asset within the financial system? What are these limitations?

11. Can you distinguish between *inflation* and *deflation?* What do they have to do with money, if anything?

12. Would you expect to find a relationship between money supply growth and inflation or deflation? What kind of a relationship would you expect to prevail?

THE EVOLUTION OF FINANCIAL TRANSACTIONS

Financial systems are never static. They change constantly in response to shifting demands from the public, the development of new technology, and changes in laws and regulations. Competition in the financial marketplace forces financial institutions to respond to public need by developing better and more convenient financial services. Over time, the global system of financial markets has evolved from simple to more complex ways of carrying out financial transactions. The growth of industrial centers with enormous capital investment needs and the emergence of a huge middle-class of savers have played major roles in the gradual evolution of the financial system.

Whether simple or complex, all financial systems perform at least one basic function. They move scarce funds from those who save and lend (surplus-budget units) to those who wish to borrow and invest (deficit-budget units). In the process, money is exchanged for financial assets. However, the transfer of funds from savers to borrowers can be accomplished in at least three different ways. We label these methods of funds transfer: (1) direct

EXHIBIT 2–4 **Direct Finance** Direct lending gives rise to direct claims against borrowers.

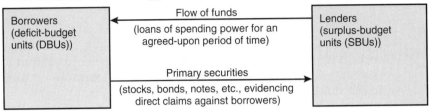

finance, (2) semidirect finance, and (3) indirect finance. Most financial systems have evolved gradually over time from direct and semidirect finance toward greater reliance on indirect finance.

Direct Finance

With the direct financing technique, borrower and lender meet each other and exchange funds in return for financial assets without the help of a third party to bring them together. You engage in **direct finance** when you borrow money from a friend and give him or her your IOU, or when you purchase stocks or bonds directly from the company issuing them. We usually call the claims arising from direct finance *primary securities* because they flow directly from the borrower to the ultimate lender of funds. (Exhibit 2–4 illustrates the process of direct financing between borrowers and lenders.)

Direct finance is the simplest method of carrying out financial transactions and most financial systems in history started out using direct finance. However, it has a number of serious limitations. For one thing, both borrower and lender must desire to exchange the *same amount* of funds at the *same time*. More important, the lender must be willing to accept the borrower's IOU, which may be quite risky or slow to mature. Clearly, there must be a coincidence of wants between surplus- and deficit-budget units in terms of the amount and form of a loan. Without that fundamental coincidence, direct finance breaks down.

Another problem is that both lender and borrower must frequently incur substantial *information costs* simply to find each other. The borrower may have to contact many lenders before finding the one surplus-budget unit (SBU) with just the right amount of funds and a willingness to take on the borrower's IOU. Not surprisingly, direct finance soon gives way to other methods of carrying out financial transactions as money and capital markets develop.

Semidirect Finance

Early in the history of most financial systems, a new form of financial transaction called **semidirect finance** soon appears. Some individuals and business firms become securities brokers and dealers whose essential function is to bring surplus-budget (SBU) and deficit-budget (DBU) units together, thereby reducing information costs (see Exhibit 2–5).

We must distinguish here between a broker and a dealer in securities. A *broker* is merely an individual or financial institution who provides information concerning possible purchases and sales of securities. Either a buyer or a seller of securities may contact a broker, whose job is simply to bring buyers and sellers together. A *dealer* also serves as an intermediary between buyers and sellers, but the dealer actually acquires the seller's securities in the hope of marketing them at a later time at a favorable price. Dealers take a "position of risk" because, by purchasing securities outright for their own portfolios, they are subject to losses if those securities decline in value.

Semidirect finance is an improvement over direct finance in a number of ways. It lowers the search (information) costs for participants in the financial markets. Frequently, a dealer will split up a large issue of primary securities into smaller units affordable by even

EXHIBIT 2–5 **Semidirect Finance** Direct lending with the aid of market makers who assist in the sale of direct claims against borrowers.

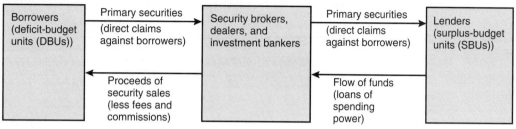

EXHIBIT 2–6
**Major Financial
Institutions Active in
the Money and
Capital Markets**

Financial Intermediaries

Depository institutions:
  Commercial banks
  Nonbank thrifts:
    Savings and loan associations
    Savings banks
    Credit unions
    Money market funds
Other financial intermediaries:
  Finance companies
  Government credit agencies
  Mortgage companies

Contractual institutions:
  Life insurance companies
  Property-casualty insurers
  Pension funds
Investment institutions:
  Investment companies (mutual funds)
  Real estate investment trusts

Other Financial Institutions

Investment bankers   Security brokers   Security dealers

---

buyers of modest means and, thereby, expand the flow of savings into investment. In addition, brokers and dealers facilitate the development of secondary markets in which securities can be offered for resale.

Despite the important contribution of brokers and dealers to the functioning of the global financial system, the semidirect finance approach is not without its limitations. The ultimate lender still winds up holding the borrower's securities, and, therefore, the lender must be willing to accept the risk and maturity characteristics of the borrower's IOUs. There still must be a fundamental coincidence of wants and needs between surplus- and deficit-budget units for semidirect financial transactions to take place.

Indirect Finance

The limitations of both direct and semidirect finance stimulated the development of **indirect finance** carried out with the help of *financial intermediaries.* Financial intermediaries active in today's global markets include commercial banks, insurance companies, credit unions, finance companies, savings and loan associations, savings banks, pension funds, mutual funds, and similar organizations. (See Exhibit 2–6.) Their fundamental role in the financial system is to serve both ultimate lenders and borrowers but in a much more complete way than brokers and dealers do. Financial intermediaries issue securities of their own—often called **secondary securities**—to ultimate lenders and at the same time accept IOUs from borrowers—**primary securities** (see Exhibit 2–7).

The secondary securities issued by financial intermediaries include such familiar financial instruments as checking and savings accounts, life insurance policies, annuities, and

EXHIBIT 2–7   **Indirect Finance**   The financial intermediation of funds.

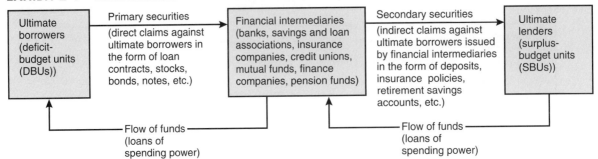

shares in a mutual fund. For the most part, these securities share several common characteristics. They generally carry *low risk of default.* For example, most deposits held in banks and credit unions are insured by an agency of government (in the United States, for amounts up to $100,000). Moreover, the majority of secondary securities can be acquired in *small denominations,* affordable by savers of limited means. For the most part, secondary securities are liquid and, therefore, can be converted quickly into cash with little risk of significant loss. Financial intermediaries in recent years have tried to make savings as convenient as possible through the mail and by plastic card, computer terminal, and telephone in order to reduce transactions costs to the saver.

Financial intermediaries accept primary securities from those who need credit and, in doing so, take on financial assets that many savers, especially those with limited funds and limited knowledge of the market, would find unacceptable. For example, many large corporations require billions of dollars in credit financing each year—sums that would make it impractical to deal directly with thousands of small savers. By pooling the resources of scores of small savings accounts, however, a large financial intermediary frequently can service the credit needs of several large firms simultaneously. In addition, many primary securities, even those issued by some of the largest borrowers, are not readily marketable and carry sizable risk of borrower default—a situation usually not acceptable to the small saver. By issuing its own securities, attractive to ultimate lenders (savers or SBUs), and accepting primary securities from ultimate borrowers (DBUs), the financial intermediary acts to satisfy the financial needs of both surplus- and deficit-budget units in the economy.

To learn more about the role of financial intermediaries in the economy see www.ny.frb.org

One of the benefits of the development of efficient financial intermediation (indirect finance) has been to smooth out consumption spending by households and investment spending by businesses over time, despite variations in income, because intermediation makes saving and borrowing easier and safer. Financial intermediation permits a given amount of saving in the global economy to finance a greater amount of investment than would have occurred without the presence of intermediation.

Interestingly enough, finance theory suggests that in a perfect world with perfect competition and where the public has perfect access to information at little or no cost, financial intermediaries probably would *not* exist. Rather, it is *imperfections* in the financial system (where, for example, some groups do not have access to relevant financial information, lack necessary financial expertise, or face prohibitive information costs) that help explain why there are financial intermediaries and why they have grown to be such huge and important institutions within the financial system. Financial intermediaries overcome inefficiencies or frictions in the financial marketplace and reduce the cost to society of moving information and wealth among households, businesses, and governments, providing access to economies of scale (information cost savings) that would otherwise not be available to many (mostly smaller) units in the economy. Financial intermediaries improve the real world efficiency of the money and capital markets in allocating the daily flow of capital through the global marketplace toward its best possible uses. How well financial intermediaries work is a key determinant of which countries have the largest and strongest economies.

RELATIVE SIZE AND IMPORTANCE OF MAJOR FINANCIAL INSTITUTIONS

Financial intermediaries and other financial institutions differ greatly in their relative importance within any nation's financial system. Measured by total financial assets, for example, *commercial banks* dominate the United States' financial system, as shown in Exhibit 2–8. The more than $6 trillion in financial assets held by U.S. banks represent about one-quarter of the total resources of all U.S. financial institutions. By some measures banks appear to have lost some of their market share to nonbank financial institutions (such as mutual funds), who are often less regulated and offer more flexible service options. In most countries, however, banks still represent the dominant financial institution. Lagging well behind banks are *savings and loans associations*—another deposit-type financial intermediary active primarily in the U.S. mortgage market.

Very similar in sources and uses of funds to savings and loans are *savings banks* (headquartered in the United States mainly along the Atlantic coast), which attract small savings deposits from individuals and families. The fourth major kind of deposit-type financial intermediary, the *credit union,* was also created to attract small savings deposits from individuals and families and make loans to credit union members.

When the assets of all four deposit-type intermediaries—commercial banks, savings and loans, savings banks, and credit unions—are combined, they make up about one-third of the total financial assets of all U.S. financial institutions. The remainder of the sector's

EXHIBIT 2–8
Total Financial Assets Held by U.S. Financial Institutions, Selected Years ($ Billions at Year-End)

Financial Institutions	1960	1970	1980	1990	2000
Financial intermediaries:					
Commercial banks	$224	$489	$1,248	$3,340	$6,488
Savings and loan associations and savings banks	111	252	794	1,358	1,219
Life insurance companies	116	201	464	1,367	3,204
Private pension funds	38	110	413	1,629	4,587
Investment companies (mutual funds)	17	47	64	602	4,457
State and local government pension funds	20	60	198	820	2,290
Finance companies	28	63	199	611	1,138
Property-casualty insurance companies	26	50	174	534	872
Money market funds	—	—	74	498	1,812
Credit unions	6	18	72	202	441
Mortgage companies	—	—	16	49	36
Real estate investment trusts	—	4	6	13	62
Other financial institutions:					
Security brokers and dealers	7	16	36	262	1,221

Source: Board of Governors of the Federal Reserve System, *Flow of Funds Accounts: Financial Assets and Liabilities,* selected years.

financial assets are held by a highly diverse group of nondeposit financial institutions. *Life insurance companies,* which protect policyholders against the risks of premature death and disability, are among the most important nondeposit institutions and rank fourth behind commercial banks in total assets. The other type of insurance firm—*property-casualty insurers*—offers a far wider array of policies to reduce the risk of loss associated with crime, weather damage, and personal negligence. Among the fastest-growing financial institutions are *pension funds,* which protect their customers against the risk of outliving their sources of income in the retirement years. Private pensions now rank second behind commercial banks in total assets held within the U.S. financial system, and pensions are also growing rapidly in other nations around the world (see again Exhibit 2–8).

Other important financial institutions include finance companies, investment companies, money market funds, and real estate investment trusts. *Finance companies* lend money to businesses and consumers to meet short-term working capital and long-term investment needs. *Investment companies* (or mutual funds) pool the funds contributed by thousands of savers by selling shares and then investing in securities sold in the open market and have represented one of the fastest growing of all financial intermediaries in recent years as more savers become concerned about preparing for retirement and other long-term financial needs. A specialized type of investment company is the *money market fund,* which accepts savings (share) accounts from businesses and individuals and places those funds in high-quality, short-term (money market) securities. Also related to investment companies are *real estate investment trusts,* one of the smallest members of the financial institutions sector, which invest mainly in commercial and residential properties. Finally, at the bottom of the list, size-wise, are *mortgage companies,* which facilitate the raising of credit to construct new businesses and homes.

CLASSIFICATION OF FINANCIAL INSTITUTIONS

Financial institutions may be grouped in a variety of different ways. One of the most important distinctions is between **depository institutions** (commercial banks, savings and loan associations, savings banks, and credit unions); **contractual institutions** (insurance companies and pension funds); and **investment institutions** (investment companies, money market funds, and real estate investment trusts). Depository institutions derive the bulk of their loanable funds from deposit accounts sold to the public. Contractual institutions attract funds by offering legal contracts to protect the saver against risk (such as an insurance policy or retirement account). Investment institutions sell shares to the public and invest the proceeds in stocks, bonds, and other assets.

PORTFOLIO (FINANCIAL-ASSET) DECISIONS BY FINANCIAL INTERMEDIARIES AND OTHER FINANCIAL INSTITUTIONS

The management of a financial institution is called on daily to make *portfolio decisions*—that is, *deciding what financial assets to buy or sell.* A number of factors affect these critical decisions. For example, the *relative rate of return and risk* attached to different financial assets will affect the composition of the institution's portfolio. Obviously, if management is interested in maximizing profits and has minimal aversion to risk, it will tend to pursue the highest yielding financial assets available, such as corporate bonds and stocks. A more risk-averse institution, on the other hand, is likely to surrender some yield in return for the greater safety available from acquiring government bonds and high-quality money market instruments.

The *cost, volatility, and maturity of incoming funds* provided by surplus-budget units also has a significant impact on the financial assets acquired by financial institutions. Commercial banks, for example, derive a substantial portion of their funds from checking accounts, which are relatively inexpensive but highly volatile. Such an institution will tend to concentrate its lending activities in short- and medium-term loans to avoid an embarrassing shortage of cash (liquidity). On the other hand, a financial institution such as a pension fund, which receives a stable and predictable inflow of savings, is largely freed from concern over short-term liquidity needs. It is able to invest heavily in long-term financial assets. Thus, the *hedging principle*—the approximate matching of the maturity of financial assets held with liabilities taken on—is an important guide for choosing those financial assets that a financial institution will hold in its portfolio.

Decisions on what financial assets to acquire and what financial assets to issue to the public are also influenced by the *size* of the individual financial institution. Larger institutions frequently can take advantage of greater *diversification* in their sources and uses of funds. This means that the overall risk of a portfolio of financial assets can be reduced by acquiring financial assets from many different borrowers. Similarly, a larger financial institution can contact a broader range of savers and achieve greater stability in its incoming flows of funds. At the same time, through *economies of scale* (size), larger financial institutions can often sell financial services at lower cost per unit and pass those cost savings along to their customers.

Finally, *regulations and competition,* two external forces, play major roles in shaping the financial assets acquired or issued by a financial institution. Because they hold the bulk of the public's savings and are so crucial to economic growth and investment activity, financial intermediaries are among the most heavily regulated of all business firms. Commercial banks are prohibited from investing in low-quality or highly volatile loans and securities in many countries. Insurance companies and pension funds must restrict any asset purchases to those a "prudent person" would most likely choose. Most government regulations in this sector pertain to the assets that can be acquired, the adequacy of net worth, and the services that can be offered to the public. Such regulations are designed to promote competition and ensure the safety of the public's funds.

DISINTERMEDIATION OF FUNDS

One factor that in recent years has influenced the financial assets selected by financial institutions for their portfolios is the phenomenon of **disintermediation.** Exactly opposite from the intermediation of funds, disintermediation means the withdrawal of funds from a financial intermediary by ultimate lenders (savers) and the lending of those funds directly to ultimate borrowers. In other words, disintermediation involves the shifting of funds from indirect finance to direct and semidirect finance (see Exhibit 2–9).

You engage in disintermediation when you remove funds from a savings account at the local bank or savings and loan association and purchase common stock, government bonds, or other financial assets through a broker. The phenomenon is more likely to occur during

EXHIBIT 2–9
Financial Disintermediation

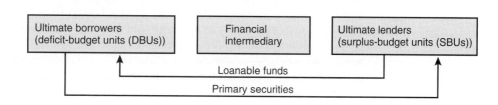

Financial Developments
The Emergence of Giant Banks within the Financial System

For many decades the U.S. financial system has been regarded as a "security-dominated financial system" rather than as a "bank-dominated financial system" like that in Japan, China, and Germany. Leading security brokers and dealers, such as Merrill Lynch, Morgan Stanley, and Goldman Sachs, accounted for a growing share of financial transactions and financial asset holdings. In contrast, U.S. banks experienced dramatic declines in the proportion of financial-system assets they held beginning in the nineteenth century and continuing almost to the end of the twentieth century.

Within the last few years, however, the biggest banking firms have moved closer to domination of *both* the U.S. and foreign banking systems (especially in Europe). Moreover, with greater freedom granted under more lenient laws and government regulations to acquire nonbank businesses, such as security dealers and insurance companies, the volume of consolidated assets and equity capital held by major banks has gained some ground on their largest nonbank business rivals, particularly security firms.

One example of banking's powerful inroads into the security underwriting and trading business occurred in 2001 when Citigroup passed Merrill Lynch as the number one security underwriting firm around the globe. Another indicator is the amount of capital invested in leading banks and in security firms of late. For example, the four top U.S. banking companies in 2000—Citigroup, Bank of America, J. P. Morgan Chase, and Credit Suisse–First Boston Corp.—held nearly three times the amount of equity (owner's) capital posted by the four largest security firms in that same year—Merrill Lynch Corporation, Morgan Stanley, Goldman Sachs, and Lehman Brothers.

In their market-share battles with nonbank financial firms banks have made heavy use of their highly diverse services to attract customers away from security firms and other nonbank service providers. For example, a corporation trying to raise new capital could be persuaded to abandon its association with a security broker or dealer in favor of working with a bank, which could not only issue new stock or bonds through its securities affiliate (i.e., provide security underwriting services) to help fund the corporation, but also grant this corporate customer new loans or lease financing agreements, manage its cash account, and assist in the control of its pension fund. Thus, the biggest banks are gaining market share today by offering their business and household customers "one-stop shopping" for financial services.

periods of high and rapidly rising interest rates, when the higher returns demanded by savers may outpace the interest rates offered by financial intermediaries. Disintermediation forces a financial institution to surrender funds and, if severe, may lead to losses of its assets and ultimate failure. A good example is provided by savings and loan associations which, during the 1980s and early 1990s, lost billions of dollars in assets due to massive withdrawals of funds by worried depositors who feared the loss of their savings. Although intermediaries are forced to be more liquid and reduce their credit-granting activities during periods of disintermediation, there is no evidence that the *total* flow of credit through the financial system is reduced during such periods.

New Types of Disintermediation

Some authorities argue that new forms of disintermediation have appeared over the past two decades, some initiated by financial intermediaries themselves and some by their borrowing customers. For example, some banks and savings and loan associations in recent years have begun to sell off their loans because of difficulties in raising capital. At the same time, some of the largest borrowing customers of these intermediaries have learned how to raise funds directly from the open market (i.e., through direct and semidirect finance) rather than borrowing from a bank or other institutional lender. These new forms of disintermediation have tended not only to shrink the size of some financial intermediaries but also to gradually reduce somewhat the overall importance of banks—still the most important financial intermediary—within the global financial system. A substantial volume of funds today flow through the financial system via direct and semidirect finance as well as through indirect finance.

BANK-DOMINATED VERSUS SECURITY-DOMINATED FINANCIAL SYSTEMS

While many lesser-developed financial systems are often referred to as *bank-dominated financial systems* because of the dominance of banks and similar financial intermediaries in supplying credit and attracting savings, many financial systems today are becoming *security-dominated financial systems,* in which traditional intermediaries play somewhat lesser roles in the lending and saving process and growing numbers of borrowers sell securities (such as stocks and bonds) directly to the public to raise the loanable funds they need. For example, several nations in Asia today find themselves in transition from being heavily bank-dominated financial systems to increasingly security-oriented financial systems, though most of these countries have a long way to go in significantly reducing bankers' current dominant position within their financial systems. In the long run, this trend toward more security-dominated financial systems may result in greater competition within the financial marketplace and, perhaps, higher returns for many savers.

Questions *to Help You Study*

13. What is *direct finance? Semidirect finance? Indirect finance?*

14. In the evolution of the financial system which came first—direct, indirect, or semidirect finance? Why do you think this is so?

15. What are the essential differences between *primary* and *secondary securities?* Why are these instruments important to the operation of the financial system?

16. In what different ways are financial institutions classified or grouped? Why are such classifications or groupings important in helping us understand what different financial institutions do and what kinds of financial assets they prefer to hold?

17. Which financial institutions are the *largest* within the financial system? Why do you think these are the largest financial institutions?

18. What factors influence the particular financial assets each financial institution acquires?

19. What is *disintermediation* and why is it important? How has disintermediation changed in recent years?

20. Please explain the difference between a *bank-dominated financial system* and a *security-dominated financial system?* Why might this distinction between types of financial systems be an important one?

Summary of the Chapter

The global financial system of money and capital markets performs the important function of channeling savings into investment. In that process a unique kind of asset in the economy—a *financial asset*—is created.

- Financial assets represent *claims against the income and assets* of the individuals and institutions issuing those claims. There are three major categories of financial assets—*money, debt,* and *equities.* A fourth instrument, *derivatives,* is closely related to financial assets, deriving its value from these assets.

- *Money* is among the most important of all financial assets in the economy because it serves as a medium of exchange to facilitate purchases of goods and services, a standard for valuing all items bought and sold, a store of value (purchasing power) when needed in the future, and a reserve of liquidity (immediate spending power). Despite all these advantages, money has a weakness—susceptibility to inflation or a rising price level, because its rate of return or yield is normally so low. In contrast, the financial assets represented by *debt* or *equity* securities, and often by *derivatives* as well, carry greater average yields but, unlike money, may incur loss when converted into immediately spendable funds.

- The creation of financial assets occurs within the financial system through three different channels—direct, semidirect, or indirect finance. *Direct finance* involves the direct exchange of financial assets for money in which the borrower and lender meet directly with each other to conduct their business. *Semidirect finance* involves the use of a broker or dealer to help bring borrower and lender together and, thereby, reduce information costs. *Indirect finance* refers to the creation of financial assets by financial intermediaries who accept primary securities from ultimate borrowers as their principal earning assets and issue secondary securities to ultimate savers to raise funds.

- *Financial intermediaries* (such as banks, pension funds, and insurance companies) have grown to dominate most financial systems today due to their greater expertise, efficiency, and capability in diversifying away some of the risks involved in lending money.

- One of the most serious management problems encountered by financial intermediaries is *disintermediation*—the loss of funds from a financial intermediary to direct or semidirect finance. Much of the disintermediation experienced by modern financial intermediaries has occurred due to financial innovation within the global financial system. Borrowers (issuers of financial assets) have found new ways to obtain the funds they need without going through a financial intermediary.

- Finally, financial systems around the world appear to fall into one of two broad categories—*bank-dominated financial systems* and *security-dominated financial systems*. In bank-dominated systems the majority of financial assets arise from the banking system and when banks get into trouble the financial system itself may experience difficulties with risk exposure and slower growth. In security-dominated financial systems, on the other hand, security brokers and dealers tend to be leaders in the financial system and often provide the greatest volume of funds to those in need of new capital. Thus, security-dominated financial systems are heavily dependent upon direct and semidirect finance (i.e., the open market), while bank-dominated financial systems tend to rely heavily upon financial intermediaries (indirect finance) for the raising of new funds.

Key Terms

Financial asset, *26*	Inflation, *37*	Secondary securities, *41*
Money, *27*	Deflation, *37*	Primary securities, *41*
Equities, *27*	Price indices, *37*	Depository institutions, *44*
Debt securities, *27*	Real value, *39*	Contractual institutions, *44*
Derivatives, *27*	Nominal value, *39*	Investment institutions, *44*
Internal financing, *29*	Direct finance, *40*	Disintermediation, *45*
Deficit-budget unit, *33*	Semidirect finance, *40*	
Surplus-budget unit, *33*	Indirect finance, *41*	

Problems

1. In a recent year, the various sectors of the economy listed below reported the following *net* changes in their financial assets and liabilities (measured in billions of dollars):

	Net Acquisitions of Financial Assets	Net Increase in Liabilities
Households	$434.6	$292.0
Farm businesses	2.7	−2.5
Nonfarm noncorporate businesses	8.7	35.0
Nonfinancial corporations	84.9	127.8
State and local governments	74.8	60.6
U.S. government	13.0	236.3
Foreign individuals and institutions	150.7	29.0
Federal Reserve System	32.0	31.2
Commercial banking	256.0	245.7
Private nonbank financial institutions	556.9	590.7

Using these figures, indicate which sectors were deficit-budget sectors and which were surplus-budget for the year under study. Were there any balanced-budget sectors? For all these sectors *combined*, were more funds loaned or more funds borrowed? Why do you think there is a discrepancy between total funds loaned and total funds borrowed?

2. Consider the balance sheets shown on page 50 for a household (individual or family), business firm, and government—the only units present in a *closed* economy. Identify which economic units above are completely self-financed. Which economic units above are deficit-budget units? Surplus-budget units? Balanced-budget units? Referring to Equations 2–4, 2–5, and 2–6 in this chapter, do these equations hold for the units depicted below? Please demonstrate.

3. In this chapter, a number of different types of financial transactions were discussed: direct finance, semidirect finance, indirect finance (intermediation), and disintermediation. Examine each of the following financial transactions and indicate which type it is. (*Note:* Some of the transactions described below involve more than one type of financial transaction. Be sure to identify *all* types of transactions involved.)

   a. Borrowing money from a bank.
   b. Purchasing a life insurance policy.
   c. Selling shares of stock through a broker.
   d. Withdrawing money from a savings deposit account and lending it to a friend.
   e. Selling shares of stock to a colleague at work.
   f. Your corporation's contracting with an investment banker to help sell its bonds.
   g. Writing a bank check to purchase stock from your broker.

HOUSEHOLD			BUSINESS FIRM			GOVERNMENT		
Assets		**Liability and Net Worth**	**Assets**		**Liability and Net Worth**	**Assets**		**Liability and Net Worth**
Cash	$ 15	Notes payable $ 20	Cash	$ 10	Bonds $ 60	Loans	$ 20	Securities $ 50
						Buildings	85	
Securities	65	Taxes payable 15	Securities	45	Taxes payable 40	Equipment	30	Money 25
Automobile	5	Net worth 135	Truck	25	Net worth 90	Tax		Net worth 140
Home	75		Plant	60		receivables	55	
			Equipment	20				
Other			Other			Other		
real assets	10		real assets	30		real assets	25	
		Total liabilities and			Total liabilities and			Total liabilities and
Total assets	$170	net worth $170	Total assets	$190	net worth $190	Total assets	$215	net worth $215

4. ITT Corporation in the most recent period reported current sales receipts of $542 million, current operating expenditures of $577 million, and net new debt issued of $5 million. What change in holdings of financial assets must have occurred over the period? Was ITT a deficit-, surplus-, or balanced-budget unit in the most recent period? Explain why.

5. Demonstrate that, for any given time period for any economic unit, current receipts plus additions (positive or negative)' to debt and equities outstanding must equal current expenditures plus additions (positive or negative) to holdings of financial assets. Please explain exactly what this statement means.

6. Ajax Corporation rejects a loan offered by its London bank and decides instead to issue Euronotes through security dealer Credit Suisse into the global financial marketplace in order to raise capital for a new project. What type of financial transaction (funds transfer) has been rejected by Ajax and what type of financial transaction (funds transfer) is Ajax going to use to raise the loanable funds it requires? If financial transactions of this latter type continue to grow in relative importance within the global financial system, how will this trend ultimately change the international system of money and capital markets? What impact do you think this might have on savers and borrowers within the global financial marketplace?

7. Suppose the GDP deflator index has a base period of 100 in 1990 and by the year 2001 the deflator had an index value of 139. What was the percentage increase in this nation's price level? Suppose the deflator, instead, had dropped to 89.6 by 2001. What change in the national price level occurred?

8. What happened to the purchasing power of the U.S. dollar if the base period for the cost of living index is 1980 = 100 and the index reached the following levels in the indicated years?
   a. 1985 — 116
   b. 1990 — 127
   c. 1995 — 134
   d. 2000 — 151

Questions about the Web and the Money and Capital Markets

1. If you wanted to track your portfolio holdings of financial assets and explore possibilities for creating a new investment portfolio, where might you look on the Web?
2. What is *inflation* as defined on the Web? If you wanted to calculate the effects of inflation on your investment portfolio or other assets you hold where could you look for the information on the World Wide Web?

Selected References

Brown, Paul M. "Experimental Evidence on Money as a Medium of Exchange." *Journal of Economic Dynamics and Control* XX, no. 4 (April 1996), pp. 583–600.

Duffy, John, and Jack Ochs. "Emergence of Money as a Medium of Exchange: An Experimental Study." *American Economic Review* LXXXII, no. 4 (September 1999), pp. 847–77.

Fitzgerald, Terry J. "Money Growth and Inflation." *Economic Commentary,* Federal Reserve Bank of Cleveland, August 1, 1999.

Gurley, John, and Edward S. Shaw. *Money in a Theory of Finance.* Washington, DC: Brookings Institution, 1960.

Revell, Jack. *The Recent Evolution of the Financial System.* New York: MacMillan, May 1997.

Teplin, Albert M. "The U.S. Flow of Funds Accounts and Their Uses." *Federal Reserve Bulletin,* July 2001, pp. 431–41.

Trejos, Alberto. "Incentives to Produce Quality and the Liquidity of Money." *Economic Theory* IX, no. 2 (February 1997), pp. 355–65.

Chapter Three

Key Sources of Financial Information

Learning Objectives in This Chapter

- You will be able to identify the most important sources of information about the money and capital markets and the global financial system.

- You will discover why the efficient distribution of information within the financial system is so important and what can happen when relevant financial information is not readily available to all market participants.

- You will understand how any individual or institution active in the financial marketplace can keep track of the prices of financial assets and changes in market interest rates.

- You will learn about both the content and the concepts behind the *Flow of Funds Accounts of the United States,* published by the Federal Reserve System, and discover what is meant by "social accounting."

What's in This Chapter? Key Topics Outline

The Efficient Markets Hypothesis: Its Assumptions and Forms

Insider Trading

Asymmetric Information

Problems of Asymmetry: Lemons, Adverse Selection, Moral Hazard

Efficiency and Asymmetry in the Real World

Remedies for Asymmetry

Sources of Information: Bonds and Notes, Corporate Stock

Information on Security Issuers and the Economy

Social Accounting Systems

The Flow of Funds Accounts: Content, Uses, and Limitations

INTRODUCTION

Every day in the money and capital markets, individuals and institutions must make important financial decisions. For those who plan to borrow, for example, key decisions must be made concerning the timing of a request for credit and exactly where the necessary funds should be raised. Lenders of funds must make decisions on when and where to invest their limited resources, considering such factors as the risk and expected return on loans and securities available in the financial marketplace. Government policymakers also are intimately involved in the financial decision-making process. It is the responsibility of government to ensure that the financial markets function smoothly in channeling savings into investment and in creating a volume of credit sufficient to support business and commerce.

Sound financial decisions require adequate and accurate *financial information.* Borrowers, lenders, and those who make financial policy require data on the prices and yields attached to individual loans and securities today and the prices and yields likely to prevail in the future. A borrower, for example, may decide to postpone taking out a loan if it appears that the cost of credit will be significantly lower six months from now than it is today. Those who wish to attempt a forecast of future interest rates and security prices need information concerning the expected supply of new securities brought to market and the expected demand for those securities. Because economic conditions exert a profound impact on the money and capital markets, the financial decision maker must also be aware of economic data series that reflect trends in employment, prices, and related types of information.

What are the principal sources of financial information? Where do financial decision makers go to find the data they need? We may divide the sources of information relied on by financial decision makers into five broad groups: (1) debt security prices and yields, (2) stock prices and dividend yields, (3) information on security issuers, (4) general economic and financial conditions, and (5) social accounting data. In this chapter, we will discuss the most important sources of each of these different kinds of information.

EFFICIENT MARKETS AND ASYMMETRIC INFORMATION

Before we examine the principal sources of information available to financial market participants, however, we need to be aware of a great debate going on in the fields of finance and economics today concerning the availability and cost of information. One view, referred to as the **efficient markets hypothesis,** contends that information relevant to the pricing (valuation) of loans, securities, and other financial assets is readily available to *all* borrowers and lenders at *negligible cost.* The other view, called **asymmetry** or the concept of asymmetric information, argues that the financial marketplace contains pockets of inefficiency in the availability and use of information. Some market players—for example, professional lenders of funds, auditors, attorneys, journalists, or members of management and the boards of directors of corporations—may possess special information that enables them to get a more accurate picture of the value and risk of certain assets. These "insiders" allegedly can earn excess returns by selectively trading assets based on the special information they have been able to acquire—information that would be costly for others to obtain.

In this chapter, we briefly sketch out these two contrasting views—efficient markets and asymmetric information—of the cost and availability of relevant information to participants and decision makers in the financial marketplace.

Information sources about the financial markets and the various institutions that operate within them is now found extensively on the World Wide Web. Indeed, we often say that the money and capital markets are among the world's most carefully watched markets every day, and the World Wide Web has made that process of "market watching" a whole lot easier than it used to be.

Among the key institutions that provide a welter of on-line information about the financial markets, their behavior, and their rules are the Securities and Exchange Commission at *www.sec.gov* and the Federal Reserve System at *www.federalreserve.gov.* The Federal Reserve and other central banks around the world also provide extensive data on the performance of national economies and financial markets, situated in their respective countries. You can usually find this central bank–supplied information for a particular country simply by entering the name of each nation's central bank (e.g., the Bank of England or the European Central Bank) in a Web search.

Many financial institutions and information sources have also made it far easier to track daily money and capital market movements. Among the more popular of these are Lycos Finance at *www.quote.com* and Stock Pick Central at *www.stockpickcentral.com.*

The Efficient Markets Hypothesis (EMH)

The efficient markets hypothesis (hereafter EMH) suggests that *all* information that has a bearing on the market value of stocks, bonds, and other financial assets will be used to value (price) those assets. *An efficient market does not waste information.* Under the terms of the EMH, the money and capital markets will not consistently ignore information that can earn profits, so there won't be any profitable trades that are not made (at least not for very long).

For example, if an individual has savings to invest in stocks and bonds, he or she will seek out information on the financial condition of the business firms issuing those securities, the quality of their management and products, the strength of each firm's industry, and the condition of the economy in which each firm operates. Each individual investor will rationally use *all* of the available information relevant to valuing the stocks and bonds he or she might wish to buy. Because all investors are likely to be seeking the same information for the same reasons, the current market price of any financial asset will reflect all relevant information that investors as a group have been able to obtain regarding that asset's true value. Because all of the information available has been used to establish the value of financial instruments, no single user of that same information can earn "excess returns" by trading on information available to all. Rather, in an efficient marketplace, each financial asset will generate an "ordinary" or "normal" rate of return commensurate with its level of risk.[1]

---

[1]By "excess returns" we mean the excess amount of actual returns earned on an asset above its "expected," "ordinary," or "normal" return, based on the amount of risk the asset carries. Thus, if AR_i represents the actual return (including interest or dividends and any price gains) and $E(R_i)$ equals the "normal" return (or the return expected on the asset given its level of risk), then the excess return (EXR) must be $EXR_i = AR_i - E(R_i)$.

Under the terms of the widely used capital asset pricing model (CAPM), the *expected return* on the *i*th financial asset will be equal to

$$E(R_i) = r_F + \beta_i[E(R_M) - r_F] \qquad \textbf{(3–1)}$$

where $E(R_i)$ measures the expected return on the *i*th asset; $E(R_M)$ is the expected return on the market's entire collection of assets (i.e., the whole market portfolio, or *M*); β_i is a measure of an individual asset's risk exposure compared to the risk exposure of the whole market portfolio; and r_F is the risk-free interest rate (often approximated by the return on government bonds). Beta (β_i) is equal to the covariance (*Cov*) between the returns on an individual asset or portfolio of assets (R_i) with the return on the market's whole portfolio of assets (R_M) divided by the variance of the return on the whole market's portfolio (*Var*). Thus,

$$\beta_i = Cov(R_i, R_M)/Var(R_M) \qquad \textbf{(3–2)}$$

The covariance (*Cov*) of the returns on an individual asset or portfolio of assets (R_i) with the return on the market's entire portfolio of assets (R_M) is the product of the correlation between asset and marketwide returns times the standard deviation of individual asset returns times the standard deviation of returns on the market's whole portfolio. Beta is sometimes called a measure of an asset's *systematic risk*—the type of risk the whole asset market faces that cannot be eliminated by simple diversification (that is, by simply buying a portfolio of different kinds of assets with varying expected returns).

The term, $\beta_i[E(R_M) - r_F]$, measures the *risk premium*—reward for risk taking—that will be demanded by investors in the money and capital markets before they are willing to buy and hold a risky asset or portfolio of risky assets (such as corporate bonds or stock) instead of holding a risk-free asset (such as a government bond). This risk premium is the product of the financial marketplace's reward for each unit of risk accepted by an investor holding the whole market portfolio (*M*) times the individual asset's own risk level, measured by β_i. (The market's entire portfolio of assets is presumed to have a beta (β) of 1.0 and an expected return of R_M.)

The line or curve described by equation 3–1 above for the CAPM is usually called the *security market line* (SML), as illustrated in Exhibit 3–1. Under the terms of the EMH, any *deviation* of an asset's actual return (AR_i) from its expected return ($E(R_i)$) results in a positive or negative excess return (EXR_i) that must be random with an expected value of zero. For example, as shown in Exhibit 3–2 asset A carries a temporary positive excess rate of return, while asset B carries a temporary negative excess return. However, the yields on all financial assets should lie along, or be very close to, the SML. *If the EMH is correct, any temporary deviation of actual returns from expected returns lying along the SML* (i.e., excess positive or excess negative returns) *should be quickly eliminated as investors react to temporary underpricing* (when an asset's actual return rises *above* its expected return along the SML) *or temporary overpricing of assets* (when an asset's actual return falls *below* its expected return on the SML) *and make changes in their asset portfolios.* Investors in the money and capital markets will react to assets they perceive to be *underpriced* (with positive excess returns) or *overpriced* (with negative excess returns) by buying or selling the temporarily mispriced assets. In short, the discovery of a financial asset whose expected return lies consistently above or below the SML would be a signal of possible market inefficiency, inconsistent with the EMH. This would be true because, according to the EMH, rational market participants use *all* relevant information available to value assets all the time. Because all asset prices instantaneously impound all relevant information concerning asset values in an efficient market, no asset trades that generate consistent excess returns will be available (at least not for very long).

EXHIBIT 3–1

The Security Market Line (SML)

A schedule of expected returns for all assets and portfolios of assets.

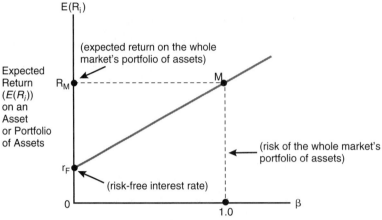

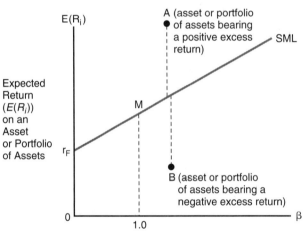

Beta (β) as an Index of Risk of an Individual Asset or Portfolio of Assets Relative to the Risk of the Whole Market's Portfolio of Assets

EXHIBIT 3–2

The Security Market Line (SML) and Assets with Temporary Positive Excess Returns (Underpricing) or Temporary Negative Excess Returns (Overpricing)

Beta (β) as an Index of the Risk of an Individual Asset or Portfolio of Assets Relative to the Risk of the Whole Market's Portfolio of Assets

Moreover, when *new* relevant information reaches the marketplace, the prices (value) of financial assets normally *will* change, and according to the EMH, they will change *quickly* as investors possessing this new information move rapidly to seize any profitable opportunities that appear, bidding up the prices of some assets and lowering the prices of others. And because market prices respond to *new* information, which by its nature is unpredictable, the value of financial assets and services cannot be predicted consistently. If we could consistently predict asset values, this would be evidence of an inefficient market in which not all information is being fully utilized.

The essential contribution that the EMH makes to our understanding of the money and capital markets is to suggest that the current prices of all financial assets represent the *optimal use* of available information. And each asset's price, determined by demand-and-supply forces in the financial marketplace, is an optimal forecast of each asset's fundamental value.

In fact, an asset's current market price is the *best estimate* of that asset's expected fundamental value. However, each asset's fundamental value will vary with the state of the world (e.g., the condition of the economy, and the current concerns of asset buyers about risk) prevailing at the time the asset is being traded. Therefore, the current price of a financial asset equals its expected fundamental value given all possible states of the world recognized by buyers and sellers actively trading in the market. Under the terms of the EMH, the price of an asset must already encompass *all* of the information relevant to the valuation of that asset, including all present and past information.

Different Forms of the EMH

In recent years, the EMH has been split into three different versions based on what each assumes to be true about the availability and cost of information. These three versions of the EMH are:

To examine the evidence for and against the efficient markets hypothesis see *www.investorhome.com*

1. *Weak form of the EMH,* which argues that the current prices of financial assets contain all information that buyers and sellers have been able to obtain on the past trading of those assets: their *price history and past volume of trading.* Moreover, this past price and trading information is publicly available and of negligible cost to obtain. No one buyer or seller of financial assets can earn excess profits beyond those that are normal for the amount of risk taken on from trading on this historical price and volume information. If this were not true, investors would have figured out long ago how to profit from such historical data and asset prices would have been adjusted accordingly, eliminating further opportunities for exceptional returns.

2. *Semistrong form of the EMH,* which contends that the current prices of stocks, bonds, and other financial assets already reflect *all publicly available information* affecting the value of these financial instruments, including information about past prices and volume, the financial condition and credit rating of each issuer, any published forecasts, the condition of the economy, and all other relevant information. All buyers and sellers are rational and use all publicly available information to help them value financial assets. No one buyer or seller will, therefore, find opportunities for exceptional profits by trading on publicly available information.

3. *Strong form of the EMH,* which argues that the current prices of financial assets capture *all* the information—*both public and private*—that is relevant to the value of financial instruments. This includes the information possessed by "insiders," such as the officers, directors, and principal owners of a corporation issuing stocks and bonds or even accountants, attorneys, or journalists who work with the company and have access to its privileged information.

Repeated research studies (several of which we will review in Chapter 22) have essentially confirmed the weak and semistrong forms of the EMH. Few opportunities for exceptional profits flowing from trading on past or present publicly available information appear to exist. The strong form of the EMH, however, has aroused the most controversy and resulted in mixed research findings, especially because of the existence of insider trading activities and because of the apparent presence of pockets of special information asymmetrically scattered throughout the financial system.

Insiders and Insider Trading

The word "insiders" has come to have a sinister meaning to most of us. It smacks of something illegal or unfair. Someone has special knowledge or special privileges and can, at will, take advantage of that knowledge or privilege and profit from it, perhaps at someone else's expense. Nowhere is the term "insider" more recognized and more often condemned than in the money and capital markets. The board of directors of a company, its officers or managers, and even many of its staff employees may know something about its condition or performance that the public doesn't know, and may be able to benefit from that knowledge, perhaps by buying or selling the firm's stock in advance before the public becomes aware of what's really going on. Section 10(b)-5 of the Securities and Exchange Act of 1934 forbids any "manipulative or deceptive device" in trading securities, and Section 16(c) of the Securities and Exchange Act requires all trading by insiders to be reported to the Securities and Exchange Commission (SEC) within the first 10 days of the month following the particular month an insider trade has occurred. These insider trades are reported in the SEC's *Official Summary of Insider Transactions.* Recent federal laws have raised the maximum criminal penalties for insider trading up to a million dollars and have allowed jail terms of up to 10 years.

Recent research suggests that **insider trading** frequently "works" in the sense that insiders often win exceptional (abnormal) returns. For example, studies by Keown and Pinkerton (1981) and by Meulbrock (1992) find that nearly half of a stock's rise in price before a major public announcement seems to come from trading by insiders or by others receiving early information. One of the most famous insider trading cases involved Michael Milken, a securities dealer and broker, who worked with numerous companies on their new bond and stock offerings and allegedly used some of the insider information he gained to earn millions of dollars in the financial markets. Ultimately, Milken paid fines in the hundreds of millions of dollars and went to prison for a time, eventually receiving a presidential pardon.

Actually, insiders can use privileged information legally if they provide that information to the public *before* they go into the market to trade securities. However, the number of insider trading cases prosecuted in court has been rising, despite the doubts expressed by some experts that people are consistently hurt by insider trading activity. For example, shouldn't managers who produce performance improvements for their company be able to benefit from the gains they can earn from trading in their firm's stock? Governments penalizing insider trading may actually discourage business managers from taking on risk and from demonstrating their superior managerial capabilities. Other experts argue that businesses themselves, not the government, should decide if they want to permit or prohibit their insiders from trading in their securities. Moreover, insider trading may actually *improve* market efficiency because it tends to result in more rapid information flows and quicker security price adjustments to new information. Securities may be more correctly priced more quickly as a result, and this tends to reduce the risk to investors from owning equity shares in a particular corporation. Thus, the overall informational efficiency of the money and capital markets in pricing assets may actually be improved as a result of some insider trading activity.

The Concept of Asymmetric Information

What if *all* relevant information about the true value of financial assets is *not* readily available or costless to obtain? What would happen if some important information pertinent to decision making were distributed *asymmetrically* so that deep pockets of special knowledge existed in the financial marketplace?

The asymmetric view says that there *are* pockets of special information—a "lumpiness" in the supply of relevant information about financial assets. These pockets may include corporate insiders, journalists, security dealers, and financial analysts who possess unique analytical skills in spotting profitable trades. These possessors of special knowledge need not be operating illegally. Indeed, they may come by their unique talents in assessing value and risk through rigorous schooling and on-the-job training or by virtue of the special location

Financial Developments
What Is Legal and Illegal Insider Trading in the Money and Capital Markets?

Defining what types of insider activity in the money and capital markets are legal and what forms are illegal is one of the toughest distinctions to make, and many experts in the field flatly disagree on the issue. One problem is deciding who an "insider" really is. Certainly the members of the board of directors, management, and employees of a company whose securities are publicly traded would qualify as privileged "insiders." These individuals are said to owe a *fiduciary duty* to their firm to act in their company's best interest and in the best interests of its stockholders (owners). If these people personally benefit from the inside information they possess, they may be charged with breaching their fiduciary duty or with *misappropriating information* that really belongs to their employer. However, most government lawyers would argue that outside consultants, investment bankers, and lawyers under contract to provide advice or other services to a firm also owe a fiduciary duty to that company and could be considered illegal "insiders," breaching their fiduciary duty if they used the information they received to engage in related security trading.

Beyond these particular groups of individuals, however, case law is badly split today on what current laws apply to whom in the insider trading field. Generally speaking, those who clearly have a fiduciary duty because they are paid to work for a firm and could benefit personally from using that firm's information to score profits in the market run the risk of prosecution. However, if you do *not* work for such a firm and

still obtain insider information that you use to score trading profits, there may be no legal violation because there may be no fiduciary responsibility to the security-issuing firm. This happened to a print shop worker in the *Chiarella vs. the United States* case (1986) because of profit-generating information that Mr. Chiarella allegedly obtained while setting copy for the corporate clients of his printing firm. However, Mr. Chiarella went free because the Supreme Court found no evidence that he had a fiduciary duty to the firms whose reports he read.

On the other hand, you might be brought to a trial on misappropriation of information if you are working for a company that has a relationship with another firm and just happen to overhear some valuable, nonpublic information and proceed to trade on it. This happened to a person in the case of *James H. O'Hagan vs. the United States* (1996). Mr. O'Hagan allegedly found out about a proposed acquisition of Pillsbury—a case being worked on by attorneys in his law firm—and allegedly used that information to generate trading profits. Ultimately, the Supreme Court ruled that misappropriation of information had occurred with respect to the defendant's law firm. Unfortunately, the Supreme Court and several circuit courts have mixed records on whether misappropriation of information or the existence of fiduciary duty can be broadly applied to individuals or groups who are not employees or owners of a business firm.

they occupy within the financial system. Every year hundreds of corporations flock to college campuses to hire graduates whom they believe have the potential to become expert judges of the quality of financial assets.

Attempts by those armed with special information to exploit asymmetries in information could have great consequences for the financial marketplace as a whole. For example, if the asymmetric distribution of relevant information exists, there will be differences of opinion (*heterogeneous expectations*) among buyers and sellers of assets. This is particularly true of any estimates of future asset returns (that is, the probability distribution of expected returns from stocks, bonds, and other financial instruments). With differing estimates of value and risk, the prices of financial assets will tend to settle at a "consensus" price, reflecting the average expectation currently prevailing in the financial marketplace.

Moreover, with asymmetrically distributed information, there will be variations in both the quantity and the quality of information available. Unfortunately, most users of financial information cannot easily assess its quality at the time they must pay for it. Thus, considerable incentive exists in the money and capital markets for sellers of information to make wild claims about the quality and value of the information they are selling. It is not clear that the financial markets have yet developed an effective mechanism for policing the quality and truthfulness of information (as exemplified recently by the financial problems of Enron Corp. and Global Crossing), although, over time, those who provide misleading information may suffer a loss of reputation and eventually exit the industry due to lack of demand for their services. In short, the presence of imperfect or "bad" information leads to market inefficiency, thwarts the making of optimal decisions, and may lead to more government intervention in the marketplace in an effort to fix the problems that asymmetrically distributed and poor quality information can create.

The asymmetric information theory does not necessarily contradict the weak and semi-strong forms of the EMH. It concedes that the value of financial assets will capture all publicly available information. Where it departs from the EMH is in believing that some market participants have sufficient access to special information that they can, at times, profit from that information, earning excess returns. Moreover where asymmetries are very strong, a financial market can misfire, misallocate resources, and even collapse.

Problems Informational Asymmetries Can Create: Lemons and Plums

Asymmetries can create many difficulties in the availability and distribution of information. One of the most familiar—often called the *lemons problem*—has confronted used car buyers ever since the automobile was invented. Everyone who has ever purchased a used car is aware of the risks involved in the process. The buyer does not know for sure whether the used automobile he or she is looking at is a real "lemon," a continuing source of trouble and grief as repair bills mount, or if the car is a "plum," a solid piece of transportation that runs and runs with few problems. The seller, in hopes of getting a higher price, has a strong incentive to misrepresent the car as a plum. Unless he or she is convinced this is true, the buyer will probably be unwilling to pay the full price for a plum due to the risk that the car will ultimately turn out to be a lemon. The seller possesses special ("inside") information built up by personal experience with the vehicle; the buyer cannot obtain this information except at considerable cost (such as by hiring a mechanic to do an inspection of the vehicle).

A similar problem confronts the loan officer of a bank. Dozens of customers come in every day asking for loans and claiming they will use the requested funds for a good (hopefully, profitable and legal) purpose that meets the lending institution's credit standards and promising that they will repay their loans on time. Clearly, the loan officer can't be sure without incurring substantial costs which of his or her customers is a lemon or a plum. Equally frustrating, some customers who were plums when they took out their first loan may now be lemons due to changing circumstances, such as the loss of a job or the failure of a business. This asymmetry problem helps us explain why credit rating agencies have become so important to lending institutions that willingly pay the added expense required to have someone accumulate and evaluate the credit histories of borrowing businesses and consumers.

One more observation concerning the lemons problem is worth noting. Given the right circumstances, it can be shown that a market divided between lemons and plums can eventually become largely a market in which only lemons are offered for sale. This can happen because buyers will be unwilling to pay a premium price for plums if there is a substantial probability they will, in fact, be purchasing lemons. However, the seller, possessed of inside information, knows whether he or she owns a plum and will usually be unwilling to sell a plum for the price of a lemon. If there is no low cost way around this asymmetry problem, the ultimate result over time is that the plums will be driven from the market and only lemons will remain to be sold. Lower-value assets will drive out higher-value assets.

What can happen to used cars also can happen to financial assets, such as loans. Unless significant informational asymmetries can be overcome, lower-quality borrowers can drive away higher-quality borrowers who are unwilling to borrow at the higher interest rates that lower-quality borrowers must pay. Instead, higher-quality borrowers may turn to other markets for funds where informational asymmetries are less of a problem. As we noted in the previous chapter, a new form of *disintermediation* has occurred in recent years in which top-quality borrowers have gone around traditional lenders, such as banks, and have gone instead directly to the open market, selling their bonds and stocks to larger and wealthier investors who may be more knowledgeable about the true quality of high-quality borrowers' IOUs. In short, the existence of information asymmetries has helped to restructure some of our most important financial markets.

Problems Asymmetries Can Create: The Problem of Adverse Selection

A related problem revolves around differences in the risk presented by different groups of customers who want to enter into contracts with financial institutions. In this case, information asymmetry exists *before* the parties to a contract reach an agreement. When an asymmetrical distribution of information is already present, it can drastically alter the nature of contracts that a business firm is willing to write in order to serve its customers.

For example, banks face an *adverse selection* problem with one of their most important services: checking accounts. To a banker, there are two principal categories of checking account customers: (1) those who hold high deposit balances and write few checks, giving the bank more money to lend while the low level of account activity keeps bank costs down, and (2) those customers who keep low balances in their account but write lots of checks, giving the bank few funds to invest while heavy account activity runs up bank costs. When a customer walks in to open a new account, the banker doesn't know what kind of checking account customer he or she will be. Only the customer has the "inside" information on what kind of checking account user he or she is likely to be.

If the banker sets *one price* for all checking account customers in such an asymmetric situation, the bank runs the risk of being *adversely selected against* by its potentially most profitable customers. The preferred high-balance, low-activity customers will leave because the one price set by the bank is likely to be too high for them, but that price may be too low to cover the bank's operating costs in serving the less preferred low-balance, high-activity checking account customers. Another bank could simply enter the market with a checking account service that is cheaper and more attractive to high-balance customers and attract away the most profitable accounts. The first bank would be "adversely selected against" by those customers it most wanted to attract.

How does the first bank mitigate this problem of adverse selection? The most common technique today is to set up a *price schedule* in which the prices charged vary based on how much money each customer keeps on deposit and how many checks are written and to let the customer pick which checking account plan to sign up for. Such a price schedule based on customer usage and deposit balances helps a bank to ensure that low-balance, high-activity deposit customers will pay higher service fees and that low-activity, high-balance customers will pay lower fees. In effect, the customer "self-selects" his or her own checking account plan according to the "inside" information he or she possesses. Moreover, the customer's choice of deposit plan signals to the banker what kind of customer he or she is likely to be.

Thus, one way to deal with the problem of asymmetrical information is through *signaling:* letting the participants in the marketplace who possess special or inside information take an action that reveals the nature of the unique information they possess. For example, an insider in a corporation who knows that his or her company is in trouble can signal the problem to the public by selling the company's stock. If the public sees insiders selling out, they too may begin to sell, driving the value of the company's stock lower in the marketplace.

The Moral Hazard Problem

Another problem in information asymmetry often arises *after* contracts are agreed to between buyers and sellers or principals and agents. One party to a contract may decide to pursue his or her own self-interest at the expense of other parties to the agreement. This is known as a **moral hazard** problem, and it often arises because of poorly drafted contracts or ineffective monitoring activity by the principal parties involved.

For example, the managers of a corporation, instead of managing the company for the benefit of the firm's stockholders, may grant themselves generous benefit packages and lavish offices, boosting their firm's expenses well beyond what is necessary to efficiently produce and sell the firm's products. Management may also conceal bad performance, excessive risk, misrepresent the outcomes of projects, or simply shirk in doing their jobs. The result is that management—the *agent* of the stockholders—optimizes its own well-being, while the stockholders—the *principals* in this instance—receive less than optimal returns on their stock. Because information on what is happening inside the firm is often difficult and expensive to obtain, the stockholders (principals) may not be aware for a long time (if ever) of the unnecessary expenses that their agent—the firm's management—is creating. (The act of running up operating costs higher than they need to be is often called *expense preference behavior.*) In this instance the agents are creating a "moral hazard" problem for a company's principals (its shareholders).

Moral hazard problems can lead to unexpected consequences. Elimination of moral hazard problems can be costly, both in discovering the problem and in rewriting the contract between principal and agent to get rid of the problem. Usually, moral hazard problems are dealt with by placing appropriate incentives in principal-agent contracts so that agents will want to act more in line with the interests of principals.

Asymmetry, Efficiency, and Real-World Markets

No market in the real world in which we live is either completely efficient or completely asymmetric. Rather, all real-world markets have elements of *both* efficiency and asymmetry.

As Peter Fortune (1991) has observed, recent research has found some evidence that appears to be inconsistent with the pure efficient markets hypothesis. For example, there is evidence that some investors earn excess returns from trading the stock of small firms or from buying shares in certain types of mutual funds (known as closed-end funds). Moreover, some market anomalies seem inconsistent with a truly efficient market, such as unusually high stock returns on Fridays and unusually low stock returns on Mondays (known as the *weekend effect*). Stock prices also appear to display exceptionally high volatility in the short run, with some traders apparently buying on the basis of a stock's past performance rather than buying on the basis of its fundamental value, temporarily driving its price higher, and then, subsequently, selling the stock as its price returns to its former level (a phenomenon called *mean reversion,* which is inconsistent with the efficient markets hypothesis). Perhaps real-world markets are split into two segments: (1) a highly efficient segment, in which well-informed individual investors and financial institutions (the "smart money") trade, and (2) a market segment in which less-well-informed small investors and small businesses trade, where information is asymmetrically distributed and much of the information that becomes public is of poorer quality.

We will see in the following chapters of this book how financial market participants have moved to counter informational asymmetries by developing special kinds of expertise, forming special kinds of organizations (such as credit rating agencies), writing unique contractual agreements (such as detailed insurance and loan contracts), and by striving continually to become more efficient and reduce operating costs. It is also useful to bear in mind that the possession of special or inside information does not always result in an advantage for its possessor. Recent research has suggested that, at times, there is a "curse of knowledge": more information is not always better. For example, better-informed market participants often find it impossible to ignore private information even if it would be advantageous for them to do so.

Possible Remedies for Informational Asymmetries

One way to deal with market asymmetries is to pass laws and regulations designed to improve the flow of information between buyers and sellers and to protect the public against deception in valuing financial assets. For example, in 1933 the United States passed the Securities Act, requiring companies selling securities across state lines to submit a *prospectus* to a federal agency, the Securities and Exchange Commission (SEC), giving detailed economic and financial information on the firm's condition and prospects. Once the prospectus is approved, the SEC requires that the security issuer supply a prospectus to any investor interested in buying those securities. Misrepresentation or fraud in a prospectus can trigger lawsuits by the SEC and by investors against a business firm selling securities, its directors, any public accounting firms involved, and even security dealers handling the sale of those securities.

In 1934 the Securities Exchange Act was passed, requiring corporate insiders to follow guidelines in trading the securities of firms with which they are affiliated in order to avoid excessive profit taking from privileged information. This law also moved to outlaw fraud and misrepresentation in trading securities already issued, requiring securities traded on exchanges and trading firms themselves to register with the SEC and to provide detailed annual reports to the SEC and to their own shareholders. Shortly thereafter, the Maloney Act was passed, requiring trade associations, such as the National Association of Securities Dealers (NASD), to register with the SEC. Today, NASD tries to discourage cheating and deception of investors by enforcing an ethics code and by licensing security dealers.

The Investment Company Act, passed in 1940, required mutual funds (investment companies) to register with the SEC and provide the shareholding public with reports on their activities and performance. The Investment Advisers Act, passed in the same year, required the registration of professional investment advisers, who also must report their procedures for analyzing and recommending investments. In 1970, the Securities Investor Protection Act set up the Securities Investor Protection Corporation (SIPC) to insure an investor from loss of up to $500,000 in securities and up to $100,000 in lost cash should his or her brokerage firm fail. The SIPC agrees to replace any assets lost due to the collapse of a brokerage firm, although it does not guarantee the value of those assets.

In the fall of 2000 the U.S. Securities and Exchange Commission passed Regulation FD (for Fair Disclosure). This required companies to disclose material financial information broadly rather than only to selected viewers. This supposedly gives all possible investors roughly equal access to market-moving information. Rules such as these help to protect the public by giving them easier access to pertinent information as an aid to sound financial decision making.

While the government regulations and controls recently put in place to mitigate the damaging effects of asymmetric information may be helpful in improving the efficiency of the financial markets, many observers think we have a long way to go in solving asymmetric information problems. They point, for example, to the case of Enron Corporation, a huge energy firm that filed for bankruptcy in 2001 and whose alleged insider dealings and questionable accounting practices cost investors billions in stock market losses and destroyed the retirement savings of many of Enron's workers. Perhaps the accounting practices of major corporations need a closer look today to make sure that capital-market investors are getting the full amount of information they need to make rational buy-sell decisions. We now turn to look at some of the most important sources of financial information currently available to the public.

Questions *to Help You Study*

1. Why is the availability and reliability of financial information important to both borrowers and lenders of funds? What can happen when relevant information is missing?

2. Can you explain why financial information that is accurate and reliable is also of great significance to government policymakers and regulators within the financial system?

3. Carefully explain what is meant by the term *efficient market.* Are there different levels of market efficiency? What are these different efficiency levels?

4. Please explain what is meant by the term *informational asymmetries.* What problems can these asymmetries create for participants in the money and capital markets and the financial system?

5. What does it mean to say an asset is "temporarily overpriced" or "temporarily underpriced"? How can such a situation happen? Why is such overpricing or underpricing likely to be temporary? Can you suggest a situation that might lead to permanent overpricing or underpricing of an asset?

6. As you look at the real world around you, can you see some examples of what seem to be efficient markets? Can you detect any real-world examples of informational asymmetries? How did you identify these market situations?

DEBT SECURITY PRICES AND YIELDS: SOURCES OF INFORMATION

Bonds and Notes

Investors can get lots of information on investing in bonds through such sources as the Bond Market Association at *www.investinginbonds.com*

Among the most important assets traded in the financial system are bonds and notes. These financial assets are debt obligations issued by governments and corporations, usually in units (par values) of $1,000. A **note** is a short-term written promissory obligation, usually not exceeding 5 years to maturity; a **bond** is a long-term promissory note, at least 5 to 10 years to maturity and often much longer. Although bonds and notes generally pay a fixed rate of return to their owner in the form of coupon income, their prices fluctuate daily as interest rates change. Therefore, although bonds and notes are often referred to as *fixed income securities,* the investor may experience significant gains or losses on these securities as their prices change. Bonds and notes generally carry a set maturity date, at which time the issuer must pay the holder the security's par value. These securities are generally identified by the name of the issuing company or governmental unit, their coupon (fixed interest) rate, and their maturity date.

Bid and Asked Prices of Bonds and Notes

Both bid and asked prices for bonds and notes are posted by dealers, who will purchase securities at the **bid price** but sell to customers at the **asked price.** Yields are computed against the asked price and are generally figured to maturity when the security is selling at a discount from its par value. When the security is selling at a premium over its par value and has various possible maturity dates, the yield is generally figured to the nearest maturity date.

Price Information

Today traders require information regarding the prices and availability of securities on an up-to-the-minute basis. Computer networks report instant prices and quotations on the most actively traded bonds and other securities, supplemented by televised reports via such channels as the CNN Financial Network and CNBC. One of the most complete listings of daily price and yield quotations appears in *The Wall Street Journal (WSJ)* published by Dow Jones. *WSJ* reports the prices of securities traded on the major securities exchanges and also the prices of issues sold over the counter (OTC). Most daily newspapers contain a list of prices for bonds traded on the New York and American Stock Exchanges as of the close of business the previous day. Many of the bond trades reported on the major securities exchanges are small-volume, odd-lot transactions. Purchases and sales of large quantities of bonds (known as *round lots*) between dealers and major institutional investors generally take place off the major exchanges, through direct negotiation or with the aid of security brokers, and often at prices different from those quoted in the daily newspaper.

Bond Yield Indexes

A number of *bond yield indexes* have been compiled in recent years. These pool several bond issues of similar quality and report the average rate of return (yield) to the investor for the entire pool of bonds. With bond yield indexes, investors and companies planning to issue new bonds can see the trend of recent price and yield changes and decide whether their plans need to be altered to reflect the latest developments. Among the most popular bond yield indexes are those compiled by Moody's Investors Service and *The Daily Bond Buyer* for both corporate and state and local government bonds. In addition, the U.S. Treasury makes available estimated average yields for its notes and bonds, arrayed by maturity. Dow Jones publishes a daily index of prices for some of the most actively traded corporate bonds.

These various bond yield indicators appear in numerous publications, including both private and governmental sources. The *Federal Reserve Bulletin,* published by the Board of Governors of the Federal Reserve System, and the *Survey of Current Business,* published by the U.S. Department of Commerce, report weekly, monthly, and annual average bond yields. Recent changes in various bond yield indexes as reported in the *Federal Reserve Bulletin* are shown in Exhibit 3–3. We note the marked fluctuations in bond yields, reflecting significant changes in economic and credit conditions during this period. This is why bond buyers pay a great deal of attention to announcements each week of new economic data, such as the release of new information on auto sales, industrial production, price inflation, or the construction of new homes. Any hint of softening in the economy or of reduced inflation often results in a short-term bond market price rally.

EXHIBIT 3–3
Indicators of Average Bond Yields (Average Annual Yields in Percent)

Yield Series	1990	1992	1994	1996	1998	2000	2001*
State and local government notes and bonds:							
Aaa-Moody's series	6.96%	6.09%	5.77%	5.52%	4.93%	5.58%	4.89%
Bond buyer series	7.29	6.48	6.18	5.76	5.09	5.71	5.03
Corporate bonds:							
Seasoned issues, all industries	9.77	8.55	8.26	7.66	6.87	7.98	7.37
Moody's corporate bond indices classified by rating:							
Aaa	9.32	8.14	7.97	7.37	6.53	7.62	7.02
Aa	9.56	8.46	8.15	7.55	6.80	7.83	7.11
A	9.82	8.62	8.28	7.69	6.93	8.11	7.48
Baa	19.36	8.98	8.63	8.05	7.22	8.36	7.85

*2001 figures for August.

Source: Board of Governors of the Federal Reserve System, *Federal Reserve Bulletin,* selected issues.

STOCK PRICES AND DIVIDEND YIELDS: SOURCES OF INFORMATION

Of all securities traded in the money and capital markets, **stocks** are among the most popular with investors. Stock prices can be extremely volatile, offering the prospect of substantial capital gains if prices rise but also significant capital losses if prices fall. Many corporations issuing stocks pay dividends regularly, thus giving the investor a reasonably steady source of income as well as the opportunity to achieve "windfall" gains if the value of the stock rises. Unlike a bond, however, a share of stock is a certificate of ownership in a corporation, not a debt obligation. No corporation need pay dividends to its stockholders, and some never do, preferring to retain all after-tax earnings in the business.

Price and Yield Information

As in the case of bonds, price and yield data on the most actively traded stocks are reported daily in the financial press as well as over television, radio, and the Internet. Most daily newspapers, along with *The Wall Street Journal* and other popular financial newssheets, list current stock prices. Each stock price quotation is identified by the abbreviated name of the company issuing it. High and low prices at which the stock has been traded during the past year and the most recent annual dividend declared by the issuing company are normally given. The dividend yield—the ratio of dividends to current price—often appears, along with the ratio of the stock's current price to the past 12 months of company earnings (the P-E ratio). Remaining entries in a financial newssheet may provide a summary of the previous business day's transactions in the markets on which that particular stock is bought and sold. The one-day sales volume, expressed in hundreds of shares, may also be shown, as well as the highest and lowest prices at which the stock was exchanged that day. The closing price for which the stock was traded in the last sale of the day is often reported, expressed in dollars and decimal fractions of a dollar.

Information on daily stock market developments for active investors may be found on the World Wide Web at such sites as *http://moneycentral. msn.com/*

Stock prices for more than 1,700 companies in over 100 industries are provided by *The Value Line Investment Survey,* published weekly by Arnold Bernhard & Company of New York. Each company's business is described, and basic financial information, such as sales, net earnings, and long-term indebtedness, is provided for at least a decade. Individual stocks are also rated by *Value Line,* from those expected to be top performers down to those expected to be the poorest performers—a service widely followed by many capital market investors. Stock prices and basic financial data for individual companies are also presented in comprehensive reports compiled by Standard & Poor's Corporation (S&P). The performance of the shares issued by mutual funds is reported by Morningstar, which rates each mutual fund's recent performance using a star system of one to five. Five-star-rated mutual funds are considered by Morningstar to be among the best-performing and best-managed investment companies.

The stock market is watched closely by investors as a barometer of expectations in the business community. A rising trend in stock prices generally signals an optimistic assessment of future business prospects and expectations of higher corporate earnings. A declining market, on the other hand, is often a harbinger of adverse economic news and may signal a cutback in business investment and lower corporate earnings. Among the most important factors watched by stock traders are reports of corporate earnings, merger and dividend announcements, changes in corporate management, announcements of new products being introduced, changes in government policy that might affect interest rates (with the prospect of lower interest rates generally favorable for stocks), and apparent changes in the strength of the economy (as reflected in such data series as new orders to manufacturers of durable goods, new housing construction, the growth of business investment expenditures, changes in the level of business inventories, and measures of inflation).

Stock Price Indexes

For further information on stocks, bonds, and mutual funds see the Investment Company Institute at *www.ici.org.*

Many students of the financial markets follow several broad stock price indexes that reflect price movements in groups of similar quality securities. One of the most popular indexes is the Dow Jones Industrial Average of 30 stocks, including such major companies as General Motors and Exxon. Dow Jones also reports a transportation average of 20 stocks (including such industry leaders as Federal Express) and a utility average of the shares of 15 leading utility companies (such as Pacific Gas and Electric). The utility average is of special importance to many investors because it appears to be highly sensitive to interest rate fluctuations, and some analysts regard it as a barometer of interest rate expectations.

To learn more about stock price indexes see such sources as That Money Show at *www.pbs.org* and through Standard & Poor's Corporation at *www.stockinfo.standard poor.com.*

Two of the most comprehensive stock market indicators available are Standard & Poor's 400 Industrial Stock Price Index and 500 Composite Stock Price Index, both of which include the most actively traded U.S. corporate equity shares. The S&P 500 includes the shares of 40 utility companies, 20 transportation firms, and 40 financial stocks not present in the S&P 400 industrial index. All five S&P stock series—the 400 Index, Utility Index, Transportation Index, Financial Stock Index, and the 500 Composite Index—are regarded as sensitive barometers of general stock price movements in the United States. An even broader price index than the S&P 500 Composite is the New York Stock Exchange Composite Index, which gives greatest weight to stocks having the highest market values. Considered a useful indicator of total market performance, the NYSE composite is often used to compare the performance of major institutional investors, such as investment companies and pension funds, against the market as a whole. One other broad market indicator is the NASDAQ OTC composite, which measures price movements in stocks sold over the counter rather than on the major exchanges.

Many newspapers and financially oriented magazines contain daily stock market diaries or summaries. Such summaries of recent market developments indicate both price movements and the volume of trading on the major exchanges. Examples may be found in *Barrons, Forbes, Fortune, Money,* and *The Wall Street Journal.* Market diaries or summaries usually report the total number of shares traded on a given day or week and the number of stocks advancing or declining in price.

Foreign Stock Prices

You can track foreign stock price movements at such sites as *www.stocksmart.com* and *www.finix.at/.*

With the spreading globalization of markets, more and more savers and borrowers are turning to foreign markets to invest their savings and raise needed funds. Therefore, key information sources increasingly are reporting daily changes in security prices and interest rates in foreign trading centers, such as London, Frankfurt, Hong Kong, Singapore, Tokyo, and Sydney. To help foreign investors who deal predominantly in their own home currencies, there are also listings of currency exchange rates in various publications (such as the *Federal Reserve Bulletin*) so that they can translate a security's current price from one currency into another.

INFORMATION ON SECURITY ISSUERS

Moody's and Standard & Poor's

Want to know more about Moody's and Standard & Poor's? Try *www.moodys.com/* or *www.standardpoor.com*

Lenders of funds have a pressing need to secure accurate financial information on those individuals and institutions that seek to borrow funds or to sell their stock. Fortunately, financial information on many individual companies and other security issuers, particularly for the largest institutions, is available from a wide variety of published sources.

Two of the most respected sources of information on major security issuers are Moody's Investors Service, Inc., and Standard and Poor's Corporation, both headquartered in New York City. In a series of annual publications, Moody's provides financial data on industrial corporations, financial institutions, utilities, and state and local units of government. The most widely known of Moody's annual publications include the *Industrial Manual, Bank and Finance Manual, Public Utility Manual, Transportation Manual,* and *Municipal and Government Manual.* In the case of individual corporations, Moody's provides information on the history of each firm, names of key officers, and recent financial statements. In addition, Moody's assigns credit ratings to selected issuers of corporate and municipal bonds, commercial paper, and preferred stock as a guide for investors. These ratings are published in Moody's *Bond Record.* Standard & Poor's provides similar credit ratings for corporate and municipal bonds, assessing the likelihood of default on a security issue and the degree of protection afforded the buyer.

SEC Reports

Even more extensive financial data are provided by the reports that corporations must file with the Securities and Exchange Commission (SEC). These SEC reports are available in many libraries on microfiche or microfilm. One company, Disclosure Incorporated, provides its subscribers with microfiche copies of more than 100,000 corporate documents filed each year by well over 10,000 companies. The most important of these corporate documents is the SEC's 10-K report, an annual statement that must be filed by most companies within 90 days after their fiscal year-end. These 10-K reports identify the principal products or services of each firm, provide a summary of its recent operations, note any securities outstanding, and list the names of key officers.

Company Histories

The backgrounds on thousands of businesses all over the world can be found by searching through a wide variety of private information sources. For example, *The International Directory of Company Histories* provides brief historical sketches of nearly 3,000 firms worldwide, while a service on CD-ROM called *Global Researcher SEC* provides information on the directors, officers, and leading shareholders for over 12,000 companies whose securities are traded in U.S. markets. A related CD-ROM source known as *Global Researcher Worldscope* provides financial data and news headlines for almost 15,000 firms that trade on leading stock exchanges around the world.

Dun & Bradstreet

Learn more about Dun & Bradstreet at *www.dnb.com*

Another useful source of data on individual business firms is Dun & Bradstreet, Inc. (D&B). This credit rating company collects information on approximately 3 million firms, making detailed financial reports available to its subscribers. Dun & Bradstreet also provides industrywide financial data so that the financial condition of an individual business borrower can be compared with that of other firms in the same industry. D&B's Key Business Ratios series includes key operating and financial ratios for more than 800 lines of business. Similar industrywide performance indicators are prepared and published in *Troy's Almanac* and in Robert Morris & Associates' *Annual Statement Studies* (which covers smaller firms in more than 400 lines of business). This information can be supplemented with news about individual industries and firms by checking *The Wall Street Journal Index,* the *New York Times Index,* and *Barron's Index.* Recently, a new Internet database called *Investext* was added, with financial reports and forecasts for more than 11,000 companies in over 50 different industries.

Financial Institutions

Information on banks and other financial institutions is available from a wide variety of sources, including trade associations in each industry and federal and state regulatory

You can reach the Federal Deposit Insurance Corporation's Web site at *www.fdic.gov*, while the Comptroller of the Currency can be contacted at *www.occ.treas.gov*. The Federal Home Loan Banks are reachable at *www.fhlbi.com*

agencies. For example, the American Bankers Association, Life Insurance Association of America, Insurance Information Institute, and Credit Union National Association frequently provide annual reports or pamphlets describing recent industry trends. Studies of financial institutions' problems are found in specialized journals and magazines, such as the *Bankers Magazine, Financial Analysts Journal, Euromoney, The Economist, Forbes, Fortune,* and the *Journal of Portfolio Management.*

Among key government agencies that provide annual reports and special studies of financial institutions' trends and problems are the Federal Deposit Insurance Corporation, Federal Reserve Board and Federal Reserve Banks, the Federal Home Loan Banks, and the Comptroller of the Currency. For example, the Federal Deposit Insurance Corporation (FDIC) has a detailed Web site that identifies all FDIC-insured depositories and provides financial data for each insured institution. Many government reports are available in university libraries or through the Superintendent of Documents in Washington, DC. There are also several popular directories that list the names of banks and other financial institutions and contain limited data on each institution, its address, and often the names of key officers. Among the most popular of these directories are *Moody's Bank and Finance Manual,* the *Thomson/Polk Bank Directory,* and *Qualisteam's List of Banks on the Internet.*

Credit Bureaus

To discover more about what credit bureaus do see The Consumer Data Industry Association at *www.acb-credit.com/*

Information on individuals and families who seek credit is assembled and disseminated to institutional lenders by *credit bureaus.* The files of these bureaus include such information as the individual's place of residence and occupation, debts owed, and the promptness with which an individual pays his or her bills. Most credit bureaus maintain files on an individual's bill-paying record for up to seven years and may release that information only to lenders, employers, or licensing agencies who have a legitimate right to know the individual's credit standing. Individuals also have a right to see their credit files and verify their accuracy.

GENERAL ECONOMIC AND FINANCIAL CONDITIONS

A number of different sources provide market participants with information on developments in the economy, prevailing trends in the money and capital markets, and actions by the government that may affect economic and financial conditions worldwide.

The Federal Reserve

Learn more about the Federal Reserve Bulletin at *www.federalreserve.gov*

The Federal Reserve System releases large quantities of financial information to the public on request. Statistical releases available on a weekly or monthly basis cover such items as interest rates, money supply measures, industrial output, and international transactions. Information of this sort is summarized each month in the *Federal Reserve Bulletin,* published by the Board of Governors of the Federal Reserve System in Washington, DC. The Board also publishes the results of internal staff studies that examine recent financial trends or address major issues of public policy. Within the Federal Reserve System, the Federal Reserve banks scattered around the United States are also major suppliers of financial and economic information. Addresses for the Federal Reserve Board and all the Federal Reserve banks appear at the back of each monthly *Federal Reserve Bulletin,* as well as on the Internet.

Other Domestic Sources

A number of published sources regularly report on the status of the economy. Daily financial newspapers, such as *The Wall Street Journal,* nearly always include important

You may contact *The Wall Street Journal* at www.wsj.com/ and *The Survey of Current Business* at the U.S. Department of Commerce at www.doc.gov

economic data. *The Survey of Current Business,* a magazine published by the U.S. Department of Commerce (USDC), contains one of the most comprehensive collections of U.S. economic data available anywhere, including the latest statistics on consumer, government, and business spending, and on exports and imports. The USDC also publishes several other convenient compilations of business data, including the annual *Statistical Abstract of the United States.*

Forecasts of *future* economic and financial developments are available from a wide variety of sources. For example, the Federal Reserve Bank of Philadelphia publishes the quarterly *Survey of Professional Forecasters,* which compiles a summary of the forecasts of leading economists regarding production, unemployment, inflation, and interest rates. Forecasts of annual capital spending based on repeated industry surveys are prepared by the U.S. Department of Commerce and McGraw-Hill Publications Company. Businesses often subscribe to the services of one or more of a number of economic consulting firms that prepare detailed forecasts of the nation's income and interest rates.

International Sources

Important and interesting international web sites include the International Monetary Fund at *www.imf.org*, the Bank for International Settlements at *www.bis.org*, the *Financial Times* at *www.ft.com*, and *Euromoney* at *www.Euromoney.com*

The growing internationalization of the financial markets has led to dramatic increases in new sources of information regarding foreign markets and institutions. Up-to-date security price and interest rate data are published in *The Wall Street Journal/Europe* from Brussels, and a corresponding *Asian Wall Street Journal* is issued from Hong Kong. *The Financial Times* of London is considered one of the finest daily newspapers in the world. *The Economist,* also published in London, deals with foreign business and political developments throughout the world. Of comparable quality is the monthly *Euromoney* (London), which monitors Europe's ongoing economic integration. For businesspersons interested in Asia and the Pacific Rim, such magazines as *Asiaweek,* the *Far Eastern Economic Review,* and *Asiamoney* offer greater understanding of Pacific economies and institutions.

Questions *to Help You Study*

7. See how many major sources of financial information you can list. Can you explain what types of information each source contains?

8. If you need to gather information for a possible stock or bond purchase, where would you go to get such information? What are the principal sources to check?

9. Suppose you wanted to evaluate the financial condition of a business firm? What major sources exist that could assist you in getting that kind of information? Why might such information be important to you?

10. Suppose you were planning to take a job with a particular business firm or company. What would you want to know about the business involved? Where could you find what you need to know?

11. If you wanted to gather information about the state of the U.S. economy, which information sources would likely be most helpful to you?

12. Where could you go to gather information and data regarding the global economy?

SOCIAL ACCOUNTING DATA

Students of the economy and the financial markets also make use of social accounting systems to keep track of broad trends in economic and financial conditions. **Social accounting** refers to a system of record keeping that reports transactions between the principal

Data on the U.S. economy may be found at such Web sites as *www.economagic.com*

sectors of the economy, such as households, financial institutions, corporations, and units of government. The two most closely followed social accounting systems in the United States are the National Income Accounts and the Flow of Funds Accounts.

National Income Accounts

The **National Income Accounts** (NIA) system is compiled and released quarterly by the U.S. Department of Commerce. It presents data on the nation's production of goods and services, income flows, investment spending, consumption, and savings. Probably the best-known account in the NIA series is gross national product (GNP), a measure of the market value of all goods and services produced by U.S.-related institutions and individuals (regardless of their location) within a year's time. Recently, the gross domestic product (GDP), a closely related but slightly smaller measure of production in the U.S. economy that includes only goods and services produced within the geographical boundaries of the United States, was introduced and has become the most popular barometer of overall economic activity. GDP may be broken down into the uses to which the nation's output of goods and services is put. For example, Exhibit 3–4, drawn from the *Survey of Current Business* and *Federal Reserve Bulletin,* indicates the size of the U.S. GDP and its major components during 2001.

The National Income Accounts system provides valuable information on the level and growth of the nation's economic activity, which have a profound impact on conditions in the money and capital markets. However, the NIA accounts provide little or no information on financial transactions themselves. For example, one component of the NIA system reports the annual amount of personal savings, but it does *not* show how those savings are allocated among purchases of bonds, stocks, and other financial assets. This task is left to the **Flow of Funds Accounts** prepared by the Board of Governors of the Federal Reserve System.

The Flow of Funds Accounts

Flow of funds data have been published quarterly by the Federal Reserve System since 1955. Monthly issues of the *Federal Reserve Bulletin* contain the latest summary reports of flow of funds transactions, and detailed breakdowns of financial transactions among major sectors of the economy are readily available on both a quarterly and an annual basis from the Federal Reserve Board in Washington, DC.

EXHIBIT 3–4

National Income and Product Accounts: The Components of U.S. Gross Domestic Product (GDP), 2001* ($ Billions, Current)

Personal consumption expenditures		$7,045
Durables	$ 845	
Nondurables and services	6,200	
Gross private domestic investment:		1,670
Fixed investment	1707	
Change in inventories	−37	
Net exports		−347
Exports	1080	
Imports	1427	
Governmental purchases		1,835
Federal	610	
State and Local	1225	
Gross domestic product (GDP)		$10,203

*Figures are for the second quarter of 2001.

Source: U.S. Department of Commerce and Board of Governors of the Federal Reserve System, *Federal Reserve Bulletin,* Table 2.16, November 2001, p. A48.

The basic purpose of the Flow of Funds Accounts are to (1) trace the flow of savings by businesses, households, and governments into purchases of financial assets; (2) show how the various parts of the financial system interact with each other; and (3) highlight the interconnections between the financial sector and the rest of the economy.

Construction of the Flow of Funds Accounts takes place in *four* basic steps.

Sectoring the Economy

More information on the Federal Reserve's Flow of Funds Accounts may be found at such sites as *www.federalreserve.gov /releases/*

The first step is to divide the economy into several broad *sectors,* each consisting of economic units (transactors) with similar balance sheets. Among the major sectors in the current account series are the following:

- Households, including personal trusts, foundations, private schools and hospitals, labor unions, churches, and charitable organizations.

- Farm businesses.

- Nonfarm noncorporate businesses, including partnerships and proprietorships engaged in nonfinancial activities.

- Nonfarm nonfinancial corporations.

- State and local governments.

- U.S. government, including government-owned agencies.

- Federally sponsored credit agencies, such as the Federal Land Banks and Federal National Mortgage Association.

- Monetary authorities, including the Federal Reserve System and certain monetary accounts of the U.S. Treasury.

- Commercial banks.

- Savings institutions, including savings and loans, credit unions, insurance companies, mutual funds, and pension funds.

- Other financial institutions, such as finance companies, mortgage companies, and security brokers and dealers.

- Rest of the world (U.S. international transactions).

Constructing Sector Balance Sheets

The second step in assembling the Flow of Funds Accounts is to construct *balance sheets* for each of the sectors listed above at the end of each quarter. Like any balance sheet for a business firm or household, sector balance sheets contain estimates of the total assets, liabilities, and net worth held by each sector at a single point in time. The assets held by each sector are divided into financial assets and real (nonfinancial) assets.

An example of such a partial balance sheet containing financial assets and liabilities for the household sector for the years 1980, 1990, and 2000 (third quarter) is shown in Exhibit 3–5. We note, for example, that U.S. households held total financial assets of more than $35 trillion in 2000 (shown in line 1), more than quadruple their financial asset holdings 20 years before. A substantial part of this total was represented by holdings of deposits—checking (demand) accounts and time and savings deposits at commercial banks and savings institutions. These liquid financial assets totaled close to $4.5 trillion in 2000 (line 2). An even larger financial asset held by households was pension fund reserves (line 19), accumulated to prepare for the retirement years, which amounted to more than $10 trillion, followed by holdings of corporate stock (equities), totaling almost $7.5 trillion in 2000

EXHIBIT 3–5
Statement of
Financial Assets and
Liabilities for the
Household Sector,
1980, 1990, and 2000
($ Billions,
Outstanding at Year-
End)

Asset and Liability Items	1980	1990	2000*
1. Total financial assets	$6,398.5	$13,901.1	$35,205.4
2. Deposits	1,562.6	3,248.3	4,456.1
3. Checkable deposits and currency	258.6	527.1	376.2
4. Time and savings deposits	1,161.1	2,308.5	3,170.6
5. Money market fund shares	63.0	412.7	909.3
6. Credit market instruments	476.9	1,454.6	2,174.1
7. U.S. government securities	216.8	550.9	729.0
8. Treasury issues	182.3	298.4	274.3
9. Savings bonds	72.5	126.2	184.3
10. Other Treasury securities	109.8	172.2	90.0
11. Federal agency securities	34.4	252.6	454.7
12. Municipal securities	80.0	468.9	530.3
13. Corporate and foreign bonds	35.2	94.9	728.9
14. Mortgages	112.0	170.4	110.4
15. Open market paper	33.0	169.5	75.4
16. Mutual fund shares	45.6	451.7	3,274.2
17. Corporate equities	975.4	1,758.7	7,447.6
18. Life insurance reserves	216.4	380.0	821.2
19. Pension fund reserves	949.3	3,400.3	10,348.6
20. Investment in bank personal trusts	218.7	509.9	1,124.5
21. Equity in noncorporate businesses	1,863.6	2,440.6	4,848.4
22. Security credit	16.2	62.4	365.3
23. Miscellaneous assets	73.5	214.6	345.5
24. Total liabilities	1,450.9	3,706.2	7,450.8
25. Credit market instruments	1,392.1	3,594.8	7,024.3
26. Home mortgages and home equity loans	904.9	2,419.4	4,930.5
27. Consumer credit	318.8	896.4	1,495.6
28. Commercial mortgages	31.5	133.5	148.2
29. Bank loans (not elsewhere classified)	27.8	33.1	67.5
30. Other loans and advances	54.7	109.8	240.6
31. Security credit	24.7	38.8	270.2
32. Trade credit	22.1	56.2	137.7
33. Deferred and unpaid life insurance reserves	12.9	16.5	18.7

Note: the definition of "households" includes personal trusts and nonprofit organizations as well as individuals and families. It excludes corporate entities.

*2000 figures are for the third quarter of the year. Checkable deposits include foreign deposits.

Source: Board of Governors of the Federal Reserve System, *Flow of Funds Accounts: Flows and Outstandings,* selected issues.

(line 17). Holdings of debt securities (credit market instruments), including Treasury notes and bonds, federal agency securities, state and local government bonds, mortgages, and similar assets, amounted to just under $2.2 trillion (line 6) in 2000.

It is interesting that the total indebtedness of individuals and families in the United States is far less than their holdings of financial assets. Exhibit 3–5 indicates that the household sector's liabilities totaled roughly $7.5 trillion in 2000 (line 24), roughly one-fourth of its total financial asset holdings. Most household indebtedness was in the form of home mortgages and home equity loans (line 26) and installment (consumer) debt obligations (line 27), such as automobile and education loans paid off in a series of payments.

Sources of Balance Sheet Data

Data needed to construct sector balance sheets in the Flow of Funds Accounts come from a wide variety of public and private sources. For example, information on lending and borrowing by nonfinancial businesses is derived from such sources as the Securities and

Exchange Commission and the U.S. Department of Commerce. Various trade groups provide financial data on their respective industries, and the Securities Industry Association provides selected information on gross offerings of securities. Inevitably, inconsistencies arise in classifying financial transactions due to differences in accounting procedures among the groups contributing data. Moreover, in an economy as vast and complex as that of the United States, some financial transactions fall between the cracks. To deal with problems in data consistency and coverage, the Federal Reserve includes a *statistical discrepancy* account that brings each sector into balance.

Preparing Sources and Uses of Funds Statements

After balance sheets are constructed for each sector of the economy, the third step in the construction of the Flow of Funds Accounts is to prepare a **sources and uses of funds statement** for each sector. This statement shows changes in net worth and changes in holdings of financial assets and liabilities taken from each sector's balance sheet at the beginning and end of a calendar quarter or year. The basic structure of a sources and uses statement is given below:

Sources and Uses of Funds Statement

Uses of Funds	Sources of Funds
Change in real assets (or net real investment) Change in financial assets (or net financial investment)	Change in liabilities outstanding (or net borrowing) Change in net worth (or net current savings)
Change in total assets = Total uses of funds	Change in liabilities and net worth = Total sources of funds

An example of such a statement for the U.S. commercial banking sector for 2000 is shown in Exhibit 3–6. The first portion of the sources and uses statement (lines 1–20) shows changes in the banking sector's net worth (gross saving), real assets (net fixed investment in plant and equipment), and net acquisitions of financial assets. The second portion of the sources and uses statement (lines 21–40) reflects net borrowing as illustrated by an increase in the liabilities carried by U.S. commercial banks and their affiliates.[2]

We note, for example, that U.S.-chartered commercial banks increased their holdings of financial assets by just over $300 billion during 2000 (line 3). Bank loans to consumers, businesses, and other borrowers rose by almost $222 billion (line 11), as the U.S. economy enjoyed a period of sustained growth after a recession at the beginning of the decade (though another recession was about to arrive in the year 2001). With the U.S. economy in 2000 experiencing relatively fast expansion more individuals and businesses demanded bank credit to help them increase their standard of living and expand the output of goods and services. To make room for the credit, demands of the public commercial bank holdings of U.S. government and federal agency securities (including issues of mortgage-backed securities guaranteed by a federal government agency) declined by about $32 billion (line 6), though banks increased their holdings of state and local government (tax-exempt) securities

---

[2]All changes on a sources and uses of funds statement are shown *net* of purchases and sales. When purchases of an asset exceed sales of that asset, the resulting figure is reported as a *positive* increase in the asset. When sales exceed purchases, an asset item will carry a *negative* sign. A nonnegative liability item on the sources and uses statement indicates that net borrowing (i.e., total borrowings larger than debt repayments) has occurred during the period under study. If a liability item is negative, debt repayments exceed new borrowings during the period covered by the statement.

EXHIBIT 3–6   Sources and Uses of Funds Statement for the U.S. Banking Sector, 2000* ($ Billions)

Asset and Liability Items			
1. Gross saving	−21.4	21. Net increase in liabilities	416.0
2. Fixed nonresidential investment	30.9	22. Net interbank liabilities	57.4
3. Net acquisition of financial assets	332.1	23. To monetary authority	0.9
4. Vault cash and reserves at Federal		24. To domestic banks	16.4
Reserve Banks	−14.9	25. To foreign banks	40.0
5. Total bank credit	324.3	26. Checkable deposits	−47.6
6. U.S. government securities	−32.4	27. Federal government	−20.3
7. Treasury	7.6	28. Rest of the world	8.7
8. Agency	−40.0	29. Private domestic	−35.9
9. Municipal securities	1.4	30. Small time and savings deposits	217.5
10. Corporate and foreign bonds	132.6	31. Large time deposits	62.3
11. Total loans	221.6	32. Federal funds and security RPs (net)	−75.5
12. Open market paper	0.3	33. Credit market instruments	−12.2
13. Bank loans not elsewhere classified	51.8	34. Open market paper	−1.8
14. Mortgages	130.9	35. Corporate bonds	9.2
15. Consumer credit	50.4	36. Other loans and advances	−19.6
16. Security credit	−11.6	37. Corporate equity issues	3.9
17. Corporate equities	1.3	38. Taxes payable	2.2
18. Mutual fund shares	−0.3	39. Miscellaneous liabilities	208.1
19. Customers' liabilities on acceptances	−1.9	40. Statistical discrepancy	31.7
20. Miscellaneous assets	24.7		

*Figures are for the third quarter of 2000.

Source: Board of Governors of the Federal Reserve System, *Flow of Funds Accounts,* December 8, 2000.

by more than $1 billion (line 9) in 2000. Meanwhile, bank holdings of vault cash and reserves held at the central bank (the Federal Reserve System inside the United States) declined by a whopping $15 billion in total (line 4) in the year 2000, reflecting changing economic conditions and new banking regulations. U.S.-chartered commercial banks invested nearly $31 billion (line 2) in new plant and equipment (fixed nonresidential investment) during the year as the industry continued to automate many of its facilities.

Where did the banking sector get the funds it needed to make new loans and security purchases and increase its investment in new plant and equipment in 2000? The necessary funds came principally from a rise of about $217 billion in small-denomination (under $100,000 each) time and savings deposits, though the largest time deposits (each over $100,000 in amount) also rose by more than $60 billion (lines 30 and 31). Banks often supplement their deposit growth with borrowings in the money market and by issuing bonds and notes to borrow in the capital markets, though these particular sources declined in 2000 (lines 32 and 33). U.S.-chartered banks also dredged up new funds by reducing their savings (shown in their gross savings account) by nearly $22 billion (line 1), thereby opening up another source of funds that bankers could draw upon to respond to their customers' needs and help their industry grow.

Balancing Out a Sources and Uses of Funds Statement

As we have seen, sources and uses of funds statements in the Flow of Funds Accounts are derived from the aggregated balance sheets of each sector of the economy. Because balance sheets must always balance, we would also expect a sources and uses of funds statement to balance (except, of course, for discrepancies in the underlying data). In a sources and uses statement,

$$\begin{array}{ccc} \begin{array}{c} \text{Net investment} \\ \text{in plant and} \\ \text{equipment} \end{array} + \begin{array}{c} \text{Net acquisitions} \\ \text{of financial} \\ \text{assets} \end{array} = \begin{array}{c} \text{Net increase in} \\ \text{liabilities} + \text{Change in} \\ \text{current surplus} \\ \text{account} \end{array} & \textbf{(3–3)} \end{array}$$

Net acquisitions of financial assets are frequently referred to as **financial investment;** net purchases of plant and equipment may be labeled **real investment.** Both are *uses of funds* for a sector or economic unit. Net increases in liabilities represent **current borrowing** in the current period, while changes in the current surplus account reflect **current savings.** These latter two items are *sources of funds.* Therefore, the relationship shown above may be written as follows:

$$\begin{array}{c} \text{Net real investment } + \text{ Net financial investment} \\ = \text{Net borrowing } + \text{Net current saving} \end{array} \qquad \textbf{(3–4)}$$

or

$$\text{Total uses of funds} = \text{Total sources of funds.} \qquad \textbf{(3–5)}$$

For each unit—business, household, or government—and for each sector of the economy, the above statement *must* be true. For example, in the commercial banking sector in 2000 we have, as shown in Exhibit 3–6:

Sources and Uses of Funds Statement
for the Banking Sector, 2000 ($ Billions)

Uses of Funds		Sources of Funds	
Net investment in plant and equipment (net increase in real assets)	$ 30.9	Net borrowing (net increase in liabilities)	$416.0
Net financial investment (net acquisitions of financial assets)	332.0	Net current saving (net change in net worth)	−21.4
Statistical discrepancy	31.7		
Total uses of funds	$394.6	Total sources of funds	$394.6

Once the statistical discrepancy account is considered, total uses and total sources of funds should be equal for this and for all other sectors of the economy (except for small remaining discrepancies in column totals due to rounding error).

Constructing a Flow of Funds Matrix for the Economy as a Whole

The final step in the construction of the Flow of Funds Accounts is to combine the sources and uses of funds statement for each sector into a flow of funds matrix for the entire U.S. economy. An example of such a matrix is shown in Exhibit 3–7, which shows borrowings by each major sector of the economy and total borrowings by all sectors combined. Another example appears in Exhibit 3–8, which shows funds loaned by each major sector to domestic nonfinancial borrowers and total credit extended by all sectors. The majority of funds sought by businesses, consumers, and governments in the financial markets clearly were raised by issuing debt instruments, as shown in Exhibit 3–7. The sum total of all debt instruments outstanding rose by just over $1.5 trillion (line 1 in Exhibit 3–7) in the year 2000 (as of the third quarter of that year, annualized). Corporations were among the heaviest borrowers of funds in the American economy, issuing almost $400 billion in debt instruments (line 5). Also among the heaviest borrowers were debtors taking on mortgage loans (both new home mortgage loans and commercial mortgages), who borrowed almost

EXHIBIT 3-7 Funds Raised in Credit and Equity Markets ($ Billions)

	1993	1994	1995	1996	1997	1998	1999	2000*	
	Credit Market Borrowing, All Sectors, by Instrument								
1. Total	952.2	1026.6	1229.0	1365.6	1529.8	2160.1	2233.6	1535.5	1.
2. Open market paper	-5.1	35.7	74.3	102.6	184.1	193.1	229.9	133.6	2.
3. U.S. government securities	421.4	448.1	348.5	376.5	235.9	418.3	520.8	285.4	3.
4. Municipal securities	74.8	-35.9	-48.2	2.6	71.4	96.8	68.2	29.8	4.
5. Corporate and foreign bonds	281.2	157.3	319.6	357.0	422.4	550.4	465.9	397.7	5.
6. Bank loans n.e.c.	-7.2	62.9	114.7	92.1	128.2	145.0	68.9	43.1	6.
7. Other loans and advances	-0.8	50.3	70.2	62.5	102.8	158.5	172.6	-46.2	7.
8. Mortgages	127.3	183.2	211.1	283.6	332.4	530.3	612.9	571.7	8.
9. Consumer credit	60.7	124.9	138.9	88.8	52.5	67.6	94.4	120.4	9.
	Funds Raised through Corporate Equities and Mutual Fund Shares								
10. Total net issues	429.7	125.2	143.9	231.9	181.2	100.0	156.5	150.0	10.
11. Corporate equities	137.7	24.6	-3.5	-5.7	-83.9	-174.6	-31.8	-111.5	11.
12. Nonfinancial	21.3	-44.9	-58.3	-69.5	-114.4	-267.0	-143.5	-87.6	12.
13. Foreign shares purchased by U.S. residents	63.4	48.1	50.4	82.8	57.6	101.2	114.4	13.0	13.
14. Financial	63.4	21.4	4.4	-19.0	-27.1	-8.9	-2.7	-36.9	14.
15. Mutual fund shares	292.0	100.6	147.4	237.6	265.1	274.6	188.3	261.5	15.

*Figures are for the third quarter at annual rates.

Source: Board of Governors of the Federal Reserve System, *Flow of Funds Accounts.*

EXHIBIT 3–8 Total Net Borrowing and Lending in Credit Markets ($ Billions)

	1993	1994	1995	1996	1997	1998	1999	2000**	
	Total Net Borrowing and Lending in Credit Markets*								
1. Total net borrowing	952.2	1026.6	1229.0	1365.6	1529.8	2160.1	2233.6	1535.5	1.
2. Domestic nonfinancial sectors	588.0	572.2	701.6	731.4	804.3	1042.9	1120.4	758.5	2.
3. Federal government	256.1	155.9	144.4	145.0	23.1	−52.6	−71.2	−219.3	3.
4. Nonfederal sectors	331.9	416.4	557.1	586.3	781.2	1095.5	1191.6	977.5	4.
5. Household sector	207.8	311.4	349.0	358.1	345.8	488.1	548.1	564.8	5.
6. Nonfinancial corporate business	52.1	143.6	232.7	148.8	266.1	416.3	480.3	292.7	6.
7. Nonfarm noncorporate business	3.2	3.3	23.9	81.4	107.0	103.2	105.7	87.2	7.
8. Farm business	2.6	4.4	2.9	4.8	6.2	7.7	5.2	7.6	8.
9. State and local governments	66.2	−46.2	−51.5	−6.8	56.1	80.3	52.3	25.2	9.
10. Rest of the world	69.8	−14.0	71.1	88.4	71.8	43.3	25.3	61.6	10.
11. Financial sectors	294.4	468.4	456.4	545.8	653.7	1073.9	1087.9	715.4	11.
12. Commercial banking	13.4	20.1	22.5	13.0	46.1	72.9	67.2	17.4	12.
13. U.S.-chartered commercial banks	9.7	12.5	11.2	11.7	29.5	52.8	41.8	−12.3	13.
14. Foreign banking offices in U.S.	−5.1	−2.6	−3.1	−0.7	−2.4	−4.8	−0.4	−0.7	14.
15. Bank holding companies	8.8	10.3	14.4	2.0	19.0	24.9	25.8	30.4	15.
16. Savings institutions	11.3	12.8	2.6	25.5	19.7	52.2	48.0	−17.2	16.
17. Credit unions	0.2	0.2	−0.1	0.1	0.1	0.6	2.2	1.1	17.
18. Life insurance companies	0.2	0.3	−0.1	1.1	0.2	0.7	0.7	−0.3	18.
19. Government-sponsored enterprises	80.6	172.1	105.9	90.4	98.4	278.3	318.2	279.3	19.
20. Federally related mortgage pools	84.7	115.4	98.2	141.1	114.5	192.6	273.8	225.1	20.
21. ABS issuers	83.6	72.9	141.1	150.8	202.2	321.4	234.0	136.8	21.
22. Finance companies	−1.4	48.7	50.2	45.9	48.7	43.0	62.4	96.9	22.
23. Mortgage companies	0.0	−11.5	0.4	4.1	−4.6	1.6	0.2	−0.3	23.
24. REITs	3.4	13.7	5.7	11.0	39.6	62.7	6.3	−2.4	24.
25. Brokers and dealers	12.0	0.5	−5.0	−2.0	8.1	7.2	−17.2	25.2	25.
26. Funding corporations	6.3	23.1	34.9	64.1	80.7	40.7	92.2	46.2	26.
27. Total net lending	952.2	1026.6	1229.0	1365.6	1529.8	2160.1	2233.6	1535.5	27.

*Excludes corporate equities and mutual fund shares.
**Figures are for the third quarter of the year at annual rates.

Source: Board of Governors of the Federal Reserve System, *Flow of Funds Accounts*.

$572 billion (line 8 in Exhibit 3–7). Borrowings by governments at all levels ranked high as well in volume at just over $300 billion (lines 3 and 4). Of course, borrowing—issuing debt—is not the only possible source of funds from the money and capital markets. Substantial funds can be raised by issuing stock (corporate equities), which, in 2000, totaled $150 billion (line 10 in Exhibit 3–7).

Exhibit 3–8 looks at borrowing in the economy from both the lenders' and borrowers' points of view. From Chapter 2 we know that what is borrowed by one sector must equal the credit extended to that sector by other sectors. For example, line 27 in Exhibit 3–8 shows that total funds loaned in U.S. credit markets during 2000 amounted to just over $1.5 trillion. This amount exactly matches the total net borrowings by all sectors reported in line 1 of Exhibit 3–8 for 2000 and the total borrowings figures given in line 1 of Exhibit 3–7. *The flow of funds matrix reminds us that, for all sectors of the economy combined into one, the amount of saving must equal the total amount of real investment in the economy, and the amount of borrowing in total must equal total financial investment* (i.e., the total amount of financial assets acquired by all sectors).

Limitations and Uses of the Flow of Funds Accounts

It should be clear by now that the Flow of Funds Accounts provide a vast amount of information on trends in the financial system. These accounts provide indispensable aid in tracing the flow of savings through the money and capital markets. Estimates of flow of funds data can be used to help make forecasts of lending, borrowing, and interest rates. However, these social accounts have a number of limitations that must be kept firmly in mind.

First, the Flow of Funds Accounts present no information on transactions among economic units *within* each sector. If a household sells stock to another household, this transaction will *not* be picked up in the accounts, because both units are in the same sector. However, if a household sells stock to a business firm, this transaction *will* be captured by the flow of funds bookkeeping system. The accounts show only *net* flows between one point in time and another point, not the changes that occur between the beginning and ending points of the period.

Finally, all flow of funds data are expressed in terms of current market values. Therefore, these accounts measure not only the flow of savings in the economy but also capital gains and losses. This market-value bias distorts estimates of the amount of actual savings and investment activity that occur from year to year.

Despite these limitations, however, the Flow of Funds Accounts are among the most comprehensive sources of information available to students of the financial system. These accounts provide vital clues on the demand and supply forces that shape movements in interest rates and security prices. The Flow of Funds Accounts indicate which types of securities are growing or declining in volume and which sectors finance other sectors. One of the principal uses of Flow of Funds data today is to forecast interest rates and build econometric models to simulate future conditions in the credit markets. Combined with other sources of information, Flow of Funds accounting provides us with the raw material from which to make important financial decisions.

Questions *to Help You Study*

13. Please explain what is meant by the term *social accounting*. Why is such an accounting system needed?

14. Compare and contrast the Flow of Funds Accounts of the United States with the National Income Accounts. What types of information does each system of accounts provide that could be useful for making financial decisions?

15. Why would information about the global economy be of significance to an investor in stocks, bonds, and other financial assets?

16. Please explain how the Flow of Funds Accounts of the United States are constructed.

17. What is a *sources and uses of funds statement?* Why is it important?

18. Discuss the principal limitations of Flow of Funds data. Why must a user of Flow of Funds information keep these limitations in mind?

Summary of the Chapter

This chapter examines the key role that *information* plays in the money and capital markets and the financial system. Among its key points are those items listed below.

- An unimpeded flow of relevant, low-cost information is vital to the efficient and effective functioning of the financial markets and the financial system. If the scarce resource of credit is to be allocated efficiently and an ample flow of savings made available for investment, accurate financial information must be made readily available at low cost to all market participants.

- There are two different types of markets operating within the financial system every day: an *information market* and a *market for financial assets.* The two different types of markets must work together in a coordinated fashion to accomplish the desired end result—directing the flow of scarce loanable funds (coming primarily from savings) toward their most profitable and beneficial uses (primarily into investments that help the economy, our standard of living, and jobs to grow).

- If the market for financial information is truly *efficient,* so that all relevant information for valuing financial assets is readily available at negligible cost, financial assets will be correctly priced based on their expected return and risk, and scarce resources will flow to those uses of funds promising the highest expected returns.

- When *asymmetries* exist in information flow and availability, however, the financial marketplace will operate imperfectly. Some market participants, armed with special information not broadly available to all market participants, will earn *excess profits* (that is, generate returns that exceed the *normal* rate of return for the amount of risk taken on). Scarce resources will then be allocated less efficiently than otherwise might be the case. Research evidence to date suggests that most financial markets are efficient but that important asymmetries still remain.

- Today there is a wide array of different information sources available to the general public. Among the more prominent examples are financial newssheets such as *The Wall Street Journal, Fortune Magazine,* and *Forbes.* Daily stock and bond market reports are not only provided extensively via the World Wide Web and through multiple Internet sources but also from local newspapers in most cities around the globe. Key sources of public information about individual companies include condition reports provided by the Securities and Exchange Commission, Standard & Poor's Corporation, and Moody's Investors Service. Economies in the United States and around the globe are tracked through such sources as *The Economist,* the *Federal Reserve Bulletin,* and *The Survey of Current Business.* Finally, data on financial transactions from the whole United States' economy is published quarterly by the Board of Governors of the Federal Reserve System through the *Flow of Funds Accounts.*

- In this chapter, our principal focus has been on five broad categories of financial information available today: debt security prices and yields, stock prices and dividend yields, the financial condition of security issuers, general conditions in the economy and financial system, and social accounting data. The purpose of this chapter has been to give the student of the financial system a broad overview of the kinds and quality of information currently available to the public. Knowing where to find relevant, up-to-date information is an essential ingredient in the process of solving economic and financial problems.

Key Terms

Efficient markets hypothesis, *53*
Asymmetry, *53*
Insider trading, *58*
Moral hazard, *62*
Note, *64*
Bond, *64*

Bid price, *64*
Asked price, *64*
Stocks, *66*
Social accounting, *70*
National Income Accounts, *71*
Flow of Funds Accounts, *71*

Sources and Uses of Funds
   Statements, *74*
Financial investment, *76*
Real investment, *76*
Current borrowing, *76*
Current savings, *76*

Problems

1. For each of the following data items, cite at least two sources (where possible) from which this information could be obtained:
   a. Stock prices of a corporation whose shares are publicly traded.
   b. Credit ratings of the bonds and notes issued by U.S. corporations.
   c. Interest rates (yields) on government bonds and notes.
   d. Financial statements of corporations.
   e. Volume of savings generated by U.S. households, businesses, and units of government.
   f. The allocation of current savings by businesses, households, and governments among various types of financial assets.
   g. Volume of investment in real assets by businesses and households.
   h. Size and rate of growth in the money supply.
   i. Current rate of inflation in consumer and producer prices.
   j. Volume of credit extended by banks and other financial institutions.
   k. Recent rate of growth in the economy's income, output, and employment.

2. Construct sources and uses of funds statements for each sector of the economy and for the whole economy using the following information:

	Households ($ Billions)	Business Firms ($ Billions)	Banks and Other Financial Institutions ($ Billions)	Governmental Units ($ Billions)
Current saving	$428.8	$280.0	$35.0	−$35.0
Current real investment	332.5	350.0	17.5	—
Current financial investment	306.3	78.8	43.8	8.8
Current borrowing	210.0	148.8	26.3	43.8

Assume that the four sectors listed above are the only sectors in the economy and that there are no international transactions. Is there a statistical discrepancy? Where? Referring to the discussion in Chapter 2, which sectors are deficit-budget sectors (DBUs) and which are surplus-budget sectors (SBUs)?

3. Suppose that you are given the data listed below for the household sector of the economy. From this information, please construct a statement of financial assets and liabilities for the household sector.

	($ Billions)		($ Billions)
Deposits in banks and savings institutions	$540	U.S. government securities	$110
Home mortgages	290	Credit extended by nonbank lending institutions	40
Installment loans extended by banks	110	Trade credit	5
Holdings of currency and coin	120	Corporate and foreign bonds	30
Security credit owed	10	Corporate equities	680
State and local government bonds	50	Life insurance reserves	130
Deferred and unpaid life insurance premiums	10	Pension fund reserves	420
Holdings of miscellaneous financial assets	50	Miscellaneous liabilities	35

4. Construct a sources and uses of funds statement for the commercial banking sector for the year immediately concluded. A check of the Federal Reserve's Flow of Funds Accounts indicates that U.S. banks reported a current earnings surplus (after paying stockholder dividends) of $12 billion and made investments in plant and equipment of $11 billion. They acquired net $120 billion in loans to their customers and purchased $4 billion in corporate bonds, $13 billion in state and local government bonds, and $25 billion in U.S. governmental securities. Miscellaneous financial assets rose $10 billion. There was a statistical discrepancy in the Flow of Funds Accounts of $8 billion on the banking sector's sources of funds side.

5. At year-end 2001, suppose the corporate business sector posted net worth of $60 billion, total investment in plant and equipment of $75 billion, total holdings of financial assets of $131 billion and total debt outstanding of $146 billion. The following year-end, 2002, suppose total corporate indebtedness climbed to $167 billion, holdings of financial assets fell to $120 billion, and net worth increased to $63 billion due to retained profits. Construct a sources and uses of funds statement for the corporate sector for 2002.

6. The following situations *may* be covered by insider trading laws in the United States. Please examine each situation described and indicate whether, in your opinion, a violation of insider trading laws might have occurred. If you think a violation occurred, what kind of violation was it?

   a. The chief financial officer of Start Corporation reads an internal memorandum criticizing the firm's recent oil field development investments and picks up his phone to call his broker, placing an order to short sell the firm's shares when the market opens in the morning.

   b. Corren Professional Corporation, a CPA firm, assists Selkirk Industrial Corporation with its quarterly and annual financial reports. Jim Roberts, a CPA with Corren, after reviewing the latest information provided by Selkirk's CEO, calls a friend and suggests making certain stock and bond trades involving Selkirk's securities. Roberts will not benefit financially from these suggested trades and refuses to be involved in the transaction.

    c. James Smith works for Cohen and Cooper, a local law firm, and while browsing in his firm's law library, he discovers a new report from a legal client of his colleague, lawyer Roscoe Adams, that predicts serious financial problems if the client proceeds with its recently drafted strategic plan. Smith subsequently discovers discreetly that the strategic plan is to be launched next week. He also learns that Roscoe is selling the client's stock short through his broker. Smith quietly advises Roscoe not to make the intended security transactions and then lets the matter drop.

    d. Samuel Joule learns from conversations with Sarah Conklin, a bartender at a local restaurant and bar, that neighboring Locket Corporation has recently developed a secret air warning device that may help prevent air collisions and may be worth tens of millions of dollars once it is announced to the government and the aircraft industry. Joule does not work for Locket, though he has been dating Miss Conklin for some time. Sarah Conklin also does not work for Locket. Both of these individuals decide to purchase 1,000 shares of Locket's common stock before Locket holds its press conference to announce the new air collision device. Joule and Conklin will use a bank loan to finance the purchase of Locket's shares. A wedding is planned if the transaction succeeds financially.

7. Please identify the key terms and concepts in this chapter as described in the phrases and sentences listed below:

    a. Change in liabilities outstanding over a specified period.

    b. Change in net worth over a particular time span.

    c. Net change in real assets over a specified time interval.

    d. Net change in financial assets over a particular time span.

    e. A financial report showing changes in financial and real assets, net worth and outstanding liabilities over a particular time period.

    f. A system of recordkeeping covering economic and/or financial activity for the whole economy or for major sectors of the economy.

    g. A system of accounts reporting on a nation's total production, spending, consumption, and savings.

    h. The price of selling securities to the public as published by dealers.

    i. A debt obligation issued by a business or governmental unit usually lasting more than 5 years.

    j. A short-term IOU usually with a maturity of less than 5 years.

    k. The price for buying securities from the public as posted by security dealers.

    l. A party to a contract or other agreement who takes advantage of the other parties involved to benefit his or her self-interest.

    m. Purchasing or selling the securities of a firm by someone having access to privileged information about the firm.

    n. The prices of securities and other assets fluctuate randomly around their intrinsic values and return quickly to equilibrium.

    o. Pockets of inefficiency in the availability and use of information.

Questions about the Web and the Money and Capital Markets

1. Government plays a key role in monitoring the financial system and in helping individuals and institutions keep abreast of market movements. Identify at least two key government agencies present on the Web that aid individuals in staying informed about some of the latest developments in the money and capital markets.

2. If you are interested in economic data pertaining to the U.S. economy as well as other major economies around the world, where might you look for useful data?

3. If you are especially concerned about your own personal portfolio of financial assets and their performance in today's financial markets, where could you go on the World Wide Web to easily keep track of the daily behavior of these assets?

Selected References

Board of Governors of the Federal Reserve System. *The Federal Reserve Bulletin,* selected monthly issues.

Board of Governors of the Federal Reserve System. *Flow of Funds Accounts of the United States.* Washington, DC, December 8, 2000.

Camerer, Colin; George Lowenstein; and Martin Weber. "The Cause of Knowledge in Economic Settings: An Experimental Analysis." *Journal of Political Economy* XXVII, no. 5 (1989), pp. 1232–1354.

Fortune, Peter. "Stock Market Efficiency: An Autopsy." *New England Economic Review.* Federal Reserve Bank of Boston, March/April 1991, pp. 17–40.

Hu, Tie, and Thomas H. Noe. "The Insider Trading Debate." *Economic Review.* Federal Reserve Bank of Atlanta, Fourth Quarter 1997, pp. 34–35.

Keown, Arthur T., and John M. Pinkerton. "Merger Announcements and Insider Trading Activity: An Empirical Investigation." *Journal of Finance* 361 (1981), pp. 855–69.

Meulbrock, Lisa N. "An Empirical Analysis of Illegal Insider Trading." *Journal of Finance* 47, no. 5 (1992), pp. 1661–66.

Teplin, Albert M. "The U.S. Flow of Funds Accounts and Their Uses." *Federal Reserve Bulletin,* July 2001, pp. 431–41.

Webb, Roy H. *Macroeconomic Data: A User's Guide.* Federal Reserve Bank of Richmond, 1990, pp. 1–48.

Chapter Four

The Future of the Financial System and the Money and Capital Markets

Learning Objectives in This Chapter

- You will be able to understand the economic, demographic, social, and technological forces reshaping financial institutions, financial markets, and the financial system today.

- You will gain an important sense of perspective on where recent trends in the financial system and the money and capital markets appear to be leading us and you will see how trends in the financial system may affect each one of us in the future, both personally and professionally.

- You will better understand how the problems that the financial system faces today may well affect its future, leading to a new and different financial marketplace of the future.

What's in This Chapter? Key Topics Outline

Forces Reshaping Today's and Tomorrow's Financial System

Financial Innovation, Technological Change, Homogenization

Consolidation, Convergence, Globalization, and Market Broadening

Deregulation and Harmonization

Demographic and Economic Trends Affecting the Financial System

New Types of Financial Institutions and New Types of Regulation

Risk in the Financial System and Some Possible Remedies

New Technologies and Financial Services

Financial Disclosure

Personal Privacy and the Gramm-Leach-Bliley Act

INTRODUCTION

The money and capital markets and the financial system that surrounds them are continually in transition, continually moving toward something *new*. As we observed in the opening chapter, you cannot step into the same river twice, for rivers are ever flowing onward; and so it is with the financial system of money and capital markets. Today's financial system differs radically from that of a decade ago and will be still more different as we move forward into our future.

Powerful forces are reshaping financial institutions and financial services today and reshaping as well the public's demand for new financial services. These forces for change include powerful new trends within the financial sector itself, major changes in the structure and functioning of the economy that surrounds the financial system, and new social and demographic trends that are altering the public's need for innovative new financial services. In this chapter we focus upon these tidal changes that are refashioning the financial system that we see today and helping to build a new financial system for the future.

FINANCIAL FORCES RESHAPING THE MONEY AND CAPITAL MARKETS TODAY

The money and capital markets that we see today will soon be very different as the financial marketplace continues to transform. Vast changes now under way within the financial system will demand that we continue to study the money and capital markets throughout our lives for our own personal benefit and for greater understanding.

One of the most important changes currently sweeping through the financial system is **financial innovation**—the development of *new* financial services and instruments. Every year new financial services and instruments expand rapidly in variety and volume. Home equity credit lines, international mutual funds, currency and interest-rate swaps, loan securitizations, and many other exotic new services and financial instruments that we may have heard about (and will discuss later in this book) are only the vanguard of a wave of invention and change sweeping through the money and capital markets in every corner of the globe. Moreover, with rapidly growing service innovation has come **service proliferation** as each financial institution expands the menu of services it is willing to offer customers.

One of the causes of the ongoing rush to innovate and develop new services and techniques is the rise of intense **competition** among financial-service providers. Banks, insurance companies, securities dealers, mutual funds, and thrift institutions are locked in an intense struggle for the customer's business that is unparalleled in history. Many of these financial institutions are engaged in *mergers and acquisitions* aimed at creating financial giants out of numerous smaller financial-service providers—giant service companies that can more effectively compete and win greater shares of the financial-services marketplace.

The rapid rise of intense competitive rivalry has been fueled, in part, by **deregulation.** Major governments around the world, especially in the United States, Japan, and Europe, are freeing the financial sector from many government rules. As government regulations are lightened or eliminated, the *private marketplace* becomes more and more important in shaping how financial-service providers compete and perform in order to serve the public. Financial-services competition is increasingly taking the place of government rules in the hope that the public will benefit in terms of more convenient services at lower cost.

The expanding competitive struggle in a deregulated financial marketplace has given rise not only to *new* services and *new* financial instruments but also to *new* types of financial institutions: large, multiproduct, multimarket, technologically sophisticated, sales-oriented organizations that are designed to weather the risks inherent in today's volatile financial marketplace. More and more, financial institutions look *alike,* offering the same services and organized in much the same ways. Traditional distinctions between one type of financial-service institution and another are becoming hopelessly blurred. This process of **homogenization** is creating a real challenge for marketing professionals trying to convince the public that their particular financial institution is really different from its rivals.

More financial institutions are establishing interstate operations and expanding their marketing programs to cover whole regions and, in many instances, the whole globe (usually referred to as **globalization**). The results are falling geographic barriers to international competition and strong pressure to consolidate smaller financial-service institutions into larger ones. More financial institutions are becoming stockholder-owned corporations in order to open up new sources of capital to fund their expansion. Under intense competitive pressure and rising costs, the number of independently owned financial institutions is declining, victims of merger or, in some cases, failure.

Financial markets that have traditionally been local in character are expanding to become regional, national, and even international in scope. This **market broadening** reflects *recent advances in communications technology.* Such breakthroughs offer the prospect of reducing service delivery costs, improving employee productivity, bringing new financial services on line more rapidly, and expanding the effective marketing area for both old and new services. Today, many commercial and consumer loans are traded in national and international markets, providing new sources of liquidity for financial institutions making these loans and improving the availability of credit to the public.

As new financial-service markets develop, businesses and governments will have less reason to borrow from traditional financial intermediaries and more reason to *sell debt and equity securities directly to investors in the open market.* Indeed, the role of the traditional financial intermediary in the channeling of savings into investment is shrinking somewhat. Moreover, the development of a market for *securitized assets*—pools of loans—allows almost any large firm with a strong market reputation to package its loans and issue new securities against them, thereby generating more cash to make *new* loans and investments. Thus, there is less need for traditional loans from traditional financial institutions, although many banks and insurance companies have learned that they can benefit from this trend by selling advice on how to effectively package new security offerings, by acting as agent for such offerings, and by issuing standby credit guarantees in case something goes wrong.

Of course, the trends we observe in today's financial system and among financial institutions is *not* a completely new story. Its roots lie deep in history. For example, today's trend toward deregulation of financial institutions counteracts the excesses of a much earlier era—the Great Depression of the 1930s—when comprehensive regulation of financial institutions promised *safety* but tended to stifle both competition and innovation. Furthermore, the current emphasis in the financial sector on new product development and research, frequent technological updating, elaborate marketing programs to sell financial services, and strategic planning is a carryover from manufacturing and industrial firms that have used such techniques for decades. There is a growing awareness that the challenges and techniques of managing a financial-service institution are *not* fundamentally different from those of managing any other business firm. The products are different, but the methods of control and decision making are essentially the same.

A number of sites on the World Wide Web are devoted to a look at the future of the financial system and changes and trends currently reshaping the money and capital markets. Prominent examples include Banking Regulations (at www.bankinfo.com), and Banking Reform (at http://fullcoverage.yahoo.com). Other useful Web sites focusing upon the unfolding trends within today's and tomorrow's domestic and global financial systems include *Financial Technology International Magazine* (at www.epinions.com) and the Bond Market Association at www.bondmarket.com. This is an area of great dynamic change and new Web sites are likely to appear more frequently as time passes in an effort to stay abreast of sweeping changes in the structure, operations, and technology of the global financial system.

SOCIAL, ECONOMIC, AND DEMOGRAPHIC FORCES RESHAPING THE FINANCIAL SYSTEM

We must recognize that much of what is happening in the financial system of markets and institutions today is a response to broad social, economic, and demographic trends that span generations. These trends are affecting not just financial institutions but also governments, businesses, and households in every corner of society and every nation on the globe.

For example, fundamental changes in the age makeup of the population are having profound effects on savings habits, consumption, and borrowing decisions worldwide. The population is *rapidly aging,* due primarily to better medical care, nutrition, and changing attitudes about childbearing. The *life-cycle hypothesis*—developed by Modigliani and Ando (1960) and expanded later by others—suggests that, as individuals age, they reduce their expectations of lifetime income, mainly because their expected time in the labor force is decreasing. With retirement looming closer, personal savings rates should rise and, correspondingly, per-capita consumption spending should fall in real terms. Thus, the long-term post–World War II boom of runaway consumer borrowing and spending may soon be moderating, resulting in a more moderate-growth economy, lower average interest rates, and less inflation. The challenge faced by banks, insurance companies, and other service providers in the future will be to find better ways to accommodate the demands of older savers, including the greater need for retirement, tax, and estate planning.

The basic family unit is also changing, with *more single-parent households, a rising age at which first marriages occur,* and *a declining fertility rate in most industrialized countries.* However, in the United States, population growth estimates have recently been revised upward due to greater-than-expected immigration, an increase in fertility, and greater longevity related to improved medical care. A high divorce rate marks many industrialized nations, although married couples make up three-quarters of all U.S. households. But less than half of these have children living in the home. People living alone make up less than one-quarter of all households in the United States today, although their numbers appear to be rising. Also on the rise are dual-earner couples with above-average incomes, who are becoming one of the most important segments of the population.

More men are responsible for household chores and child care today, making them more conscious of the problems of household budgeting and the need to build savings capital. In contrast, women are entering the labor force in greater numbers and are also getting stronger educational backgrounds than at any other time in history. Today, a roughly *equal* proportion of young women and young men (ages 25 to 29) have completed at least four

- Aging population (with wealthier retirees and a growing volume of funds transfers over time to their heirs and to charities).

- Larger corporate customers going directly to the open market to raise funds, bypassing traditional financial institutions.

- Growing demands for retirement planning and long-term saving by millions of workers and their families not covered adequately by existing retirement plans.

- Increasing numbers of nontraditional families (including single-parent homes) who have credit-access problems and a need for lower-cost financial services.

- Growing need for financial planning programs to aid individuals and families in need of help with managing debt, retirement assets, and their inheritances.

- Greater ethnic diversity in the populations of the world's leading countries, resulting in a range of different customer attitudes and philosophies about managing money, the work ethic, citizenship responsibilities, taxation, and the need for a range of lower-cost financial services.

- More volatile job markets, with customers switching jobs, careers, and residential locations more frequently so that financial-service providers need greater product-line and geographic flexibility.

---

years of college. Moreover, in these younger age groups, the gap between the earnings of men and women has closed significantly, though not completely. In general, educational levels have risen so much that today almost half of the U.S. labor force (in the 25 to 64 age group) has been enrolled in college at one time or another. High school diplomas are becoming the minimal educational achievement an individual needs to avoid poverty.

For further discussion of recent demographic trends see U.S. Bureau of the Census at www.census.gov.

Although many of these demographic trends have slowed or paused recently, most demographers do not anticipate a significant *reversal* anytime soon, and so demands will continue to grow for new forms of housing, daycare facilities, flexible work schedules, and less expensive medical care. The result is a new matrix of financial-service needs, including demands for new savings instruments and loans that support retraining and relocation, provide college educations, and supply more venture capital to support new businesses that are struggling to be born.

Added to the demographic changes are broad *economic* movements. For example, manufacturing industries are being displaced by service industries in more developed economies. The computer has transformed the economy from a system primarily reliant on manufacturing to one centered increasingly upon the flow of *information*. The expansion of service firms is creating most of the new jobs, and these businesses have their own unique financing needs. Accelerated growth in automation, computer systems, telecommunications, and biotechnology is creating the need for new kinds of credit and risk protection that financial-service providers must respond to.

The broader and faster dissemination of information today is contributing to the *internationalization* of markets, which spurs competition and heightens the need for international cooperation among financial institutions and among the government agencies that regulate them. One of the most dramatic examples is the formation of the European Community (EC), creating a common market with more than 300 million customers. Banks, insurance companies, and other financial firms are licensed to offer their services throughout Western Europe, leading to the free and open marketing of financial services. These reforms have already set in motion a wave of mergers and joint ventures among leading European banks, insurance companies, and other firms in order to survive in a more open financial marketplace.

Financial Developments   Social, Economic, Financial, Technological, and Demographic Forces Affecting the Financial System of the Future

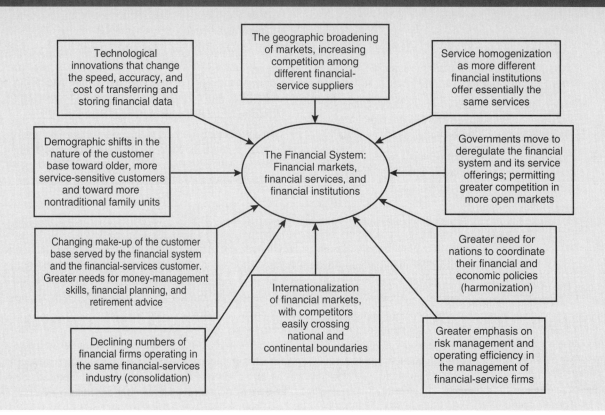

Similar developments loom on the horizon for Eastern Europe and the nations that make up the former Soviet Union now that the Cold War has ended. Huge amounts of venture capital and funding for education are desperately needed in Russia and the other nations that once belonged to the old Warsaw Pact in order to improve their living standards and retrain their workers in an effort to reduce high rates of unemployment and modernize production methods. Several Eastern European nations are seeking entry into the European Community.

As *internationalization* proceeds along with continuing advances in communications technology, there will be a whole range of benefits for the financial system and the public. More savings and investment opportunities will be opened. Investing in foreign corporations and institutions may eventually become less risky because more information will be available on their financial condition, and the markets serviced by these institutions will be better known and better understood. The result should be a more efficient allocation of scarce resources and increases in the real output of goods and services. Arbitrage opportunities due to discrepancies in prices between markets should be less frequent and shorter in duration.

However, increasing globalization of the financial and economic system will not be without its cost. Economic conditions within any one nation will become increasingly sensitive to foreign developments and harder for domestic policymakers to control or influence. Confirmation of security trades (*clearing*) and getting proper payment and timely delivery of securities bought and sold (*settlement*) will be more challenging in a globalized financial system, at least until advances in communications technology and international cooperation among governments and regulatory agencies catch up with rapidly advancing globalization.

So powerful are the foregoing trends that *none* can be ignored by the management and owners of financial-service firms today. The choice now for those who work in or use the services of the financial system is either to recognize and adapt to such trends or to become a victim, rather than a beneficiary, of change.

Questions *to Help You Study*

1. Please explain the meaning of the term *financial innovation*. How about *deregulation*? *Service proliferation*?

2. Why are financial innovation and deregulation significant factors in today's money and capital markets? Are they also likely to be important to the future of the financial system?

3. What is meant by the term *market broadening*? Why is this phenomenon taking place inside today's financial marketplace?

4. Do you think market broadening will be an important force in shaping the future of the financial-services marketplace? Please explain why you think so.

5. Please explain the reasoning behind the concept known as the *life-cycle hypothesis*? How will the life-cycle idea affect the financial system of the future, in your opinion?

6. How is the character of the *customer base* that demands financial services changing today? What changes in the financial markets' customer base do you anticipate for the future? What are the implications of these projected changes in the customer base for managers of financial-service institutions?

7. What is meant by the term *homogenization*? What do you think is motivating this trend toward service homogenization today? Why is it likely to be more important in the future?

THE CHALLENGES AND OPPORTUNITIES PRESENTED BY RECENT TRENDS

There is little question now that the demographic, economic, and financial-service trends mentioned above will continue into the foreseeable future. But we must recognize that these trends have unleashed new problems of their own—great unresolved issues that must somehow be dealt with as we rush toward the future. We turn now to these critical issues for the future of the financial system in the sections that follow.

Dealing with Risk in the Financial System: Ensuring the Strength and Viability of Financial Institutions

The money and capital markets and the financial institutions that operate within them depend heavily on *public confidence*. The financial system works to channel scarce loanable funds (credit) to their most productive uses only if individuals and businesses are willing to save and trust those savings to financial institutions, and only if other businesses and individuals are willing to rely on the financial system to provide credit to support their consumption and investment. When *any* financial institution develops serious problems that reach public notice, the public's confidence in other financial institutions may be damaged as well. The result can be a smaller flow of savings through *all* financial institutions and restrictions on the availability of credit. Jobs and economic growth could be adversely affected.

The Consequences of Reduced Public Confidence

Many members of the public regard financial institutions as less secure today than in the past, especially in the wake of failing banks, securities firms, and other financial institutions in a number of countries around the world (especially in Japan, Argentina, Asia, and the former Soviet Union). These failures appear to have contributed to a decrease in public confidence in the financial system in some markets. Financial-service customers today appear to be more sensitive to the risk of losing their funds and are, therefore, less loyal in dealing with any *one* financial institution. Financial-service *reliability* has become as important as price to many customers today.

Loss of public confidence not only produces adverse consequences for individual institutions but also damages the *efficiency* of financial market processes. A flight of funds from financial institutions reduces their size, threatening to make them less efficient in using resources. That portion of the public continuing to rely on the financial system is forced to pay higher prices for financial services that may be less in quantity and inferior in quality.

Ways to Promote Public Confidence

How can we ensure the continued viability of existing financial institutions and promote public confidence in them? Both government and the private sector may offer effective remedies.

Government Insurance Systems   Governments have taken major steps over the years to ensure the safety of banks and other financial institutions in order to protect the public's funds. For example, during the 1930s, with thousands of banks failing, the U.S. Congress created the Federal Deposit Insurance Corporation (FDIC) to provide insurance coverage for small deposits. When federal deregulation of depository institutions was launched in the United States in 1980, Congress anticipated the public's concern about deposit safety and raised federal insurance maximums from $40,000 to $100,000 per depositor. In 1974, Congress created the Pension Benefit Guaranty Corporation (PBGC) to insure retirement plans promised to the employees of some private businesses. Certainly, the public-sponsored insurance idea could be extended to include other financial instruments in which the public saves its money, such as life insurance policies or annuities.

To learn more about government insurance systems for financial institutions in the United States see, for example, *www.fdic.gov* and *www.pbgc.gov*

One problem with government-provided insurance that must be faced, however, is how to avoid distorting risk-taking decisions by the managers of privately owned financial institutions. Federal deposit insurance, for example, has protected small depositors but led many banks and thrifts in prior decades to take on greater risk because, for most of the FDIC's history, insurance premiums were the same for *all* depository institutions, resulting in riskier depository institutions being subsidized by safer institutions (see the *moral hazard* problem discussed in Chapter 3).

One solution mandated by the U.S. Congress for the FDIC (beginning in 1993) was to tie the size of government insurance premiums directly to the amount of risk taken on by each insured institution so that risk exposure to the insurance fund becomes the determinant of the cost of government-sponsored insurance to private financial institutions. Unfortunately, we aren't sure yet how to accurately measure the failure risk of an individual financial institution. Ideally, we would like to have a risk index that correctly *ranks* insured institutions from most risky to least risky every time. This way, we could be sure that the most risky financial-service firms pay the highest insurance premiums. Our preferred risk index ought to tell us that if one financial firm is twice as risky as another, the former will pay insurance premiums twice as high as the latter. Moreover, the difference in risk premiums must be significant enough to modify the behavior of riskier financial institutions.

Unfortunately, no such ideal risk measure has yet been identified. Moreover, history indicates that private entrepreneurs possess great skill in finding loopholes in nearly all the regulatory formulas that have ever been devised.

Another step governments can take to promote greater public confidence in financial institutions is to impose at least minimum *equity capital requirements* on financial-service industries. The stockholders' equity (net worth) in each financial institution provides a cushion to absorb losses until management can correct weaknesses. When a financial institution has insufficient capital to cover its current and anticipated risk exposure, it faces a *capital adequacy problem.* By imposing minimum equity capital requirements on a financial institution, regulators can force a financial firm's *stockholders* to accept a substantial share of the risks taken on by their firm. The bigger the stockholders' share of each financial institution's total capital, presumably the more watchful the stockholders will be over the firm's risk exposure and the policies pursued by its management. In this instance, the burden of controlling risk would be vested in a financial institution's stockholders, who must supply more high-cost capital if the institution suffers so many losses that it has a capital adequacy problem.

For further discussion of trends in the financial system see such sources as *www.apra.gov.au* and *www.gcn.com/*

Governments must be careful in imposing capital requirements on financial institutions, however. The international financial markets have become so competitive that if financial institutions in one nation face high minimum capital requirements while those in another nation face low or no capital requirements, the latter institutions possess an unfair competitive advantage. This fact of international life led the 12 leading industrialized nations to adopt the Basle Agreement on Bank Capital Standards in July 1988 (discussed in Chapter 18). This agreement pledged bank supervisory authorities in each nation to achieve a minimum overall bank capital-to-risk-adjusted-assets ratio of at least 8 percent. A unique feature of the Basle Agreement is that risk weights were applied to each category of assets a bank holds so that riskier banks were forced to hold additional capital in order to protect their depositors. Important breakthroughs in cooperative international financial regulation like the Basle Agreement must continue in the future if public confidence in the increasingly global financial system is to be maintained.

Private Responses to the Safety Issue   Can the private financial sector satisfactorily ensure its own financial strength and stability? Is the *market* a competent police officer to control institutional risk taking?

In theory at least, the private marketplace *is* its own regulator. Financial institutions choosing to accept greater risk in managing their customers' and their owners' funds must pay the penalty for risk that the market imposes: a higher cost for any funds raised and often a less reliable supply of funds, particularly in periods of economic recession when capital market investors display a heightened sensitivity to risk. Thus, the financial markets will squeeze the earnings of riskier financial institutions through the mechanism of a rising cost of capital. This phenomenon is called *market discipline.*

One of the most important ways the private market is dealing with greater risk of failure today is by encouraging the development of *larger* financial institutions that diversify themselves geographically and by product line in order to spread risk over a greater number of markets and services. This development has been most evident, as we will see in Part Four of this text, in the rise of interstate banking in the United States (partly the result of the passage of the Riegle-Neal Interstate Banking and Branching Efficiency Act of 1994) and the emergence of highly service-diversified financial holding companies (partly the result of passage of the Gramm-Leach-Bliley Financial Services Modernization Act of 1999). This trend toward market-expanding operations has encompassed not only financial firms that have traditionally served broad regional, national, and international markets (such as insurance companies, money-center banks, and security brokerage firms) but also locally oriented financial institutions (such as credit unions and savings banks).

Developing Better Management Tools to Deal with Risk

For a discussion of risk management techniques in the modern world see especially *http://ideas. uqam.ca* and *www.finpipe.com/ derivglossary.htm*

Another way for private financial institutions to deal with risk in the financial system is to develop and use better **risk-management tools.** Managers of successful financial institutions today must be intimately familiar with such risk-management tools as:

- *Interest rate SWAPs,* which permit institutions to trade interest payments for better matching of inflows and outflows of cash (discussed in Chapter 9).

- *Currency swaps,* which permit borrowers to trade currencies with each other and avoid exchange rate risk (discussed in Chapter 25).

- *Financial futures and option contracts,* which allow the setting of prices today for future security purchases or sales (discussed in Chapter 9).

Although these risk-management tools are useful, *new* tools must be added to the financial manager's arsenal in the future in order to effectively hedge against the risks that will challenge tomorrow's financial-service institutions. The fact that new risk-management tools are still needed was made glaringly clear to financial market investors when Long-Term Capital Management (LTCM), one of the world's largest hedge funds, virtually collapsed in 1998. Even though LTCM was previously considered to be among the best-managed hedge funds in the world, it had to be rescued by the Federal Reserve Bank of New York, which brought together a consortium of Wall Street bank and securities firms to help. Mere knowledge of existing risk-management tools does not guarantee that all risk exposures will be adequately dealt with. Continuing innovation in the risk-management field is absolutely essential to the future smooth operation of the financial system and to the continuing maintenance of public confidence in that system.

The Information Problem

Unfortunately, relying *exclusively* on the private marketplace to ensure the strength of financial institutions is open to serious question. Given adequate information, an efficient market can correctly value individual financial institutions. But does the financial marketplace receive *all* of the information it needs to generate optimal decisions? The answer is probably *no.* Depository institutions, for example, still provide only limited information to buyers of the claims they issue. Key information regarding the quality of their assets (particularly their loans) is often known in detail only to government regulatory agencies.

Capital market investors can only *approximately* price the securities of financial institutions that do not fully disclose their financial condition and prospects. Serious consideration needs to be given to greater financial disclosure of the risk exposure of individual financial institutions, especially for the protection of retirement savings. In 1991, the U.S. Congress passed the FDIC Improvement Act requiring regular full-scope, on-site examinations of each U.S.-insured depository institution. Moreover, federally insured depository institutions must supply regulatory agencies with annual reports, including an annual audit by an independent public accountant. The FDIC Improvement Act also called for more public disclosure of auditor information and of the market values of institutional assets and capital. In combination with a strong, risk-adjusted insurance program, increased public information about the true condition of financial-service firms could unleash the powerful economic force of informed investing to more effectively control risk taking by financial institutions, enhance the stability of the financial marketplace, and promote public confidence in the financial system.

Questions *to Help You Study*

8. How can we reduce *risk* in the financial sector?

9. Can we really reduce risk exposure or simply shift exposure to risk? Why?

10. What are the principal types of risk encountered by financial institutions?

11. In what ways can we promote and protect *public confidence* in the financial-services sector of the economy? Why is this important to the public and to financial institutions?

12. Can publicly provided *insurance* help to preserve and protect public confidence in our financial institutions? What are its advantages? How can we as a society be damaged by overly generous, publicly provided insurance plans?

The Effect of New Technology on the Design and Delivery of Financial Services

The Information Revolution

Providing financial services to the public involves the analysis, storage, and transfer of *financial information.* A checking account, for example, conveys the information that an individual or a business firm has claim to assets managed by a depository institution or other checkbook service–offering financial institution. The writing of a check is a new information item, designating what amount of funds is to be removed from one account and transferred to another account. The advent of computers and the Internet has taught us that information can be transferred in microseconds via computer and through Web sites, wire, satellite or other electronic networks that offer greater speed, lower cost, and greater accuracy. The technological revolution in information analysis, storage, and transfer is moving at an accelerating pace. Newer, smaller, and faster electronic-based communications systems appear every year, continually impacting the money and capital markets and the financial-services industry.

Recent Technological Advances

For a good example of an extensive Web site maintained by a financial-service institution see *www.wellsfargo.com*

One area of continuing growth will be in *networking,* or *systems integration,* in which computers and other electronic devices are linked via a global communications network. The *Internet,* or *World Wide Web,* offers banks and other financial-service firms a low-cost channel through which to advertise their services and offer routine service packages that need not be personalized to the special needs of each customer. Leading financial firms today typically have extensive home pages on the Internet that describe the services they offer and their facilities. Web customers can file requests for transfers of funds, pay bills electronically, file loan applications, receive price or rate quotes, check on available balances, and, in many cases, carry out online purchases of certain goods and services. Once fully adequate safety measures are in place to protect the customer's privacy and funds, access to an even wider array of goods and services will be available instantly through the nearest networked computer in the future.

Also beginning to have a real impact on financial-market transactions are *cellular* or *pocket telephones,* no bigger than a deck of playing cards, which allow financial-service customers to communicate from any location, 24 hours a day. Accompanying the development of full-service pocket telephones is the *pocket* or *handheld computer.* As faster and lighter computer chips are developed, pocket-size and palm-size PCs will be able to merge information storage, information retrieval, telecommunications, and extensive computing power into one lightweight, eminently portable, information-gathering resource, eventually available to almost everyone at low cost. *Pocket* and *handheld* computers will allow more managers of financial-service firms and more of their customers to instantly record transactions, notes, and memos; to fax documents; and to send and retrieve data over wireless networks. Financial decision makers increasingly are being equipped with a powerful new tool, permitting 24-hour market monitoring and decision making and the rapid implementation of financial decisions from anywhere.

New financial technologies are making it possible for more and more customers to literally do away with their checkbooks. Growing numbers of depository institutions are offering telephone-bill-paying services as well as home and office personal computer (PC) links to a financial institution's computer through which the customer can authorize payments from his or her account with the touch of a button. Equally significant is the spread of "smart cards" encoded with a certain amount of "digitized cash" that allow the customer to pay for goods and services at the point of sale by merely presenting a plastic card. When inserted into a suitable terminal, the amount of a purchase is automatically subtracted from the remaining balance of "digitized cash." Smart cards have grown rapidly in Europe, but more slowly in the United States, though these cards seem to have a bright future almost everywhere.

These and other technological advances in information technology literally make every financial-service customer into a mobile "branch office." There will be less and less need to ever visit the brick-and-mortar office facilities of a financial institution. Fewer employees will be needed in the financial institutions sector and, eventually thousands of full-service branch offices may be closed. The financial-services business clearly is in transition from a labor-intensive industry to a capital-intensive one that relies more and more upon automation and electronic processing.

Public Attitudes and Cost

The adjustment of people and institutions to the unfolding technological revolution probably will be slower than the revolution itself. Many consumers and businesses still prefer the security and privacy of cash and checkbook transactions. Personal communication between financial institutions and their customers will always be important in the delivery of some financial services, especially to older customers and smaller businesses. However, the cost of these traditional communications methods is rising, so their economic advantage over electronic methods continues to decline.

All financial institutions must be prepared for the continuing spread of new information technology. Otherwise, their competitors will wrest the "high ground" of new markets and new services away from them. But there are major challenges in this technological high ground for financial institutions, including the following:

- Customer access to financial information and the transfer of financial information must be as user friendly and as nonthreatening as possible (especially for older customers, who grew up in an era when computers and electronic processing were less in evidence).

- Operating costs and service prices must be kept low relative to more conventional paper-based or in-person information systems so that there is sufficient economic incentive for the customer to use the most cost-efficient delivery systems available.

- Adequate technological flexibility must be built in so that, as improved technologies for service production and delivery appear, they can be quickly pressed into service in order to keep each financial-service institution current and competitive. At today's rapid rate of technological innovation, new computer systems and software packages become outdated within two to three years, on average.

- Finally, auditing and internal control programs must be strengthened to reduce the probability of loss due to computer error or computer fraud, which can drive away customers and endanger the viability of any financial institution (as illustrated by the multiple system break-ins into Citibank's portion of Citigroup's operations that occurred in the former Soviet Union during 1997 and the more recent upsurge in identity theft).

The Changing Mix of Financial-Service Suppliers in the Financial System

Who will offer the financial services of the future? When the customer wishes to purchase a life insurance policy, a retirement plan, or a checking account, who will be the most likely provider? One thing that is clear now is that the traditional walls between different financial-service industries have eroded so far that they are almost nonexistent today. For example, the cash management accounts and annuities that an insurance company sells to its customers are fully competitive with the cash-management and savings instruments offered by banks and securities firms. Most of the remaining vestiges of the traditional distinctions between one type of financial-service institution and another will be swept away in the years ahead— a process we have called *homogenization.*

Price Sensitivity and Local Competition

Financial services will be purchased from the financial firm offering the lowest price and the best nonprice features. That low-cost supplier may differ from one market to another, depending on the level and intensity of competition in each local financial marketplace. In smaller cities and rural communities, the local bank may turn out to be the most advantageous supplier of most financial services, as was the case in many local communities before elaborate regulatory restrictions were placed on the banking industry during the 1930s. Larger urban markets, in contrast, will continue to be characterized by multiple financial-service suppliers usually locked in an intense competitive struggle. Moreover, financial-service firms will face a customer increasingly sensitized to differing terms of sale and more ready to transfer his or her business to the cheapest source for the quantity and quality of service desired.

Importance of Established Delivery Systems

Because cost control and productivity will be key factors for the future success of financial-service firms, financial institutions with extensive service delivery systems (including electronic delivery channels) already in place will have a competitive advantage. This feature will clearly favor financial-service institutions possessing established computer, telephone, and office networks. These cost and productivity advantages are likely to lead to still more mergers and consolidations among smaller financial-service companies so that service providers converge and consolidate into larger and larger producing units.

New Financial Institutions and Instruments

The future will usher in *new* financial institutions to deal with the newly emerging financial-service needs. For example, additional secondary (resale) markets for many loans and securities will emerge so that lenders of funds can readily sell their older assets and gain the cash needed to make new loans and investments. Just as high-grade common stocks, bonds, and futures and options contracts are traded on national exchanges or in the open market today, freer and more open trading of many other financial instruments will eventually become a reality. The unfolding new markets will require new types of financial institutions and new financial services. A few of the newer financial instruments and services that appear to have good prospects for rapid market development in the future include:

1. Loans to remodel residential dwellings (due to the aging of existing homes and greater availability of home equity credit).

2. Small business loans.

3. Credit risk derivatives (including credit swaps), which permit a lending institution to seek protection against loan defaults and depreciation in asset values (as discussed in Chapter 8).

Securitization

There will be a need for new institutions to facilitate the continuing trend toward **securitization** of many of the credit-related assets held by lending institutions and other corporations. The success of mortgage-backed securities over the past three decades demonstrates that a financial institution can more easily take some of the loans it has made and use them as collateral for borrowing money through the sale of securities. Investors purchasing the securities receive their earnings from the interest and principal payments generated by the mortgages in the pool. Today, there are loan-backed securities collateralized by such diverse assets as commercial and residential mortgage loans, mobile home loans, credit-card receivables, auto and boat loans, home equity loans, and computer equipment leases, to name just a few (see, for example, Chapters 8, 15, and 24).

The future may bring even greater use of loan-backed securities because this device opens up additional funding sources for financial institutions and for many of their customers, adding liquidity and diversification. Securitization is also likely to accelerate an ongoing shift of nonfinancial companies away from traditional types of credit obtained through a financial intermediary (such as a bank or savings and loan association) and toward self-financing and self-borrowing directly from investors in the open market. Banks, insurance companies, and other traditional intermediaries will have to develop new services to offset the potentially damaging effects of this trend away from their traditional services on their future profitability.

Consolidation and Convergence Trends within the Financial System

As we noted at this chapter's beginning, mergers have recently come to dominate the financial-services business, as the largest banks, insurance and finance companies, security dealers, and other financial firms have moved to expand toward giant size in the fastest way possible, usually through megamergers involving multibillion-dollar institutions. These megamergers are generally of two types: *consolidations,* which bring together financial firms serving the same industry; and *convergences,* where firms from two or more different financial industries combine their operations. Familiar examples as the twentieth century drew to a close include Travelers Insurance and Citicorp, which converged into a nearly $800 billion banking-securities-insurance firm called Citigroup; and Nations Bank and BankAmerica, which consolidated into BankAmerica Corp., a $600 billion, coast-to-coast banking firm with service facilities in at least 35 states. Meanwhile, giant financial firms in Canada, Germany, Great Britain, Italy, Spain and other leading nations are following a similar trend toward *consolidation* and *convergence* into fewer, but far larger entities with a wide menu of new and old services in an effort to capture the largest customer base possible, cut costs, and lower risk.

Many strong economic and technological forces are also propelling these changes—increased customer wealth, the globalization of financial transactions, better-informed financial-service customers, the rapidly changing technology of information storage and transfer, and the development of many new financial instruments and services. Some of the key players in this race for market size and dominance argue that these financial-firm consolidation and convergence trends will bring about the following changes:

- Substantial operating cost savings (through the elimination of duplicate office facilities and other overlapping resources).

- Acceleration of revenue growth (as new services are developed and offered in both new and old markets in order to reach out to broader customer segments).

- Greater diversification and, therefore, reduction of risk by widening the service lines offered to the public and spreading out geographically into many different local markets, with each product and location possessing somewhat different cash-flow patterns over time.

- Increased professional expertise, developed by combining the best talents of two or more companies, so that customers get higher-quality services.

- Increased affordability of the latest information storage and transfer technology so that financial-service firms of a wide variety of types and sizes can remain up-to-date in developing new services and in reaching their customers, no matter how distant those customers may be.

- Greater efficiency in producing and selling a mix of services that can be jointly marketed and cross-sold so that the same customers are encouraged to buy more than one service from the same financial firm, helping to tie a larger proportion of customers more closely to the particular financial-service companies with which they trade.

However, other experts in the field warn that today's trend toward consolidation and convergence is definitely a "mixed blessing." There are key *disadvantages* that may prove to be as powerful as the alleged advantages of these major structural trends among financial-service institutions. These possible disadvantages include the following:

- Higher operating costs may result due to the greater complexities of managing and controlling a highly diversified, giant company that may have grown too fast, going well beyond the optimum (lowest) production cost point for its type of product mix or industry.

- There may be an overestimation of the public's real demand for "one stop" financial shopping, because many consumers seem less interested in the convenience of receiving all their financial services from one supplier and more interested in shopping around for the best terms available for each major service that they buy, even if that requires trading with several different financial firms.

- The possibility of damaging competition for the largest financial firms from smaller financial-service companies (including many newly chartered banks and other financial firms) who can provide more personalized financial services and superior individualized service quality (including making the most sensitive customers seem like valued clients, more than simply a number in a computer file).

- The ability of smaller financial companies to compete effectively in the range of services they are able to offer, even with financial-service giants, by using *outsourcing*— that is, selling services provided to the offering firm by other suppliers (similar to the franchising concept in retailing)—in order to offer more service variety than a smaller firm operating exclusively on its own can usually provide.

The foregoing potential disadvantages of consolidation and convergence suggest that not every financial firm needs to be huge or national or international in scope. Smaller, specialized financial-service companies may still be able to hold onto a solid niche in to-morrow's financial marketplace. This will be especially true if the smaller and more specialized firms can keep their operating costs under tight control and not be undersold by the more wealthy financial-service giants. Indeed, there is little evidence that economies of scale in financial services favor only the largest firms. Often, the most profitable and best-run financial-service companies lie in the middle ground, being neither the largest nor the smallest suppliers of financial services.

Questions *to Help You Study*

13. What *technological changes* are likely to have the greatest impact on the production and delivery of financial services to the public in future years?

14. Please explain what the terms *consolidation* and *convergence* mean.

15. Why do you think consolidation and convergence are taking place today in the financial-services sector of the economy? What are their consequences for the managers of financial institutions?

16. What are the possible *disadvantages* of consolidation and convergence among financial-service institutions?

A NEW ROLE FOR FINANCIAL-SERVICES REGULATION IN AN AGE OF FINANCIAL-SERVICE CONSOLIDATION AND CONVERGENCE

The growing consolidation and convergence of financial-service companies pose major new challenges for the regulators and regulatory agencies charged with maintaining a safer and more stable financial system. Regulators cannot stop the powerful market forces that are bringing about the rise of massive financial-service conglomerates, such as Citigroup, Bank America, or Deutsche Bank, because the financial-services industry is now world-wide and much of its growth is technologically driven, which recognizes no artificially erected boundaries. However, government regulators must find a way to make safety and soundness principles work and preserve at least something of the "safety net" that protects less financially sophisticated consumers from mistreatment and the loss of their savings.

This dual concern—letting markets and competition do their essential work to benefit consumers, while preserving safety and soundness to protect the most vulnerable customers—has led to the development of several different regulatory approaches, any one of which may come to dominate the future of the financial-services business. For example, the recent Financial-Services Modernization (Gramm-Leach-Bliley) Act, passed in the United States in November 1999, now allows banks, thrifts, insurance companies, and securities firms to enter each other's backyard through a well-known type of financial structure, the *holding company,* where different affiliated firms offer different groups of services, but all are owned by one controlling company at the top of the organization. (See Exhibit 4–1.) Yet another possibility permitted under the new Gramm-Leach-Bliley Act is to allow one financial-service provider (e.g., a bank) to sell other services through its own *subsidiary firms.* (See Exhibit 4–2.)

In the financial holding company model, each financial firm has its own capital and management and its own net earnings or earnings losses, which are independent of the earnings or losses of other affiliated companies belonging to the same holding company. With the subsidiary approach, on the other hand, the earnings or losses of each subsidiary company also affect the parent firm. Nevertheless, intelligent regulators can develop walls of protection to shelter those financial firms they wish to insulate, such as by insisting upon stronger capitalization for all of the businesses belonging to the same parent company (especially any

EXHIBIT 4–1
Financial Holding Company Model

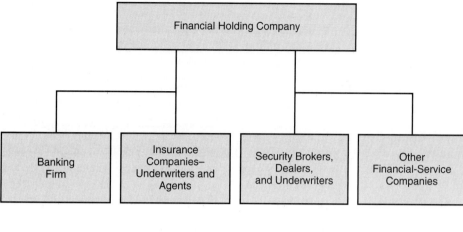

EXHIBIT 4–2
Subsidiary Model

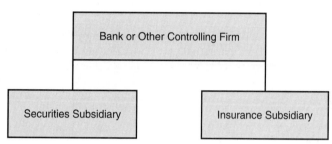

banks or other financial firms that serve small savers) or by legally limiting transactions between more-regulated and less-regulated affiliates of the same holding company.

There are also different models that may be used in the future to help fashion new regulatory regimes—that is, to create new organizational structures for regulators that match the changing features of the financial-services industry. One such model—known as the *single regulator* approach—calls upon one regulatory agency to oversee an entire financial-services company with all of its component parts. The challenge here is that such a regulator has to know many different financial businesses well in order to do a good job of supervising the safety of complex financial institutions. Nevertheless, the "single regulator" strategy may work well in certain situations—for example, in the oversight of small banks, credit unions, and insurance companies. (See Exhibit 4–3.)

For further discussion of the Gramm-Leach-Bliley Act and its implications for financial institutions and their regulators see, for example, *www.bankinfo.com* and *www.federalreserve.gov*

A different approach, adopted in the Financial Services Modernization (Gramm-Leach-Bliley) Act, calls for *functional regulation* in the future—letting specialized regulators oversee those financial firms about which they know the most and then pooling their regulatory reports to get an overall picture of the condition of a large, complex financial company. For example, state insurance commissions could regulate and supervise a bank holding company's insurance affiliates or subsidiaries, while the Securities and Exchange Commission could oversee the activities of the securities dealers and brokers belonging to that same banking company, and the Comptroller of the Currency or the Office of Thrift Supervision could track the soundness of any commercial bank or savings bank that belongs to the large, complex financial firm we are describing. Finally, one regulatory agency (such as the Federal Reserve System) may act as overall or "umbrella" supervisor, receiving regulatory reports from the different regulatory agencies involved and making a general assessment of the strength or weakness of the entire financial-services company. (See Exhibit 4–4.)

Unfortunately, each of these regulatory models is somewhat cumbersome, may be costly, and could lead to regulatory conflicts. In the case of the single regulator model, the

EXHIBIT 4–3
The Single Regulator Model

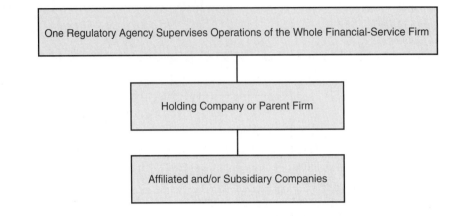

EXHIBIT 4–4
The Functional Regulator Model

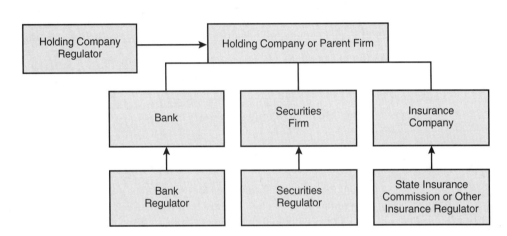

same government agency must learn how to examine and supervise many different types of firms in different industries—a potentially costly endeavor—and could easily miss major problems or be misled. On the other hand, functional regulation may not allow any one supervisor to get an accurate picture of the true condition of the *whole* financial-services organization. This is one of the reasons the U.S. Congress, when it passed the Financial Services Modernization (Gramm-Leach-Bliley) Act in 1999, adopted a portion of *both* the single regulator model (with the Federal Reserve System normally serving as overall or "umbrella" regulatory supervisor for each financial-services company as a whole) and a form of functional regulation (with two or more different regulators looking at different units within the same financial-services company).

There is also the danger that some financial firms, if allowed to acquire many different types of companies without safeguards and checks on the quality of management they are hiring, will simply become "too big to fail," requiring governments and regulators to spread out (and possibly thin down) the government's safety net, which was originally set up to protect small savers. If the biggest financial-service providers are not allowed by government to fail, not only does this give financial companies an incentive to expand their size as fast as possible, it also does not fully allow the discipline of the marketplace to work effectively to control the assumption of risk by financial institutions. We may easily lose sight of the fact that the most vulnerable financial institutions are probably those who manage the public's savings deposits and carry out payments for businesses, households, and governments—two financial-service areas that we can ill afford to have break down due to reckless management and risk seeking because these services impact the whole economy and, if poorly done, threaten the public's confidence in the financial system.

We need more disclosure of information to the public on the true condition of financial institutions, and we also need more international regulatory cooperation (known as **harmonization**) to prevent global contagion and panics by investors and the public at large. We need to use recent technological advances to improve monitoring and warning systems so that regulators can spot troubled financial firms earlier and have a chance to quickly head off service problems. We need to have the owners of financial institutions bear more of their institutions' risk and encourage large account holders to play a bigger role in market disciplining poorly managed financial firms, stimulating the management and owners of financial-service companies to pay increasing attention to measuring and managing risk in order to protect the public from spreading panic and needless financial losses.

THE FUTURE OF THE PAYMENTS SYSTEM

Tomorrow's economy and financial marketplace will depend crucially upon the continuing ability of the world's *payments system* to function efficiently, speedily, and accurately. Unless businesses that sell goods and services can be confident they will be paid accurately and promptly for what they sell, the economy will begin to slow down, production will fall, and unemployment will rise. A good example of partial payment system breakdown occurred when terror attacks in September 2001 caused many businesses to shut down temporarily. Ultimately, unless restored, the economy may collapse, because a well-functioning payments system is the essential lifeblood of a modern economy. A major breakdown in the flow of payments can result in economic disaster for millions of people who will lose their incomes and their standard of living.

There are, in reality, *two* payments systems continually at work in the economy today—one for *retail* (or small) payments flowing largely between individuals, families, and business firms; and one for *wholesale* (or large) transactions that flow mainly between banks, business firms, and agencies of government and typically pass through automated clearinghouses (ACHs), the Federal Reserve's wire network (Fedwire), and regional clearing institutions (such as the New York Clearinghouse known as CHIPS). Technological change has affected *both* of these payment systems, as a growing volume of payments are being made today electronically through computers, via telephone, with plastic cards inserted in point-of-sale terminals in stores, through electronic wire networks between depository institutions, and through the Internet. By the year 2000 at least 3000 U.S. banks had Internet sites, mostly just to provide information or to initiate PC banking. However, more than 500 U.S. banking firms today offer fully interactive electronic banking services (with the typical Internet transaction costing about a penny compared to $0.25 to $0.30 per ATM use, and over a dollar for those who carry out financial transactions through a human teller). Still, the Internet is mainly focused on information and shifting funds from one account to another, not upon the taking of deposits. Moreover, fewer than 10 percent of U.S. families do Internet or electronic banking today, only about half of these using the service on a regular basis.

Thus, the retail payments system in the United States continues to lag significantly behind the wholesale payments system in converting from expensive paper transactions to electronic systems. Americans, for example, still write about 70 billion checks a year, roughly a quarter of all their transactions—a veritable mountain of paper—though smart cards (plastic wafers with an encoded computer chip aboard that lists how much is available to spend and identifies the account owner) are gaining ground, as are online accounts inside the Internet, the use of automated teller machines, and telephone payments via verbal authorization or through the use of a credit card number. What the public must have for the future, if our financial system and economy is to avoid being overwhelmed by the crush of paper transactions, is a retail payments network that is fast, cheap, and convenient. Countries such as Norway have raised their use of electronic payments media to account for a majority of their daily payments from less than 10 percent of all their transactions a decade ago, and Denmark now operates a debit card system (called DanKort) that has reduced checks written by its citizens from 280 million a year in the 1980s to under 100 million annually in recent years. Meanwhile, the United States remains mired in paper, perhaps due to the fact that the prices of several financial services are often bundled together and U.S. customers frequently have no idea how much their paper-based checking account service costs by itself.

You can explore further the trends unfolding in the payments system through such sites as *www.buscom.com*

To be sure, all of the problems of the future in our payments system do not reside exclusively on the retail side of that system. Within the wholesale payments system, where transactions typically total well over a trillion dollars a day, it is the *size* of individual wholesale transactions—most of these denominated in multimillions of dollars apiece—that poses a substantial threat for the future. If a few of these supersize transactions fail to *settle* (clear) because of credit risk (i.e., failure of one party to fully comply), liquidity risk (i.e., a temporary cash shortage on the part of one or more large transactors), Herstatt risk (where payments are made by one party but are not yet received by another), or unwinding risk (where payment instructions are subsequently reversed and, therefore, someone is left unpaid), the result could be a panicky chain reaction of failed payments transactions spreading around the globe.

For example, suppose a large buyer cannot pay a large seller because the buyer himself or herself was not paid. Eventually, the *whole* payments system could break down, like falling dominos, as institutions expecting payments do not receive them and, because of that, cannot meet all of their own promises to pay. Security trading suddenly collapses because dealers and other sellers can no longer be sure that buyers have successfully avoided the settlement crisis or cannot be sure how much damage has been done to their customers' available liquidity. To help head off such a calamity in the United States, the Federal Reserve has set limits upon how much in total a payments-system participant can owe to everyone else who belongs to the same clearing system. They have also placed limitations upon the maximum payment a participant can accept from every other institution that is part of the same clearing system.

Questions *to Help You Study*

17. What exactly is meant by the concept of *functional regulation*? What are its advantages and disadvantages for financial institutions and their customers?

18. In what ways is regulation of the financial-services sector changing? What new types of regulation and deregulation can be expected in the future?

19. What is happening to the global *payments system* today? What changes in the payment system seem likely for the future? Why are these changes important to both financial institutions and to their customers?

20. How can we avoid a breakdown of the payments system? What damage would a full-scale payments breakdown do?

21. Why was passage of the Gramm-Leach-Bliley (Financial Services Modernization) Act so important for American banks and other financial-service institutions?

The Future Need for Regulation of Financial Institutions

The recent trend toward *deregulation*—the removal of government restrictions on the freedom of the financial markets to trade and allocate resources—of the worldwide financial sector is likely to continue. Governments will be under continuing pressure to amend and relax regulations against product-line and geographic diversification and to lift or liberalize any restrictions placed on the cost of credit (interest rates) and currency prices. If governments do not act to free more completely the financial institutions they supervise from today's product-line and geographic restrictions, nonregulated financial intermediaries will move in and eventually drive out the more regulated financial institutions from one market after another.

The more likely future developments in deregulation will be the following:

- Reduced barriers to geographic diversification in order to allow financial institutions to find new customers anywhere (as happened during the 1990s in the United States when interstate banking became permissible under federal and state laws).

- Reduced restrictions on the portfolio choices made by financial institutions except as may be required to preserve public confidence in financial institutions and the financial system, allowing the private marketplace to play a larger role in shaping a financial-service firm's portfolio choices.

- Reorganization of regulatory agencies to avoid duplication and to minimize the burden of regulation on financial institutions.

- Reduced barriers to product-line diversification (especially in securities underwriting and sales and in the underwriting of insurance, merchant banking, and real estate brokerage).

Within the United States, one of the most contentious regulatory debates will focus on the issue of what *new services* commercial banks and other depository institutions should be allowed to offer, consistent with the public's interest in a sound banking and financial system. For example, in the fall of 1999 the U.S. Congress lifted restrictions in place since the 1930s and allowed banks and financial-service holding companies the power to combine menus of banking, insurance, and security underwriting services under the same financial-services organization. The Gramm-Leach-Bliley Act also allowed regulators to expand the permissible list of financial services for banks and financial holding companies as market conditions change in the future. For example, in 2001 the Federal Reserve Board invited public comment on the possibility of allowing banking companies to provide real estate brokerage services.

Overall, the pace of financial deregulation appears to be accelerating. For example, at the recent Uruguay Round of the General Agreement on Tariffs and Trade (GATT), with 105 nations participating, both Australia and the United States proposed a global free-trade agreement in financial services. In 1993 Mexico, Canada, and the United States crafted a free-trade agreement (NAFTA) parallel to the one signed by the United States and Canada in 1987. These moves toward freer trade in financial services have been accompanied by banking and securities deregulation in Britain; the phaseout of foreign exchange restrictions in France, Italy, Greece, Portugal, Belgium, and Spain; recent liberalization of bank service offerings in Germany; and the licensing of European financial firms to offer their services throughout Western Europe as part of the continuing expansion of the European Economic Community.

Regulations That Could Grow

But all regulations in the financial-services field will *not* be eliminated. Indeed, the regulation of financial institutions is shifting to a different ground, with a new emphasis in some cases and a reemphasis on traditional regulatory goals in others. There will continue to be great concern over the safety of the public's savings and over maintaining public confidence in the smooth and efficient functioning of financial institutions and the money and capital markets in which they operate. Regulators are likely to be looking closely in the years ahead at rules applying to the adequacy of owners' equity capital, loan-loss reserves, eligibility for low-cost government insurance, and the permissible risk exposure for each financial institution. The recent collapse of Enron has set in motion a huge public debate about making all businesses more transparent in revealing their true financial condition.

Financial Disclosure

Information on financial disclosure protection for the modern consumer may be found at such Web sites as *www. consumerlaw.org* and *www.fdic.gov/ consumers*

One important area of emphasis for the future will be **financial disclosure.** Financial institutions will be expected to divulge more completely their terms of service and their financial condition to investors and to the customers they serve in order to promote better financial decision making. Good examples of this trend in the United States in the recent past are the Competitive Banking Equality Act (1987), the Truth in Savings Act (1991), and the FDIC Improvement Act (1991). These laws require increased public disclosure of deposit terms and withdrawal penalties, as well as guaranteeing customers more rapid credit for their deposits so they will have quicker access to spendable funds and greater disclosure concerning the risks of losing one's home if it is used as collateral for a loan.

There is potential gain here as well as risk. With greater disclosure, more financial institutions will be subject to the risk of public disfavor. Ultimately the "discipline of the market" will be more completely unleashed to help ensure prudent management and to control risk taking. However, increased disclosure will enable both investors in and customers of financial institutions to make more intelligent decisions about expected return and risk and the most economical use of available resources.

Privacy Protection

The 1990s and the beginning of the new century ushered in a hotly debated issue centered around the disclosure of individuals' personal information (such as their social security number, credit and deposit account numbers, etc.). Scores of proposed new laws were introduced at federal and state levels to protect so-called "nonpublic information" about individuals and families.

One cause of this explosion in privacy legislation was "identity theft." Tens of thousands of credit card holders and other consumers were becoming victims each year of fraud and theft as their personal information was stolen and used to access their accounts in banks and other financial-service entities. Frequently before the thieves could be stopped, victimized consumers might lose their access to credit, find that their credit reputation and rating had been severely damaged, and discover that their savings had disappeared.

For further discussion of consumer privacy issues see especially *http:// www.aba.com/Industry+ Issues/Issue . . .* and *www.ftc.gov*

Under the terms of the Gramm-Leach-Bliley (Financial Services Modernization) Act banks and other covered financial-service entities (such as credit counselors and credit bureaus) were ordered to develop procedures to protect the privacy of their customers' nonpublic information. Moreover, customers were granted the authority to stop a financial institution from sharing their private information with nonaffiliated firms if those customers did so in writing or by some other acceptable method. However, the new law permitted companies that are part of the same overall organization to share private customer information with each other unless they voluntarily agreed not to do so.

The future is likely to bring much more debate over *privacy protection* for the customers of financial institutions. The 1999 Gramm-Leach-Bliley Act specified that consumers of financial services had to "opt out" if they didn't want financial-services companies sharing their "nonpublic" (private) information with others. Moreover, as we noted above, financial-service institutions affiliated with each other may share private customer information even if customers specify in writing that they do not want their private data shared with any other businesses. Opposition to this new law's information provisions grew substantially as the new century dawned with proposed new laws introduced at state and federal levels proposing to give individuals and families greater authority to control their own private information.

For example, several of the proposed new privacy laws call for requiring financial firms to protect consumer information and not share it *unless the customer grants permission to do so.* This would be a far more strict standard than the current rule which allows information sharing unless customers notify their financial-service institution that they wish to put a stop to this practice. While consumer groups tended to support such strict privacy legislation, many financial-service firms oppose these proposals because of the added cost and risk involved. Indeed, the debate over protecting the privacy of financial-service consumers is likely to persist far into the foreseeable future as consumer interests are balanced against the demands for efficiency, innovation, and cost control within the financial-services marketplace.

Social Responsibility

Another area of regulatory emphasis likely to grow in the future is the *social responsibility* of financial institutions. The financial-services industry will find itself under increasing regulatory scrutiny concerning the fairness of its use of resources and the distribution of its services, particularly access to credit. For example, are all loan customers subjected to the same credit standards? Is there any evidence that the age, race, religion, the neighborhood where someone lives or does business, or other irrelevant characteristics of a credit customer have entered into the decisions of what loans a financial institution has chosen to make or not to make, resulting in illegal discrimination? Are some communities and neighborhoods losing convenient access to financial services as their offices and other facilities are closed, forcing some household residents and businesses to travel great distances in order to obtain the financial services they require? Are these closings due solely to economic factors or do they reflect hidden discrimination? How can the regulatory agencies who supervise these changes balance economic forces with social issues? Pressure will grow on *all* financial service firms to make an "affirmative effort" to serve *all* of their customers, consistent with sound financial practice but with due regard for economic necessity and the fact that most financial-service firms are privately owned and must earn competitive returns for their owners in order to survive.

Promoting a Level Playing Field

Finally, the fair and *equal* regulatory treatment of all financial institutions offering essentially the same services will continue to be a burning issue in future years. Bankers, who have labeled this the *level playing field* issue, will continue to be among its strongest advocates, pressing for more equal taxation of the earnings of different financial institutions and more equal powers to offer a full range of services competitive with other financial-service firms. As long as some financial firms are taxed and regulated differently than other financial firms, the so-called "level playing field" issue will never go away. It will continue to be a bone of contention that divides the financial sector into the "more regulated" and the "less regulated" financial firms. Inevitably, financial-services businesses that are "more regulated" and see these added rules as a real burden will strive to bend or change the rules in order to close the gap with their less-regulated competitors.

Questions *to Help You Study*

22. What regulations in the financial sector are likely to grow in the future?

23. What is the *disclosure* issue and what is its significance?

24. What is the *privacy protection* issue all about? Why is it important to customers of financial institutions? To financial-service institutions themselves?

25. What does the concept of a *level playing field* mean to financial institutions and the public? Who is most likely to be impacted when a level playing field exists?

Summary of the Chapter

The focus of this chapter is the future of the money and capital markets and the financial system that surrounds them. We have highlighted several powerful financial, economic, demographic, regulatory, and technological trends that are reshaping the financial marketplace today and helping to determine the future of the money and capital markets.

- Among the most important broad trends affecting the financial system today are *service innovation* (i.e., the development of many new financial services), *service proliferation* (as the service menu offered by most financial firms grows), *deregulation* (as governments pull back and let the private marketplace play a bigger role in shaping the financial system), *globalization* (as financial-service companies more frequently reach across national borders), *consolidation* (as financial firms grow individually large but there are fewer of them), and *competition* (as broader markets, better technology, and longer service menus bring more financial institutions into direct competitive rivalry with each other).

- This chapter also tackles the broad *social, economic,* and *demographic* trends that are restructuring financial services and financial institutions today. The chapter highlights major shifts in the character of the population—the consumers of today's and tomorrow's financial services. That population is not only growing older with a need for a somewhat different menu of services, but is also more focused on risk exposure and the need for long-term, relatively stable sources of income. Financial institutions must learn to better serve this most rapidly growing segment of the world's population who are living longer and need larger reservoirs of savings to live a decent life.

- This chapter examines the broad *technological* and *economic* changes that are likely to make the financial markets look very different in the era ahead. Service-oriented industries, such as those active in the money and capital markets, are expanding, while manufacturing units are becoming less important, particularly in the United States and in Europe. Automation, expansion of telecommunications, and the emergence of remarkable advances in biotechnology have opened up new areas for capital investment and for accelerated economic growth provided the financial system can generate more savings to fund them in the future.

- Each of the foregoing trends must be dealt with by the management and owners of financial institutions. The foregoing trends call for new managerial methods and new technical skills. These include greater knowledge of marketing and planning techniques, more sensitivity to older customers' financial needs, knowledge of how to integrate new technology into the financial-services business, and the capacity to deal with the information revolution, making effective use of the incredible flow of information we are experiencing and turning it into sound financial decisions.

- No one knows for sure what the financial system of the future will look like. Only the broadest outline seems clear at this point and the details are still hazy. It seems safe for us to predict fewer, but larger financial-service institutions and more highly diversified financial firms, growing competition, and the likelihood of some failures within an increasingly competitive financial system.

- Financial institutions of the future almost certainly will come to pay more attention to the tasks of risk management and to training their employees to be more effective salesmen and women. Managers and their staffs inside financial institutions will have to work harder to control expenses, improve productivity, be more price conscious and make better pricing decisions, and strive for great reliability in serving the customer.

Key Terms

Financial innovation, *86*
Service proliferation, *86*
Competition, *86*
Deregulation, *86*

Homogenization, *87*
Globalization, *87*
Market broadening, *87*
Risk management tools, *94*

Securitization, *98*
Harmonization, *103*
Financial disclosure, *106*

Problems

1. List the principal trends in the economy, society, and population that you believe will affect financial institutions and financial services the most over the next five years. How about the next 10 years? For each trend listed, describe at least one response the management of a financial-service firm might make to that trend.

2. If you were managing a small bank or insurance agency in your local community, what future trends in financial services and financial institutions would be likely to have the greatest impact on your institution? Why? What response or responses could you make to each trend you have listed?

3. Please identify from the descriptions listed below several of the key terms and concepts discussed in this chapter:
   a. The development of new financial-service products.
   b. The lifting or liberalizing of rules imposed by governments on the financial marketplace and financial institutions.
   c. Financial-service firms becoming more alike in the services they offer.
   d. The spreading of financial-service markets across borders and around the globe.
   e. The tendency of markets to expand territorially due to the advancing technology of communications and growing competition.
   f. Making the public feel more secure in dealing with financial institutions.
   g. Key focus or target of regulation for banks and other financial firms in recent years.
   h. Financial devices to control and manage risk exposure in the financial sector.
   i. The principal purpose and function of any financial service.
   j. Linking computers to globally integrated systems in order to store, process, and transfer financial information over great distances.
   k. The number of new financial services being offered today is growing rapidly.
   l. Financial firms become more and more alike in their service menus and all offer broader service menus over time.
   m. Smaller financial firms increasingly are being combined into larger financial firms.
   n. The pooling of loans and issuing securities for public sale based on the expected cash flows out of the loan pool.

o. Federal law permitting banks, insurance companies, and security firms to merge into consolidated financial firms.

p. Allowing different regulatory agencies to examine the particular elements or components of a financial firm that they know the most about with the reports being pooled and given to an overall or umbrella regulatory supervisor.

q. Different nations agreeing on common regulatory rules.

r. Requiring financial-service firms to divulge more information to the customer about the features and terms of a financial service.

s. Protecting customers' personal information and allowing customers to decide if they wish their personal data to be shared among different financial-service providers.

t. Using law and regulation to promote competition among financial-service firms by equalizing the rules to which different types of financial firms are subjected.

Questions about the Web and the Money and Capital Markets

1. Suppose you wanted to keep up with the latest changes in the regulation of banks and other financial institutions? What Web site or sites might be most helpful to you?

2. The forces for reform of the financial system in order to make the money and capital markets more responsive to changing financial-service laws, regulations, technology, and financial products are frequently represented on the World Wide Web. Find one or more key Web sites that discuss financial-services or financial-institutions reform.

3. If you wanted to find out how changing technology is affecting financial services, financial institutions, and the money and capital markets today and tomorrow what important Web site(s) would be helpful to you in explaining what is happening?

Selected References

Baily, Martin Neil, and Robert Z. Lawrence. "Do We Have a New E-conomy?" *American Economic Review* 91 (May 2001), pp. 308–312.

Craig, Ben. "Resisting Electronic Payment Systems: Burning Down the House?" *Economic Commentary,* Federal Reserve Bank of Cleveland, July 1999, pp. 1–4.

Cyberstates 2001: A State-by-State Overview of the High-Technology Industry. American Electronics Association, 2001.

Duca, John C. "The Democratization of America's Capital Markets." *Economic and Financial Review,* Federal Reserve Bank of Dallas, Second Quarter 2001, pp. 10–19.

Good, Barbara. "Electronic Money." *Working Paper 97-16,* Federal Reserve Bank of Cleveland, 1997.

Holmes, Thomas J. "The Location of Industry: Do States' Policies Matter?" *Regulation* 23, no. 1 (2000), pp. 47–50.

Litan, Robert E., and Alice M. Rivlin. "Projecting the Economic Impact of the Internet." *American Economic Review* 91 (May 2001), pp. 313–17.

Modigliani, Franco, and Albert Ando. "The Permanent Income and the Life Cycle Hypothesis of Saving Behavior." In *Proceedings of the Conference on Consumption and Saving,* The University of Pennsylvania, 1960, pp. 49–174.

Nunes, Paul F.; Diane Wilson; and Ajit Kambil. "The All-in-One Market." *Harvard Business Review* 78 (May/June 2000), pp. 19–20.

Orrenius, Pia M., and Alan D. Viard. "The Second Great Migration: Economic and Policy Implications." *Southwest Economy,* Issue no. 3 (May/June 2000), pp. 1–8.

Saving, Jason L. "Census Data Show the Economy Matters." *Southwest Economy,* Federal Reserve Bank of Dallas, Issue no. 4 (July/August 2001).

Siems, Thomas F. "B2B E-Commerce: Why the New Economy Lives." *Southwest Economy,* Federal Reserve Bank of Dallas, Issue no. 4 (July/August 2001).

Part **Two**

Interest Rates and the Prices of Financial Assets

This section of the text tackles one of the most fundamental and important issues in the field of money and capital markets—what determines the *price of credit* within the financial system? Why are *interest rates*—the price of credit—high or low at any particular moment in time? And what causes them to change? What about the prices of financial assets? Why do the prices of these assets rise and fall over time?

And beyond these basic questions is another fundamental issue—can market interest rates be predicted or forecasted? Or, if not, can we at least find effective ways of protecting ourselves from loss through various hedging strategies when interest rates and asset prices begin to move?

The first four chapters of this part of the text focus upon the forces that determine the level of interest rates and the market prices of financial assets. Each of these opening chapters of Part Two fills in a piece of the puzzle about changing asset prices and interest rates. For example, we begin in Chapter 5 with an exploration of the fundamental forces of the demand and supply for credit and how these forces bring about shifts in the pure or risk-free rate of interest. Then, in Chapter 6, we discuss how both interest rates and security prices are measured in the real world—knowledge that will serve us well as we progress further into Part Two. In Chapter 7 we examine the impact of inflation and deflation and the length or term of a loan on one interest rate versus another. Chapter 8 brings us to the influence of borrower default risk, taxes, call privileges, prepayment and event risk, and other interest rate and asset-price-determining factors.

The final chapter in Part Two turns our attention toward efforts to predict (forecast) interest rates and to hedge against loss from shifting market rates of interest and fluctuating asset prices. The controversies surrounding interest-rate forecasting and interest-rate hedging (risk protection) have taken front and center stage in finance for the past three decades. We will discover why interest-rate forecasting is so difficult (many would say, virtually impossible) and why interest-rate hedging (risk protection) has become so popular and widely used. Chapter 9 introduces us to the most important risk protection tools in the financial marketplace today, including financial futures, options, and swaps. Each rate-hedging instrument has its own unique story to tell—one that we must learn if we are to participate fully in tomorrow's financial marketplace.

Chapter **Five**

The Determinants of Interest Rates: Competing Ideas

Learning Objectives in This Chapter

- You will be able to see the important roles and functions that *interest rates* perform within the economy and inside the money and capital markets.

- You will have the opportunity to explore the most important ideas about what determines the level of interest rates and asset prices within the financial system.

- You will be able to draw up a list for easy reference of the key forces that economists believe set market interest rates and asset prices in motion.

What's in This Chapter? Key Topics Outline

Interest Rates: Nature and Roles within the Financial System

The Classical Theory of Interest: Assumptions and Conclusions

The Substitution Effect and Investment Demand

Liquidity Preference Theory and Demands for Money

The Role of the Money Supply and the Liquidity Trap

Central Banking and Interest Rates

Limitations of Interest-Rate Theories

The Credit Theory of Interest Rates: Loanable Funds

Elements of the Demand for Loanable Funds

The Supply of Loanable Funds: The Components

Rational Expectations and the Public's Changing Outlook

INTRODUCTION

In the opening chapter of this book, we described the money and capital markets as one vast pool of funds, depleted by the borrowing activities of households, businesses, and governments and replenished by the savings these sectors supply to the financial system. The money and capital markets make saving possible by offering the individual saver a wide menu of choices where funds may be placed at attractive rates of return. By committing funds to one or more financial instruments (assets), the saver, in effect, becomes a lender of funds. The financial markets also make borrowing possible by giving the borrower a channel through which securities (IOUs) can be issued to lenders. And the money and capital markets make investment and economic growth possible by providing the funds needed for the purchase of machinery and equipment and the construction of buildings, highways, and other productive facilities.

Clearly, then the acts of saving and lending, borrowing and investing are intimately linked through the financial system. And one factor that significantly influences and ties all of them together is the **rate of interest.** The rate of interest is the price a borrower must pay to secure scarce loanable funds from a lender for an agreed-upon time period. It is the **price of credit.** But unlike other prices in the economy, the rate of interest is really a *ratio* of two quantities: the money cost of borrowing divided by the amount of money actually borrowed, usually expressed on an annual percentage basis.

Interest rates send *price signals* to borrowers, lenders, savers, and investors. For example, higher interest rates generally bring forth a greater volume of savings and stimulate the lending of funds. Lower rates of interest, on the other hand, tend to dampen the flow of savings and reduce lending activity. Higher interest rates tend to reduce the volume of borrowing and capital investment, and lower interest rates stimulate borrowing and investment spending. In this chapter, we will discuss in more detail the forces that are believed by economists and financial analysts to determine rates of interest in the financial system.

FUNCTIONS OF THE RATE OF INTEREST IN THE ECONOMY

The *rate of interest* performs several important functions in the economy:

- It helps guarantee that current savings will flow into investment to promote economic growth.

- It rations the available supply of credit, generally providing loanable funds to those investment projects with the highest expected returns.

- It brings the supply of money into balance with the public's demand for money.

- It is an important tool of government policy through its influence on the volume of saving and investment. If the economy is growing too slowly and unemployment is rising, the government can use its policy tools to lower interest rates in order to stimulate borrowing and investment. On the other hand, an economy experiencing rapid inflation has traditionally called for a government policy of higher interest rates to slow borrowing and spending and encourage more saving.

In the pages of the financial press, the phrase "the interest rate" is frequently used. In truth, there is no such thing as "*the* interest rate," for there are thousands of different interest rates in the financial system. Even securities issued by the same borrower often carry a variety of interest rates. In Chapters 7 and 8, the most important factors that cause interest rates to vary among different loans and securities and over time are examined in detail. In this chapter, we focus upon those basic forces that influence the level of *all* interest rates.

To uncover these basic rate-determining forces, however, we must make a simplifying assumption. We assume in this chapter that there *is* one fundamental interest rate, known as the *pure* or **risk-free rate of interest,** which is a component of *all* interest rates. While the pure or risk-free rate of interest exists only in theory, the closest real-world approximation to this pure rate of return is the market interest rate on government bonds. It is a rate of return presenting little or no risk of financial loss to the investor and representing the opportunity cost of holding idle cash because the investor can always invest in government bonds of lowest risk and earn this minimum rate of return.

Once we explain the pure rate of interest in this chapter, the interest rates we normally see in the real world will be explored in the chapters that follow. Only the government can borrow at approximately the risk-free rate of interest. Other borrowers in the real world must pay higher interest rates for borrowed funds than the risk-free rate due to several different risk factors—for example credit or default risk, maturity or term risk, marketability risk, and so on. In Chapters 7 and 8 we will add these risk factors onto the pure or risk-free rate of interest to determine the level of and changes in real-world interest rates that we see every day.

First, however, we must examine the forces that determine the pure or risk-free interest rate itself. In this chapter we present the four most popular views—The Classical Theory, The Liquidity Preference Theory, The Loanable Funds Theory, and The Rational Expectations Theory of Interest—about how the fundamental pure or risk-free rate of interest is determined. We will also note which of these interest rate theories is the most widely followed today by practitioners and active investors "on the street," keeping in mind, however, that there are some important truths to consider in every one of the interest-rate theories discussed in this chapter.

THE CLASSICAL THEORY OF INTEREST RATES

One of the oldest theories concerning the determinants of the pure or risk-free interest rate is the **classical theory of interest rates,** developed during the eighteenth and nineteenth centuries by a number of British economists and elaborated by Irving Fisher (1930) and others more recently. The classical theory argues that the rate of interest is determined by two forces: (1) the supply of savings, derived mainly from households, and (2) the demand for investment capital, coming mainly from the business sector. Let us examine these rate-determining forces of savings and investment demand in detail.

Saving by Households

What is the relationship between the rate of interest and the volume of savings in the economy? Most saving in modern industrialized economies is carried out by individuals and families. For these households, saving is simply abstinence from consumption spending. *Current savings, therefore, are equal to the difference between current income and current consumption expenditures.*

In making the decision on the timing and amount of saving to be done, households typically consider several factors: the size of current and long-term income, the desired savings target, and the desired proportion of income to be set aside in the form of savings (i.e., the propensity to save). Generally, the volume of household saving rises with income. Higher-income families and individuals tend to save more and consume less relative to their total income than families with lower incomes.

Although income levels probably dominate saving decisions, interest rates also play an important role. Interest rates affect an individual's choice between current consumption and saving for future consumption. The classical theory of interest assumes that individuals have a definite *time preference* for current over future consumption. A rational individual, it is assumed, will always prefer current enjoyment of goods and services over future enjoyment. Therefore, the only way to encourage an individual or family to consume less now and save more is to offer a higher rate of interest on current savings. If more were saved in the current period at a higher rate of return, future consumption would be increased. For example, if the current rate of interest is 10 percent and a household saves $100 instead of spending it on current consumption, it will be able to consume $110 in goods and services a year from now.

The classical theory considers the payment of interest a reward for *waiting*—the postponement of current consumption in favor of greater future consumption. Higher interest rates increase the attractiveness of saving relative to consumption spending, encouraging more individuals to substitute current saving (and future consumption) for some quantity of current consumption. This so-called **substitution effect** calls for a *positive* relationship between interest rates and the volume of savings. Higher interest rates bring forth a greater volume of current savings. Exhibit 5–1 illustrates the substitution effect: If the rate of interest in the financial markets rises from 5 to 10 percent, the volume of current savings by households is assumed to increase from $100 to $200 billion.

EXHIBIT 5–1
The Substitution Effect Relating Savings and Interest Rates

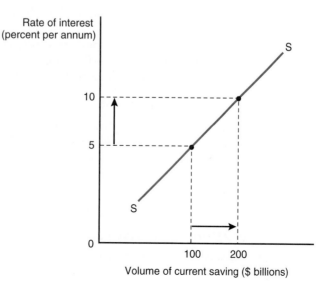

Financial Developments   Are Americans Really Saving More These Days Than We Think?

American scientist and diplomat Benjamin Franklin once noted that "a penny saved is a penny earned." Recently with the U.S. personal savings rate (i.e., the ratio of personal savings to disposable personal income) falling to its lowest level in over half a century, many observers think that Americans no longer believe Ben Franklin was right. Some analysts of our financial system believe, however, that the U.S. savings rate is, in truth, substantially larger than many people realize. For example, the *personal savings rate*—or ratio of personal disposable income less personal consumption spending divided by personal disposable (after-tax) income—does *not* record savings by corporations and other institutions or pick up the purchase of capital goods by households (such as the purchase of new homes) or capture any increases occurring in human capital (e.g., a college education). America's savings rate jumps to about 10 percent (from less than 1 percent recently) when the above elements are added on to personal savings.

Another key element of overall savings is *capital appreciation*—that is, when the value of our holdings of financial assets (stocks, bonds, etc.) and of nonfinancial assets (such as a home) rises, increasing net worth. If our assets are rising in value, there is less need to save out of current income in order to achieve our savings goals. In brief, if we look at *all* sources of savings, rather than just one type of savings, the performance of America (and other countries as well) looks better, though the U.S. savings rate is still low.

Saving by Business Firms

Not only households but also businesses save. Most businesses hold savings balances in the form of retained earnings (as reflected in their equity or net worth accounts). In fact, the increase in retained earnings reported by businesses each year is a key measure of the volume of current business saving, which supplies most of the money for annual investment spending by business firms.

The critical element in determining the amount of business savings is the level of business profits. If profits are expected to rise, businesses will be able to draw more heavily on earnings retained in the firm and less heavily on the money and capital markets for funds. The result is a reduction in the demand for credit and a tendency toward lower interest rates. On the other hand, when profits fall but firms do not cut back on their investment plans, they are forced to make heavier use of the money and capital markets for investment funds. The demand for credit rises, and interest rates may rise as well.

Although the principal determinant of business saving is profits, interest rates also play a role in the decision of what proportion of current operating costs and long-term investment expenditures should be financed internally and what proportion externally. Higher interest rates in the money and capital markets typically encourage firms to use internally generated funds more heavily in financing projects. Conversely, lower interest rates encourage greater use of external funds from the money and capital markets.

Saving by Government

Governments also save, though usually less frequently than households and businesses. In fact, most government saving (i.e., a budget surplus) appears to be unintended saving that arises when government receipts unexpectedly exceed the actual amount of expenditures. Income flows in the economy (out of which government tax revenues arise) and the pacing of government spending programs are the dominant factors affecting government savings. Interest rates are probably *not* a key factor here.

The Demand for Investment Funds

Business, household, and government savings are important determinants of interest rates according to the classical theory of interest, but they are not the only ones. The other critical rate-determining factor is *investment spending*, most of it carried out by business firms.

Certainly, businesses, as the leading investment sector in the economy, require huge amounts of funds each year to purchase equipment, machinery, and inventories, and to support the construction of new buildings and other physical facilities. The majority of business expenditures for these purposes consists of *replacement investment;* that is, expenditures to replace equipment and facilities that are wearing out or are technologically obsolete. A smaller but more dynamic form of business capital spending is labeled *net investment:* expenditures to acquire new equipment and facilities in order to increase output. The sum of replacement investment plus net investment equals *gross investment.*

Replacement investment usually is more predictable and grows at a more even rate than net investment. This is due to the fact that such expenditures are financed almost exclusively from inside the firm and frequently follow a routine pattern based on depreciation formulas. Expenditures for new equipment and facilities (net investment), on the other hand, depend on the business community's outlook for future sales, changes in technology, industrial capacity, and the cost of raising funds. Because these factors are subject to frequent changes, it is not surprising that net investment is highly volatile and a driving force in the economy. Changes in net investment are closely linked to fluctuations in the nation's output of goods and services, employment, and prices.

The Investment Decision-Making Process

The process of investment decision making by business firms is complex and depends on a host of qualitative and quantitative factors. The firm must compare its current level of production with the capacity of its existing facilities and decide whether it has sufficient capacity to handle anticipated demand for its product. If expected future demand will strain the firm's existing facilities, it will consider expanding its operating capacity through net investment.

Most business firms have several investment projects under consideration at any one time. Although the investment decision-making process varies from firm to firm, each business generally makes some estimate of net cash flows (i.e., revenues minus all expenses, including taxes) that each project will generate over its useful life. From this information, plus knowledge of each investment project's acquisition cost, management can calculate its expected net rate of return and compare that expected return with anticipated returns from alternative projects, as well as with market rates of interest.

One common method for performing this calculation is the *internal rate of return method,* which equates the total cost of an investment project with the future net cash flows (NCF) expected from that project discounted back to their present values. Thus,

$$\text{Cost of project} = \frac{NCF_1}{(1 + r)^1} + \frac{NCF_2}{(1 + r)^2} + \ldots + \frac{NCF_n}{(1 + r)^n} \quad \textbf{(5–1)}$$

where each *NCF* represents the expected annual net cash flow from the project and *r* is its expected internal rate of return. The internal rate performs two functions: (1) it measures the annual yield the firm expects from an investment project, and (2) it reduces the value of all future cash flows expected over the economic life of the project down to their present value to the firm. In general, if the firm must choose among several investment projects, it will choose the one with the *highest* expected internal rate of return.

Although the internal rate of return provides a yardstick for selecting potentially profitable investment projects, how does a business decide how much to spend on investment at any point in time? How many projects should be chosen? It is here that the money and capital markets play a key role in the investment decision-making process.

Suppose a business firm is considering the following projects with their associated expected internal rates of return:

Project	Expected Internal Rate of Return (annualized)
A	15%
B	12
C	10
D	9
E	8

How many of these projects will be adopted? The firm must compare each project's expected internal return with the cost of raising capital—the interest rate—in the money and capital markets to finance the project.

Assume that funds must be borrowed in the financial marketplace to complete any of the above projects and that the current cost of borrowing—the rate of interest—is 10 percent. Which projects are acceptable from an economic standpoint? As shown in Exhibit 5–2, projects A and B clearly are acceptable because their expected returns exceed the current cost of borrowing capital (10 percent) to finance them. The firm would be indifferent about project C because its expected return is no more than the cost of borrowed funds. Projects D and E, on the other hand, are unprofitable at this time.

It is through changes in the cost of raising funds that the financial markets can exert a powerful influence on the investment decisions of business firms. As credit becomes scarcer and more expensive, the cost of borrowed capital rises, eliminating some investment projects from consideration. For example, if the cost of borrowed funds rises from 10 to 13 percent, it is obvious that only project A in our earlier example would then be economically viable. On the other hand, if credit becomes more abundant and less costly, the cost of capital for the individual firm will tend to decline and more projects will become profitable. In our example, a decline in the cost of borrowed funds from 10 to 8½ percent would make all but project E economically viable and probably acceptable to the firm.

Investment Demand and the Rate of Interest

This reasoning explains, in part, why the demand for investment capital by business firms was regarded by the classical economists as *negatively* related to the rate of interest. Exhibit 5–3 depicts the business investment demand schedule as drawn in the classical theory, sloping downward and to the right. At low rates of interest, more investment projects become economically viable and firms require more funds to finance a longer list of projects.

EXHIBIT 5–2
The Cost of Capital and the Investment Decision

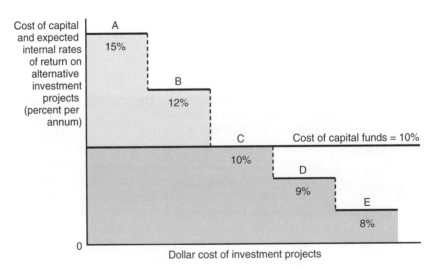

On the other hand, if the rate of interest rises to high levels, fewer investment projects will be pursued and fewer funds will be required from the financial markets. For example, at a 12 percent rate of interest, only $150 billion in funds for investment spending might be demanded by business firms in the economy. If the rate of interest drops to 10 percent, however, the volume of desired investment by firms might rise to $200 billion.

The Equilibrium Rate of Interest in the Classical Theory of Interest

The classical economists believed that interest rates in the financial markets were determined by the interplay of the supply of saving and the demand for investment. Specifically, the equilibrium rate of interest is determined at the point where the quantity of savings supplied to the market is exactly equal to the quantity of funds demanded for investment. As shown in Exhibit 5–4, this occurs at point *E,* where the equilibrium rate of interest is i_E and the equilibrium quantity of capital funds traded in the financial markets is Q_E.

EXHIBIT 5–3
The Investment Demand Schedule in the Classical Theory of Interest Rates

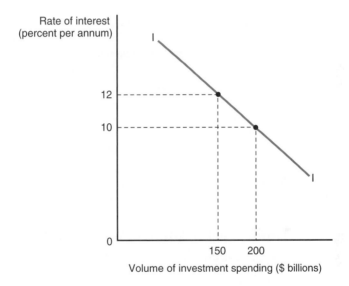

EXHIBIT 5–4
The Equilibrium Rate of Interest in the Classical Theory

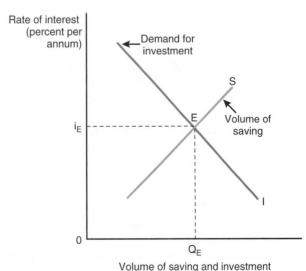

Data on interest rates may be found at a wide variety of sites on the World Wide Web such as *www.bankrate.com* and *www.investinginbonds.com*

To illustrate, suppose the total volume of savings supplied by businesses, households, and governments in the economy at an interest rate of 10 percent is $200 billion. Moreover, at this same 10 percent rate, businesses would also demand $200 billion in funds for investment purposes. Then 10 percent must be the equilibrium rate of interest, and $200 billion is the equilibrium quantity of funds that would be traded in the money and capital markets.

The market rate of interest moves toward its equilibrium level. However, supply and demand forces change so fast that the interest rate rarely has an opportunity to settle in at a specific equilibrium level. At any given time, the interest rate is probably above or below its true equilibrium level but moving *toward* that equilibrium. If the market rate is temporarily above equilibrium, the volume of savings exceeds the demand for investment capital, creating an excess supply of savings. Savers will offer their funds at lower and lower rates until the market interest rate approaches equilibrium. Similarly, if the market interest rate lies temporarily below equilibrium, investment demand exceeds the quantity of savings available. Business firms will bid up the interest rate until it approaches the level at which the quantity saved equals the quantity of funds demanded for investment purposes.

The classical theory of interest rates helps us to understand some of the *long-term forces* driving interest rates. For example, several economists (e.g., Bryan and Byrne, 1990) have argued that, in the future, interest rates may average lower than today's interest rates. This may be true because the populations of the United States and most other nations are aging, shifting heavily toward those age groups in which individuals spend less of their current income and save more (in part to prepare for retirement). This viewpoint assumes that people's consumption and savings habits tend to follow a predictable *life cycle,* with younger workers borrowing heavily in anticipation of higher incomes in the future and older workers, who have reached their maximum annual earnings, saving heavily in anticipation of lower incomes in the future. The money and capital markets make a vital contribution to this process, directing the savings of older individuals into the hands of younger people who desire to improve their current standard of living by borrowing.

Limitations of the Classical Theory of Interest

The classical theory sheds light on the factors affecting interest rates. However, it has serious limitations. The central problem is that the theory ignores factors other than saving and investment that affect interest rates. For example, many financial institutions have the power to create money today by making loans to the public. When borrowers repay their loans, money is destroyed. The volume of money created or destroyed affects the total amount of credit available in the financial system and, therefore, must be considered in any explanation of interest rates. In addition, the classical theory assumes that interest rates are the principal determinant of the quantity of savings available. Today economists recognize that *income* is actually more important in determining the volume of saving. Finally, the classical theory contends that the demand for borrowed funds comes principally from the business sector. Today, however, both consumers and governments are also important borrowers. As we will see in the rest of this chapter, more recent theories about interest rates address a number of these limitations of the classical theory.

Questions *to Help You Study*

1. What are the functions or roles played by the rate of interest in the economy and financial system? Can you explain why each function or role that you list is important to the well-being of individuals, businesses, and governments?

2. Explain the meaning of the term *pure* or *risk-free **rate of interest.*** Why is this interest rate important and what is its relationship to other interest rates in the money and capital markets?

3. If we could identify the forces shaping the level of and changes in the risk-free or pure rate of interest, what advantage could this give to us in trying to explain the many different interest rates we see every day in the real world?

4. In the so-called classical theory of interest rates, what major forces determine the market rate of interest? What assumptions does the classical theory of interest rest upon?

5. Explain why the supply curve in the classical theory of interest rates has a positive slope. Why does the demand curve in the classical theory have a negative slope?

THE LIQUIDITY PREFERENCE OR CASH BALANCES THEORY OF INTEREST RATES

The classical theory of interest has been called a *long-term* explanation of interest rates because it focuses on the public's thrift habits and the productivity of capital—factors that tend to change slowly. During the 1930s, British economist John Maynard Keynes (1936) developed a short-term theory of the rate of interest that, he argued, was more relevant for policymakers and for explaining near-term changes in interest rates. This theory is known as the **liquidity preference** (or *cash balances*) **theory of interest rates.**

The Demand for Liquidity

Keynes argued that the rate of interest is really a payment for the use of a scarce resource, *money* (cash balances). Businesses and individuals prefer to hold money for carrying out daily transactions and also as a precaution against future cash needs even though money's yield is usually low or even nonexistent. Investors in fixed-income securities, such as government bonds, frequently desire to hold money or cash balances as a haven against declining asset prices. Interest rates, therefore, are the price that must be paid to induce money holders to surrender a perfectly liquid asset (cash balances) and hold other assets that carry more risk. At times the preference for liquidity grows very strong. Unless the government expands the money supply, interest rates will rise.

In the theory of liquidity preference, only two outlets for investor funds are considered: *bonds* and *money* or *cash balances* (including bank deposits). Money provides perfect liquidity (instant spending power). Bonds pay interest but cannot be spent until converted into cash. If interest rates rise, the market value of bonds paying a fixed rate of interest falls; the investor would suffer a capital loss if those bonds were converted into cash. On the other hand, a fall in interest rates results in higher bond prices; the bondholder will experience a capital gain if his or her bonds are sold for cash. To the classical theorists, it was irrational to hold money because it provided little or no return. To Keynes, however, the holding of money (cash balances) could be a perfectly rational act if interest rates were expected to rise, because rising rates can result in substantial losses for investors in bonds.

Motives for Holding Money (Cash Balances)

Keynes observed that the public demands money for three different purposes (motives). The *transactions motive* represents the demand for money (cash balances) to purchase goods and services. Because inflows and outflows of money are not perfectly synchronized in either timing or amount and because it is costly to shift back and forth between money

Our discussion of how interest rates affect business investment decisions earlier in this chapter focused upon the internal rate of return (IRR) method for comparing interest rates with the expected return on an investment project. Actually, the IRR method for evaluating investments is less widely used by investment decision makers today than another method of investment analysis—the *net present value* (NPV) approach.

For example, suppose that we operate a business that is considering an investment project costing $1,000 and generating expected net cash flows (cash revenues less cash expenses) of:

Year	Net Cash Flow
1	$100
2	$100
3	$300
4	$400
5	$500
6	$600

after which point in time the project becomes worthless. Thus, its internal rate of return (IRR) can be found from the formula:

$$\$1,000 = \frac{\$100}{(1+r)^1} + \frac{\$200}{(1+r)^2} + \frac{\$300}{(1+r)^3} +$$

$$\frac{\$400}{(1+r)^4} + \frac{\$500}{(1+r)^5} + \frac{\$600}{(1+r)^6}$$

where the internal rate of return (*r*) turns out to be about 10 percent. If the going market rate on borrowed funds in the money and capital markets is 8 percent, this project is clearly acceptable because its expected internal rate of return exceeds the cost of raising borrowed funds. Now suppose the

firm believes that its stockholders demand a minimum required after-tax return of 12 percent. Then the proposed project's net present value must be:

$$NPV = \$1,000 + \frac{\$100}{(1+.12)^1} + \frac{\$200}{(1+.12)^2} + \frac{\$300}{(1+.12)^3} +$$

$$\frac{\$400}{(1+.12)^4} + \frac{\$500}{(1+.12)^5} + \frac{\$600}{(1+.12)^6} \approx \$304$$

This proposed investment project is acceptable because its NPV is positive (*NPV* > 0) at about + $304.

With IRR, the implied reinvestment rate of return for each project's cash flows is equal to the calculated internal rate of return and, therefore, is likely to be different for each proposed project. However, under the NPV method, the implied reinvestment rate is the *same* for *all* projects—investors' required rate of return (i.e., the minimum necessary return on the investment opportunity available to an investor to keep a business's stock price unchanged). Thus, NPV tends to be a correct measure of the true opportunity cost of a given project for an investor whose goal is value maximization (i.e., maximizing the value of each business firm's stock price).

As interest rates in the money and capital markets rise, offering investors higher returns on other investment alternatives of comparable risk, then investors will tend to raise the required return they demand from an investment project. Fewer projects will be acceptable. Conversely, when interest rates in the money and capital markets fall, investors' required rates of return will tend to decline. Investment spending will tend to rise. No matter what method is used to evaluate investment projects, interest rates in the money and capital markets play a vital role in determining the volume of investment and in attracting savings to make investment possible.

and other assets, businesses, households, and governments must keep some cash in the till or in demand accounts simply to meet daily expenses. Some money also must be held as a reserve for future emergencies and to cover extraordinary expenses. This *precautionary motive* arises because we live in a world of uncertainty and cannot predict exactly what expenses or investment opportunities will arise in the future.

Keynes assumed that money demanded for transactions and precautionary purposes is dependent on the level of national income, business sales, and prices. Reflecting money's role as a medium of exchange, higher levels of income, sales, or prices increase the need for cash balances to carry out transactions and to respond to future opportunities. However, neither the precautionary nor the transactions demand for money was assumed to be affected by changes in interest rates. In fact, Keynes assumed money demand for precautionary and transactions purposes to be fixed in the short term. In the longer term, however, transactions and precautionary demands change as income changes.

Short-term changes in interest rates were attributed by Keynes to a third motive for holding money or cash balances—the *speculative motive*—that stems from uncertainty about the future prices of bonds. To illustrate, suppose an investor has recently purchased a corporate bond for $1,000. The company issuing the bond promises to pay $100 a year in interest income. To simplify matters, assume the bond is a *perpetual security.* This means the investor will receive $100 a year for as long as the security is held. The annual rate of return (or yield) on the bond, then, is 10 percent ($100/$1,000). Suppose now that the interest rate on bonds of similar quality rises to 12 percent. What happens to the price of the 10 percent bond? Its price in the marketplace will *fall* because its annual promised yield at a price of $1,000 is *less* than 12 percent. The 10 percent bond's price will approach $833 because at this price the bond's $100 annual interest payment gives the investor an approximate annual yield of 12 percent ($100/$833). In the reverse situation, if interest rates were to decline— say, to 9 percent—the 10 percent bond would experience a rise in its market price.[1]

If investors expect rising interest rates, many of them will demand money or near-money assets instead of bonds because they believe bond prices will fall. As the expectation that interest rates will rise grows strong in the marketplace, the demand for cash balances as a secure store of value increases. We may represent this speculative demand for money by a line or curve that slopes downward and to the right, as shown in Exhibit 5–5, reflecting a *negative* relationship between the speculative demand for money and the level of interest rates. At low rates of interest, many investors believe that interest rates are soon to rise (i.e., bond prices are going to fall), and, therefore, more money is demanded. At high rates of interest, on the other hand, many investors will conclude that interest rates soon will fall and bond prices rise, so the demand for cash balances decreases while the demand for bonds increases.

From another vantage point, when interest rates are high, the opportunity cost (loss) from holding idle cash increases. Thus, high interest rates encourage investors to reduce their cash balances and buy bonds. In contrast, when interest rates are low, the opportunity cost of holding idle cash is also low, but the expected capital loss from holding bonds is high should interest rates rise. Thus, there is more incentive to hold money rather than bonds when interest rates are low.

Total Demand for Money (Cash Balances)

The total demand for money or cash balances in the economy is simply the sum of transactions, precautionary, and speculative demands. Because the principal determinant of transactions and precautionary demand is income, not interest rates, these money demands

---

[1]The price of a perpetual bond (*P*) is related to its market interest rate (*r*) by the formula

$$P = R/r$$

where *R* is the annual income in dollars paid by the security. Clearly, as interest rate *r* increases, market price *P* falls. As we will see in Chapter 6, the same *inverse* relationship between the price and interest yield on a fixed-income security holds even if we assume the security is not perpetual but has a finite maturity.

EXHIBIT 5–5
Speculative Demand for Money or Cash Balances

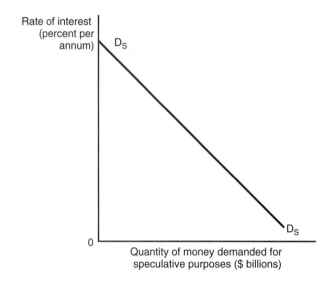

EXHIBIT 5–6
The Total Demand for Money or Cash Balances in the Economy

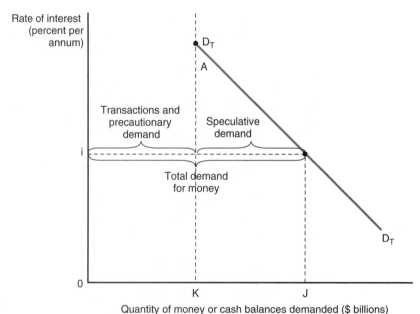

are fixed at a certain level of national income. Let this demand be represented by the quantity $0K$ shown along the horizontal axis in Exhibit 5–6. Then, any amount of cash demanded in excess of $0K$ represents speculative demand. The total demand for money is represented along curve D_T. Therefore, if the rate of interest lies at the moment at i, Exhibit 5–6 shows that the speculative demand for money will be KJ and the total demand for money will be $0J$.

The Supply of Money (Cash Balances)

The other major element determining interest rates in liquidity preference theory is the supply of money. In modern economies, the money supply is controlled, or at least closely regulated, by government. Because government decisions concerning the size of the money

EXHIBIT 5–7
**The Equilibrium
Rate of Interest in the
Liquidity Preference
Theory**

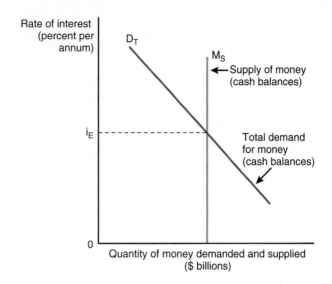

supply presumably are guided by the public welfare, not by the level of interest rates, we assume that the supply of cash balances is *inelastic* with respect to the rate of interest. Such a money supply curve is represented in Exhibit 5–7 by the vertical line M_S.

The Equilibrium Rate of Interest in Liquidity Preference Theory

The interplay of the total demand for and the supply of money or cash balances determines the equilibrium rate of interest in the short run. As shown in Exhibit 5–7, the equilibrium rate is found at point i_E, where the quantity of money demanded by the public equals the quantity of money supplied. Above this equilibrium rate, the supply of money exceeds the quantity demanded, and some businesses, households, and units of government will try to dispose of their unwanted cash balances by purchasing bonds. The prices of bonds will rise, driving interest rates down toward equilibrium at i_E. On the other hand, at rates below equilibrium, the quantity of money demanded exceeds the supply. Some decision makers in the economy will sell their bonds to raise additional cash, driving bond prices down and interest rates up toward equilibrium.

Liquidity preference theory provides some useful insights into investor behavior and the influence of government policy on the economy and financial system. For example, the theory suggests that it is rational at certain times for the public to hoard money (cash balances) and at other times to "dishoard" (spend away) unwanted cash. If the public disposes of some of its cash by purchasing securities, this action increases the quantity of loanable funds available in the money and capital markets. Other things being equal, interest rates will fall. On the other hand, if the public tries to "hoard" more money (expanding its cash balances by selling securities), less money will be available for loans. Interest rates will rise, *ceteris paribus*.

Liquidity preference theory illustrates how central banks such as the Federal Reserve System can influence interest rates in the financial markets, at least in the short term. For example, if higher interest rates are desired, the central bank can contract the size of the money supply and interest rates will tend to rise (assuming the demand for money is unchanged). If the demand for money is increasing, the central bank can bring about higher interest rates by ensuring that the money supply grows more slowly than money demand. In contrast, if the central bank expands the money supply, interest rates will decline in the short term (provided the demand for money does not increase).

International Focus   Convergence of Interest Rates and "The Liquidity Trap"

As the 1990s drew to a close and the new century was beginning, students of interest rates were greeted with two remarkable and somewhat hard to explain phenomena. One was a so-called "convergence" of market interest rates in Western Europe as yields on securities issued by governments about to enter the new European Monetary Union (EMU) began to fall and gradually move much closer toward each other. The same interest rate "convergence" trend began to show itself in Europe's private security markets.

A wide variety of explanations for this trend soon surfaced. One factor was a perceived decline in risk by many investors who anticipated that currency risk inside the new European Community (EC) would likely soon fall dramatically as the Euro—the European Community's new single currency—replaced many traditional European currencies. Some market participants also saw the possibility that the newly expanded common European economy would tend to be more stable overall than were the separate economies of the individual nations making up the new EC.

For its part, Japan's financial system illustrated a second rare phenomenon in the field of interest rates—a "liquidity trap." Market interest rates in Japan fell to record lows (in some cases, below 1 percent—the lowest level seen in several centuries) due, in part, to a weak Japanese economy and a flood of savings as Japanese families and businesses moved to protect themselves against the risks of early retirement, rising unemployment and fears of more bank failures. Japanese interest rates dropped so low that many investors in Japanese securities became convinced they must eventually rise, resulting in eventual losses for holders of those securities. Efforts by the Japanese government to push interest rates even lower in an effort to stimulate their lagging economy by encouraging more borrowing and spending met with little success. Market interest rates seemed to have reached a rock bottom below which they would not fall. The "liquidity trap" concept, based on the liquidity preference theory of interest rates, implies that the demand for money (cash balances) curve may become *perfectly horizontal* at some very low interest rate. This means that no matter how much the government tries to expand the supply of money and credit, interest rates simply cannot be driven any lower. Market investors seem convinced the only likely change is an eventual interest rate *increase*. In this instance, other policy measures (such as changes in tax rates) may be needed if the government hopes to stimulate a struggling economy.

For further information about the European Monetary Union (EMU) see the Web site of the European Central Bank at *www.ecb.int/*

Limitations of the Liquidity Preference Theory

Like the classical theory of interest, liquidity preference theory has limitations. It is a short-term approach to interest rate determination unless modified because it assumes that income remains stable. In the longer term, interest rates are affected by changes in the level of income and by inflationary expectations. Indeed, it is impossible to have a stable equilibrium interest rate without also reaching an equilibrium level of income, saving, and investment in the economy. Also, liquidity preference considers only the supply and demand for the stock of money, whereas business, consumer, and government demands for credit clearly have an impact on the cost of credit. A more comprehensive view of interest rates is needed that considers the important roles played by *all* actors in the financial system: businesses, households, and governments.

Questions *to Help You Study*

6. What are the origins of the *liquidity preference theory of interest*? What main assumptions seem to underlie this important idea about what determines the level of and changes in market rates of interest?

7. The demand for money is one of the most important concepts in the *liquidity prefer-ence theory of interest.* What are the three main components of the demand for money in this idea about how interest rates are determined?

8. What factors appear to determine the *transactions demand* for money? How about the *precautionary motive* for demanding and holding money? The *speculative motive*?

9. What makes up the *total demand for money*? What is the shape of the relationship be-tween the total demand for money and the market rate of interest?

10. What determines the equilibrium interest rate under the liquidity preference theory of interest? Please draw what this equilibrium interest rate looks like. Explain what forces cause the equilibrium interest rate to move, according to the liquidity preference idea?

11. What are the principal limitations of the liquidity preference theory of interest?

THE LOANABLE FUNDS THEORY OF INTEREST

A view that overcomes many of the limitations of earlier theories is the **loanable funds theory of interest rates.** It is the most popular interest-rate theory among practitioners and those who follow interest rates "on the street." The loanable funds view argues that the risk-free interest rate is determined by the interplay of two forces: the demand for and sup-ply of *credit* (loanable funds). The demand for loanable funds consists of credit demands from domestic businesses, consumers, and governments, and also borrowing in the domes-tic market by foreigners. The supply of loanable funds stems from four sources: domestic savings, dishoarding of money balances, money creation by the banking system, and lend-ing in the domestic market by foreign individuals and institutions. We consider each of these demand and supply factors in turn.

The Demand for Loanable Funds

Consumer (Household) Demand for Loanable Funds

Domestic consumers demand loanable funds to purchase a wide variety of goods and ser-vices on credit. Recent research indicates that consumers (households) are not particularly responsive to the rate of interest when they seek credit but focus instead principally on the nonprice terms of a loan, such as the down payment, maturity, and size of installment pay-ments. This implies that consumer demand for credit is relatively *inelastic* with respect to the rate of interest. Certainly a rise in interest rates leads to some reduction in the quantity of consumer demand for loanable funds, whereas a decline in interest rates stimulates some additional consumer borrowing. However, along the consumer's relatively inelastic de-mand schedule, a substantial change in the rate of interest must occur before the quantity of consumer demand for funds changes significantly.

Domestic Business Demand for Loanable Funds

The credit demands of domestic businesses generally are more responsive to changes in the rate of interest than is consumer borrowing. Most business credit is for such investment purposes as the purchase of inventories and new plant and equipment. As noted earlier in our discussion of the classical theory of interest, a high interest rate eliminates some busi-ness investment projects from consideration because their expected rate of return is lower than the cost of borrowed funds. On the other hand, at lower rates of interest, many invest-ment projects look profitable, with their expected returns exceeding the cost of funds.

Therefore, the quantity of loanable funds demanded by the business sector increases as the rate of interest falls.

Government Demand for Loanable Funds

Government demand for loanable funds is a growing factor in the financial markets but does not depend significantly upon the level of interest rates. This is especially true of borrowing by the federal government. Federal decisions on spending and borrowing are made by Congress in response to social needs and the public welfare, not the rate of interest. Moreover, the federal government has the power both to tax and to create money to pay its debts. State and local government demand, on the other hand, is slightly interest elastic because many local governments are limited in their borrowing activities by legal ceilings. When open market rates rise above these legal ceilings, some state and local governments are prevented from offering their securities to the public.

Foreign Demand for Loanable Funds

In recent years, foreign banks and corporations, as well as foreign governments, have increasingly entered the huge U.S. financial marketplace to borrow billions of dollars. This huge foreign credit demand is sensitive to the spread between domestic lending rates and interest rates in foreign markets. If U.S. interest rates decline relative to foreign rates, foreign borrowers will be inclined to borrow more in the United States and less abroad. At the same time, with higher foreign interest rates, U.S. lending institutions will increase their foreign lending and reduce the availability of loanable funds to domestic borrowers. The net result, then, is a *negative* or *inverse relationship* between foreign borrowing and domestic interest rates relative to foreign interest rates.

Total Demand for Loanable Funds

The total demand for loanable funds is the sum of domestic consumer, business, and government credit demands plus foreign credit demands. This demand curve slopes downward and to the right with respect to the rate of interest, as shown in Exhibit 5–8. Higher rates of interest lead some businesses, consumers, and governments to curtail their borrowing plans; lower rates bring forth more credit demand. However, the demand for loanable funds

EXHIBIT 5–8
Total Demand for Loanable Funds (Credit)

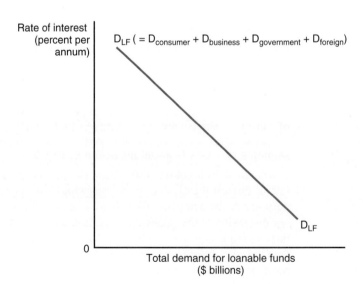

does not determine the rate of interest by itself. The supply of loanable funds must be added to complete the picture.

The Supply of Loanable Funds

Loanable funds flow into the money and capital markets from at least four different sources: (1) domestic saving by businesses, consumers, and governments; (2) dishoarding (spending down) of excess money balances held by the public; (3) creation of money by the domestic banking system; and (4) lending to domestic borrowers by foreigners. We consider each of these sources of funds in turn.

Domestic Saving

The supply of domestic savings is the principal source of loanable funds. As noted earlier, most saving is done by households and is simply the difference between current income and current consumption. Businesses, however, also save, by retaining a portion of current earnings and by adding to their depreciation reserves. Government saving, while relatively rare, occurs when current revenues exceed current expenditures.

Most economists today believe that income levels, rather than interest rates, are the dominant factor in the decision of how much and when to save. But there is evidence that business and household saving may be goal oriented: the so-called **income effect.** For example, suppose an individual wishes to accumulate $100,000 in anticipation of retirement. Interest rates subsequently rise from 5 to 10 percent. Will this individual save more out of each period's income or less? Probably *less*, because the higher interest rates will enable the saver to reach the $100,000 goal with less sacrifice of current income. At higher interest rates, savings accumulate faster. On the other hand, a lower interest rate might lead to a greater volume of saving because a business firm or household then must accumulate savings at a faster rate to achieve its savings goal.

Clearly, then, the income effect would have the opposite result for the volume of saving than the substitution effect described earlier in our discussion of the classical theory of interest. The substitution effect argues for a *positive* relationship between the rate of interest and the volume of savings, while the income effect suggests a *negative* relationship between interest rates and savings volume. Thus, these two effects pull aggregate saving in opposite directions as interest rates change. It should not be surprising, therefore, that the annual volume of saving in the economy is difficult to forecast.

Recent research using econometric models has suggested the importance of another factor—the **wealth effect**—in influencing savings decisions. Individuals accumulate wealth in many different forms: real assets (e.g., automobiles, houses, land) and financial assets (e.g., stocks, bonds). What happens to the value of financial assets as interest rates change? If rates rise, for example, the market value of many financial assets will fall until their yield approaches market-determined levels. Therefore, a rise in interest rates will result in decreases in the value of wealth held in some financial assets, forcing the individual to save more to protect his or her wealth position. Conversely, a decrease in interest rates will increase the value of many financial assets, increasing wealth and necessitating a lower volume of current saving.

For businesses and individuals heavily in debt, however, the *opposite* effects may ensue. When interest rates rise, debt contracted in earlier periods, when interest rates were lower, seems less of a burden. For example, a home mortgage taken by a family when interest rates in the mortgage market were 10 percent seems a less burdensome drain on income when rates on new mortgages have risen to 15 percent. Therefore, a rise in interest rates tends to make those economic units carrying a large volume of debt relative to their financial assets

For a discussion of savings goals and how to achieve them, consult such sources as the National Endowment for Financial Education (NEFE) at *www.nefe.org/*

feel better off. They may tend to save *less* as a result. A decrease in interest rates, on the other hand, may result in *more* savings due to the wealth effect.

The *net* effect of the income, substitution, and wealth effects leads to a relatively *interest-inelastic* supply of savings curve. Substantial changes in interest rates usually are required to bring about significant changes in the volume of aggregate saving in the economy.

Dishoarding of Money Balances

Still another source of loanable funds is centered on the public's demand for money relative to the available supply of money. As noted earlier, the public's demand for money (cash balances) varies with interest rates and income levels. The supply of money, on the other hand, is closely controlled by the government. Clearly the two—money demand and money supply—need not be the same. The difference between the public's total demand for money and the money supply is known as *hoarding*. When the public's demand for cash balances exceeds the supply, *positive hoarding* of money takes place as some individuals and businesses attempt to increase their cash balances at the expense of others. Hoarding *reduces* the volume of loanable funds available in the financial markets. On the other hand, when the public's demand for money is less than the supply available, *negative hoarding (dishoarding)* occurs. Some individuals and businesses will dispose of their excess cash holdings, *increasing* the supply of loanable funds available to others in the financial system.

Creation of Credit by the Domestic Banking System

Commercial banks and nonbank thrift institutions offering payments accounts have the unique ability to create credit by lending and investing their excess reserves (a process described in Chapter 15). Credit created by the domestic banking system represents an additional source of loanable funds, which must be added to the amount of savings and the dishoarding of money balances (or minus the amount of hoarding demand) to derive the total supply of loanable funds in the economy.

Foreign Lending to the Domestic Funds Market

Finally, foreign lenders provide large amounts of credit to domestic borrowers in the United States. These inflowing loanable funds are particularly sensitive to the difference between U.S. interest rates and interest rates overseas. If domestic rates rise relative to interest rates offered abroad, the supply of foreign funds to domestic markets will tend to rise. Foreign lenders will find it more attractive to make loans to domestic borrowers. At the same time, domestic borrowers will turn more to foreign markets for loanable funds as domestic interest rates climb relative to foreign rates. The combined result is to make the net foreign supply of loanable funds to the domestic credit market *positively* related to the spread between domestic and foreign rates of interest.

Total Supply of Loanable Funds

The total supply of loanable funds, including domestic saving, foreign lending, dishoarding of money, and new credit created by the domestic banking system, is depicted in Exhibit 5–9. The curve rises with higher rates of interest, indicating that a greater supply of loanable funds will flow into the money and capital markets when the returns from lending increase.

The Equilibrium Rate of Interest in the Loanable Funds Theory

The two forces of supply and demand for loanable funds determine not only the volume of lending and borrowing going on in the economy but also the rate of interest. *The interest*

EXHIBIT 5–9
The Supply of
Loanable Funds
(Credit)

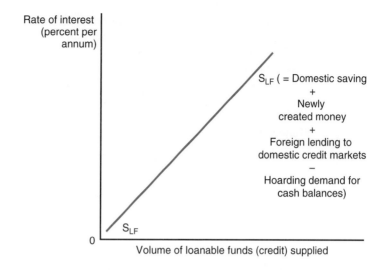

Rate of interest
(percent per
annum)

S_{LF} (= Domestic saving
+
Newly
created money
+
Foreign lending to
domestic credit markets
−
Hoarding demand for
cash balances)

S_{LF}

Volume of loanable funds (credit) supplied

EXHIBIT 5–10
The Equilibrium
Rate of Interest in the
Loanable Funds
Theory

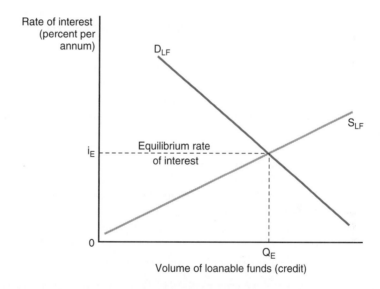

Rate of interest
(percent per
annum)

D_{LF}

S_{LF}

i_E

Equilibrium rate
of interest

Q_E

Volume of loanable funds (credit)

rate tends toward the equilibrium point at which the supply of loanable funds equals the demand for loanable funds. This point of equilibrium is shown in Exhibit 5–10 at i_E.

If the interest rate is temporarily *above* equilibrium, the quantity of loanable funds supplied by domestic savers and foreign lenders, by the banking system, and from the dishoarding of money (or minus hoarding demand) exceeds the total demand for loanable funds, and the rate of interest will be bid down. On the other hand, if the interest rate is temporarily *below* equilibrium, loanable funds demand will exceed the supply. The interest rate will be bid up by borrowers until it settles at equilibrium once again.

The equilibrium depicted in Exhibit 5–10 is only a *partial* equilibrium position, however. This is due to the fact that interest rates are affected by conditions in *both* the domestic and world economies. For the economy to be in equilibrium, planned saving must equal planned investment across the whole economic system. For example, if planned investment exceeds planned saving at the equilibrium interest rate shown in Exhibit 5–10, investment demands will push interest rates higher in the short term. However, as additional investment spending occurs, incomes will rise, generating a greater volume of savings.

Eventually, interest rates will fall. Similarly, if exchange rates between dollars, yen, and other world currencies are not in equilibrium with each other, there will be further opportunities for profit available to foreign and domestic lenders by moving loanable funds from one country to another.

Only when the economy, the money market, the loanable funds market, and foreign currency markets are *simultaneously* in equilibrium will interest rates remain stable. Thus, a completely *stable* equilibrium interest rate over the long run will be characterized by the following set of circumstances:

1. Planned saving = Planned investment (including business, household, and government investment) across the whole economic system (i.e., equilibrium in the economy).

2. Money supply = Money demand (i.e., equilibrium in the money market).

3. Quantity of loanable funds supplied = Quantity of loanable funds demanded (i.e., equilibrium in the loanable funds market).

4. The difference between foreign demand for loanable funds and the volume of loanable funds supplied by foreigners to the domestic economy = The difference between current exports from and imports into the domestic economy (i.e., equilibrium in the balance of payments and foreign currency markets).

This simple demand-supply framework is useful for analyzing broad movements in interest rates. For example, if the total supply of loanable funds is increasing and the total demand for loanable funds remains unchanged or rises more slowly, the volume of credit extended in the money and capital markets must increase. Interest rates will fall. This is illustrated in Exhibit 5–11A, which shows the supply schedule sliding outward and to the right when S_{LF} increases to S'_{LF}, resulting in a decline in the equilibrium rate of interest from i_1 to i_2. The equilibrium quantity of loanable funds traded in the financial system increases from C_1 to C_2.

What happens when the demand for loanable funds increases with no change in the total supply of funds available? In this instance, the volume of credit extended will increase, but loans will be made at higher interest rates. Exhibit 5–11B illustrates this. The loanable funds demand curve rises from D_{LF}, to D'_{LF}, driving the interest rate upward from i_1 to i_2.

Questions *to Help You Study*

12. What are *loanable funds*? Why is this term important?

13. What factors make up the total *demand* for loanable funds? The total *supply* of loanable funds? Please list and define each of these demand and supply factors in the Loanable Funds Theory of Interest.

14. Explain how the equilibrium loanable funds interest rate is determined. Please draw a picture of what the equilibrium rate of interest might look like under the loanable funds theory.

15. Suppose the demand for loanable funds increases relative to the supply. What happens to the equilibrium rate of interest? Suppose, on the other hand, the supply of loanable funds expands with loanable funds demand unchanged. What does the equilibrium loanable funds interest rate look like under these circumstances? Can you draw a picture of these changes in the equilibrium interest rate?

16. What does it take to have a *permanently stable equilibrium interest rate* under the loanable funds theory of interest? How does this differ from a *temporary* or *partial* equilibrium loanable funds rate?

17. What are the principal *limitations* of the loanable funds theory of interest?

EXHIBIT 5–11
Changes in the Demand for and Supply of Loanable Funds

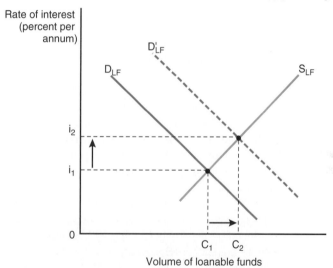

A. Effects of increased supply of loanable funds with demand unchanged

B. Effects of increased demand for loanable funds with supply unchanged

THE RATIONAL EXPECTATIONS THEORY OF INTEREST

In recent years, a fourth major theory about the forces determining interest rates has appeared: the **rational expectations theory of interest rates.** This theory builds on a growing body of research evidence that the money and capital markets are highly efficient institutions in digesting *new information* affecting interest rates and security prices.

For example, when new information appears about investment, saving, or the money supply, investors begin immediately to translate that new information into decisions to borrow or lend funds. So rapid is this process of the market digesting new information that asset prices and interest rates presumably impound the new data from virtually the moment they appear. As we saw in Chapter 3, in a perfectly efficient market, it is impossible to win excess returns consistently by trading on publicly available information.

This expectations theory assumes that businesses and individuals are *rational agents* who form expectations about the distribution of future asset prices and interest rates that do not differ significantly from optimal forecasts made from using all the available information that the marketplace provides. Rational agents attempt to make optimal use of the resources at their disposal to maximize their returns. Moreover, a rational agent will tend to make *unbiased* forecasts of future asset prices, interest rates, and other variables. That is, he or she will make no systematic forecasting errors and will easily spot past patterns in forecast errors and correct them quickly.

If the money and capital markets are highly efficient in the way we have described, this implies that interest rates will always be very near their equilibrium levels. Any deviation from the equilibrium interest rate dictated by demand and supply forces will be almost instantly eliminated. Security traders who hope to *consistently* earn windfall profits from correctly guessing whether interest rates are "too high" (and therefore will probably fall) or are "too low" (and therefore will probably rise) are unlikely to be successful in the long term. Interest rate fluctuations around equilibrium are likely to be random and momentary. Moreover, knowledge of *past* interest rates—for example, those that prevailed yesterday or last month—will *not* be a reliable forecast of where those rates are likely to be in the future. Indeed, the rational expectations theory suggests that, in the absence of new information, the *optimal forecast* of next period's interest rate would probably be equal to the current period's interest rate (i.e., $E(r_{t+1}) = r_t$) because there is no particular reason for next period's interest rate to be either higher or lower than today's interest rate until new information causes market participants to revise their expectations.

Old news will *not* affect today's interest rates because those rates already have impounded the old news. Interest rates will change only if entirely *new and unexpected* information appears. For example, if the federal government announces for several weeks running that it must borrow an additional $10 billion next month, interest rates probably reacted to that information the first time it appeared. In fact, interest rates probably *increased* at that time, because many investors would view the government's additional need for credit as adding to other demands for credit in the economy and, with the supply of funds unchanged, interest rates would be expected to rise. However, if the government merely repeated that same announcement again, interest rates probably would *not* change a second time; it would be old information already reflected in today's interest rates.

Imagine a new scenario, however. The government suddenly reveals that, contrary to expectations, tax revenues are now being collected in greater amounts than first forecast and therefore no new borrowing will be needed. Interest rates probably will fall immediately as market participants are forced to revise their borrowing and lending plans to deal with a new situation. How do we know which *direction* rates will move? Clearly, the path interest rates take depends on *what market participants expected to begin with.* Thus, if market participants were expecting increased demand for credit (with supply unchanged), an unexpected announcement of reduced credit demand implies lower interest rates in the future. Similarly, a market expectation of less credit demand in the future (supply unchanged) when confronted with an unexpected announcement of higher credit demand implies that interest rates will rise.

We can illustrate the foregoing points about the rational expectations theory of interest by modifying the loanable funds theory of interest so that its demand and supply schedules reflect not just actual demand and supply but also the *expected* demand for and supply of loanable funds. For example, referring to Exhibit 5–12, suppose D_0 and S_0 reflect the *actual* supply and demand for loanable funds in the current period, while D_F reflects the *actual* demand for loanable funds that will prevail in the next (future) time period. The supply of loanable funds is assumed to be the same in both time periods ($S_0 = S_F$).

EXHIBIT 5–12
Expected Demand for and Supply of Loanable Funds under the Rational Expectations Theory

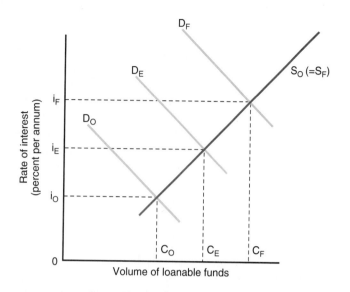

Now imagine that during the current period, the government makes an unexpected announcement of its increased need to borrow more money in future period *F* due to an unusually large budget deficit. The result is a new expected demand for loanable funds curve D_E, projected to prevail in the next (future) period *F* but as viewed by borrowers and lenders today in time period *0*. In this case, the equilibrium interest rate in the current period will not be i_o, but rather i_E, where the expected demand curve (D_E) intersects the actual supply curve S_0. The equilibrium quantity of loanable funds traded in the current period then will be C_E not C_0. This is because, according to the rational expectations theory, borrowers and lenders will act as rational agents, using all the information they possess (including expected events, such as the government announcing it will need to borrow more money in a future period) to price assets *today*. When the future period arrives, the equilibrium interest rate will rise to rate i_F and the quantity of loanable funds traded then will be C_F. The equilibrium rate moves upward because the demand for loanable funds in period *F* is more than the expected future loanable funds demand as seen by market participants in period *0*.

Suppose, on the other hand, that actual loanable funds demand in period *F* increases upward and beyond D_0 but by a smaller amount than was anticipated by investors in the market in period *0*. Demand schedule D_F would then fall somewhere between D_0 and D_E. The equilibrium interest rate (with the supply curve unchanged) would be *lower* than i_E, lying somewhere between i_0 and i_E.

But this is a startling conclusion! Actual demand *increased* (above D_0, but not to D_E) in the next period with supply held constant. Still, the equilibrium interest rate *fell*! How could this be? Clearly, it makes sense only when we assume that the real world works the way the rational expectations theory says it should. *To know which way interest rates will go, we must know what the market expects to begin with.* In this example, demand for loanable funds rose but not as high as the market expected. Therefore, interest rates will *decline,* other factors held constant.

The rational expectations view argues that forecasting interest rates requires knowledge of the public's *current set of expectations.* If new information is sufficient to alter those expectations, interest rates and asset prices *must* change. If correct, this portion of the rational expectations theory creates significant problems for government policymakers. It implies that policymakers cannot cause interest rates to move in any particular direction without knowing what the public already expects to happen and, indeed, cannot change interest rates and asset prices at all unless government officials can convince the public that a new set of expectations is warranted. Moreover, because guessing what the public's expectations are is treacherous at best, rational expectations theorists suggest that *rate hedging*—using various tools to reduce the risk of loss from changing interest rates—*is preferable to rate forecasting*. Indeed, to be a consistently correct interest rate forecaster under the rational expectations theory you must know (1) what market participants expect to happen and (2) what new information will arrive in the market before that information actually arrives. That's a tall order!

A growing number of studies today imply that at least some elements of the rational expectations/efficient markets view *do* show up in actual market behavior. For example, studies by Mishkin (1978) and Phillips and Pippenger (1976) find that past interest-rate movements are *not* significantly related to current rates of return on bonds or stock, as the theory predicts. Other studies (e.g., Rozeff, 1974) have found that past information on economic conditions and money supply movements also appears to bear little correlation to today's interest rate levels or to observed changes in current interest rates. However, *unanticipated* growth in the money supply, income, and the price level *do* appear to be correlated with some bond and stock returns, especially with short-term interest rates. Moreover, adjustments in interest rates and asset prices to *new* information appear to be very rapid.

Nevertheless, the rational expectations view is still in the development stage. One key problem is that we do not know very much about how the public forms its expectations—what data are used, what weights are applied to individual bits of data, and how fast people learn from their forecasting mistakes. Moreover, several characteristics of real-world markets seem at odds with the assumptions of the expectations theory. For example, the cost of gathering and analyzing information relevant to the pricing of assets is not always negligible, as assumed by the theory, tempting many lenders and borrowers of funds to form their expectations by rules of thumb (trading rules) that are *not* fully rational. Although rationally formed expectations appear to exist in large auction markets (such as the markets for government securities or listed common stock), it is not clear that such is the case for other financial markets, such as those for consumer loans. Thus, not all interest rates and security prices appear to display the kind of behavior implied by the rational expectations theory.

Questions *to Help You Study*

18. Can you explain what is meant by *rational expectations*?

19. What, then, is the *rational expectations theory of interest rates*? How does it differ from earlier interest-rate determination theories, such as the classical, liquidity preference, and loanable funds ideas?

20. What key *assumptions* underlie the rational expectations view of interest?

21. What are the implications of the rational expectations theory of interest for those who try to *forecast* changes in market rates of interest? Based on this view of interest rates what would you recommend to interest-rate forecasters?

Summary of the Chapter

This important chapter focuses on the leading ideas today of what determines the level of and changes in market interest rates and asset prices. Its specific target is the *pure* or *risk-free rate of interest* (such as that interest rate attached to a government bond). Each theory of interest presented in this chapter attempts to account for the changes we see everyday in this pure or risk-free market interest rate.

- The chapter explores the critical roles played by interest rates in the functioning of the money and capital markets and the economy. These fundamental interest-rate roles include (a) generating an adequate volume of savings in order to fund investment and growth in the economy; (b) directing the flow of credit in the economy toward those investment projects carrying the highest expected rates of return; (c) bringing the supply of money (cash balances) into alignment with the demand for money so the money market will achieve a stable equilibrium; and (d) serving as a tool of government economic policy so that the nation can better achieve its broad economic goals of full employment, avoidance of serious inflation, sustainable economic growth, and a stable equilibrium in the nation's balance of payments with the rest of the world.

- The so-called *classical theory* of interest rates emphasizes the critical roles of savings and investment demand in determining market interest rates. The supply of savings is assumed to be positively related to the market interest rate, while the demand for investment is negatively related to the level of interest rates. The equilibrium interest rate in this long-run interest rate model is established at the point where the total supply of savings and the quantity of investment demand are in balance with each other.

- The *liquidity preference theory of interest,* on the other hand, looks at the demand and supply for money (cash balances), fixing the equilibrium interest rate in the money market at the point where the quantity of money in supply matches the total demand for money. Demand for money consists of money demands for transactions, precautionary savings, and speculation about the future course of interest rates and security prices. The supply of money is heavily influenced by actions of the government, principally the central bank.

- The popular *loanable funds theory of interest* brings together elements of *both* the classical and liquidity preference theories, focusing upon the total demand for credit (loanable funds) and the total supply of credit (loanable funds). The aggregate demand for loanable funds includes credit demands from all sectors of the economy—businesses, consumers, and governments. The aggregate supply of loanable funds includes domestic and foreign savings, the creation of money by the banking system, and the hoarding or dishoarding of cash balances by the public. The equilibrium loanable funds interest rate tends to settle at the point where total demand for credit matches total credit supply.

- The *rational expectations theory of interest* focuses upon the total *expected* supply of credit relative to the *expected* demand for credit. This view of interest rates and asset prices assumes that the money and capital markets are highly efficient in the use of information in determining the public's expectations regarding future changes in interest rates and asset prices. Equilibrium interest rates impound all relevant information very quickly and change only when relevant *new* information appears. Forecasting market interest rates is presumed to be virtually impossible on a consistent basis because interest-rate forecasters must know what new information is likely to arrive before that information appears and must assess how that new information will influence interest rates and security prices when it does arrive.

- Collectively, the different views of interest-rate determination discussed in this chapter help guide us toward those fundamental forces that shape the level of and changes in market rates of interest. These include such critical forces as domestic and foreign savings, the demand for investment, the money supply, the demand for cash balances, and government economic policy (including the workings of central banks around the world). This chapter sets the stage for future chapters in Part Two of the text where we attempt to discover what factors cause one interest rate to differ from another (including inflation, the term or length of a loan, credit or default risk, and many other causal elements).

Key Terms

Rate of interest, *113*
Price of credit, *113*
Risk-free rate of interest, *114*
Classical theory
  of interest rates, *114*
Substitution effect, *115*

Liquidity preference theory
  of interest rates, *121*
Loanable funds theory
  of interest rates, *127*
Income effect, *129*

Wealth effect, *129*
Rational expectations theory
  of interest rates, *133*

Problems

1. Construct a supply of savings schedule (with all schedules and axes correctly labeled) that illustrates the *income effect.* Do the same to illustrate the *wealth effect* and the *substitution effect.* Explain the differences you observe.

2. Suppose the going market rate of interest on high-quality corporate bonds is 12 percent. FORTRAN Corporation is considering an investment project that will last 10 years and requires an initial cash outlay of $1.5 million but will generate estimated revenues of $500,000 per year for 10 years. Would you recommend that this project be adopted? Explain why.

3. A government securities dealer has purchased a 10-year bond bearing a coupon rate of 9 percent. The bond was purchased at par ($1,000). Interest rates on *new* bonds with comparable terms rise to 11 percent. What will happen to the 9 percent bond's market price? What price will it approach? Answer these same questions in the case in which bond rates decline to 7 percent. Explain the price changes you have calculated.

4. The statements listed below were gathered from recent issues of financial news sheets. Read each statement carefully and then *(a)* identify which theory or theories of interest rate determination is implicit in each statement and *(b)* indicate which *direction* interest rates should move if the statement is a correct analysis of the current market situation. Use appropriate supply-demand diagrams, where possible, to show the reasoning behind your answers to part b.

   a. The factor which is likely to dominate interest rate changes in the weeks ahead is a tighter credit policy at the Federal Reserve.

   b. The White House unexpectedly disclosed today that budget negotiations with Capitol Hill have broken down. Market analysts are fearful of the effects on the bond and stock markets when trading begins tomorrow morning.

   c. Corporate profits have declined significantly in the quarter just concluded, following a year of substantial growth. Financial experts expect this negative trend to continue for at least the next six months.

   d. Personal consumption expenditures are rising rapidly, fueled by an unprecedented level of borrowing. Personal savings are up in real dollar terms, but the national savings rate dropped significantly this past year and further declines are expected. Economists believe this recent change in the savings rate explains the current trend in interest rates—a trend likely to continue into next autumn.

5. Suppose that total savings and business investment demand in the economy behave as follows (dollars are in billions):

Total Business Investment Demand	Volume of Total Savings Expected	Alternative Market Interest Rates
$170	$ 80	5%
155	96	6
142	103	7
135	135	8
128	178	9
111	207	10
92	249	11
86	285	12

According to the classical theory of interest, what equilibrium interest rate will prevail given the above schedules of planned saving and investment? What could cause the equilibrium rate to change?

6. Suppose the total demand for money is described by the following equation:

$$MD = 30 - 2i$$

where i is the prevailing market interest rate. The total supply of money is described by the following equation:

$$MS = 3 + 7i$$

According to the liquidity preference theory of interest rates, what is the prevailing equilibrium rate of interest?

7. A new drill press is considered a possible new investment for EXRON Corporation if it generates an expected return of $2,000 per year for 10 years. Its expected purchase price (including installation) is $9,400. What is the drill press project's expected internal rate of return?

   Suppose that EXRON can borrow the necessary funds in the money and capital markets to make this investment at a cost of 15 percent. Should it proceed with the project?

   If EXRON's investors' required rate of return is 16 percent, what is the NPV of the drill press project? Based upon your calculation of the NPV, should EXRON pursue this project any further?

8. INLAC Company, Ltd, is examining two investment projects as a part of its expansion plan for the coming year. These two projects are *not* mutually exclusive. The cost of project A is $9,870, while the second project (B) is expected to cost $17,850. INLAC's cost of capital (required rate of return) is 12 percent. Expected annual cash flows are projected to be as follows:

Year	Project A	Project B
1	$3,310	$6,525
2	3,310	6,525
3	3,310	6,525
4	3,310	6,525
5	3,310	6,525

Each project will last an estimated 5 years with no remaining significant scrap value. Determine the IRR and the NPV for each of these two projects. What should INLAC decide about each proposed project, assuming the above figures are truly accurate?

9. Please indicate which key term or concept presented in this chapter goes with each of the sentences or phrases listed below:

a. A theory of interest rates based upon changing views on the future behavior of interest rates and the value of financial assets.

b. People may save less as interest rates rise due to expected higher rates of return.

c. A saver's asset and debt position affects his or her response to changing market interest rates.

d. The credit view of what determines the level of and changes in interest rates.

e. Interest rates change as changes occur in the supply and demand for cash balances.

f. Market interest rates depend upon savings and investment demand.

g. Higher interest rates increase the volume of savings.

h. Rate of return on a riskless security.

i. The price paid to gain access to credit.

Questions about the Web and the Money and Capital Markets

1. If you wanted to keep track of domestic interest rates inside the United States where would you look on the World Wide Web?

2. Suppose you wanted to track global interest rates. Where on the Web might you look?

3. What type of Web site talking about interest rates is most common on the Web? How could such a site be helpful to you or possibly to your business?

Selected References

Ando, A., and Franco Modigliani. "The Life Cycle Hypothesis of Saving." *American Economic Review,* March 1963, pp. 55–84.

Boskin, M.J. "Taxation, Savings, and the Rate of Interest." *Journal of Political Economy,* April 1978, pp. S3–S27.

Bryan, Michael F., and Susan Byrne. "Don't Worry, We'll Grow Out of It: An Analysis of Demographics, Consumer Spending, and Foreign Debt." *Economic Commentary.* Federal Reserve Bank of Cleveland, October 1, 1990, pp. 1–4.

Bullard, James B. "Learning, Rational Expectations, and Policy: A Summary of Recent Research." *Review,* Federal Reserve Bank of St. Louis, January/February 1991, pp. 50–60.

Dynan, Karen E.; Jonathan Skinner; and Stephen P. Zeldes. "Do the Rich Save More?" *Finance and Economics Discussion Series,* Board of Governors of the Federal Reserve System, no. 2000-52, 2000.

Fisher, Irving. *The Theory of Interest.* New York: Macmillan, 1930.

Justen, F. T., and L. D. Taylor. "Towards a Theory of Saving Behavior." *American Economic Review,* May 1975, pp. 203–9.

Keynes, John M. *The General Theory of Employment, Interest and Money.* New York: Harcourt Brace Jovanovich, 1936.

Marquis, Milt. "What's Behind the Low U.S. Personal Saving Rate?" *FRBSF Economic Letter,* Federal Reserve Bank of San Francisco, March 2002, pp. 1–3.

Mishkin, Frederick. "Efficient-Markets Theory: Implications for Monetary Policy." *Brookings Papers on Economic Activity* 3 (1978), pp. 707–52.

Neely, Christopher J. "International Interest Rate Linkages." *International Economic Conditions,* Federal Reserve Bank of St. Louis, August 2001.

Peach, Richard, and Charles Steindel. "A Nation of Spendthrifts? An Analysis of Trends in Personal and Gross Saving." *Current Issues in Economics and Finance,* Federal Reserve Bank of New York, September 2000.

Phillips, Llad, and John Pippenger. "Preferred Habitat vs. Efficient Markets: A Test of Alternative Hypotheses." *Review,* Federal Reserve Bank of St. Louis, May 1976, pp. 11–39.

Rozeff, Michael S. "Money and Stock Prices: Market Efficiency and the Lag in Effect of Monetary Policy." *Journal of Financial Economics* 1 (September 1974), pp. 245–302.

Chapter **Six**

Measuring and Calculating Interest Rates and Financial Asset Prices

Learning Objectives in This Chapter

- You will learn how to measure and calculate interest rates and the prices of financial assets.

- You will be able to see more clearly the important relationship between the interest rate on a bond or other financial instrument and its market value or price.

- You will be introduced to the many different ways that banks and other lending institutions calculate the interest rates they charge borrowers for loans.

- You will be able to determine how interest rates or yields on deposits in banks, credit unions, and other depository institutions are figured.

What's in This Chapter? Key Topics Outline

Measures of Interest Rates

Quoting Prices on Stocks and Bonds

Measures of the Rate of Return or Yield on Financial Assets

The Yield to Maturity and Holding-Period Yields

The Relationship between Yields and Asset Prices

Interest Rates Quoted by Institutional Lenders: Simple Interest, Add-on Rate, Discount Method, the APR

Home Mortgage Loan Rates

Compounding of Interest

The APY

INTRODUCTION

Theories of the rate of interest, such as those we sketched out in the preceding chapter, help us understand the forces that cause interest rates and the prices of assets to change. However, these theories provide little or no information on how interest rates should be *measured* in the real world. As a result, many different measures of interest rates on securities and loans have been developed, leading to some confusion, especially for small borrowers and savers. In this chapter, the methods most frequently used to measure interest rates and security prices in today's financial markets are examined. We also consider the relationship between asset prices and interest rates and how they impact each other.

UNITS OF MEASUREMENT FOR INTEREST RATES AND SECURITY PRICES

Definition of Interest Rates

The **interest rate** is the price charged a borrower for the loan of money. This price is unique because it is really a *ratio* of two quantities: the total required fee a borrower must pay a lender to obtain the use of credit for a stipulated time period divided by the total amount of credit made available to the borrower. By convention, the interest rate is usually expressed in *percent per annum.* Thus,

$$
\begin{matrix}
\text{Annual} \\
\text{rate of} \\
\text{interest on} \\
\text{loanable} \\
\text{funds (in} \\
\text{percent)}
\end{matrix}
=
\frac{
\begin{matrix}
\text{Fee required by the} \\
\text{lender for the} \\
\text{borrower to obtain credit}
\end{matrix}
}{
\begin{matrix}
\text{Amount of credit made} \\
\text{available to the} \\
\text{borrower}
\end{matrix}
}
\times 100
\qquad \textbf{(6–1)}
$$

For example, an interest rate of 10 percent per annum on a $1,000, one-year car loan implies that the lender of funds has received a borrower's promise to pay a fee of $100 (10 percent of $1,000) in return for the use of $1,000 in credit for a year. The promised fee of $100 is in addition to the repayment of the loan principal ($1,000), which must occur sometime during the year.

Interest rates are usually expressed as *annualized percentages* even for loans and investments shorter than a year. For example, in the federal funds market, commercial banks frequently loan reserves to each other overnight, with the loan being repaid the next day. Even in this market the interest rate quoted daily by lenders is expressed in percent per annum, as though the loan were for a year's time. However, various types of loans and securities display important differences in how interest fees and amounts borrowed are valued or accounted for, leading to several different methods for determining interest rates. Some interest-rate measures use a 360-day year, while others use a 365-day year. Some employ compound rates of return, with interest income earned on accumulated interest, and some do not use compounding.[1]

---

[1] Interest rates on U.S. Treasury bills, commercial paper, and a few other short-term financial instruments are based on a 360-day year and do not compound interest. See Part Three (especially Chapter 11) for a discussion of these instruments and the basis for calculating their rates of return to the investor, known as the *bank discount method.*

The measurement or calculation of interest rates is a popular subject on the Web with hundreds of sites available. There are, for example, scores of sites to help you calculate how much you can save or how much it will cost you in terms of interest payments to take out a loan. Most focus on consumer-oriented loans, such as a loan to buy a new home. Many other sites focus on determining the rate of return you can expect from a variety of savings instruments, such as bank deposits.

Examples of the foregoing Web sites include the Interest-rate Calculator for determining the savings you would experience if you refinanced your home mortgage loan (at www. financialpowertools.com or at www.interestratecalculator.com). Others compare one lender's interest rate offerings to those posted by other lenders. For example, CompareInterestRates.com produces a listing of home mortgage loan rates in all 50 states (at www.compareinterestrates .com), while Local Bank Rates on Loans and Savings (at www.digitalcitv.com) permits you to compare and contrast loan rates and savings returns in dozens of cities around the United States.

Basis Points

Interest rates on securities traded in the open market rarely are quoted in whole percentage points, such as 5 percent or 8 percent. The typical case is a rate expressed in hundredths of a percent: for example, 5.36 percent or 7.62 percent. Moreover, most interest rates change by only fractions of a whole percentage point in a single day or week. To deal with this situation, the concept of the basis point was developed. A *basis point* equals 1/100 of a percentage point. Thus, an interest rate of 10.5 percent may be expressed as 10 percent plus 50 basis points, or 1,050 basis points. Similarly, an increase in a loan or security rate from 5.25 percent to 5.30 percent represents an increase of 5 basis points.

Security Prices

The prices of common and preferred *stock* are measured today in many markets in terms of dollars and decimal fractions of a dollar (or other currency unit). This is a relatively recent development because stocks used to be quoted in the marketplace in standard fractions— for example, at a price of $40¼ per share. Today, however, such a stock's market price will usually be expressed as $40.25 or whatever its prevailing market value happens to be. An example of a typical stock price quotation as it often appears in financial newspapers and magazines is shown below. In this case the shares issued are common stock of Wells Fargo Corporation (stock symbol: WFC), one of the largest banking firms in the world.

Example of a Stock Price Quotation as Typically Reported in the Financial Press Each Day

STOCK LISTING	YTD %Chg.	52 week range High	Low	Yield Div.	%	PE Ratio	Volume (in 100s)	Closing Bid	Net Change
Wells Fargo (WFC)	−22.1	56.38	38.25	1.04	2.4	22x	48795	43.38	+0.40

We notice from the data above that stock market investors are given several useful pieces of information about the trading of Wells Fargo's stock as of the close of trading the previous day. This information includes the percentage change in its price thus far in the current year (in this instance, a decline of just over 22 percent). During the past 52 weeks the stock ranged in market value at the close of each day from a high of $56.38 per share to a low of $38.25 per share. The most recent shareholder dividend payment was $1.04 per share, which represented a dividend yield—or ratio of current dividends to current price—of 2.4 percent when yesterday's trading ended. The concluding price bid was $43.38—a rise of 40 cents over the previous day's closing value. The stock's ratio of current market price to current earnings was 22—a high "price multiple" by historical standards. Nearly $5 million in Wells Fargo shares were traded in yesterday's market.

Bond prices are expressed in points and fractions of a point, with each point equal to $1 on a $100 basis or $10 for a $1,000 bond. For example, a U.S. government bond priced at 97 points is selling for $97 on a $100 basis or for $970 for each $1,000 in face value. Fractions of a point are typically measured in 32nds, sixteenths, eighths, quarters, and halves of a point.

Example of a Bond Price Quotation as Typically Reported in the Financial Press Each Day

Bonds Listed	Current Yield	Volume Traded	Closing Price	Net Change
ATT 8⅝ 31	8.3	85	103½	−½

An example of a typical bond price quotation as it often appears in the newspaper or in magazines each day is shown for some bonds issued by American Telephone and Telegraph Corporation (ATT). In this instance the AT&T bonds are long-term debt scheduled to reach maturity in the year 2031 and bear an annual coupon (promised) interest return of 8⅝ percent (or 8.625%). Their current yield—or ratio of annual interest income to current market price—was 8.3 percent. The volume of these AT&T bonds trading hands on the day represented here amounted to $85,000. The closing price on this bond was $103.50 on a $100 basis or $1,035 for a bond bearing a face value of $1,000. This latest closing price represented a drop in market value from the previous day of $0.50 per $100 or $5 on a $1,000 face-value bond.

Security dealers usually quote *two* prices for an asset rather than just one. The higher of the two is the *asked* price, which indicates what the dealer will *sell* the security for. The *bid* price is the price at which the dealer is willing to *purchase* the security. The difference between bid and asked prices—known as the *spread*—provides the dealer's return for creating a market for the security. Generally, the longer the maturity of a security, the greater the spread between its bid and asked prices. This is due, at least in part, to the added risks associated with trading in long-term securities. For example, short-term securities may trade with a spread as low as $312.50 for a sale of $1 million in securities while long-term bonds may be trading on spreads of about $2,500 for every $1 million sold. For small transactions, a commission fee is usually added to cover the cost of executing the transaction. On large sales, however, dealers often forgo commissions and quote a *net* price.

MEASURES OF THE RATE OF RETURN, OR YIELD, ON A LOAN, SECURITY, OR OTHER FINANCIAL ASSET

The interest rate on a loan is the annual rate of return promised by the borrower to the lender as a condition for obtaining a loan. However, that rate is not necessarily a true reflection of the yield or rate of return actually earned by the lender during the life of the loan. Some borrowers will default on all or a portion of their promised payments. The market value of the security evidencing the loan may rise or fall, adding to or subtracting from the lender's total rate of return (yield) on the transaction. Thus, the interest rate measures the "price" the borrower has promised to pay for a loan, but the actual *yield,* or rate of return, on the loan from the lender's viewpoint may be quite different. In this section, a number of the most widely used measures of the yield or rate of return on a loan or security are discussed.

Coupon Rate

One of the best-known measures of the rate of return on a debt security is the **coupon rate.** The coupon rate is the contracted interest rate that the security issuer agrees to pay at the time a security is issued and often is set close to prevailing interest rates on comparable securities at the time a debt security is sold (unless the debt security is a zero coupon instrument). If, for example, a company issues a bond with a coupon rate printed on its face of 9 percent, the borrower has promised the lender an annual interest payment of 9 percent of the bond's par value. Most bonds are issued with $1,000 par values, and interest payments are semiannual.

The amount of promised annual interest income paid by a bond is called its *coupon.* The annual coupon may be determined from the formula

$$\text{Coupon rate} \times \text{Par value} = \text{Coupon} \qquad \textbf{(6–2)}$$

Thus, a bond with par value of $1,000 bearing a coupon rate of 9 percent pays an annual coupon of $90.

The coupon rate is *not* an adequate measure of the return on a debt security unless the investor purchases the security at a price equal to its par value, the borrower makes all of the promised payments on time, and the investor sells or redeems the instrument at its par value. However, the prices of bonds or other debt securities fluctuate with market conditions; rarely does a bond trade exactly at par, for example.

Current Yield

Another popular measure of the return on a loan or security is its **current yield.** This is simply the ratio of the annual income (dividends or interest) generated by the loan or security to its current market value. Thus, a share of common stock selling in the market for $30 and paying an annual dividend to the shareholder of $3 would have a current yield calculated as follows:

$$\text{Current yield} = \frac{\text{Annual income}}{\text{Market price of security}} = \frac{\$3}{\$30} = 0.10, \text{ or } 10\% \qquad \textbf{(6–3)}$$

Frequently, the yields reported on stocks and bonds in the financial press are current yields. Like the coupon rate, the current yield is usually a poor reflection of the rate of return actually received by the lender or investor. It ignores the stream of actual and anticipated payments and the price at which the investor will be able to sell or redeem an asset.

Questions *to Help You Study*

1. Interest rates are often called the most important "price" within the financial system. Why do you think this is so?

2. What is different about interest rates, or *the price of credit,* from other prices in the economy?

3. What exactly is a *basis point?* Why is it an important interest-rate measure?

4. How are bond and stock prices measured today?

5. In your opinion are the coupon rate and the current yield good measures of the rate of return on a bond or other financial instrument? Why or why not?

Yield to Maturity

The most widely accepted measure of the rate of return on a loan or security is its **yield to maturity.** It is the rate of interest the market is prepared to pay for a financial asset to exchange present dollars for future dollars. Specifically, the yield to maturity is the rate that equates the purchase price of a security or other financial asset (P) with the present value of *all* of its expected annual net cash inflows (income). In general terms,

$$P = \frac{I_1}{(1 + y)^1} + \frac{I_2}{(1 + y)^2} + \ldots + \frac{I_n}{(1 + y)^n} \qquad \text{(6–4)}$$

where *y* is the yield to maturity and each *I* represents the expected annual income from the security, presumed to last for *n* years and terminate when the financial asset is retired. The *I* terms in the formula include both receipts of income and repayments of principal.

To illustrate the use of this formula, assume that the investor is considering the purchase of a bond due to mature in 20 years, carrying a 10 percent coupon rate. This security is available for purchase at a current market price of $850. If the bond has a par value of $1,000, which will be paid to the investor when the security reaches maturity, the bond's yield to maturity, *y*, may be found by solving the equation:

$$\$850 = \frac{\$100}{(1 + y)^1} + \frac{\$100}{(1 + y)^2} + \ldots + \frac{\$100}{(1 + y)^{20}} + \frac{\$1,000}{(1 + y)^{20}} \qquad \text{(6–5)}$$

In this instance, *y* equals 12 percent, a rate higher than its 10 percent coupon rate, because the bond is currently selling at a *discount* from par.

Suppose this same $1,000, 10 percent coupon bond were selling at a *premium* over par. For example, if this 20-year security has a current market price of $1,200, its yield to maturity could be found from the following equation:

$$\$1,200 = \frac{\$100}{(1 + y)^1} + \ldots + \frac{\$100}{(1 + y)^{20}} + \frac{\$1,000}{(1 + y)^{20}} \qquad \text{(6–6)}$$

In this case, *y* equals 8 percent. Because the investor must pay a higher current market price than par value (the amount the investor will receive back when the bond matures) this bond's yield to maturity must be *less* than its coupon rate.

From these two examples, it should be clear that the *value of a debt security depends on the size of its promised rate of return (coupon rate) relative to prevailing market interest rates on securities of comparable quality and terms.* If a security's coupon rate equals the current market interest rate on comparable securities, that security will trade at par. If the security's coupon rate is less than the prevailing market rate, it will sell at a *discount* from par. Finally, if the security's coupon rate exceeds the current interest rate in the market, it will sell at a *premium* above its par value.

The yield to maturity has a number of significant advantages as a measure of the rate of return or yield on a financial asset. In fact, security dealers typically use the yield to maturity in quoting rates of return to investors. Unlike the current yield, this return measure considers the time distribution of expected cash flows from a financial asset. Of course, the yield-to-maturity measure does assume that the investor will hold a security until it reaches final maturity. Moreover, yield to maturity is *not* an appropriate measure for most stocks, the majority of which are perpetual instruments, or even for some bonds, because the investor may sell them prior to their termination date or the bonds may pay a variable return. Another problem is that this measure assumes that all cash flowing to the investor can be reinvested at the computed yield to maturity.[2] And we have not yet considered the impact of taxes on the investor's true return, a subject taken up in Chapter 8.

Holding-Period Yield

A slight modification of the yield-to-maturity formula results in a return measure for those situations in which an investor holds a financial asset for a time and then sells it to another investor in advance of the asset's maturity. This so-called **holding-period yield** is simply

$$P = \frac{I_1}{(1 + h)^1} + \frac{I_2}{(1 + h)^2} + \ldots + \frac{I_m}{(1 + h)^m} + \frac{P_m}{(1 + h)^m} \qquad \textbf{(6–7)}$$

where h is the holding-period yield and the investor's holding period covers m time periods. Thus, the holding-period yield is simply the rate of discount (h) equalizing the market price of a financial asset (P) with all net cash flows between the time the asset is purchased and the time it is sold (including the selling price, P_m). If the asset is held to maturity, its holding-period yield equals its yield to maturity.

Calculating Yields to Maturity and Holding-Period Yields

Holding-period yields and yields to maturity can be calculated in several different ways. One method is to employ present value tables identical to those presented in most finance and accounting texts.

Suppose, for example, that an investor is contemplating the purchase of a corporate bond, $1,000 par value, with a coupon rate of 10 percent. To simplify the problem, assume that the bond pays interest of $100 just once each year. Currently, the bond is selling for $900. The investor plans to hold the bond to maturity in five years. We have

$$\$900 = \frac{\$100}{(1 + y)^1} + \frac{\$100}{(1 + y)^2} + \frac{\$100}{(1 + y)^3} + \frac{\$100}{(1 + y)^4} + \frac{\$100}{(1 + y)^5} + \frac{\$1,000}{(1 + y)^5} \qquad \textbf{(6–8)}$$

It is useful at this point to consider what each term in Equation 6–8 means. Both the yield-to-maturity and holding-period-yield formulas are based on the concept of *present value:* Funds to be received in the future are worth less than funds received today. Present dollars may be used to purchase and enjoy goods and services today, but future dollars are

---

[2]The examples shown assume that interest is paid once a year; however, most bonds pay interest semiannually and some even more frequently. In this instance, the yield-to-maturity formula needs to be modified to include the parameter k, the number of times during the year that interest is paid to the bondholder. The formula thus becomes:

$$Purchase\ price = \frac{I_1/k}{(1 + y/k)^1} + \frac{I_2/k}{(1 + y/k)^2} + \ldots + \frac{I_{nk}/k}{(1 + y/k)^{nk}} + \frac{Final\ price}{(1 + y/k)^{nk}}$$

Thus, for a 10-year government bond paying $50 interest twice each year, $k = 2$ and there would be 20 periods ($n \times k = 10 \times 2$) in which the investor receives $50 in interest income. Solution of the yield-to-maturity formula proceeds the same way as before except that you need to look up y/k percent in the present value and annuity tables (instead of y) and discount over $n \times k$ rather than n time periods.

only *promises* to pay and force us to postpone consumption until the funds actually are received. Equation 6–8 indicates that a bond promising to pay $100 for five successive years in the future plus a lump sum of $1,000 at maturity is worth only $900 in present value dollars. The yield, *y*, serves as a rate of discount reducing each payment of future dollars back to its present value in today's market. The further into the future the payment is to be made, the larger the discount factor, $(1 + y)^n$, becomes.

Turning the concept around, the purchase of a security in today's market represents the investment of present dollars in the expectation of a higher return in the form of future dollars. The familiar *compound interest formula* (discussed later in this chapter) applies here. This formula

$$FV = P(1 + y)^t \qquad \textbf{(6–9)}$$

indicates that the amount of funds accumulated *t* years from now (*FV*) depends on the principal originally invested (*P*), the investor's expected rate of return or yield (*y*), and the number of years the principal is invested (*t*). Thus, a principal of $1,000 invested today at a 10 percent annual rate will amount to $1,100 a year from now [i.e., $1,000 \times (1 + 0.10)^1$]. Rearrangement of the compound interest formula gives

$$P = \frac{FV}{(1 + y)^t} \qquad \textbf{(6–10)}$$

Equation 6–10 states that the present value of *FV* dollars to be received in the future is *P* if the promised interest rate is *y*. If we expect to receive $1,100 one year from now and the promised interest rate is 10 percent, the present value of that $1,100 must be $1,000.

Each term on the right-hand side of the yield-to-maturity and holding-period-yield formulas is a form of Equation 6–10. Solving Equation 6–8 for the yield to maturity of a bond simply means finding a value for *y*, which brings both right- and left-hand sides of the yield formula into balance, equating the current price (*P*) of a financial asset with the stream of future dollars it will generate for the investor. When all expected cash flows are not the same in amount, trial and error may be used to find the solution. Fortunately, in the case of the bond represented in Equation 6–8, the solution is not complicated. Rewrite Equation 6–8 in the following form:

$$\$900 = \$100\left[\frac{1}{(1 + y)^1} + \frac{1}{(1 + y)^2} + \ldots + \frac{1}{(1 + y)^5}\right] + \$1,000\left[\frac{1}{(1 + y)^5}\right] \qquad \textbf{(6–11)}$$

This indicates that the bond will pay an annuity of $1 per year (multiplied by $100) for five years, plus a lump-sum payment of $1 (multiplied by $1,000) at the end of the fifth year.

Use of Present Value Tables

What is the yield on this bond? A reasonable initial guess is 10 percent. To determine how accurate a guess it is, we need to consult the present value and annuity tables in the appendix at the back of this book. The annuity table indicates the present value of $1 received annually for five years at a discount yield of 10 percent is $3.791. The present value table shows that the present value of $1 to be received five years from today at 10 percent is $0.621. Inserting these figures into Equation 6–11 yields

$$\$100\,[3.791] + \$1,000\,[0.621] = \$1,000.1 > \$900 \qquad \textbf{(6–12)}$$

An annual yield of 10 percent is obviously too small because it results in a present value for the bond far in excess of its current price of $900. A 12 percent yield gives a present value of $927.50, and a 14 percent yield results in a present value for the bond of $862.30. Clearly, the true yield to maturity of this $900 bond lies between 12 percent and 14 percent, but closer to 12 percent. Linear interpolation fixes this yield at 12.84 percent.[3] The investor interested in maximizing return would compare this yield to maturity with the yields to maturity available on other assets of comparable risk.

Present value tables may also be used to calculate the holding-period yield on corporate stock. To illustrate, suppose an investor is considering the purchase of common stock issued by General Electric Corporation currently selling for $40 per share. He plans to hold the stock for two years and sell out at an expected price of $50 per share. If dividends of $2 per share are expected each year, what holding-period yield does the investor expect to earn? Following the form of Equation 6–6, we have

$$\$40 = \frac{\$2}{(1 + h)^1} + \frac{\$2}{(1 + h)^2} + \frac{\$50}{(1 + h)^2} \qquad \textbf{(6–13)}$$

The reader may wish to verify from the present value and annuity tables in the appendix at the back of this book that the holding period yield on GE's stock is 16.54 percent.

Bond Yield Tables

Present value tables provide a reasonably accurate method for calculating maturity and holding-period yields. However, use of the tables is a trial and error process and can be time consuming. To save time, securities dealers and experienced investors may use bond yield tables, which give the appropriate yield for bonds of a given coupon rate, maturity, and price. These tables may be stored in computer files or appear in book form. An example of data taken from a bond yield table is shown in Exhibit 6–1.

To illustrate, suppose that the investor holds a corporate bond, bearing a 10 percent coupon rate, with 10 years remaining until maturity. The bond's purchase price may be found in the table under the correct number of years (or, for more detailed bond yield tables, number of months and years) to maturity. The correct yield to maturity will be found along the same line as the price in the extreme left-hand column of the table. For example, if the 10-year bond's purchase price were $88.53 (on a $100 basis), then its yield to maturity would be 12 percent, as shown in Exhibit 6–1.

---

[3]The present value and annuity tables provide the following information for the bond described above:

Difference in Yield to Maturity	Difference in Present Value of Bond
14%	$ 862.3
12	927.5
2%	$−65.2

There is a difference of $27.5 between the current $900 price of the bond and its present value at a yield of 12 percent, which is $927.50. Therefore, the bond's approximate actual yield to maturity may be found from

$$12\% + \frac{\$27.5}{\$65.2} \times 2\% = 12\% + 0.8436\% \approx 12.84\%$$

Linear interpolation of this sort must be used with care, especially when yield differentials are substantial, because the yield-price relationship is *not* linear.

EXHIBIT 6–1
Bond Yield Table
Prices of a bond with a 10 percent coupon rate

Yield to Maturity In Percent	Maturity of a Bond in Years				
	5	10	15	20	25
5%	121.88	138.97	152.33	162.76	170.91
6	117.06	129.75	139.20	164.23	151.46
7	112.47	121.32	127.59	132.03	135.18
8	108.11	113.59	117.29	119.79	121.48
9	103.96	106.50	108.14	109.20	109.88
10	100.00	100.00	100.00	100.00	100.00
11	96.23	94.02	92.73	91.98	91.53
12	92.64	88.53	86.24	84.95	84.24
13	89.22	83.47	80.41	78.78	77.91
14	85.95	78.81	75.18	73.34	72.40
15	82.84	74.51	70.47	68.51	67.56

Note: Prices expressed on the basis of $100 par value.

Questions *to Help You Study*

6. Explain the meaning of the interest rate measure known as the *yield to maturity.*

7. What *assumptions* underlie the calculation of the yield to maturity?

8. How does the interest rate measure known as the *holding-period yield* differ from the yield to maturity?

9. Why are yields on bonds and other debt securities typically quoted on a yield-to-maturity basis, while stock yields are usually expressed as current yields or holding-period yields?

YIELD–ASSET PRICE RELATIONSHIPS

The foregoing yield-to-maturity and holding-period-yield formulas illustrate a number of important relationships between security prices and yields or interest rates that prevail in the financial system. One of these important relationships is expressed as follows:

> The price of a security and its yield or rate of return are *inversely* related—a rise in yield implies a decline in price; conversely, a fall in yield is associated with a rise in the security's price.

We note that investing funds in financial assets can be viewed from two different perspectives, the borrowing and lending of money or the buying and selling of securities. As noted in Chapter 5, the equilibrium rate of interest from the lending of funds can be determined by the interaction of the supply of loanable funds and the demand for loanable funds. Demanders of loanable funds (borrowers) supply securities to the financial marketplace, and suppliers of loanable funds (lenders) demand securities as an investment. Therefore, the equilibrium rate of return or yield on a security and the equilibrium price of that security are determined at one and the same instant and are simply different aspects of the same phenomenon, the borrowing and lending of loanable funds.

This point is depicted in Exhibit 6–2, which shows demand and supply curves for both the rate of interest (yield) and the price of securities. The supply of loanable funds curve (representing lending) in the interest rate diagram (Exhibit 6–2A) is analogous to the demand for securities curve (also representing lending) in the price of securities diagram (Exhibit 6–2B). Similarly, the demand for loanable funds curve (representing borrowing) in the

EXHIBIT 6–2 **Equilibrium Security Prices and Interest Rates (Yields)**

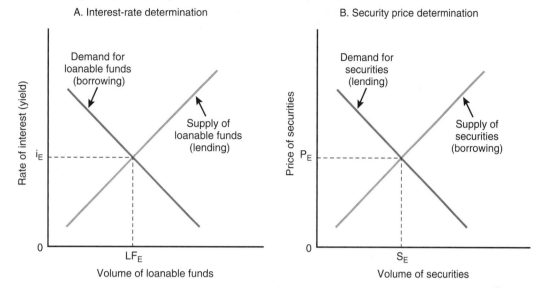

interest rate diagram is analogous to the supply of securities curve (also representing borrowing) in the price of securities diagram.

We note in Exhibit 6–2B that borrowers are assumed to issue a larger volume of securities at a higher price and that lenders will demand more securities at a lower price. In Exhibit 6–2A, on the other hand, borrowers demand a smaller quantity of loanable funds at a higher interest rate, while lenders supply fewer loanable funds at a lower interest rate (yield). The *equilibrium interest rate* (yield) in Exhibit 6–2A is determined at point i_E, where the demand for loanable funds equals the supply of loanable funds. Similarly, in Exhibit 6–2B, the *equilibrium price* for securities lies at point P_E, where the demand for and supply of securities are equal. Only at the equilibrium interest rate and equilibrium security price will *both* borrowers and lenders be content with the volume of lending and borrowing taking place within the financial system.

The *inverse* relationship between interest rates and security prices can be seen quite clearly when we allow the supply and demand curves depicted in Exhibit 6–2 to change. This is illustrated in Exhibit 6–3. For example, suppose that, in the face of continuing inflation, consumers and business firms accelerate their borrowings, increasing the demand for loanable funds. As shown in the upper left-hand portion of Exhibit 6–3, the demand for loanable funds curve slides upward and to the right with the supply of loanable funds unchanged. This increasing demand for loanable funds also means that the supply of securities must expand, as shown in the upper right-hand portion of Exhibit 6–3 by a shift in the supply curve from *S* to *S'*. Both a new *lower* equilibrium price for securities and a *higher* equilibrium interest rate for loanable funds result.

Conversely, suppose that consumers decide to save more, expanding the supply of loanable funds. As shown in the lower left-hand panel of Exhibit 6–3, the supply of loanable funds curve slides downward and to the right from *S* to *S'*. But with more savings, the demand for securities curve must rise, sliding upward and to the right from *D* to *D'* as those added savings are invested in securities. The result is a *rise* in the equilibrium price of securities and a *decline* in the equilibrium interest rate.

While the previous discussion describes the inverse relationship between interest rates and debt security prices, we should also note that interest rates and stock (equity) prices

EXHIBIT 6–3 **Effects of Changing Supply and Demand on Security Rates (Yields) and Prices**

A. Effects of an increase in the demand for loanable funds: higher interest rates and lower security prices

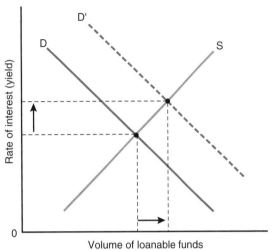

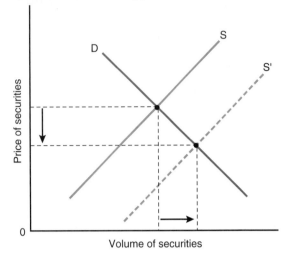

B. Effects of an increase in the supply of loanable funds: lower interest rates and higher security prices

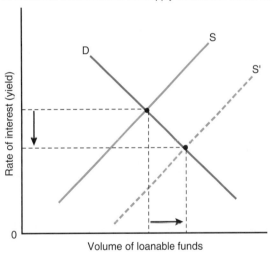

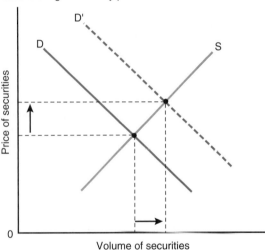

also frequently move in opposite directions (though by no means is this always the case). For example, if interest rates rise, debt instruments now offering higher yields become more attractive relative to some stocks, resulting in increased stock sales and declining equity prices (all other factors held equal). Conversely, a period of falling interest rates often leads investors to dump their lower-yielding debt securities and switch to equities, driving stock prices upward. Then, too, lower market interest rates tend to lower the overall cost of capital for businesses issuing stock, resulting in a rise in stock prices if expected corporate dividends do not fall.

What actually happens to stock prices when market interest rates change can often be understood by tracking changes in two fundamental factors that appear to influence all stock prices—the stream of shareholder dividends a company is expected to pay in current and future time periods ($E(D)$) and the minimum rate of return required by a company's stockholders (k). Thus, a corporation's stock price per share (SP) is:

$$SP = \sum_{t=0}^{\infty} E(D_t) / (1 + k)^t \qquad \textbf{(6–14)}$$

Clearly, a rise in *E(D)* or a fall in the required risk-adjusted rate of return for the company's stockholders (*k*) leads to higher stock prices per share (*SP*), other factors held equal. However, there are *no* guarantees surrounding the stock price–interest rate relationship we have just described because *both* expected dividends and the required discount rate of return (*k*) may change at the same time, offsetting one another and leaving stock prices unchanged or causing them to move in an unexpected direction.

INTEREST RATES CHARGED BY INSTITUTIONAL LENDERS

In this chapter, we have examined several different measures of the rate of return, or yield, on financial assets. Our list is not complete, however, for institutional lenders of funds— banks, credit unions, insurance companies, and finance companies, to name the most important—often employ very different methods to calculate the rate of interest charged on their loans. Six commonly used methods for calculating institutional loan rates are discussed on the following pages.

The Simple Interest Method

The widely used **simple interest method** assesses interest charges on a loan for only the period of time the borrower actually has use of borrowed funds. The total interest bill *decreases* the more frequently a borrower must make payments on a loan because the borrower has less money to work with each time the repayment of part of a loan is made to the lender. This definition of a *simple interest loan* follows the U.S. government's Truth-in-Lending law passed originally in 1968.

For example, suppose you borrow $1,000 for a year at simple interest. If the interest rate is 10 percent, your interest bill will be $100 for the year. This figure is derived from the formula

$$I = P \times r \times t \qquad \textbf{(6–15)}$$

where *I* represents the interest charge (in dollars), *P* is the principal amount of the loan, *r* is the annual rate of interest, and *t* is the term (maturity) of the loan expressed in years or fractions of a year. (In this example, $1,000 \times 0.10 \times 1 = $100.)

If the $1,000 loan is repaid in one lump sum at the end of the year,

$$\underbrace{\frac{\text{Principal} + \text{Interest}}{\$1,000 + \$100}}_{} = \frac{\text{Total payment}}{\$1,100}$$

Suppose, however, that this loan principal is paid off in two equal installments of $500 each, every six months. Then you will pay

First
installment: $\dfrac{\text{Principal} + \text{Interest}}{\$500 + \$50 \text{ (i.e., 6 months' interest on \$1,000 at 10\%)}}$ = Total payment
= $ 550

Second
installment: $500 + $25 (i.e., 6 months' interest on $500 at 10%)   = $ 525
                                                                        $1,075

Clearly, you pay a lower interest bill ($75 versus $100) with two installment payments instead of one. This happens because with two installment payments you effectively have use of the full $1,000 for only six months. For the remaining six months of the year you have use of only $500.

A shorthand formula for determining the total payment (interest plus principal) on a simple interest loan is

$$\text{Total payment due} = P + P \times r \times t = P(1 + r \times t) \qquad \textbf{(6–16)}$$

For example, borrowing $1,000 for 6 months at a 10 percent loan rate means the borrower owes:

$$\text{Total payment due} = \$1,000 + \$1,000 \times 0.10 \times 6/12 = \$50$$

The simple interest method is still popular with many mortgage lenders, credit unions, and banks.

Add-On Rate of Interest

A method for calculating loan interest rates often used by finance companies and banks is the **add-on rate** approach. In this instance, interest is calculated on the full principal of the loan, and the sum of interest and principal payments is divided by the number of payments to determine the dollar amount of each payment. For example, suppose you borrow $1,000 for one year at an interest rate of 10 percent. You agree to make two equal installment payments six months apart. The total amount to be repaid is $1,100 ($1,000 principal + $100 interest). At the end of the first six months, you will pay half ($550), and the remaining half ($550) will be paid at the end of the year.

If money is borrowed and repaid in one lump sum (a single payment loan), the simple interest and add-on methods give the same interest rate. However, as the number of installment payments increases, the borrower pays a higher effective interest rate under the add-on method. This happens because the average amount of money borrowed declines with the greater frequency of installment payments, yet the borrower pays the *same* total interest bill. In fact, the effective rate of interest nearly doubles when monthly installment payments are required. For example, if you borrow $1,000 for a year at 10 percent simple interest but repay the loan in 12 equal monthly installments, you have only about $500 available for use, on average, over the year. Because the total interest bill is still $100, the interest rate exceeds 18 percent.

Discount Method

Many commercial loans, especially those used to raise working capital, are extended on a discount basis. This so-called **discount method** for calculating loan rates determines the total interest charge to the customer on the basis of the amount to be repaid. However, the borrower receives as proceeds of the loan only the *difference* between the total amount owed and the interest bill. For example, suppose you borrow $1,000 for one year at 10 percent, for a total interest bill of $100. Using the discount method, you actually receive for your use only $900 (i.e., $1,000 − $100) in net loan proceeds. The effective interest rate, then, is

$$\frac{\text{Interest paid}}{\text{Net loan proceeds}} = \frac{\$100}{\$900} \times 100 = 11.11\% \qquad \textbf{(6–17)}$$

Some lenders grant the borrower the full amount of money required but add the amount of discount to the face amount of the borrower's note. For example, if you need the full $1,000, the lender under this method will multiply the effective interest rate (11.11 percent) times $1,000 to derive a total interest bill of $111.11. The face value of the borrower's note and, therefore, the amount that must be repaid becomes $1,111.11. However, the borrower receives only $1,000 for use during the year. Most discount loans are for terms of one year or less and usually do not require installment payments. Instead, these loans generally are settled in a lump sum when the note comes due. Discount rate loans are quite popular today in Latin America.

Home Mortgage Interest Rate

One of the most confusing of all rates charged by lenders is the interest rate on a home mortgage loan. Many home buyers have heard that under the terms of most mortgage loans, their monthly payments early in the life of the loan go almost entirely to pay the interest on the loan. Only later is a substantial part of each monthly payment devoted to reducing the principal amount of a home loan. Is this true?

To broaden your understanding about home mortgage interest rates you may find the Web site *www.bankrate.com* useful.

Yes, and we can illustrate it quite easily. Suppose that you find a new home you want to buy and borrow $100,000 to close the deal. The mortgage lender quotes you an annual interest rate of 12 percent on the loan. If we divide this annual interest rate by 12 months, we derive a monthly mortgage loan rate of 1 percent. The lender tells you that your monthly payment will be $1,100 each month (to cover property taxes, insurance, interest, and principal on the loan). This means that the first month's payment of $1,100 will be divided by the lender as follows: (1) $1,000 for the interest payment (or 1% per month × $100,000); and (2) $100 to be applied to the principal of the loan, insurance premiums, taxes, and so forth. For simplicity, let's assume the $100 left over after the $1,000 interest payment goes entirely to help repay the $100,000 loan principal. This means that next month your loan now totals just $99,900 (or $100,000 − $100). When you send in that next monthly payment of $1,000, the interest payment will drop to $999, and, therefore, $101 will now be left over to help reduce the loan principal. Gradually, the monthly interest payment will fall and the amount left over to help retire the loan's principal will rise. After several years, as the mortgage loan's maturity date gets near, each monthly payment will consist mostly of repaying the loan principal itself.

How do mortgage lenders figure the amount of the monthly payment new home buyers must make on their home loan? The usual formula is

$$\text{Total amount borrowed} \times \frac{\left[\dfrac{\text{Loan interest rate}}{12}\right] \times \left[1 + \dfrac{\text{Loan interest rate}}{12}\right]^{t \times 12}}{\left[1 + \left(\dfrac{\text{Loan interest rate}}{12}\right)\right]^{t \times 12} - 1} \qquad \textbf{(6–18)}$$

where *t* stands for the number of years the money is borrowed by the home buyer, and the annual interest rate charged on the mortgage loan is divided by 12 to restate that interest rate on a monthly basis.

To see how this formula works, suppose a family takes out a $50,000 loan for 25 years at an interest rate of 12 percent to buy its new home. In this case, the required payment on the loan each month would be

$$\$50,000 \times \frac{\left[\dfrac{0.12}{12}\right] \times \left[1 + \dfrac{0.12}{12}\right]^{25 \times 12}}{\left[1 + \dfrac{0.12}{12}\right]^{25 \times 12} - 1} = \frac{\$9,894.23}{18.7885} = \$526.62$$

Actually, there is an easier way to calculate the required monthly payment on a home mortgage using the annual percentage rate (APR) table given in the appendix at the back of this book. With an annual loan rate of 12 percent and 25 years multiplied by 12, or 300 monthly payments, the APR table gives us the following information:

$$\text{Total finance charge per \$100 financed} = \$215.97$$

$$\text{Total finance charge on a \$50,000 loan} = \frac{\$50,000}{\$100} \times \$215.97 = \$107,985$$

Then the monthly home mortgage payment will be as follows:

$$\frac{\text{Total finance charge} + \text{Loan amount}}{\text{Number of loan payments}} = \frac{\$107,985 + \$50,000}{300} = \$526.62$$

Note that the borrower in this case pays a total amount of interest ($107,985) that is more than *double* the amount of money borrowed ($50,000)!

Annual Percentage Rate (APR)

The wide diversity of rates quoted by lenders is often confusing and discourages shopping around for credit. With this in mind, the U.S. Congress passed the Consumer Credit Protection Act in 1968. More popularly known as *Truth in Lending,* this law requires institutions regularly extending credit to consumers to tell the borrower what interest rate he or she is actually paying and to use a prescribed method for calculating that rate.[4] Specifically, banks, credit unions, and other lending institutions are required to calculate an **annual percentage rate (APR)** and inform the loan customer what this rate is *before* the loan contract is signed. The APR, which measures the yearly cost of credit, includes not only interest costs but also any transaction fees or service charges imposed by a lender of funds. The actuarial method is used to determine the APR, and loan officers usually have computerized tables or books of tables at hand to translate a simple interest or add-on rate into the APR.

The constant ratio formula, shown below, usually gives a close approximation to the true APR:

$$\text{APR} = \frac{\begin{array}{c}2 \times \text{Number of payment periods in a year} \\ \times \text{ Annual interest cost in dollars}\end{array}}{\begin{array}{c}(\text{Total number of loan payments} + 1) \\ \times \text{ Principal of the loan}\end{array}} \times 100 \quad \textbf{(6–19)}$$

To illustrate, suppose you borrow $1,000 at 10 percent simple interest but must repay your loan in 12 equal monthly installments. The APR for this loan is approximately:

$$\text{APR} = \frac{2(12)(\$100)}{(12 + 1)(\$1,000)} \times 100 = 18.46\%$$

Regulatory agencies have developed APR tables, such as the one shown in the appendix at the back of this book, to aid lenders in figuring a borrower's required monthly payment and total finance charge on an installment loan. For example, consider the loan described above. The borrower is asked to pay a 10 percent simple interest rate on a loan of $1,000, or $100 in annual interest. The APR table shows us that an annual percentage rate of 18

---

[4]See Chapter 23 for a discussion of consumer credit laws.

percent (last column in the APR table) comes closest to the true annual interest rate for this loan. At an 18 percent APR, the borrower must pay $10.02 per $100 loaned if repayment is to be made in 12 equal monthly payments. On a $1,000 loan, this means the total finance charge will be $10.02 × $1,000 ÷ $100 = $10.02 × 10 = $100.20. Therefore, the borrower's required monthly payment will be the sum of the total finance charge plus the total amount of the loan divided by the required number of payments:

$$\text{Monthly payment} = \frac{\$100.02 + \$1,000}{12} = \$91.67$$

For further information about the APR see Consumer Credit and Credit Protection Laws at *www.federal reserve.gov*

Congress hoped that introduction of the APR would encourage consumers to exercise greater care in the use of credit and to shop around to obtain the best terms on a loan. It is not at all clear that either goal has been realized, however. Most consumers appear to give primary weight to the size of installment payments in deciding how much, when, and where to borrow. If their budget can afford principal and interest charges on a loan, most consumers seem little influenced by the reported size of the APR and are often not inclined to ask other lenders for their rates on the same loan. Consumer education is vital to intelligent financial decision making, but progress in that direction has been slow. However, there is some evidence that with growing use of the Internet more borrowers are shopping around for credit today.

Compound Interest

Some lenders and loan situations require the borrower to pay **compound interest** on a loan. In addition, most interest-bearing deposits at banks, credit unions, savings and loans, and money market funds pay compound interest on the balance in the account as of a certain date. The compounding of interest simply means that the lender or depositor earns interest income on both the principal amount and on any accumulated interest. Thus, the longer the period over which interest earnings are compounded, the more rapidly does interest earned on interest and interest earned on principal grow.

The conventional formula for calculating the future value of a financial asset earning compound interest is simply

$$FV = P(1 + r)^t \qquad \textbf{(6–20)}$$

Many different Web site sources discuss compounding of interest —for example, see *www.finaid.org*

where *FV* is the sum of principal plus all accumulated interest over the life of the loan or deposit, *P* is the asset's principal value, *r* is the annual rate of interest, and *t* is the time expressed in years. For example, suppose $1,000 is borrowed for three years at 10 percent a year, compounded annually. Using a computer program, an electronic calculator, or a compound interest table (see the appendix tables at the back of this book) to find the compounding factor, $(1 + r)^t$, gives

$$FV = \$1,000(1 + 0.10)^3 = \$1,000(1.331) = \$1,331$$

which is the lump-sum amount the borrower must pay back at the end of three years.[5] The amount of accumulated compound interest on this loan must be

$$\text{Compound interest} = FV - P = \$1,331 - \$1,000 = \$331 \quad \textbf{(6–21)}$$

---

[5]The compound interest table may be used to derive the compound interest factor in this problem. Simply check along the top row of the table for the appropriate annual percentage rate (10 percent in the above problem) and then check the number of time periods (in this case, three years) in the extreme left-hand column. The figures in the body of the compound interest table indicate the total future value (*FV*)—principal plus interest—repaid or earned per $1 of principal at alternative annual rates and time periods.

Increased competition in the financial institutions' sector has encouraged most deposit-type institutions to offer their depositors interest compounded more frequently than annually, as assumed in the formula above. To determine the future value of accumulated interest from such a deposit, two changes must be made in the formula: (1) the quoted annual interest rate (r) must be divided by the number of periods during the year for which interest is compounded, and (2) the number of years involved (t) must be multiplied by the number of compounding periods within a year. For example, suppose you hold a $1,000 deposit, earning a 12 percent annual rate of interest, with interest compounded monthly, and you plan to hold the deposit for three years. At the end of three years, you will receive back the lump sum of

$$FV = P(1 + r/12)^{t \times 12} = \$1,000(1 + 0.12/12)^{3 \times 12} \qquad \textbf{(6–22)}$$
$$= \$1,000(1.431) = \$1,431$$

Total interest earned will be $1,431 − $1,000, or $431. Compounding on a more frequent basis increases the depositor's accumulated interest and therefore the deposit's future value.[6]

The Annual Percentage Yield (APY)

In 1991 the U.S. Congress passed the Truth in Savings Act in response to customer complaints about the way some depository institutions were calculating their customers' interest returns on deposits. Instead of giving customers credit for the average balance in their deposit accounts, some depository institutions were figuring a customer's interest return on the amount of the *lowest* balance in their account. The U.S. Congress responded to this practice by requiring depository institutions to calculate the *daily average* balance in a customer's deposit over each interest-crediting period and to use that daily average balance to determine the customer's **annual percentage yield (APY)** from the deposit account.

The annual percentage yield (APY) is discussed on the Web at *www.federalreserve.gov* under the Truth in Savings Act.

For example, suppose a customer deposits $2,000 in a one-year bank savings account for 6 months (180 days) but then withdraws $1,000 to help meet personal expenses, leaving $1,000 for the remainder of the year (185 days). Then the customer's daily average balance would be:

$$\text{Daily average balance} = \frac{\$2,000 \times 180 \text{ days} + \$1,000 \times 185 \text{ days}}{365 \text{ days}} = \$1,493.15$$

Suppose the bank credits the customer's account with $100 in interest. If the account has a term of 365 days (a full year) or has no stated maturity, then the customer's annual percentage yield can be calculated from the simple formula:

$$\text{APY} = 100 \text{ [Annual interest earned/Daily average balance]} \qquad \textbf{(6–23)}$$

In this case,

$$\text{APY} = 100 \text{ [\$100/\$1493.15]} = 6.70 \text{ percent}$$

[6]The reader can look up the 1.431 compounding factor in the compound interest table simply by checking under the 1 percent (i.e., 12%/12 months) annual percentage rate column and checking the rows for 36 (3 × 12 months) payment periods. Many financial institutions quote deposit rates compounded *daily*. In this case, the annual interest rate (r) is divided by 360 for simplicity and the number of years (t) in the formula is multiplied by 365. Thus, the formula for *daily* interest rate compounding is

$$FV = P(1 + r/360)^{t \times 365}$$

See the table of compounding factors in the appendix at the back of this book for daily interest-rate compounding.

On the other hand, if the deposit account runs for less *than* a year, a depository institution subject to the provisions of the Truth in Savings Act must use the formula:

$$\text{APY} = 100\left[\left(1 + \frac{\text{Amount of interest earned/Daily average balance}}\right)^{365/\text{days in term}} - 1\right] \quad \textbf{(6–24)}$$

For data on credit card plans and the interest rates and other terms they impose on customers, see the credit card analyzer at *www. creditcardanalyzer.com/*

For example, suppose that a customer opens a savings account with a maturity of 182 days (6 months) and leaves $1,000 in the account for the whole period. Suppose too that at the end of the deposit's term the bank credits the customer with $30.37 in interest earned. Then, the annual percentage yield (APY) that must be reported to the customer under the Truth in Savings Act would be

$$\text{APY} = 100[(1 + \$30.37/\$1,000)^{365/182} - 1] \approx 6.18 \text{ percent.}$$

Whenever a customer opens a new deposit account in the United States, he or she must be informed about how interest will be computed on his or her account, what fees will be charged that could reduce the customer's interest earnings, and what must be done to earn the full APY promised on the deposit.

Questions *to Help You Study*

10. Please explain why debt security prices, such as the prices attached to bonds, and interest rates are *inversely related*. Illustrate this inverse relationship with an appropriate diagram.

11. Explain the meaning of the following terms and, where a formula is involved, explain the components of each formula:

   a. Simple interest

   b. Add-on interest

c. Discount method

d. APR

e. Compound interest

f. APY

12. How is the monthly payment that a *home mortgage borrower* must meet determined? Why is it that payments made early in the life of a typical home mortgage go largely to pay interest rather than to repay principal?

Summary of the Chapter

Interest rates and security prices are among the most important ingredients needed to help make sound financial decisions. Over the years, a number of methods have been developed to aid in the measurement and calculation of interest rates and security prices within the financial system. The intelligent participant in the financial markets today must learn how to distinguish one interest rate and price measure from another.

- Two of the most widely used and conceptually sound measures of the rate of return on a security or other financial asset are the *yield to maturity* and the *holding-period yield*. Both take into account the size and timing of all payments expected to be received from a financial instrument and consider the time value of money (that is, payments to be received sooner are more valuable, dollar for dollar, than payments to be received later).

- In contrast, other interest-rate or return measures, such as the *coupon rate* (or annual rate of return printed on a financial asset's face and set by contract) or the *current yield* (consisting of annual interest payments or dividends divided by the price of a financial instrument) do *not* consider the present value of any income or principal payments received by the holder of a financial instrument.

- In this chapter, we have highlighted one of the fundamental principles of finance: the mandatory *inverse relationship between the prices of debt securities and interest rates*. Falling bond prices, for example, are associated with rising interest rates in the money and capital markets.

- Often we observe stock prices falling during a period of rising interest rates as well, although this need not always be so because stock prices are sensitive to several other factors besides interest rates (such as the condition of the economy and business profits).

- Banks and other lending institutions often calculate the interest (loan) rates they quote borrowers according to different interest-rate measures. Examples include the *simple interest rate* (where interest owed is adjusted for repayments of the principal of a loan), and the *add-on interest rate* (where interest owed is added to the principal of a loan and the payments made by the borrower are calculated by dividing the sum of principal and interest by the number of payments called for in a loan agreement). Other loan-rate measures include the *discount method* (where interest is deducted at the beginning of a loan) and the *APR* (or annual percentage rate) which adjusts interest owed for repayments of loan principal. The APR is subject to regulation so that lenders calculate it in the same way and borrowers can more meaningfully compare one loan agreement against another in order to find the best deal available.

- Interest rates or yields on deposits today are increasingly quoted as the *annual percentage yield* or *APY*. Regulations require that depositors receive APY information when taking out a new deposit or renewing an existing deposit so that the depositor can make an informed decision.

- Most banks and other depository institutions pay *compound interest* on their deposits. This means that interest is earned on accumulated interest as well as on the principal invested in a deposit. Increasingly deposits accrue compound interest on a daily or other, more frequent basis than in the past.

- One of the most complicated interest rate and loan payment methods is the procedure used to figure loan rates and payment amounts on *home mortgage loans.* Under most home mortgage contracts payments made early in the life of such a loan go largely to pay interest; only after several years are substantial portions of home mortgage payments directed to help repay the loan principal.

In the next two chapters various factors that significantly impact the interest rate attached to a loan or security are examined. These factors—inflation, maturity or term of a loan, default risk, taxation, and other influences—often have a significant impact upon the price of credit in the money and capital markets.

Key Terms

Interest rate, *142*	Holding-period yield, *147*	Annual percentage rate (APR), *156*
Coupon rate, *145*	Simple interest method, *153*	Compound interest, *157*
Current yield, *145*	Add-on rate, *154*	Annual percentage yield
Yield to maturity, *146*	Discount method, *154*	(APY), *158*

Problems

1. Suppose a 10-year bond is issued with a coupon rate of 8 percent when the market rate of interest is also 8 percent. If the market rate rises to 9 percent, what happens to the price of this bond? What happens to the bond's price if the market rate falls to 6 percent? Explain why.

2. Preferred stock for XYZ corporation is issued at par for $50 per share. If stockholders are promised an 8 percent annual dividend, what was the stock's current yield at time of issue? If the stock's market price has risen to $60 per share, what is its new current yield?

3. An AAA-rated corporate bond has a current market price of $800 and will pay $100 in interest for 10 years. If its par value is $1,000, what is its yield to maturity? Suppose the investor plans to sell it in five years for $900. What would his or her holding-period yield be?

4. You plan to borrow $2,000 to take a vacation and want to repay the loan in a year. The banker offers you a simple interest rate of 12 percent with repayment of principal in two equal installments, 6 months and 12 months from now. What is your total interest bill? What is the APR? Would you prefer an add-on interest rate with one payment at the end of the year? If the bank applied the discount method to your loan, what are the net proceeds of the loan? What is your effective rate of interest?

5. An investor is interested in purchasing a new 20-year government bond carrying a 10 percent coupon rate. The bond's current market price is $875 for a $1,000 par value instrument. If the investor buys the bond at the going price and holds to maturity, what will be his or her yield to maturity? Suppose the investor sells the bond at the end of 10 years for $950. What is the investor's holding-period yield?

6. You discover a $1,000 par value bond just issued by XYZ corporation that pays interest semiannually at a coupon rate of 12 percent. The bond will mature in 10 years and can be purchased today at a price of $900 including the broker's commission. What is the bond's yield to maturity if all interest payments are made on time?

7. You borrow $2,500 for five years at a rate of 12 percent per annum, compounded annually. What is the lump-sum amount due at the end of five years? What is the total amount of interest owed?

8. In Problem 7, if interest were compounded monthly instead of annually, what lump-sum amount would be due in five years and how much total interest must be paid?

9. You have just placed $1,500 in a bank savings deposit and plan to hold that deposit for eight years, earning 5½ percent per annum. If the bank compounds interest daily, what will be the total value of the deposit in eight years? How does your answer change if the bank switches to monthly compounding? Quarterly compounding?

10. You decide to take out a 30-year mortgage loan to buy the home of your dreams. The home's purchase price is $120,000. You manage to scrape together a $20,000 down payment and plan to borrow the balance of the purchase price. Hardy Savings and Loan Association quotes you a fixed annual loan rate of 12 percent. What will your monthly payment be? How much total interest will you have paid at the end of 30 years?

11. A home mortgage loan for $60,000 is available from the neighboring bank at an interest rate of 1 percent per month. The loan will mature in 25 years. What payment must the borrower make each month under the terms of this loan agreement?

12. A depositor leaves her funds in the amount of $5,000 in a credit union deposit account for a full year but then withdraws $1,000 after 270 days. At the end of the year, the credit union pays her $300 in interest. What is this depositor's daily average balance and APY?

13. A bank customer takes out a CD from his principal bank for 90 days in the amount of $2,500 and earns $99 in interest for the 90-day period. What is the depositor's APY?

14. A commercial loan extended to CIBER-LAND Corporation for $2.5 million assesses an interest charge of $350,000 up front. Using the discount method of calculating loan rates, what is the effective interest rate on this loan? Suppose that instead of deducting the interest owed up front, the company's lender agrees to extend the full $2.5 million and add the amount of interest owed to the face amount of CIBER's note. What, then, is the loan's effective interest rate?

15. The Pine family borrows $1,500 for a year at an 11 percent simple interest rate, but the loan is to be repaid in 12 equal monthly installments. What is the loan's APR? Please check the APR table at the back of this book and try to confirm your estimate of the loan's true APR.

16. Please identify each of the key terms or concepts described below that were discussed in this chapter:
    a. Rate of return on a savings account that depository institutions must report to their customers.
    b. Earning interest on interest income.
    c. Interest rate attached to a consumer loan that, U.S. laws stipulate, must be reported to the borrowing customer before he or she agrees to a loan.
    d. Interest is charged only for the period that loanable funds (credit) is actually available.
    e. Interest on a loan is paid up front before the borrower has the use of the funds.

f. Interest owed by the borrower is figured on the full initial loan balance.

g. Ratio of a financial asset's expected annual income to its market value or price.

h. Includes the present value of all expected cash flows from a financial instrument.

i. Rate of return expected from a financial asset based on the expected cash flows generated by the asset between the purchase date and the asset's sale date.

j. Promised interest rate usually printed on the face of a bond or note.

k. Known as the price of credit and usually measured by the ratio of two values.

Questions about the Web and the Money and Capital Markets

1. How could you determine, using the World Wide Web, the best loan rates available to you if you wanted to purchase a new home? A new automobile?

2. How can you use the Web to find out if local interest rates in your area are competitive with interest rates in other areas of the United States?

3. How much can you save if you decide to refinance your current home mortgage loan? How can the Web be of help to you here?

Selected References

Rose, Peter S. *Commercial Bank Management,* 5th ed. New York: McGraw-Hill, 2001.

Sundaresan, Suresh. *Fixed Income Markets and Their Derivatives.* New York: International Thomson, 1997.

Trainer, Richard D. C. *The Arithmetic of Interest Rates.* New York: Federal Reserve Bank of New York, 1980.

Chapter **Seven**

The Impact of Inflation and Deflation, Yield Curves, and Duration on Interest Rates and Asset Prices

Learning Objectives in This Chapter

- You will discover what *inflation* is all about and how inflation can impact interest rates and the prices of loans, securities, and other financial assets.

- You will understand why there is greater concern today than in the past about the prospect of *deflation—the* reverse of inflation—and how it might affect the economy and the financial system.

- You will see how *yield curves* arise and view the controversy over what determines the shape of the yield curve at any moment in time.

- You will discover how yield curves can be a useful tool for those interested in investing their money and in tracking the health of the economy.

- You will explore the concept of *duration—a* popular measure of the maturity of a financial instrument—and see how it can be used to assist in making investment choices and in protecting against the risk of changes in interest rates.

What's in This Chapter? Key Topics Outline

Inflation: What Is It? How Does It Affect Interest Rates?

The Fisher Effect

Alternative Views: Inflation, Changes in the Economy, and Interest Rates

Price Deflation and Its Effects

Inflation and Stock Prices: What Are the Links?

INTRODUCTION

In Chapter 5 we examined demand and supply forces believed to determine the rate of interest on a loan or security. We know, however, that there is not just one interest rate in the financial system, but thousands. And many of these rates differ substantially from one another. For example, early in 2002 six-month maturity U.S. Treasury bills were being auctioned at an annual interest rate of 1.80 percent, while long-term Treasury bonds were offering investors a 5.75 percent annual return. The market yield on high-quality corporate bonds averaged almost 7 percent. At the same time, major banks were quoting average loan rates to their most financially sound (prime) customers of 4.75 percent. Meanwhile, investors in the market for state and local government (municipal) long-term bonds were being promised an annual rate of return of about 5.20 percent.

Why are all these interest rates so different from one another? Are these rate differences purely random, or can we attribute them to a limited number of factors that can be studied and perhaps predicted? Understanding the factors that cause interest rates to differ among themselves is an indispensable aid to the investor and saver in choosing financial assets for a portfolio. It is not always advisable, for example, to reach for the highest yield available in the financial marketplace. The investor who does so may assume an unacceptable level of risk, have his or her securities called in by the issuer in advance of maturity, pay an unacceptably high tax bill, accept a rate of return whose value is seriously eroded by inflation, or suffer other undesirable consequences. Without question, the intelligent saver and investor must have a working knowledge of the factors affecting interest rates and be able to anticipate possible future changes in those factors. In this chapter and the next, we address these important issues.

INFLATION AND INTEREST RATES

One of the most serious problems confronting several economies around the globe in recent years has been **inflation.** Inflation is defined as *a rise in the average level of prices for all goods and services.* Some prices of individual goods and services are always rising while others are declining. However, inflation occurs when the *average* level of all prices in the economy rises.[1] Interest rates represent the "price" of credit. Are they also affected by inflation? The answer is *yes,* though there is considerable debate as to exactly *how* and by *how much* inflation affects interest rates.

The Correlation between Inflation and Interest Rates

To be sure, the apparent correlation in recent years between the rate of inflation in the United States and both long-term and short-term interest rates appears to be fairly strong. Exhibit 7–1, which reports two popular measures of the rate of inflation—the consumer

---

[1]See Chapter 14 for a discussion of the nature, causes, and recent public policy responses to inflation.

Factors that influence interest rates and cause one interest rate to be different from another are discussed in numerous places on the World Wide Web. In this chapter our focus is upon two very important interest-rate determining factors—inflation in the prices of goods and services and time or duration which influences the relative size of interest rates attached to short-term securities versus interest rates on long-term securities.

Numerous sources of interest-rate data lie out on the Web and there are key sources that frequently link interest rates and inflation rates. One example is Global Financial Data at www.globalfindata.com. In addition, there are financial newssheets and research papers posted that frequently take up the issue of how inflation impacts market rates of interest. Prominent examples include *The Economist* (at www.economist.com) and the Federal Reserve Bank of Cleveland Working Paper Series (at www.clev.frb.org/Research). In addition, there are discussions of the pros and cons of investing in inflation-adjusted securities, such as those issued today by the United States Treasury (at www.savingsbond.com).

The impact of duration or calendar time on the size of interest rates, and especially the process by which yield curves are created and interpreted, is discussed in numerous Web sites. There are, for example, software systems to aid in the construction of yield curves at such sites as Mathematical Finance Company (at www.mathematical-finance.com) or at Securities Math (at www.pvlinton.com/securiti.htm).

price index and the GDP deflator—and a key money market interest rate—the yield on six-month commercial paper—suggests a relatively close association between inflation and interest rates, especially during the 1970s and 1980s. History reveals, for example, that there was a sharp run-up in the rate of inflation between 1971 and 1974 and a parallel upward surge in the commercial paper rate, which reached an average yield of nearly 10 percent in 1974. Similarly, between 1974 and 1980, the inflation rate soared into double digits before falling back in the early 1980s, and interest rates did the same. Between 1980 and 2000, both inflation and U.S. interest rates generally declined, before rising slightly as the decade of the 1990s ended. Finally, in the wake of terrorist attacks and a weakening economy as the new century opened, interest rates sank to 40-year lows while inflation remained relatively modest.

In summary, then, interest rates and inflation appear to be at least moderately correlated with one another. But is there really a causal connection between them?

The Nominal and Real Interest Rates

To explore the possible relationship between inflation and interest rates, several key terms must be defined. First, we must distinguish between nominal and real interest rates. The **nominal interest rate** is the published or quoted interest rate on a security or loan. For example, an announcement in the financial press that major commercial banks have raised their prime lending rate to 10 percent per annum indicates what nominal interest rate is now being quoted by banks to some of their best loan customers. In contrast, the **real interest rate** is the return to the lender or investor measured in terms of its actual purchasing power. In a period of inflation, of course, the real rate will be lower than the nominal rate. Another important concept is the **inflation premium,** which measures the rate of inflation *expected* by lenders and investors in the marketplace during the life of a particular financial instrument.

EXHIBIT 7–1
Inflation and Interest Rates (Annual Rates, Percent)

| Year | Rate of Inflation Measured by Percentage Change in | | Interest Rate on Prime Commercial Paper (Six-Month Maturities) |
	Consumer Price Index	GDP Deflator	
1960	1.6%	1.7%	3.85%
1970	5.9	5.4	7.72
1980	13.5	8.8	12.29
1990	6.2	4.0	7.83
2000	3.4	2.3	6.50
2001*	2.7	2.3	1.84

*Consumer price index is from August 2001 to August of preceding year. GDP deflator is for the first two quarters of 2001. The 2001 commercial paper interest rate is for directly placed paper, last day of the year.

Source: U.S. Department of Commerce and Board of Governors of the Federal Reserve System.

These three concepts *are* related. Obviously, a lender of funds is most interested in the *real rate of return* on a loan; that is, the purchasing power of any interest earned. For example, suppose you loan $1,000 to a business firm for a year and expect the prices of goods and services to rise 10 percent during the year. If you charge a nominal interest rate of 12 percent on the loan, your *real* rate of return on the $1,000 loan is only 2 percent, or $20. However, if the actual rate of inflation during the period of the loan turns out to be 13 percent, you have actually suffered a real decline in the purchasing power of the monies loaned. In general, lenders will attempt to charge nominal rates of interest that give them desired *real* rates of return on their loanable funds based upon their expectations regarding inflation.

The Fisher Effect

In a classic article written just before the end of the nineteenth century, economist Irving Fisher (1896) argued that the nominal interest rate was related to the real interest rate by the following equation:

$$\begin{matrix} \text{Expected} \\ \text{Nominal} \\ \text{Interest Rate} \end{matrix} = \begin{matrix} \text{Expected} \\ \text{real} \\ \text{rate} \end{matrix} + \begin{matrix} \text{Inflation} \\ \text{Premium} \end{matrix} + \begin{matrix} \text{Expected} \\ \text{real} \\ \text{rate} \end{matrix} \times \begin{matrix} \text{Inflation} \\ \text{Premium} \end{matrix} \qquad \textbf{(7–1)}$$

Clearly, if the expected real interest rate is held fixed, changes in expected nominal rates will reflect shifting inflation premiums (i.e., changes in the public's views on expected inflation). The cross-product term in the above equation (expected real rate × inflation premium) is often eliminated because it is usually quite small except in countries experiencing severe inflation.[2]

Does Equation 7–1 suggest that an increase in expected inflation *automatically* increases expected nominal interest rates? Not necessarily. There are several different views on the matter. Fisher argued that the expected real rate of return tends to be relatively stable over time because it depends on such long-term factors as the productivity of capital and the volume of savings in the economy. Therefore, changes in the expected nominal interest rate are most likely to reflect changes in the inflation premium, not the expected real rate, at least in the short run. The expected nominal rate will rise by close to the full amount of the expected increase in the rate of inflation. For example, suppose the expected real rate

[2]For example, if inflation is running 5 percent a year and the real rate of interest is 3 percent, the cross-product term in Equation 7–1 is only 0.05 × 0.03, or 0.0015. Equation 7–1 is derived from the relationship (1 + Nominal rate) = (1 + Real rate) × (1 + Inflation premium).

is 3 percent and the expected rate of inflation is 10 percent. Then the expected nominal rate would be close to:

$$\text{Expected nominal interest rate} = 3\% + 10\% = 13\% \qquad \textbf{(7–2)}$$

According to Fisher's hypothesis, if the expected rate of inflation now rises to 12 percent, the expected real rate will remain essentially unchanged at 3 percent, but the expected nominal rate will rise to about 15 percent.

If this view, known today as the **Fisher effect,** is correct, it suggests a method of judging at least the *direction* of future interest rate changes. To the extent that a rise in the actual rate of inflation causes investors to expect greater inflation in the future, higher nominal interest rates will soon result. Conversely, a decline in the actual inflation rate may cause investors to revise downward their expectations of future inflation, leading eventually to lower nominal rates. This will happen because, in an efficient market, investors will seek full compensation for the risk of expected changes in the purchasing power of their money.

The Harrod-Keynes Effect of Inflation

The Fisher effect conflicts directly with another view of the inflation/interest rate phenomenon, developed originally by British economist Sir Roy Harrod. It is based upon the Keynesian liquidity preference theory of interest discussed in Chapter 5. Harrod argues that the *real* rate *will* be affected by inflation but the nominal interest rate may not be. Following the liquidity preference theory, the nominal interest rate is determined by the demand for and supply of money. Therefore, unless inflation affects either the demand for or supply of money, the expected nominal interest rate must remain unchanged regardless of what happens to inflationary expectations.

What, then, is the link between inflation and interest rates according to this view? Harrod argues that a rise in inflationary expectations will lower the *real* rate of interest. In liquidity preference theory, the real rate measures the inflation-adjusted return on bonds. However, conventional bonds, like money, are *not* a hedge against inflation, because their rate of return is usually fixed by contract. Therefore, a rise in the expected rate of inflation lowers investors' expected real return from holding bonds. If the nominal rate of return on bonds remains unchanged, the expected real rate *must* be squeezed by expectations of rising prices.

This so-called **Harrod-Keynes effect** does not stop with bonds, however. There are two other groups of assets in the economy that, unlike bonds, may provide a hedge against inflation: *common stocks* and *real estate.* Inflationary expectations often lead to rising prices for homes, farmland, and commercial structures and occasionally to rallies in the stock market. Proponents of the Harrod-Keynes view argue that an increase in the rate of inflation causes the demand for these inflation-hedged assets to increase. Real estate and stock prices rise and, therefore, their nominal rates of return will fall until an equilibrium set of returns on bonds, real estate, and other assets is achieved.

Alternative Views on Inflation and Interest Rates

The simple one-to-one relationship between the expected inflation rate and the expected nominal rate of interest proposed by Irving Fisher was the majority view for decades until researchers began to find problems with it. For example, the Fisher effect assumes that inflation is *fully anticipated.* As an example, let us imagine that both borrowers and lenders of funds expect an inflation rate for the next year of 10 percent and the real interest rate is

EXHIBIT 7–2

The Impact of Fully Anticipated Inflation on Real and Nominal Interest Rates

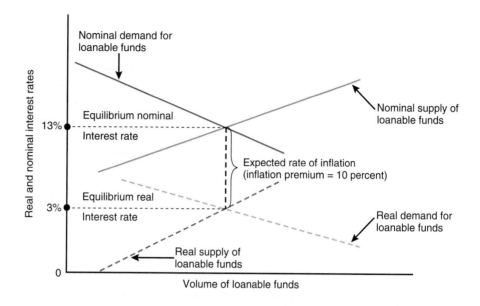

3 percent. We can illustrate this using Exhibit 7–2, which shows two sets of demand and supply curves for loanable funds: a set of *real* demand and supply curves intersecting at a 3 percent real interest rate, and a set of *nominal* demand and supply curves intersecting at a point just high enough to fully reflect the expected inflation rate (in this example, 10 percentage points higher than the real rate). The nominal supply and demand curves for loanable funds both shift upward just enough to ensure that the going nominal interest rate on a one-year loan is 3 percent plus 10 percent, or 13 percent. Lenders will be unwilling to lend money at any rate lower than 13 percent because they expect the prices of the goods and services they plan to purchase to increase by 10 percent during the life span of the loan.

Suppose however, that all or a portion of the increase in inflation is *unanticipated*. In this case, there is no way to be certain about what the equilibrium nominal interest rate will be, for the nominal rate may not fully reflect the amount of inflation expected. The simple one-for-one change in the expected nominal rate in response to changing inflationary expectations breaks down.

The Inflation-Caused Wealth Effect

Another problem with the Fisher effect centers on its assumption that people will borrow and lend the *same* amount of funds at *any* expected real interest rate, regardless of the expected inflation rate. However, inflation can affect incomes, wealth, saving and investment, the burden of taxes, and so on. Suppose, for example, that people come to expect a higher inflation rate and they perceive this change as lowering the value of their inflation-adjusted (real) wealth. In response to this inflation-caused wealth effect, people may decide to save more, lowering the equilibrium expected real rate of interest. Therefore, the expected nominal interest rate will rise by *less* than the expected increase in inflation because of the offsetting decline in the expected real rate. Similarly, a decrease in expected inflation might lead to a perceived increase in the real value of wealth holdings, reduce current saving, and cause the expected real interest rate to rise. Thus, the nominal interest rate will fall by less than the decrease in expected inflation. Clearly, with the **inflation-caused wealth effect,** there is *less* than a one-to-one relationship between changes in expected inflation and expected nominal interest rates.

The Inflation-Caused Income Effect

The wealth effect may be joined by an **inflation-caused income effect.** A rise in expected inflation, for example, may lead to an increase in real (inflation-adjusted) income. This may happen because a declining expected real interest rate associated with the reduced value of wealth may cause consumers to reduce their supply of savings to the financial markets and to step up their current spending on goods and services. In response, businesses will borrow more to increase production and stock their shelves with additional goods to sell. The expanded consumption and production will increase employment, and both businesses and consumers will experience a rise in their incomes. Out of that higher income more savings will eventually flow into the financial system, expanding the supply of loanable funds. Other factors held equal, borrowing and lending will take place at a lower real rate of interest, and the expected nominal rate will again rise by *less* than the increase in expected inflation.

Similarly, a decrease in expected inflation may stimulate more saving and less consumption, reducing business investment and incomes. Eventually, savings flowing into the financial markets will begin to fall with the decline in incomes, and the expected real interest rate will rise even as expected nominal rates fall due to lower expected inflation. As before, there is *less* than a one-to-one relationship between changes in expected inflation and the expected nominal interest rate.

Both the inflation-caused income effect and the wealth effect take *time* to exert their influence on real and nominal interest rates, and this time factor can distort the inflation-interest rate linkage. Unless we adopt a pure rational expectations-efficient markets approach to explaining interest rates (as discussed in Chapter 5), nominal interest rates will reach equilibrium only after a series of rate-determining adjustments have been made. For example, suppose the central bank increases the nation's money supply. The liquidity preference theory of interest discussed in Chapter 5 suggests that nominal rates will fall at first due to the expansion in the available money stock relative to the public's money demands. However, the growing money stock may kindle both expectations of inflation and rising incomes, eventually putting upward pressure on nominal rates. Thus, the nominal interest rate we observe at any single point in time may not fully reflect the public's inflationary expectations because it is being buffeted by several other forces in its journey toward equilibrium.

The Inflation-Caused Depreciation Effect

Still another factor to consider in the inflation/interest rate story is **the inflation-caused depreciation effect.** Inflation drives up the cost of new capital goods—buildings and machinery—that must be purchased to replace old capital items that are wearing out. However, old capital must be depreciated by formulas (such as the straight-line method) dictated by federal and state tax laws. In periods of rapid inflation, the true cost of using up existing capital equipment is understated, so that taxable business income is inflated. As a result, *after-tax* income from business investment projects is *less* than would be true with lower or no inflation. With less income after taxes, businesses will cut back on their plans to purchase new capital goods, and the resulting fall in the demand for loanable funds will decrease the equilibrium real interest rate. Clearly, then, if the expected rate of inflation rises and the real interest rate falls at the same time, the nominal interest rate is likely to rise by *less* than the increase in expected inflation.

The Inflation-Caused Income Tax Effect

The depreciation effect brings taxes into the picture. Recent research suggests that the tax impact may work in *both directions;* that is, while the depreciation effect tends to dampen changes in the expected nominal interest rate, the **inflation-caused income tax effect** may widen movements in the nominal rate so that it changes by *more* than any given change in expected inflation. The heart of this argument is that lenders and investors not exempt from income taxes make lending and investing decisions on the basis of their expected real rate of return *after taxes*. If an investor desires to protect (i.e., hold constant) his or her expected real after-tax rate of return, then the expected nominal rate has to increase by a *greater* amount than any rise in the expected inflation rate because otherwise real after-tax returns will decline when expected inflation increases.

To see the validity of this argument, we observe that

$$
\begin{array}{c}
\text{Expected after-tax} \\
\text{real rate of return} \\
\text{earned by a} \\
\text{taxpaying} \\
\text{investor}
\end{array}
=
\begin{array}{c}
\text{Expected} \\
\text{nominal} \\
\text{rate}
\end{array}
-
\left[
\begin{array}{c}
\text{Expected} \\
\text{nominal} \\
\text{rate}
\end{array}
\times
\begin{array}{c}
\text{Taxpayer's} \\
\text{income tax} \\
\text{bracket rate}
\end{array}
\right]
-
\begin{array}{c}
\text{Inflation} \\
\text{premium}
\end{array}
\quad \textbf{(7–3)}
$$

Suppose an investor is in the 28 percent income tax bracket, so that a little more than a quarter of any additional income he or she earns is taxed. Moreover, suppose the current expected nominal interest rate on a one-year taxable security this investor is interested in buying is 12 percent, and the inflation premium (expected inflation rate) over the coming year is 5 percent. Then this investor's expected real after-tax return from the security must be

$$
\begin{array}{c}
\text{Expected after-tax} \\
\text{real rate of return} \\
\text{earned by a tax-} \\
\text{paying investor}
\end{array}
= 12\% - [12\%\,(0.28)] - 5\% = 3.64\% \quad \textbf{(7–4)}
$$

Now suppose the expected rate of inflation rises from 5 to 6 percent. By how much must the *expected nominal rate* on the taxable security rise to yield this investor the *same* expected real return after taxes? The answer must be that the nominal rate must rise to 13.39 percent, for

$$
\begin{array}{c}
\text{Expected after-tax} \\
\text{real rate of return} \\
\text{earned by a tax-} \\
\text{paying investor}
\end{array}
= 13.39\% - [13.39\%\,(0.28)] - 6\% = 3.64\% \quad \textbf{(7–5)}
$$

Thus, a change of 1 percent in expected inflation required a 1.39 percent change in the expected nominal rate to leave this taxed investor in the same place in terms of a real (purchasing-power) return from his or her investment.

The arithmetic shown above works both ways: a *reduction* in expected inflation by 1 percent requires a 1.39 percent *decline* in the nominal rate to leave the expected real after-tax return where it is. While investors in lower tax brackets would not require as numerically large a change in expected nominal rates to leave after-tax real returns unaltered, inflation tends to force most investors into higher and higher tax brackets as both prices and nominal incomes rise, unless government tax schedules are indexed to change with inflation.

Conclusions from Recent Research on Inflation and Interest Rates

With all the foregoing *possible* effects from inflation, what actually happens to nominal rates when the expected rate of inflation shifts? The bulk of recent research suggests *nominal rates rise by less than any given increase in the expected inflation rate and decline by less than any given decrease in the expected inflation rate.* In essence, the inflation-caused income, wealth, and depreciation effects appear to outweigh influences pulling in the opposite direction, such as the income tax effect. Estimates vary but generally suggest that nominal interest rates change by 60 to perhaps 90 percent of the calculated change in the expected inflation rate.

The relationship between interest rates and inflation is discussed in numerous Web sites, including *www. interestratecalculator .com* and *www.finpipe.com.*

The response of interest rates to inflation seems to depend crucially on whether inflation is anticipated or unanticipated by the public. Hayford (1990), for example, finds that if an increase in inflation was *not* expected by the marketplace, the value of investor wealth will decline and total spending in the economy will fall, which subsequently will lead to *lower* real interest rates. This linkage suggests that those who have argued that nominal interest rates do *not* change point-for-point with changes in inflation are probably right. However, the reader should retain a healthy skepticism about research in this field. The topic of inflation and interest rates is plagued by numerous measurement problems.

For example, there are no direct, widely accepted measures of the two key actors in the drama—the expected real rate and the expected rate of inflation. Because the underlying theory speaks of *expected* inflation and the *expected* real interest rate, there is the obvious problem of measuring people's expectations. We cannot, as a practical matter, survey all investors, and the results of such a survey would soon be irrelevant anyway, because expectations can change fast. Note, too, that we cannot automatically derive the expected real interest rate merely by subtracting the current inflation rate from the current nominal rate; this gives us a measure of the actual (ex post) real rate at a single point in time, not necessarily the *expected* real rate. Moreover, none of these approaches takes into account *time lags* as interest rates, buffeted by numerous forces, strive over time to reach long-run equilibrium.[3]

The Impact of Price Deflation

For the past 50 years and more inflation—a rising average level of prices of good and services—has been a key economic and financial problem. However, as the twentieth century drew to a close and the twenty-first century began there was growing concern that *deflation*—a falling average level of prices—might soon replace inflation as one of the key problems nations might face in the future. Indeed, Japan for much of the past decade has experienced falling prices to go along with rising unemployment and nominal interest rates hovering close to zero.

If inflation tends to result in rising interest rates, what can we say about *deflation?* Would it lead to falling interest rates?

We cannot say for sure because periods of deflation in prices—at least during the past century—have been relatively rare. The last time the United States experienced a sustained deflation was during the Great Depression of the 1930s. Nominal prices of goods and ser-

---

[3]Recent research has suggested that the nominal rate-real rate (or Fisher) equation should be modified as follows:

Nominal rate = Real rate + Expected inflation rate (or inflation premium) + Inflation risk premium.

The final, newly added term—the inflation risk premium—represents compensation to an investor for that component of inflation that is not expected. Thus, this last term represents future uncertainty about what the actual inflation rate will turn out to be during the life of a loan or security. The inflation risk premium generally rises with the maturity of a nominal financial instrument because the longer the period until final payment on a loan or security the greater the likelihood of unexpected inflation occurring. It is more difficult to forecast inflation over a longer period of time. Moreover, the longer the future period before final payment the greater the cost of any inflation forecasting error the investor might make. Recent research by Shen (1998) for the United Kingdom suggests that the inflation risk premium can be sizable—a percentage point or more added to the rate of return on inflation-risk-exposed financial instruments.

vices fell nearly *25* percent and real output (i.e., the production of goods and services) dropped almost 40 percent during the 1929–33 period. More recently, consumer prices and manufacturers' output fell slightly in the wake of the September 2001 terrorist attacks against New York City and Washington, DC.

Were these two economic series—a falling price level and declining real output— connected somehow? We think so, because deflation can be damaging to production and to people's well-being. For one thing, deflation tends to force real interest rates higher even as nominal interest rates drop toward zero. These elevated real interest rates tend to slow investment spending and decrease the development of new jobs. Real economic output will decline as factories come to produce less and business profits fall. At the same time lenders gain at the expense of borrowers because the former's purchasing power rises, and businesses trying to borrow money have to struggle to raise the capital they require to grow and put people back to work

In summary, price deflation can result in lower output (production) of goods and services, but force real interest rates upward. However, businesses and the financial system are much better positioned today to deal with moderate deflation, in part because of the development of so many risk management tools (such as financial futures contracts, swaps, and options). It would probably take a major deflationary period, such as the one that impacted the United States during the Great Depression of the 1930s and Japan late in the twentieth century and early in this century, to cause serious economic and financial disruption.

Inflation and Stock Prices

The discussion so far has centered on the public's expectations about the prices of goods and services and their possible impact on interest rates attached to bonds and other debt securities. However, another interesting question centers on the relationship between expectations of inflation and stock prices. Does inflation cause the prices of corporate stock (equities) to rise? The conventional wisdom says *yes*. Common stock, for example, is widely viewed as a hedge against inflation—a place to park your money if you want to preserve the purchasing power of your savings over the long haul.

Unfortunately, the facts often contradict what everybody "knows." For example, the stock market rose to unprecedented highs in the mid-1980s and again in the late 1990s, yet the U.S. inflation rate *fell* during these periods. One useful way to view this issue is to decide what factors determine the prices of corporate stock and see if those factors are likely to be affected by inflation.

In basic terms, the stock price of any corporation (SP) is positively related to the dividends investors expect the company to pay to shareholders in future periods and is negatively related to the risk attached to that stream of expected dividends. That is,

$$\text{Price per share of corporate stock} \quad (\text{SP}) = \sum_{t=0}^{\infty} \frac{E(D_t)}{(1 + k)^t} \qquad \textbf{(7–6)}$$

where $E(D_t)$ are expected dividend payments in each period t, and k is the rate of discount applied to those expected dividends to express them in terms of their present value. The riskier the corporation's dividend stream, the higher the required rate of discount, k, because investors demand a higher rate of return to compensate them for the added risk of holding stock (which promises no specific rate of return).

Clearly, if a rise in expected inflation raises stock prices, it must increase the amount of dividends shareholders expect each company to pay them [$E(D)$], or lower the perceived risk of holding stock (k), or both. On the other hand, stock prices will tend to fall if more

Deflation—a decline in the average level of prices attached to goods and services—has been a rare occurrence in most industrialized countries in the past century, especially since the end of World War II. However, Japan has been experiencing just that—a declining price level—since the early 1990s. By late 1994 the percentage change in Japan's GDP deflator price index became negative, recovered briefly in 1997, and then fell precipitously again as the new century approached.

Japan's price deflation has been associated with all kinds of damage to their economy and financial system. Since 1997 real output and income levels inside Japan have either declined or increased only weakly. The supply of credit appears to be falling as well and many banks have either failed or merged with other banks in order to head off impending failure. Bad loans have reached record levels. Nominal interest rates, in some cases averaging less than two-tenths of one percent, have reached the lowest level since the seventeenth century. Japanese deflation has been associated with falling business profits and revenues, eroding business asset values and stock prices.

The nation's central bank—the Bank of Japan—has attempted to "reinflate" the Japanese economy and financial system by flooding the banking system with liquid reserves and by pumping up the money supply in an effort to stimulate borrowing and spending. Thus far, however, there is not much to show for these efforts. Gross domestic product (GDP), measured in real terms, has increased only slightly. Unemployment remains unusually high for Japan and many Japanese workers fear eventual loss of their jobs. In short, severe deflation of prices, just like very rapid price inflation, can damage a nation's standard of living and reduce the economic welfare of its citizens.

inflation causes investors to lower their dividend expectations, increases the perceived risk to stockholders, or both. Is there any research evidence on which way the relationship goes?

There are several conflicting views. One line of argument says that if inflation is fully expected by all investors, nominal (published) stock prices may rise but *real* stock prices will not change at all. This is because corporate revenues and expenses will grow equally fast and the size of each firm's net income and dividend payments probably will *not* be affected (assuming the company's board of directors does not change the dividend rate). On the other hand, if inflation is only partly expected, the amount of unexpected inflation may be captured by company stockholders, as opposed to debt holders, in the form of increased earnings, and real stock prices will rise. Conversely, if the company's depreciation expenses on worn-out equipment are inadequate to offset the rising cost of new equipment in a period of inflation, current before-tax corporate income will be overstated, resulting in higher taxes against the firm, lowering its after-tax income and reducing stockholder dividend payments. In this instance, more rapid inflation would tend to *lower* stock prices. Indeed, studies by Ammer (1994), Solnik (1983), and others find a *negative* relationship between stock prices and inflation for several countries.

Recently the concept of **nominal contracts** has emerged to explain the inflation/stock price connection. What are nominal contracts? They are agreements between parties, such as a company and its workers or customers, that fix prices or costs in terms of current dollar (nominal) values for a stipulated time period. For example, corporations and labor unions may agree to increase wages 10 percent a year until current labor-management contracts expire or pledge to deliver their products to customers at a fixed price during the coming year. Corporate rules for valuing inventories or calculating depreciation expenses are other examples of nominal contracts. If inflation subsequently rises faster or slower than a company expected when it entered into its current nominal contracts, its profits may be squeezed or enhanced and its stock price may decrease or increase depending upon the circumstances. Thus, *the impact of inflation on stock prices may vary from firm to firm and*

Management Insight   The Nominal Contracts Hypothesis for Explaining the Links between Inflation and Stock Prices

Nominal contracts are formal agreements that *fix* the time and terms in current (nominal) dollars under which a business firm will compensate its employees, creditors, and other suppliers of productive resources and the prices at which it will deliver its product or service to customers. Examples include business contracts with labor unions that fix wage rates or wage increases, the issue of bonds at a fixed interest cost, or the valuing of business inventories and the depreciation of capital equipment using prespecified, unchanging formulas. A business firm can be hurt by inflation, experiencing a fall in its stock price, if actual inflation turns out to be different from what it expected when it agreed to a nominal contract. However, some nominal contracts can benefit a firm experiencing inflation, particularly if the company correctly anticipated future price changes or, by using well-structured nominal contracts, managed to hold down its expenses or enhance its revenues. For example:

If a business firm enters into nominal contracts that:	Then, if inflation turns out to be *greater than expected:*	However, suppose inflation turns out to be *less than expected.* Then:
A. Fix its expenses at a constant level or constant rate of growth (e.g., borrowing money at a fixed rate or paying employees a guaranteed wage) based on its current expectations for inflation.	Business revenues may grow faster than expenses, increasing profits; the firm's stock price may *rise.*	Business expenses may increase faster than revenues, reducing profits; the firm's stock price may *fall.*
B. Fix its revenues at a constant level or constant rate of growth (e.g., selling to customers at a guaranteed price for the coming year) based on its current inflationary expectations.	Business expenses may grow faster than revenues, reducing profits; the firm's stock price may *fall.*	Business revenues may grow faster than expenses, increasing profits; the firm's stock price may *rise.*

from industry to industry depending upon the actual rate of inflation and the terms of existing nominal contracts.

An alternative view—called the *proxy effect*—argues for a *negative* relationship between inflation and stock prices but claims that relationship is *spurious,* not real. Fama (1981) and Geske and Roll (1983) contend, for example, that changes in expected inflation are inversely related to fluctuations in expected output in the economy. If the public comes to believe that living costs will rise and the nation's economic output will decline at about the same time, then real stock prices may fall due to a more pessimistic outlook for business profits. However, it is the expected decrease in the economy's output, not the expected change in living costs (inflation), that leads to a decline in stock prices. Similarly, inflation and stock prices may have a spurious relationship due to monetary policy. If the economy's output falls and the central bank expands the nation's money supply to fight the output decline, inflation may accelerate because more money is in circulation. However, if stock prices subsequently fall, the public may blame inflation for the decline, when, in fact, the cause was the economy's declining production. Research evidence on these newer views is decidedly mixed but seems to favor the nominal contracts approach. Either way, the issue of stock prices and inflation remains in doubt, awaiting further research to find the right answers.

Summary of the Debate over Inflation, Interest Rates, and Stock Prices: Have We Found the Answers?

With so many competing ideas about what inflation (or deflation) does to interest rates and stock prices it's easy to emerge from this ongoing debate badly bruised and confused! The truth is we know nothing for sure, and this is especially true of stock prices and inflation.

Most researchers and practitioners on the street seem to believe the *Fisher Effect* is essentially true: expected nominal interest rates closely follow expected inflation and both tend to move in the same direction. Still, there is some "slippage" in this link between expected nominal interest rates and inflation; they don't move perfectly together, leaving at least some room for the idea that inflation affects how people spend and save their money and, therefore, real interest rates also change somewhat in the face of rising prices for goods and services. Expected nominal rates and inflation seem to be positively related, while real interest rates and inflation tend to be negatively related.

Far more research needs to be done on how inflation (or deflation) affects the level of stock prices and the yields on stock portfolios. Stocks do seem to be one of those assets that help savers and investors deal with the problems created by inflation. However, this certainly doesn't apply to all stocks indiscriminantly. Perhaps the most hopeful theory for the future is the *nominal contracts hypothesis* because it asks us to examine each company's stock separately and determine what kinds of contracts the company issuing the stock has entered into in order to produce and sell its goods or services. Some businesses are better hedged against inflation than others due to their contractual relationships with customers and suppliers.

THE DEVELOPMENT OF INFLATION-ADJUSTED SECURITIES

In 1997 the U.S. Treasury offered a possible way for investors buying government securities—considered one of the safest of all conventional debt obligations—to gain some protection against inflation. The Treasury began to issue inflation-indexed bonds called **TIPS** (Treasury Inflation Protection Securities), following the lead of such nations as Brazil and Great Britain, who experimented with inflation-indexed securities in earlier years.

Five- and 10-year TIPS were sold initially in the Treasury's experiment with these newly designed instruments. The Treasury also sells so-called "I bonds" that are inflation-adjusted as part of its savings bond program. Investors buying these innovative new bonds could literally separate out inflation risk exposure from interest-rate risk exposure because TIPS adjust the payment of income to the investor to the actual amount of inflation experienced during the life of the bonds (in contrast to traditional bonds that pay a fixed rate of interest regardless of what is happening to inflation).

The inflation measure used to adjust the investor's return from TIPS is the Consumer Price Index (CPI), published by the U.S. Bureau of Labor Statistics and designed to reflect changes in the cost of living each month for an urban family of four. Thus, the real value of the interest payments from a TIPS will be constant in purchasing power for those goods and services included in the CPI. This happens because the bond's nominal (face) value will increase at the same rate as the actual CPI inflation rate.

For example, suppose the rate of inflation in the CPI is zero right now and the U.S. Treasury issues a new TIPS that has a nominal (face) value of $1,000 and promises a real annual coupon rate of 3.5 percent for five years. If inflation remains at zero, this bond will pay $35 a year in real interest income and, at maturity, when it is redeemed by the U.S. Treasury, its nominal value will remain at $1,000. Suppose, however, that inflation suddenly increases to 4 percent (annual rate) the day after the bond is issued and remains at that level for all five years of the bond's life. Then, the Treasury will calculate the bond's nominal value from the following formula:

$$\text{TIPS inflation-adjusted nominal value at maturity} = \text{Original face value} \left[1 + \text{Annual rate of inflation} \right]^{\text{Time to maturity in years}} \quad \textbf{(7-7)}$$

In this example, the TIPS bond would have an inflation-adjusted nominal value at the end of its first year of:

$$\text{TIPS inflation-adjusted nominal value at the end of the first year} = \$1,000\,(1 + .04)^{1\text{ year}} = \$1,040.00$$

If the inflation rate remains at 4 percent over the next four years until the above bond reaches maturity, this TIPS would have a nominal value at the end of five years of:

$$\text{TIPS inflation-adjusted nominal value at the end of the 5 years} = \$1,000\,(1 + .04)^{5\text{ years}} = \$1,216.65$$

The TIPS bond holder's annual nominal interest payment can be found from the simple formula:

$$\text{TIPS inflation-adjusted nominal value} \times \text{Promised coupon rate} = \text{Annual nominal interest payment from a TIPS} \quad \textbf{(7-8)}$$

If the bond's promised (coupon) rate is 3.5 percent, as in the example above, by the end of the bond's first year, the amount of nominal interest earned by an investor would be:

$$\$1,040 \times .035 = \$36.40$$

instead of just $1,000 × 0.035, or $35, for a conventional bond whose principal is *not* adjusted for inflation. By the fifth year, when the TIPS described above reaches maturity, it will pay in annual nominal interest:

$$\$1,216.65 \times .035 = \$42.58$$

In summary, with an annual inflation rate of 4 percent a year, the inflation-adjusted bond just described would have increased its nominal principal and interest payments each year as follows:

Period	Actual Annual Rate of Inflation (%)	TIPS's Principal Nominal Value at the End of Each Year	Nominal Interest Payment to the TIPS Bond's Holder at Year-End	Nominal Interest Payment from a Conventional (Non-inflation-Adjusted) Bond
First year	4%	$1,040.00	$36.40	$35
Second year	4	1,081.60	37.86	35
Third year	4	1,124.86	39.37	35
Fourth year	4	1,169.86	40.95	35
Fifth year	4	1,216.65	42.58	35

We must hasten to add, however, that even though the foregoing gains look impressive, the TIPS investor's real rate of return (that is, what he or she can actually buy with the earnings received) has *not* changed. The investor's *real* interest return must be:

$$\begin{array}{c} \text{Actual real rate} \\ \text{of return on} \\ \text{the TIPS} \end{array} = \begin{array}{c} \text{Nominal rate} \\ \text{of return on} \\ \text{the TIPS} \end{array} - \begin{array}{c} \text{Actual} \\ \text{annual CPI} \\ \text{inflation rate} \end{array} \qquad \textbf{(7–9)}$$

Or, in the example traced out above:

Actual annual real rate of return on the 5-year TIPS bond = 7.5% − 4% = 3.5%

The nominal return on the TIPS rises to 7.5 percent if inflation persists for five years at a 4 percent annual rate because *both* the face value of the bond and its interest earnings are adjusted upward. In contrast, a conventional bond would have to fall in value to about:

$$\begin{array}{c} \text{Adjusted real value} \\ \text{of a conventional} \\ \text{bond under inflation} \end{array} = \frac{\text{Face value of conventional bond}}{\left[1 + \begin{array}{c} \text{Actual} \\ \text{annual rate} \\ \text{of inflation} \end{array} \right]^{\text{Years to maturity}}} = \frac{\$1,000}{(1 + .04)^5} = \$821.93 \quad \textbf{(7–10)}$$

in order to remain competitive in the market with TIPS and other inflation-adjusted assets available for purchase. The result for the conventional bond is an inflation-caused loss of $178.07 (or $1,000 − $821.93) if the investor sells the conventional bond prior to its maturity. Moreover, by the fifth year the investor's real annual interest income from the conventional bond would have dropped to only $28.77 [or $35/(1 + .04)^5] with inflation running at 4 percent a year. In contrast, as we saw in the table above, by holding a TIPS instead, this investor would receive a principal payment of $1,216.65 at the end of five years, gaining an additional $216.65 in nominal principal over a five-year period, or an average gain in principal of $43.33 per year. (Remember, however, that the investor's real principal value of the bond held at the end of five years would still be just $1,000, assuming a 4 percent annual inflation rate.) The TIPS's nominal price gain of $216.65 (or $1,216.65 − $1,000) plus its additional nominal interest revenues (which over five years will result in a total of $22.16 in additional interest income) would result in a nominal yield of about 7.5 percent.

Thus, Treasury inflation-index bonds (TIPS) are a relatively safe type of asset whose remaining risk is largely the danger that the real interest rate prevailing in the market will change (i.e., exposure to real interest rate risk). For example, real interest rates may rise and erode the real value of any bond; however, these new inflation-adjusted bonds make the management of risk more efficient by at least limiting an investor's overall risk exposure.

The coupon (interest) income and the principal payment from these indexed bonds are both fixed in terms of purchasing power.

We should note, however, that not all inflation risk is eliminated by TIPS because rising inflation can drive an investor into a higher tax bracket, resulting in an after-tax rate of return somewhat less than the full inflation-adjusted real interest income from these special Treasury bonds. Moreover, TIPS are subject to market risk if an investor wishes to sell them ahead of their maturity date. However, Shen (1998) has recently demonstrated that the overall market risk for inflation-indexed bonds appears to be smaller than the market risk on conventional bonds. Still, most investors in the financial markets have been lukewarm in their response to TIPS offerings, possibly because these innovative instruments appeared during a period when inflation was relatively low inside the U.S. Recently the U.S. Treasury has considered suspending further issues of TIPS.

Exhibit 7–3 illustrates the interesting relationship over time between the interest rates or yields on inflation-adjusted versus non-inflation-adjusted Treasury securities and the public's expectations regarding price inflation. As theory would suggest, when the public comes to expect faster inflation, TIPS and other inflation-adjusted securities become more valuable. Their prices rise and their interest rates or yields fall relative to the rates or yields on securities not bearing an inflation-adjustment mechanism.

Questions *to Help You Study*

1. What is *inflation?* Why is it important?

2. Explain how inflation affects interest rates. What is the *Fisher effect?* What does it assume?

3. Explain how the following connect inflation to changes in interest rates:

   a. The inflation-caused income effect.

   b. The inflation-caused wealth effect.

   c. The inflation-caused depreciation effect.

   d. The inflation-caused tax effect.

4. What is meant by *deflation?* How does deflation appear to impact interest rates and the economy? Which nation has experienced deflation on a significant scale in recent years?

5. What are *TIPS?* What advantages do they offer investors? Any disadvantages?

THE MATURITY OF A LOAN

One of the most important factors causing interest rates to differ from one another is differences in the **maturity** (or term) of securities and loans. Financial assets traded today in the world's financial markets have a wide variety of maturities. In the federal funds and U.S. government securities markets, for example, some loans are overnight or over-the-weekend transactions, with the borrower repaying the loan in a matter of hours. At the other end of the spectrum, bonds and mortgages used to finance the purchase of new homes often stretch out 25 to 30 years. Between these extremes lie thousands of securities issued by large and small borrowers with a tremendous variety of maturities.

The Yield Curve and the Term Structure of Interest Rates

The relationship between the rates of return (yields) on financial instruments and their maturity is called the *term structure of interest rates.* This term structure may be represented

EXHIBIT 7–3

Relationship between Inflation and Yield Spreads for Inflation-Adjusted versus Unadjusted Securities

Source: Federal Reserve Bank of Cleveland, Research Department, *Economic Trends,* July and August 2001.

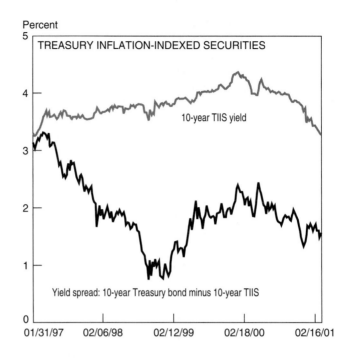

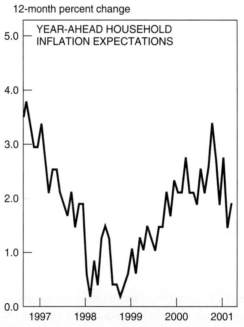

Note: Inflationary expectations are based upon the monthly University of Michigan Household Survey.

visually by drawing a **yield curve** for all securities having the same credit quality. An example of several recent yield curves for U.S. government securities as they appeared in a recent issue of *Economic Trends,* published by the Federal Reserve Bank of Cleveland, is shown in Exhibit 7–4. We note that yield to maturity (measured by the annual percentage rate of return) is plotted along the vertical axis, and the horizontal scale shows the length of time (term) to final maturity (measured in months and years).

EXHIBIT 7–4

A Variety of Yield Curves for U.S. Treasury Securities

Source: U.S. Treasury Department and Federal Reserve Bank of Cleveland, Research Department, *Economic Trends,* June 2001.

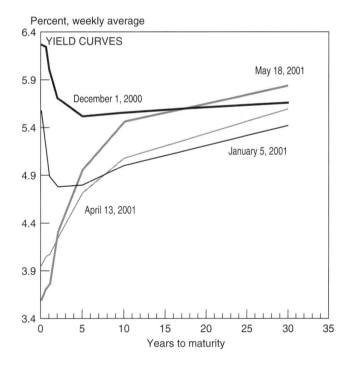

The yield curve considers only the relationship between the maturity or term of a loan or security and its yield at one moment in time (all other influential factors held constant). For example, we cannot draw a yield curve for securities bearing different degrees of credit risk or subject to different tax laws because both risk and tax laws affect relative yields along with maturity. We may, however, draw a yield curve for U.S. government securities of varying maturity because they all have minimal credit risk, the same tax status, and so on. Similarly, yield curves could be constructed for all corporate bonds or for all municipal bonds having the same credit rating.

Types of Yield Curves

To follow the daily yield curve, see *www. investinginbonds.com*

Several different shapes of yield curve have been observed, but most may be described as upward sloping, downward sloping, or horizontal (flat). An upward-sloping yield curve indicates that borrowers must pay higher interest rates for longer-term loans than for shorter-term loans. A downward-sloping yield curve means that longer-term loans and securities presently carry lower interest rates than shorter-term financial assets. Exhibit 7–4 illustrates a wide variety of yield curve shapes that prevailed as the new century began. Each shape of the yield curve has important implications for lenders, borrowers, and the financial institutions that serve them.

The Unbiased Expectations Hypothesis

What determines the shape or slope of the yield curve? One view is the **unbiased expectations hypothesis,** which argues that investor expectations regarding future changes in short-term interest rates determine the shape of the curve. For example, a rising yield curve is presumed to be an indication that investors expect short-term interest rates to rise above their current levels in the future. A declining yield curve suggests declining short-term interest rates in the future. Finally, a horizontal yield curve implies that investors in the market expect interest rates to remain essentially unchanged from their present levels. If the unbiased expectations hypothesis is true, the yield curve becomes an important forecasting tool, because it suggests the direction of future movements in short-term interest rates as viewed by the financial marketplace today.

Many economists believe that the yield curve is a useful economic indicator. For example, economic history suggests that an upward-sloping yield curve is associated with a growing economy, rising incomes, and declining unemployment. In contrast, a negatively sloped yield curve appears to be associated frequently with a recession in the economy, declining output, and rising unemployment.

The unbiased expectations hypothesis assumes that investors act as *profit maximizers* over their planned holding periods and have no maturity preferences. All securities in a given risk class, regardless of maturity, are perfect substitutes for each other in the minds of investors. Under this theory, all investors are *risk neutral.* That is, they do not care about the character of the distribution of possible returns from a security, only about its expected (mean) return. Each investor will seek those individual securities or combinations of securities offering the highest expected (mean) rates of return. For example, it is immaterial to investors with a planned 10-year investment horizon whether they buy a 10-year security, two 5-year securities, or a series of 1-year securities until their 10-year holding period terminates. Each investor will pursue that investment strategy that offers the highest expected rate of return or yield over the length of his or her planned holding period.

Profit-maximizing behavior on the part of thousands of investors interacting in the marketplace ensures that holding-period yields on all securities move toward equality.

Once equilibrium is achieved, and assuming no transactions costs, the investor should earn the *same* yield from buying a long-term security as from purchasing a series of short-term securities whose combined maturities equal that of the long-term security. If the rate of return on long-term securities rises above or falls below the return the investor expects to receive from buying and selling several short-term securities, forces are quickly set in motion to restore equilibrium. Investors at the margin will practice *arbitrage* (moving funds from one security market to another) until long-term yields once again are brought into balance with short-term yields.

The Role of Expectations in Shaping the Yield Curve

How can a factor as intangible as expectations determine the shape of the yield curve? Expectations are a potent force in the financial marketplace because *investors act on their expectations.* For example, if interest rates are expected to rise in the future, this can be disturbing news to investors in long-term bonds. As we noted in Chapter 6, rising interest rates mean falling prices for bonds and other debt securities. Moreover, the longer the term of a bond, the more sensitive tends to be its price to changes in market interest rates. Faced with the possibility of falling bond prices, many investors will sell their long-term bonds and buy short-term securities or hold cash instead. As a result, the prices of long-term bonds will plummet, driving their interest rates (yields) higher. At the same time, increased investor purchases of short-term securities will send the prices of these securities higher and their yields lower. With rising long-term interest rates and falling short-term interest rates, the yield curve will gradually assume an upward slope. The yield curve's prophecy of rising interest rates will have come true simply because investors responded to their expectations by making changes in their asset portfolios.

Relative Changes in Long-Term Interest Rates versus Short-Term Interest Rates

One assumption of the expectations theory does help to explain an interesting phenomenon in the financial markets. Long-term rates tend to change gradually over time, while short-term interest rates are highly volatile and often move over wide ranges. The expectations hypothesis, like many other views of the yield curve, rests on the premise that the expected long-term interest rate may be represented as a *geometric* average of a series of interest rates on current and future (forward) short-term loans whose combined maturities equal that of the long-term loan. In terms of conventional symbols

$$(1 + {_tR_n})^n = (1 + {_tR_1})(1 + {_{t+1}r_{1t}}) \ldots (1 + {_{t+n-1}r_{1t}}) \qquad \textbf{(7–11)}$$

where

$_tR_n$ = The rate of interest prevailing at time t on a long-term loan covering n periods of time

$_tR_1$ = The one-period loan rate prevailing at time period t

$_{t+1}r_{1t}$ = Forward interest rate as quoted at time t on a one-period loan to start in time period $t+1$

$_{t+2}r_{1t}$ = Forward interest rate as quoted at time t on a one-period loan to start in time period $t+2$

$\vdots$

$_{t+n-1}r_{1t}$ = Forward interest rate as quoted at time t on a one-period loan to start in time period $t+n-1$

The unbiased expectations hypothesis presumes that each of the forward rates—$_{t+1}r_{1t}$, $_{t+2}r_{1t}$, $\ldots$, $_{1+n-1}r_{1t}$—is equal to the future interest rate the market expects to exist in each future time period from $t+1$ through $t+n-1$. Equation 7–11 illustrates a fundamental principle in the expectations theory: *An investor expects the same holding-period yield regardless of whether he or she purchases one long-term security or a series of short-term securities whose combined maturities make up the maturity of the long-term security. This is true because all markets are presumed to be perfectly competitive without significant barriers between them and all securities, whatever their maturity, are presumed to be perfect substitutes for each other in the minds of investors.*

The rate of interest on a 20-year bond, for example, may be viewed as equivalent to the geometric average of the interest rate on a current 1-year loan plus the rates expected to be attached in future periods to a series of 19 separate 1-year loans, together adding up to 20 years. Experience teaches us that an *average* changes much more slowly than the individual components making up that average. If the long-term interest rate is really a geometric average of current and expected future short-term rates, then this helps to explain why, in real-world markets, long-term interest rates tend to lag behind short-term interest rates and are less volatile.

Policy Implications of the Unbiased Expectations Hypothesis

The unbiased expectations hypothesis has important implications for public policy. The theory implies that changes in the relative amounts of long-term versus short-term securities do *not* influence the shape of the yield curve *unless* investor expectations also are affected. For example, suppose the U.S. Treasury decided to refinance $100 billion of its maturing short-term IOUs by issuing $100 billion in long-term bonds. Would this government action affect the shape of the yield curve? Certainly, the supply of long-term bonds would be increased, while the supply of short-term securities would be reduced. However, according to the expectations theory, the yield curve itself would not be changed *unless* investors altered their expectations about the future course of short-term interest rates.

To cite one more example, the Federal Reserve System buys and sells government securities almost daily in the money and capital markets to promote the economic goals of the

United States. Can the Fed (or, for that matter, any other central bank around the world) influence the shape of the yield curve by buying one maturity of securities and selling another? Once again, the answer is "no" *unless* the central bank can influence the interest-rate expectations of investors. Why? The reason lies in the underlying assumption of the unbiased expectations hypothesis: *Investors regard all securities, whatever their maturity, as perfect substitutes.* Therefore, the relative amounts of long-term bonds versus short-term securities simply should *not* matter.

The Liquidity Premium View of the Yield Curve

The strong assumptions underlying the unbiased expectations hypothesis coupled with the real-world behavior of investors have caused many financial analysts to question that theory's veracity. Securities dealers who trade actively in the financial markets frequently argue that other factors besides interest rate expectations also exert a significant impact on the character and shape of the yield curve.

For example, in recent years, most yield curves have sloped *upward.* Is there a *built-in bias* toward positively sloped yield curves due to factors other than interest rate expectations? The liquidity premium view of the yield curve suggests that such a *bias* exists.

Long-term securities tend to have more volatile market prices than short-term securities. Therefore, the investor faces greater risk of capital loss when buying long-term financial instruments. This greater risk of loss will be important to an investor who is *risk averse* (not risk neutral as in the expectations theory). To overcome the risk of capital loss, investors must be paid an extra return in the form of an interest rate (term) premium to encourage them to purchase long-term financial instruments. This additional rate or yield premium for surrendering liquidity—known as the **liquidity premium**—would tend to give yield curves a bias towards a *positive slope.*

Why then do some yield curves slope downward? In such instances, expectations of declining interest rates plus other factors simply overcome the liquidity premium effect. The liquidity premium view does not preclude the important role of interest rate expectations in influencing the shape of the yield curve. Rather, it argues that other factors, such as liquidity and price risk, play an important role as well.

The liquidity argument may help explain why yield curves tend to *flatten out* at the longest maturities. (Note that this flattening out at the long-term end of the maturity spectrum is characteristic of all the yield curves shown in Exhibit 7–4.) There are obvious differences in liquidity between a 1 year and a 10 year bond, but it is not clear that major differences in liquidity exist between a 10-year bond and a 20-year bond, for example. Therefore, the size of the required liquidity (or term) premium may decrease for securities bearing longer maturities.

THE SEGMENTED-MARKETS OR HEDGING-PRESSURE ARGUMENT

A strong challenge to the expectations theory appeared several years ago in the form of the **market segmentation argument** or *hedging-pressure theory* of the term structure of interest rates. The underlying assumption is that all securities are *not* perfect substitutes in the minds of investors. *Maturity preferences* exist among some investor groups, and these investors will not stray from their desired maturity range unless induced to do so by higher yields or other favorable terms on longer- or shorter-term securities.

Why would some investors *prefer* one maturity of security over another? Market segmentation theorists find the answer in a fundamental assumption concerning investor behavior, especially the investment behavior of financial intermediaries, such as mutual funds, pension funds, and banks. These investor groups, it is argued, often act as *risk minimizers* rather than profit maximizers as assumed under the expectations hypothesis. They prefer to *hedge* against the risk of fluctuations in the prices and yields of securities by balancing the maturity structure of their assets with the maturity structure of their liabilities.

For example, pension funds have stable and predictable long-term liabilities. Therefore, these intermediaries prefer to invest in bonds, stocks, and other long-term assets. Commercial banks, on the other hand, with volatile money market liabilities prefer to confine the majority of their investments to short-term loans and securities. These investor groups use the *hedging principle* of portfolio management: correlating the maturities of their liabilities with the maturities of their assets to ensure the ready availability of liquid funds when those funds are most needed. This portfolio strategy reduces the risks of fluctuating income and loss of principal.

The existence of maturity preferences among investor groups implies that the financial markets are *not* one large pool of loanable funds but rather are segmented by maturity into a series of submarkets. Thus, the market for securities of medium maturity (5- to 10-year securities) attracts different investor groups than the market for long-term (over 10-year) securities. Demand and supply curves within each maturity range are held to be the dominant factors shaping the level and structure of interest rates within that maturity range. However, interest rates prevailing in one maturity range are little influenced by demand and supply forces at work in other maturity ranges.

The segmented-markets or hedging-pressure theory does *not* rule out the possible influence of expectations in shaping the term structure of interest rates, but it argues that other factors related to maturity-specific demand and supply forces are also important.

Policy Implications of the Segmented-Markets Theory

The segmented-markets theory, like the expectations theory, has significant implications for public policy. If markets along the maturity spectrum are relatively isolated from each other due to investor maturity preferences, government policymakers can alter the shape of the yield curve merely by influencing supply and demand in one or more market segments.

For example, if a positively sloped yield curve were desired, the government could flood the market with long-term bonds. Simultaneously, the government could purchase large quantities of short-term securities. The expanded supply of bonds would drive long-term interest rates higher, while government purchases of short-term securities would push short-term interest rates down, other factors held equal. Therefore, the government could alter the shape of the yield curve merely by shifting the supplies available of different maturities of securities relative to the demand for those securities. This conclusion directly contradicts the unbiased expectations hypothesis.

The Preferred Habitat or Composite Theory of the Yield Curve

During the 1960s and 1970s, an expanded model of the determinants of the yield curve appeared that attempted to combine the expectations, liquidity premium, and market segmentation arguments into a single theory. This composite view argues that investors seek out their **preferred habitat** along the scale of varying maturities of securities that matches their risk preferences, tax exposure, liquidity needs, regulatory requirements, and planned holding periods. Normally, an investor will not stray from his or her preferred habitat unless rates of return on longer- or shorter-term securities are high enough to overcome each investor's preferences. The result is that security markets are divided into distinct submarkets by these multifaceted investor preferences. Thus, according to the preferred habitat theory, factors other than expectations alone play a role in shaping the character of the yield curve.

Proponents of preferred habitat argue that investors derive their expectations about future interest rates on the basis of *historical experience*—the recent trend of interest rates and what history suggests is a "normal" range for rates. In the short term, the majority of investors expect current interest-rate trends to persist into the future; thus, rising interest rates in recent weeks often lead to the expectation that rates will continue to rise in the near term. However, investors generally expect that, given sufficient time (months or years), interest rates will return to their historical averages. An important implication here is that more recent movements in interest rates are linked to *past* interest rate behavior—a conclusion that tends to contradict the expectations and efficient markets theories of how the financial markets operate.

Research Evidence on Yield-Curve Theories

Which view of the yield curve is correct? A number of recent studies (e.g., Campbell, 1986; and Mankiw, 1986) seem to reject the unbiased expectations hypothesis and find that the yield curve does *not* have significant predictive power in forecasting interest rates. However, these findings are contradicted by other studies (e.g., Froot, 1989; and Longstaff, 1990) that find evidence consistent with the unbiased expectations hypothesis. Some of these studies find significant forecasting power from the yield curve over certain time periods.

For example, Froot (1989) finds that the expectations hypothesis does *not* seem to work for interest rates on short-term securities, but for long maturities of bonds, the yield curve appears to move, point for point, with changes in expected future rates. Also consistent with the unbiased exceptions hypothesis, long-term interest rates appear to "underreact" to changes in short-term interest rates. Fama (1984) observes that the term structure of rates can be used to forecast one-month interest rates one month ahead; and Fama and Bliss (1987) found that one-year forward interest rates could forecast changes in the one-year interest rate two to four years in advance. Moreover, as Abken (1993) notes, there is some evidence that yield curves can provide useful forecasts of inflation over periods of one year or longer.

This longer-term forecasting power of the yield curve may be due to the tendency of interest rates to move back toward their historic mean levels over a sufficiently long period of time (known as *mean reversion*). Although all investors clearly do not regard all maturities of securities as perfect substitutes, there are sufficient numbers of traders in the financial marketplace who do *not* have specific maturity preferences. These investors are guided principally by the relative expected returns on different securities. Their beliefs and actions can bring about the results generally predicted by the expectations theory.

Nevertheless, there is evidence that nonexpectational factors, especially the demand for liquidity, do affect the shape of the yield curve. Studies by Van Horne (1965) and others point to the existence of a liquidity premium attached to the yields on longer-term securities, compensating investors for added risk. Moreover, liquidity premiums appear to get smaller as we move toward longer maturities of securities. In fact, Fama and Bliss (1987) have found that liquidity premiums (or, more generally, *term premiums*) are *not* constant. Rather, term premiums seem to vary with business conditions. Fama and French (1989), for example, find that term premiums move opposite to business conditions, rising in recessions and falling in business expansions. Moreover, term premiums do *not* appear to increase or decrease *uniformly* as maturity increases or decreases. More recently, Kiely, Kolari, and Rose (1994) confirmed that liquidity premiums vary over time, rising and falling with the business cycle.

There is also evidence that changes in the supply of securities in any particular maturity range can, at least temporarily, alter the shape of the yield curve, offering some support for the segmented-markets theory. For example, at certain phases of the business cycle, banks become heavy sellers of medium-term government securities to raise cash and make more loans. The yield curve may take a bowed or humped shape at those times. In this instance, a sudden massive increase in the supply of medium-term bonds seems to briefly alter the yield curve's shape.

Traditional models of the yield curve are giving way today to *new* term-structure models. These newer models are being created in response to recent developments in finance centered around option pricing (see Chapter 9) and the rational expectations theory (see Chapter 5). Traditional yield-curve theories do not appear to explain easily the more volatile movements in stock and bond prices observed in recent years or help in valuing some of the newest financial instruments, such as securitized assets and swap agreements (see Chapters 8 and 9). Newer models of the term structure incorporate the presence of *uncertainty* in the financial markets about future movements in interest rates. Recent modeling has brought measures of economic activity into the process of determining the yield curve's shape, arguing that the term structure of interest rates is influenced by the economy and cannot be fully explained without including measures of the economy's performance.

Uses of the Yield Curve

The controversy surrounding the determinants of the yield curve should not obscure the fact that this curve can be an extremely useful tool for borrowers and lenders.

Forecasting Interest Rates

If the expectations hypothesis is correct, the yield curve gives the investor a clue concerning the future course of interest rates. If the curve has an upward slope, for example, the investor may be well advised to look for opportunities to move away from long-term securities into investments whose market price is less sensitive to interest rate changes. A downward-sloping yield curve, on the other hand, suggests the likelihood of near-term declines in interest rates and a rally in bond prices if the market's forecast of lower rates turns out to be true.

One version of the yield curve—the so-called *yield spread* between long-term and short-term government securities—has been found in the United States to aid in the prediction of real growth in the economy and to seemingly forecast coming recessions in economic activity. For example, a study by Stojanovic and Vaughan (1997) finds that an inverted yield curve—where short-term interest rates are higher than long-term interest rates—has preceded U.S. economic recessions since 1960 and has generally out-predicted other widely used forecasting data series, such as common stock prices and the U.S. Commerce Department's Index of Leading Economic Indicators. In general, the *smaller* the interest rate spread between long- and short-term interest rates, the *greater* the probability of a recession in the United States over the next four quarters. Moreover, recent studies by Kozicki (1997) and Bonser-Neal and Morley (1997), looking at several different countries (including Australia, Canada, Japan, the United States, and the nations of Western Europe) suggest that the yield spread seems to predict growth in GDP (gross domestic product) for these nations over the next year or so with greater accuracy than other popular economic indicators. The yield spread appears to be an especially powerful economic forecaster in Canada, Germany, and the United States.

Uses for Financial Intermediaries

The slope of the yield curve is critical for financial intermediaries, especially banks, credit unions, and saving and loan associations. A rising yield curve is generally favorable for these institutions because they borrow most of their funds by selling short-term deposits and lend a major portion of those funds long term. The more steeply the yield curve slopes upward, the wider the spread between borrowing and lending rates and the greater the potential profit for a financial intermediary. However, if the yield curve begins to flatten out or slopes downward, this should serve as a warning signal to managers of these institutions.

A flattening or downward-sloping yield curve squeezes the earnings of financial intermediaries and calls for an entirely different portfolio management strategy than an upward-sloping curve. For example, if an upward-sloping yield curve starts to flatten out, portfolio managers of financial institutions might try to lock in relatively cheap sources of funds by getting long-term commitments from depositors and other funds-supplying customers. Borrowers, on the other hand, might be encouraged to take out long-term loans at fixed rates of interest. Of course, the institution's customers also may be aware of impending changes in the yield curve and resist accepting loans or deposits with terms heavily favoring financial intermediaries.

Detecting Overpriced and Underpriced Securities

Yield curves can be used as an aid to investors in deciding which securities are temporarily overpriced or underpriced. This use of the curve derives from the fact that, in equilibrium, the yields on all securities of comparable risk should come to rest along the yield curve at their appropriate maturity levels. In an efficiently functioning market, however, any deviations of individual securities from the yield curve will be short lived, so the investor must act quickly.

If a security's rate of return lies *above* the yield curve, this sends a signal to investors: The security is temporarily *underpriced* relative to other securities bearing the same maturity. Other things equal, this is a *buy* signal some investors will take advantage of, driving the price of the purchased security upward and its yield back down toward the curve. On the other hand, if a security's rate of return is temporarily *below* the yield curve, this indicates a temporarily *overpriced* financial instrument, because its yield is below that of securities bearing the same maturity. Some investors holding this asset will *sell,* pushing its price down and its yield back up toward the curve.

Indicating Trade-Offs between Maturity and Yield

Still another use of the yield curve is to indicate the current trade-off between maturity and yield confronting the investor. If an investor wishes to alter the maturity of her portfolio, the yield curve indicates what gain or loss in rate of return may be expected for each change in the portfolio's average maturity.

With an upward-sloping yield curve, for example, an investor may be able to increase a bond portfolio's expected annual yield from 7 percent to 9 percent by extending the portfolio's average maturity from 1 to 10 years. However, the prices of longer-term bonds are more volatile, creating greater risk of capital loss. Longer-term securities tend to be less liquid than short-term securities. Therefore, the investor must weigh the gain in yield from extending the maturity of his or her portfolio against added price and liquidity risk. Because yield curves tend to flatten out for the longest maturities, the investor bent on lengthening the maturity of a portfolio eventually discovers that gains in yield get smaller for each additional unit of maturity. At some point along the yield curve, it no longer pays, in terms of extra yield, to further extend the maturity of an investor's asset portfolio.

Riding the Yield Curve

Finally, some active investors, especially dealers in government securities, have learned to "ride" the yield curve for profit. If the curve is positively sloped, with a slope steep enough to offset transactions costs, the investor may gain by timely portfolio switching.

A prime example of a "riding the yield curve" strategy appeared in the wake of the September 11, 2001, terror attacks in New York and Washington, DC. A steep, positively sloped yield curve prevailed in the financial markets before the attacks, offering the opportunity for substantial profits if active investors played their cards right! In the aftermath of the attacks many investors expected that the yield curve would become *even steeper* than it already was. Thus, short-term interest rates were expected to move even lower while long-term interest rates were expected to head skyward, further steepening the prevailing yield curve.

In times of crisis many investors come to believe the yield curve will turn steeper because a crisis often creates greater uncertainties about the long run. Result: Investors will tend to move toward shorter-term investments, driving their prices up and interest rates down, and sell off longer-term investments, pushing their prices down and their associated interest rates higher. Long-term investors simply demand an extra yield premium before they will hold longer-term financial instruments. The yield curve may tilt sharply upward.

In the fall of 2001 sophisticated institutional investors (such as government security dealers and hedge funds) borrowed heavily to buy short-term securities (particularly shorter-term Treasury notes), whose prices were expected to rise, and sold off longer-term bonds (especially Treasury bonds over 10 years to maturity) whose prices dropped for a time.

What might lead investors toward such expectations about the future course of interest rates? One big factor is monetary policy and another is inflation. If a crisis threatens to slow down the economy and create substantial unemployment, the central bank (e.g., the Federal Reserve System) is likely to push short-term interest rates lower. With easier credit conditions setting in, fears begin to rise in the investment community that inflation will accelerate. Because inflation tends to hurt long-term bond holders the most, they quickly begin to sell off their holdings of longer-term issues. Long-term interest rates rise and the prices of these instruments decline. The yield curve simply becomes steeper for a time, offering profit opportunities to those who understand what is happening.

For example, if a security dealer purchases U.S. Treasury bills six months from maturity, holds them for three months and converts the bills into cash, and then buys new six-month bills, he can profit in two ways from a positively sloped yield curve. Because the yield is lower (and the price higher) on the three-month than the six-month bills, the dealer experiences a capital (price) gain on the sale. Moreover, the purchase of new six-month bills replaces a lower-yielding asset with a higher-yielding one at a lower price. Riding the yield curve can be risky, however, because yield curves are constantly changing their shape. If the curve suddenly gets flatter or turns down, a potential gain can be turned into a realized loss. In this case, riding the yield curve may be less profitable than a simple "buy and hold" strategy. Experience and good judgment are indispensable in using the yield curve for profitable investment decision making.

Summary of the Debate over the Yield Curve's Shape: What Do We Really Know?

With so many competing views on what determines the shape of the yield curve, it's not easy to draw any firm conclusions about what we currently know and don't know. Among all the theories it seems clear that the *unbiased expectations hypothesis* is the most popular among academic researchers and theorists. Public expectations regarding the future behavior of interest rates do seem to be a powerful force in reshaping interest rates, asset prices, and the yield curve's shape or slope.

Still, there remains much disagreement and there is credible research evidence that yield curves do have a bias toward a positive slope, at least in the modern era. This implies that a combination of theories—both the *unbiased expectations hypothesis plus the liquidity premium view*—merged together has the best explanatory power in accounting for how the yield curve changes over time.

However, among practitioners on the street and active investors groups the *segmented markets view* seems to be the most popular, supplemented at times by factors discussed in the *preferred habitat* approach. Followers of these theories tend to cite special, real-world factors that frequently impact the yield curve, such as changes in central bank policy, the presence of inflation, new security auctions, changes in tax laws, and shifts in the rules that govern investment activity by financial institutions.

Questions *to Help You Study*

6. Explain the meaning of the phrase *term structure of interest rates*. What is a *yield curve*? What *assumptions* are necessary to construct a yield curve?

7. Explain the difference between the *expectations, market segmentation, preferred habitat*, and *liquidity premium* views of the yield curve. What does each of these theories assume and what is the principal conclusion of each?

8. What are the implications for investors and for public policy of each of the yield-curve ideas mentioned in the preceding question?

9. What *uses* does the yield curve have? Why is each possible use of potential value to borrowers and lenders of funds?

10. What conclusions can you draw from recent research regarding the determinants of the yield curve? Which theory of the yield curve discussed in this chapter appears to be most supported by recent research studies?

DURATION: A DIFFERENT APPROACH TO MATURITY

The Price Elasticity of a Debt Security

Theories of the yield curve remind us that longer-maturity securities tend to be more volatile in price. That is, for the same change in interest rates, the price of a longer-term bond generally changes more than the price of a shorter-term bond. A popular measure of how responsive a debt security's price is to changes in interest rates is its **price elasticity.** Thus:

$$\text{Price elasticity of a debt security (E)} = \frac{\text{Percentage change over time in a security's price}}{\text{Percentage change over time in a security's yield}} = \frac{\dfrac{P_1 - P_0}{P_0}}{\dfrac{y_1 - y_0}{y_0}} \qquad \text{(7–12)}$$

where P_0 and y_0 represent a debt security's price and yield at some initial point in time, while P_1 and y_1 represent the security's price and yield at a subsequent point in time. Price elasticity is generally measured from the debt security's par value and coupon rate and is larger for downward price movements than for upward price movements.[4] Security price elasticity must be negative, because rising interest rates (yields) result in falling debt security prices, and conversely.

For example, suppose we are interested in purchasing a 10-year bond, par value of $1,000, promising its holder a 10 percent annual coupon rate ($100 a year in interest). Information in a computer file containing a bond yield table (see Chapter 6) tells us that if

---

[4]That is, for the same change in yield, capital gains generally are larger than capital losses on the same security.

interest rates on comparable securities sold in the open market are at 10 percent, this bond will sell for exactly $1,000. If interest rates fall to 5 percent, this 10 percent bond will have a price of about $1,389.70, and if rates climb to 15 percent, the bond's price will drop to just $745.10. What is the price elasticity of this bond, measured from par? From Equation 7–12, we have for the *downward* movement in interest rates from 10 to 5 percent:

$$\text{Price elasticity of 10 percent bond (E)} = \frac{\dfrac{(\$1,389.70 - \$1,000)}{\$1,000}}{\dfrac{5\% - 10\%}{10\%}} = \frac{0.3897}{-0.5} = -0.779 \quad \textbf{(7–13)}$$

On the other hand, for an upward movement in interest rates from 10 to 15 percent, this bond's elasticity is −0.510. (The reader should verify this.) Clearly, *E* is greater in absolute terms for the downward movement in interest rates (from 10 to 5 percent) than it is for the rise in interest rates (from 10 to 15 percent).

Greater price elasticity means that an asset goes through a greater price change for a given change in market rates of interest. And, as we noted above, longer-term debt securities generally carry greater price risk (their price elasticity, *E,* is larger) than shorter-term securities. However, this relationship between maturity and price elasticity is *not* linear (i.e., not strictly proportional). It is *not* true, for example, that 10-year bonds are twice as price elastic (and price volatile) as 5-year bonds. One important reason for this nonlinear relationship is that the price volatility and elasticity of a debt security depend upon the size of its *coupon rate*—the annual rate of return promised by the borrower—as well as its maturity.

The Impact of Varying Coupon Rates

The lower a debt security's annual coupon (promised) rate, the more volatile (and elastic) its price tends to be. Investors buying lower coupon securities generally take on greater risk of price fluctuations. In effect, a debt security promising lower annual coupon payments behaves as though it has a longer maturity even if it is due to mature on the same date as a security carrying a higher coupon rate. With a low coupon (promised) rate, the investor must wait longer for a substantial return on her funds because a greater proportion of the low-coupon security's total dollar return lies in the final payment at maturity, when the bond's face value is returned to the investor. And the further in the future cash payments are to be received, the more sensitive is the present value of that stream of payments to changes in interest rates.

The relationship we have been describing is called the **coupon effect.** It says simply that the prices of low-coupon securities tend to rise *faster* than the prices of high-coupon securities when market interest rates decline. Similarly, a period of rising interest rates will cause the prices of low-coupon securities to fall *faster* than the prices of high-coupon securities. Thus, the potential for capital gains and capital losses is greater for low-coupon than for high-coupon securities.

An Alternative Maturity Index for a Security: Duration

Knowledge of the impact of varying coupon (promised) rates on security price volatility and elasticity resulted in the search for a new index of maturity other than straight calendar time (years and months)—the maturity measure used in conventional yield curves. What was needed was a measure of the term of a bond that would allow financial analysts to construct a *linear* (strictly proportional) relationship between maturity and security price volatility or elasticity, regardless of differing coupon rates. Such a measure would have the property, for example, that a doubling of maturity would mean a doubling of a security's price elasticity, thereby giving us a direct measure of the price risk faced by an investor. This maturity measure is known as **duration** (D):

$$D = \frac{\begin{array}{c}\text{Present value of interest and}\\\text{principal payments from a}\\\text{security weighted by the}\\\text{timing of those payments}\end{array}}{\begin{array}{c}\text{Present value of the security's}\\\text{promised stream of interest}\\\text{and principal payments}\end{array}} = \frac{\displaystyle\sum_{t=1}^{n} \frac{I_t(t)}{(1+y)^t}}{\displaystyle\sum_{t=1}^{n} \frac{I_t}{(1+y)^t}} \qquad \textbf{(7–14)}$$

In the duration formula above, I represents each expected payment of principal and interest income from the security and t represents the time period in which each payment is to be received. The discount factor, y, is the security's yield to maturity, with final maturity reached at the end of n periods. Duration reflects the price elasticity of a debt instrument with respect to changes in the instrument's yield to maturity. As the formula indicates, D is a *weighted average* measure of maturity in which each payment of interest and principal is multiplied by the time period in which it is expected to be received by the investor.

We can explain the use of duration through an example. Let us imagine that an investor is interested in purchasing a $1,000 par value bond that has a term to maturity of 10 years, a 10 percent annual coupon rate (with interest paid once a year), and a 12 percent yield to maturity based on its current price of $887.10. Then its duration must be

$$\text{Duration (D)} = \frac{\dfrac{\$100(1)}{(1.12)^1} + \dfrac{\$100(2)}{(1.12)^2} + \ldots + \dfrac{\$100(10)}{(1.12)^{10}} + \dfrac{\$1,000(10)}{(1.12)^{10}}}{\dfrac{\$100}{(1.12)^1} + \dfrac{\$100}{(1.12)^2} + \ldots + \dfrac{\$100}{(1.12)^{10}} + \dfrac{\$1,000}{(1.12)^{10}}} \qquad \textbf{(7–15)}$$

or

$$D = \frac{\$5810.90}{\$887.10} = 6.55 \text{ years}$$

There is a simple way to calculate D that has the added value of making it easy to check your figures. Using the example above of the 10-year bond with a 12 percent yield to maturity, we can set up the following table:

Period	Expected Cash Flows from Security	Present Values of Expected Cash Flows (at 12% Rate of Discount)	Time Period Cash Is to Be Received (t)	Present Value of Expected Cash Flows × t
1	$ 100	$ 89.30	1	$ 89.30
2	100	79.70	2	159.40
3	100	71.20	3	213.60
4	100	63.60	4	254.40
5	100	56.70	5	283.50
6	100	50.70	6	304.20
7	100	45.20	7	316.40
8	100	40.40	8	323.20
9	100	36.10	9	324.90
10	100	32.20	10	322.00
10	1,000	322.00	10	3,220.00
		$887.10		$5,810.90

Then, as above, the duration of this bond must be

$$D = \frac{\text{Sum of present values of cash flow} \times t}{\text{Sum of present values of cash flow}} = \frac{\$5810.90}{\$887.10} = 6.55 \text{ years}$$

Note that the denominator of the ratio above ($887.10) is the same value as the bond's current price.

A number of duration's features are evident from this example. For example, duration is always *less* than the time to maturity for a coupon-paying security.[5] Duration increases with a longer stream of future payments, but the rate of increase in D decreases as time to maturity increases. The larger an asset's yield to maturity, y, the lower its duration.

Duration reflects the amount and timing of *all* payments expected during the life of an asset, unlike the conventional measure of maturity—calendar time—which shows only the length of time until the final cash payment. In simplest terms, duration is an index of the average amount of time required for the investor to recover the original cash outlay used to buy the asset. Assets bearing higher values of D are more volatile in price and, therefore, carry increased price risk. Low-coupon bonds, for example, have longer durations and, therefore, display more price risk than high-coupon bonds.

The Convexity Factor

The relationship between an asset's change in market price and its change in yield or interest rate is called **convexity.** Research has shown that convexity increases with an asset's duration. Moreover, an asset's change in market price for any given change in interest rates will vary with the prevailing level of market interest rates.

In general, an asset's change in price is greater at lower market interest rates than it is at higher market interest rates. Thus, an asset's price risk tends to be greater at lower rates of interest than it does at higher interest rates. Moreover, the convexity of a financial asset tends to decline as that asset's promised rate of return (coupon rate) increases. In summary, the market prices of assets change in different ways depending upon their durations, promised rates of return (coupons), and the level of interest rates in the financial marketplace.

Uses of Duration

Estimating Asset Price Changes

To learn more about duration, see *www.finpipe.com* or *www.contingencyanalysis.com*
.

Because duration is directly related to the price volatility of an asset, there is a useful approximate relationship between changes in market interest rates and percentage changes in asset prices. This relationship may be written:

$$\begin{matrix}\text{Percent change in} \\ \text{the price of an} \\ \text{asset (such as a} \\ \text{debt security)}\end{matrix} \approx -D\left[\frac{\Delta r}{1 + r}\right] \times 100 \qquad \textbf{(7–16)}$$

where D is duration and Δr is the change in interest rates. For example, consider the bond whose duration was calculated above to be 6.55 years. The bond's price at the coupon rate of 10 percent is $1,000; and at an r of 12 percent, its price is $887.10. Thus, if the interest

---

[5]See Chapter 6 for a discussion of yield to maturity and calculating discounted present values such as required in the above duration formula. Any security carrying installment payments of principal and/or interest will have a duration shorter than its calendar maturity. Only for zero-coupon bonds or for any loan in which principal and accumulated interest are paid in a lump sum at maturity will duration and maturity be the same.

rate changes from 10 to 12 percent, the bond's approximate percentage decline in price would be

$$\text{Percent change in bond's price} \approx -6.55 \times \left[\frac{.02}{1 + 0.10}\right] \times 100 = -11.91\% \quad \textbf{(7–17)}$$

In this instance, if interest rates rise by two percentage points, the bond's price declines by almost 12 percent (measured from the bond's par value and coupon rate). An investor who expects interest rates to rise would find this information helpful in deciding whether to continue holding this bond. In general, investors concerned about the risk of loss due to rising interest rates tend to move toward assets of shorter duration, while falling interest rates usually lead investors toward assets of longer duration.

Portfolio Immunization

Today, duration has aroused great interest among portfolio managers. The reason is its possible usefulness as a device to insulate (or, in the terminology of finance, *immunize*) asset portfolios against the risk of changing interest rates. In theory, **portfolio immunization** against interest rate changes can be achieved by simply acquiring a portfolio of assets whose average duration equals the length of the investor's desired holding period. If this is done, the effect is to hold the investor's total return *constant* regardless of whether interest rates rise or fall. In the absence of borrower default, the investor's realized return can be no less than the return he has been promised by the borrower. Only if the future course of interest rates is known for certain would portfolio immunization be a less than optimal strategy.

Let's consider an example of how portfolio immunization with duration works. Suppose we are interested in purchasing a bond with a $1,000 par value that will mature in two years. The bond has a coupon rate of 8 percent, paying $80 in interest at the end of each year. Interest rates on comparable bonds also are currently at 8 percent but may fall to as low as 6 percent or rise as high as 10 percent. The buyer knows he or she will receive $1,000 at maturity, but in the meantime this buyer must face the uncertainty of having to reinvest the annual $80 in interest earnings from this bond at 6 percent, 8 percent, or 10 percent, depending on whether interest rates rise or fall.

Suppose interest rates decline to 6 percent. This bond will earn $80 in interest payments for year one, $80 for year two, but only $4.80 (or $80 × 0.06) when the $80 interest income received the first year is reinvested at 6 percent during year 2. With interest rates falling to 6 percent, the investor will earn only $1,164.80 in total over the two-year period:

First year's interest earnings		Second year's interest earnings		Interest earned reinvesting the first year's interest earnings at a 6 percent interest rate		Par value of security returned to investor at maturity		Total return
$80	+	$80	+	$4.80	+	$1,000	=	$1,164.80

On the other hand, what if interest rates rise to 10 percent after the first year? Again, the investor holding this bond earns $80 interest in each of the next two years but will also earn $8 in interest when he reinvests the $80 in interest income received at the end of the first year at the new rate of 10 percent ($80 × .10). In this case, the investor's total return from the bond will be $1,168 after two years:

First year's interest earnings		Second year's interest earnings		Interest earned reinvesting the first year's interest earnings at a 10 percent interest rate		Par value of security returned to investor at maturity		Total return
$80	+	$80	+	$8.00	+	$1,000	=	$1,168.00

Clearly, the bond buyer's earnings could drop as low as $1,164.80 (with a 6 percent interest rate) or rise as high as $1,168 (with a 10 percent interest rate). Is there a way to avoid this kind of fluctuation in earnings and stabilize the total return received regardless of what happens to interest rates? Yes, if the buyer finds a bond whose *duration matches his or her planned holding period.* For example, suppose the buyer finds a $1,000 bond that also carries an 8 percent coupon rate whose maturity exceeds two years but whose duration is exactly two years, matching the buyer's planned holding period. This means that, at the end of two years, the buyer will have to *sell* the bond at the price then prevailing in the market, because it will not yet have reached maturity.

What will happen to the buyer's total earnings with a bond whose duration is exactly two years? First, if interest rates fall to 6 percent, the bond will earn $80 interest at the end of year 1 and another $80 at the end of year 2, but as before, only $4.80 will be earned when the first year's interest income is invested during the second year at the low rate of 6 percent ($80 × 0.06). However, the bond's market price will *rise* to $1,001.60 due to the drop in interest rates. Therefore, the investor will receive in two years a total of $1,166.40 in cash:

First year's interest earnings		Second year's interest earnings		Interest earned reinvesting the first year's interest earnings at a 6 percent interest rate		Market price received when selling bond at the end of the investor's planned holding period		Total return
$80	+	$80	+	$4.80	+	$1,001.60	=	$1,166.40

Suppose instead that interest rates rise to 10 percent. Clearly, interest earnings will go up, but the bond's market price will be lower because of the rise in interest rates. In this case, the investor also receives a total return of $1,166.40:

First year's interest earnings		Second year's interest earnings		Interest earned reinvesting the first year's interest earnings at a 10 percent interest rate		Market price received when selling bond at the end of the investor's planned holding period		Total return
$80	+	$80	+	$8.00	+	$998.40	=	$1,166.40

In the foregoing example, *the buyer earns identical total earnings whether interest rates go up or down!* This happens because, with duration set equal to the buyer's planned holding period, a fall in the reinvestment rate (in this case, down to 6 percent) is completely offset by an increase in the bond's price (in this instance, the bond's market value climbs from $1,000 to $1.001.60). Conversely, a rise in the reinvestment rate (up to 10 percent in the second case) is counterbalanced by a fall in the bond's market price (down to $998.40). The bond buyer's total return is fully protected regardless of the future path followed by interest rates.

Of course, there is a price to be paid for reducing risk exposure. Duration, like any interest rate hedging tool, is *not* free. Suppose in the example above that the bond buyer had chosen not to worry about duration and just purchased a bond with a calendar maturity of two years. Suppose also that interest rates rose to 10 percent during the second year. Clearly, this investor would have earned a larger total return ($1,168) without using portfolio immunization. *The cost of immunization is a lower, but more stable, expected return.*

Limitations of Duration

All this sounds easy: *To protect the return from a portfolio of assets against changes in interest rates, merely select a portfolio whose duration equals the time remaining in your planned holding period.* In practice, it does not work out quite this easily. For example, it is often difficult to find a collection of assets whose average portfolio duration exactly matches the investor's planned holding period. As time passes, the investor's planned holding period grows shorter, as does the average duration of the investor's portfolio. However, these two items—the remaining holding period and the duration of the investor's portfolio—are not likely to decline at the same speed. Therefore, an investor must constantly make portfolio adjustments to ensure that duration still equals the remaining length of the investor's planned holding period. And because many bonds are callable in advance of their maturity, bondholders may find themselves with a sudden and unexpected change in their portfolio's average duration.

Another problem with duration matching arises if the slope of the yield curve changes during the investor's planned holding period. In general, different patterns of interest rate movements require somewhat different measures of duration—a complex problem. Because the future path of interest rates cannot be perfectly forecast, immunization with duration cannot be perfect without developing a complicated model that takes account of a wide range of factors. Thus, there is always some risk associated with the use of conventional measures of duration due to uncertainty about future interest-rate movements: a type of risk called *stochastic process risk.*[6]

Immunization using duration seems to work well because (as a recent factor analysis study by Bliss (1997) shows) the largest single element seen in most interest rate movements is a parallel change in *all* interest rates (a factor that explains about 80 percent of the variability we see in interest-rate movements over time). Thus, the assumption of duration models that interest rates tend to move in parallel (i.e., the slope of the yield curve does not change significantly over time) is not exactly true, but it represents a reasonably close approximation of what we often see in real-world markets over time. Thus, there is evidence that investors can achieve reasonably effective immunization by *approximately* matching the duration of their portfolios with their planned holding periods. The duration model, in other words, seems to be quite robust under a variety of different market conditions.

Questions *to Help You Study*

11. What is the *coupon effect?* How does it relate to the concept of *security price elasticity?*

12. What is the relationship between the coupon rate on an asset and the volatility of its price as interest rates change?

13. Explain the meaning and importance of the concept of *duration?*

14. What is *portfolio immunization?* How does it work?

15. What are the *limitations* of duration and the portfolio immunization technique?

---

[6]For a discussion of stochastic process risk see, for example, Bierwag, Kaufman, and Toevs (1983).

Summary of the Chapter

While theories of how interest rates are determined usually focus upon a single interest rate in the economy, there are in fact thousands of different interest rates confronting savers and borrowers every day. This chapter has focused our attention upon two major factors that cause interest rates to differ from security to security and loan to loan: (a) *inflationary expectations:* and (b) the *maturity, term,* or *duration* of a financial instrument. Knowledge of these two important rate-determining factors is critical if we are to make intelligent saving and borrowing decisions and understand how the money and capital markets work.

- One key factor affecting interest rates is *expectations about inflation.* If lenders expect a higher rate of inflation to prevail during the life of a financial instrument they will demand a higher nominal interest return before making a loan. The *Fisher effect* argues that the expected nominal interest rate attached to a loan or security is the sum of the expected real rate plus the inflation premium (or expected rate of inflation). Fisher believed that the real rate would be relatively stable; therefore, changes in the nominal interest rate were due largely to changes in inflationary expectations.

- More recent research suggests that the relationship between inflation and interest rates may not be as simple as implied by the Fisher effect. For example, the *Harrod-Keynes effect* suggests that changes in the expected inflation rate may result, not in changes in the nominal rate, but changes in the real rate of return instead. Moreover, the economy and the public's spending and investment habits may significantly impact the linkages between inflation and interest rates. For example, the *inflation-caused wealth, income,* and *depreciation* effects argue that a rise in expected inflation can reduce the expected real rate of return, causing the expected nominal interest rate to rise by less than the full expected change in the rate of inflation. In contrast, the *taxation* of interest income may force the expected nominal interest rate to increase by more than expected inflation so that savers can protect their after-tax return.

- There is great controversy today surrounding the possible linkages between inflation and *stock prices.* Rising inflation doesn't necessarily lead to rising stock prices. The stock-price impact from inflation may depend on *nominal contracts*—that is, whether revenues and expenses are favorably or unfavorably affected by inflation as a result of agreements having to do with such things as wages and salaries, goods sold to customers, and borrowing costs. Inflation doesn't affect all stocks the same way because different businesses and individuals are involved in different nominal contracts shaping their cash inflows (revenues) and outflows (expenses).

- This chapter has also emphasized the usefulness of the *yield curve* in explaining interest-rate movements. The yield curve visually captures the relationship between the annual rate of return on financial instruments and their term to maturity. Yield curves have sloped upward most frequently in recent years, with long-term interest rates higher than short-term rates. However, yield curves may also slope downward or become relatively flat (horizontal).

- Why does the yield curve change its shape? The *unbiased expectations hypothesis* contends that yield curves reflect predominantly the interest-rate expectations of the financial marketplace. A rising yield curve suggests that market interest rates are expected to rise, while a declining yield curve points to lower expected interest rates in the future.

- Other viewpoints on the yield curve stem from the *liquidity premium, market segmentation,* and *preferred habitat* theories. For example, the *liquidity premium view* contends that the greater risk associated with longer-term financial instruments results in these longer-maturity assets bearing higher average returns, giving an upward bias to the slope of yield curves.

- The *market segmentation* and *preferred habitat* views of the yield curve suggest that the supply of securities of different maturities available to investors can affect the yield curve's shape. For example, a sudden increase in the supply of longer-term financial instruments may cause long-term security prices to fall and their yields to rise, tipping the yield curve toward an upward slope.

- Regardless of which yield-curve theory may be valid, yield curves can play a key role in the management of financial institutions, which borrow a substantial portion of their funds at the short end of the maturity spectrum and lend heavily at longer maturities. Yield curves can be used to help forecast interest rates, with upward-sloping curves implying rising interest rates and downward-sloping yield curves implying falling interest rates in the future.

- Yield curves may help identify underpriced or overpriced assets whose yields will lie above or below the curve at any moment in time. Moreover, some security traders "ride the yield curve," taking advantage of opportunities to sell short-term seurities bearing the lowest yields and purchasing securities at longer maturity bearing higher interest rates.

- In recent years financial analysts have become somewhat dissatisfied with one of the two key factors making up the yield-curve relationship—the *term to maturity* or number of months and years until a security is due to be retired. An alternative measure of the maturity of a financial instrument—*duration*—has become popular in recent years because it is a weighted average measure of the maturity or length of a financial instrument, capturing both the size and the timing of all cash payments from an individual income-generating asset or portfolio of assets. Duration has grown in popularity among portfolio managers because it can be used, at least partially, to *immunize* a single asset or an asset portfolio against changing market interest rates.

- Duration is also linked to the price volatility (or *price elasticity)* of a financial instrument in a directly proportional way. Duration connects the percentage change in price of a financial instrument to the change in its interest return or yield. Longer-term assets tend to have longer durations and, therefore, greater price instability than do shorter-term assets.

Key Terms

Problems

1. According to the Fisher effect, if the real interest rate is currently 3 percent and the nominal interest rate is 8 percent, what rate of inflation is the financial marketplace predicting? Explain the reasoning behind your answer. If the nominal rate rises to 11 percent and follows the assumptions of the Fisher effect, what would you conclude about the expected inflation rate? The real rate?

2. Suppose the real interest rate in the economy is 4 percent and the nominal interest rate is 9 percent. Now investors in the financial marketplace expect a sudden doubling in the rate of inflation. According to the Fisher effect, what new rate of inflation is expected? If the depreciation, income, or wealth effects are at work, what do you conclude is the new expected rate of inflation?

3. Calculate the expected after-tax rate of return for an investor in the 28 percent marginal income tax bracket if she purchases a bond whose nominal rate is 12 percent and the expected rate of inflation is 4 percent.

4. An investor buys a U.S. Treasury bond whose current yield to maturity as reported in the daily newspaper is 10 percent. The investor is subject to a 33 percent federal income tax rate on any new income received. His real after-tax return from this bond is 2 percent. What is the expected inflation rate in the financial marketplace?

5. Calculate the price elasticity of a 15-year bond around its $1,000 par value and 10 percent coupon rate if market interest rates on comparable securities drop to 6 percent. The market price of the bond at a 6 percent yield to maturity is $1,392. Suppose now that the yield to maturity climbs to 14 percent. If the bond's price falls to $751.80, what is the bond's price elasticity?

6. Calculate the value of duration for a four-year, $1,000 par value U.S. government bond purchased today at a yield to maturity of 15 percent. The bond's coupon rate is 12 percent, and it pays interest once a year at year's end. Now suppose the market interest rate on comparable securities falls to 14 percent. What percentage change in this bond's price will result?

7. A government bond is scheduled to mature in five years. Its coupon rate is 10 percent, with interest paid to holders of record at the conclusion of each year. This $1,000 par value carries a current yield to maturity of 10 percent. What is its duration?

8. For the bond described in Problem 7, calculate the percentage change in its price if interest rates on comparable securities in the market decline to 9 percent. What percentage change will occur if interest rates jump to 11 percent?

9. A bank buying bonds is concerned about possible fluctuations in earnings due to changes in interest rates. Currently the bank's investment officer is looking at a $1,000 par-value bond that matures in four years and carries a coupon rate of 12 percent. Market interest rates are also currently at 12 percent, but the bank's officer believes there is a significant probability that interest rates could drop to 10 percent or rise to 14 percent during the first year and stay there until the bond matures. What would be this bond's total earnings for the bank over the next four years if interest rates rise to 14 percent? Fall to 10 percent? Remain at 12 percent? What will happen to total earnings if the bank's investment officer finds another bond whose maturity is reached in five years but whose duration is four years, the same as the bank's planned holding period?

10. A bank grants a loan to AXTEL Corporation for three years to cover repairs at one of its production units. The terms of this $10 million loan call for the accrual of interest by the bank at a compound interest rate of 9 percent. However, the interest and the principal owed on this loan are due and payable when the loan matures at the end of the third year. What is the duration of this loan?

11. The 10-year Treasury bond rate is currently trading at 6.08 percent, while the 1-year bond rate carries a yield to maturity of 5.35 percent. What is the current yield spread between these instruments? What is this yield spread forecasting for the economy in the period ahead? Please explain.

    Suppose the 10-year T-bond rate falls to 5.57 percent, while the 1-year T-bond yield rises to 6.04 percent. What change in the yield spread has occurred? What is the expected outlook for economic conditions following this particular change in the yield spread? Can you explain why?

12. Synchron Corporation borrows long-term capital at an interest rate of 8.5 percent under the expectation that the annual inflation rate over the life of this borrowing was likely to be about 5 percent. However, shortly after the loan contract was signed, the actual inflation rate climbed to 5.5 percent and is expected to remain at that level until Synchron's loan reaches maturity. Other factors held constant, what is likely to happen to the market value per share of Synchron's common stock? Please explain your reasoning.

13. A four-year TIPS government bond promises a real annual coupon return to investors of 4 percent and its face value is $1,000. While the annual inflation rate was approximately zero when the bond was first issued, the inflation rate suddenly accelerated to 3 percent and is expected to remain at that level for the four-year term of the bond. What will be the amount of interest paid in nominal dollars each year of the bond's life? What will be the face (nominal) value of the bond at the end of each year of its life?

14. A TIPS issued five years ago for $1,000 with a 10 percent coupon rate and maturing today had the following inflation history:

Year in Life of the TIPS Bond	Actual Inflation Rate (Measured by the CPI)
1	2%
2	3
3	4
4	3
5	2

    How did the nominal principal value and nominal interest payment associated with this bond change over its lifetime?

15. Please identify the key term or concept that goes with each of the descriptions given below.
    a. Duration matches the length of the investor's planned holding period.
    b. Weighted average maturity of a financial asset.
    c. Ratio of changes in the price of a financial instrument relative to changes in its yield.
    d. The size of an asset's promised yield influences how rapidly its price changes as market interest rates move.
    e. Investors prefer certain asset maturities due to such factors as their liquidity needs, tax exposure, and risk.
    f. Maturity preferences of active investors divide up the financial markets into different submarkets.
    g. Investors must receive an extra component of yield or return in order to accept the risk of longer-term financial instruments.
    h. Graphical representation of yield to maturity versus calendar time.

   i. Dominant determinant of a yield curve's shape is investors' anticipation of future interest rate movements.
   j. Adjusts payment of income to an investor based upon the actual rate of inflation.
   k. Agreements between parties that fix prices, rates, or costs.
   l. Declining net value of plant and equipment over time does not match its actual replacement cost.
   m. Change in the value of assets held affects real versus nominal rates and savings.
   n. Change in consumption habits due to inflation causes a shift in expected real and nominal interest rates.
   o. Real interest rates, rather than nominal rates, are affected by shifts in expected inflation.
   p. Nominal interest rates change one-for-one with changes in the inflation premium.
   q. The published rate of interest on a loan or security.
   r. The purchasing power rate of return on a loan or security.
   s. The expected rate of inflation as viewed by investors in the market.
   t. A rise in the average level of prices for goods and services.

Questions about the Web and the Money and Capital Markets

1. If you wanted to obtain data on the differing inflation rates of countries around the globe and their relative interest rates what World Wide Web sources could be of help to you?
2. Where on the Web might you be able to find discussions of the various possible linkages between inflation in the prices of goods and services and the level of market interest rates?
3. If you wanted help in learning how to construct yield curves where could you look on the Web?
4. If you were in search of help in interpreting the meaning and implication of the yield curves you see in the financial press every day, where on the Web could you go for assistance?

Selected References

Abken, Peter A. "Inflation and the Yield Curve." *Economic Review,* Federal Reserve Bank of Atlanta, May/June 1993, pp. 13–31.

Ammer, John. "Inflation, Inflation Risk, and Stock Returns." International Finance Discussion Paper 464, Board of Governors of the Federal Reserve System, April 1994.

Bierwag, G. O.; George G. Kaufman; and Alden Toevs. "Duration: Its Development and Use in Bond Portfolio Management." *Financial Analysts Journal,* July–August 1983, pp. 15–35.

Bliss, Robert R. "Movements in the Term Structure of Interest Rates." *Economic Review,* Federal Reserve Bank of Atlanta, Fourth Quarter 1997, pp. 16–32.

Bonser-Neal, Catherine, and Timothy R. Morley. "Does the Yield Spread Predict Real Economic Activity? A Multi-Country Analysis." *Economic Review,* Federal Reserve Bank of Kansas City, Third Quarter 1997, pp. 37–53.

Campbell, J. Y. "A Defense of Traditional Hypotheses about the Term Structure of Interest Rates." *Journal of Finance* 41 (1986), pp. 183–93.

Campbell, John Y.; Andrew W. Lo; and A. Craig MacKinlay. *The Econometrics of Financial Markets.* Princeton, NJ: Princeton University Press, 1997.

Carlstrom, Charles T., and Timothy S. Fuerst. "Perils of Price Deflations: An Analysis of the Great Depression." *Economic Commentary,* Federal Reserve Bank of Cleveland, February 15, 2001.

Fama, Eugene F. "Stock Returns, Real Activity, Inflation and Money." *American Economic Review,* September 1981, pp. 545–65.

————— . "The Information in the Term Structure." *Journal of Financial Economics* 13 (December 1984), pp. 509–28.

Fama, Eugene F., and R. R. Bliss. "The Information in Long-Maturity Forward Rates." *American Economic Review* 72 (1987), pp. 680–92.

Fama, Eugene F., and Kenneth R. French. "Business Conditions and Expected Returns on Stocks and Bonds." *Journal of Financial Economics* 25 (November 1989), pp. 23–49.

Fisher, Irving. "Appreciation and Interest." *Publication of the American Economics Association,* August 1896.

Froot, R. A. "New Hope for the Expectations Hypothesis of the Term Structure of Interest Rates." *Journal of Finance* 44 (1989), pp. 283–305.

Geske, Robert, and Richard Roll. "The Fiscal and Monetary Linkages between Stock Returns and Inflation." *Journal of Finance,* March 1983, pp. 1–33.

Haubrick, Joseph G. "The Term Structure from A to B." *Economic Review* XL, no. 3 (1999), Federal Reserve Bank of Cleveland, pp. 2–9.

————— . "Productivity and the Term Structure." *Economic Review* XL, no. 4 (2000), Federal Reserve Bank of Cleveland, pp. 2–9.

Hayford, Marc. "Real Interest Rates and the Distribution Effects of Unanticipated Inflation." *Journal of Macroeconomics* 12, no. 1 (Winter 1990), pp. 1–22.

Kiely, Joseph K.; James W. Kolari; and Peter S. Rose. "A Re-examination of the Relationship between Liquidity Premiums and the Level of Interest Rates." *Journal of Business Research,* 1994.

Kozicki, Sharon. "Predicting Real Growth and Inflation with the Yield Spread." *Economic Review,* Federal Reserve Bank of Kansas City, Fourth Quarter 1997.

Longstaff, Francis A. "Time Varying Term Premia and Traditional Hypotheses about the Term Structure." *Journal of Finance* 41, no. 4 (September 1990), pp. 1307–14.

McNees, Stephen K. "How Well Do Financial Markets Predict the Inflation Rate?" *New England Economic Review,* Federal Reserve Bank of Boston, September/October 1989, pp. 31–46.

Mankiw, N. G. "The Term Structure of Interest Rates Revisited." *Brookings Papers on Economic Activity,* 1986, pp. 61–96.

Shen, Pu. "How Important Is The Inflation Risk Premium?" *Economic Review,* Federal Reserve Bank of Kansas City, Fourth Quarter 1998, pp. 35–47.

Shiller, R. J.; J. Y. Campbell; and R. K. Schoenholtz. "Forward Rates and Future Policy: Interpreting the Term Structure of Interest Rates." *Brookings Papers on Economic Activity,* 1983, pp. 173–217.

Solnik, Bruno. "The Relation between Stock Prices and Inflationary Expectations: The International Evidence." *Journal of Finance* 38 (1983), pp. 35–48.

Startz, Richard. "Do Forecast Errors or Term Premia Really Make the Difference between Long and Short Rates?" *Journal of Financial Economics* 10 (November 1982), pp. 323–29.

Stojanovic, Dusan, and Mark D. Vaughn. "Yielding Clues about Recessions: The Yield Curve as a Forecasting Tool." *Economic Review,* Federal Reserve Bank of Boston, 1997, pp. 10–21.

Terrell, William T., and William J. Frazier, Jr. "Interest Rates, Portfolio Behavior, and Marketable Government Securities." *Journal of Finance,* March 1972, pp. 1–35.

Van Horne, James. "Interest-Rate Risk and the Term Structure of Interest Rates." *Journal of Political Economy,* August 1965, pp. 344–51.

Chapter Eight

Marketability, Default Risk, Call Privileges, Prepayment Risk, Taxes, and Other Factors Affecting Interest Rates

Learning Objectives in This Chapter

- You will see the effect of several different features of various loans and securities—such as their marketability, liquidity, default risk, call privileges, prepayment risk, convertibility, and taxability—upon their interest rates or yields.

- You will learn why we have, not one, but, in fact, thousands of different interest rates within the global economy.

- You will discover how the "structure of interest rates" is built and why that rate structure is constantly undergoing change.

- You will see more clearly why it is so difficult to accurately forecast interest rates and financial asset prices.

What's in This Chapter? Key Topics Outline

Marketability and Liquidity

Default Risk Premiums Attached to Interest Rates

Credit Ratings and Bankruptcies

The Rise and Fall of Junk Bonds

Call Privileges and Call Risk

INTRODUCTION

In the preceding chapter, we examined two factors that cause the interest rate or yield on one asset to be different from the interest rate or yield on another. These factors include the maturity or term of a loan or security and expected inflation. In this chapter, our focus is upon a different set of elements influencing relative interest rates: (1) marketability, (2) default risk, (3) call privileges, (4) taxation of security income, (5) prepayment risk, and (6) convertibility. The impact of each of these factors is analyzed separately, but it should be noted that yields on securities are influenced by several factors acting *simultaneously*. For example, the market yield on a 20-year corporate bond may be 8 percent, while the yield on a 10-year municipal bond may be 6 percent. The difference in yield between these two assets reflects not only the difference in their maturities but also any differences in their degree of default risk, marketability, callability, and tax status. To analyze yield differentials between various financial assets, therefore, we must understand thoroughly *all* of the factors that shape interest rates in the global money and capital markets.

MARKETABILITY

One of the most important considerations for an investor is *whether a market exists for those assets he or she would like to acquire.* Can an asset be sold quickly, or must the investor wait some time before suitable buyers can be found? This is the question of **marketability,** and financial instruments traded around the world vary widely in terms of the ease and speed with which they can be converted into cash.

For example, Treasury bills, notes, and bonds have one of the most active and deep markets in the world. Large lots of marketable Treasury securities in multiples of a million dollars are bought and sold daily, with the trades taking place in a matter of minutes. Small lots (under $1 million) of these same securities are more difficult to sell. However, there is usually no difficulty in marketing even a handful of Treasury securities provided the seller can wait a few hours. Similarly, common stock actively traded on the New York, London, Frankfurt, or Tokyo exchanges typically can be moved in minutes, depending on the number of shares being sold. In active markets like these, negotiations are usually conducted by telephone or E-mail and confirmed by wire. Frequently, payment for any securities purchased is made the same day by wire or within one or two days by check.

For thousands of lesser-known financial assets not actively traded each day, however, marketability can be a problem. Stocks and bonds issued by smaller companies usually have a narrow market, often confined to the local community or region. Trades occur infrequently, and it is difficult to establish a consistent market price. A seller may have to wait months to secure a desired price or, if the security must be sold immediately, its price may have to be discounted substantially.

As we will see in this chapter powerful forces shape the level and structure of interest rates, including fear of borrower bankruptcy and failure to repay a loan (usually referred to as default risk), the degree of liquidity attached to a financial instrument, whether previously issued debt securities can be recalled (known as a call privilege), the taxation of asset gains and losses and interest income from securities, and shifts in the strength or weakness of the economy. Some financial instruments are more susceptible to these forces than others and, therefore, the structure of interest rates will change over time.

The World Wide Web addresses a number of the foregoing issues in a variety of Web sites. Examples include a discussion of the risks attached to bond investing in the United States (at www.investinginbonds.com and www.bondmarket.com) and of tax policy at the Urban Institute—Research on Economics (at www.urban.org/economics.htm). Additional material, including daily interest rate series, may be found at the Federal Reserve's data releases site at FRB: Statistical Releases (www.federalreserve.gov/releases/) and occasional research articles on interest rate structure are featured in the FRB Cleveland Economics Working Paper Series (at www.clev.frb.org/Research).

Marketability is positively related to the *size* (total sales or total assets) and *reputation* of the institution issuing the securities and to the number of similar securities outstanding. Not surprisingly, stocks and bonds issued in large blocks by the largest corporations and governmental units tend to find acceptance more readily in the global financial markets. With a larger number of similar assets available, buy-sell transactions are more frequent, and a consistent market price can be established.

Marketability is a decided advantage to the asset purchaser (lender of funds). In contrast, the issuer of assets is not particularly concerned about any difficulties the purchaser may encounter in the resale (secondary) market unless lack of marketability significantly influences asset sales in the primary market. And where marketability is a problem, it does influence the yield the issuer must pay in the primary market. In fact, there is a *negative* relationship between marketability and yield. More marketable assets generally carry *lower* expected returns than less marketable assets, other things being equal. Purchasers of assets that can be sold in the secondary market only with difficulty must be compensated for this inconvenience by a higher promised rate of return.

LIQUIDITY

Marketability is closely related to another feature of financial assets that influences their interest rate or yield: their degree of **liquidity.** A liquid financial asset is *readily marketable.* In addition, its price tends to be *stable* over time and it is *reversible,* meaning the holder of the asset can usually recover her funds upon resale with little risk of loss. Because the liquidity feature of financial assets tends to lower their risk, liquid assets carry lower interest rates than illiquid assets. Investors strongly interested in maximum profitability try to minimize their holdings of liquid assets. Examples of highly liquid assets, bearing relatively low rates of return (yields), include most bank deposits, shares in money market mutual funds, and marketable U.S. Treasury securities.

DEFAULT RISK AND INTEREST RATES

Another important factor causing one interest rate to differ from another in the global marketplace is the degree of default risk carried by individual assets. Investors in financial assets face many different kinds of risk, but one of the most important is **default risk**—the risk that a borrower will not make all promised payments at the agreed-upon times. All debt except some government securities is subject to varying degrees of default risk. If you purchase a 10-year corporate bond with a $1,000 par value and a coupon rate of 9 percent, the issuing company promises in the indenture (bond contract) to pay you $90 a year (or more commonly, $45 every six months) for 10 years plus $1,000 at the end of the 10-year period. Failure to meet any of these promised payments on time puts the borrower in default, and the lender may have to go to court to recover the monies owed.

The Premium for Default Risk

The promised yield on a risky asset is positively related to the risk of borrower default as perceived by investors. Specifically, the promised yield on a risky asset is composed of at least two elements:

$$\text{Promised yield on a risky asset} = \text{Risk-free interest rate} + \text{Default risk premium} \quad \textbf{(8–1)}$$

where:

$$\text{Default risk premium} = \text{Promised yield on a risky asset} - \text{Risk-free interest rate} \quad \textbf{(8–2)}$$

The promised yield on a risky debt security is the yield to maturity that will be earned by the investor if the borrower makes all promised payments when they are due. As Exhibit 8–1 illustrates, the higher the degree of default risk associated with a risky debt security, the higher the default risk premium on that security and the greater the required rate of return (yield) that must be attached to that asset as demanded by investors in the global financial marketplace. Any adverse development, such as a downturn in the economy or serious financial difficulties, that makes a borrower appear riskier will lead the market to assign a higher default risk premium to his debt security. And if the risk-free rate remains unchanged, the financial asset's promised risky yield must rise and its price must decline.

The Expected Rate of Return or Yield on a Risky Asset

Increasingly in recent years some of the largest business firms on the planet have been forced into default and subsequently declared bankruptcy. Among the leading U.S. bankruptcy filers in modern history are such firms as:

Enron Corporation (2001) with $49.5 billion in assets

Texaco, Inc. (1987) with $35.9 billion in assets

Financial Corporation of America (1988) with $33.9 billion in assets

Pacific Gas and Electric Company (2001) with $21.5 billion in assets

MCorp (1989) with $20.2 billion in assets

Not even governments have been exempt from default and ultimate bankruptcy, including Argentina, Russia, and Orange County, California. Volatile changes in business and consumer spending, interest rates, and commodity prices frequently have led to serious miscalculations by both large and small businesses and governments with sometimes fatal results. For this reason, many investors around the globe today have learned to look at the *expected* rate of return, or yield, on a risky asset as well as its *promised* yield.

EXHIBIT 8–1
The Relationship between Default Risk and the Promised Yield on Risky Assets

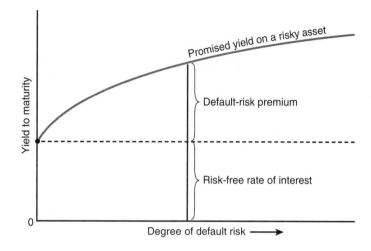

The **expected yield** is the weighted average of all possible yields to maturity from a risky asset. Each possible yield is weighted by the probability that it will occur. Thus, if there are *m* possible yields from a risky asset:

$$\text{Expected yield} = \sum_{i=1}^{m} p_i y_i \qquad (8–3)$$

where y_i represents the *i*th possible yield on a risky asset and p_i is the probability that the *i*th possible risky yield will be obtained.

Anticipated Loss and Default-Risk Premiums

For a risk-free asset held to maturity, the expected yield equals the promised yield. However, in the case of a risky asset, the promised yield may be greater than the expected yield, and the yield spread between them is usually labeled the *anticipated default loss.* That is,

Anticipated default loss on a risky asset = Promised yield − Expected yield **(8–4)**

The concept of *anticipated default loss* is important because it represents each investor's view of what the appropriate default risk premium on a risky asset should be. Let's suppose that an investor carries out a careful financial analysis of a company in preparation for purchasing its bonds and decides that the firm is a less risky borrower default-wise than perceived by the market as a whole. Perhaps the market has assigned the firm's bonds a default-risk premium of 4 percent; the investor believes, however, that the true anticipated loss due to default is only 3 percent. Because the market's default-risk premium exceeds this investor's anticipated default loss, she would be inclined to *buy* the company's bonds. As she sees it, the risky asset's promised yield (including its market-assigned default-risk premium) is too high and, therefore, its price is too low. To this investor, the company's bonds appear to be a bargain—a temporarily underpriced financial asset.

Consider the opposite case. An investor calculates the anticipated default loss on bonds issued by a government toll road project. He concludes that a default-risk premium of 5 percent is justified because of a significant number of uncertainties associated with the future success of the project. However, the current promised yield on the risky asset is only 10 percent, and the risk-free interest rate is 6 percent. Because the market has assigned only a 4 percent default-risk premium, and the investor prefers a 5 percent default-risk premium, it is unlikely that he will purchase the bond. As the investor views this bond, its promised risky yield is too low and, therefore, its price is too high.

Major financial institutions, especially insurance companies, banks, and pension funds, employ a large number of credit analysts for the express purpose of assessing the anticipated default loss on a wide range of assets they would like to acquire. These institutions believe they have a definite advantage over the average investor in assessing the true degree of default risk associated with any particular asset. This high level of technical expertise may permit major institutional investors to take advantage of underpriced assets where, in their judgment, the market has overestimated the true level of default risk.

Factors Influencing Default-Risk Premiums

What factors influence the default-risk premiums assigned by the market to different assets? For many years, privately owned rating companies have exercised a dominant influence on investor perceptions of the riskiness of individual security issues. Among the most widely consulted investment rating companies are Moody's Investors Service—a division of Dun & Bradstreet—and Standard & Poor's Corporation—a subsidiary of McGraw-Hill, Inc. Both companies rate individual security issues according to their perceived probability of default (based on the borrower's financial condition and business prospects) and publish the ratings as letter grades. A summary of the letter grades used by these companies for rating corporate and municipal bonds is shown in Exhibit 8–2.

For nearly a century, Moody's and Standard & Poor's (S&P) have automatically assigned credit ratings to thousands of companies selling bonds and other forms of debt. Two other rating agencies—Fitch and Duff & Phelps—often issue their ratings when someone requests a "second opinion" concerning a new bond issue. The Securities and Exchange Commission has labeled Moody's, S&P, Fitch, and Duff & Phelps as "nationally recognized" raters for U.S. corporate bonds, while Thomson Bankwatch and IBCA are nationally recognized as raters for debt instruments issued by financial institutions. Recently, new credit rating agencies have appeared all over the globe to match the growing globalization of the money and capital markets.

EXHIBIT 8–2
Bond-Rating Categories Employed by Moody's Investors Service and Standard & Poor's Corporation

Quality Level of Bonds	Moody's Rating Categories	Standard & Poor's Rating Categories	Default-Risk Premium
High-quality or high-grade bonds	Aaa	AAA	Lowest
	Aa	AA	
	A	A	
Medium-quality or medium-grade bonds	Baa	BBB	
	Ba	BB	
	B	B	
Lowest grade, speculative, or poor-quality bonds	Caa	CCC	
	Ca	CC	
	C	C	
Defaulted bonds and bonds issued by bankrupt companies	—	DDD	Highest
	—	DD	
	—	D	

The economic basis for the rise of credit rating companies has to do with economies of scale in collecting credit information. Presumably, large rating agencies can do credit evaluations cheaper and more conveniently than can small investors who lack the necessary data and market contacts. Allegedly, large credit rating companies have lower agency costs (because investors have developed confidence in the rating agencies' independence and competence at assessing the degree of risk exposure investors may face with any particular bond issue).

While theory might lead us to suspect that all credit agencies assign about the same ratings along equivalent credit risk scales, recent research by Cantor and Packer (1996), suggests that this is not always true. Even the same level of rating at two different credit agencies does not necessarily imply the same level of perceived default risk exposure. Moreover, Moody's and Standard & Poor's tend to assign lower credit ratings, on average, than other, less-well-known agencies, like Fitch and Duff & Phelps. One explanation may be that Moody's and S&P have tougher credit standards, or it may be that those bond issuers requesting third and fourth credit ratings expect to get a higher rating from a third or fourth credit reviewer and, thereby, save on their borrowing costs. When ratings are different, either the highest rating or the second-highest rating is often generally recognized in the market as the correct risk level, no matter which agency happens to assign the one rating chosen as "representative." Larger debt issuers also tend to get third or even fourth ratings because they face lower percentage rating costs, as Cantor and Packer (1996) explain.

Moody's investment ratings range from Aaa, for the highest-quality securities with negligible default risk, to C, for those securities deemed to be speculative and carrying a significant prospect of borrower default. Quality ratings assigned by Standard & Poor's range from AAA, for high-grade ("gilt-edged") securities, to those financial instruments actually in default (D) or issued by bankrupt firms. Bonds falling in the four top rating categories—Aaa to Baa for Moody's and AAA to BBB for Standard & Poor's—are called *investment-grade issues.* Laws and regulations frequently require commercial banks, insurance companies, and other financial institutions to purchase only those securities rated in these four categories. Lower-rated securities are referred to as *speculative issues.*

Exhibit 8–3 illustrates how the yields on bonds bearing different degrees of default risk (for example: 30-year U.S. Treasury bonds versus corporate, municipal, and mortgage securities) change relative to each other with the progression of time, fluctuations in the economy, and other factors. Exhibit 8–4 compares market yields on long-term U.S. Treasury bonds with those on corporate bonds in the four top rating categories, Aaa to Baa. It is interesting to note that these yield relationships are all in the direction theory would lead us to expect. For example, the yield on Aaa corporate bonds—the least risky securities rated by Moody's and Standard & Poor's—is consistently lower than yields attached to lower-rated (Baa) bonds. This suggests that investors in the marketplace tend to rank securities in the same relative default risk order as the credit rating agencies do. This seems to be an appropriate strategy, because there appears to be a high (though by no means perfect) correlation between the ratings assigned by the agencies and the actual default record of corporate bonds.

Recent research has found that there is a pronounced association between market-assigned default-risk premiums and fluctuations (cycles) in business activity (recessions versus expansions or boom periods). For example, the yield spread between Aaa- and Baa-rated securities rises during economic recessions and decreases during periods of economic expansion. The correlation is not perfect, though. Fluctuations in output and income do not always influence the default-risk premium on one security versus another in the same way or to the same degree. However, when economic and financial conditions suggest to

EXHIBIT 8–3
**The Behavior of
Interest Rates
Attached to Risky
versus Riskless
Capital Market
Securities**

Source: Federal Reserve Bank
of Cleveland, Research
Department, *Economic Trends,*
April 2001.

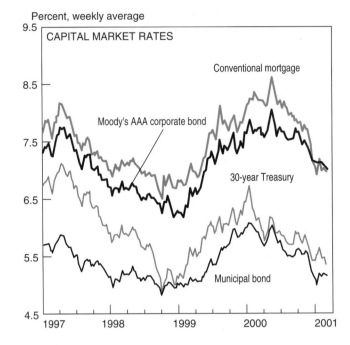

investors that uncertainty has increased and that business prospects are less robust, the market generally translates these opinions into higher default-risk premiums.

Several studies in recent years have addressed the question of what factors influence default-risk premiums on securities and what factors rating firms use to evaluate default risk. Among the factors identified for corporate securities are variability in company earnings, the period of time a firm has been in operation, and the amount of leverage employed (i.e., amount of debt relative to equity).[1]

A company with volatile earnings runs a greater risk of experiencing periods when losses will exceed the firm's ability to raise funds. The longer a firm has been operating without default, the more investors come to expect continued successful performance. Greater use of financial leverage in the capital structure of a firm offers the potential for greater earnings per share of stock, because debt is a relatively cheap source of funds (especially when measured on an after-tax basis). However, financial leverage is a two-edged sword. As the proportion of borrowed funds rises relative to equity, the risk of significant declines in net earnings increases.[2]

[1]See especially the study by Fisher (1959). We do not know for sure what factors the security rating companies use to assign default risk ratings, but we do know that they consider at least three levels of factors: (1) condition of the economy, (2) industry conditions, and (3) borrower-specific factors, including coverage ratios (earnings before interest and taxes to interest and principal payments owed), leverage ratios (debt-to-equity ratios), liquidity indicators (such as the current ratio), and profitability measures (such as return on assets and equity). Studies of corporate bankruptcy, as noted by Scott (1981), have found some of these factors—especially liquidity or cash flow, earnings, debt exposure, and stock prices—to be effective discriminators between corporations eventually declaring bankruptcy and healthy firms. Moreover, a study by Holthausen and Leftwich (1986) finds that when Moody's or Standard & Poor's downgrades a firm's credit rating, the affected company's stock returns tend to fall immediately following the announcement.

[2]A study by Ederington, Yawitz, and Roberts (1987) found that *both* ratings assigned by the credit rating agencies and company financial reports are used by investors to assess the credit quality of bonds and to derive the appropriate default-risk premium.

EXHIBIT 8–4
Market Yield on Rated Corporate Bonds and Long-Term U.S. Treasury Bonds, 1990–2001

Type of Bond	Average Yields (Percent per Annum)						
	1990	**1992**	**1994**	**1996**	**1998**	**2000**	**2001****
Long-term U.S. Treasury bonds	8.74%	7.52%	7.41%	6.80%	5.69%	6.03%	4.97%
Aaa corporate bonds*	9.32	8.14	7.97	7.37	6.53	7.62	7.02
Aa corporate bonds*	9.57	8.46	8.15	7.55	6.80	7.83	7.11
A corporate bonds*	9.82	8.62	8.28	7.69	6.93	8.11	7.48
Baa corporate bonds*	10.36	8.98	8.63	8.05	7.22	8.36	7.85

*Corporate bond ratings are from Moody's Investors Service.
**2001 rates are for the month of August.
Source: Board of Governors of the Federal Reserve System, *Federal Reserve Bulletin,* selected issues.

Inflation and Default-Risk Premiums

Earlier, in Chapter 7, we saw that inflation can cause interest rates to rise as investors in the financial markets demand to be compensated with higher nominal returns when the level of expected inflation or uncertainty about future inflation goes up. However, *inflation also appears to affect the size of default-risk premiums on risky securities.* Default-risk premiums (often called "quality spreads") tend to be higher and more volatile when inflation is high and volatile. Greater uncertainty about inflation, as Wheelock (1997) notes, tends to produce a "flight to quality" in the financial markets, and investors simply become more cautious about buying default-risk-exposed financial instruments, as we have seen most recently in Asian and Latin American markets. This is one of the many ways in which high and volatile price inflation can disrupt the efficient functioning of a market-oriented economy.

Yield Curves for Risky Securities

Finance theory suggests that yield curves on higher-risk (speculative) corporate bonds tend to have a downward (negative) slope or are humped or bowed in shape. However, yield curves on government securities and for high-grade corporate bonds have a tendency to display a positive slope, trending upward with advancing maturity. This may be due, in part, to the fact that junk bonds issued by poorer-credit-quality firms are generally at their riskiest when they are first issued and appear to improve in quality, the longer the issuing company survives. While some studies (e.g., Fons, 1994) tend to support this version of finance theory, recent work by Helwege and Turner (1997), which appears to control better for the credit quality of bond issuers, finds quite the opposite—the yield curve for the majority of speculative-grade bond issues *rises* with increasing maturity just like it does for most other bonds.

The Rise and Fall of Junk Bonds

The decades of the 1980s and 1990s ushered in the rapid growth and development of the market for **junk bonds**—long-term debt securities whose repayment is judged to be significantly less certain than bonds rated as investment quality, as shown in the following table:

Corporate and municipal debt securities sold in the financial markets generally must carry a credit rating assigned by one or more rating agencies. The two most widely respected credit rating agencies over the years have been Moody's Investors Service and Standard & Poor's Corporation, both headquartered in New York City.

Other prominent security rating companies operating today include Fitch Investors Service, Thomson Bank Watch, and Duff and Phelps Credit Rating Co. in the U.S., as well as the Canadian Bond Rating Service, Japanese Bond Rating Institute, Dominion Bond Rating Service, IBCA, Ltd., the Japanese Credit Rating Agency, and Nippon Investor Service Inc. The ratings assigned by these firms are generally regarded in the investment community as an objective evaluation of the probability that a borrower will *default* on a security issue.

Each rating assigned to a security issue is a reflection of at least three factors: (1) the character and terms of the particular security being issued; (2) the ability and willingness of the issuer to make timely payments; and (3) the degree of protection afforded investors if the security issuer is liquidated, reorganized, or declares bankruptcy. The credit rating agencies focus principally on (1) the past and probable future cash flows of the security issuer as an indication of the institution's ability to service its debt, (2) the volume and composition of outstanding debt, and (3) the stability of the issuer's cash flows over time. Other factors influencing quality ratings are the value of assets pledged as collateral and the securities' priority of claim against the issuing firm's assets.

The rating agencies stress that their evaluations of security issues are not recommendations to buy or sell or an indication of the suitability of any particular security for the investor. The agencies do not act as financial advisors to the businesses or units of government whose securities they rate, which helps to promote objectivity in assigning quality ratings. Fees are assessed for ratings based on the time and effort involved. These fees are usually paid either by the security issuer or the underwriter.

While credit rating agencies have a good record ranking the default-risk exposure of most security issuers, the interpretation of the ratings seems to vary across time and across different rating agencies. Because the number of credit-rating companies seems to be growing, there is some fear that security issuers in the future will "shop around" even more than they do today for the best ratings they can get. Fortunately, credit-rating firms have a strong incentive to preserve their reputation for publishing accurate risk ratings. Otherwise, security issuers and investors will tend to avoid agencies that lose their reputation for quality and objectivity and, undoubtedly, investors who lose money from faulty ratings may seek relief in the courts.

To discover how credit ratings are assigned and how buyers of securities can find out about changes in companies' credit ratings see Moody's Investors Service at *www.moodys.com/* and Standard and Poor's Corporation at *www.standardpoor.com*

Junk versus Investment-Grade Corporate Bonds	
Investment-grade bond issues	All those debt securities rated: Aaa, Aa, A, or Baa by Moody's Investors Service AAA, AA, A, or BBB by Standard & Poor's Corporation
Junk Bonds	All those debt securities rated: Ba, B, Caa, Ca, or C by Moody's Investors Service BB, B, CCC, CC, C by Standard & Poor's Corporation

The term *junk bonds* arose years ago when several companies that were trapped in serious financial problems with low credit ratings ("fallen angels") were forced to issue inferior-quality bonds to stay alive. More recently, new companies and small established companies have also been able to reach the bond market, which previously was closed to them, by issuing these speculative-grade securities. Junk bonds have also been issued to facilitate mergers and, in the opposite situation, to prevent corporate takeovers. Many junk bonds are "zeros," which pay no interest, and others are "pics," which pay interest not in cash but in the form of new bonds—both ideal for companies with low or uncertain earning power. Such low-rated bonds may trade at interest yields of 4 or 5 percentage points or more over yields on comparable government securities.

The number of individual investors and financial institutions interested in purchasing junk bonds grew rapidly during the 1980s due to few actual defaults on these bonds. At the same time, a leading investment banking firm, Drexel Burnham Lambert, Inc., pioneered

Developments in the "junk bond" market may be followed through such sources as *www.encyclopedia.com, www.finpipe.com/bndjunk.htm,* and *www.speculativebubble.com*

new techniques to sell junk bonds that rapidly expanded the scope of the market. Many investors discovered that a diversified portfolio of junk bonds (e.g., about 12 different issues) appeared to lower overall portfolio risk to a level comparable to many higher-rated bonds. Thus, the yields offered on junk bonds appeared to be higher than their actual degree of default risk. Moreover, the development of an active market for junk bonds gave many small and new firms access to another source of financing besides borrowing from banks and finance companies. Certainly, the tax deductibility of interest expenses on corporate debt and the more recent development of sophisticated hedging instruments (such as Swaps, credit derivatives, financial futures, and options) to combat market risk encouraged private corporations to make greater use of junk securities in order to raise new capital.

On the negative side, however, the rapid growth of junk bonds has aroused concern among government policymakers over the declining credit quality of corporate debt. For example, insurance company regulators from New York state acted to limit junk bond investments by insurance firms selling policies in that state, a move soon followed by other insurance regulators across the United States. The use of junk bonds to finance hostile takeovers and the failure of hundreds of savings and loans that had purchased junk securities finally captured the attention of the U.S. Congress. Passage of the Financial Institutions Reform, Recovery, and Enforcement Act of 1989 outlawed further purchases of junk bonds by federally supervised depository institutions. In 1990, the king of junk bond dealers, Drexel Burnham Lambert, declared bankruptcy, as junk bond prices plummeted.

Moreover, a recession in the U.S. economy in 1991 resulted in a wave of defaults by firms that had previously issued junk bonds, climbing up to a default rate as high as 11 percent, though by 1994 the mean default rate on junk bonds had dropped back to less than 2 percent. However, in 2001 a recession in the economy sent junk bond interest rates and business bankruptcies rising again. Research by Fons (1991) and Helwege and Kleimen (1996) suggests that junk bond default rates vary over time due to (1) the strength of the economy (with default rates dropping when the economy is strong); (2) the proportion of lower-rated bonds issued each year (with more lower-rated issues increasing the average default rate); and (3) an "aging effect" (with defaults more likely within the first three years of a junk bond issue).

Higher yields available on junk bonds coupled with a declining supply of these securities later in the 1990s sparked a market rally in junk bond prices and an upward surge in new offerings as a new century was beginning. Much of the price gain appeared to be due to the emergence of junk bond mutual funds that often buy half or more of available new junk issues. The rise in new junk bond offerings can be traced to more borrowing companies bypassing rigid and expensive bank loans as a source of credit and to an upward surge of corporate mergers financed by junk bond issues. In addition, the formation of the European Community (EC) has recently acted as a spur to international junk bond offerings, as firms move to expand and take advantage of a huge new common market, using a common currency with sharply reduced trade barriers.

The Junk-Bond Spread and the Economy

The behavior of yields on junk bonds have attracted the attention of economists trying to forecast changes in the strength or weakness of the economy. They have recently begun to focus on the so-called *junk-bond-spread:*

Junk-bond spread = Junk-bond yields − Average yield on Aaa-rated coporate bonds

The basic argument concerning this measure of economic conditions is that a rise in the junk-bond spread indicates a growing fear among bond market investors that marginal-

Financial Developments   Default Risk in Action: The Failures of Argentina and of Enron Corporation— Largest in History

The buyers of bonds and other financial instruments must be ever watchful of *default risk*—failure to pay interest owed or to pay back the principal of a loan—which can occur in some unexpected places. Two dramatic examples of the dangers of lending funds to risky borrowers occurred in 2001—one involving Enron Corporation in the United States (the largest corporate bankruptcy in U.S. history) and the other in Argentina (the largest international credit default in world history).

In the case of Enron Corporation—a U.S. company with about $50 billion in assets—the ship went down fast with a jolting effect on the financial markets and on many individual investors. Enron was one of the largest energy companies in the United States, involved not only in the marketing and distribution of natural gas and other energy resources around the globe but also in trading derivatives that allowed producers and consumers to reduce the risk of energy price fluctuations. For years Enron scored one market success after another, generating excess returns for its shareholders, many of which were employees and officers of the company.

Unfortunately, a combination of events threw Enron into bankruptcy court as the year 2001 drew to a close. The company had begun borrowing heavily to support its trading activities and the pile-up of corporate debt coupled with the sell-off of many of its most valuable assets made Enron very vulnerable to adverse movements in energy prices. Slumping energy prices in the recession of 2001 wreaked havoc with Enron's revenues and asset values and, as the marketplace became aware of its growing financial troubles, the firm's borrowing costs soared. At the same time investors in the market became aware of questionable accounting practices at the company which tended to inflate the value of its assets and overestimate its gains from market trading activities. Enron's bankruptcy threatened huge losses for many of its employees who had invested their personal savings and pension monies in the firm's stock. Remarkably Enron's credit rating remained at investment grade until 5 days before it filed a federal bankruptcy petition.

Even larger in magnitude was Argentina's default on much of its $141 billion in debt in January of 2002. A decade before this massive default occurred the Argentine government began tying the value of its national currency, the peso, to the U.S. dollar, one for one, in the hope of stopping serious inflation and strengthening the country's position in global trade. If the government wanted to print more money it had to post an equivalent amount of dollar reserves. This device worked for a few years in helping to stabilize the Argentine economy but eventually became too restrictive and inflexible. The global recession that occurred as the new century opened coupled with a resurgence of domestic inflation and unemployment proved to be more than Argentina's central government could deal with. Riots in the streets and the flight of capital from the country's financial system finally forced the Argentine government into default.

quality corporate borrowers are more likely to default on their debts. Thus, greater risk among corporate borrowers signals a weakening economy. In contrast, a decline in the junk-bond spread suggests fewer likely corporate bond defaults and, therefore, an improving economy.

There is some anecdotal evidence favoring the junk-bond-spread concept. For example, during the year 1999—a period of economic expansion in the United States—the yield spread between Ba corporate bonds—the highest quality junk bond issues—and Aaa (top-quality) corporate bonds was only about three-quarters of a percentage point (75 basis points). Capital market investors were pricing the risk of corporate business failures fairly low. In contrast, by August of 2001—when the U.S. economy was in a recession—this junk-bond yield spread was more than a full percentage point (100 basis points) as capital market investors began to express concern that a weakening economy might sink a number of weaker companies. More research is needed on this so-called "economic forecaster," however, before we accept its predictions about business conditions and the strength of the economy.

NEW WAYS OF DEALING WITH DEFAULT (CREDIT) RISK

Rising concern over defaults and business bankruptcies in the 1980s and 1990s led to new techniques for protecting lenders against default risk. These so-called *credit derivatives* are financial contracts that provide at least some positive rate of return to the beneficiaries of each contract.

Among the most popular of these default risk–protection instruments are *credit swaps* in which two or more investors in risky loans and securities agree to exchange at least a portion of their expected payments due from the borrowers. For example, a swap dealer may draw up an agreement involving two lenders, located in different regions, who pledge to deliver all or part of the stream of loan payments expected from their customers. Because the contracting lenders serve different market areas, each lender, in effect, is no longer completely dependent on his or her local loan market for revenue. Each has geographically diversified its sources of revenue to a greater extent than before.

Another example of a credit derivative is the *total return swap*. Under this arrangement a swap dealer may provide assurance that parties to this swap receive a minimum rate of return on the credit they have extended to borrowers. For example, the dealer may guarantee a lender a rate of return on its loans at least 2 percentage points higher than the prevailing market yield on long-term Treasury bonds. There is still risk here due to fluctuating interest rates, but the lender's credit risk has been at least partially reduced (unless, of course, the guarantor fails).

Under a so-called *credit option* an investor in risky assets may protect itself against such risks as rising borrowing costs or a decline in value of the risky assets it holds in its asset portfolio. For example, a risk-exposed lender may contact a swap dealer about an option contract that pays off if a loan or other credit asset begins to lose value. If the covered loan pays out as expected, however, the option becomes worthless and the lender loses the option fee that he or she paid. Alternatively, a financial institution about to borrow a large amount of funds and fearing a drop in its credit rating may seek an option contract that reimburses the institution if its borrowing cost rises above some maximum amount (often determined by a maximum "base rate spread" of the risky loan rate over the riskless rate on government bonds).

Credit derivatives help to reduce default risk by shifting that risk to someone else willing to accept it for a fee. They have opened up the money and capital markets to a wider range of risky borrowers. However, this is a comparatively young financial marketplace that remains largely untested. Standardization of credit derivative contracts is under way, but many legal issues are open to controversy. Some credit-risk contracts have provisions that are vague about what represents a true default on a loan contract and, therefore, may result in confusion about what must be paid and when. Then, too, the market is still relatively small and no one is sure that it can withstand a major downturn in the economy.

A Summary of the Default Risk–Interest Rate Relationship

In summary, careful study of the relationship between default risk and interest rates points to a fundamental principle in the field of finance: *default risk and expected return are positively related.* The investor seeking higher expected returns must also be willing to accept higher risk of ruin. Default risk is correlated with both *internal* (borrower-specific) factors associated with a loan and *external* factors (especially the state of the economy and changing demands for industry products and services).

CALL PRIVILEGES AND CALL RISK

Some corporate bonds, mortgages, municipal revenue bonds, and federal government bonds carry a **call privilege.** This provision of a bond contract (indenture) grants the borrower the option to retire all or a portion of a bond issue by buying back the securities in advance of maturity. Bondholders usually are informed of a call through a notice in a newspaper of general circulation, while holders of record of registered bonds are notified directly. Normally, when the call privilege is exercised, the security issuer will pay the investor the *call price,* which equals the securities' face value plus a call penalty. The size of the *call penalty* is set forth in the indenture (contract) and generally varies inversely with the number of years remaining to maturity and the length of the call deferment period. In the case of a bond, one year's worth of coupon income is often the minimum call penalty required.

Calculating the Yields on Called Securities

Bonds may be callable immediately, or the privilege may be deferred (postponed) for a time. In the corporate sector, bonds usually are not eligible for call for a period of 5 to 10 years after issue (known as a *call deferment*) to give investors at least some protection against early redemption. Of course, calling a security in advance of its final maturity can have a significant impact on the investor's effective yield, resulting in substantial *call risk.*

To demonstrate this, we recall from Chapter 6 that the yield to maturity of any security is that discount rate, y, which equates the security's price, P, with the present value of all its future cash flows, I_t. In symbols:

$$P = \frac{I_1}{(1 + y)^1} + \frac{I_2}{(1 + y)^2} + \ldots + \frac{I_n}{(1 + y)^n} \qquad \textbf{(8–5)}$$

where n is the number of periods until maturity. Suppose that after k periods (with $k < n$), the borrower exercises the call option and redeems the security. The investor will receive the call price (C) for the security, which can be reinvested at current market interest rate, i. If the investor's planned holding period ends in time period n, the expected holding-period yield (h) can be calculated using the formula:

$$P = \frac{I_1}{(1+h)^1} + \frac{I_2}{(1+h)^2} + \ldots + \frac{I_k}{(1+h)^k} + \frac{i \times C_{k+1}}{(1+h)^{k+1}}$$
$$+ \frac{i \times C_{k+2}}{(1+h)^{k+2}} + \ldots + \frac{i \times C_n}{(1+h)^n} + \frac{C}{(1+h)^n} \qquad \text{(8–6)}$$

Using summation signs, this reduces to

$$P = \sum_{t=1}^{k} \frac{I_t}{(1+h)^t} + \sum_{t=k+1}^{n} \frac{i \times C_t}{(1+h)^t} + \frac{C}{(1+h)^n} \qquad \text{(8–7)}$$

The first term in Equation 8–7 gives the present value of all expected cash flows (*I*) from the security until it is called in time period *k*. The second term captures the present value of income received by the investor after he or she reinvests at interest rate *i* the call price (*C*) received from the security issuer. The third and final term in the equation shows the current discounted value of the call price the investor expects to receive when the holding period ends in time period *n*.

As an example, let's suppose that a corporate bond, originally offering investors an 8 percent coupon rate for 10 years and issued at $1,000 par, is called 5 years after its issue date when going market interest rates on investments of comparable risk are 6 percent. What is this bond's 10-year holding-period yield (*h*) if its call price equals par ($1,000) plus one year's worth of coupon income ($80)? We have:

$$1,000 = \sum_{t=1}^{5} \frac{\$80}{(1+h)^t} + \sum_{t=6}^{10} \frac{\$1,080 \times .06}{(1+h)^t} + \frac{\$1,080}{(1+h)^{10}} \qquad \text{(8–8)}$$

The reader, using the present value and annuity tables in the appendix, should verify that *h*, the 10-year holding-period yield, is 7.94 percent in this example.[3] Thus, the investor holding this bond received 0.06 percent *less* in yield than if the bond had *not* been called, but had instead been held to maturity.

Equation 8–7 shows clearly that the investor in callable securities encounters two major uncertainties:

1. The investor does not know if or when the securities might be called (i.e., the value of *k*).

2. The investor does not know the market yield (reinvestment rate, *i*) that might prevail at the time the security is called.

Therefore, how aggressively the investor chooses to bid for a callable instrument will depend upon:

1. The investor's expectations regarding future changes in interest rates, especially decreases in rates, during the term of the security.

2. The length of the deferment period before the security is eligible to be called.

3. The call price (par value plus call penalty) the issuer is willing to pay to redeem the security.

---

[3]Note that the middle term in Equation 8–8 may be found by first determining 10 year's worth of the $1,080 × 0.06 cash flow amount; then assume that this same cash flow occurs for just years 1 through 5; and finally, take the difference between the above two cash flows to derive the contribution made by the middle term in the equation to the bond's face (par) value.

Advantages and Disadvantages of the Call Privilege

Clearly, the call privilege (which is a type of *option*) is an advantage to the security issuer because it grants greater financial flexibility and the potential for reducing future interest costs. On the other hand, the call privilege is a distinct disadvantage to the security buyer, who may suffer a decline in expected holding-period yield if the security is called. The issuer will call in a security if the market rate of interest falls far enough so that the savings from issuing a new security at lower interest rates more than offset the call penalty plus flotation costs of a new security issue. This means, however, that the investor who is paid off will be forced to reinvest the call price in lower-yielding securities.

Another disadvantage for the investor is that call privileges limit the potential increase in a security's market price. In general, the market price of a security will not rise significantly above its call price. The reason is that the issuer can call in a security at its call price, presenting the investor with a loss equal to the difference between the prevailing market price and the call price. Thus, callable securities tend to have more limited potential for capital gains than noncallable securities.

The Call Premium and Interest Rate Expectations

For all these reasons, securities that carry a call privilege generally sell at lower prices and higher interest rates than noncallable securities. Moreover, there is an inverse relationship between the length of the call deferment period and the required rate of interest on callable securities. The longer the period of deferment and, therefore, the longer the investor is protected against early redemption and possible loss of yield, the lower the interest rate the borrower must pay. Issuers of callable securities must pay a *call premium* in the form of a higher rate of interest for the option of early redemption and for a shorter deferment period.

The key determinant of the size of the call premium is the *interest rate expectations* of investors in the marketplace. If interest rates are expected to rise, the risk that the security will be called is low. Borrowers are unlikely to call in their securities and issue new ones at a higher interest rate. As a result, the yield differential between callable and noncallable securities normally will be minimal. The same conclusions apply even if interest rates are expected to decline moderately but not enough to entice borrowers to call in already-issued securities and issue new ones.

Securities are most likely to be called when interest rates are expected to fall substantially. In this instance, security issuers can save large amounts of money—more than enough to cover the call penalty plus flotation costs of issuing new securities—by exercising the call privilege. Thus, the call premium is likely to be significant, as investors demand a higher yield on callable issues to compensate them for increased *call risk*. The yield spreads between bonds with long call deferments widen during such periods as investors come to value more highly the call deferment feature.

Research Evidence

Is there evidence of an expected *inverse* relationship between interest rate expectations and the value of the call privilege? Research studies answer in the affirmative. For example, Cook (1973) found that when interest rates are high, the call premium rises, because investors expect interest rates to fall in the future, resulting in more securities being called in. He points out that call provisions also influence yield spreads between corporate bonds, some of which have the call privilege attached, and government bonds, which generally are *not* subject to call. For example, when interest rates are expected to fall, the spread between corporate and government bond rates tends to widen. Pye (1966) and Jen and Wert (1966,

1967) found evidence that bonds carrying a call deferment have lower rates of return than bonds that are callable immediately.

Research by Kraus (1973) and others suggests that calling in bonds to save on interest costs may be a "zero sum game" between the bondholders and the stockholders of a company issuing callable bonds. Gains by stockholders (due to higher earnings from savings on interest costs) may be offset by losses for the bondholders (in the form of a lower effective holding-period yield). Generally, a call will occur when the owners of the issuing firm believe they will benefit at the expense of the firm's creditors. In an efficient market, with all participants possessing identical interest rate expectations, callable securities will sell at a price and yield just sufficient to compensate buyers for call risk. Therefore, in theory at least, management of the issuing firm should be indifferent between issuing callable or noncallable securities. Under some circumstances, however, call provisions may be beneficial to the callable security issuer where management has greater knowledge of the future course of interest rates than does the market as a whole, where a call provision prevents security holders from blocking beneficial investments that a security-issuing entity might make, or where a call privilege lowers the sensitivity of a callable security's market value to changes in interest rates. Additional research is needed to clarify more precisely who the winners and losers are likely to be from transactions involving callable securities.

In recent years, the proportion of corporate bonds issued with call privileges attached has been declining significantly. One reason is the large number of shorter bond maturities, which means that issuing companies have less need to call in their outstanding bonds before they reach maturity. Then, too, there has been a virtual explosion in new financial instruments to hedge bond issues against interest rate risk, including financial futures, options, and swaps, also reducing the need for the interest rate protection afforded by the call privilege. Finally, the yield premium associated with issuing callable bonds, rather than noncallable bonds, appears to have increased over the years, discouraging many corporations from issuing bonds bearing a call feature.

PREPAYMENT RISK AND THE INTEREST RATES ON LOAN-BACKED SECURITIES

A newer form of risk affecting the relative interest rates confronting modern investors arises when they acquire so-called *loan-backed securities,* such as mortgage passthroughs, collateralized mortgage obligations (CMOs), auto-loan-backed securities, and credit-card-backed securities. These instruments are usually created when a lending institution, such as a bank or mortgage company, removes a group of similar loans from its balance sheet and places them with a trustee (such as a security dealer) who, using the loans as collateral, sells securities to raise new capital for the lending institution. Each of these securities derives its value from the income-earning potential of the pool of loans that backs the securities. As the loans in the pool generate interest and principal payments, these payments flow through to holders of the loan-backed securities.

Unlike ordinary bonds, which usually pay nothing but interest until they finally reach maturity, loan-backed securities pay their purchasers a stream of income that includes *both* repayments of loan principal and interest. In this case, the purchaser may receive higher-than-expected repayments of principal early in the life of the pooled loans, possibly lowering his or her expected return from loan-backed securities. Investors in those loan-backed securities that carry substantial **prepayment risk** will demand higher yields to compensate them for the risk associated with early prepayment of the loans backing the securities they hold.

Prepayment risk is especially troublesome for investors purchasing securities that are backed by pools of home mortgage loans. The pool of loans serving as collateral for these securities generally consists of 25- and 30-year loans to purchase new homes. Many of these home loans will be retired early due to: (1) *refinancing of loans,* as homeowners try to get new, cheaper mortgage loans in order to lower their monthly mortgage payments as market interest rates fall; and (2) *home-owner turnover,* as families move and need to sell their homes or simply default on their loans.

The investor interested in purchasing loan-backed securities needs to make certain assumptions about the likely prepayment behavior of the loans in the pool in order to decide what the true value of the loan-backed securities must be. Each package of pooled loans would have somewhat different characteristics due to variations in loan quality and location, the condition of the economy, and other factors. The current value of a loan-backed security can be determined from:

$$\begin{matrix} \text{Market value} \\ \text{(price) of} \\ \text{loan-backed} \\ \text{security} \end{matrix} = \frac{\begin{matrix}\text{Expected} \\ \text{cash flow} \\ \text{including projected} \\ \text{prepayments of} \\ \text{loans in period 1}\end{matrix}}{(1 + y/m)^1} + \frac{\begin{matrix}\text{Expected} \\ \text{cash flow} \\ \text{including projected} \\ \text{prepayments of} \\ \text{loans in period 2}\end{matrix}}{(1 + y/m)^2} + \ldots + \frac{\begin{matrix}\text{Expected} \\ \text{cash flow} \\ \text{including projected} \\ \text{prepayments of} \\ \text{loans in period n}\end{matrix}}{(1 + y/m)^{m \times n}}$$

where y is the security's yield to maturity, m is the number of times during a year that interest and principal payments occur, and n is the total number of years covered by the pooled loans. Note that each expected cash flow from a loan-backed security must be adjusted to reflect the risk that some loans will pay out early, increasing cash flows to an investor in these securities in the early years and, thus, reducing an investor's expected cash flow from these securities in later years. The greater the prepayment risk, the higher the yield tends to rise and the lower the loan-backed security's price tends to go.[4]

Questions *to Help You Study*

7. What is a *call privilege?* Why is this privilege an advantage to a security issuer and a disadvantage to a buyer of financial instruments?

8. What types of *risk* are encountered by a purchaser of callable securities?

9. What exactly is *prepayment risk?* What factors lead to an increase in prepayment risk?

10. How can a buyer of loan-backed securities reduce prepayment risk? Why would this be important?

11. What is meant by the term *event risk?* What factors appear to contribute to an increase in a corporation's stock price? A decrease in its stock price?

---

[4]Actually, the relationship between the value of a loan-backed security and changes in market interest rates is quite complicated. For example, when interest rates fall, investors in loan-backed securities will experience quicker recovery of their invested funds, as more borrowers repay their loans early and the lower interest rates increase the present value of the securities' cash flow. On the other hand, with more loans paid off early, the investor loses future interest payments that will never be received, and the funds received by the security holder will have to be reinvested at lower market interest rates, reducing future earnings from the security. Generally, a loan-backed security will fall in value when lost interest payments and reduced reinvestment income offset the benefits from quicker recovery of principal and a lower discount rate applied to future cash flows.

Management Insight   Event Risk—Another Risk Factor Affecting Interest Rates and Security Prices

Money and capital markets research in recent years has revealed another risk factor that often affects the market value of debt and equity securities issued by corporations and other units raising funds in the money and capital markets. This so-called **event risk** factor consists of news announcements that reflect decisions by the management of a corporation or other fund-raising unit. Examples include announcements of new stock or bond offerings, increases or decreases in corporate dividend payments, stock splits, mergers and acquisitions, replacement of old with new management, new product offerings, and so forth.

Financial research suggests that announcements of events like these tend to have fairly predictable impacts on security values and borrowing costs. For example,

Event	Usual Market Response
Announcement of a new security issue	The issuer's security prices usually fall, at least temporarily.
Announcement of an increased stock dividend	The issuer's security prices usually rise, at least temporarily.
Announcement of a stock split	The issuer's security prices usually rise, at least temporarily.
Debt-equity swap (a company's bonds are replaced by stock)	The company's stock price usually falls, at least temporarily.

Many financial analysts believe that events such as the foregoing trigger changes in security prices and interest rates for the affected institutions because they convey new information about the probable future performance of these institutions. For example, the management of a business firm possesses inside (asymmetric) information on the firm's true financial condition, investment prospects, and potential earnings. Presumably, management draws on this inside information when it elects to go ahead with an event such as a new security offering, increasing or decreasing dividends paid to stockholders, launching a new product, and so forth. Investors in the financial marketplace regard the announcements of such "events" as a revelation of how management views the firm's future prospects. (For example, management may issue new stock because it wants to increase a company's future borrowing capacity.) The result is a reevaluation by investors of the value of a security issuer's stocks and bonds; the market prices and yields of those securities will change with the appearance of this new information.

Sources: See, for example, Stewart Myers and Nicholas Majluf, "Corporate Financing and Investment Decisions When Firms Have Information That Investors Do Not Have," *Journal of Financial Economics* XIII, no. 2 (1984); and Merton Miller and Kevin Bock, "Dividend Policy Under Asymmetric Information," *Journal of Finance*, 1985.

TAXATION OF SECURITY RETURNS

For information about tax policy and filling out U.S. tax forms see especially *www.federaltaxreturn.com* and *www.irs.gov*

Taxes imposed by federal, state, and local governments have a profound effect on the returns earned by investors on financial assets. The income from most securities—interest or dividends and capital gains—is subject to taxation at the federal level and by many state and local governments as well. Government uses its taxing power to encourage the purchase of certain financial assets and, thereby, redirect the flow of savings and investment toward areas of critical social need.

In 1986, the U.S. Congress enacted the Tax Reform Act, which resulted in major changes in personal and business tax rates in the United States, with major redistributive effects on the financial markets, the supply of savings, and the demand for loanable funds. Further changes were made in the federal tax code in 1990 and 1993 as the result of budget compromises between the president and Congress. The 1986 Tax Reform Law had reduced both personal and corporate tax rates; however, tax rates on high-income individuals and corporations went up again during the 1990s. Capital gains tax rates (previously as low as 20 percent) were first increased, and then late in the 1990s were scaled back with passage of the so-called 1997 Taxpayer Relief Act, which was designed to stimulate additional saving and investment. As a result, the longest-held investments faced considerably lower capital gains tax rates. For example, short-term capital gains on assets held less than one year were to be taxed at the individual investor's ordinary marginal income tax bracket rate, which at the time could range as high as 39.6 percent for those with the highest taxable incomes. For example, a top-tax-bracket investor, buying the stock of XYZ Corporation for $1,900 and later selling it during the same year for $3,100, would experience a taxable short-term gain of $1,200. This top-income-earner would have incurred a tax liability of $1,200 × 0.396, or $475.20.

However, long-term capital gains received after holding an asset for at least 18 months could be assessed no more than a 20 percent tax rate (and for assets held more than 12 months but less than 18 months, a maximum of 28 percent) up through the year 2000. After the year 2000, long-term capital gains tax rates were set at a maximum of only 18 percent. Thus, the top-bracket taxpayer who previously owed $475.20 on the $1,200 gain described above then faced a maximum tax of only $1,200 × 0.18, or $216.00, if the $1,200 gain was a long-term capital gain. For investors in one of the lowest positive income tax brackets (15 percent) the capital gains rate would be as small as only 8 percent of any long-term gains scored by these taxpayers.

The Taxpayer Relief Act of 1997 also endeavored to encourage individuals and families to save more by awarding tax exemptions to people (1) selling their homes; (2) setting aside savings for a college education; (3) buying a new home; (4) preparing for retirement; or (5) who might die with substantial accumulations of retirement savings left over and wish to pass more of those savings along to surviving loved ones or to other individuals or institutions. Estate taxes were substantially lowered, allowing tax-free transfers of up to a million dollars to a deceased person's beneficiaries by the year 2006.

Then, in the spring of 2001 the latest major U.S. tax legislation—The Economic Growth and Tax Relief Reconciliation Act—was passed by Congress and signed into law by President George W. Bush. This sweeping new law was aimed at stimulating the economy and encouraging saving by lowering the tax rates carried by households (individuals and families) and allowing greater use of retirement and educational savings instruments (such as IRAs and Keoghs) than in the past. Among other major changes, the new tax bill created a new low 10 percent tax bracket and gradually adjusted other income tax rates downward, increased the permissible tax credit for children, and called for a phaseout of estate taxes to be completed in the year 2010. However, most of these changes were stretched out over the first decade of the twentieth century and the Tax Relief Act contained an unusual "sunset provision" which mandated that all the new law's provisions will expire on December 31, 2010. Congress and the president must bring forward new legislation no later than the year 2010 in order to continue the tax reforms brought about by this newest federal tax law.

Treatment of Capital Losses

For further discussion of the latest U.S. tax law see, for example, such sources as *www.tax planet.com/prez* and *www. taxes.about.com*

Net losses on investments in financial assets are deductible for tax purposes within well-defined limits. For the individual taxpayer, a net capital loss is deductible up to the amount of the capital loss, the size of ordinary income, or $3,000, whichever is smaller. For example, suppose an investor experiences a net loss on securities held and then sold of $8,000. Suppose this person receives other taxable income of $20,000. How much of the capital loss can be deducted? What is this taxpayer's total taxable income? The maximum loss deduction in this case is $3,000, and therefore the taxpayer's net taxable income is $17,000 ($20,000 minus the $3,000 in deductible losses). Current federal law allows the taxpayer to carry forward into subsequent years the remaining portion of the loss ($5,000 in this example) until all of the loss has been deducted from ordinary income, but the loss cannot be carried backward.

Tax-Exempt Securities

One of the most controversial tax rules affecting securities is the tax-exemption privilege granted investors in state and local government (municipal) bonds. The interest income earned on municipal bonds is exempt from federal income taxes.[5] **Tax-exempt securities** represent a subsidy to induce investors to support local government by financing the construction of schools, highways, airports, and other needed public projects. The exemption privilege shifts the burden of federal taxation from buyers of municipal bonds to other taxpayers.

What investors benefit from buying municipals? The critical factor here is the marginal tax rate (tax bracket) of the investor—the tax rate he or she must pay on the last dollar of income received during the tax year. For individual investors, these marginal tax rates range from zero for nontaxpayers to as high as about 39 percent for the highest income-earning couples, though by 2006 this top tax bracket will be reduced to just 35 percent (see Exhibit 8–5 for an example of recent tax rates for individuals and corporations). The marginal tax rate for corporations is 15 percent on the first $50,000 in taxable profits up to as high as 39 percent on net income above $100,000 to $335,000 and up to 38 percent for corporations earning $15 million to about $18⅓ million annually. In recent years, marginal tax rates of approximately 20 to 30 percent have represented a break-even level for investors interested in municipal bonds. Investors carrying marginal tax rates above this range often receive higher after-tax yields from buying tax-exempt securities instead of taxable securities. Below this range, taxable securities often yield a better after-tax return.

The Effect of Marginal Tax Rates on After-Tax Yields

To illustrate the importance of knowing the investor's marginal tax rate in deciding whether to purchase tax-exempt assets, consider the following example. Assume the current yield to maturity on taxable corporate bonds is 12 percent, while the current tax-exempt yield on municipal bonds of comparable quality and rating is 9 percent. The after-tax yield on these two securities can be compared using the following formula:

$$\text{Before-tax yield } (1 - \text{Investor's marginal tax rate}) = \text{After-tax yield} \quad \textbf{(8–9)}$$

For example, for an investor in the 27.5 percent tax bracket (see Exhibit 8–5), the after-tax yields on these bonds are as follows:

Taxable Corporate Bond	Tax-Exempt Municipal Bond
12% (1 − 0.275) = 8.70%	9% before and after taxes

On the basis of yield alone, the investor in the 27.5 percent tax bracket would prefer the tax-exempt municipal bond.[6]

[5]Although the interest income from municipals is federal income tax exempt, capital gains on municipals are generally taxable as ordinary income. In addition, most states do not tax income from their own bonds or from the bonds issued by local governments within their borders. Income from U.S. government securities is usually exempt from state and local taxes but not from federal taxes.
[6]The particular tax brackets favoring the purchase of municipals versus taxable securities change over time due to changes in tax laws and variations in the yield spread between taxable and tax-exempt securities.

EXHIBIT 8–5   Examples of Recent Marginal Federal Income Tax Rates (Individual and Corporate Tax Brackets Shown)

INCOME TAX BRACKETS AND TAX RATES FOR SINGLE AND MARRIED TAXPAYERS: (Effective January 1, 2001)			INCOME TAX BRACKETS AND TAX RATES FOR CORPORATIONS PAYING TAXES: (Effective January 1, 2000)		
Single Taxpayers' Taxable Incomes	Married Taxpayers' Taxable Incomes	Marginal Tax Brackets (percent)	Taxable Income Bracket	Base Amount Owed	Marginal Tax Rate Applied to Excess over Base
$ 0–6,000	$ 0–12,000	10%	Less than $50,000	$ 0	15%
$ 6,000–27,050	$ 12,000–45,200	15	$50,000–$75,000	$ 7,500	25
$ 27,050–65,550	$ 45,200–109,250	27.5	$75,000–$100,000	$ 13,750	34
$ 65,550–136,750	$109,250–166,500	30.5	$100,000–$335,000	$ 22,250	39
$136,750–297,350	$166,500–297,350	35.5	$335,000–$10 million	$113,900	34
$297,350 and over	$297,350 and over	39.1	$10 million–$15 million	$3.4 million	35
			$15 million–$18.33⅓million	$5.15 million	38
			Over $18.33⅓ million	$6.416⅔ million	35

Source: U.S. Treasury Department

How would an individual figure his or her income tax? Suppose you are single and have taxable annual income (that is, gross income receipts less all exemptions and deductions allowable under tax law) of $30,000. Then you would owe:

Base amount owed	+	Excess income above preceding tax bracket × Marginal tax rate
$3,600	+	($30,000 − $27,050) × 0.275, or
$3,600	+	$811.25
	=	$4,411.25 in total federal income taxes owed

What about a corporation? Suppose the company had annual net income (earnings) before taxes of $250,000. Then the company would owe federal taxes in the amount of:

Base amount owed	+	Excess earnings above preceding tax bracket × Marginal tax rate
$22,250	+	($250,000 − $100,000) × 0.39, or
$22,250	+	$19,500
	=	$41,750 in taxes owed

Note: The tax rates given above applied in 2000 and 2001. However, the taxable individual income brackets shown change each year as the inflation rate moves because the federal tax structure in the United States is indexed to inflation in order to at least partially prevent taxpayers from paying higher and higher taxes due solely to rising prices for goods and services. The above marginal tax rates do not reflect the Social Security Program's tax structure which stands at 6.2 percent for up to $62,700 of annual earned income or 12.4 percent for a self-employed individual. There is also a 1.45 percent Medicare payroll tax levy against all of a person's annual earned income and, if you are self-employed, this Medicare tax rate jumps to 2.9 percent of annual earned income.

At what rate would an investor be *indifferent* as to whether securities are taxable or tax exempt? In other words, what is the break-even point between these two types of financial instruments?

This point is easily calculated from the formula

$$\text{Tax-exempt yield} = (1 - t) \times \text{Taxable yield} \qquad \textbf{(8–10)}$$

where t is the investor's marginal tax rate. Solving for the break-even tax rate gives

Financial Developments Selected Provisions of the 2001 Economic Growth and Tax Relief Reconciliation Act

- A new 10 percent personal income tax rate is created applying to the first $6,000 in taxable income for an individual taxpayer or the first $12,000 earned by a married couple filing jointly.

- The highest income tax bracket for U.S. personal taxpayers will decrease from 39.6 percent in the year 2000 to 35 percent by 2006.

- In order to boost saving by individuals and families for educational purposes the permissible annual contribution into Educational IRA accounts will rise from $500 to $2,000. Beginning in 2002 parents or guardians can make withdrawals from state-sponsored educational savings plans (so-called 529 programs) that are free of federal tax liabilities when used to cover the costs of education.

- In order to better prepare for their future retirement individuals will be allowed to contribute up to $3,000 to Individual Retirement Accounts (IRAs) in 2002 and gradually increase their annual contributions to these retirement accounts up to $5,000 in 2008.

- Individuals with employer or business-related retirement plans (Keoghs or 401ks) can increase their annual contri-

butions to these retirement plans from $10,500 in 2001 to, eventually, $15,000 by the year 2006.

- Estate taxes will be phased out over the next 10 years and will have a tax rate of zero in 2010.

- Unless Congress and the president renew the above provisions and bring forward new tax laws no later than December 31, 2010, all the foregoing provisions will disappear in the year 2011. The old U.S. tax structure will then be reactivated in the absence of any new legislation that might appear.

Changing Tax Bracket Rates under the 2001 Economic Growth and Tax Relief Reconciliation Act

2001	2002–03	2004–05	2006–10
39.1%	38 6%	37.6%	35.0%
35.5	35.0	34.0	33.0
30.5	30.0	29.0	28.0
27.5	27.0	26.0	25.0
15.0	15.0	15.0	15.0
10.0	10.0	10.0	10.0

Source: U.S. Treasury Department.

$$t = 1 - \frac{\text{Tax-exempt yield}}{\text{Taxable yield}} \qquad \textbf{(8–11)}$$

Clearly, if the current yield on tax-exempt securities is 8 percent and 10 percent on taxable issues, the break-even tax rate is $1 - 0.80$, or 20 percent. An investor in a marginal tax bracket *above* 20 percent would prefer the yield on a tax-exempt security to a taxable one at these prevailing interest rates, other factors held equal.

Comparing Taxable and Tax-Exempt Securities

The Bond Market Association provides a free online calculator to aid investors to compare tax-exempt bond yields with yields on taxable securities at *www. investinginbonds.com*

The existence of both taxable and tax-exempt securities complicates the investor's task in trying to choose a suitable portfolio to buy and hold. To make valid comparisons between taxable and tax-exempt issues, the taxed investor must convert all expected yields to an *after-tax basis*.

In the case of the yield to maturity on a security, this can be done by using the following formula:

$$P_0 = \sum_{i=1}^{n} \frac{I_i(1-t)}{(1+a)^i} + \frac{(P_n - P_0)(1-t)}{(1+a)^n} + \frac{P_0}{(1+a)^n} \qquad \textbf{(8–12)}$$

which equates the current market value (P_0) of the security to the present value of all after-tax returns promised in the future. If the security is to be held for n years, I_i is the amount of interest or other income expected each year, and t is the marginal income tax rate of the investor. If we assume the security will be sold or redeemed for price P_n at maturity, then ($P_n - P_0$) measures the expected capital gain on the instrument, which will be taxed at the taxpayer's ordinary income tax rate—let's say about 27 percent under the most recent U.S. tax laws. Provided investors know their marginal income tax rate, the current price of the security, and the expected distribution of future income from the security, they can easily calculate discount rate a—the after-tax yield to maturity.

For example, consider the case of a $1,000 corporate bond selling for $900 (with par value of $1,000), maturing in 10 years, with a 10 percent coupon rate. If an investor in the 27 percent federal income tax bracket buys and holds the bond to maturity, her after-tax yield, a, could be found from evaluating the following:

$$\$900 = \sum_{i=1}^{10} \frac{\$100(1 - 0.27)}{(1 + a)^i} + \frac{(\$1,000 - \$900)(1 - 0.18)}{(1 + a)^{10}} + \frac{\$900}{(1 + a)^{10}}$$

In this instance, the reader should verify, using the annuity and present value tables at the back of this book, that the after-tax yield, a, is 8.38 percent, assuming an 18 percent capital gains tax rate.

Certainly, the tax-exempt privilege has lowered the interest rates at which municipals can be sold in the open market relative to taxable bonds and, therefore, the amount of interest costs borne by local taxpayers. For example, in January 2002, municipal bonds carried an average yield to maturity of about 5.20 percent, compared to 6.87 percent on comparable quality (taxable) corporate bonds—a yield spread of close to 2 percentage points. However, the primary beneficiaries of the exemption privilege are investors who can profitably purchase municipals and escape some portion of the federal tax burden. Other taxpayers must pay higher federal taxes in order to make up for those lost tax revenues. By limiting the municipal market to these high tax-bracket investors, the tax-exempt feature has probably increased the volatility of municipal bond interest rates and made the job of fiscal management for state and local governments more difficult.

CONVERTIBLE SECURITIES

Another factor that affects relative rates of return on different securities is **convertibility.** Convertible securities consist of special issues of corporate bonds or preferred stock that entitle the holder to exchange these securities for a specific number of shares of the issuing firm's common stock. Convertibles are frequently called *hybrid securities* because they offer the investor the prospect of stable income in the form of interest or dividends plus capital gains on common stock once conversion occurs. The timing of a conversion is usually at the option of the investor. However, an issuing firm often can "force" conversion of its securities by either calling them in or by encouraging a rise in the price of its common stock (such as by announcing a merger offer) because conversion is most likely in a rising market.

Recent growth of convertible securities has led to the appearance of many new Web sites discussing convertibles. One example is *www.convertbond.com*

Investors generally pay a premium for convertible securities over nonconvertible securities in the form of a higher price. Thus, convertibles will carry a lower rate of return than other securities of comparable quality and maturity issued by the same company. This occurs because the investor in convertibles is granted a hedge against future risk. If security prices fall, the investor still earns a fixed rate of return in the form of interest income from a convertible bond or dividend income from convertible preferred stock. On the other hand, if stock prices rise, the investor can exercise his or her option and share in any capital gains earned on the company's common stock.

Convertible bonds offer several significant advantages to the company that decides to issue them. Due to the conversion feature, they can be issued at a lower net interest cost than conventional (nonconvertible) bonds. Convertibles offer an alternative to issuing more common stock, which a firm may wish to avoid because additional stock could dilute the equity interest of current stockholders and reduce earnings per share. Dividends on stock are not deductible from federal income taxes, but interest on convertible bonds *is* a tax-deductible expense.

Key advantages to the investor include the fact that convertible bonds guarantee the payment of interest and generally appreciate in value when the company's common stock is also rising in price. Moreover, there is a floor under the price of a convertible bond—known as its *investment value*—below which its price normally will not fall. This is the price that would produce a yield on the convertible equal to the yield on nonconvertible bonds of the same quality. However, investors are often counseled by financial analysts not to buy convertibles unless they would be happy holding the issuing company's stock, because the issuer may call in the securities early, forcing conversion. This situation may present the investor with a substantially reduced rate of return.

THE STRUCTURE OF INTEREST RATES

As we conclude this chapter, it is important to gain some perspective on the fundamental purpose of this section of the book. In reality, Chapters 5, 6, 7, and 8 should be viewed as a unit, tied together by a common subject: what determines the level of and changes in interest rates and asset yields. In Chapter 5, we argued that there is *one* interest rate that underlies all interest rates and is a component of all rates. This is the *risk-free* (or pure) rate of interest, which is a measure of the opportunity cost of holding cash and a measure of the reward for saving rather than spending all of our income on consumption. All other interest rates are scaled upward by varying degrees from the risk-free rate, depending on such factors as inflation, the term (maturity) of a loan, the risk of borrower default, the risk of prepayment, and the marketability, liquidity, convertibility, and tax status of the securities to which those rates apply.

There is, then, a structure to interest rates whose foundation is the risk-free rate (as determined by the demand and supply for loanable funds described in Chapter 5). Perhaps one picture of that **interest rate structure** is worth a thousand words. Recently, the yield to maturity on long-term U.S. Treasury bonds was reported as close to 5.75 percent, while corporate Baa bonds were quoted at an average yield of about 7.60 percent. As Exhibit 8–6 indicates, each of these rates, like *all* interest rates, is a summation of rewards (premiums) paid to lenders of funds to get those investors to hold a particular security. Each reward or premium is merely compensation for bearing some kind of *risk,* for example: (1) the risk of giving up liquidity and accepting greater price risk from buying a longer maturity security, (2) the risk of inflation over the term of a security, (3) the risk that the borrower will default on some or all of his promised payments, (4) the risk that some securities can be called in before they mature and the investor may have to reinvest her money at a lower interest rate, and (5) the risk of taking on a security with a weak resale market (low marketability). Each interest rate or yield that we see in today's market is the *sum* of all of these risk premium factors plus the real risk-free interest rate. And when interest rates change, that change may be due to a change in the risk-free rate or to a change in any of the risk premium factors cited above.

EXHIBIT 8–6

An Example of the Structure of Interest Rates in the Financial System

Source: Bond rates derived from *Federal Reserve Bulletin*, November 2001, Table 1.35; interest-rate components estimated by the author.

During the month of January 2002:
The long-term
U.S. Treasury bond rate averaged 5.75% + 1.85% = 7.60%

while the Corporate Baa bond rate averaged:

Estimated components of the rate on long-term U.S. Treasury bonds		
Rate premium for buying long-term security rather than short-term security	Liquidity premium	+0.75%
Rate premium for inflation risk	Expected inflation	+2.00%
Rate premium for forgoing consumption and saving money	Risk-free real rate of interest	+3.00%
	Total	5.75%

Estimated components of the rate or yield spread between corporate Baa bond rate and long-term Treasury bond rate		
Rate premium for accepting less marketable security	Premium for lower marketability	+0.35%
Rate premium for accepting risk security might be called	Call risk premium	+0.25%
Rate premium for accepting risk of borrower default	Default risk premium	+1.25%
	Total	1.85%

Truly, interest rates are a complex phenomenon, affected by many factors. We need to keep this complexity in mind as we proceed to the next chapter and take on the difficult task of trying to anticipate and forecast interest rate changes and discover how to hedge against possible losses due to interest rate movements.

Questions *to Help You Study*

12. What types of securities and other financial instruments are most favored by tax laws?

13. What portion of the income generated by municipal bonds is considered tax-exempt and what portion is taxable income? Why do you think United States' laws are structured in this way?

14. Explain the relationship between a taxpayer's marginal tax rate and the after-tax rates of return on corporate and municipal bonds. Would municipals be a worthwhile investment for you today? Please explain why or why not.

15. What does *convertibility* refer to in Finance? Why are convertibles sometimes called hybrid securities?

16. Convertibles typically carry lower yields than nonconvertibles of the same maturity and risk class. Can you explain why?

17. What do we mean by the term *interest rate structure?* What does the structure of interest rates tell us about the difficulties involved in trying to forecast movements in interest rates?

Summary of the Chapter

This chapter has focused our attention upon multiple factors that cause interest rates or yields to differ between one type of financial asset and another. Its special target has been such rate-determining elements as marketability, liquidity, default risk, call privileges, and taxation.

Among the principal conclusions of the chapter are the following:

- *Marketability,* or the capacity to be sold readily, is positively related to an asset's price and negatively related to its rate of return or yield. More marketable financial instruments generally carry lower rates of return or lower yields.

- *Liquid* financial instruments also tend to carry lower yields, but possess the advantages of ready marketability, stable price, and reversibility (i.e., the capacity to fully recover the funds originally invested in an asset).

- *Default risk*—the danger that a borrower will not make all promised payments at agreed-upon times—typically results in the promised yields of risky securities rising above the yields on riskless financial instruments. Potential buyers of these instruments compare their estimated (subjective) probability of loss from a risky security to the market's assigned default-risk premium. If a potential buyer anticipates less risk of loss than suggested by the market's assigned risk premium he or she will tend to purchase the financial instrument in question because its risky yield appears to be too high and its price too low (i.e., the security in question looks like a bargain). Conversely, a potential purchaser expecting greater probability of loss due to default than the market's assigned risk premium will tend to avoid or sell such an instrument because its price seems too high and its yield too low for the amount of risk involved.

- Default-risk premiums attached by the financial marketplace to the promised yields on risky securities tend to be heavily influenced by the *credit ratings* assigned by various credit rating agencies (such as Moody's Investors Service or Standard & Poor's Corporation) and by the condition of the economy. An expanding economy tends to result in lower default-risk premiums, while an economy trapped in a recession with rising business bankruptcies tends to generate higher default-risk premiums on risky securities.

- Many lower-rated companies with questionable credit ratings began to issue speculative or *junk bonds* in large quantities during the 1980s and 1990s. The rapid rise of junk bonds broadened the market for corporate bonds greatly, offering participating investors substantially higher yields than were previously available.

- Debt securities with *call privileges* attached tend to carry higher promised rates of return than financial instruments not bearing a call privilege. The right of a security issuer to call away the security he or she has previously issued and retire it in return for paying a prespecified price gives borrowers greater flexibility in adapting their capital structure to changing economic and financial conditions. Most recently, call privileges have been declining in use as corporate borrowers have discovered other ways of protecting their financial structure and sources of funds.

- The rapid growth of *loan-backed securities* (such as mortgage-backed instruments) has given rise to *prepayment risk.* This is the danger that loans used to back loan-backed securities may be paid back early, lowering an investor's expected yield from these loan-backed instruments. The rapid expansion of loan-backed security issues has made prepayment risk more important with time. Issuers of these instruments have sought to make them more attractive to buyers by such devices as creating different maturity classes so that potential buyers can select how much prepayment risk they are willing to take on.

- *Event risk* has long been a potentially significant factor in the pricing of corporate stock and debt securities. Among the *events* that appear to have an especially significant impact upon corporate security values include announcements of new security issues, stock dividends, stock splits, and management changes within a particular business firm.

- Financial assets generate interest or dividend payments and capital gains or losses—any or all of which may be subject to *taxation* at federal and state levels. Investors, therefore, must be cognizant of changes in tax laws and regulations. It is also important to be able to calculate tax-exempt yields versus taxable returns from financial assets because some financial instruments (such as municipal bonds) generate tax-exempt income and some investing institutions (such as credit unions and pension funds) are tax-exempt investors.

- Some corporate debt and stock instruments carry a *convertibility* feature which allows them to be exchanged for a certain number of shares of common stock. These are often called "hybrid securities" because they offer not only relatively stable or guaranteed income (interest payments or fixed dividends) but also the prospect of substantial capital gains when once converted into common stock. Thus, financial instruments with convertibility features attached tend to sell at a higher price and a lower promised yield due to their potential for exceptional capital gains upon conversion.

- Finally, the chapter closes with an overview of the *interest rate structure* model which aids us in understanding why there are so many different interest rates in the real world. Each different interest rate or yield is viewed in this model as the sum of the risk-free interest rate plus a series of risk premia dependent on the different degrees of risk exposure of each financial instrument. Among the possible risk premiums included in this model are liquidity and term (or maturity) risk, inflation risk, default risk, call risk, and exposure to tax risk. Because any of these risk premia can change at any time, interest rates themselves may change at any time and the causes of any interest-rate movement can be very complex.

Key Terms

Marketability, *204*
Liquidity, *205*
Default risk, *206*
Expected yield, *207*

Junk bonds, *211*
Call privilege, *216*
Prepayment risk, *219*
Event risk, *221*

Tax-exempt securities, *223*
Convertibility, *226*
Interest rate structure, *227*

Problems

1. In a recent Federal Reserve publication, the following market interest rates or yields were reported:

Three-month Treasury bills	7.62%
One-year Treasury bills	7.40
Five-year Treasury bonds	8.33

Long-term Treasury bonds	8.64
Corporate Baa bonds	10.20
Aaa municipal bonds	9.24

Calculate the difference in percentage points and basis points between these rates. Explain the rate differences you derive in terms of the factors discussed in Chapters 7 and 8.

2. The market yield to maturity on a risky bond is currently listed at 14.50 percent. The risk-free interest rate is estimated to be 9.25 percent. What is the default risk premium, all other factors removed? The promised yield on this bond is 15 percent. A certain investor, looking at this bond, estimates there is a 25 percent probability the bond will pay 15 percent at maturity, a 50 percent probability it will pay a 10 percent return, and a 25 percent probability it will yield only 5 percent. What is the bond's expected yield? What is this investor's anticipated default loss? Will the investor buy this bond?

3. A 10-year corporate bond was issued on January 1, 1999, with call privilege attached. The bond was sold to investors at $1,000 par value with a 10 percent coupon rate. The bond was called on January 1, 2002, at a call price paid to holders of par plus one year's coupon income. At the time, the prevailing market interest rate on securities of comparable quality was 8 percent. If a holder of this bond reinvested the call price at 8 percent for 7 years, calculate this investor's holding-period yield for the entire period of 10 years. How much yield did the investor lose as a result of the call?

4. Aaa-rated municipal bonds are carrying a market yield today of 5.25 percent, while Aaa rated corporate bonds have current market yields of 11.50 percent. What is the break-even tax rate that would make a taxable investor indifferent between these two types of bonds?

5. An investor purchases a 10-year U.S. government bond for $800. The bond's coupon rate is 10 percent and, at time of purchase, it still had five years remaining until maturity. If the investor holds the bond until it matures and collects the $1,000 par value from the Treasury and his marginal tax rate remains at 28 percent, what will be his after-tax yield to maturity?

6. The current market yield on U.S. Treasury bills (three-month maturities) is 5.38 percent. Investors are expecting zero inflation over the next three months, but the expected rate of long-term inflation is determined to be 2.25 percent and the long-term U.S. Treasury borrowing rate stands at 8.16 percent. The premium for accepting less marketability in a security is 25 basis points; the default risk premium for lower-grade (Baa) corporate bonds is 105 basis points, and the call risk premium is 29 basis points. Using this information and the concept of the structure of interest rates developed in this chapter, what is the liquidity premium? What is the yield on Baa corporate bonds?

7. A pool of credit-card loans is expected to pay the following stream of cash flows for each quarter of the year indicated:

Time Period	Expected Cash Flow Including Projected Prepayments
Year 1, quarter 1	$ 82 million
Year 1, quarter 2	80 million
Year 1, quarter 3	72 million
Year 1, quarter 4	60 million
Year 2, quarter 1	48 million
Year 2, quarter 2	36 million
Year 2, quarter 3	27 million
Year 2, quarter 4	18 million
Year 3, quarter 1	6 million
Year 3, quarter 2	1 million
Total expected cash flows	$430 million

If the yield to maturity on comparable quality instruments is 14 percent, what should be the market value (price) of each security issued against this particular pool of credit-card loans?

8. If the following *events* happened to Alvernon Way Corporation, what is likely to happen to the company's stock price, all other factors held constant?

   a. Alvernon retires a bond issue with the issuance of new preferred stock.

   b. Alvernon announces a dividend payment to holders of its common stock of $2.36 per share; security analysts had expected a dividend of $2.45 per share.

   c. Alvernon is selling 270,000 new shares of common stock today.

   d. Alvernon Class A common stock shares, currently priced at $140 per share, are splitting 2 for 1 next week.

   e. Alvernon announces the development and marketing of a new medical device that promises significant relief for persons suffering from severe arthritis and stiffness of the joints.

   f. Six weeks after receiving her largest salary bonus in history, Alvernon's chief operating officer announced early retirement today due to family and medical problems.

   g. Alvernon has just been sued in federal court by the U.S. Department of Justice for alleged price fixing and antitrust violations.

9. Please identity the term or concept described by each of the phrases or sentences listed below.

   a. Capacity of a loan or security to find a market where it can be sold quickly.

   b. Stable value with little risk of loss on resale of a financial asset.

   c. Potential for missing some promised debt repayments.

   d. Weighted average return on a risky security.

   e. Corporate debt rated below investment grade.

   f. A bond may be repurchased and retired early by the borrower.

   g. Expected yield falls as some loans in a pool are paid off ahead of schedule.

   h. Probability that the changing environment inside a borrowing entity impacts the market's assessment of the value of its financial instruments.

   i. Ordinary interest income is not subject to taxation.

   j. Investor is granted privilege under certain circumstances to trade securities he or she holds for common stock.

   k. Any market interest rate includes risk premia.

Questions about the Web and the Money and Capital Markets

1. How does risk in its various forms appear to affect the relative prices and interest rates on bonds in the United States? In other parts of the world?

2. If you wanted to measure the risk structure of interest rates at any moment in time, where could you go on the Web to get the data you needed?

3. How does the tax structure appear to affect the relative sizes and changes in interest rates? Where on the Web can you find information about how the taxation of securities affects their value and relative interest rates?

4. Is a corporation's credit rating related to its performance, especially to its profitability, stock price, or growth of sales revenue net of expenses? Select several companies with different credit ratings from a database on the Web (such as Standard and Poor's Market Insight, Educational Version) to see if such a relationship exists. Can you explain why or why not?

Selected References

Cantor, Richard, and Frank Packer. "Municipal Ratings and Credit Standards: Differences of Opinion in the Credit Rating Industry." Staff Report no. 12, Federal Reserve Bank of New York, April 1996.

Cook, Timothy Q. "Some Factors Affecting Long-Term Yield Spreads in Recent Years." *Monthly Review,* Federal Reserve Bank of Richmond, September 1973, pp. 2–14.

Ederington, L. H.; J. B. Yawitz; and B. E. Roberts. "The Informational Content of Bond Ratings." *Journal of Financial Research* 10 (Fall 1987), pp. 211–26.

Fisher, Lawrence. "Determinants of Risk Premiums on Corporate Bonds." *Journal of Political Economy,* June 1959, pp. 217–37.

Fons, Jerome S. "An Approach to Forecasting Default Rates." *Moody's Special Report,* August 1991.

Fons, J. "Using Default Rates to Model the Term Structure of Credit Risk." *Financial Analysts Journal* L (1994), pp. 25–32.

Helwege, Jean, and Paul Kleimen. "Understanding Aggregate Default Rates of High Yield Bonds." *Current Issues in Economics and Finance.* Federal Reserve Bank of New York, May 1996, pp. 1–6.

Helwege, Jean, and Christopher M. Turner. "The Slope of the Credit Yield Curve for Speculative-Grade Issuers." Research Paper no. 9725, Federal Reserve Bank of New York, August 1997.

Holthausen, Robert W., and Richard W. Leftwich. "The Effect of Bond Rating Changes on Common Stock Prices." *Journal of Financial Economics* 17 (1986), pp. 57–89.

Jen, Frank C., and James E. Wert. "The Value of the Deferred Call Privilege." *The National Banking Review,* March 1966, pp. 269–78.

———. "The Effect of Call Risk on Corporate Bond Yields." *Journal of Finance,* December 1967, pp. 637–51.

Kraus, Alan. "The Bond Refunding Decision in an Efficient Market." *Journal of Financial and Quantitative Analysis* 8, no. 5 (1973).

Pye, Gordon. "The Value of the Call Option on a Bond." *Journal of Political Economy,* April 1966, pp. 200–5.

Rose, Peter S. *Commercial Bank Management.* New York: McGraw-Hill, 5th ed., 2001.

Scott, James. "The Probability of Bankruptcy: A Comparison of Empirical Predictions and Theoretical Models." *Journal of Banking and Finance* 5 (1981), pp. 317–44.

Wheelock, David C. "Inflation and Quality Spreads." *Monetary Trends,* Federal Reserve Bank of St. Louis, November 1997.

Chapter **Nine**

Interest-Rate Forecasting and Hedging: Swaps, Financial Futures, and Options

Learning Objectives in This Chapter

- You will see the possible benefits, but also the challenging problems someone faces when they attempt to forecast market interest rates.

- You will discover why financial analysts today usually choose hedging against losses from changing interest rates rather than attempting to forecast interest rates or the prices of financial assets (such as stocks and bonds).

- You will explore several of the most popular tools currently in use to protect borrowers and lenders from losses due to movements in market interest rates, including interest-rate swaps, financial futures, and option contracts.

What's in This Chapter? Key Topics Outline

The Business Cycle and Interest Rates

Seasonal Pressures on Interest Rates

Interest-Rate Forecasting: Advantages, Problems, Possible Approaches

Interest-Rate Hedging with Swaps: Features and Examples

Financial Futures Contracts: Types, Trading Hedges, and Their Effects

Option Contracts: Possible Payoffs and Profits

Derivatives: Their Costs and Risks

INTRODUCTION

In this section of the book, we have looked, thus far, at several of the most important factors that cause interest rates and asset prices to change over time. Included in our survey have been such powerful rate- and price-determining factors as savings, investment demand, inflation, default risk, taxes, call features, and marketability. Yet even this impressive list of influential factors does not account for all of the changes in interest rates and asset prices we observe daily in the real world. Political developments at home and abroad, changes in government policy, changes in corporate earnings and business conditions, announcements of new security offerings, and thousands of other bits of information flood the money and capital markets daily and bring about fluctuations in interest rates and asset prices. In fact, for actively traded assets, demand and supply forces are continually shifting, minute by minute, so that investors interested in these assets must constantly stay abreast of the latest developments in the financial marketplace.

INTEREST-RATE FORECASTING[1]

For many decades some economists and financial analysts believed that it was possible to forecast (predict) market interest rates and perhaps the prices of financial assets (such as stocks and bonds) as well. What an advantage this would bring to the correct forecaster! For example, if you knew when interest rates were likely to be the lowest, you could wait for that low point and borrow more cheaply. Likewise, if you knew when stock and bond prices were going to rise, you could position yourself in the market to make a great deal of money.

The Business Cycle and Seasonality

To understand how business cycles are defined in the United States see the National Bureau of Economic Research at www.nber.org/

Moreover, there seemed to be some basis for this belief in interest-rate forecasting. For example, economists often point out that market interest rates frequently follow the **business cycle**—the pattern of expansion (boom) and contraction (recession) periods in the economy. (See Exhibit 9–1.) *Market interest rates tend to rise when the economy is expanding toward its peak or highest point and fall when the economy is contracting toward the trough of a recession or its lowest point.* This is particularly true for short-term interest rates, which tend to move rapidly up or down with the business cycle, while long-term interest rates change more gradually and follow the business cycle less closely.[2] (See Exhibit 9–2)

---

[1] Portions of this section are based on Rose's earlier article in *Canadian Banker* (1984) and are used with the permission of that journal.

[2] We should note that this difference in the speed of up and down movements in long-term versus short-term market interest rates means that *yield curves* (discussed in Chapter 7) also tend to change with the business cycle. In particular, yield curves tend to slope upward (with long-term interest rates higher than short-term rates) during periods of economic expansion and tend to slope downward (with higher short-term than long-term interest rates) in a recession. This implies that yield curves *may* have some forecasting power in predicting changes in the economy.

Another interesting aspect of long-term versus short-term interest rate behavior is that the market *prices* of longer-term assets tend to be more volatile than the market *prices* of shorter-term assets. Thus, the maturity-asset price volatility relationship tends to be opposite that of the maturity-interest rate relationship. Investors in longer-term financial instruments usually face greater risk of capital loss (increased *principal risk)* due to price fluctuations than do investors in shorter-term assets. Of course, the investor in longer-term assets has the offsetting advantage of generally receiving a more stable rate of return (reduced *income risk)* than is true for investors in shorter-term assets.

Markets on the Net

Numerous sites on the World Wide Web publish their own forecasts of interest rates and asset prices. Examples include the Federal Reserve Bank of Philadelphia's Livingston survey (at *www.phil.frb.org/*) which issues forecasts of a wide range of both short-term and long-term interest rates and the economy and Stock Market Index Forecasts (at *http://www.stock-forecast.com*), which attempts to predict broad movements in equity price indices for a subscription fee. As always, with the great difficulties that exist in achieving consistently correct forecasts, readers are cautioned in relying upon sites like these. If you are interested in interest-rate forecasting it is wise to examine several different forecasts from a variety of professional sources.

Interest-rate hedging tools also appear extensively on the Web. Many of these Web sites represent advertising by firms and professional consultants who advise investors exposed to interest-rate and asset price risk. Other hedging sites explain how various hedging tools may be used. One prominent example is Derivatives Concepts A-Z (at *www.finpipe.com*).

Information on trading financial futures and options and on how to use these financial instruments to combat investment risks has blossomed on the World Wide Web in recent years. One of the most interesting routes to pursue on the Web is to tour major futures and options exchanges. All have Web sites and invite the public as well as practioners to take a look. Examples of prominent exchange Web sites include the Chicago Mercantile Exchange or CME at *http://www.cme.com*, the Chicago Board Options Exchange (CBOE) at *www.cboe.com*, and the New Zealand Futures and Options Exchange incorporated in the SFE Corporation web site at *www.sfe.com.au/*.

For new investors who need extra help in understanding the use of futures and options as well as the special risks they present, there are additional help sites. One useful example here is About.com: Options and Futures at *www.about.com/finance*.

EXHIBIT 9–1
The Modern Business Cycle

To examine fluctuations over time in the economy and interest rates see the extensive collection of economic and financial data series at the Federal Reserve's site, *www.economagic.com/fedbog.htm*

The "ups and downs" of business activity—particularly fluctuations in businesses hiring new workers and making new investments in plant, equipment, and inventories—are known as *business cycles*. The downward phase of the business cycle is better known as a *recession*—an event that has afflicted the U.S. economy about every 4 to 5 years since World War II. Today a business recession is defined by the National Bureau of Economic Research as a widespread decline in economic activity (measured by such indicators as industrial production, employment, and sales) that lasts for more than a few months. Fortunately, business recessions have averaged considerably shorter than the *expansion* (or "up") phase of the modern business cycle, lasting only about 11 months, on average. Interest rates, stock prices, and many other financial data series are *strongly* affected by these cycles in the economy and often move in the same direction (but with a lead or lag) that the business cycle is moving.

Another potentially useful time pattern among market interest rates is that some of these interest rates tend to display **seasonality.** At certain times of the year market rates appear to experience upward pressure and, at other times, seasonal pressures appear to push interest rates down. For example, short-term rates tend to feel upward pressure in the second half of the year as businesses borrow more heavily to stock their shelves with goods for the Fall and Winter seasons. In contrast, long-term interest rates often seem to experience an upward push in the late Spring and Summer, possibly related to borrowing to support construction activity.

EXHIBIT 9–2   **Interest Rates over the Course of a Business Cycle**

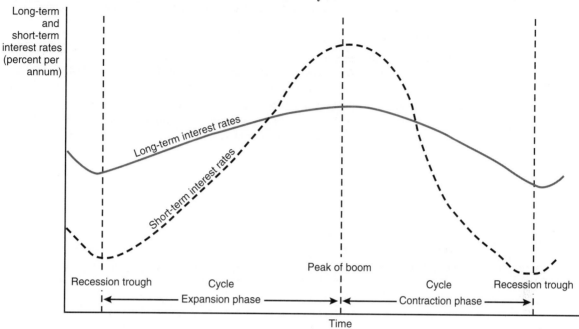

The foregoing interest-rate patterns seem to suggest that if someone could forecast changes in the economy, interest rates (and at least some asset prices) would follow a similar path. This has turned out to be a treacherous path, however, because the economy is so difficult to forecast, often changing direction abruptly. Moreover, seasonal patterns tend to be overshadowed by other forces, such as changes in political conditions or monetary policy actions by the central bank, which are often unpredictable. Then, too, as we saw in Chapter 5, market interest rates are influenced by thousands of borrowing and lending decisions by thousands of individual decision makers. We do not yet have a computer program big enough to tackle all of these individual borrowing and lending decisions.

The Fisher Effect

Nevertheless, some analysts thought there might still be a way to get a handle on the interest-rate forecasting problem using some familiar models from Finance. For example, as we saw in Chapter 7, the Fisher effect suggests that nominal (published) interest rates change as the public's inflationary expectations change. If we could forecast shifts in inflationary expectations, then changes in market interest rates might be more predictable. Unfortunately, inflation forecasting turns out to be nearly as hard to do as interest-rate forecasting.

Money Supply Effects

Similarly, the public's money holdings (the money supply, as discussed in Chapter 2) seems to be related to interest-rate and asset-price movements at times. According to the **money-supply expectations effect,** if the public expects money-supply growth to accelerate, interest rates may rise, perhaps due to fear of inflation. Moreover, the **money-supply income effect** suggests that rising incomes cause the public's demand for money to increase as well, pushing interest rates higher. In contrast, the **money-supply liquidity effect** suggests that higher money growth (particularly if it isn't expected to trigger more inflation) will actually *lower* market interest rates. Notice that, unfortunately for the forecaster, these so-called "money supply" effects pull in opposite and confusing directions.

Implied Forecasting

Another forecasting approach is called **implied rate forecasting,** relying upon changing public expectations to predict the future. In this case analysts look at such data as the shape of the yield curve (discussed earlier in Chapter 7). For example, rising yield curves (with long-term market interest rates higher than short-term rates) imply a public expectation of rising interest rates in the future, while a declining yield curve suggests lower future rates. Similarly, the prices of financial futures contracts (to be discussed later in this chapter) appear to reflect the public's expectation about whether future interest rates and asset prices are likely to be higher or lower than they are today. Unfortunately, implied forecasts seem to change very quickly for unknown reasons and may be inherently biased.

Econometric Models and Consensus

For further discussion of econometrics and econometric models see, for example, *www. encyclopedia.com* and *www.worldbank.org/ data*

While some economists and financial analysts still attempt interest-rate forecasting using sophisticated **econometric models**—systems of equations relying upon multiple interacting variables (e.g., inflation, the money supply, unemployment, production, income, etc.) to jointly predict interest rates and other economic data series—most appear to recognize the great uncertainties and hazards in the forecasting process. Some analysts today recommend **consensus forecasts**, using several different forecasting methods in the hope that these differing approaches will lead to the same general prediction about the future.

Questions *to Help You Study*

1. For what *reasons* are interest rates so difficult to forecast accurately?

2. Suppose you could forecast interest rates correctly on a consistent basis. What advantages would this give to you?

3. Explain the meaning of the following terms:

   a. Liquidity effect

   b. Expectations effect

   c. Income effect

   d. Fisher effect

4. What variables are used most frequently in *econometric models* to predict changes in interest rates?

5. How can public opinion affect interest rates? Why might public opinion be important in interest-rate forecasting?

6. How can the marketplace's *expectations* be used as a guide to anticipate future changes in interest rates? What are the pitfalls in using such an expectations approach as a forecasting tool?

7. Please explain the meaning of the term *consensus forecast*.

INTEREST-RATE AND ASSET-PRICE HEDGING STRATEGIES

Volatile interest rates and security prices in recent years, coupled with the difficulties inherent in interest-rate and asset-price forecasting, have led many individuals and institutions to search for ways to insulate themselves from these interest-rate and value changes.

If rate and price changes cannot be reliably forecast, is it possible to at least *hedge* against (reduce) the damaging effects of increasing or decreasing interest rates and asset prices? Although several hedging methods have been developed, there is a price for this form of value or rate "insurance." *Hedging tends to lower interest-rate and price risk but also tends to reduce the profit potential that could be recovered from correctly anticipating the direction and magnitude of future interest-rate and asset-price changes.* In the sections that follow we look at the most popular tools for controlling interest-rate and asset-price risk —swaps, futures and options.

INTEREST RATE SWAPS

Early in the 1980s a new interest-rate and value hedging tool—the **interest rate swap**—became popular. In an interest rate swap, two participating business firms independently borrow from two different lenders and then exchange interest payments with each other for a stipulated period of time. In effect, each company helps to pay off a portion of the interest cost owed by the other firm. The result is usually *lower* interest expense for both firms and a better *balance* between cash inflows and outflows for both firms. (See, for example, Exhibit 9–3.) Swaps give a company a powerful tool in managing its liabilities, helping to offset any maturity mismatches that may exist between its assets and liabilities.

EXHIBIT 9–3   **Using Interest Rate Swaps to Hedge against Fluctuating Interest Rates**

The Swap Market

The situation:

| Low-credit-rated (BB) borrower:
– Wants lower interest costs
– Prefers fixed-rate, long-term borrowing (such as by issuing bonds) to match the cash-flow characteristics of its long-term assets. | High-credit-rated (AAA) borrower:
– Wants lower interest costs
– Prefers flexible, short-term rate on its borrowings (such as a loan from a bank or finance company) to match the cash-flow characteristics of its short-term assets. |

The swap agreement:

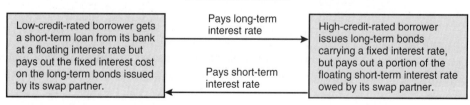

| Low-credit-rated borrower gets a short-term loan from its bank at a floating interest rate but pays out the fixed interest cost on the long-term bonds issued by its swap partner. | Pays long-term interest rate →

 Pays short-term interest rate ← | High-credit-rated borrower issues long-term bonds carrying a fixed interest rate, but pays out a portion of the floating short-term interest rate owed by its swap partner. |

Result: Both companies save on interest costs and better match the maturity structure of their assets and their liabilities. In reality, the two parties to the swap exchange only the *net difference* in their borrowing rates, with the party owing the highest interest rate in the market on the payment date paying the other party the rate difference.

Swaps were first used by multinational banks in the Eurocurrency markets beginning in 1982. These huge banks generally possess excellent credit ratings. This means that, if they wish to, multinational banks can borrow at low, fixed long-term interest rates. However, these international lending institutions may decide to "sell" their ability to borrow long term at low cost in exchange for what they want most: access to low-cost, short-term funds carrying floating interest rates in order to match their short-term, floating-rate assets. The development of interest rate swaps has made maturity matchups like this possible. The first domestic U.S. interest rate swap occurred when the Student Loan Marketing Association, a federal agency that guarantees college student loans, and ITT Corporation exchanged interest rate payments on some of their debt. Most swaps today range from $25 to $100 million in dollar volume (usually called the *notional* amount of the swap because this dollar amount never changes hands). They usually cover periods ranging from about 3 years to 10 years and involve both fixed- and floating-rate loans, with the floating rate often tied to the London Interbank Offer Rate on Eurodollar deposits (LIBOR), the prime rate, or the market yield on Treasury securities.

The LIBOR rate that is the reference interest rate for most swaps is set daily by the British Bankers Association following a survey of leading banks. See *www.bba.org.uk/*

Swaps work because the interest-rate spreads related to default risk (called *quality spreads*) are generally greater in the long-term capital market than they are in the short-term money market. To see how swaps can simultaneously fulfill two goals—lower interest costs and better matching of the maturities of a firm's assets with the maturities of its liabilities—consider the following example. A top-rated corporation with a AAA credit rating can borrow in the long-term bond market at a 10 percent interest rate. However, this company prefers to borrow short-term money at a floating interest rate because it holds mainly short-term assets that roll over into cash just about the time its short-term borrowings come due. Because of the firm's top credit rating, it can borrow short-term funds at prime. Currently, the prime rate is 10 percent, but prime can rise or fall at any time.

A second company is interested in being the first company's swap partner, but this second firm has a credit rating no better than average. This firm has been told by its investment banker that it could issue long-term bonds at an interest rate of 11 percent. Alternatively, this lower-credit-rated firm could borrow short-term funds at prime plus 0.50 percent (making a current short-term loan cost of 10% + 0.50%, or 10.50%). However, the lower-rated firm would prefer to issue long-term bonds because it holds primarily long-term assets.

In summary, these two companies face the following situation:

The Two Parties to the Swap:	Could Borrow in the Long-Term Bond Market at	Could Borrow in the Short-Term Loan Market at	
Low-credit-rated borrower	11%	Prime rate + 0.50%	**(9–1)**
High-credit-rated borrower	<u>10</u>	<u>Prime rate</u>	
Quality spread	1%	0.50%	

In this case, *both* firms can save on interest costs if each company borrows in that financial market—long-term or short-term—in which it has the *greatest comparative interest cost advantage.*

A bank or securities dealer might aid these two firms by helping the top-rated firm sell long-term bonds in the open market at 10 percent, while the lower-rated company agrees to make the top-rated firm's bond interest payments. In the meantime, the lower-rated firm takes out a floating-rate bank loan in the same amount at an interest rate of prime plus 0.50 percent. The top-rated company agrees to pay this second firm a rate of prime less one quarter of a percentage point (25 basis points), which would cover most of the lower-rated company's interest cost. If the prime rate remains at its current level of 10 percent, each firm would owe its swap partner the following:

- Low-credit-rated borrower pays the high-rated borrower the fixed 10 percent interest rate it owes on its long-term bonds.

- High-credit-rated borrower pays the low-rated borrower prime minus one quarter point, or 10 percent − 0.25 percent.

- Low-credit-rated borrower saves 11 − 10, or 1 percent in long-term interest cost less 0.75 percent additional cost on the prime rate loan, or 0.25 percent.

- High-credit-rated borrower saves 0.25 percent in interest cost (prime less 0.25 percent).

Today, borrowers often negotiate swap agreements with lenders at the same time they reach an agreement on a loan. For example, if a borrower is granted a floating-rate loan based on the prime rate but fears that interest rates are going up, he or she can convert that floating-rate loan into a *synthetic fixed-rate loan* through a swap agreement. Although the swap and the loan are usually separate contracts, together they have the net effect of giving the borrower a fixed borrowing cost. As the diagram in Exhibit 9–4 shows, when the borrower pays a floating rate to the lender, the borrower also pays a fixed interest rate to the lender under a swap agreement. Simultaneously under the swap agreement, the lender sends the borrower a floating-rate payment. Therefore, the floating-rate payment from the borrower under the loan agreement is offset by the lender's floating-rate payment to the borrower under the swap agreement. What's left over is the borrower's fixed-rate payment to the lender under the swap.

Thus, a floating-rate loan agreement has been transformed by a swap into a fixed-rate loan, even though the borrower remains legally committed to make all the scheduled floating interest rate payments called for by the loan agreement.

Recently the International Swaps and Derivatives Association (ISDA) has begun to survey daily the fixed interest rates on swaps of varying maturity traded in the global marketplace. Not surprisingly, this new data source reveals that *the longer the term of a swap agreement, the higher the interest rate attached.* Thus, like most other financial instruments, swaps generally display an upward-sloping yield curve. Interest-rate risk increases with longer-term swap contracts and swap partners have had to find ways of dealing effectively with this form of risk exposure.

During the 1990s a new variety of swap contract appeared called the *index amortizing rate (IAR)* swap. An IAR swap, like most other swaps, is an over-the-counter contract calling for two parties to agree to exchange fixed-rate and floating-rate interest payments based upon a certain fixed principal (notional) value of a loan. However, unlike conventional

EXHIBIT 9–4
The Synthetic Fixed-Rate Loan

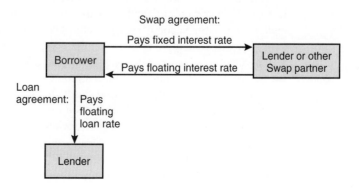

("plain vanilla") swaps, the principal or notional value of an IAR *decreases* over the swap's life at a rate that varies with changes in short-term interest rates. The pace at which the principal of the IAR swap decreases will be affected by an amortization schedule agreed upon by the two parties to the swap. The notional principal underlying the IAR swap will decline (amortize) more quickly if short-term interest rates fall and amortize more slowly if short-term interest rates rise. Actually not all swaps involve a fixed interest rate exchanged for a floating interest rate (now often called "coupon" swaps); the market has broadened to include "basis" swaps in which the parties exchange two different floating—rate payment streams (such as a 3-month interest rate exchanged for a 6-month rate).

Interest rate swaps have become much easier to arrange in recent years with the appearance of swap *brokers*. These financial firms—most often investment banks or commercial banks—usually charge a finder's fee of about ¼ of 1 percent of the principal (notional) amount of the swap to bring the two parties together under the swap agreement. Swap brokers charge more than this if they also are asked to administer the swap—that is, calculate the amount of interest owed by each party to the agreement, collect the monies owed, and distribute the required payments. The swap broker or another financial intermediary may also be asked to issue a *guarantee* in case either party to the swap cannot meet its obligation. These guarantees may cost from 1 to 15 basis points of the notional amount of the swap or more, depending on the credit record of each swap partner. In recent years, swap dealers have developed inventories of "unmatched" swaps—requests from customers who are willing to enter into swap agreements but need a counterparty to make the swap complete.

Swaps are never without risk. Either party to the agreement may go bankrupt or even steal the funds owed to its counterparty, leaving its swap partner exposed to interest-rate risk. Swaps help to cover interest-rate risk but do not necessarily reduce *credit (default) risk*. A few swaps call for one or both parties to post collateral, but this is usually not done. Unfortunately, without collateral requirements, it is easy for a swap partner to overdo the use of swaps and get itself into trouble. One dramatic example of this occurred during the 1990s, when several municipalities in Great Britain took on far more swaps than their revenues could accommodate. In fact, one local government near London faced a swap interest bill so huge that, had a British court not intervened and negated its swap agreements, it would have had to tax each of its citizens thousands of pounds merely to pay off the interest owed on all of its swaps! However, because the notional amount of a swap is not at risk, typically a swap is less risky than a bond.

Swaps are themselves subject to *interest-rate risk* due to the fact that shifts in market interest rates can alter the value of existing swap agreements and, therefore, affect a swap's replacement cost. As Simons (1993) shows, *rising* market interest rates result in greater risk of default on a swap than do stable interest rates. For example, Procter & Gamble Co. lost close to $160 million during the 1990s on interest rate swaps entered into on the assumption that interest rates would fall; they rose instead. A swap can be hedged against interest-rate risk by entering into another swap agreement that is the mirror image of the first (a *matched pair*). Some companies use futures contracts or other hedging tools to counter interest-rate risk from their swaps rather than proliferating still more swaps.

One notable advantage of swaps is the largely unregulated character of the market. Swaps are private agreements with minimal government interference. There is no regulatory commission to restrict the use of this hedging tool. Many firms do not even report the amount of swaps they have outstanding on their balance sheets. This means that investors interested in buying their bonds or their stock may not know how much risk exposure these companies carry in the form of swap obligations. However, recently the Financial Accounting Standards Board (FASB) tightened up on its rules applying to swaps and other derivatives, asking corporations to report the fair-market value of derivatives on their bal-

Financial Developments
The Terminology of the Swap Market

As we have seen, the parties to an interest rate swap merely exchange interest payments (cash flows), with one party paying a short-term, floating interest rate and the other paying a long-term, fixed interest rate. A swap partner that pays out a floating (variable) interest rate is said to be in a *short position*, sending a variable interest rate to its swap partner and receiving a fixed interest rate in return. In contrast, the swap partner that pays out a fixed interest rate and receives, in return, a floating interest rate is said to be in a *long position* in the swap market.

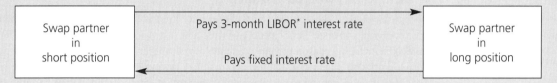

Financial intermediaries and other institutions frequently occupy a *hedged position,* meaning that the hedged institution pays and receives both floating and fixed interest rates. The diagram below shows a financial intermediary, for example, occupying a hedged position in swaps:

In this case, the intermediary is often a swap dealer, aiding two of its corporate customers with their interest rate risk exposure. The dealer can make money on this hedged position in several different ways. First, a fee is often charged to bring these two counterparties together. Moreover, there may be a difference in the fixed interest rate or floating interest rate payments that the dealer receives and pays out. For example, this swap intermediary may collect an annual fixed interest rate of 8 percent from the counterparty in the long position and pay out only a fixed interest rate of 7.75 percent to the counterparty in the short position. The hedged institution pockets the 0.25 percent difference in fixed interest rates received and paid out.

*London Interbank Offer Rate on short-term dollar deposits traded by international banks.

Information on swaps and other derivative instruments may be found at such sites as *www.finpipe.com/ derivglossary.htm*

ance sheets. Nevertheless, disclosure by companies of their commitments under swaps and other derivative obligations remains a serious problem as indicated by the recent collapse of Enron Corporation.

Questions *to Help You Study*

8. What is *interest-rate hedging?* What is its *goal?*

9. What are *interest rate swaps?* Why were these instruments developed?

10. What *risks* are associated with swap contracts? Can any of these risks be reduced?

11. When is a partner to a swap in *long position?* A *short position?* To what kinds of risk is each exposed?

FINANCIAL FUTURES AND OPTION CONTRACTS

Among the most innovative markets to be developed in recent years are the markets for *financial futures* and *options*. In the financial futures and option markets, the risk of future changes in market prices or yields attached to various assets is transferred to someone else—an individual or an institution—willing to bear that risk. Financial futures and options are used in both the short-term money market and the long-term capital market to protect both borrowers and lenders against changing interest rates and shifting asset prices.

The Nature of Futures Trading

For a review of the history of futures and options see *www.cbot.com*

In the futures market, buyers and sellers enter into contracts for the delivery of commodities or securities at a specific location and time and at a price that is set when the contract is made. The principal reason for the existence of the futures market is **hedging,** the act of coordinating the buying and selling of a commodity or financial claim to protect against the risk of future price fluctuations. In the futures market, investors interested in hedging trade futures contracts with investors interested in speculating (i.e., profiting from favorable market movements).

Hedging in futures does not reduce risk. It is a low-cost method of *transferring* the risk of unanticipated changes in prices or interest rates from one investor or institution to another. Ultimately, some investor must bear the risk of fluctuations in the prices and yields of commodities or securities. The hedger who successfully transfers risk through a futures contract can protect an acceptable selling price for a commodity or a desired yield on a security weeks or months ahead of the sale or purchase of that item.

Why Hedging Can Be Effective

The hedging process can be effective in transferring risk because prices in the spot (or cash) market for commodities and securities are generally correlated with prices in the futures (or forward) market. Indeed, the price of a futures contract in today's market represents an estimate of what the spot (or cash) market price will be on the contract's delivery date (less any storage, insurance, and financing costs). *Hedging essentially involves adopting equal and opposite positions in the spot and futures markets for the same assets.*

The relationship between the price of a commodity or security in the cash or spot market and its price in the futures market is captured in the concept of **basis.** Specifically,

$$\begin{array}{l}\text{Basis for a} \\ \text{futures contract}\end{array} = \begin{array}{l}\text{Spread between the cash (spot) price of a commodity} \\ \text{or security and the futures (forward) price for that} \\ \text{same commodity or security at the same point in time.}\end{array} \qquad \textbf{(9–2)}$$

For example, if long-term Treasury bonds are selling in today's cash market for immediate delivery at a price of $98 per bond (assuming a $100 par value) but are selling in the futures market today for forward delivery in three months at $88 per bond, the basis for this T-bond futures contract purchased today is $98 − $88, or $10. We can also define basis in terms of interest rates; it is the difference between the interest rate attached to an asset in the cash market and the interest rate on that same asset in the futures market.

One important principle of futures trading is the *principle of convergence.* As the delivery date specified in a futures contract draws nearer, the gap (basis) between the futures and spot prices for the same security or commodity narrows. At the moment of delivery, the futures price and spot price on the same security or commodity must be identical (except for transactions costs), so that the basis of the futures contract becomes zero. Whether a futures trade ultimately turns out to be profitable depends on what happens to its basis now and when the contract ends. *It is changes in basis that create risk in the trading of futures contracts.*

Hedging through futures converts price or interest rate risk into basis risk. One useful measure of basis risk in financial futures is the *volatility ratio:*

$$\begin{array}{c} \text{Volatility ratio} \\ \text{for a} \\ \text{futures contract} \\ \text{(basis risk measure)} \end{array} = \frac{\begin{array}{c}\text{Percentage change in cash (spot) price} \\ \text{of a commodity or security}\end{array}}{\begin{array}{c}\text{Percentage change in the price of the} \\ \text{futures instrument used for hedging} \\ \text{the commodity or security}\end{array}} \quad \textbf{(9–3)}$$

The more stable the basis associated with a given futures trade—that is, the closer the volatility ratio is to 1—the greater the reduction of risk achieved by the futures trader. When cash and futures prices or interest rates move in parallel, basis risk is zero. The futures markets "work" to offset risk, because the risk of changes in basis is generally less than the risk of changes in the price or yield from an asset.

The Purpose of Trading in Financial Futures

A securities dealer, bank, or other investor may sell **financial futures contracts** on selected assets in order to protect against the risk of falling prices (rising interest rates) and, therefore, a decline in the rate of return or yield from an investment. If the price of the asset in question does fall, the investor can lock in the desired yield, because a profit on the futures contract may offset the capital loss incurred when selling the asset itself. On the other hand, a rise in the market price of an asset (fall in interest rates) may be offset by a loss in the futures market. Either way, the investor may be able to maintain his or her desired holding-period yield.

Under a financial futures contract, for example, the seller agrees to deliver a specific security at a fixed price at a specific time in the future. Delivery under the shortest contracts is usually in 3 months from today's date; a few contracts stretch out to 18 months or even 2 years. When the delivery date arrives, the security's seller can do one of three things: (1) make delivery of the security if he or she holds it; (2) buy the security in the spot (cash) market and deliver it as called for in the futures contract; or (3) purchase a futures contract for the same security with a delivery date exactly matching the first contract. This last option would result in a buy and sell order maturing on the same day, canceling each other out ("zeroing out") and eliminating the necessity of making delivery. In reality, settlement of contracts generally occurs in the futures market by using offsetting buy and sell orders rather than making actual delivery.

Securities Used in Financial Futures Contracts

The number of futures markets and the types of securities and contracts traded in those markets have been expanding in recent years, both inside the United States and on exchanges in London, Western Europe, Japan, and around the Pacific Rim. In 1975 only one type of contract was traded at the Chicago Board of Trade. By the beginning of the twenty-first century many different futures contracts were being traded. However, most trading in financial futures today centers upon contracts calling for the delivery of:

Domestic and foreign government notes and bonds

Eurodollar and other Eurocurrency deposits

Federal funds

Common stock indices (such as the S&P 500 index)

Foreign currencies (such as the yen and the Euro)

International Focus
Leading Futures and Options Exchanges That Have Operated around the World

Chicago Board of Trade (CBT)
Chicago Board Options Exchange (CBOE)
London International Financial Futures
   Exchange (LIFFE)
New York Futures Exchange (NYFE)
New York Financial Exchange (FINEX)
New York Mercantile Exchange (NYM)
Singapore International Monetary
   Exchange, Ltd. (SIMEX)
Sydney Futures Exchange (SFE)
Tokyo International Financial Futures
   Exchange (TIFFE)

Chicago Mercantile Exchange (CME)
Deutsche Boerse (DTB of Frankfurt)
Marché à Terme International de France (MATIF)
Montreal Exchange (ME)
Osaka Stock Exchange (OSE)
Swedish Options and Futures Exchange (SOFE)
Toronto Futures Exchange (TFE)
Tokyo Stock Exchange (TSE)
Pacific Exchange (in San Francisco)
International Securities Exchange
   (electronic exchange)

To explore some interesting facts about futures and options exchanges see such web sites as *www.nyce.com, www.pacificex.com, www.amex.com*, and *www.belfox.be*

While the number of exchanges where trading of these and other contracts proliferated rapidly for a time, there is a strong trend today toward the merging of exchanges in order to lower operating costs and increase trading volume, leading to faster and electronic trading settlement of exchange transactions. Each exchange controls which contracts may be offered for sale and their acceptable delivery dates, delivery methods, posting of prices, contract par values, and other essential terms of trade.[3]

Examples of Daily Futures Price Quotations: U.S. Treasury Notes and Bonds

The futures market for U.S. Treasury bonds and notes is one of the most active markets for the forward delivery of an asset to be found anywhere in the world. Treasury bonds and notes are a popular investment medium for individuals and financial institutions because of their safety and liquidity. Nevertheless, there is substantial market risk involved with longer-term Treasury bonds and notes due to their lengthy maturities and relatively thin market. Because the market for U.S. Treasury bonds is thinner than for Treasury bills and Treasury bond durations are longer, T-bond prices are more volatile, creating greater uncertainty for investors. Not surprisingly, then, U.S. Treasury bonds were among the first financial instruments for which a futures market was developed for hedging risk. Today there are parallel markets for contracts covering foreign government bonds centered on exchanges in London, Paris, Frankfurt, Tokyo, and elsewhere around the globe.

All U.S. Treasury bonds delivered under a futures contract must come from the same issue. The basic trading unit is a $100,000 bond (measured at par) with a minimum maturity

[3]The contract exchanges carry a heavy burden of responsibility in preserving the integrity of futures trading and the orderliness of markets. Each exchange stands behind the transactions conducted on its floor and imposes strict rules to minimize risk to the investor. For example, daily price fluctuations are not permitted to go beyond defined limits. Qualifications of floor traders and standards for member firms are monitored by management and the governing board. The U.S. government regulates futures trading through the Commodity Futures Trading Commission and the Securities and Exchange Commission.

EXHIBIT 9–5 **Examples of Daily Price Quotations on Financial Futures Exchanges**

						U.S. Treasury Bond Financial Futures Contracts (in Denominations of $100,000; Prices in 32nds of 100 Percent)		

Month When Maturity Is Reached	Opening Price	High Trading Price	Low Trading Price	Settlement Price	Change from Previous Trading Day	Lifetime Extreme Prices		Volume of Open Interest
						High Price	Low Price	
September	122–08	122–16	122–0	122–12	+4	125–01	118–2	950,655
December	122–04	122–10	121–31	122–04	+6	125–12	118–4	120,448

Estimated most recent trading volume: 320,000.
Previous day's trading volume: 366,580.

of 15 years and a coupon rate of 8 percent. Bonds with coupon rates above or below 8 percent are deliverable at a premium or discount from par in the months of March, June, September, and December. Delivery of Treasury bonds is accomplished by book entry, and accrued interest is prorated. Price quotes in the market are often expressed as a percentage of par value. The minimum price change that is recorded on published lists or in dealer quotations is ½₂ of a point, or $31.25 per $100,000 face-value contract.[4]

Sample data on financial futures prices for U.S. Treasury bond contracts appear in many financial news sheets and computer screens all over the world. As shown in Exhibit 9–5, the first column indicates the months when each futures contract matures. The next four columns show the opening price for the September and December T-bond contracts when trading began in yesterday's market. The September contract, for example, opened at a price of 122–08 (or $122 and ⁸⁄₃₂ on a $100 par value T-bond, or about $122,250 for a T-bond with a $100,000 face value). The September T-bond's futures price fluctuated during yesterday's trading from a high of $122,500 (or 122 and ¹⁶⁄₃₂) to a low of $122,000 (or 122 and ⁰⁄₃₂). Trading in the September bond contract closed (settled) at a price of 122 and ¹²⁄₃₂ (or $122,375 for a $100,000 par-value bond) at the end of the day. This settlement price was ⁴⁄₃₂ (or $125) higher than the previous trading day. During the life of this particular futures contract, the T-bond's futures price has fluctuated between a high of $125,031.25 (or 125 and ¹⁄₃₂) and a low of $118,062.50 (or 118 and ²⁄₃₂). The final data column, labeled "Volume of Open Interest," reveals the number of outstanding September futures contracts—in this case, more than 950,000—not yet "zeroed out," indicating delivery of T-bonds must still be made when the contract matures unless the contract is canceled out before it reaches maturity. At the bottom of the table information is often provided to interested investors on the volume of trading (number of contracts) for the most recent day and the preceding day.

Eurodollar Time Deposits

Futures trading in Eurobank dollar-denominated time deposits (which are described in Chapter 12) began in 1981 at the International Monetary Market (IMM) of the Chicago Mercantile Exchange (CME). The next year the London International Financial Futures Exchange (LIFFE) introduced a similar contract, and more recently, it introduced Eurodeposits based on leading international currencies traded on leading futures exchanges in

---

[4]See Chapter 6 on asset prices and interest rates for the meaning of 32nds and points and how bonds and other financial asset prices and yields are measured.

Tokyo (TIFFE), Singapore (SIMEX), and Paris (MATIF). The Eurodollar futures market offers investors the opportunity to hedge against changing interest rates on commercial loans, bank deposits, and other money market instruments. Eurodollar futures are settled in cash with the exchange clearinghouse. Prices are expressed as an index equal to 100 minus the prevailing London Interbank Offer Rate (LIBOR) on short-term deposits that day. In addition to the Eurodollar time deposit futures contract there are contracts for the delivery of Euros, Swiss Francs, Japanese yen, the British pound, Mexican pesos, and Canadian and Australian dollars designed to help guard against fluctuations in the value of these particular currencies.

Other Money Market Futures Contracts

For money market investors such as commercial banks, a popular financial futures contract is the 30-day Fed funds futures contract, trading in $5 million units at the Chicago Board of Trade. This device for hedging short-term money market borrowing costs and investment returns is priced at 100 minus the prevailing average Fed funds market interest rate for the delivery month. In the international money market, interest-rate risk associated with large commercial loans can also be dealt with by using the one-month LIBOR futures contract, which trades in $3 million units at the Chicago Mercantile Exchange.

Stock Index Futures

In February 1982, futures contracts on the index value of those common stocks making up the Value Line Stock Index were first offered by the Kansas City Board of Trade. Two months later, the Chicago Mercantile Exchange offered its own version of these "pin-stripe pork bellies" by opening trading in a contract tied to the Standard & Poor's (S&P) 500 Stock Index. And in May 1982, the New York Futures Exchange inaugurated trading in the New York Stock Exchange's (NYSE's) Composite Stock Price Index. Later Dow Jones' Industrials, S&P Mid-Cap, Nasdaq 100, and Russel 2000 stock-index contracts were developed.

To learn more about the nature of financial futures, options, swaps and other derivatives see such web sources as *www.encyclopedia.com*

The advantage of these composite contracts is that they permit an investor to participate in the "action" of the stock market without buying individual stocks. The investor merely risks his cash on whether the stock or bond index will rise or fall in value. This is accomplished by buying or selling a futures contract a few points above or below the current stock index value. For example, one popular S&P 500 contract has a value based on the level of the S&P 500 stock index multiplied by $250. If the S&P stock index rises to 400 points, the S&P futures contract would have a value of 400 × $250 or $160,000. If an investor purchased the S&P index contract at 400 and then sold a similar contract later at 410 for $162,500, he would receive a trading profit of $2,500 from the exchange clearinghouse. Current exchange rules require all stock index contracts to be zeroed out so that no exchange of stock occurs; the difference between buying and selling prices is settled in cash alone. Buyers of stock index futures bet on rising stock prices; sellers are usually forecasting declining stock prices.

Questions *to Help You Study*

12. What is the basic purpose of futures and options trading in securities? Where is most futures and options trading carried out?

13. How do the spot (cash) markets differ from futures (forward) markets?

14. What is *basis?* Explain how the basis for a futures contract relates to trading risk.

15. For what specific kinds of securities is there now an active futures market? Who issues these securities?

Financial futures and option contracts as well as swaps belong to a broad class of financial instruments called *derivatives*. These unique instruments depend for their value on one or more underlying securities or variables, such as stock prices, interest rates, currency, or commodity prices. Recent experience has shown that derivatives pose their own special brand of risk for both buyers and sellers.

For one thing, derivatives involve at least two parties to the contract that creates them and either party may fail to deliver what is agreed to, exposing the other party to loss (*counterparty risk*). Other forms of risk associated with derivatives include *price risk* (as their market values change), *liquidity risk* (because traders may be prevented from carrying out risk-covering transactions due to halts in trading activity or other problems), *settlement risk* (when securities are delivered before payment is received), *operating risk* (due to faulty internal controls on trading activity), *legal risk* (if customers sue to recover their losses), and *regulatory risk* (when regulations are changed or violated). Derivatives can become so complex that it's easy for a trader to become entangled in multiple contracts and lose track of his or her true position and exposure to loss.

Still, it's important not to overlook the potential *benefits* that properly managed derivatives trading offers. These include saving money on interest costs or on foreign currency purchases and better balancing of a business firm's cash inflows with its outflows. Moreover, with relatively low cash margins required by most brokers, it is possible to control large amounts of capital with the investment of only limited amounts of cash. And, thanks to a 1993 change in IRS regulations, losses from hedging transactions may be treated as "ordinary" losses and, therefore, are deductible from taxable income as long as the hedges and the items hedged are clearly identified. However, the fair market value of derivative holdings must be reported on a trader's financial statements and any earnings must be adjusted accordingly.

TYPES OF HEDGING IN THE FINANCIAL FUTURES MARKET

Basically *three* types of hedges are used in the financial futures market today: the *long hedge,* the *short hedge,* and the *cross hedge.* Each type of hedge meets the unique trading needs of a particular group of investors.

The Long (or Buying) Hedge

A **long hedge** involves the *purchase* of futures contracts today before the investor must buy the actual securities desired at a later date. The purpose of the long hedge is to guarantee (lock in) a desired yield in case interest rates decline before assets are actually purchased in the cash market.

As an example of a typical long hedge transaction, suppose that a bank or other institutional investor anticipates receiving $1 million 90 days from today. Assume that today is April 1 and funds are expected on July 2. The current yield to maturity on securities the investor hopes to purchase in July is 12.26 percent. We might imagine that these securities are long-term U.S. Treasury bonds, which appeal to this investor because of their high liquidity and zero default risk. Suppose, however, that interest rates are expected to decline over the next three months. If the investor waits until the $1 million in cash is actually available 90 days from now, the yield on Treasury bonds may well be lower than 12.26 percent. Is there a way to lock in the higher yield available now even though funds will not be available for another three months?

Yes, if a suitable long hedge can be negotiated with another trader. In this case, the investor can *purchase* ("go long") 10 September Treasury bond futures contracts at their current market price. The number of bond futures contracts required can be figured as follows:

$$\frac{\text{Value of securities to be hedged}}{\begin{array}{c}\text{Denomination of the}\\ \text{appropriate futures contract}\end{array}} = \frac{\$1 \text{ million}}{\$100,000} = 10 \text{ contracts} \quad \textbf{(9–4)}$$

Cash payment on these contracts will not be due until September.

In many practical situations, the asset to be hedged and the time for risk protection will not exactly match available futures contracts. These differences introduce uncertainty into the process of determining exactly how many futures contracts will be needed. A formula that takes some of these problems into account is the following:

$$\begin{matrix} \text{Number of} \\ \text{futures} \\ \text{contracts} \\ \text{needed} \end{matrix} = \frac{\begin{matrix} \text{Value of} \\ \text{securities or} \\ \text{loans to be} \\ \text{hedged} \end{matrix}}{\begin{matrix} \text{Denomination} \\ \text{of futures} \\ \text{contracts} \end{matrix}} \times \begin{matrix} \text{Volatility ratio} \\ \text{of price} \\ \text{movements in} \\ \text{the cash (spot)} \\ \text{security relative} \\ \text{to the price of} \\ \text{the futures} \\ \text{contract} \end{matrix} \times \frac{\begin{matrix} \text{Days exposed to} \\ \text{risk in the cash} \\ \text{(spot) market} \end{matrix}}{\begin{matrix} \text{Term of futures} \\ \text{contracts} \end{matrix}} \qquad \textbf{(9–5)}$$

where the volatility ratio is the percentage change in market price of the cash (spot) asset relative to the percentage change in price of the desired futures contract over the most recent period. For example, if we wish to hedge $1 million in corporate bonds for 60 days with $100,000-denominated Treasury bond futures contracts covering 90 days and recent price movements of corporate bonds and T-bond futures have displayed a volatility ratio of 0.75, then

$$\text{Number of futures contracts needed} = \frac{\$1\ \text{million}}{\$100,000} \times 0.75 \times \frac{60}{90} \approx 5\ \text{contracts} \ \textbf{(9–6)}$$

Suppose the price of T-bond futures contracts currently is 68–10, which is 68 and $^{10}\!/_{32}$, or $68,312.50 on a $100,000 face-value contract. Assume too that, as expected, bond prices rise and interest rates fall. At some later point, the investor may be able to sell these futures contracts at a profit, because their prices tend to rise along with rising bond prices in the cash market. Selling bond futures at a profit will help this investor offset the lower yields on Treasury bonds that will prevail in the cash market once the $1 million actually becomes available for investing on July 2nd.

The details of this long hedge transaction are given in Exhibit 9–6. We note that on July 1, the investor goes into the spot market and buys $1 million in 8¼ percent, 20-year U.S. Treasury bonds at a price of 82–13. At the same time, the investor sells 10 September Treasury bond futures at 80–07. Due to higher bond prices (lower yields) in July, the investor loses $139,687.50, because the market price of Treasury bonds has risen from 68–14 to 82–13. This represents an opportunity loss because the $1 million in investable funds was not available in April when interest rates were high and bond prices low. However, this loss is at least partially offset by a gain in the futures market of $119,062.50, because the 10 September bond futures purchased on April 1 were sold at a profit on July 2. Over this period, bond futures rose in price from 68–10 to 80–07. In effect, this investor will pay only $705,000 for the Treasury bonds bought in the cash market on July 2. The market price of these bonds will be $824,062.50 (or 82 and $^{13}\!/_{32}$) per bond, but the investor's net cost is lower by $119,062.50 due to a gain in the futures market.

The Short (or Selling) Hedge

A financial device designed to deal with rising interest rates is the **short hedge.** This hedge involves the immediate *sale* of financial futures until the actual securities must be sold in the cash market at some later point. Short hedges are especially useful to investors who may hold a large portfolio of assets they plan to sell in the future but, in the meantime,

EXHIBIT 9–6
An Example of a Long Futures Hedge Using U.S. Treasury Bonds

Spot (or Cash) Market Transactions	Futures (or Forward) Market Transactions
April 1:	April 1:
A portfolio manager for a financial institution wished to "lock in" a yield of 12.26 percent on $1 million of 20-year, 8¼ percent U.S. Treasury bonds at 68–14.	The portfolio manager purchases 10 September Treasury bond futures contracts at 68–10.
July 2:	July 2:
The portfolio manager purchases $1 million of 20-year, 8¼ percent U.S. Treasury bonds at 82–13 for a yield of 10.14 percent.	The portfolio manager sells 10 September Treasury bond futures contracts at 80–07.
Results:	Results:
Opportunity loss of $139,687.50 due to lower Treasury bond yields and higher bond prices.	Gain of $119,062.50 on futures trading (less brokerage commissions, interest cost on funds tied up in required cash margin, and taxes).

Source: Based on an example developed by the Chicago Board of Trade in an *Introduction to Financial Futures*, February 1981. Reprinted by permission of the Chicago Board of Trade.

must be protected against the risk of declining prices. We examine a typical situation in which a securities dealer might employ the short hedge.

Suppose the dealer holds $1 million in U.S. Treasury bonds carrying an 8¾ percent coupon and a maturity of 20 years. The current price of these bonds is 94–26 (or 94 and ²⁶⁄₃₂ which is $948.125 per $1,000 par value), which amounts to a yield of 9.25 percent. However, the dealer is concerned that interest rates may rise. Any increase in interest rates would bring about lower bond prices and therefore reduce the value of the dealer's portfolio. A possible remedy in this case is to *sell* bond futures to counteract the anticipated decline in bond prices. For example, suppose the dealer decides to sell 10 Treasury bond futures at 86–28 and 30 days later is able to sell $1 million of 20-year, 8¾ percent Treasury bonds at a price of 86 and ¹⁹⁄₃₂ for a yield of 10.29 percent. At the same time, the dealer goes into the futures market and *buys* 10 Treasury bond contracts at 79–26 to offset the previous forward sale of bond futures.

The financial consequences of these combined trades in spot and futures markets are offsetting, as shown in Exhibit 9–7. The dealer has lost $83,125 in the cash market due to the price decline in bonds. However, a gain of $70,625 (less brokerage commissions, interest on cash margins held, and any tax liability) has resulted from the fall in the futures price. This dealer has helped insulate the value of his asset portfolio from the risk of price fluctuations through a short hedge.

Cross Hedging

Another approach to minimizing risk is the **cross hedge**—a combined transaction between the spot market and the futures market using *different types of assets* in each market. This device rests on the assumption that the prices of most financial instruments tend to move in the same direction and by roughly the same proportion. Because this is only approximately true in the real world, profits or losses in the cash market will not exactly offset losses or profits in the futures market because *basis risk is greater with a cross hedge.* Nevertheless, if the investor's goal is to minimize risk, cross hedging is usually preferable to a completely unhedged position.

EXHIBIT 9–7
An Example of a Short Futures Hedge Using U.S. Treasury Bonds

Spot (or Cash) Market Transactions	Futures (or Forward) Market Transactions
October 1: A securities dealer owns $1 million of 20-year, 8¾ percent U.S. Treasury bonds priced at 94–26 to yield 9.25%.	October 1: The dealer sells 10 Treasury bond futures contracts at 86–28.
October 31: The dealer sells $1 million of 20-year, 8¾ percent U.S. Treasury bonds at 86–16 to yield 10.29%.	October 31: The dealer purchases 10 Treasury bond futures contracts at 79–26.
Results: Loss of $83,125 in spot (cash) market.	Results: Gain of $70,625 on futures trading (less brokerage commissions, interest cost on cash margin maintained, and tax obligation).

Source: Based on an example developed by the Chicago Board of Trade in an *Introduction to Financial Futures*, February 1981. Reprinted by permission of the Chicago Board of Trade.

As an example, consider the case of a bank that holds corporate bonds carrying a face value of $5 million and an average maturity of 20 years. The bank's portfolio manager anticipates a rise in interest rates, which will reduce the value of the bonds. Unfortunately, there is only a limited futures market for corporate bonds, and the portfolio manager fears that he or she cannot construct an effective hedge for these securities. However, futures contracts exist for U.S. Treasury bonds, providing a short cross hedge against the risk of a decline in the value of the corporate bonds.

To illustrate how such a cross hedge might take place, suppose that on January 2 the total market value of the bank's corporate bonds is $3,673,437.50. This means that each $1,000 par value bond currently carries a market price of $734.69 (73–15 on a $100 basis). The portfolio manager decides to sell 50 Treasury bond futures contracts at 81 and $^{20}\!/_{32}$ ($816.25 per $1,000 face value). About two months later, on March 14, interest rates have risen significantly. The value of each corporate bond has fallen to 64–13 ($644.06 per $1,000 bond). At this point, the bank's portfolio manager decides to sell these bonds, receiving $3,220,312.50 from the buyer. This represents a loss of $453,125. At the same time, however, the portfolio manager buys back 50 U.S. Treasury bond futures contracts at 69–20. The result is a gain from futures trading of $600,000. In this particular transaction, the gain from futures more than offsets the loss in the cash market. (See Exhibit 9–8 for a summary of this transaction.)

Executing a Trade and the Cash Margin

Information on the trading and pricing of financial futures contracts appears in many places on the web, including the National Futures Association at *www.nfa.futures.org*, the Commodity Futures Trading Commission at *www.CFTC.com*, and *www.citylink-uk.com*

Most trading in financial futures contracts takes place through a broker or dealer who may find another party interested in participating in the trade or, more commonly, will contact a *floor trader* working on an organized futures exchange. The floor trader will attempt to place the customer's order, either *electronically* or via *open outcry* on the floor of the exchange, seeking a counterparty interested in the terms being offered. If a trade is successful the customer will be asked to post a *cash margin* (equal to a specified percentage of the value of the contracts traded) with his or her broker.

What is the purpose of the *cash margin* that each investor must post? It protects the customers, brokers, and traders against market risk. At the end of each trading day, the exchange clearinghouse is required to *mark to market* (value) each contract outstanding based

EXHIBIT 9–8
An Example of a Short Cross Futures Hedge Involving Corporate and U.S. Treasury Bonds

Spot (or Cash) Market Transactions	Futures (or Forward) Market Transactions

January 2:
  A commercial bank holds a diversified portfolio of $5 million in high-grade corporate bonds with an average maturity of 20 years and a current market value of 73–15 per bond. The market value of the total portfolio is, therefore, $3,673,437.50.
	January 2:
	  The bank's portfolio manager sells 50 U.S. Treasury bond futures contracts at 81–20.

March 14:
  The market price per bond falls to 64–13, for a total value of the portfolio of $3,220,312.50 when sold.
	March 14:
	  The portfolio manager purchases 50 U.S. Treasury bond futures contracts at 69–20.

Results:
  The total loss in value of the corporate bonds is $453,125.
	Results:
	  Gain of $600,000 on the Treasury bond futures contracts (less brokerage commissions, interest cost on cash margins maintained, and taxes owed).

Source: Based on an example developed by the Chicago Board of Trade in *An Introduction to Financial Futures*, February 1981. Reprinted by permission of the Chicago Board of Trade.

on its closing price that day. The cash margin covers the loss when a futures contract falls in price. If the price decline is more than a specified percentage of the margin, the investor may get a *margin call* to post additional cash or securities for protection.

Payoff Diagrams for Long and Short Futures Contracts

We can represent losses or gains from trading in futures and from taking long or short hedging positions by using payoff diagrams of the type shown in Exhibit 9–9. In these diagrams, the different possible prices of futures (F_t) are shown along the horizontal axis. The vertical axis records any profits or losses (not including taxes and transactions costs) that result when futures prices move up or down.

A 45° line is drawn through the original purchase price (F_B) of the contract marked on both horizontal and vertical axes. Because the line through F_B has an angle of 45°, this means that along this line, a change of $1 in the futures price, up or down, also results in a $1 profit or loss to the holder of the contract. Note, too, that there is no profit or loss when the futures contract price equals its original, or base, purchase price, F_B.

As the left-hand diagram in Exhibit 9–9 illustrates, the buyer of a long hedge in futures scores a profit if the price of the underlying asset and the value of the associated futures contract rise. This happens if interest rates fall, causing subsequent futures prices to climb above their base price ($F_t > F_B$). On the other hand, suppose that futures prices fall below the original purchase price, so that $F_t < F_B$ because interest rates have risen. Then the holder of a long hedge will suffer a loss.

The right-hand diagram in Exhibit 9–9 shows that the holder of a short futures position suffers losses when interest rates decline. In this case, the prices of the futures contract and of the assets named in that contract increase, forcing the holder of a short hedge to buy assets or futures at a higher price ($F_t > F_B$) to make delivery or to cancel out the short position. On the other hand, if interest rates rise, then the prices of futures (and the associated assets) eventually may drop below their original purchase price ($F_t < F_B$), handing the short hedger a profit.

EXHIBIT 9–9 **Payoffs for Long and Short Futures Positions**

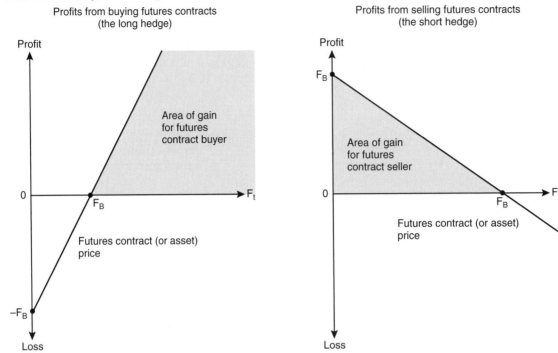

OPTION CONTRACTS ON FINANCIAL FUTURES

In addition to financial futures contracts themselves, there is also active trading in options on financial futures contracts. An **option contract** is an agreement between a buyer and seller to grant the holder of the contract the right to buy or sell a futures contract or asset at a specified price on or before the day the contract expires. Options on farm commodities and on selected common stock have been traded for decades. There was an explosion of new options products in the 1980s, led by options on $100,000 in Treasury bond futures introduced in October 1982. Then, in 1985, the International Monetary Market (IMM), a division of the Chicago Mercantile Exchange (CME), began trading option contracts on financial futures for Eurodollar deposits. As more investors began to take an interest in options trading, major exchanges around the world began developing many new option contracts on stock, foreign currencies, and financial futures contracts.

Basic Types of Option Contracts

There are two basic types of option contracts. **Call options** give the contract buyer the right, but not the obligation, to buy ("call away") futures contracts or assets at a set price called the **strike price.** The seller of the contract is called the *option writer.* Under the terms of U.S. options, the buyer may exercise the option and purchase the futures or assets specified from the writer at any time on or before the expiration date of the option. European options, on the other hand, can be exercised only on their expiration date. An option that is not used by its expiration date becomes worthless.

Put options grant the contract purchaser the right, but not the obligation, to sell ("put," or deliver) futures contracts or securities to the option writer at a set (strike) price on or before the option's expiration date. Buyers of both call and put options must pay an **option**

Recently more options and other securities have been traded electronically for greater speed and efficiency. A prominent example is the International Securities Exchange at *www.iseoptions.com* which has been trading options beginning in 2000.

premium for the privilege of being able to buy or sell futures or securities at a guaranteed price. By fixing the price of a financial transaction for a stipulated period, options provide an alternative way of hedging against market risk. Their principal advantage over futures contracts is that hedging with futures contracts limits the hedger's profits. Options, in contrast, can be used to limit losses while preserving the opportunity to make unlimited profits.

Most options on financial instruments are traded today on organized exchanges such as the IMM or the Chicago Board Options Exchange (CBOE). Exchange-traded options are standardized contracts with uniform terms that enhance the marketability of options. The options exchange sets rules for trading and pricing options: the exchange clearinghouse keeps a record of all trades and guarantees performance on all exchange-traded options. In effect, the clearinghouse becomes the ultimate seller to all option buyers and the ultimate buyer for all option sellers.

Most option contracts are liquidated before they expire by each trader making an offsetting purchase or sale. For example, the buyer of a call option can "erase" his or her contract by selling a call option involving the same security with the same expiration date and strike price. Put options are liquidated in the same fashion with the buyer (seller) of the put selling (buying) a comparable put on or before the expiration date.

Examples of Price Quotes on Options Contracts

One of the most popular exchange-traded options is the Treasury bond option contract, traded on the Chicago Board of Trade's Options Exchange in units of $100,000. The T-Bond options' current price is quoted in points ($1 on a base of $100) and 64ths of a point. Its future popularity is somewhat in doubt, however, due to the possible long-run decline in the volume of the U.S. Treasury securities provided the United States' government can achieve sustainable budget surpluses and retire more of its outstanding debt.

An example of the data most investors usually see on option prices and trading volume on their computers and in financial newspapers is shown in Exhibit 9–10. We note, for example, that the option to call U.S. Treasury bond futures contracts between now and their maturity date in September and carrying a strike price of 120 (that is, $120,000 for a $100,000 futures contract) was trading at a market price of 1–60 (that is, 1 and $^{60}\!/_{64}$ for a $100 par value option, or $1,937.50 on a $100,000 face value call option contract). The prices of put options on T-bonds expiring in September and December appear in a companion table to the right of the table of call options. Trading volume information and the volume of uncancelled (open interest) options appears as a final item on many option price tables appearing in the financial press.

As Exhibit 9–10 makes clear, the higher an option's strike price, the lower the call option's price (premium) tends to be, because there is less likelihood the call will be exercised. Moreover, call options expiring at a later date sell for higher premiums than those expiring sooner because there is more time in the case of the former options for security prices to change in a way that favors their exercise by the option buyer.

Uses of Options on Futures Contracts

Options have many uses. Their two most common ones involve (1) protecting a future investment's yield against falling interest rates by using call options and (2) protecting against rising interest rates by using put options.

Protecting against Declining Investment Yields

A major concern of most asset buyers is how to protect against falling yields and rising prices on bonds and other assets that will be purchased in the future. Options offer a way to

EXHIBIT 9–10
Examples of Daily Price Quotations on Option Contracts

Strike (Exercise) Price	Call Options Settlement Prices		Put Options Settlement Prices	
	September	December	September	December
120	1–60	2–01	0–16	0–42
121	1–32	1–58	0–32	0–60
122	1–16	1–48	0–48	1–12

U.S. Treasury Bond Futures Options
(in Denominations of $100,000; Prices in 64ths of 100 Percent)

Estimated volume of trading: 120,000 contracts.
Open interest volume in call options: 485,776.
Open interest volume in put options: 250,715.

To learn more about options pricing and trading consider such sources as In the Money at *www.in-the-money.com* and CityLink at *www.citylink-uk.com*

prepare for a future investment, even if the investor doesn't yet have sufficient cash to make the investment, by carrying out a temporary transaction that helps guarantee future yields. An option contract enables an investor to set a maximum price for assets targeted for future purchase.

For example, suppose a security dealer plans to buy $100 million in U.S. Treasury bonds in a few days and hopes to earn an interest yield of at least 7 percent. However, fearful of a substantial drop in interest rates before the dealer is ready to buy, he executes a call option on T-bond futures at a strike price of 120. If T-bond futures rise in value above 120 (i.e., fall below 7 percent in yield), the dealer probably will exercise the option because it is now "in the money." When the market price of a futures contract or security rises above the strike price in the associated option contract, the buyer of the call option is said to be "in the money," because he or she can buy the futures contract or security from the option writer at the strike price (in this case, at 120) and sell at a higher price (perhaps at 121) in futures or cash markets. The resulting profit (after paying the option's premium, taxes, and transactions costs) offsets the loss in yield on the planned investment due to a decline in market interest rates.

If interest rates go against the dealer's forecast, however, and rise instead, the call option will be "out of the money." Its strike price will be above the market's current price for the securities or futures covered by the option. In this case, the call will *not* be exercised, and the dealer will lose the premium he or she paid for the option. However, the fact that interest rates rose (and, therefore, Treasury bond prices fell) means the dealer can now purchase Treasury bonds at a cheaper price and a more desirable yield.

Incidentally, the profit on an exercised *call option* can be found by using the equation:

$$\text{Profit} = F - S - Pr - T \tag{9–7}$$

where F is the current futures or security price, S is the strike price agreed upon in the option contract, Pr is the premium paid by the call option buyer, and T represents any taxes owed as a result of the transaction. If the futures or security price, F, rises high enough, the buyer can call away futures contracts or securities from the option writer at price S and still have some profit left over after paying the premium (Pr) and any taxes incurred (T). However, if the futures price, F, declines, the option will go unexercised and the buyer's loss will equal $-Pr$. The seller of the unexercised call will then reap a profit of $+Pr$.

Protecting against Rising Interest Rates

In contrast to lenders, who often worry about falling yields, borrowers' concerns usually are to keep borrowing costs from rising. Consider a bank, for example, that must borrow millions of dollars daily and fears rising money market interest rates. Perhaps market rates on deposits are currently at 8 percent and the bank fears a substantial rise in deposit interest costs to 9 percent. Accordingly, the bank's deposit manager purchases a put option on Eurodollar futures at a strike price of 92. If these futures fall below 92 in price due to rising interest rates, the bank's liability manager may decide to exercise the put option and sell Eurodollar futures to the option writer at the strike price. The manager will then liquidate the bank's futures position by buying equivalent futures contracts at the now lower market price and profit from the spread between the strike price of 92 and the current lower market price. This profit will at least partially offset the bank's higher borrowing costs.

On the other hand, if interest rates do not rise, the bank's deposit manager will not exercise the put option. This will mean losing the full amount of the option premium, but the bank's borrowing costs will stay low. In this instance, it paid a premium for interest rate insurance that turned out not to be needed.

The profit to the buyer of a *put option* can be calculated from the following equation:

$$\text{Profit} = S - F - Pr - T \qquad \textbf{(9–8)}$$

where S is the strike price, F the market price of the futures or securities mentioned in the option, Pr the premium paid for the option, and T taxes owed. If the futures or security price, F, falls far enough below strike price S, the put buyer will show a profit $S - F$. On the other hand, if the futures or security price rises, the put will go unexercised, and the buyer's loss will be measured by $-Pr$. The seller of the unexercised put will then experience a corresponding profit of $+Pr$.

Payoff Diagrams for Valuing Options

We can diagram how options are valued by looking first at the value of a put option to the investor who holds it (the option buyer) on the date or dates the option can be exercised. Exhibit 9–11 illustrates the relationship between a put option's value and the value of the underlying futures contract or asset named in the option. Point S marked on the horizontal axis in Exhibit 9–11 represents the strike price, the price at which the futures contract or asset can be sold by the option's holder.

EXHIBIT 9–11
Payoffs to the Option Buyer from Put Options

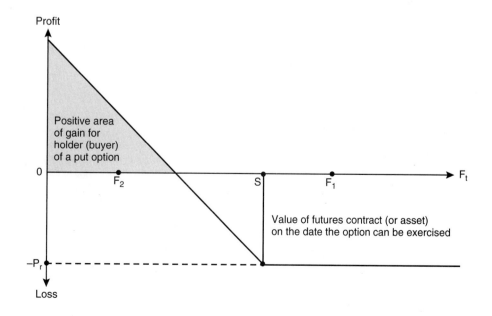

Suppose the futures contract or asset in question currently is selling for price F_1, which is more than its strike price, S (i.e., $F_1 > S$). In this case, the option has a current value of zero (actually less than zero because the option buyer had to pay premium Pr, which is lost if the option goes unexercised). The holder of the option would prefer to sell the futures contracts she holds at current market price F_1 rather than deliver them to the option writer for a price of only S. If current price F_1 is significantly larger than S, however, the option buyer may still reap a substantial gain despite losing the option premium.

In contrast, suppose that the futures contract has a current price of F_2, where $F_2 < S$. In this instance, with a market price lower than the strike price, exercise of the option results in a profit for its buyer. The option buyer will deliver the futures to the option writer and receive strike price S for a net profit per contract of $S - F_2 - Pr - T$. Clearly for the holder of a put option, when $S > F_t$, the option will normally be exercised for a profit and be "in the money" as long as $S - F_t$ exceeds the option premium, taxes, and transaction costs. When $S < F_t$, the option will expire unexercised; the profit will be zero or negative and clearly will be "out of the money." Only within the triangle in the upper left-hand corner of Exhibit 9–11 will the holder of a put option reap positive gains.

From the standpoint of the writer (seller) of a put option, the writer benefits if the option is *not* exercised. This happens if the market value of the futures contract or security remains higher than the option's strike price, as at $F_1 > S$. Exhibit 9–12 shows that the area of gain for the writer of a put option lies around and to the right of strike price S. In this region, the option currently is "out of the money" from the buyer's standpoint, and the writer pockets the premium paid by the option holder.

In the case of *call options*, the writer agrees to sell securities to the buyer of the option at a stipulated strike price. If, as shown in Exhibit 9–13, the market price of the underlying futures contract or asset rises above the strike price to F_1, the holder of the call option will exercise that option and call away the futures contract or asset from the option writer at strike price S. Exercise of this now "in the money" call option will enable the option buyer to resell each of the newly acquired futures contracts or assets for a profit of $F_1 - S - Pr - T$. If, on the other hand, the market value of futures contracts or securities falls *below* the option's strike price, as at F_2, the option holder would be better off purchasing the futures contracts or assets in the open market rather than exercising his or her option to buy at price S. The call will expire unused ("out of the money"), and the option buyer will suffer a loss

EXHIBIT 9–12
Payoffs for Put Options to the Option Writer

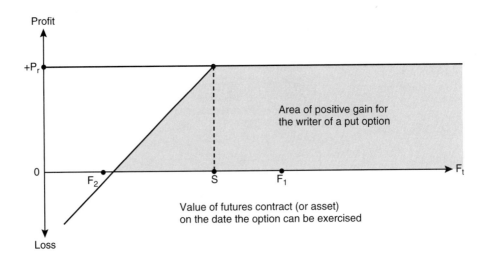

due to the premium (Pr) he or she has paid. Thus, the area of positive gain to the holder of a call option generally lies to the right of the strike price in Exhibit 9–13 and in the upper right-hand portion of that diagram.

The writer of a call option, on the other hand, gains when the market value of the futures contract or asset falls below the strike price, as at $F_2 < S$ in Exhibit 9–14. At this price and at all prices below S, the call option is "out of the money" for the option buyer and will go unexercised, allowing the option writer to earn the option premium, Pr. However, if the futures' or asset's market value climbs above S, as at price F_1 in Exhibit 9–14, the writer must sell off from his portfolio currently higher-valued assets to the option buyer at the low contract price S, taking a loss equal to $F_1 - S$. The call option clearly has become "in the money" for the option buyer. As shown in Exhibit 9–14, the region of positive gain for the writer of a call option lies in the upper left-hand portion of the price diagram (including price F_2). In contrast, futures or asset prices increasingly to the right of point S result in decreasing profits or increasing losses for the option writer.

EXHIBIT 9–13
Payoffs to the Option Buyer from Call Options

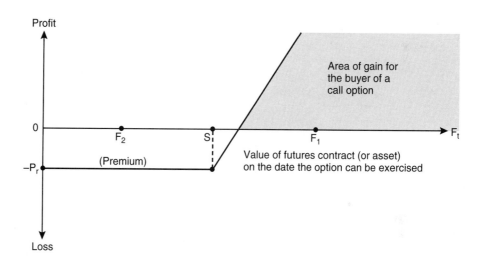

EXHIBIT 9–14
Payoffs to the Option Writer from Call Options

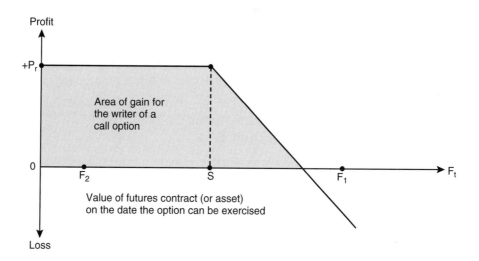

Risks and Costs Associated with Futures and Options

Futures and options trading is not without its own special risks and costs. The risk of price and yield fluctuations is reduced through negotiating these contracts, but the investor faces the risk of changing interest rates and security prices between futures and spot markets (basis risk). It is rare that gains and losses from simultaneous trading in spot, futures, or options markets exactly offset each other, resulting in a perfect hedge. There is also the risk of broker cash margin calls on the trader due to adverse price changes (margin risk) and possible problems in liquidating an open position in futures or options (liquidity risk). Moreover, there are substantial brokerage fees for executing futures contracts and required minimum deposits for margin accounts that tie up cash in non-interest-bearing assets.

Questions *to Help You Study*

16. Define and explain the use of the following:

    Long hedge

    Short hedge

    Cross hedge

17. Which type of hedge named above works best in an environment of *rising* interest rates? Of *falling* interest rates? Can you illustrate this using a payoff diagram?

18. Explain the uses of the following instruments:

    Call options

    Put options

19. What type of option contract is appropriate in an environment of *rising* interest rates? *Falling* interest rates? Please illustrate this using payoff diagrams.

20. What risks and costs are inherent in financial futures and options trading?

Appendix

The Black-Scholes Model for Valuing Options

In the real world, we have discovered that not one, but several, variables influence the prices of options. These variables include the following:

Rf = The *risk-free rate of interest* (that investors can approximately achieve by purchasing default-free government securities), which is positively related to option prices.

P = The *current market value* (price) of the futures contract or security that is the subject of the option contract, which is positively related to the option's price.

σ = The *degree of volatility* in the value of the underlying futures contract or security, measured by the variance (σ^2) or standard deviation (σ) of its rate of return, which is also positively related to the price of the option.

S = The *strike price* specified in the option contract, which is negatively related to the price of the option.

t = The *length of time* between now and the point in time when the option expires, also positively related to the option's price.

In 1973, a major breakthrough occurred in the field of finance when researchers Fisher Black and Myron Scholes developed a model that explained the price of a call option (C) using continuous-time mathematics. They determined that the call option's price could be found by solving the following differential equation:

$$C = P \times Nr\,(Y_A) - Se^{-Rft} \times Nr\,(Y_B) \qquad \textbf{(A–1)}$$

where

$$Y_A = [\ln(P/S) + Rft + \sigma^2 t/2]\sigma t^{1/2} \qquad \textbf{(A–2)}$$

and

$$Y_B = [\ln(P/S) + Rft - \sigma^2 t/2]\sigma t^{1/2} \qquad \textbf{(A–3)}$$

In the preceding formula, ln represents the log of a quantity relative to the base *e,* and *Nr* stands for the normal cumulative probability density function, measuring the probability that a normally distributed random variable will be equal to or less then *Y.* Several brokers operating today on Wall Street use high-speed computer programs that calculate the expected value of an option as figured from the above formula and then buy or sell options or securities until option prices approach their expected levels. (See the accompanying box for an example of how to use the Black-Scholes Formula to calculate an option's expected value.)

Reduced to nonmathematical terms, the preceding equation suggests that option prices depend on the expected value of the underlying futures contract or security named in the option and the expected value of the strike price on the day the option expires, both expressed in present-value terms. The discount rate used is the risk-free interest rate because, Black and Scholes assumed, there are enough informed and technically sophisticated investors to effectively reduce risk close to the risk-free rate of return by constructing an adequately hedged investment portfolio. In such a portfolio, movements in the value of options, futures, and securities will offset each other, leaving the value of the investor's total portfolio better protected against adverse price and rate movements (though there always remains some unhedgeable volatility risk). Subsequent testing of the Black-Scholes model suggests that it performs reasonably well at calculating the true value of European options (which can be exercised only on a single day), making significant errors only when the underlying securities have especially large or small variability in rates of return or, in the case of options on stock, when a stock's dividend payments are significant.[1]

---

[1] The Black-Scholes formula in Equation A–1 measures the expected value of a *call* option (*C*). We can find the expected value of the corresponding *put* option having the same strike price and time to maturity by solving:

$$\text{Expected value of put} = C + Se^{-Rf \times t} - P$$

where *P* is the price of the underlying security or futures contract and *S, Rf,* and *t* are the same as defined in Equation A–1.

The Black-Scholes option pricing model rests on some strong assumptions. It assumes that there are no transactions costs or taxes, that the underlying asset does not pay out income during the life of an option, that the standard deviation of return is constant, that security prices follow a continuous random process, homogenous expectations among investors, and that the risk-free interest rate is constant over time and the same regardless of maturity. However, repeated testing suggests that even if these assumptions are violated, the option value estimates generated by the Black-Scholes model usually are remarkably close to real-world values.

PRICING OPTIONS: AN EXAMPLE

To illustrate how to price an option on financial futures or other securities using the Black-Scholes pricing model let's suppose that the current price of the futures contract or security in which we are interested is $100 with a standard deviation around its expected rate of return of 0.50, or 50 percent; that the option on this security has a strike price of $95; and that the risk-free interest rate is currently 10 percent. If the option will expire in three months (0.25 years), what is its expected price according to the Black-Scholes model?

The expected current price of a *call option* (C) on this security can be found from:

$$\text{Expected call option price (C)} = P \times Nr(Y_A) - Se^{-Rf \times t} \times Nr(Y_B)$$

where P is the current market price, S the strike price, Rf the risk-free rate, and t the option's time to maturity. The terms $Nr(Y_A)$ and $Nr(Y_B)$ measure the probability that the option will have value to the buyer (i.e., the probability the option will eventually be exercised because it is "in the money"). The higher the probability that an option will be "in the money," the higher must be its price to the option buyer. Nr represents the normal distribution; the security's return is assumed to be normally distributed.

We can calculate the probability that this option will pay off from:

$$Y_A = [1n(P/S) + Rf \times t + \sigma^2 t/2]/\sigma t^{1/2}$$

Substituting in the figures from our example,

$$Y_A = (1n[100/95] + [0.10 \times 0.25] + 0.25 \times (0.50)^2/2)/0.50 \times (.25)^{1/2} = 0.43$$

We can derive the second probability estimate in the equation, Y_B, from:

$$Y_B = Y_A - \sigma t^{1/2} = (0.43) - (0.50) \times (0.25)^{1/2} = 0.18$$

Next, we find the corresponding values from the assumed normal distribution of security prices, represented by $Nr(Y_A)$ and $Nr(Y_B)$. These we can look up in a table for the cumulative normal distribution, which is contained in most statistics books. A portion of such a table is given below:

Cumulative Normal Distribution Table							
Y	**Nr(Y)**	**Y**	**Nr(Y)**	**Y**	**Nr(Y)**	**Y**	**Nr(Y)**
−0.50	.3085	−0.20	.4207	0.12	.5478	0.20	.5793
−0.40	.3446	−0.10	.4602	0.14	.5557	0.30	.6179
−0.30	.3821	0.00	.5000	0.16	.5636	0.40	.6554
−0.25	.4013	0.10	.5398	0.18	.5714	0.50	.6915

Checking the above table and interpolating if necessary for the normal probabilities associated with Y_A and Y_B gives:

$$Nr(0.43) = .6664$$

$$Nr(0.18) = .5714$$

continued

concluded

Then, the expected value of the call option must be:

$$\text{Expected call option price (C)} = \$100 \times (.6664) - \$95 \times e^{-10 \times 0.25} \times (.5714) = \$13.70$$

Could we also find the value of a put option for this same security? Assuming the same option strike price and option maturity, the expected value of the corresponding put option would be:

$$\text{Expected put option price} = C + Se^{-Rf \times t} - P$$

Substituting in the calculated call option price (*C*) of $13.70, the security's price (*P*) of $100, the strike price (*S*) of $95, the risk-free interest rate (*Rf*) of 10 percent, and 0.25 years time to maturity (*t*) from the example above, we get an expected put option price of:

$$\text{Expected put option price} = \$13.70 + \$95e^{(-.10 \times 0.25)} - 100$$

Checking the value of $e^{(-.10 \times 0.25)}$ on a calculator gives:

$$\text{Expected put option price} = \$13.7 + \$95(0.9753) - \$100 = \$6.35$$

Summary of the Chapter

This chapter is devoted to the forecasting (predicting) and hedging (risk protection activities) associated with changing interest rates and changes in the prices of securities and other financial assets. It also examines basic patterns in the behavior of market interest rates, exploring the linkages between interest rates, asset prices, and the economy.

- Interest rates appear to bear a close relationship to the *economy,* tending to rise in periods of economic expansion and fall in economic recessions.

- Short-term interest rates tend to change more rapidly than long-term interest rates, moving over a much wider range than long-term interest rates as economic conditions change.

- Several different methods of interest-rate forecasting have been employed in recent years, though none have been consistently successful. Most forecasting approaches today rely upon linkages in the economy and financial system, predictions of inflation, money-supply changes, and changing expectations of borrowers and lenders in the financial marketplace as reflected in such indicators as the yield curve and the prices and yields attached to financial futures contracts.

- The great difficulties inherent in forecasting interest rates have led many borrowers and lenders of funds to practice *hedging,* insulating themselves at least partially from the ravages of fluctuating interest rates and asset prices in the financial marketplace.

- In recent years one of the most popular of all interest-rate and asset-price hedging tools has been the interest-rate swap in which borrowing institutions exchange interest payments with each other. The net effect of a well-drawn swap agreement is to achieve a better balance between interest revenue inflows and interest cost outflows. Frequently such transactions also result in lower interest costs for both participants in a swap agreement.

- During the 1970s and 1980s *financial futures* and *option contracts* on a variety of debt securities, stocks, and stock indices (such as the Standard & Poor's 500-stock index) began trading in the United States at the Chicago Board of Trade and the Chicago Mercantile Exchange and, subsequently, spread around the world on multiple exchanges. Both futures and options are contracts calling for the future delivery of securities or cash at an agreed-upon price in an effort to set the price or yield on a future trade and, thereby, lessen the risk associated with future price and interest-rate fluctuations.

- Hedging with financial futures contracts and options transfers risk from one investor to another willing to bear that risk. The hedger contracts away all or a portion of the risk of asset-price and interest-rate fluctuations in order to lock in a targeted rate of return. This is accomplished by taking equal and opposite positions in the spot (cash) market and in the forward (or futures) market or by purchasing put or call options to deliver or take delivery of designated assets or futures contracts at a stipulated price on or before a specific date.

- If interest rates are expected to *fall* and an investor desires to lock in a current high yield on a security or other financial asset, he or she would buy a contract calling for the future delivery of the security (or other financial asset) at a set price (i.e., take on a *long hedge*) or purchase a *call option* contract. An opposite set of buy-sell transactions in the futures market (i.e., a *short hedge*) or in the options market (i.e., a *put option*) would generally be used if interest rates were expected to *rise*.

Key Terms

Business cycle, *235*	Econometric models, *238*	Short hedge, *250*
Seasonality, *236*	Consensus forecast, *238*	Cross hedge, *251*
Money-supply expectations effect, *237*	Interest rate swaps, *239*	Option contract, *254*
Money-supply income effect, *237*	Hedging, *244*	Call options, *254*
Money-supply liquidity effect, *237*	Basis, *244*	Strike price, *254*
Implied rate forecasting, *238*	Financial futures contracts, *245*	Put options, *254*
	Long hedge, *249*	Option premium, *254*

Problems

1. In an interest rate swap transaction, a large corporation can borrow in the bond market at a current fixed rate of 9 percent and could also obtain a floating-rate loan in the short-term market at the prime bank rate. However, this firm wishes to borrow short term because it has a large block of assets that roll over into cash each month. The other party to the swap is a company with a lower credit rating that can borrow in the bond market at an interest rate of 11.5 percent and in the short-term market at prime plus 1.50 percent. This lower-rated company has long-term predictable cash inflows, however. The higher-credit-rated company wishes to pay for its part in the swap an interest rate of prime less 50 basis points. The lower-rated company is willing to pay the underwriting cost associated with the higher-rated company's security issue, which is estimated to be 25 basis points. The swap transaction is valued at $100 million. What kind of interest

rate swap can be arranged here? Which company will borrow short term and which long term? If the prime bank rate is currently 10 percent, who will pay what interest cost to whom? Explain what the benefit is to each party in this swap.

2. Suppose that a top-quality firm with an A-1 or AAA credit rating can borrow at a fixed coupon rate attached to its bonds of 12 percent. Moreover, this firm's bank is willing to extend it a LIBOR-based loan in London at a rate of 9.5 percent that will change weekly as LIBOR moves. Working through its principal banker, this top-rated company makes contact with a firm whose credit rating is considerably lower (rated only BB). The lower-rated firm has been informed by its investment banker that it probably could sell bonds at a 14 percent coupon rate, and the finance company from which it receives short-term money has promised a LIBOR-based floating-rate loan of 11.25 percent. Could these two firms benefit from a swap under the interest rates given above? Which firm would save the most, and under what circumstances? Will the company with the lower credit rating have to offer the top-credit-quality firm an added inducement to participate in a rate swap? What inducement or inducements could be used to equalize the interest savings for both parties?

3. What position in the swap market does each of the following parties occupy?
   a. INTEX Corporation pays a fixed interest rate of 9 percent and receives a floating interest rate equal to the 3-month Treasury bill rate.
   b. CrossTimbers International, Ltd. pays out an interest rate based on the 6-month LIBOR rate and receives a long-term, fixed rate of 10 percent.
   c. Montgomery Securities pays out and also receives an interest rate based upon a flexible 12-month LIBOR interest rate; it also receives a fixed interest rate of 9.5 percent, while paying out a fixed rate of 9.3 percent.

4. An insurance company during the month of March committed itself to buy a block of home mortgages at a fixed price from a mortgage banker in September. The mortgages have a face value of $10 million. The insurer has recently prepared a forecast that indicates that mortgage interest rates will rise between now and September by a full percentage point. What kind of futures transaction would you recommend to protect the insurance company against a sizable loss on its mortgage commitment, particularly if it has to sell the mortgages shortly after they are taken into its portfolio? Indicate specifically what buy and sell transactions you would undertake in the futures market. Which futures contract would you most likely use? Why? What options contract seems best and why?

5. A large money center bank plans to offer money market CDs in substantial volume (at least $100 million) in six months due to a projected upsurge in credit deals from some of its most valued corporate customers. Unfortunately, the bank's economist has just predicted that money market interest rates should rise over the next year (with perhaps a full 1.5 percentage point increase within the next six months). Explain why the bank's management would be concerned about this development. Suppose management expects its corporate loan customers to resist any loan terms that would automatically result in loan rates being immediately adjusted upward to reflect any rate increases in the money market. What futures market transaction would you recommend? What is the best options contract alternative for the bank?

6. An investment banking firm discovers that 90 days from today it is due to receive a cash payment from one of its corporate clients of $972,500. The firm's portfolio manager is instructed to plan to invest this new cash for a horizon of three months, after which it will need to be liquidated. Interest rates are attractive today at 10 percent, but a steep decline is forecast due to a developing recession. The portfolio manager decides to try to guarantee a 9 percent rate of return today on this planned three-month investment of cash.

    a. Describe what the manager should do today in the financial futures market. Then, indicate how he will close out the futures position eventually.

    b. What are the appropriate (buy-sell) steps for the manager if options on financial futures are to be used?

7. During the month just concluded, the prices of U.S. Treasury bonds fluctuated between a price of $95 (based on a $100 par value) and a price of $93. Treasury bond futures over the same period fluctuated between $92 and $88 (based on a $100 par value). How did the *basis* for T-bond futures contracts change over this period? What was the *volatility ratio* for T-bond futures for the month just ended? Using the volatility ratio you have just calculated and assuming you wish to hedge for the next 30 days $25 million in Treasury bonds that you currently hold with $100,000 denomination T-bond futures contracts maturing in 90 days, how many T-bond futures contracts will you need to buy to fully cover the $25 million in securities at risk?

8. Please identify each of the terms and concepts presented in this chapter that are defined or described below:

    a. Fluctuations in economic activity.

    b. Patterns in market interest rates during the year.

    c. Money supply increases push interest rates downward.

    d. Actual money growth versus expected money growth.

    e. Changes in spending and income receipts result in interest rate movements in the same direction.

    f. Systems of equations designed to predict or explain interest rate movements.

    g. Securities expected to be offered for sale in future periods.

    h. Market's expectation concerning future interest rate levels.

    i. Use of several different forecasting approaches.

    j. Two borrowers exchange interest payments.

    k. Using financial tools to protect against fluctuations in financial asset prices or interest rates.

    l. The spread between the spot and forward prices of a financial asset.

    m. Contracts applying to the forward sale of assets at a price set when the contract is made.

    n. Simultaneous purchase and sale of stocks and futures contracts in order to profit from temporary price differences.

    o. Purchase of futures contracts.

    p. Sale of futures contracts.

    q. Trading different financial assets in futures and cash (spot) markets.

    r. Price of acquiring financial assets listed in an option contract.

    s. Right to purchase a specified volume of assets at a specified price before expiration.

    t. Right to sell a specified volume of financial assets at a specified price before expiration.

    u. Price of an option.

Questions about the Web and the Money and Capital Markets

1. If you wanted to discover what interest-rate forecasters are predicting to happen to money and capital market interest rates next quarter and next year where could you go on the Web to find out?

2. Suppose you were interested in learning how to use interest-rate hedging tools. What different sites are available on the Web to help you get the information you need?

3. If you had to explain to someone who doesn't know the differences between various interest-rate derivatives, often used in interest-rate hedging, where would you advise that person to look on the Web?

4. Identify at least six of the world's top futures and options exchanges. Based on their Web sites do these exchanges appear to be about the same and do they differ from one another?

5. What main services does a futures and options exchange provide?

6. Describe three dealer/broker sites in the area of futures and options trading. Do these dealers or brokers appear to be similar or different from one another? Which sites most appeal to you?

Selected References

Anderson, Leonall C., and Keith M. Carlson. "A Monetarist Model for Economic Stabilization." *Review,* Federal Reserve Bank of St. Louis, April 1970, pp. 7–25.

Barth, James R., and James T. Bennett. "Seasonal Variation in Interest Rates." *Review of Economics and Statistics,* February 1975, pp. 80–83.

Black, Fisher, and M. Scholes. "The Valuation of Option Contracts and a Test of Market Efficiency." *Journal of Finance,* May 1972.

———. "The Pricing of Options and Corporate Liabilities." *Journal of Political Economy* 81 (May–June 1973), pp. 637–54.

Galaif, Lisa N. "Index Amortizing Rate Swaps." *Quarterly Review,* Federal Reserve Bank of New York, Winter 1993–94, pp. 63–70.

Haubrich, Joseph G. "Swaps and the Swaps Yield Curve," *Economic Commentary,* Federal Reserve Bank of Cleveland, December 2001, pp. 1–4.

Parkin, Michael. *Macroeconomics,* 2nd ed. New York: Addison-Wesley, 1993.

Rose, Peter S. *Commercial Bank Management,* 5th ed. New York: McGraw-Hill, 2002.

———. "Interest Rates, Economics Forecasting, and Bank Profits." *Canadian Banker,* 91, no. 3 (June 1984), pp. 38–44.

Sill, Keith. "The Cyclical Volatility of Interest Rates." *Business Review,* Federal Reserve Bank of Philadelphia, January/February 1996, pp. 15–29.

Sundaresan, Suresh. *Fixed Income Markets and Their Derivatives.* Cincinnati: Southwestern, 1997.

Part **Three**

The Money Market and Central Banking

This section of the text examines one of the most important of all markets in the world—the market for short-term loans, securities, and other near-money financial instruments, known as the *money market.* This highly visible and widely respected institution attracts temporary cash surpluses from savers for brief periods of time and grants short-term loans to borrowers facing temporary cash deficits.

In this portion of the book we not only present an overview of the money market, but also explore in some depth its principal financial instruments. These highly popular short-term financial assets include such well-known instruments as Treasury bills, repurchase agreements (RPs), Federal funds, bank certificates of deposit (CDs), commercial paper, federal agency securities, bankers acceptances, and Eurodeposits.

Part Three also explores the history and makeup of one of the most important financial-service institutions ever invented—the *central bank.* This centuries-old banking institution not only works to stabilize and protect the value of a nation's currency but also strives to combat inflation, promote economic growth, and pursue full employment. In the concluding two chapters of Part Three, we focus upon both central banking in general and the unique characteristics of the Federal Reserve System—the most powerful and most respected central bank in the world.

Chapter **Ten**

Introduction to the Money Market

Learning Objectives in This Chapter

- You will understand the many roles and functions performed by the money market in order to aid the financial system and the economy.

- You will also be able to determine who the key actors—individuals and institutions—are in the workings of the money market.

- You will see how money market loans and securities differ from other financial services and instruments in the financial system.

- You will discover how the money market handles the fears of borrowers and lenders regarding risk in the financial marketplace and why speed and efficiency matter so much to money market participants.

What's in This Chapter? Key Topics Outline

Nature and Characteristics of the Money Market

Why the Money Market Is Needed

Key Borrowers and Lenders and the Structure of the Market

Investor Goals and Investment Risks

Global Money Markets

Federal Funds and Clearinghouse Funds

Volume of Money Market Securities

Pattern of Money Market Interest Rates

INTRODUCTION

To the casual observer, the financial markets appear to be one vast cauldron of borrowing and lending activity in which some individuals and institutions are seeking credit while others supply the funds needed to make lending possible. All transactions carried out in the financial markets seem to be basically the same: borrowers issue securities (financial assets) that lenders purchase. When the loan is repaid, the borrower retrieves the securities and returns borrowed funds to the lender. Closer examination of our financial system reveals,

The money market is one of the world's largest and most established financial systems—populated by the largest banks and security firms around the globe—providing short-term saving and lending services to hundreds of thousands of corporations, governments, and wealthy investors. Governed largely by verbal agreements and understandings, rather than rigid, written rules, it is also the key vehicle today for the transmission of government policy to the economy as a whole.

As the money market has grown in size, it has attracted great attention on the World Wide Web. Explanations of money market trading, instruments, and interest rates may be found in such sites as *www.enth.com/ask.asp*, *www.investinginbonds.com*, and *www.bondmarket.com*. Extensive data on money market behavior over time may be found in the Federal Reserve Board's databank at *www.economagic.com/fedbog.htm*. There are also extensive advertisements posted on the Web by leading banks and security dealers who traffic daily in the money market, including such institutions as Citigroup, J. P. Morgan Chase, Wells Fargo Bank, Goldman Sachs, Merrill Lynch, and dozens of other money market–focused institutions.

however, that beyond the simple act of exchanging financial assets and funds, there are major differences between one financial transaction and another. For example, an individual may borrow $100,000 for 30 years to purchase a new home, whereas another's financing need may be for a six-month loan of $3,000 to cover a federal income tax obligation. A corporation may enter the financial markets this week to offer a new issue of 20-year bonds to finance the construction of an office building, and next week find itself in need of funds for just 60 days to purchase raw materials so that production can continue.

Clearly, then, the purposes for which money is borrowed within the financial system vary greatly from person to person and transaction to transaction. And the different purposes for which money is borrowed result in the creation of different kinds of financial assets, having different maturities, risks, and other features. In this chapter and the others in Part Three, we will be focusing on a collection of financial markets that share a common purpose in their trading activity and deal in financial instruments with similar features. Our particular focus is on the *money market*—the market for short-term credit.

In the money market, loans have an original maturity of one year or less. Money market loans are used to help corporations and governments pay the wages and salaries of their workers, make repairs, purchase inventories, pay dividends and taxes, and satisfy other short-term, working capital needs. In this respect, the money market stands in sharp contrast to the capital market. The capital market deals in long-term credit—that is, loans and securities over a year to maturity, typically used to finance long-term investment projects. There are important similarities between the money and capital markets, as we will see in subsequent chapters, but there are also important differences that make each of these two markets unique.

CHARACTERISTICS OF THE MONEY MARKET

The money market, like all financial markets, provides a channel for the exchange of financial assets for money. However, it differs from other parts of the financial system in its emphasis on loans to meet purely short-term cash needs (i.e., current account, rather than capital account, transactions). The **money market** is the mechanism through which *holders of temporary cash surpluses meet holders of temporary cash deficits*. It is designed, on the one hand, to meet the short-term cash requirements of corporations, financial institutions, and governments, providing a mechanism for granting loans as short as overnight and as long as one year to maturity. At the same time, the money market provides an investment outlet for those spending units (also principally corporations, financial institutions, and governments) that hold surplus cash for short periods of time and wish to earn at least some return on temporarily idle funds. The essential function of the money market is to bring these two groups into contact to make borrowing and lending possible.

The Need for a Money Market

Why is such a market needed? There are several reasons. First, for most individuals and institutions, inflows and outflows of cash are rarely in perfect harmony with each other. Governments, for example, collect taxes from the public only at certain times of the year, such as in April when personal and corporate income tax payments are due. Disbursements of cash must be made throughout the year, however, to cover the wages and salaries of government employees, office supplies, repairs, and fuel costs, as well as unexpected expenses. When taxes are collected, governments usually are flush with funds that far exceed their immediate cash needs. At these times, they frequently enter the money market as lenders and purchase Treasury bills, bank deposits, and other attractive financial assets. Later, however, as cash runs low relative to current expenditures, these same governmental units must once again enter the money market as borrowers of funds, issuing short-term notes attractive to money market investors.

Business firms, too, collect sales revenues from customers at one point in time and dispense cash at other points in time to cover wages and salaries, make repairs, and meet other operating expenses. The checking account of an active business firm fluctuates daily between large cash surpluses and low or nonexistent cash balances. A surplus cash position frequently brings such a firm into the money market as a net lender of funds, investing idle funds in the hope of earning at least a modest rate of return. Cash deficits force it onto the borrowing side of the market, however, seeking other institutions with temporary cash surpluses. Clearly, then, the money market serves to bridge the gap between receipts and expenditures of funds, covering cash deficits with short-term borrowing when current expenditures exceed receipts and providing an investment outlet to earn interest income for units whose current receipts exceed their current expenditures.

To fully appreciate the workings of the money market, we must remember that *money* is one of the most perishable of all commodities. The holding of idle surplus cash is expensive, because cash balances earn little or no income for their owners. When idle cash is not invested, the holder incurs an opportunity cost in the form of interest income that is forgone. Moreover, each day that idle funds are not invested is a day's income lost forever. When large amounts of funds are involved, the income lost from not profitably investing idle funds for even 24 hours can be substantial. For example, the interest income from a loan of $10 million for one day at a 10 percent annual rate of interest amounts to about $2,800.[1] In a week's time, nearly $20,000 in interest would be lost from not investing $10

---

[1]As we saw in Chapter 6, the amount of interest income from a simple interest loan may be calculated from the formula:

$$I = P \times r \times t$$

where *I* is interest income, *P* is the principal amount loaned, *r* is the annual rate of interest, and *t* is the maturity of the loan. In the example given above, we have

$$I = (\$10,000,000)(0.10)(1/360) = \$2,777.78$$

Note that for purposes of simplifying the calculation, we have assumed a 360-day year—a common assumption in determining yields on money market instruments.

million in idle funds. Many students of the financial system find it hard to believe that investment outlets exist for loans as short as one day. However, billions of dollars in credit are extended in the money market overnight or for only a few daylight hours to securities dealers, banks, and nonfinancial corporations to cover temporary shortfalls of cash. As we will see in the next chapter, one important money market instrument—the federal funds loan—is designed mainly for extending credit within a day or less or over a weekend.

Borrowers and Lenders in the Money Market

Who are the principal lenders of funds in the money market? Who are the principal borrowers? (See Exhibit 10–1 for an overview of the structure of the money market.) These questions are difficult to answer, because the same institutions frequently operate on *both* sides of the money market. For example, a large commercial bank operating in the money market (such as Citibank or the Bank of Montreal) will borrow funds aggressively through CDs, federal funds, and other short-term instruments while lending short-term funds to corporations that have temporary cash shortages. Frequently, large nonfinancial corporations borrow millions of dollars on a single day, only to come back into the money market later in the week as a lender of funds due to a sudden upsurge in cash receipts. Institutions that typically play *both sides* of the money market include large banks, finance companies, major nonfinancial corporations, and units of government. Even central banks, such as the Federal Reserve System, the European Central Bank (ECB), the Bank of England, or the Bank of Japan, may be aggressive suppliers of funds to the money market on one day and reverse themselves the day following, demanding funds through the sale of securities in the open market. One institution that is virtually always on the demand side of the market, however, is the government. The U.S. Treasury, for example, is among the largest of all money market borrowers (even though its current borrowing demands have slowed appreciably in recent years as the United States moved toward a substantial budget surplus, at least until a business recession struck as the twenty-first century began and the government's budget surplus began to ebb away).

The Goals of Money Market Investors

Investors in the money market seek mainly *safety* and *liquidity,* plus the opportunity to earn some interest income. This is because funds invested in the money market represent only temporary cash surpluses and are usually needed in the near future to meet tax obligations, cover wage and salary costs, pay stockholder dividends, and so on. For this reason, money market investors are especially *sensitive to risk.*

The strong aversion to risk among money market investors is especially evident when there is even a hint of trouble concerning the financial condition of a major money market borrower. For example, when the huge Penn Central Transportation Company collapsed in 1970 and defaulted on its short-term commercial notes, the short-term commercial paper market virtually ground to a halt because many investors refused to buy even the notes offered by top-grade companies. Similarly, during the 1980s, when the huge Continental Illinois Bank had to be propped up by government loans, the rates on short-term certificates of deposit (CDs) issued by other big banks surged upward due to fears on the part of money market investors that *all* large-bank CDs had become more risky. (See Exhibit 10–2 for a summary of the goals and instruments of the money market.)

Types of Investment Risk

What kinds of risk do investors face in the financial markets? And how do money market instruments rank in terms of these different kinds of risk?

EXHIBIT 10–1 Money Market Structure

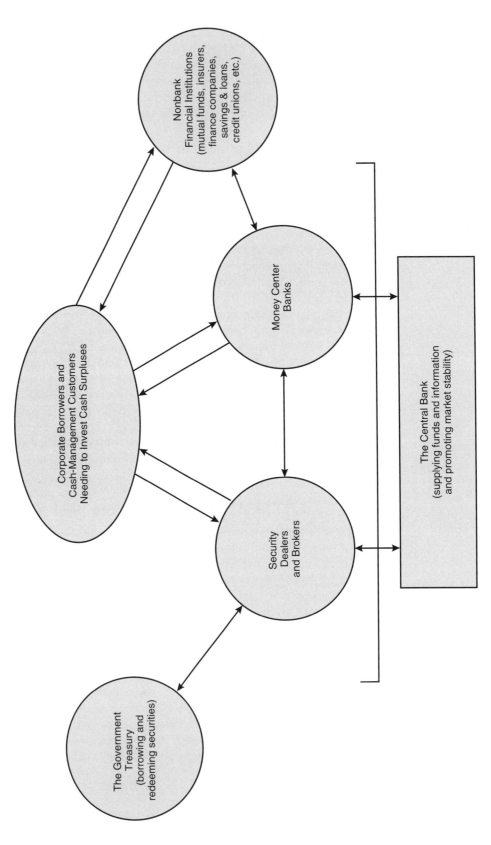

EXHIBIT 10–2 The Goals and Instruments of the Money Market

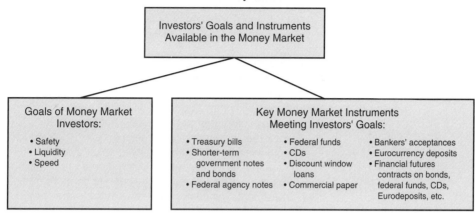

First, all securities, including money market instruments, carry **market risk** (sometimes called *interest rate risk*), which refers to the danger that their prices will fall (and interest rates rise), subjecting the investor to a capital loss. Even Treasury notes and bonds decline in price when interest rates rise. Not only can security prices fall, but so can interest rates. This latter development increases an investor's **reinvestment risk,** the risk that earnings from a financial asset will have to be reinvested in lower-yielding assets at some point in the future. Even government securities carry reinvestment risk.

Securities issued by private firms and state and local governments carry **default risk.** For such securities, there is always some positive probability that the borrower will fail to meet some or all of his or her promised principal and/or interest payments (as happened to Orange County, California, in 1995, and to Enron Corporation and Argentina in 2001, for example, as discussed earlier in Chapter 8).

Lenders of funds face the possibility that increases in the average level of prices for all goods and services will reduce the purchasing power of their income. This is known as **inflation risk** (sometimes called *purchasing power risk*). Lenders usually attempt to offset anticipated inflation by demanding higher contract rates on their loans.

International investors also face **currency risk:** possible loss due to unfavorable changes in the value of foreign currencies. For example, if a U.S. investor purchases British Treasury bills on the London money market, the return from these bills may be severely reduced if the value of the British pound falls relative to the dollar during the life of the investment.

Finally, **political risk** refers to the possibility that changes in government laws or regulations will result in a diminished rate of return to the investor or, in the extreme case, a total loss of invested capital. For example, the windfall profits tax on U.S. petroleum companies levied by Congress during the 1980s generally reduced the earnings of petroleum stockholders. Investors in industries that are closely regulated, such as banking and public utilities, continually run the risk that new price controls, output quotas, or other restrictions will be imposed, reducing their earnings potential. In some foreign countries, facilities and equipment owned by U.S. corporations have been expropriated by national governments, resulting in total loss for the investors involved. A summary of each of the foregoing kinds of risk is shown in Exhibit 10–3.

Money market instruments generally offer more protection against such risks than most other investments. The prices of money market securities tend to be remarkably stable over time compared to the prices of bonds, stocks, real estate, and commodities, such as wheat

EXHIBIT 10–3
Types of Risk Confronting Investors in the Money and Capital Markets

Type of Risk	Definition
Market risk	The risk that the market price (value) of an asset will decline, resulting in a capital loss when sold. Sometimes referred to as *interest rate risk.*
Reinvestment risk	The risk that an investor will be forced to place earnings from a loan or security into a lower-yielding investment because interest rates have fallen.
Default risk	The probability that a borrower will fail to meet one or more promised principal or interest payments on a loan or security.
Inflation risk	The risk that increases in the general price level will reduce the purchasing power of earnings from a loan, security, or other investment.
Currency risk	The risk that adverse movements in the price of one national currency vis-à-vis another will reduce the net rate of return from a foreign investment. Sometimes referred to as *exchange rate risk.*
Political risk	The probability that changes in government laws or regulations will reduce an investor's expected return from an investment.

and gold. Money market instruments generally do not offer the prospect of significant capital gains for the investor, but neither do they normally raise the specter of substantial capital losses. Similarly, default risk is minimal in the money market. In fact, money market borrowers must be well-established institutions with impeccable credit ratings before their securities can even be offered for sale in this market.

Few investments today adequately protect the investor against inflation risk. Money market securities are no exception. However, they do offer superior **liquidity,** allowing the investor to quickly cash them in, with little risk of loss of principal, when a promising inflation-hedged investment opportunity comes along.

Currency risk concerns the international investor who frequently must convert one currency into another. That risk has increased dramatically in recent years due to the increase in foreign exchange rates that float with market conditions. Investors who purchase securities in foreign markets cannot completely escape currency risk, but they are probably less prone to such losses when buying money market instruments due to the short-term nature of money market assets. These assets also provide some hedge against political risk because they are short-term investments and fewer dramatic changes in government policy are likely over brief intervals of time. Moreover, the appearance of the Euro in the European money market as the twentieth century ended and the twenty-first century began is likely to reduce some forms of currency risk in one of the world's largest international markets for goods and services.

Questions *to Help You Study*

1. What exactly do we mean by the term *money market*?

2. Please explain why there is a critical need within the economy and financial system to have money market instruments available to anyone who can afford them.

3. What are the principal *goals* usually pursued by money market investors?

4. The money market is characterized by very large financial institutions. Who are the principal borrowers and lenders in this market?

5. Please define the following types of *risk:*

Market risk

Default risk

Inflation risk

Currency risk

Political risk

Which of the risks listed above are *minimized* by purchasing money market instruments? Does investing in the money market avoid *all* of the foregoing risks?

Money Market Maturities

Despite the fact that money market securities cover a narrow range of maturities—one year or less—there are maturities available within this range to meet just about every short-term investment need. We must distinguish here between original maturity and actual maturity, however. The interval of time between the issue date of a security and the date on which the borrower promises to redeem it is the security's **original maturity. Actual maturity,** on the other hand, refers to the number of days, months, or years between today and the date the security is actually retired.

Original maturities on money market instruments range from as short as one day on many loans to banks and security dealers to a full year on some bank deposits and Treasury bills. Obviously, once a money market instrument is issued, it grows shorter in actual maturity every day. Because there are thousands of money market securities outstanding, some of which reach maturity each day, investors have a wide menu from which to select the precise number of days they need to invest their cash.

Depth and Breadth of the Money Market

The money market is extremely *broad* and *deep,* meaning it can absorb a large volume of transactions with only small effects on security prices and interest rates. Investors can easily sell most money market instruments on short notice, often in a matter of minutes. This is one of the most efficient markets in the world, containing a vast network of securities dealers, major banks, and funds brokers in constant touch with one another and alert to any bargains. The slightest hint that a security is underpriced (i.e., carries an exceptionally high yield) usually brings a flood of buy orders, but money market traders are quick to dump or avoid overpriced securities. This market is dominated by active traders who constantly search their video display screens for opportunities to arbitrage funds; that is, they move money from one corner of the market with relatively low yields to another where investments offer the highest returns available. Overseeing the whole market is the Federal Reserve System and other central banks around the globe, who try to ensure that trading is orderly and prices are reasonably stable.

There is no centralized trading arena in the money market as there is on a stock exchange, for example. The money market is a telephone and computer market, in which participants arrange trades over the phone or through computer networks and usually confirm their transactions by wire. Speed is of the essence in this market because, as we observed earlier, money is a highly perishable commodity. Each day that passes means thousands of dollars in lost interest income if newly received funds are not immediately invested. Most business between traders, therefore, is conducted in seconds or minutes, and payment is made almost instantaneously.

Money markets around the world share several common characteristics. They reconcile cash imbalances for public and private businesses, individuals, and institutions and do so at low levels of risk for both borrowers and lenders. Money markets also transmit government economic policies, aiding governments in financing their deficits (fiscal policy) and in managing the growth of money and credit (monetary policy).

Each nation has its own money market, though some are poorly developed and others reach far beyond the boundaries of one country or continent to involve traders on many continents. There is an *international money market* that arches over all the domestic money markets and ties them all together, trading in under-one-year credit instruments that are bought and sold all over the globe. The heart of the international money market is the Eurocurrency market, where large bank deposits are traded outside the boundaries of the country where a particular currency is issued. Increasingly, domestic money markets are being integrated into the international money market; *no* nation's money market today is unaffected by movements in interest rates and security prices in the international money market.

As Dufey and Giddy (1993) have observed, national money markets around the globe tend to fall into one of two types— those (such as the United States and Great Britain) that are *securities market dominated,* where most borrowing and lending is through open-market trading of financial instru-

ments, and those that are *bank dominated,* where bank borrowing and lending is at the center of most transactions (as in Japan and China). However, worldwide deregulation of many financial institutions is under way, with the probable outcome that more money markets of the future will become more security trading oriented and less dominated by a few large financial institutions.

In developing countries, money markets are usually dominated by large banks because their securities markets usually are not well developed. In these settings, money market trading usually starts with interbank trading of deposits. In some cases, the banks involved are government owned and at least some money market interest rates may be regulated so the government can issue debt more cheaply. Moreover, the government may play a major role in allocating credit, reducing the efficiency of the financial marketplace in allocating savings and credit. Bank-dominated money markets have a potential weakness, as economic problems experienced in Asia during the late 1990s suggest; they can yield more easily to government pressure, resulting in many bad loans, and they may slow the development of long-term capital markets, which promote greater economic stability. Central banks, such as the Federal Reserve and the European Central Bank, are usually the single most important institution in money markets, no matter whether they are security dominated or bank dominated.

Federal Funds versus Clearinghouse Funds

How can funds move so fast in the money market? The reason is that money market traders usually deal in **federal funds.** These funds are mainly deposit balances of commercial banks held at the regional Federal Reserve banks and at larger correspondent banks across the nation. When a dealer firm buys securities from an investor, for example, it immediately contacts its bank and requests that funds be transferred from its account to the investor's account at another bank. Many of these transactions move via a public or private wire network (such as the Federal Reserve's electronic wire transfer network in the United States). In this case, the central bank or funds transfer firm removes funds from the reserve account of the buyer's bank and transfers these reserves to the seller's bank. The transaction is so quick that the seller of securities has funds available to make new investments, pay bills, or to use for other purposes the same day a trade is carried out or a loan is made. Federal funds are often called *immediately available* funds because of the speed with which money moves from one bank's reserve account to that of another.

Contrast this method of payment with that used generally in the capital market and by most businesses and households. When most of us purchase goods and services— especially purchases involving a large amount of money—a check or a credit card (followed by issuing a check) is the most desirable means of paying the bill. Funds transferred by check are known as **clearinghouse funds,** because once the buyer writes a check, it goes to the seller's depository institution, which forwards that check eventually to the deposit-type institution upon which it was drawn. If the two depositories are in the same community, they exchange bundles of checks drawn against each other every day through the local clearinghouse—an agreed-upon location where checks and other cash items are delivered and passed from one depository institution to another.

Clearinghouse funds are an acceptable means of payment for most purposes, but not in the money market, where speed is of the essence. It takes at least a day to clear local checks and two to three days for checks moving between cities. For money market transactions, this is far too slow, because no interest can be earned until the check is collected. Clearinghouse funds also have an element of *risk,* because a check may be returned as fraudulent or for insufficient funds. Federal funds transactions, however, are both speedy and safe.

A Market for Large Borrowers and Lenders

The money market is dominated by a relatively small number of large financial institutions. No more than a hundred banks in New York, London, Tokyo, Singapore, and a handful of other money centers are at the heart of the market. These large institutions account for the bulk of federal funds trading through which many money market transactions are carried out. In addition, securities move readily from sellers to buyers through the market-making activities of major security dealers and brokers. And, of course, governments and central banks around the world play major roles in this market as the largest borrowers and as regulators, setting the rules of the game. For example, the Federal Reserve System, operating principally through the trading desk at the Federal Reserve Bank of New York, is in the market nearly every day, either supplying funds to banks and security dealers or absorbing funds through security sales.

Individual transactions in the money market involve huge amounts of funds. Most trading occurs in multiples of a million dollars. For this reason, the money market is often referred to as a *wholesale market* for funds, as opposed to the retail market where most households and small businesses borrow and save.

Questions *to Help You Study*

6. What is the difference between *actual maturity* and *original maturity* of a financial asset? Why is this difference important in the money market?

7. How do money markets around the world differ from one another?

8. What danger do *bank-dominated money markets* face that may be less of a problem in *security-dominated money markets*?

9. What are *federal funds* and how do they differ from *clearinghouse funds*?

10. Which of these two types of funds—federal funds versus clearinghouse funds—are most important in the money market and why is this so?

THE VOLUME OF MONEY MARKET SECURITIES

The principal financial instruments traded in the money market are Treasury bills, federal agency securities, dealer loans, repurchase agreements, bank certificates of deposit (CDs), federal funds, commercial paper, bankers' acceptances, financial futures, and Eurocurrency deposits. Each of these instruments is discussed in detail in the next several chapters, but it is useful at this point to examine the relative importance, measured by the dollar volume outstanding, of each of these instruments in the U.S. portion of the money market.

In fact, the volume of money market securities has grown rapidly in recent years. One reason is the international economy's growing need for liquid, readily marketable, and relatively safe securities, particularly during periods when banks are failing and some national currencies are tumbling in value. Another factor in the money market's growth has been the attractive yields offered investors.

As shown in Exhibit 10–4, two of the most important money market instruments (measured by dollar volume) are *Treasury bills* and *certificates of deposit (CDs)*. By 2000, nearly $650 billion in U.S. Treasury bills were outstanding, representing just over 10 percent of the United States government's total debt. However, T-bills outstanding fell back somewhat in 2001 to $620 billion due to reduced government borrowing needs.

Even larger in total amount were $100,000-plus certificates of deposit issued by banks operating in the United States. These large-denomination CDs totaled more than $700 billion in 2000 before slipping back slightly below $700 billion during the recession in the economy in 2001. Thus, like most other money market instruments, the volume of the CDs fluctuates with economic and credit-market conditions, with corporate earnings fluctuations, and with changes in the interest rates (yields) available on other financial assets.

The largest sector in today's money market consists of securities issued by U.S. *federal agencies.* These high-quality securities—a substantial portion of which fall due within a year and, therefore, are true money market instruments—totaled more than $1.9 trillion in 2001. Over half of all agency IOUs are issued by just three federally sponsored organizations: the Federal Home Loan banks, the Federal National Mortgage Association, and the Federal Home Loan Mortgage Corporation. The remaining agency issues come from a variety of government-related enterprises and organizations, including the Department of Defense, the Export-Import Bank, the Postal Service, the Student Loan Marketing Association, and the Farm Credit banks.

Commercial paper issued by topflight corporations also totaled well over a trillion dollars in 2001 and represented one of the most rapidly growing money market instruments. Many large corporations have found the commercial paper market a cheaper and more flexible place to obtain credit than borrowing from banks (though the market dipped after the terror attacks of September 2001). *Bankers' acceptances*—time drafts against large multinational banks—have fluctuated with the growth of world trade and declined in recent years, but they totaled close to $10 billion in 2001.

EXHIBIT 10–4
Volume of Selected Money Market Instruments ($ Billions at Year-End)

Financial Instruments	1990	1992	1994	1996	1998	2000	2001*
U.S. Treasury bills	$527	$658	$734	$777	$ 691	$ 647	$ 620
Federal agency securities	435	484	742	926	1,296	1,852	1,920
Commercial paper	561	549	595	775	1,163	1,624	1,454
Bankers' acceptances	55	38	30	26	14	10	10
Federal funds borrowings and repurchase agreements	409	448	482	610	572	618	660
Net Eurodollar borrowings by domestic banks from their own branches	37	71	76	114	152	191	215
Certificates of deposit ($100,000 or more)	432	367	364	413	576	720	688

*2001 figures are mostly August outstandings.
.Source: Board of Governors of the Federal Reserve System, *Federal Reserve Bulletin*, selected issues.

The volume of *federal funds loans*—the principal means of payment in the money market—is difficult to estimate because thousands of banks and other very large companies are active in this market every day and not all transactions are reported. Moreover, the federal funds market is extremely volatile, reflecting wide swings in the flow of funds through the banking system. Estimates by the Federal Reserve System indicate that Federal funds loans outstanding (including repurchase agreements) amounted to about $660 billion in 2001.

The true size of the *Eurodollar market* (dollar-denominated deposits in banks outside U.S. territory) is also unknown, principally because this market spans so many nations and is not regulated. The amount shown in Exhibit 10–4 of over $200 billion in 2001 includes only time deposits owned by foreigners but held by U.S. banks abroad. Conservative estimates of total Eurodollar deposits worldwide place the net figure at more than $3 trillion.

THE PATTERN OF INTEREST RATES IN THE MONEY MARKET

The rates of return on money market securities vary over time and among different securities. The foundation of the market's structure is the level of yields on *Treasury bills.* These securities are considered to have zero default risk and minimal market risk as well. The resale market for Treasury bills is among the most active and deep of all securities markets, making bills readily marketable should the investor need cash in a hurry. Because of this combination of low risk and ready marketability, Treasury bills typically carry one of the lowest yields in the money market. The importance of T-bills as an "anchor" of the money market may decline in the future, however, if government budget surpluses reduce the government's need for borrowed funds.

Most other yields in the money market are scaled upward from Treasury bill rates. One set of yields that hovers very close to T-bill rates is the yield on *federal agency securities,* considered virtually riskless by many investors. Nevertheless, agency securities are less marketable than bills, though their quantity has increased rapidly in recent years. As a result, the yield spread between agencies and bills in recent periods averages more than half a percentage point in favor of agency securities.

Another yield in the money market that stays close to the Treasury bill rate is the rate charged on *federal funds loans.* The low risk of these essentially interbank loans, coupled with their short maturities (usually covering only a few daylight hours or overnight), helps to explain their relatively low yields. As shown in Exhibit 10–5, Federal funds carried an average interest rate of just over 1.60 percent early in 2002, while the shortest (3-month) Treasury bills carried a yield (auction average) of about 1.65 percent. Thus, the Federal funds rate and the Treasury bill rate were almost identical with the Federal funds rate (an overnight lending rate), just slightly lower than the prevailing interest rate on 3-month Treasury bills. In the language of the money market, the

$$
\begin{array}{c}
\text{Yield spread} \\
\text{between money} \\
\text{market instruments} \\
\text{(in this case, T-bills} \\
\text{and Federal funds)}
\end{array}
=
\begin{array}{c}
\text{Federal} \\
\text{funds} \\
\text{rate}
\end{array}
-
\begin{array}{c}
\text{Treasury} \\
\text{bill} \\
\text{rate}
\end{array}
=
\begin{array}{c}
1.63 \\
\text{percent}
\end{array}
-
\begin{array}{c}
1.65 \\
\text{percent}
\end{array}
=
\begin{array}{c}
-0.02 \text{ percent} \\
\text{or } -2 \text{ basis} \\
\text{points}
\end{array}
$$

Because *yield spreads* between money market instruments typically are *less* than a full percentage point, they are nearly always expressed in terms of *basis points* (1/100 of a percentage point—a measure we discussed earlier in Chapter 6). However, the size of these basis-point yield spreads varies continually, as the perceptions of money market investors

EXHIBIT 10–5
Money Market Interest Rates (Reported Daily in the U.S.)

Money Market Instrument	Interest Rate (Percent per Year, Reported First Week of January 2002)	Money Market Instrument	Interest Rate (Percent per Year, Reported First Week of January 2002)
Federal funds loans	1.63 %	Certificates of deposit: secondary market ($100,000+, negotiable):	
Borrowings from the Federal Reserve Banks' discount window	1.25	1-month	1.81%
		3-month	1.80
		6-month	1.94
Commercial paper:		Eurodollar deposits, 3-month	1.80
Issued by nonfinancial companies for:		U.S. Treasury bills:	
1 month	1.76	Secondary market:	
2 months	1.75	3-month bill	1.69
3 months	1.78	6-month bill	1.78
Issued by finance companies for:		1-year bill	2.24
30–89 days	1.76	Auction average:	
99–149 days	1.77	3-month bill	1.65
150–179 days	1.78	6-month bill	1.75
Bankers' acceptances:		Overnight repurchase agreements(RPs)	1.73
3-month	1.80		
6-month	1.91		

Source: Board of Governors of the Federal Reserve System.

regarding risk and other rate-determining factors shift frequently and the relative supplies of different money market instruments change daily.

The interest rates on two bank-related financial instruments—*negotiable CDs* and *bankers' acceptances*—also tend to follow changes in the market yield on Treasury bills and hover close to prevailing bill rates for the same maturities. As shown in Exhibit 10–5, the secondary market yield on three-month CDs was just slightly above the three-month Treasury bill rate (by 15 basis points). The yield spread between the T-bill rate and the interest rate on three-month *bankers' acceptances* was about the same as the Treasury bill–bank CD spread. Acceptances are considered to be a high-quality financial instrument, guaranteed by a money-center bank and by everyone who endorses the instrument, and therefore are viewed almost as safe as Treasury bills. However, the resale market for acceptances is not as active or as deep as the T-bill market, and this difference in marketability helps to explain why acceptances must carry a slightly higher yield than T-bills. In addition, T-bill interest earnings are tax free from state and local taxes, while income from most privately issued securities is not, so this specific tax exemption helps to explain a portion of many money market yield spreads.

Another money market interest rate that lies very close to the T-bill rate is the yield on overnight *repurchase agreements*. Known more popularly as REPOs or RPs, these loan contracts generally last for only 24 hours to a few days and are collateralized by high-quality government securities. Because of the quality collateral behind an RP, its interest return typically lies only a few basis points higher than the prevailing interest rate on short-term T-bills.

Large, well-established corporations in need of credit can, of course, draw on many different sources of funds. However, when short-term credit is needed, two of the most popular sources are borrowing from commercial banks and issuing marketable IOUs in the

Management Insight   Key Determinants of the Price and Yield of Money Market Instruments

Key Price and Yield Determinants in the Money Market	Associated Characteristics of Money Market Securities
Safety	Degree of default risk Size and reputation of issuer
Liquidity	Depth and breadth of secondary market Price stability
Marketability	Denominations and maturities offered the public Supply of new securities and frequency of issue Ability to sell and acquire rapidly
Taxability	Exposure to federal, state, and local taxes After-tax rate of return

commercial paper market. The largest and best-known corporations generally qualify for the prime bank lending rate or for even lower loan rates. Thus, the market for *prime-rated bank loans* is a direct competitor with the commercial paper market. As shown in Exhibit 10–5, for those corporations able to tap either market, it is generally cheaper to borrow in the commercial paper market. This spread in rates on short-term corporate loans favoring commercial paper helps explain why the commercial paper market has been one of the most rapidly growing segments of the U.S. money market (until the recession of 2001).

Another important money market interest rate shown in Exhibit 10–5 is the *discount rate* charged depository institutions when they borrow from the Federal Reserve banks. In contrast to the other yields discussed to this point, the discount rate is not determined by demand and supply forces in the marketplace but is set by the Federal Reserve banks with the approval of the Board of Governors of the Federal Reserve System. The level of the discount rate is governed by the Federal Reserve's assessment of the state of the economy and credit market conditions. When possible, however, the Fed tries to keep the discount rate reasonably close to market interest rates on Treasury bills. An unusually low discount rate may result in excessive borrowing at the Fed's discount window. In contrast, an excessively high discount rate forces banks to borrow heavily in the open market, increasing the volatility of interest rates and sometimes creating unstable market conditions for all borrowers.

Questions *to Help You Study*

11. Why has the money market grown so rapidly in recent years? Why have its services been in heavy demand?

12. Describe the *structure of interest rates* in the money market. What instrument anchors the market and appears to be the foundation of other interest rates? Can you explain why this is so? Could the "anchor" of today's money market change in the future? Why?

13. How are *yield spreads* figured in the money market? Why is this important to know?

14. What are some of the most important determinants of the prices and yields attached to money market instruments? Can you explain why?

Summary of the Chapter

This chapter has presented a broad overview of one of the most important components of any financial system, the *money market*. Money markets are among the largest of all financial system components and provide numerous services that modern savers and borrowers cannot do without in the modern world.

- *Money markets* are defined as the collection of institutions and trading relationships that move short-term funds from lenders to borrowers and back again.

- All money market loans have an original maturity of *one year or less*. Thus, money market transactions typically consist of credit flows from lenders and borrowers that last for only hours, days, weeks, or months, unlike the capital markets where credit transactions may cover many years.

- Most loans extended in the money market are designed to provide short-term working capital to businesses and governments so they can purchase inventories, pay dividends and taxes, and deal with other immediate needs for cash. Their short-term cash needs arise from the fact that inflows and outflows of cash are *not* perfectly synchronized. In the real world, even with the best planning available, temporary cash deficits and temporary cash surpluses are more often the rule rather than the exception.

- The money market simultaneously answers the needs of borrowers for short-term credit and the needs of lenders of funds (savers) for temporary interest-bearing outlets for their surplus funds.

- Money market investors are typically extremely conservative when it comes to placing their savings in financial instruments. They usually will accept little or no risk of borrower default, prefer financial instruments whose prices are stable, and usually require an investment from which their funds can be recaptured quickly (i.e., they prefer assets with high liquidity and marketability).

- Nearly all money market instruments are of *prime quality*—among the safest, most liquid, and most readily marketable assets that are available anywhere within the financial system.

Key Terms

Money market, *271*	Inflation (or purchasing power) risk, *275*	Original maturity, *277*
Market or interest rate risk, *275*	Currency risk, *275*	Actual maturity, *277*
Reinvestment risk, *275*	Political risk, *275*	Federal funds, *278*
Default risk, *275*	Liquidity, *276*	Clearinghouse funds, *278*

Problems

1. How much interest would be earned (on a simple interest basis) from a three-day money market loan for $1 million at an interest rate of 12 percent (annual rate)? Suppose the loan were extended on the third day for an additional day at the going market rate of 11 percent. How much total interest income would the money market lender receive?

2. Check the most recent issue of *The Wall Street Journal* you can find. Calculate the yield spreads in basis points between U.S. Treasury bills of varying maturity, the federal funds rate, and commercial paper, CD, and bankers' acceptance rates. How do your calculated yield spreads compare with those shown in Exhibit 10–5? Can you explain the observed differences in yield spreads using your knowledge of the factors explaining movements in interest rates discussed in Chapters 5 through 9?

3. Suppose the yield spread between the three-month U.S. Treasury bill rate and the three-month bank CD rate were 35 basis points. An investor has $250,000 to invest in either of these instruments for three months. How much does the investor surrender in total interest income for three months if he or she invests in Treasury bills instead of CDs? Does the investor receive any offsetting benefits by buying the bills and not the CDs?

4. Please identify each of the key terms and concepts discussed in this chapter whose definition or description is listed below.

   a. Money transferred by writing a check and presenting it for collection.
   b. Funds available for immediate payment.
   c. Time span between issue date and redemption date for a financial asset.
   d. Time span between today's date and the date of retirement for a financial asset.
   e. Probability of changes in government laws and regulations lowering the expected rate of return on a financial asset.
   f. Probability of loss in the expected return for a financial asset due to adverse movements in currency prices.
   g. Probability of loss in expected return due to rising or falling interest rates.
   h. Probability of lowering the expected return on a financial asset due to the necessity of investing the asset's earnings stream in lower yielding financial assets.
   i. Probability that a rising average price level will reduce the purchasing power of the income expected from a financial asset.
   j. Institution created by society to channel temporary cash surpluses in order to meet temporary cash deficits.

Questions about the Web and the Money and Capital Markets

1. If you wanted to gather data about changes going on in the money market, such as movements in the volume of trading and prevailing interest rates, what would be a good source to check out on the Web? Do you think the source you have chosen is likely to be reliable? Why?

2. Suppose you wanted to find out what services an active money market trader offers to the public. How could you use the World Wide Web to gather this information?

3. If you wanted to learn more about the different types of money market instruments, what Web sources could be helpful to you?

Selected References

Allen, Linda. *Capital Markets and Institutions: A Global View.* New York: John Wiley & Sons, 1997.

Diamond, D. "Liquidity, Banks, and Markets." *Journal of Political Economy* 105 (1997), pp. 928–56.

Dufey, Gunter, and Ian H. Giddy. "Money Markets of the Pacific Basin." Working Paper 93-10, Mitsui Life Financial Research Center, The University of Michigan, 1993.

Federal Reserve Bank of Richmond, *Instruments of the Money Market,* 1995.

Livingston, Miles. *Money and Capital Markets,* 2nd ed. Miami, FL: Kolb, 1993.

Rose, Peter S. *Commercial Bank Management,* 5th ed. New York: McGraw-Hill, 2002.

Chapter **Eleven**

Money Market Instruments: Treasury Bills, Repurchase Agreements, Federal Funds, and Bank CDs

Learning Objectives in This Chapter

- You will examine the characteristics of *Treasury bills* and the workings of the *government securities market.*

- You will see how Treasury bills (as well as other government securities) are auctioned off and how their rate or return (yield) is determined.

- You will explore the reasons why *security dealers* are so important to the functioning of the money market and how these dealers raise money to carry on their daily operations.

- You will discover two of the most important ways leading *banks* borrow and lend funds in the money market—through *federal funds trading* and the *issuance of CDs.*

- You will see what significant changes the managerial strategy known as *liability management* has made in bank performance and practice in recent years.

What's in This Chapter? Key Topics Outline

Treasury Bills: Features, Growth, and Types

The Controversy over Modern Bill Auctions

Calculating Treasury Bill Yields and Returns

Primary Security Dealers: Sources of Income and Risk

Repurchase Agreements (RPs)

The Federal Funds Market and Bank Money Management

The Federal Funds Rate and Government Policy

Negotiable CDs: Origins, Growth, and Innovations

Liability Management: Importance to the Money Market

INTRODUCTION

As we noted in the previous chapter, the money market is an institution designed to supply the cash needs of short-term borrowers and provide savers who hold temporary cash surpluses with an interest-bearing outlet for their funds. In this chapter we focus upon two of the most important of all institutions in the money market—security dealers and banks—and explore in detail four of the most popular of all money market instruments—Treasury bills, repurchase agreements (RPs), federal funds, and bank CDs. We will focus not only upon the basic characteristics of these key money market institutions and instruments, but also on the critical role each institution and instrument fulfills in assuring a ready supply of short-term credit to governments and private institutions and in offering an attractive outlet for the public's near-term savings.

U.S. TREASURY BILLS

Purchases and sales of *Treasury bills* often represent one of the largest volumes of daily transactions in the money market. Interest rates on government bills tend to be, in most countries that issue them, the anchor for all other money market interest rates. Trading in T-bills, as these instruments are usually called, is one component of a vast international market for securities issued by the U.S. government and by other governments around the world. These government-guaranteed IOUs, which include bills, notes, and bonds, carry great weight in the financial system due to their zero (or nearly zero) default risk, ready marketability, and high liquidity. At the heart of the market for Treasury bills, notes, and bonds is a handful of *securities dealers* who make the market go and aid the government in selling billions of dollars in new securities each year. In this chapter, we examine the activities of these securities dealers and how they finance their daily trading operations in T-bills and other high-quality financial instruments.

U.S. Treasury bills are direct obligations of the United States government, indicating that tax revenues or any other source of government funds can be used to repay holders of these financial instruments. By law, Treasury bills must have an original maturity of one year or less. T-bills were first issued by the U.S. Treasury in 1929 to cover the federal government's frequent short-term cash deficits.

In the United States the federal government's fiscal year runs from October 1 to September 30. However, individual income taxes—the largest single source of U.S. federal revenue—are not fully collected until April of each year. Therefore, even in those rare years when a sizable budget surplus is expected, the government is likely to be short of cash during the fall and winter months and often in the summer as well. During the spring, personal and corporate tax collections are usually at high levels, and the resulting inflow of funds can be used to retire some portion of the securities issued earlier in the fiscal year. T-bills are suited to this seasonal ebb and flow of government cash because their maturities are short, they find a ready market among investors, and their prices adjust readily to changing market conditions.

The major financial instruments of the money market discussed in this chapter include Treasury bills, security repurchase agreements (RPs), federal funds, and bank negotiable CDs—some of the most popular financial instruments in the world. Because of the great importance of these instruments, the World Wide Web began a number of years ago to gather and present detailed information about these widely used financial assets.

Among the most popular Web sites to help you understand these financial instruments in greater depth are such locations as *www.publicdebt.treas.gov* and *www.treasurydirect.gov* which provide information about Treasury bills and auctions of government securities. Additional information of an educational nature about these key money market securities appears in *www.toerien.com*. An outstanding source of data concerning the above money market instruments and many others as well is contained in the Federal Reserve Board's economic data bank at *www.economagic.com/fedbog.htm*.

Volume of Bills Outstanding

The volume of U.S. Treasury bills outstanding grew rapidly until the late 1990s. As shown in Exhibit 11–1, the total volume of bills outstanding climbed over $760 billion in 1995 and then moved further upward to almost $780 billion in 1996, compared to slightly over $200 billion in 1980. Subsequently the volume of T-bills outstanding began to fall. The major factors behind the growth of T-bills were record federal budget deficits, occasional economic recessions that reduced tax revenues, and the rapid expansion of certain federal programs (such as national defense during the Cold War). Moreover, the global economy has grown rapidly in recent years, creating a greater need for liquid assets such as T-bills to aid banks and other investors in the efficient management of their cash positions. More recently, T-bills began to fall in volume as the federal government began to experience at least some budget surpluses and, therefore, reduced cash needs.

Types of Treasury Bills

There are several different types of Treasury bills. *Regular-series bills* are issued routinely every week or month in competitive auctions. Bills issued in regular series have carried original maturities of three months (13 weeks), six months (26 weeks), and one year (52 weeks). Today three- and six-month bills are auctioned weekly. The six-month bill provides the largest amount of revenue for the U.S. Treasury.

On the other hand, *irregular-series bills* are issued only when the Treasury has a special cash need. These instruments include strip bills and cash management bills. A package offering of bills requiring investors to bid for an entire series of different bill maturities is known as a *strip bill*. Investors who bid successfully must accept bills at their bid price each week for several weeks running. *Cash management bills,* on the other hand, consist simply of reopened issues of bills that were sold in prior weeks. The reopening of a bill issue normally occurs when there is an unexpected Treasury need for cash.

How Bills Are Sold

Treasury bills are sold using the **auction** technique. The marketplace, not the U.S. Treasury, sets bill prices and yields. A new regular bill issue is announced by the Treasury on Thursday of each week (except for holidays) with bids from investors due the following Monday before 1 P.M. New York time. Interested investors fill out a form tendering an offer to the Treasury for a specific bill issue at a specific price. These forms must be filed by the

EXHIBIT 11–1

U.S. Treasury Bills: Total Amount Outstanding and Their Proportion of the Marketable Public Debt of the United States, 1960–2001

End of Year	Total Volume of Bills Outstanding ($ Billions)	Marketable Public Debt of the United States ($ Billions)	T-Bills as a Percent of the Total Marketable Public Debt
1960	$ 39.4	$ 189.0	20.8%
1965	60.2	214.6	28.1
1970	87.9	247.7	35.5
1975	157.5	263.2	43.4
1980	216.1	623.2	34.7
1985	399.9	1,437.7	27.8
1990	527.4	2,195.8	24.0
1995	760.7	3,307.2	23.0
2000	646.9	2,966.9	21.8
2001*	620.1	2,822.3	22.0

*2001 figures are for the second quarter of the year.
Source: Board of Governors of the Federal Reserve System, *Federal Reserve Bulletin*, selected issues.

Monday deadline with one of the 37 regional Federal Reserve banks or branches or with the Treasury's Bureau of the Public Debt. The interested investor can appear in person at a Federal Reserve bank or branch to fill out a tender form, submit it by mail, or place an order in person or electronically through a security broker or depository institution. T-bills are now also traded online and usually issued the Thursday following Monday's auction.

The Treasury entertains both competitive and noncompetitive tenders for bills. *Competitive* tenders typically are submitted by large investors, including banks and securities dealers, who bid for several million dollars' worth at one time. Although anyone can submit a bid for his or her own account, depository institutions and registered government security brokers and dealers (about 2,000 in number) may also bid on behalf of their customers. Institutions submitting competitive tenders bid aggressively for bills, trying to offer the Treasury a "price"—expressed as a discount rate of interest (DR)—high enough to win an allotment of bills. In contrast, *noncompetitive* tenders (normally less than about $1 million each) are submitted by small investors who agree to accept the price determined by the auction. Generally, the Treasury fills all noncompetitive orders for bills.

In the typical bill auction, Federal Reserve officials array all the bids received from the highest price bid to the lowest price. All competitive bids must be expressed as a DR or discount rate—a measure of a bill's rate of return that we will discuss shortly. For example, a typical series of bids in a Treasury auction might appear as follows:

Hypothetical Prices and Discount Rates Bid for Three-Month U.S. Treasury Bills	
Equivalent Treasury Bill Prices	**Treasury Bill Discount Rates Bid**
$96.460	3.540%
96.455	3.545
96.450	3.550
96.445	3.555
96.440	3.560
96.435	3.565
96.430	3.570

Note in the above table that the column measuring possible T-bill prices expresses each bill's price as though it had a $100 par (face) value. In fact, the minimum denomination for U.S. Treasury bills is $1,000 and they are issued in multiples of $1,000 above that minimum. The highest competitive bidder receives bills and those who bid successively lower prices also receive bills until all available securities have been awarded. The lowest successful price bid, known as the "stop-out"(or market-clearing) price, becomes the common price that all successful bidders actually pay to the Treasury.

Once bills are acquired by successful bidders, many of them will be sold right away in the secondary market, giving unsuccessful bidders a chance to add to their own T-bill portfolios. Payments for bills won in the auction must be made in federal funds, cash, cashier's check, certified personal check, by redeeming maturing Treasury securities or coupon payments, or, when permitted by the Treasury, through crediting Treasury tax and loan accounts at banks.[1]

All bills today are issued only in *book-entry form*—a computerized record of ownership maintained at the Federal Reserve banks, through private depository institutions, and at the Treasury Department. The Federal Reserve manages the National Book-Entry System (NBES), which keeps records of Treasury security purchases for depository institutions, and the depository institutions, in turn, keep records on their customers' purchases. Alternatively, a purchaser of Treasuries can keep an electronic account with the Treasury Department's *Treasury Direct* system, showing all the buyer's holdings of Treasury obligations. Settlement of transactions involving purchases and sales of new bills or other Treasury securities takes place mainly through depository institutions, led by a few large clearing banks that process a large volume of transactions daily.

Results of a Recent Bill Auction

A summary of the results from each T-bill auction is published in financial newssheets all over the world. The results of a recent Treasury bill auction are illustrated in Exhibit 11–2. In this particular example, two maturities of bills—13 and 26 weeks—were offered to the public, and both issues were heavily oversubscribed. More than $37 billion in 13-week bills and $30 billion in 26-week bills were requested by the public; however, the Treasury only awarded about $6 billion of the shorter-term bills and $7.5 billion of the 26-week bills.

Noncompetitive tenders in the amount of $1.3 billion for the 13-week issue and about $1.1 billion for the 26-week issue received their bills. The market-clearing auction price for the 13-week bill was $98.50 per $100 par value. The 26-week issue sold for an auction price of $96.50 for a $100-denominated instrument. This works out to a 5.93 percent discount rate of return (DR) on the 13-week bill and a 6.92 percent discount rate of return (DR) on the 26-week issue. On a yield-to-maturity [investment return (IR)] basis—a rate of return measure for bills we will also discuss shortly—the 13-week bill carried a market-clearing investment return of 6.10 percent, while the 26-week bill posted an investment (IR) yield of 7.27 percent.

---

[1]These so-called T&L accounts are Treasury deposits kept in about 10,000 of the nation's depository institutions. The purpose of these accounts is to minimize the impact on the financial system of Treasury tax collections and debt-financing operations. As taxes are collected or securities are sold, the Treasury deposits the funds received in these T&L accounts and withdraws money from them as needed into its checking accounts held at the Federal Reserve banks.

EXHIBIT 11–2   **An Example of the Outcome of an Auction of U.S. Treasury Bills***

	13 Week or 91-Day Bills	26 Week or 182-Day Bills
Volume of bills requested	$37.5 billion	$30.1 billion
Volume of bids accepted by the U.S. Treasury Department	$5.9 billion	$7.5 billion
Noncompetitive tender offers accepted by the U.S. Treasury Department	$1.3 billion	$1.1 billion
The bill price established in this auction	98.500	96.500
	(on a $100 basis)	(on a $100 basis)
The discount yield established in this auction (DR)	5.93%	6.92%
Percentage of bids at the market's yield or rate of return	70%	85%
Investment rate of return (IR)[†]	6.10%	7.27%

*All successful Treasury bill bids are filled at a single price as determined by the bill yield that clears the market. Competitive bids must be submitted in paper form, and competitive bidders may have their bids rejected. A competitive bidder whose bid rate or yield is the highest rate or yield (lowest price) accepted may not receive the full amount of bills he or she requested. Competitive bidders who bid too low a price (i.e., filed too high a yield bid) may have their bids rejected depending upon the market-determined outcome of each Treasury auction.

[†]Sometimes referred to as the yield to maturity or coupon-equivalent bill rate of return.

Questions *to Help You Study*

1. Why did the volume of *Treasury bills* grow rapidly in earlier decades and then during the most recent decade level off and then decline?

2. Please explain why Treasury bills are so popular with investors (savers) all over the world.

3. Why have governments found the Treasury bill such an effective instrument for raising new funds?

4. List and define the various *types* of Treasury bills. Why are there so many different types?

5. Please explain how a Treasury bill *auction* works in the United States. Can you find some advantages stemming from this type of sale?

Calculating the Yield on Bills

Treasury bills do not carry a promised interest rate but instead are sold at a discount from their par or face value. Thus, their yield is based on their appreciation in price between time of issue and the time they mature or are sold by the investor. Any price gain realized by the investor is treated for federal tax purposes not as a capital gain but as ordinary income received during the year the bill matures.[2] We saw in Chapter 6 that the rate or yield on most debt instruments is calculated as a yield to maturity. However, bill yields are determined by the **bank discount method,** which ignores the compounding of interest rates and uses a 360-day year for simplicity.

The bank discount rate (DR) on bills is given by the formula:

$$ DR = \frac{\text{Par value} - \text{Purchase price}}{\text{Par value}} \times \frac{360}{\text{Number of days to maturity}} \qquad \textbf{(11–1)} $$

For example, suppose you purchased a Treasury bill at auction for $97 on a $100 basis (par value) and the bill matures in 180 days. Then the discount rate on this bill would be

---

[2]The income earned from investing in T-bills is *not* exempt from federal taxes, but it *is* exempt from state and local income taxes. Income from U.S. Treasury securities is subject to federal and state inheritance, gift, estate, and certain excise taxes, however.

$$DR = \frac{(100 - 97)}{100} \times \frac{360}{180} = 6\%$$

Because the rate of return on T-bills is figured in a different way from the rate of return on most other debt instruments, the investor must convert bill yields to an investment (bond or coupon-equivalent) yield to make realistic comparisons with other securities. The investment yield or rate (IR) on Treasury bills can be obtained from the following formula:

$$IR = \frac{Par\ value - Purchase\ price}{Purchase\ price} \times \frac{365}{Days\ to\ maturity} \quad \textbf{(11–2)}$$

The IR on the bill discussed above having a purchase price of $97 is

$$IR = \frac{100 - 97}{97} \times \frac{365}{180} = 0.0627,\ or\ 6.27\%$$

Notice that this IR formula explicitly recognizes that each bill is purchased at a discounted price, which should be used instead of par value as the basis for figuring the bill's true return. Because of the compounding of interest and the use of a 365-day year, the investment yield (IR) on a bill is always higher than its discount rate (DR).

Several other formulas have become popular among investors for calculating yields on Treasury bills when the bills are *not* held to maturity. Both Equations 11–1 and 11–2 assume that the investor buys a T-bill and ultimately redeems it with the Treasury on its due date. But what if the investor needs cash right away and sells the bill to another investor in advance of its maturity? In this instance, we may use the following formulas:

$$Holding\text{-}period\ yield\ on\ bill = DR\ when\ purchased \\ \pm\ Change\ in\ DR\ over\ the\ holding\ period \quad \textbf{(11–3)}$$

where:

$$\begin{array}{c} Change\ in\ DR \\ over\ the\ investor's \\ holding\ period \end{array} = \frac{\begin{array}{c}(Days\ to\ maturity\ when \\ purchased - Days\ held)\end{array}}{Days\ held} \times \begin{array}{c} Difference\ in\ DR \\ on\ date\ purchased \\ and\ date\ sold \end{array} \quad \textbf{(11–4)}$$

Key Web sites for government security trading in the money market are:

U.S. Treasury Department
http://www.publicdebt. treas.gov

Federal Reserve Bank of New York
http://www.ny.frb.org

Board of Governors of the Federal Reserve System
http://www.federal reserve.gov

Federal Deposit Insurance Corporation
http://www.fdic.gov

For example, suppose the investor buys a new six-month (180-day) bill at a price that results in a discount rate (DR) of 6 percent. As is typical, the bill's price begins to rise (and DR to fall) as it approaches maturity. Thirty days after purchase, the investor needs immediate cash and is forced to sell at a price that results in a DR of 5.80 percent. What is the investor's holding-period yield? Using Equation 11–4:

$$Change\ in\ DR\ over\ the\ holding\ period = \frac{180 - 30}{30} \times (6.00\% - 5.80\%)$$

$$= \frac{150}{30} \times 0.20\% = 1.00\%$$

Then, using Equation 11–3:

$$Holding\text{-}period\ yield\ on\ bill = 6.00\% + 1.00\% = 7.00\%$$

Because this T-bill rose in price, the investor experienced a gain that increased the bill's holding-period yield by 1 percent over the original discount rate of 6 percent.

Market Interest Rates on Treasury Bills

Due to the absence of default risk and because of the superior marketability of T-bills, the yields on these popular financial instruments are typically the lowest in the money market. And because of the tremendous size of the bill market, conditions there tend to set the tone in other segments of the money market. A rise in T-bill rates, for example, usually is quickly translated into increases in interest rates attached to other money market instruments.

Although the prices of Treasury bills tend to be stable, yields on bills fluctuate widely in response to changes in economic conditions, government policy, and a host of other factors. This can be seen clearly in Exhibit 11–3, which gives annual averages for the secondary market yields on 3-, 6-, and 12-month bills. T-bill rates typically fall during periods of recession and sluggish economic activity as borrowing and spending sag. Note, for example, the decline in bill yields in 1975, 1982, 1991–1992 and 2001. All of these years were periods in which the economy reached the peak of a boom period and then dropped into a recession or near-recession. During periods of economic expansion, on the other hand, T-bill rates frequently surge upward, as happened between 1976 and 1981, 1986 and 1989, and 1993 and 1997.

It is interesting to examine the shape of the *yield curve* for bills. As Exhibit 11–3 suggests, that curve usually *slopes upward,* with 12-month bill maturities generally carrying the highest yields, 6-month bills the next highest, and 3-month maturities the lowest yields of all. This is not always the case, however. During certain periods—1979–1981, 1989–1990, and 2001 are good examples—the bill yield curve seems to signal the onset of a recession by sloping downward or lying relatively flat. Occasionally, too, the yield curve for bills assumes a pronounced humped or inverted U shape, with middle maturities carrying the highest rates of return.

EXHIBIT 11–3   **Market Interest Rates on U.S. Treasury Bills, 3-, 6-, and 12-Month Maturities (Annual Percentage Rates)**

Year	3-Month	6-Month	12-Month	Year	3-Month	6-Month	12-Month
1974	7.84	7.95	7.71	1989	8.11	8.03	7.92
1975	5.80	6.11	6.30	1990	7.50	7.46	7.35
1976	4.98	5.26	5.52	1991	5.38	5.44	5.52
1977	5.27	5.53	5.71	1992	3.43	3.54	3.71
1978	7.19	7.58	7.74	1993	2.95	3.05	3.20
1979	10.07	10.06	9.75	1994	4.25	4.64	5.02
1980	11.43	11.37	10.89	1995	5.49	5.56	5.60
1981	14.03	13.80	13.14	1996	5.01	5.08	5.22
1982	10.61	11.07	11.07	1997	5.06	5.18	5.32
1983	8.61	8.73	8.80	1998	4.78	4.83	4.80
1984	9.52	9.76	9.92	1999	4.64	4.75	4.81
1985	7.48	7.65	7.81	2000	5.87	5.90	5.78
1986	5.98	6.02	6.07	2001*	3.51	3.45	3.39
1987	5.78	6.03	6.33	2002†	1.65	1.75	NA
1988	6.67	6.91	7.13				

*Figures are averages for July of 2001.
†Auction averages for first week of January.
Source: Board of Governors of the Federal Reserve System; *Federal Reserve Bulletin,* selected monthly issues.

International Focus   Treasury Bills Worldwide

U.S. Treasury bills and other U.S. government securities are traded 24 hours a day around the globe. But many people are not aware that governments in Europe, Asia, and the Americas also issue their own Treasury bills. For example, the Bank of Canada, acting as agent for the Canadian government, auctions bills to a select list of banks and dealers authorized to bid for themselves and their customers. Canadian central government bills are issued in maturities of 3 months, 6 months, and 364 days. In addition, Canada's provinces borrow through Provincial Bills, normally issued in denominations up to $100,000 (expressed in Canadian dollars) for maturities of 3 months or less.

In Europe, Treasury bills are issued by several governments and widely traded. Bills issued by the United Kingdom rank among the most popular in Western Europe. Leading central banks in Europe regularly trade in the bill market and monitor T-bill rates as a barometer of credit market conditions.

Treasury bills are a relatively recent government financing instrument in Japan, first appearing in 1986, but they are now sold regularly in three- and six-month maturities. Somewhat shorter instruments (with two-month maturities), called Financing Bills, help to cover the emergency cash needs of the Japanese government. T-bills are considered to be in short supply in Japan because the Japanese government borrows principally through longer-term bonds, and an active secondary market for T-bills has been slow to develop. Similarly, in Korea the government issues Treasury bills irregularly, and thus, the secondary market for this money market instrument is not yet fully developed. In the Philippines, the government began issuing Treasury bills in 1966, and bills now represent one of the largest components of the Philippine money market.

The Treasury bill market is one of the most important for the development of an efficient and fluid financial system in any nation. The bill market is a natural channel for government economic policy and can aid in the development of a strong central banking and financial market system.

Investors in Treasury Bills

Principal holders of Treasury bills include commercial banks, nonfinancial corporations, state and local governments, and the Federal Reserve banks. Commercial banks and private corporations hold large quantities of bills as a reserve of liquidity until cash is needed. The most attractive feature of bills for these institutions is their ready marketability and stable price. The Federal Reserve banks conduct many of their open market operations in T-bills because of the depth and volume of activity in this market. The Fed purchases and sells bills in an effort to influence other money market interest rates, alter the volume and growth of bank credit, and ultimately affect the volume of investment spending and borrowing in the economy.

Questions *to Help You Study*

6. How are the yields on Treasury bills calculated?

7. How does the method for determining Treasury bill yields differ from the primary method used to calculate yields on most bonds? Why is this difference important?

8. What is the "normal" or "typical" shape of the yield curve for T-bills? What other shapes have been observed and why do you think these occur?

9. Who are the principal *buyers* of Treasury bills today? Make a list of the key factors that you believe motivate these investors to buy bills.

PRIMARY DEALERS, DEMAND LOANS, AND REPURCHASE AGREEMENTS

The money market depends heavily on the buying and selling activities of securities dealers to move funds from cash-rich units to those with cash shortages. Today, 25 **primary dealers** in government securities trade in both new and previously issued Treasury bills, bonds, and notes. These firms include such market leaders as Merrill Lynch, Goldman Sachs, Salomon Brothers, Inc., and Bear Stearns. About half are banks or securities affiliates of banks.

The role of government security dealers in supporting the market for government securities is discussed in the publications of the Federal Reserve Bank of New York, listed at Web site *www.ny.frb.org*

The term *primary dealer* simply means that a dealer firm is qualified to trade securities directly with the Federal Reserve Bank of New York. To join the Fed's primary dealer list, the firm must agree to be available to trade securities at all times and to post adequate capital. About one-third of all primary dealer firms are controlled by corporations located outside the United States, including dealers in Canada, Japan, and Great Britain. Many customers prefer to trade only with primary dealers. Moreover, achieving primary dealership status gives foreign dealers a solid foothold in U.S. markets. The primary dealers agree to "meaningfully participate" in trading with the Federal Reserve at any time the Fed wishes, to make "realistic" bids, and to trade continuously in the full range of government securities.

Scandal Rocks the Market for Government Securities

Due in part to competition and the nature of Treasury auction methods used prior to November 1998, the primary dealers had a significant incentive to attempt to "corner" the government securities market and to "collude" and place common bids, so that all dealers could get some share of new securities in order to be able to fill their customers' orders and make a profit. In such a huge and highly competitive market, dealers could easily overbid, eliminating potential profits by either posting bid prices that were too high or by underbidding, receiving no securities from the government to meet their obligations to their customers. Thus, the dealers had a strong incentive to share information with each other on the size of the orders they planned to place with the government and even on the prices they hoped to bid. In 1991 rumors swept through the financial markets that collusion was rampant. After several weeks of investigation, officials at the Federal Reserve and the Securities and Exchange Commission alleged that they had evidence of improper trading practices on the part of the old-line primary dealer, Salomon Brothers.

It was alleged that Salomon cornered a $12-billion-plus auction of U.S. Treasury notes in May 1991, inflating the amount of its bid to the Treasury well beyond the 35 percent maximum share of a new issue normally allowed. When Salomon wound up with nearly 90 percent of the new Treasury notes, other dealers filed complaints that they were being "squeezed" by Salomon—forced to pay exorbitant prices to purchase the new notes in order to meet their own customers' orders. Subsequently, Salomon itself, cooperating with government investigators, revealed evidence of manipulation of at least seven other government auctions. There was also evidence that the government wound up paying higher borrowing costs as a result of the manipulation of the market.

In the wake of the Salomon scandal, the U.S. Treasury and the Federal Reserve Bank of New York set up new rules by which government securities would be auctioned in the future. For one thing, customers purchasing large amounts of government securities through dealers were thereafter required to *verify in writing* the amounts they bid before they could receive any new securities. The Treasury announced that any security dealer or broker registered with the SEC, not just primary dealers, could file bids on behalf of its customers without putting up a deposit or a guarantee. The U.S. Treasury promised that it would stop giving primary dealers an advance look at its borrowing plans before the same information was released to the public and to move swiftly to automate the bidding process for U.S. government securities rather than relying on traditional handwritten bids. These steps were reinforced by the U.S. Congress when it enacted the Government Securities Act Amendments of 1993, broadening the U.S. Treasury's authority in the government securities market.

EXHIBIT 11–4 **The Problems Dealers Can Face in the Market for New Treasury Securities**

When-Issued Market

In the "when-issued" market for Treasury securities, dealers take customer orders for the new securities before they are auctioned off.

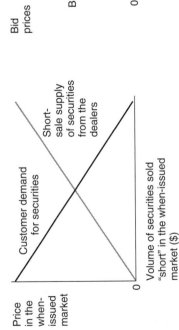

Auction Market

Dealers place bids for securities at the auction, hoping to bid high enough to win but not so high as to eliminate profit when the securities are sold to customers in the resale market.

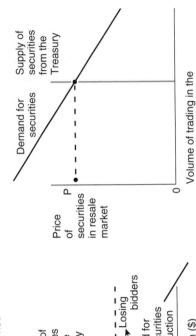

Resale (or Secondary) Market

Dealers sell and deliver securities to customers in the resale market at a price they hope exceeds the auction's market-clearing price.

Finally, the rules of government security auctions were to be written and published for the first time and a market-surveillance committee was created, composed of representatives from the U.S. Treasury, the Securities and Exchange Commission, and the Federal Reserve System. The Treasury pledged it would reopen previous security offerings and issue more new securities if it detected that a market "squeeze" was developing with some dealers unable to find reasonably priced securities to satisfy the needs of their customers.

Proposals for New Ways to Auction Government Securities

The scandal that rocked the government security market in the early 1990s gave rise to a multitude of proposals to change the way the Treasury auctions off its IOUs. The auction method then in use by the U.S. Treasury to sell T-bills was called a *first-price sealed-bid auction,* or English auction. Although it possessed the advantage of allowing the market to set the prices of Treasury securities, the English auction had definite weaknesses. It encouraged dealers to bid high to increase their probability of winning some of the auctioned securities. However, the higher the price that was bid, the lower the expected profit when any Treasury securities won in the auction were sold in the secondary market, because the highest bidders had to follow through on their commitment and pay the Treasury what they had bid even though other successful bidders were paying a lower amount for the same securities. Moreover, the high bidders could sell their securities for no more later in the resale market than those who bid less. (See Exhibit 11–4.) In effect, dealers bidding the highest prices faced a real "winner's curse," because they incurred greater probability of loss when they attempted to resell the securities won in the auction to their customers. At best, the "winner's curse" brought on by the use of the first-price sealed-bid auction method reduced the aggressiveness of competitive bidding by the dealers and probably resulted in the Treasury getting a lower price for its securities.

Several experts suggested remedies for this situation by making changes in the design of Treasury auctions. One popular recommendation was to set up a *Dutch* or *uniform-price auction,* in which bids are arrayed by price from highest to lowest but all the securities in the auction are then sold for just *one price,* the highest bid that is just sufficient to sell out the whole security issue. Thus, the price paid by every successful participant in a Dutch auction is identical and usually comes fairly close to the market consensus price, meaning that the winner's curse has been alleviated to a certain extent. There was some fear, however, that such an approach could reduce Treasury revenues because high bidders would then pay less for their securities. However, Dutch auctions tend to incite more aggressive bidding and to encourage more individuals and institutions to participate.

Beginning in November 1998 the U.S. Treasury abandoned its first-price or English auction approach in which different bidders paid different prices and adopted the *uniform price* auction method. All successful bidders receive securities at the same price, mitigating the "winner's curse" problem discussed earlier. This uniform price is sometimes referred to as the "market-clearing" or "stop-out" price.

DEALERS IN THE MONEY MARKET

Government Security Dealers' Reliance on Borrowed Funds

Although government security dealers supply a huge volume of securities daily to the financial marketplace, these dealers depend heavily on the money market for borrowed funds. Most dealer houses invest little of their own equity in the business. The bulk of operating capital is obtained through borrowings from commercial banks and other institutions. A major dealer firm carries hundreds of millions of dollars in securities in its trading portfolio, with 95 percent or more of that portfolio supported by short-term loans, some carrying only 24-hour maturities.

Demand Loans

The two most heavily used sources of dealer funds are demand loans from the largest banks and repurchase agreements (RPs) with banks and other lenders. Every day major banks post interest rates at which they are willing to make short-term loans to dealers. Generally, one rate is quoted on new loans and a second (lower) rate is posted for renewals of existing loans. A **demand loan** may be called in at any time if the banks need cash in a hurry. Such loans are virtually riskless, however, because they usually are collateralized by U.S. government securities, which may be transferred temporarily to the lending bank or to its agent.

Repurchase Agreements

A popular alternative to the demand loan is the **repurchase agreement (RP).** Under this agreement, the dealer sells securities to a lender but makes a commitment to buy back the securities at a later date at a fixed price plus interest. Thus, *RPs are simply a temporary extension of credit collateralized by marketable securities.* Some RPs are for a set length of time (*term RPs*), while others, known as *continuing contracts,* carry no explicit maturity date but may be terminated by either party on short notice. Larger banks provide both demand loans and RPs to dealers, while nonfinancial corporations have provided a growing volume of funds to dealers through RPs in recent years. Other lenders active in the RP market include state and local governments, insurance companies, and foreign financial institutions who find the market a convenient, relatively low-risk way to invest temporary cash surpluses that may be retrieved quickly when the need arises.

The typical RP loan transaction can be described easily through the use of T accounts (an abbreviated balance sheet) for a dealer and for the lender of funds. Exhibit 11–5 presents a typical example of such a loan. In this case, we assume a manufacturing company has a temporary $1 million cash surplus. The company is eager to loan its temporary cash surplus right away to avoid losing even a single day's interest, while the dealer wishes to borrow at the low-cost RP loan rate in order to purchase interest-bearing securities. The borrowing dealer and the lending company agree on a $1 million RP loan—the minimum loan usually made in this market—collateralized by Treasury bills, with the dealer agreeing to buy back the bills within a few days and to pay the interest on the loan. Normally, the securities that form the collateral for the RP are supposed to be placed in a custodial account held by a third party. When the loan is repaid, the dealer's RP liability is automatically canceled and the securities are returned to the dealer.

There is evidence that this safety device of placing securities involved in an RP agreement into a separate custodial account has not always been scrupulously followed in the past. Moreover, because the majority of outstanding RP loans are simply recorded as book entries at the Federal Reserve banks, verification of what has been done with the pledged securities can be difficult. The result is that if a government securities dealer goes out of business, a customer lending money under an RP to that dealer may have difficulty recovering the securities pledged as collateral behind the loan. Following the collapse of several dealer firms and the failure of several savings and loan associations that lost millions of dollars from inadequately collateralized security loans to those same dealers, federal authorities imposed stricter reporting requirements on the dealers. The Government Securities Act was passed in 1986, granting the U.S. Treasury oversight authority to protect the public from "unscrupulous" dealers with new rules that require written contracts between dealers and investors lending them money that describe where the securities in the RP are

EXHIBIT 11–5 **Example of a Typical RP Loan Transaction**

	Security Dealer		Manufacturing Company	
	Assets	**Liabilities**	**Assets**	**Liabilities**
a. Lender of funds—a manufacturing company—has a $1 million surplus in its cash account.			Deposit at bank + $1 million	
b. A security dealer and the company settle on an RP with the dealer using the borrowed funds to buy securities.	Securities held + $1 million	RP borrowing from manufacturer + $1 million	Deposit at bank − $1 million RP loan to security dealer + $1 million	
c. The RP agreement is concluded and the funds returned (plus interest).	Dealer's cash account − $1 million	RP borrowing from manufacturer − $1 million	Deposit at bank + $1 million RP loan to security dealer − $1 million	

held, specify whether other securities can be substituted for those held as loan collateral, and note that RPs are not protected by federal deposit insurance. The Securities and Exchange Commission and the federal banking agencies must enforce any rules for the government securities market that the Treasury Department writes.

Until recently, RPs were principally overnight transactions or expired in a few days. Today, however, there is a substantial volume of one- to three-month agreements, and some carry even longer maturities. The interest rate on RPs is the return that a dealer must pay a lender for the temporary use of money and is closely related to other money market interest rates. The RP (or repo) rate is based on the differences between the underlying security's current price and the agreed-upon future repurchase price. Usually, the securities pledged behind an RP are valued at their current market prices plus accrued interest (on coupon-bearing securities) less a small "haircut" (discount) to reduce the lender's exposure to market risk. The longer the term and the riskier and less liquid are the securities pledged behind an RP, the larger the "haircut" will be to protect the lender in case security prices fall. Periodically, RPs are "marked to market," and if the price of the pledged securities has dropped, the borrower may have to pledge additional collateral.

Interest income from repurchase agreements is determined from the formula:

$$\begin{array}{c} \text{RP interest} \\ \text{income} \end{array} = \begin{array}{c} \text{Amount of} \\ \text{loan} \end{array} \times \begin{array}{c} \text{Current RP} \\ \text{rate} \end{array} \times \frac{\text{Number of days loaned}}{360 \text{ days}} \quad \textbf{(11–5)}$$

For example, an overnight loan of $100 million to a dealer at a 7 percent RP rate would yield interest income of $19,444.44. That is,

$$\text{RP interest income} = \$100,000,000 \times .07 \times \frac{1}{360} = \$19,444.44$$

The interest rates on repurchase agreements (RPs) and other developments in the RP market may be traced through such Web sites as *www.toerien.com* and the Federal Reserve Bank of New York at *www.ny.frb.org*

Under a continuing contract RP, the interest rate changes daily, so the calculation above would be made for each day the funds were loaned, and the total interest owed would be paid to the lender when the contract is ended by either party. The current RP rate is usually close to the federal funds interest rate (which we will discuss shortly) as well as the prevailing Treasury bill rate.

Financial Developments   The Repo Market Feels the Impact of Terror and Fights Back

The terrorist attacks of September 2001 affected many areas of the financial system, not the least of which was the market for repurchase agreements (RPs). In the immediate wake of the attacks in New York and Washington, DC, thousands of investors rushed to buy government securities as a "safe haven" for their funds. This action resulted in a serious shortage of Treasury notes in the dealer market, particularly for government security dealers who needed these instruments to serve as collateral for their borrowings carried out through RPs.

The RP market soon began to experience "failed" trades. Security dealers who had promised to return government securities that they had borrowed could not do so. Many investors holding government securities simply declined to lend them to anyone, including dealers desperately in need of borrowing money to finance their portfolio positions.

The result was a form of "systemic risk"—similar to the game of dominoes. When one dealer couldn't deliver the securities it had promised to provide to another dealer, the second dealer couldn't honor its own delivery commitments, and so on.

The U.S. Treasury quickly responded to this problem with a rarely used move—it borrowed money when it didn't need to! The Treasury simply held emergency auctions and sold Treasury notes. The result was an expansion in the supply of available T-notes, making it easier for dealers to cover their positions and raise funds. Simultaneously, the Federal Reserve began lending T-notes out of its own portfolio to the primary dealers it works with on a regular basis. A potentially serious financial crisis was avoided.

Sources of Dealer Income

Securities dealers take substantial risks to make a market for Treasury bills and other financial instruments. To be sure, the securities they deal in are among the highest-quality instruments available in the financial marketplace. However, the prices of even top-quality securities can experience rapid declines if interest rates rise. Moreover, established dealer houses cannot run and hide but are obliged to stand ready at all times to buy and sell on customer demand, regardless of the condition of the market. In contrast to securities brokers, who merely bring buyers and sellers together, dealers take a *position of risk,* which means that they act as principals in the buying and selling of securities, adding any securities purchased to their own portfolios.

Dealers stand ready to buy specified types of securities at an announced *bid* price and to sell them at an announced *asked* price. This is called *making a market* in a particular financial instrument. The dealer hopes to earn a profit from such market-making activities in part from the positive spread between bid and asked prices for the same security. This spread varies with market activity and the outlook for interest rates but is narrow on bills (often about $50 per $1 million or less). Spreads range higher on longer-term securities, on small transactions, and on securities not actively traded due to greater risk and greater cost.

As we have seen, the dealers' holdings of securities are financed by borrowing, so their portfolio positions are extremely sensitive to fluctuations in interest rates. For this reason, dealers frequently shift from long positions to short positions, depending on the outlook for interest rates. A **long position** means that the dealers have purchased securities outright, taken title to them, and will hold them in their portfolios until a customer comes along. Long positions typically increase in a period of falling interest rates. A **short position,** on the other hand, means that dealers have sold securities they do not presently own to a customer. In doing so, they hope the prices of those securities will fall (and interest rates rise) before they must acquire the securities and make delivery. Obviously, if interest rates fall (and security prices rise), the dealer will experience capital gains on a long position but losses on a short position. On the other hand, if interest rates rise (resulting in a drop in

EXHIBIT 11–6
Repurchase Agreements (RPs) as a Vehicle for Dealers in Securities and Other Financial Institutions to Borrow and Lend Money

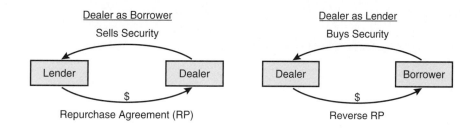

security prices), the dealer's long position will experience capital losses, and the short position will post a gain.

In periods when interest rates are expected to rise, dealers typically reduce their long positions and go short. Conversely, expectations of falling rates lead dealers to increase their long positions and avoid short sales. By correctly anticipating interest-rate movements, the dealer can earn sizable *position profits.* Dealers also receive **carry income**, the difference between interest earned on securities they hold and their cost of borrowing funds. Generally, dealers earn higher rates of return on the securities they hold than the interest rates they pay for loans, but this is not always so. Because most dealer borrowings are short term, they normally are better off if the yield curve is positively sloped.

To help reduce exposure to risk, security dealers have recently diversified the revenue-generating services they offer. Some dealer firms now trade in foreign currencies, commodities (such as oil), security options, futures contracts, and swap contracts. Leading dealers—for example, Merrill Lynch & Co. and Salomon Brothers—offer cash management services in which they hold the funds of customers and invest them in securities, earning cash management fees from those same customers. Dealers have also tried to stabilize their income by acting as financial intermediaries, simultaneously borrowing and lending money through a technique known as *matched book,* in which funds are borrowed through low-cost short-term RPs and then are loaned out through longer-term, higher-yielding RPs. (See, for example, Exhibit 11–6.) The yield spread between these "matched" RPs gives the dealer a net profit unless, of course, the slope of the yield curve suddenly changes and the dealer is forced to borrow short-term money at significantly higher interest rates.

Dealer Positions in Securities

Dealer holdings of U.S. government and other securities are both huge and subject to erratic fluctuations. For example, in 1991 the dealers held a massive net long position in U.S. government securities of nearly $20 billion before falling to a sizable net short position of −$3.3 billion early in 1992. Late in 2000, on the other hand, the government security dealers held substantial net long positions in U.S. Treasury bills and federal agency securities but also held a huge short position in longer-term Treasury notes and bonds of nearly $40 billion.

Why is there often such a tremendous difference in the size and direction of dealer portfolios from year to year? Interest rate movements and interest rate expectations explain a substantial proportion of the changes observed. For example, in 1991 and 1992 a deep recession drove market interest rates sharply lower, holding out the lure of higher profits if the dealers could shift their holdings into a long position. During 2000, however, short-term interest rates were rising modestly before dropping at year's end, and there was considerable fear among market participants that inflation and a growing economy might eventually send long-term interest rates higher, creating losses on notes and bonds held in a long position.

Dealers make heavy use of interest-rate hedging tools today to further protect their portfolios from losses due to changes in interest rates. They are active participants in the

Sources of Funds	Uses of Funds
Borrowings from money market banks, other dealers, nonfinancial companies, etc. in the form of direct loans and repurchase agreements	Purchases of securities at auction and in the secondary market for the dealer and his/her customers
Dealer revenue sources:	Loans to other dealers, banks, and other money market customers
Bid-ask spreads	
Carry income	
Position profits	Payment of dealers' salaries and bonuses
Miscellaneous service fees for advice and assistance to customers	Dividends to owners of dealer firms
Owners' capital	

financial futures markets and also are making increased use of *forward commitments,* in which a dealer sells securities but does not deliver to the customer until more than five business days have elapsed. A dealer often does not hold the securities to be delivered under the forward commitment but waits to acquire them near the promised delivery date. This strategy minimizes the risk of loss due to interest rate changes because the dealer is exposed to risk for only a brief period before delivery is made.

Dealer Transactions and Government Security Brokers

Trading among dealers and between dealers and their customers amounts to billions of dollars each day. Indeed, so large is the government securities market that the volume of trading often exceeds the total volume of trading on many of the world's stock exchanges. Government securities dealers trade among themselves usually through *brokers.* Government security brokers do not take investment positions themselves but try to match bids and offers placed with them by dealers and other investors. Each broker operates a closed-circuit TV network showing dealer prices and quantities available. These half-dozen inter-dealer brokers make price and trade information efficiently available and allow the dealers to remain anonymous in their trading.

Intense competition generally exists among government-security brokers. In 1992, for example, a "price war" broke out among leading brokerage houses in which commissions were cut by 50 percent or more and volume discounts were offered to the largest dealers. In some cases, dealers were told that if they placed a specified minimum volume of orders each month, any subsequent trades during that same month would be handled free of charge by the advertising broker. The principal motivation for the sudden appearance of "bargain" brokerage rates was a sharp decline in trading volume, related to a slowdown in the economy.

Dealerships are a cutthroat business in which each dealer firm is out to maximize its returns from trading, even if gains must be made at the expense of competing dealers. Indeed, market analysts housed within each dealer firm study the daily price quotations of competitors. If one dealer temporarily underprices securities (offering excessively generous yields), other dealers are likely to rush in before the offering firm has a chance to correct its mistake. It is a business with little room for the inexperienced or slow-moving trader and fraught with low margins and unstable earnings. For example, in 1982 two major firms—Drysdale Government Securities, Inc., and Lombard-Wall, Inc.—collapsed. These closings were soon followed by four more dealer failures: Lion Capital Group, RTD Securities, E.S.M. Government Securities, and Bevill, Bresler & Schulman Asset Management Corporation. In 1989 and 1990, several foreign-owned dealers, including Britain's National Westminster Bank PLC, Lloyds Bank PLC, Midland Bank PLC, and L.F. Rothchilds & Co., as well as Australia's Westpac Banking Corporaton, withdrew from the Fed's primary dealer list due to falling trading volume and declining profit margins. U.S. primary dealer Drexel Burnham Lambert also withdrew from that list in 1990 and filed for protection under the federal bankruptcy code. With soaring competition both at home and abroad, several primary dealers have posted substantial net losses in recent years. Moreover, government security prices and interest rates appeared to become somewhat less volatile in the 1990s and in the opening of the new century. Unfortunately for the dealers, it is generally in periods of high price and rate volatility that these firms generate the most revenue, because the volume of security trading rises and there is more demand for interest rate risk protection at that time.

One of the most remarkable features of the dealer's business is how rapidly market conditions and the dealer's financial position can deteriorate. Large losses in tens of millions of dollars can be recorded in a few hours. Moreover, dealers may buy large quantities of bonds that are not yet issued (*when-issued securities*) without any money down and payment not due until delivery a week or so later, only to discover that within minutes the market values of these securities have dropped like a stone. Yet the dealers are *essential* to the smooth functioning of the financial markets and to the successful placement of billions of dollars in securities issued each year by the Treasury Department and by a host of federal and federally sponsored agencies.

Questions *to Help You Study*

10. Explain why security dealers are essential to the smooth functioning of the securities markets and especially the money market.

11. What is a *demand loan?* How does it help security dealers obtain the financing they need?

12. What is a *repurchase agreement* or *RP?* Explain what an RP's role is in financing the operations of security dealers?

13. In what different ways do security dealers generate *income* and possibly make a profit?

14. To what types of *risk* is each form or source of dealer income subject? How might a dealer handle these different forms of risk exposure?

15. What causes the positions in securities that dealers hold to change over time?

BANKS IN THE MONEY MARKET

The single most important financial institution in most money markets is the *commercial bank.* Large money center banks, such as those headquartered in New York City, London, Paris, Tokyo, and a handful of other major cities around the globe, provide billions of dollars in funds daily through the money market to governments and corporations in need of cash. As we saw in the previous section, bank loans and repurchase agreements are a

Banks' Money Market Roles

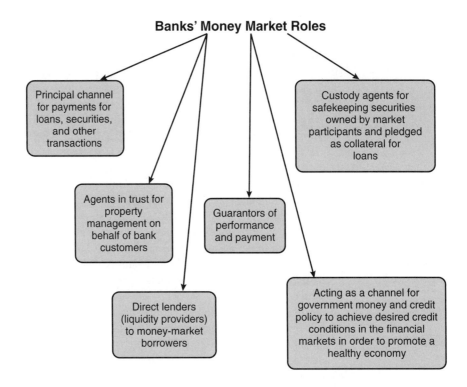

principal source of financing for dealers in securities, while banks also make large purchases of Treasury bills and other money market securities. Commercial banks support private corporations borrowing in the money market, both by purchasing their securities and by granting lines of credit to backstop a new security issue. Banks supply credit to support the movement of goods in domestic and international trade. And both large and small banks today readily lend their cash reserves to other financial institutions and to industrial corporations to cover short-term liquidity needs.

For banks to lend huge amounts of funds daily in the money market, they must also borrow heavily in that market. The owners (stockholders) supply only a minor portion of a commercial bank's total resources; the bulk of bank funds must be *borrowed.* The majority of borrowed funds (nearly 80 percent for most banks) come from deposits, but a growing portion of the industry's financing needs is supplied by the *money market.* However, bank managers today are often cautious in their use of money market borrowings. Such funds can be expensive to use, and their interest cost is more volatile than for most kinds of deposits. Many banks follow the strategy of maintaining a roughly equal balance between their lending and borrowing activities in the money market: The volume of short-term bank debt is counterbalanced by a nearly equal volume of short-term bank assets.[3]

In this chapter, we examine two of the most important money market sources of funds for banks and other deposit-type financial institutions: federal funds and certificates of deposit (CDs). In Chapter 12, we discuss still another important source of funds for many of the largest depository institutions, Eurocurrency deposits.

---

[3]The idea of maintaining a roughly *equal* balance between borrowing and lending in the money market follows one of the oldest concepts in the field of finance: the *hedging principle.* As discussed in Chapter 7, in a world of uncertainty, borrowers of funds can reduce their liquidity risk by matching the maturity of their assets and liabilities. This approach reduces the risk of borrowing when funds are not needed and lowers the risk of not having sufficient cash when bills come due.

FEDERAL FUNDS

As we saw in the introductory chapter to the money market (Chapter 10), **federal funds** are among the most important of all money market instruments for one key reason: *Fed funds are the principal means of making payments in the money market.* By definition, federal funds are any monies available for immediate payment ("same-day money"). They are generally transferred from one depository institution to another by simple bookkeeping entries requested by online computer, by wire, or by telephone after a purchase of securities is made or a loan is granted or repaid.

Nature of Federal Funds

The name *federal funds* came about because, early in the development of the market, the principal source of immediately available money was the reserve balance that each member bank of the Federal Reserve System had to keep at the Federal Reserve bank in its region of the United States. If one bank needed to transfer funds to another, it needed only to contact the Federal Reserve bank in its district, and funds were readily transferred into the appropriate reserve account—a transaction accomplished in seconds by telephone, telegraph, or, later, computer.

Today, however, the Fed funds market is far broader in scope than just reserves on deposit with the Federal Reserve banks. For example, virtually all banks maintain deposits with large correspondent banks in central cities; these deposits may be transferred readily by telephone, by computer, or by wire from the account of one bank to that of another. They may also be borrowed by the institution that holds the correspondent deposit, simply by transferring funds from the correspondent deposit to an account titled "Federal funds purchased" and reversing these entries when the loan matures. Savings and loan associations, credit unions, and savings banks maintain deposits with commercial banks or with the Federal Reserve banks that also are available for immediate transfer to a customer or to another financial institution. Business corporations and state and local governments can lend federal funds by executing repurchase agreements with securities dealers, banks, and other funds traders. Securities dealers who have received payment for securities sold can turn around and make their funds immediately available to borrowers through the federal funds market.

Borrowers of federal funds include securities dealers, corporations, state and local governments, and nonbank financial intermediaries, such as savings and loan associations and insurance companies. Without question, however, the most important of all borrowers in the Fed funds market are commercial banks, which use this instrument as the principal way to adjust their legal reserve account at the Federal Reserve bank in their district.

Use of the Federal Funds Market to Meet Deposit Reserve Requirements

Banks and other depository institutions must hold in a special reserve account liquid assets equal to a fraction of the funds deposited with them by the public. Only vault cash held on the premises and reserve balances kept with the Federal Reserve bank in the district count in meeting a U.S. bank's requirement to hold **legal reserves.** Frequently, some banks hold more legal reserves than the law requires. Because these reserves earn little or no income, most bankers active in the money market try to lend out any excess reserves in their possession, even if they lend the funds only overnight.

Banks are aided in this endeavor by the fact that their legal reserve requirement is calculated on a daily average basis over a two-week period, known as the *reserve computation period.* For example, the reserve computation period for *transaction deposits* (e.g., checking accounts and NOWs) stretches from a Tuesday through a Monday two weeks later. The Federal Reserve calculates the daily average level of transaction deposits held by each depository institution over this two-week period and then multiplies that average by the required reserve percentage (3 percent for smaller banks and 10 percent for larger banks, for example) to determine the amount of legal reserves that must be held by each institution. These legal reserves must average the required amount over a two-week period known as the *reserve maintenance period.* For transaction (checkable) deposits, the reserve maintenance period starts on a Thursday—30 days after the transaction-deposit reserve computation period begins for the largest U.S. banks—and ends on a Wednesday two weeks later. Thus, the reserve computation and reserve maintenance periods for transaction deposits no longer overlap each other as they used to. This time-delay feature explains why this reserve accounting system is often called **lagged reserve accounting** or LRA. Furthermore, each depository institution is allowed to count its average vault cash holdings over the same two-week computation period as is used for transaction deposits and then deduct that daily average vault cash figure from its required reserves.

The manager of each depository institution's money desk—the department responsible for keeping track of the depository's legal reserve position—must adjust each institution's reserve balance at the district Federal Reserve bank to the right level over the two-week reserve maintenance period. The federal funds market is an indispensable tool for this kind of daily reserve management, especially for the largest and most aggressive banks which hold few reserves of their own. Indeed, many large U.S. banks today borrow virtually all of the legal reserves behind their deposits from the federal funds market.

Mechanics of Federal Funds Trading

The mechanics of federal funds trading vary depending on the locations of the buying (borrowing) and selling (lending) institutions. For example, suppose two commercial banks involved in a federal funds transaction are located in the heart of the New York money market. These banks could simply exchange checks. The borrowing bank could be handed a check drawn on the lending bank's reserve account at the Federal Reserve Bank of New York City. This check is payable immediately ("same-day money"), and therefore Fed funds would be transferred to the borrower's reserve account before the close of business that same day. The lender, on the other hand, may be given a check drawn on the borrower. This last check is "one-day money" (payable the following day) because it must pass through the New York clearinghouse for settlement. Thus, funds flow instantly to the borrowing bank's reserve account and are automatically returned to the lending bank's reserve account the next day or whenever the loan agreement terminates. Alternatively, the lending bank can simply contact the Federal Reserve Bank of New York directly and ask it to electronically move funds from the lender's reserve account to the borrower's reserve account immediately, with the transaction usually reversed the next day. Interest on the Fed funds loan may be included when the funds are returned, paid by separate check, or settled by debiting and crediting the appropriate correspondent balances.

If the transacting institutions are not both located within the same Federal Reserve district, the loan transaction proceeds in much the same way except that *two* Federal Reserve banks are involved. Once borrower and lender agree on the terms of a loan, the lending institution directly, or indirectly through a correspondent bank, contacts the Federal Reserve bank in its district, requesting a wire transfer of federal funds. The Reserve bank then transfers reserves through the Fed's wire network (FEDWIRE) to the Federal Reserve bank serving the region where the borrowing institution is located. Funds travel the reverse route when the loan is terminated.

International Focus   The Interbank Loan Market in Russia

The federal funds market in the United States is not the only market for interbank loans. Banks in many other countries have established a market for making loans of reserves to each other. While the U.S. Fed funds market is highly efficient and works very well, sometimes these foreign interbank markets run into trouble and this can have serious consequences for the rest of the economy. A dramatic example of how troubles in interbank lending can send tremors through a country's financial system occurred in Russia in 1995.

Newspaper stories and rumors spread through Russia's commercial banking system to the effect that several Russian banks were not sound. As this tale spread, many of Russia's more than 2,500 banks then in operation simply stopped extending loans to one another. Because there is only limited information available on any bank's true condition in Russia and their regulatory system is still rudimentary, many Russian bankers indicated they could not get enough information on other banks to decide whether these banks were solvent

enough to pay back their interbank loans. As a result, the overnight market for ruble-denominated deposits ground to a halt, and some banks offered interest rates as high as 1,000 percent in an effort to get a loan of reserves! Moreover, with bankers not trusting each other, the Russian public began to mistrust their banks, resulting in scores of depositors demanding to retrieve their funds.

Many observers were concerned that, should such a condition continue, the Russian banking system might collapse. One possible solution was to have Russia's central bank grant loans to any banks in trouble, thus encouraging private bankers to begin lending again. Only a few days into the crisis, the central bank began buying government bonds held by banks and other investors in order to flood the system with liquidity. However, over the longer term, reform of the Russian banking system to clarify regulations, install risk-management systems, and require banks to release more information to the public about their true financial condition is in order.

Incidentally, how do Fed funds borrowers and lenders contact each other to find out who has surplus funds to lend and who is short of funds? Computer networks and the telephone are the most common media for communicating between institutions in need of funds and those with surplus funds. In addition, a handful of *Fed funds brokers* active in the money market work to bring buying and selling institutions together, indicating by telephone and computer screen what funds are available and at what interest rate.

Volume of Borrowings in the Funds Market

Commercial banks borrow billions of dollars each day in the funds market. Total federal funds borrowings by banks in all 50 states (including security repurchase agreements with nonbank institutions) exceeded $600 billion as the twenty-first century began. The federal funds market probably extends at least $300 billion to occasionally as much as $700 billion in credit *daily*. The large banks in New York City, by virtue of their strategic location at the heart of the domestic money market, still account for a disproportionate share of all Fed funds transactions. However, the market has broadened considerably in recent years to include both domestic and foreign banks in Atlanta, Chicago, San Francisco, and other major U.S. cities, as well as thousands of smaller banks in outlying areas.

Most federal funds loans are *overnight* (one-day) transactions or *continuing contracts* that have no specific maturity and can be terminated without advance notice by either party. One-day loans carry a fixed rate of interest, but continuing contracts often do not. There is a growing volume of loans lasting beyond one day, often arising from security repurchase agreements. These longer-maturity interbank loans are usually called *term* federal funds and are being supplied increasingly by foreign banks, savings and loan associations, insurance companies, pension funds, and finance companies as a safe and profitable way to warehouse funds until they are needed for longer-term commitments.

307

Rates on Federal Funds

The federal funds interest rate is highly volatile from day to day, although on an annual basis, it tends to move roughly in line with other money market interest rates (see Exhibit 11–7). The short-term volatility of the funds rate arises from substantial variations in the volume of funds made available by lenders each day and the size of daily cash deficits experienced by banks and other money market participants. The funds rate tends to be most volatile toward the close of the reserve maintenance period, depending on whether larger banks are flush with or short of reserves. There are also seasonal patterns, with the funds rate tending to rise around holiday periods, when loan demand and deposit withdrawals are often heavy.

Federal Funds and Government Economic Policy

Key sources on the Web for following developments in the federal funds market include *www.ny.frb.org* and *www.frbatlanta.org/ publica*

The federal funds market is an easy and riskless way to invest excess reserves for short periods and still earn some interest income. It is essential to the daily management of bank reserves, because credit can be obtained in a matter of minutes to cover emergency situations. As we have seen, Fed funds are also critical to the whole money market, because these funds serve as the principal means of payment for securities and loans. Moreover, the funds market transmits the effects of Federal Reserve monetary policy quickly throughout the banking system.

Beginning in 1989 the Federal Reserve has routinely set target levels for the federal funds rate and raised or lowered those targets, depending on whether the Fed wishes to slow down borrowing and spending in the economy or speed it up. Using daily open market operations—buying and selling securities—the Fed is able to push the funds rate in the desired direction on any given day. A recent study by Dueker and Fischer (1996) suggests the existence of a close relationship between the federal funds interest rate target and the Federal Reserve's inflation target. The U.S. central bank tends to increase the federal funds rate when inflation in the prices of goods and services rises above a given target level that the Federal Reserve finds unacceptable and to lower the federal funds rate when inflation declines.

EXHIBIT 11–7
Effective Interest Rates on Federal Funds Transactions, 1980–2002 (Percent per Annum)

Year	Average Daily Rate on Federal Funds	Year	Average Daily Rate on Federal Funds
1980	13.36%	1992	3.52%
1981	16.38	1993	3.02
1982	12.26	1994	4.21
1983	9.09	1995	5.83
1984	10.22	1996	5.30
1985	8.10	1997	5.46
1986	6.80	1998	5.35
1987	6.66	1999	4.97
1988	7.57	2000	6.24
1989	9.21	2001[*]	3.65
1990	8.10	2002[†]	1.25
1991	5.69		

[*]Average for August 2001.
[†]Closing bid on January 7, 2002.
Source: Board of Governors of the Federal Reserve System. *Federal Reserve Bulletin*, selected monthly issues.

Recently, the volume of legal reserves that U.S. banks hold at the Federal Reserve banks has decreased substantially. Many banks have discovered a way to reduce their required reserve balances by rapidly switching funds out of customers' demand deposit accounts, which still carry legal reserve requirements, into time and saving deposits, which carry *no* reserve requirements, often returning the funds to demand deposits the next day. These contractual switching arrangements—known as *sweep accounts*—not only reduce a U.S. bank's required legal reserve levels but also allow some customers to earn interest on checking account balances. More than $200 billion in sweep account arrangements were in place by the beginning of the twenty-first century, and partly as a result, U.S. bank legal reserve balances fell by more than half.

Unfortunately, one consequence of the decline in required legal reserve balances is an increase in the volatility of the federal funds interest rate because there are fewer reserves to be traded in the federal funds market. Since 1995, in particular, according to a recent study by Bennett and Hilton (1997), the daily volatility of the federal funds interest rate has increased as much as 200 basis points on some days. This increased volatility is of concern because the federal funds rate is the Federal Reserve's prime instrumental target for achieving the goals of U.S. monetary policy. If the Fed funds rate becomes too difficult to control, the Fed will have greater difficulty hitting its desired interest rate targets. The financial markets and the economy might become more difficult to control, and the public could become more confused about the central bank's true goals for U.S. money and credit policy.

It should be noted, however, that the apparent increased volatility of the federal funds interest rate has been relatively modest and bank managers seem to have adjusted well to a more volatile Fed funds rate environment. In part, this is due to the improved technology of communications between the Federal Reserve and the banks that keep reserve balances at the Federal Reserve's regional banks. For exarnple, in recent years, the Fed has made it possible for bankers to monitor on their computer screens, on a real-time basis, most debits and credits to individual bank legal reserve accounts so that bank managers can see more clearly how their legal reserve position stands and can better anticipate developing surpluses and deficits.

The key role of the federal funds market in aiding the central bank of the United States, the Federal Reserve System, in the conduct of monetary policy is discussed in several Web sites, especially the Intended Federal Funds Rate at *www. federalreserve.gov/fomc*

Questions *to Help You Study*

16. Define the term *federal funds.* Why are federal funds so important to the functioning of the money market?

17. Who are the principal *borrowers* active in the federal funds market? Why are they attracted to this market for the funds they require?

18. Who are the principal *lenders* active in the federal funds market? Why do they find this market a good place to lend money?

19. Describe the process of legal reserve position adjustment that depository institutions go through. What role does the federal funds market play in helping depository institutions manage their so-called *money* or *legal reserve* position?

20. Why has the federal funds market become so important to the United States' central bank, the Federal Reserve System, in carrying out the government's *monetary policy* operations?

NEGOTIABLE CERTIFICATES OF DEPOSIT

One of the largest of all money market instruments, measured by dollar volume, is the **negotiable certificate of deposit (CD).** A CD is an interest-bearing receipt for funds left with a depository institution for a set period of time.[4] Banks and other deposit-type institutions issue many types of CDs, but true money market CDs are negotiable instruments that may be sold any number of times before reaching maturity and carry a minimum denomination of $100,000. The usual round-lot trading unit for money market CDs is $1 million.

The interest rate on a large negotiable CD is set by negotiation between the issuing institution and its customer and generally reflects prevailing market conditions. Therefore, like the interest rates on other money market securities, CD interest rates rise in periods of tight money, when loanable funds are scarce, and fall in periods of easy money, when loanable funds are more abundant.

The negotiable CD is one of the youngest of all U.S. money market instruments. It dates from 1961, when First National City Bank of New York (later Citibank) began offering the instrument to its largest corporate customers. Simultaneously, a small group of dealers agreed to make a secondary (resale) market for CDs of $100,000 or more. Other money center banks soon entered the competition for corporate funds and began to offer their own CDs.

The decision to sell this new money market instrument was an agonizing one for banks because CDs tended to increase the average cost and the volatility of bank funds. However, commercial banks had little choice but to offer the new instrument or face the loss of billions of dollars in interest-sensitive deposits. The cash management departments of major corporations have become increasingly aware of the many profitable ways available to invest their short-term funds. Prior to the introduction of the negotiable CD, many bankers found that their biggest corporate customers were reducing their deposits and buying Treasury bills, RPs, and other money market instruments. The CD was developed to attract those lost deposits back into the banking system.

Negotiable CDs are a real success story for most banks. In December of 2000, large ($100,000+) time deposits outstanding at banks and thrifts operating in the United States totaled more than $720 billion. This compares with only about $100 billion in large CDs about 15 years earlier.

Terms Attached to CDs

Negotiable CDs may be *registered* on the books of the issuing depository institution or issued in *bearer form* to the purchasing investor. CDs issued in bearer form are more convenient for resale in the secondary market because they are in the hands of the investors who own them. Denominations range from $25,000 to $10 million, although CDs actively traded in the money market carry a minimum denomination of $100,000. Maturities range upward to around 18 months, depending on the customer's needs. However, most negotiable CDs have maturities of six months or less. CDs with maturities beyond one year are called *term* CDs.

Interest rates in the CD market are computed as a yield to maturity but are quoted on a 360-day basis (except in secondary market trading, where the bank discount rate is used as a measure of CD yields). The general formula to use is:

$$\text{Funds owed the depositor} = D + \frac{n}{360} \times D \times i \qquad \textbf{(11–6)}$$

where D is the original deposit principal; i is the promised yield to maturity based upon a 360-day year; and n is the number of days that interest is earned. For example, if a business

---

[4]The minimum maturity permitted for CDs under federal regulation is seven days. There is no legal upper limit on CD maturities, however. CDs must be issued at par and trade on an interest-bearing basis, unlike Treasury bills. Payment is made in federal funds on the day each CD matures.

Current yields available on negotiable CDs and the latest developments in the CD market can be followed daily via such Web sites as *www.torien.com* and *www.bankrate.com*

firm purchases a $100,000 negotiable CD for six months at an interest rate of 7.50 percent, it would receive back at the end of 180 days:

$$\$100{,}000 \times (1 + \frac{180}{360} \times 0.075) = \$103{,}750$$

To convert the yield on newly issued CDs to a true coupon-equivalent yield for a full 365-day year, that is, to determine the CD's true yield to maturity (YTM), we must multiply the 360-day-based yield (i) by the ratio 365:360. That is,

$$\text{YTM}_{\text{CDs}} = i \times \frac{365}{360} \qquad \textbf{(11–7)}$$

For example, a 360-day yield (i) of 6.25 percent for a CD would mean a coupon-equivalent return (YTM) for that same CD of:

$$\text{YTM} = 6.25 \text{ percent} \times \frac{365}{360} = 6.33 \text{ percent}$$

In the secondary (resale) market, yields on negotiable CDs are figured by the bank discount rate (DR) method discussed earlier. That is,

$$\text{DR} = \frac{\begin{array}{c}\text{(Par value of CD – Purchase price}\\\text{of CD in the secondary market)}\end{array}}{\text{Par value of CD}} \times \frac{360}{n} \qquad \textbf{(11–8)}$$

where n is the number of days until the CD matures or is sold in advance of its maturity to another investor. For example, a 6-month CD bearing a 7.50 percent promised interest rate at maturity but sold 3 months (90 days) early for $98,200 would carry a discount yield (DR) of:

$$\text{DR}_{\text{CD}} = \frac{\$100{,}000 - \$98{,}200}{\$100{,}000} \times \frac{360}{90} = 7.20 \text{ percent}$$

The yield on CDs normally is slightly above the Treasury bill rate due to greater default risk, a thinner resale market, and the state and local government tax exemption on earnings from Treasury bills. Because investors can easily *arbitrage* between short-term markets, moving funds toward the highest yields, the CD interest rate hovers close to the average of current and future federal funds interest rates expected by investors to prevail over the life of the CD. However, as Exhibit 11–8 shows, in 1984 and again in 1988, following severe problems at some of the largest banks, risk premiums attached to CDs rose, driving them well above the prevailing federal funds rate. During the 1990s and into the twenty-first century, however, CD risk premiums were lower due to a strong U.S. economy into the year 2000 and improved bank capital positions. The yield spread between CDs and other money market instruments varies over time, depending on investor preferences, the supply of CDs and other money market instruments, and the financial condition of issuing banks.

One of the most interesting developments in recent years has been the appearance of a *multitiered* (segmented) market for CDs. Investors have grouped issuing banks into different risk categories, and yields in the market are scaled accordingly. This development is a legacy of the collapse of such banking giants as Franklin National Bank of New York in 1974 and Continental Illinois Bank of Chicago in 1984. Faced with the spector of major

EXHIBIT 11–8   **Recent Interest Rates on Money Market CDs ($100,000 or More) versus Rates on Treasury Bills, Federal Funds, Eurodollars, and the Federal Reserve Bank of New York's Discount Rate (Year-End)**

Instrument	Period					
	1984	**1988**	**1990**	**1995**	**2000**	**2002***
Certificates of deposit:						
Three month	10.37%	7.73%	8.15%	5.92%	6.46%	1.80%
Six month	10.68	7.91	8.17	5.98	6.59	1.94
U.S. Treasury bills:						
Three-month	9.52	6.67	7.50	5.49	5.82	1.65
Six-month	9.76	6.91	7.46	5.56	5.90	1.75
Federal funds	10.22	7.57	8.10	5.83	6.74	1.25
Eurodollars, Three-month	10.73	7.85	8.16	5.93	6.45	1.87
Discount rate, FRB New York	8.00	6.50	6.50	5.25	5.73	1.25

Note: Based on weekly average rates as quoted by five dealers. Bill yields in the secondary market on a bank discount basis from daily closing bids.
*Interest rates of January 7th.
Source: Board of Governors of the Federal Reserve System, *Federal Reserve Bulletin,* selected issues.

bank failures, banks viewed as less stable by investors are usually compelled to issue their CDs at significantly higher interest rates.

CDs from the largest and most financially sound banks are rated *prime;* smaller banks or those viewed as less stable issue *nonprime* CDs at higher interest rates. As is true for any depositor in a U.S. insured bank, the holder of a CD is covered against loss up to $100,000 if the issuing bank fails. Unfortunately, this insurance is of limited value to a corporation holding a million-dollar or larger CD. However, holders of large CDs do help to discipline their banks from taking on excessive risk.

Buyers of CDs

The principal buyers of negotiable CDs include corporations, state and local governments, foreign central banks and governments, wealthy individuals, and a wide variety of financial institutions. The latter include insurance companies, pension funds, investment companies, savings banks, credit unions, and money market funds. Large CDs appeal to these investors because they are readily marketable at low risk, may be issued in any desired maturity, and carry a somewhat higher yield than that on Treasury bills. However, the investor gives up some marketability in comparison with T-bills because the resale market for CDs operates well below the average daily volume of trading in bills.

Most buyers hold CDs until they mature. However, prime-rate CDs issued by billion-dollar banks are actively traded in the secondary market. The purpose of the secondary market is principally to accommodate corporations that need cash quickly or see profitable opportunities from the sale of their deposits. Also, buyers of CDs who want shorter maturities or higher yields than are available on *new* CDs will enter the secondary market or redeem them in advance of maturity. Moreover, banks usually will not lend money on their own CDs as collateral because of the risk the borrower may default on the loan, in which case the bank would wind up owning its own CD and redeeming it before it matures.

New Types of CDs

Bankers are becoming increasingly innovative in packaging CDs to meet the needs of customers. One notable innovation occurred in 1975 when the *variable-rate CD* was introduced. Variable, or floating-rate, CDs generally carry maturities out to five years, with an interest rate that is adjusted every 30, 90, or 180 days (known as a *leg* or *roll* period). The

International Focus   CD Markets around the Globe

Inside the United States, the market for bank certificates of deposit (CDs) has grown slowly at times and, in some years, declined due to a variety of regulatory restrictions. However, an international market for CDs in the form of EuroCDs has grown rapidly, and many CD markets abroad have developed into active financial marketplaces.

In Canada, for example, the big chartered banks (such as the Bank of Montreal or Scotiabank) issue chartered bank CDs and chartered bank bearer deposit notes with maturities ranging from 30 days to 12 months in units of $100,000 and higher. These instruments are sold at a discount from par and are usually obtained directly from the issuing bank. Some Canadian-bank CDs are available in both Canadian and U.S. dollars.

In Japan, bank CDs were first permitted by the Japanese Ministry of Finance at the beginning of the 1980s. Gradually, restrictions on maturities and minimum account sizes have been relaxed as the Japanese CD market has grown. Many Japanese loans today are priced on the basis of prevailing CD interest rates, though there is only a weak secondary market for these instruments due, in part, to Japanese regulation and a troubled Japanese economy.

The Asian area of the world also spawned *Asian* dollar CDs. These interest-sensitive bank deposits may carry fixed or floating interest yields based upon the prevailing level of the Singapore interbank offer rate (known as SIBOR). Asian CDs normally trade in $1 million units.

Half a world away in Europe, Eurodollar CDs were developed in 1966. Eurodollar CDs are negotiable, dollar-denominated time deposits issued by the foreign branches of U.S. banks and foreign-owned banks worldwide. These instruments generally carry higher yields than comparable domestic CDs due to greater perceived risk. Most Eurodollar CDs carry fixed rates, but floating-rate instruments were introduced in 1977. Eurodollar CDs can carry maturities longer than one year, and their interest rate may be adjusted every three to six months to match changes in the London Interbank Offer Rate (LIBOR)

If a country is to have a strong money market, the development of an active market for bank deposits appears to be a critical early step. Indeed, most money markets seem to owe their earliest origins to the trading of bank deposits. The key to the success of such a market seems to be a stable banking system with a minimum of government interference with the terms on deposits sold to the public.

floating interest rate is usually tied to movements in the secondary-market yield on fixed-rate CDs, the prevailing federal funds interest rate, the prime bank rate, or the going market interest rate on Eurodollar deposits. A variable-rate CD may give the investor a higher return than normally would be obtained by continually renewing short-term CDs and is a popular investment for money market mutual funds.

Another innovation occurred in the 1970s when Morgan Guaranty Trust in New York City introduced the *rollover* or *roly-poly CD*. Because six-month CDs are the maximum maturity usually traded in the secondary market, Morgan offered its customers longer term CDs with higher rates, but in packages composed of a series of six-month CDs extending for at least two years. Thus, the rolypoly CD promised higher returns plus the ability to market some CDs in the package early to meet emergency cash needs. However, the bank's customer was still obligated to purchase the remaining certificates on each six-month anniversary date until the contract expired.

Recent years have ushered in still more CD innovations: for example, *jumbo CDs, Yankee CDs, brokered CDs, bear and bull CDs, installments CDs, rising-rate CDs, and foreign-index CDs. Jumbo CDs* are large ($100,000+), negotiable CDs issued by nonbank thrift institutions such as savings and loan associations and savings banks. *Yankee CDs* are issued in the United States by foreign banks (mainly Japanese, Canadian, and European institutions) that usually have offices in U.S. cities. *Brokered CDs* consist of CDs sold through brokers or dealers in maximum $100,000 denominations to qualify for federal deposit insurance. *Bear and bull CDs*, whose rates of return are linked to stock market performance, appeared in the mid-1980s. However, these instruments fell out of favor with the Great Global Stock Market Crash of 1987. *Installment CDs*, in contrast, allow customers to make a small initial deposit and then gradually build up the balance in the account to some target level. *Rising-rate CDs* are usually longer-term deposits whose promised yield increases over time with penalty-free withdrawals permitted on selected anniversary dates. Further innovations in CDs are likely in the future as banks struggle to adjust their fund-raising efforts in the face of increasingly stiff competition for funds.

COMPARING MONEY MARKET COSTS OF FUNDS NEEDED BY BANKERS

It is useful to conclude our discussion about banks' borrowing funds in the money market by illustrating how a banker evaluates the choices among federal funds, negotiable CDs, and other sources of borrowed funds. Among other key factors, a banker must keep in close touch with money market developments each day, paying particular attention both to current money market interest rates and to forecasts about future interest rates.

Consider an example: During a portion of the year 2001 federal funds were trading at an annual interest rate of 5.50 percent and the average rate that New York money-center banks were paying to bring in deposits of large, negotiable CDs from their customers was 5.47 percent on one-month maturities. Even though reserve requirements had been set at zero on CDs several years earlier by the Federal Reserve Board, a bank raising money through the issuance of CDs would still have been compelled to pay deposit insurance fees to the Federal Deposit Insurance Corporation (FDIC) equal to the full amount of the CD (not just the $100,000 portion that is insured). The U.S. deposit insurance fee at the time was set at zero, but let's assume for purposes of illustration that the FDIC's insurance fee was 0.0004 cents per dollar (or four cents per $100) on any deposits received from the public, as it had been during much of the 1990s.

Suppose a money-center bank needed to borrow $1 million for at least one day. Its daily cost for funds derived from each of these sources would be:

$$\text{Federal funds: } \$1 \text{ million} \times 0.0550 \times \frac{1}{360} = \$152.78$$

$$\underbrace{\text{Negotiable CDs: } \$1 \text{ million} \times .0547 \times \frac{1}{360}}_{\text{Deposit interest cost}} + \underbrace{\$1 \text{ million} \times .0004 \times \frac{1}{360}}_{\text{Deposit insurance cost}} = \$153.05$$

On this particular day, the cheapest money market funds source was borrowing from the Federal Reserve banks, followed by borrowing added funds in the federal funds market. However, because the CD interest rate is fixed for 30 days in this instance, if the Fed funds rate is expected to rise significantly, this borrowing bank might well decide to borrow at the currently more expensive CD rate. Clearly, a banker must consider not only current money market interest rates but expected *future* interest rates and government regulations as well when choosing a source of money market funding.

CONCLUDING COMMENT ON BANK ACTIVITY IN THE MONEY MARKET

The money market has not always been as important a source of funds for banks and other depository institutions as it is today. Prior to the 1960s, even many of the largest money-center banks regarded borrowings from the money market as only a secondary source of funds. Bankers were aware that heavy dependence on money market borrowing would make their earnings more sensitive to fluctuations in interest rates. However, the force of competition intervened in the 1960s and 1970s. Major corporations began to seek out alternative investments for their short-term funds rather than holding most of their money in bank deposits. Bankers were forced to turn to the money market for additional funds. As we have seen in this chapter, the banking community approached the problem in several different ways. One was to offer a new financial instrument—the negotiable certificate of deposit—to compete directly for short-term corporate funds. Another approach was to draw more intensively on existing sources of money market funds, especially the federal funds market.

Prior to the 1960s and 1970s, the federal funds market was confined principally to the largest banks, which swapped reserves with each other. As bankers turned more and more to the funds market, however, it broadened tremendously. Thousands of small depository institutions in towns and rural areas across the United States began supplying their excess reserves to larger banks in the central cities, hoping to boost their earnings. In turn, the greater supply of Fed funds encouraged the largest banks to rely even more heavily on the money market and less on customer deposits as a source of reserves. The federal funds market had become an accepted innovation for both the smallest and largest financial institutions.

The rapid expansion of the CD and federal funds markets was just the beginning of banking's *money market strategy*. When the Federal Reserve became concerned over the rapid growth of CDs and federal funds and clamped down with tight-money policies, innovative financial managers were forced to find new sources of reserves or face a real cutback in their lending activities. Many turned to the Eurocurrency market, borrowing deposits from abroad, or to organizing holding companies and issuing commercial paper through subsidiary corporations. Still others found innovative ways to use repurchase agreements backed by government securities to raise new funds.

All of these clever maneuvers form part of a technique called **liability management.** Bankers quickly came to realize that simply by varying the daily interest rates they were willing to offer on CDs and other funds sources, they could gain a measure of control over their liabilities. If more funds were needed on a given day to accommodate customer loan demand, a bank active in the money market would simply offer a higher yield on the particular money market instrument it desired to use. If a smaller volume of funds were required at another time, the institution could lower its offer rate on money market borrowings.

To learn more about modern liability management see, for example, such web sites as *www. almprofessional. com* and *www. contingencyanalysis. com*

What is especially fascinating about liability management strategies is that they have had precisely the effects many analysts predicted from the start. The earnings of financial institutions *have* become more sensitive to fluctuations in interest rates; and in periods of rapidly escalating market interest rates, profit margins have often been squeezed. Whether this adverse impact on the earnings of banks will continue into the future remains to be seen due to changing technology and the growing use of risk-management techniques. The great innovative abilities of these institutions, freed in recent years by deregulation, will do much to shape their earnings performance in the years ahead. But whatever the future holds, bankers have transformed the money market into a far larger and more dynamic institution than at any other time in history.

Questions *to Help You Study*

21. What is a large *negotiable CD?*

22. When were CDS first offered in the money market? By what financial institution? Why were these instruments developed?

23. What factors appear to influence the interest rate offered on CDs issued by a depository institution?

24. What is meant by the term *multitiered market?*

25. What role do large negotiable CDs play in *liability management?*

26. What is a variable-rate CD? A Eurodollar CD? Is it likely that banks and other depository institutions will continue to develop and bring forward new types of CDs in the future? Why?

27. What factors influence a banker's choice among negotiable CDs and federal funds as important sources of borrowed reserves for banking institutions?

28. What exactly is meant by the term *liability management?* What changes has it brought to the depository institutions' industry?

Summary of the Chapter

In this chapter we have examined some of the most important of all securities markets—the marketplaces where Treasury bills, repurchase agreements (RPs), federal funds, and bank CDs are traded.

- The U.S. Government securities market began about 200 years ago when the first Secretary of the Treasury, Alexander Hamilton, organized the market and began to sell debt securities to selected individuals and financial houses. This market grew with tremendous speed during and after World War II in response to high government borrowing needs and the needs of savers for highly liquid, readily marketable financial instruments, though its growth slowed appreciably as the twentieth century drew to a close and the new century opened. Most recently the federal government has reduced the volume of its deficit spending and begun to repay a portion of its debt.

- It is difficult to underestimate the importance of the government securities market in anchoring the world's financial system. This market sets the tone for the whole financial system in terms of interest rates, security prices, and the availability of credit to both governments and private borrowers. It is an indispensable tool for the government to finance its large volume of debt, and interest rates on government securities serve as reference rates for thousands of private loan contracts.

- Moreover, investors all over the globe rely upon government securities as a safe haven for their cash reserves. This is especially true of *Treasury bills,* which are direct government debt obligations with an original maturity of a year or less. And it is in this same market today that most government economic policy changes begin, in the form of Treasury and government agency issues of new securities and in central bank operations in the open market.

- At the heart of the government security market are dealer houses that actively make markets for a broad range of government, agency, and private security issues. These dealers actively raise funds to support their purchases of government and other securities from their customers. Among their most important funds sources are *demand loans* from banks and other lenders and *repurchase agreements* negotiated with financial and nonfinancial corporations. Demand loans can be canceled at any time by borrower or lender and carry daily posted interest rates. Repurchase agreements are collateralized loans, using high-quality securities as loan collateral.

- Security dealers active in the money market generate income through such sources as commissions and fees charged for carrying out transactions or giving advice, gains on their security positions if interest rates move favorably, and carry income based on the spread between their borrowing costs and the yields on the securities they hold as assets.

- *Security dealers* are in a risky position. Interest rates and security prices are constantly changing, exposing their security holdings and sources of profit to rapid and sometimes drastic changes. Many have failed over the years and today these institutions are making increasing use of hedging tools, such as trading in financial futures contracts, to protect the value of their assets and profitability.

- *Banks* are among the most important financial institutions in the money market, providing credit to security dealers, industrial firms, and other money market participants. Banks are also the principal channel for making payments in the money market, acting as guarantors of payments and as custodians for the safekeeping of financial instruments. Finally, banks serve as a key channel for government economic policy, particularly in regulating the supply and cost of money and credit.

- Two of the most important sources of funds in the money market to support the activities of banks are federal funds and negotiable CDs (certificates of deposit). *Federal funds* represent "immediately available" money in the form of large-denomination deposits that can be wired the same day from lenders to borrowers and then back again. *Negotiable CDs* are savings deposits with fixed or variable interest rates that are issued in denominations of $100,000 or more.

- Both federal funds and negotiable CDs help banks meet the *legal reserve requirements* that the central bank (in the United States, the Federal Reserve System) imposes upon their deposit holdings. Bankers must continually compare the cost and availability of federal funds, CDs, and other sources of bank funds in order to secure the reserves they require.

- Finally, interest rates attached to money market instruments are key barometers of credit conditions and have a powerful impact on the strength of the economy. One of these money market interest rates, the daily federal funds interest rate, has become a key indicator and channel for the impact of government economic policy upon the U.S. economy.

Key Terms

Problems

1. From the following sets of figures, (1) calculate the bank discount rate on each T-bill and (2) convert that rate to the appropriate investment (or coupon-equivalent) yield.

   a. A new three-month T-bill sells for $98.25 on a $100 basis.

   b. The investor can buy a new 12-month T-bill for $96 on a $100 basis.

c. A 30-day bill is available from a U.S. government securities dealer at a price of $97.50 (per $100).

2. Calculate the holding-period yield for the following situations:

a. The investor buys a new 12-month T-bill at a discount rate of $7\frac{1}{2}$ percent. Sixty days later, the bill is sold at a price that results in a discount rate of 7 percent.

b. A large manufacturing corporation acquired a T-bill in the secondary market 30 days from its maturity but is forced to sell the bill 15 days later. At time of purchase, the bill carried a discount rate of 8 percent, but it was sold at a discount rate of $7\frac{3}{4}$ percent.

3. A dealer in government securities currently holds $875 million in 10-year Treasury bonds and $1,410 million in six-month Treasury bills. Current yields on the T-bonds average 7.15 percent, while six-month T-bill yields average 3.28 percent. The dealer is currently borrowing $2,300 million through one-week repurchase agreements at an interest rate of 3.20 percent. What is the dealer's expected (annualized) *carry income?* Suppose that 10-year T-bond rates suddenly rise to 7.30 percent, T-bill rates climb to 5.40 percent, and interest rates on comparable maturity RPs increase to 5.55 percent. What will happen to the dealer's expected (annualized) carry income and why? Should this dealer have moved to a long position or a short position before the interest rate change just described? Should the dealer alter his or her borrowing plans in any way? Please explain your answer.

4. A government securities dealer is currently borrowing $25 million from a money center bank using repurchase agreements based on Treasury bills. If today's RP rate is 6.25 percent, how much in interest will the dealer owe the bank for a 24-hour loan?

5. Suppose that a dealer borrows cash through a $40 million RP from a manufacturing corporation for one day. If the dealer will have to pay $3,500 in interest on this loan, what is the current RP loan rate?

6. An automobile company, NISSAN, has a temporary cash surplus and lends its funds overnight through a repurchase agreement to a government securities dealer, earning $55,600 in interest income when the RP loan rate stood at 5.70 percent. What was the size of the loan that NISSAN granted to the securities dealer?

7. Ninety-one-day Treasury bills carry an investment yield (IR) of 6.25 percent. What is their purchase price? What is their discount rate?

8. Security State Bank has just verified by checking with the Federal Reserve bank in its district that its daily average reserve balance for the current reserve maintenance period is $1.25 million. Today is the final day of the current reserve maintenance period, and the bank's money market officer is concerned that Security might be running a large deficit in its legal reserve account. Checking the bank's own records, the officer discovers that transaction deposits averaged $43 million and nontransaction deposits averaged $16 million over the relevant two-week reserve computation period. Vault cash holdings averaged $250,000. Suppose that currently the Federal Reserve imposes a 3 percent reserve requirement on the total of a depository institution's transaction deposits below $41 million and 12 percent for any amount of transaction deposits over $41 million. Suppose that nontransaction deposits are subject to a 3 percent required reserve. Does Security State have a reserve deficiency? If so, is it required to cover the reserve shortfall before this current reserve maintenance period ends today? Explain your answer.

9. A money-center bank is trying to decide which source of funding to rely upon to cover loans being made today. It needs to borrow $10 million in either the federal funds market or in the negotiable CD market. Funds are needed for at least a week, but the bank's money desk manager is most concerned about the next 24 hours. Federal funds

are currently trading at 4.80 percent; rates on new negotiable CDs posted by leading banks have reached 4.70 percent. FDIC insurance fees are currently 27 cents per $100.

Calculate the cost to the bank for each of these funds sources. If you were a banker facing this decision, which source would you prefer to use?

10. Glenwood National Bank is short of required legal reserves. The bank's money manager estimates it will need to raise an additional $50 million in funds to cover its reserve requirement over the next three days. Federal funds are trading today at 5.90 percent, and the bank's economist has forecast a federal funds rate of 6.15 percent tomorrow and 6.20 percent the next day. Negotiable CDs in minimum maturities of seven days have been trading in New York this morning at 5.85 percent, with a forecast of 5.90 percent tomorrow and 5.98 percent the next day. The FDIC charges 30 cents per $100 for insurance coverage.

Please calculate the lowest-cost source of funding for Glenwood National Bank and the next cheapest source for borrowing over the next three days (today, tomorrow, and the next day). What are the relative advantages and disadvantages of each of these funding sources?

11. If Sterling Corporation purchases a $5 million bank CD that matures in 90 days and promises an interest return of 6.25 percent, how much in total will Sterling receive back when this CD matures?

12. What is the coupon-equivalent yield to maturity (YTM) on a 30-day negotiable CD promising an annualized interest return (i) of 5.95 percent?

13. Please calculate the bank discount rate (DR) attached to a 60-day, $1 million CD selling in the secondary market for $990,000.

14. J . P . Morgan Chase Bank is short cash reserves in the amount of $225 million—a condition expected to last for the next five business days—and is weighing securing a loan in the domestic federal funds market where the interest rate prevailing today is 5.45 percent, or issuing seven-day domestic negotiable CDs at a current market rate of 5.50 percent, or tapping its foreign branch offices for 30-day Eurodollars at a market rate of 5.58 percent. The estimated noninterest cost of all of these various funding sources is approximately the same, except that the domestic CDs currently carry an annual FDIC insurance fee of $0.04 per every $100 in deposits received from the public. Which source of funds would you recommend the bank make use of? What factors should the bank's funds management division weigh in making this borrowing decision?

15. Please identify each of the key terms or concepts that are described by the phrases or sentences listed below.

   a. The purchase of financial assets outright from a seller.
   b. The promise of delivery of financial assets not currently owned in the hope asset prices subsequently will fall.
   c. Borrowing funds subject to recall on demand by the lender.
   d. A loan collateralized by high-quality securities.
   e. Security firms that deal directly with the Federal Reserve.
   f. Procedure by which yields on Treasury bills, commercial paper, and acceptances are calculated.
   g. A mechanism for buying and selling financial assets with the highest bidders gaining access to those assets.
   h. A debt obligation issued by the U.S. government that has an original maturity of one year or less.

    i. Technique employed mainly by banks to control the amount, cost, and composition of their borrowed funds.

    j. A marketable interest-bearing receipt for the deposit of funds in a bank.

    k. A method for determining the volume of legal reserves a depository institution must hold behind its deposits.

    l. Funds available for immediate payment.

Questions about the Web and the Money and Capital Markets

1. If you were interested in purchasing *Treasury bills* for your own portfolio, how would you find out on the Web about the procedure you would need to follow? How could you use the Web to stay abreast of what's happening to prices and yields in the bill market?

2. Using the Web, find out what is meant by the "intended" federal funds rate? Why is the "intended" funds rate important? How could you track it?

3. Data on the interest rates or yields attached to Treasury bills, security repurchase agreements, federal funds, and bank negotiable certificates of deposit can be found where on the Web? Which source do you prefer and why?

Selected References

Bennett, Paul, and Spence Hilton. "Falling Reserve Balances and the Federal Funds Rate." *Current Issues in Economics and Finance,* Federal Reserve Bank of New York, April 1997, pp. 1–6.

Duecker, Michael J., and Andreas M. Fischer. "Are Federal Funds Rate Changes Consistent with Price Stability? Results from an Indicator Model." *Review,* Federal Reserve Bank of St. Louis, January–February 1996, pp. 45–51.

Duffie, Darrell. "Special Repo Rates." *Journal of Finance* 51 (June 1996), pp. 493–526.

Dupoint, Dominique, and Brian Sack. "The Treasury Securities Market: Overview and Recent Developments." *Federal Reserve Bulletin,* December 1999, pp. 785–806.

Evans, Charles L. "Real-Time Taylor Rules and the Federal Funds Futures Market." *Economic Perspectives,* Federal Reserve Bank of Chicago, June 1998, pp. 44–55.

Federal Reserve Bank of New York. *Basic Information on Treasury Securities.* 1990.

Fleming, Michael J. "The Round-the-Clock Market for U.S. Treasury Securities." *Economic Policy Review,* Federal Reserve Bank of New York, July 1997, pp. 9–32.

Jones, David S., and V. Vance Roley. "Rational Expectations, the Expectations Hypothesis, and Treasury Bill Yields: An Economic Analysis." Research Working Paper 82-01. Federal Reserve Bank of Kansas City, February 1982.

Keane, Frank. "Repo Rate Patterns for New Treasury Notes." *Current Issues in Economics and Finance,* Federal Reserve Bank of New York, September 1996, pp. 1–6.

Krueger, J., and K. Kuttner. "The Fed Funds Futures Rate as a Predictor of Federal Reserve Policy." *Journal of Futures Markets* 16 (1996), pp. 865–79.

Nandi, Saikat. "Treasury Auction: What Do the Recent Models and Results Tell Us?" *Economic Review,* Federal Reserve Bank of Atlanta, Fourth Quarter 1997, pp. 4–14.

Nosal, Ed. "How Well Does the Federal Funds Futures Rate Predict the Future Federal Funds Rate?" *Economic Commentary,* Federal Reserve Bank of Cleveland, October 1, 2001.

Reinhart, Vincent. "An Analysis of Potential Treasury Auction Techniques." *Federal Reserve Bulletin,* June 1992, pp. 403–13.

Rose, Peter S. *Commercial Bank Management.* 5th edition. New York: McGraw-Hill, 2002.

Rowe, Timothy D; Thomas A. Lawler; and Timothy Q. Cook. "Treasury Bill versus Private Money Market Yield Curves." *Economic Review,* Federal Reserve Bank of Richmond, July–August 1986, pp. 3–12.

Chapter **Twelve**

Money Market Instruments: Commercial Paper, Federal Agency Securities, Bankers' Acceptances, and Eurocurrency Deposits

Learning Objectives in This Chapter

- You will discover the important role that large corporations and government agencies play in the domestic U.S. money market and that banks play in the international money market through the issuance of *bankers' acceptances* and *Eurodollar deposits.*

- You will explore the nature and characteristics of one of the oldest of all money market instruments—*commercial paper.*

- You will learn how *federal agencies,* by borrowing many of their outside funds in the money market, aid several different sectors of the economy (including agriculture, home buyers, and small businesses) to find low-cost credit.

- You will discover the trend toward *internationalization* of the money market, which now reaches around the globe, helping to efficiently allocate capital and other resources nearly everywhere on the planet.

- You will understand how bankers' acceptances and Eurodeposits are employed, not only to provide credit within the borders of a single nation, but also to aid international trade by flowing credit across national borders.

- You will see how transfers of money from spending unit to spending unit across international boundaries impact the economy of a particular nation.

What's in This Chapter? Key Topics Outline

Commercial Paper: Nature and Recent Growth

Credit Ratings and Credit Enhancements

Advantages and Disadvantages for Commercial Paper Issuers

Government-Sponsored and Federal Agencies in the Financial Marketplace

Key Borrowers in the Agency Market

Agency Notes and Bonds: Terms and Uses

How Bankers' Acceptances Are Born and Why

Recent Decline in the Acceptance Market

Eurocurrency Deposits: Definition and Origins

Creation and Destruction of Eurocurrency Deposits

Benefits and Costs of the Eurocurrency Markets

INTRODUCTION

In this chapter we conclude our survey of the major money market instruments in use today by exploring the sources and uses of four very popular short-term lending tools—commercial paper, federal agency securities, bankers' acceptances, and Eurocurrency deposits.

The first of these, *commercial paper,* arises from the short-term borrowings of some of the largest corporations. Each year, companies like American Telephone & Telegraph, General Motors, Marriott Corp., MCI Communications, and Philip Morris borrow billions of dollars in the money market through the sale of unsecured promissory notes known as *commercial paper.* A study at the Federal Reserve Board a decade ago found that well over 1,000 corporations were regularly selling their commercial notes to money market investors and that number appears to have more than doubled recently. Commercial paper issued by large corporations and bought principally by other large corporations has become one of the most dynamic and rapidly growing segments of the money market, and it now leads all other securities in the domestic money market in terms of total volume.

During the 1960s and 1970s several key units within the United States government's huge structure, known as *federal agencies,* came to be major buyers of money market funds. Many of these agencies, such as the Farm Credit System, Small Business Administration, and Federal National Mortgage Association, have become familiar names to active investors worldwide, who are regularly offered a menu of attractive certificates, notes, and bonds so that these agencies can carry out their mission of assisting "disadvantaged" sectors of the economy. The growth of so-called "agency debt" has been remarkable in recent years and, if large federal government budget surpluses emerge again in the future as some experts believe, may come to replace the U.S. public debt as a principal investment vehicle for safety-conscious investors.

Information on changing money market conditions and on specific money market instruments is growing slowly on the world wide web as more and more financial newssheets go online. Selected internet sites explore the four main financial instruments discussed in this chapter—commercial paper, federal agency securities, bankers' acceptances, and Eurocurrency deposits.

For example, information on commercial paper can be found at *www.encyclopedia.com,* while for those interested in federal agency securities one of the best sources is to dial up each issuing federal or government-sponsored agency. Prominent examples include the web sites of the Federal National Mortgage Association at *www.fanniemae.com* and the Federal Home Loan Mortgage Corporation at *www.freddiemac.com.*

Information about bankers' acceptances and Eurocurrency deposits is a bit harder to find. A few relevant web sites on these instruments appear at *www.clev.frb.org/research* and at *www.bondresources.com.* Often useful information may be found among the web sites of major security dealers, such as Merrill Lynch and Goldman Sachs, who trade in many of these money market instruments for themselves and for their customers. Also, extensive data on rates of return (yields) and trading volume for a wide variety of money market instruments is available through the Federal Reserve Board's web databank at *www.economagic.com/fedbog.htm.*

In the final half of this chapter we learn that the money market today is not confined within the boundaries of a single nation. Money flows around the globe, seeking out those investments offering the highest expected returns for a given degree of risk. Moreover, world trade has expanded in recent years at a rapid pace, especially between the United States, the nations of Central and South America, the Pacific Basin, Europe, and the Middle East. Further increases in international commerce are expected in the decade ahead, including a significant expansion of trade between East and West. China, the nations that formerly were part of the Soviet Union, and Eastern Europe are developing close economic ties with several Western countries. The exporting of agricultural products and advanced technology by the United States, Japan, and Western Europe to Third World countries constitutes one of the major venues for trade in the modern world.

And, of course, the growth and development of international commerce requires a concomitant expansion in both long- and short-term sources of financing. Long-term capital is needed to build new factories, transportation systems, and energy-producing and refining facilities. Short-term capital from the money market is needed to finance the annual export and import of goods and to provide other working capital needs. In this chapter, we focus on two of the best-known international money market instruments: *bankers' acceptances* and *Eurocurrency deposits.*

COMMERCIAL PAPER

What Is Commercial Paper?

Commercial paper is one of the oldest of all money market instruments, dating back to the eighteenth century in the United States. By definition, commercial paper consists of short-term, unsecured promissory notes issued by well-known companies that are financially strong and carry high credit ratings.[1] The funds raised from a paper issue normally are used for *current transactions*—to purchase inventories, pay taxes, meet payrolls, and cover other short-term obligations—rather than for *capital transactions* (long-term investments). However, a substantial number of paper issues today are used to provide "bridge financing" for such long-term projects as building pipelines, office buildings, and manufacturing assembly lines. In these instances, issuing companies usually plan to convert their short-term paper into more permanent financing when the capital market looks more favorable.

Commercial paper is generally issued in multiples of $1,000 and in denominations designed to meet the needs of the buyer. It is traded mainly in the primary market. Opportunities for resale in the secondary market are more limited, although dealers today will often work to redeem the notes they sell and others trade paper issued by large finance companies and bank holding companies. Because of the limited resale possibilities, investors are usually careful to purchase those paper issues whose maturity matches their planned holding periods, though resale opportunities (liquidity) have increased in recent years.

Types of Commercial Paper

There are two major types of commercial paper—direct paper and dealer paper. The main issuers of **direct paper** are large finance companies and bank holding companies that deal directly with the investor rather than using a securities dealer as an intermediary. These companies, which regularly extend installment credit to consumers and large working capital loans and leases to business firms, announce the rates they are currently paying on various maturities of their paper. For example, not long ago, the largest finance company borrowers in this market offered the following yields to interested investors:

Paper Maturity	Recent Direct or Finance Company Paper Yields (Percent)
1 month	5.41%
2 month	5.29
3 month	5.19

Source: Board of Governors of the Federal Reserve System.

Investors select maturities that most closely approximate their expected holding periods and buy the securities directly from the issuer. Interest rates may be adjusted during the day the paper is being sold to regulate the inflow of investor funds.

---

[1]As a further backstop to reduce investor risk, borrowers in the commercial paper market nearly always secure a *line of credit* at a commercial bank for a small fee or hold a compensating deposit at their bank. However, because the line of credit cannot be used to directly guarantee payment if the company goes bankrupt and the lender may renege on the credit line if the borrowing company has had a "material adverse change" in its condition, many issuers also take out irrevocable letters of credit prepared by their banks. Such a letter makes the bank unconditionally responsible for repayment if the corporation defaults on its paper. The lending institution usually charges a fee of ½ percent to 1½ percent of the amount of the guarantee it issues. Insurance companies and parent companies of paper-issuing firms also guarantee commercial paper. In 2001 and 2002 several major companies, including Tyco International Ltd., Qwest Communications International, and Computer Associates International, found themselves having to draw upon their backup bank lines of credit to pay their day-to-day bills when they ran into problems trying to sell their commercial paper in the money market.

Additional information on commercial paper instruments and their market may be uncovered in several key Web sites, including *www.federalreserve.gov /releases*, *www.sec.gov*, *www.economagic.com/ fedbog.htm*, and *www.toerien.com*

Leading finance company borrowers in the direct paper market include General Motors Acceptance Corporation (GMAC), General Electric Capital Corporation (GE Capital), CIT Financial Corporation, and Commercial Credit Corporation. The leading U.S. bank holding companies that issue commercial paper are centered around the largest banks in New York, Chicago, San Francisco, and other major U.S. cities.[2] Today, about 70 financially oriented U.S. companies account for nearly all directly placed paper, with finance companies issuing approximately three-fourths of the total. All of these firms have an ongoing need for huge amounts of short-term money, possess top credit ratings, and have established working relationships with major institutional investors in order to place new paper issues rapidly.

Directly placed paper must be sold in large volume to cover the substantial costs of distribution and marketing. On average, each direct issuer will borrow at least $1 billion per month. Issuers of direct paper do not have to pay dealers' commissions, but these companies must operate a marketing division to maintain constant contact with active investors. Selected issuers, like New York's Citigroup, sell commercial paper in weekly auctions in which buyers bid and the issuing company accepts the highest price (lowest yield) bid. Sometimes direct issuers must sell their paper even when they have no need for funds in order to maintain a good working relationship with active investor groups. These companies also cannot escape paying fees to banks for supporting lines of credit, to rating agencies that rate their paper issues, and to agents (such as trust departments or trust companies) that dispense required payments and collect funds.

The other major variety of commercial paper is **dealer paper,** issued by security dealers on behalf of their corporate customers. Also known as *industrial paper,* dealer paper is issued mainly by nonfinancial companies (including public utilities, manufacturers, retailers, and transportation companies), as well as by smaller bank holding companies and finance companies, all of which borrow less frequently than firms issuing direct paper. The issuing company may sell the paper directly to the dealer, who buys it less discount and commission and then attempts to resell it at the highest possible price in the market. Alternatively, the issuing company may carry all the risk, with the dealer agreeing only to sell the issue at the best price available less commission, referred to as a *best efforts basis.* Finally, the open-rate method may be used in which the borrowing company receives some money in advance but the balance depends on how well the issue sells in the open market. Companies using dealers to place their paper are generally smaller, less frequent borrowers than are issuers of direct paper. Not long ago dealers were posting the following short-term yields in the primary paper market:

Paper Maturity	Recent Nonfinancial or Dealer Paper Yields (Percent)
1 month	5.39%
2 month	5.25
3 month	5.14

Source: Board of Governors of the Federal Reserve System.

[2]Bank holding companies issue *both* direct and dealer paper, with the largest companies going the direct placement route. Much of this bank-related paper comes from finance company subsidiaries of large bank holding companies. Frequently, a holding company will issue paper through a nonbank subsidiary and then funnel the proceeds to one or more of its subsidiary banks by purchasing some of the banks' assets. This gives the banks additional funds to lend and may be especially helpful when a bank is having difficulty attracting deposits through normal channels.

Recent Growth of Commercial Paper

As Exhibit 12–1 indicates, the volume of commercial paper has more than doubled since 1990. Indeed, as Exhibit 12–2 shows, commercial paper issues have doubled, tripled, or quadrupled in volume in every decade since 1960. By 2000, more than 1,200 companies had over $1.6 trillion dollars in commercial notes outstanding. About one-fifth of the total was placed directly with investors by large finance companies and bank holding companies; the rest reached the market through the efforts of security dealers. Subsequently, paper volume fell in a weakened economy.

What factors explain the rapid growth of commercial paper? One factor is the relative cost of other sources of credit compared to interest rates prevailing on commercial paper. For the largest, best-known corporations, commercial paper is usually a cost-effective substitute for bank loans and other forms of borrowing. This is especially true for nonfinancial companies issuing paper through dealers. These firms usually come to the paper market when it is significantly cheaper to borrow there than to tap bank lines of credit. In recent years, paper has also frequently been a cheaper funds source than issuing long-term bonds or selling stock. Also, many companies use the paper market today to participate in interest rate swaps, which are designed to hedge against losses from fluctuating interest rates.[3]

Another reason for the market's rapid growth is the high quality of most commercial paper obligations. Many investors regard this instrument as a close substitute for Treasury bills and other money market instruments. As a result, market yields on commercial paper tend to move in the same direction and by similar amounts as the yields on other money market securities. This fact is shown clearly in Exhibit 12–3, which compares market yields on three-month maturities of commercial paper, Treasury bills, negotiable CDs, and bankers' acceptances. Rates on these four money market instruments tend to stay close to

EXHIBIT 12–1   **Volume of Commercial Paper Outstanding ($ Billions, End of Period)**

Instrument	1984	1988	1990	1994	1998	2000	2001*
All issuers	$237.6	$458.5	$562.7	$595.4	$1,163.0	$1,615.3	$1,453.8
Financial companies issuing paper							
Dealer placed—Total	56.5	159.8	214.7	223.0	614.1	973.1	958.9
Directly placed paper—Total	110.5	194.9	200.0	207.7	322.0	298.8	265.8
Nonfinancial companies issuing paper	70.6	103.8	147.9	164.6	227.1	343.4	229.0

NA = not available
*Figures for 2001 are for the month of July.
Source: Board of Governors of the Federal Reserve System, *Federal Reserve Bulletin,* selected issues.

EXHIBIT 12–2
Growth of Commercial Paper Issues in the United States

Year	Outstanding Volume of Paper in Billions of Dollars
1960	$ 4.5
1970	33.4
1980	124.4
1990	562.7
2000	1,615.3
2001*	1,453.8

*Figure as of July 2001.
Source: Board of Governors of the Federal Reserve System, *Federal Reserve Bulletin,* selected issues.

[3]Chapter 9 contains an explanation of interest rate swaps.

EXHIBIT 12–3   **Market Yields on Commercial Paper Compared to Yields on Other Money Market Instruments (Average Yields on Three-Month Maturities; Percent per Annum)**

Instruments	1984	1988	1994	1996	1998	2000	2002*
Commercial paper	10.10%	7.66%	4.66%	5.41%	5.34%	6.29%	1.80%
U.S. Treasury bills	9.52	6.67	4.25	5.01	4.78	5.82	1.73
Certificates of deposit	10.37	7.73	4.63	5.39	5.47	6.46	1.82
Prime bankers' acceptances	10.14	7.56	4.56	5.31	5.39	6.23	1.85

Note: Commercial paper yields are unweighted averages of interest rates quoted by at least five dealers. Treasury bills are secondary-market yields computed from daily closing bid prices. CD rates are secondary-market yields quoted as five-day averages by five dealers. Bankers' acceptance rates are on 90-day maturities and are based on daily closing rates on domestic issues. All yields except CDs are quoted on a bank discount basis.
*Figures for the first week of May.
Source: Board of Governors of the Federal Reserve System, *Federal Reserve Bulletin,* selected issues.

each other. We note that commercial paper yields are usually higher than market rates on comparable maturity Treasury bills due to the greater risk and lower marketability of paper and the fact that Treasury bills are exempt from state and local taxation.

Still another key factor in the market's recent growth is the expanding use of **credit enhancements,** in the form of standby letters of credit, indemnity bonds, and other irrevocable payment guarantees. For example, a bank or other lending institution may issue a certificate that promises repayment of principal and/or interest on a customer's paper if the borrowing company fails to do so. The result is that such paper, often called *documented notes,* usually carries the higher credit rating of the guarantor rather than the lower credit rating of the issuing firm. Through these guarantees, mortgage companies, utilities, and small manufacturers in large numbers have been attracted into a market that otherwise would be closed to them, still saving on interest costs even after paying the guarantor's fee.

Other groups recently entering the market include foreign banks and industrial companies, international financial conglomerates, and state and local governments (which offer *tax-exempt* commercial paper). Paper issued in the United States by foreign firms is called *Yankee paper* and frequently can be sold at lower interest costs in the United States than abroad. However, foreign borrowers in the U.S. market generally must pay higher interest costs than U.S. companies of comparable credit rating to compensate U.S. buyers for the added difficulty of gathering information on foreign borrowers and the lack of name recognition.

Maturities and Rates of Return on Commercial Paper

Maturities of U.S. commercial paper range from three days ("weekend paper") to nine months. Most commercial notes carry an original maturity of 60 days or less, with an average maturity ranging from 20 to 45 days. U.S. paper is generally not issued for maturities longer than 270 days because, under the provisions of the Securities Act of 1933, any security sold in U.S. markets for a longer term must be registered with the Securities and Exchange Commission. Yields to the investor are calculated by the *bank discount method,* just like Treasury bills. As in the case of T-bills, most commercial paper is issued at a discount from par; the investor's yield arises from the price appreciation of the security between its purchase date and maturity date.

For example, if a million-dollar commercial note with a maturity of 180 days is acquired by an investor at a discounted price of $980,000, the discount rate of return (DR) is:

$$DR = \frac{\text{Par value} - \text{Purchase price}}{\text{Par value}} \times \frac{360}{\text{Days to maturity}}$$

$$= \frac{\$1,000,000 - \$980,000}{\$1,000,000} \times \frac{360}{180} = 0.04, \text{ or 4 percent}$$

The commercial paper market in the United States has been copied abroad for many years now, though other countries have added their own special features to this market for corporate IOUs. Among the leading national commercial paper markets today are those of Japan, France, Canada, and Sweden.

One of the most dramatic developments in the history of commercial paper markets has been the relatively recent development of the Japanese yen-denominated paper market. Yen-denominated commercial paper was first allowed to be offered in domestic Japanese markets by the Ministry of Finance in 1987. Many Japanese companies had threatened to move their short-term borrowing abroad unless the Japanese government relaxed its regulations. A year later, foreign businesses were given permission to sell "Samurai paper" inside Japan.

With so many U.S. companies operating in Canada and many Canadian firms having money market access inside the United States, the Canadian commercial paper market has relatively modest dimensions. Like U.S. paper, Canadian paper must be backed by a bank line of credit to catch the attention of money market investors. It has a broader range of maturities (usually from demand notes, cashable in 24 hours, out to about one year) than in the United States and also tends to be issued in larger denominations (usually $100,000 or more), suggesting that most Canadian paper is purchased by large corporations.

In the mid-1980s a new commercial paper market emerged —the *Europaper market*. Europaper soared in volume because borrowing companies were able to tap a larger reservoir of foreign cash. Many U.S. corporations that have had difficulty borrowing in the domestic market, often because of declining credit quality, have turned to the Euromarket, which appears to be less quality conscious. The heaviest investors in Europaper are international banks, private corporations, and central banks.

Europaper is priced below its face value and appreciates in value as maturity approaches. The interest rate quoted to investors is expressed as a discount rate (DR) like that attached to Treasury bills. For example, suppose we are interested in a $100 million Europaper issue with 90 days remaining until maturity that bears a discount rate today of 6 percent. The price the Europaper investor must pay is:

$$\text{Price of Europaper issue} = 100 - DR \times \frac{\text{Days to maturity}}{360 \text{ days}}$$

$$\text{Price} = 100 - 6 \times \frac{90}{360} = 98.50$$

In this instance, the $100 million Europaper issue would be priced today to sell at $98.5 million. There appears to be an active resale market for Europaper, which has an average maturity almost double the average maturity of U.S. paper. The bulk of Europaper is sold through dealers with interest rates linked to Eurobank deposit rates.

If this commercial note's rate of return were figured like that of a regular bond, its coupon-equivalent yield (or investment rate of return, IR) would be

$$IR = \frac{\text{Par value} - \text{Purchase price}}{\text{Par value}} \times \frac{365}{\text{Days to maturity}}$$

$$= \frac{\$1,000,000 - \$980,000}{\$980,000} \times \frac{365}{180} = 0.0414, \text{ or } 4.14 \text{ percent}$$

This second formula helps an investor compare prospective returns on paper against the returns available on other securities available for purchase. In addition to discount paper, some corporations also sell interest-bearing (coupon) paper.

The minimum denomination of commercial paper issues is usually $25,000, although among institutional investors, who dominate the market, the usual minimum denomination is $1 million. Payment is made at maturity on presentation to the particular bank listed as agent on the note. Settlement in federal funds is usually made the same day the note is presented for payment by its holder.

Changing Yields on Paper Issues

Because yields on commercial paper are open market rates, they fluctuate with the daily ebb and flow of supply and demand forces in the marketplace. In the wide swings between easy and tight money, between depressed and resurgent economic activity in recent years, commercial paper rates have fluctuated between extreme highs and lows. For example, in 1986 and in the years 1992–98—years of moderate credit demands and moderate inflation—the paper rates averaged less than 4 percent to only about 6 percent. (See again Exhibit 12–3.) In the early 1980s, however, when intense credit demands and rapid inflation characterized the economy, the paper rates averaged more than 10 percent. The commercial paper market is highly volatile and difficult to predict. This is the reason that many corporations eligible to borrow there still maintain close working relationships with banks and other institutional lenders and employ interest-rate hedging techniques (such as financial futures contracts).

Questions *to Help You Study*

1. What do we mean by the term *commercial paper?*

2. Why is commercial paper attractive to such money market investors as banks, insurance companies, money market funds, and industrial companies?

3. Please describe the functions that *dealers* perform in the functioning of the commercial paper market. In what market segment are they most active? Least active?

4. Why do some investors (savers) find commercial paper unsatisfactory for their investment needs?

5. Exactly how is the *rate of return* on commercial paper figured? Is the method used to determine paper's rate of return similar to the return calculation for any other money market instrument? Which one?

Advantages of Issuing Commercial Paper

There are several financial advantages to a company able to tap the paper market for funds. Generally, interest rates on paper are lower than on corporate loans extended by banks. This is evident from the data shown in Exhibit 12–4. In 2002, for example, the bank prime rate averaged about three percentage points higher than the rate on three-month dealer paper.

Moreover, the effective rate on many commercial loans granted by banks is even higher than the quoted prime rate, due to the fact that corporate borrowers usually are required to keep a percentage of their loans in a bank deposit. This *compensating balance* requirement is generally 15 to 20 percent of the amount of the loan. Suppose a corporation borrows $100,000 at a prime interest rate of 8.50 percent but must keep 20 percent of this amount ($20,000) on deposit with the bank granting the loan. Then the effective annual loan rate is 10.625 percent [or $8,500/($100,000−$20,000)].

Another advantage of borrowing in the paper market is that interest rates there are often more flexible than bank loan rates. A company in need of funds can raise money quickly through either dealer or direct paper. Dealers maintain close contact with the market and generally know where cash may be found. Frequently, notes can be issued and funds raised the same day.

Generally, larger amounts of funds may be borrowed more conveniently through the paper market than from other sources, particularly bank loans. This situation arises due to federal and state regulations that limit the amount of money a bank can lend to a single borrower. For national banks, the maximum unsecured loan is 15 percent of the bank's capital and surplus account. Corporate credit needs frequently exceed an individual bank's

EXHIBIT 12–4

Spread between the Average Prime Rate Quoted by Major U.S. Banks and the Three-Month Commercial Paper Rate, Selected Years

Year	Bank Prime Lending Rate	Three-Month Commercial Paper Rate	Rate Spread in Percentage Points
1995	8.83%	5.93%	2.90%
1996	8.27	5.41	2.86
1997	8.44	5.58	2.86
1998	8.35	5.34	3.01
1999	8.00	5.18	2.82
2000	9.23	6.31	2.92
2001*	6.67	3.42	3.25
2002†	4.75	1.75	3.00

Note: The prime rate is the average of rates posted by major U.S. banks. The three-month commercial paper rate is the unweighted average of offer rates quoted by at least five dealers. The prime rate is averaged for each year.
*August 2001.
†January 7th figures.
Source: Board of Governors of the Federal Reserve System, *Federal Reserve Bulletin,* selected issues.

loan limit, and a group of banks (consortium) has to be assembled to make the loan. However, this takes time and often requires lengthy negotiations. The paper market is generally much faster than trying to hammer out a loan agreement among several parties, though some experts believe that the current consolidation of the banking industry worldwide, creating fewer, but much larger, banks, could limit the growth of the paper market in future years.

The ability to issue commercial paper gives a corporation considerable leverage when negotiating with banks. A banker who knows that a customer can draw on the paper market for funds is more likely to offer advantageous terms on a loan and be more receptive to future customer credit needs.

Possible Disadvantages from Issuing Commercial Paper

Despite the advantages, there are some risks for corporations that choose to borrow frequently in the commercial paper market. One of these is the risk of alienating banks whose loans might be needed when a real emergency develops. The paper market is sensitive to financial and economic problems. This fact was demonstrated convincingly in 1980 when Chrysler Financial, the finance company subsidiary of Chrysler Corporation, was forced to cut back its borrowings in the paper market due to the widely publicized troubles of its parent company, which sought government assistance. However, the paper market appears to have strengthened and become so broad in recent years that it may be more tolerant of defaults and corporate failures. For example, in January and February 1997 when the huge auto lender Mercury Finance Company defaulted on more than $300 million in paper, there was little effect outside the automobile industry on the commercial paper market as a whole, though Enron's collapse in 2001 did depress this market.

At times, it is difficult even for companies in sound financial condition to raise funds in the paper market at reasonable rates of interest. It helps to have a friendly banker available to supply emergency credit when this market turns sour. Another problem lies in the fact that commercial paper cannot usually be paid off at the issuer's discretion, but generally must remain outstanding until maturity. In contrast, many bank loans permit early retirement without penalty.

Principal Investors

The most important investors in the commercial paper market include nonfinancial corporations, money market mutual funds, bank trust departments, small banks, pension funds, insurance companies, and state and local governments. In effect, this is a market in which corporations borrow from other corporations. These investor groups generally regard commercial paper as a low-risk outlet for their surplus funds, although recent financial problems and a few defaults among paper issuers have caused some investor groups, such as money market funds, to sharply cut back their purchases of lower-quality paper.

In 1991, the U.S. Securities and Exchange Commission (SEC) became particularly concerned about the safety of money market funds and the risk to the savings of thousands of investors who, by that time, had placed nearly $500 billion with the money market fund industry. More than half the industry's assets had been invested in commercial paper, with an increasing proportion of these investments in lower-quality issues bearing higher but riskier yields. These lower-quality commercial notes are often acquired by more aggressive money fund managers interested in attracting more savings deposits by offering higher returns. Following several commercial paper defaults, the SEC ruled that money market funds could hold no more than 5 percent of their total assets in less than top-quality (not prime-rated) commercial paper, nor could they place any more than 1 percent of their assets in the paper of any one non-prime-rated corporate issuer. Money funds must inform investors that their shares are not insured or guaranteed by the U.S. government. The new rules appear to enhance the safety of savings held with money market funds, which now hold over a third of all paper outstanding, but they may also have placed a future restraint on the growth of the commercial paper market, making it more difficult for many companies, especially those with less-than-top credit ratings, to sell their paper.

Continuing Innovation in the Paper Market

One important innovation in the direct paper market is the **master note,** most frequently issued to bank trust departments and other permanent money market investors by finance companies. Under a master note agreement, the investing firm agrees to take some paper each day up to an agreed-upon maximum amount. Interest owed is figured on the average daily volume of paper taken on by the investor during the current month. The prevailing interest rate on six-month commercial paper is generally used to determine the appropriate rate of return.

An extension of the paper market has appeared in the form of *medium-term notes* (MTNs). These 9-month to 10-year notes are issued by investment-grade corporations, normally carry a fixed interest rate, and are generally noncallable, unsecured obligations marketed through dealers. They are particularly suited to companies with substantial quantities of medium-term assets who wish to balance these assets with IOUs that are longer than the short maturities attached to conventional commercial paper. First sold by automobile finance companies in the 1970s, the MTN market has attracted industrial and utility companies and a secondary market has developed with several investment banking firms trading in these medium-length instruments.

Beginning in the 1980s, a new form of paper began to appear—*asset-backed commercial paper*—in which loans or credit receivables are pooled into packages and paper is then issued as claims against that pool (that is, the credit receivables are *securitized*). The loans or receivables are removed from the issuing company's balance sheet and placed in a *special-purpose entity* (SPE), which issues the paper and uses the proceeds to purchase the receivables. Among the most popular assets pooled to back these unique commercial paper issues are credit-card receivables, installment sales contracts, and lease receivables. Participants in these programs include banks, finance companies, and retail dealers. Banks find them a handy vehicle for assisting their corporate customers to obtain financing without having to loan them money and, thereby, increase the bank's capital requirements. A bank can earn fees for advising the paper-issuing customer, reviewing the quality of the assets to be pooled, and supplying credit enhancements (usually in the form of letters of credit, surety bonds, etc.) and liquidity enhancements (to help retire maturing paper in case of temporary cash shortfalls) for outstanding paper issues.

Asset-backed commercial paper gives issuing corporations a low and stable cost of financing that is often far cheaper than direct financing through a bank or finance company, or than using *factoring*, in which a company sells its accounts receivable to a lender at a sizable discount from their face value. For those asset-backed paper issues backed by credit and liquidity guarantees, any change of fortune at the customer's business should not appreciably affect the firm's actual funding costs. The SPE normally issues enough commercial paper to cover the discounted purchase price of the company's receivables and uses the proceeds from the paper issue to purchase the firm's receivables. The issuing customer usually services the underlying receivables, collecting interest and principal payments and passing the funds along to the SPE, or a bank chosen by the customer may service the receivables supporting the paper issue. The fact that paper is issued for less than the full nondiscounted value of the receivables generates a margin of value to protect investors.

COMMERCIAL PAPER RATINGS

Commercial paper is rated *prime, desirable,* or *satisfactory,* depending on the credit standing of the issuing company. Firms desiring to issue paper generally will seek a credit rating from one or more of several rating services, including such firms as Moody's Investors Service; Standard & Poor's Corporation; Fitch Investors Service; Duff and Phelps; Canadian Bond Rating Service; Japanese Bond Rating Institute; Dominion Bond Rating Service; and IBCA, Ltd.—with the first two rating companies especially prominent. Moody's assigns a rating of Prime–1 (P–1) for the highest-quality paper, with lower-quality issues designated as Prime–2 (P–2) or Prime–3 (P–3). Standard & Poor's assigns ratings of A–1+ or A–1, A–2, and A–3; Fitch uses F–1, F–2, or F–3. Any issue rated below P–2, A–2, or F–2 usually sells poorly or not at all.

Generally, commercial notes bearing credit ratings from at least two rating agencies are preferred by investors. The rating assigned to an issue often depends heavily on the liquidity position and the amount of backup lines of credit held by the issuing company. Moreover, there is evidence—for example, Crabbe and Post (1992)—that when a paper issuer's credit rating is lowered, large reductions occur in its volume of paper outstanding within a few weeks, reflecting declining demand for the downgraded issues. Eloyan, Maris, and Young (1996) find that a company's stock price tends to fall if its commercial paper is downgraded in quality or if its paper is placed on Standard and Poor's Credit Watch (i.e., review) list because of possible financial problems.

Dealers in Paper

The market is concentrated among a handful of dealers that account for the bulk of all trading activity. Top commercial paper dealers today include Citicorp (or Citigroup) Investment Bank; Goldman Sachs & Co.; the Credit-Suisse-First Boston Corporation; Morgan Stanley Dean Witter; Salomon Smith Barney; and Merrill Lynch. Dealer firms charge varying fees to borrowing companies, depending on the size of an issue and how much paper the company has issued through the dealer recently. The dealer market has become more intensely competitive in recent years as many new foreign dealers have emerged. And dealer activities have further increased in the wake of passage of the Gramm-Leach-Bliley Act in 1999 that allowed U.S. financial holding companies to underwrite more securities through their affiliated securities firms.

Dealers maintain inventories of unsold issues and repurchased paper, but they usually expect to turn over most of a new issue within 24 hours. Like dealers in government securities, paper dealers draw on repurchase agreements (RPs) and demand loans from banks to help finance their inventory positions. They generally pay interest costs only a few basis points higher than on RPs collateralized by government securities.

Questions *to Help You Study*

6. What are the principal *advantages* accruing to a company large enough to tap the commercial paper market for funds? Please make a list of these advantages.

7. What are the principal *disadvantages* of commercial paper to an issuer? To potential buyers?

8. Who are the *principal investors* in commercial paper? Why do the types of investor institutions you have named find commercial paper particularly attractive?

9. How is commercial paper *rated?* Why does its rating matter?

10. Please explain what *credit enhancements* are. What specifically is *asset-backed* commercial paper? How have these financial devices aided the growth of the paper market?

FEDERAL AGENCY SECURITIES

For nearly a century now, the federal government has attempted to aid certain sectors of the economy that appear to have an unusually difficult time raising funds in the money and capital markets. These "disadvantaged sectors" include agriculture, housing, small businesses, and college students. Dominated by smaller, less creditworthy borrowers, these sectors allegedly are pushed aside in the race for scarce funds by large corporations and governments, especially in periods of tight money. Beginning in 1916, the federal government created special agencies to make direct loans to or guarantee private loans to these disadvantaged borrowers. Several of these agencies buy selected assets from private lenders (creating a secondary market), which gives the lenders funds to make new loans to disadvantaged borrowers. Exhibit 12–5 depicts this process. Today, federal credit agencies are large enough and, with the government's blessing, financially strong enough to compete successfully for funds in the open market and channel those funds to areas of social need.

Types of Federal Credit Agencies

There are two types of federal credit agencies: government-sponsored agencies and true federal agencies. **Government-sponsored agencies** are *not* officially a part of the federal government's structure but are quasi-private institutions. They are federally chartered

EXHIBIT 12–5
Government Agencies: Performing the Roles of a Financial Intermediary

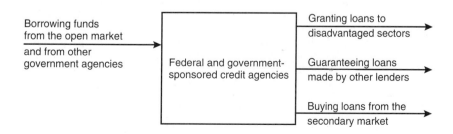

Borrowing funds from the open market and from other government agencies →	Federal and government-sponsored credit agencies	→ Granting loans to disadvantaged sectors
		→ Guaranteeing loans made by other lenders
		→ Buying loans from the secondary market

but privately owned; in some instances, their stock is traded on major securities exchanges. The borrowing and lending activities of government-sponsored agencies are *not* reflected in the federal government's budget. This has aroused the ire of many fiscal conservatives who regard the credit-granting operations of government-sponsored agencies as a disguised form of government spending. Some critics contend that the agencies have been used to get around limits on federal spending. Because these agencies are omitted from the federal government's books, annual federal deficits look considerably smaller and conceal the full extent of federal deficit financing.[4] True **federal agencies,** on the other hand, are legally a part of the government structure, and their borrowing and lending activities are included in the federal budget. Exhibit 12–6 lists the principal federal and government-sponsored agencies that borrow in the money and capital markets.

In their borrowing and lending activities, federal and government-sponsored agencies act as true **financial intermediaries.** They issue attractively packaged notes and bonds to capture funds from savers, and they direct the resulting flow of funds into loans and loan guarantees to farmers, small business owners, home mortgage borrowers, and other sectors. The securities issued by government-sponsored agencies are usually *not* guaranteed by the federal government, but most investors believe that the government is "only a step away" in the event that any agency gets into serious trouble.[5]

Growth of the Agency Market

Armed with this implied government support, the agency market has soared in recent years, with the volume of outstanding securities climbing from about $2 billion during the 1950s to almost $2 trillion today. Estimates place the total of all agency obligations—both those issued inside the federal government's huge structure and those issued from outside agencies, many having stock that is privately owned—at well over $5 trillion, or close to the overall size of the federal government's direct debt. On an average day, the leading

[4]Public concern over the growth of federal agency activities has increased in recent years. To the extent that agency borrowing and lending increase the total amount of credit available in the economy and add to aggregate spending for goods and services, they may add to inflationary pressures. Agency borrowing is not generally limited by restrictions that apply to direct debt obligations of the U.S. government. Moreover, there is a tendency to create a new agency each time a new problem rears its head, increasing the cost of government activities. For example, in 1987, the Financing Corporation (FICO) was established to bail out the failing Federal Savings and Loan Insurance Corporation (FSLIC), and in 1989, the Resolution Funding Corporation (REFCO) was created to support the liquidation of hundreds of failing savings and loans that the FSLIC could no longer handle.

The creation of these and many other special agencies has raised a number of significant issues concerning government involvement in the private sector of the economy. How many other firms should the federal government guarantee against failure in the future? Upon what basis are such guarantees to be made? What happens to the efficiency of the market system when some firms are not allowed to fail?

[5]Government-sponsored agencies are permitted to draw on the U.S. Treasury for funds up to a specified limit with Treasury approval. However, neither the principal nor the interest on the debt of government-sponsored agencies is guaranteed by the federal government, although the issuing agency guarantees its own securities. In contrast, securities of agencies operated by the federal government are fully guaranteed by the credit of the U.S. government. The government-sponsored agencies generally have capitalization requirements which limit to some extent the rate of growth of their debt obligations, but the sponsored agencies operate with considerably less capital per dollar of debt than do private lending institutions and other corporations, giving them a distinct advantage in the money and capital markets over private borrowers. The relatively lower capitalization of the government-sponsored agencies aroused some concerns as the new century began due to their heavier use of financial derivatives and apparent increases in their risk exposure. The financial condition of FNMA (FannieMae) and FHLMC (FreddieMac) came under heavier scrutiny in the financial press as new regulations required greater disclosure of their financial position.

EXHIBIT 12–6
Principal Borrowers in the Federal Agency Market

Agencies of the Federal Government

Export-Import Bank (EXIM)	Postal Service (PS)
U.S. Railway Association	Tennessee Valley Authority (TVA)
Farmers Home Administration (FMHA)	Federal Deposit Insurance Corporation (FDIC)
General Services Administration (GSA)	
Government National Mortgage Association (GNMA, or Ginnie Mae)	

Government-Sponsored Agencies

Banks for Cooperatives (BC)	Federal Land Banks (FLB)
College Construction Loan Insurance Association (CCLIA, or Connie Lee)	Federal National Mortgage Association (FNMA, or Fannie Mae)
Federal Farm Credit Banks (FFCB)	Student Loan Marketing Association (SLMA, or Sallie Mae)
Federal Home Loan Banks (FHLB)	Financing Corporation (FICO)
Federal Home Loan Mortgage Corporation (FHLMC, or Freddie Mac)	Financing Assistance Corporation (FAC)
Federal Intermediate Credit Banks (FICB)	Resolution Funding Corporation (REFCO)
Federal Agricultural Mortgage Corporation (FAMC, or Farmer Mac)	

federal agency borrowers (especially the federal mortgage-market agencies) borrow up to a third of a percentage point cheaper in interest cost than do the largest and best-known private borrowers, due primarily to the federal government's implied financial support. Moreover, the government-sponsored agencies consistently have been profitable in recent years, though they do face both credit (default) risk and interest rate risk on the loans they issue or buy and the debt they sell.

The agency market is dominated by the government-sponsored agencies, which have restricted access to government coffers and must rely mainly on the open market to raise money. The federal agencies, part of the federal government, in contrast, are financed through the **Federal Financing Bank (FFB),** which borrows money from the Treasury. The FFB is closely supervised by the Treasury Department and, in fact, is staffed by Treasury employees.[6]

Money market borrowing is usually done by issuing discount notes, which, like Treasury bills and commercial paper, have no promised interest rate but are sold at a price below their par value. Dealers sell the notes for a small fee, with banks, mutual funds, insurance companies, thrifts, and pension funds purchasing most of them. The sponsored agencies also issue short-term coupon securities and variable-rate notes. Long-term borrowing in the capital market is usually accomplished by issuing debentures, either on a monthly basis or irregularly as the need for funds arises.

Longer-term agency securities are available in denominations as small as $1,000, while the shorter-term notes traded in the money market generally come in minimum

---

[6]Due to FFB activities, the Treasury has to add a certain amount to its regular borrowings each year to cover any FFB drawings. The FFB was created by Congress in 1973. Up to that time each federal agency did its own borrowing. As a result, the number of different agency issues was proliferating at a rapid rate, creating confusion among investors. Centralization of borrowing in one agency, it was hoped, would increase efficiency in the funding process, improve the marketability of agency securities, and give Congress a more adequate measure of the growth of agency activities. All FFB obligations are fully guaranteed by the U.S. government. The FFB, in turn, purchases only those securities fully guaranteed as to principal and interest by the issuing agency.

denominations of $50,000 or more. They are subject to federal income taxes, but many are exempt from state and local taxes. However, state and local government estate, gift, and inheritance taxes do apply to agency obligations. Depository institutions may use agency securities as collateral for loans from the Federal Reserve's discount window and as backing for government deposits.

The heaviest agency borrowers in recent years, as indicated in Exhibit 12–7, have been the Federal National Mortgage Association (FNMA), the Federal Home Loan Banks (FHLB), the Federal Home Loan Mortgage Corporation (FHLMC), the Student Loan Marketing Association (which has converted to a private firm), and the Farm Credit Banks. These agencies account for well over three-quarters of the outstanding debt issued by all federal and government-sponsored agencies, and an active secondary market exists for the short-term debt of these agencies. Most agency borrowing goes to support, directly or indirectly, the housing market and agriculture.

The securities of all government-sponsored agencies are regarded as highly similar by investors. Comparable maturities tend to have about the same yield, regardless of the issuing agency. Each agency is able to borrow at interest rates below the average yield on its asset portfolio due to government support but pays a slightly higher interest rate than the U.S. Treasury. Most of this small difference in interest cost is due to the fact that agency securities are less marketable than Treasury IOUs. The Treasury issues a security homogeneous in quality and other characteristics, but the agency market is splintered into many pieces. The yields on agency securities are lower than yields on private debt issues, however, due to their superior credit standing.

EXHIBIT 12–7 **Total Debt** **Outstanding of** **Federal and** **Government-** **Sponsored Agencies,** **2000* ($ Billions)**	

Agency	Total Debt Outstanding
Federal agencies:	
Export-Import Bank	$ 0.1
Federal Housing Administration	0.2
Postal Service**	—
Tennessee Valley Authority	26.0
Other agencies	0.1
Total federal agency debt[†]	$ 26.4
Government-sponsored agencies:	
Federal Home Loan Banks	580.6
Federal Home Loan Mortgage Corporation	406.9
Federal National Mortgage Association	607.0
Farm Credit Banks[§]	71.1
Student Loan Marketing Association	42.4
Resolution Funding Corporation	30.0
Other agencies	12.3
Total government-sponsored debt[†]	$1,750.3
Total agency debt outstanding	$1,776.7

*Data as of September 2000.
**Off-budget agency.
[†]Figures may not add to column totals due to rounding.
[§]In January 1979, the Farm Credit Banks began issuing consolidated bonds to replace those securities previously issued by the Federal Land Banks, the Federal Intermediate Credit Banks, and the Banks for Cooperatives. The Resolution Funding Corporation was established by the Financial Institutions Reform, Recovery, and Enforcement Act of 1989.

Source: Board of Governors of the Federal Reserve System, *Federal Reserve Bulletin,* June 2001, Table 1.44.

Financial Developments   A Federal Agency (Fannie Mae) Fights Back!

As the 21st century dawned, one of the largest and best-known U.S. government-sponsored agencies—Fannie Mae or the Federal National Mortgage Association (FNMA)—faced a powerful group of real or potential enemies. Officials from the U.S. Treasury and Federal Reserve System raised questions about whether Fannie Mae—the nation's largest mortgage trading and lending institution—really deserved to have all of its special privileges. Other (mainly private) mortgage lending institutions competing against Fannie Mae complained about what they saw as unfair competition.

To add to the developing storm some members of Congress began discussing new legislation to slow Fannie Mae down. One of the key proposals was to require Fannie Mae to hold more equity capital behind its assets, thus making its stockholders bear more risk and reducing the amount of leverage (debt) that it could use. And, in fact, the recently created Office of Federal Housing Enterprise Oversight required Fannie Mae and its sister mortgage agency Freddie Mac, to undergo "stress testing" to make sure these agencies could withstand greater risk should the home mortgage market suffer serious losses.

Then, quite suddenly, the storm seemed to blow over. Fannie Mae—at least for now—appears to have sailed through with few scratches. Why? What magic did it work?

No one seems to know for sure, but a few recent developments may help explain what happened. One of these factors was "success"—recently the home mortgage loan market has performed extremely well. Mortgage loan rates have remained relatively low, permitting more families to afford a new home. Today more families own their own homes than at any other time in American history.

Then, too, Fannie Mae, like so many federal agencies, seems to possess strong political connections. It used its contacts all across the United States to lobby Congress and the Treasury to adopt its point of view. No one can say for sure that Fannie won't face an onslaught again in the future. However, like most government agencies working in the financial sector, it seems to know how to defend its territory politically.

Terms on Agency Securities

Agency securities are generally short to medium term in maturity (running out to about 10 years), but the most rapidly growing segment is the money market segment—agency securities under one year to maturity. One reason for the explosion in new money market agency securities is the gap opening up in the supply of new short-term direct government IOUs because the U.S. government's debt in public hands is declining and the government has less need today to issue huge amounts of new Treasury bills and other federal IOUs. Many money market investors now feel compelled to search around for alternative liquid investments. Shorter-term agency securities are often the next best alternative in terms of safety and yield to Treasury bills and notes, for example. In the future, if the volume of long-term Treasury bonds continues to fall due to possible government budget surpluses and a government decision to issue shorter-term debt, long-term agency securities may move in to take up the slack as money market investors continue to demand high-quality, liquid instruments in which to invest their money.

The Marketing of Agency Issues

Among the most active buyers of agency securities are banks, state and local governments, government trust funds, and the Federal Reserve System. The Federal Reserve has been authorized to conduct open market operations in agency IOUs since 1966. Fed buying and selling of these securities has helped to improve their marketability and stature among private investors. Major securities dealers who handle U.S. government securities also generally trade in agency issues and, in fact, if the federal debt declines in the twenty-first century due to greater likelihood of government budget surpluses and more federal debt retirement, dealers may anticipate gradual substitution of agency securities for direct Treasury debt in both the portfolios of dealers and their customers.

Government-sponsored agencies have become innovative borrowers in recent years. For example, FNMA and SLMA have sold securities in foreign markets, some of these denominated in foreign currencies or sold in "dual currency" form in which interest is paid in a foreign currency and the principal is repaid at maturity in U.S. dollars. These agencies have also used interest rate swaps and currency swaps to protect themselves against the risk of fluctuating interest rates and currency prices.

Questions *to Help You Study*

11. Federal agencies active in the financial markets were usually set up to aid so-called *disadvantaged sectors* of the economy. Who are these? Please give some examples.

12. What is the difference between a *government-sponsored agency* and a *federal agency?* Is there a practical difference between the two?

13. What are the principal investment characteristics of federal agency securities? Which groups of investors are attracted to them and why?

14. Can you explain how federal agency securities are marketed?

BANKERS' ACCEPTANCES

A **bankers' acceptance** is a *time draft* drawn on a bank by an exporter or an importer to pay for merchandise or to buy foreign currencies. If the bank honors the draft, it will stamp "Accepted" on its face and endorse the instrument. By so doing, the issuing bank has unconditionally guaranteed to pay the face value of the acceptance at maturity, shielding exporters and investors in international markets from default risk. Acceptances carry maturities ranging from 30 to 270 days (with 90 days being the most common) and are considered prime-quality money market instruments. They are traded among financial institutions, industrial corporations, and securities dealers as a high-quality investment and source of ready cash. An illustration of a typical bankers' acceptance, prepared for illustration by the Federal Reserve Bank of New York, is shown in Exhibit 12–8.

EXHIBIT 12–8
Illustration of a Bankers' Acceptance

Source: Federal Reserve Bank of New York.

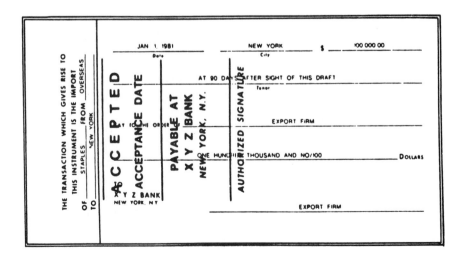

International Focus

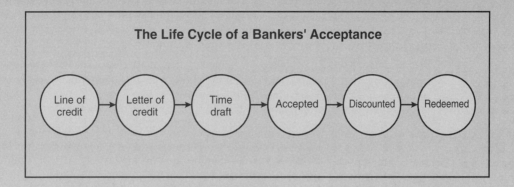

The Life Cycle of a Bankers' Acceptance

Line of credit → Letter of credit → Time draft → Accepted → Discounted → Redeemed

Why Acceptances Are Used in International Trade

Additional information on the nature of bankers' acceptances may be found in *www.ny.frb.org*

Acceptances are used in the import and export trade because most exporters are uncertain of the credit standing of the importers to whom they ship goods. Exporters may also be concerned about business conditions or political developments in foreign countries. Nations experiencing terrorist violence or even civil war have serious problems in attracting financing for imports of goods and services because of the obvious risks of extending credit inside their territory. However, exporters usually are quite content to rely on acceptance financing by a well-regarded domestic or foreign bank. Thus, an acceptance is a financial instrument designed to shift the risk of international trade to a third party willing to take on that risk for a known cost. Banks are willing to take on such a risk because they are specialists in assessing credit risk and spread that risk over thousands of different loans.

How Acceptances Arise

Trade acceptances usually begin when an importer goes to a bank to secure a line of credit to pay for a shipment of goods from abroad. Once the line of credit is approved, the bank issues a letter of credit in favor of the foreign exporter. This document authorizes the exporter to draw a time draft for a specified amount against the issuing bank, provided that the exporter agrees to send appropriate shipping documents giving the issuing bank temporary title to the exported goods.

Because the letter of credit authorizes the drawing of a **time draft**—not a sight draft, which is payable immediately upon presentation—the exporter must wait until the draft matures (perhaps as long as six months) to be paid. Such a delay is unacceptable for most export firms, which must meet payrolls and satisfy other near-term obligations.

Moreover, the time draft generally is redeemed in the home currency of the issuing bank, and this particular currency may not be needed by the exporter. A French exporter holding a time draft from a U.S. bank, for example, would be paid in dollars on its maturity date, even though the exporter probably needs Euros to pay employees and meet other local expenses. Typically, then, the exporter *discounts* the time draft in advance of maturity through his or her principal bank. The exporter then receives timely payment in local currency and avoids the risk of trading in foreign currencies.

The foreign bank that has now acquired the time draft from the exporter forwards it (plus shipping documents if goods are being traded) to the bank issuing the original letter of credit. The issuing bank checks to see that the draft and any accompanying documents are correctly drawn and then stamps "Accepted" on its face. Two things happen as a result

339

of this action: (1) a bankers' acceptance has been created and (2) the issuing bank has acknowledged an absolute liability, which must be paid in full at maturity. Frequently, the issuing bank discounts the new acceptance for the foreign bank that sent it and credits that bank's correspondent account for the proceeds. The acceptance may then be held by the issuing bank as an asset or sold to a dealer. Meanwhile, shipping documents for any goods that accompanied the acceptance are handed to the importer against a trust receipt, permitting the importer to pick up and market the goods. However, under the terms of the letter of credit, the importer must deposit the proceeds from selling those goods at the issuing bank in sufficient time to pay for the acceptance. When the time draft matures, the acceptance will be presented to the issuing bank for payment by its current holder.

It should be clear that all three principal parties to the acceptance transaction—the exporter, importer, and the issuing bank—benefit from this method of financing international trade. The exporter receives good funds with little or no delay. The importer may delay payment for a time until the related bank line of credit expires. The issuing bank regards the acceptance as a readily marketable financial instrument that can be sold before maturity through an acceptance dealer in order to cover short-term cash needs.

However, there are costs associated with all these benefits. A discount fee is charged off the face value of the acceptance whenever it is discounted in advance of maturity. The accepting bank earns a commission (usually 50 to 100 basis points of the face amount), which may be paid by either exporter or importer, in addition to the fees associated with the original letter of credit.

The Growth and Decline of Acceptance Financing

Given the significant advantages of acceptance financing for exporters, importers, and banks, it is not surprising that the volume of bankers' acceptances outstanding grew rapidly, at least until the mid-1980s. The volume of U.S. dollar acceptances increased from less than $400 million in 1950 to just over $2 billion in 1960 and then tripled in 1970 to slightly more than $7 billion outstanding. However, even these rapid rates of growth look pale compared with the virtual explosion of acceptance financing during the 1970s and early 1980s. By December 1984, the volume of bankers' acceptances outstanding reached almost $80 billion—more than a tenfold increase in about 15 years.

Then the growth of acceptances in U.S. dollars leveled out and turned sharply downward. Part of the reason for the turnaround was a slowing in trade as several leading export nations entered a recession at the beginning of the 1990s and subsequently their economies grew slowly. In the late 1990s, economic problems in Asia further dampened the need for traditional forms of trade financing. In addition, a wider variety of foreign currencies today are being readily accepted in payment for international purchases, and thus there is less need for dollar-denominated acceptances. Another factor has been greater use of direct bank loans bearing low money market interest rates for both exporters and importers. Moreover, many corporations involved in international trade have turned from banks toward the open market to borrow the funds they need, particularly through issues of bonds and commercial paper.

The majority of acceptances created by U.S. banks arise from four types of financial transactions: (1) the financing of imports into the United States; (2) the financing of exports from the United States; (3) the acquisition of dollars to add to foreign exchange reserves; and (4) the financing of goods stored in or transported between countries other than the United States. Acceptances arising from the last source are called **third-country bills.** Third-country bills are the largest acceptance category. In fact, more than half of all dollar acceptances outstanding are accounted for by non-U.S. banks, primarily banks in France, Great Britain, Germany, Switzerland, Australia, Canada, and Japan.

Acceptances are *not* widely used inside the United States for purely domestic trade. A small amount of domestic acceptance financing is carried out to support the storage of staple commodities such as cotton and tobacco or the domestic shipment of goods. However, if a company can borrow at close to the prime interest rate, it will usually do so rather than use acceptance financing. It is usually much easier for a domestic firm to assess the financial condition of its domestic customers than to evaluate the credit standing of a foreign firm thousands of miles away. For this reason, suppliers of goods in the domestic market usually extend short-term credit (accounts receivable) directly to customers rather than insisting on the use of acceptances. Moreover, in domestic commerce, no exchange of foreign currencies is necessary, eliminating one important type of risk that motivated the growth of acceptances.

Acceptance Rates

Acceptances do not carry a fixed rate of interest but are sold at a discount in the open market like Treasury bills. The prime borrower under an acceptance is charged a commitment fee for this line of credit, which is usually about 1½ percent (⅛ of 1 percent per month) for top-quality customers. U.S. banks are limited in the dollar amount of acceptances they can create to 150 percent of their paid-in capital and surplus (or by special permission from the Federal Reserve Board, up to 200 percent of their capital and surplus).

If the bank wishes to sell the acceptance in advance of its maturity, the rate of discount it must pay is determined by the current bid rate on acceptances of similar maturity in the open market. The yield on acceptances is usually only slightly higher than on Treasury bills because banks that issue them are among the largest and have solid international reputations. Acceptance rates hover close to negotiable CD rates offered by major banks because both acceptances and CDs are unconditional obligations of the issuing bank to pay. Adding to the stature of acceptances, depository institutions are permitted to borrow reserves from the Fed's discount window using certain types of acceptances as collateral.[7]

Investors in Acceptances

Commercial banks regard acceptances as high-grade instruments suitable for liquidity management purposes. In addition, the essential safety of acceptances is recognized by the U.S. Treasury, which permits banks to use them as collateral to back the Treasury's tax and loan accounts held in a majority of the nation's commercial banks. U.S. banks are also allowed to discount any "eligible" acceptances they hold with the Federal Reserve banks in order to borrow emergency funds. An acceptance is considered "eligible" by the Federal Reserve if it matures within six months and grows out of domestic or international trading or storage of goods. Smaller banks often participate in acceptance financing with money center banks to gain added income, spread out their risk, and accommodate their largest customers.

Other important investors in the acceptance market include industrial corporations, savings banks, money market mutual funds, foreign banks, local governments, federal agencies, and insurance companies. To many investors, acceptances are a close substitute for

[7]The bankers' acceptance is one of me safest of all financial instruments. It is an irrevocable primary debt of the bank that stamps "accepted" on its face, as well as a contingent liability of the drawing firm and of any other bank, firm, or individual who endorses the document. Moreover, domestic banks are limited in the volume of acceptances they can have outstanding relative to the size of their capital. At the same time, the customer who has requested the initiating letter of credit that gives rise to the acceptance has guaranteed payment by the maturity date. Then too, any goods shipped under the letter of credit are nearly always insured and accompanied by trust and warehouse receipts specifying value and ownership.

Treasury bills, negotiable CDs, or commercial paper in terms of quality, although the acceptance market is far smaller in volume of trading.

Only a few dealers regularly trade acceptances, usually as an adjunct to their trading activities in Treasury bills, notes, and bonds. Trading is carried out purely on a negotiated basis, with most daily volume accounted for by swaps of holdings among accepting banks. The dealers call accepting banks and place bids for acceptances on behalf of their customers. Although a variety of denominations is available for both large and small investors, nonbank investors often find the menu of fresh offerings very limited. Nevertheless, an investor who is willing to accept the odd-lot denominations in which acceptances are issued generally finds the investment rewarding in terms of competitive rate of return and low risk.

Questions *to Help You Study*

15. What exactly is a *bankers' acceptance?* What is the meaning of the word "accepted"?

16. Explain why acceptances over the years have been attractive to exporters and importers of goods moving between different countries. Why has the volume of acceptances declined in recent years?

17. Why are acceptances not as widely used inside the United States as they are in international markets?

18. Please evaluate bankers' acceptances as an investment instrument. What are their principal advantages and disadvantages to savers interested in finding a secure financial asset that is readily marketable?

EUROCURRENCY DEPOSITS

Comparable to the domestic CD market, a chain of international money markets trading in deposits denominated in the world's most convertible currencies stretches around the globe. This so-called **Eurocurrency market** has arisen because of a tremendous need worldwide for funds denominated in dollars, Euros, pounds, and other relatively stable currencies. For example, as U.S. corporations have expanded their operations in Europe, Asia, and the Middle East, they have needed huge amounts of U.S. dollars to purchase machinery and other goods in the United States and to pay federal and state taxes. The same companies have also required large volumes of other national currencies to carry out transactions in the countries where they are represented. To meet these financial needs, international banks headquartered in the world's key financial centers began during the 1950s to accept deposits from businesses, individuals, and governments denominated in currencies other than that of the host country and to make loans in those same currencies.

The nature and origins of the Eurocurrency markets are discussed in a wide range of publications prepared by the staff of the Federal Reserve Bank of New York at *www.ny.frb.org*, and for the Federal Reserve System as a whole at *www.federalreserve. gov*

One of the earliest sources of Eurodollar deposits was the former Soviet Union, which, in the 1950s, moved huge amounts of dollar-denominated assets out of the United States in order to avoid sequestration (capture) of its funds by U.S. authorities. Anti-Soviet sentiment was then running very high in the United States, and a number of highly publicized court trials and Congressional hearings had aroused the interest of the American public. A short time later, several large American banks themselves moved some of their dollar deposits abroad to avoid restrictive U.S. banking regulations. Thus, the Eurocurrency market was born.

What Is a Eurodollar?

Because the dollar remains the chief international currency today, the market for Eurodollars dominates the Eurocurrency markets. What are **Eurodollars?** They are deposits of

U.S. dollars in banks located outside the United States. The banks in question record the deposits on their books in U.S. dollars, not in the home currency. The large majority of Eurodollar (and other Eurocurrency) deposits are held in Europe, but these deposits have spread worldwide. Europe's share of the total is declining.

Frequently, banks accepting Eurodollar deposits are foreign branches of U.S. banks. For example, in London, the center of the Eurocurrency market today, branches of U.S. banks outnumber British banks and bid aggressively for deposits denominated in U.S. dollars. Many of these funds are then loaned to the banks' home offices in the United States to meet reserve requirements and other liquidity needs. The remaining funds are loaned to private corporations and governments abroad that need U.S. dollars. No one knows exactly how large the Eurodollar market is. One reason is that the market is unregulated. Many banks refuse to disclose publicly their deposit balances in various currencies. Another reason for the relative lack of information on market activity is that Eurocurrencies are merely bookkeeping entries on a bank's ledger and not currencies. You cannot put Eurocurrency deposits in your pocket like bank notes or coins.

Eurodollars and other Eurocurrency deposits are continually on the move in the form of loans. They are employed to finance the import and export of goods, to supplement government tax revenues, to provide working capital for the foreign operations of multinational corporations, and to provide liquid reserves for the largest banks. In total, the Eurocurrency and Eurodollar markets represent the largest of all money markets worldwide, with total funds probably in excess of $4 trillion.

Some experts believe that Eurodollar growth may slow appreciably or the volume of Eurodollar deposits may even decline as the European Union matures, creating a potentially strong rival to U.S. dollars and dollar deposits. European central banks, for example, may have less need for U.S. dollar reserves in a united Europe and begin to dump some of their huge holdings of dollar-denominated assets, reducing the value of the U.S. dollar and U.S.-issued securities in international markets. Much depends upon the success of the new European Monetary Union and the new European Central Bank in controlling inflation and maintaining a strong and vibrant European economy and Eurocurrency.

The Creation of Eurocurrency Deposits

To illustrate how Eurocurrency deposits arise, we trace through a simple but typical example. Our discussion is in terms of Eurodollars, but the reader should be aware that the process being described really applies to *any* Eurocurrency.

Suppose a French exporter of fine wines ships cases of champagne to a New York importer, accompanied by a bill for $10,000. The importing firm pays for the champagne by issuing a check denominated in dollars and deposits it right away in a U.S. bank—First American Bank—where the French firm maintains a checking account. After this check clears, the results of the transaction are as follows:

French Exporter		First American Bank	
Assets	*Liabilities*	*Assets*	*Liabilities*
Demand deposit in U.S. bank +$10,000			Demand deposit owed French exporter +$10,000

Is the deposit shown above a Eurodollar deposit? *No,* because the deposit of dollars occurred in the United States, where the dollar is the official monetary unit. Suppose, however, that the French exporter is offered an attractive rate of return on its dollar deposit by its own local bank in Paris and decides to move the dollar deposit there. The Paris bank wants to loan these dollars to other customers who need them to pay bills or make purchases in the United States. After the wine exporter and its Paris bank have negotiated the terms of the deposit and the funds are transferred, the French exporter receives a receipt for a dollar-denominated time deposit in its Paris bank. That bank, in return, now holds claim to the original dollar deposit in the United States. The Paris bank has at least one U.S. correspondent bank and asks to have the original dollar deposit transferred there. We show these transactions as follows:

French Exporter	
Assets	*Liabilities*
Demand deposit in U.S. bank −$10,000	
Time depoit in Paris bank +$10,000	

First American Bank	
Assets	*Liabilities*
Reserves transferred to U.S. correspondent bank −$10,000	Demand deposit owed French exporter −$10,000

U.S. Correspondent Bank	
Assets	*Liabilities*
Reserves received from First American Bank +$10,000	Demand deposit owed Paris bank +$10,000

Paris Bank	
Assets	*Liabilities*
Deposit with U.S. correspondent bank +$10,000	Time deposit owed French exporter +$10,000

Do we now have a Eurodollar deposit? *Yes* in the form of a $10,000 time deposit in a Paris bank. The wine exporter's deposit has been accepted and recorded on the Paris bank's books in U.S. dollars, even though the official monetary unit in France is now the euro).[8] Let us follow this Eurodollar deposit through one more step. Assume now that the Paris bank makes a loan of $10,000 to a small oil company based in Manchester, England. The British company needs dollars to pay for a shipment of petroleum drilling equipment from Houston, Texas. By securing a dollar credit from the Paris bank, the British oil firm, in effect, receives a claim against dollars deposited in U.S. banks. The appropriate entries would be as follows:

Paris Bank	
Assets	*Liabilities*
Loan to British oil company +$10,000	
Deposit in U.S. correspondent bank −$10,000	

British Oil Company	
Assets	*Liabilities*
Demand deposit in U.S. correspondent bank +$10,000	Loan owed to Paris bank +$10,000

---

[8]The $10,000 time deposit is used here for illustrative purposes only. The vast majority of Eurocurrency deposits are far larger. In fact, the normal trading unit in this market is l million currency units.

U.S. Correspondent Bank	
Assets	*Liabilities*
	Deposit owed to Paris bank −$10,000
	Deposit owed to British oil company +$10,000

Note that we have assumed that the British oil company held a deposit account in the same U.S. bank where the Paris bank held its deposits. This, of course, is often not the case, but it was done here to reduce the number of accounting entries. If another U.S. bank were involved, we would simply transfer deposits and reserves to it from the U.S. correspondent bank that held the account of the Paris bank. The result would be exactly the same as in our example: *The total amount of dollar deposits and U.S. bank reserves remains unchanged.* These funds are merely passed from U.S. bank to U.S. bank as loans are extended and deposits made in the Eurodollar market. Thus, Eurodollar activity does *not* alter the total reserves of the U.S. banking system. In fact, the workings of the Eurocurrency markets remind us of a fundamental principle of international finance: *Money itself usually does not leave the country where it originates; only the ownership of money is transferred across international boundaries.*

The chain of Eurocurrency loans and deposits started in our example by the wine exporter's bank in Paris will go on unbroken as long as such loans are in demand and the funds are continually redeposited somewhere in the international banking system. Some economists believe that Eurobanks, like domestic U.S. banks, can create a multiple volume of deposits and loans for each Eurocurrency deposit they receive. However, this view has been disputed by a number of analysts who point out that major Eurobanks in their borrowing and lending activities are closer to nonbank financial institutions than to commercial banks. Eurobanks appear to closely match the maturities of their assets (principally loans) with the maturities of their liabilities (principally Eurocurrency deposits and money market borrowings); thus, funds raised in the Eurocurrency markets flow through Eurobanks back into those same markets. Rather than creating money, Eurobanks appear to function more as "efficient distributors of liquidity." If there is any actual credit or money creation in the Eurosystem, leading to a multiplication of deposits, the deposit multiplier must be close to one.[9]

Just as Eurocurrency deposits are created by making loans, they are also destroyed as loans are repaid. In our example, suppose the British oil company trades pounds for dollars with a foreign currency dealer and uses the dollars purchased to repay its loan from the

[9]See Chapters 13, 14, and 15 for discussions of the deposit multiplier. The granting of a Eurocurrency loan to a borrower does not give the borrower "money" in a strict sense. Eurocurrency deposits are not generally acceptable as a medium of exchange to pay for goods and services. They are more like regular time deposits. The holder of a Eurocurrency deposit must convert that deposit into some national currency unit before using it for spending. Thus, Eurocurrency deposits are *not* negotiable instruments. The Eurocurrency system does not create money in the traditional sense. A lender of Eurocurrency who needs liquid funds before a deposit matures must go back into the market and negotiate a separate loan.

Interest usually is paid only at maturity unless the Eurodeposit has a term of more than one year. Most deposit interest rates are tied to the London Interbank Offer Rate (LIBOR), the rate at which major international banks offer term Eurocurrency deposits to each other. The rate is usually fixed for the life of the deposit, though floating rates tied to semiannual changes in LIBOR are not uncommon on longer-term deposits, with promised interest rates reset every three to six months at a spread over LIBOR.

Paris bank. At about the same time, the dollar time deposit held by the French exporter matures, and the exporter spends those dollars in the United States. As far as U.S. banks are concerned, total deposits and reserves remain unchanged. However, as a result of these transactions, all dollar deposits are now held in the United States and, therefore, have ceased to be Eurocurrency deposits.

Eurocurrency Maturities and Risks

Eurocurrency deposits are short-term time deposits (ranging from overnight to call money loaned for a few days out to one year) and therefore are true money market instruments. However, a small percentage are long-term time deposits, extending in some instances to about five years. Most Eurocurrency deposits carry one-month maturities to coincide with payments for shipments of goods. Other common maturities are 2, 3, 6, and 12 months.[10] The majority are interbank liabilities that pay a fixed interest rate.

Even though Eurobanks do not issue demand deposits, funds move rapidly in the Eurocurrency market from bank to bank in response to demands for short-term liquidity from corporations, governments, and Eurobanks themselves. There is no central trading location in the market. Traders thousands of miles distant may conduct negotiations by satellite, cable, computer networks, telephone, or telex, with written confirmation coming later. Funds normally are transferred on the second business day after an agreement is reached through correspondent banks.

Eurocurrency deposits are known to be volatile and highly sensitive to fluctuations in interest rates and currency prices. A slight difference in interest rates or currency values between two countries can cause a massive flow of Eurocurrencies across national boundaries. One of the most famous examples of this phenomenon occurred in Germany in 1971 when speculation that the German mark would be upvalued brought an inflow into Germany of billions in dollar deposits within hours, forcing the German government to cut the mark loose from its official exchange value and allow that currency to float upward.

Eurocurrecy deposits are not without risk. There is *political risk* because governments may restrict or prohibit the movement of funds across national borders, as the United States did for a time during the Iranian crisis and more recently following the terrorist attacks in September of 2001. There may be disputes between nations over the legal jurisdiction and control of deposits. *Default risk* may also be a factor because banks in the Eurobank system may fail; Eurocurrency deposits usually are *not* insured. This problem is compounded by the fact that it is more costly to secure information on the financial condition of foreign banks than on domestic banks. However, on the positive side, Eurobanks are among the largest and most stable banking institutions in the world. Moreover, most foreign nations have tried to encourage the growth of Eurocurrency markets through lenient regulation and taxation.

The Supply of Eurocurrency Deposits

Where do Eurocurrency deposits come from? The sources of Eurodollar deposits provide a good example of how and why this market grows. For example, a major factor in the Eurodollar market's growth has been the enormous balance-of-payments deficits the United

---

[10]Banks active in the Eurocurrency market for liquidity-adjustment purposes use *short-date* deposits. Comparable to federal funds in the domestic U.S. money market, short dates represent deposits available for as long as 14 days, though generally they are weekend or 2-day money, with some 7-day maturities as well. Short dates may carry fixed maturities or simply be payable on demand with minimal notice (such as 24 or 48 hours).

States has run in nearly every year since the late 1950s.[11] U.S. firms building factories and purchasing goods and services abroad have transferred ownership of dollar deposits to foreign companies and banks. Domestic shortages of oil and natural gas have forced the United States to import about half or more of its petroleum needs, generating enormous outflows of dollars to oil-producing nations. The OPEC countries, for example, accept dollars in payment for crude oil and use the dollar as a standard for valuing the oil they sell. U.S. tourists visiting Europe, Japan, and the Middle East frequently use dollar-denominated traveler's checks or take U.S. currency with them and convert it into local currency overseas. Dollar loans made by U.S. corporations and foreign-based firms have added to the vast Eurodollar pool. Many of these dollar deposits have gravitated to foreign central banks, such as the Bank of England, as these institutions have attempted to support the dollar and their own currencies in international markets.

Eurodollars in U.S. Domestic Bank Operations

Since the late 1960s, U.S. banks have drawn heavily on Eurodollar deposits as a means of adjusting their domestic reserve positions. Thus, the manager of the money desk at a large U.S. bank, knowing the bank will need extra cash reserves in a few days, can contact foreign banks holding dollar deposits and arrange a loan. The manager can also contact other U.S. banks with branches abroad and borrow Eurodollars from them. Alternatively, if the money manager's own bank operates foreign branches accepting dollar deposits, these can be placed at the disposal of the home office.

Eurodollar borrowing of bank reserves has been especially heavy during periods of rapidly rising interest rates in the United States. Such borrowings are extremely interest-rate sensitive, however. When U.S. money market rates fell precipitously from record highs during the 1980s and 1990s and domestic sources of reserves became much less expensive, American banks repaid their Eurodollar borrowings nearly as fast as they borrowed these international deposits in the earlier periods when interest rates were at record highs.

Eurodollars usually carry *higher* reported interest rates than many other sources of bank reserves, such as domestic certificates of deposit, due to perceptions of higher risk, although this is not always the case. (See Exhibit 12–9.) However, there are fewer legal restrictions on the borrowing of Eurodollars and other Eurocurrency deposits. For example, Eurodollar deposits have no reserve requirements or insurance fees today. In contrast, U.S. banks must pay assessments to the Federal Deposit Insurance Corporation on domestic nonbank deposits to cover the costs of deposit insurance.

For further discussion of the London Interbank Offer Rate (LIBOR) see the British Bankers Association at *www.bba.com.uk/*

In addition to meeting their own reserve needs from the Eurodollar market, U.S. banks have aided their corporate customers in acquiring Eurocurrency deposits. Direct loans in Eurocurrencies are made by U.S. banks, and these banks will readily swap Eurocurrencies at the customer's request. Although most Eurocurrency loans to nonbank customers are short-term credits to provide working capital, a sizable percentage in recent years has consisted of medium-term (one- to five-year) loans for equipment purchases, frequently set up under a revolving credit agreement. Both borrowers and lenders in the Eurocurrency market can more effectively hedge against interest rate risk on these international loans today due to the recent rapid growth of Eurocurrency interest rate futures markets centered in London, Chicago, and other leading international financial centers.

Eurodollar loan rates have two components: (1) the cost of acquiring Eurocurrency deposits (usually measured by the **London Interbank Offer Rate (LIBOR)** on three- or six-month Eurodeposits) and (2) a profit margin ("spread") based on the riskiness of the

---

[11]See Chapter 25 for a discussion of the causes and effects of U.S. balance-of-payment deficits.

EXHIBIT 12–9
Interest Rates on
Eurodollar Deposits
and Other Money
Market Instruments

Year	Eurodollar Deposits, Three-Month Maturities	U.S.-Issued Certificates of Deposit, Three-Month Maturities	Federal Funds Interest Rate
1990	8.16%	8.15%	8.10%
1993	3.18	3.17	3.02
1995	5.93	5.92	5.83
1997	5.61	5.54	5.46
1999	5.31	5.33	4.97
2000	6.45	6.46	6.24
2001*	3.47	3.48	3.65
2002†	1.87	1.80	1.25

*Figures as of August 2001.
†Figures as of January 7th.

Source: U.S. Department of Commerce, *Business Statistics,* selected editions; and Board of Governors of the Federal Reserve System, *Federal Reserve Bulletin,* selected monthly issues.

loan and the intensity of competition. Profit margins are low on Eurocurrency loans (often a percentage point or less) because the market is highly competitive, lending costs are low, and the risk is normally low as well. Borrowers are generally well-known institutions with substantial net worth and solid credit standing. Market transactions are usually carried out in large denominations, ranging from about $500,000 to $100 million or more.

In deciding whether to tap the Eurocurrency market for funds, banks and other borrowers compare Eurodeposit interest rates with alternative borrowing costs available in their domestic financial systems. For example, U.S. banks during a recent week were looking at the following alternative borrowing costs:

Cost rate on 30-Day Eurodollar deposits (Quoted by international banks in London)	5.60%
Domestic negotiable 30-Day CDs (Average yield posted by leading New York City banks)	5.55
Federal funds (Average rate quoted by brokers in New York City)	5.45

The rate spreads shown above seem to favor borrowing domestically through federal funds or by using negotiable CDs (even though the domestic CDs carry an added insurance fee that would bring their cost up closer to that of comparable-maturity Eurocurrency deposits). For a nonbank corporation borrowing money, the critical issue would be the size of the margin or spread a lender would ask for over and above the Eurocurrency deposit rate versus the domestic money market rate on Fed funds or CDs. For example, one lender might quote the borrowing company a LIBOR-based loan rate priced off the cost of 30-day Eurodollar deposits as follows:

$$\text{Loan rate} = \text{30-day LIBOR rate} + \tfrac{1}{8}\% \text{ margin} = 5.60\% + 0.125\% = 5.725\%$$

while another lender might ask for

$$\text{Loan rate} = \text{30-day domestic CD rate} + \tfrac{1}{2}\% \text{ margin} = 5.55\% + 0.50\% = 6.05\%$$

or

$$\text{Loan rate} = \text{Federal funds rate} + \tfrac{3}{4}\% \text{ margin} = 5.45\% + 0.75\% = 6.20\%$$

In this particular example, a loan priced off the 30-day Eurodollar deposit rate (LIBOR) appears to be cheaper for the borrowing corporation than a loan based on the Federal Funds rate or based on the domestic CD interest rate. However, all of these market interest rates change every day, making one or another source of funds cheaper or more expensive on any given day that a borrower might need loanable funds. Borrowers need to keep a close eye on both domestic and international financial markets in order to make sure they are getting the best deal currently available.

Recent Innovations in the Eurocurrency Markets

Beginning in the 1980s, the Eurocurrency market witnessed rapid growth in medium-term credit arrangements between international banks and their corporate and governmental customers. These so-called *note issuance facilities* (NIFs) often span five to seven years and allow the customer to borrow in his or her own name by selling short-term IOUs (typically maturing in three to six months) to investors. The underwriting bank or banks backstop this customer paper either by purchasing any paper that remains unsold or by providing standby credit at an interest rate spread over LIBOR. The notes issued are usually denominated in U.S. dollars with par values of $100,000 or higher. With bank support, NIFs are roughly equivalent to Eurocurrency CDs and compete with them for investor funds.

Benefits and Costs of the Eurocurrency Markets

For the most part, the development of Eurocurrency trading has resulted in substantial benefits to the international community, especially to banks and multinational corporations. The market ensures a high degree of funds mobility between international capital markets and provides a true international market for bank and nonbank liquidity adjustments. It has provided a mechanism for absorbing huge amounts of U.S. dollars flowing overseas and lessened international pressure to forsake the dollar for gold and other currencies. The market reduces the cost of international trade by providing an efficient method of economizing on transactions balances.[12] Moreover, it acts as a check on domestic monetary and fiscal policies and encourages international cooperation in economic policies, because interest-sensitive traders in the market will quickly spot interest rates that are out of line and move huge amounts of funds toward any point on the globe. Central banks, such as the Bank of England and the new European Central Bank created by the European Economic Community, monitor the Eurocurrency markets continuously in order to moderate inflows or outflows of funds that may damage their domestic economies.

The capacity of Eurocurrency markets to mobilize massive amounts of funds has occasionally brought severe criticism from regulators in Europe, the United States, and Asia. They sometimes see the market as contributing to instability in currency values. Moreover, the market can wreak havoc with monetary and fiscal policies designed to cure domestic economic problems. This is especially true if a nation is experiencing severe inflation and massive inflows of Eurocurrency occur at the same time. The net effect of Eurocurrency expansion, other things being equal, is to push domestic interest rates down, stimulate credit expansion, and accelerate the rate of inflation (which may ultimately result in higher market interest rates). The ability of local authorities to deal with inflationary problems might be overwhelmed by a Eurocurrency glut. This danger is really the price of freedom, for an unregulated market will not always conform to the plans of government policymakers.

[12]See Balbach and Resler (1980) on this point. In effect, the Eurodollar market lowers the cost of dollar-denominated financial intermediation worldwide.

Questions *to Help You Study*

19. What is the *Eurocurrency market* and why is it needed?

20. Please define the term *Eurodollar*. Can a U.S. bank create Eurodollars? How?

21. Describe the process by which Eurocurrency deposits are created. What happens to the total volume of domestic bank reserves and deposits in the process of creating Eurocurrency deposits?

22. Can Eurocurrency deposits be *destroyed?* How can this happen?

23. What are the principal *sources* of Eurocurrency deposits? Please make a list.

24. What role do Eurodollar deposits play in *reserve management operations* of U.S. banking firms? What are the advantages of Eurodollar borrowings over other sources of reserves for banks? What about the disadvantages?

25. Evaluate the Eurocurrency markets from a social point of view. What are their major benefits and costs to the public and to market participants? In your opinion should these markets be more closely regulated or be relatively free of regulation?

Summary of the Chapter

This chapter has focused upon four widely known financial instruments traded in domestic and global money markets. These key instruments are commercial paper, federal agency securities, bankers' acceptances, and Eurocurrency deposits.

- The *commercial paper* market has grown rapidly in recent years as major industrial corporations and financial-service companies, facing rapidly advancing demands for their products and services, have turned increasingly to the open market for the capital they require. They have seen in the commercial paper market a relatively low cost and flexible vehicle for raising short-term cash.

- Commercial paper has offered several distinct *advantages* over other sources of corporate funds, including ready access to new funds, lower interest rates than on most other sources of capital, and providing leverage to use against other lenders of funds when seeking new financing. A borrowing company that can tap the paper market for funding can always threaten to go to that market if a lending institution refuses to make a loan on reasonable terms. However, the paper market has some *disadvantages* as well, being highly volatile at times with a scarce supply of available credit.

- Nearly matching the rapid growth of the commercial paper market has been the market for the IOUs issued by *federal agencies*, such as the Federal National Mortgage Association or the Farm Credit System. These agencies, either owned or sponsored by the federal government, were set up to provide credit or help develop a market for loans to disadvantaged sectors of the economy, such as farms and ranches, new home buyers, and small businesses.

- Federal and government-sponsored agencies act like financial intermediaries, borrowing and lending funds at the same time. They rely upon the government's implied or expressed guarantee to give them an advantage in the competition for funds, lowering their cost of financing. With the government's implicit or explicit backing these agencies issue securities almost as attractive as government securities to most investors, but with slightly higher yields than are available on direct government obligations.

- *Bankers' acceptances* are time drafts drawn against a bank. The accepting bank pledges payment upon a specific date in the future. Widely used for many years to fund exports and imports of goods in international markets, the volume of acceptances has recently been declining as other financial instruments have moved in to take over the same role. Moreover, information flows between countries are much more ample today, reducing some of the risk of foreign trade that acceptances were designed originally to deal with.

- *Eurocurrency deposits* consist of bank time deposits denominated in a currency other than the currency of the country where the bank accepting these deposits is located. Thus, a deposit of U.S. dollars in Great Britain is a Eurodollar deposit. They are not immediately spendable funds but constitute a reservoir of liquidity that can be used as a basis for expanding the volume of credit available within the international financial system.

- Among the most important sources of Eurocurrency deposits are tourist travel, balance-of-payments deficits with other nations, and investments made overseas. Banks also use Eurocurrency deposits to help supply liquid reserves they need for lending or for raising new funds.

Key Terms

Commerical paper, *323*	Government-sponsored	Time draft, *339*
Direct paper, *324*	agencies, *333*	Third-country bills, *340*
Dealer paper, *325*	Federal agencies, *334*	Eurocurrency market, *342*
Credit enhancements. 327	Financial intermediaries, *334*	Eurodollars, *342*
Master note, *331*	Federal Financing Bank (FFB), *335*	London Interbank Offer Rate
	Bankers' acceptances, *338*	(LIBOR), *347*

Problems

1. A new issue of 90-day commercial paper is available from a dealer in New York City at a price of $97.60 on a $100 basis. What is the bank discount yield on this note if held to maturity?

2. A note traded in the commercial paper market will mature in 15 days. The dealer will sell it to you at $98.35 on a $100 basis. What is the note's discount rate of return?

3. Commercial paper was purchased in the secondary market 30 days from maturity at a bank discount yield of 9 percent. Ten days later, it was sold to a dealer at an 8 percent discount rate. What was the investor's holding-period yield?

4. What is the difference in basis points between the discount rate of return (DR) and the investment rate of return (IR) on a $10 million commercial paper note purchased at a price of $9.85 million and scheduled to mature in 25 days?

5. A commercial paper note with $1 million par value and maturing in 60 days has an expected discount return (DR) at maturity of 6 percent. What was its purchase price? What is this note's expected coupon-equivalent (investment return) yield (IR)?

6. Alamo Corporation requests a $20 million, 90-day loan from its banks, which proposes to make the requested loan at an interest rate of 6 percent and a compensating balance requirement of 10 percent of the amount of the loan. What will Alamo's effective loan rate be under these terms? Suppose 90-day commercial paper sold by dealers is currently trading at an interest rate of 6.0 percent. What is the interest rate spread between

the effective loan rate quoted by the bank and the current commercial paper rate? Does the bank's proposed loan carry any advantages that borrowing through the commercial paper market won't necessarily provide Alamo Corporation?

7. What price would attach today to Europaper issued at par (100) with a maturity of 180 days and carrying a discount rate of 7 percent?

8. What is the appropriate discount rate for a 270-day Europaper issue priced at par (100) and expected to sell today at a discounted price of 96?

9. A bank is willing to issue a line of credit to fully back a $25 million issue of commercial paper for a fee of 1 percent. If any portion of the line is used, an interest rate of 8 percent will be assessed. The compensating balance requirement for the line of credit is 5 percent, while the portion of the line that is used carries a 20 percent compensating balance requirement. How much will the borrowing company pay for the full unused line? Suppose $1.5 million is actually drawn upon for unexpected expenses and the balance of the credit line is used merely to back the paper issue. How much will the borrowing firm pay in total bank charges?

10. What is the discount rate (DR) and the investment return (IR) on the following commercial notes?

	Face Value	Purchase Price	Maturity in Days
a.	$10,000,000	$ 9,750,000	60
b.	$22,500,000	$21,350,000	45
c.	$48,750,000	$46,975,000	30
d.	$60,175,000	$48,850,985	15

11. A German manufacturer of furniture sells a large order of home furnishings to an outlet store in Houston. The Houston firm pays for the shipment by wiring funds from its local bank through Fedwire to the German firm's account at J. P. Morgan/Chase Bank in New York City. Subsequently, the German manufacturer decides to invest half of the funds received in a dollar deposit offered by Barclays Bank in London, where interest rates are particularly attractive. No sooner are the funds deposited in London than a Japanese auto company, shipping cars to the U.S. and Europe, asks the London bank for a loan to purchase raw materials in the United States.

Later, when the loan falls due, the Japanese firm will go into the currency market to purchase dollars in order to retire its Eurodollar loan at Barclays Bank, receiving a dollar deposit at a U.S. bank. When the loan is repaid, Barclays gains the dollar deposit in the United States and uses the deposit to pay off the German firm when its time deposit matures. The German firm chooses to deposit the funds received from Barclays in its demand deposit account at J. P. Morgan/Chase Bank in New York City because it now needs to buy goods and services in the United States.

Construct T accounts that reflect the foregoing transactions. In particular, show the proper entries for: (1) payment by the Houston firm to the German furniture company; (2) deposit of the funds in London; (3) the loan to the Japanese automaker; (4) repayment of the loan; and (5) return of funds to the United States. Indicate which deposit is a Eurodollar deposit and if any Eurodollars are destroyed at any particular stage.

12. A company known as Standard Quality Importing ships videocassette recorders made in Japan to retail dealers in the United States and Western Europe. It decides to place an order with its Japanese supplier for 10,000 Hi-Fi VCRs at $575 each after securing a line of credit from Guaranty Security Bank in Los Angeles. Guaranty issues a credit letter to the Japanese supplier promising payment in U.S. dollars 90 days hence. However, the Japanese firm needs the promised funds within seven days from receipt of the

credit letter to make purchases of technical components from an electronics firm in Phoenix, Arizona. Explain and illustrate with T accounts and diagrams how a bankers' acceptance would arise from the foregoing transactions, how the Japanese supplier could receive the dollars she needs in timely fashion, and what would happen to the acceptance at the end of the 90-day period. Use T account entries to show the movement of funds from the importer to the Japanese supplier, to the electronics firm, and to money market investors.

13. Instel Corporation has been offered a $100 million, 3-month loan at a fixed rate of 90-day LIBOR plus ⅜% margin or at the prevailing federal funds rate plus ½% margin with the loan rate adjusted every 24 hours to the federal funds rate prevailing at the close of business each day. These rates, along with prevailing yields on U.S. Treasury bills, are posted in London and New York as follows:

90-Day LIBOR rate on Eurodollar deposits	4.275%	3-month U.S. Treasury bill rate	4.12%
Federal funds rate	4.08	6-month U.S. Treasury bill rate	4.20
One-month (30 day) U.S. Treasury bills	4.05	1-year U.S. Treasury bill rate	4.30

   Which set of loan terms would you recommend to Instel's treasurer? Why?

14. A British investor withdraws her million-dollar deposit from Citicorp Bank, N.A. and converts the deposit into a dollar-denominated, 30-day CD in a Belgian commercial bank at the going market rate (LIBOR) of 5.85 percent. Almost immediately, the Belgian bank makes a loan of $750,000 to an aluminum frames manufacturer at LIBOR plus 30 basis points for 21 days. When the CD matures and the deposit is returned to Citicorp, how much in interest income will the depositor receive? How much will the aluminum frame manufacturer pay in total interest expense for its 21-day bank loan? Please show the proper accounting entries for all of the foregoing transactions (including the return of funds to the original depositor).

15. ABC Corporation receives a letter of credit for 90 days from Republic Bank of New York to guarantee payment of $1.35 million for a shipment of goods from an Italian manufacturer. Republic Bank charges a fee of 0.75 percentage points on the face value of the credit letter in return for its services of issuing the letter and, if properly presented, accepting a draft for payment that will eventually be sent by the foreign manufacturer. What is the total amount of the fee that ABC must pay Republic Bank for this service?

16. Please identify the key terms or concepts discussed in this chapter whose descriptions or definitions appear below.

   a. A short-term debt security issued by a corporation with a superior credit rating.
   b. Commercial paper sold directly to investors without the aid of a broker or dealer.
   c. Commercial paper sold through security dealers.
   d. Financial devices used to upgrade the credit rating of a borrower.
   e. Continuous borrowing agreement involving the daily issuance of commercial paper.
   f. Institutions originally government owned but now privately owned that lend and guarantee loans in the private sector.
   g. Divisions of the federal government empowered to borrow and make credit available to the private sector.
   h. A unit of the federal government that loans money through the U.S. Treasury Department.
   i. A method for marketing agency securities.
   j. A time draft against a bank.

k. Acceptances issued by banks in one nation that finance the transport or storage of goods traded between two other nations.

l. An international money market where deposits are traded.

m. Deposits of U.S. dollars in foreign banks or branches.

n. The short-term interest rate attached to Eurocurrency deposits.

Questions about the Web and the Money and Capital Markets

1. Where on the Web could you look for useful information about commercial paper, federal agency securities, bankers' acceptances, and Eurodollars and other Eurocurrency deposits?

2. Suppose you wanted to track the yield spread between commercial paper issues, federal agency securities, bankers' acceptances, and Eurocurrency deposits. Where on the Web could you turn for data to help you construct these yield spreads? See if you can construct a yield spread chart for the most recent quarter of the year. How did these yield spreads change over time?

3. Do businesses that make the greatest use of commercial paper and other short-term debt tend to display superior performance in terms of profitability, stock values, and revenue growth compared to companies that tend to emphasize using longer-term debt (such as bonds)? Using data provided by several companies represented on the Web (such as the data base provided by Standard and Poor's Market Insight) see if you can detect a relationship between the use of short-term, money market debt and business performance.

Selected References

Balbach, Anatol B., and David H. Resler. "Eurodollars and the U.S. Money Supply." *Review,* Federal Reserve Bank of St. Louis, June–July 1980, pp. 2–12.

Board of Governors of the Federal Reserve System. *Federal Reserve Bulletin,* Washington, DC, selected monthly issues.

Crabbe, Leland, and Mitchell A. Post. "The Effect of SEC Amendments to Rule 2A–7 on the Commercial Paper Market." *Finance and Economics Discussion Series #199.* Board of Governors of the Federal Reserve System, May 1992.

Eloyan, Fayez A.; Brian A. Maris; and Philip J. Young. "The Effect of Commercial Paper Rating Changes and Credit-Watch Placement on Common Stock Prices." *The Financial Review* 31, no. 1 (February 1996), pp. 149–67.

Ferderer, J. Peter; Stephen C. Vogt; and Ravi Chahil. "Increasing Liquidity and the Declining Informational Content of the Paper-Bill Spread." *Journal of Economics and Business* 50 (1998), pp. 361–77.

Goodfriend, Marvin. "Eurodollars." *Economic Review,* Federal Reserve Bank of Richmond, May–June 1981, pp. 12–18.

Puglisi, Donald J. and Anthony J. Vignola, Jr. "An Examination of Federal Agency Debt Pricing Practices." *Journal of Financial Research* 6, no.2 (Summer 1983), pp. 83–92.

Rose, Peter S. *Commercial Bank Management,* 5th ed. New York: McGraw-Hill, 2002.

Schmid, Frank A. "The Future of the Euro." *International Economic Trends,* Federal Reserve Bank of St. Louis, July1998.

Schnure, Calvin D. "Debt Maturity Choice and Risk-Free Assets: The 'Clientele Effect' and the Commercial Paper Market." *Finance and Economics Discussion Series #944.* Board of Governors of the Federal Reserve System, April 1994.

Stojanovic, Dusan, and Mark D. Vaughan. "The Commercial Paper Market: Who's Minding the Shop?" *The Regional Economist,* Federal Reserve Bank of Boston, April 1998, pp. 5–9.

Chapter **Thirteen**

The Roles and Services of the Federal Reserve and Other Central Banks around the World

Learning Objectives in This Chapter

- You will explore the many different roles played and the functions performed by *central banks* around the world.

- You will see how and why the *Federal Reserve System* came to be established as the U.S. central bank.

- You will examine how the Federal Reserve System is organized to carry out the many tasks it must perform, not only domestically but also as part of the global financial system.

- You will discover how important *central bank independence* from the dictates of governments is in designing and carrying out an effective central banking (monetary) policy.

- You will understand the concept of *legal reserves* and how actions taken by the U.S. central bank, the *Federal Reserve System,* influence the level and growth of legal reserves.

What's in This Chapter? Key Topics Outline

Roles and Functions of Central Banking

Goals Pursued by Central Banks around the World

Channels of Central Banking Influence on the Economy and Financial Markets

The Fed and the European Central Bank: How Do They Compare?

INTRODUCTION

One of the most important financial institutions in any modern economy is the **central bank.** Basically, a central bank is an agency of government that has important public policy functions in monitoring the operation of the financial system and controlling the growth of its money supply. Central banks ordinarily do not deal directly with the public; rather, they are "bankers' banks," communicating with commercial banks and securities dealers in carrying out their essential policymaking functions. (For a list of the world's leading central banks, see the accompanying box.) The central bank of the United States is the **Federal Reserve System,** a creation of the U.S. Congress charged with issuing currency, regulating the banking system, and taking measures to protect the value of the dollar and promote full employment. In this and the following chapter, we examine in detail the nature and impact of central bank operations and the major problems of policymaking faced by central bank money managers today.

THE ROLES OF CENTRAL BANKS IN THE ECONOMY AND FINANCIAL SYSTEM

Control of the Money Supply

Central banks, including the Federal Reserve System, perform several important functions in a modern economy. (See Exhibit 13-1.) The first and most important of their functions is *control of the money supply.*

What is money? Money is anything that serves as a *medium of exchange* in the purchase of goods and services. Money, however, has another important function—serving as a *store of value,* for money is a financial asset that may be used to store purchasing power until it is needed by the owner. If we define money exclusively as a medium of exchange, the sum of all currency and coin held by the public plus the value of all publicly held checking accounts and other deposits against which drafts may be made (such as NOWs and money market accounts) would constitute the money supply. If we define money as a store of value, on the other hand, then time and savings accounts at banks and nonbank financial intermediaries would also be considered important components of the money supply.

However we define money, the power to regulate its quantity and value in the United States was delegated by the Congress early in this century to the Federal Reserve System. The Fed has become not only the principal source of currency and coin (pocket money) used by the U.S. public but also the principal government agency responsible for stabilizing the value of the dollar and protecting its integrity in international markets. Why is control of the money supply so important? One reason is that changes in the money supply appear to be closely linked to changes in economic activity. A number of studies in recent years have found a statistically significant relationship between current and lagged changes in the money supply and changes in nominal gross domestic product (GDP).[1] The implica-

---

[1] See, for example, the studies by Carlson (1980) and Faust (1992).

Markets on the Net

Extensive information exists on the World Wide Web today on central banking and the policies and policy tools of central banks all over the world. The Federal Reserve System, in particular, is very well represented on the Web with such important sites as the Board of Governors of the Federal Reserve System at *www.federalreserve.gov,* the Federal Reserve Bank of New York at *www.ny.frb.org,* the Federal Reserve Bank of Cleveland at *www.clev.frb.org,* and the Federal Reserve Bank of San Francisco at *www.sf.frb.org.*

Other central banks around the world are likewise well represented on the Web. You may contact the Web sites of any of these institutions by simply entering their names in a search program—for example, the European Central Bank(ECB), the Bank of England, or the Bank of Japan. Most of these central banking sites are extensive, providing information on national economies and the structure and organization of each central bank as well as its goals and responsibilities.

EXHIBIT 13-1
Roles Usually Played by Central Banks in the Financial System

- Market stabilization
- Control of the money supply
- Lender of last resort
- Supervisor of the banking system
- Protecting and improving the flow of payments

tion of these studies is that, if the central bank can control the rate of growth of money, it can influence the nominal growth rate of the economy as a whole.

Another important reason for controlling the money supply is that, in the absence of effective controls, money in the form of paper notes or bank deposits could expand virtually without limit. The marginal cost of creating additional units of money is nearly zero. Therefore, the banking system or the government or both are capable of increasing the money supply well beyond the economy's capacity to produce goods and services. Because this action would result in severe price inflation and eventually bring business activity to a halt, it is not surprising that modern governments have come to rely so heavily on central banks as guardians of the quantity and value of their currencies. For example, the Federal Reserve System and other central banks enter the financial markets frequently in an attempt to control domestic price inflation in order to protect the purchasing power of the dollar.

Today there appears to be growing recognition that central banks cannot significantly influence real variables, such as the economy's output and employment in the long run. However, they are a major influence on the rate of inflation in the long run. Thus, it is often argued today that price level stability *must* be the principal long-run goal of central bank policy, and therefore, central banks *must* pay close attention to how fast money and credit are allowed to grow in order to avoid serious inflation.

Stabilizing the Money and Capital Markets

A second vital function of central banking is *stabilization of the money and capital markets.* The financial system must transmit savings to those who require funds for investment so the economy can grow. If the system of money and capital markets is to work efficiently, however, the public must have confidence in financial institutions and be willing to commit

For a review of the structure, laws, and performance of central banks around the world see the web site of the Center for the Study of Central Banks at *www.law.nyu.edu/ centralbankscenter*

its savings to them. If the financial markets are unruly, with volatile fluctuations in interest rates and security prices, or if financial institutions are prone to frequent collapse, public confidence in the financial system might well be lost. The flow of investment capital would dry up, resulting in a drastic slowing in the rate of economic growth and a rise in unemployment. All central banks play a vital role in fostering the mature development of financial markets and in ensuring a stable flow of funds through those markets. Pursuing this objective, a central bank may, from time to time, provide funds to major securities dealers and/or depository institutions when they have difficulty financing their portfolios or providing an adequate supply of credit so that buyers and sellers may easily acquire or sell securities and borrowers interested in making investments can find adequate funding. When the money supply and interest rates rise or fall more rapidly than seems consistent with economic goals and the desired volume of saving and investment in the economy, a central bank may again intervene in the financial marketplace.

Lender of Last Resort

Another essential function of many central banks is to serve as a *lender of last resort*. This means providing liquid funds to those financial institutions in need, especially when alternative sources of funds have dried up. For example, through its discount window, the Federal Reserve will provide funds to selected deposit-type financial institutions to cover their short-term cash deficiencies. The central bank's discount window can supply large amounts of emergency funds very quickly, as occurred, for example, in the wake of the September 11, 2001, terrorist attacks when the Federal Reserve moved rapidly to supply liquidity to the struggling U.S. economy. As we will see, before the Federal Reserve System was created, one of the weaknesses in the financial system of the United States was the absence of a lender of last resort to aid financial institutions squeezed by severe liquidity pressures.

Maintaining and Improving the Payments Mechanism

Finally, central banks have a role to play in *maintaining and improving the payments mechanism*. This may involve the central bank helping to clear checks, providing an adequate supply of currency and coin, wiring funds, and preserving confidence in the value of the fundamental monetary unit. A smoothly functioning and efficient payments mechanism is vital for business and commerce. If checks or electronic payments cannot be cleared in timely fashion (as happened in the immediate wake of the terrorist crisis in September 2001) or if the public cannot get the currency and coin it needs to carry out transactions, business activity will be severely curtailed. The result might well be large-scale unemployment and a decline in the nation's rate of economic growth.

THE GOALS AND CHANNELS OF CENTRAL BANKING

Central banking is *goal oriented*. Since World War II, the United States and other industrialized nations have accepted the premise that government is responsible to its citizens for maintaining high levels of employment, combating inflation, and supporting sustained growth in the economy. Specifically, central banking in the United States and in most other nations is directed toward four major goals:

1. Full employment of resources.

2. Reasonable stability in the general price level for all goods and services.

International Focus   The World's Leading Central Banks

Bank of England	European Central Bank (ECB)	Federal Reserve System
Bank of Japan	Deutsche Bundesbank (Germany)	Banque de France
Bank of Switzerland	Banca D'Italia	Reserve Bank of New Zealand
Bank of Canada	Reserve Bank of Australia	De Nederlandsche Bank NV (The Netherlands)
Banque Nationale de Belgique (Belgium)	Banco Central do Brasil	The People's Bank of China

Articles and speeches by central banking officials around the world are compiled by the Bank for International Settlements at *www.bis.org/review*

3. Sustained economic growth.

4. A stable balance-of-payments position for the nation vis-à-vis the rest of the world.[2]

Through its influence over interest rates and the growth of the money supply, the central bank is able to influence the economy's progress toward each of these goals. Achievement of all of these goals simultaneously has proven to be exceedingly difficult, however. One reason is that the goals often *conflict*. Pursuit of price stability and an improved balance-of-payments position, for example, may require higher interest rates and restricted credit availability—policies that tend to increase unemployment and slow economic growth. Central bank policymaking is a matter of accepting *trade-offs* (compromises) among multiple goals. For example, the central bank can pursue policies leading to a lower rate of inflation and a stronger dollar in international markets, but probably at the price of some additional unemployment and slower economic growth in the short run.

Central banking in most major nations today operates principally through the *marketplace*. Modern central banks operate as a balance wheel in promoting and stabilizing the flow of savings from surplus-spending units to deficit-spending units. They try to ensure a smooth and orderly flow of funds through the money and capital markets so that adequate financing is available for worthwhile investment projects. This means, among other things, avoiding panics due to sudden shortages of available credit or sharp declines in security prices. However, most of the actions taken by the central bank to promote a smooth flow of funds are carried out through the marketplace rather than by government order. For example, the central bank may encourage interest rates to rise in order to reduce borrowing and spending and combat inflation, but it does not usually allocate credit to particular borrowers. The private sector, working through supply and demand forces in the marketplace,

[2]In the United States, two laws were passed in the 1970s in an effort to specifically define the goals to be pursued by the U.S. central bank, the Federal Reserve. The Full Employment and Balanced Growth Act of 1978 listed full employment and production, increased real income, balanced growth, adequate productivity growth, an improved trade balance, and reasonable price stability as primary objectives for monetary and fiscal policy. The Federal Reserve Reform Act of 1977 amended the 1913 Federal Reserve Act to require the Fed to promote maximum employment, stable prices, and moderate long-term interest rates. Unfortunately, none of these laws contained any hint or suggestion as to how best to achieve these goals or, in the case of conflicts between the goals, which goal was to have priority. In contrast, some central banks have their priorities carefully spelled out by their governments. For example, the new European Central Bank (ECB) has been instructed to pursue *price stability* as its primary goal.

is left to make its own decisions about how much borrowing and spending will take place and who is to receive credit.

The Channels through Which Central Banks Work

It is useful at this point to give a brief overview of the channels through which modern central banks influence conditions in the economy and financial system. Central bank policy affects the economy as a whole by making the following adjustments:

1. Changes in the cost and availability of credit to businesses, consumers, and governments.

2. Changes in the volume and rate of growth of the money supply.

3. Changes in the financial wealth of investors as reflected in the market value of their stocks, bonds, and other security holdings.

4. Changes in the relative prices of domestic and foreign currencies (currency exchange rates).

5. Changes in the public's expectations regarding future money and credit conditions and currency values (see Exhibit 13-2).

The central bank has a number of policy tools at its command to influence the cost of credit (interest rates); the value (prices) of securities; money supply volume and growth; the relative prices (exchange rates) of world currencies; and the public's expectations regarding future interest rates, currency prices, and credit conditions. In the United States, the principal policy tools used by the central bank are open market operations, changes in

EXHIBIT 13-2   **The Impact of Central Bank Policy: How Central Banks Influence the Economy and the Global Financial System**

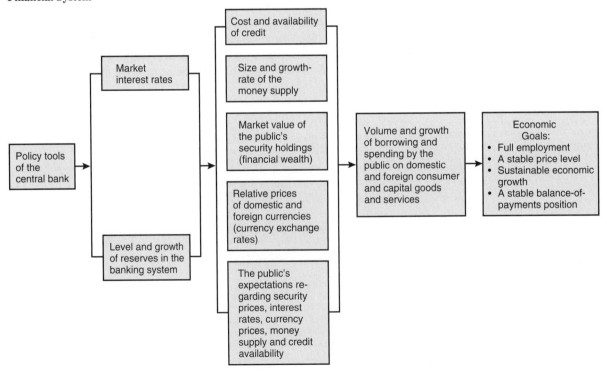

required reserves held by depository institutions, and changes in the discount rate on central bank loans. Many of these same tools are used by other central banks around the world, with a growing use of open market operations, which appears to be becoming the most popular monetary tool across the globe.

Changes in interest rates, security prices, and bank reserves that result from the use of the central bank's policy tools influence, first of all, the cost and availability of credit. If borrowers find that credit is less available and more expensive to obtain, they are likely to restrain their borrowing and spending for both capital and consumer goods at home and abroad. This results in a slowing in the economy's rate of growth and perhaps a reduction in inflationary pressures. Second, if the central bank can reduce the rate of growth of the money supply, this policy will eventually slow the growth of income and production in the economy due to a reduction in the public's demand for goods and services.

Third, if the central bank raises interest rates and thereby lowers security prices, this will tend to reduce the market value of the public's holdings of stocks, bonds, and other securities. The result is a decline in the value of investors' financial wealth, altering the public's borrowing and spending plans and ultimately influencing employment, prices, and the economy's rate of growth. Fourth, the central bank can make changes in domestic interest rates relative to foreign interest rates, which will affect the exchange ratios (relative prices) in world markets between domestic and foreign currencies. If the price of the home currency falls relative to foreign currency prices, the home country's exports will become cheaper and more sought after abroad, stimulating domestic production and creating more jobs.

In recent years, economic research has suggested a fifth channel for central bank policy to affect the economy: *its impact on the public's expectations* regarding future credit costs, money supply growth, the value of loans and securities, and relative currency values. If central bank operations result in shifting public expectations, businesses and consumers will alter their borrowing, spending, and investing plans (unfortunately, not always in the direction the central bank wishes), which can have profound effects on the economy's rate of growth and the creation of jobs. We will have more to say about these important channels of central bank policy in Chapter 14.

Questions *to Help You Study*

1. What *functions* do central banks perform in a market-oriented economy? Explain why each function you have listed is important in the functioning of a market-oriented economic system.

2. What are the principal *goals* that central banks pursue as they work to carry out monetary policy?

3. To what extent are the principal goals of central bank monetary policy consistent or inconsistent with each other? What does a central bank do when the goals it wishes to pursue directly conflict with each other?

4. What are the principal *channels* through which central banks, including the Federal Reserve System, work to influence the economy and achieve their goals?

THE HISTORY OF THE FEDERAL RESERVE SYSTEM—CENTRAL BANK OF THE UNITED STATES

The United States was one of the last major nations in the Western world to permanently charter a central bank. The Bank of England was established in 1694; the Bank of France

International Focus   The World's Newest Major Central Bank: The ECB

In 1998 a new central bank—the ECB, or European Central Bank—joined the world's list of key financial institutions devoted to pursuing monetary policy and stabilizing economies. Formed as a result of the European Union (EU), the new central bank, headquartered in Frankfurt, Germany, and representing all 11 initial member nations of the EU as well as affecting the economic lives of nearly 300 million European citizens, will begin to shape the structure of interest rates on the European continent and assist in the conversion to a common EU currency, the Euro. It will be aided in this task by the 11 central banks of the EU countries, which represent the new European System of Central Banks (ESCB). The principal goal of the ECB, as defined by the Masstricht Treaty, is to pursue *price stability,* unlike many other central banks (such as the Federal Reserve) that pursue other economic goals (such as full employment and sustainable economic growth) as well. The ECB will assist the European Monetary Institute and the central banks of EU member nations in developing a new electronic payments network comparable to the Federal Reserve's FEDWIRE that will be called TARGET—the Trans-European Automated Real-Time Gross Settlement Express Transfer—allowing cross-border payments to be processed in Europe's new currency, the *Euro.*

The ECB faces multiple challenges as it operates in the 21st century. It must finalize the design and power of its organizational structure and governing council, decide on the policy tools it will use, establish credibility with international traders and investors as well as its own citizens, and figure out how to maintain a uniform monetary policy for multiple European nations, each with a different mix of industries and varying social and political customs and systems. It will supervise the eventual achievement of uniform interest rates throughout its territory, though the central banks of EU member states by law retain the right to set their own nations' interest rate levels. Each member state, regardless of its size, has only one vote on the ECB's Governing Council, which contains the governors of the member countries' central banks and is chaired by the ECB's president—a position comparable to the Chairman of the Board of Governors of the Federal Reserve System. The ECB will not be as clearly dominated by its president as is the Fed with its Board chairman, and therefore, the ECB may be somewhat slower to respond to crises than is the Federal Reserve System. The ECB's Executive Board, which runs its daily operations, is appointed by the European Council of Ministers and confirmed by the European Parliament. In principle at least, the European central banking system should be one of the most independent central banks in the world, as its charter can be modified only by unanimous consent of all member nations.

and the central banks of Switzerland and Italy were founded during the eighteenth century. Most major industrialized nations early in their histories recognized the need for an institution that would provide a measure of stability and control over the growth of money and credit. Public officials in the United States were hesitant to charter a central bank, for fear that it would possess great financial power and restrict the availability of credit to a growing nation. However, a series of economic and financial crises in the late nineteenth and early twentieth centuries forced the U.S. Congress to create the Federal Reserve System.

Problems in the Early U.S. Banking System

To fully understand why the Federal Reserve System was created, we must understand the problems that plagued the U.S. financial system throughout much of this nation's early history. Many of these problems were born in the years prior to the Civil War, when the states, not the federal government, controlled the banking system. Unfortunately, with a few notable exceptions, the states did a poor job. Charters for new banks frequently were awarded by state legislatures and were therefore subject to political lobbying and influence peddling. If a new bank's organizers had the right political connections, a charter could be obtained by individuals with little banking experience and with minimal capital invested in the business.

Deposit banking was not as popular then as it is today. Most people preferred hard money (currency and coin) to deposits. As a result, banks made loans simply by printing and issuing their own paper notes, which circulated as currency. Because few controls existed, there was a tendency to issue these notes well beyond the financial strength of the bank making the loan. Frequently, charters were granted to "wildcat banks" that would issue a large quantity of notes and then disappear. Some banks, promising to redeem their notes in gold or silver coin, set up "redemption centers" in locations nearly impossible for the public to reach, such as in the middle of a swamp. Needless to say, there was a high failure rate among these poorly capitalized, ill-managed institutions, resulting in substantial losses to unlucky depositors.

Responding to these problems and also to the tremendous financial strain imposed by the Civil War, Congress passed the National Banking Act of 1863. This act authorized the establishment of federally licensed commercial banks, subject to regulations imposed by a newly created office, the Comptroller of the Currency, a part of the U.S. Treasury Department. Any group of businesspeople could organize a *national bank,* provided they could show that the new bank would be profitable within a reasonable period of time (usually within three years), meet minimum equity capital requirements imposed by the Comptroller's office, and not endanger the viability of banks already operating in the local area. Under the provisions of the National Banking Act, the chartering of commercial banks was, in the main, removed from the political sphere and made subject to carefully spelled-out rules. At the same time, Congress attempted to drive state-chartered banks into the national banking system by imposing a 10 percent tax on state bank notes. It was argued that most bankers would prefer the more liberal state regulations and avoid applying for national bank charters unless they were forced to do so.

To help finance the Civil War, Congress authorized national banks to issue their own notes as circulating currency. However, these notes had to be collateralized by U.S. government securities. Under the terms of the National Banking Act, federally chartered banks could issue notes up to 90 percent of the value of Treasury securities they deposited with the Comptroller of the Currency. The result was to create a money medium under federal control to help pay for the Civil War by creating a demand from banks for U.S. government securities. Even more important, the National Banking Act created a *dual banking system,* with both federal and state authorities having important regulatory powers over commercial banks. Unfortunately, these authorities were given overlapping powers, and in recent years competition between federal and state bank regulatory agencies has sometimes resulted in actions detrimental to the public interest.

Creation of the Federal Reserve System

Several festering problems (including some traceable to the provisions of the National Banking Act) resulted in the creation of the Federal Reserve System. For one thing, the new national bank notes proved to be unresponsive to the nation's growing need for a money or cash medium. The need for money and credit grew rapidly as the United States became more heavily industrialized and the Midwest and Far West opened up to immigration. Farmers and ranchers in these areas demanded an "elastic" supply of money and credit—adequate to their needs at relatively low cost. As we will soon see, the new Federal Reserve System would attempt to deal with this problem by issuing a currency of its own and by exercising closer control over the growth of money and credit.

As deposit banking and the writing of checks became increasingly popular, another serious problem appeared. The process of clearing and collecting checks was too slow and expensive. Then, as now, most checks written by the public were local in character, moving funds from the account of one local customer to that of another. These checks normally are cleared routinely through the local clearinghouse, which is simply a location where representatives of local banks meet daily to exchange bundles of checks drawn on each other's banks. For checks sent outside the local area, however, the collection process is more complicated, with some checks passing through several banks before reaching their final destination.

To learn more about the history of the Federal Reserve System see such web sites as Fed101 at *www.kc.frb. org/fed101* and the Federal Reserve Bank of Minneapolis at *www.mpls.frb.org*

Before the Federal Reserve System was created, many banks charged a fee (*exchange charge*) for the clearing and redemption of checks. This fee was usually calculated as a percentage of the par (or face) value of each check. Banks levying the fee were called *no-par* banks because they refused to honor checks at their full face value. To avoid exchange fees, bankers would try to route the checks they received only through banks accepting and redeeming them at par. Often this meant routing a check through scores of banks in distant cities until days or weeks had elapsed before the check was finally cleared. Such a delay was not just annoying, but also served as an impediment to commercial transactions. Exchange charges resulted in needless inefficiency and increased the true cost of business transactions far above their nominal cost. A new national check-clearing system was needed that honored checks at par and moved them swiftly between payee and payer. This responsibility too was given to the Federal Reserve System, which insisted that all checks cleared through its system be honored at full face (par) value.

A third problem with the banking and financial system of that time was recurring liquidity crises. Then, as now, money and bank reserves tended to concentrate in leading financial centers, such as New York City or San Francisco, where the greatest need for loanable funds existed. Bank reserves flowed into the major cities as smaller banks in outlying areas deposited their reserves with larger banking institutions to earn greater returns. However, when the pressures for agricultural credit increased in rural areas, many country banks had to sell securities and call in their loans to city banks in the nation's financial centers to come up with the necessary funds. Thus, when the reserve demands of country banks were larger than expected, security prices in leading financial centers plummeted due to massive sell-offs of bank-held securities. Panic selling by other investors soon followed, leading to chaos in the marketplace.

The banking system clearly needed a lender of ready cash to provide liquidity to those banks with heavy cash drains and to protect the stability of the financial system. A serious financial panic in 1907 finally led to the creation of the Federal Reserve System. In 1908, Congress created the National Monetary Commission to study the financial needs of the nation. The commission's recommendations were forwarded to Congress and ultimately resulted in passage of the Federal Reserve Act, signed into law by President Wilson in December 1913. The Federal Reserve banks opened for business as World War I began in Europe.

The Early Structure of the Federal Reserve System

The first Federal Reserve System was quite different from the Fed of today. The original Federal Reserve Act reflected a mix of diverse viewpoints: an effort to reconcile competing political and economic interests. There was great fear that the Fed would have too much control over financial affairs and operate against the best interest of important segments of U.S. society. For example, small businesses, consumer groups, and farmers were concerned that the Fed might pursue restrictive credit policies, leading to high interest rates. In addition, it was recognized that the Federal Reserve would become a major financial institution wherever it was located. Any city that housed a Federal Reserve bank was likely to become a major financial center.

Responding to these various needs and interest groups, Congress created a truly "decentralized" central bank. Not 1 but 12 Federal Reserve banks were chartered, stretching across the continental United States. Each Reserve bank was assigned its own district, over which it possessed important regulatory powers. A supervisory board of seven members was set up in Washington, DC, to promote a common monetary policy for the nation. In fact, however, the regional Federal Reserve banks possessed the essential monetary tools and made the key policy decisions during the Fed's early years.

Goals and Policy Tools of the Federal Reserve System

To deal with the financial problems of that day, the Federal Reserve Act permitted each regional Reserve bank to open a *discount window* where eligible banks could borrow reserves for short periods of time. However, borrowing banks were required to present high-quality, short-term business loans (commercial paper) to secure the loans they needed. The Fed's chief policy tool of the day was the *discount rate* charged on these loans, with each Reserve bank having the authority to set its own rate. By varying this rate, the Reserve banks could encourage or discourage banks' propensity to discount commercial paper and borrow reserves. Central bankers could promote easy or tight credit conditions and influence the overall volume of bank loans.

The Federal Reserve banks were given authority to issue their own paper notes to serve as a circulating currency, but these notes had to be 100 percent backed by Fed holdings of commercial paper plus a 40 percent gold reserve. Almost as an afterthought, Congress authorized the Reserve banks to trade U.S. government securities in the open market, known as *open market operations,* the Fed's principal policy tool today. Reserve requirements were imposed on deposits held by member banks of the system, but the Fed could not readily change these requirements.

Slowly but surely, economic, financial, and political forces combined to amend the original Federal Reserve Act and remake the character and methods of the central bank. The leading causes of change were war, economic recessions, and more recently, persistent inflation. For example, to combat economic recession, fight wars, and pursue desired programs, the U.S. government issued billions of dollars in debt. As the debt began to grow, it seemed only "logical" to permit greater use of U.S. government securities in the Federal Reserve's operations. Banks were authorized to use government securities as backing for loans from the Fed's discount window. The Fed itself was called on to play a major role in stabilizing the market for U.S. government securities to ensure that the Treasury would have little difficulty in refinancing its maturing debt. Government securities were made eligible as collateral for the issue of new Federal Reserve bank notes.

More than any other historical event, however, it was the Great Depression of the 1930s that changed the character of the Federal Reserve. Faced with the collapse of the banking system and unprecedented unemployment—at least a quarter of the U.S. labor force was thrown out of work during the 1930s—Congress entrusted the Fed with sweeping monetary powers as a result of the passage of the Banking Acts of 1933 and 1935. Significant changes also were made in the central bank's operating structure and lines of authority.

The seven-member Board of Governors in Washington, DC, became the central administrative and policymaking group for the Fed. Thereafter, any changes in discount rates charged by the Reserve banks had to be approved in advance by the Board of Governors. The Board was granted authority to set minimum reserve requirements on deposits and maximum interest rates that banks could pay on those deposits. To control speculative buying of stocks, the Reserve Board was empowered to set margin requirements specifying what proportion of a security's market value the investor could borrow to buy that security. Recognizing that open market operations in U.S. government securities were rapidly becoming the Fed's main policy tool, a powerful policymaking body—the Federal Open Market Committee—was created to oversee the conduct of open market operations. In summary, the Great Depression brought about a *concentration of power* within the Federal Reserve System so that the Fed could pursue unified policies and speak with one voice concerning monetary affairs.

HOW THE FED IS ORGANIZED

The Federal Reserve System today has an organizational structure that resembles a *pyramid.* As Exhibit 13-3 shows, the apex of the pyramid is the **Board of Governors,** the Federal Reserve's chief policymaking and administrative group. At the middle level of the pyramid are the Federal Reserve banks, which carry out system policy and provide essential services to banks and other depository financial institutions in their particular regions, and the Federal Open Market Committee. The bottom of the pyramid contains the member banks of the system, which the Fed supervises and regulates, and the manager of the System Open Market Account, who is responsible for buying and selling securities to achieve the goals of Fed monetary policy.

Board of Governors of the Federal Reserve System

The key administrative body within the Federal Reserve System is the Board of Governors. The board consists of seven persons appointed by the president of the United States and confirmed by the Senate for maximum 14-years terms. Terms of office are staggered, with one board member's appointment ending every even-numbered year. When a member of the Federal Reserve Board resigns or dies, the president may appoint a new person to complete the remainder of the unexpired term, and that member may be reappointed to a subsequent full term. However, no member who completes a full term can be reappointed to the Board of Governors. The president designates one member of the board as its chairperson and another as vice chairperson, and both serve four-year terms in those positions. In selecting new board members, the president is required to seek a fair representation of the financial, agricultural, industrial, and commercial interests and geographical divisions of the country and may not choose more than one member from any one Federal Reserve district.

See Board of Governors at *www.federalreserve. gov* for additional information about the Federal Reserve Board.

The powers of the Federal Reserve Board are extensive. The board sets reserve requirements on deposits held by depository institutions subject to its rules, reviews and determines the discount rate charged on loans to depository institutions, sets margin requirements on the public's purchases of securities, and provides leadership in the conduct of open market operations through the Federal Open Market Committee. Besides its monetary policy functions, the Board supervises the activities of the 12 Reserve banks and has supervisory and regulatory control over member banks of the system. It regulates financial holding companies, foreign banks entering the United States, and the overseas activities of U.S. banks.

EXHIBIT 13-3
How the Federal Reserve System is Organized

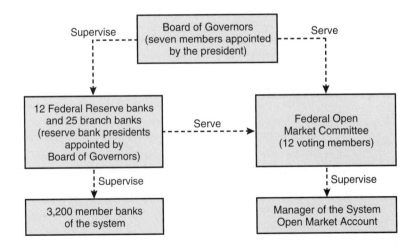

In principle, the Board is independent of both legislative and executive branches of the federal government. This independence is supported by terms of office much longer than the president's (up to 14 years) and by the fact that the Fed does not depend on the U.S. Congress for operating funds. The Federal Reserve supports itself from revenue generated by selling its services (such as clearing checks), making loans through the discount window, and earning interest on government securities the Fed holds. These monies are not retained by the Fed, because it is operated in the public interest and not for profit. All monies left over after expenses, dividends paid to member banks, and minimal allocations to equity reserves are transferred to the U.S. Treasury. For example, in 2001 the Fed reported operating income of about $32 billion, of which about $27 billion was paid to the U.S. Treasury, helping to reduce tax collections from the private sector.

The Federal Open Market Committee and Manager of the System Open Market Account

The Federal Open Market Committee— known as the FOMC— is widely followed by active investors around the globe. Greater understanding on why the FOMC is so important to interest rates and credit conditions may be found in such Web sites as *www.federalreserve. gov/fomc* and through the publications of the Federal Reserve Bank of New York at *www.ny.frb.org*

Aside from the Federal Reserve Board, the other key policymaking group within the system is the **Federal Open Market Committee (FOMC).** It has been called the most important committee of individuals in the United States because its decisions concerning the conduct of monetary policy and the cost and availability of credit affect the lives of millions of people. Membership on the FOMC consists of the seven members of the Federal Reserve Board and the presidents or first vice presidents of the Reserve banks. Only the seven members of the Board and five of the Reserve bank presidents or their representatives may vote when a final decision is reached on the future conduct of monetary policy, however. The president of the Federal Reserve Bank of New York is a permanent voting member of the FOMC, the presidents of the Chicago and Cleveland Federal Reserve banks alternate in filling one other voting seat, and the remaining three voting positions on the FOMC are rotated annually among the presidents of the nine remaining Federal Reserve banks. Each Reserve bank representative occupying a rotating seat serves a voting term of one year.

By tradition, the chairperson of the Federal Reserve Board and the president of the New York Federal Reserve bank serve as chairperson and vice chairperson of the FOMC. The law stipulates that the FOMC will meet in Washington, DC, at least four times a year. In practice, however, the committee meets about eight times a year and more frequently if emergencies develop. Between regularly scheduled meetings, telephone conferences may occur, and the members of the FOMC may be asked to cast votes by telephone or telegram. FOMC meetings are *not* open to the public because confidential financial information frequently is discussed and also because the Fed wants to avoid sending false signals to the financial marketplace. Only Federal Reserve Board members, selected board staff, the Reserve bank presidents and their aides, and the manager and deputy manager of the System Open Market Account are permitted to attend FOMC meetings.

The name Federal Open Market Committee implies that this committee's sole concern is with the conduct of Federal Reserve open market operations in securities, a power granted to it by the Banking Act of 1935. In fact, the FOMC reviews current economic and financial conditions and considers *all* aspects of monetary policy at its meetings. It also directs Fed operations in the foreign exchange markets. Once a consensus is reached concerning the appropriate future course for monetary policy, a directive is given to the manager of the System Open Market Account (SOMA), who is a vice president of the Federal Reserve Bank of New York. The SOMA manager is told in general terms how open market operations should be conducted in the weeks ahead and what the FOMC's targets for money supply growth and interest rates are. Decisions made by the FOMC and actions of the SOMA manager at the securities trading desk in New York are binding on the entire Federal Reserve System.

The Federal Reserve Banks

When the Federal Reserve System was created in 1913, the nation was divided into 12 districts, with one **Federal Reserve bank** in each district responsible for supervising and providing services to the member banks located there. Reserve banks were established in the cities of Atlanta, Boston, Chicago, Cleveland, Dallas, Kansas City, Minneapolis, New York, Philadelphia, Richmond, San Francisco, and St. Louis. In addition, 24 branches (later expanded to 25) were created to serve particular regions within the 12 districts.

Using computers and high-speed sorting machines, the regional Reserve banks route checks and other cash items drawn on financial institutions in one city and deposited in another city back to the institutions on which they were drawn for proper crediting of the amounts involved. Although the Fed processes only about 40 percent of all checks written in the United States, it still handles billions of checks and other paper items that reflect billions of transactions carried out by businesses and individuals each year. The Federal Reserve maintains an electronic network (known as FEDWIRE), which transfers millions of dollars daily in money and securities among banking institutions in the United States that maintain reserves or clearing accounts with the Fed. Approximately 30 automated clearinghouses (ACHs) are operated by the Reserve banks and their branches to handle the direct deposit of payrolls, mortgage payments, and other funds transfer requests electronically. The Reserve banks ship currency and coin to banks and other depository institutions at those times when the public needs more pocket money and store excess currency and coin in their vaults when less pocket money is needed.

The Reserve banks serve as the federal government's *fiscal agent.* This involves keeping the financial accounts of the U.S. Treasury and delivering and redeeming U.S. government securities. The Reserve banks also accept deposits for federal income, excise, and unemployment taxes. In addition to serving as the federal government's fiscal agent, the Reserve banks closely supervise the activities of member banks within their districts. They conduct field examinations of all state-chartered member banks and supervise bank holding companies headquartered in their region.

The Reserve banks play a significant role in the conduct of money and credit policy. Each Reserve bank houses a research division to study regional economic and financial developments and conveys this information to the Board of Governors and to the Federal Open Market Committee. Only 5 of the 12 Reserve banks have voting seats on the FOMC, but all 12 Reserve bank presidents or first vice presidents attend FOMC meetings to report on conditions in their region and give their views on the appropriate course for monetary policy. The Reserve banks also administer the discount windows where loans are made to financial institutions in their district.

Each Federal Reserve bank is a corporation chartered by Congress. Officially, the Reserve banks are owned by the member banks of their districts, which select a majority of each bank's board of directors. Each Reserve bank president is nominated by that Reserve bank's board of directors, and the appointment is confirmed or denied by the Federal Reserve Board. Under federal law, the board of directors of each Federal Reserve bank must consist of nine directors, six elected by bankers in the district (with three of these directors representing bankers and three the general public or nonbank interests in the same district) and three directors selected by the Federal Reserve Board. The regional Reserve banks are closely controlled by the Federal Reserve Board, which not only reviews officer appointments but also may remove any officer or director of a Federal Reserve bank and examine,

EXHIBIT 13–4
The Balance Sheet of the Federal Reserve System

The Federal Reserve System's Consolidated Assets and Liabilities, Year-end 2000*
($ Billions)

Assets		Liabilities and Capital Accounts	
Gold and special drawing rights certificates	$ 13.2	Liabilities:	
		Federal Reserve notes	$563.5
Coins	0.9	Deposits from banks & thrifts	19.0
Loans to depository institutions	0.1	U.S. Treasury account	5.1
U.S. government and federal agency securities held	511.7	Foreign and other accounts	0.2
		Deferred availability cash items	6.3
Cash items in process of collection	7.1	Other liabilities	5.6
Other assets	80.5	Capital:	13.8
Total assets	$613.5	Total liabilities and capital	$613.5

Note: End-of-month estimates: slight inaccuracies may exist because of rounding.
*Consolidated for all 12 regional Federal Reserve Banks.
Source: Board of Governors of the Federal Reserve System, Release H.4.1(a), March 2001.

reorganize, or even liquidate a Reserve bank if this appears to be necessary to serve the public interest.

Although under the terms of the original Federal Reserve Act the Reserve banks could set the discount rate on loans to depository institutions, these rate changes must now be approved by the Federal Reserve Board in Washington. The regional banks are required to participate in all open market transactions on behalf of the system. These purchases and sales are carried out through the FOMC, but the Reserve banks must provide the securities needed for open market sales and must also take their *pro rata* share of any security purchases the Federal Reserve System makes. As Exhibit 13-4 reveals, the Federal Reserve banks collectively held nearly $512 billion in securities—their principal asset—and had issued nearly $564 billion in Federal Reserve notes, the principal circulating currency of the United States, at year-end 2000.

The Member Banks of the Federal Reserve System

The **member banks** of the Federal Reserve System consist of national banks, which are required to join the system, and state-chartered banks that agree to conform to the Fed's rules. Today, Federal Reserve member banks constitute a minority of all U.S. banks, about 40 percent of the total. There are about 2,200 national banks and just under 1,000 state-chartered banks registered as members of the Federal Reserve System, compared to approximately 5,000 nonmember banks.

The structure of the Federal Reserve System is also discussed at some length at *www.banx.com*

Member banks must subscribe to the stock of the Reserve bank in their district in an amount equal to 6 percent of their paid-in capital and surplus accounts. However, only half this amount must actually be paid, with the rest payable on call. Member banks are bound by Federal Reserve rules regarding capital, deposits, loans, branch operations, formation of holding companies, and policies regarding the conduct of officers and boards of directors. These banks are subject to supervision and examination by the Federal Reserve at any time. Moreover, member banks must hold reserves behind their deposits at levels specified by the Federal Reserve Board.

A number of important privileges are granted to member banks. Legally, they are "owners" of the Federal Reserve banks because they hold the stock of these institutions and elect six of their nine directors. A 6 percent annual dividend is paid to member banks on their

International Focus   The Issue of Central Bank Independence

The issue of central bank independence from government has become a center of controversy in recent years. Early studies by Alesina (1988) and Bade and Parkin (1987) found a significant negative correlation between the inflation rate experienced by leading industrial countries and the degree of independence from the political process enjoyed by their central banks. For example, Germany and Switzerland, whose central banks operate under greater freedom from government control than most other nations, had average annual inflation rates of only about 3.5 percent between 1974 and 1990, while Italy, whose central bank appeared to be more closely tied to the Italian government, experienced a 12.4 percent annual inflation rate over the same time period. These researchers concluded that economies generally perform better where central banks enjoy greater independence from government. Central banks regulate the money stock and there is often a strong political temptation to overissue money (thereby igniting inflation) in order to combat a lagging economy or to fund extravagant government programs.

The independence from government control enjoyed by central banks varies widely around the world. In the new European Central Bank, representing the entire European Community (EC), board members have eight-year terms, but the ECB has the additional protection that its charter cannot be changed without the unanimous vote of all of its member nations. In the United States, members of the Federal Reserve's Board of Governors can serve for up to 14 years, which limits the power of Congress or the president to alter Fed policy in the short run. Moreover, the Federal Reserve does not depend upon Congress for income—it generates its own revenues through security trading and service fees.

Several bills have been introduced in the U.S. Congress in recent years to restrict the freedom of action of the Federal Reserve System. One proposal would expand the authority of the Government Accounting Office (GAO) to audit *all* phases of Federal Reserve operations. Another proposal would require congressional approval of anyone who wishes to serve as president of a Federal Reserve Bank.

Still another proposed change calls for denying Federal Reserve bank presidents any voting seats on the Federal Open Market Committee (FOMC), the Fed's chief policymaking body. Moreover, some members of Congress have recently demanded that the Fed fully and immediately disclose to the public the minutes from all FOMC meetings. There has even been a call for videotaping FOMC meetings as is now done for many congressional sessions and court trials. Recent presidential administrations have proposed stripping the Fed of its bank examination functions in order to allow it to concentrate on money and credit policy. For its part, the Federal Reserve has argued that these changes would render monetary policy weak and ineffective.

Some experts have argued that the whole structure of the Fed needs revamping in an age of electronics and in an era when the banking system is increasingly being dominated by a few huge banks. They argue that some of the Federal Reserve banks are no longer really needed and should be closed. In many ways, the geographic distribution of the Federal Reserve banks no longer reflects the vast population shifts that have occurred in the United States since the Fed was founded in 1914. In a new era of computers and satellite communications the Fed's vast network of banks and branches *may* be an increasingly inefficient system. However, the Fed argues that its regional offices will likely always be needed to provide convenient services to local areas and to more thoroughly monitor regional conditions.

See, in particular, Alberto Alesina, "Macroeconomics and Politics," in *NBER Macroeconomic Annual, 1988* (Cambridge, MA: MIT Press, 1988); Robin Bade and Michael Parkin, "Central Bank Laws and Monetary Policy," Unpublished Mimeograph, Department of Economics, University of Western Ontario, 1987; and Bruce Kasman, "A Comparison of Monetary Policy Operating Procedures in Six Industrial Countries," *Quarterly Review,* Federal Reserve Bank of New York, Summer, 1992, pp. 5-24.

holdings of Federal Reserve bank stock. Member banks may borrow reserves through the discount window of the Reserve bank in their district and use the Fed's check-clearing system to process checks coming from distant cities. However, this is not an exclusive privilege, because nonmember banks and thrifts may also use the Fed's check-clearing facilities, provided that they agree to maintain a clearing account with the Reserve bank in the region. An intangible benefit of membership is the prestige that comes from belonging to the Federal Reserve System. Many bankers believe that membership in the system attracts large business deposits and correspondent accounts from smaller banks that otherwise might go elsewhere.

Management Insight   Transparency in Monetary Policy: A Concept Whose Time Has Come?

Major central banks around the world, led by such central banks as the Federal Reserve System, the Bank of England, and the Bank of Japan, have worked recently to bring an old idea into modern reality. It's called **transparency**—making the monetary policymaker's intentions about current and future policy very clear so that borrowers and lenders in the money and capital markets come to expect the same policy actions as the policymaker does. If, for example, monetary policy is transparent, members of the public can develop more accurate forecasts of where that policy is headed in the future. Transparency has the great virtue of minimizing the waste of resources caused by market players' decisions that are misguided due to uncertainty about policymakers' intentions.

Recently the Federal Reserve has been following a transparent policy with its conduct of *open market operations*—its principal policy tool. When the Fed makes a new policy decision, like changing the federal funds interest rate, it quickly announces its new target interest rate and gives an explanation of why it is making a change and how it views the economy's condition and response to that change.

The Bank of Japan has been following in a similar vein since the Japanese government granted that bank greater in-dependence. The Bank of Japan Law, passed in 1997, states that "after each Board meeting for monetary control matters, the chairman shall, without delay, prepare a document which contains an outline of the discussion at the meeting in accordance with the decisions made by the Board, and publish the document upon its approval at another Board meeting for monetary control matters." The Bank of Japan also pledged to release the minutes of its policy meetings (usually within five weeks after those meetings), announce to the public its key policy decisions right after each such meeting, publish reports on the Japanese economy each month, and publish schedules of its future policy meetings at least six months in advance. The Bank's Web site (*www.boj.or.jp*) provides daily reports of its account balances. Collectively, all these recent changes in the bank's method of operation suggest the BOJ has recently become one of the globe's most transparent central banks.

Source: See especially Ed Stevens, "Beyond Zero: Transparency in the Bank of Japan's Monetary Policy," *Economic Commentary,* Federal Reserve Bank of Cleveland, March 15,2001.

Questions *to Help You Study*

5. What major problems in the late nineteenth and early twentieth century led to the creation of the Federal Reserve System? How did the creation of the Fed help to solve these problems?

6. In what important ways did the early Federal Reserve System differ from the Federal Reserve we see today?

7. What are the principal responsibilities assigned to the *Board of Governors of the Federal Reserve System?* To the *Federal Open Market Committee?*

8. What are the *Federal Reserve banks* expected to do in serving the public and the banking system?

9. What duties are assigned to the *manager of the System Open Market Account* within the Federal Reserve System?

ROLES OF THE FEDERAL RESERVE SYSTEM TODAY

In the course of this chapter we have talked about the many roles the Federal Reserve plays in the financial system and how these roles have changed over time. In this section we attempt to pull together all of the Fed's responsibilities and roles to give a more complete view of how the central bank interfaces with the financial markets and the banking system.

The Clearing and Collection of Checks and Other Means of Payment

As we saw earlier in this chapter, one of the earliest tasks of the Federal Reserve System was to establish a nationwide system for clearing and collecting checks. When a depository institution receives a check drawn on another institution in a distant city, it can route this check directly through the Federal Reserve banks. The Fed credits an account called Deferred Availability Items on behalf of the institution sending in the check and routes that check to the institution on which it was drawn for eventual collection. At the end of a specified period, the depository institution sending in the check will receive credit in its legal reserve account for the amount of that check. Eventually, the check reaches the institution on which it was drawn and is deducted from that institution's reserve account.

Issuing Currency and Coin and Providing Other Services

Brief descriptions of Federal Reserve services may be found at *www.kc.frb.org* and *www.frbservices.org*

The Fed helps to promote an efficient payments mechanism not just through the clearing of checks but also by issuing its own currency in response to public need. Today, nearly all of the paper money in circulation consists of Federal Reserve notes, issued by all 12 of the Reserve banks and backed mainly by Federal Reserve holdings of government securities. These notes are liabilities of the Federal Reserve bank issuing them. In fact, Federal Reserve notes are a lien against the assets of the Fed, payable to the holder in the event the Reserve banks are ever liquidated. When the public demands more currency, financial institutions request a shipment of new currency and coin from the Federal Reserve bank in the region, which maintains an ample supply in its vault. Payment for the shipment is made simply by charging the legal reserve account of the institution requesting the shipment. In the opposite situation, when depository institutions receive deposits of currency and coin from the public beyond what they wish to hold in their vaults, the surplus is shipped back to the Reserve banks. Depository institutions receive credit for these return shipments through an increase in their legal reserve accounts at the Reserve bank.

Prior to 1981, most Federal Reserve services, including the clearing of checks and shipments of currency and coin, were provided free of charge. However, the Depository Institutions Deregulation and Monetary Control Act (DIDMCA) of 1980 required the Fed to assess fees for such services as transportation of currency and coin, check clearing, wire transfer of funds, the use of Federal Reserve automated clearinghouse facilities, and the safekeeping and redemption of government securities. All fees set by the Fed are to be reviewed annually and set at levels that, over the long term, recover the total costs of providing each service.

Maintaining a Sound Banking and Financial System

Another important function of the Federal Reserve System today is to maintain a sound banking and financial system. It contributes to this goal by serving as a lender of last resort—providing loans of reserves to depository institutions that hold their legal reserve accounts with the Fed through the discount window of each Reserve bank. The window represents a source of funds that can be drawn on without taking reserves away from other banks, and it helps to avoid a liquidity squeeze brought about by sudden changes in economic and financial conditions (as occurred following the terrorist attacks in New York and Washington, DC, on September 11, 2001). The Fed also promotes a sound banking system by regularly examining member banks, reviewing the quality and quantity of their assets and capital, and making sure that federal and state laws are followed.

- Monetary policy—control of the nation's money and credit supply and the pursuit of interest rate levels that optimize economic welfare
- Stabilization of the financial markets—promoting orderly changes in security prices and interest rates
- Improving the payments process to insure greater accuracy and speed in settling the purchase and sale of goods, services, and financial instruments
- Supervision of banks, financial holding companies, and international offices of domestic and foreign banks
- Fiscal agent for the government in dispersing and collecting monies for the federal government and federal agencies
- Information source for the public about economic, financial, and regulatory matters

Serving as the Federal Government's Fiscal Agent

The Fed serves as the government's chief **fiscal agent.** In this role, it holds the Treasury's checking account and clears any checks written against that account. The Fed supervises the thousands of Treasury Tax and Loan Accounts (TT&L) maintained in banks across the United States, which hold the bulk of the Treasury's cash balances until the Treasury needs these monies for spending. The Fed also makes recurring payments (for example, salary checks for government employees) for the federal government through its electronic network of automated clearing houses. The Federal Reserve banks receive bids when new Treasury securities are offered and provide securities to the purchasers. They redeem maturing U.S. government securities as well. In general, the Fed is responsible for maintaining reasonable stability in the government securities market so that any new Treasury offerings sell quickly and the government raises the amount of money that it needs.

Providing Information to the Public

Another critical function that the Federal Reserve has performed particularly well in recent years is to provide *information* to the public. Each Reserve bank has its own research staff, and the Board of Governors maintains a large staff of economists who follow current economic and financial developments and recommend changes in policy. The Fed makes available on a daily, weekly, and monthly basis an impressive volume of statistical releases, special reports, and studies concerning the financial markets and the condition of the economy. This information function is one of the more important contributions of the central bank.

Carrying Out Monetary Policy

The most critical job of the Federal Reserve is to carry out **monetary policy.** Monetary policy may be defined as the use of various tools by the central bank to control the availability of loanable funds in an effort to achieve national economic goals, such as full employment and reasonable price stability. The policy tools reserved for the Federal Reserve include deposit reserve requirements, discount rates, open market operations, and margin requirements on purchases of securities. We will examine the Fed's policy tools in detail in Chapter 14.

THE KEY FOCUS OF CENTRAL BANK MONETARY POLICY: INTEREST RATES, RESERVES, AND MONEY

If the Federal Reserve's most critical job is *monetary policy*—regulating money and credit conditions in an effort to strengthen the economy, what target or targets does the Fed pursue in order to impact the money and capital markets and, ultimately, the economy as a whole?

Today the principal target of most central banks around the globe is *market interest rates,* pushing them higher in order to slow borrowing and spending in the economy and pushing them lower if the economy needs to grow faster. However, to impact market interest rates the Federal Reserve and other central banks must have a "lever" to pull—a device or tool to use over which the central bank has relatively close control.

The central bank's "lever"—its principal immediate monetary policy target—is usually the volume of *reserves available to the banking system.* In the United States, these consist mainly of deposits held at the Federal Reserve banks plus currency and coin held in bank vaults. These reserves are the raw material out of which banks and other depository institutions create credit and cause the money supply to grow. And because the growth of the money supply is closely linked to changes in income, production, prices, and employment, the Federal Reserve and other central banks pay close attention on a daily basis to fluctuations in the quantity of reserves that depository institutions have at their disposal. The total supply of reserves can be changed directly by open market operations—the Federal Reserve's principal policy tool and a growing central bank tool worldwide—and by making loans to depository institutions through the central bank's credit or discount window. The Fed can also exert a powerful effect on the growth of money and credit by changing the legal reserve requirements applicable to deposits held by depository institutions.

Central banks like the Fed can nudge market interest rates in any desired direction by manipulating the legal reserve balances with which depository institutions work. When the supply of reserves is reduced relative to the demand for reserves, interest rates tend to rise as scarce funds are rationed among competing financial institutions. Conversely, an expansion in the supply of reserves usually leads to lower interest rates because of the increased availability of loanable funds. Why do these changes occur? What are the specific links between bank reserves and the money supply?

THE COMPOSITION OF RESERVES FOR DEPOSITORY INSTITUTIONS

To answer the preceding questions, we need to look closely at what makes up the supply of reserves at depository institutions. All U.S. depository institutions offering selected kinds of deposits are required to hold a small percentage of those deposits in an asset account known as **legal reserves.** Legal reserves in the United States consist of the amount of deposits each institution keeps with the Federal Reserve bank in its district plus the amount of currency and coin held in its vault. (Other central banks often include other types of assets in their definitions of legal reserves—for example, government securities.)

Legal reserves may be divided into two parts: *required reserves* and *excess reserves,* as we noted in Chapter 11. In particular,

$$\text{Total legal reserves} = \text{Required reserves} + \text{Excess reserves} \qquad \textbf{(13–1)}$$

In the United States,

$$\text{Total legal reserves} = \begin{array}{c}\text{Deposits at the}\\ \text{Federal Reserve}\\ \text{banks}\end{array} + \begin{array}{c}\text{Vault cash held on the}\\ \text{premises of depository}\\ \text{institutions}\end{array} \qquad \textbf{(13–2)}$$

Required reserves are those holdings of cash and deposits at the Fed that a depository institution *must* hold to back the public's deposits. **Excess reserves** are the amount of reserves left over after we deduct required reserves from total legal reserves. Excess reserves may be used to make loans, purchase securities, or for other purposes. Because legal reserve assets earn little or no income, most depository institutions try to keep their excess reserves close to zero. For example, the largest banks today frequently run reserve deficits and must borrow additional legal reserves in the money market to avoid costly penalties.

THE DEPOSIT MULTIPLIER

The distinction between excess and required reserves is important because it plays a key role in the growth of money and credit in the economy. Depository institutions offering checkable deposits have the unique ability to create and destroy deposits—which are the bulk of the money supply—at the stroke of a pen. Although an individual depository institution cannot create more deposit money than the volume of excess reserves it holds, the banking system as a whole can create a multiple amount of deposit money from any given injection of reserves by using its excess reserves to make loans and purchase securities.

How much in deposits can the banking system create if it has excess reserves available? The banking system's deposit-creating potential can be estimated using a concept known as the **deposit multiplier,** or coefficient of deposit expansion. The deposit multiplier indicates how many dollars of deposits (and loans) will result from any given injection of new excess reserves into the financial system. If we assume the existence of a very simple financial system in which the public makes all of its payments by check and does not convert any checkbook (transaction deposit) money into savings deposits and in which depository institutions do not wish to hold any excess reserves, then the transaction deposit multiplier is

$$\frac{1}{\text{Reserve requirement on transaction deposits}} \qquad \textbf{(13–3)}$$

For example, if the Federal Reserve insists that depository institutions keep $0.12 in required reserves for each new dollar of transaction (checkbook) deposits they receive, the deposit multiplier must be 1/0.12, or 8.33.

Then how much in new deposit money can the banking system create under these circumstances? If all depository institutions continually make loans with any excess reserves they receive, the maximum amount of new deposits (and loans) that can be created by the entire banking system may be found from the following equation:

$$\text{Transaction deposit multiplier} \times \text{Excess reserves} = \text{Maximum volume of new deposits and loans} \qquad \textbf{(13–4)}$$

If banks and other depository institutions receive additional excess reserves in the amount of $1 million and the reserve requirement behind transaction deposits is 12 percent, we have the following:

$$1/0.12 \times \$1 \text{ million} = 8.33 \times \$1 \text{ million}$$

$$= \$8.33 \text{ million in new deposits and loans}$$

A *withdrawal* of reserves from depository institutions can work in the opposite direction, destroying deposits and loans. For example, a withdrawal of deposits by the public that causes depository institutions to have a $1 million deficiency in their required reserves would eventually lead to an $8.33 million *decline* in deposits, assuming a 12 percent reserve requirement.

Of course, the real world is quite different from the simple deposit expansion model outlined above. Leakages of funds from the banking system greatly reduce the size of the deposit multiplier, so that its actual value is probably somewhat less than 2. Among the most important leakages are the public's desire to convert some portion of new checkbook money into pocket money (currency and coin) or into savings deposits and the presence of unutilized lending capacity. Banks may choose to hold substantial excess reserves and not lend out all their excess funds because they cannot find enough qualified borrowers or wish to hold a protective "cushion" of reserves.

These various leakages of funds from transaction deposit balances suggest the need for a slightly more complex model of the deposit and loan expansion process. In this model, the deposit multiplier would be represented by the following expression:

$$\text{Transaction deposit multiplier assuming drains of funds into cash, time and savings deposits, and excess reserves} = \frac{1}{RR_D + CASH + EXR + RR_T \times TIME} \qquad \textbf{(13–5)}$$

In this instance, RR_D represents the required legal reserve ratio for transaction (demand) accounts, and RR_T is the required legal reserve ratio for time and savings deposits. *CASH* and *TIME* represent the amounts of additional currency and coin and time and savings deposits the public wishes to hold for each dollar of new transaction deposits they receive, and *EXR* stands for the quantity of excess reserves depository institutions desire to hold for precautionary purposes out of each dollar of new transaction deposits. The largest amount of transaction deposits and loans that the banking system can create, assuming all of the above drains of funds occur, would be given by:

$$\frac{1}{RR_D + CASH + EXR + RR_T \times TIME} \times \text{Excess reserves} = \text{Maximum volume of new deposits and loans} \quad \textbf{(13–6)}$$

To illustrate the use of this formula, assume that depository institutions have just received an additional $1 million in excess reserves from some source outside the banking system.

(One possible source is the central bank lowering deposit reserve requirements or buying securities from the public.) We further assume that, for each new dollar of transaction deposits received, the public will convert $0.25 into pocket money (*CASH* = 0.25), and $0.60 will be placed in time and savings deposits (*TIME* = .60). Further, suppose depository institutions elect to hold $0.05 of every new checkable deposit dollar received as excess reserves *(EXR* = 0.05)* to protect against future contingencies. The reserve requirement on transaction deposits (*RR$_D$*) is assumed to be 10 percent, and on time and savings deposits (*RR$_T$*), 3 percent. Thus, the maximum amount of new deposits and loans that depository institutions as a group can create with $1 million in excess reserves is calculated as follows:

$$\frac{1}{0.10 + 0.25 + 0.05 + (0.03 \times 0.60)} \times \$1 \text{ million} = \frac{1}{0.418} \times \$1 \text{ million}$$

$$= 2.39 \times \$1 \text{ million}$$

$$= \$2.39 \text{ million in new deposits and loans}$$

Clearly, the deposit multiplier is far smaller when we allow for the conversion of checkable deposits into currency, coin, and savings deposits, and when banks and other depository institutions are unwilling to lend all of their excess reserves. This would appear to be good news for the central bank charged with controlling the growth of the money supply. A numerically small deposit multiplier implies that the banking system will not be able to significantly increase the size of the deposit money supply unless the supply of excess reserves is also greatly increased.

Unfortunately the existence of cash drains, time and savings deposits, and other reserve-absorbing factors, while reducing the size of the deposit multiplier, also makes forecasting deposit flows much more difficult. The central bank must be constantly alert to shifts in the public's demand (preferences) for currency and coin and savings deposits as well as to the changing demands of depository institutions for excess reserves. If the central bank cannot accurately forecast changes in the public's money preferences, control of the money and credit supply will be less precise, so that the achievement of economic goals will be much more difficult for a central bank.

The Money Multiplier

Although the concept of the deposit multiplier is useful for some purposes, central bankers are usually more interested in a related concept known as the **money multiplier,** which defines the relationship between the size of the money supply (including deposits, currency and coin, and other readily spendable funds) and the size of the total reserve base available to depository institutions. The money multiplier is defined as follows:

$$\text{Money multiplier} = \frac{1 + \text{CASH}}{\text{RR}_D + \text{CASH} + \text{EXR} + (\text{RR}_T \times \text{TIME})} \quad \textbf{(13–7)}$$

The terms *CASH, EXR, RR$_D$, RR$_T$* and *TIME* are defined as they were in the deposit multiplier formula.

We note that the money multiplier differs from the deposit multiplier only in the addition of *CASH*—the proportion of new transaction deposits the public desires to hold in the form of currency and coin—to the numerator of the multiplier ratio. This change is made because currency and coin held by the public also forms an important component of the money supply and must be accounted for in measuring how fast the money supply grows

The U.S. money supply and the monetary base are key indicators for the economy and the Federal Reserve System and are actively followed on such Web sites as *www.stls.frb.org/research* and *www.federalreserve.gov/releases*

over time. With the rapid spread of coin-operated machines, the amount of currency and coin outstanding has been growing faster than the volume of regular checking accounts.

Another important point to note about currency and coin is that fluctuations in the volume held by the public have a direct bearing on the reserves held by depository institutions, affecting both the size and rate of growth of transaction accounts and reserves. If the public desires to hold less pocket money, the excess currency and coin typically is redeposited in transaction accounts, increasing both reserves and demand deposits. Recognizing this important link between currency and bank reserves, economists have developed the concept of the **monetary base,** which is simply the sum of legal reserves plus the amount of currency and coin held by the public.

Why is the monetary base important? It is one of the principal determinants of the nation's money supply. Specifically,

$$\text{Money multiplier} \times \text{Monetary base} = \text{Money supply}$$

or,

$$\frac{1 + \text{CASH}}{\text{RR}_\text{D} + \text{CASH} + \text{EXR} + (\text{RR}_\text{T} \times \text{TIME})} \times \frac{\text{Monetary}}{\text{base}} = \frac{\text{Money}}{\text{supply}} \quad \textbf{(13–8)}$$

We may use this formula as a device to estimate the size of the money multiplier. For example, in August 2001 the U.S. monetary base was about \$615 billion and the sum of transaction deposits (e.g., demand deposits, NOWs, Super NOWs, and travelers' checks) and currency and coin held outside banks stood at \$1,143 billion. The money multiplier for transaction accounts was as follows:

$$\text{Money multiplier} = \$1,143 \text{ billion}/\$615 \text{ billion} = 1.86$$

On average, each \$1 increase in the monetary base resulted in a rise in the narrowly defined (transaction-based) U.S. money supply of about \$1.86. This is one reason the monetary base is often referred to as *high-powered money;* a change in the base, working through the money multiplier, produces a magnified change in the nation's money supply.

The monetary base–money multiplier relationship identifies the most important factors that explain changes in the money supply, and it also helps us understand how a central bank like the Federal Reserve System can influence the money and credit creation process. In the United States, the Fed is one of the principal determinants of the size of the monetary base, along with the public and the U.S Treasury. It can increase or decrease the total supply of reserves to change the size of that base. Alternatively, the Fed may choose merely to offset actions taken by the public or the Treasury to keep the size of the monetary base unchanged. Finally, the central bank can change the required reserve ratios behind transaction (RR_D) and time (RR_T) deposits, which will affect the magnitude of the money multiplier. Occasionally, when the central bank wishes to exert a potent impact on economic and financial conditions, it makes changes in *both* the monetary base and the money multiplier. In the next chapter, we take a close look at the tools the Federal Reserve System uses to influence the size of the monetary base, the money multiplier, and, ultimately, the nation's supply and cost of money and credit.

Questions *to Help You Study*

15. What is/are the principal target(s) of monetary policy?

16. What are *legal reserves? Required reserves? Excess reserves?* Why are these concepts important?

17. Why are deposit-type intermediaries able to create money? What factors increase the amount of deposits the banking system can create with any given injection of new reserves?

18. What factors *reduce* the *money-creating abilities of the banking system?*

19. In what ways can the Federal Reserve System or any central bank influence the *money and credit creation process?*

20. Why should a central bank like the Federal Reserve worry about money and credit growth?

Summary of the Chapter

In this chapter, we have examined the important roles played by *central banks* in the global financial system and the economy.

- Central banks must function to control the money and credit supply, maintain stable conditions in the financial markets, serve as a lender of last resort to aid financial institutions in trouble, and maintain and improve the mechanism for making payments for goods and services.

- In most industrialized countries, central banking is *goal-oriented,* aimed principally at the major economic goals of full employment, reasonable stability in the prices of goods and services, sustainable economic growth, and a stable balance-of-payments position with the rest of the world. In the Western world, central banks operate to achieve the foregoing goals principally by working in the *private financial marketplace*, influencing credit conditions but leaving to private borrowers and lenders the basic decision of whether to create credit, borrow, and spend.

- Central banks appear to influence the spending, saving, and borrowing decisions of millions of individuals and businesses through at least five interrelated *channels*—the cost and availability of credit, the volume and rate of growth of the money supply, the market value of assets held by the public, the relative prices of world currencies, and the public's expectations regarding domestic and international economic conditions.

- The central bank of the United States is the *Federal Reserve System,* whose chief administrative body is the *Board of Governors* which controls such important policy tools as deposit reserve requirements, margin requirements on purchasing stocks and other securities, and changes in the discount rate on loans made by the Fed to depository institutions.

- Another important policy-making unit within the Federal Reserve System is the *Federal Open Market Committee (FOMC),* composed of the seven members of the Federal Reserve Board and the presidents of the 12 Federal Reserve Banks, which oversees the use of the Fed's chief monetary policy tool—open market operations.

- The 12 *Federal Reserve banks* represent the Fed's regional presence across the United States. These banks supervise private banks and financial holding companies within their individual districts, decide which depository institutions can borrow reserves from the Fed, and provide such services as clearing and collecting checks, shipping currency and coin, wiring funds to effect payments, and the safekeeping of securities.

- Each Federal Reserve bank also serves as a *fiscal agent* for the U.S. government and performs such services as dispensing and collecting the government's funds, selling and redeeming government securities, and helping to maintain an orderly marketplace so the federal government can borrow and refinance its debt.

- The Federal Reserve's most critical task in the financial markets today is the conduct of *monetary policy* in order to achieve the nation's economic goals. Today the Fed primarily targets market interest rates by manipulating the volume of reserves available to the banking system, which, in turn, affect the supply of deposits and money through the *deposit* and *money multipliers*. By creating or absorbing excess reserves available to depository institutions the central bank can impact the growth and cost of money and credit and, ultimately, the economy as a whole.

Key Terms

Central bank, *356*

Federal Reserve System, *356*

Board of Governors, *366*

Federal Open Market Committee (FOMC), *367*

Federal Reserve bank, *368*

Member banks, *369*

Transparency, *371*

Fiscal agent, *373*

Monetary policy, *373*

Legal reserves, *375*

Required reserves, *375*

Excess reserves, *375*

Deposit multiplier, *375*

Money multiplier, *377*

Monetary base, *378*

Problems

1. Which *channel* of central bank policy do each of the following events or situations represent?
   a. Stock prices decline rapidly following an increase in market interest rates.
   b. Recent speeches by central bank officials have cautioned the public about an apparently excessive rise in debt-financed spending.
   c. Several major corporations were recently denied direct loans by their principal banks.
   d. Following a heavy purchase of pounds by the Bank of England, that bank moves to offset the domestic effects of the purchase by slightly tightening credit conditions.
   e. Concerned about the recent increase in checkable deposits, the central bank moves to increase the proportion of legal reserves that depository institutions must post behind these deposits.

2. Which roles of central banks are described below?
   a. Shipments of currency are being made to banks in the region due to unusually heavy withdrawals by the public.
   b. Several banks in the region are being subjected to a follow-up examination due to problems unearthed by central bank examiners on a visit last month.
   c. Unexpectedly heavy demand for funds by the public associated with a decline in stock prices resulted in a significant increase in depository institutions' seeking loans from the central bank.
   d. Concerned over an apparent increase in the cost of living (consumer price index) and an above-average rate of growth in transaction deposits, the central bank moves to slow the latter through a combination of restrictive policy-directed actions in the financial markets.
   e. Dealers in government securities suddenly face a shortage of available loans and a rise in borrowing costs, which the central bank moves to counteract immediately.

3. Suppose the public wishes to hold $0.40 in pocket money (currency and coin) and $0.15 in excess reserves for each new dollar of transaction money received. If reserve requirements on transaction deposits and time and savings deposits are 3 percent, what is

the size of the transaction deposit multiplier? The money multiplier? Suppose $5 million in new excess reserves appear in the banking system. How much will be created in the form of new deposits and loans?

Total legal reserves currently amount to $40 billion, while currency and coin in public hands total $160 billion. The narrowly defined (transaction) money supply is $525 billion. How large is the money multiplier?

4. A bank holds $130 million in the form of transaction and time and savings deposits. Its reserve deposit at the Federal Reserve bank during the current reserve maintenance period contains a daily average balance of $0.40 million for several weeks running. Calculate its required reserves and excess reserves if deposits are subject to a 5 percent legal reserve requirement. Now suppose that the bank elects to buy $1 million in Treasury bills from the Fed. Do you see any problems with this?

5. Suppose that legal reserve requirements imposed on all public deposits held by depository institutions increase from 10 to 15 percent. What change occurs in the transaction deposit multiplier? How would this change affect the maximum volume of new deposits and loans that the entire banking system could create? Would there be any impact on the money multiplier? Under what circumstances?

6. If the reserve requirement applicable to the deposits held by all depository institutions in the financial system is reduced from 10 percent to 5 percent, how does the transaction deposit multiplier change? Would there be a shift in the maximum volume of new deposits and loans that could be generated inside the banking system? How do you know?

7. Suppose the central bank injects $15 million in new reserves into the banking system and that the current legal reserve requirement on deposits held by the banking system is 8 percent. Moreover, the banking system is perfectly efficient and there are no leakages of funds from that system except for the current legal reserve requirement. Please set up an EXCEL spreadsheet that shows how much in total required reserves and new deposits can be created in this banking system as a result of the injection of the $15 million in new legal reserves.

Now suppose the central bank subsequently withdraws $20 million in legal reserves from this same banking system. What level of deposits and legal reserves would ultimately result? Please demonstrate on your EXCEL spreadsheet.

8. Please identify the key terms and concepts presented in this chapter whose description or definition appears below.

   a. An agency of government that controls money and credit growth and monitors the condition of the financial system.
   b. The central bank of the United States.
   c. Chief policy-making and administrative body within the Federal Reserve System.
   d. Chief group within the Federal Reserve System for setting money and credit policy.
   e. One of 12 regional financial institutions chartered by the U.S. Congress.
   f. Banks that have joined the Federal Reserve System and bought stock in the Federal Reserve banks.
   g. Services supplied by the central bank to the government.
   h. An effort made by central banks to influence the cost and availability of credit in order to achieve the nation's economic goals.
   i. The volume of assets depository institutions are required to hold based upon central bank rules.
   j. Total legal reserves less required reserves.
   k. Volume of new deposit creation from a specific volume of excess reserves.

l. Ratio of the size of the money supply relative to the total reserve base of depository institutions.

m. Sum of legal reserves in the banking system.

Questions about the Web and the Money and Capital Markets

1. If you wanted to find detailed information about one of the more than 100 central banks around the world, how could you use the Web to help you get that information?

2. Where on the Web would you go to find out more details about the Federal Reserve System?

3. Using the Web as your key research tool, what is the principal governing body for the Bank of England? the Bank of Japan? the European Central Bank? How do these central banks seem to differ in major ways from the Federal Reserve System?

Selected References

Board of Governors of the Federal Reserve System, "Monetary Policy Report to the Congress." *Federal Reserve Bulletin,* March 2000, pp. 103-31.

Carlson, Keith M. "Money, Inflation, and Economic Growth: Some Updated Reduced Form Results and Their Implications." *Review,* Federal Reserve Bank of St. Louis, April 1980.

Cukierman, Alex. *Central Bank Strategies, Credibility and Independence.* Cambridge, MA: MIT Press, 1992.

Faust, Jon. *Whom Can We Trust to Run the Fed? Theoretical Support for the Founders' Views.* International Finance Discussion Papers, K. 7. Board of Governors of the Federal Reserve System, April 1992.

Rupert, Peter; Martin Schindler; Andrei Shevchen Ko; and Randall Wright. "The Search-Theoretic Approach to Monetary Economics: A Primer." *Economic Review,* Federal Reserve Bank of Kansas City, Quarter 4, 2000, pp. 10-28.

Stevens, Ed. "Beyond Zero: Transparency in the Bank of Japan's Monetary Policy." *Economic Commentary,* Federal Reserve Bank of Cleveland, March 15, 2001.

Wallace, Neil, and Ruilin Zhow. "A Model of a Currency Shortage." *Journal of Monetary Economics* XL, no. 3 (December 1997), pp. 555-72.

Wright, Randall. "Search, Evolution, and Money." *Journal of Economic Dynamics and Control* XIX, no. 2 (January-February 1995), pp. 181-206.

Chapter **Fourteen**

The Tools and Goals of Central Bank Monetary Policy

Learning Objectives in This Chapter

- You will understand how the policy tools available to the Federal Reserve and other central banks around the world really work in carrying out a nation's money and credit policies and in affecting the cost and availability of loanable funds.

- You will explore the strengths and weaknesses of the monetary policy tools used by the Fed and other central banks to achieve their objectives.

- You will discover how the Federal Reserve System controls credit and interest rate levels inside the United States.

- You will see the various ways in which central bank policy actions affect a nation's economic goals of achieving full employment, controlling inflation, sustaining adequate economic growth, and achieving a stable balance-of-payments position.

What's in This Chapter? Key Topics Outline

Tools of Central Banking

General and Selective Credit Controls

Reserve Requirements and the Discount Rate: Effects and Limitations

Open Market Operations: Nature, Types, and Impact

Policy Tools Used by Central Bankers around the World

Interest-Rate Targeting and the Federal Funds Rate

Economic Goals of the Fed and Other Central Banks

Central Bank Inflation Targeting

Goal Trade-offs and Monetary Policy Limitations

All central banks have one or more policy tools, such as reserve requirements, lending (discount) rates, and open market operations, to carry out their monetary policy objectives. And there is great variety around the world as to what tools are being used by any given central bank. However, among the prominent trends in this area is a general movement away from non-market-oriented tools to those that interact with the private marketplace, such as open market operations.

It's easy to find out which tools any given central bank has at its disposal and is using at the present time. Simply dial up the name of a central bank that interests you and find out what tools they normally use to carry out money and credit policy and who has authority over the use of those tools. Among the most interesting today in this respect are the banks of Canada, New Zealand, and Great Britain (the Bank of England) who have recently changed their set of policy tools and are experimenting with new policy approaches. Type in their names on your Web search engine and take a look at the unique changes recently adopted by these powerful central banks.

INTRODUCTION

As we discussed in the preceding chapter, central banks like the Federal Reserve System have been given the task of regulating the money and credit system in order to achieve economic goals. Prominent among these goals are the achievement of full employment, a stable price level, sustainable economic growth, and a stable balance-of-payments position with the rest of the world. As recent experience has demonstrated, these objectives are not easy to achieve and frequently conflict. Still, the central bank has powerful policy tools at its disposal with which to pursue these economic goals. Our purpose in this chapter is to examine the policy tools available to the Federal Reserve (and many other central banks as well) in carrying out its task of controlling the supply of credit and affecting the cost of borrowed funds in order to achieve the nation's economic goals.

GENERAL VERSUS SELECTIVE CREDIT CONTROLS

To change the volume of reserves available to depository institutions for lending and investing and to influence interest rates in the economy, the Federal Reserve System (as well as other central banks) uses a variety of policy tools. Some of these tools are **general credit controls,** which affect the entire banking and financial system. Included in this list are reserve requirements, the discount rate, and open market operations. A second set of policy tools may be labeled **selective credit controls** because they affect specific groups or sectors of the financial system. Moral suasion and margin requirements on the purchase of listed securities are examples of selective credit controls.

GENERAL CREDIT CONTROLS OF THE FED

Reserve Requirements

Since the 1930s in the United States, the Federal Reserve Board has had the power to vary the amount of required legal reserves that member banks must hold behind the deposits they receive from the public, as we saw earlier in Chapters 11 and 13. With passage of the

Depository Institutions Deregulation and Monetary Control Act (DIDMCA) in 1980, non-member banks and other depository financial institutions (including credit unions and savings and loan associations) were required to conform to the deposit **reserve requirements** set by the Fed. Early in the Fed's history, it was believed that the primary purpose of reserve requirements was to safeguard the public's deposits. Most recently, we have come to realize that their principal use is to give the central bank a powerful tool for emergency situations. Indeed, reserve requirements are probably the most potent policy tool the Federal Reserve System has at its disposal today. However, changes in reserve requirements are a little-used tool, as we will soon see, and recently, reserve requirements have been reduced in the United States and eliminated in some other nations (for example, Canada, New Zealand, and the United Kingdom).

Effects of a Change in Deposit Reserve Requirements

A change in deposit reserve requirements has at least *three* different effects on the financial system. First, it *changes the deposit multiplier* (or coefficient of expansion), which affects the amount of deposits and new loans the banking system can create for any given injection of new reserves. A change in reserve requirements also *affects the size of the money multiplier,* as we saw in the preceding chapter, influencing the rate of increase in the money supply. If the Fed increases reserve requirements, the deposit multiplier and the money multiplier are *reduced,* slowing the growth of money, deposits, and loans. On the other hand, a decrease in reserve requirements increases the size of both the deposit multiplier and the money multiplier. In this instance, each dollar of additional reserves will lead to accelerated growth in money, deposits, and loans.

Second, a change in reserve requirements affects the *mix* between excess and required legal reserves. Suppose all depository institutions are fully loaned up and excess reserves are zero. If reserve requirements are *reduced,* a portion of what were required reserves now becomes excess reserves. Depository institutions will soon convert all or a portion of these newly created excess reserves into loans and investments, expanding the money supply. Similarly, if all institutions are fully loaned up, with zero excess reserves, an *increase* in reserve requirements will mean that some depository institutions will be short required legal reserves. These institutions will be forced to sell securities, cut back on loans, and borrow reserves from other financial institutions to meet their reserve requirements. The money supply will grow more slowly and may even decline.

Third, *interest rates* also respond to a change in reserve requirements. A move by the central bank toward higher reserve requirements may soon lead to higher interest rates, particularly in the money market, as depository institutions scramble to cover any reserve deficiencies. Credit becomes less available and more costly. In contrast, a lowering of reserve requirements tends to bring interest rates down and increase investment spending and incomes. Flush with excess reserves, depository institutions are willing to make more loans at lower interest rates, and fewer institutions will have to sell securities or borrow to meet their reserve requirements.

An Illustration   Exhibit 14–1 illustrates the effects of changes in reserve requirements. Suppose depository institutions are required to keep 10 percent of their deposits in legal reserves: $100 of legal reserves will then be needed to support each $1,000 in deposits. If there is sufficient demand for loanable funds, institutions will probably loan or invest the remaining $900. Suppose that the Federal Reserve increases reserve requirements from 10 to 15 percent. As a result, more legal reserves are necessary to support the same volume of deposits, and institutions have a $50 reserve deficit for each $1,000 of deposits. This deficit may be covered by selling loans or investment securities, borrowing funds, or reducing deposits.

EXHIBIT 14–1   **Effects of Changes in Reserve Requirements on Deposits, Loans, and Investments**

With a 10 percent reserve requirement, $100 of reserves is needed to support each $1,000 of deposits.

Depository Institution			
Assets		*Liabilities*	
Loans and		Deposits	$1,000
investments	$ 900		
Legal reserves	100		
Required	100⌉		
Excess	0⌋		
	$1,000		$1,000

Increase in reserve requirements:

If required reserves are increased from 10 to 15 percent, more reserves are needed against the same volume of deposits. Any deficiencies (negative excess reserves) must be covered by liquidating loans and investments or by borrowing.

Depository Institution			
Assets		*Liabilities*	
Legal		Deposits	$1,000
reserves	$ 100		
Required	150⌉		
Excess	−50⌋		
Loans and			
investments	900		
	$1,000		$1,000

Decrease in reserve requirements:

If required reserves are reduced from 10 to 8 percent, excess reserves are created which can be loaned to the public or invested in securities.

Depository Institution			
Assets		*Liabilities*	
Legal		Deposits	$1,000
reserves	$ 100		
Required	80⌉		
Excess	20⌋		
Loans and			
investments	900		
	$1,000		$1,000

On the other hand, suppose required reserves are lowered from 10 to 8 percent. There are now $20 in excess reserves for each $1,000 in deposits, and that excess can be loaned or invested, creating new deposits. We should note that *total* legal reserves available to the banking system are *not* affected by changes in reserve requirements. A shift in reserve requirements affects only the *mix* of legal reserves between required and excess.

Current Levels of Reserve Requirements

In the United States, reserve requirements are imposed by the Federal Reserve Board on all depository institutions that are federally insured or eligible to apply for federal deposit insurance. Three types of deposits are, potentially at least, subject to legal reserve requirements:

1. *Transaction accounts,* which are deposits used to make payments by negotiable or transferable instruments and include regular checking accounts, NOW accounts, and any account subject to automatic transfer of funds.

EXHIBIT 14–2

Reserve Requirements of Depository Institutions (Percent of Deposits)

Source: Board of Governors of the Federal Reserve System, *Federal Reserve Bulletin,* February 2002, Table 1.15.

Type of Deposit and Deposit Interval	Percentage Reserve Requirement	Permissible Statutory Range
Net transaction accounts:		
$0–$42.8 million	3%	3%
Over $42.8 million	10	8–14
Nonpersonal time deposits:		
Original maturity of:		
Less than 1½ years	0	0–9
1½ years or more	0	0–9
Eurocurrency liabilities:		
All types	0	None

Note: Required reserves must be held in deposits with the Federal Reserve banks or in vault cash. Nonmember institutions may maintain reserve balances with a Federal Reserve bank indirectly on a pass-through basis with certain approved institutions. Depository institutions subject to reserve requirements include commercial banks, mutual savings banks, savings and loan associations, credit unions, agencies and branch offices of foreign banks, and Edge Act corporations that offer checkable deposits or business time deposits.

2. *Nonpersonal time deposits,* which are interest-bearing time deposits—including savings deposits and money market deposit accounts (MMDAs)—held by businesses and governmental units but not individuals.

3. *Eurocurrency liabilities,* which are borrowings of deposits from banks and bank branches located outside the United States.

As shown in Exhibit 14–2, the current reserve requirements on transaction accounts of $42.8 million or less is 3 percent, and the net amount of transaction deposits over $42.8 million is subject to a 10 percent reserve requirement.[1] Time and savings deposits currently carry *no* reserve requirements, although the Federal Reserve Board could impose new reserve requirements on these deposits at any time. Average reserve requirements usually have been higher on transaction accounts than on time and savings accounts because transaction balances are considered to be less stable than time and savings deposits.

The largest *depository institutions* carry the heaviest reserve requirements. This is due to the fact that larger financial institutions hold the deposits of thousands of smaller deposit intermediaries. The failure of a large depository institution can send shock waves through the entire financial system and threaten the economic viability of many other institutions as well.

Changes in reserve requirements can be used to carry out major shifts in government economic policy. The reserve requirement tool is exceedingly powerful, so that even a small change affects hundreds of millions of dollars in legal reserves. Moreover, it is an inflexible tool. Required reserve ratios cannot be changed frequently because this would disrupt the banking system. Not surprisingly, changes in reserve requirements do not occur very often, averaging no more than once every two or three years since World War II.

[1]The Federal Reserve Board is empowered to vary reserve requirements on transaction accounts over $42.8 million between 8 and 14 percent. The $42.8 million dividing line (known as *the tranche*) is indexed and changes each calendar year by 80 percent of the percentage change in total transaction accounts of all depository institutions during the previous year ended June 30. In addition, the Garn-St Germain Depository Institutions Act of 1982 stipulated that some minimum amount of reservable liabilities (transaction accounts, nonpersonal time deposits, and Eurocurrency liabilities) of each depository institution be subject to a zero reserve requirement, adjusted by the Federal Reserve Board each year by 80 percent of the percentage increase in total reservable liabilities. By 2002, this zero reserve requirement base had been expanded to $5.5 million.

Today in the United States, legal reserves apply only to checkable-type deposits and are being gradually reduced. Depository institutions have also found innovative new ways (such as "sweep accounts" that temporarily move customer funds out of a deposit account subject to reserve requirements) to lower their required reserve levels. Indeed, most depositories now meet their reserve requirements by holding vault cash rather than keeping large balances at the Federal Reserve banks. Recently, the new European Central Bank (ECB) imposed a 2 percent reserve requirement on the short-term deposits and debt of financial institutions subject to its authority. Unlike the Federal Reserve, however, the ECB pays interest on required reserve balances.

Changes in the Federal Reserve's Discount Rate

Any depository institution that accepts transaction accounts or nonpersonal time deposits and holds a legal reserve account at the Fed may borrow reserves from the discount window of the Federal Reserve bank in its region. The Fed's Regulation A states, however, that these loans must be a *temporary* source of funds. In fact, Federal Reserve regulations require depository institutions to alternate their borrowings from the discount window with drawings from other sources, such as the federal funds market. Frequent borrowing is discouraged and may be penalized with a higher interest rate.

The **discount rate** is the annual percentage interest charge levied against those institutions choosing to borrow from the Fed. The board of directors of each Federal Reserve bank votes to determine what the discount rate should be in its region of the country. However, the Federal Reserve Board in Washington, DC, must approve the rate charged in each of the 12 Federal Reserve districts. As shown in Exhibit 14–3, the basic rate on short-term loans of reserves early in 2002 was 1.25 percent. Depository institutions with marked seasonal changes in deposits or those with long-term (extended) liquidity problems could apply for loans at interest rates ranging from 1.70 percent to 2.20 percent, depending upon seasonal pressures, how long funds are needed, and market conditions.

Borrowing and Repaying Discount Window Loans

Depository institutions that borrow regularly at the discount window keep a signed loan authorization form at the Federal Reserve bank in their district and keep U.S. government securities or other acceptable collateral on deposit there. When a loan is needed, the officer responsible for managing the borrowing institution's legal reserve position contacts the district Federal Reserve bank and requests that the necessary funds be deposited in that institution's reserve account.

In Exhibit 14–4, we illustrate the borrowing process by supposing that a depository institution has requested a loan of $1 million and the Fed has agreed to make the loan. The borrowing bank receives an increase in its account, Reserves Held at Federal Reserve Bank, of $1 million. At the same time, the bank's liability account, Bills Payable, increases by $1 million. On the Federal Reserve bank's balance sheet, the loan is entered as an increase in Bank Reserves of $1 million—a liability of the Federal Reserve System—and also as an increase in a Fed asset account, Discounts and Advances. When the loan is repaid, the transaction is reversed.

Quite clearly, borrowings from the Fed's discount window *increase* the total reserves available to the banking system. Repayments of those borrowings cause total reserves to *fall*.

Effects of a Discount Rate Change

Most observers today believe that at least *three* effects follow from a change in the Federal Reserve's discount rate or in the lending rates of most other central banks. One is the *cost*

EXHIBIT 14–3

The Discount Rates Charged by the Federal Reserve Banks on Loans to Depository Institutions (Percent per Annum)

Source: Board of Governors of the Federal Reserve System, *Federal Reserve Bulletin,* February 2002, Table 1.14.

Type of Loan	Short-Term Adjustment Credit	Seasonal Credit	Extended Credit Borrowing
Discount rates	1.25%	1.70%	2.20%

Note: Credit at a flexible rate somewhat above existing market rates may be extended for longer periods of time after the first 30 days of borrowing when a particular borrowing institution needs support due to exceptional circumstances. Adjustment credit is available on a short-term basis to help depository institutions meet temporary needs for funds that cannot be met through reasonable alternative sources. Seasonal credit is available to help smaller depository institutions meet seasonal needs for funds that cannot be met through other lenders. Extended credit is available when an institution is experiencing difficulties adjusting to changing market conditions over a longer period of time.

EXHIBIT 14–4

Borrowing and Repaying Loans from the Central Bank

Borrowing from a Federal Reserve Bank:

Federal Reserve		Commercial Bank or Other Depository Institution	
Assets	*Liabilities*	*Assets*	*Liabilities*
Discounts +$1 million and advances	Bank +$1 million reserves	Reserves +$1 million held at Federal Reserve bank	Bills +$1 million payable

Repayment of Borrowings from the Fed:

Federal Reserve		Commercial Bank or Other Depository Institution	
Assets	*Liabilities*	*Assets*	*Liabilities*
Discounts −$1 million and advances	Bank −$1 million reserves	Reserves −$1 million held at Federal Reserve bank	Bills −$1 million payable

effect. An increase in the discount rate means that it is more costly to borrow reserves from the central bank than to use some other source of funds. Other things being equal, loans from the discount window and the total volume of borrowed reserves will decline. Conversely, a lower discount rate should result in an acceleration of borrowing from the Federal Reserve and more reserves flowing into the banking system.

Of course, the strength of the cost effect depends on the spread between the discount rate and other money market interest rates. If the Fed's rate remains below other interest rates even after it is increased, then it would still be cheaper to draw on the Fed for funds. There would be little reduction in loans from the discount window. This has happened frequently in recent years, with the discount rate usually lagging well behind other interest rates in the money market.

A second consequence of changes in the discount rate is called the *substitution effect.* A change in the discount rate usually causes other interest rates to change as well. This is due to the fact that the central bank is one source of borrowed reserves, but it is certainly not the only source. An increase in the discount rate, for example, makes borrowing from the Fed less attractive, but borrowing from other sources, such as the Eurodollar market, becomes relatively more attractive. Banks and other borrowers will shift their attention to these other markets, causing interest rates there to rise as well.

A lowering of the central bank's discount rate, on the other hand, frequently causes a downward movement in market interest rates. This happens because deposit-type financial institutions will begin borrowing more from the Federal Reserve, reducing the demand for credit in other segments of the financial marketplace.

The final effect of a discount rate change is called the *announcement effect.* The discount rate has a psychological impact on the financial markets because the central bank's lending rate is widely regarded as an indicator of monetary policy. If, for example, the Federal Reserve raises its discount rate, many observers regard this as a signal that the Fed is pushing for tighter credit conditions. Market participants may respond by reducing their borrowings and curtailing their spending plans.

For a more detailed overview of the discount windows and discount rates of the Federal Reserve Banks see especially www.frbdiscountwindow.org and www.chicagofed.org/discountwindow

Unfortunately, the psychological impact of the discount rate may work *against* the central bank as well as *for* it. It is quite likely, for example, that if the Federal Reserve raises its discount rate, borrowers will respond by accelerating their borrowings in an effort to secure the credit they need before interest rates move even higher. Such an action would thwart the Fed's objective of slowing the growth of borrowing and spending. Because of the possibility of *negative psychological effects,* the discount rate is changed infrequently and often lags behind interest rates in the open market. The Fed, however, sometimes makes a technical adjustment in the discount rate just to bring it closer into line with other interest rates. Even so, market participants may "read into" discount rate changes a new central bank policy position.

Since the middle of 1999 the Fed's discount rate has followed the federal funds interest rate (discussed earlier in Chapter 11). Each time the target federal funds rate—the Federal Reserve's principal policy target today—has been changed by the Federal Open Market Committee the discount rate has been moved in parallel fashion. Typically, the discount rate has been set half-a-point lower than the Fed funds rate. The result of this new policy has been to turn the discount rate and the discount window into a passive tool in the conduct of U.S. monetary policy. This new minimal role for the discount rate (plus the very small amount of borrowing recently taking place through the discount window) has led to proposals to eliminate this policy weapon. Yet, as the terrorist attacks in September 2001 demonstrated, access to the discount window can help to stabilize the economy in times of crisis and provide badly needed liquidity in a hurry. History teaches us that policy tools that may have little importance today can suddenly become important again in the future.

Questions *to Help You Study*

1. How does the *reserve requirement* tool affect the ability of deposit-type financial institutions to create money? What are the principal advantages and disadvantages of the reserve requirement tool?

2. How and why does a depository institution borrow from the central bank? Explain what happens when a central bank changes its *discount or lending rate.* What are the principal advantages and disadvantages of the discount policy tool?

3. Why do you think reserve requirements and discount rates are being phased out as policy tools by many central banks around the world? Are reserve requirements and the discount rate a general credit control or a selective credit control? Why?

Open Market Operations

The limitations of the discount rate and reserve requirement policy tools have led the Federal Reserve (and many other central banks as well) to rely more heavily in recent years upon **open market operations** to accomplish their goals. By definition, open market operations in the United States consist of buying and selling U.S. government and other securities by the Federal Reserve System to affect the quantity and growth of legal reserves and, ultimately, general credit conditions. Open market operations are the most flexible policy tool available to the Fed, suitable for fine-tuning the financial markets when this is necessary. Other central banks around the world may use different types of securities to buy or sell in conducting their open market operations. Among the more common financial instruments traded by many central banks today are bank deposits, derivative securities, and central bank debt. Open market operations are rapidly becoming the most popular tool of leading central banks around the globe. Recently, the new European Central Bank (ECB) was granted the open market tool; it selects which financial instruments can be used and under what terms and conditions, but the ECB's operations must be carried out through the central banks of its member countries.

Effects of Open Market Operations on Interest Rates

The open market tool has two major effects on the banking system and credit conditions. First, it has an *interest rate effect.* For example, in the United States, the Fed usually buys or sells a large quantity (several hundred million dollars worth) of government securities in the financial marketplace at any one time. If the Fed is *purchasing* securities, this adds additional demand for these securities in the market, which tends to increase their prices and lower their yields. In this case, interest rates decline. If the Federal Reserve is *selling* securities from its portfolio, this action increases the supply of securities available in the market, tending to depress their prices and raise their yields. In this case, interest rates tend to rise.

Effects of Open Market Operations on Reserves

The principal day-to-day effect of central bank open market operations is to change the level and growth of *legal reserves.* For example, a Federal Reserve *purchase* of government securities *increases* the reserves of the banking system and expands its ability to make loans and create deposits, increasing the growth of money and credit. In contrast, a *sale* of securities by the Federal Reserve *decreases* the level and growth of reserves and ultimately reduces the growth of money and credit. The impact of Federal Reserve open market operations on the reserve positions of depository institutions with accounts in the United States is illustrated in Exhibit 14–5.

Fed Purchases   In the top portion of Exhibit 14–5, we assume that the Fed is making *purchases* of U.S. government securities in the open market from either depository institutions, which keep their reserve accounts at the Federal Reserve banks, or from other institutions and individuals. In the case of purchases from depository institutions, the Federal Reserve System records the acquisition of securities in the System's asset account—U.S. securities—and pays for the securities by increasing the reserve accounts of the selling institutions. Thus, reserves of depository institutions at the Fed *rise,* while institutional holdings of securities fall by the same amount. Note that *both* total and excess reserves rise in the wake of a Fed purchase, assuming that depository institutions have no reserve deficiencies to begin with. With these extra reserves, additional loans can be made and deposits created that will have an expansionary impact on the availability of credit in the economy.

EXHIBIT 14–5   Central Bank Open Market Operations

The Federal Reserve Buys Securities

Open Market Purchase from a Bank or Other Deposit-Type Financial Institution:

Depository Financial Institution			Federal Reserve Bank			Effects
Assets		*Liabilities*	*Assets*		*Liabilities*	Total and excess legal reserves increase.
U.S. securities	−1,000		U.S. securities	+1,000	Reserves +1,000	
Reserves at Fed	+1,000					

Open Market Purchase not from a Depository Financial Institution:

Depository Financial Institution			Federal Reserve Bank			Effects
Assets		*Liabilities*	*Assets*		*Liabilities*	Total and excess legal reserves increase; deposits increase.
Reserves at Fed	+1,000	Deposits +1,000	U.S. securities	+1,000	Reserves +1,000	

The Federal Reserve Sells Securities

Open Market Sale to a Bank or Other Deposit-Type Financial Institution:

Depository Financial Institution			Federal Reserve Bank			Effects
Assets		*Liabilities*	*Assets*		*Liabilities*	Total and excess legal reserves decrease.
U.S. securities	+1,000		U.S. securities	−1,000	Reserves −1,000	
Reserves at Fed	−1,000					

Open Market Sale not to a Depository Financial Institution:

Depository Financial Institution			Federal Reserve Bank			Effects
Assets		*Liabilities*	*Assets*		*Liabilities*	Total and excess legal reserves decrease; deposits decrease.
Reserves at Fed	−1,000	Deposits −1,000	U.S. securities	−1,000	Reserves −1,000	

An expansionary effect also takes place when the Federal Reserve buys securities from an institution or individual other than a depository institution. Legal reserves increase, but total deposits—a component of the money supply—increase as well. Deposits rise because the central bank issues a check to pay for the securities it purchases, and that check will be deposited in some financial institution. Excess reserves rise, making possible an expansion of deposits and loans on the part of depository institutions. Note, however, that the rise in excess reserves is *less* in this case than would occur if the Fed bought securities only from depository institutions that maintain reserve accounts with the Federal Reserve banks. This is due to the fact that some of the new legal reserves created by the Fed purchase must be pledged as required reserves behind the newly created deposits. Therefore, Federal Reserve open market purchases of securities have *less* of an effect on total credit and deposit expansion if the Fed's transaction involves only nondeposit financial institutions and individuals.

Fed Sales   Central bank *sales* of securities *reduce* the growth of reserves, deposits, and loans. For example, shown in the bottom half of Exhibit 14–5, when the Federal Reserve sells U.S. government securities from its portfolio to a depository institution, that institution must pay for those securities by letting the Fed deduct the amount of the purchase from its reserve account. Both total reserves and excess reserves *fall*. If deposit institutions were fully loaned up with no excess reserves available, the open market sale would result in a reserve deficiency. Some institutions would be forced to sell loans and securities or borrow funds in order to bring in additional reserves, reducing the availability of credit.

The central bank may also sell securities to an individual or a nondeposit institution. As Exhibit 14–5 reveals, in this instance, *both* reserves and deposits fall. Credit becomes less available and usually more expensive.

How Open Market Operations Are Conducted in the United States

All trading in securities by the Federal Reserve System is carried out through the System's Trading Desk, located at the Federal Reserve Bank of New York. The Trading Desk is supervised by the manager of the System Open Market Account (SOMA), a vice president of the New York Fed. The SOMA manager's activities are, in turn, supervised and directed by the Federal Open Market Committee. All Fed security purchases and sales are made through a select list of primary U.S. government securities dealers who agree to buy or sell in amounts called for by the Trading Desk at the time the Fed wishes to trade. Many of these dealers are commercial banks that have securities departments. The rest are exclusively dealers in U.S. government and selected private securities.[2]

The Policy Directive   How does the SOMA manager decide whether or not to buy or sell securities in the open market on a given day? The manager is guided, first of all, by a *policy directive* issued to the Federal Reserve Bank of New York following the conclusion of each meeting of the Federal Open Market Committee (FOMC). The SOMA manager attends each FOMC meeting and participates in its policy discussions. He or she listens to the views of each member of the Federal Reserve Board and the Reserve bank presidents, who describe economic conditions in their region of the country. The manager also receives the benefit of a presentation by staff economists of the Federal Reserve Board that analyzes current economic and financial developments.

An example of a recent Federal Reserve policy directive to the SOMA manager is shown in Exhibit 14–6. This directive summarizes the Federal Reserve's view of current economic developments, particularly those that pertain to the growth of output in the economy and to movements in prices and employment. The FOMC asks the SOMA manager to use the open market policy tool in an effort to achieve a target range or level for a key money market interest rate—the average rate on federal funds loans. In the event that the federal funds rate drifts outside this range, the SOMA manager must notify the chairperson of the Federal Reserve Board for further instructions.

We note that the directive issued to the SOMA manager is extremely *general* in nature, giving specific targets or target ranges but recognizing the need for flexibility as market

---

[2]See Chapter 11 for a discussion of the characteristics and activities of primary security dealers. U.S. government securities held by the public are falling, forcing the Fed to consider trading other types of securities.

EXHIBIT 14–6
Domestic Policy Directive Issued to the Federal Reserve Bank of New York Following the Federal Open Market Committee Meeting, December 19, 2000

Source: *Federal Reserve Bulletin*, April 2001.

The information reviewed at this meeting provided evidence that economic activity might have slowed further in recent months. Consumer spending and business purchases of equipment and software had decelerated markedly after having registered extraordinary gains in the first half of the year. With final spending rising at a reduced rate, inventory overhangs had emerged in a number of goods-producing industries, most visibly in the motor vehicle sector. Manufacturing production had declined as a consequence. Evidence on core price inflation was mixed; by one measure, it appeared to be increasing very gradually but by another it had remained at a relatively subdued level.

Manufacturing payrolls changed little over the two months, and job gains in the construction, retail trade, and services industries were smaller than those of earlier in the year. With growth in the demand for labor slowing, initial claims for unemployment insurance continued to trend upward, and the civilian unemployment rate edged up to 4 percent in November.

At the conclusion of this discussion, the Committee voted to direct the Federal Reserve Bank of New York to execute transactions in the System Account in accordance with the following domestic policy directive:

> The Federal Open Market Committee seeks monetary and financial conditions that will foster price stability and promote sustainable growth in output. To further its long-run objectives, the Committee in the immediate future seeks conditions in reserve markets consistent with maintaining the federal funds rate at an average of around 6½ percent.
>
> Against the background of its long-run goals of price stability and sustainable economic growth and of the information currently available, the Committee believes that the risks are weighted mainly toward conditions that may generate economic weakness in the foreseeable future.
>
> Votes for this action: Messrs. Greenspan, McDonough, Broaddus, Ferguson, Gramlich, Guynn, Jordan, Kelley, Meyer, and Parry. Votes against this action: None.

conditions change. This is a reflection of the crude state of the art in trying to control credit market conditions. Many factors other than Federal Reserve operations affect interest rates and credit availability. Although the Federal Reserve can have a significant impact on the *direction* of change, it has considerable difficulty in trying to hit specific targets, especially interest rate and credit targets. The Federal Open Market Committee must be flexible and trust the SOMA manager's judgment in responding to daily conditions in the money market, which subsequently may be quite different from those anticipated when the FOMC held its last meeting.

For a more complete overview of the structure and operations of the Federal Open Market Committee (FOMC) and the SOMA manager see especially *www.federalreserve.gov/fomc*

The Conference Call As an added check on the decisions of the SOMA manager, a conference call between staff economists at the Federal Reserve Board, a member of the FOMC, and the SOMA manager is held each day before trading occurs. The SOMA manager updates those sitting in on the conference call on current conditions in the money market and then makes a recommendation on the type and volume of securities to be bought or sold that day. At this point, the conference call participants may make alternative recommendations. Usually, however, the SOMA manager's recommendation is taken and trading proceeds.

Types of Open Market Operations

There are four basic types of Federal Reserve open market operations. (See Exhibit 14–7.) The so-called *straight,* or *outright, transaction* refers to the sale or purchase of securities in which outright title passes to the buyer on a permanent basis. In this case, a permanent change occurs in the level of legal reserves, up or down. Thus, when the Federal Reserve wants to bring about a *once-and-for-all* change in reserves, it tends to use the straight, or outright, type of transaction.

In contrast, when the Fed wishes to have a *temporary* effect on bank reserves, it employs a *repurchase agreement* with a securities dealer. Under a repurchase agreement (RP), the Fed buys securities from dealers but agrees to sell them back after a few days.[3] The result is a temporary increase in legal reserves that will be reversed when the Fed sells the securities back to the dealers. Such RPs frequently are used during holiday periods or when factors are at work that have resulted in a temporary shortfall in reserves.

A good example of how the RP can be used to deal with temporary emergencies appeared in September 2001 when, in the wake of a terror attack on the United States, the Fed injected about $80 billion in additional liquidity into the U.S. financial system using repurchase agreements with primary security dealers. A week later as market conditions stabilized it withdrew most of these extra funds.

The Fed can also deal with a temporary excess quantity of reserves by using a matched-sale purchase transaction, commonly called a *reverse RP*. In this instance, the Fed agrees to sell securities to dealers for a brief period and then to buy them back. Frequently, when mail deliveries are slowed by weather or strikes, the result is a sharp increase in the volume of uncollected checks (float), giving banks and other depository institutions millions of dollars in excess reserves until the checks are cleared. The Fed can absorb these excess reserves using reverse RPs until the situation returns to normal.

The third type of open market operation is the *runoff*. The Federal Reserve may deal directly with the U.S. Treasury in acquiring and redeeming securities. Suppose the Fed has some maturing U.S. Treasury securities and wishes to replace them with new securities currently being offered by the Treasury in its latest public auction. The amount of securities that the Fed takes will *not* then be available to the public, reducing the quantity of securities sold in the marketplace. Other things being equal, this would tend to raise security prices and lower interest rates.[4]

On the other hand, the Fed may decide *not* to acquire new securities from the Treasury to replace those that are maturing. This would mean the Treasury would be forced to sell an increased volume of securities in the open market to raise cash in order to pay off the Fed. At the same time, the Treasury would draw funds from its deposits held at private banks, reducing bank reserves, to redeem the Fed's maturing securities. Other things being equal, security prices would fall and interest rates rise. Credit market conditions would tighten up. Moreover, the Federal Reserve saves on transactions costs (in the form of dealer fees) by dealing directly with the Treasury and not conducting a regular open market transaction through private security dealers.

Finally, the Fed also conducts purchases and sales of securities on behalf of foreign central banks and other official agencies and institutions that hold accounts with the New York Federal Reserve Bank, known as *agency operations*. The Fed may buy or sell securities from its own portfolio to accommodate these foreign accounts or merely act as an intermediary between the foreign accounts and security dealers. For example, suppose that the Federal Reserve Bank in New York has just received a request from the Bank of Japan to purchase U.S. government securities. That central bank has probably built up too much cash in its U.S. accounts and decides to earn some interest on that cash by buying some U.S. Treasury bonds. To pay for the securities, the Bank of Japan transfers a portion of its deposit at a U.S. bank to its deposit account at the New York Fed. The Fed's Trading Desk may contact private dealers and make the purchase on behalf of the Bank of Japan, crediting the dealers' banks for the purchase price of the securities and reducing the Bank of Japan's deposit at the Fed. In this case, the total reserves of the U.S. banking system do *not change,* falling initially but then rising back to their original levels.

---

[3]See Chapter 11 for an explanation of how these repurchase agreements are used as a source of funds for securities dealers.

[4]The Fed is prohibited by law from purchasing government securities directly from the Treasury Department out of concern that such transactions could lead to government abuse of Federal Reserve credit and result in serious inflation in the economy.

EXHIBIT 14–7

**Types of Federal
Reserve Open
Market Transactions**

Outright or Straight Open Market Transaction
(permanent change in the level of reserves held by depository institutions)

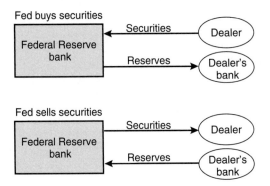

RP or Reverse RP Transaction
(temporary change in the level of reserves held by depository institutions)

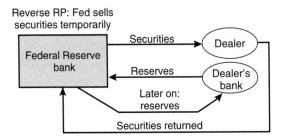

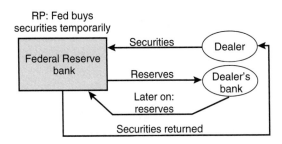

Run-Off Transaction
(permanent reduction in the level of reserves held by depository institutions)

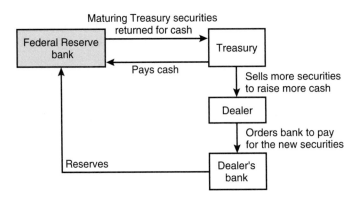

EXHIBIT 14–7
(Continued)

Agency Transaction
(may or may not affect the level of reserves held by depository institutions depending on the type of transaction)

A. First Type of Agency Transaction

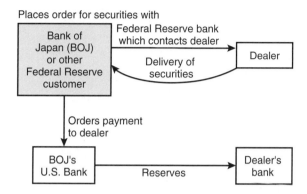

Net Effect: *No* change in total reserves held by all depository institutions as reserves merely shift from one depository institution to another; Fed acts only as a broker, contacting a dealer to complete the security transaction.

B. Second Type of Agency Transaction

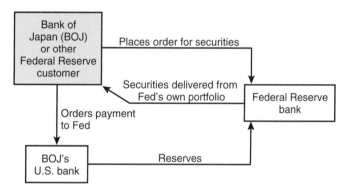

Net Effect: Total reserves of depository institutions fall in this particular transaction as payment for the securities acquired is made to the Fed; Fed acts as a dealer, itself.

However, the Fed may decide to sell the Bank of Japan securities from its *own* portfolio (that is "from System account"). In this case, bank reserves fall initially, as the Bank of Japan pays for its purchase, but do not rise again. The money received from this Fed sale is "locked up" within the Federal Reserve System and does not flow out to private banks. In general, sales of Federal Reserve-held securities to foreign accounts reduce U.S. bank reserves; purchases of securities from foreign accounts that go into the Fed's own security account increase U.S. bank reserves.

Goals of Open Market Operations: Defensive and Dynamic   In the use of any of its policy tools, the Federal Reserve, like other central banks, always has in mind the basic economic goals of full employment, a stable price level, sustainable economic growth, and a stable international balance-of-payments position for the United States. However, only a

Management Insight   The Open Market Policy Process in the United States

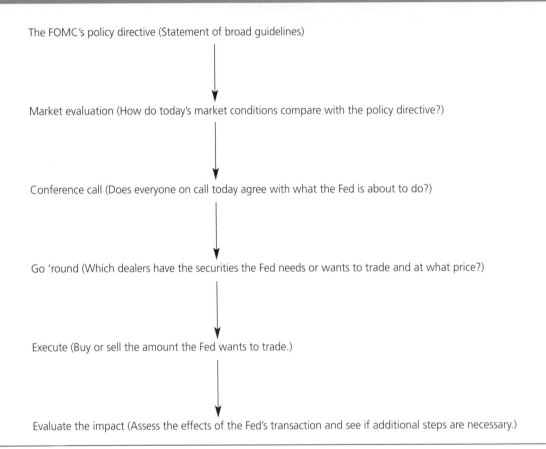

The FOMC's policy directive (Statement of broad guidelines)

Market evaluation (How do today's market conditions compare with the policy directive?)

Conference call (Does everyone on call today agree with what the Fed is about to do?)

Go 'round (Which dealers have the securities the Fed needs or wants to trade and at what price?)

Execute (Buy or sell the amount the Fed wants to trade.)

Evaluate the impact (Assess the effects of the Fed's transaction and see if additional steps are necessary.)

portion of the Federal Reserve's daily open market activity is directed toward those particular goals. The Fed is also responsible on a day-to-day basis for stabilizing the money and capital markets and avoiding sharp changes in interest rates to help keep the financial markets functioning smoothly. These technical adjustments in market conditions are often referred to as *defensive* open market operations. Their basic purpose is to preserve the *status quo* and to keep the present pattern of interest rates and credit availability about where it is.

For example, suppose that the Fed believes that the current level of reserves held by the banking system of about $38 billion is just right to hold interest rates and credit conditions where they are. However, due to changes in other factors affecting bank reserves (such as the public demanding more currency and coin from banks to spend over the holidays), total reserves in the system are expected to fall to $37 billion. The Fed is likely to buy about $1 billion in securities so that total reserves remain at $38 billion—a *defensive operation.*

In contrast, when the Federal Reserve is interested in the pursuit of broader economic goals, it engages in *dynamic* open market operations. These operations are designed to upset the status quo and to change interest rates and credit conditions to a level the Fed believes to be more consistent with its economic goals. For example, if the Fed believes the economy needs to grow faster to create more jobs, it may come to the conclusion that total reserves in the banking system must increase from $38 to $40 billion. In this case, the Fed's trading

International Focus   Policy Tools Used by Central Banks around the World

Different central banks around the world emphasize different policy tools. For example, the Bank of England (BOE) relies primarily upon purchases of British Treasury and commercial bills from discount houses to affect interest rates and the availability of credit. The BOE also may make changes in the basic lending rate that it charges borrowing banks and securities houses.

The Bank of Canada (BOC) focuses its energies mainly on the buying and selling of short-term Treasury bills and repurchase agreements. The Canadian central bank also impacts reserves in the banking system by moving government deposits between the BOC and private banks within the Canadian system. Canada's central bank phased out its use of legal reserve requirements in 1994.

The new European Central Bank (the ECB) may use a variety of open market instruments (including repurchase agreements, outright purchases and sales of securities, currency swaps, and the issuance of debt). The ECB also has the power to loan funds to financial institutions in need of liquidity and it has imposed reserve requirements on short-term deposits and other forms of short-term debt. However, the use of the ECB's open market policy tool is somewhat dispersed because the central banks of the European Community's member states actually carry out open market operations.

The Bank of Japan (BOJ) uses security trading, primarily in commercial bills but also increasingly in Japanese government securities, to influence domestic credit conditions. The BOJ makes loans to banks through its discount window. In several other Asian countries—Indonesia, Korea, Taiwan, Hong Kong, and the Philippines—central banks issue and trade in their own IOUs in order to control credit growth and influence economic conditions.

Central banks do not change their policy tools very often. However, with deregulation of financial markets and financial institutions becoming more alike all over the world, more and more central banks are choosing to work through the *private marketplace* to accomplish their goals, increasingly emphasizing the buying and selling of government and corporate financial instruments to change or maintain existing credit conditions. Such arbitrary, non-market-determined tools as interest rate and credit ceilings, currency (exchange-rate) controls, reserve requirements, and central bank loan or discount rates are increasingly being phased out. The discount (loan) windows of leading central banks today are more often used to relieve temporary stresses faced by individual financial institutions rather than to achieve broad policy goals.

desk is likely to launch an aggressive program of buying securities until reserve levels reach $40 billion. Open market operations have now become *dynamic,* not merely defensive.

The fact that open market operations are carried out for a wide variety of purposes makes it difficult to follow a central bank's daily transactions in the marketplace and to draw any firm conclusions about the direction of monetary policy. On any given day, the central bank may be buying or selling securities merely to defensively stabilize market conditions without any longer-term objectives in mind. The central bank is really a balance wheel in the financial system, supplying or subtracting reserves as needed on any given day. Although experienced central bank watchers find the daily pattern of open market operations meaningful, unless the investor possesses inside information on the motivation of central bank actions, it is exceedingly difficult to "read" daily open market operations. A longer-term view is usually needed to see the direction in which the central bank is trying to move the financial system.

SELECTIVE CREDIT CONTROLS USED BY THE FED

The discount rate, reserve requirements, and open market operations are often called *general credit controls* because each has an impact on the whole financial system. Another set of policy tools available to the Federal Reserve and other central banks, however, is more *selective* in its impact, focusing on particular sectors of the economy. Nevertheless, use of some of these selective tools can contribute toward the overall objectives of the central bank to minimize unemployment, stabilize prices, and sustain economic growth.

Moral Suasion by Central Bank Officials

A widely used selective policy tool is known as **moral suasion.** This refers to the use of "arm-twisting" or "jawboning" by central bank officials to encourage banks and other lending institutions to conform with the spirit of its policies. For example, if the Federal Reserve wishes to tighten credit controls and slow the growth of credit, Fed officials issue letters and public statements urging financial institutions operating in the United States to use more restraint in granting loans. These public statements may be supplemented by personal phone calls from top Federal Reserve officials to individual lending institutions, stressing the need for more conservative policies. Some central banks, such as the Bank of Japan, use the moral suasion tool as an important supplement to their other policy weapons.

Margin Requirements

To learn more about security margin requirements see such sources as *www.nyse.com*, *www.speculative bubble.com*, and *www.nasdr.com*

A selective credit control still under the exclusive control of the Federal Reserve Board is **margin requirements** on the purchase of stocks and convertible bonds and on short sales of those same securities. Margin requirements were enacted into law with passage of the Securities Exchange Act of 1934. This federal law limited the amount of credit that could be used as collateral for a loan. Regulations G, T, and U of the Federal Reserve Board prescribe a maximum loan value for marginable stocks, convertible bonds, and short sales. That maximum loan value is expressed as a specified percentage of the market value of the securities at the time they are used as loan collateral. The margin requirement on a regulated security, then, is simply the difference between its market value (100 percent) and the maximum loan value of that security.

For example, as shown in Exhibit 14–8, the current margin requirement on stock is 50 percent. This means that common and preferred stock can be purchased on credit with the stock itself used as collateral. However, the purchaser can borrow only up to a maximum of 50 percent of the stock's current market value. He or she must put up the remainder of the stock's purchase price in cash money.

As Exhibit 14–8 suggests, margin requirements are not often changed. In fact, the current U.S. margin requirements on stocks, convertible bonds, and short sales of these securities have remained unchanged since January 1974. Most observers of the financial markets believe that the imposition of margin requirements was unnecessary. These requirements arose out of the turmoil of the Great Depression, when many believed that speculative buying and selling of stocks had contributed to the U.S. economy's sudden collapse. This was

EXHIBIT 14–8 Federal Reserve Margin Requirements on Stocks, Convertible Bonds, and Short Sales (Percent of Market Value and Effective Date)

Security	March 11, 1968	June 8, 1968	May 6, 1970	Dec. 6, 1971	Nov. 24, 1972	Jan. 3, 1974
Margin stocks	70%	80%	65%	55%	65%	50%
Convertible bonds	50	60	50	50	50	50
Short sales	70	80	65	55	65	50

Note: Regulations G, T, and U published by the Board of Governors of the Federal Reserve System, in accordance with the Securities Exchange Act of 1934, limit the amount of credit to purchase or carry margin stocks when the securities to be purchased are used as collateral. Margin requirements specify the maximum loan value of the securities expressed as a percentage of their market value at the time a loan is made.

Source: Board of Governors of the Federal Reserve System, *Federal Reserve Bulletin,* February 2002, Table 1.36.

For a further review of the Federal Reserve's credit controls and policy-making see *www.kc.frb.org/fed101*

probably *not* the case, but margin requirements do ensure that a substantial amount of cash will be contributed by the buyer of securities, keeping borrowing against these securities within reasonable limits. One serious limitation of this selective tool is that it does *not* cover purchases of *all* types of stocks and bonds. For this reason, its future use as a tool of Federal Reserve monetary policy is likely to remain very limited.

Questions *to Help You Study*

4. Why are *open market operations* increasingly the most popular and frequently used monetary policy tool? What are the principal effects of open market operations on the financial system?

5. Describe the relationship between the SOMA manager and the FOMC. What is a *policy directive?* What types of policy targets does the Federal Reserve use?

6. Explain the difference between an *RP* and a *straight* (or outright) open market transaction. Why is each used? What is a *runoff?* An *agency* operation?

7. Explain the difference between *defensive* and *dynamic* open market operations.

8. What is *moral suasion?* Do you believe this tool can be effective?

9. Explain how *margin requirements* affect the financial system. Why were these requirements instituted by the U.S. Congress during the 1930s?

INTEREST-RATE TARGETING

The Federal Reserve and other central banks around the world have given increasing weight in recent years to targeting *the cost and availability of credit in the money market.* One reason is that central banks are charged with the responsibility of stabilizing conditions in the financial markets to assure a smooth flow of funds from savers (lenders) to borrowers. In addition, central banks must ensure that the government securities market functions smoothly so that adequate supplies of credit are available to security dealers and that the federal government can market its billions of dollars in debt securities without serious difficulty. But to what dimension of the money market does a central bank like the Federal Reserve pay the most attention today?

The Federal Funds Rate

As we saw earlier in Chapter 11, the money market indicator that usually feels the first impact from Federal Reserve policy moves is the *daily average interest rate on federal funds transactions.* Beginning in 1989 the Fed adopted a *federal funds interest rate targeting procedure*—the monetary policy approach it uses today. When the Fed sells securities, the supply of reserves available to depository institutions is reduced and, other things held equal, the Fed funds rate, which is the "price" of overnight borrowings of reserves in the banking system, tends to rise. On the other hand, a Federal Reserve purchase of securities increases available reserves to depository institutions, which tends to push the Fed funds rate down.

Recently, the Federal Reserve adopted a new policy of "openness" when it comes to announcing its target for the federal funds interest rate, letting the public know right away when it is moving the funds-rate target level. For example, in January 2001, following a meeting of the Federal Open Market Committee, the Fed announced that it was dropping its target for the federal funds interest rate from 6 percent to 5½ percent because the economy appeared to be slowing and inflation seemed to be under control. When the markets opened the next morning, the Fed funds rate moved quickly toward its new target level. A similar experience greeted the movement of the federal funds rate late in 2001 as the Federal Reserve battled a possible recession in the U.S. economy, made worse by tragic terrorist bombings in September of that year. On September 17, 2001, the Fed dropped the federal funds target rate one-half point to 3 percent in order to make it cheaper for individuals and institutions to raise more liquid funds and to increase public confidence as the New York Stock Exchange opened after the terrorist attacks of September 11th.

How is the Federal Reserve's Trading Desk able to maintain the federal funds rate at or close to its announced interest rate target? Exhibit 14–9 provides us with an illustration of the process. Suppose the Fed has targeted a Fed funds rate of 5 percent and the funds rate currently sits at the 5 percent level, where the total demand for reserves by depository institutions, represented by schedule *D*, in Exhibit 14–9, intersects the supply of total reserves, represented by schedule *S*, achieving an equilibrium rate of interest at *E*.

We note that the supply of total reserves consists of the sum of borrowed and nonborrowed reserves:

$$\text{Total reserves} = \text{Borrowed reserves} + \text{Nonborrowed reserves}$$

Borrowed reserves (labeled *BR* in Exhibit 14–9) are loans made to depository institutions by the Federal Reserve banks. **Nonborrowed reserves** are legal reserves that belong to depository institutions (labeled *SNBR* in Exhibit 14–9). Through open market operations the central bank impacts primarily nonborrowed reserves which, in turn, affect total reserves available to the banking system.

Now, suppose that depository institutions increase their demand for total reserves to *D'*. If the Federal Reserve does nothing to the supply of reserves, the Fed funds rate must rise above its current equilibrium 5 percent target level to accommodate the new higher level of demand for total reserves, perhaps rising to equilibrium level *E'*, well above the old 5

EXHIBIT 14–9 **The Federal Reserve's Impact on the Federal Funds Interest Rate**

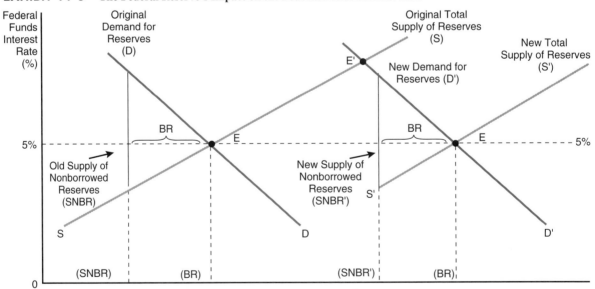

Financial Developments Open Market Operations— The Lever That Keeps Total Reserves of the Banking System at the Level Desired

(Figures in $ Billions for Week Ended December 27, 2000)

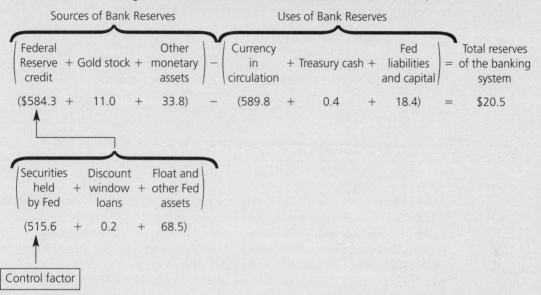

Sources of Bank Reserves   Uses of Bank Reserves

$$\begin{pmatrix} \text{Federal} \\ \text{Reserve} \\ \text{credit} \end{pmatrix} + \text{Gold stock} + \begin{pmatrix} \text{Other} \\ \text{monetary} \\ \text{assets} \end{pmatrix} - \begin{pmatrix} \text{Currency} \\ \text{in} \\ \text{circulation} \end{pmatrix} + \text{Treasury cash} + \begin{pmatrix} \text{Fed} \\ \text{liabilities} \\ \text{and capital} \end{pmatrix} = \begin{pmatrix} \text{Total reserves} \\ \text{of the banking} \\ \text{system} \end{pmatrix}$$

$$(\$584.3 + 11.0 + 33.8) - (589.8 + 0.4 + 18.4) = \$20.5$$

$$\begin{pmatrix} \text{Securities} \\ \text{held} \\ \text{by Fed} \end{pmatrix} + \begin{pmatrix} \text{Discount} \\ \text{window} \\ \text{loans} \end{pmatrix} + \begin{pmatrix} \text{Float and} \\ \text{other Fed} \\ \text{assets} \end{pmatrix}$$

$$(515.6 + 0.2 + 68.5)$$

Control factor

An example: The Fed's current target might be to keep total legal reserves at $20.5 billion in order to stabilize interest rates.

The Problem: Currency in circulation in the public's hands is expected to increase by $1 billion over the next two-week period, all other factors held constant. Bank reserves will fall and interest rates are likely to rise as the public withdraws this pocket money from banks unless the Federal Reserve acts.

Possible Solution: Use open market operations to purchase $1 billion in U.S. government securities (the Fed's open-market control factor) through the trading desk of the New York Federal Reserve Bank.

percent Fed funds rate. If the Fed doesn't want this to happen, it will increase the supply of nonborrowed reserves by using open market operations, sliding the old schedule *SNBR* over to a new schedule, *SNBR'*. This action moves the supply of total reserves, *S,* over to a new schedule *S'*. If the amount of borrowed reserves doesn't change, we now have a *new* intersection of supply and demand for reserves, but the level of the Fed funds rate stays at the old equilibrium point *E,* and the old 5 percent interest rate. Thus, *the Federal Reserve can keep the Fed funds interest rate at or near its desired level so long as the central bank is willing to offset changes in the demand for total reserves and in the demand for borrowed reserves by making appropriate adjustments in the supply of nonborrowed reserves through open market operations.*

Of course, the central bank cannot maintain the Fed funds rate exactly at its target level every hour of every day. This is because depository institutions are constantly changing their demands for reserves and their attitudes about borrowing reserves from the Federal

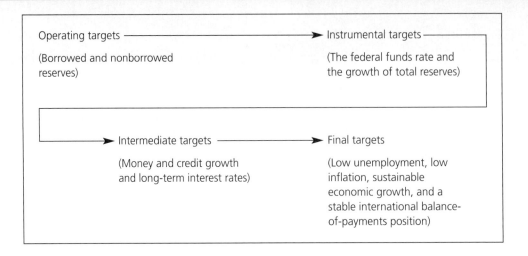

One way to follow interest-rate targeting in the United States is to check frequently with such Web site as *www.federalreserve.gov/fomc* and *www.economagic.com*

Reserve banks. Moreover, interest rates are impacted by the public's expectations for inflation and by the total demand for and supply of credit within the financial system.

Finally, one important point about targeting the federal funds rate should be noted. Just because the Fed can manipulate the federal funds rate—a key money market interest rate—does not mean that long-term capital market interest rates will also respond in the same way. For example, even though the Federal Reserve nudged the Fed funds rate downward in 2001 to try to head off a recession in the U.S. economy, long-term interest rates on Treasury bonds actually increased in the first six months of that year. Why do long-term interest rates sometimes change quite differently than the federal funds rate?

One factor is *inflation*. When the central bank cuts short-term interest rates investors in the capital market may come to believe that prices will rise. Thus, easier monetary policy lowers short-term interest rates in the near term, but may lead longer-term investors to expect higher interest rates in the future. Ultimately, higher inflationary expectations may push long-term interest rates upward as capital market investors seek compensation for the fear of greater inflation.

The key point to remember is that the central bank does *not* have direct control over longer-term interest rates. And, unfortunately, it is long-term interest rates that appear to have the greatest impact on investment spending in the economy and the creation of new jobs. The central bank must be patient. Short-term interest rates, like the Fed funds rate, react quickly to changes in central bank policy, but long-term interest rates may take several months to respond to what the central bank is trying to do. Monetary policy often operates with long and variable time lags.

THE FEDERAL RESERVE AND ECONOMIC GOALS

For many years, the Federal Reserve System, along with other central banks around the world, has played an active role in the stabilization of the economy and the pursuit of economic goals. These goals include controlling inflation, promoting full employment and sustainable economic growth, and achieving a stable international balance-of-payments position for the United States. In recent years, these goals have proved to be extremely

Financial Developments   The Federal Funds Futures Market—An Aid to Market Participants Trying to Guess Which Way the Central Bank Is Headed

Since early in 1994 the Federal Reserve has been setting target levels for the daily average federal funds interest rate. Moreover, when the Fed announces a new target level for the effective federal funds rate, usually following a meeting of its Federal Open Market Committee (FOMC), the effective Fed funds rate moves quickly toward the new target level. This relatively new procedure of setting clear and explicit federal funds interest-rate targets and doing it right away has helped to make it easier for investors to "tune in"on what the central bank is trying to do.

In October 1988 the Chicago Board of Trade (CBOT) began public trading on its exchange floor of a federal funds futures contract in the amount of $5 million per contract for 30 days and priced on the basis of 100 less the overnight federal funds rate for the delivery month. For example, if the prevailing federal funds interest rate is 5 percent, the contracts value is 100−5 or 95 (on a $100 basis). These futures contract's are usually traded for the current month out to about six or seven months ahead. The federal funds interest rate on these contracts may be readily found any time during the trading day through radio, television, and the Internet.

The futures contracts' funds rate is a forecast of what the Federal Reserve is likely to do with its *target federal funds rate* in the near future. Thus, investors can put together a forecast of the future direction of the federal funds rate and of the decisions likely to be made by the FOMC to change that interest rate at little cost. The creation of the new futures contract and the Fed's willingness to be more open with its plans for the federal funds interest rate and with how it views the economy's condition has made Federal Reserve monetary policy much more transparent and more helpful to active market investors than ever before.

Recent research suggests the CBOT's futures contract for federal funds is a reliable and generally accurate (unbiased) forecaster of what the actual funds rate is likely to do. It is particularly accurate in anticipating the *direction* toward which the funds rate is likely to go. Moreover, the marketplace's prediction of the effective Fed funds rate seems particularly accurate when it is made right before the next scheduled FOMC meeting.

Sources: Raymond Owens and Roy Webb, "Using the Federal Funds Futures Market to Predict Monetary Policy Actions," *Economic Quarterly,* Federal Reserve Bank of Richmond, Spring 2001, pp. 69–77; and Ed Nosal, "How Well Does the Federal Funds Futures Rate Predict the Future Federal Funds Rate?" *Economic Commentary,* Federal Reserve Bank of Cleveland, October 1, 2001.

difficult to achieve in practice and, in fact, have often required conflicting policies. Nevertheless, the Fed remains committed to them, particularly to maintaining long-run price stability.

The Goal of Controlling Inflation

Inflation—a rise in the general price level of all goods and services produced in the economy—has been among the more serious economic problems of the world during the past half century, with many nations experiencing far higher annual rates of inflation than those currently prevailing in the United States. Moreover, inflation is *not* new; price levels have been generally rising since the beginning of the Industrial Revolution in Europe nearly 300 years ago. There is also evidence of outbreaks of rampant inflation during the Middle Ages and in ancient times.

What are the *causes* of inflation? During the 1960s and 1970s, war and government spending were certainly contributing factors. Soaring energy and food costs, higher home mortgage rates, and rapid increases in labor and medical care costs also played key roles until the 1980s brought a turnaround, as Exhibit 14–10 reveals. Another contributing factor was the decline in the value of the U S. dollar in international markets. The dollar's weakness relative to other major currencies (particularly the German mark and the Japanese yen) raised the prices of imports into the United States and lessened the impact of foreign competition on domestic producers until the dollar strengthened significantly during

EXHIBIT 14–10
Measures of the Rate of Inflation in the United States (Compound Annual Rates of Change)

	Period										
	1960–65	1965–70	1970–75	1975–80	1980–85	1985–90	1990–95	1996	1998	2000	2001
Consumer price index (CPI)	1.3%	4.2%	7.7%	8.9%	5.5%	4.0%	2.3%	2.9%	1.5%	3.4%	2.8%
Producer price index, finished goods (PPI)	0.4	2.9	8.6	8.6	3.5	2.6	1.4	2.6	−0.9	3.7	2.0
Implicit price deflator for gross domestic product	1.6	4.2	6.6	7.2	5.4	3.6	2.8	2.3	1.2	2.3	2.2

Source: Federal Reserve Bank of St. Louis, *Annual U.S. Economic Data;* U.S. Department of Commerce; and Board of Governors of the Federal Reserve System, *Federal Reserve Bulletin,* Table 2.15, selected issues.

the 1990s. With the turn of the century increasing production costs and continuing strength in the U.S. economy seemed to result in a slight rise in inflationary pressures. However, inflation slowed substantially as the U.S. economy weakened during 2001—a situation made even worse by the terrorist attacks in the fall of that year.

Still another causal factor is *inflationary expectations:* the anticipation of continued inflation by businesses and households. Once underway, inflation seems to develop a momentum of its own, as consumers spend more and borrow more freely to stay ahead of rising prices, sending those prices still higher. Businesses and labor unions begin to build inflation into their price and wage decisions, passing higher costs along in the form of higher prices for goods and services. The result may be a wage-price spiral in which each plateau of increased costs is used as a basis for justifying further price increases.

Inflation creates distortions in the allocation of scarce resources and definitely hurts certain groups. For example, it tends to discourage saving and encourages consumption at a faster rate to stay ahead of rising prices. Moreover, the decline in the savings rate tends to discourage capital investment. Unfortunately, this means that the economy's growth in productivity (output per worker-hour) tends to slow. The fall in productivity means that the supply of new goods and services cannot keep pace with rising demands, putting further upward pressure on prices. At the same time, workers usually seek cost-of-living adjustments in wages and salaries, leading to an increase in labor costs. Some workers represented by strong unions or in growth industries usually manage to keep pace with inflation, but other groups, including retired persons and government employees, whose income is fixed or rises slowly, often experience a decline in their real standard of living when inflation is on the rise.

Central-Bank Targeting of Inflation

Beginning in the 1990s several central banks around the world began setting *target inflation rates* or target inflation rate *ranges* to shoot at with their policy weapons. New Zealand was the first nation to establish a formal inflation-targeting regime. Canada followed in 1991, Great Britain in 1992, and Australia and Sweden in 1993. Before they joined the European Community, Spain and Finland adopted an inflation-targeting approach and the European

Central Bank (ECB) soon declared that price stability was its primary goal. In contrast, the United States has set no explicit inflation rate target, though it seeks to drive inflation so low it doesn't affect business and consumer decisions.

Inflation targets vary among the nations that have set them—some are *point targets* and others are *inflation rate ranges.* For example, New Zealand's central bank has expressed its determination to keep inflation within a 0 to 3 percent annual rate range. (The New Zealand central bank's governor can be fired if he or she misses the inflation target range!) Most other countries seek to hold inflation near 2 percent annually and the target inflation-rate range is normally 1 to 3 percent. The key inflation measure most widely used is some index of consumer prices—such as the Consumer Price Index (CPI) in the United States. If the target or target range is missed, some nations give their central banks a specific time period to get the inflation rate back on track—for example, 18 months to 2 years.

The jury is still out on the success or failure of central bank inflation targeting. Certainly the central bank is the most likely institution to successfully pursue inflation targets. But some central bankers are hesitant to set specific numerical inflation-rate targets, fearing a loss of flexibility and possible adverse consequences if the public becomes aware that the announced target has been missed. Might a missed inflation target lead to even greater inflation? More evidence is needed on the actual benefits and costs of inflation targeting.

Deflation

Some experts believe that inflation may be giving way to **deflation**—declining price levels—in some key countries (such as Japan). As we saw earlier in Chapter 7, this too can create serious problems, resulting in falling production and incomes and higher real interest rates which further slow the economy. Under a true deflationary situation a nation's central bank must find ways to guard against a tailspin in the economy, as spending and earnings contract and unemployment begins to rise. As bad as inflation can be, deflation may result in even greater problems for a central bank to control.

The Goal of Full Employment

The Employment Act of 1946 committed the United States government for the first time to *minimizing unemployment* as a major national goal. The Federal Reserve, as part of the government's structure, is therefore committed to this goal as well. In recent years, the U.S. unemployment rate as determined from monthly surveys conducted by the U.S. Department of Labor has hovered mainly in the 4 to 10 percent range. (See Exhibit 14–11.) In terms of numbers of people, between 6 and 11 million workers have been actively seeking jobs but have been unable to find them. The nation's output of goods and services and its real standard of living are reduced by unemployment, which also breeds social unrest, increased crime, and higher tax burdens on those who are working.

Is it possible to have zero unemployment? What is full employment? In a market-oriented economy, where workers are free to change jobs and business people are free to hire and fire, some unemployment is inevitable. There is a minimum level of unemployment, known as *frictional unemployment,* which arises from the temporary unemployment of persons who are changing jobs in response to higher wages or better working conditions. *Full employment,* therefore, refers to a situation in which the only significant amount of unemployment is frictional in nature. In a fully employed economy, everyone actively seeking work finds it in a relatively short period. During the 1960s, the President's Council of Economic Advisers defined full employment as a situation in which only 4 percent of the civilian labor force is unemployed. Today the U.S. target seems to fall somewhere within the 4–5 percent unemployment range.

EXHIBIT 14–11
U.S. Civilian
Unemployment Rate
(Percent of Civilian
Labor Force)

1970	4.9%	1994	6.1%
1975	8.5	1996	5.4
1980	7.1	1998	4.5
1985	7.2	2000	4.0
1990	5.5	2001*	5.8
1992	7.4	2002**	5.5

Begining in 1994, a new unemployment survey was adopted that slightly increased the unemployment rate over previous levels.
*2001 figure is for December.
**The 2002 figure is for February.

Source: *Economic Report of the President* and *Federal Reserve Bulletin,* Table 2.11, selected issues.

Until recently, economists had raised their estimates of the amount of irreducible frictional unemployment. A key factor was the massive shifts that occurred in the composition of the U.S. labor force, especially the rapid increase in the number of adult women seeking jobs. Women 20 years of age and older, in fact, have accounted for more than half of the net increase in the U.S. labor force in recent years. This upward surge in women's employment may be attributed to a decline in fertility rates, more varied jobs available to women, and the erosion of family incomes due to inflation. Teenage participation in the labor force also has expanded under the pressure of inflation, the rising cost of college education, and the spread of vocational schools. Historically, these two groups (women and teenagers) have reported higher average unemployment rates than most other workers, moving in and out of the job market with greater fluidity than adult male workers due to family needs and schooling opportunities, thus tending to increase the average unemployment rate. Other groups also increasing in importance and who traditionally report higher average unemployment rates include nonwhite workers and unskilled laborers.

In the most recent period the average unemployment rate inside the United States fell substantially to one of the lowest levels—about 4 percent—in modern history. One of the key factors in this period of declining unemployment, which lasted through much of the 1990s, was strong demand for consumer and business goods and services and a shortage of skilled workers. Another key force was demographics—a rise in the proportion of older workers who tend to experience less unemployment and greater job stability. Unfortunately, this downward movement in unemployment did not last as the U.S. economy subsequently entered a period of economic weakness and experienced terrorist attacks as the new century began. Once again unemployment began to climb for a brief period.

The Goal of Sustainable Economic Growth

The Federal Reserve has declared that one of its important long-term goals is to *keep the economy growing at a relatively steady and stable rate*—that is, a rate high enough to absorb increases in the labor force and prevent the unemployment rate from rising but slow enough to avoid runaway inflation. Most economists believe that this implies a rate of growth in GNP or GDP of about 2 to 3 percent annually on a real (inflation-adjusted) basis. Periodically, the economy grows more slowly than this or turns down into a recession, resulting in rising unemployment. (See especially Exhibit 14–12.) Although most economic recessions have been relatively brief and mild, they have averaged two each decade, or about one recession every four to five years.

Forecasting the actual starting point of each recession and its duration has proved to be an exceedingly difficult problem for the Federal Reserve. Each downturn in the economy springs from somewhat different causes, although most recessions involve a sharp cutback in business inventories. Fears of being caught with a large quantity of unsold goods lead to

EXHIBIT 14–12

Rates of Growth in Real U.S. GNP or Real GDP (Compounded Annual Rates of Change)

Time Period	Annual Rate of Change in Real GNP	Time Period	Annual Rate of Change in Real GDP
1960-69	3.9%	1996	3.9
1970–79	3.5	1997	4.4
1980–89	3.0	1998	4.3
1990–95	2.1	1999	4.1
1996–2000	4.2	2000	4.1
		2001	1.1

Source: Federal Reserve Bank of St. Louis, *National Economic Trends* and *Annual U.S. Economic Data,* various issues; and Board of Governors of the Federal Reserve System, *Federal Reserve Bulletin,* various issues.

periodic cutbacks in new orders, throwing people out of work. At the same time, interest rates usually rise to peak levels before a recession begins, gradually choking off private investment in new capital goods and inventories.

Traditional economic theory suggests that a decline in the rate of economic growth should lead to a lower rate of inflation. This follows from the observation that recessions are marked by reduced demand for goods and services and falling incomes. Thus, in theory at least, a recession and slower economic growth are short-term cures for severe inflation, although for those without jobs, they are certainly high-cost cures. Interestingly enough, some recent recessions have been accompanied by substantial inflation. Many observers believe there is some bias in the U.S. economy toward inflation, even during recessionary periods, that may be due to the rapid growth of service industries relative to the manufacturing sector, escalator clauses in wage contracts, and the expectation that government policy will always respond quickly to protect jobs whenever economic problems appear.

Equilibrium in the U.S. Balance of Payments and Protecting the Dollar

The Federal Reserve, like all central banks, must be concerned not only with economic conditions but also with developments in the international sector. In this area, the Fed pursues two interrelated goals: (1) protecting the value of the dollar in foreign currency markets and (2) achieving an equilibrium position in the U.S. balance of payments.

When the United States buys more of the goods, services, and securities offered by other nations than those countries spend for what the United States sells, the difference must be made up by giving foreigners claims against U.S. resources. If the United States persists in purchasing or acquiring more abroad than foreigners purchase or acquire here, a disequilibrium position in the balance of payments results. This means that the United States cannot continue to draw down its reserve assets (primarily gold, foreign currencies, and special drawing rights at the International Monetary Fund) indefinitely, nor is it likely to find foreigners willing to accept unlimited amounts of dollars.[5] At some point, the federal government and the Federal Reserve must adopt policies that slow down the outflow of U.S. dollars and encourage foreigners to buy more U.S. goods, services, and securities. Failing this, the value of the dollar in international markets will begin to weaken.

In recent years, the United States has experienced some deep deficits in its merchandise trade with other nations and in its international balance-of-payments position (see Exhibit 14–13). One cause of these international deficits has been massive imports of foreign oil. Other foreign imports into the United States experiencing considerable growth include

[5]See Chapter 25 for a discussion of reserve assets and disequilibrium problems in the U.S. balance of payments.

EXHIBIT 14–13
Merchandise Trade Balance of the United States

Year	FOB Exports Minus CIF Imports ($ Billions)	Year	FOB Exports Minus CIF Imports ($ Billions)
1965	$ 4.3	1990	−108.1
1970	0.5	1995	−173.6
1975	2.2	2000	−375.7
1980	−36.2	2001	−347.8
1985	−122.1		

Source: U.S. Department of Commerce and Board of Governors of the Federal Reserve System, *Federal Reserve Bulletin,* Table 3.10, selected issues.

European and Asian autos, steel products, building materials, electronic equipment, crude rubber, textiles, and toys. At the same time, foreign investors have sharply increased their investments in the United States, making the United States a debtor nation and leading to large outflows of earnings to foreign investors. Early in the 1990s, foreign investment in the United States slowed due to economic problems and stock market crises abroad, especially in Japan, before resuming a faster pace later in the 1990s due to the comparatively stable U.S. investment environment and economic and political problems in Asia.

The sizable trade deficits and current net debtor position of the United States has presented Federal Reserve policymakers with a major dilemma. Should they push up domestic interest rates and limit credit growth to protect the dollar, slow imports, and prevent future inflation? Perhaps, but this would probably slow domestic economic growth and increase unemployment. This is not an easy dilemma to solve. There are substantial costs no matter which way the central bank chooses to go.

THE TRADE-OFFS AMONG ECONOMIC GOALS

As we have seen in this chapter, the United States and other nations face some serious economic problems. Inflation is less severe today in North America than in the turbulent 1970s or than in other parts of the world today, particularly in portions of South America, Europe, and Asia, where price increases remain a problem. In the United States, balance-of-payments problems present imposing difficulties, while in Asia, unemployment and weakened asset values in several countries threaten economic and political stability. Does this mean that the Federal Reserve System and other central banks have simply failed to do their jobs?

Unfortunately, the problem is not that simple. For one thing, economic goals *conflict.* For example, controlling inflation and stabilizing the U.S. international payments situation usually require the Fed to slow down the economy through restricted money supply growth and higher interest rates. However, this policy threatens to generate more unemployment and subdue economic growth. Evidence that economic goals may conflict was provided by British economist A. W. Phillips (1958) and U.S. economists Paul Samuelson and Robert Solow (1960) more than four decades ago. These economists uncovered an *inverse* relationship between price-level increases (inflation) and unemployment. For example, Samuelson and Solow, using data collected from the 1950s, found that stable prices could be achieved only if unemployment remained as high as 5 to 6 percent of the civilian labor force. In recent years, U.S. unemployment has hovered in the 4 to 6 percent range, while price increases have usually ranged between 2 and 4 percent a year.

Such policy trade-offs may not be valid in the longer term, as Laidler (1990) and others have recently observed. Indeed, there is growing research evidence that full employment and price stability (absence of serious inflation) can be compatible with each other. The central bank can reach a point of low unemployment that can be maintained over fairly long periods of time without triggering rising inflation. This definition of sustainable long-run full employment is often referred to by economists as the NAIRU—the non-accelerating inflation rate of unemployment. However, in the short run maintaining *both* stable prices and full employment can conflict with one another, forcing central bankers into making some tough choices. Worse still, governments frequently fail to prioritize their nation's economic goals so that central bank policymakers may not have a clear idea of which goal or goals are most important. There does appear to be a growing consensus, however, that the most feasible, long-term goal for monetary policy is probably to *control inflation* (i.e., maintain reasonable price stability). Several governments (for example: Canada, New Zealand, Great Britain, and the new European Community) have recently moved to spell out policy priorities for their central banks, particularly when it comes to controlling inflation.

THE LIMITATIONS OF MONETARY POLICY

In addition to conflicts among economic goals, central banks like the Federal Reserve find that they cannot completely control financial conditions, interest rates, or the money supply. Changes in the economy itself feed back on the money supply and the financial markets. It becomes exceedingly difficult, especially on a weekly or monthly basis, to sort out the effects of monetary policy from the impact of broad economic forces. Moreover, the structure of the economy itself is changing—as Mauskopf (1990) observes—due to deregulation of interest rates and financial services, the abandonment of fixed exchange rates, the increasing integration of global money and capital markets, and the breath-taking speed of new technological developments. As a result, international markets have come to exert a greater impact on the domestic economy and on central bank policymaking, while changes in domestic interest rates are probably not as potent a factor affecting the economy as they were a decade ago. The Federal Reserve and other central banks must learn how to deal with these changes in fundamental economic relationships.

Questions *to Help You Study*

10. What is *interest-rate targeting?* Which interest rate does the Federal Reserve focus upon in its conduct of monetary policy?

11. If the Federal Reserve wishes to put upward pressure on market interest rates, what would it be most likely to do? How would it proceed to push the federal funds rate in an upward direction? How would it lower the funds rate?

12. What are the principal economic *goals* of the Federal Reserve System? How could the Fed cause changes in the rate of inflation? In unemployment and economic growth? In the nation's balance-of-payments position?

13. Describe the *trade-offs* that appear to exist among the nation's economic goals. How do these trade-offs influence the central bank's ability to achieve the nation's economic goals?

14. What are the principal *limitations* of monetary policy?

Summary of the Chapter

The policy tools used by central banks, such as the Federal Reserve System, impact the quantity and rate of growth of legal reserves in the banking system and, in turn, the cost and availability of credit.

- The principal immediate target of Federal Reserve policy today is the *federal funds interest rate,* which, in turn, affects interest rates in both the money market and the capital market and, ultimately, the strength of the economy as a whole.

- The main policy tool used by the Federal Reserve to influence the cost and availability of credit is *open market operations*—the buying and selling of securities through the Trading Desk of the Federal Reserve Bank of New York. Open-market *sales* tend to raise interest rates and restrict the supply of credit available, while open-market *purchases* tend to lower interest rates and expand the supply of credit.

- The Fed, like many other central banks around the globe, has other broad policy tools at its disposal in the form of *deposit reserve requirements* and the *discount rates* of the individual Federal Reserve banks. An increase in reserve requirements or in the discount rate tends to tighten money and credit policy, slowing borrowing and spending, while a reduction in reserve requirements and Federal Reserve bank discount rates tends to ease monetary policy, leading to an expansion of money and credit at lower cost.

- While open market operations, reserve requirements, and discount rates represent *general credit controls,* most central banks also have *selective credit controls* that impact specific groups or sectors of the financial system and the economy. The Federal Reserve's selective controls include moral suasion (or psychological pressure applied by central bank officials) and margin requirements (which restrict purchases of selected securities on credit).

- As open market operations have become the central tool of the Federal Reserve and other central banks around the globe, different varieties of this important central bank tool have been developed. Examples include straight or outright open market operations (where actual title to security ownership changes hands), repurchase agreements (where only temporary transfer of security ownership occurs), run-off transactions (where the central bank demands cash for maturing securities), and agency transactions (where the central bank acts to buy or sell securities on behalf of a central bank customer, such as a foreign government or foreign central bank).

- Besides central bank monetary policy other important groups acting in the economy and financial system also affect interest rates and the reserves of the banking system, including actions of the public (such as demanding additional supplies of currency and coin) and operations of the government's treasury (as when the government sells or redeems securities or collects taxes). The central bank must often act *defensively* to counteract these other sources of change in the financial marketplace, using its policy tools as a counterweight to actions taken by the public and the government.

- When the Federal Reserve decides to change the desired level of the federal funds interest rate it uses open market operations to change the quantity of *nonborrowed reserves* held by depository institutions. Nonborrowed reserves plus borrowed reserves (loaned to depository institutions by the Federal Reserve banks) make up the supply of total reserves at the disposal of the banking system.

- The principal economic goals pursued by most central banks include the *control of inflation,* achieving *full employment,* achieving *sustainable economic growth,* and attaining a *stable equilibrium in the nation's balance of payments* with other nations. Unfortunately the policy goals often conflict, requiring the central bank to compromise, sometimes achieving only a portion of one sought-after goal (such as combating inflation) in order to avoid doing too much damage to another desired goal (such as achieving full employment for all those willing to work).

Key Terms

General credit controls, *384*

Selective credit controls, *384*

Reserve requirements, *385*

Discount rate, *388*

Open market operations, *391*

Moral suasion, *400*

Margin requirements, *400*

Borrowed reserves, *402*

Nonborrowed reserves, *402*

Deflation, *407*

Problems

1. Describe what is likely to happen to interest rates, deposits, and total bank reserves as a result of the transactions listed below:

   a. The Federal Reserve sells $50 million in securities outright to a bank.

   b. The Federal Reserve buys $85 million in securities outright from a bank.

   c. The Federal Reserve sells $93 million in securities outright to a nonbank security dealer.

   d. The Federal Reserve buys $42 million in securities outright from a nonbank security dealer.

   e. The Federal Reserve sells $21 million in securities from its own portfolio to a foreign central bank.

   f. The Federal Reserve buys $37 million in securities for its own portfolio that are being offered for sale by a foreign central bank.

   g. The Federal Reserve declines the U.S. Treasury's offer to roll over $150 million in Treasury notes that are maturing in the Fed's own portfolio in exchange for new Treasury notes; instead the Federal Reserve demands cash from the Treasury.

2. Suppose the banking system's nonborrowed reserves total $48.3 billion, with total legal reserves standing at $51.2 billion. What must borrowed reserves be? This morning the Federal Reserve decided to undertake the sale of $500 million in government securities through open market operations. What will be the new level of nonborrowed reserves? If interest rates do not change, what will be the new level of total reserves? What must you assume to make this calculation? If interest rates do change, which way are they likely to move?

3. If the total supply of nonborrowed reserves equals $500 million and borrowed reserves are $50 million at the current equilibrium federal funds rate (FFR), and if the supply of total reserves is described by the following equation:

$$S = \$530 \text{ million} + 4 \text{ FFR}$$

What is the equilibrium federal funds rate (FFR)? What could the central bank do to increase the federal funds rate above its current equilibrium level? How could it reduce the funds rate below its current equilibrium level?

4. In Problem 3 above, suppose the supply of nonborrowed reserves falls to $490 million due to open market sales by the central bank. Holding all other factors constant, what happens to the equilibrium federal funds interest rate? If nonborrowed reserves drop to $490 million while borrowed reserves increase to $56 million, all else held equal, what happens to the equilibrium funds rate?

5. First National Bank of Elderidge borrowed $550,000 from the Federal Reserve Bank of St. Louis last Friday. The bank received short-term adjustment credit for three days and plans to repay its loan at the close of business Monday. Show the proper accounting (T-account) entries for this transaction when the loan was taken out on Friday and when it is repaid Monday afternoon. How much did total bank reserves rise when this loan was made? Are reserve requirements a factor here?

6. Please identify each of the key terms or concepts presented in this chapter as they are defined or described below:

   a. Monetary policy tools affecting the whole economy and financial system.
   b. Monetary policy tools that affect specific groups or sectors of the economy.
   c. Percentage of legal reserves depository institutions must hold behind the deposits they receive from the public.
   d. Annual percentage loan rate quoted by each of the Federal Reserve banks.
   e. Buying and selling of securities by a central bank in order to influence general credit conditions.
   f. A central bank tool dependent upon psychological pressure and persuasion.
   g. Difference between the market value of a financial asset and its loan value.
   h. Deposits kept at the central bank plus currency and coin held in the vaults of depository institutions.
   i. Legal reserves loaned to depository institutions by the Federal Reserve banks.
   j. Legal reserves owned by depository institutions.

Questions about the Web and the Money and Capital Markets

1. According to the Federal Reserve Web sites what is the *principal policy tool* of the Federal Reserve System in pursuing monetary policy? Why?

2. How do the policy tools of the Bank of Canada differ from those of the Federal Reserve System? Where on the Web can you find the answer to this question?

3. How do the policy tools and policy goals of the European Central Bank (ECB) differ from those of the Federal Reserve System? From the Bank of Japan? Where on the Web did you go to find the answers to these questions?

Selected References

Board of Governnors of the Federal Reserve System. "Monetary Policy Report to Congress." *Federal Reserve Bulletin,* March 2001, pp. 103–31.

Kozicki, Sharon. "Why Do Central Banks Monitor So Many Inflation Indicators." *Economic Review,* Federal Reserve Bank of Kansas City, Third Quarter 2001, pp 5–42.

Laidler, David. "The Legacy of the Monetarist Controversy." *Review,* Federal Reserve Bank of St. Louis, March–April 1990, pp. 49–64.

Long, Richard W. "The FOMC in 1979: Introducing Reserve Targeting." *Review,* Federal Reserve Bank of St. Louis, March 1980.

Loungani, Prakash, and Mark Rush. "The Effects of Changes in Reserve Requirements on Investment and GNP." *International Finance Discussion Papers,* No. 471. Board of Governors of the Federal Reserve System, June 1994.

Mauskopf, Eileen. "'The Transmission Channels of Monetary Policy: How Have They Changed?" *Federal Reserve Bulletin,* December 1990, pp. 985–l008.

Meyer, Laurence H. "Inflation Targets and Inflation Targeting." *Review,* Federal Reserve Bank of St. Louis, November–December 2001, pp. 1–13.

Neely, Christopher J. "International Interest Rate Linkages." *International Economic Conditions,* Federal Reserve Bank of St. Louis, August 2001.

Nosal, Ed. "How Well Does the Federal Funds Futures Rate Predict the Future Federal Funds Rate?" *Economic Commentary,* Federal Reserve Bank of Cleveland, October 2001.

Owens, Raymond, and Roy Webb. "Using the Federal Funds Futures Market to Predict Monetary Policy Action." *Economic Quarterly,* Federal Reserve Bank of Richmond, Spring 2001, pp. 69–77.

Owyang, Michael. "Persistence, Excess Volatility, and Volatility Clusters in Inflation." *Review,* Federal Reserve Bank of St. Louis, November–December 2001, pp. 41–50.

Phillips, A. W. "The Relation between Unemployment and the Rate of Change of Money Wage Rates in the United Kingdom, 1957–1961." *Economica,* November 1958.

Roth, Howard L. "Federal Reserve Open Market Techniques." *Economic Review,* Federal Reserve Bank of Kansas City, March 1986, pp. 2–15.

Rudebusch, Glenn D., and Carl E. Walsh. "Central Bank Inflation Targeting." *Economic Letter,* Federal Reserve Bank of San Francisco, May 22, 1998.

Rush, Mark; Gordon Sellon; and Li Zhu. "The Role of the Discount Rate in Monetary Policy." Research Working Paper 94-1. Federal Reserve Bank of Kansas City, April 1994.

Samuelson, Paul A., and Robert M. Solow. "'The Problem of Achieving and Maintaining a Stable Price Level: Analytical Aspects of Anti-Inflation Policy." *American Economic Review,* May 1960.

Financial Institutions within the Financial System: Nature, Management, and Regulation

Part Four directs a spotlight upon the most important units in any financial system—the financial-service providers, including banks, credit unions, mutual funds, insurance companies, pension funds, security dealers, and other financial institutions. Three of the four chapters (Chapters 15 through 17) describe each type of major financial-service institution, including its principal services, history, and problems, while the fourth chapter (Chapter 18) examines government regulation of the financial-services industry.

Chapter 15 focuses upon the *commercial banking industry*—the number one financial-service provider in most financial systems around the globe. The banking industry is going through great change as a result of increased competition from bank and nonbank financial firms and gradual government deregulation of this vitally important service sector. In this opening chapter we explore the many different services that banks offer, look at the structure and organization of their industry, discover how to read their financial statements, and explain how it is that their transactions with bank customers result in the creation and destruction of money and credit within the financial system.

Chapter 16 switches our attention to *thrift institutions*—financial-service providers that compete most directly with commercial banks. The thrifts include such popular financial firms as savings and loan associations, savings banks, and credit unions. These private businesses are among the leading providers of individual and family checking and savings services, household installment loans, and home mortgage loans in the financial system. A fourth thriftlike institution is also discussed here—the money market mutual fund. As we will see, money market funds are hard to classify, with some authorities labeling them as "thrifts" and others putting them in the mutual fund or investment company category.

Chapter 17 explores the services, history, and problems of the remaining major nonbank financial-service firms. Included in this chapter are such financial-service providers as mutual funds, insurance companies, and pension funds. This portion of the financial institutions' sector is heavily oriented toward the long-term capital markets, providing huge amounts of funds annually to finance the expansion of businesses and the acquisition of new homes by individuals and families.

Finally, Chapter 18 closes Part Four with an overview of the government agencies and the rules of the game that make up *regulation* of the financial-services industry. The financial institutions' sector is one of the most heavily regulated industries on the planet, due, in part, to its importance in collecting and safeguarding the public's savings and in providing credit to support business and household economic activity. Government regulation is a critical factor in shaping how financial institutions perform and grow and is constantly undergoing change. For this reason Chapter 18 is one of the most important chapters in this book.

Chapter **Fifteen**

The Commercial Banking Industry

Learning Objectives in This Chapter

- In this chapter you will understand how important commercial banks are to the functioning of a modern economy and financial system.

- You will have the opportunity to explore the makeup (structure) of the United States' banking industry—one of the most important in the world.

- You will learn about the content of bank financial statements and discover how to read them.

- You will see how banks create and destroy money and credit and why this activity is so vital to the operation of both the economy and the financial system.

What's in This Chapter? Key Topics Outline

The Organizational Structure of Modern Commercial Banking

Economies of Scale and Consolidation within the Banking Industry

Branch, Holding Company, and International Banking

Industry Convergence and the Gramm-Leach-Bliley Act

Automation and the Changing Technology of Banking

Portfolio Characteristics of Banks: Balance Sheets and Income/Expense Statements

Worldwide Trends in Banking

Money Creation and Destruction by Banks and Bank Accounting

INTRODUCTION

The dominant privately owned financial institution in the United States and in the economies of most major countries is the *commercial bank*. This institution offers the public both deposit and credit services, as well as a growing list of newer and more innovative services, such as investment advice, security underwriting, selling insurance, and financial planning. The name *commercial* implies that banks devote most of their resources to meeting the financial needs of business firms. In recent decades, however, commercial banks

The number of Web sites focusing on the commercial banking industry has mushroomed in recent years. Thousands of domestic and foreign banks have established individual sites describing their services and location—Web sites that usually can easily be called up simply by typing in the bank's name and location. In addition, a wide variety of bank regulatory agencies are also represented on the World Wide Web.

Bank regulators' Web sites typically include a brief history of each regulatory agency, its principal responsibilities, how it is organized, and how the public may make contact. Examples include the extensive Web sites presented by the Board of Governors of the Federal Reserve System (at *www.federalreserve.gov*), the Federal Deposit Insurance Corporation (at *www.fdic.gov*), and the Comptroller of the Currency (at *www.occ.treas.gov*). State bank regulatory agencies may usually be found by entering the state's name in front of the term "banking commission" or "banking board."

Information on potential jobs in the banking sector can be found on such sites as the FDIC's career Web site (at *www.fdic.gov*) and the Comptroller of the Currency's Web site (at *www.occ.treas.gov*). Descriptions of the content of bank financial reports may be found at the Web site of the Federal Financial Institutions Examination Council (at *www.ffiec.gov*).

have significantly expanded their offerings of financial services to consumers and units of government around the world. The result is the emergence of a financial institution that has been called a *financial department store* because it satisfies the broadest range of financial service needs in the global economy.

The importance of commercial banks may be measured in a number of ways. They hold about one-quarter of the total assets of all financial institutions headquartered in the United States, as well as a major share of financial assets abroad. Banks are still the principal means of making payments, through the checking accounts (demand deposits), credit cards, and electronic transfer services they offer. And banks are important because of their ability to create money from excess reserves made available from the public's deposits. The banking system can take a given volume of excess cash reserves and, by making loans and investments, generate a multiple amount of credit—a process explored later in this chapter.

Banks today are the principal channel for government monetary policy. In the United States, the Federal Reserve System implements policies to affect interest rates and the availability of credit in the economy mainly through altering the level and growth of reserves held by banks and other depository institutions. The same is true in Canada, Great Britain, the European Community, Japan, and many other nations. Today, commercial banks are the most important source of consumer credit (i.e., loans to individuals and families) and one of the major sources of loans to small businesses. Banks are major buyers of debt securities issued by federal, state, and local governments. For all of these reasons, commercial banks play a dominant role in the money and capital markets and are worthy of detailed study if we are to understand more fully how the financial system works.

THE STRUCTURE OF U.S. COMMERCIAL BANKING

The structure of U.S. banking is unique in comparison with other banking systems around the globe. The term **banking structure** focuses on the number and different sizes of commercial banks operating in thousands of local communities across the nation. Although the banking systems of most other nations consist of a few large banking organizations operating hundreds or thousands of branch offices, the U.S. system is dominated by thousands of small commercial banks. For example, in the year 2000, about 8,300 commercial banking institutions were operating in the United States, compared to less than a dozen domestically chartered banks in Canada and less than three dozen domestically owned banks in the United Kingdom and Mexico.

Not surprisingly, most U.S. banks are modest in size compared to banks in other countries. Roughly three-fifths of all U.S. commercial banks hold total assets of under $100 million each; only about 5 percent hold assets of a billion dollars or more and actively compete in global markets for loans and deposits. Smaller banks predominate in numbers, but the larger banks have a disproportionate share of the industry's assets. For example, the small handful of all U.S. banks with $1 billion or more in total assets hold just over four-fifths of all assets in the industry.

Most commercial banks in the United States are chartered by the states rather than by the federal government. As shown in Exhibit 15–1, of the roughly 8,300 U.S. commercial banks in operation in the year 2000, just under three quarters were **state-chartered banks.** The remaining banks, classified as **national banks,** were chartered by the federal government. National banks, on average, are larger and include nearly all of the nation's billion-dollar banking institutions. All national banks must be insured by the Federal Deposit Insurance Corporation (FDIC) and must also be members of the Federal Reserve System ("the Fed"). State-chartered banks may elect to become members of the Fed and also seek FDIC deposit insurance protection if they are willing to conform to the regulations laid down by these two federal agencies. The vast majority of U.S. banks (more than 98 percent) are FDIC insured, but only a minority have elected to join the Fed. Nevertheless, Fed member banks hold at least two-thirds of all bank deposits in the United States. (We will have more to say about the roles of the Federal Reserve, the FDIC, and other bank regulatory agencies in Chapter 18.)

A Trend toward Consolidation

A number of structural changes have affected the banking industry in recent years. One of the most important is the drive toward **consolidation** of industry assets into fewer, but larger, banking organizations.

The United States is still essentially a nation of small banks. But great pressures are operating to form larger banking organizations in order to make more efficient use of resources. During the past 25 years the number of U.S. commercial banks dropped from more than 14, 000 to less than 9,000; at year-end 2000 there were 8,315; and by the year 2002 there were less than 8,200 U.S. commercial banks in operation. Consequently, the average U.S. bank is substantially larger today than in the past.

Research studies suggest that, as banks grow, their costs increase more slowly than output, resulting in cost savings. For example, a 100 percent rise in deposit and loan accounts may result in only a 92 percent increase in the cost of bank operations. When automated

EXHIBIT 15–1

Number of Operating Commercial Banks and Branch Offices in the United States, Year-End 2000

Source: Federal Deposit Insurance Corporation, *Statistics on Banking*, 2000.

Type of Bank	Number of Banks	Number of Branch Offices
National banks	2,230	32,808
State-chartered member banks	990	12,954
Total member banks of the Federal Reserve System	3,220	45,762
Nonmember state-chartered banks	5,095	18,317
Total of all U.S.-insured commercial banks	8,315	64,079

bookkeeping and computer processing of accounts are used, substantial economies of scale characterize bank lending and the offering of checking accounts. Under pressure from a cost squeeze and increased competition from other financial institutions, many U.S. bankers view the strategy of growing into larger-sized banking organizations as a competitive response to these pressures.

We hasten to add, however, that scale economies resulting from bank growth appear to be modest—once a bank reaches perhaps $500 million or so in total assets, its unit production costs appear to approximately level out. In fact, some analysts argue that production costs begin rising when banks approach $1–$10 billion in size because of the tendency of larger banks to multiply their service offerings. Others argue, however, that large banks enjoy lower fund-raising costs and enjoy risk reduction from diversification across many different services and geographic areas, giving them a significant advantage over smaller banks.

BRANCH BANKING

The drive toward consolidation of banks into larger organizations is most evident in the long-term historical shift toward **branch banking.** Until the 1940s and 1950s, the United States was basically a nation of *unit banks,* each housed in only a single office. For example, in 1900 there were 12,427 banks, but only 87 of these had any branches. By 2001, however, there were less than 8,000 independently owned U.S. commercial banks, the majority of which were branch banking organizations. The number of branch offices has increased dramatically in recent years: In 1950 there were approximately 4,700 branch banking offices in operation; by 2000, the number of total U.S. full-service branches had climbed to well over 60,000 offices, as shown in Exhibit 15–1.

The growth of branching has been aided by the liberalization of many state and federal laws to permit greater use of branch offices as a means of bank growth. As we will see more fully in Chapter 18, interstate bank expansion should become more common in future years due to the passage of the Riegle-Neal Interstate Banking bill by the U.S. Congress in 1994 which allows branching throughout the United States. The spread of branching across the United States has also been aided by a massive population shift over the last three decades to suburban and rural areas and to the sunbelt states. Many of the nation's largest banks have followed their customers to distant markets through branching and mergers to protect their sources of funds and their earnings and gradually spread across the nation. Recent research suggests that the development of interstate banking has had a *stabilizing* impact on the banking industry with less volatile revenues and earnings than in the past.

The principal trade association representing the U.S. banking industry is the American Bankers Association which has a useful Web site about the industry at *www.aba.com*

Banks have also pursued greater geographic expansion through the establishment of branch offices because of the strong competitive challenge they face from a host of nonbank financial-service firms, including security brokers and dealers, mutual funds, insurance companies, credit unions, and dozens of other financial institutions. Many of these nonbank financial institutions (especially mutual funds and pension plans) appear to have gained market share at the expense of commercial banks, often by offering better returns and more flexible services. The rise of this form of outside competition for commercial banks has brought strong protests from the banking community for faster government deregulation of the industry and for permission to offer many new services.

Bank Holding Companies

Paralleling the rapid growth of branch banking has been the growth of bank holding companies, which originated in the nineteenth century. A **bank holding company** is a

Financial Developments   Top-Ranked U.S. Commercial Banks and Bank Holding Companies (Figures are for the year 2000)

Name of Commercial Bank	Total Assets in $ Billions	Name of Bank Holding Company	Total Assets in $ Billions
Bank of America, Charlotte	$607	Citigroup, New York City	$790
Citibank, New York City	370	Bank America, Charlotte	680
J.P. Morgan/Chase Bank, New York City	346	J.P. Morgan/Chase, New York City	662
First Union National Bank, Charlotte	228	Bank One Corp., Chicago	273
Morgan Guaranty Trust Co., New York City	178	First Union Corp., Charlotte	258
Fleet National Bank, Providence	162	Wells Fargo Corp., San Francisco	234
Wells Fargo Bank, San Francisco	104	Fleet Boston Financial Corp., Boston	180
Bank One, Chicago	98	SunTrust Banks, Atlanta	100
SunTrust Bank, Atlanta	97		
HSBC Bank USA, Buffalo	84		

Source: Board of Governors of the Federal Reserve System.

The size, acquisitions, and recent performance of leading U.S. bank holding companies may be traced through the National Information Center at *www.ffiec.gov/nic*

corporation organized to acquire and hold the stock of one or more banks. The company may also hold stock in nonbank business ventures. Holding companies have become popular as vehicles to avoid laws prohibiting the extension of branch banking and as a way to offer services that banks themselves cannot offer.

Bank holding companies have grown rapidly in the United States. In 1960 there were just 47 registered holding company organizations, controlling only about 8 percent of the total assets of U.S.-insured banks. By the 1990s, U.S. holding companies numbered more than 6,000 and held over 90 percent of U.S. bank assets and that share has continued to rise in the new century. In the international markets as well, holding companies have become the predominant bank organizational form because of their advantages in raising capital, spreading out their risk exposure, and allowing entry into new business opportunities.

The growth of nonbank business activities of holding companies has been rapid. Insurance agencies, finance companies, mortgage companies, consulting firms, and other businesses have been started or acquired in large numbers by bank holding companies in recent years. These ventures represent an attempt to diversify banking operations to reduce risk and gain access to a broader market. Unfortunately, many bankers have found that, often, they cannot effectively manage a highly diverse set of nonbank businesses. In recent years several large holding companies sold off some of their nonbank business ventures in an effort to cut costs and raise more capital for their banks (e.g., Citigroup and Travelers).

International Banking

The growth of banking organizations at home has been paralleled by the growth of banks abroad. This expansion overseas has not been confined to the largest institutions in such established money centers as New York, Chicago, and San Francisco but also includes leading banks in regional financial centers such as Atlanta, Charlotte, and Miami. Several of the largest U.S. banks receive half or more of their net income from foreign sources, although many U.S. banks have reduced their overseas activity recently due to poorly performing international loans and high operating costs.

423

International Focus   Banking and the Drive toward a Unified Europe

The international market for banking services is likely to feel a significant impact in the years ahead as Europe, with more than 300 million consumers, moves toward economic unity. A giant step toward European unity was taken in December 1991 when leaders of the European Community (EC) signed the Maastricht Treaty, which set forth a process to achieve one economy with a single currency and a unified financial system. European integration is now well along with monetary policy cooperation among member countries now a fact of life. The European system of central banks is now conducting coordinated operations under one European Central Bank (the ECB) and employing just one European currency unit (the Euro). Indeed, the Euro has become a major tradeable currency in its own right, replacing the franc, the lira, the mark, and other traditional currencies issued by individual EC nations.

Eleven nations make up the initial European Union—Austria, Belgium, Finland, France, Germany, Ireland, Italy, Luxembourg, the Netherlands, Portugal, and Spain; others will likely join later as they come to conform with the community's membership requirements. Potential benefits include: (1) reduced currency risk for banks, investors, and traders in goods and services because of having to deal in only one currency inside the EC; (2) a more stable economy overall due to greater mobility of productive resources across the EC's various national borders; and (3) increased competition between European banks and other suppliers of goods and services as one huge market (comparable to the United States in overall size) gradually emerges out of many relatively independent, national marketplaces.

The road to complete European economic and financial unity will not be an easy journey, however. Differences in national economies, concern over unemployment and the welfare needs of citizens, and strong feelings of national identity and independence pose major problems for the newly formed European Union of 11 nations. Moreover, unlike the United States, the new union currently has no common fiscal policy that can redistribute income and productive resources out of economically robust areas toward economically depressed areas. Considerable planning will be required if European financial and economic integration is to really be of benefit to the public it is supposed to serve.

While branch banks and bank holding companies have dominated the expansion of banking inside the United States, bank expansion into international markets has taken place through a wide variety of unique organizational forms. *Representative offices,* the simplest form, represent the "eyes and ears" of a bank in foreign markets, helping to market each bank's services to both old and new customers, but these limited-service facilities cannot take deposits or book loans. In contrast, a *branch office* offers all or most of the services the home office provides, including the taking of deposits and the booking of loans. International banks sometimes find it less expensive to acquire an existing bank overseas with an established clientele than to set up their own branch office. The acquired institution becomes a *subsidiary* of the international bank, retaining its own charter and capital stock. Alternatively, a bank may establish a *joint venture* with a foreign firm, sharing expenses but gaining access to the expertise and customer contacts already made by the foreign company.

Banks today penetrate overseas markets for a wide variety of reasons. In many cases, their corporate customers expanding abroad demand access to multinational banking facilities. The huge Eurocurrency market, which spans the globe, also offers an attractive source of bank funds when domestic funding sources are less available or more costly. Foreign markets frequently offer fewer regulatory barriers and less competition than may be found at home, but also more risk (as in Argentina).

Foreign banks have grown rapidly in the United States, with many of the largest Canadian, European, and Asian banks viewing the 50 states as a huge economically and politically stable common market. (See Exhibit 15–2 for a list of some of the world's largest banks and their financial-service competitors.) Moreover, foreign banks were able to offer some services, such as underwriting corporate securities or selling insurance, that U.S. banking organizations were restrained from offering until the Financial Services

Modernization (Gramm-Leach-Bliley) Act was passed in 1999. Congress initially responded to this invasion by passing the International Banking Act in 1978, bringing foreign banks under federal regulation for the first time. Passage of the FDIC Improvement Act in 1991 also ushered in even greater regulatory powers over foreign bank activity inside the United States, granting the Federal Reserve authority to close the U.S. offices of foreign banks if they are operated in an unsafe manner or are violating U.S. laws.[1]

THE CONVERGENCE TREND IN BANKING

Perhaps the most common characteristic of all international banks today is their striving to offer a full line of services to all customers. Thus, *commercial banks,* which specialize predominantly in lending and deposit taking, are combining with *investment banks,* which deal in securities issued by their customers. Many banks in Canada, Great Britain, and Western Europe long ago took an additional step to become *universal* or *merchant banks.* Universal banks, like Germany's Deutsche Bank and Britain's Barclays Bank, provide not only deposit, loan, and security underwriting services but also consulting, insurance, and real estate sales. Merchant banks make private equity investments in businesses, investing some of their owners' capital in their customers' projects, thus becoming principals as well as creditors in business investment projects. As a result, merchant and universal banks tend to make longer-term investments than traditional banks and are active in both the money market and the capital market simultaneously.

In 1999 with passage of the Gramm-Leach-Bliley Act, leading banks in the United States began to move toward universal banking more aggressively, establishing financial holding companies (FHCs), combining banking, securities, insurance, and other affiliates under one corporate umbrella. Nineteen of the 20 largest U.S. banks now belong to an FHC. Many large and small U.S. banks have created FHCs because their traditional deposits and loans are declining and they feel the need to find new services and new revenue sources.

[1]The current provisions of the International Banking Act and the recent growth of international banking are discussed more fully in Chapter 26.

EXHIBIT 15–2
Some of the Largest Banks and Other Financial Institutions That Have Operated in the World

Sources: Board of Governors of the Federal Reserve System and various central banks.

Citigroup, United States	Swiss Bank Corporation, Switzerland
Nomura Securities, Japan	Bank of China
Dai-Ichi Kangyo Bank, Japan	National Westmister Bank, United Kingdom
Fuji Bank, Japan	Aetna Life and Casualty Insurers, United States
Bank of Tokyo–Mitsubishi	
Industrial Bank of Japan	BankAmerica, United States
Sanwa Bank, Japan	Münchner Ruckversicherungsgesellschaft, Germany
Sumitomo Mitsui Banking Corp., Japan	
Long-Term Credit Bank of Japan	Credit Suisse, Switzerland
Daiwa Bank, Japan	Bank One Corp., United States
Nikko Securities, Japan	Barclays Bank, United Kingdom
Tokoi Marine and Fire, Japan	Credit Agricole Mutuel, France
Assicurazioni Generali, Italy	Dresdner Bank, Germany
Industrial and Commerce Bank of China	Banque Nationale de Paris, France
ABN AMRO Bank, N.V., Netherlands	Midland Bank, Great Britain
American Express, United States	Hong Kong Bank, Hong Kong
HSBC Holdings PLC, United Kingdom	Credit Lyonnais, France
Merrill Lynch and Company, United States	Royal Bank of Canada, Canada
Yasuda Trust and Banking Co., Japan	Canadian Imperial Bank, Canada
Union Bank of Switzerland (UBS)	Internationale Nederlanden, Netherlands
Deutsche Bank, Germany	Wells Fargo, United States
J.P. Morgan/Chase Bank, United States	Toronto–Dominion Bank, Canada

Thus, one of the most important structural changes occurring in banking today is **convergence.** This means that banking organizations are looking more and more like other financial-service providers, offering many of the same services as security firms, insurance companies, and other service suppliers. In turn, the public is finding it much tougher today to distinguish banks from other financial-service businesses. Competition between banks and nonbank service companies is intensifying, forcing many bank and nonbank companies to consolidate into fewer, but much larger organizations.

Bank Failures

The rapid expansion of bank services has not protected some banks and banking systems from getting into serious trouble, however, due to declining economies and falling real estate and stock prices coupled with excessive government control over who does and does not receive loans. For example, late in the 1990s banks in Japan, Korea, and other parts of Asia as well as in Russia were forced to grapple with a financial crisis, with many banks collapsing or being swept up into mergers to add vitally needed capital and experienced management. More recently, Japan has been pasting together new bail-out plans (with the help of the International Monetary Fund and other public and private institutions) to stem the tide of bank failures and restore public confidence in its banking system. Bad loans and declining stock prices continue to threaten many Japanese banks and other financial institutions with failure.

In contrast, for most of the history of the United States, the American banking industry has experienced an extremely low failure rate (only about 1 or 2 percent of the U.S. banking population failing each year, on average) due to extensive regulatory supervision, a relatively strong economy, and conservative management on the part of most banks. However, the number of U.S. bank failures and the average size of U.S. failing banks advanced sharply during the 1980s due to a weak economic environment and excessive risk-taking before the bank failure rate slowed dramatically again and returned to a more normal pace as the twenty-first century approached.

The reasons behind most bank failures are numerous. Many bankers today are willing to accept greater risk in their operations, in part because of intensified competition and government insurance of bank deposits. Moreover, a worldwide movement toward banking **deregulation** (which we will discuss more fully in Chapter 18) has given banks greater opportunities to market new services and expand geographically without such strict government controls, but it has also increased their opportunities for failure. Some analysts argue that even more important is the *increased volatility of economic and financial conditions,* especially the prices of many foreign currencies which fluctuate with market conditions. This volatility has made bank earnings and stock prices more unstable and forced bankers to devote more time to the control and management of risk. An additional factor in bank failure is crime—fraud, embezzlement, and outright theft—which banks and bank regulators are working to combat with stronger security measures.

Information about U.S. bank failures each year can be found at www.fdic.gov/bank

Changing Technology

Banking today is passing through a technological revolution. Computer terminals and high-speed information processing are transforming the industry, stressing convenience and speed in handling such routine transactions as making deposits and paying for purchases. Most of the new technology is designed to reduce labor and paper costs, making the banking industry less labor intensive and more capital intensive.

Among the most important pieces of technology in the industry are automated teller machines (ATMs). ATMs accept deposits, dispense cash, and accept payments on loans and other bills owed by customers. For many banking transactions, they perform as well as human tellers do, with the added advantage of 24-hour availability. Initially, ATMs were placed on bank premises, but their growth has extended widely to shopping centers, gasoline stations, airports, and train terminals. In these locations, they are known as *remote service units* (RSUs). Most ATMs promote lower transactions costs for the customer and reduce the need for conventional branch banking offices. Related to ATMs are point-of-sale (POS) terminals located in retail stores and other commercial establishments. Connected online to the bank's computer, POS terminals accept plastic credit and debit cards, permitting the customer to pay instantly for a purchase without the necessity of cashing a check.

Another important new piece of electronic banking machinery is the automated clearinghouse (ACH). An ACH transfers information from one financial institution to another and from account to account via computer tape. The majority of banks and other financial-service institutions offering payments services are members of about three dozen ACHs serving the United States. They are used principally for handling business payrolls and processing federal government transactions. Check truncation systems are being used alongside the ACH. Such a system transmits images of checks electronically from one financial institution to another, eliminating the need to transfer paper.

Finally, banking over the *Internet* through home and office computers is expanding rapidly, allowing customers to quickly and easily enter their requests for information or to conduct remote financial transactions. While most banks' Web sites provide only information today, nearly 2,000 are offering 24-hour, Web-based transactional services, such as bill paying, transferring funds, and applying for new loans. Several Internet-only ("virtual") banks have been started recently, seeking to take advantage of low overhead, convenience, and speed. Unfortunately, this form of banking model has not been highly successful despite the savings on brick and mortar over conventional banks. One reason for the comparatively weak performance of Internet-only banking institutions appears to be their lack of volume and relatively high operating costs. However, virtual banks may become competitive in the future as more and more customers go online with their transactions and as the cost of conventional banking transactions continues to rise.

To learn about possible careers in banking see especially *www.aba. careersite.com*

These recent technological changes have profound implications for bank costs, employment, and profitability. In the future, customers will have less need to enter a bank building, and the need for brick-and-mortar branches will decline. Indeed, many branch offices have recently been closed, suggesting that future needs will be met mainly by electronically transferring information rather than by requiring people to move from one location to another. The banker's principal function will be one of providing the necessary equipment and letting customers conduct their own transactions. This development implies fewer but more highly skilled bank employees and more equipment. Heavy investment in computers and money machines will result in substantial fixed costs, requiring a large volume of transactions and favoring the largest banking organizations. The new technology of banking should further intensify pressures for consolidation of the industry into banks smaller in number but much larger in size.

Questions *to Help You Study*

1. In what ways are commercial banks of special importance to the functioning of the money and capital markets and the economy?

2. Four dominant movements in the structure of U.S. banking in recent years have been:

   a. The spread of branch banking.

   b. The growth of financial holding companies.

   c. The rise of interstate banking.

   d. The convergence of banks and nonbank firms.

   Explain what has happened in these four areas and why.

3. What is *consolidation* in banking? What appears to be driving this particular trend in the banking industry?

4. How numerous are bank failures and what seem to be their most important causes?

5. What changes are under way in bank technology and why?

PORTFOLIO CHARACTERISTICS OF COMMERCIAL BANKS

Commercial banks are the financial department stores of the financial system. They offer a wider array of financial services than any other financial institution, meeting the credit, payments, and savings needs of individuals, businesses, and governments. This characteristic of financial diversity is reflected in the basic financial statement of the industry, its balance sheet (or statement of condition). Exhibit 15–3 provides a list of the principal uses of funds (assets) and the major sources of funds (liabilities and equity capital) for all FDIC-insured U.S. commercial banks.

Cash and Due from Banks (Primary Reserves)

All commercial banks hold a substantial part of their assets in **primary reserves,** consisting of cash and deposits held with other banks. These reserves are the banker's first line of defense against withdrawals by depositors and customer demand for loans. Banks generally hold no more cash than is absolutely required to meet short-term contingencies, however, because the yield on cash assets is minimal. The deposits held with other banks do

EXHIBIT 15–3 Bank Report of Condition (Balance Sheet): Assets, Liabilities, and Capital of Insured Commercial Banks in the United States ($ Billions, Year-End Figures)

	1980		1990		2000	
	Billions of Dollars	Percent of Total Assets	Billions of Dollars	Percent of Total Assets	Billions of Dollars	Percent of Total Assets
Assets:						
Cash and deposits due from banks	$ 331.9	17.9%	$ 318.0	9.4%	$ 369.8	5.9%
Investment securities:						
U.S. Treasury securities	104.5	5.6	150.8	4.4	75.7	1.2
Federal agency securities	59.1	3.2	275.6	8.2	634.7	10.2
State and local govt. securities	146.3	7.9	83.5	2.5	92.6	1.5
Corporate bonds	13.4	0.7	85.9	2.5	233.5	3.7
Corporate stock	1.8	0.1	8.8	0.3	41.1	0.7
Investment Totals	$ 325.0	17.5%	$ 604.6	17.8%	$1,077.6	17.3%
Total loans and leases, gross	1,016.5	54.8	2,110.2	62.3	3,819.1	61.2
Real estate loans	269.1	14.5	829.8	24.5	1,670.3	26.8
Commercial and industrial loans	391.0	21.1	615.0	18.1	1,048.2	16.8
Loans to individuals	187.4	10.1	403.5	11.9	609.7	9.8
Agricultural loans	32.3	3.2	33.3	1.0	48.1	0.8
Loans to depository institutions	81.2	8.1	51.2	1.5	120.5	1.9
All other loans and leases	55.5	5.5	177.4	5.2	322.3	5.2
Less: Unearned income	−21.0	−2.1	−13.7	−0.4	−3.0	−0.1
Allowance for loan and lease losses	−10.1	−0.5	−55.5	−1.6	−64.1	−1.0
Net loans and leases	1,006.4	54.2	2,054.6	60.6	3,752.1	60.4
Bank premises and equipment	26.7	1.4	51.4	1.5	75.7	1.2
Other real estate owned	2.2	0.1	21.6	0.6	3.2	0.1
Intangible assets	NA	NA	10.6	0.3	102.7	1.6
All other assets	163.4	8.8	328.5	9.7	857.6	13.5
Total assets	$1,855.7	100.0%	$3,389.5	100.0%	$6,238.7	100.0%
Liabilities:						
Total deposits	$1,481.2	79.8%	$2,650.1	78.2%	$4,176.6	66.9%
Demand deposits	431.5	23.3	463.9	13.7	679.3	10.9
Savings deposits	200.9	10.8	798.1	23.5	1,567.0	25.1
Time deposits	554.7	29.9	1,094.7	32.3	1,371.5	22.0
Other deposits	294.1	15.8	293.4	8.7	558.8	9.0
Borrowings in the money market	177.7	9.6	385.3	11.4	1,256.2	20.1
Subordinated capital notes and debentures	6.5	0.4	23.9	0.7	87.0	1.4
Other liabilities	82.7	4.5	111.5	3.3	189.4	3.0
Total liabilities	$1,748.1	94.2%	$3,170.8	93.5%	$5,709.1	91.5%
Equity capital:						
Preferred stock	$ 0.1	0.0*	$ 1.7	0.1	$ 3.4	0.1
Common stock	21.7	1.2	30.9	0.9	31.2	0.5
Surplus	37.8	2.0	92.4	2.7	259.4	4.2
Undivided profits	48.0	2.6	93.7	2.8	236.9	3.8
Total equity capital	107.6	5.8	218.6	6.4	529.6	8.5
Total liabilities and capital	$1,855.7	100.0%	$3,389.5	100.0%	$6,238.7	100.0%

*Less than $50 million.

Source: Federal Deposit Insurance Corporation, *Historical Statistics on Banking, 1934–1992*, and *Statistics on Banking*.

provide an implicit return, however, because they are a means of "paying" for correspondent banking services. In return for the deposits of smaller banks, larger U.S. correspondent banks provide such important services as clearing checks and processing records by computer. Thousands of smaller banks across the United States invest their excess cash reserves in loans to other banks (called *federal funds*) with the help of their larger correspondents.[2]

Security Holdings and Secondary Reserves

Commercial banks hold securities acquired in the open market as a long-term investment and as a secondary reserve to help meet short-term cash needs. Many banks still hold sizable quantities of municipal securities—bonds and notes issued by state, city, and other local governments—because their interest income is tax exempt, although recent tax reform legislation has substantially limited the tax advantages of municipal notes and bonds for banks. However, holdings of U.S. Treasury obligations and debt obligations of federal agencies (such as the Federal National Mortgage Association ("Fannie Mae") or the Farm Credit System) are much larger in volume today than municipal securities in U.S. bank portfolios. Banks generally favor shorter-term government securities because these securities can be marketed readily to cover short-term cash needs and are free of default risk. In the most recent period banks have been shifting more heavily toward federal agency-issued securities not only due to their higher yields, but also because, in the United States at least, the volume of marketable U.S. Treasury securities has been falling recently as federal government revenues have risen.

A related type of security purchased in large volume by banks are loan-backed securities, each representing an interest in a pool of previously made loans, which pay interest and principal to investors as the loans are paid out. Most loan-backed securities held by banks are backed by government-guaranteed real estate mortgages or credit-card receivables. By the turn of the century mortgage-backed securities accounted for more than half of all investment securities held by U.S. banks.

Commercial banks also hold small amounts of corporate bonds and notes, although they generally prefer to make direct loans to businesses as opposed to purchasing their securities in the open market. Under existing regulations, U. S. commercial banks are forbidden to purchase most types of corporate stock. However, banks do hold small amounts of corporate stock as collateral for some of their loans and are allowed to invest in selected equities, such as the stock of small business investment companies, community development corporations, and the Federal Reserve banks.

Recently, American banks have been under strong regulatory pressure to value their security holdings and selected other assets and liabilities at current market value rather than at book value on the day they were acquired. The long-range goal is to make bank balance sheets reflect more accurately the true condition of a bank so that capital-market investors and depositors can make a more informed judgment about the bank's true financial standing. Unfortunately, this step has done little, thus far, to improve the quality of information coming from bank financial reports.

---

[2]A more complete discussion of the operations of the federal funds market is presented in Chapter 11. Primary reserves also include reserves held behind deposits as required by Federal Reserve System. Recently banks have been reducing their primary reserves, especially the portion held with the central bank, known as legally required reserves. Not only are banks becoming more efficient in managing their cash positions, but by using so-called "sweep accounts" they have been able to transfer funds out of deposits bearing legal reserve requirements into reserve-free deposits, thereby reducing some of their funding costs.

Loans

The principal business of commercial banks is to make *loans* to qualified borrowers (or at least make it easier for their customers to find credit from some source (with a bank perhaps agreeing to underwrite a customer's security issue or guarantee a loan from a third-party lender). Loans are among the highest yielding assets a bank can add to its portfolio, and they often provide the largest portion of traditional banks' operating revenue.

Banks make loans of reserves to other banks through the federal funds market and to securities dealers through repurchase agreements. Far more important in dollar volume, however, are direct loans to businesses and individuals. These loans arise from negotiation between the bank and its customer and result in a written agreement designed to meet the specific credit needs of the customer and the requirements of the bank for adequate security and income.

As shown in Exhibit 15–3, a substantial portion of bank credit is extended to commercial and industrial customers in the form of direct loans. Historically, commercial banks have preferred to make *short-term loans* to businesses, principally to support purchases of inventory. Recently, however, banks have lengthened the maturity of their business loans to include *term loans* (which have maturities over one year) to finance the purchase of buildings, machinery, and equipment. Moreover, longer-term loans to business firms have been supplanted to some extent in recent years by equipment leasing plans. These leases are the functional equivalent of a loan—that is, the customer not only makes the required lease payments while using the equipment but is also responsible for repairs and maintenance and for any taxes due. Lease financing carries not only significant cost and tax advantages for the customer but also substantial tax advantages for a bank, because it can depreciate leased equipment.

Commercial banks are also important lenders in the real estate field, supporting the construction of residential and commercial structures. In fact, real estate loans are, by volume, the most important bank loan category. Major types of loans in the real estate category include farm and real estate credit, conventional government-guaranteed (FHA and VA) single-family residential home loans, conventional and government-guaranteed loans on multifamily residences (such as apartments), and mortgage loans on nonfarm commercial properties. Today, commercial banks are the most important source of construction financing in the economy.

To learn more about trends in bank balance sheets (reports of condition) and other financial reports for the banking industry as a whole see *www.fdic.gov/ bank* and for individual banking firms see *www. fdic.gov/bank/individual*

One of the most dynamic areas in bank lending today is the making of installment loans to individuals and families, particularly loans secured by a property owner's equity in his or her home (i.e., *home equity loans,* the interest costs of which may be tax deductible to the borrower). Home equity loans can be used to finance a college education, start a new business, or to cover a variety of other financial needs not related to housing. While banks began making home equity loans equal to a fraction of a home owner's equity, intense competition among lenders has resulted in many home equity loans and lines of credit today exceeding the value of the home owner's equity investment in a home, increasing lenders' risk. Banks also finance the purchase of automobiles, home furnishings, and appliances and provide funds to modernize homes and other properties and to pay for education and travel.

There is a growing concern today that consumer loans, particularly of the credit-card variety, have become more risky for banks due to higher default rates. Many banks and credit card companies have increased their issue of new credit cards explosively, democratizing debt in order to reach millions of new customers, many of whom represent serious risks for lenders. Intense competition has encouraged many banks to give credit cards to customers who may have little or no credit history, some of whom turn out to be poor credit risks.

Recently bankers have faced the necessity of closely examining the *quality,* not just the quantity, of their loans, especially in the wake of the terrorist attacks in 2001. Recent events have demonstrated the great sensitivity of bank loan performance to changes in the economy. Problem loans reduce bank loan revenues, raise operating expenses, and force bankers to reexamine their relationships with customers and redesign and renegotiate the terms they are offering on loan contracts.

Deposits

To carry out their extensive lending and investing operations, banks draw on a wide variety of deposit and nondeposit sources of funds. The bulk of commercial bank funds—more than three fourths of the total—comes from *deposits.* There are three main types of deposits: demand, savings, and time. *Demand deposits,* more commonly known as *checking accounts,* are still the principal means of making payments because they are safer than cash and are widely accepted (although outside the United States smart cards, credit cards, and transfers by electronic means have generally outstripped demand deposits as payments media). *Savings deposits* generally are in small dollar amounts; they bear a relatively low interest rate but may be withdrawn by the depositor with no notice. *Time deposits* carry a fixed maturity, a penalty for early withdrawal, and usually offer the highest interest rates a bank can pay. Time deposits may be divided into nonnegotiable certificates of deposit (CDs), which are usually small, consumer-type accounts, and negotiable CDs that may be traded in the open market in million-dollar amounts and are purchased mainly by corporations all over the world.

During the past three decades, new forms of checkable (demand) deposits appeared, combining the essential features of both demand and savings deposits. These **transaction accounts** include negotiable orders of withdrawal (NOWs) and automatic transfer services (ATS). NOW accounts may be drafted to pay bills but also earn interest, while ATS is a preauthorized payment service in which the bank transfers funds from an interest-bearing savings account to a checking account as necessary to cover checks written by the customer. Two newer types of transaction accounts—money market deposit accounts (MMDAs) and Super NOWs—are designed to compete directly with the high-yielding share accounts offered by money market mutual funds, carry prevailing market rates on short-term funds, and can be drafted via check, automatic withdrawal, or telephone transfer.

In recent years banks have experienced a shift in their deposits toward more costly interest-bearing accounts, such as MMDAs. These newer deposits are generally *market-linked accounts,* the returns of which are tied to movements in interest rates and security prices, reflecting prevailing credit conditions in the financial system. This shift toward more expensive, market-responsive deposits reflects the growing sophistication of bank customers, who have developed efficient cash management practices and insist on maximum returns on their funds.

Moreover, the cost of attracting customer funds has been further increased in recent years by the tendency of bankers to expand their services in an effort to offer their customers "one-stop" financial convenience. Thus, to retain old customers and attract new ones, many banks have developed or are working through franchise agreements to offer (1) security brokerage services so that customers can purchase stocks, bonds, and shares in mutual funds and pay by charging their deposit accounts; (2) insurance counters to make life, health, and property-casualty insurance coverage available (often through joint ventures with affiliated or cooperating nonbank firms); (3) account relocation services and real estate brokerage of homes and other properties for customers who move; (4) financial and tax counseling centers to aid customers with important personal and business decisions; and (5) merchant banking services that aid major corporations with mergers and long-term financing requirements. These new services may have opened up new markets for banks, but they have also created new risks for bank management and demanded greater efficiency in bank operations.

Nondeposit Sources of Funds

One of the most marked trends in banking in recent years is greater use of **nondeposit funds** (borrowings), especially as competition for deposits increases. Principal nondeposit sources of funds for banks today include purchases of reserves (federal funds) from other banks, security repurchase agreements (when securities are sold temporarily by a bank and then bought back later), and the issuance of capital notes. Capital notes are of particular interest because many of these securities may be counted under current regulations as capital for purposes of determining how much a bank can lend (i.e., its *loan limit*). Both state and federal laws limit the amount of money a commercial bank can lend to any one borrower to a fraction of the bank's capital. To be counted as capital, however, capital notes must be subordinated to deposits, so that if a bank is liquidated, the depositors have first claim to its assets.

Recently banks have turned to new nondeposit funds sources, including floating-rate CDs and notes sold in international markets, sales of blocks of loans, securitizations of selected assets, and standby credit guarantees. The floating-rate securities tend to be longer-

EXHIBIT 15–4
Securitizations of Bank Loans to Raise Funds

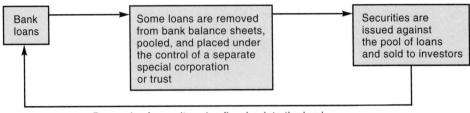

Proceeds of security sales flow back to the bank
as a new source of funds

term borrowings of funds, stretching out beyond one year, with an interest rate that is adjusted periodically to reflect changing conditions in international markets. Larger banks (such as J.P. Morgan/Chase and Citicorp) have expanded their sales of short-term business loans from their books, usually selling these credits in million-dollar blocks to raise new funds. Better-quality loans have been packaged into asset pools and *securitized*—that is, used as collateral for bank security issues that are sold to investors through a broker or dealer. (See Exhibit 15–4.) The bank secures additional funds to make new loans and investments from these **securitized assets,** which have included packages of auto, credit-card, home mortgage, and other loan types. The packaged loans generate interest and principal payments, which are passed through to investors who purchased the securities backed by these loans.

Finally, many large banks today are issuing **standby credit letters** on behalf of their customers who borrow from another lender or sell securities in the open market. As illustrated in Exhibit 15–5, standbys contain the bank's pledge to pay (guarantee) if its customer cannot pay a third party. They generate fee income for the bank without using up scarce funds or booking more assets that would require a bank to pledge more capital behind them.

Many of these activities are *off-balance-sheet transactions*—not recorded on a bank's balance sheet and using up little or no bank capital. However, securitizations, standby credits, and other off-balance-sheet activities help banks provide services to their customers and earn *fee income*—the fastest growing form of bank revenue. The result is an expansion in bank net earnings without booking additional assets on the bank's balance sheet. One possible problem for the future, however, is the prospect of significant new restrictions and stiffer reporting requirements on off-balance-sheet activities in the wake of the collapse of Enron Corporation.

Equity Capital

Equity capital (or net worth) supplied by a bank's stockholders provides only a minor portion (only about 8 percent, on average) of total funds for most banks today. In fact, while the ratio of equity capital to bank loans and deposits has risen recently, it previously had been in a decline for several decades due to falling profit margins, inflation, and efforts by bank managers to employ greater financial leverage. This concerned many financial experts because one of the most important functions of equity capital is to keep a bank open in the face of operating losses until management can correct its problems. Recently, federal law has mandated minimum capital-to-asset ratios for banks, and many banks have recently expanded their equity capital positions. There is also a set of cooperative international capital regulations for major banks in the United States, Great Britain, Japan, and the nations of Western Europe, imposing minimum capital requirements on all banks in leading industrialized countries based on the degree of risk exposure that each of these banks faces.[3]

[3]See Chapter 18 for a fuller discussion of the Basle Agreement on bank capital requirements.

EXHIBIT 15–5
**Bank Standby
Letters of Credit
Issued on Behalf of
Their Customers**

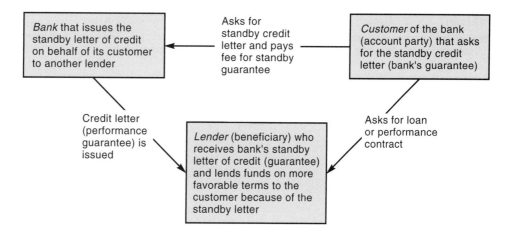

Revenues and Expenses

The majority of bank revenues come from interest and fees on loans, as shown by the industry's statement of earnings and expenses presented in Exhibit 15–6. Interest and dividends on security holdings are the second most important source of bank revenues after loans. Other minor sources of income include earnings from trust (fiduciary) activities and service charges on deposit accounts.

Bank expenses have risen rapidly in recent years, threatening to squeeze the industry's operating income. Greater competition from bank and *nonbank financial institutions* has resulted in increases in the real cost of raising funds, and the expense of upgrading computers and automated equipment has placed an added drain on bank revenues. Interest on deposits and other borrowed funds is the principal expense item for most commercial banks, followed by the salaries and wages of their employees. Recently, however, interest expenses on bank deposits and other borrowings have declined in percentage terms, as banks have carried on a growing share of their service operations off of their balance sheets.

A careful perusal of the statement of earnings and expenses (Report of Income) for all U.S. insured banks in Exhibit 15–6 shows an interesting arrangement of revenue and expense accounts. First, bankers record all of their bank's interest income from loans and security investments. Then the total interest paid out on borrowed funds is subtracted to derive each bank's net interest income or *interest margin.* The interest margin measures how efficiently a bank is performing its function of borrowing and lending funds. For many banks the interest margin is the principal determinant of their profitability.

Of increasing importance in the industry, however, is the *noninterest margin,* which is the difference between total noninterest income (such as service fees on deposits) and noninterest expenses (such as employee salaries and wages). The noninterest margin is growing in importance as a determinant of bank profits because commercial banks are developing more and more new services that generate noninterest fees, such as security underwriting services, guaranteeing the credit a customer has gotten from another lender, managing pension plans for corporations, and so forth. Because bankers face stiff competition for funding, they have little influence over the interest expenses on their borrowed funds. Accordingly, they work especially hard to minimize their *noninterest expenses,* particularly employee costs, by substituting automated equipment for labor.

In summary, bankers today must contend with increasing competition from both foreign and domestic financial institutions; a shifting customer base of older, higher-income, and better-educated consumers; the ever-changing technology of service production and delivery; and greater risk of failure in a more competitive and volatile environment.

You can track recent trends in U.S. bank earnings and expenses through *FYI* and *Bank Trends,* two publications appearing on the Federal Deposit Insurance Corporation's web site at *www.fdic.gov*

EXHIBIT 15–6 **Bank Report of Income (Earnings and Expense Statement):**
Income and Expenses of Insured Commercial Banks in the United States, 1980,1990, and 2000

	1980		1990		2000	
	Billions of Dollars	Percent of Total Operating Income	Billions of Dollars	Percent of Total Operating Income	Billions of Dollars	Percent of Total Operating Income
Total interest income:	$176.4	92.5%	$320.5	85.4%	$428.0	73.7%
Interest and fees on loans	127.0	66.7	234.4	62.4	319.4	55.0
Lease income	1.4	0.7	4.4	1.2	10.8	1.7
Income from investment securities	23.1	12.1	51.1	13.6	68.5	11.8
Trading account income	NA	NA	5.4	1.4	9.4	1.6
Income from federal funds loans and security RPs	8.8	4.6	12.5	3.3	13.5	2.3
Other interest income	16.3	8.5	12.7	3.4	17.2	3.0
Total interest expense:	$120.1	63.0%	$205.0	54.6%	$224.2	38.6%
Interest on deposits	34.9	18.3	161.5	43.0	151.7	26.1
Interest on federal funds and security RPs	16.8	8.8	22.7	6.0	27.4	4.7
Interest on subordinated capital notes and debentures	0.5	0.3	1.8	0.5	5.9	1.0
Interest on other borrowed funds	4.4	2.3	18.9	5.0	39.2	6.8
Net interest income	$ 56.3	29.5%	$715.5	30.8%	$203.8	35.1%
Total noninterest income:	14.3	7.5	54.9	14.6	152.8	26.3
Service charges on deposits	3.2	1.7	11.4	3.0	23.8	4.1
Other noninterest income	11.2	5.9	43.4	11.6	129.0	22.2
Total noninterest expense:	46.7	24.5	115.8	30.8	215.8	37.2
Employee salary and benefits	24.7	13.0	51.8	13.8	88.5	15.2
Occupancy expenses	7.4	3.9	17.4	4.6	26.8	4.6
All other noninterest expenses	14.6	7.7	46.6	12.4	100.5	17.3
Net noninterest income	−32.4	−17.0	−60.9	−16.2	−63.0	−10.8
Provision for loan and lease losses	4.5	2.4	−32.1	8.6	29.3	5.0
Pretax net operating income	19.5	10.2	22.6	6.0	111.5	19.2
Securities gains (or losses)	−0.9	−0.5	0.5	0.1	−2.3	−0.4
Applicable income taxes	4.7	2.5	7.7	2.1	38.0	6.5
Net extraordinary items	0.0*	0.0**	0.6	0.2	−0.3	0.1
Net income after taxes	$ 14.0	7.3%	$ 16.0	4.3%	$ 71.2	12.3%

*Less than $50 million.
**Less than 0.05 percent.

Source: Federal Deposit Insurance Corporation.

Questions *to Help You Study*

6. What are the principal *uses* of commercial bank funds? Major *sources* of funds?

7. What new sources and uses of funds have been developed in the banking industry in recent years?

8. Please explain how *securitization* of loans helps a bank raise new funds.

9. What benefits do *standby credit letters* provide for banks and their customers?

10. What are a bank's principal *revenue* and *expense* items?

11. What is the *net interest margin?* The *noninterest margin?* Why are they important to banks?

Powerful trends are reshaping banking around the globe:

1. *Deregulation* of banking in the United States, Canada, Great Britain, Japan, and in many other nations around the globe, permitting private markets to determine bank prices and services instead of governments.

2. Increased *penetration of foreign markets* by major banks, securities firms, and other financial institutions in most countries, so that banking and financial services are increasingly becoming a global industry with few territorial boundaries.

3. Growing *proliferation of services* (i.e., financial innovation) as bankers respond to increased competition, including the spread of securities underwriting, insurance services, and real estate development and brokerage services.

4. A spreading *technological revolution* with more banking transactions carried out via teller machines, satellites, "smart" cards, fax machines, the internet and worldwide web, and other innovative devices instead of through human labor, transforming banking into an increasingly automated, fixed-cost, capital-intensive industry.

5. *Changing sources and uses of bank funds* as banking's customer base changes toward older, more financially sophisticated, and more interest-sensitive depositors. New sources of bank funds include loan sales, securitized loans, and market-linked accounts (where yields to the depositor fluctuate with market conditions). In addition, banks are doing more "off-balance-sheet" support of their customers' financial-service needs, providing guarantees behind customer borrowings and other support services, such as financial advice and consulting. These support services usually earn fee income for banks but avoid draining scarce bank capital.

6. Growing *international cooperation* between governments and regulatory agencies from different countries to promote uniform regulation and supervision of banks, regardless of country.

MONEY CREATION AND DESTRUCTION BY BANKS AND BANK ACCOUNTING

Commercial banks differ from many other financial institutions in one critical respect: *Banks have the power to create money in the form of new checkable deposits, credit card lines, debit cards, and other immediately spendable funds.* The banking system creates and destroys billions of dollars in money each day.

Money creation by banks is made possible because the public readily accepts claims on bank deposits (mainly checks, credit and debit cards, and computer entries) in payment for goods and services. In addition, the law requires individual banks to hold only a fraction of the amount of deposits received from the public as cash reserves, thus freeing up a majority of incoming funds for making loans and purchasing securities.

As we saw previously in Chapters 13 and 14, vault cash and deposits at the Fed constitute a U.S. bank's holdings of **legal reserves**—those assets acceptable for meeting legal reserve requirements behind the public's deposits. In turn, each bank's legal reserves may be divided into required reserves and excess reserves. *Required reserves* are equal to the legal reserve requirement percentage ratio times the volume of deposits subject to reserve requirements. For example, if a bank holds $50 million in checkable (transaction) deposits and the law requires it to hold 3 percent of its transaction accounts in legal reserves, the reserve requirement for this bank would be $50 million $\times$ 3%, or $1.5 million.

On the other hand, **excess reserves** equal the difference between the total legal reserves actually held by a bank and the amount of its required reserves. For example, if a bank is required to hold legal reserves equal to $1.5 million but finds on a given date that it has $500,000 in cash on the premises and $1.5 million on deposit with the Federal Reserve bank in its region, this bank holds $500,000 in excess reserves.

The Creation of Money and Credit

The distinction between excess and required reserves is important because it plays a key role in the growth of bank loans and the creation of money by the banking system. To understand why, we need to make certain assumptions concerning how banks account for their transactions with customers and the regulations they face. To simplify the arithmetic, assume that one of the banking system's key regulators, the Federal Reserve, has set a basic legal reserve requirement of 20 percent behind the public's deposits.[4] Therefore, for every dollar that the public deposits in the banking system, each bank must put aside in either vault cash or deposits at the Federal Reserve 20 cents as required reserves. Assume also that, initially, the banking system is "loaned up"—that is, bankers have loaned out all excess reserves available to them. In addition, assume that all bankers are profit maximizers and attempt to loan out immediately any excess funds available to earn the most income possible.

Suppose that a deposit of $1,000 is made from some source outside the banking system. For example, the public may decide to convert a portion of its currency and coin holdings ("pocket money") into bank deposits for greater convenience and safety. Suppose a deposit of $1,000 appears at Bank A as shown in Exhibit 15–7. This exhibit contains an abbreviated balance sheet (T account) for Bank A with changes in its assets shown on the left-hand side and changes in its liabilities and net worth shown on the right-hand side.

Under the assumed Federal Reserve regulations, Bank A is required to place $200 aside as required legal reserves (i.e., 20 percent of the $1,000 deposit), leaving excess reserves of $800. Because the $800 in cash earns no interest income, the banker will immediately try to loan out these excess reserves. Banks make loans today by a simple accounting entry. The borrower signs a note indicating how much is borrowed, at what rate of interest, and when the note will come due. In return, the banker creates a checking account in the borrower's name. In our example, assume that Bank A has received a loan request from one of its customers and decides to grant the customer a loan of $800—exactly the amount of excess reserves it holds.

Banks find that, when they make loans, the borrowed funds are withdrawn rapidly as borrowers spend the proceeds of their loans. Moreover, it is likely that most of the borrowed funds will wind up as deposits in other banks as borrowing customers write checks against their loan balances. For this reason, Bank A will not loan out any more than the $800 in excess reserves it currently holds. This way, when a borrower spends his or her funds and the money flows to other banks, Bank A will have sufficient funds in reserve to cover the cash letters demanding payment that it will receive from other banks.

Assume that the $800 loaned by Bank A eventually winds up as a deposit in Bank B. As indicated in Exhibit 15–7, Bank B must place $160 (20 percent) of this deposit in required reserves; it then has excess reserves of $640, which are quickly loaned out. As the new borrowers spend their funds, the $640 in loans will find its way into deposits at Bank C. After setting aside required reserves of $128, Bank C has excess reserves of $512. It too will move rapidly to loan out these funds if suitable borrowers can be found.

The pattern of these changes in deposits, loans, and reserves should now be clear. The results are summarized in the bottom portion of Exhibit 15–7. Note that the total volume of bank deposits has been considerably expanded by the time it reaches the third or fourth

---

[4]Commercial banks' current reserve requirements and the role that they play in government monetary policy are discussed in Chapter 14.

EXHIBIT 15–7
The Creation of
Credit and Deposits
by the Banking
System

1. Bank A Receives New Deposit			
Assets		*Liabilities*	
Required reserves	200	Deposits	1,000
Cash	800		

4. Loan Made by Bank B			
Assets		*Liabilities*	
Required reserves	160	Deposits	800
Loans	640		

2. Loan Made by Bank A			
Assets		*Liabilities*	
Required reserves	200	Deposits	1,000
Loans	800		

5. Deposit of Loan Funds in Bank C			
Assets		*Liabilities*	
Required reserves	128	Deposits from Bank B	640
Cash	512		

3. Deposit of Loan Funds in Bank B			
Assets		*Liabilities*	
Required reserves	160	Deposits from Bank A	800
Cash	640		

6. Loan Made by Bank C			
Assets		*Liabilities*	
Required reserves	128	Deposits	640
Loans	512		

By making loans whenever there are excess reserves, the banking system will ultimately generate a volume of deposits several times larger than the amount of the initial deposit received by Bank A.

Transactions within the Banking System			
Name of Bank	**Deposits Received**	**Loans Made**	**Required Reserves**
A	$1,000	$ 800	$ 200
B	800	640	160
C	640	512	128
D	512	410	102
—	—	—	—
—	—	—	—
Final amounts for all banks in the system	$5,000	$4,000	$1,000

bank. Similarly, the total volume of new loans grows rapidly as funds flow from bank to bank within the system. By making loans whenever excess reserves appear, the banking system eventually creates money in the form of deposits and loans several times larger than the original volume of new funds received.

Destruction of Deposits and Reserves

Not only can banks expand deposits and money by a multiple amount, but they can also contract deposits and money by a multiple amount. This is illustrated in Exhibit 15–8, in which a depositor has decided to withdraw $1,000 from a transaction account at Bank A and not to place the money on deposit in another bank. Recall that behind the $1,000 deposit, Bank A holds only $200 in required reserves. This means that when the deposit is

EXHIBIT 15–8
Deposit and Credit Destruction in the Banking System

Depositor withdraws funds

Federal Reserve Bank		Bank A	
Assets	*Liabilities*	*Assets*	*Liabilities*
	Member bank reserves −1,000	Required reserves −1,000	Deposits −1,000

If Bank A was loaded up when the withdrawal occurred, it will now have a reserve deficiency of $800 as indicated below:

Total reserves lost at Bank A when depositor withdrew funds	$1,000
Required reserves no longer needed due to deposit withdrawals	−200
Net reserve deficit at Bank A	$ 800

Bank A		Bank B	
Assets	*Liabilities*	*Assets*	*Liabilities*
Securities −800		Required reserves −800	Deposits −800
Required reserves +800 from Bank B			

The sale of securities in the amount of $800 enables Bank A to cover its reserve deficit. However, assume that customers of Bank B bought those securities and that bank was already loaned up. Therefore, Bank B now has a reserve deficiency of $640. Thus:

Total reserves lost at Bank B after deposit withdrawals to purchase Bank A's securities	$800
Required reserves no longer needed due to deposit withdrawal	−160
Net reserve deficit at Bank B	$640

withdrawn, that bank will have a net deficiency of $800. If Bank A is loaned up and has used all of its cash to make loans and investments, it will have to raise the necessary funds through the sale of securities or through borrowing.

Suppose that Bank A decides to sell securities in the amount of $800. As indicated in Exhibit 15–8, the sale of securities increases Bank A's legal reserves by the necessary amount. However, the individuals and institutions that purchase those securities pay for them by wiring funds or writing checks against their deposits in other banks, reducing the legal reserves of those institutions.

For example, assume that Bank B loses deposits of $800 and required legal reserves of $800 as Bank A gains these funds. Considering Bank A and Bank B together, total deposits have fallen by $1,800. This deposit contraction has freed up $360 ($200 + $160) in required reserves. However, if Bank B is also loaned up and has a net reserve deficiency of $640, further contraction of deposits will occur as Bank B attempts to cover its reserve deficiency by drawing reserves from other banks. Ultimately, deposits will contract by a multiple amount as banks try to cover their reserve deficits by raising funds at the expense of other banks.

Implications of Money Creation and Destruction

This capacity of banks to create and destroy money and deposits has a number of important implications for the financial system and the economy. Creation of money by banks is one of the most important sources of credit funds in the global economy—an important supplement to the supply of savings in providing funds for investment so the economy can grow faster. Money created by banks is instantly available for spending and, therefore, unless carefully controlled by government action, can fuel inflation. As we saw earlier in Chapters 13 and 14, that is why the Federal Reserve System and other central banks around the globe regulate interest rates and the growth of credit principally by influencing the growth of bank reserves and deposits.

Questions *to Help You Study*

12. How are banks able to *create money?*

13. Is the ability of banks to create money of significance for the economy and the creation of new jobs?

14. What are the dangers of money creation by banks?

15. How do banks *destroy money?*

16. Why is money creation and destruction of importance in the pursuit of public policy?

Summary of the Chapter

The banking industry has undergone significant financial and structural changes in recent years as well as expanding the number of services that banks offer to the public.

- One key trend reshaping the global banking industry is *consolidation* into fewer, but larger, banks serving geographically broader markets. Banking is one of the leading industries in mergers and acquisitions each year.

- Inside the United States the spread of larger banks has been accomplished through the rapid expansion of branch banks, bank holding companies, and interstate banking firms. In Europe banking units are spreading throughout the European Community, crossing national boundaries and also investing in banking facilities inside the United States.

- Leading banks around the globe have reached out to become *universal banks,* offering not only traditional services (including checking and savings deposits and loans) but also securities underwriting, insurance policy sales and underwriting, real estate services, and longer-term corporate funding, generating new sources of revenue but also new risks for the banking community. Large banks increasingly are experiencing *convergence,* offering many of the same services as other financial industries, such as insurance companies and security firms.

- *Cost pressures* have encouraged banks not only to grow larger, but to automate as many of their services as possible. This has enabled many banks to reduce the number of their employees and close many full-service branch offices.

- A growing list of bank services are now being offered through automated teller machines (ATMs), through computer networks, and via telephones, satellites, and cable television systems. In short, banking is becoming a more heavily *fixed-cost industry* (based on greater volumes of capital equipment) with a smaller proportion of variable costs (especially labor time).

- The industry's financial statements are undergoing changes paralleling the above-noted structural changes. More of a bank's resources today typically are devoted to loans and to nontraditional fee-generating services (such as assisting customers with purchases and sales of securities and with financial planning). At the same time nondeposit borrowings and bank stockholders' capital have grown as sources of bank funds while deposits—the traditional main source of bank funding—have become somewhat less important as a key source of bank funding.

- Finally, banks are still the most important institution in most financial systems around the globe. And they remain the leading financial institution in creating money. Banks create money both by offering checkable deposits and by granting loans (credit). However, more and more nonbank financial institutions are competing with banks in money and credit creation, offering parallel services and posing increasingly intense competition for the banking industry.

Key Terms

Banking structure, *420*
State-chartered banks, *421*
National banks, *421*
Consolidation, *421*
Branch banking, *422*
Bank holding company, *422*

Convergence, *426*
Deregulation, *427*
Primary reserves, *428*
Transaction accounts, *433*
Nondeposit funds, *433*
Securitized assets, *434*

Standby credit letters, *434*
Money creation, *437*
Legal reserves, *437*
Excess reserves, *437*

Problems

1. Given the following information on the revenues and expenses of First National Bank, determine the bank's net income after taxes for the year just concluded:

Salaries and employee benefits	$ 80,000	Applicable income taxes	$ 50,000
Interest on deposits	170,000	Occupancy costs	11,000
Interest on loans	320,000	Provision for loan losses	22,000
Income from U.S. Treasury		Miscellaneous expenses	8,000
securities	75,000	Interest on municipal securities	86,000
Extraordinary items, net	-0-	Service charges on deposits	10,000
Interest on nondeposit borrowings	30,000	Miscellaneous operating	
Net securities gains	-0-	revenues	13,000

2. Construct the report of condition (balance sheet) for First National Bank for December 31 of the year just ended from the following information:

Equity capital	$ 50 million	Real estate loans	$ 60 million
Demand deposits	100 million	U.S. Treasury securities	25 million
Savings deposits	150 million	Commercial and	
Time deposits	200 million	industrial loans	300 million
Federal funds borrowings	12 million	Other liabilities	38 million
Cash and due from banks	20 million	Municipal securities	55 million
Other assets	50 million	Loans to individuals	40 million

3. See if you can fill in correctly the missing items from the balance sheet (report of condition) and the statement of earnings and expenses (report of income) of the bank whose financial accounts are listed below:

Balance Sheet		**Statement of Earnings and Expenses**	
Cash and interbank deposits	$ 11	Revenue sources:	
Investment securities	?	Domestic loan interest and fees	$?
Federal funds sold	8	Foreign loan interest and fees	6
Loans, gross	81	Income from security investments	4
Allowance for loan losses	(6)	Miscellaneous revenues	1
Unearned discount on loans	(1)	Total revenues	?
Net loans	?		
Premises and fixed assets	2	Expenses:	
Miscellaneous assets	5	Interest on deposits	?
Total assets	$110	Interest on nondeposit borrowings	1
Demand deposits	?	Salaries and wages	2
Savings deposits	20	Occupancy costs	1
Time deposits	65	Provision for loan losses	1
Nondeposit borrowings	12	Miscellaneous expenses	2
Total liabilities	?	Total expenses	15
Stockholder's equity capital	4	Net operating income	3
		Income taxes	?
		Net income (or loss) after taxes	1

4. Suppose you have been given the financial information below for a commercial bank:

Income taxes owed	$ 13	Interest on nondeposit borrowings	$ 8
Noninterest revenues from service fees	70	Salaries and wages	
Interest revenues from loans	129	of bank employees	27
Interest and dividends from		Overhead costs	3
investments in securities	26	Loan-loss provision	2
Dividends paid to stockholders	4	Securities gains (or losses)	0
Interest paid to depositors	64		

a. Please calculate this bank's net interest income, net noninterest income, pretax net operating income, net income after taxes, undivided profits (or retained earnings), total revenues, and total expenses.

b. Suppose the above bank's return on assets—the ratio of its net income after taxes to total assets—is 0.85 percent. What is the total of the bank's assets in dollars?

c. Suppose this bank's return on stockholder's equity capital—the ratio of its net income after taxes to total equity capital—is 12 percent. What is the bank's total equity capital in dollars?

d. Suppose the above bank's total deposits equal 75 percent of its total liabilities. How many deposits in total dollar volume does the bank hold?

5. Please identify each of the terms and concepts from this chapter that are described or defined below.

a. The number, relative sizes, and types of banks in a given market or in the industry as a whole.

b. Charter of incorporation issued by a state.

c. Charter of incorporation from the Comptroller of the Currency.

d. Smaller financial institutions combined into larger financial institutions.

e. A corporation owning stock in one or more banks.

f. Banking organization that sells services through multiple offices.

g. Liberalizing any government rules that restrict what private businesses, including financial institutions, can do.

h. Cash and deposits held with other banks.

i. Deposits used to make payments.

j. Loans packaged together in a pool.

k. Deposits held at the Federal Reserve banks plus currency and coin in bank vaults.

Questions about the Web and the Money and Capital Markets

1. If you wanted to find the individual Web sites of banks in your local community how would you go about it? In your opinion which bank serving your local area has the best Web site? Why?

2. What is the difference between the Comptroller of the Currency and the Federal Reserve System according to their Web sites? Which is the oldest of these two regulatory agencies?

3. Where is the banking commission of your home state located according to their Web site?

4. If you were interested in pursuing a career in the banking industry how could you find out what jobs are available by exploring the Web?

5. How do the financial statements of a bank differ from those of a nonbank company? Using a Web-based database (such as Standard and Poor's Market Insight) compare the financial statements of a banking firm (like Citigroup) with those of a nonbank business of comparable size.

Selected References

Canner, Glenn B. "Recent Developments in Home Equity Lending." *Federal Reserve Bulletin*, April 1998, pp. 241–51.

De Nicolo, Gianni. "Size, Charter Value, and Risk in Banking: An International Perspective." *International Finance Discussion Papers*, No. 689. Board of Governors of the Federal Reserve System, December 2000.

Lopez, Jose A. "Patterns in the Foreign Ownership of U.S. Banking Assets." *Economic Letter*, Federal Reserve Bank of San Francisco, November 24, 2000, pp. 1–3.

Marion, Justin. "Europe: Risk and Reward under Monetary Unification." *Southwest Economy*, Federal Reserve Bank of Dallas, November–December 1998, pp. 4–8.

Rose, Peter S. "The Quest for Bank Funds: New Directions in a New Market." *The Canadian Banker*, December 1987, pp. 56–61.

———— *Commercial Bank Management*, 5th ed. New York: Irwin/McGraw-Hill, 2002.

———— *Banking across State Lines: Public and Private Consequences*, Westport, CT: Quorum Books, 1997.

Santomero, Anthony M. "The Causes and Effect of Financial Modernization." *Business Review*, Federal Reserve Bank of Philadelphia, Fourth Quarter 2001.

Treacy, William F., and Mark S. Carey. "Credit Risk Rating at Large U.S. Banks." *Federal Reserve Bulletin*, November 1998, pp. 897–921.

Woosley, Lynn. "Store Branching: A Part in Banking's Future." *Financial Update*, Federal Reserve Bank of Atlanta, January 1997, pp. 1–2, 4.

Chapter **Sixteen**

Nonbank Thrift Institutions: Savings and Loan Associations, Savings Banks, Credit Unions, and Money Market Funds

Learning Objectives In This Chapter

- You will see how significant *thrift institutions* are in the functioning of a modern economy and financial system.

- You will discover what types of *services* thrift institutions offer to the public and who their principal competitors are.

- You will come to understand the principal differences between major types of thrift institutions—savings and loan associations, savings banks, credit unions, and money market funds—as well as their principal similarities and why these differences and similarities are important.

What's in This Chapter? Key Topics Outline

The Savings and Loan and Savings Bank Industries: Origins and Characteristics

Mutuals versus Stock Companies

Deregulation and Sources and Uses of Funds

Maturity Mismatch and Other Industry Problems

INTRODUCTION

There is a tendency in discussions of the financial system to minimize the role of nonbank financial institutions and to emphasize the part played by commercial banks in the flow of money and credit. For many years, financial experts did not consider the liabilities of nonbank financial institutions—including deposits in savings and loan associations, savings banks, money market funds, and credit unions—as really close substitutes for bank deposits. It was argued that interindustry competition between commercial banks and other financial institutions was slight and, for all practical purposes, could be ignored. Today, however, an entirely different view prevails concerning the relative importance of nonbank financial institutions. We now recognize that these institutions play a vital role in the flow of money and credit within the financial system and that they are particularly important in selected markets, such as the home mortgage market and the market for personal savings.

In truth, many nonbank financial institutions are becoming increasingly like commercial banks and are competing for many of the same customers. Moreover, banks themselves are offering many of the services traditionally offered by nonbank financial firms, such as brokering securities and selling insurance (often through joint ventures with nonbank firms). Thus, both bank and nonbank financial institutions are rushing toward each other in the services they offer and the markets they serve—a phenomenon known as *convergence*. This is why financial analysts today stress the importance of studying the *whole* financial institutions' sector to understand how the financial system works. In this chapter and the next, we examine the major types of nonbank financial institutions that channel the public's savings into loans and investments.

SAVINGS AND LOAN ASSOCIATIONS

Savings and loan associations (S&Ls) are among the largest of all thrift institutions, accepting deposits and extending loans and other services primarily to *household customers.* S&Ls emphasize longer-term loans to individuals and families in contrast to the shorter-term lending focus of most other deposit-type financial institutions. In particular, savings and loans are a major source in the United States of mortgage loans to finance the purchase of single-family homes and multifamily dwellings (such as apartments and duplexes). At the same time, savings and loans today are developing many new financial services to attract customers and boost their earnings. However, these associations today continue to face a challenge to their long-run survival. Hundreds of S&Ls failed during the 1980s and early 1990s, and many have since converted into commercial bank and savings bank charters, some becoming branch offices of other depository institutions. We will discuss some of the causes of the most recent industry problems in the sections that follow.

Web site information on thrift institutions has expanded significantly in recent years as consumers have sought out a broader menu of financial services. Thousands of thrifts have established their own individual Internet sites, listing their service offerings and contact information. You can nearly always find these by typing in the name of each thrift institution supplemented by the principal city that it serves.

Among the more interesting Web sites for credit unions are those posted by various state-level credit union leagues (such as the New York State Credit Union League at *www.nyscul.org*). There is also a Credit Union Journal (at *www.cujournal.com*) which keeps track of daily news bulletins on the state of the industry and a site known as Credit Union Land (at *www.culand.com*) which serves as a possible locator for any credit union you may be trying to find inside the United States.

Two important lobby groups for the credit union industry include the Credit Union National Association (CUNA at *www.cuna.org*) and the World Council of Credit Unions (at *www.woccu.org*). One of the credit union industry's best known regulatory agencies is the National Credit Union Administration in Washington, D.C. (known as NCUA at *www.ncua.gov*) which supervises more than 10,000 federal and state-chartered U.S. credit unions that offer federally insured deposits to the public.

The savings and loan and savings bank industries fall under the supervision of the Office of Thrift Supervision (OTS), a part of the U.S. Treasury Department (at *www.ots.treas.gov*), and the Federal Deposit Insurance Corporation (at *www.fdic.gov*).

Finally, the newest of thrift institutions, money market funds, show up in more than 3,000 Web sites, most of them focusing on a single money market fund. An overview of many different money funds is provided by such sources as Smart Money at *www.smartmoney.com* and Money.com at *www.pathfinder.com/money*. A good general discussion of the nature of money market funds may be found at *www.encyclopedia.com*.

Origins

The first savings and loans were started early in the nineteenth century as building and loan associations. Money was solicited from individuals and families so that certain members of the group could finance the building of new homes. The same individuals and families who provided loanable funds were also borrowers from the association. Today, however, savers and borrowers are frequently different individuals.

Savings and loan associations began essentially as a *single-product industry,* accepting savings deposits from middle-income individuals and families and lending those funds to home buyers. More recently, however, competition from commercial banks, credit unions, and mutual funds, coupled with deregulation and many failures, has forced savings and loans to diversify their operations and aggressively solicit new customers.

The history of the S&L industry is traced out in *www.encyclopedia.com*

Many savings and loans are **mutuals** and therefore have *no stockholders.* Technically, they are owned by their depositors. However, a growing number of associations are converting to stock form. *Stockholder-owned S&Ls* can issue capital stock to increase their net worth—a privilege that is particularly important when a savings and loan is growing rapidly and needs an additional source of long-term capital. Stockholder-owned associations, on average, are much larger in size than mutuals.

How Funds Are Raised and Allocated

Savings and loans, like credit unions, are gradually broadening their role, with many choosing to offer a full line of financial services for individuals and families. Other S&Ls are branching out into business credit and commercial real estate lending.

Asset Portfolios

Residential mortgage loans dominate the asset side of the savings and loan business. Exhibit 16–1 shows the combined financial assets and liabilities of both savings and loans and savings banks (which we will discuss next in this chapter).

As revealed in the exhibit, direct mortgage credit (predominantly loans to purchase new homes) accounts for more than half of all industry assets. But the current era has brought rapid growth in other housing-related investments, such as mortgage-backed securities, mobile home loans, and home equity loans. Mortgage-backed securities include pass-throughs issued by the Government National Mortgage Association, participation certificates (PCs) issued by the Federal Home Loan Mortgage Corporation, and collateralized mortgage obligations (CMOs). Pass-throughs, PCs, and CMOs are investor shares in the earnings generated by pools of mortgage loans, backed by the issuing government agency or put together by a private lender. As discussed earlier in Chapter 15, these forms of *loan securitizations* allow S&Ls and other thrifts to package many of their housing-related loans, remove them from their balance sheets, and generate new sources of fee income. CMOs are a little more flexible than other types of loan-backed securities because they can be found in short, medium, and long maturities, helping S&Ls minimize their risk exposure from changing interest rates and from mortgage loans being paid off too early.

As we will see in Chapter 18, the savings and loan industry was first deregulated in the early 1980s and given broad new service powers, including checking accounts, credit cards and other consumer lending powers, trust services, investments in mutual funds, and the power to invest in riskier corporate and government bonds. Predictably, many S&Ls went overboard, bought too many "junk" bonds, and launched into new services with very little preparation, while interest-rate changes added to their losses. Hundreds collapsed, so that by the 1990s, new legislation pushed S&Ls back heavily toward the home mortgage market, where they reside today with the majority of their loans.

Liabilities of S&Ls

Savings deposits provide the bulk of funds available to the savings and loan industry. However, there has been a significant shift in deposit mix in recent years from those savings accounts earning the lowest interest rate to deposits earning higher and more flexible returns. Particularly important among the newer higher-yield savings deposit plans offered by the industry are money market deposit accounts, CDs, NOW and Super NOW accounts, and Keogh and IRA retirement accounts. **Money market deposit accounts (MMDAs)** and Super NOWs were authorized for banks and S&Ls in 1982. Both of these new deposit accounts are draftable by check and carry interest rates that change with market conditions. One unfortunate side effect of these newer deposits is that savings and loans today are faced with a costlier deposit base.

Savings and loans also rely on several nondeposit sources of funds to support their loans and investments. One of the most important consists of advances (loans) from the Federal Home Loan Bank System, which provides extra liquidity in periods when deposit withdrawals are heavy or when loan demand exceeds incoming deposits. As we saw above, another rapidly growing source of funds is securitized assets, when mortgages or other S&L loans are packaged together into a pool of loans (often backed by the guarantee of a government agency), and debt securities are issued against these pooled assets and sold to investors to raise longer-term, lower-cost funds. Thrift institutions continue to make widen-

EXHIBIT 16–1

Combined Financial Balance Sheet of Savings and Loans and Savings Banks, 2000* ($ Billions)

Source: Board of Governors of the Federal Reserve System.

Balance Sheet Item	Amount	Percentage of Total Assets
Assets:		
Checkable deposits and currency	$ 17.5	1.5%
Reserves held at the Federal Reserve banks	1.1	0.1
Time and savings deposits	1.1	0.1
Federal funds and security RPs	14.7	1.2
Corporate equities	24.4	2.0
U.S. government and federal agency securities	148.4	12.3
State and local government (tax-exempt) securities	3.0	0.2
Corporate and foreign bonds	107.3	8.9
Mortgage loans	721.7	60.0
Consumer credit	62.6	5.2
Loans to business firms and others	37.9	3.2
Miscellaneous assets	63.2	5.3
Total financial assets	$1,202.9	100.0%
Liabilities:		
Checkable deposits	$ 254.9	21.8%
Small time and savings deposits	324.1	27.7
Large ($100,000 +) time deposits	139.4	11.9
Borrowings through security repurchase agreements	81.2	6.9
Borrowings from the Federal Home Loan banks and other loans and advances	253.4	21.7
Borrowings from banks (not elsewhere classified)	20.8	1.8
Corporate bonds	3.4	0.3
Investments by parent companies	6.4	0.5
Taxes payable	2.1	0.2
Miscellaneous liabilities	84.7	7.2
Total liabilities	$1,170.4	97.0%

*Figures are for third quarter of 2000.

ing use of *securitized assets,* issued against a growing list of home mortgage and consumer installment loans, to supplement their deposit flows and keep funding costs down. The ability of an S&L or other loan-securitizing institution to remove securitized assets from an S&L's balance sheet tends to lower its total assets and improves its ratio of capital to assets, possibly lessening regulatory pressure on the institution to raise more capital.

Another popular nondeposit funds source is *loan sales*—sales of existing loans to investors in the secondary (resale) market. These sales of S&L assets tend to be heaviest in periods when loan demand is high and deposit growth is sluggish, and they give savings and loans the opportunity to invest in new, higher-yielding loans. They also help S&Ls better diversify their assets and avoid an increased regulatory burden (such as government demands for more owners' capital). One danger, however, is that S&Ls and other financial institutions will sell their best-quality loans, leaving them with a riskier loan portfolio overall.

Equity capital or net worth (i.e., the retained earnings and reserves held by individual associations) presently makes up only about 3 to 4 percent of total S&L funds sources but is very important to the public. The net worth account absorbs losses and keeps the doors open until management can correct any problems. Some S&Ls, particularly in those regions of the nation hit hard by a weak real estate market, have had a net worth close to zero. In the early 1990s the federal government of the United States received the power to close banks and thrifts if their net worth had fallen near zero. Since then, the S&L industry's net worth position has improved somewhat.

Trends in Revenues and Costs

Recently, savings and loans experienced one of the darkest periods in their long history. Many savings associations were unprofitable or had very little net worth. Dozens of ailing associations were helped into mergers by the **Federal Deposit Insurance Corporation (FDIC),** which purchased sizable amounts of questionable industry assets. The industry's former deposit insurance agency (the FSLIC) went bankrupt during the 1980s, to be replaced at the beginning of the 1990s by the Savings Association Insurance Fund (SAIF) managed by the FDIC. At the same time, Congress moved to authorize agency-assisted mergers in which a troubled S&L could be merged with a stronger association or with another depository institution (such as a commercial bank) through its holding company.

One indication of the industry's recent problems is the situation regarding its assets, deposits, and net earnings in recent years:

	Trends in Assets, Deposits, and Net Income after Taxes of U.S. Savings and Loans and Savings Banks		
Year	Total Financial Assets Reported at Year-End ($ Billions)	Total Deposits Reported at Year-End ($ Billions)	Net Income after Taxes of U.S. Savings and Loans and Savings Banks ($ Millions)
1980	$ 792	$ 665	$ 781
1984	1,180	1,172	1,013
1988	1,641	1,605	−12,057
1990	1,358	1,342	1,800e
1994	1,009	734	4,200e
1996	1,032	721	10,174e
2000	1,219	727	NA
2001*	1,288	769	3,500

eEstimates by author based on figures from the Office of Thrift Supervision and the Federal Deposit Insurance Corporation. N/A means not available.

*2001 Figures are for the third quarter annualized.

Source: Board of Governors of the Federal Reserve System, *Flow of Funds Accounts;* Federal Deposit Insurance Corporation; and Office of Thrift Supervision.

As the preceding figures suggest, the industry's overall asset and deposit size peaked in 1988 and then began to contract until near the end of the twentieth century, the result of large numbers of failures and the conversion of some S&Ls into other kinds of financial institutions (most notably commercial banks and savings banks). By 1995 S&Ls were earning an average return on their equity (owners') capital of just over 8 percent and more than 90 percent of the industry had positive profits—a much better performance record than in earlier years, but not yet competitive with most other financial-service industries. Then, in more recent periods, industry profitability continued to improve, climbing above a 10 percent average rate of return on equity capital with more than 90 percent of these thrifts reporting positive profits, though the industry still lagged well behind commercial banks in terms of average profitability. Commercial bank holding companies began to purchase growing numbers of these thrifts, converting many to commercial bank charters or to branch offices of existing banks.

Financial Developments   Principal Regulators of Nonbank Thrifts

Trends in the performance of the savings and loan industry may be followed in several Web sites, such as *www.ots.treas.gov*

Industry earnings would have been higher except for mandates from the U.S. government that thrifts help recapitalize the struggling Savings Association Insurance Fund (SAIF) in the late 1990s in order to bring its deposit insurance reserves up to the levels required by the U.S. Congress. Moreover, like banks, thrift institutions have developed many new fee-based income-generating services (including servicing outstanding home mortgage loans, selling loans in the secondary market, and offering credit card plans). Recently, savings institutions have made (originated) fewer new home mortgage loans and have sometimes sold off more old mortgages than the volume of new home mortgage loans being added to their portfolios. Many S&Ls are directing their lending into other areas—such as construction loans, commercial real estate loans, and consumer loans used for purposes other than buying a new home (including financing college educations, starting new businesses, or purchasing new or used automobiles)—which have generally grown faster than S&L home mortgage loans. Moreover, these thrift institutions have turned increasingly to the Federal Home Loan Banks (FHLB)—a federal agency designed to help the thrift industry—and to new security issues to fund their operations, as their deposits have tended to decline or grow slowly.

What factors got the savings and loan industry into such serious trouble during the 1980s and 1990s? Why did the industry nearly collapse and so many S&Ls sink beneath the waves? One primary cause was the fact that savings and loans, historically, have issued mortgage loans carrying mostly fixed interest rates while selling deposits to the public whose interest rates closely mirror changing market conditions. In short, many S&L assets were interest-rate *insensitive* in earlier years (and many still are), while most of their liabilities have been (and still are) highly interest-rate *sensitive*. During periods of rapidly rising market interest rates, the industry's net interest margin—the difference between its interest earnings on assets and its interest costs on borrowed funds—has been severely squeezed. Indeed, in several recent periods, short-term interest rates paid on deposits exceeded interest rates earned on long-term loans, and the industry's net interest margin turned *negative.*

Other recent trends have also hurt S&L profitability. The individuals and families whose savings provide the bulk of association funds have become more financially sophisticated, withdrawing deposits whenever high returns are available elsewhere or whenever there is even a hint of trouble in the thrift industry. Unquestionably, the savings and loan industry has been damaged by the growth of money market funds—aggressive institutions that offer

Management Insight   The Thrifts' Principal Problem: Portfolio Maturity Mismatch

Savings and loan associations, savings banks, and credit unions face a common problem that, at several times in the past, has caused many of them to fail. *The maturities* (and, therefore, the expected streams of future cash payments) *of many of their assets and their liabilities do not match.* In particular, asset maturities are usually considerably longer than the maturities attached to their liabilities. For example, the bulk of savings and loans' assets are long-term home mortgage loans, which usually take years to pay out, while the bulk of their liabilities are savings deposits and checking accounts that are often turned into cash by a thrift's depositors in a matter of hours, days, or weeks. This means that thrifts must be prepared to pay out large amounts of cash on short notice. Moreover, the interest costs on their borrowed funds (including interest owed on deposits) tend to change faster, up or down, than the interest revenues from their assets.

If we use what has become conventional terminology when talking about thrift institutions, their volume of *interest-rate-sensitive liabilities (ISL)* (consisting largely of short-term savings and checkable deposits) exceeds their volume of *interest-rate-sensitive assets (ISA)* (such as floating-rate loans or short-term loans about to mature). That is, for most thrift institutions, ISA < ISL. A liability or an asset is interest sensitive if its rate of return changes with market conditions. This difference in the thrifts' volume of interest-rate-sensitive assets and liabilities is usually called the GAP:

$$GAP = ISA - ISL$$

If rate-sensitive liabilities are larger than the volume of rate-sensitive assets, the GAP is *negative,* which is the usual situation for most thrift institutions.

The GAP concept tells us that a thrift with a negative GAP will lose interest income if interest rates rise. Interest costs attached to the thrifts' rate-sensitive liabilities will move upward faster than the revenues derived from rate-sensitive assets. The thrifts' net interest income (i.e., their interest revenues less interest expenses) will fall.

We can represent this classic maturity mismatch problem faced by thrift institutions by means of a diagram like that shown below. Deposit rates, like most other short-term interest rates, change rapidly and move over a wide range, rising as the economy expands and inflation increases and falling as the economy slows down or inflation weakens. In contrast, the average rate of return on a thrift's long-term assets changes much more slowly. Losses build up when short-term interest rates exceed long-term interest rates.

The Maturity Mismatch Problem for a Thrift Institution

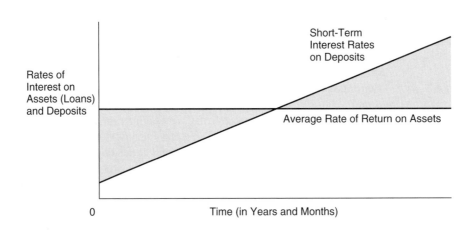

small savers higher and more flexible yields—and, more recently, by the public's growing interest in stock and bond mutual funds. At the same time, government rules have prevented S&Ls from introducing more flexibility into their investments so their revenues can grow as fast as their rising operating costs.

Financial Developments Top-Ranked U.S. Thrift Institution Financial Holding Companies Arrayed by Total Assets

(Figures Listed in Total Assets, Measured in Billions of Dollars in 1999)

Name of Holding Company	Total Assets in $ Billions
Washington Mutual, Seattle	$181
Golden State Bancorp, San Francisco	56
Golden West Financial Corp., Oakland	40
Sovereign Bancorp., Philadelphia	25
Astoria Financial Corp., Lake Success	23
Dime Bancorp., New York City	23
Bank United Corp., Houston	16
Greenpoint Financial Corp., New York City	16
Peoples Heritage Financial Group, Portland	14
Commercial Federal Corp., Omaha	13

Sources: Board of Governors of the Federal Reserve System and Office of Thrift Supervision.

The pressure of rising costs and the resulting squeeze on earnings and net worth have caused many savings and loans to merge or be absorbed by larger institutions. As a result, the number of independently owned associations in the United States has been declining for more than four decades. The S&L population decreased from about 6,300 in 1960 to only about 1,200 by the beginning of the new century. More savings and loans are likely to be absorbed into larger financial institutions (especially bank holding companies) in the future, and many will have their thrift charters converted into bank charters in order to be able to offer a wider range of financial services.

Possible Remedies for the Industry's Problems

If savings and loans are to become more successful institutions in the future, they will need help from at least four sources: (1) sound decision making by S&L management to further diversify their activities by geographic areas and by services offered, (2) careful management of the loan portfolio to put good loans on the books and minimize future loan losses, (3) better use of risk-management tools (such as financial futures, swaps, and options), and (4) a further relaxation of government regulations to permit the offering of new services and the merging of smaller associations into larger financial-service companies. The classic savings and loan association—investing the bulk of its assets in long-term fixed-rate mortgages and offering relatively low-yielding savings accounts to the public—is unlikely to perform well in the long run.

More aggressive S&Ls today are branching out in at least three different directions. Some have followed a *real estate model,* literally becoming mortgage banking firms. These savings associations are selling off their long-term mortgages and converting into real estate service organizations, managing and developing property and brokering mortgages. Many have become *family financial centers,* offering a full range of retail banking services to the consumer. Home mortgages continue to dominate their asset portfolios, but most S&Ls today offer adjustable-rate mortgages (ARMs), whose yield adjusts more readily to changing market conditions, as well as fixed-rate mortgages (FRMs) and a wide variety of other consumer-oriented loans. Other S&Ls have adopted a *diversified model,* becoming holding company organizations with ownership and control over retail-oriented consumer banks, mortgage banking firms, commercial credit affiliates, and other businesses. Only time will tell which of these models can adapt successfully to the changing character of the financial system. One hopeful sign recently has been the return to profitability of many S&Ls that survived the debacle of the 1980s and 1990s and managed to direct their assets into better-quality investments and achieve greater operating efficiency.

SAVINGS BANKS

Savings banks actually began in Scotland early in the nineteenth century and then took root in the United States approximately 150 years ago to meet the financial needs of the small saver. These institutions play an active role in the residential mortgage market, as do savings and loans, but they are more diversified in their investments, purchasing corporate bonds and common stock, making consumer loans, and investing in commercial mortgages.

In 1982 the U.S. Congress voted to allow savings and loan associations to convert readily into federally chartered savings banks, and savings banks to convert readily into S&Ls if they wished to do so. In 1989 Congress decided to allow S&Ls that qualify to become commercial banks. Recently, substantial numbers of S&Ls have converted to savings banks (along with a number of conversions to commercial bank charters) in an effort to lower their regulatory costs. For this reason, the distinction between savings and loans, savings banks, and commercial banks is becoming very blurred. The public often cannot tell these depository institutions apart.

From their earliest origins, savings banks have designed their financial services to appeal to individuals and families. Deposit accounts can be opened for amounts as small as $1, with transactions carried out by mail, electronically, or, in many instances, at 24-hour automated tellers in convenient locations. Savings banks in Massachusetts and New Hampshire were the first to develop the interest-bearing and checkable NOW account, one of the most important new consumer financial services of the past generation. Many savings banks advertise the availability of family financial counseling services, home equity loans, and travel planning, as well as a wide variety of savings instruments.

Number and Distribution of Savings Banks

The number of savings banks operating today is relatively small. The combined total of FDIC-insured savings and loans and savings banks fell from 3,626 in 1985 to 1,552 in 2001. The U.S. Congress authorized the chartering of federal savings banks (FSBs) in 1978, which led to an increase for a time in the savings bank population. Unfortunately, many of these institutions failed in the economic dislocations of the late 1980s and early 1990s. Savings banks today are scattered throughout the United States, though they are most prominent in the New England and the Middle Atlantic states. Massachusetts leads the list, followed by New York. Other states in which savings banks are particularly important include California, Connecticut, Maine, New Hampshire, New Jersey, Pennsylvania, Rhode Island, Texas, and Wisconsin.

How Funds Are Raised and Allocated

Technically, savings banks are owned by their depositors. All earnings available after funds are set aside to provide adequate reserves must be paid to the depositors as owners' dividends. The industry's role in the financial system can be seen by looking at its financial

Financial Developments   Dangers for Banks and Thrifts in Subprime Lending

One of the more alarming developments in the financial institutions' sector as the twentieth century gave way to the twenty-first century was the rapid rise of *subprime lending* by banks and thrift institutions. This form of credit consists mainly of consumer and small business loans extended to poor credit risks at relatively lofty interest rates.

Subprime lending rests on the principle that if you as a lender price a loan correctly in order to account for its risk exposure, you can still make money from such a loan despite the risks involved. The higher the degree of risk exposure (i.e., the lower the borrower's credit rating), the more the lender charges to compensate for the estimated risk exposure—sometimes well above a 20 percent interest rate. Some authorities refer to the highest-cost subprime loans as "predatory lending" because borrowers facing a very high loan rate are more likely to default on such loans.

Unfortunately for many financial institutions, especially banks and thrifts over the past decade, the expansion of loan losses outstripped revenue growth as loan defaults soared. Moreover, many high-risk borrowers were able to get their high-rate loans refinanced, paying off their subprime lenders sooner than expected. Subprime lending proved to be highly sensitive to economic conditions; a weaker economy generated a large volume of defaults among subprime loans and also failures among the lenders who granted them.

An added cause of problems in this field was so-called "loan residuals" in which certain loans were packaged together and securities representing claims against the pool of loans were sold to investors in the capital market. Because the loan package was, on the whole, less risky than individual loans would be, the lender was able to borrow more cheaply using securitized loans as collateral and profit from a more favorable interest-rate spread. This spread or "residual" was recorded on the lender's balance sheet as an asset, though it proved to be a volatile one. Higher interest rates often have caused these "residual" assets to plunge in value.

Some of the largest depository institutions ran into trouble as a result of subprime lending, such as First Union Corp.'s Money Store, which was closed in 1998. These events suggest that a prolonged economic slump can create serious losses on subprime loans. For this reason bank and thrift regulators recently have been discouraging loans of this type.

balance sheet, which is shown for both savings and loans and savings banks combined in Exhibit 16–1. On the asset side, the key instruments are mortgages and mortgage-related instruments, which account for the majority of industry assets.

Most of the mortgage total represents direct mortgage loans to build single-family homes, apartments, shopping centers, and other commercial and residential structures. The remainder of the mortgage asset total is devoted to mortgage-backed securities, such as Government National Mortgage Association (GNMA) pass-through securities (also known as Ginnie Maes), and similar mortgage-related securities backed by a pool of mortgages.[1]

A distant second in importance to mortgages are savings bank investments in nonmortgage loans (mainly consumer installment credit), corporate bonds, corporate stock, and government bonds. Due to the pressures of inflation and higher deposit costs, many states have liberalized their regulations to allow savings banks to make increased purchases of common and preferred stock. Another factor favoring investments in stock has been the industry's growing federal tax burden. Because most of their stock dividend income is exempt from federal taxation, savings banks have taken greater interest in the stock market. State law and tradition, however, limit the growth of savings bank investments in the stock market. Savings banks also make loans for the support of education, to fund home improvements, and to cover household expenses.

The principal source of funds for savings banks is *deposits.* Savings deposits have no specific maturity but may be withdrawn at any time by the customer, and they carry the lowest rate of interest. Time deposits, on the other hand, have fixed maturities, and savings banks pay higher interest rates on these deposit accounts, depending on their maturity date.

[1]See Chapter 24 for a discussion of GNMA pass-through and other mortgage-related securities.

Industry deposits have grown rapidly over the past four decades, reflecting the ability of savings banks to appeal to the financial needs of individuals and families. The larger savings banks have established extensive branch office systems and have been highly innovative in offering new services. Nearly all savings banks today offer checkable NOW accounts, money orders, loans against savings accounts, and home equity and home improvement loans. Many savings banks also offer life insurance policies to their customers when permitted by law.

Like savings and loan associations, savings banks have discovered that the customers they serve have become more financially sophisticated in recent years. The highest-yielding deposit accounts have grown much faster than lower-yielding savings plans. The most pronounced shift has been from regular passbook savings accounts to fixed-maturity time deposits and money market accounts that carry contract interest rates that float with conditions in the market. The net result of all of these changes has been to push up overall interest expenses, put pressure on savings bank earnings, and, at times, increase the volatility of their funds flows. Savings banks today must also be more concerned with changing electronic technology, which is forcing them to automate more of their routine services and make customer access to their facilities and services more convenient than ever before.

Current Trends and Future Problems

The savings bank industry faces a number of problems that will significantly affect its future as a conduit for savings and investment. One factor is increasing competition with savings and loan associations, credit unions, and commercial banks offering similar services. Because of the heavy concentration of savings bank assets in mortgage-related investments, savings banks are less flexible than commercial banks in adjusting to changing financial conditions and to the changing service needs of their customers. Many have earnings problems due to inflexible asset structures and bad loans, coupled with higher fund-raising costs. On the other hand, many savings banks have countered this relative inflexibility in their asset structures with aggressive competition for funds and innovative new services. The future growth of this industry, like that of most other financial institutions, will depend heavily on the ability of savings banks to gain the necessary changes in government regulations to allow them to respond to changing financial market conditions.

Questions *to Help You Study*

1. How did *savings and loans* get started? How does the history of savings and loans compare with the history of savings banks? Which is the oldest financial institution?

2. What exactly are *mutuals?* How do these institutions differ from stockholder-owned depository institutions?

3. Why has the savings and loan industry been in trouble in recent years?

4. What solutions have been developed to deal with the savings and loan industry's problems? Do these actual and proposed solutions seem reasonable to you?

CREDIT UNIONS

The characteristics and operations of **credit unions** have been a neglected area of research in the financial system. Recently, however, there has been a revival of interest in credit union behavior. One reason has been the rapid growth of this financial intermediary. For example, credit union assets have more than doubled since 1990 (see Exhibit 16–2),

EXHIBIT 16–2
Credit Unions in the United States and around the Globe

Source: Credit Union National Association, *Credit Union Report 2000*; World Council of Credit Unions, Inc., *2000 Statistical Report;* and Board of Governors of the Federal Reserve System, *Flow of Funds Accounts.*

Year	Number of Credit Unions in the United States	Number of Credit Union Members in the United States	U.S. Credit Union Assets ($Millions)
1940	9,023	2,806,612	$ 253
1950	10,586	4,617,086	1,005
1960	20,094	12,025,393	5,651
1970	23,687	22,775,511	17,872
1980	21,465	43,930,569	68,974
1990	14,549	61,610,957	221,759
1995	12,230	69,305,876	316,170
1998	11,392	75,616,434	391,500
2000	10,684	79,751,853	449,799
2001*	10,628	NA	496,400

Credit Unions around the Globe

Number of credit unions belonging to the World Council of Credit Unions, 2000: 36,512 CUs
Worldwide membership, 2000: 108,261,819 people
Worldwide assets (in U.S. dollars): $536.2 billion

Note: *Figures for 2001 as of third quarter of the year.

though a combination of failures and mergers among smaller credit unions has recently slowed overall credit union growth. U.S. credit unions are the third-largest institutional supplier of nonmortgage installment credit to individuals and families, trailing only commercial banks and finance companies. These institutions are household-oriented intermediaries, offering deposit and credit services to individuals and families. Their long-run survival stems mainly from being able to offer low loan rates and high deposit interest rates to their customers and from their relatively low operating costs.

Credit unions are cooperative, self-help associations of individuals rather than profit-motivated financial institutions. Savings deposits and loans are offered only to members of each association and not to the general public. The members of a credit union are technically the *owners,* receiving dividends and sharing in any losses that occur. Each member gets one vote regardless of the size of his or her credit union account. Credit unions began in nineteenth-century Germany in order to serve low-income individuals and families, working primarily in industrial jobs, by providing them with inexpensive credit and a ready outlet for their savings. They came to the United States (beginning in the state of New Hampshire) in 1909. Early growth was modest until the 1950s, when these institutions broadened their appeal to middle-income individuals by offering many new financial services.

The credit union sector remains small compared to other major financial institutions, accounting for less than 10 percent of all consumer savings in the United States. However, worldwide, the industry's potential for future growth appears promising due to its innovative character and solid public acceptance. The credit union has become an aggressive competitor of banks and savings associations for both savings deposits and consumer installment loans. Beginning in 1978, credit unions were authorized to offer money market certificates, which can carry the same terms as the money market deposit plans sold by banks. In addition, many credit unions offer payroll savings plans by which employees can automatically set aside a portion of their salary in a savings account.

Credit union loans have kept pace with the growth of their deposits and today account for about 12 percent of all consumer installment loans in the United States and a substantial portion of these loans worldwide. Consumer loan rates charged by credit unions are fully competitive with loan rates charged by most other major consumer lenders. Moreover, credit unions frequently grant their borrowing members interest refunds up to 20 percent of the amount of a loan. Many credit unions provide life insurance free to their borrowing customers, a service charged for by most other lending institutions. Thus, credit unions often accept a smaller spread between their loan and deposit interest rates. This is possible because their operating costs are among the lowest of all financial-service firms. Frequently, the sponsoring employer or association provides free office facilities, and credit union members elect officers and directors who frequently serve with no compensation at all.

Interestingly enough, credit unions usually report one of the lowest default and delinquency rates on their loans of any lending institution in the financial system. Why? One reason is that they make relatively few business loans, which, particularly during downturns in the economy, can be a very risky credit. Another factor is something we are about to discuss—the common bond between credit union members which seems to encourage borrowing members to repay their loans in timely fashion.

Credit Union Membership

Credit unions are organized around a common affiliation or *common bond* among their members. Most members work for the same employer or for one of a group of related employers. Moreover, if one family member belongs to a credit union, other family members are eligible as well. Occupation-related credit unions account for about two-thirds of all U.S. credit unions. About one-fifth are organized around nonprofit associations, such as a labor union, a church, or a fraternal or social organization. Common area of residence, such as a city or state, and age (e.g., an association for retired persons) have also been used to get credit unions started. The Federal Credit Union Act permits these types of credit unions: (1) common bond (members from a single group); (2) community (members from a single area); and (3) multiple bond (members from several groups).

In recent years, credit unions have been allowed to define their members' common bond so liberally that millions of people have become eligible for credit union membership, and the industry in the United States has recently come under attack in court by bankers' groups for its lenient membership rules and special tax advantages. In 1997, the U.S. Supreme Court voted to limit membership in federally chartered credit unions to members working for a single employer or to individuals residing in the same community (i.e., individuals sharing a single common bond). Recent legislation introduced in the U.S. Congress has now overridden key parts of that court ruling, however, allowing most credit unions to keep their existing membership base.

Size of Credit Unions

There is a strong shift today toward fewer, but larger, credit unions. For example, the number of associations reached an all-time high in 1969 at almost 24,000 but now totals less than 11,000 in the United States, with the decline due primarily to mergers, failures, and a structural shift in the U.S. economy away from manufacturing industries (where credit unions have concentrated historically) toward more service industries (where credit union activity tends to be more subdued). With fewer credit unions but continued industry growth, the average-size credit union has risen substantially in recent years.

For example, although only about one-sixth of credit unions held more than $1 million in assets in 1970, today the majority of all U. S. credit unions exceed $2 million in total

Financial Developments   The Credit Union Membership Access Act of 1997

Financial institutions do battle not only within the market areas they serve, fighting for the attention of customers, but also in courts and legislative bodies over differences in the rules and regulations they face. For example, when the set of rules applying to banks grows tougher and more restrictive than the set of rules applying to credit unions, a phenomenon called "regulatory arbitrage" may occur. Credit unions may grow faster than banks in both numbers and services; in response, bankers can and will fight back, both in the marketplace and through the legal process.

Bankers fought back in the courts and by 1997 had won a considerable victory in the U.S. Supreme Court, forcing future credit union membership to be limited more closely to traditional common-bond boundaries. Unfortunately for the banks, however, U.S. credit unions appealed this court decision to their supporters in the U.S. Congress and overturned much of it via legislation—the new Credit Union Membership Access Act. This bill, signed into law by President Clinton in August 1998, divides credit unions into several different groups:

1. Single-common-bond credit unions whose members share a common occupation or association.

2. Multiple-common-bond credit unions with members arising from more than one group having a common bond.

3. Community credit union members, living in or joining an organization that is part of a well-defined local area or neighborhood.

This latest credit-union law limits multiple-common-bond credit unions to 3,000 members except in cases where the National Credit Union Administration (NCUA) finds that achieving efficiency or safety and soundness requires the formation of a larger organization. Moreover, the NCUA can approve larger multiple-common-bond unions if a particular area seems to be underserved—that is, the public does not have access to adequate and reasonably priced financial services. Moreover, existing credit union memberships are grandfathered under this most recent law, thereby allowing previously diverse credit unions to be able to continue operating with their current members.

Credit unions can expand their membership if they are adequately capitalized, are capable of managing and serving larger numbers of people, provide affordable services to their current members, are operating in safety, and would not harm existing credit unions. However, as they expand, credit unions must now conform to capitalization (net worth) rules similar to those faced by banks and other thrift institutions, and the largest unions must have annual independent audits. Finally, credit unions were granted an avenue of escape from their industry if they so desire—they can convert themselves into other types of depository institutions.

assets. The smallest credit unions are declining in numbers, while the largest credit unions are growing in numbers. Nevertheless, the average-size credit union remains very small compared to other kinds of depository institutions.

Still, worldwide membership in credit unions has not stopped its upward climb. Around the globe more than 108 million people belong to one or more of nearly 37,000 credit unions scattered across close to 100 different countries. Inside the United States credit union members grew from fewer than 5 million in 1950 to almost 80 million as the twenty-first century began. Nearly 100 percent of U.S. credit union deposits are either federally or privately insured.

New Services Offered

Credit unions are expanding the number of services they offer. Some sell life insurance. Others act as brokers for group insurance plans where state law permits. Many credit unions are active in offering 24-hour automated or telephone and Internet services, travelers checks, financial planning services, retirement savings, credit cards, home equity and first-mortgage loans, and money orders. Larger credit unions compete directly with banks for transaction accounts by offering **share drafts**—interest-bearing checkbook deposits. A substantial proportion of U.S. credit unions also offer credit cards and automated teller machines (many of which are linked nationwide through an electronic exchange network in order to accommodate members who travel). Several recently began to take loan applications via fax and personal computers and to offer preauthorized drafts as well as telephone bill paying.

U.S. credit unions are under intense pressure to develop new services and penetrate new markets due to increasing competition from other financial institutions and a decline in the demand for their historically most important credit service—automobile loans—where they face fierce competition from banks and finance companies (such as GMAC and Ford Motor Credit). In addition, because a larger proportion of family income today is spent on food, fuel, education, and other necessities, credit unions have been shifting many of their loans into these areas. First-mortgage loans to purchase new homes and second-mortgage loans to repair or improve existing homes, as well as home equity credit to fund a wide variety of household purchases, have grown rapidly and now account for about a third of all credit union loans. (See Exhibit 16–3.) Finally, loans to small businesses have recently been added to many credit union service menus, along with auto and equipment leases. As the new century began credit unions' most rapidly growing loans included new auto loans, adjustable-rate first home mortgages, and second mortgage loans.

Like banks, credit unions have a dual (federal and state) regulatory structure. First chartered only by the states, the federal government entered the picture in 1934 with passage of the Federal Credit Union Act, which issues charters of incorporation for federally supervised credit unions. There is a second layer in the industry today known as corporate credit unions (CCUs) that make loans to credit unions in need of financial help and process their checks as well as professionally invest credit union funds.

Under current federal government rules in the United States, credit unions are permitted to make unsecured loans to members (including credit card loans) not exceeding 5 years to maturity and to grant secured loans out to 30 years. Their permissible investments in

EXHIBIT 16–3
Financial Assets and Liabilities Held by U.S. Credit Unions, 1980–2000 ($ Billions)

Source: Board of Governors of the Federal Reserve System, *Flow of Funds Accounts,* selected issues.

Item	1980	1990	2000*
Financial Assets:			
Checkable deposits and currency	$ 1.2	$ 4.8	$ 25.2
Time and savings deposits	7.1	21.7	16.7
Federal funds loans and security RPs	0.7	14.6	7.8
U.S. government and federal agency securities	4.3	23.0	75.4
Home mortgage and equity loans	4.7	48.2	123.7
Consumer installment loans	44.0	93.1	181.6
Open-market paper	—	2.3	1.2
Miscellaneous assets	5.7	9.3	3.6
Total financial assets	$67.6	$217.0	$435.2
Liabilities:			
Checkable deposits/shares	$ 3.3	$ 22.2	$ 50.9
Small time and savings deposits/shares	57.9	175.3	309.9
Large ($100,000+) deposits/shares	0.5	3.3	23.0
Loans from the Federal Home Loan banks and other advances	—	—	3.1
Miscellaneous liabilities	3.1	3.9	6.8
Total liabilities	$64.8	$204.7	$393.7

*Figures for 2000 are as of the third quarter.

Examples of Leading Credit Unions

Navy Federal Credit Union, Virginia	Corporate One Federal Credit Union, Ohio
Capital City Savings, Canada	Municipal Credit Union, New York
USA Federal Credit Union, California	Lockheed Federal Credit Union, California
Global Credit Union, Washington	IBM Credit Union, Minnesota

Up-to-date news about developments in the credit union industry may be found in www.cujournal.com and in the Credit Union Times at www.cutimes.com

securities are limited to a list prescribed by either state or federal regulations. In the main, credit unions are permitted to acquire U.S. government securities; to hold savings deposits at banks, savings and loan associations, and federally insured credit unions; and to purchase selected federal agency securities. They rely heavily on U.S. government securities and on savings deposits to provide liquidity to meet deposit withdrawals and accommodate member credit needs. Credit unions pay dividends to their members, but they are considered *nonprofit associations,* doing business only with their owners, and, therefore, are classified as *tax-exempt mutual organizations.*

A Strong Competitive Force

Credit unions represent stiff competition for commercial banks, savings banks, and other financial institutions serving consumers. Today, one of every five Americans belongs to a credit union—roughly double the proportion of a decade earlier. True, the total number of credit unions is down in some areas, such as in the United States; however, this industry has repeatedly demonstrated its capacity for service innovation and its ability to compete successfully for both consumer loans and savings accounts against some of the largest financial-service competitors in the world.

MONEY MARKET FUNDS

A fourth major nonbank thrift institution appeared on the scene as recently as 1972. In that year, the first **money market mutual fund**—a financial intermediary pooling the savings of thousands of individuals and businesses and investing those monies in short-term, high-quality money market instruments—opened for business. Taking advantage of the fact that interest rates on most deposits offered by commercial and savings banks were then restrained by government regulation, the money fund offered share accounts whose yields were free to reflect prevailing interest rates in the money market. Thus, the money fund represents the classic case of profit-seeking entrepreneurs finding a loophole around ill-conceived government regulations.

The growth of money market funds was explosive. As of year-end 1973, there were only four in existence, with assets totaling just $100 million. Money funds appeared to peak in 1982, when more than 200 of them held over $200 billion in assets (see Exhibit 16–4). Beginning in late 1982 and 1983, a decline in their assets set in as banks and other depository institutions fought back with Super NOWs and money market deposit accounts (MMDAs), both authorized by the U.S. government in 1982 to carry unregulated interest rates. Subsequently, however, money market funds resumed their rapid growth, making share gains during the late 1980s, the 1990s, and into the twenty-first century. In fact, 2001 was the best year ever in money market fund history with their assets spiraling upward to a record of nearly $2.3 trillion late in that year. This recent growth probably reflects several factors, including increased public concerns about saving and preparing for the retirement years and the public's concerns about risks in the economy and the financial sector, particularly after the recession and the terrorist attacks of 2001. Another factor boosting money funds

The most frequently asked questions about money market funds are answered by The Investment Company Institute at www.ici.org/aboutfunds

EXHIBIT 16–4
Money Market Funds: Assets Held and Total Shares Outstanding, 1974–2000*
($ Billions)

Source: Board of Governors of the Federal Reserve System, *Flow of Funds Accounts; Financial Assets and Liabilities,* selected issues.

Item	1974	1980	1990	2000*
Financial Assets:				
Checkable deposits and currency	$ —	$ 0.2	$ 11.4	$ —
Time and savings deposits	1.6	21.0	21.0	129.3
Loans made through security RPs	0.1	5.6	59.0	172.0
Foreign deposits	—	6.8	27.1	75.5
U.S. government and federal agency securities	0.1	8.2	82.4	241.7
State and local government (tax-exempt) securities	—	1.9	83.6	227.6
Open-market paper	0.6	31.6	206.7	589.3
Miscellaneous assets	−0.1	1.2	7.3	262.4
Total assets	$ 2.4	$76.4	$498.4	$1,697.8
Total shares outstanding	2.4	76.4	498.4	1,697.8

Note: Columns may not add to totals because of rounding.
*2000 figures are for third quarter of the year.

is the comparative absence of regulations tying the industry down. There are no legal interest-rate ceilings limiting what a money fund can pay to its shareholders and, unless a money fund happens to impose them, no penalties for early withdrawal of funds, as is required of customers by many banks and nonbank thrift institutions.

However, money market funds are not without their limitations. For example, during the 1980s and 1990s a number of these thrift institutions reached out for riskier, but higher yielding, issues of commercial paper (i.e., short-term corporate notes) so they could offer high returns to savers. Unfortunately, massive losses soon occurred for some money funds. These losses on investments in commercial paper led the U.S. Securities and Exchange Commission (SEC) in 1991 to impose limits on money market fund investments in less than top-quality securities, restricting their investments in lower-quality financial instruments to no more than 5 percent of total assets. No more than 1 percent of a money fund's assets may be placed in securities coming from a single corporate issuer.

Moreover, future money market fund investments were restricted to securities that are rated in one of the two highest rating categories by at least two nationally recognized credit-rating companies (such as Moody's and Standard & Poor's). In the same year, the SEC allowed money funds to reach for somewhat longer-maturity financial instruments, allowing them to buy securities with maturities up to 13 months compared to a 12-month maximum under previous rules. However, the SEC reduced the permissible average maturity of a money fund's investment portfolio from a maximum of 120 days to a maximum of only 90 days. In 1996 the SEC tightened restrictions on money funds investing in risky derivative securities (such as futures or options) to reduce the risk that changing interest rates might threaten a money fund's stability and solvency. These new restrictions were accompanied by widely publicized reminders from the SEC to the general public that savings left with money market funds are *not* protected by federal insurance.

On the whole, however, money market funds hold high-quality assets—primarily U.S. Treasury bills, bank certificates of deposit, bankers' acceptances, commercial paper, and securities issued by federal government agencies[2]—which helps explain why money market funds remain so popular with millions of investors. The interest-bearing securities they acquire generally carry low risk of borrower default and limited fluctuations in price.

---

[2]These various money market securities are discussed in depth in Part Three of this text.

Management Insight Raising Funds for a Financial Institution

As we have seen in these chapters on financial institutions, different institutions rely upon different sources of funds. For banks and thrifts, for example, the principal sources of funds are deposits, money market borrowings, and equity capital provided by their owners; for insurance companies, policyholder premiums usually provide a steady inflow of funds. Regardless of the sources of funds a financial institution relies upon, several common problems are faced by *all* financial institutions attempting to raise new funds. Each institution must decide which of multiple sources of funds to draw upon, how to measure the cost of those funds, and how to price its services to cover its funding costs.

Among the most important factors the managers of the fund-raising departments of a financial institution must consider are:

1. The relative cost of raising funds from each source.

2. The risk (volatility or dependability) of each fund's source.

3. The length of time (term) for which a source of funds will be needed.

4. The size and market access of the financial institution attempting to raise funds.

5. Laws and regulations that may limit a financial institution's access to funds.

The *relative cost* factor is particularly important because, other factors held equal, a financial institution would prefer to borrow from the cheapest sources of funds available. Moreover, if an institution is to maintain consistent profitability, its cost of fund raising must somehow be kept below the returns earned on the sales of its services. One common method for assessing a financial institution's costs is called the *pooled-funds approach*. For example, suppose a financial institution plans to draw upon the following funds sources to make new loans and investments:

Sources of New Funds	Volume of New Funds Generated	Interest Costs and Other Expenses Involved in Raising the New Funds
Deposits	$200	$20
Money market borrowings	50	5
Equity capital	50	5
Total new funds raised	$300	Total cost of fund-raising $30

Suppose that only $250 of the $300 in funds raised can be used to invest in new loans and investments (earning assets), with the remaining $50 going into the cash account. We can get an estimate of the minimum amount this financial institution must earn on its earning assets (loans and investments) just to cover its cost of raising funds. In this case:

$$\text{Minimum rate of return required on a financial institution's earning assets to cover its fund-raising costs} = \frac{\text{All expected fund-raising costs}}{\text{Amount of funds available to invest in earning assets}} = \frac{\$30}{\$250} = 0.12 \text{ or } 12\%$$

This financial institution will have to earn at least a 12 percent return on its loans, securities, and other earning assets just to cover its fund-raising costs.

Trends in the money market funds industry can be followed via iMoneyNet at *www.imoneynet.com* Contributing to the low-risk character of money fund investments is their short average maturity of only a few weeks or months. The short maturity of fund investments results in a highly liquid security portfolio that can be adjusted quickly to changing market conditions. Many funds declare dividends on a daily basis, crediting their earnings to customer accounts and often notifying the customer by mail monthly of any additional shares purchased with the dividends earned. Most are "no load" funds that do not charge their customers commissions for opening an account, purchasing additional shares, or redeeming shares for cash.

Examples of Leading Money Market Funds

Merrill Lynch CMA Money Fund	Vanguard MMR Prime Portfolio
Fidelity Cash Reserves	Schwab Money Market Fund
Dean Witter Liquid Asset Fund	Merrill Lynch Ready Assets
Prudential MoneyMart Assets	Bunker Hill Money Market Fund
TouchStone Money Market Fund	Vanguard Tax-exempt Money Market Fund

EXHIBIT 16–5

An Example of Typical Money Market Fund Information Reported Daily by Security Brokers, Dealers, and in Daily Newspapers

Name or Abbreviation of Money Market Fund	Average Maturity of Fund's Portfolio in Days	Weekly Average Annualized Yield on the Fund's Assets	Millions of Dollars in Assets Held by the Fund (on the Date Indicated)
KPR Municipal Money Market Fund (KPRM)	54	2.97%	878
Z.Row Money Market Assets (ZRMA)	43	4.68	1651

Another outstanding advantage of the money funds for many investors is the ease with which their accounts can be accessed. Most funds allow the customer to write checks to redeem shares, provided the amount of each check exceeds a designated minimum ($500 is common). The customer is issued a book of checks and can write and deposit checks in his or her local bank account, often receiving credit for the deposited check from the local bank the same day, even though it may take several days for the money fund check to be collected. Meantime, daily interest is still being earned on the monies waiting in the customer's share account. Most money funds also offer customers the option of purchasing or redeeming shares by wire or by telephone. Today, as was true when they began their operations in the 1970s, money market funds serve as: (1) cash-management vehicles where market rates of return can be earned on funds used for daily transactions; (2) tax-sheltering vehicles for those investors who choose shares in tax-exempt money market funds; (3) a temporary repository for liquid funds waiting for a major purchase or waiting for the appearance of higher-return investments expected to appear later in the marketplace; and (4) a haven of safety for savings when the rest of the financial marketplace appears to be too volatile and risky for a conservative saver to immediately commit his or her funds.

Many local newspapers and financial newssheets, as well as brokers' screens, report the current rates of return (yields) being posted by the largest money market funds, as well as the volume of assets currently held by each of these funds. We can see an illustration of a typical daily newspaper report on a couple of money market funds in Exhibit 16–5. Most money funds manage their assets with the goal of keeping their NAV (i.e., net asset value, or selling price) fixed at $1 per share. They carry no extra sales charge (that is, are not front-end loaded) and must stand ready to redeem the saver's shares for cash each business day. Shareholder dividends are earned every day in proportion to the number of shares each saver owns in the fund. All money market funds must register with the Securities and Exchange Commission and abide by its rules in offering shares to the public.

Despite their numerous advantages for customers interested in professional management of their short-term funds, money market funds today possess some competitive disadvantages that must be overcome if their rapid growth is to continue. Their share accounts

Management Insight   Managing a Financial Institution's Liquidity Position

Banks, thrifts, and other financial institutions face more serious *liquidity problems*—that is, making sure they have sufficient cash available at reasonable cost to meet all cash demands on time—than almost any other business firm. One reason is that financial institutions rarely can perfectly match the maturities of their assets and the maturities of their liabilities. Therefore, the volume of cash flowing in rarely matches exactly the volume of cash flowing out. Moreover, some of a financial institution's liabilities (such as checkable deposits) are payable immediately upon demand, resulting in the outflow of cash with little or no notice. Financial institutions are especially sensitive to interest-rate movements, which affect both the flow of savings they attract from the public and the earnings from the loans and securities they acquire.

Liquidity managers usually meet their institutions' cash needs through two different methods: (a) asset conversion or (b) liability management. *Asset conversion* refers to selling selected assets (preferably those that are closest to cash, such as deposits or government securities) that a financial institution holds in order to cover a pending cash need. Unfortunately, asset conversion results in a financial institution losing future earnings from the assets it must sell. Moreover, conversion requires a financial institution to "store" liquidity in low-yielding assets that can easily be liquidated, generating an *opportunity*

cost in the form of reduced earnings. As a result, liquidity managers try to sell those assets carrying the least profit potential.

Liability management, on the other hand, calls for borrowing enough liquidity to cover a financial institution's cash demands as they arise. The borrowing institution simply uses interest rates to bid in the financial marketplace for the cash it needs, and it borrows liquidity only as needed. Among the most popular sources of borrowed liquidity are selling deposits, borrowing in the money market, or, in the case of depository institutions, borrowing from the central bank. Most financial institutions today use a combination of asset conversion and liability management, known as a *balanced* liquidity management approach.

Liquidity managers of financial institutions must pay special attention to their institutions' largest customers, trying to find out in advance what these biggest customers plan to do with their money (for example, if a large depositor is planning to withdraw his or her deposit any time soon). By knowing ahead of time when the institution's liquidity position is likely to change, the liquidity manager can make a good decision on when and where to raise new cash in order to cover a liquidity deficit or invest wisely the cash made available by a liquidity surplus.

are *not* government insured, although many of the funds have attempted to deal with this problem by arranging for private insurance or by creating funds invested solely in default-free government securities, which attracted thousands of small investors during the 1980s and 1990s as concerns about risk in the banking system mounted. Moreover, the yield differential between posted yields on money market fund share accounts and money market deposits at banks has narrowed in recent years. Certainly, the money market funds are not likely to go away. They are a potent competitor for both small individual savings accounts and businesses' liquid funds. However, barring further restrictive federal regulation of bank and thrift deposits, all bank and nonbank thrift institutions, including money market funds, will continue to compete for savings and transaction accounts on relatively equal terms, leading to intense competition and, perhaps, some failures among competing financial institutions in future years.

Questions *to Help You Study*

5. *Credit unions* are one of the fastest-growing financial intermediaries in the United States and in many other parts of the world as well. What factors have contributed to this rapid growth?

6. What *services* do credit unions offer that compete with the services offered by banks and savings and loan associations?

7. What advantages do credit unions have over banks? What disadvantages do they face?

Summary **of Nonbank Thrifts**

Key Characteristics of Different Thrift Institutions

Savings and Loan Associations—Depository institutions created in local communities throughout the United States, beginning in the 1830s, to encourage savings by individuals and families and to provide credit for the construction and ownership of new homes. The earliest S&Ls were mostly mutuals—owned by their depositors—but the stockholder-owned S&L corporation has come to dominate the industry's recent growth, attracting both savings and checking accounts and extending not only home loans but a wide variety of other forms of credit to consumers.

Savings Banks—Depository institutions that first appeared in Scotland in the early nineteenth century and then spread around the world, including the United States, shortly thereafter. Their basic purpose has been to stimulate savings by individuals and families and to invest those savings in interest-bearing assets (such as government and corporate bonds, consumer installment loans, and mortgage loans) that can generate competitive returns for the saver. Like savings and loans, government deregulation of savings banks has greatly expanded the services they can offer, including interest-bearing checking accounts, credit cards, insurance policies, and investments in mutual funds.

Credit Unions—Depository institutions first developed in Germany in the middle of the nineteenth century, spreading to Canada and the United States early in the twentieth century. These mutual (depositor-owned), nonprofit institutions originally were aimed primarily at workers in industry, offering low- and middle-income wage earners an interest-bearing outlet for their savings and reasonably priced loans to cover household needs. Today's credit union has become a financial department store of household finance, offering a wide variety of consumer-oriented financial services that are fully competitive with banks and other thrift institutions serving the same markets.

Money Market Funds—A form of investment company (mutual fund) that first appeared during the 1970s to offer savers higher, market-sensitive rates of return on their cash balances rather than the government-regulated interest rates that banks and other thrifts were then offering on their deposits. A money market fund sells shares to the public that are claims against a pool of assets made up of short-term (money market) securities, including Treasury bills, commercial paper, bank CDs, repurchase agreements, and other money market instruments. By law a money fund cannot invest in assets having a maturity of more than 13 months nor have an average weighted asset portfolio maturity of more than 90 days. A shareholder's funds may be withdrawn at any time, usually without penalty, and checks of minimum denomination (usually $100 or $500) may be written against the balance left in each shareholder's account.

8. How and why did *money market funds* begin to appear during the 1970s? What factors have contributed to their recent growth?

9. Exactly how are money market funds different from banks and credit unions in their behavior and the assets they hold?

10. If you are a small saver what advantages do money market funds appear to offer you relative to banks and credit unions? What disadvantages?

Summary of the Chapter

Thrift institutions—savings and loan associations, savings banks, credit unions, and money market funds—are among the most popular financial institutions within the financial system. They are especially well-known to individuals and families (households)—their principal customer base.

- Thrift institutions began their history primarily to reach small savers (individuals and small businesses) and help this group of customers achieve home ownership, a better education, satisfactory preparation for retirement, and other personal financial goals. Over time, however, thrifts have diversified their services and attempted to reach out to a broader customer base, including both households and some business enterprises.

- Some thrift institutions (particularly money market funds) have experienced rapid growth, while others (especially savings and loan associations) have experienced relatively slow or even negative growth at times. Many of the more troubled thrift institutions have been merged into larger and healthier financial-service companies (including banks and financial holding companies) or simply closed their doors.

- Nevertheless, thrift institutions have continued to be tough competitors with banks, often outbidding banks for their customers' checking accounts, savings deposits, home mortgages, and personal installment loans. Unlike many other financial intermediaries they are primarily *local* service providers, though some thrifts have grown to become nationally and internationally known institutions.

- Like the banking industry (discussed in the previous chapter) the thrift industry is experiencing waves of changing technology as they seek to provide more electronic financial services in order to lower overhead and personnel costs and improve customer service.

- Thrifts have paralleled banks in a trend toward *consolidation* with these financial-service industries contracting into smaller numbers of thrifts, but the average thrift institution has increased substantially in overall size. In turn, these larger thrifts have broadened their service menus and are reaching out to expand their beach front within the global financial marketplace.

Key Terms

Savings and loan associations, *446*
Mutuals, *447*
Money market deposit accounts (MMDAs), *448*

Federal Deposit Insurance Corporation (FDIC), *450*
Savings banks, *454*
Credit unions, *456*

Share drafts, *460*
Money market mutual fund, *461*

Problems

1. Axtell Credit Union elects to draw upon the following new sources of funds to support the $40 million in new automobile loan requests it is expecting from its customers next week:

Expected Sources of New Funds	Interest and Noninterest Costs Incurred in Raising New Funds ($ Millions)	Amount of New Funds Raised ($ Millions)
Member share-draft deposits	$0.6	$10
Member savings deposits	1.4	20
Member time deposits	1.6	20

If only 80 percent of the total of new funds raised will actually be available for making new auto loans, what is the minimum rate of return Axtell must earn in order to at least break even on these new loans?

2. Stronghold Money Fund Assets is a relatively new money market fund with about $400 million in total financial assets and shares outstanding (each maintained at a value of $1.00 per share). Most of the fund's accounts represent the savings of high-income, interest-sensitive financial market investors. Stronghold's current distribution of financial assets currently is as follows:

U.S. Treasury securities	$170 million
Federal agency securities	115 million
Prime bank CDs	85 million
Prime commercial paper issues	30 million

Interest rates are expected to rise substantially in the money market over the next several weeks or months and Stronghold's management is concerned that its relatively low current yield (a seven-day average of 4.05 percent, one of the lowest yields among existing money funds) may result in the loss of many of its more interest-sensitive share accounts. The fund's average maturity is currently at 34 days, also substantially less than the industry's current average maturity of about 45 days.

What steps would you recommend to help Stronghold Money Fund prepare for an apparent impending change in money market conditions?

3. Please identify the terms and concepts defined or described below as discussed in this chapter.

a. Investment company investing only in short-term financial instruments.
b. Interest-bearing checking accounts offered by a credit union.
c. Nonprofit associations providing financial services only to their members.
d. Depository institutions owned by their depositors.
e. Insures deposits placed in U.S. banks and savings and loan associations.
f. Deposits bearing market-sensitive interest rates and subject to withdrawal by check.
g. A leading home mortgage lender in the United States.

Questions about the Web and the Money and Capital Markets

1. If you wanted to find the individual Web site of a thrift institution how would you find it on the World Wide Web? Which thrifts are located in your community? Are all of them visible on the Web?

2. According to the Web what are credit union leagues and how can you find them?

3. How can you locate the credit union or other thrift institution nearest to your home?

4. According to the Web what is the role and purpose of such institutions as CUNA? the World Council of Credit Unions? the NCUA?

5. How can you find the Web sites of a savings and loan or savings bank?

6. Who regulates savings and loans and savings banks? According to the Web who are their principal federal regulators and when were these agencies started?

7. If you wanted to explore the policies and performance of any particular money market fund how could you do so on the Web? Suppose you wanted to compare the performance of two or more money market funds. Where could you go on the Web?

Selected References

Good, Barbara A. "The Credit Union Industry—An Overview." *Economic Commentary.* Federal Reserve Bank of Cleveland, May 15, 1996, pp. 1–4.

Investment Company Institute. *Money Market Mutual Funds.* Washington, DC, May 1991.

Jordan, Jerry L. "Effective Supervision and the Evolving Financial Services Industry." *Economic Commentary,* Federal Reserve Bank of Cleveland, June 2001.

Rose, Peter S. *Commercial Bank Management,* 5th ed. New York: Irwin/McGraw-Hill, 2002.

World Council of Credit Unions. *Statistical Report 2000*, Madison, Wisconsin.

Chapter **Seventeen**

Mutual Funds, Pension Funds, Insurance Companies, Finance Companies, and Other Financial Institutions

Learning Objectives in This Chapter

- You will explore the many roles played by a variety of financial institutions ranging from mutual funds (investment companies), pension funds, and insurance companies to finance companies, mortgage banks, and security dealers.

- You will discover the different *services* each of these nonbank financial institutions offers to the public.

- You will examine the principal *sources and uses of funds* that these nonbank institutions draw upon to carry out their daily activities.

- You will be able to understand more fully many of the key problems that financial institutions operating in today's money and capital markets face.

What's in This Chapter? Key Topics Outline

Mutual Funds: Advantages for the Small Investor

New Types of Mutual Funds

Goals, Earnings, and Tax Status of Mutual Funds

Pension Funds: Purpose and Types of Retirement Plans

Cash Balance Pensions and Efforts to Reduce Employer Costs

Pensions' Investment Strategies and Government Regulation (ERISA)

Life and Property-Casualty Insurers: Old and New Services Provided

Investment Policies and Insurable Risks

Terrorism and the Insurance Industry

Finance Companies: Types of Companies, Asset Portfolios, and Funding Sources

New Consumer Finance Options: Pawn, Title, and Check-Cashing Credit Providers

Investment Bankers, Mortgage Banks, REITs, Venture Capital and Leasing Companies

Trends Affecting All Financial Institutions

INTRODUCTION

We now turn to a highly diverse group of financial institutions that attract savings mainly from individuals and families and, for the most part, make long-term loans in the capital market. Included in this group are mutual funds (sometimes called investment companies), pension funds (or, as they are sometimes called, retirement plans), and life and property-casualty insurers, which today are the leading institutional buyers of bonds and stocks. Finance companies, another member of this group of financial institutions, are active lenders to both business firms and consumers (households) and borrow heavily in the money market. As we will soon see, the majority of these institutions provide important services to participants in the markets for both business and consumer credit.

MUTUAL FUNDS (OR INVESTMENT COMPANIES)

One of the most rapidly growing of all financial institutions over the past two decades is the **mutual fund** or, as it is more properly called, the investment company. **Investment companies** provide an outlet for the savings of thousands of individual investors, directing their funds into bonds, stocks, and money market securities. These companies are especially attractive to the small investor, to whom they offer continuous management services for a large and varied security portfolio. By purchasing shares offered by an investment company, the small saver gains greater diversification, risk sharing, lower transactions costs, opportunities for capital gains, and indirect access to higher-yielding securities that can be purchased only in large blocks. In addition, most investment company stock is highly liquid, because these companies stand ready at all times to repurchase their outstanding shares at current market prices. The bulk of mutual fund shares are held by individuals and families rather than by institutional investors.

The Background of Investment Companies

Investment companies, first developed in Great Britain, made their appearance in the United States in 1924 as a vehicle for buying and monitoring subsidiary corporations. Many were unsuccessful in the early years, and the Great Depression of the 1930s forced scores of these firms into bankruptcy. New life was breathed into the industry after World War II, however, when investment companies appealed to a rapidly growing middle class of savers. They were also buoyed by rising stock prices that attracted millions of investors, most of whom had only modest amounts to invest and little knowledge of how the financial markets work. The industry launched an aggressive advertising campaign that attracted more than 40 million shareholders during the 1960s alone.

Markets on the Net

The financial-services firms—life insurers, property-casualty insurers, pension funds, mutual funds, finance companies, and investment banks—represented in this chapter are also heavily represented on the World Wide Web. Because hundreds of these firms have Web sites the easiest way to gather information about each industry is to enter the names of major financial firms, which usually tells you a great deal about the services offered and about whom you can contact for added information.

However, several of these financial-service industries also have trade groups to represent their interests with government and the public. These trade associations include the American Council of Life Insurers (*www.acli.com*), the Insurance Information Institute (representing the property-casualty insurance industry at *www.iii.org*), and the Investment Company Institute (representing the mutual fund industry at *www.ici.org*). Further information about property-casualty insurers is available through the National Association of Mutual Insurance Companies at *www.namic.org* and there is a directory of over one thousand insurance companies on the Internet at *www.iiin.com/iiincompanies.html*. These trade associations distribute a wide variety of publications, many of which are listed on their Web sites.

Pension funds have been growing rapidly in importance within the financial system and also on the Web where many are represented by name. News and data on the pension fund industry appears in the Pension and Investments newsletter at *www.pionline.com*. Also extensively represented on the Web is the mutual fund industry with hundreds of sites. Among the most interesting is that maintained by the Securities and Exchange Commission (SEC) at *www.sec.gov*. If you are a potential online mutual fund investor you can get some help from the Wall Street Journal at *www.investing.wsj.com*.

Finance companies are listed on the Web primarily by their individual names such as Citifinancial and CIT Group. The same is true of investment banks with such old-line firms as Morgan Stanley Group, Lehman Brothers, and Goldman Sachs maintaining good sites. Another interesting Web location with information on investment banking is *www.encyclopedia.com*.

Then the roof fell in as the long postwar bull market in stocks collapsed in the late 1960s and again in the 1970s. Small investors began to pull out of the stock market in droves. Many investment companies disappeared in this shakeout period, most of them consolidated into larger firms.

The future of the industry seemed in doubt until a new element appeared: *innovation*. Managers began to develop new types of investment companies designed to appeal to groups of investors with specialized financial needs. By tradition, investment companies had stressed investments in common stock, offering investors capital appreciation as well as current income. With the stock market performing poorly, these firms turned their focus increasingly to bonds and money market instruments. New *bond funds* directed the majority of the funds into corporate debt obligations or tax-exempt municipal bonds. Their principal objectives in recent years have been to generate current income and, in the case of the municipal bond fund, a higher after-tax rate of return for the investor. Capital appreciation is normally a secondary consideration to bond funds.

Money market funds, discussed earlier in Chapter 16, began in 1972 with the announced intent of holding money market securities, mainly bank certificates of deposit (CDs), commercial paper, and government bills. They were created in response to record-high interest rates and the desire of the small investor to skirt around federal interest rate ceilings on time and savings deposits offered by banks and thrift institutions. In addition, the money funds have offered investors professional management of their liquid funds (cash) and reduced risk through diversification.

The traditional stock-investing mutual funds began to grow rapidly again during the 1980s and 1990s. Although money market funds rescued the investment companies during the turbulent 1970s, equity-oriented mutual funds outpaced the money market funds more recently, with money flowing in from individual retirement accounts (IRAs) and from investors eager to take advantage of higher expected long-term yields on selected stocks versus the relatively low yields available on deposits and other short-term investment instruments. Moreover, several stock funds outperformed the market as a whole by purchasing stocks from smaller, rapidly growing firms dealing in high-tech products, health care, and other specialty areas.

By the fall of 2000 mutual funds of all types approached the $5 trillion in assets mark, compared to barely more than $1 trillion in assets in1990. Nevertheless, many stock funds did *not* outperform the market and soon began to plummet in value. This increased the popularity of *index funds* that invest in a portfolio of stocks and bonds reflective of the whole market and that tend to move synchronously with that market.[1]

Equally important in the 1980s and 1990s was the rapid growth of *global funds.* These are stock and bond funds whose income-earning securities come from all over the world. These funds have access to security trading 24 hours a day through active exchanges in London, Tokyo, Singapore, Hong Kong, and other financial centers around the globe. Managers of these funds believe that higher returns are achievable with a balanced international portfolio, rather than from just holding domestic securities. Unfortunately, the risk attached to these global funds has often proven to be higher than expected (as in Asia and Japan, for example). Currently more than 80 percent of equity (stock) mutual funds are *domestic* in their focus rather than global. Another innovative investment company developed recently is the *vulture fund,* which purchases securities from firms in trouble in the hope of scoring exceptional returns should these firms recover or when their more valuable assets are liquidated.

Another group of funds experiencing considerable popularity in recent years are so-called *small-cap, mid-cap,* and *large-cap* investment companies. These mutual funds specialize in the stocks of companies that occupy different size groups. For example, the smallest-size firms, in terms of total capitalization, are called "small caps" while the largest companies are referred to as "large caps." There has been some research evidence in recent years that small- and mid-cap firms represent riskier investments but often provide higher average returns than do large-cap companies. In contrast, the large-cap funds frequently claim they offer more stable long-run returns than small-cap and mid-cap funds.

Finally, during the 1990s and early into the new century *hedge funds* became prominent. These mutual funds are really private partnerships that sell shares to only a limited number of investors in the hope of reaping large returns from pursuing high-risk investments. In

---

[1]*Index funds* are based on the theory of efficient markets, which argues that in the long run, active money managers cannot beat the market as a whole. Thus, index funds tend to hold their investments longer and charge lower brokerage and service fees than do investment companies that turn over their security portfolios more rapidly. Many index funds are tied to movements in the Dow-Jones Industrials, Standard and Poor's 500 Stock Index, or other popular stock indices. (See Chapters 3 and 22 for further discussion of market efficiency.)

Recently a version of index funds, known as Exchange-Traded Funds (ETFs), appeared, offering investors mutual funds that trade like stocks on an exchange. These baskets of stocks mirror a popular stock index (such as the S&P 500 index) and may be traded at any time, giving investors somewhat greater control over their portfolios compared to standard mutual funds.

Investment companies—the fastest-growing major financial institution of the past decade—have also been a source of controversy among investors, regulators, and the general public. These mutual funds provide savers with multiple benefits—easy access to the financial marketplace, professional asset management services, greater liquidity, and ready marketability.

While benefits such as these are appreciated by most investors, there is growing research evidence that many mutual fund investors *may* pay too much for the service they receive from many of these financial intermediaries. One of the most significant of the fees paid by mutual funds' customers are *advisory fees,* which range, on average, between 0.50 percent and 0.60 percent of the "typical" mutual fund's total assets. Advisory fees compensate professional fund managers for the research and investment decisions they carry out on behalf of the mutual fund that hires them.

Of course, advisory fees are not the only charges that mutual fund investors often wind up paying. Many funds charge a front-end or back-end *load,* comparable to a brokerage fee or sales commission, which may range upwards of 6 to 8 percent of the total amount of funds contributed. And there may be *administrative costs* and *trading fees* on top of that.

It does appear, however, that operating costs decline as a mutual fund grows larger so that investors may benefit more from investing in larger mutual funds—one reason industry mergers are soaring. In any event, knowing what fees and other expenses a mutual fund charges or experiences is one of the wisest things a mutual fund investor can do.

this case, the word "hedge" refers to an investment strategy that splits the money being invested between those assets expected to increase in value if the market goes up and those assets believed to benefit if the market goes down. Many hedge funds gamble on the market's direction by betting that they know better than the market as a whole which way interest rates and security prices are likely to go. The high risk posed by these funds gave rise in the 1990s to public calls for closer regulation of investment company behavior, especially after the collapse of the huge Long-Term Capital Management hedge fund. However, many market observers oppose such regulation because it might limit the options currently available to investors.

Tax and Regulatory Status of the Industry

Investment companies have a favorable tax situation. As long as they conform to certain rules to qualify as an investment company (such as those spelled out in the Investment Company Act of 1940), they pay *no* federal taxes on income generated by their security holdings. However, no less than half of their resources must be devoted to securities and cash assets. Investment companies must maintain a highly diversified portfolio: a maximum of one quarter of their total resources can be devoted to securities issued by any one business firm. Only a small portion of net income (no more than 10 percent) can be retained in the company. The rest must be distributed to shareholders. Investment companies and the securities they issue must be registered with the Securities and Exchange Commission.

Open-End and Closed-End Investment Companies

There are two basic kinds of investment companies. *Open-end investment companies*—often called *mutual funds*—buy back (redeem) their shares any time the customer wishes, and sell shares in any quantity demanded. Thus, the amount of their outstanding shares changes continually in response to public demand. The price of each open-end company share is equal to the *net asset value* of the fund—that is, the difference between the values of its assets and liabilities divided by the volume of shares issued.

EXHIBIT 17-1

Financial Assets Held by Mutual Funds (Open-End Investment Companies)

Source: Board of Governors of the Federal Reserve System, *Flow of Funds Accounts.*

Asset Holdings	Amount in 2000* ($ Billions)	Percent of Total Assets
Security repurchase agreements	$ 101.5	2.1%
Corporate stock (equities)	3,622.4	75.2
U.S. Treasury securities	238.5	5.0
Federal agency securities	154.0	3.2
State and local government (municipal) securities	228.3	4.7
Corporate and foreign bonds	368.4	7.6
Open-market paper	101.5	2.1
Miscellaneous assets	1.8	0.1
Total financial assets held	$4,816.4	100.0%
Total mutual fund shares outstanding	$4,816.4	

Note: Columns may not add to totals due to rounding error.
*Figures through the third quarter of 2000.

Open-end companies may be either *load* or *no-load* funds. Load funds offer shares to the public at net asset value plus a commission to brokers marketing their shares. No-load funds sell shares purely at their net asset value. The investor must contact the no-load company directly, however. Whether load or no-load, open-end investment companies are heavily invested in common stock, with corporate bonds running a distant second. As Exhibit 17–1 shows, corporate stock represents about three-quarters of mutual-fund industry's assets, with government bonds and corporate bonds accounting for most of the remaining assets.

Closed-end investment companies sell only a specific number of ownership shares, which usually trade on an exchange. An investor wanting to acquire closed-end shares must find another investor who wishes to sell; the investment company itself does not take part in the transaction. These funds often attract investors by offering "double discounts," which consist of discounted prices on the stocks they hold and discounted share prices to buy into the fund itself. Closed-end companies issue a variety of securities to raise funds, including preferred stock, regular and convertible bonds, and stock warrants. In contrast, open-end companies rely almost exclusively on the sale of equity shares to the public in order to raise the funds they need.

Goals and Earnings of Investment Companies

Investment companies adopt many different goals. *Growth funds* are interested primarily in long-term capital appreciation and tend to invest mainly in common stocks offering strong growth potential. *Income funds* stress current income in their portfolio choices rather than growth of capital, and they typically purchase stocks and bonds paying high dividends and interest. *Balanced funds* attempt to bridge the gap between growth and income, acquiring bonds, preferred stock, and common stock that offer both capital gains (growth) and current income.

The majority of investment companies give priority to capital growth over current income. However, the industry's growth in recent years has centered primarily on funds that tend to stress current income, such as bond funds, money market funds, and option funds (which issue options against a portfolio of common stocks). Although most investment companies hold a highly diversified portfolio of securities, a few specialize in stocks and bonds from a single industry or sector (such as precious metals or oil and natural gas).

Management Insight Rating and Selecting Mutual Funds: Morningstar

One of the best-known sources of information for investors interested in purchasing shares in mutual fund companies is *Morningstar,* which provides detailed data for more than 8,000 investment companies today. This investor service describes each fund's asset portfolio and its investment objective, explains the fund's type (i.e., whether it is a *load* or *no load* fund), and assesses its recent total returns and risk exposure. *Morningstar* also assigns a rating based upon each company's reward-to-risk ratio. *Morningstar* is now available on CD Rom with a quarterly updated database called *Principia Plus,* which helps a potential investor develop a hypothetical portfolio that might meet his or her particular investment needs. One word of caution for anyone using any mutual fund or stock or bond rating service: most such services rate these investment vehicles according to their *past performance.* Unfortunately, when it comes to most stocks, bonds, and mutual funds, past performance is not necessarily a reliable guide to future performance.

Keeping track of daily developments in the mutual fund industry can be done by following such Web sites as Mutual Fund Investor's Center at *www.mfea.com,* and the Mutual Fund Investing Newsletter at *www.funds-newsletter.com*

Policies and goals for investing funds are determined by an investment company's board of directors, which is elected by its shareholders. Its assets, however, are managed by an *investment advisory service* in return for an annual fee (usually 0.5 to 2 percent of a fund's assets). The contract between investment advisor and mutual fund must generally be approved by the fund's stockholders. Most funds have very few employees; most of their services (such as record keeping and investment advice) are contracted out to other firms. A mutual fund's price per share (or net asset value (NAV)) is often published in daily newspapers. As illustrated below, newspapers usually print the abbreviated name of the fund, its price or net asset value per share the preceding business day, the net change in price from the day before, and the change in yield occurring thus far in the current year. Thus:

Name	NAV per Share	Net Chg	Yield Chg
Balanced Equity Fund	$15.60	+0.08	+3.9

It is not at all clear that mutual funds hold a significant advantage over other investors in seeking the highest returns available in the financial marketplace. Moreover, there is evidence that, with the possible exception of index funds, these companies may roll over their portfolios too rapidly, which runs up the cost of managing the fund and reduces earnings. Less frequent trading activity on the part of investment companies might well result in greater long-term benefits for the saver. Research evidence has been mounting for a number of years that security markets are highly efficient. Overvaluation or undervaluation of securities is, at most, a temporary phenomenon. In this kind of environment, it is doubtful that investment companies are of significant benefit to the large investor, though they may aid the small investor in reducing information and transactions costs and opening up investment opportunities not otherwise available. As the new century began, many investment companies began to raise their account fees and require customers to put up larger minimum investments, thereby increasing the burden on the small investor. The industry has cited declining investment volume and higher operating costs as the course of these adjustments. And, indeed, recent research evidence suggests that there are significant economies of scale in the investment-company industry with larger funds reporting substantially lower operating costs per dollar of assets held.

Examples of Leading Investment Companies (Mutual Funds)

Growth Fund of America	Putnam Voyager Fund
USAA Income Stock	INVESCO Equity Inc.
Vanguard Equity Inc.	Fidelity Magellan Fund
T.Rowe Price Equity Income Fund	Janus Venture Fund
AIM Equity Constellation Fund	Vanguard 500 Index Fund

PENSION FUNDS

Pension funds protect individuals and families against loss of income in their retirement years by allowing workers to set aside and invest a portion of their current income. A pension plan places current savings in a portfolio of stocks, bonds, and other assets in the expectation of building an even larger pool of funds in the future. In this way, the pension plan member can balance planned consumption after retirement with the amount of savings set aside today.

Two main types of pension plans exist today. *Defined benefit* plans promise a specific monthly or annual payment to workers when they retire based upon the size of their salary during the working years and their length of employment. In contrast, *defined contribution* plans (such as a 401(K) plan) specify how much must be contributed each year in the name of each worker but the amount to be received when retirement is reached will vary depending upon the amount saved and the returns earned on accumulated savings. Defined-benefit pension programs have the advantage of guaranteed income if the employee remains with a particular employer for a relatively long period of time, but an employee who leaves early or is dismissed before retirement may get little or nothing. Under the defined contribution approach, however, the funds saved belong to the employee and are portable provided the employee stays on the job long enough (usually 1 to 2 years) for the savings to be "vested" in his or her name. Defined benefit plans are declining as a percentage of all pension programs, while defined contribution plans are rising and now account for the majority of private pension programs.

Growth of Pension Funds

Pension funds have been among the most rapidly growing of all financial intermediaries. Between 1980 and 2000, the assets of all private and public pension funds multiplied more than ten times over, reaching more than $9 trillion in the United States alone in 2000. (See Exhibit 17–2.) Approximately half of all full-time workers in private businesses and three-quarters of all civilian government employees are protected by pension plans other than the U.S. social security program (OASDI). Nearly 200 million persons are insured under the U.S. social security program.

Pension fund growth in the past has been spurred on by the relatively few retirees drawing pensions compared to the number of people working and contributing to a pension program. That situation is changing rapidly, however; individuals over 65 years of age now

---

Examples of Leading Pension Funds

Calilfornia Public Employees' Retirement System	New York City Pension Funds
Ontario Pension Board	TIAA-CREF Pension Plan
British Columbia Municipal Superannuation Fund	Wisconsin Retirement System

---

EXHIBIT 17–2   Total Assets of Private and Public Pension Funds, Selected Years ($ Billions)

Type of Pension Plan or Program	1940	1950	1960	1970	1980	1990	2000*
Private pension programs:	$2.0	$12.1	$ 52.0	$138.2	$422.7	$2,324.8	$5,129.0
Insured plans	0.6	5.6	18.8	41.2	165.8	695.7	—
Noninsured plans	1.4	6.5	33.2	97.0	286.8	1,629.1	—
Government pension programs:	$4.3	$25.8	$ 56.1	$125.9	$289.8	$1,203.5	$4,032.7
State/local retirement systems	1.6	5.3	19.3	60.3	185.2	720.8	3,034.1
Federal civilian systems	0.6	4.2	10.5	23.1	75.8	247.5	416.7*
Railroad retirement program	0.1	2.6	3.7	4.4	2.1	9.9	14.9**
Social security program (OASDI)	2.0	13.7	22.6	38.1	26.5	225.3	567.0**
Total assets of all funds	$6.3	$37.9	$108.2	$262.0	$712.3	$3,528.3	$9,161.7

Note: Columns may not add to totals due to rounding.
*2000 figures are for the third quarter.
**Indicated figures are for 1996.

Source: Securities and Exchange Commission; Railroad Retirement Board; U.S. Department of Health and Human Services; the American Council of Life Insurance; and the Federal Reserve Board.

represent one of the fastest growing segments of the world's population. The growing proportion of retired individuals will threaten the solvency of many private pension funds and has already created major funding problems for various government programs (such as the U.S. medicare and medicaid programs) designed primarily to aid the elderly.[2]

Competition among employers for skilled management personnel has also spurred pension fund growth, as firms have tried to attract top-notch employees by offering attractive fringe benefits. This growth factor is likely to persist into the future due to a possible shortage of skilled entry-level workers as the population ages. Some experts foresee a real problem in this area, stemming from recent difficulties pension plans have had in keeping up with inflation and with the increasing number of retirees. Workers in the future are likely to demand better performance from their retirement plans and greater control over how their long-term savings are invested.

Recently, a highly controversial form of pension plan, a so-called *cash balance plan,* has appeared. These new plans appear to save employers money and to favor younger workers, but they may actually reduce older workers' benefits. With a cash balance plan, employers typically make a hypothetical contribution to an employee's retirement account equal to a percentage of the employee's annual salary and credit the employee's account with an annual interest credit based upon a reference interest rate (such as the U.S. Treasury bond rate). At retirement, the participating employee receives periodic payments based on his or her accumulated funds. One controversial limitation is that an employee typically cannot take all of his or her funds upon departure from the sponsoring employer's place of work.

Moreover, under many such retirement plans, you have to be a plan participant for at least five years in order to receive any benefits at all. When an employer converts from a traditional pension to a cash balance plan, that employer determines the accumulated value held in the old pension under each employee's name and may transfer all or only a portion of that accumulated value into the employee's new plan account. In short, employers have considerable discretion over how much built-up credit each employee receives upon conversion to a cash balance plan; older workers, in particular, seem most vulnerable to losing some of their accumulated retirement earnings and may have to work several additional

[2]The present ratio of working adults to retired persons in the U.S. population is about 3:1. This ratio is projected to shrink to about 2:1 during the next century. When the U.S. Social Security Act was passed in 1935, there were 11 working adults for each retired individual.

Management Insight   Managing a Financial Institution's Investment Portfolio

Most financial institutions, including insurance companies, pension funds, and banks, actively buy securities sold through brokers and dealers in the money and capital markets. Examples include purchases of common and preferred stock, corporate and government bonds, Treasury bills, commercial paper, and other marketable securities.

The purpose of adding security-type assets to a financial institution's portfolio varies from institution to institution but generally includes a desire to (a) add new sources of income; (b) stabilize a financial institution's income flow (for example, when loan revenues decline, security income may be increasing); (c) offset the risks presented by riskier assets (such as real estate holdings); (d) provide additional liquidity (with securities that can be readily sold for cash); and (e) reduce tax exposure (such as by purchasing tax-exempt securities). Most financial institutions today have written investment policies describing the goals they expect to achieve with their security investments, the quality or risk exposure they are willing to accept, and the maturities and other terms that they consider most desirable.

Different types of financial institutions often hold very different kinds of investment securities. Banks, for example, tend to favor short-term and medium-term government securities, while pension funds, mutual funds, and insurance companies tend to buy large quantities of longer-term corporate bonds and stock. Among the principal factors that affect which types of investment securities a financial institution will buy are:

1. The *expected rate of return* on the security and how that return correlates with the returns from other assets that the financial institution already holds (because a negative or low positive correlation will help to stabilize an institution's overall income).

2. *Degree of tax exposure,* with heavily taxed financial institutions (such as banks and insurance companies) generally preferring those securities with zero or low tax exposure.

3. *Exposure to credit or default risk,* with regulations often limiting such institutions as banks, pension funds, and insurance companies to higher-quality financial investments.

4. *Exposure to interest rate risk,* indicating how strongly the market price of a security reacts to changes in interest rates.

5. *Exposure to liquidity risk,* indicating how much of a loss the institution might be forced to take if a security must be sold quickly.

6. *Exposure to prepayment risk,* on loan-backed securities, where some loans in the pool of loans backing the securities are paid off early, lowering expected yield.

7. *Exposure to inflation risk,* with some securities perhaps rising in value when inflation threatens.

8. *Desired maturity range,* with financial institutions holding relatively short-term liabilities generally preferring to match these with shorter-term security investments.

Clearly, the choice of what types of investment securities to hold is not an easy one for the manager of a financial institution. Several factors must be weighed before a decision is made.

You can keep track of ongoing developments in the pension fund industry through such Web sites as that established by the International Foundation for Employee Benefit Plans at *www.ifebp.org*

years to catch up to where they were when their employer converted to a cash-balance-type pension. Clearly, the prime beneficiary of the cash-balance-type plan is the *employer,* as the ultimate impact is usually to keep business costs down. Fortunately for most U.S. employees with employer-sponsored pension programs, federal law entitles covered employees to request and receive a statement of vested benefits accrued to date. Such a request may be made once each year in writing. Once a request is received, the employer must reply within 30 days.

Investment Strategies of Pension Funds

Pension funds are long-term investors with limited need for liquidity. Their incoming cash receipts are known with considerable accuracy because a fixed percentage of each employee's salary is usually contributed to the fund. At the same time, cash outflows are not difficult to forecast, because the formula for figuring benefit payments is stipulated in the contract between the fund and its members. This situation encourages pensions to purchase

Pension funds set aside current savings in a pool of earning assets (stocks, bonds, etc.) in the hope of accumulating a larger amount of savings that will provide a stream of income during the retirement years. For example, suppose an employee of a company with a pension plan who is scheduled to retire in five years has $2,500 deposited in her retirement account this year. If the pension plan promises her a 6 percent annual yield on each dollar set aside for retirement, the $2,500 she sets aside today will be worth:

$$
\begin{array}{l}
\text{Value of funds} \\
\text{contributed today} \\
\text{at retirement}
\end{array}
=
\begin{array}{l}
\text{Amount set} \\
\text{aside today}
\end{array}
\left(1 + \frac{\text{Promised}}{\text{rate of return}}\right)^{\text{Years invested}}
$$

$$
= \$2{,}500(1+.06)^5 = \$3{,}345.57
$$

in five years. Suppose this same employee who plans to retire in five years has $2,500 contributed every year between now and retirement and earns 6 percent on each dollar saved. Then her total savings pool at retirement will be:

$$
\begin{array}{l}
\text{Total funds} \\
\text{available at} \\
\text{retirement}
\end{array}
=
\begin{array}{l}
\text{Amount of savings} \\
\text{contributed} \\
\text{each year}
\end{array}
\times
\begin{array}{l}
\text{Sum of compound interest factors} \\
\text{for savings contributed each year} \\
\text{up to retirement at interest rate } i
\end{array}
$$

$$
= \$2{,}500[(1 + .06)^5 + (1 + .06)^4 + \ldots + (1.06)^1]
$$

$$
= \$14{,}937.50
$$

How much in annual income can this employee look forward to in retirement from this one pension plan? The answer depends on the annual annuity rate promised and whether the employee has access to (i.e., is vested with) all funds contributed in her name. Suppose this employee is vested with the full amount shown above (i.e., a vesting ratio of 1.00) and is promised an annual annuity (income) rate of 5.5 percent based on her life expectancy. Then her expected annual retirement income from this pension plan will be:

$$
\begin{array}{l}
\text{Expected annual} \\
\text{retirement} \\
\text{income}
\end{array}
=
\begin{array}{l}
\text{Annual} \\
\text{annuity} \\
\text{rate}
\end{array}
\times
\begin{array}{l}
\text{Total funds available} \\
\text{to employee at} \\
\text{retirement}
\end{array}
\times \text{Vesting ratio}
$$

$$
= 0.055 \times \$14{,}937.50 \times 1.0 = \$821.56
$$

(*Note:* To verify the figures above please see Chapter 6 and the compound interest table at the back of this book.)

common stock, long-term bonds, and real estate and to hold these assets on a permanent basis. In addition, interest income and capital gains from investments are exempt from federal income taxes, and pension plan members are not taxed on their contributions unless benefits are actually paid out.

Although favorable taxation and predictable cash flows favor longer-term, somewhat riskier investments, the pension fund industry is closely regulated in all its activities. The Employee Retirement Income Security Act (ERISA) requires all U.S. defined-benefit private plans to be *funded*, which means that any assets held plus investment income must be adequate to cover all promised benefits. ERISA also requires that investments must be made in a "prudent" manner, which is usually interpreted to mean that they be invested in highly diversified holdings of high-grade common stock, corporate bonds, and government securities and only limited real estate investments.

Although existing regulations emphasize conservatism in pension investments, private pensions have been under intense pressure in recent years by management and employees of sponsoring companies to be more liberal in their investment policies. The sponsoring

EXHIBIT 17–3

Financial Assets Held by Private Pension Funds and State and Local Government Employee Retirement Funds

Source: Board of Governors of the Federal Reserve System, *Flow of Funds Accounts.*

Assets Held by Private Pension Plans	Amount in 2000* ($ Billions)	Percent of Total Assets
Checkable deposits and currency	$ 10.7	0.2%
Time and savings deposits	114.1	2.2
Money market fund shares	91.8	1.8
Security repurchase agreements	26.6	0.5
Open market paper	33.5	0.7
U.S. Treasury securities	182.0	3.5
Federal agency securities	275.0	5.4
Corporate and foreign bonds	286.8	5.6
Mortgage loans	16.0	0.3
Corporate stock (equities)	2,451.2	47.8
Shares in mutual funds	918.0	17.9
Miscellaneous assets	723.3	14.1
Total financial assets held	$5,129.0	100.0%

Assets Held by State and Local Government Pension Plans	Amount in 2000* ($ Billions)	Percent of Total Assets
Checkable deposits and currency	$ 10.8	0.4%
Time and savings deposits	2.3	0.1
Security repurchase agreements	51.1	1.7
Open market paper	51.1	1.7
U.S. Treasury securities	208.9	6.9
Federal agency securities	173.6	5.7
State and local government (tax-exempt) securities	1.7	0.1
Corporate and foreign bonds	324.4	10.7
Mortgage loans	21.5	0.7
Corporate stock (equities)	1,953.7	64.4
Miscellaneous assets	235.0	7.7
Total financial assets held	$3,034.1	100.0%

*Figures are for the end of the third quarter of 2000.

employer has a strong incentive to encourage its affiliated pension plan to reduce operating expenses and earn the highest possible returns on its investments. This permits the company to minimize its contributions to the plan. However, in 1985 the Financial Accounting Standards Board issued SFAS 87, which required *defined-benefit pension plans* to more fully disclose their funding status, asking businesses to make projections of their future pension obligations, publish estimates of how much in benefits employees will receive, and report any *unfunded* portion of pension benefits on each business's balance sheet as a liability. These accounting requirements have made some business firms offering pension plans look weaker and, along with strict government regulations, have caused many businesses to abandon their pension programs, leaving it to their employees to develop and manage their own retirement plans.

Pension Fund Assets

The particular assets held as investments by pension funds depend heavily on whether the fund is government controlled or a private venture. As shown in Exhibit 17–3, private funds emphasize investments in corporate stock, which represent about 50 percent of their assets. Corporate bonds rank a distant second, accounting for about 6 percent of all private

Management Insight   Will Pension Rules Look Different after the Enron Case?

The startling collapse of Enron Corporation of Houston—the largest bankruptcy filing in U.S. history—in 2001 and 2002 aroused a storm of controversy about how employee retirement plans are set up and managed. The Enron case led some authorities to conclude that pension law in the United States may be too heavily tilted toward favoring employers rather than employees.

When the Employee Retirement Income Security Act was passed by the U.S. Congress in 1974 it permitted companies to contribute their own stock to their employees' retirement plan with few limitations. The loophole granted many employer-sponsored retirement plans soon led to many businesses placing 50 percent or more of their employees' retirement account in the company's stock. Clearly, employees in these situations received little or no risk-reducing benefits from asset portfolio diversification.

Why were firms like Enron tempted to put so much of their own stock in their employee retirement plans? These "inside" stock sales created more demand for the company's stock and drove its price higher. Moreover, contributing stock instead of cash helped conserve the employer's cash reserves.

Even more controversial, pension law also allowed these corporate retirement plans to block employee sales of company stock until an employee reached a certain age. (In Enron's case apparently this was 50 years of age.) Thus, many Enron employees watched helplessly as the company's stock declined drastically in value but were unable to "unlock" their holdings. These awkward limits on retirement portfolio diversification and early stock sales may lead to significant new pension reform legislation in the years ahead, including possibly stricter limits on investing workers' pensions in their employer's stock and greater disclosure of insider transactions.

pensions' assets. With few liquidity needs, private pension funds held relatively small amounts of cash and bank deposits, although their holdings of U.S. government and federal agency securities have remained substantial (almost 10 percent of their total assets) due to the relatively high yields and safety of these financial instruments. Many of the largest pension plans also hold substantial real estate investments for asset diversification and as a hedge against inflation.

Corporate stock recently has become more important in the portfolios of government pensions than among many private pension plans. As Exhibit 17–3 shows, state and local government pension programs held about 60 percent of their assets in corporate stock. Stock investments are followed in government pension plans by holdings of corporate bonds, which represent about 10 percent of their assets. The pressure of regulation falls more heavily upon government (public) pensions than upon private plans. As a result, the investments of government pensions tend to be somewhat more conservative with heavier concentrations in higher-grade assets.

Factors Affecting the Future Growth of Pension Funds

Most experts believe that pension fund growth may continue to be quite rapid in the future, particularly due to the uncertainty surrounding the U.S. Social Security program. With government and business playing a smaller role, individual workers will be compelled to rely more heavily upon their own resources to finance their retirement years. Still, there appear to be serious problems ahead for both the growth and the stability of pension plans. One concern is the rising proportion of pension beneficiaries to working contributors, related to the aging of the population. At the same time, the cost of maintaining pension programs has increased dramatically. The full funding of a defined benefit plan to cover all promised benefits may place extreme pressure on corporate profits, particularly if declining security markets or falling interest rates diminish investment returns.

Even more significant is the rising cost of government regulation, which has imposed costly reporting requirements on the industry, granted employees the right to join pension programs soon after they are hired, and allowed pension plan members to acquire owner-ship and control more quickly of monies contributed on their behalf. These government regulations have forced many private pension plans to close. The control of others has been turned over to a financial institution—typically a bank trust department or life insurance company—that is better able to deal with the current rules. Many defined-benefit private pension plans are in weak financial condition, especially those connected to corporations that are in serious trouble. In addition, some of the best pension plans have been terminated because their sponsoring employers are trying to recapture their assets, the value of which has risen in recent years.

In short, the pension fund sector faces some serious problems that will require creative solutions in the future, including a redefining of the role of public and private institutions in assuring an equitable and adequate distribution of retirement monies to those who have earned them.

Questions *to Help You Study*

1. What advantages do *investment companies* (mutual funds) offer the small saver? Why has their growth been so erratic in recent years?

2. Define the following terms:

   a. *Open-end company*   e. *Growth funds*
   b. *Closed-end company*   f. *Balanced funds*
   c. *Bond fund*   g. *Global funds*
   d. *Money market fund*   h. *Index funds*

3. What is the principal function of *pension funds?* Explain why these institutions have been among the most rapidly growing financial institutions in recent years. Do you expect their growth to be faster or slower in the future? Why? What is the difference between a defined-benefit and a defined-contribution pension plan?

4. What are the principal assets acquired by pension funds? What factors guide their selection of assets to hold?

LIFE INSURANCE COMPANIES

The recent rapid growth of mutual funds and pension funds contrasts sharply with the more moderate growth of one of the oldest financial-service firms—the **life insurance company.** Life insurers have been operating for centuries in Europe, and the life insurance company was one of the first financial institutions founded in the American colonies. The Corporation for Relief of Poor and Distressed Presbyterian Ministers and of the Poor and Distressed Widows and Children of Presbyterian Ministers, established in 1759, was the first U.S.-based life insurer.

Life insurance companies offer their customers a hedge against the risk of earnings losses that often follow death, disability, or retirement. Policyholders receive risk protection in return for the payment of policy premiums that are set high enough to cover estimated benefit claims against the company, all operating expenses, and a target profit margin. Additional funds to cover claims and expenses are provided by the earnings from investments made by life insurance companies in bonds, stocks, and other assets approved by law and government regulation. Figures on the volume of insurance in force in the United States are shown in Exhibit 17–4, and the principal kinds of insurance policies sold by U.S. life insurers are listed in Exhibit 17–5.

EXHIBIT 17–4
Life Insurance in Force in the United States, 1989 and 1999 ($ Billions)

Source: American Council of Life Insurance.

Category	1989	1999
Individual life insurance	$ 4,964	$ 9,172
Credit life insurance	260	214
Group life insurance	3,470	6,110
Total	$ 8,694	$ 15,496
Average amount of coverage in value of life insurance per insured family:	$112,400	$189,800

Note: Columns may not add to totals due to rounding.

EXHIBIT 17–5
The Principal Kinds of Insurance Policies Sold by Life Insurance Companies

Source: American Council of Life Insurance.

Ordinary or whole life insurance	Insurance protection that covers the entire lifetime of the policyholder. Premiums build up cash values that may be borrowed by the policyholder.
Term life insurance	Insurance coverage for a certain number of years so that the policyholder's beneficiaries receive benefit payments only if death occurs within the period of coverage.
Endowment policy	A policy with benefits payable to the living policyholder on a specified future date or to the policyholder's beneficiaries if death occurs before the date specified in the policy.
Group life insurance	Master insurance policy covering a group of people, usually all working for the same employer or members of the same organization.
Industrial life insurance	Small-denomination life policies with premium payments collected monthly or weekly by a company agent.
Universal life insurance	Insurance protection with premium payments whose amount and timing can be changed by the policyholder and including a savings account with a flexible rate of return.
Variable life insurance	Insurance protection whose benefits vary in amount with the value of assets pledged behind the policy contract.
Adjustable life insurance	A flexible form of insurance protection that permits the policyholder to alter some of the policy's terms, period of coverage, or face value.
Credit life insurance	A policy pledged to pay off a loan in the event the borrower dies or becomes disabled before the debt is retired.

The Insurance Principle

The insurance business is founded upon the *law of large numbers*. This mathematical principle states that a risk that is not predictable for one person can be forecast accurately for a sufficiently large group of people with similar characteristics. No insurance company can accurately forecast when any one person will die, but its actuarial estimates of the total number of policyholders who will die in any given year are usually quite accurate.

Life insurance companies today insure policyholders against three basic kinds of risk: premature death, the danger of living too long and outlasting one's accumulated assets, and serious illness or accident. Many policies combine financial protection against death, disability, and retirement with savings plans to help the policyholder prepare for some important future financial need, such as the purchase of a home or meeting the costs of a college education. Actually, most benefit payments are made primarily to living, rather than deceased, policyholders, who receive annuities or health insurance benefits.

Life insurance companies are among the leading sources of retirement (pension) benefit payments for older citizens, and today more than 60 million U.S. citizens are enrolled in pension programs managed by life insurers. Many life-insurer-managed pension plans consist of *fixed annuity accounts* or *variable annuity accounts.* The fixed annuities pay out a stable stream of income to the customer, based upon the amount saved, the expected rate of return on those savings, and the withdrawal rate agreed to between the annuitant and the insurance company. Variable annuities, in contrast, pay out a variable stream of income to the customer that changes over time as the value of the accumulated savings in the annuitant's account changes with market conditions.

Investments of Life Insurance Companies

Life insurers invest the bulk of their funds in long-term securities such as bonds, stocks, and mortgages, thus helping to fund real capital investment by businesses and governments. They are inclined to commit their funds long term due to the high predictability of their cash inflows and outflows. This predictability normally would permit a life insurance company to accept considerable risk in the securities it acquires. However, both law and tradition require a life insurer to act as a "prudent person." This restriction is imposed to ensure that sufficient funds are available to meet all legitimate claims from policyholders or their beneficiaries at precisely the time those claims come due.

The life insurance industry and the current trends reshaping that industry can be followed through such Web sites as the U.S. Business Reporter at *www.activemedia-guide.com* and through the site of *Risk and Insurance Magazine* at *www.riskandinsurance. com*

Life insurance companies generally pursue *income certainty* and *safety of principal* in their investments. The majority of corporate securities they purchase are in the top four credit-rating categories.[3] Life insurers frequently follow a "buy and hold" strategy, acting as long-term holders of securities rather than rapidly turning over their portfolios. This investment approach reduces the risk of fluctuations in income and avoids having to rely as heavily on forecasting interest rates. We should note, however, that some life insurers have become more active traders in securities. Emphasizing performance more than permanence in their investments, larger life insurance companies have set up trading rooms to more closely monitor the performance of their investment holdings, selling out and reinvesting in higher-yielding alternatives when circumstances warrant. Because this new investment strategy creates additional risk, many larger insurers now use financial futures, options, and other risk-hedging tools and more closely match asset and liability maturities to protect themselves against losses from fluctuating interest rates.[4]

Exhibit 17–6 shows the kinds of investments held by U.S. life insurance companies as the twenty-first century was beginning. The primary investment is in *corporate bonds* issued by both domestic and foreign companies. Several companies ran into trouble recently from heavy purchases of high-risk ("junk") corporate bonds as well as poorly performing real estate investments. During the 1990s Mutual Benefit Life Insurance Company and Executive Life Insurance Company were taken over by state regulators, both firms among the largest U.S. insurers ever to fail. Several state regulators restricted further purchases of junk bonds. Holdings of common and preferred stock, although smaller, have become significant in recent years. Life insurance companies have shown renewed interest in corporate stock due to the growing importance of variable annuity and variable life insurance policies in their sales programs.

Another important asset held by life insurance companies is *mortgage loans* on farm, residential, and commercial properties. Substantial changes have occurred in life insurer mortgage investments in recent years. The industry has reduced its holdings of farm and residential mortgages on one-to four-family homes and increased its holdings of commercial

[3]See Chapter 8 for an explanation of security ratings.
[4]See Chapter 9 for a detailed discussion of various interest-rate hedging methods.

EXHIBIT 17–6

Financial Assets and Liabilities of Life Insurers

Source: Board of Governors of the Federal Reserve System, *Flow of Funds Accounts.*

Asset and Liability Items Outstanding	Amount in 2000[*] ($ Billions)	Percent of Total Assets
Assets held:		
Checkable deposits and currency	$ 3.7	0.1%
Money market fund shares	136.6	4.3
Open market paper	79.5	2.5
U.S. Treasury securities	59.3	1.9
Federal agency securities	229.4	7.2
State and local government (municipal) securities	20.8	0.7
Corporate and foreign bonds	1,204.4	37.7
Loans to policyholders	100.9	3.2
Mortgage loans	233.5	7.3
Corporate stock (equities)	1,028.3	32.1
Mutual funds shares	51.1	1.6
Miscellaneous assets	51.4	1.6
Total financial assets held	$3,198.9	100.0%
Liabilities outstanding:		
Loans and advances	$ 2.7	0.1%
Life insurance reserves	785.2	26.2
Pension fund reserves	1,389.2	46.3
Taxes payable	17.3	0.6
Miscellaneous liabilities	805.4	26.8
Total liabilities outstanding	$2,999.7	100.0%

[*]Figures are for the end of the third quarter of 2000.

mortgages, including loans on retail stores, shopping centers, office buildings, apartments, hospitals, and factories. The higher yields and shorter maturities of the latter loans explain much of the recent growth of commercial mortgage lending by the life insurance industry. However, life insurers continue to provide indirect support to the residential mortgage market by making heavy purchases of federal agency securities, most of which come from government agencies aiding the home mortgage loan market.

Government securities play a secondary but still important role in the portfolios of life insurance companies. These securities serve the important function of providing a reservoir of *liquidity* because they may be sold with little difficulty when funds are required. U.S. life insurers buy mostly federal government securities rather than state and local government obligations. The industry has only a limited need for the tax-exempt income provided by state and local bonds because its effective tax rate is relatively low.

One asset whose importance increased dramatically in earlier years, though it has slowed recently, is *loans to policyholders.* The holder of an ordinary (whole life) insurance policy can borrow against the accumulated cash value of that policy, which increases each year. The interest rate on policy loans is stated in the policy contract and in some policies is quite low. Policy loans tend to follow the business cycle, rising in periods when economic activity and interest rates are increasing, and declining when the economy or interest rates are headed down. Because of this cyclical characteristic, policy loans represent a volatile claim on the industry's resources. When policy loan demand is high, life insurance companies frequently are forced to reduce their purchases of bonds and stocks. In recent years, however, most new whole life policies have had floating loan rates tied to an index of corporate bond yields, and policyholder borrowing has settled into a relatively small percentage of industry assets.

Sources of Life Insurance Company Funds

The primary income source for life insurers comes from *premium receipts* from sales of insurance policies. Premiums from sales of annuity plans and health insurance policies have actually grown faster than sales of traditional life insurance policies. Annual net income from investments in bonds, stocks, and other assets averages only about a third of premium receipts. The industry's net earnings after expenses roughly equal its net investment income each year, because virtually all premiums from the sale of policies are ultimately returned to policyholders or their beneficiaries. This means that, on balance, the industry hopes to break even from its insurance underwriting operations (with premiums flowing in roughly equal to benefits paid out) while earning its profits from its investment income.

This normal expectation of greater total insurance income than insurance-industry claims and expenses sometimes goes awry when tragic events occur. A dramatic example of such an "exogenous shock" to the life insurance industry struck on September 11, 2001, when terrorist attacks on the United States resulted in great losses of life as well as huge property damage. Actually, life insurers often have built-in protections against such costly events should they decide to use them. For example, many life insurance policies exclude the payment of insurance claims resulting from acts of war unless, as happened frequently following the events of September 2001, the companies involved waive such exclusions.

Structure and Growth of the Life Insurance Industry

The majority of the close to 1,700 U.S. life insurance companies are corporations owned by their stockholders. The rest are *mutuals,* which issue ownership shares to their policyholders. However, mutuals are bigger, on average, and typically were established much earlier than stockholder-owned companies. Most new insurance companies in recent years have been stockholder owned, and a substantial number of mutuals have converted to *stock* companies (such as Prudential Insurance) to gain greater financial flexibility and open up new sources of capital. Recently, several big life insurers have converted to stockholder form by creating mutual holding companies, attracting new stockholder capital and issuing stock options to their employees.

Health insurance companies are often part of or closely related to life insurers. You can follow developments in the health insurance industry via such Web sites as the Healthcare Insurers at *www. plunkettresearch.com*

The U.S. life insurance industry's population reached a high of almost 2,350 in 1988 and has been falling ever since. Most recently worldwide many of the biggest life insurers are merging with banks and securities firms, diversifying their services, and reaching across continents. One of the most notable is the recent merger of Travelers Insurance with Citibank of New York to form Citigroup, Inc., one of the largest financial conglomerates in the world (though Travelers may soon be sold). Thus the largest life insurers today are *converging* with other financial-service industries to form huge multiproduct businesses.

New Services

Life insurers are under increasing pressure to develop *new services* due to a long-term decline in their share of household savings and pressure on their earnings caused by new high-cost, more-automated service delivery systems. Many analysts argue that life insurance is becoming less attractive a product as the population ages, while retirement planning and retirement savings instruments are likely to grow in importance. Increasing competition from other financial intermediaries, especially mutual funds, has also played a major role in encouraging the development of new services. Among the most important recent developments are the offering of such innovative services as universal and adjustable life insurance, variable premium and variable life insurance, mutual funds, tax shelters, venture capital loans, corporate cash management systems, and deferred annuities.

Management Insight   How the Premiums Charged by Insurance Companies Are Computed

When insurance companies agree to provide risk protection services to their customers, how do they decide how much to charge?

Let's consider an example. Suppose a life insurer has 100,000 policyholders, each 40 years of age with a $1 million life insurance policy. The company must set an annual premium so it will have sufficient cash to pay off the beneficiaries of any customers who die this year.

$$\text{Expected deaths} = \text{Number of policyholders in age group} \times \text{Expected mortality rate} = \frac{100}{\text{thousand}} \times \frac{4 \text{ per}}{\text{thousand}} = \frac{400 \text{ deaths}}{\text{expected}}$$

If each policyholder has a $1 million policy, the insurance company must prepare for expected claims of:

$$\text{Expected claims} = \text{Expected deaths} \times \text{Policy amounts promised} = 400 \times \$1 \text{ million} = \$400 \text{ million}$$

How much should the insurance company charge each policyholder in premiums? Suppose the 400 deaths expected will occur toward the end of this year. We want to determine how much to charge all policyholders at the beginning of this year to be ready for $400 million in claims at year's end. We need to estimate how much the insurance company will earn when it invests the premiums paid by its policyholders in stocks, bonds, and other financial assets. Let's suppose the company estimates it will earn an average of 8 percent on its portfolio of investments in the coming year. Thus, to have $400 million available at year's end, the company needs the following

The first thing the insurer must do is determine the expected number of deaths among the 100,000 policyholders this year. Actuarial science has produced mortality tables that predict how many individuals of any age are expected to die each year out of every 1,000 persons. If the expected death rate for 40-year-olds is 4 per 1,000, the expected number of deaths in the coming year from this group of 100,000 policyholders is:

amount from its policyholders at the beginning of the year: $400 million/$(1 + .08)^1$ or $370.4 million or $3,704 per policyholder.

However, this calculation does not include operating costs (salaries of sales personnel, etc.), including the need to earn a normal profit for the company's stockholders. Suppose it will cost $2.6 million to service the insurance needs of policyholders this year. This operating cost is called the *loading*, which must be added to the net premium to drive the *gross premium* charged policyholders:

$$\text{Gross premium} = \frac{\$370.4 \text{ million} + \$2.6 \text{ million}}{100,000} = \$3,730 \text{ per policyholder}$$

The insurance premium rates charged are also shaped by *competition*, which tends to hold premium rates down and encourages insurers to be more efficient.

Begun as far back as 1979, *universal life insurance* allows the customer to change the face amount of his or her policy and the size and timing of premium payments, as well as earn higher investment returns from any premiums paid in. Premium payments on a universal life insurance policy usually are invested in a money market fund. Another example of the newer and more flexible life insurance products emerging in recent years is *adjustable life insurance,* which permits the policyholder to change periodically from a whole life policy to term insurance (which offers protection only for a designated period) and back again to deal with changing circumstances. Adjustable policies allow the policyholder to increase or decrease the face value of a policy, the period of insurance protection, and the size of premium payments within limits spelled out in the policy contract. A variation of this idea is *variable premium life insurance,* which grants the policyholder lower premium payments when investments made by the life insurer earn a greater return. *Variable life insurance* pays benefits according to the value of assets pledged behind the policy rather than paying a fixed amount of money. There is normally a guaranteed minimum benefit for the policyholder's beneficiary, however—a form of inflation-hedged life insurance.

Life insurers have also been active in venture capital loans to help start new businesses and in offering professional funds management services to many businesses that have neither the time nor the experience to manage their own cash accounts. Life insurers have also found success in attracting *deferred annuity* accounts in which an individual will deposit funds with the insurer under an agreement to receive a future stream of income flowing from those deposited funds beginning on a stipulated future date. The insurer agrees to invest the funds in earning assets that will grow over time and escape taxation until the customer actually begins receiving income.

In recent years, insurance companies have found a way to supplement their cash inflows from insurance premiums by selling *guaranteed investment contracts* (GICs) to large institutional investors such as pension funds and state and local governments. Similar to deposits, GICs promise investors a fixed rate of return for a stipulated period. Many corporations and governmental units that have sold bonds in the open market have in turn purchased GICs with the proceeds of those bond issues. GICs have increased insurance company risk somewhat because of their relatively high fixed cost.

One area of growing insurance needs is coverage for small businesses. New businesses are being formed today in record numbers, with more than 30 million uninsured persons currently working for them in the United States alone. The provision of life and health insurance for owners and employees of small firms has become a promising service area for those insurers able to correctly price the coverages they provide. Another area of need for the future is health and life insurance for individuals, such as retired citizens, who are no longer members of group insurance plans. Without question, the new services offered by life insurers in future years will depend heavily upon favorable changes in government laws and regulations. One prominent example is expanded entry into Japan and China, two of the largest insurance and pension plan markets in the world, but this opportunity is dependent upon the willingness of the Japanese and Chinese governments to let more foreign financial firms come in. Life insurers must also continue to lower the cost of marketing and delivering their services, such as through increased use of telephone sales, automation, and joint-venture sales of policies through banks and stockbrokers. Correspondingly, the industry recently has made major cuts in its traditional vehicle for the delivery of services—local insurance agencies.

PROPERTY-CASUALTY INSURANCE COMPANIES

Property-casualty (P/C) insurers offer protection against fire, theft, bad weather, negligence, and other acts and events that result in injury to persons or property. So broad is the range of risk for which these companies provide protection that P/C insurers are referred to as *insurance supermarkets.* In addition to their traditional insurance lines—automobile, fire, marine, personal liability, and property coverage—many of these firms have branched into the health and medical insurance fields, clashing head-on with life insurers offering the same services. Others, like Travelers Insurance, have reached out to merge with whole new industries (such as Travelers' alliance with Citicorp in 1998) and, thereby, reach out to large numbers of potential new customers with a sharply expanded menu of new services.

Financial Developments Top-Ranked Life and Property-Casualty Insurers in the United States (Ranked by Total Assets as of Year-End 1999)

Name of Life Insurance Company	Total Assets in Billions of Dollars	Name of Property-Casualty Insurance Company	Total Assets in Billions of Dollars
Prudential of America	$212	State Farm Insurance	$95
Metropolitan Life Insurance	199	Berkshire Hathaway	69
Hartford Life	134	American International	46
Aegon USA, Inc.	123	Allstate Insurance	39
TIAA Group	111	Travelers PC	35
American General	97	CNA Insurance	35
American International Group	96	Liberty Mutual	31
New York Life Insurance Company	96	Nationwide Group	23
Equitable Group	95	Hartford Insurance	23
Nationwide	90	St. Paul Insurance Companies	22
Aetna Company Group	89		

Sources: Federal Reserve Board and A. M. Best Company.

Makeup of the Property-Casualty (P/C) Insurance Industry

The property-casualty insurance business has grown rapidly in recent years due to the effects of inflation, rising crime rates, and an increasing number of lawsuits arising from product liability and professional negligence claims. There were nearly 3,000 P/C companies in the United States as the twentieth century drew to a close, holding nearly $600 billion in total assets. Stockholder-owner companies are dominant, holding about three-fourths of the industry's total resources. Mutual companies—owned by their policyholders—command roughly one-fourth of all industry resources.

Property-casualty insurers are also grouped by whether they are *agency companies* or *direct writers.* Agency firms sell policies primarily through local agents who earn commissions on their sales of policies from many different insurance companies. Direct writers sell directly to the public (often via telephone or television) or have their own dedicated agents to promote their products. In recent years direct writers have captured a growing share of the insurance industry.

Changing Risk Patterns in Property/Liability Coverage

Property-casualty insurance is a riskier business than life insurance. The risk of policyholder claims arising from crime, fire, personal negligence, and similar causes is less predictable than is the risk of death. Moreover, inflation has had a potent impact on the cost of property and services for which this form of insurance pays. For example, the cost of medical care and repair of automobiles has increased significantly more rapidly than the overall cost of living in recent years.

Equally important, basic changes now seem to be under way in the risk patterns of many large insurance programs, creating problems in forecasting policyholder claims and in setting new premium rates. Examples include a rapid rise in medical malpractice suits; a virtual explosion in product liability claims against manufacturers of automobiles, tires, home

Financial Developments   Insurance Companies Deal with a Torrent of Terror-Related Policyholder Claims

The terrorist attacks in September 2001 subjected insurance companies to one of the most panicky episodes in their history. The attacks on the New York City World Trade Center and the Pentagon cost more than 3,000 lives and millions of dollars in property damage. Fears of possible collapse ran rampant through the insurance industry (with the stock prices of leading insurers falling precipitously) in the wake of these tragedies.

Because the terror attacks came from outside the normal purview of the financial system, this huge external shock to the insurance industry was completely unexpected. Insurance companies had no time to adjust the premiums they charge to cover the potential claims they face. Many insurers feared that they would have inadequate reserves to pay off a flood of policyholder claims.

The insurance industry was quick to respond to these huge pressures with several initiatives. First, proposals were made to the U.S. government to setup an "insurance pool" that could handle certain terrorist-related claims or backstop those insurance companies feeling the greatest financial pressure. In other words, under the "pool" proposal the government would become the "insurer of last resort" should such a proposal ever become law.

A number of insurers indicated that they had little choice but to include new terror-exclusion clauses in policies sold to the public. Reason: a number of leading *reinsurers*—companies that accept some of the risks taken on by primary insurance providers—declared that, with the dawning of the new policy year, they would no longer underwrite terrorist-related risks. At the same time several insurance companies debated whether or not to enforce a standard exclusion that has been included in most insurance policies for many years—denial of any claims arising from "acts of war." Regardless, some companies have recently begun to offer anti-terror coverage.

appliances, and other goods; a recent rise in civilian fire deaths and losses due to airplane crashes and weather damage; a rapid increase in terrorist-related losses; and the emergence of billions of dollars in claims from so-called *toxic torts,* arising from individuals suffering from illness or injury caused by exposure to asbestos, lead, nuclear radiation, and other hazardous substances. To reduce risk, more P/C insurers have become *multiple-line companies,* diversifying into many different lines of insurance. Another risk-reducing device of growing importance is the *reinsurance* market, in which an insurer contracts with other companies to share some of the risks of its insurance underwriting in return for a share of the insurer's premium income.

Will my insurance company be around when I need it? One way to answer that question is to check with the company that provides quality ratings for insurance companies, A. M. Best Company at *www.bestweek.com*

It is interesting to compare the distribution of assets held by life insurance companies against those assets held by P/C companies. The net cash flows of the two industries—their annual premium income—are roughly comparable. Yet life insurers hold about six times the assets of P/C insurers. Much of the difference is explained by the fact that life insurance is a highly predictable business, whereas property and personal injury risks are not. Most life insurance policies are long-term contracts, and claims against the insurer are not normally expected for several years. In contrast, P/C claims are payable from the day a policy is written because an accident or injury may occur at any time. Therefore, although life insurers can stay almost fully invested, P/C insurers must be ready at all times to meet the claims of their policyholders. In addition, claims against P/C companies are directly affected by inflation, which drives up repair costs. Most life insurance policies, in contrast, pay the policyholder or beneficiary a fixed sum of money or an amount based upon the market value of investments that back the policies.

Investments by Property-Casualty (P/C) Companies

The majority of funds received by P/C companies are invested in state and local government bonds and common stock. P/C insurers, unlike most financial institutions, are subject to the full federal corporate income tax (except that policyholder dividends are tax

Management Insight Measuring and Evaluating the Performance of a Financial Institution

Financial institutions today are closely watched by their customers, regulators, and the financial markets. The performance of a financial institution is evaluated not only relative to the institution's own goals but also relative to the performance of other businesses competing for capital and other productive resources in the global marketplace.

What measures of a financial institution's performance are the most widely used? Most performance measures employed focus upon four different dimensions of a financial institution's behavior:

1. The *stock price* (market value) of a stockholder-owned financial institution.

2. The *rate of return* or *profitability* of a financial institution.

3. The *risk exposure* of a financial institution, which encompasses multiple aspects of its financial condition and behavior.

4. The *operating efficiency* of a financial institution, measuring how well the institution uses the resources at its command to produce and deliver its services.

In a market-driven economy, stock price is usually the single best indicator of how well a stockholder-owned financial institution is performing. However, many financial institutions (such as mutual savings banks, credit unions, and mutual insurance companies) do *not* have stockholders; for these institutions, measures of profitability are needed to evaluate how well these financial firms are performing. Return on assets and return on equity capital are the most comprehensive measures of a financial-service firm's profitability.

Financial institutions are subject to *multiple* types of *risk,* including risk to the solvency (survival) of the institution as reflected in how much capital the owners have placed in the institution relative to its risk-exposed assets. If an institution's risky assets decline in value by more than the volume of its owners' capital (net worth), it will become *insolvent.* Similarly, financial institutions that make loans may face serious trouble if a substantial proportion of their loans must be written off as uncollectible and overwhelm the owners' stake in the firm.

Financial institutions also face significant *liquidity* risks in the form of "cash outs" and are exposed to *interest rate risk*—the danger of loss due to changing market interest rates. Any financial institution will suffer loss if its assets and liabilities cannot be successfully adjusted to a new interest rate environment.

Intense competition in recent years has pressured financial institutions into watching their expenses very closely to ensure that operating costs don't completely eat away the revenues generated from service sales. Many institutions have recently reduced their staff sizes in the hope that the remaining employees will be highly productive. Finally, increased emphasis has been placed in recent years on generating *noninterest* (fee) income from services not directly tied to the borrowing and lending of money (including fees for managing a customer's asset or retirement portfolio). Managers of financial institutions recently have attempted to minimize the amount by which their noninterest expenses (including salaries, wages, and overhead costs) exceed their noninterest (fee) income.

---

deductible for the issuing company). Faced with a potentially heavy tax burden, these companies find tax-exempt state and local government bonds an attractive investment. As shown in Exhibit 17–7, industry holdings of state and local bonds represented almost a quarter of its total financial assets, although property-casualty insurers have placed less emphasis on purchases of municipal bonds in recent years, due in part to their sluggish earnings and recent changes in tax laws. Another important asset—corporate stock, also representing close to a quarter of all industry assets—is intended to protect industry earnings and net worth against inflation. Other significant investments include U.S. government securities, federal agency securities, and corporate bonds. P/C insurers have maintained heavy purchases of government securities and corporate bonds in recent years due to their higher yields and, in the case of government bonds, their greater safety and liquidity.

Sources of Income

Like life insurance firms, P/C insurers plan to break even on their insurance product lines and earn most of their net return from their investments. Achieving the break-even point in

EXHIBIT 17–7
Financial Assets and Liabilities of Property-Casualty Insurers

Source: Board of Governors of the Federal Reserve System, *Flow of Funds Accounts.*

Asset and Liability Items Outstanding	Amount in 2000* ($ Billions)	Percent of Total Assets
Assets held:		
Checkable deposits and currency	$ 3.4	0.4%
Security repurchase agreements	35.4	4.0
U.S. Treasury securities	61.1	6.8
Federal agency securities	78.5	8.8
State and local government (municipal) securities	199.2	22.2
Corporate and foreign bonds	185.1	20.7
Commercial mortgage loans	1.8	0.2
Corporate stock (equities)	203.4	22.7
Trade receivables	68.9	7.7
Miscellaneous assets	58.6	6.5
Total financial assets outstanding	$895.3	100.0%
Liabilities outstanding:		
Taxes payable	19.0	3.3%
Miscellaneous liabilities	560.2	96.7
Total liabilities outstanding	$579.3	100.0%

*Figures are for the end of the third quarter of 2000.

insurance underwriting has been difficult, however, due to rising costs, increased litigation, the reluctance of state insurance commissions to boost policy premiums, and new forms of risk. In fact, property-casualty insurers have experienced billions of dollars in underwriting losses in recent years, and the recent terror attacks have added to their problems.

Business Cycles, Inflation, and Competition

Property-casualty insurance is an industry whose earnings and sales revenue reflect the ups and downs of the business cycle. This cyclical sensitivity, coupled with the vulnerability of P/C insurers to inflation, has created a difficult environment for insurance managers. Inflation pushes up the cost of claims, while intense competition holds premium rates down. Among U.S. P/C companies, a key challenge today is the rapid growth of foreign insurance underwriters who have entered the United States in large numbers. Moreover, many U.S. corporations have started their own *captive* insurance companies. To improve their situation for the future, P/C insurers must become more innovative in developing new services, and more determined to eliminate those services that result in underwriting losses and to reduce their operating costs.. This will not be easy due to extensive regulations and public pressure for lower insurance rates.

Questions *to Help You Study*

5. Against what kinds of *risk* do life insurance companies protect their policyholders? What about property-casualty insurers?

6. Compare and contrast the asset portfolios of life insurance companies with the asset portfolios of property-casualty insurers. Please try to explain any differences you are able to observe.

7. What principal factors influence the *premiums* that insurers charge their policy-holding customers?

8. What is happening to the mix of services offered by life insurers and property-casualty insurance companies? Why?

One of the best examples of the struggles insurance companies have faced in recent years to preserve their profitability and capital is Lloyds of London—the three-centuries-old insurance market in which individual investors (called "names"), underwrite the risks taken on by their clients in return for premiums and investment income. Lloyds has insured some unusual risks, including actress Elizabeth Taylor's eyes, while also underwriting the reward for corralling the Loch Ness monster! But what is equally unusual about Lloyds is that their "names" (underwriters) pledge their entire net worth, if necessary, to cover their share of any losses that may occur.

Unfortunately for Lloyds, the risks associated with a volatile economy, political upheaval and war, as well as extremes in weather, environmental damage, and other sources of loss, have resulted in burgeoning claims that have threatened Lloyds' financial stability at times. One point in Lloyds' favor is that it requires full (100 percent) setting aside of reserves behind any possible future claims, whereas most regular insurance companies set aside fewer reserves and count on other income (mainly investment earnings) to help cover any claims received. Moreover, Lloyds has imposed special levies on its members and, for the first time in its history, allowed corporate capital to come in. The venerable insurer has also turned more heavily to the reinsurance market (where policies are written to back up any excess risk presented by conventional insurance contracts). These recent steps by Lloyds illustrate how creative the managers of insurance companies must be to deal with the risks and the intense global competition that confront the insurance industry today.

FINANCE COMPANIES

Finance companies are sometimes called d*epartment stores of consumer and business credit.* These institutions grant credit to businesses and consumers for a wide variety of purposes, including the purchase of business equipment, automobiles, vacations, and home appliances. Most authorities divide firms in the industry into one of three groups—consumer finance companies, sales finance companies, and commercial finance companies.

Different Finance Companies for Different Purposes

Consumer finance companies make personal cash loans to individuals. The majority of their loans are home equity loans and loans to support the purchase of passenger cars, home appliances, and mobile homes. However, a growing proportion of consumer-finance-company loans centers on aiding customers with medical and hospital expenses, educational costs, vacations, and household expenses. Loans made by consumer finance companies are considered to be riskier than other consumer installment loans and, therefore, generally carry steeper finance charges than those assessed by most other lending institutions.

Sales finance companies make indirect loans to consumers by purchasing installment paper from dealers selling automobiles and other consumer durables. Many of these firms are captive finance companies controlled by a dealer or manufacturer. Their principal function is to promote sales of the sponsoring firm's products by providing credit. Firms having captive finance company affiliates include such industry leaders as General Motors, Ford Motor Company, and General Electric. Generally, sales finance companies specify in advance to retail dealers the terms of installment contracts they are willing to accept.

Examples of Leading Finance Companies

GE Capital Corporation	GMAC Financial Services
Household Finance Corp.	Ford Motor Credit Co.
Morgan Stanley Dean Witter Credit Corp.	CIT Group
Beneficial Finance Corp.	Citifinancial Inc.

Frequently they will give the retail dealer sample contract forms, which the dealer fills out when a sale is made. The contract is then sold to the finance company.

Commercial finance companies focus principally on extending credit to business firms. Most of these companies provide accounts receivable financing or factoring services to small- or medium-sized manufacturers and wholesalers. With accounts receivable financing, the commercial finance company may extend credit against the borrower's receivables in the form of a direct cash loan. Alternatively, a factoring arrangement may be used in which the finance company acquires the borrowing firm's credit accounts at an appropriate discount rate to cover the risk of loss. Most commercial finance companies today do not confine their credit-granting activities to the financing of receivables but also make loans secured by business inventories and fixed assets. In addition, they offer lease financing for the purchase of capital equipment and rolling stock (such as airplanes and railroad cars) and make short-term unsecured cash loans.

We should not overdramatize the differences among these three types of finance companies. The larger companies are active in all three areas. In addition, most finance companies today are extremely diversified in their credit-granting activities, offering a wide range of installment and working capital loans, leasing plans, and long-term credit to support capital investment. Exhibit 17–8 shows that business loans are the most important financial assets held by finance companies, accounting for almost half of their assets, followed by loans to individuals and families (consumers), accounting for nearly one-fifth of industry assets. Real estate mortgage loans are also significant, representing one of the fastest growing finance-company assets in recent years. Smaller amounts of funds are held in cash to provide immediate liquidity.

Trends in the finance company industry can be traced through the Web sites of leading finance companies, such as GE Capital, at www. gecommercialfinance. com

Growth of Finance Companies

Finance companies have been profoundly affected by recent changes in the character of competition among all financial intermediaries. The lack of an intensive network of branch

EXHIBIT 17–8
Financial Assets and Liabilities Held by Finance Companies

Source: Board of Governors of the Federal Reserve System.

Asset and Liability Items Outstanding	Amount in 2000[*] ($ Billions)	Percent of Total Assets
Assets held:		
Checkable deposits and currency	$ 27.2	2.5%
Mortgage loans	142.4	13.3
Consumer credit	197.3	18.4
Business loans and advances	455.7	42.6
Miscellaneous assets	248.0	23.2
Total financial assets held[**]	$1,070.7	100.0%
Liabilities outstanding:		
Open market paper	$ 215.6	19.6%
Corporate bonds	465.5	42.9
Bank loans (not elsewhere classified)	35.4	3.2
Taxes payable	8.8	0.8
Miscellaneous liabilities (including foreign direct investment in the United States and investments by parent companies)	373.1	34.8
Total liabilities outstanding	$1,098.4	100.0%

[*]Figures shown are for end of third quarter of 2000.
[**]Financial assets held do not include receivables from operating leases granted by finance companies, such as consumer auto loans that are booked to operating income. The leased equipment is *not* a financial asset.

offices has put many finance companies at a disadvantage in reaching the household borrower who values convenience. As a result, both banks and nonbank thrifts have been able to capture a larger share of the consumer loan market at the expense of finance companies. For example, data compiled by the Federal Reserve Board show that finance companies held about 45 percent of consumer installment loans extended by financial institutions in 1950 but less than 15 percent in 2000, although captive finance companies of automobile firms (such as Ford Motor Credit) have done well vis-à-vis their competitors by offering discount-rate loans. Over the same time interval, however, credit unions have more than tripled their share of the consumer installment loan market.

Many experts now believe that the fastest growing market for finance companies in future years will be in business-oriented, not consumer-oriented, financial services. Revolving credit, working capital loans, merger and acquisition loans, and equipment leasing are among the fastest growing forms of credit extended by finance companies today. Recently, finance companies have expanded their lending programs to include small- and medium-sized businesses, making loans to and accepting some of the stock of these firms. However, home equity lending to consumers has also grown rapidly in recent years.

Methods of Industry Financing

Finance companies are heavy users of *debt* in financing their operations. Principal sources of borrowed funds include bank loans, commercial paper, and debentures (bonds) sold primarily to banks, insurance companies, and nonfinancial corporations. (See Exhibit 17–8.) The source of funds that these companies emphasize most heavily at any given time depends on the structure of interest rates. When long-term rates are high, these companies tend to emphasize commercial paper and short-term bank loans as sources of funds. In years when long-term rates are relatively low, bonds are likely to be drawn on more heavily. The only source of industry funds that has not grown significantly in recent years is borrowings from parent companies, as finance companies have come to borrow more heavily in the open market rather than relying as heavily upon internally generated funds.

Recent Changes in the Character of the Finance Company Industry

The structure of the finance industry has changed markedly in recent years. As in the case of banks, credit unions, and savings and loans, the number of finance companies has been trending *downward,* although the average size of such companies has grown considerably. A survey by the Federal Reserve Board revealed that in 1960 there were more than 6,400 finance companies operating in the United States, but by the beginning of the new century, only about 1,000 finance companies could be found, many of these operating as finance company subsidiaries belonging to holding companies. The industry is concentrated; the 20 top firms hold about 70 percent of all receivables.

This long-term downtrend in the industry's total population of firms reflects a number of powerful economic forces at work. Rising cost pressures, the broadening of markets, the need to innovate, and intensified competition have encouraged finance companies to strive for larger size and greater operating efficiency. Many smaller companies have sold out to larger conglomerates. Despite their declining numbers, however, finance companies continue to be a potent force in the markets for business and consumer credit.

Indeed, new forms of consumer-oriented finance companies have been emerging recently in the form of *pawnshop, title loan,* and *check-cashing companies.* These small finance firms invite customers to pledge their personal assets (such as an automobile, home, television set, or future paycheck) in return for a loan at a relatively high rate of interest (often the loan rates exceed 50 or even 100 percent). These businesses open up the financial system to a whole new tier of customers (mainly lower-income individuals and families) who are short of immediate cash and often have poor credit histories. The result is that pawnshop, title loan, and check-cashing companies most frequently seem to serve those customers who have few other places from which they can borrow money.

OTHER FINANCIAL INSTITUTIONS

In addition to the foregoing, a number of other financial institutions have developed over the years to meet the specialized financial needs of their customers. For example, **security dealers** provide a conduit for buyers and sellers of marketable securities to adjust their holdings of these securities. These dealer houses stand ready at all times to buy selected private and government securities or to sell from a list of securities to their customers at posted "bid" and "asked" prices. The best known of the dealers are the 25 primary government securities dealers that aid the U.S. Treasury in selling new issues of federal debt and trade securities regularly with the Federal Reserve System. (See Exhibit 17–9 for a list of the largest security dealer/broker firms.)

If you are interested in a career in investment banking check out the site *www.careers-in-finance.com*

Many of these dealers also serve as **investment bankers,** who market large amounts of new securities on behalf of governments and corporations. These specialized "banks" are especially prominent in the offering of *new* corporate securities, state and local government bonds and notes, and securities issued by federal government agencies such as the Federal National Mortgage Association (Fannie Mae). They *underwrite* new offerings of these securities, purchasing them from the original issuer and placing them in the hands of investors at a higher price. When a new issue of securities involves substantial risk, several investment banking firms band together to form a *syndicate* to bid for and market the issue, thus spreading the risk. Investment banks also give advice on the best terms and times to sell new securities and on how to finance corporate mergers and acquisitions. These firms are among the best-known names in the financial world and include such prominent companies as Morgan Stanley Dean Witter, Salomon Brothers, First Boston-Credit Suisse, and Merrill Lynch Capital Markets. Competition between these investment firms has become intense, as capital markets have become global and investment bankers must be prepared to market new securities worldwide.

To learn more about venture capital firms see the Web site of the National Venture Capital Association at *www.nvca.org*

A rising but highly volatile financial-service industry today consists of **venture capital firms.** These businesses gather funds from private investors and other sources and then look for promising new businesses or rapidly emerging companies to invest in. They often fund the development of innovative new products or services, such as new computer software or medicines, in the hope of earning exceptional returns if these new products or services succeed. Many large banks, insurance companies, and other traditional financial

EXHIBIT 17–9
Top-Ranked Security Brokers and Dealers (Listed According to Total Revenues Received during 1999)

Source: Federal Reserve Board.

Name of Broker-Dealer Firm	Total Revenues in Billions of Dollars
Merrill Lynch & Co.	$35
Morgan Stanley Dean Witter	34
Goldman Sachs	25
Lehman Brothers	19
Bear Stearns	8
Paine Webber	8
Charles Schwab Co.	5
A. G. Edwards & Co.	2

intermediaries have set up affiliated venture-capital companies to make these risky investments and hold the stock of promising new or rapidly growing businesses.

Additional information about the mortgage banking industry is available from the Web site of the Mortgage Bankers Association at *www.mbaa.org*

A related type of dealer firm is the **mortgage bank.** Mortgage bankers commit themselves to take on new mortgage loans used to fund the construction of homes, office buildings, and other structures. They carry these loans for a short time until the mortgages can be sold to a long-term (permanent) lender such as an insurance company or savings bank. As in the case with other dealer operations, the financial risks to the mortgage banker are substantial. A rise in interest rates sharply reduces the market value of existing fixed-rate mortgage loans, presenting the mortgage banker with a loss when it sells the loans out of its portfolio. The risk of rising interest rates and falling mortgage prices encourages mortgage banks to turn over their portfolios rapidly and to arrange lines of credit from lending institutions to backstop their operations. These firms also service the mortgage loans they sell to other lenders, collecting loan payments and inspecting mortgaged property.

You can learn more about REITs from the National Association of Real Estate Investment Trusts at *www.nareit.com* and to explore trends in the leasing company industry see such sites as The Association for Equipment Leasing and Finance at *www.elaonline.com*

Authorized by federal law in 1960, **real estate investment trusts (REITs)** are publicly held, tax-exempt corporations that must receive at least three quarters of their gross income from real estate transactions (such as rental income, mortgage interest, and sales of property). They also must devote at least three quarters of their assets to real estate property loans, cash, and government securities. REITs raise funds by selling stock and debt securities and invest most of their available funds in mortgage loans to finance the building of apartments, housing tracts, office buildings, shopping centers, and other commercial ventures.

Leasing companies represent still another kind of specialized financial institution that provides customers with access to productive assets, such as airplanes, automobiles, and equipment through the writing of leases. These leases allow a business or household to use assets sometimes at a lower cost than borrowing money and owning those same assets. The leasing company, on the other hand, benefits from the stream of lease payments and gains substantial tax benefits from depreciating the leased assets. Competition is intense in this industry because of the entry of scores of banks and bank holding companies, insurance companies, and manufacturing firms that have either opened leasing departments or formed subsidiary leasing companies.

TRENDS AFFECTING ALL FINANCIAL INSTITUTIONS TODAY

There are several major trends affecting virtually all financial institutions today. One of these trends is *increasing cost pressures* resulting from the considerable expense associated with raising funds for lending and investing and burgeoning land, labor, and equipment costs that have narrowed profit margins. Another trend is *consolidation,* in which each financial institution tries to expand its size to improve efficiency and ease its growing cost burden. A key result of the consolidation movement is declining numbers of independent financial institutions, while the remaining institutions average much larger in size and organizational complexity.

Still a third trend is *service diversification,* as all major financial institutions have invaded each other's traditional markets with new services in an effort to offset rising costs and protect thinning profit margins. Service diversification has led to a blurring of functions among the different institutions to such an extent that it is becoming increasingly difficult to distinguish between different financial institutions—a phenomenon known as *homogenization.*

Service diversification has led to *convergence* as banks, insurance companies, security firms, and other types of financial institutions rush toward one another and, increasingly, are merging with each other to become large financial conglomerates. This convergence trend has been aided considerably by the passage of the Financial Services Modernization (Gramm-Leach-Bliley) Act passed in the United States in 1999. This new law permits banks, insurers, and securities firms (as well as selected other financial firms) to reach across industry boundaries and link up with each other.

The offering of many new services over wider market areas has been made possible by another trend in the financial institutions' sector: a *technological revolution,* particularly in the growing adoption of automated electronic equipment for making payments and transferring financial information. Increasingly, there is little need to walk into the offices of a financial institution, because many transactions can be handled more efficiently via home and office computers linked online to each financial institution's computer network. The technological revolution has made possible a global financial system and unleashed a trend toward *global competition* in which all financial institutions find themselves increasingly in a common market, competing for many of the same customers. Distance and geography no longer shelter financial institutions from the forces of demand and supply in the financial system as they once did. Accompanying the rise of global competition is a drive toward *regulatory cooperation,* so that financial institutions headquartered in different countries face essentially the *same* regulatory rules. There is a trend toward harmonizing laws and regulations so that no one country's financial institutions operate at a competitive disadvantage vis-à-vis those of another country.

Many of the new services, technological innovations, and the development of global competition have come into existence because of a trend toward *deregulation,* in which the content and prices of financial services increasingly are being determined by the marketplace rather than by government rules. Most of the deregulation movement, thus far, has centered in banking and among nonbank depository institutions as well as leading security dealers and brokers in Canada, the United States, Japan, Great Britain, Australia, and Western Europe. However, as depository institutions and securities firms continue to receive new service powers and expand their markets, it is quite likely that the whole panoply of financial institutions will seek to further loosen the regulatory rules that bind them today. It is hoped that the public will be the ultimate beneficiary in terms of more and better financial services at lower cost.

Questions *to Help You Study*

9. What role do *finance companies* play in supplying funds to the financial marketplace? How many different kinds of finance companies are there?

10. A growing sector within the general finance company industry consists of *small-loan companies,* which include *pawnshops, title loan firms,* and *check-cashing companies,* among others. What do these firms do? What kinds of customers do they serve primarily?

11. What is a *REIT?* A *mortgage bank?* A *leasing company?* Why do you think these specialized lenders came into being? Have they faced any serious problems of late?

12. What functions do security brokers and dealers perform within the financial system? Why are these security companies so important to the effective functioning of the money and capital markets?

13. In the concluding section of this chapter, several major trends affecting all financial institutions today were discussed. Identify these trends. Which ones do you see as long-term trends likely to continue indefinitely into the future? Which may be short lived (if any)? Please explain your answer.

Investment Companies (or Mutual Funds)—Businesses owned by their shareholders that invest incoming share purchases in stocks or other financial assets, paying each shareholder a portion of investment earnings based upon the number of shares held.

Pension Funds—Plans that assist business owners and workers in preparing for the retirement years by accumulating and investing savings in order to pay out retirement income in future years.

Life Insurance Companies—Financial institutions that shelter their policyholders against the risk of death, disability, or ill health by collecting policyholder premiums and investing these funds until claims are made.

Property-Casualty Insurers—Financial firms that protect their policyholders against loss or damage arising from accidents, negligence, dangerous products or hazardous substances, medical or legal malpractice, or other causes by collecting premium payments from policyholders, investing those premiums, and paying off any loss or damage claims that qualify.

Finance Companies—Business and consumer lending institutions that fund a wide variety of needs, especially the purchase of automobiles, household furniture and appliances, and business equipment.

Security Dealers—Firms that "take a position of risk" in government and privately issued securities, purchasing these instruments from sellers and selling them to buyers with the expectation of a profitable spread between purchases and sales.

Investment Bankers—Capital-market firms that assist businesses and governments to issue debt and stock in order to raise new capital.

Mortgage Banks—Intermediaries that work with other businesses on real estate development projects and sell the mortgage loan instruments that arise from these projects to other investors, such as pension funds and insurance companies.

Venture Capital Firms—Institutional investors that provide long-term capital financing for new businesses and rapidly emerging companies.

Real Estate Investment Trusts—Specialized lenders and equity investors that fund commercial and residential real estate projects.

Leasing Companies—Financial firms that purchase business equipment and other assets and then make the purchased items available for use by others in return for rental fees.

Summary of the Chapter

This chapter has examined the services offered by and the portfolio characteristics of a variety of different financial institutions, including mutual funds or investment companies, pension funds, life and property-casualty insurance companies, finance companies, security firms, mortgage banks, real estate investment trusts, leasing companies, venture capital firms, and financial conglomerates of various types.

- Several of the financial institutions discussed in this chapter—particularly *pension funds* and *insurance companies*—provide risk protection for their customers against death, ill health, negligence, loss of property, and the danger of outliving one's savings in retirement. In addition, pension funds, insurance companies, and most of the other financial-service institutions examined in this chapter make loans in the money and capital markets to businesses, individuals, and governments. They are predominantly *capital market institutions,* focused mainly upon providing long-term credit.

- The most rapidly growing financial institution of the past decade has been the *investment company*—most often referred to as a *mutual fund.* Investment companies sell shares to the public and use the proceeds of those sales to buy various types of stocks, bonds, and other securities. Shareholders in a mutual fund receive earnings based on the performance of the securities held by the company. Mutual funds have grown rapidly in recent years, in part because they offer small savers access to the financial marketplace, provide professional funds management and portfolio diversification, and supply liquidity if a customer needs to quickly convert his or her investments into cash.

- Among the more rapidly growing sectors in this financial-services field are *finance companies,* which provide credit to businesses and households. Finance companies too are merging into fewer but larger firms with a growing menu of loans and other financial services. However, this financial-services industry is also developing numerous small-loan companies (in the form of pawn shops, title loan companies, and check-cashing facilities) that cater to individuals and families, particularly those credit customers presenting higher risk.

- The chapter concludes its survey of major financial institutions with an overview of such key industries as *real estate investment trusts (REITs)* and *mortgage banks* that serve the home loan industry and also provide funds for commercial building projects. Another key sector is *security brokers and dealers* who make it possible for corporations, governments, and other institutions in need of funds to reach the security markets and raise new capital. Finally, financial support of businesses stemming from *leasing companies* and *venture capital companies* has been rising in recent years, particularly for new firms and rapidly growing enterprises that have limited sources of funding available to them.

- All of the financial institutions discussed in this chapter are undergoing major changes in the form of *consolidation* of smaller financial-service firms into larger financial-service providers. Not only are financial firms in the same industry growing larger, but many are reaching across several industries and combining different service providers under one corporate umbrella—a phenomenon known as *convergence.* This convergence trend has been helped along by new government legislation (such as the Financial Services Modernization (Gramm-Leach-Bliley) Act passed in the United States in 1999).

- In an effort to lower production costs and reduce risk exposure most financial institutions are diversifying their services—developing and adding new services in order to reduce the overall risk exposure of their revenues and net earnings. One result of this *service diversification* trend is to make more and more financial companies look alike (*homogenization*) because they are offering many of the same services as their neighbors.

- Changes in the *technology of information gathering and distribution* have had a greater impact on financial institutions than most other industries, permitting these institutions to serve their customers with greater accuracy and speed over wider geographic areas. New computer-based technology has allowed financial-service firms to reduce their personnel expenses and become less labor-intensive, but more capital-intensive in their production and service distribution activities.

- More financial-service institutions have become *international* in their focus, reaching across national borders with their services. This trend toward *globalization* has contributed to the emergence of much larger financial institutions and broader financial service menus. Globalization has also encouraged government regulatory agencies in various countries to reach out to each other and cooperate in their oversight of the activities and performance of the financial-services sector.

Key Terms

Mutual funds, *471*
Investment companies, *471*
Pension funds, *477*
Life insurance companies, *483*
Property-casualty insurers, *489*

Finance companies, *494*
Security dealers, *497*
Investment bankers, *497*
Venture capital firms, *497*
Mortgage bank, *498*

Real estate investment trusts (REITs), *498*
Leasing companies, *498*

Problems

1. The manager of a life insurance company is trying to decide what annual premium to charge a group of policyholders, each of whom has just reached his or her 40th birthday. A check of mortality tables indicates that, for every million persons born 40 years ago, 3 percent die, on average, sometime during their 40th year. If the company has 10,000 policyholders in this age bracket and each has taken out a $50,000 life insurance policy, estimate the probable amount of death benefit claims against the company. How much must be charged in premiums from each policyholder just to cover these expected claims? Suppose the company has operating expenses (plus a target profit) on sales to these policyholders of $500,000. What annual premium must be charged each policyholder to recover expenses and meet expected benefit claims?

2. A pension fund has accumulated $1 million in a retirement plan for James B. Smith, who retires this month at age 65. If Mr. Smith has a life expectancy of 75 years, what is the minimum size of annual annuity check the pension plan will be able to send him each year (assuming that the value of the pension fund's investments remains stable)? Should he insist on receiving that size payment each year? Why or why not? What other kinds of information would be helpful in analyzing Mr. Smith's financial situation at retirement?

3. An employee has just joined SONY Corporation and a pension plan is set up in her name under which the company will contribute $5,000 per year and the employee herself will contribute $1,000 per year. How much will this year's contributed funds be worth in 10 years if the pension plan pledges a 7 percent annual return on each dollar saved? Suppose the employee plans to retire in 10 years. How much will be available in total at retirement if the company and the employee contribute the amounts noted above each year for the next 10 years and this employee owns (is vested with) the full amount of savings contributed to the pension plan? If the pension promises an annual annuity

rate of 6 percent given this employee's life expectancy, what annual retirement income can she expect?

4. Delbert Ray is planning to retire this year and draw upon the accumulated savings in his pension plan, which amount to $205,800. Mr. Ray is vested with 80 percent of the accumulated funds and, based on his life expectancy, has been promised an annual annuity (income) rate of 3.5 percent. What is Delbert Ray's expected annual retirement income from his pension plan?

5. A financial institution reports the following figures in its latest annual report:

Net after-tax income	$ 15 million	Equity capital	$145 million
Total assets	996 million	Interest revenues	42 million
Earning assets	775 million	Interest expenses	28 million
Risky assets	685 million	Noninterest sources	
Allowance for loan losses	38 million	of revenue	5 million
Cash and government		Noninterest expenses	19 million
securities	250 million	Interest-sensitive liabilities	493 million
Interest-sensitive assets	382 million		
Number of employees	185		

Drawing upon the discussion in this chapter on measuring and evaluating the performance of a financial institution, please calculate as many measures of this firm's performance as you can. Do you notice any performance measures that the management of this institution might wish to investigate for possible problems?

6. You are examining the profitability of five different financial institutions as measured by their ROE (return on equity capital) and ROA (return on assets). The table below reports the ROE and ROA for each of these five institutions. Using the data below, can you determine what proportion of each institution's total assets is financed by equity (owners') capital and what proportion is financed by debt?

Financial Institution	Return on Equity Capital (ROE)	Return on Total Assets (ROA)
A	15%	1.25%
B	12	0.75
C	10	1.00
D	8	1.60
E	20	2.00

7. Please identify the key term or concept used in this chapter that is described or defined by each of the phrases or sentences below.

a. Sells as many ownership shares as the public demands.

b. Financial-service firms offering and managing retirement plans.

c. Financial-service companies selling their customers protection against loss related to death, disability, and old age.

d. Protecting their customers against losses or damage to persons and/or property.

e. Financial-service companies supplying various forms of credit to businesses and consumers, whose loan rates often rank among the highest.

f. Financial-service firm that assists corporations and governments in raising new funds.

g. Places long-term loans with long-term lenders.

h. Receive most of their income from real estate transactions.

i. Financial-service firms providing access to equipment and other assets to their customers for a stipulated period of time.

Questions about the Web and the Money and Capital Markets

1. What is the best way to find information about a leading insurance company, mutual fund, finance company, or investment bank on the World Wide Web?

2. What is the difference in financial services offered by such firms as Prudential, Travelers, CNA, Scudder, and Beneficial? Do these companies, representing different industries, seem to be becoming more alike? How can the Web help you answer these questions?

3. What are trade associations in the financial-services sector? Which ones representing financial-service providers can you find on the Web? Which association, in your opinion, best represents its industry? Why?

4. If you were an investor possibly interested in becoming a customer of one of the financial-service firms discussed in this chapter, where could you go on the Web to get more assistance to help you in your investment decision making?

Selected References

Ambachtsbeer, Keith P. "How Should Pension Funds Manage Risk?" *Journal of Applied Corporate Finance* 11, no. 2 (Summer 1998), pp. 122–27.

August, James D.; Michael R. Grupe; Charles Luckett; and Samuel M. Slowinski. "Survey of Finance Companies." *Federal Reserve Bulletin,* July 1997, pp. 543–56.

Berlin, Mitchell. "That Thing Venture Capitalists Do." *Business Review,* Federal Reserve Bank of Philadelphia, January–February 1998, pp. 15–26.

Dynan, Karen E.; Kathleen W. Johnson; and Samuel M. Slowinski. "Survey of Finance Companies." *Federal Reserve Bulletin,* January 2002, pp. 1–14.

Engen, Eric M., and Andrew Lehnert. "Mutual Funds and the U.S. Equity Market." *Federal Reserve Bulletin,* December 2000, pp. 797–812.

Friedberg, Leora, and Michael T. Owyang. "Not Your Father's Pension Plan: The Rise of 401(K) and Other Defined Contribution Plans." *Review,* Federal Reserve Bank of St. Louis, January–February 2002, pp. 23–34.

Rose, Peter S. *Commercial Bank Management,* 5th ed. New York: Irwin/McGraw-Hill, 2002.

———— "Symbiotics: Financial Supermarkets in the Making." *The Canadian Banker,* April 1982, pp. 77–84.

Simons, Katerina. "Risk-Adjusted Performance of Mutual Funds." *New England Economic Review,* Federal Reserve Bank of Boston, September–October 1998, pp. 33–48.

Chapter **Eighteen**

The Regulation of the Financial Institutions' Sector

Learning Objectives in This Chapter

- You will explore the reasons why financial institutions represent one of the most regulated sectors in the modern world.

- You will discover the many types of *regulation* (government rule-making) affecting the behavior and performance of financial institutions.

- You will understand how regulation has influenced and shaped the structure of financial-services industries.

- You will examine the recent global trend toward *deregulation* of financial institutions and learn why this trend is under way and what its effects may be.

What's in This Chapter? Key Topics Outline

Why Financial Institutions Are Regulated

The Deregulation Movement

Do Regulations Help or Harm Financial Institutions?

The Structure of Banking Regulation in the United States

Changing the Rules on Interstate Banking and Investment Banking: The Riegle-Neal and Gramm-Leach-Bliley Acts

Basle Agreement and Controlling Bank Capital

Market Discipline as a Regulator of Financial Institutions

Regulating Thrift Institutions: Federal and State Agencies

Insurance and Pension Fund Regulation: Institutions and Issues

The Regulation of Finance Companies

Trends in the Regulation of Financial-Service Firms

INTRODUCTION

Financial institutions are one of the most heavily regulated of all businesses in the world. Around the globe, these financial-service firms face stringent government rules limiting the services they can offer; the territories they can enter or not enter; the makeup of their portfolios of assets, liabilities, and capital; and even how they price and deliver their services to the public. As we will see in this chapter, a variety of reasons have been offered for heavy government intrusion into the financial institutions' sector, including protecting the public's savings and ensuring that consumers receive an adequate quantity and quality of reasonably priced financial services.

Many economists, financial analysts, and financial institutions have argued over the years that **regulation** has done more harm than good for both financial institutions themselves and for the public they serve. In particular, government restrictions allegedly have allowed nonregulated or less-regulated financial-service firms to invade the markets and capture many of the customers of highly regulated financial institutions, who are not sufficiently free to compete effectively. Moreover, regulations are often backward looking, addressing problems that have long since disappeared, and they may compound this problem of "relevancy" by changing much more slowly than the free marketplace, inhibiting the ability of regulated financial institutions to stay abreast of new technologies and changing customer tastes. Other observers, however, argue that government regulations have achieved some positive results in the financial institutions' sector, reducing the number of failed financial-service firms, promoting more stable financial markets, and reducing the incidence of racial, religious, age, and sex discrimination in public access to financial services.

In this chapter we explore these and many other issues as we examine the variety of government regulations and regulatory agencies that oversee financial institutions today, assess the reasons for and the effectiveness of existing regulations, and explore recent efforts to deregulate the financial institutions' sector.

THE REASONS BEHIND THE REGULATION OF FINANCIAL INSTITUTIONS

Elaborate government rules controlling what financial institutions can and cannot do arise from multiple causes. One is a concern about the *safety of the public's funds,* especially the safety of the savings owned by millions of individuals and families. The reckless management and ultimate loss of personal savings can have devastating consequences for a family's future economic well-being and lifestyle, particularly at retirement. While savers have a responsibility to carefully evaluate the quality and stability of a financial institution before committing their savings to it, governments have long expressed a special concern for small savers who may lack the financial expertise and access to quality information necessary to be able to correctly judge the true condition of a financial institution. Moreover, many of the reasons that cause financial institutions to fail—such as fraud, embezzlement, deteriorating loans, or manipulation of the books by insiders—are often concealed from the public.

Related to the desire for safety is a government's goal of *promoting public confidence* in the financial system. Unless the public is confident enough in the safety and security of their funds placed under the management of financial institutions, they will withdraw their savings and thereby reduce the volume of funds available for productive investment to construct new buildings, purchase new equipment, set up new businesses, and create new jobs. The economy's growth will slow and, over time, the public's standard of living will fall.

The government commissions and agencies that regulate financial institutions have become increasingly visible on the World Wide Web. These regulatory bodies have a responsibility to assist both the public and the financial institutions they supervise and, therefore, have come to view the Internet as a key vehicle for reaching both of these audiences. Indeed, financial institution regulatory bodies maintain some of the most extensive of all sites on the World Wide Web.

Among the most prominent examples are the bank regulatory agencies in the United States. These include the Federal Reserve System (at *www.federalreserve.gov*), the Comptroller of the Currency (at *www.occ.treas.gov*), and the Federal Deposit Insurance Corporation (at *www.fdic.gov*). For a parallel description of European regulatory agencies see the European Union at *http://europa.eu.int/inst-en.htm*. These sites help the reader understand the different roles these agencies play within the financial system and how both consumers and financial institution managers can use regulatory agency information to help resolve problems.

Paralleling the federal regulatory system is a state or provincial regulatory system in many countries. Inside the United States, for example, are many state regulatory commissions and nearly all have established Web sites. Examples include the Wisconsin Department of Financial Institutions (at *www.wdfi.org*) and the New York State Banking Department (at *www.banking.state.ny.us/ccs.htm*).

Among the most important state regulatory agencies are insurance commissions, because almost all insurance regulation in the United States is done at the state level. See, for example, the Pennsylvania Insurance Commission at *www.insurance.state.pa.us*.

Securities regulation, including the regulation of the activities of security brokers and dealers, mutual funds, and security issuers, is conducted through national securities' agencies or commissions. In the United States, the Securities and Exchange Commission (SEC) maintains an extensive Web presence to aid both regulated institutions and investors, using such Web sites as *www.sec.gov*.

Government rules are also aimed at ensuring *equal opportunity and fairness* in the public's access to financial services. For example, in an earlier era many groups of customers—women, members of racial minority groups, the elderly, and those of foreign birth—found that their ability to borrow money on convenient terms was often severely restricted. Consumers of financial services were not well organized then, and the discriminatory policies of lending institutions seemed to change very slowly, particularly in markets where competition was subdued. While many economists believed that the potent force of competition generated by both domestic and foreign service suppliers would eventually kill off the vestiges of discrimination, other observers argued that such an event might take a very long time, particularly in those markets where financial firms colluded with each other and agreed not to compete.

Many regulations in the financial institutions' sector spring from the ability of some financial institutions to create money in the form of credit cards, checkable deposits, and other accounts that can be used to make payments for purchases of goods and services. History has shown that the creation of money is closely associated with inflation. If uncontrolled money growth outstrips growth in the economy's production of goods and services, prices will begin to rise, damaging especially those consumers on fixed incomes, as their money balances can buy fewer and fewer goods and services. Thus, the regulation of *money creation* has become a key objective of government activity in the financial sector.

Regulation is often justified as the most direct way to aid so-called "disadvantaged" sectors in the economy—those groups that appear to need special help in the competition for scarce funds. Examples include new home buyers, farmers, small businesses, and low-income families. Governments often place high social value on subsidizing or guaranteeing loans made to these sectors and on supporting financial institutions that lend money to these sectors of the economy.

Finally, the enforcement of government rules for financial institutions has arisen because governments depend upon these institutions for many important services. Governments borrow money and depend upon financial institutions to buy a substantial proportion of government IOUs. Financial institutions also aid governments in the collection and dispersal of tax revenues and in the pursuit of economic policy through the manipulation of interest rates and the money supply. Thus, governments frequently regulate financial institutions simply to ensure that these important financial services will continue to be provided at a reasonable cost and in a reliable manner.

What are we to make of these reasons so often posed for the extensive government regulations applied to many financial institutions? Few of them can go unchallenged. For example, while safety is important for many savers, no government can completely remove risk for savers. Indeed, in the long run, it may be more efficient and far less costly for governments to promote full disclosure of the financial condition of individual financial institutions and let competition in a free marketplace discipline poorly managed, excessively risky financial-service firms. Similarly, there is no question that discrimination on the basis of sex, race, religious affiliation, or other irrelevant factors is repugnant, but can we be more effective in eliminating discrimination by some method other than by struggling to enforce complicated rule books and by requiring endless compliance reports? Perhaps the same ends could be achieved by lowering the regulatory barriers to competition and by making it easier for customers hurt by discrimination to recover their damages in court.

Certainly the ability of financial institutions to create money needs to be monitored carefully, because excessive money growth can easily generate inflation and weaken the economy. But aren't there already enough tools available to control money growth? For example, when money grows too fast, a central bank like the Federal Reserve System can use its powerful tools to slow money growth. And wouldn't it be more efficient to pay direct money subsidies to disadvantaged groups (such as new home buyers) rather than to indirectly reach these groups by regulating financial institutions and interfering with the free operation of the financial services markets? As for providing a reliable stream of financial services to governments, wouldn't profit-motivated financial institutions be likely to provide these services if it were profitable to do so?

In brief, there are no absolutely irrefutable arguments justifying the regulation of financial institutions. Much depends on your personal political philosophy regarding society's goals and whether those goals are each more likely to be achieved by an unfettered marketplace or by collective action through government laws and regulations. As we shall see shortly, there is a trend today toward gradually allowing private markets to discipline risk taking by financial institutions and to minimize the role of government. Progress toward **deregulation** of the financial sector is slow, however, and can easily be derailed if financial institutions abuse the new liberties that come their way.

Does Regulation Benefit or Harm Financial Institutions?

For many years a controversy has been brewing as to whether government regulations help or hurt financial institutions. One of the earliest arguments on the positive side was propounded by economist George Stigler (1965), who suggested that regulated industries, far from dreading regulation, actually *invite* government intrusion, expecting to benefit from it. In the early history of the United States, for example, the railroads often prospered because government subsidized their growth and protected them from competition. Because regulators may prevent or restrict entry into an industry, the firms involved may earn excess profits ("monopoly rents") due to the absence of strong competitors. Therefore, the lifting of regulatory rules (deregulation) may bring about decreased profits for financial institutions.

A more balanced view of the benefits and the costs of regulation has been offered by Edward Kane (1981). He suggests that, on the positive side, regulation tends to increase public confidence in the regulated industry. Thus, customers may trust their banks' stability and reliability more because they are regulated, increasing customer loyalty to regulated firms and helping to shelter them from risk. Moreover, regulation may lead to a curious form of "innovation," which Kane labels the *regulatory dialectic.* He believes that regulated firms are constantly searching for ways around government rules in order to increase the market value of their business. Once they find a regulatory loophole that attracts the regulators' attention, new regulations are imposed to close the gap. But this leads to still more "innovation" by regulated businesses in order to escape the new restrictions. The result is a continuing chain reaction: Regulations spawn innovative escapes that, in turn, give rise to new rules in a never-ending struggle between the regulators and the regulated.

Notice, too, that the so-called "innovation" brought on by the regulatory dialectic is not the most productive form of innovation from society's point of view. Instead of developing ways to lower costs and deliver financial services more efficiently to the public, financial institutions are spending their time and energy looking for regulatory loopholes—something they wouldn't do if the regulations weren't there in the first place. This "wasted" time and energy, Kane believes, places regulated firms at a disadvantage vis-à-vis their unregulated competitors. Other factors held equal, the market share of regulated firms begins to fall. Many economists believe that this has happened to banks and other depository institutions in recent decades, as security dealers and mutual funds, facing fewer regulations, have captured many of the banking industry's biggest and most profitable customers, reducing the share of the financial-services marketplace controlled by depository institutions.

Thus, regulations are costly and can reduce the competitiveness of regulated financial institutions relative to nonregulated or lesser-regulated businesses. For example, a recent study of the banking industry by Ellihousen (1998) estimates that regulatory costs for this particular financial-service industry amounted to between 12 and 13 percent of all banks' noninterest costs, or about $15 to $16 billion per year. Moreover, some regulations, such as compliance with disclosure rules regarding suspicious customer transactions under the Bank Secrecy Act, are particularly costly. Regulatory costs are labor intensive, particularly the costs of making sure each institution is in compliance with all the rules. Financial institution managers devote great amounts of time to regulatory compliance activities. However, there do appear to be economies of scale associated with regulatory compliance costs, so financial institutions tend to save on these costs as they grow larger. This cost factor may limit the entry of new institutions into the financial-services field, discourage the development of new services, and encourage consolidation of smaller financial-service companies into bigger ones. Regulators should be especially cautious about making frequent minor changes in regulatory rules, which appears to be a more costly practice than making major, but infrequent, rule changes.

On balance, then, regulation of financial institutions may be a "tale of two cities," delivering both the best of times and the worst of times. Regulation may increase regulated institutions' profitability and shelter them from risk, resulting in fewer failures, but perhaps at the price of less efficient financial firms. In return for greater stability and public confidence in financial institutions, customers may be less well served in terms of prices charged and quality of services delivered.

THE REGULATION OF COMMERCIAL BANKS

Due to their importance in the financial system, *commercial banks* are typically the most regulated of all financial institutions. Moreover, in the United States, banking is more heavily regulated than in most other industrialized countries. From earliest history, there has been a fear of concentrated power in banking because bank credit and other banking services are so vital to the well-being of businesses and households.

Responsibility for regulating U.S. banks today is divided among three federal banking agencies and the 50 state governments. These regulatory agencies have overlapping responsibilities, so most banks are subject to multiple jurisdictions. The regulatory agencies responsible for enforcing banking's ground rules include the Federal Reserve System, the Comptroller of the Currency, and the Federal Deposit Insurance Corporation—all at the federal level—and the state banking commissions of the 50 states. Exhibit 18–1 provides a summary of the principal regulatory powers exercised by these federal and state agencies in the United States.

The Federal Reserve System

The **Federal Reserve System** is responsible for examining and supervising the activities of all its member banks. When a member bank wishes to merge with another bank or establish a branch office, it must notify the Fed. The Fed must review and approve the acquisition of bank and nonbank businesses by holding companies. The Federal Reserve is responsible for supervising U.S.-based international banking corporations, for overseeing the operations of member banks in foreign countries, and for regulating the activities of foreign banks inside the United States. The Fed also sets reserve requirements on deposits for all depository institutions.

The Comptroller of the Currency

The **Comptroller of the Currency**—also known as the Administrator of National Banks—is a division of the U.S. Treasury established under the National Banking Act of 1863. The Comptroller has the power to issue federal charters for the creation of new *national banks*. These banks, once chartered, are subject to an impressive array of regulations, most of which pertain to the kinds of loans and investments that may be made and the amount and types of capital each bank must hold. All national banks are examined periodically by the Comptroller's staff and may be liquidated or consolidated with another financial institution if deemed to be in the public interest.

Federal Deposit Insurance Corporation

The **Federal Deposit Insurance Corporation (FDIC)** insures deposits of commercial banks, savings banks, and savings and loans that meet its regulations. As a result of passage of the Financial Institutions Reform, Recovery and Enforcement Act of 1989, the FDIC's insurance reserves are divided between the Bank Insurance Fund (BIF), backing commercial bank deposits; and the Savings Association Insurance Fund (SAIF) for the deposits of savings and loans and savings banks. With passage of the FDIC Improvement Act of 1991, each depositor is limited to a maximum of $100,000 in insurance coverage should a bank

EXHIBIT 18–1   Principal Bank Regulatory Agencies

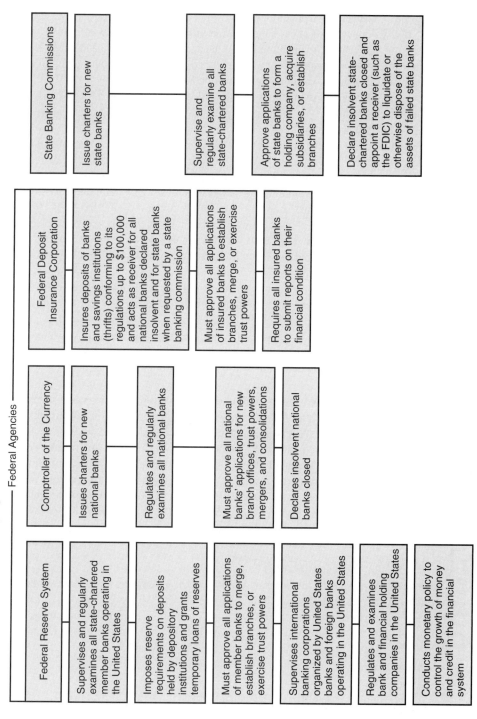

Federal Agencies

Federal Reserve System

- Supervises and regularly examines all state-chartered member banks operating in the United States
- Imposes reserve requirements on deposits held by depository institutions and grants temporary loans of reserves
- Must approve all applications of member banks to merge, establish branches, or exercise trust powers
- Supervises international banking corporations organized by United States banks and foreign banks operating in the United States
- Regulates and examines bank and financial holding companies in the United States
- Conducts monetary policy to control the growth of money and credit in the financial system

Comptroller of the Currency

- Issues charters for new national banks
- Regulates and regularly examines all national banks
- Must approve all national banks' applications for new branch offices, trust powers, mergers, and consolidations
- Declares insolvent national banks closed

Federal Deposit Insurance Corporation

- Insures deposits of banks and savings institutions (thrifts) conforming to its regulations up to $100,000 and acts as receiver for all national banks declared insolvent and for state banks when requested by a state banking commission
- Must approve all applications of insured banks to establish branches, merge, or exercise trust powers
- Requires all insured banks to submit reports on their financial condition

State Banking Commissions

- Issue charters for new state banks
- Supervise and regularly examine all state-chartered banks
- Approve applications of state banks to form a holding company, acquire subsidiaries, or establish branches
- Declare insolvent state-chartered banks closed and appoint a receiver (such as the FDIC) to liquidate or otherwise dispose of the assets of failed state banks

If you're interested in the examination process and examination procedures used by the federal banking agencies please see the Web site maintained by the Federal Financial Institutions Examination Council, which co-ordinates examination standards by the various federal banking agencies, at *www.ffiec.gov*

or savings institution fail. Each participating bank is assessed a fee equal to a fraction of its eligible deposits to build and maintain the national insurance fund.

One of the most important functions of the FDIC is to act as a check on state banking commissions, because few banks today—even those with state charters—open their doors without FDIC deposit insurance. The FDIC reviews the adequacy of capital, earnings prospects, the character of management, and the public convenience and needs aspects of each application before granting deposit insurance. This agency is also charged with ex-amining insured banks that are *not* members of the Federal Reserve System. The FDIC acts as receiver for all failed national banks and for failed state-chartered banks when requested by a state banking commission. In most cases, an insolvent bank will be merged with or ab-sorbed by a healthy one.

The savings and loan debacle of the 1980s, coupled with the failure of hundreds of banks eventually led to the realization that the federal deposit insurance system as origi-nally created was flawed. Until the mid-1990s, each bank, no matter how risky, paid the *same* insurance premium per dollar of the public's deposits. Moreover, until passage of the Financial Institutions Reform, Recovery, and Enforcement Act (FIRREA) of 1989, there was lax enforcement of federal bank capital standards, which led to excessive risk exposure to the federal insurance fund. The result was the appearance of a "moral hazard" problem in which banks and savings and loans could attract low-cost deposits (due to the benefit of cheap insurance coverage) and then invest in highly risky assets, knowing the government would, in effect, underwrite their gamble. Because the FDIC's reserves began declining in the 1980s, numerous proposals were brought forward to strengthen the deposit insurance system. Finally, with the deposit insurance fund almost drained away, the FDIC Improve-ment Act of 1991 put Congress on record in favor of risk-adjusted deposit insurance pre-miums. The FDIC was ordered to charge riskier banks higher deposit insurance fees. Moreover, the FDIC was given authority to borrow additional funds through the U.S. Trea-sury Department.

Recently several bankers' associations and government policymakers proposed raising the U.S. deposit insurance limit from $100,000 to $200,000. Supporting arguments include concern over inflation because the insurance limit of $100,000 was set back in 1980 and has not been increased since that time. Moreover, there is concern that banking risk may have increased with banks being allowed to affiliate more aggressively now with nonbank businesses. Opponents argue, on the other hand, that raising the insurance limit would not benefit small savers—the group it was principally designed to aid—and might well expand the "moral hazard" problem, making depositors even less inclined to monitor the risky be-havior of their banks. This issue remains unresolved.

State Banking Commissions

The regulatory powers of the federal banking agencies overlap with those of the **state banking commissions** that regularly examine all state-chartered banks. The states also have rules prescribing the minimum amount of equity capital for individual state-chartered banks and issue charters for new banks. As we shall see in the next section, the states have historically played a major role in regulating the geographic and services expansion of banks.

Regulations Controlling the Geographic Expansion of Banks

One of the areas where state and federal regulators have exercised the most influence over banking is in controlling what new *geographic* markets banks can enter. Until the begin-ning of this century, few U.S. banks operated branch offices and most authorities believed that banks chartered by the federal government (national banks) could not branch at all under the terms of the National Bank Act of 1863–64. (See Exhibit 18–2.) Later, in the Banking Act of 1933, national banks were permitted to set up branch offices throughout their home state if state law permitted state-chartered banks to do the same. However, branching across state lines was forbidden unless the states involved expressly permitted interstate branching. As the years rolled by, more and more states voted to allow branch banking within their borders. By the 1990s, all U.S. states allowed branching in one form or another within their borders, reflecting the combined influence of a wave of bank mergers, failures, and a more mobile population.

State regulation of banks and other financial institutions is traceable through Web sites maintained by all state regulatory agencies—for example, *www.banking.state.tx.us* for the state of Texas and *www.azbanking. com* for the Arizona Banking Department.

When bank branching was prohibited or restricted by many states, holding companies—corporations controlling the stock of one or more banks—were developed in order to tie together groups of banks serving different geographic markets. Each holding company could issue debt or stock and use the proceeds to buy up a network of banks in a single state or even make acquisitions across state lines. In response to a chorus of complaints from bankers and state legislatures, the U.S. Congress passed the Bank Holding Company Act in 1956. Thereafter, holding company activities could be restricted by state law if individual states chose to do so. Moreover, Congress stipulated in the Douglas Amendment that no bank holding company could acquire more than 5 percent of the voting stock of a bank located outside its home state without express permission from the state entered.

When the Bank Holding Company Act effectively blocked bank expansion across state lines, bankers soon found loopholes in this law. The original Bank Holding Company Act left an unregulated opening for holding companies that held stock in only one bank. As a result, many of the largest banks formed one-bank holding companies and began to acquire nonbank businesses far removed from the business of banking, including steel mills and meat packing plants. Congress closed this loophole with passage of the 1966 and 1970 amendments to the Bank Holding Company Act. From this point on, all holding companies seeking to acquire even a single bank had to register with the Federal Reserve Board and gain approval before purchasing any new bank or nonbank business. Nonbank business ventures acquired now had to be "closely related" to banking.

What business activities are "closely related to banking" and, therefore, are legal for bank holding companies to acquire or start? As the 1970s, 1980s, and 1990s unfolded the Federal Reserve Board approved holding company acquisitions of those businesses engaged in such activities as making loans (such as finance, mortgage, or credit-card companies); writing property leases (e.g., equipment leasing companies); insuring credit repayment (such as firms selling credit life insurance); recording financial information (such as data processing firms); giving financial advice (i.e., through a trust company, consulting firm, or investment adviser); executing security trades (such as discount brokerage services); and, on a case-by-case basis, underwriting corporate stocks and bonds (i.e., buying these securities from their issuers and reselling them). Passage of the Financial Institutions Reform, Recovery, and Enforcement Act of 1989 permitted holding company acquisitions of savings and loan associations and savings banks as well, thus making it possible for bank holding companies to purchase nonbank thrifts across state lines.

Information and data on bank mergers appears at multiple Web sites, such as *www.clev.frb.org/ research* and at *www.fdic.gov*

Banks also sought to expand their market territory by outright *mergers* with other institutions. When the industry seemed on the verge of being transformed by a tidal wave of merger activity, the U.S. Congress stepped in once again and, in the Bank Merger Act of 1960, required each bank involved in a merger to receive the approval of its principal federal regulatory agency. For national banks this means that the Comptroller of the Currency must approve the merger transaction, while state-chartered banks who are members of the Federal Reserve System must secure the approval of the Fed and state-chartered nonmember banks must get approval from the Federal Deposit Insurance Corporation. The

EXHIBIT 18–2   Key Federal Laws That Have Affected the Structure and Regulation of the U.S. Banking Industry and Foreign Banks Operating in the United States

National Bank Act (1863–1964)	Authorized federal chartering and supervision of banks by the Comptroller of the Currency.
Federal Reserve Act (1913)	Created the Federal Reserve System as central bank and guarantor of the banking system's liquidity.
Banking Act of 1933	Created the FDIC to insure the public's deposits and denied banks the power to underwrite corporate securities; allowed national banks to branch statewide if allowed by state law.
Bank Holding Company Act (1956)	Required holding companies controlling two or more banks to register with the Federal Reserve Board; prohibited control by out-of-state holding companies of banks within a given state without the state's express permission.
Bank Merger Act (1960)	Required mergers involving federally supervised banks to have the approval of their principal federal regulatory agency.
Bank Merger Act and Bank Holding Company Act Amendments (1966)	Called for mergers and holding-company acquisitions to be approved by federal banking agencies if their anticompetitive effects are outweighed by public benefits, such as offering more convenient services.
Bank Holding Company Act Amendments (1970)	Made holding companies controlling only one bank subject to Federal Reserve regulation; confined nonbank business ventures of holding companies to bank-related services.
International Banking Act (1978)	Brought foreign banks operating in the United States under federal regulation for the first time.
Depository Institutions Deregulation and Monetary Control Act (1980)	Granted nonbank thrift institutions broader deposit and credit powers like those possessed by banks, began the phaseout of federal deposit rate ceilings, and imposed uniform deposit reserve requirements on banks and thrifts.
Garn–St Germain Depository Institutions Act (1982)	Authorized banks and savings and loans to offer money market deposit accounts, granted savings and loans additional commercial and consumer lending powers, and granted federal regulators new powers to deal with troubled depository institutions.
Financial Institutions Reform, Recovery, and Enforcement Act (1989)	Restructured the federal supervisory agencies responsible for monitoring savings and loan associations, allowed bank holding companies to acquire savings and loans, and created two deposit insurance funds, one for banks (BIF) and the other for savings and loans (SAIF) under the FDIC.
Federal Deposit Insurance Corporation Improvement Act (1991)	Provided additional funding and borrowing authority for the federal deposit insurance fund (FDIC); gave federal regulatory agencies the power to close an undercapitalized bank or thrift; required the FDIC to set deposit insurance fees based on a bank's risk exposure; and imposed new regulations on foreign bank expansion inside the United States.
Riegle-Neal Interstate Banking and Branching Efficiency Act (1994)	Allowed holding companies to acquire banks in any state and banks to branch across state lines if the states do not "opt out" of interstate branching.
Financial Services Modernization (Gramm-Leach-Bliley) Act (1999)	Permitted financial-service providers to form financial holding companies (FHCs) offering banking, insurance, securities, and other services under one controlling corporation and regulated the sharing of private consumer data.

Department of Justice must review each proposed merger and can sue in federal court to block it if competition would be damaged significantly. Amendments to the Bank Merger Act in 1966 allowed U.S. bank regulatory agencies to approve mergers even if competition was slightly damaged provided there were other benefits stemming from a merger, such as expanding the quality or quantity of services or rescuing a troubled bank. Recently, as consolidation gathers momentum, the U.S. banking industry has experienced a wave of mega-mergers, including such leading banks as Chase Manhattan Bank, J. P. Morgan (which recently merged with Chase), Banc One Corporation, First Union Corp., First Fidelity, and BankAmerica.

Interstate Banking

Few states granted out-of-state bank holding companies permission to enter their territory through mergers or acquisitions until the 1980s. However, a massive wave of bank failures coupled with pressures from bankers' associations soon led to state after state voting to permit interstate holding company acquisitions. By the 1990s, 49 of the 50 states had voted to permit interstate holding companies to come in, but under a wide variety of entry conditions. For example, many states would permit entry only from neighboring states (so-called *regional* interstate banking) and insisted that their own banks be given reciprocal entry privileges by other states (so-called *reciprocity* laws). However, gradually over time, more and more states expanded their regional entry laws, many allowing entry from any other state in the nation.

Clearly, holding company banking had opened the door to the interstate expansion of banks, but this approach proved to be an expensive way for a banking organization to reach into new markets. Every bank acquired by a holding company had to be kept open as a separate corporation with its own capital, management, and board of directors. Establishing branch offices might be considerably less expensive because of less duplication of personnel and resources, but federal law prohibited interstate branch banking unless the individual states approved.

The final step at the federal level toward interstate branching was finally taken in August 1994 when the U.S. Congress passed the Riegle-Neal Interstate Banking and Branching Efficiency Act. (See Exhibit 18–3.) This law arose out of concern for the more than 60 million Americans who commute to work or shop across state lines each day but often find that their bank account relationships are not as easily transportable. It also sprang from the long-standing complaint among the largest banks that using holding companies as a vehicle to cross state lines was inefficient and expensive. The Riegle-Neal Act permits holding companies to acquire banks in *any* of the remaining 49 states, thus rendering ineffective those state laws limiting bank entry to regions or requiring reciprocal entry privileges. The new law took an additional important step, however, in allowing banks acquired across state lines to be converted into branch offices unless the states involved voted before June 1, 1997 to "opt out" of interstate branching. Nearly all states elected to allow interstate banking, subject to a variety of special conditions.

The Riegle-Neal Interstate Banking Act helped to *concentrate* the U.S. banking industry into fewer, but much larger banks. By 2000 the largest 10 percent of all U.S. banks held nearly 90 percent of the industry's assets. By 2001 more than two-thirds of the 50 states found that over 15 percent of their branch offices belonged to out-of-state banks or savings associations. In an effort to guard against an excessive concentration of banking industry resources into the hands of only a few banks, the Riegle-Neal law held that no one banking organization would be allowed to control more than 10 percent of nationwide deposits nor more than 30 percent of all deposits in a single state (unless the state involved chooses to

EXHIBIT 18–3
The Riegle-Neal Interstate Banking and Branching Efficiency Act of 1994

President Bill Clinton signed this nationwide bank holding company and interstate branching law on September 29, 1994. This sweeping banking law included the following provisions:

Nationwide Holding-Company Banking

1. Beginning September 30, 1995 holding companies could acquire banks in any state even if state law prohibits such acquisitions.
2. However, no one banking organization can control more than 10 percent of nationwide deposits or more than 30 percent of the deposits in a single state unless a state chooses to waive this latter limit.

Interstate Branch Banking

1. A banking organization can merge with banks in other states and convert those acquired banks into branch offices unless the state or states involved chose to "opt out" of the interstate branching portions of the new law.
2. A state could enact legislation that exempts that state from interstate branching. However, its own banks could not participate in further interstate banking acquisitions.
3. States can vote to permit *de novo* interstate branching, allowing a bank to branch into their territory without having previously acquired any banks there.

Community Reinvestment Requirements

Branch offices established by national banks must conform to local laws requiring consumer protection, fair lending, and investments in local communities. Federal regulatory agencies must consider the views of local community organizations prior to closing an interstate banking organization's branch office situated in a low-income neighborhood.

Foreign Banking Provisions

1. If a foreign-owned bank has established a subsidiary corporation based in the United States, it can acquire banks and branches across state lines to the same extent as U.S. banks.
2. Foreign-owned banks acquiring domestic U.S. banks subject to the Community Reinvestment Act must conform to all the provisions of that law.

waive this upper limit). And to ensure against the draining away of local deposits by a large interstate company, banks expanding across state lines were required to commit a minimum percentage of their incoming funds to locally based loans.

Regulation of the Services Banks Can Offer

Even as banks have sought greater freedom to expand geographically, they have also fought for, but only occasionally won, new service powers in order to retain their existing customers and attract new ones. Unfortunately, regulations have been tight and sometimes unyielding in this area out of concern for bank safety (as service innovation can be highly risky) and because of a desire to protect certain nonbank financial institutions, such as credit unions and savings and loans, from tough bank competition.

Probably the most influential law in American history in defining bank service powers was the **Glass-Steagall Act** (or Banking Act) of 1933. This sweeping law confined bank service powers essentially to the making of loans and the taking of deposits, while insurance services were largely relegated to insurance companies, and home lending was centered in savings and loan associations and savings banks. U.S. bankers also lost an important service power they possessed in the decades before Glass-Steagall—the power to assist their largest corporate customers by purchasing corporate stock and then reselling it in the open market. Foreign banks continued to offer corporate bond and stock *underwriting services* to American companies, and U.S. banks were active in the security underwriting business overseas through a variety of affiliated organizations, but until recently they clearly lost customers to security dealers and foreign banks (principally from Canada and Western Europe) in domestic securities' underwriting, except where exceptions were granted from federal restrictions. Bankers have avidly sought security underwriting powers because this business can be highly profitable and it complements traditional lending services.

Beginning in the late 1980s, the Federal Reserve Board began to permit individual banking organizations on a case-by-case basis to underwrite selected types of securities through separate subsidiaries. For example, individual institutions such as Bankers Trust of New York, Citicorp (now Citigroup), and Security Pacific Corporation (now part of BankAmerica) were granted authority to underwrite certain loan-backed securities and some forms of corporate debt. Finally, in September 1990, J.P. Morgan (now J.P. Morgan Chase, Inc.) was extended the power to underwrite new issues of corporate stock. By 1998, the year before federal laws were changed to formally permit bank-sponsored corporate securities underwriting, about 40 U.S. and foreign banking corporations had been approved by the Federal Reserve Board to offer selected debt security underwriting services, while close to a dozen banking companies had received approval to underwrite corporate stock. However, tight restrictions were imposed upon all participating banks. For example, the underwriting of previously forbidden types of securities had to be carried out through a special subsidiary, not by the bank itself, and revenue generated from these previously forbidden underwriting activities could represent only a minor proportion of the total revenues of the underwriting subsidiary.

Despite such restrictions, however, U.S. banks' share of all corporate security underwriting activities grew quite rapidly and many bankers continued to ask for further expansion of their underwriting powers. However, any proposed changes in the law faced stiff opposition from trade groups, representing those industries banks most wanted to enter, and from public interest groups concerned about consumer rights. There was also concern among bank regulators that affiliation with nonbank industries would stretch the so-called "federal safety net" (e.g., the protection provided by deposit insurance from the FDIC and low-interest loans from the Federal Reserve) to the breaking point.

The Gramm-Leach-Bliley Act

Finally, in November 1999 the **Financial Services Modernization (Gramm-Leach-Bliley) Act** was passed, permitting banks to affiliate with securities firms, insurance companies, and selected other types of businesses. This could be done by creating a financial holding company (FHC) that owns the shares of all of the above businesses or through a subsidiary structure in which a bank or other financial firm operates securities firms and other subsidiaries. This new law opens up the United States for the first time in more than half a century to *universal* or *multidimensional* banking. However, surprisingly few financial-service providers rushed out to form FHCs right away—less than a fifth of the largest bank holding companies and a few securities houses, insurance companies, and smaller commercial banking organizations, though 19 of the 20 largest U.S. banks belong to an FHC. Most financial institutions seem content with the organizational structures they already operate and many are waiting to see what the final rules for operating an FHC are going to look like.

As we saw earlier in Chapter 4, each business affiliated with an FHC is regulated and supervised by its *traditional functional regulator.* For example, the insurance company affiliate of an FHC is regulated by a state insurance commission, while the securities affiliate would be supervised by the Securities and Exchange Commission (SEC). If the FHC contains a national bank, that bank's primary regulatory supervisor would be the Comptroller of the Currency. Supervision of the FHC as a whole, however, is the responsibility of the

Federal Reserve. Any banks involved in an FHC must be rated "well-capitalized" and "well-managed."

The debate over banks being allowed to offer new services is a reminder of the difficulties the banking industry has always faced when it tries to develop and offer new services. Bankers have argued that new services could *reduce* bank risk, because the earnings generated by these new services may have a low positive, or even a negative, correlation with the earnings from traditional bank services. Moreover, they argue, unless banks can keep up with shifting public demand for financial services, they are in danger of becoming irrelevant to the workings of the financial system. Regulators, however, generally adopt a "go slow" approach in order to assess the risks involved for depositor safety. Bankers who wish to retain federal deposit insurance coverage must expect that regulations are likely to continue to be a significant hurdle to bank service innovation for the foreseeable future.

The Rise of Disclosure Laws in Banking

One of the most rapidly expanding areas of U.S. banking regulation today centers around *disclosure rules*—regulations requiring financial institutions to reveal certain information to customers (in an effort to encourage shopping around and avoid deception) and to regulators (to improve supervision of the banking industry). Among the most prominent examples are the Truth in Lending Act (1968) and the Truth in Savings Act (1991), which require disclosure of all the interest and fees associated with selling loans and deposits to individuals. Similarly, the Home Mortgage Disclosure Act (1975) requires banks to report to the public and to regulators the locations of both their approved and rejected applications for loans to purchase or improve homes as a check on possible discrimination in lending. The FDIC Improvement Act (1991) requires banks and other depositories to notify customers and regulators in advance when branch offices are to be closed. Finally, the Community Reinvestment Act (1977) stipulates that bankers must make an affirmative effort to serve *all* segments of their trade territory, including low-income neighborhoods, and to disclose to the public their community service performance ratings. Regulators must review a bank's community service record before approving its request to offer new services, merge or acquire other businesses, or set up new facilities.

A "reverse disclosure" law appeared in the U.S. in 1999 under the label of the Financial Services Modernization (Gramm-Leach-Bliley) Act. This new set of government rules permits customers of banks and selected other financial-service providers to stop the sharing of at least some of their *nonpublic personal information* with other businesses, except that the customer must contact his or her financial institution and indicate that they do not wish their personal data conveyed to others (such as telemarketing firms). Otherwise, information sharing is generally permitted. Under a strict interpretation of the Gramm-Leach-Bliley Act information sharing about customers can occur among affiliates of the *same company* and the customer involved cannot legally stop that. However, each covered financial-service provider must publish at least once a year a *privacy policy statement* and offer its customers the right to "opt out" of at least some personal information sharing. The firm issuing this statement can decide not even to share its customers' personal data with affiliates of the same company if it wishes to do so, thereby placing tougher restrictions on itself than the law requires.

For a review of the new rules on customer privacy and the sharing of personal information please see the Web site maintained by the Federal Trade Commission (FTC) at *www.ftc.gov*

These and other disclosure rules have aroused a storm of controversy. For most such rules, it is not clear that the benefits of greater disclosure outweigh the costs involved. For example, the U.S. Office of Management and Budget has estimated that U.S. bankers commit an average of at least 7.5 million hours each year just to comply with the Truth in Lending Act. Nor is it clear that the public pays much attention to these disclosure requirements.

The Growing Importance of Capital Regulation in Banking

In addition to the spread of interstate banking and the explosion in branching activity by banks, another major trend reshaping the regulation of banks and other financial institutions today centers upon their *capital*—the long-term funds invested in a financial institution, mainly by its owners. For example, when stockholders buy ownership shares in a bank, they have a claim against the bank's earnings and assets. However, a bank's stockholders bear all the risks of ownership. If the bank fails to generate sufficient earnings, the stockholders may receive no dividend income, and if the bank fails, they could lose everything.

Beginning in the 1980s, bank regulators in leading industrialized countries (including the United States, Canada, Japan, and the nations of Western Europe) came to the conclusion that regulatory control of risk taking by banks is best centered upon a bank's *owners*. When a bank chooses to take on more risk, its owners should be asked to increase their financial commitment to the bank by supplying more capital. Because stockholder capital is expensive to raise and could be lost completely if the bank fails, the owners of the bank are likely to monitor the bank's risk taking more closely, pressuring management to be more prudent in taking on risk.

Additional information regarding the terms of the Basle Agreement on bank capital and its importance for the banking industry may be found at *www.bis.org*

This concept of making the owners more responsible for the consequences of risk taking by their banks led in June 1988 to the adoption of *minimum capital standards* for all banks by the leading countries of Western Europe, Canada, Japan, and the United States. The so-called **Basle Agreement** (named for Basle, Switzerland, where it was adopted) stipulated that banks in all the participating nations must have a minimum ratio of total capital to risk-weighted assets and other related risk-exposed items of 8 percent. Risk-weighted assets are determined by classifying each of a bank's assets listed on its balance sheet into categories based on each asset's degree of risk exposure and then multiplying the volume of assets in each risk category by a risk weight ranging from 0 for cash and government securities to 1.00 for commercial loans and other high-risk assets. Thus:

$$\text{Total risk-weighted assets on a bank's balance sheet} = \begin{array}{l} 0 \times (\text{Cash and U.S. government securities}) + 0.20 \times (\text{Other} \\ \text{types of government securities and interbank deposits}) + \\ 0.50 \times (\text{Residential mortgage loans, government revenue} \\ \text{bonds, and selected types of mortgage-backed securities}) + \\ 1.00 \times (\text{Commercial and consumer loans and other assets} \\ \text{of the highest risk exposure}) \end{array}$$

The Basle Agreement was unique in also including off-balance-sheet commitments that banks often make to their largest customers and to hedge themselves against risk, including credit commitments to grant future loans, loans sold with recourse, and futures, options, and swap contracts. The amount of each off-balance-sheet item is multiplied by a fractional amount known as its "credit-equivalent" value, which is, in turn, multiplied by a risk weight based on its assumed degree of risk exposure. The volume of risk-weighted off-balance-sheet items is then added to a bank's total risk-weighted on-balance-sheet assets. Thus:

$$\begin{array}{l} \text{Total risk-weighted} \\ \text{on- and off-balance-} \\ \text{sheet items} \end{array} = \begin{array}{l} \text{Total risk-weighted} \\ \text{assets on a bank's} \\ \text{balance sheet} \end{array} + \begin{array}{l} \text{Total risk-weighted} \\ \text{off-balance-sheet} \\ \text{items} \end{array}$$

To determine a bank's total capital, its longer-maturity liabilities and its equity (owners') capital are classified into two broad categories:

$$\begin{array}{l} \text{Tier-one, or} \\ \text{permanent (core)} \\ \text{bank capital} \end{array} = \begin{array}{l} \text{Tangible equity including common stock} + \text{Perpetual} \\ \text{preferred stock} + \text{Surplus} + \text{Retained earnings} + \\ \text{Capital reserves less Intangibles} \end{array}$$

$$\begin{array}{l} \text{Tier-two, or} \\ \text{supplemental} \\ \text{capital} \end{array} = \begin{array}{l} \text{Subordinated capital notes and debentures over} \\ \text{5 years to maturity + Limited-life preferred} \\ \text{stock + Loan-loss reserves} \end{array}$$

The Basle Agreement required each bank in all participating countries to achieve and hold the following *capital minimums:*

$$\frac{\text{Tier-one capital}}{\begin{array}{c}\text{Total risk-weighted on- and}\\\text{off-balance-sheet items}\end{array}} = \text{At least 0.04, or 4 percent}$$

$$\frac{\text{Total tier-one plus tier-two capital}}{\begin{array}{c}\text{Total risk-weighted on- and off-}\\\text{balance-sheet items}\end{array}} = \text{No less than 0.08, or 8 percent}$$

Thus, a bank with a 4 percent tier-one capital ratio and a 5 percent tier-two capital ratio would have a ratio of total capital to risk-weighted on- and off-balance-sheet items of 9 percent, 1 percent above the minimum required. However, if a bank had only a 3 percent tier-one capital ratio and a tier-two capital ratio of 5 percent, it would actually fall *below* the minimum 8 percent total capital ratio. This is because it had to have at least a 4 percent tier-one capital ratio and could count toward meeting the Basle capital requirements only an amount of tier-two capital up to the amount of its tier-one capital. Thus, this last bank would be short 1 percent in tier-one capital and would have to work out a plan with its principal regulatory agency to raise the additional amount of required tier-one capital.

In the United States and selected other countries, a bank holding more than the required minimum amount of capital is allowed to expand its services and service facilities with few or no regulatory restrictions imposed. However, if bank capital drops below the minimum percentage of risk-exposed assets, regulatory restrictions become increasingly stiff, restraining the bank's growth and subjecting its operations to greater supervision. This regulatory policy, called *prompt corrective action,* was adopted in the United States with passage of the FDIC Improvement Act of 1991. In addition, as we saw earlier, the FDIC Improvement Act required riskier, inadequately capitalized U.S. banks to pay higher fees for government deposit insurance.

The Unfinished Agenda for Banking Regulation

The tremendous changes in banking regulation in recent years—including the adoption of nationwide banking and universal banking with multiple financial services in the United States and the spreading internationalization of bank regulation as evidenced by the Basle Agreement on bank capital—might lead us to think that there is little left to do in reshaping the future structure of bank regulation. Nothing could be further from the truth! Banking in the United States and in most other countries of the world remains heavily burdened by constraining government rules. Slowly, and along something of a zig-zag path, banking is experiencing an era of *deregulation,* as legal constraints are being lifted on a variety of banking activities.

More and more regulators of financial institutions are handing over a large share of the regulation and supervision of financial-service providers and the financial system to the *private marketplace.* If a financial institution is viewed as too risky the marketplace will make it pay for that added risk taking by increasing its funding costs. Moreover, financial institutions' regulation is focusing increasingly upon the quality and comprehensiveness of the financial firm's *risk management systems,* making sure each financial-service provider understands the risk it faces and has adequate internal controls to deal with that risk. The largest banks in the world are now required to develop their own in-house models of risk assessment and to conduct frequent "stress tests" to determine how effective each bank's risk defenses really are. A key element in managing risk is making sure each financial institution has *adequate capital* (particularly the capital supplied by its owners) to protect itself from large and unexpected losses due to risk.

In short, it seems clear that *market data* will be used much more heavily in the future to assess the condition and performance of banks and other financial-service providers. The marketplace will be used as a supplement to the work of regulatory supervisors in order to yield a more complete picture of the financial firm's risk exposure. Among the key market data items regulators will likely watch are:

1. A financial institution's stock price and stock price volatility (equity risk).

2. The market value and interest rate attached to senior debt instruments issued by a bank or other financial institution (such as subordinated notes and debentures).

3. The volume and interest cost attached to uninsured liabilities (such as deposits not covered by federal deposit insurance).

4. Changes in the proportion of uninsured liabilities (such as uninsured deposits) relative to other sources of funding for a financial firm.

In brief, *market-based information* seems to offer for the future a low-cost method of evaluating the condition and riskiness of banks and other financial-service firms, aiding supervisory and regulatory agencies to do their job better. *Supervision of financial institutions in the future will rest primarily upon three main pillars: government examinations, capital requirements, and the discipline provided by the private marketplace.*

Questions *to Help You Study*

1. What are the principal *purposes* or *goals* of financial institutions?

2. What impact does regulation appear to have upon the availability and cost of financial services to the public? Upon financial institutions themselves?

3. Who are the principal regulatory agencies responsible for the regulation and supervision of commercial banks? What aspects of banking does each agency regulate and supervise?

4. How is the nature of government regulation of financial institutions changing today? What is the new focus of recent regulation? Why do you think this change is occurring?

5. What are the principal features of the Financial Services Modernization (Gramm-Leach-Bliley) Act? Why was it passed?

6. How will Gramm-Leach-Bliley likely affect the structure of the banking and financial-services industries? Why?

7. How will Gramm-Leach-Bliley affect the disclosure of financial information and the privacy rights of the customers of financial-service firms? Do you think additional legislation is needed in this field?

THE REGULATION OF NONBANK THRIFT INSTITUTIONS

As we saw in Chapter 16, nonbank thrift institutions include credit unions, savings and loan associations, savings banks, and money market mutual funds. Like commercial banks, each of these institutions also faces an impressive array of federal or state regulations, or both.

Information about credit union regulations may be found at the federal level through the National Credit Union Administration site at *www.ncua.gov*. If you are interested in state regulatory agency information call up the particular state in question. If you want to find out about financial institutions' regulation in foreign countries you may want to call up their names—for example, in Canada look at the Department of Finance at *www.fin.gc.ca*

Credit Unions

In the United States, credit unions are chartered and regulated at both the state and federal levels (see Exhibit 18–4). Today about three-fifths of all credit unions are chartered by the federal government; the remainder are chartered by the states. Federal credit unions have been regulated since 1970 by the **National Credit Union Administration (NCUA),** an independent agency within the federal government. Deposits are insured by the National Credit Union Share Insurance Fund (NCUSIF) up to $100,000. State-chartered credit unions may qualify for federal insurance if they conform to NCUA's regulations.

Credit unions, like banks, are closely regulated in the services they can offer the public, the investments they can make with their depositors' money, and the types of deposits they can sell. Fortunately for the industry, regulations have been liberalized in recent years through such federal deregulation laws as the **Depository Institutions Deregulation and Monetary Control Act (DIDMCA)** (1980), which gave U.S. credit unions the power to offer checkable deposits (share drafts) and home mortgage (real estate) loans in order to be able to compete effectively against commercial banks. (See Exhibits 18–5 and 18–6.)

EXHIBIT 18–4   **Government Agencies That Regulate the Nonbank Thrifts (Federal and State Agencies)**

Nonbank Thrift Institution	Chartering and Licensing of Thrifts	Setting Up New Branches	Mergers and Acquisitions	Deposit Insurance	Supervision and Examination
Credit unions	National Credit Union Administration (NCUA)/state credit union or banking departments	No approval required	NCUA/state credit union or banking departments	NCUA Share Insurance Fund/state deposit insurance departments	NCUA/state credit union or banking departments
Savings and loan associations	Office of Thrift Supervision/state banking or savings and loan departments	Office of Thrift Supervision/Federal Deposit Insurance Corporation (FDIC)/state banking or savings and loan departments	Office of Thrift Supervision/FDIC/state banking or savings and loan departments	FDIC's Savings Association Insurance Fund/state insurance departments	Office of Thrift Supervision/state banking or savings and loan departments
Savings banks	Office of Thrift Supervision/state banking departments	Office of Thrift Supervision/state banking departments	Office of Thrift Supervision/FDIC/state banking departments	FDIC/state insurance departments	FDIC/state banking departments
Money market funds	Securities and Exchange Commission (SEC)	No approval required	No approval required	No government insurance; some funds have private insurance	SEC for selected activities

Source: Federal Reserve Bank of New York, and the author.

Savings and Loans

Savings and loan associations are also regulated and can receive their charter of incorporation from either state or federal government agencies. About half have charters from state authorities who supervise their activities and regularly examine their books, while the remainder have federal charters. Federal savings and loans are insured (up to a maximum of $100,000 per depositor) by the Savings Association Insurance Fund (SAIF) managed by the Federal Deposit Insurance Corporation (FDIC). (See Exhibit 18–7.)

S&Ls chartered by the states also may qualify for insurance coverage from the FDIC. Both federally chartered and federally insured state associations are supervised and examined by the **Office of Thrift Supervision (OTS)** of the U.S. Treasury Department, and the FDIC also has certain S&L supervisory powers, such as regulating the capital positions of these savings associations. Qualified S&Ls can borrow emergency funds from the Federal Home Loan banks and from the discount windows of the Federal Reserve banks.

Regulation of the savings and loan industry over the past two decades has resembled a roller coaster, with wide swings from deregulating the industry to imposing much tougher restrictions. For example, as Exhibits 18–5 and 18–6 illustrate, two major laws passed in the early 1980s—the Depository Institutions Deregulation and Monetary Control Act of 1980 and the **Garn–St Germain Depository Institutions Act** of 1982—granted federally supervised savings and loans major new service powers (such as credit cards and consumer installment loans) so they could compete directly with commercial banks. Then, after hundreds of S&Ls failed in the 1980s and early 1990s, in part because they sometimes moved too quickly to offer new services, the federal government substantially tightened the rules surrounding savings and loan operations with passage of the **Financial Institutions Reform, Recovery and Enforcement Act (FIRREA)** of 1989. No longer could S&Ls buy low-quality (junk) bonds, and the majority of their lending had to be focused on the housing industry. Designed to restore public confidence in savings and loans, this new law stipulated that to be a "qualified thrift lender" (QTL), eligible for special tax benefits and to borrow funds at low cost from the Federal Home Loan banks—a lender of last resort for the industry—S&Ls must hold a minimum of 70 percent of their total assets in real estate mortgage loans, mortgage-backed securities, and other qualifying assets.

EXHIBIT 18–5
Provisions of the Depository Institutions Deregulation and Monetary Control Act (DIDMCA) of 1980 Applying to Credit Unions, Savings and Loan Associations, and Savings Banks

New Deposit Powers

1. Interest-rate ceilings on deposits were to be phased out, permitting interest yields offered the public to respond to competition and market forces.
2. NOW accounts, which bear interest and can be used to make payments, could be offered to individuals and nonprofit organizations by all federally insured depository institutions.
3. Federally insured credit unions were authorized to offer share drafts (interest-bearing checking accounts) to their members.
4. Savings banks were empowered to offer demand deposits to business customers.

New Loan and Investment Powers

1. Federally insured credit unions were approved to offer real estate loans.
2. Federally chartered savings and loan associations could issue credit cards, offer trust services, and make investments in consumer loans, commercial paper, and corporate bonds up to 20 percent of their assets.
3. Savings banks with federal charters could invest up to 5 percent of their total assets in commercial, corporate, and business loans within their home state or within 75 miles of their home office.

EXHIBIT 18–6

Provisions of the Garn–St Germain Depository Institutions Act of 1982 (Garn bill; HR-6267) Applying to Credit Unions, Savings and Loan Associations, and Savings Banks

New Deposit Powers

1. Depository Institutions Deregulation Commission (DIDC) was authorized to develop a deposit account for banks and nonbank thrifts competitive with shares in money market funds.
2. Federally chartered savings associations could accept regular checkbook deposits from businesses having a long-term relationship to a savings association or could serve as a repository for business payments.
3. All deposit-type institutions are permitted to offer NOW accounts to governmental units.

New Loan and Investment Powers

1. Federal savings associations may make secured or unsecured loans to businesses totaling up to 10 percent of their assets.
2. Commercial real estate loans may be increased from 20 to 40 percent of the total assets at federal savings associations and required loan-value minimum ratios are eliminated. Federal credit unions are granted broader real estate loan powers.
3. Federal savings associations may purchase municipal revenue bonds (up to 10 percent of their capital) as well as general-obligation municipal bonds and invest in insured time deposits.
4. Federal savings associations may invest in consumer loans up to 30 percent of their total assets.
5. Federal savings associations may lease or lend against personal property up to 10 percent of their total assets.
6. State laws and court decisions restricting enforcement of due-on-sale clauses in real property loans are preempted so that when a mortgaged home is sold, the outstanding mortgage loan becomes due and payable.

Other Provisions

Depository institutions could freely change organizational form from mutual to stockholder owned and change their federal or state supervisory agency.

This latter provision of the Financial Institutions Reform, Recovery, and Enforcement Act proved to be severely constraining on S&Ls that chose to remain in the thrift industry. Many converted to commercial or savings banks to enjoy more freedom and flexibility. In November 1991, these restrictive rules limiting S&L asset diversification were eased somewhat with passage of the FDIC Improvement Act, allowing savings associations to become qualified thrift lenders (QTLs) if a minimum of 65 percent of their portfolio assets were in mortgage-related investments or other qualified assets. Moreover, a portion of consumer loans and mortgage loans previously sold could be counted toward meeting the new requirements to qualify for special federal tax benefits as a QTL. (See Exhibit 18–8.)

The savings and loan industry was further jolted by tough new *regulatory forbearance* rules when the Financial Institutions Reform, Recovery, and Enforcement Act was passed in 1989 and when the FDIC Improvement Act (FDICIA) appeared in 1991. Prior to these laws, regulatory agencies often allowed insolvent S&Ls, banks, and other depository institutions to keep their doors open, and permitted them to pay higher and higher interest rates in an effort to keep the public's deposits invested in these troubled institutions. This form of regulatory forbearance drove up deposit costs for all depository institutions and, on occasion, drove some healthy banks and S&Ls to the point of failure. Moreover, if the regulators were eventually forced to close the insolvent institutions, the delay in taking action made it difficult to sell the failed institutions to healthy companies for enough money to

A New Insurance and Regulatory Plan for Depository Institutions

1. The Federal Savings and Loan Insurance Corporation, created originally to insure S&L deposits, is replaced by the Savings Association Insurance Fund (SAIF) to insure the public's deposits up to $100,000. SAIF is placed under the management of the Federal Deposit Insurance Corporation (FDIC), which also manages the Bank Insurance Fund (BIF) to insure commercial banks' deposits.
2. Supervisory powers over the U.S. savings and loan industry are transferred from the Federal Home Loan Bank (FHLB) Board to the Office of Thrift Supervision (OTS), a division of the U.S. Treasury Department, and the FDIC. The OTS can limit the growth of thrift institutions that are inadequately capitalized and prevent these institutions from accepting deposits brokered by security dealers, thus reducing possible future drains on federal insurance reserves.
3. The FDIC is empowered to increase deposit insurance assessments against thrifts until federal insurance reserves rise to at least 1.25 percent of all insured deposits.
4. Federal regulators were given greater power to restrict risky investments by savings and loans and greater flexibility in closing insolvent depository institutions. The FDIC can become a conservator (operating a depository institution as a going concern) or a receiver (closing and liquidating a depository institution) for any insured depository chartered under either federal or state law that has been declared insolvent or can suspend insurance coverage for a risky depository institution.
5. Responsibility for disposing of the assets of closed depository institutions was given to the Resolution Trust Corporation (RTC), which has authority to borrow in the financial markets.

Changes in Capital, Investment, and Service Powers

1. To promote greater safety among depository institutions, new minimum capital standards are imposed on depository institutions so that core capital provided by their owners equals at least 3 percent of their total assets and tangible capital must amount to at least 1.5 percent of their assets.
2. Thrift institutions are prohibited from purchasing junk bonds.
3. Depository institutions desiring to be "qualified thrift lenders" (and, therefore, receive tax benefits and FHLB low-interest loans) must increase the proportion of their assets placed in mortgage-related investments up to at least 70 percent of their total assets.

recover all the costs involved. While regulatory forbearance was originally designed to save deposit insurance money, it often wound up costing the government's insurance fund more in the long run.

Congress put a stop to regulatory forbearance when the **FDIC Improvement Act (FDICIA)** was passed. Under the new law, a bank or thrift could be closed if its ratio of tangible equity capital to total assets fell below two percent for more than 90 days. The troubled institution *must* be closed down or sold to a healthy firm if its undercapitalized condition lasts for more than 270 days. Thus, bank and thrift regulators do not have to wait until a depository institution has zero capital (i.e., is technically bankrupt) to close it, permitting the regulators to sell the troubled institution while it still retains enough value to interest potential buyers.

One final regulatory problem facing the savings and loan industry over the past decade centered upon SAIF—the Federal Savings Association Insurance Fund administered by the FDIC. When Congress passed the Financial Institutions Reform, Recovery, and Enforcement Act of 1989, it mandated that all federal deposit insurance pools must be built up to a point where $1.25 in insurance reserves are available to cover each $100 in insured

EXHIBIT 18–8
Provisions of the Federal Deposit Insurance Corporation Improvement Act of 1991 Applying to Savings and Loan Associations, Other Thrifts, and Banks (Passed in November 1991)

Recapitalization of the FDIC and Protecting Federal Insurance Reserves

1. The Federal Deposit Insurance Corporation (FDIC) is empowered to borrow an additional $30 billion from the U.S. Treasury to be repaid from future insurance premiums. The FDIC may also borrow using the assets of the failed institutions it has taken over as collateral.
2. Federal regulators may close an undercapitalized bank or thrift institution that is not yet insolvent. Critically undercapitalized institutions (with capital/asset ratios below 2 percent) may be placed in receivership. Regulations become increasingly strict as a depository institution's capital position weakens and may include requiring a merger, restricting growth, replacing management, or prohibiting stockholder dividends.
3. Riskier depository institutions will be assessed higher insurance fees. The FDIC must assess sufficient fees to bring federal insurance reserves up to at least 1.25 percent of all insured deposits by the year 2006.
4. The FDIC may prohibit undercapitalized depository institutions or those with no more than average capital from accepting deposits placed with them by brokers unless the FDIC finds this is not unsafe.
5. Deposit insurance coverage of personal retirement accounts is limited to a maximum of $100,000 for any one retirement account holder in any one insured depository institution.

Restrictions on Services Offered

1. State-chartered branches and agency offices operated by insured depository institutions cannot engage in activities that federally chartered depository institutions cannot legally offer unless approved by the Federal Reserve or the FDIC.
2. State-chartered banks are subject to the same lending limits as federally chartered banks and cannot offer insurance underwriting services or make equity investments if national banks are not permitted to do so.
3. Depository institutions must retain a licensed or certified appraiser to evaluate real estate purchases involving large investments or loans. Federal regulators must adopt uniform standards for real estate lending.
4. Misleading advertising of deposits is prohibited and any adverse change in deposit terms must be communicated to depositors 30 days prior to the change. Moreover, any insured depository institution must notify its customers and its principal regulator at least 90 days before closing any branch office.
5. Savings and loans may qualify for special benefits (e.g., tax benefits and borrowing from the Federal Home Loan banks at low cost) if at least 65 percent of their total assets are in mortgage-related assets or other qualified assets.

New Restrictions on Foreign Banks

The Federal Reserve Board must approve new offices and service activities of foreign banks and can revoke a foreign bank's license to operate in the United States if it is pursuing unsafe or illegal activities or is not adequately supervised by regulators in its home country.

Other Provisions

1. Federal savings associations can loan up to 35 percent of their total assets to individuals and families.
2. Savings associations and banks can merge with each other, subject to regulatory approval.

deposits by no later than 2006. The Bank Insurance Fund (BIF) reached the mandated insurance coverage goal in 1995, and bankers were told that their federal insurance fees would be reduced from about 24 cents per $100 of insured deposits to about 4 cents per $100. (Subsequently, adequately capitalized banks with acceptable examiner ratings had their insurance fees set at zero.) SAIF, on the other hand, was far away from the minimum-coverage goal, meaning savings and loans and other thrifts insured by SAIF would have to pay much larger federal insurance fees than commercial banks for a time. Eventually, Congress levied a special assessment against thrift institutions to bring their federal insurance reserves closer to required government standards and to level deposit insurance costs so that banks and thrifts faced more nearly equal insurance fees.

Savings Banks

Savings banks, like savings and loans, can be chartered by either the states or the federal government. State and federal governments also share responsibility for insuring savings bank deposits (see again Exhibit 18–4). However, most savings banks have deposits insured by the Federal Deposit Insurance Corporation up to $100,000. Regulations are designed to insure maximum safety of deposits. This is accomplished principally through close control over the types of assets a savings bank is permitted to acquire. For example, state law and the "prudent person" rule enforced by the courts generally limit savings bank investments to first-mortgage loans, U.S. government and federal agency securities, high-grade corporate bonds and stocks, and municipal bonds. Investment powers are heavily restricted in this industry, because it focuses upon small depositors who may not be able to evaluate the riskiness of these institutions. On the negative side, however, these strict regulations limit the flexibility of savings banks in responding to shifting customer service needs.

One regulatory issue involving savings banks that has rocketed into public prominence recently concerns the trend toward converting mutuals into stockholder-owned savings associations. As we saw in Chapter 16, the purpose of these mutual-to-stock conversions is to infuse new capital into these organizations and force them to become more profit and cost conscious and act in the interest of their owners. Unfortunately, these conversions have sometimes led to multi-million-dollar windfalls for the managements and boards of directors of mutuals with few gains for the depositors, who, legally at least, own a mutual savings bank. Employees and trustees of these associations sometimes award themselves options to buy a major proportion of the converted savings banks' new stock. The management of the converting bank may pick an appraisal firm that underprices the initial stock offering. When trading begins in the new stock, its price rises rapidly to its true market value and insiders may score substantial capital gains.

Recently, U.S. regulators began to clamp down on these mutual-to-stock conversions. In the case of savings banks, the FDIC requires the submission of a conversion plan, which that agency can approve or disapprove in an effort to make sure that depositors are not cheated and that "insiders" in a mutual are not "unjustly enriched."

Money Market Funds

The final type of nonbank thrift institution is the *money market mutual fund.* Because this financial intermediary sells shares in pools of securities, it is primarily regulated by the U.S. Securities and Exchange Commission (SEC), which limits money market fund investments primarily (95 percent or more) to top-quality securities and restricts the maximum and average maturity of money market fund security holdings. The SEC requires money funds to issue a prospectus to any potential buyer of their shares detailing the objectives of the fund, describing its recent performance, and revealing in what assets the shareholders' money has been invested. Today, in an effort to protect the small individual saver, money funds must remind their customers that their shares are *not* government insured and, therefore, may not always be able to maintain their par (usually $1.00) value.

THE REGULATION OF INSURANCE COMPANIES

While not quite as heavily regulated as commercial banks, insurance intermediaries face tough regulations that are imposed primarily by state insurance commissions. The fundamental purpose of insurance company regulation is to ensure that the public is not overcharged or poorly served and to guarantee adequate compensation to insurance companies themselves. A new insurance company must be chartered under the rules of a particular home state (with most selecting states that have the most lenient rules, such as Arizona or Delaware). Once chartered, each company must submit periodic reports to state commissions, its agents must be licensed by the states, and the terms of its policies (including the premium rates it charges policyholders) must be approved.

Both the courts and state commissions insist that any investments of incoming policyholder premiums must conform to the common law standard of a "prudent person." While, as we saw in Chapter 17, speculative investments by insurance companies rose considerably in the 1980s, recent periods have ushered in a more conservative standard, with state insurance commissions inside the United States and regulators in other countries putting great pressure on insurance companies to significantly increase the quality of their asset portfolios and to maintain minimum levels of capital as protection against risk. Finally, federal law at the end of the twentieth century permitted banks and insurance companies to affiliate with each other inside the United States, similar to what other nations (especially those in Western Europe) have allowed for some time. To facilitate such mergers between banks and insurers an increased number of insurers have recently converted from mutual to stockholder-owned insurance firms.

THE REGULATION OF PENSION FUNDS

Because pension funds have risen rapidly to hold the bulk of the retirement savings of millions of workers, they have been subject to much heavier regulation by the courts and government agencies in recent years. Because employers—the principal creators and managers of pension plans—have an incentive to take on considerable risk in an effort to minimize the cost burden they must carry, many pension plans even today remain only *partially funded;* that is, the market value of their assets plus expected investment income does *not* fully cover all the benefits promised to pension plan members. While English common law requires pension plans to be "prudent" managers of their members' retirement savings, many pensions have branched out into riskier investments, including real estate development projects and derivative securities contracts.

Responding to concerns about pension safety and employee accessibility, the U.S. Congress during the 1970s passed the Employee Retirement Income Security Act (ERISA), which requires full funding of all private pensions and prudent investment policies. ERISA granted employees the right to join a pension program, in most cases, after only one year on the job. More rapid *vesting* of accumulated benefits was also required so that employees can recover a higher proportion of their past contributions should they decide to retire early or move to another job. Trying to eliminate the danger that pensions may not have adequate funds to pay future claims against them, Congress now requires employers eventually to cover any past liabilities not fully funded at present. In addition, a federal agency, the Pension Benefit Guaranty Corporation (PBGC or "Penny Benny") was created to insure some vested employee benefits. Currently, Penny Benny insures the pension benefits of approximately 40 million U.S. workers who belong to about 85,000 defined-benefit pension programs.

Penny Benny was expected to be self-supporting, receiving inflows of cash from insurance premiums, from its own investments, and from the assets received from companies turning their pension plans over to Penny Benny. By the early 1990s, however, Penny Benny had taken over more than 1,600 pension plans, and its liabilities were larger than its assets. Some experts fear a financial crisis in the future as the number of retired persons continues to increase, demanding an increasing volume of pension benefits.

Under the law, Penny Benny must insure all *defined benefit plans* (that is, those promising a fixed amount of income at retirement). This has meant that Penny Benny has become relatively less important with the passage of time because more and more pension programs are becoming *defined-contribution* retirement plans where no specific level of retirement benefits is promised. Nevertheless, to insure the pension plans it is responsible for, Penny Benny assesses a flat insurance premium for each pension plan and does not charge riskier pension plans a higher insurance fee. This creates a "moral hazard," with riskier pensions being subsidized by safer ones. Moreover, Penny Benny currently has no legal authority to regulate pension funds, nor does it receive any substantial financial support from the government, having only a small line of credit with the U.S. Treasury.

Clearly, there is a pressing need for pension plan reform so that *all* pension plan members can have reasonable assurance of receiving their benefits. Recently proposed reforms include charging higher insurance premiums and placing a freeze on additional Penny Benny guarantees for those corporate pension plans that have been severely underfunded for a long period of time. Other recent reform proposals in the pension sector, particularly since the collapse of Enron Corporation, are aimed at providing greater protection for employees who have defined-contribution retirement plans. Of special concern are those pension plans heavily invested in their sponsoring company's own stock. Under strong consideration are reforms that would require employers sponsoring a pension plan to more frequently update their employees on the condition and performance of their pension accounts, mandate greater diversification of pension-plan portfolios to promote increased risk protection for employees, provide easier access to investment advice for pension account holders, and allow employees to sell company stock more quickly.

THE REGULATION OF FINANCE COMPANIES

As we saw in Chapter 17, finance companies rank among the most important lenders to consumers and businesses in recent years. The bulk of regulation of this industry is at the state level and focuses principally upon the making of consumer loans. Several states impose maximum loan rates so that finance companies are limited in the amount of interest they can charge consumers, which tends to limit the volume of credit extended to riskier households. The states, trying to protect consumers, also usually spell out the rules for installment loan contracts and the conditions under which automobiles, furniture, home appliances, or other household assets can be repossessed for nonpayment of a loan extended by a finance company.

New forms of small-loan companies have, in recent years, spread across the United States, making the riskiest of consumer loans. These so-called "payday loan companies" and "title loan companies" (along with "check-cashing" firms) are regulated by state governments with some states placing ceilings on the loan rates they may charge and imposing minimum capital requirements on each small-loan company. Several other states have either outlawed these institutions or restricted their growth due to concerns that they may take advantage of small borrowers who often have to surrender their property when they cannot meet the high interest rates these firms often charge.

THE REGULATION OF INVESTMENT COMPANIES

Investment companies or mutual funds, which invest primarily in pools of stocks or bonds on behalf of individuals and institutional customers, are regulated predominantly by the federal government in the United States. Among the most important laws are the Investment Company Act and Investment Advisers Act, passed by the U.S. Congress in 1940. Registration of investment company ownership shares and the submission of periodic reports to the Securities and Exchange Commission (SEC) are mandatory under U.S. law. The SEC requires investment companies to provide their customers with a *prospectus* that describes each company's goals, performance, and financial condition. It is the SEC's duty to make sure the rights of investment company shareholders are fully protected, including the shareholders' right to elect at least two thirds of an investment company's board of directors and the right to approve the choice of an investment advisory service that will manage the investment company's asset portfolio and make buy/sell decisions.

AN OVERVIEW OF TRENDS IN THE REGULATION OF FINANCIAL INSTITUTIONS

In this chapter we have tried to convey at least a sense of the great complexity of regulations that surround the financial institutions' sector and the rationale for those regulations. We have seen that regulation is rooted in the belief that financial institutions occupy a special place in the economy and that the behavior and performance of financial institutions can profoundly affect the welfare of businesses, governments, and households. Thus, regulation seeks to promote the safety and stability of financial institutions in order to preserve the confidence of the public and avoid institutional failures.

Unfortunately, the regulation of financial institutions has not proceeded at a measured pace over time. New regulations often have been piled on top of old regulations, in many cases set up to deal with problems that are no longer important in today's economy. Thus, regulations can become a costly burden that significantly increases financial institutions' operating costs and limits the cleansing effects of failure and competition. The research evidence suggests that the ultimate impact of regulation is to restrict the entry of new competitors, raising financial service prices but also reducing the likelihood of institutional failures.

The thrust of regulation is changing. It is seeking a lower profile as governments around the world seek to pull back from the financial marketplace somewhat and allow the management and owners of financial institutions to face more fully the competition of the marketplace and to respond directly to customers' demands rather than to just regulators' demands. Instead of seeking to wall off and protect one type of financial institution from another, there is growing recognition that the distinctions between financial institutions are blurring and that, eventually, all financial firms must learn how to compete with one another and how to be efficient enough to survive without government support.

Regulators are letting *markets* do more of the regulation of financial firms and they are also learning how to *cooperate* more because the financial-service companies they oversee are becoming more alike and acquiring each other, so that regulators must share more information with each other in order to be effective. Indeed, there is a trend in Europe toward creating just one regulator to supervise *all* financial-service providers. As financial-service industries are gradually being deregulated, the focus of regulation is moving away from control over services offered and geographic expansion to *controlling risk taking*. As we have seen in this chapter, more regulatory attention has recently been focused upon the

Management Insight   A Key Regulatory Agency for Financial Institutions Selling Securities: The SEC

One of the most important regulators of mutual funds and other financial institutions in the United States is the **Securities and Exchange Commission (SEC),** created by the Securities Act of 1933 and the Securities Exchange Act of 1934. The SEC requires that a mutual fund or other business selling new securities to the public provide a potential investor with a *prospectus* that truthfully describes the nature of the operations of the offering company, its management and financial condition, the purpose of the new security offering, and any legal actions pending against the company. All mutual funds and other security issuers must also file a *registration statement* with the SEC. Any false or misleading information in an SEC registration statement may subject the offending security issuer to criminal penalties and lawsuits from investors who may have relied on such statements and lost money in the process.

The SEC also sets rules for the operation of securities exchanges, such as the New York Stock Exchange and the American Stock Exchange. Each security exchange must set its own rules consistent with SEC guidelines and enforce those rules to ensure fair practices, including rules designed to discipline or expel exchange members who break the exchange's rules. If any exchange fails to effectively regulate itself, the SEC may step in to enforce federal securities laws. Passage of the Maloney Act of 1939 extended the SEC's regulatory power to regulate the over-the-counter securities market as well as the securities exchanges. The SEC limits the amount of debt a securities dealer can take on in an effort to protect the public against losses on security trading resulting from the failure of a dealer firm.

With passage of the Investment Advisers and Investment Company Acts of 1940, the SEC was granted power to regulate both those who give investment advice for pay—so-called investment advisers—and investment companies or mutual funds. A professional adviser must register with the SEC; however, the SEC doesn't usually investigate to determine if an investment adviser is competent or competitive.

For mutual funds, the Investment Company Act requires that these intermediaries invest no more than 5 percent of their assets in securities issued by any one firm, nor may they hold more than 10 percent of the voting shares of a single company (though these restrictions apply to only three-quarters of an investment company's portfolio, with the remaining 25 percent not subject to the foregoing rules in an effort to stimulate investments in small businesses). The SEC's Rule 126-1 requires mutual funds to disclose to investors how they account for sales expenses and what impact brokerage commissions and other operating expenses can have on an investor's return.

The SEC is governed by five commissioners, each appointed by the president of the United States for 5-year terms. One of its most highly publicized activities is control over corporate *insider trading* activity. When insider trading activity places outside investors at a disadvantage, the SEC may move in to stop such trading under the terms of the Insider Trading Act of 1988. Every stockholder that holds more than 10 percent of a corporation's outstanding shares and any officers and directors of that company must report their transactions in that firm's stock, as we saw earlier in Chapter 3.

---

amount of *capital* contributed by a financial institution's owners relative to the amount of risk accepted in a financial institution's assets and in its off-balance-sheet activities. Regulators increasingly are insisting that financial institutions have in place written plans describing their policies and procedures for managing exposure to a wide variety of risks, especially credit risk, interest rate risk, and currency and commodity risk.

At the same time, there is increasing attention to *public disclosure*—making sure the public is fully informed on the prices, service fees, risk exposures, and possible penalties they may pay for loans, deposits, and other key financial services. The fundamental idea is that an informed consumer will make better decisions regarding the use of financial services. Fuller disclosure stimulates competition as informed consumers shop around for the best terms available.

This issue moved closer to the front of the current regulatory agenda in 2001 when Enron Corporation filed for bankruptcy—the largest such filing in U.S. history—amid allegations of deceptive accounting practices, illegal insider trading, and lax oversight of its activities in the commodities and securities markets. Several authorities have recommended

Management Insight Self-Regulation of the Securities Industry in the United States

Shortly after the principal regulator of the securities industry, the Securities and Exchange Commission (SEC), was created with passage of the Securities and Exchange Act in 1934 the U.S. Congress enacted the Maloney Act in 1939 giving the SEC power to *delegate* securities industry regulation to various professional groups and organizations. National securities associations of brokers and dealers were authorized to self-regulate their own member firms, subject to SEC review.

For example, under current rules any broker or dealer required by law to register with the Securities and Exchange Commission must also become a member of the National Association of Securities Dealers (NASD) unless the broker or dealer firm does its business only on a national exchange (such as the New York Stock Exchange) where it is a member of that exchange. Professional self-regulatory groups like NASD must make sure their members are dealing fairly with their customers, determine if member businesses have sufficient capital and well-designed operating procedures to protect against failure, look for violations of securities law, arbitrate disputes between member firms or between securities businesses and their customers, and license professional traders who deal with the public. The major exchanges, such as the New York Stock Exchange, the American Stock Exchange, and the Chicago Board Options Exchange, are examples of other self-regulatory institutions aiding the SEC in supervising the securities business.

closer scrutiny of business accounting practices and increased regulation of corporations' use of off-balance-sheet transactions by such government agencies as the Securities and Exchange Commission (SEC) and the Commodities Futures Trading Commission (CFTC). New legislation may be needed in the future to accomplish these objectives.

Finally, for the first time in more than a century, the future of government regulation of the financial-services sector is in doubt. We are beginning to question seriously the benefits and the costs of letting governments set rules for financial institutions. We are asking more frequently: What purpose is served by both old and proposed new rules? Do the costs of both old and new regulations outweigh their benefits? How will market forces be distorted, and what will society gain or lose as a result of government interference with market forces? And, do we really need *multiple* regulatory agencies when financial-service firms are looking more similar to each other, offering many of the same services, and merging with each other in growing numbers? Shouldn't fewer numbers of financial institutions be matched by fewer regulators? It is the answers to these questions that will form the guideposts to the future of financial institutions' regulation around the world.

Questions *to Help You Study*

8. Who are the particular government agencies that regulate the following financial institutions: credit unions, savings and loan associations, savings banks, insurance companies, finance companies, investment companies, pension funds, and security brokers and dealers?

9. What major trends are reshaping financial institutions' regulation today? Why has *capital regulation* become so important?

10. What new *disclosure rules* have recently appeared? Do you think these disclosure requirements help or hurt financial institutions? Why or why not?

11. Why might there be a need for *fewer* regulatory agencies in the financial sector today?

12. Based on your reading of this chapter how has *globalization* of the financial sector impacted the regulatory agencies that oversee financial institutions? What do you think will happen in the future as the financial-services industry becomes more "globalized"?

In recent years, nations around the globe have often copied each other's regulations applying to financial institutions—in effect, learning from one another's mistakes and successes. For example, when Mexico and the nations of Asia got into trouble with bad loans and extensive numbers of failures in their banking systems, these countries selected recovery models that often seemed to bear a close relationship to the recovery approach used by the United States to resolve its hundreds of bank and thrift institution failures during the 1980s and early 1990s. Nevertheless, important differences still remain in how the regulation and supervision of banking and other financial institutions takes place around the globe.

One key international difference lies in providing the public with deposit insurance coverage. Many nations have no formal deposit insurance plans at all. Others (e.g., Switzerland) have no fund that accumulates over time to prepare for future bank failures (as happens in the U.S. with the FDIC, for example). Rather, if a bank failure occurs, the remaining solvent banks are asked to contribute sufficient funds to cover any deposits that have to be paid off.

Many *common* trends in the structure of financial-service industries do show up around the world, however. For example, most financial systems are consolidating into fewer but larger financial firms (i.e., more concentration on the supply side of these markets), and banks are generally losing market share to nonbank firms (such as security dealers and brokers, insurers, mutual funds, and pension funds). Yet some nations' financial systems (such as Germany, Japan, and France) remain dominated by banks, which hold the bulk of the nation's financial assets, while in other countries security brokers and dealers are very important (as in Great Britain and the United States). In the latter nations, securities regulation and supervision has become as important a regulatory activity and area of concern as bank regulation, while the reverse is typically true for bank-dominated national financial systems.

Countries with security-dominated financial systems—most notably, the United States—often lag behind other nations in freeing their banks to venture into new lines of business. The relatively slow response of legislators and regulators in these particular countries in modifying older, outmoded rules has probably contributed to the generally declining market share of banks relative to nonbank service providers worldwide.

Of course, just as important differences exist in financial institutions' regulation and supervision from country to country, there is a definite trend toward greater international cooperation and more common rules (e.g., the Basle Agreement on Capital Standards for banks in industrialized countries). Some experts believe that this *coordination* and *homogenization* of regulatory rules across nations will grow and may result ultimately in true multinational regulatory and supervisory agencies that "level the playing field" so that leading financial institutions around the world all play by essentially the same rules.

Summary of the Chapter

Because financial institutions provide essential services to the public and can have a potent impact on the economy, regulation of the financial sector is extensive over much of the globe. Government rules encompass nearly every aspect of the behavior and performance of financial institutions, including the services they offer, their management policies, financial condition, and their ability to expand geographically.

- *Regulation* involves governments setting rules that bind financial institutions to obey laws and to protect the public interest. These rules are enforced by agencies and commissions that operate at state and federal levels.

- *Deregulation* is becoming a reality for many financial institutions as more and more governments eliminate some rules or ease some regulations to allow the behavior and performance of financial-service institutions to be governed more by the private marketplace and less by government dictation.

- Among the key bank regulatory agencies active in the United States are the Federal Reserve System, the Office of the Comptroller of the Currency, the Federal Deposit

Insurance Corporation, and the 50 state banking commissions. The Federal Reserve oversees the performance and regulatory compliance of member banks of the Federal Reserve System and financial holding companies. The Comptroller of the Currency is responsible for the oversight of national (i.e., federally chartered) banks. The Federal Deposit Insurance Corporation supervises nonmember banks and insures the deposits of more than 98 percent of all banks selling deposits to the public in the United States. The 50 state banking commissions supervise banks that have state charters of incorporation and often are assigned regulatory responsibility for other types of financial institutions, such as state-chartered credit unions or savings institutions.

- Recent laws have dramatically changed the shape of the banking industry and other financial-service industries. Examples include the Depository Institutions Deregulation and Monetary Control Act (1980), the Riegle-Neal Interstate Banking Act (1994), and the Financial Services Modernization (Gramm-Leach-Bliley) Act (1999). These laws have brought about such changes as giving more service powers to banks and thrift institutions so they can compete more freely with each other, permitting banks to branch across state lines, and allowing banking firms to affiliate with insurance companies, security firms, and other financial-service businesses just as banks have done in Europe for decades.

- Key regulatory agencies for nonbank financial institutions include the Office of Thrift Supervision which supervises savings and loan associations; the National Credit Union Administration which oversees federally chartered credit unions and supervises the credit union deposit insurance fund (NCUSIF); the Securities and Exchange Commission which focuses principally on the behavior of security brokers and dealers and on the activities of corporations borrowing money in the open market; and the state insurance and financial-services commissions present in each of the 50 U.S. states.

- The nature of government regulation of the financial sector is changing today with the *private marketplace* gradually substituting for government rules. Today regulators are paying less attention to making and enforcing new rules and are pulling back to permit the discipline of the financial marketplace to play a greater role in controlling risk taking by financial-service firms. Regulators are also insisting that the owners of financial institutions (principally their stockholders) supply more of the capital these firms need to operate and serve the public. The result is some shifting of financial institutions' risk from the public to the private owners of these businesses.

Key Terms

Regulation, *506*

Deregulation, *508*

Federal Reserve System, *510*

Comptroller of the Currency, *510*

Federal Deposit Insurance Corporation (FDIC), *510*

State banking commissions, *512*

Glass-Steagall Act, *516*

Financial Services Modernization (Gramm-Leach-Bliley) Act, *517*

Basle Agreement, *519*

National Credit Union Administration (NCUA), *522*

Depository Institutions Deregulation and Monetary Control Act (DIDMCA), *522*

Office of Thrift Supervision (OTS), *523*

Garn–St Germain Depository Institutions Act, *523*

Financial Institutions Reform, Recovery, and Enforcement Act (FIRREA), *523*

Federal Deposit Insurance Corporation Improvement Act (FDICIA), *525*

Securities and Exchange Commission (SEC), *531*

Problems

1. A commercial bank has the following components in its capital account:

Common stock	$110	10-year subordinated debt	$25
Undivided profits	160	Loan-loss reserves	280
Perpetual preferred stock	15	Equity reserves	50
Surplus	35	Limited-life preferred stock	5

How much tier-one (or core) capital does this bank have? Tier-two capital?

2. First National Bank of Wimbley reports tier-one capital of $60 million and tier-two capital of $70 million. First National has assets of $10 million with a risk weight of zero, assets of $350 million with a 0.2 risk weight, assets of $680 million with a 0.5 risk weight, and assets of $1,010 million with a risk weight of 1.00. What is First National's total risk-weighted assets? Does the bank have enough tier-one capital? Enough total capital? Why or why not?

3. Please indicate what type of financial institution is being described by each of the following items:

   a. SEC regulations require that at least two thirds of this financial institution's board of directors must be elected by its stockholders.
   b. Insurance coverage is based upon the number of plan members.
   c. Regulated almost entirely by state commissions.
   d. Most of the regulation of this financial institution focuses upon its policies and procedures for making consumer loans.
   e. Deposits are insured by NCUSIF.
   f. This financial institution's principal regulatory agency is the OTS.
   g. All of these financial-service firms were originally mutual in form, but many have recently become stockholder owned, filing conversion plans with their principal federal regulatory agency.
   h. This financial institution must warn individual savers that their shares are not government insured and they may not always be able to maintain their fixed par value.
   i. This financial service organization receives its corporate charter (certificate of association) from the Comptroller of the Currency.
   j. This financial institution is chartered by the states but belongs to the Federal Reserve System.

4. Please identify each of the key terms or concepts that are described or defined below.

   a. Monitors the activities of security brokers, dealers, and investment institutions.
   b. Granted the FDIC additional borrowing authority.
   c. Deregulated the depository institutions' sector.
   d. Authorized a bailout of the savings and loan industry.
   e. Charters and supervises savings and loans.
   f. Supervises federal credit unions.
   g. Agreement among central banking agencies in leading countries to regulate bank capital.
   h. U.S. law passed in the 1930s to separate commercial from investment banking.
   i. Federal government agency established in 1934 in order to increase the confidence of the public in banks.
   j. Charter and supervise banks headquartered in a given state.
   k. Created by Congress originally to issue currency and coin and protect the U.S. dollar in international markets.
   l. Charters and supervises national banks.
   m. Government enforcement of rules applying to financial-service businesses.

Questions about the Web and the Money and Capital Markets

1. If you wanted to find out who is the principal federal regulator for the bank in your neighborhood how could the Web be of help to you?

2. How do the services and functions of the Federal Reserve differ from those of the Comptroller of the Currency based on their Web site information?

3. How would you find the location of the bank regulatory agency in your home state, using the World Wide Web? What is the name and location of the bank regulatory commission in the home state or province where you are now located?

4. According to its Web site what functions or services does the Securities and Exchange Commission provide to the public? To the financial institutions it regulates?

5. How does the regulatory structure of the European Union seem to differ from that of the United States according to the Web?

6. What does the Web tell you about the role of the *states* in the regulation of financial institutions inside the United States?

Selected References

Berger, Allen; Sally Davies; and Mark Flannery. "Comparing Market and Regulatory Assessments of Bank Performance: Who Knows What When?" *Journal of Money Credit and Banking* XXXII, no. 3 (August 2000), Part II, pp. 641–70.

Cecchetti, Stephen G. "The Future of Financial Intermediation and Regulation: An Overview." *Current Issues in Economics and Finance,* Federal Reserve Bank of New York, May 1999.

Ellihousen, Gregory. *The Cost of Banking Regulation: A Review of the Evidence.* Staff Study 171, Board of Governors of the Federal Reserve System, April 1998.

Emmons, William R.; R. Alton Gilbert; and Mark D. Vaughn. "A Third Pillar of Bank Supervision." *The Regional Economist,* Federal Reserve Bank of St. Louis, October 2001, pp. 5–9.

Engen, Eric M., and Andreas Lehnert. "Mutual Funds and the U.S. Equity Market." *Federal Reserve Bulletin,* December 2000, pp. 797–812.

Feldman, Ron, and Mark Levonian. "Market Data and Bank Supervision: The Transition to Practical Use." *The Region,* Federal Reserve Bank of Minneapolis, September 2001, pp. 11–13 and 46–54.

Gunther, Jeffrey W.; Mark E. Levonian; and Robert R. Moore. "Can the Stock Market Tell Bank Supervisors Anything They Don't Already Know?" *Economic and Financial Review,* Federal Reserve Bank of Dallas, Second Quarter 2001, pp. 2–8.

Jordan, Jerry L. "Effective Supervision and the Evolving Financial Services Industry." *Economic Commentary,* Federal Reserve Bank of Cleveland, June 2001.

Kane, Edward J. "Accelerating Inflation, Technological Innovation and the Decreasing Effectiveness of Banking Regulation." *The Journal of Finance,* May 1981, pp. 355–67.

Peach, Richard, and Charles Steindel. "A Nation of Spendthrifts? An Analysis of Trends in Personal and Gross Saving." In *Current Issues in Economics and Finance,* Federal Reserve Bank of New York, September 2000.

Stigler, George J. "The Theory of Oligopoly." *Journal of Political Economy,* February 1965, pp. 44–61.

Thomson, James B. "Who Benefits from Increasing the Federal Deposit Insurance Limit?" *Economic Commentary,* Federal Reserve Bank of Cleveland, September 15, 2001, pp. 1–4.

Walleghem, Joe Van. "Financial Modernization: A New World or Status Quo?" *Financial Industry Perspectives,* Federal Reserve Bank of Kansas City, 2001, pp. 49–56.

Part Five

Governments in the Financial Markets

This section of the book focuses our attention upon the financial market activities of federal, state, and local governments. It explores the ways in which government operations influence the financial system, financial institutions, and the money and capital markets.

We often divide the financial-market activities of governmental units into two broad areas—fiscal policy and debt management policy. The concept of *fiscal policy* centers around the taxing and spending activities of governmental bodies. Taxes tend to draw funds out of the financial system, at least until the taxing government spends those newly raised monies. Government spending, on the other hand, tends to expand the volume of savings flowing into the financial system because government spending generates income out of which savings appear.

In the area of fiscal policy governments must make crucial decisions about how to raise new capital to finance daily government operations and whether or not to build new public facilities, such as office buildings and airports. They may choose to levy taxes to collect the funds needed or engage in deficit spending which requires them to borrow funds from the financial marketplace. As we will soon discover, taxation and borrowing have different impacts upon interest rates, financial asset prices, financial market conditions, and the economy.

Government managers must choose carefully which of those impacts appear to be most desirable given the present condition of the economy. For example, raising taxes may be optimal in a period of inflation and rapid economic expansion because it tends to slow the economy down and take pressure off prices. In contrast, borrowing money may turn out to be the best option when the economy is in a recession because the spending of those borrowed funds adds to the nation's income stream, stimulating new construction and spending by the public.

Debt management policy focuses upon the decisions governments must make in controlling the composition and structure of debt they have issued as a result of past decisions to borrow money. Of the more than 80,000 units of government in the United States, for example, the great majority possess the authority to borrow money and, therefore, must manage any debt they have taken on. These governmental units must decide what types of new securities to issue and what to do when previously issued securities are about to mature and must be retired.

Debt management, like fiscal policy, can exert a powerful impact upon the financial marketplace and upon the economy as a whole. For example, the decision to borrow short-term money tends to provide additional liquidity in the economy, fostering additional public spending. With added spending pouring into the economy incomes and savings tend to rise. Inflation may eventually become a problem. In contrast, borrowing long-term money tends to boost the cost of investment spending by all borrowers—private and public—and may slow economic growth. Clearly, we cannot ignore the roles played by governments as they interact with the financial markets and financial institutions.

Chapter Nineteen

The Treasury in the Financial Markets

Learning Objectives in This Chapter

- You will examine the many important roles played by the government's Treasury Department in supporting government programs and in pursuing the government's goals and objectives.

- You will be able to identify how the government raises new funding and how it manages to spend the funds that it raises.

- You will understand how the activities of the Treasury Department impact the money and capital markets and the economy.

- You will explore the meaning, purpose, and effect of two key government policy tools—*fiscal policy* and *debt management*.

What's in This Chapter? Key Topics Outline

The Fiscal Policy Activities of the United States Government

Sources and Uses of Government Funds

Effects of Government Borrowing and Debt Retirement

Debt Management: A Tool of Economic Policy

Size and Growth of the Public Debt

Composition and Ownership of the U.S. Public Debt

Rise of Foreign Investors in U.S. Securities

Auctioning Treasury Securities

The Housekeeping and Stabilization Goals of Debt Management

INTRODUCTION

One of the most important financial institutions in any economy is the government treasury. In the United States, the Treasury Department exerts a powerful impact on the financial system because of two activities that it pursues on a continuing basis. One of these is **fiscal policy,** which refers to the taxing and spending programs of the federal government designed to promote high employment, sustainable economic growth, and other worthwhile economic goals. A second area in which the Treasury exerts a potent effect on financial conditions is **debt management policy,** which involves the refunding or refinancing of the federal government's debt in a way that contributes to broad economic goals and minimizes the burden of the federal debt. These Treasury policymaking activities influence interest rates and the availability of credit for all sectors of the economy. In general, the Treasury pursues policies designed to achieve its economic goals but not to disturb the functioning of the financial markets or unduly interfere with the operations of the Federal Reserve System, the nation's central bank.

THE FISCAL POLICY ACTIVITIES OF THE U.S. TREASURY

Congress dictates the amount of funds the federal government will spend each year for a variety of programs ranging from welfare to national defense. Congress also determines the sources of tax revenue and the tax rates that must be paid by individuals and businesses. Frequently, Congress votes for a higher amount of spending than can be supported by tax revenues. Alternatively, due to a slowdown in the economy, tax revenues may fall short of projections and not be sufficient to cover planned expenditures. Either way, the result is a **budget deficit,** requiring the U.S. Treasury to borrow additional funds in the financial markets. On the other hand, government revenues may exceed expenditures, resulting in a **budget surplus,** which the Treasury may use to build up its cash balances or to retire debt previously issued.

As shown in Exhibit 19–1, U.S. Treasury budget surpluses have been very infrequent. In fact, until 1998, the federal budget had been in surplus in only eight fiscal years since 1931. However, an agreement between the U.S. Congress and President Clinton led to more slowly growing federal expenditures, while a generally strong economy resulted in steadily advancing tax receipts. Federal budget deficits fell from a peak of close to $300 billion in 1992 to only about $22 billion in fiscal 1997. A federal budget surplus finally appeared late in the 1990s and into the opening of the twenty-first century.

Does the advent of federal budget surpluses during the most recent period mean the federal government of the United States will never need to borrow money again? Hardly. For one thing, a sudden downturn in the economy could lower tax receipts and reduce or eliminate projected budget surpluses, as appeared to occur when an economic recession and terrorist attacks struck the U.S. economy in the year 2001. (In fact, there is recent evidence

EXHIBIT 19–1
Federal Government Revenues, Expenditures, and Net Budget Surplus or Deficit, Selected Fiscal Years, 1969–2001

Sources: The President's Council of Economic Advisers, *Economic Report of the President,* selected years; and Board of Governors of the Federal Reserve System, *Federal Reserve Bulletin,* selected monthly issues.

Fiscal Years	Total Revenues	Total Expenditures	Net Budget Surplus or Deficit
1969	$ 186.9	$ 183.6	+$3.2
1970	192.8	195.6	−2.8
1980	517.1	590.9	−73.8
1990	1,031.3	1,251.8	−220.5
1997	1,579.3	1,601.2	−21.9
1998*	1,721.8	1,652.6	+69.2
1999*	1,827.5	1,702.9	+124.6
2000*	2,025.2	1,789.0	+236.2
2001*	1,990.9	1,863.9	+127.0

*Estimates by the U.S. Department of the Treasury and the Office of Management and Budget.
Note: Figures based on the unified budget for fiscal years. Before 1977, fiscal years ran from July 1 through June 30. Thereafter, the federal government's fiscal year covered the October 1–September 30 period.

the U.S. federal budget was back in deficit as early as fiscal 2002.) Moreover, as we move deeper into the new century sizeable federal budget deficits are possible again due to the growing burden imposed by the Social Security and Medicare programs. Moreover, Congress and the president could enact tax cuts and new federal spending programs in the future, leading once again to budget deficits.

Finally, it must be noted that, just like you and me, the government experiences periods of cash shortages in certain weeks and months even if the fiscal year as a whole is expected to end in a budget surplus. For example, in October 2000 federal receipts totaled $135 billion while expenditures reached $146 billion. In contrast, by December, two months later, federal receipts exceeded $200 billion and expenditures totaled only about $168 billion. The Treasury will continue to need to borrow money in order to cover temporary cash shortages and to refund outstanding debt even in years of rising net revenues.

Sources of Federal Government Funds

It is interesting to analyze the sources of revenue the federal government draws upon to fund its activities. Exhibit 19–2 presents information on the principal sources of federal revenue and spending programs. On the revenue side, the bulk of incoming funds is derived from taxes levied against individual and family incomes. In fiscal 2000, for example, individuals were expected to pay an estimated $1 trillion in income taxes, representing almost 50 percent of all federal revenues that year. Social Security taxes were forecast to supply $650 billion—roughly a third of all federal revenues. Corporate income taxes were projected a distant third at about 11 percent, and other taxes and fees for government services were expected to provide about 7 percent of all federal revenues.

During the 1970s and early 1980s, the share of federal revenues produced by personal income taxes declined. This was due to efforts by Congress to reduce withholding taxes and increase personal deductions against individual income taxes. Later, in the 1990s, personal income tax revenue rose or held steady as a proportion of all government receipts, reflecting Congress' desire to shift the tax burden more heavily onto the more wealthy citizens. At the same time, payroll taxes for social insurance increased as Congress moved to rescue the Social Security system from deepening deficits. Corporate taxes were increased in an effort

EXHIBIT 19–2
Federal Government Revenues, Expenditures, and Net Budget Surplus or Deficit, 2000 (Estimates, $ Billions)

Sources: President's Council of Economic Advisers, *Economic Report of the President*, selected years; and Board of Governors of the Federal Reserve System, *Federal Reserve Bulletin*, selected monthly issues.

Budget Item	Amount	Percent of Total
On- and off-budget *receipts* by source:		
Individual income taxes	$1,004.5	49.6%
Corporation income taxes	235.7	11.4
Social insurance taxes & contributions	652.9	32.2
Other sources of revenue	160.6	6.9
Total revenues	$2,025.2	100.0%
On- and off-budget *expenditures* by function:		
National defense	$ 294.5	16.5%
International affairs	17.2	0.1
Health care	154.5	8.6
Income security programs	247.9	13.9
Social Security and Medicare	606.5	33.9
Net interest payments on the federal debt	223.2	12.5
Other expenditures	245.2	14.5
Total expenditures	$1,789.0	100.0%
Net surplus (+) or deficit (−)	+$236.2	

Note: Columns may not add to totals due to rounding.

to offset declining personal tax rates and help to reduce budget deficits. As the twenty-first century began, a new presidential administration guided by George W. Bush sought to lower tax rates to stimulate the economy and increase saving and investment.

These changes in tax rates suggest that the federal government has attempted in recent years to make the tax structure more responsive to the nation's economic problems. When the economy headed down into a recession, or inflation pushed individuals into higher tax brackets, Congress generally responded (though often with considerable lags) and made appropriate income tax adjustments.

Federal Government Expenditures

Reflecting the effects of rising taxes and inflation, the U.S. government today collects an enormous volume of revenue from its citizens. For example, federal revenues were expected to reach more than $2 trillion in 2000. Where does the federal government spend this money?

The most recently compiled budget of the U.S. Government is available from the Office of Management and Budget at *www.gpo.gov/usbudget*

Exhibit 19–2 indicates that slightly more than half of all federal spending goes for national defense and various income security programs, including Social Security, Medicare, and unemployment compensation. The latter programs are designed to sustain the spending power of individuals who are retired, ill or disabled, or temporarily unemployed. The collapse of the Warsaw Pact in Europe and economic and political problems inside the states of the former Soviet Union stimulated the U.S. government to begin cutting back on spending for national defense (as a "peace dividend" from the end of the Cold War) and to shift more resources toward social programs and environmental protection (including more funds for medical research, improved educational opportunities for children, an upgrading of public housing and rental assistance programs, stronger antidrug programs, improved facilities for safeguarding air travel, and more aggressive efforts to clean up the environment). As the twenty-first century opened, a new and more conservative presidential administration took control and spending priorities began shifting again toward national defense, guarding against terrorism at home and abroad, and educational programs with fewer monies likely to be directed toward other social programs, such as debt reduction, Social Security, and Medicare.

Recent Tax and Expenditure Legislation

Confronted with inflation and deepening federal deficits for many years until the middle and late 1990s, Congress and the president responded in the 1980s with major pieces of fiscal legislation that continue to affect the financial markets today. For example, in August 1981, Congress passed the Economic Recovery Tax Act, which brought about significant cuts in individual income tax rates. In addition, accelerated depreciation allowances, investment tax credits, and tax incentives for business research expenditures were included in the Economic Recovery Act in an attempt to increase investment spending and create jobs. Income tax brackets and personal exemptions were adjusted for the effects of inflation. This last provision, known as *indexing,* is designed to eliminate bracket creep—the tendency for inflation to push individual incomes into higher tax brackets.

In 1997, the U.S. Congress made more major changes in the federal tax code, expanding tax credits for children, lifting somewhat the burden of estate taxes, lowering capital gains tax rates on longer-term investments, and providing new incentives to save money in the form of more liberal individual retirement accounts (the Roth IRA, which promises to accumulate savings and then pay them out tax free) and special educational tax credits. One purpose of these changes was to stimulate saving and business investment in order to reduce inflationary pressures in the economy.

Although the Economic Recovery Act may have made a significant contribution toward reducing inflation, it also contributed to deepening federal budget deficits. As Exhibit 19–1 shows, the federal budget deficit nearly tripled between 1980 and 1990, forcing the U.S. Treasury to borrow unprecedented amounts in the financial markets and confronting private borrowers with both higher interest rates and more limited availability of credit. The most notable legislation during this period was the Gramm-Rudman-Hollings bill (known officially as the Balanced Budget and Emergency Deficit Control Act), which mandated reduced budget deficits until the deficit could be completely eliminated in fiscal 1991. However, Congress soon found loopholes in Gramm-Rudman and a more slowly growing economy generated sharply reduced tax collections. During the 1990s, Congress debated a balanced budget amendment to the U.S. Constitution that would have required a careful balance between revenues and expenditures each year, but the measure failed to pass. However, due in part to continuing public support for deficit reductions, the federal government's deficit fell as a percentage of the U.S. GDP from about 5 percent in 1985 to about 2 percent in 1995. At this point, President Bill Clinton and a Republican-led Congress sought out compromise legislation in an effort to gradually eliminate federal deficits as the twenty-first century approached, mandating budget surpluses beginning no later than 2002.

Great strength in the economy led, however, to budget surpluses earlier than anticipated as tax collections grew faster than projected. When budget surpluses approached record levels in the new century, President George W. Bush asked the U.S. Congress for major personal tax cuts in order to redirect surplus tax revenues back into the private sector and, hopefully, lead to a strong growth trend in the economy. The Economic Growth and Tax Relief Reconciliation Act of 2001 lowered personal tax brackets so that the top income-tax bracket rate would fall to as low as 35 percent by the year 2006, while estate taxes were gradually phased out and retirement and educational savings plans were expanded in order to encourage the public to save more.

Unfortunately, these attempts at fiscal stimulus appeared to be stymied by the terrible attacks on September 11, 2001, upon the World Trade Center and the Pentagon. Despite the prospect of lower taxes the public cut back on its spending, especially for travel and the purchase of durable goods, and the economy entered a recession as the new century moved forward. In response, Congress and the President passed a new fiscal stimulus law in March of 2002 to halt the recession by extending unemployment benefits and increasing tax benefits from additional business investment. Certainly, government taxing and spending activities can exert a powerful impact upon the public's spending and saving habits, although other factors can override that impact from time to time, creating a whole new and unexpected budgetary situation for government planners to deal with.

Questions *to Help You Study*

1. What exactly is *fiscal policy? Debt management policy?*

2. Please explain how fiscal and debt management policy might be used to help fight inflation and unemployment. Can you see any weaknesses or potential problems with the frequent use of these policy tools?

3. Please list from the largest to the smallest the principal sources of federal government revenue. What are the principal federal spending programs?

Effects of Government Borrowing on the Financial System and the Economy

What are the effects of government borrowing on the economy and the financial markets? If the federal government runs a *small* budget deficit, it is possible for the Treasury to cover the shortfall in revenues by drawing on its accumulated cash balances held at the Federal Reserve banks or even by issuing new currency. However, when government deficits are large, substantial amounts of new debt securities have to be issued. The impact of these massive borrowings on the money and capital markets and the economy depends, in part, on the *source* of borrowed funds. Exhibit 19–3 summarizes the probable effects of government borrowing designed to cover a budget deficit.

Borrowing from the Nonbank Public

For example, suppose the Treasury needs to borrow $20 billion, which it raises by selling government bonds to the nonbank public. As the public pays for these securities, it writes checks against its deposits held with depository institutions, initially reducing the size of the money supply. As these checks are deposited in the Treasury's accounts at the Federal Reserve banks, legal reserves held by depository institutions decline by $20 billion.

To gauge the full effects of government borrowing, however, we must consider the fact that the government plans to *spend* its borrowed funds. In our example, the Treasury will write checks totaling $20 billion against its Federal Reserve accounts and distribute those checks to the public. Deposits of the public rise by $20 billion, also increasing the legal reserves held by depository institutions.

On balance, after all transactions are completed, there is no change in the money supply or in the total amount of reserves held by the banking system. However, there is likely to be an *increase* in total spending and income in the economy due to the fact that funds are transferred from those who purchase securities to members of the public receiving government checks. Presumably, recipients of government checks have a higher marginal propensity to spend new income than do security investors, who have a higher marginal propensity to save any new income received. Aggregate consumption spending will probably increase, and if the economy is at or near full employment, inflation may rise. Initially, the increased sale of Treasury securities should put upward pressure on interest rates. Over a longer-term period, however, it is quite possible that interest rates will eventually fall due to the higher levels of income and increased saving out of that income.

EXHIBIT 19–3 **Effects of Government Borrowing on the Financial Markets and the Economy**

USUAL IMPACT: Higher incomes, spending, and interest rates.

Borrowing from the Nonbank Public

	Federal Reserve Banks		Depository Financial Institutions	
	Assets	*Liabilities*	*Assets*	*Liabilities*
Sale of securities		Legal reserves −20 of depository institutions Government +20 deposits	Legal reserves −20	Deposits of −20 the public
Spending of borrowed funds		Government −20 deposits Legal reserves +20 of depository institutions	Legal reserves +20	Deposits of +20 the public

EFFECTS: No change in the money supply or total reserves; total spending and income in the economy and interest rates rise.

Borrowing from Depository Institutions

	Federal Reserve Banks		Depository Financial Institutions	
	Assets	*Liabilities*	*Assets*	*Liabilities*
Sale of securities		Legal reserves −20 of depository institutions Government +20 deposits	Government +20 securities Legal reserves −20	
Spending of borrowed funds		Legal reserves +20 of depository institutions Government −20 deposits	Legal reserves +20	Deposits of +20 the public

EFFECTS: The money supply increases; total reserves are unchanged, but excess reserves fall due to increases in deposits; total spending, income, and interest rates rise.

Borrowing from the Federal Reserve Banks

	Federal Reserve Banks		Depository Financial Institutions	
	Assets	*Liabilities*	*Assets*	*Liabilities*
Sale of securities	Government +20 securities	Government +20 deposits		
Spending of borrowed funds		Government −20 deposits Legal reserves +20 of depository institutions	Legal reserves +20	Deposits of +20 the public

EFFECTS: The money supply and total reserves increase, while total spending and income in the economy rise and interest rates tend to fall.

Borrowing from Depository Institutions

The effects of government borrowing are somewhat different if the borrowing takes place entirely from depository institutions. If we assume that the Treasury borrows $20 billion, deposit-type institutions pay for the securities they purchase by drafts against their legal reserve accounts held at the Federal Reserve banks. Reserves of depository institutions drop by $20 billion, as shown in Exhibit 19–3, and the Treasury's deposits rise by a like amount. However, the Treasury spends these borrowed funds, resulting in an increase in deposits held by the public and in legal reserves. The money supply rises because the public's deposits increase.

On balance, after all transactions are completed, legal reserves remain unchanged, but excess reserves fall because of the increase in deposits. There is also likely to be an increase in spending and income as the public gains additional funds. Prices may rise if unemployment is low. Interest rates may increase in the short run with the increased quantity of government securities available and because of inflation. However, the gain in total spending should lead eventually to a decline in interest rates due to the expansion of savings.

Borrowing from the Federal Reserve Banks

A third route for government borrowing would be to secure credit directly from the central bank. For example, in the United States, this might be done by having the Treasury issue securities directly to the Federal Reserve banks. However, this is a highly *inflationary* way for the federal government to raise money. Financially speaking, it is the equivalent of printing money. Therefore, borrowing directly from the central bank is severely restricted by law in the United States, as it is in many other nations around the globe. Nevertheless, in a severe national emergency such as a serious depression, the central bank would probably be called upon to provide greater support for Treasury borrowing activities.

How would borrowing from the central bank work? The Federal Reserve banks acquire securities and increase the Treasury's deposits by the same amount. Initially, there is no withdrawal of reserves from the banking system, nor does the public lose deposits. Instead, both legal reserves and the public's deposits rise by the amount of any borrowed funds spent by the Treasury. In the example shown in Exhibit 19–3, the Treasury sells $20 billion in securities to the Federal Reserve banks, and its deposit accounts at the Fed rise by a like amount. As the Treasury spends the $20 billion, public deposits and reserves rise, causing increases in the money supply, total spending, and income. Interest rates tend to fall due to the increased growth in the money supply and to growth in savings over the long run, unless, of course, the government's actions lead to expectations of greater inflation and higher nominal interest rates.

Effects of the Retirement of Government Debt from a Budget Surplus on the Financial System and the Economy

Suppose the federal government runs a budget *surplus,* as it did when the 1990s ended and a new century unfolded. By definition, a budget surplus implies that the government withdraws a greater amount of funds from the economy in the form of tax collections than it puts back into the economy through government expenditures. The Treasury simply could save these surplus funds to cover possible deficits in later years or possibly seek tax reductions from Congress and the Administration. However, this may be unpopular from a political standpoint. It is more likely that a government budget surplus would be used to retire debt previously issued, especially debt carrying the highest interest rates. For example, in 2000, the U.S. Treasury reduced the federal government's marketable debt by just over

$300 billion. But the impact of government debt retirement on the economy and the financial system depends, in part, on who happens to hold the debt securities the government plans to retire.

Retiring Government Debt Held by the Nonbank Public

Suppose the securities scheduled for retirement are held by individuals and institutions *not* a part of the banking system. In this case, there will be little or no change in the money supply or in the reserves held by depository institutions.

This is illustrated in Exhibit 19–4, where the act of retiring government debt is separated into two steps. In the first step, we assume that the Treasury collects a surplus of $20 billion in tax revenues. This might arise, for example, if the federal government spent $100 billion, but collected $120 billion in taxes from the public. Clearly, the public's deposits drop a *net* $20 billion. Moreover, as members of the public write checks against their transaction deposits to pay taxes, legal reserves of depository institutions also fall a net $20 billion. The Treasury's deposits at the Federal Reserve banks rise by a like amount.

Assume that the Treasury uses its surplus funds to retire securities held by the nonbank public. Security holders receive government checks totaling $20 billion, which are deposited in banks and thrifts. Legal reserves of these institutions rise by $20 billion. Of course, the Treasury loses the same amount of money from its deposits at the Federal Reserve as the government's checks are cleared. The public's deposits and money supply first decline and then rise by $20 billion, with reserves following the same path. Is there no effect, then, from retiring securities held by the nonbank public? Not likely, because the government has transferred money from the general public (taxpayers), with a high propensity to spend, to security investors who tend to be heavy savers. The net effect is probably to *reduce* total spending and income in the economy. Prices of goods and services may fall and unemployment may rise. It is likely, too, that interest rates will decline as the total supply of securities is reduced, while the volume of investible savings rises in the short run.

Retiring Government Debt Held by Depository Institutions

What happens if the government uses its budget surplus to retire securities held by banks and other depository institutions? Initially the effects are much the same as discussed above. Funds are withdrawn from taxpayer deposit accounts and transferred to the Treasury's deposits at the Federal Reserve. Legal reserves of depository institutions fall by the amount of the tax surplus (in Exhibit 19–4 by $20 billion). Now, however, the surplus funds are paid to depository institutions, who turn in their securities to the Treasury. Legal reserves rise as the government spends its $20 billion deposit.

In the short term, the money supply is reduced due to the drain on taxpayer funds. Total legal reserves are unchanged, first falling and then rising. Note, however, that excess reserves increase because total legal reserves are unchanged when deposits fall. In the long term, the money supply expands due to the gain in excess reserves. With fewer taxpayer funds, however, spending in the economy should decline, which may increase unemployment. Interest rates, too, will probably decline in the short run because fewer securities are now available to investors.

Budget surpluses and the retirement of government debt tend to slow down economic activity and, therefore, could be used as a vehicle to combat inflation. If the federal government wanted to have a maximum deflationary impact on the economy, whose securities should it retire? The Treasury could have the greatest anti-inflationary impact by retiring government securities held by the Federal Reserve banks. This approach would be the equivalent of destroying money.

EXHIBIT 19–4 **Effects of Retiring Government Debt on the Financial Markets and the Economy**

USUAL IMPACT: Total spending, incomes, and interest rates tend to decrease.

Retiring Government Securities Held by the Nonbank Public

	Federal Reserve Banks		Depository Financial Institutions	
	Assets	Liabilities	Assets	Liabilities
Collection of tax surplus		Legal reserves −20 of depository institutions Government +20 deposits	Legal reserves −20	Deposits of −20 the public
Retiring government securities		Government −20 deposits Legal reserves +20 of depository institutions	Legal reserves +20	Deposits of +20 the public

EFFECTS: No change in the money supply or in bank reserves; total spending and income tend to fall because funds move from active to passive spenders; interest rates tend to decline.

Retiring Government Securities Held by Depository Institutions

	Federal Reserve Banks		Depository Financial Institutions	
	Assets	Liabilities	Assets	Liabilities
Collection of tax surplus		Legal reserves −20 of depository institutions Government +20 deposits	Legal reserves −20	Deposits −20 of taxpayers
Retiring government securities		Legal reserves +20 of depository institutions Government −20 deposits	Government −20 securities Legal reserves +20	

EFFECTS: Money supply falls in short run, while total bank reserves are unchanged. Excess reserves increase due to a fall in deposits. Total spending, income, and interest rates decline.

Retiring Government Securities Held by the Federal Reserve Banks

	Federal Reserve Banks		Depository Financial Institutions	
	Assets	Liabilities	Assets	Liabilities
Collection of tax surplus		Legal reserves −20 of depository institutions Government +20 deposits	Legal reserves −20	Deposits of −20 taxpayers
Retiring government securities	Government −20 securities	Government −20 deposits		

EFFECTS: Money supply and total reserves decrease by the amount of the budget surplus; total spending, income, and interest rates decline.

Retiring Government Debt Held by the Federal Reserve Banks

As the bottom panel of Exhibit 19–4 shows, retiring government securities held by the Federal Reserve drains funds from taxpayers. However, those funds are *not* returned to the private spending stream. Instead, the government uses its increased deposits to pay off the Federal Reserve banks and retrieve the securities they hold. Legal reserves of the banking system and the money supply decline by the full amount of the budget surplus. Spending, income, interest rates, and the prices of goods and services are likely to fall as well.

OVERALL IMPACT OF GOVERNMENT BORROWING AND SPENDING

The foregoing T-account presentation helps us to glimpse the likely effects when a government enters the money and capital markets to borrow money and then to spend it on government programs and services. We may summarize these governmental impacts on the financial system and the economy as follows:

- Added government borrowing (followed by the spending of those new government monies) adds to planned private investment spending by businesses and households, tending to increase an economy's production and income levels and create more jobs.

- Added government borrowing also tends to push interest rates higher in the money and capital markets, slowing some private borrowing by businesses and households. Thus, governmental borrowing may offset private borrowing to some extent.

- Eventually the additional government borrowing and spending could set in motion great inflation, causing the prices of goods and services to increase and tending as well to force nominal interest rates upward.

This conventional view of government borrowing adding to income and possibly driving up interest rates and inflation has been challenged in recent years. One counterargument is that interest rates and security prices in an *efficient* market simply may not respond to increased borrowing and spending, either because an equal amount of *private* borrowing and spending are crowded out of the marketplace or because the added government borrowing is already anticipated by the market and has been discounted by investors. Thus, there may be little *net* gain in terms of economic activity or change in interest rates from deficit spending.

Research studies support at least some of the foregoing arguments about the government's debt and its impact on the economy, the financial markets, and financial institutions. For example, increased investment spending by the government tends to reduce private investment to some extent, but the net decline in private investment is often less than the full amount of new government investment because some forms of government investment spending actually enhance private investment (for example, building bridges and airports). Most research studies seem to find a *positive* relationship between the size of government budget deficits and nominal long-term interest rates, suggesting that, as government borrows, this tends to "crowd out" some private investment due to higher borrowing costs. Finally, government deficits do not appear to be a principal cause of inflation except in severe cases. Rather, budget deficits appear to be more influenced by past inflation, rather than the other way around. Thus, inflation tends to force the government to borrow more.

In total, research studies seem to provide at least weak support for what is called the *equivalence theorem*—changes in government borrowing and spending tend to be offset by roughly equal and offsetting adjustments in private borrowing and spending, resulting in a relatively weak *net* effect from government fiscal policy on the economy and the financial markets. However, there is considerable controversy today about the true effects of government deficits, borrowing, and government budget surpluses on the financial markets and the economy. More research on this important issue clearly is needed.

Questions *to Help You Study*

4. Please describe the impact of *government borrowing* upon the financial system and the economy. If the federal government wished to increase total spending in the economy the most, from *whom* should it most likely borrow funds?

5. Please describe the effects of *retiring government securities* on the financial system and the economy. Whose securities should be paid off if the federal government wants to have the maximum negative (contractionary) impact on the economy?

6. What is meant by the term *crowding out effect?* What does recent research say about the link between government deficits, interest rates, and inflation?

MANAGEMENT OF THE FEDERAL DEBT

As we noted at the beginning of this chapter, one of the most important activities of the Treasury is managing the huge **public debt** of the United States. The U.S. public debt is the largest single collection of securities available in the financial system today. Securities issued by the Treasury are regarded by investors as having zero *default risk* because the federal government possesses power both to tax and to create money. The government, unless it is overthrown by war or revolution, can always pay its bills.

Government securities do carry *market risk,* however, because their prices fluctuate with changes in demand and supply. In fact, the longer the term to maturity of a government security, the more market risk it tends to possess.

The principal role of government securities in the financial system is to provide *liquidity.* Corporations, commercial banks, and other institutional investors rely heavily on government securities as a readily marketable reserve to be drawn upon when cash is needed quickly. Although private securities do carry higher explicit yields than government debt of comparable maturity, the greater liquidity of government securities represents an added (implicit) return to the investor.

THE SIZE AND GROWTH OF THE PUBLIC DEBT

How much money does the federal government owe? As shown in Exhibit 19–5, the gross public debt of the United States exceeded $5.6 trillion in 2000. On a per capita basis, the public debt amounts to more than $20,000 for every man, woman, and child living in the United States.

How did the federal debt become so large? Wars, economic depressions or recessions, and the rapid expansion of military expenditures and social programs have been among the principal causes. The federal government's debt began during the American Revolution as the United States needed money to fight for its independence. However, the central government's debt was relatively insignificant until the Great Depression of the 1930s when the administration of President Franklin D. Roosevelt chose to borrow heavily to fund government programs and provide more jobs. Even so, the public debt amounted to scarcely more than $50 billion at the beginning of World War II. The public debt multiplied five times over during the war years, approaching $260 billion by the end of World War II.

EXHIBIT 19–5
The Public Debt of the United States, 2000 ($ Billions)

Sources: Board of Governors of the Federal Reserve and the U.S. Treasury Department.

Type of Securities	Amounts
Interest-bearing public debt	$5,618.1
Marketable debt	2,966.9
Bills	646.9
Notes	1,557.3
Bonds	626.5
Nonmarketable debt	2,651.2
State and local government series	151.0
Foreign issues	27.2
Savings bonds and notes	176.9
Government account series	2,266.1
Non-interest-bearing debt	44.2
Total gross public debt	$5,662.2

Note: Columns may not add to totals due to rounding.

Embroiled in the most destructive and costly war in history, the U.S. government borrowed resources from the private sector to build planes, ships, and other war materials in enormous quantities.

For a brief period following World War II, it appeared that much of the public debt might be repaid. However, the Korean War intervened in the early 1950s, followed by a series of deep recessions when government tax revenues declined. The advent of the Vietnam War and rapid inflation during the late 1960s and 1970s sent the debt soaring (see Exhibit 19–6). Between 1970 and 1980, the public debt of the United States more than doubled; it then tripled to more than $3 trillion during the 1980-1990 period. Between 1990 and 1999, the federal government's debt expanded again, this time by more than $2 trillion. However, the total debt of the United States government began to decline in fiscal 2000 as budget surpluses emerged and some government debt could be repaid. Lower interest rates on the federal debt, the end of the Cold War, and a long-term economic boom extending through much of the 1990s made it possible for the federal budget to approach a surplus position as the new century began—a true federal budget surplus for the first time since 1969. However, the new budget surplus was soon threatened by a new economic recession in 2001, made worse by the terrorist attacks, possibly throwing the United States' federal budget back into a deficit.

How much government debt is simply too much? Opinions vary greatly on the answer to this question. For example, James Madison, fourth president of the United States, once declared: "A public debt is a public curse." In contrast, Alexander Hamilton, the first U.S. Treasury Secretary under the Constitution, wrote: "A national debt, if it is not excessive, will be to us a national blessing." Who is right?

The answer depends, in part, on the standard used to gauge the size of the public debt. Measured against the national income (the earnings of individuals and businesses that can be taxed to repay the debt), the public debt is lower now than it was a generation ago. For example, in 2000, the gross public debt amounted to about 60 percent of the U.S. Gross Domestic Product (GDP), compared to well over 100 percent at the end of World War II. Moreover, other forms of debt in the U.S. economy total as much or more than the public debt. For example, total mortgage debt outstanding in 2000 was about $6.7 trillion and the combined debt of the private sector and state and local governments was almost double that of the federal government. It should be remembered that U.S. government securities are at one and the same time both debt obligations of the government and also highly desirable marketable, liquid assets to the millions of investors who hold them.

EXHIBIT 19–6

The Public Debt of the United States in Selected Years, 1950–2001 ($ Billions at Year-End)

Sources: Board of Governors of the Federal Reserve System and the U.S. Treasury Department.

Year	Total Gross Public Debt	Year	Total Gross Public Debt
1950	$225.4	1990	$3,364.8
1960	287.7	2000	5,662.2
1970	388.3	2001*	5,726.8
1980	930.2		

*As of second quarter of 2001.

Another issue to keep in mind about today's large federal debt and its possible burden on the economy and the financial marketplace concerns the difficulties we face in trying to accurately measure the true *size* of the debt. It turns out that the answer to the question— How big is the federal debt?—is not all that easy. For example, *inflation* increases the size of the debt because it tends to increase government deficits. In an inflationary period, the government typically must borrow more, but this does not necessarily mean that the burden of the debt has increased: government may not be exerting a greater impact on the economy. Moreover, the size of the public debt is typically measured in terms of the *par value* of government securities outstanding. But when interest rates rise, the *market value* of government debt falls. Thus, a significant rise in interest rates will cause the value of that portion of the government's debt held by private investors to decline.

Accurate measurement of the burden imposed by government debt also means that we must consider the value of the *assets* held by government. Most national governments hold a reserve of gold and foreign currencies. We might also add the estimated value of government buildings, military hardware, highways, and airports. Thus, we may distinguish between *gross liabilities* of the federal government and its *net liabilities*—government debt minus government assets. Including all of the government's assets at their fair market value would yield substantially smaller net government liabilities. Of course, to be fair, we also have to consider the amount of debt owed by off-budget federal agencies (such as the farm credit agencies or the federal mortgage agencies), which amounts to almost one-third of the gross public debt. And *contingent liabilities* might be added to the government's debt total, such as deposit insurance like that offered by the FDIC to guarantee bank deposits or the Social Security Fund which must eventually pay retirement benefits to millions of citizens. Clearly, measuring the true size of the government's debt is a difficult job. For this reason, we must be careful before jumping to any hasty conclusions about how large or significant the debt is or what its impact on the economy and financial markets might be.

The Composition of the Public Debt

The U.S. public debt as it is traditionally measured consists of a wide variety of government IOUs with differing maturities, interest rates, and other features. A small amount— less than 1 percent—carries no interest rate at all. This *non-interest-bearing debt* consists of paper currency and coins previously issued by the U.S. Treasury Department. However, virtually all paper money in circulation today is in Federal Reserve notes, which are not officially a part of the public debt but are obligations of the Federal Reserve banks.

More than 99 percent of all federal debt securities are *interest bearing* and may be divided into two broad groups: marketable securities and nonmarketable securities. By definition, *marketable securities* may be traded any number of times before they reach maturity. In contrast, *nonmarketable securities* must be held by the original purchaser until they mature or are redeemed by the Treasury. It is marketable debt that has the greatest impact on the cost and availability of credit in the money and capital markets, and it is these securities over which the Treasury exercises the greatest control.

Marketable Public Debt

The marketable public debt totaled almost $3 trillion in 2000, representing about two-thirds of all interest-bearing U.S. government obligations. The marketable public debt today is composed of just three types of securities: Treasury bills, notes, and bonds. By law, a U.S. Treasury bill must mature within one year. In contrast, U.S. Treasury notes range in original maturity from 1 to 10 years, and Treasury bonds may carry any maturity, although generally they have a maturity of more than 10 years.[1] With their greater liquidity and marketability, Treasury bills, notes, and bonds have been attractive savings outlets to investors for many years. Recently however, these types of securities have fallen somewhat in dollar amount due to the recent appearance of government budget surpluses, though a recession and terrorist attacks in 2001 threatened the continuation of budget surpluses and raised the prospect of more government deficits.

Nonmarketable Public Debt

The nonmarketable public debt consists mainly of Government Account series securities issued by the Treasury to various government agencies and trust funds (see again Exhibit 19–5). These agencies and trust funds include the Social Security Administration, the Tennessee Valley Authority, the Government National Mortgage Association, the Postal Service, and several smaller government agencies. As these governmental units accumulate funds, they turn them over to the Treasury in exchange for nonmarketable IOUs, thus reducing the federal government's borrowing activity in the open market. Another component of the nonmarketable debt is U.S. savings bonds sold to the general public in small denominations, which represent less than 5 percent of the public debt.

Holdings of U.S. dollars by foreign governments and foreign investors have remained at a relatively high level in recent years due to oil imports and the flow of U.S. capital to Europe, Asia, and the Middle East. Because large foreign holdings of dollars represent a constant threat to the value of the U.S. dollar in international markets, the Treasury periodically issues nonmarketable dollar-denominated securities to attract these foreign funds. To increase U.S. government holdings of foreign currencies that can be used to settle international claims, the Treasury can sell foreign-currency-denominated securities to investors abroad as well. The Treasury also issues special securities to state and local governments. These securities provide a temporary investment outlet for the funds raised by local governments when they borrow in the open market.

Investors in U.S. Government Securities

Who *holds* the public debt of the United States? Each month, the Treasury makes estimates of the distribution of its securities among various groups of investors, drawing on data

---

[1]Both Treasury notes and bonds bear interest at a fixed interest rate payable semiannually, while bills do not carry a fixed interest rate but earn price gains instead as their market price rises over time. Treasury bonds can carry a call option, allowing the Treasury to redeem them early provided the Treasury gives at least four months' notice (though the U.S. government has issued only noncallable securities since 1985). Notes and bonds are issued in multiples of $1,000 and $5,000 depending upon maturity. Bills are available in multiples of $1,000. Payment for purchases of new Treasuries generally must be made in cash, immediately available funds, the exchange of eligible securities, or by check to the Federal Reserve banks or the U.S. Treasury.

EXHIBIT 19–7
Investors in the U.S. Public Debt, 2000*
($ Billions at End of First Quarter)

Sources: Board of Governors of the Federal Reserve System and the U.S. Treasury Department.

Investor Group	Amount Held in 2000	Percent of Total Ownership
Federal government:		
U.S. government agencies and trust funds	$2,235.7	
Federal Reserve banks	511.4	
Total for federal government investors	$2,747.1	48.1%
Private investors:		
Depository institutions	$219.7	
Mutual funds	318.6	
Insurance companies	120.9	
Pension funds	384.5	
State and local governments	256.4	
Individuals:		
Savings bonds	184.7	
Foreign and international	1,225.2	
Other miscellaneous investors**	253.8	
Total for private investors	2,963.8	51.9
Total for all investor groups	$5,710.9	100.0%

*Figures are for third quarter of 2000.
**The miscellaneous investor group includes savings and loan associations, nonprofit institutions, credit unions, mutual savings banks, corporate pension funds, security dealers, and selected federal deposits and agencies.

supplied by the Federal Reserve banks, government agencies, and private trade organizations. The results from a recent Treasury ownership survey are shown in Exhibit 19–7.

It is evident from the survey that most Treasury debt—slightly more than half—is held by private individuals and institutions. Rather surprising to many observers, however, is the relatively large proportion of the federal government's debt—almost half—that is held by the government itself. For example, in 2000 U.S. government agencies and trust funds, including the Social Security Trust Fund and other federal departments, held about 40 percent of the total federal debt. In addition, the Federal Reserve banks held almost 10 percent of all public debt securities outstanding.

The sheer size of the government's holdings of its own debt is viewed with alarm by some analysts. A large volume of government debt held out of circulation in federal vaults tends to thin the market for government securities, reducing the volume of trading. Moreover, this problem of a more volatile public debt could be exacerbated by the recent movement of the federal government toward some budget surpluses, which can result in a gradually declining federal government debt, giving private investors and the Federal Reserve banks fewer sources of highly marketable, liquid securities to trade. Other factors held constant, interest rates and security prices become more volatile and unpredictable, discouraging investment. This could be critical, because the market for government securities is currently the anchor of the financial system.

Among private holders of the federal government's debt, pension funds, mutual funds, state and local governments, and individuals are at or near the top of the list. In 2000, for example, individual investors held about 3 percent of the public debt—the majority of these holdings in U.S. savings bonds. Pension funds held almost double this proportion at 6 percent, closely followed by mutual funds holding about 5.6 percent of all Treasury-issued securities.

The proportion of the U.S. public debt held by foreign investors, including foreign central banks, governments, and other international investors, has declined slightly in recent

According to a recent U.S. Treasury survey foreign investors held more than a trillion dollars in U.S. government securities of various kinds! Why are foreign and international investors such heavy buyers of United States government securities?

Part of the cause centers upon the decline of the public debt itself, as a portion of federal budget surpluses around the turn of the century were used to retire outstanding securities, increasing the relative importance of foreign debt holders. Another force has been U.S. trade deficits with Americans paying for what they buy abroad by contributing dollars and dollar-denominated securities to foreign companies and individuals.

Then, too, the United States appears to many foreigners to be a "safe haven" compared to many foreign markets.

Many overseas territories are often in turmoil with weaker economies and, in some cases, unstable governments. By way of contrast, American businesses, bank deposits, stocks, and bonds look like havens of safety as well as good sources of profitability.

This story is not all positive, however. Some analysts fear that certain foreign investors may be more "fickle" than domestic buyers of government securities. Any sign of trouble inside the United States may send many foreign investors racing for the exits, dumping Treasuries along the way. The result could be a sharp decline in the value of the dollar in international markets and an upsurge in the cost of borrowing money.

years to about one-fifth of all issues outstanding in 2000. Nevertheless, the foreign contingent of investors is still very important—they hold well over a trillion dollars in U.S. Treasuries!

The bulk of foreign holdings of U.S. securities seems to be centered in Great Britain and Japan. Foreign holdings of government securities result, in part, from a rise in U.S. imports that lead foreign investors to build up dollar deposits in banks abroad. These investors have converted many of their dollars into purchases of Treasury securities in the money market and into foreign-currency-denominated securities purchased directly from the U.S. Treasury. Foreign holdings of U.S. Treasury securities have remained relatively high recently due to the development of active over-the-counter markets for longer-term Treasuries in London, Tokyo, and other financial centers. These overseas U.S. Treasury security markets have given Treasuries round-the-clock liquidity and are especially attractive to such investors as multinational corporations and others who find U.S. trading hours inconvenient. In the interdealer market, trading in Treasury bills worldwide starts at a minimum size of about $5 million, while T-notes and bonds trade in units of a million dollars. Daily trading in the resale market averages well over $100 billion, carried out through hundreds of brokers and dealers. Trading centered in Tokyo and London appears to generate some new information that subsequently affects the main market in New York.

Questions *to Help You Study*

7. Please describe the principal types of securities that make up the *public debt* of the United States. What portions of this debt can the U.S. Treasury Department most closely control?

8. What problems exist when you try to measure the true *size* of the government's debt? Do you have any suggestions on how to deal with this measurement problem?

9. List the principal *holders* of the United States' public debt. What are some of the most important trends that seem to be under way in the ownership of federally issued securities?

Methods of Offering Treasury Securities

Management of the public debt is a complicated task. Treasury debt managers are called on continually to make decisions about raising new money and refunding maturing securities. They must decide what kinds of securities to issue, which maturities will appeal to investors, and the form in which an offering of securities should be made.

The Auction Method

Today, the **auction method** is the principal means of selling Treasury notes, bonds, and bills. Although several different methods have been used over time, all such techniques have a number of features in common. Both competitive and noncompetitive tenders for new securities, whose dollar amount and maturity are announced about one week in advance, are invited from the public. Competitive bidders usually include money center banks and securities houses. About 2000 security brokers and dealers are registered to trade in the U.S. government securities market. Noncompetitive bidders, including smaller financial institutions and individuals, number an average of 20,000 or more per Treasury auction. Noncompetitive bidders receive an allotment of securities at the average or prevailing auction price up to a maximum amount determined by the Treasury. As we have seen, federal agencies and trust funds purchase large amounts of Treasury issues. These agencies participate in virtually every auction but pay the price charged noncompetitive bidders. They receive a special allotment of securities in exchange for their maturing issues after the regular auction is concluded.

Types of Treasury Auctions

The Treasury has used several different auction methods over the years. Today, however, the auction method used most often for Treasury notes, bonds, and bills is known as a *yield auction.* The Treasury announces the amount of securities available and calls for yield bids accurate to three decimal places (e.g., 6.105%). Treasury bill bids must be based upon the discount rate (DR), discussed in Chapter 11. Investors submitting competitive bids for Treasury notes and bonds must express their offers on an annual percentage yield basis. Those bidding the lowest annual percentage yield (the highest price) normally will be awarded securities. Awards may continue to be made at successively higher yields (lower bid prices) until the issue is exhausted. Today, however, in what is called a *uniform price auction,* all successful bidders for federal government securities wind up paying *the same price*—the lowest price that ultimately clears the market of all available securities (the *stop-out price*).

As we saw earlier, the U.S. government began running budget surpluses after many years of deficits just as the twentieth century drew to a close and a new century began. Thus, instead of always holding auctions and inviting bids to sell new government securities, the Treasury began to hold "reverse auctions" in which security holders were asked to indicate the prices at which they wished to sell some of their security holdings back to the government. However, future Treasury "reverse auctions" may be less likely in the near future in the wake of the economic recession and terror attacks of 2001.

Marketing Techniques

The Treasury places new securities *directly* with the investing public. New Treasury bills, notes, and bonds can be bought directly from the Treasury Department or from the Treasury's agents—the Federal Reserve banks—either in person, by mail, or online. Competitive tender offers are accepted from private and government investors at the Federal Reserve banks until 1 P.M. Eastern Standard Time, the day the new securities are sold. Individuals may also file bids for new Treasury securities with the Bureau of Public Debt in

Washington, DC. Many investors place orders for new Treasury issues through a security broker or dealer, bank, or nonbank financial institution.

Book Entry

The marketable public debt is issued today only in **book-entry form.** This means that the investor does *not* receive an engraved certificate representing the Treasury's debt obligation but instead receives a statement of account. The investor's name and amount of securities purchased are recorded in an Account Master Record in the automated book-entry TREASURYDIRECT System maintained by the Bureau of the Public Debt or in what is called the *commercial book-entry system* maintained by financial institutions and government security brokers and dealers on behalf of their customers. Depository institutions are permitted to hold security safekeeping accounts at the Federal Reserve banks as part of the commercial book-entry system where their own security holdings and those of their customers are recorded. As interest is received or securities are sold or purchased, banks credit or debit their own or their customers' accounts and the TREASURYDIRECT System. Book entry is the safest form in which to hold any security because this method significantly reduces the risk of theft.

Other Services Offered Investors

To encourage greater participation in the government securities market and stimulate demand for new Treasury issues, both the Federal Reserve and the Treasury offer a number of other services to investors. For example, securities held in book-entry accounts at the Federal Reserve banks may be transferred by wire almost anywhere using the Fed's electronic wire transfer network. Interest and principal payments are electronically deposited on the due date into the deposit account each investor designates for that purpose. This device makes it easy to sell Treasury securities before maturity on a same-day basis.

Price Quotations on Treasury Securities

The widespread popularity of U.S. Treasury securities to investors around the world means that their prices and yields are closely watched every day. Newspapers carry price and yield information for Treasury bonds, notes, and bills, which usually include the following information:

Rate	Maturity	Bid	Asked	Change	Asked Yield
6½	Aug 05n	105:16	105:18	+13	5.73
9⅜	Feb 06	127:15	127:19	+16	5.75
11¾	Nov 09–14	153:26	153:30	+22	5.92

Treasury security prices and yields are available from many Web sites, including Bloomberg at *www.bloomberg.com* and the Bond Market Association at *www. investinginbonds.com*

We note from the preceding that Treasury securities are usually listed in order of the dates they will mature, from the most recent to the most distant maturities. The promised coupon rates are shown under the column marked *Rate.* Thus, in the list the first security, which matures in August 2005, promises a 6½ percent annual return, or $6.50 per year for each $100 in face value. The letter *n* next to the first entry indicates that the security in question is a Treasury note. The absence of *n* means that the security listed is a Treasury bond, as is the case with the 9⅜ and 11¾ percent bonds maturing in the years 2006 and from 2009 to 2114.

The *bid* price in the next column (expressed in dollars and 32nds of a dollar) is the price for which a dealer is willing to *buy* the security. For example, the August 2005 note has a bid price of $105¹⁶⁄₃₂, or $105.50 on a $100 basis. The *asked* price is the price the security's current holder (usually a security dealer) is willing to sell it for. Any investor interested in

For the first time in more than three decades the U.S. Government achieved a *budget surplus,* with the Treasury collecting more funds than it spent, as the twentieth century ended and a new century began. At that point a decision was made to begin repurchasing and retiring a portion of the U.S. government's marketable debt, which then totaled close to $3 trillion.

The Treasury's purchases of its own debt securities are called *reverse auctions.* In these invitations to holders of government securities the Treasury designates certain issues eligible for repurchasing. Usually the repurchased securities are relatively long-term obligations (for example, bonds maturing in 2019 through 2023).

Typically, more offers are submitted for Treasury repurchases than the Treasury is willing to accept, yielding what is known as the *offer-to-cover ratio*—an indicator of the financial marketplace's demand for Treasury repurchases. For example, if the Treasury received $8 billion in offers to sell back

its IOUs and it accepted just $2 billion of these offers from the public, the offer-to-cover ratio would be $8 billion/$2 billion or 4, suggesting a margin of excess demand.

The impact of the Treasury's buyback operations soon began to be felt in the money and capital markets. By the second quarter of 2001 the marketable public debt of the United States had declined by about $635 million from its level in 1997.

Many active marketmakers expressed concern that the liquidity and marketability of the public debt would be severely damaged as a result of Treasury reverse auctions, forcing traders to look for a new financial instrument to buy and sell. However, some of these fears may have been alleviated as a result of the unfortunate events of 2001 when terrorism and an economic recession in the United States forced extra government spending, eroding a substantial portion and perhaps eliminating the government's budget surplus.

purchasing the security in question will probably seek to buy it for a price somewhere between the current bid and asked prices. The column labeled *Change* indicates the change in bid price between yesterday's closing price and the day before's closing price, expressed in 32nds of a dollar. Thus, a change of +13 indicates a price rise yesterday of $^{13}/_{32}$ of a dollar, or $0.40625 per $100 par value security. The yield to maturity the purchaser would receive if he or she bought the security at yesterday's asked price is shown in the last column. For example, if the August 2005 note were purchased for 105:18, the investor buying at this price and holding the bond to its maturity date in August 2005 would receive a yield of 5.73 percent. Trading in new Treasury securities begins in the "when-issued" market several days before the new securities actually are issued and right after the Treasury releases information on the forthcoming auction date and the amount to be issued.

The Goals of Federal Debt Management

Over the years, the Treasury has pursued several different goals in the management of the public debt. These goals may be divided into two broad groups: (1) *housekeeping goals,* which pertain to the cost and composition of the public debt; and (2) *stabilization goals,* which have to do with the impact of the debt on the economy and the financial markets.

Minimize Interest Costs

The most important housekeeping goal is to keep the interest burden of the public debt as low as possible. The Treasury has not always been successful in the pursuit of this goal, however. Today, the interest burden of the public debt is the fourth largest category of federal expenditures after welfare payments, Social Security payments, and national defense. This interest burden on the U.S. taxpayer increases when interest rates rise or the volume of debt increases faster than the nation's income.

Reduce the Frequency of Refundings

The Treasury also tries to minimize the number of trips it must make to market to refund old securities or issue new ones. This housekeeping goal is particularly important to the Federal Reserve's conduct of monetary policy.

Frequently in the past, the Fed has followed a loosely defined policy known as *even keel* when the Treasury is in the market offering a substantial volume of notes or bonds. Even-keel policy calls for the Fed to exert a *steadying* influence on the financial markets, making sure that security trading is orderly and changes in interest rates are moderate. In principle, even-keel policy protects the Treasury's financing operations from catastrophic failure, as might occur if security prices plunged at the time of a Treasury refunding, but it can limit the Fed's freedom of action.

Economic Stabilization

A much broader goal of debt management is to stabilize the economy, promoting high employment and sustainable growth while avoiding rampant inflation. In strict terms, this would involve issuing *long-term* Treasury securities in a period of *economic expansion* and issuing *short-term* securities in a period of *recession.* The long-term securities would tend to increase long-term interest rates and therefore act as a brake on private investment spending, slowing the economy down. On the other hand, issuing short-term securities during a recession may take the pressure off long-term interest rates and avoid discouraging investment spending that is needed to provide jobs.

Unfortunately, the goal of economic stabilization often conflicts with other debt management goals, particularly the goal of minimizing the interest burden of the debt. If the Treasury sells short-term securities in a period of expansion when interest rates are high and then rolls over those short-term securities into long-term bonds during a recession when rates are low, this strategy tends to minimize the debt's average interest cost. The Treasury is able to lock in cheap long-term rates. From a stabilization point of view, however, this is exactly the wrong thing to do. The short-term debt may fuel inflation during an economic expansion; long-term debt issued during a recession may drive up interest rates and reduce private investment. Treasury debt managers are confronted with tough choices among conflicting goals.

The Impact of Federal Debt Management on the Financial Markets and the Economy

What effect do Treasury debt management activities have on the financial markets and the economy? This is a subject of heated debate among financial analysts. Most experts agree that in the short run, the financial markets become more agitated and interest rates tend to rise when the Treasury is borrowing, especially when *new money* is involved. A mere exchange of new for old securities usually has minimal effects, however, unless the offering is very large.

The longer-run impact of Treasury debt management operations is less clear. Certainly the *liquidity* of the public's portfolio of securities changes. For example, suppose $10 billion in Treasury bonds are maturing next month. Treasury debt managers decide to offer investors $10 billion in 10-year notes in exchange for the maturing bonds. The bonds, regardless of what their original maturity might have been, are now short-term securities (with one-month maturities). If investors accept the new 10-year notes in exchange for the one-month bonds, the average maturity of the public's security holdings obviously has lengthened, all else being equal. Longer-term securities, as a rule, are less liquid than shorter-term securities.

Will this reduction in public liquidity affect spending habits and interest rates? The research evidence on this question is conflicting, with many studies finding little effect from debt management activities. However, there is some evidence that *lengthening debt maturities* increases the public's demand for money and *raises interest rates.* In contrast, if the

Treasury offers shorter-term securities, this tends to make the public's portfolio of securities more liquid and may reduce the demand for money. The result would be an increase in spending for goods and services and, for a time, *lower* interest rates.

Still another possible debt management impact is on the *shape of the yield curve*. *Lengthening* the average maturity of the debt tends to increase long-term interest rates relative to short rates. The yield curve assumes a *steeper positive slope,* favoring short-term investment over long-term investment. On the other hand, *shortening* the debt's maturity tends to reduce longer-term interest rates and raise short-term rates. The yield curve tends to *flatten out, i*f positively sloped, or even turn down, favoring long-term investment over short-term investment. The net impact on total investment spending would depend on whether private investment is more responsive to short-term interest rates or long-term interest rates.

On balance, most authorities are convinced that the debt management activities of the Treasury do *not* have a major impact on economic conditions. The effects of debt management operations appear to be secondary compared to the powerful impact of monetary and fiscal policy on the economy and financial markets. The optimal policy is probably one that makes Treasury refunding operations as unobtrusive as possible, especially when these operations might interfere with the monetary policy activities of the central bank. Nevertheless, debt management represents yet another policy tool that can be used by government in the face of serious economic problems.

Questions *to Help You Study*

10. Please describe the current auction method or methods for selling U.S. Treasury securities.

11. What are *reverse auctions?* Why are they relatively rare?

12. List the principal *goals* of Treasury debt management. What is the essential difference between housekeeping goals and stabilization goals? To what extent could these goals conflict with each other?

13. Please explain how changes in the maturity structure of the public debt can affect interest rates, the yield curve, and spending and saving in the economy.

Summary of the Chapter

In this chapter, we examined the many roles played by the Treasury Department in financing federal expenditures and managing the public debt of the United States.

- The federal government affects the financial system and the economy through its taxing and spending activities which are known as *fiscal policy.*

- The government can also set in motion changes in the financial system (particularly in interest rates and the volume of credit) and changes in the economy through *debt management policy* which involves changing the mix or composition of the government's debt (e.g., changes in the ratio of short-term to long-term securities outstanding).

- When the government increases its borrowing and spending activity interest rates tend to rise. Income and spending also tend to move higher unless the central bank offsets the government's *fiscal policy* action. The money supply will tend to rise, resulting in interest rates falling at least for a time. Should inflation subsequently pick up, however, interest rates may rise again as nominal interest rates move higher to reflect additional expected inflationary pressures.

- Should the government run a *budget surplus* and, therefore, need to borrow less money, interest rates would tend to decline as will income and spending in the economy. If the budget surplus is relatively large, a substantial portion of that surplus may be used to retire outstanding government debt. Not only will income and market interest rates tend to fall, but so will the nation's money supply unless the central bank acts to offset the impact of the government's debt retirement program. Inflation may be lessened, but unemployment may rise.

- The government can also use *debt management policy* to change conditions in the financial markets and the economy. For example, suppose the Treasury refunds maturing short-term securities with new long-term securities. This action will tend to reduce the liquidity of the public's security holdings. Interest rates would tend to rise, while income (spending and production) and employment would tend to fall. Long-term government borrowing, therefore, tends to slow the economy's growth rate and reduce inflationary pressures.

- In contrast, a government policy that emphasizes short-term borrowing often leads to rapid economic expansion and less unemployment. However, these benefits of a short-term debt policy are sometimes purchased at the price of greater inflation and, therefore, higher interest rates eventually.

- Fiscal policy and debt management policy, like central bank monetary policy, focus upon promoting full employment and economic growth and in keeping inflation under control. But these different forms of public policy must be coordinated for maximum effectiveness; otherwise, they may offset each other with little positive impact.

Key Terms

Fiscal policy, *539*
Debt management policy, *540*
Budget deficit, *540*

Budget surplus, *540*
Public debt, *550*
Auction method, *556*

Book-entry form, *557*

Problems

1. Due to an unexpected decline in federal income tax collections, the Treasury is compelled to borrow an extra $40 billion to cover planned expenditures in the current government budget. Using T accounts discussed in this chapter, trace through the likely effects of this additional borrowing on the financial markets and on the economy. Assume that 50 percent of the securities to be issued will be absorbed by nonbank institutions and private individuals and 50 percent by depository institutions. How would your analysis change if the economy were at full employment?

2. Due to drastic cuts in federal spending and strong economic growth, it now appears that the federal government will experience a $10 billion budget surplus during the current fiscal year. If the Treasury plans to retain $2 billion of this surplus in its cash account at the Federal Reserve and to use the balance to retire $5 billion in government securities held by depository institutions and $3 billion held by the general public, use T accounts to show the effects of this debt retirement operation.

3. Suppose the U.S. federal government's revenues and expenditure accounts displayed the amounts shown in this fiscal year (each item in billions of U.S. dollars):

Social Security benefits	$400	Social insurance	$600
Individual income tax collections	850	taxes & contributions	
National defense	275	International affairs	20
Net interest payments		Corporate income taxes	200
on the federal debt	250	Health care and Medicare	350
Miscellaneous revenue sources	160	Miscellaneous expenditures	220
Income security programs	260		

What were the government's total revenues and expenditures in the most recent fiscal year? Was the budget in surplus or deficit? All other factors held constant, what is likely to happen to the economy's level of income and interest rates as a result of this year's government budget position? Please explain the reasoning behind your answer to this last question.

4. Suppose the public debt of the United States consisted of the following types of security issues (all figures in billions of dollars):

Treasury bills	$ 750
Savings bonds and notes	180
Government account series	1,500
Federal government currency	6
Treasury bonds	600
Special notes issued to foreign investors	45
Treasury notes	2,200
Special bonds and notes sold to states and local governments	165

Please calculate the following: the total marketable debt, the total nonmarketable debt, the total interest-bearing debt, and the gross public debt.

5. Please identify each of the key terms or concepts listed below and discussed in this chapter.
   a. The taxing and spending activities carried out by the government in order to achieve the nation's economic goals.
   b. Activities of the government's Treasury Department that consist of refunding and refinancing the government's debt.
   c. Volume of debt obligations that are the responsibility of the government and, therefore, its taxpayers.
   d. Method by which marketable U.S. Treasury securities are issued and sold.
   e. Portion of the government debt that is actively traded each day.
   f. A government budget position that tends to expand economic activity and may necessitate the borrowing of money to sustain that position.
   g. A government budget position in which collections from taxpayers exceed aggregate government spending.
   h. The term most often used to label the longest-term government securities issued.
   i. A term most often used for medium-term (or intermediate term) government securities.
   j. The shortest-term government securities sold to the public are usually labeled with this term.

Questions about the Web and the Money and Capital Markets

1. According to the Web what different roles does the U.S. Treasury Department perform?
2. Where could you find information on the Web concerning the impact of *fiscal policy* upon the economy and interest rates?
3. According to the Web what types of U.S. Treasury securities are currently available for purchase by the public?
4. What impact does *debt management* have on the economy and the financial markets according to various foreign and domestic sites on the World Wide Web?

Selected References

Board of Governors of the Federal Reserve System. *Federal Reserve Bulletin,* Washington, DC, selected monthly issues.

Daniel, Betty C. "Fiscal Policy and Inflation." *FRBSF Economic Letter,* Federal Reserve Bank of San Francisco, July 13, 2001.

DuPont, Dominique, and Brian Sack. "The Treasury Securities Market: Overview and Recent Developments." *Federal Reserve Bulletin,* December 1999, pp. 785–806.

Fleming, Michael J. "The Round the Clock Market for U.S. Treasury Securities." *Economic Policy Review.* Federal Reserve Bank of New York, July 1997, pp. 9–31.

Gokhale, Jaagadeesh. "Fiscal Policy in an Era of Surpluses." *Economic Commentary,* Federal Reserve Bank of Cleveland, April 15, 2001.

Viard, Alan D. "The Federal Budget: What a Difference a Year Makes." *Southwest Economy,* Federal Reserve Bank of Dallas, January/February 2002, pp. 1, 6–10.

Chapter **Twenty**

State and Local Governments in the Financial Markets

Learning Objectives in This Chapter

- You will explore the various ways in which state, county, city, and other local units of government raise the funds needed to supply government services to the public.

- You will come to understand why state and local government borrowing has grown so rapidly in recent years and why rapid growth in the future is likely.

- You will be able to describe the different instruments that state and local governments use to raise money and why these instruments are attractive to millions of investors.

- You will examine the marketing process through which state and local government bonds and notes reach the hands of investors.

What's in This Chapter? Key Topics Outline

Why State and Local Government Debt Is Growing

Local Governments' Revenues and Expenditures

Privatization and Devolution

Motivations for Borrowing in the Financial Markets

Types of Securities Issued by State and Local Governments

The Key Features of Municipal Debt

Credit Ratings and Defaults

Insurance and Serialization

Marketing through Dealers

The Outlook for State and Local Governments

INTRODUCTION

The borrowing and spending activities of state and local governments have been one of the most dynamic, rapidly growing segments of the financial system in recent years. Pressured by rising populations and inflated costs, states, counties, cities, school districts, and other local units of government have been forced to borrow in growing numbers to meet increased demands for their services. As we will see later in this chapter, the volume of state and local government debt has more than doubled over the past decade.

Despite the rapid growth in borrowing by state and local governments, many investors consider state and local debt obligations a highly desirable investment medium due to their high quality, ready marketability, and tax exemption feature. The interest income generated by state and local securities is exempt from federal income taxes, and most states exempt their own securities from state income taxes. As a result, these high-quality debt obligations—known as **municipals**—appeal to heavily taxed investors such as top-income-bracket individuals and large corporations. In addition, an active secondary market permits the early resale of many higher-quality state and local government bonds.

GROWTH OF STATE AND LOCAL GOVERNMENT BORROWING

The rapid growth of state and local government borrowing is reflected in Exhibit 20–1, which shows the total volume of municipal securities outstanding between the years 1940 and 2001. State and local government indebtedness grew slowly until the 1950s, when it nearly tripled. The volume of municipal debt doubled again during the 1960s and more than doubled during the 1970s and 1980s. By 2000, state and local debt outstanding had climbed to well over a trillion dollars.

What factors account for this strong record of growth in municipal borrowing? *Rapid population* and *income growth* are two of the most important causes. The U.S. population rose from less than 132 million in 1940 to an estimated 280 million by the beginning of the twenty-first century—a gain of nearly 150 million people. Rapid population growth implies that many local government services, such as schools, highways, and fire protection, must also expand rapidly. Tax revenues cannot provide all of the monies needed to fund these facilities and services.

Another factor pushing state and local borrowing higher is the *uneven distribution of population growth across the nation.* Beginning in the 1950s, a massive shift of the U.S. population out of the central cities into suburban areas began to take place. This demographic change was augmented during the 1970s, 1980s and 1990s by a movement of population and industry into small towns and rural areas to escape the social and environmental

EXHIBIT 20–1

Total Debt Issued by State and Local Governments in the United States, 1940–2001 ($Billions)

Year	Debt Outstanding at Year-End	Year	Debt Outstanding at Year-End
1940	$ 20.3	1980	$ 302.8
1950	24.1	1990	848.6
1960	70.8	2000	1,270.6
1970	145.5	2001*	1,331.7

*Figure as of the third quarter of 2001.

Sources: U.S. Department of Commerce: Board of Governors of the Federal System, *Flow of Funds: Assets and Liabilities Outstanding* and the *Federal Reserve Bulletin,* selected issues.

State and local government activity in the financial markets has become a popular topic on the World Wide Web. Thousands of investors rely on this particular securities market for income, especially during their retirement years. Moreover, high-tax-bracket investors in almost any adult age group seek out municipal securities to shield them from greater income tax exposure. Thus, there is keen and continuing interest in the performance of the state and local government securities marketplace.

One of the most effective ways to follow the municipal market is through the Web sites of established dealer firms. Examples include the Internet sites maintained by John Nuveen & Co., Stoever Glass & Co., Delphis Hanover, and Merrill Lynch. Active investors like to research changing conditions in the municipal market through such Web sites as Investor's Guide to Muni's at *www.investinginbonds.com*. A look at broader trends affecting state and local governmental units and their marketplace can be found at State and Local Governments on the Net at *www.piperinfo.com* and through the U.S. Census Bureau at *www.census.gov*.

problems of urban living, and toward the western and southern states in search of a warmer climate and new business opportunities. Smaller outlying communities were transformed into cities with a corresponding need for new streets, schools, airports, and freeways to commute back to the central cities for work, recreation, and shopping. The result was an upsurge in borrowing by existing local units of government and the creation of thousands of *new* borrowing units in the form of sewer and lighting districts, power and water authorities, airport and toll-road boards, and public housing authorities. Today, the United States has more than 83,000 state, county, municipal, and other units of local government. And the majority of them have the authority to issue debt, although most have constitutional prohibitions against budget deficits or limits on how much they can borrow.

Accompanying the growth and shift of the U.S. population has come an *upgrading of citizens' expectations* concerning the quality of government services. We expect much more from government today than we did a generation ago. Particularly noticeable is an increased demand for government services that directly affect the quality of life, such as better-designed schools, and improved medical and health care facilities. Instead of gravel roads and narrow highways, local citizens demand paved and guttered streets and all-weather, controlled-access highways. Many municipal governments are active in providing cultural facilities, such as libraries and museums, and are expected to play leading roles in controlling environmental pollution.

All of these public demands have had to be financed in an era of rising construction and labor costs, exacerbating the money burdens of local governments. Moreover, in the early 1990s, many local governments were faced with sluggish economic growth and the loss of a tax base upon which to build for the future, though later during the 1990s economic growth accelerated and many state and local governments racked up sizable budget surpluses until the terrorist crisis in 2001. State and local governments are expected to continue to borrow heavily in future years, in part because the federal government seems intent on reducing its contributions to local funding and because of expected lower interest rates. In fact, the so-called "new federalism" marks an ongoing trend toward turning more and more social services over to the states to fund and manage. The states, in turn, seem to be passing more program responsibilities on to counties, cities, and other local governmental units, putting additional financial stress on these smallest units of government.

SOURCES OF REVENUE FOR STATE AND LOCAL GOVERNMENTS

Borrowing by state and local governments supplements their tax revenues and income from fees charged to users of government services. When tax and fee revenues fail to grow as fast as public demands, municipal borrowings rise. Moreover, when long-term capital projects are undertaken, long-term borrowing rather than taxation is the preferred method of governmental finance.

As we study state and local governmental borrowing in the financial markets, it is useful to have in mind the principal sources and uses of state and local funds. Where do the majority of state and local government revenues come from? And where does most of the money go? Exhibits 20–2 and 20–3, drawn from a recent census of state and local units of government, provide some answers to these questions.

As expected, most state and local government *revenues* are derived from *local* sources of funds: the citizens these governments serve. About four-fifths of state and local government revenues normally are derived from local sources, according to a U.S. Department of Commerce census. However, intergovernmental transfers of funds, including state aid to local schools and federal aid to the states, also provide a significant share of total revenues, but such intergovernmental transfers have declined in recent years, particularly because the federal government is transferring more social programs to the states. Local governments, however, still receive about a third of their revenues from state governments, on average.

Not surprisingly, *taxes* are the largest single revenue source for state and local governments. Property taxes are the mainstay of *local* government support, providing just over one-quarter of general revenues, followed by sales taxes. *State* governments, in contrast, rely principally upon sales and income taxes, each accounting for about 15 percent of state revenues. Selective sales taxes on alcoholic beverages, entertainment, gasoline, tobacco, and other specialized products and services are levied almost entirely at the state level and

EXHIBIT 20–2 Sources of Revenue and Expenditures for State and Local Governments ($ Billions for Fiscal 1996–1997)

Revenue Sources:	Amounts	Percentage of Total	Expenditures by Function:	Amounts	Percentage of Total
Property taxes	$218.8	17.0%	Education	$419.1	33.5%
Sales and gross receipts taxes	261.7	20.3	Highways	82.1	6.6
Individual income taxes	159.1	12.3	Public welfare		
Corporate profits taxes	33.8	2.6	spending	203.8	16.3
Revenue from the federal government	244.6	19.0	All other state and local government spending (including expenses for		
All other sources of revenue (including user fees and miscellaneous general revenues)	371.2	28.8	public safety, housing, environmental cleanup and pollution prevention, administration, interest on debt and general and miscellaneous expenditures)	546.4	43.7
Total revenues	$1,289.2	100.0%	Total expenditures	$1,251.3	100.0%

Source: Economic Report of the President, February 1998.

EXHIBIT 20–3
State and Local Government Finances: Major Cash Inflows and Outflows

Source: U.S. Bureau of the Census, *Census of Governments.*

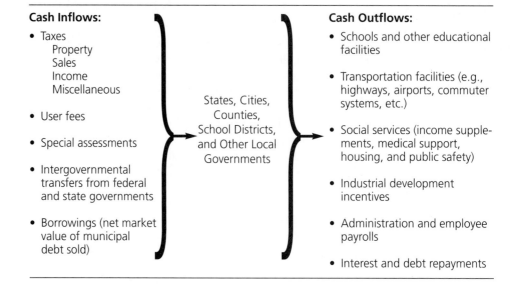

Cash Inflows:

- Taxes
    Property
    Sales
    Income
    Miscellaneous

- User fees

- Special assessments

- Intergovernmental transfers from federal and state governments

- Borrowings (net market value of municipal debt sold)

States, Cities, Counties, School Districts, and Other Local Governments

Cash Outflows:

- Schools and other educational facilities

- Transportation facilities (e.g., highways, airports, commuter systems, etc.)

- Social services (income supplements, medical support, housing, and public safety)

- Industrial development incentives

- Administration and employee payrolls

- Interest and debt repayments

have increased significantly in recent years. User fees have also grown rapidly, with more than three-quarters of U.S. cities and counties increasing their charges and fees for government services and for access to public facilities in recent years. Income taxes are imposed almost exclusively at the state level and are levied mainly against individuals rather than corporations. Income taxes contribute about one-fifth of state government revenues. In the mid-1990s, many states moved to reduce taxes due to improved revenue growth and a more conservative electorate, only to face serious revenue shortages again following the terrorist crisis in the fall of 2001.

Not shown separately in Exhibits 20–2 and 20–3 is the growing use of lotteries and taxation of gambling that close to 40 states have either set in motion or are seriously considering. State-run lotteries often dedicate net revenues from ticket sales to the support of a specific government service, such as education, which the public seems anxious to support. Lotteries have become a popular alternative to higher taxes or to slicing government services because they are a voluntary form of taxation, but they incur high administrative costs and usually contribute only a small portion of needed funds.

State and Local Government Expenditures

Trends in state and local government spending for a single state can usually be dialed up by visiting an individual state's Web site—for example, for the state of Minnesota use *www. auditor.leg.state.mn.us*

Where do state and local governments *spend* most of their funds? As Exhibit 20–2 suggests, *education* is the single largest item on the budgets of local governmental units and usually ranks number one or two on state budgets as well. *Social services,* including public welfare and medical care, occupies second place in local government spending but often ranks first in some state budgets at about a quarter of total spending. *Transportation services,* especially highway construction and maintenance, ranked third in state spending and sixth for local governments. Overall, education, Medicare and general health care, public welfare, highway construction, sanitation, and correctional facilities represent close to two-thirds of state and local government spending today.

Some of the most important government services account for only a minor share of annual public budgets. For example, the cost of ensuring public safety—police and fire protection—generally accounts for less than 10 percent of local government expenditures, although recently expenditures for police departments and jail facilities have taken up an increased share of all local spending. Sewer and sanitation services, protection of the

Financial Developments State and Local Government Revenues Are Sensitive to the Economy

Governments must carefully monitor the economy because changing economic conditions can have a profound impact on how much any unit of government will be able to collect in tax revenues and service fees and, therefore, whether a unit of government will experience a budget surplus or a budget deficit. State and local governments are certainly no exception to this rule because so much of their revenue comes from taxing consumer income and business sales, which fluctuate significantly with changing economic conditions.

A prime example occurred as the twenty-first century opened. A soft economy with rising unemployment and numerous business and household bankruptcies led to declining state revenues and tightening budgets. The situation was made worse by terrorism in the fall of 2001 and negatively impacted business and consumer spending. State budget surpluses, which had built up to unprecedented levels during the long expansion of the 1990s, suddenly decreased by the greatest margin in more than two decades.

Some states, like Arizona and New Hampshire, fought back by raising taxes. However this strategy can sometimes backfire as higher taxes depress economic activity even further. Most states simply halted or scaled back their planned building programs and some were forced to make cutbacks in their largest programs—education and health insurance. Still, because the economy was strong through most of the decade of the 1990s, more than three dozen states reported holdings of emergency cash reserves equal to 5 percent or more of their total annual spending. These states had acted wisely in managing their budgets and had stashed away substantial savings to prepare for the "rainy day" that struck as the new century opened and a global struggle against terrorism began to unfold.

Financial planners and treasurers for state and local governments must monitor changing economic conditions and be prepared to make budget adjustments and draft new plans when old budgets no longer match what reality has brought to their doorstep.

The economic condition of states, metropolitan areas, and counties may be traced through a new FDIC Web site called RECON at *www.fdic.gov*

Data revealing the fiscal condition of state and local governments in the United States is readily available through a key Web site of the U.S. Bureau of Economic Analysis at *www.bea.doc.gov*

environment, and housing programs to aid the poor normally represent about 10 percent of local government costs, but a much smaller share of state government spending.

State and local government expenditures have grown rapidly in recent years. In 1997, expenditures by state and local units topped the $1¼ trillion level. This figure was five times larger than the level of state and local government spending in 1980. Local tax revenues have simply been inadequate to handle this kind of growth in current (short-term) and capital (long-term) expenditures. Moreover, there is a growing perception that many municipal facilities need modernizing. Accordingly, borrowing in the money and capital markets against future government revenues in order to accommodate local needs for renovation, modernization, and expansion of facilities has soared. In the 1990s, several states (led by New York) began aggressive infrastructure spending programs to create more jobs, taking over a portion of the fiscal function that traditionally has been the province of the federal government, and in the late 1990s into the turn of the new century, the federal government began to pass a bigger share of welfare and social programs back to the states.

State and local governments experienced a marked upward surge in revenues and most had substantial surpluses as the 1990s drew to a close and the twenty-first century began. In 1998, for example, the 50 states closed that fiscal year with a combined surplus of close to $25 billion, or about 6 percent of their annual expenses, even after several had made tax cuts in 1996 and 1997. Even New York City—with a long history of financial troubles—achieved a budget surplus of nearly $2 billion in 1998. Indeed, some states did so well with an expanding economy and rising tax collections that they were debating whether or not to award rebates to their taxpayers or whether to retire debt or to expand their savings to deal with possible future emergencies. Some state governments decided to conserve their budget surpluses in order to protect their bond ratings and, thus, keep future borrowing costs as low as possible.

Management Insight   Privatization of Government Services

The 1980s and 1990s ushered in a strong movement toward *privatization*—that is, letting privately owned businesses produce and offer some local government services. Among the most common government services turned over to private suppliers in recent years have been the following:

Hospitals	Sewer systems
Landfills	Natural gas retail
Stadiums, auditoriums,	services
convention centers,	Water supplies
and other	Electric power services
recreational facilities	Fire protection
Airports	Libraries
Public transportation	Prisons and other
systems	correctional facilities

By 1987, when the first census of U.S. governments to inquire about privatization took place, almost 40 percent of all cities and towns with populations of at least 25,000 had contracted out to a private business at least one former government-provided service. By the 1992 government census, the percentage of cities and towns over 25,000 in population with at least some privatized services had jumped to 47 percent. Many state and local officials have seen privatization as a way to lower the cost of government, promote greater efficiency, and reduce taxes to their citizens. The theory is that private competition replacing government monopolies should improve both service quality and cost. Some local governments see the private sourcing route as a way to offer services—stadiums or utilities, for example—that the local area could not otherwise afford to offer.

Whatever the motivations have been, the privatization trend lost much of its steam in the late 1990s as the new century approached. No one knows for sure why this has occurred most recently, but it seems clear that only a fraction of cities and towns previously involved in private outsourcing appear to still be doing so. One reason may be resistance from local government workers who fear loss of their jobs. Moreover, private production of government services seems to be more seriously considered when a local community is facing a fiscal crisis and needs to stop providing some of its more costly services. However, when times improve, fewer local governments seem to be as interested in the privatization of services route.

Then, in the year 2000 an economic slowdown began, with an actual decline in economic activity in 2001, following the terrorist attacks in September of that year. State and local sales and income tax revenues sagged for many states while the cost of social programs and of providing protection against possible future terrorism soared. Many states were forced to dip deeply into their previously accumulated surpluses and others raised taxes in an attempt to cover their cash shortages.

The fiscal situation at the local level—cities, counties, and school districts—is often less "rosy" than for many states due to pressure from citizens for lower taxes and the prospect of cutbacks in federal financial aid. Many local governments face populations of jail inmates, school-age children, and indigent individuals and families who need subsidized housing and health care. Added to these fiscal problems are many government employee retirement funds that are not yet fully funded, requiring local governments to set aside more funds or even borrow using pension-obligation bonds to insure that their employees receive the pensions they have been promised.

MOTIVATIONS FOR STATE AND LOCAL GOVERNMENT BORROWING

State and local governments borrow money for several reasons. The first is to *satisfy short-term cash needs;* that is, meet payrolls, make repairs, purchase supplies, cover fuel costs, and maintain adequate levels of working capital. Most state and local governments use tax-anticipation notes (to be discussed later) and other forms of short-term borrowing as a supplement to tax revenues to meet these immediate cash needs. Frequently, the construction phase of a building project is financed from short-term funds, and then permanent financing is obtained by selling long-term bonds.

The second major reason for state and local government borrowing is to *finance long-term capital investment;* that is, to build schools, highways, and similar permanent facilities. Long-term projects of this sort account for the bulk of all municipal securities issued each year. Some governmental units try to anticipate future financial needs by borrowing when interest rates are low even though project construction will not begin for a substantial period of time. Funds raised through anticipatory borrowing are then "warehoused" in various investments (such as Treasury bills and notes) until actual construction begins.

In recent years, local governments have occasionally employed *advance refunding* of securities. Advance refundings occur when a governmental unit has been granted a higher credit rating on its bonds by a rating agency, such as Moody's Investors Service or Standard & Poor's Corporation. Bonds issued previously with lower credit ratings (higher interest rates) are called in, and new securities are issued at lower cost. Any significant decline in market interest rates usually gives rise to more advance refunding activity by state and local governments—a practice that has sometimes led to alleged "pay to play" activities in which security underwriters have tried to persuade local government officials (by making contributions to local political campaigns) to refund outstanding debt and thereby generate more underwriting fees.

Questions *to Help You Study*

1. The market for state and local government bonds and notes has been among the most rapidly growing financial markets over the past half century. Why has this growth occurred?

2. Can you foresee any serious problems on the horizon as state and local governments work to deal with the rapid growth of public demands on their budgets?

3. What are the principal sources of *revenue* for state and local governments today? Where do they spend the bulk of their incoming funds?

4. For what principal reasons do state and local governments borrow money?

5. Why is the economy of special importance to state and local governments in planning their revenues and expenditures?

TYPES OF SECURITIES ISSUED BY STATE AND LOCAL GOVERNMENTS

Many different types of securities are issued by state and local governments, and the variety of municipal securities available to investors is expanding rapidly. (See, for example, Exhibit 20–4.) One useful distinction is between short-term securities, which are generally issued to provide working capital, and long-term securities, used mainly to fund capital projects (such as the construction of new buildings or highways).

Short-Term Securities

The most popular short-term securities issued by state and local governments are **tax-anticipation notes (TANs), revenue-anticipation notes (RANs),** and **bond-anticipation notes (BANs).**

Tax-Anticipation and Revenue-Anticipation Notes

These notes are used to attract funds in lieu of tax receipts or other revenues expected to be received in the near future. Governments, like businesses and households, have a daily need for cash to meet payrolls and purchase supplies. However, funds raised through taxes

EXHIBIT 20–4
New Security Issues of Tax-Exempt State and Local Governments, 2000 ($ Billions)

Source: Board of Governors of the Federal Reserve System, *Federal Reserve Bulletin*, selected issues.

Types of Issue and Issuer or Use of Funds	2000	Use of Funds	2000
All issues	$180.4	Use of proceeds from new capital issues:	
Type of issue:			
General obligation	64.5	Education	$38.7
Revenue	115.9	Transportation	19.7
Type of issuer		Utilities and conservation	11.9
State governments	19.9	Social welfare	NA
Special districts	111.7	Industrial aid	7.1
Municipalities, counties and townships	39.3	Other purposes	47.3
Issues for new capital, total	154.3		

Note: Issues represented in the table are to raise new capital and refund outstanding debt.

usually flow in only at certain times of the year. To satisfy their continuing need for cash between tax dates, state and local governments issue short-term notes with maturities ranging from a few days to a few months. Most of these short-term issues are acquired by local banks. When tax funds are received, the issuing government pays off the note holders and retires any outstanding securities.

Bond-Anticipation Notes

These short-term IOUs, also called *BANs,* are used to provide temporary financing of a long-term project until the time is right to sell long-term bonds. A school district, for example, may need to start construction on new school facilities due to pressure from rising enrollments. If market interest rates currently are too high to permit the issue of bonds, then construction can start from funds raised from bond-anticipation notes. Once the project is under way and interest rates decline to more modest levels, the school district then sells its long-term bonds and retires the bond-anticipation notes.

Long-Term Securities

The most common type of municipal borrowing is through long-term bonds. There are two major types of municipal bonds issued today—**general obligation bonds** and **revenue bonds**—and both are used principally to finance construction.

General Obligation Bonds

These bonds, known as *GOs,* are the most secure form of municipal borrowing from the standpoint of the investor because they are backed by the "full faith and credit" of the issuing government and may be paid from *any* revenue source. State, county, and city governments, along with school districts, have the power to tax citizens to meet principal and interest payments on any debt issued. GOs are fully backed by this taxing power and often must be approved by public referendum before issue. The quality or level of risk of GOs depends on the economic base (income and property values) of local communities and the total amount of debt issued.

Revenue Bonds

In contrast, *revenue bonds* are payable only from a specified source of revenue, such as a toll road or a sewer project, and usually do not require a public referendum before they can be issued. These securities are not guaranteed or backed by the taxing power of government. Instead, revenue bonds depend for their value on the revenue-generating capacity of the particular project they support.[1]

Both general obligation and revenue bonds have grown rapidly over the past decade, and there has been a virtual explosion of different types of revenue bonds. Much of the growth of revenue issues is due to programs of the federal government designed to provide housing for low-income groups, improved medical facilities, and student loans, as well as efforts by local governments to modernize their facilities.

Types of Revenue Bonds

Among the best-known revenue issues are *student-loan revenue bonds* (SLRBs), which are issued by state government agencies that lend money to college students. The federal government guarantees 100 percent of the principal and interest of an SLRB, provided the issuing agency's loan-default ratio is low. If a high percentage of students default on their loans, federal guarantees are limited to only a certain portion (usually 80 to 90 percent) of principal and interest payments on the bonds.

In the housing field, several new forms of state and local revenue bonds have appeared. For example, *life-care bonds* are issued by state and local development agencies to provide housing for the elderly. Frequently, nonprofit agencies organized by religious groups administer the property. Investor funds are secured by lease rentals and mortgages against the property.

Construction of hospital facilities is frequently supported by *hospital revenue bonds*. These bonds are issued by state authorities to build hospitals for lease to public or private operating agencies. Hospital revenue bonds have their principal and interest secured by lease rentals and a mortgage against hospital property.

An unusual type of municipal security that serves both public and private interests is the *industrial development bond* (IDB). These securities originally were used to finance plant construction and the purchase of land, which is then leased to a private company. More recently, IDBs have financed the construction of industrial parks, electric-generating plants, pollution control equipment, and other capital items. Their purpose is to attract industry into the local area and increase jobs and tax revenues. However, the use of public funds raised through the tax-exempt borrowing privilege for private purposes soon disturbed many members of Congress. The Deficit Reduction Act of 1984 listed several prohibited uses of IDB money, placed a ceiling on IDBs stemming from a single issuer, and restricted the total amount that could be issued from each state based upon its population. Accordingly, issuers of IDBs must plan much farther in advance and work to get their new issues approved and sold early in the new year before a local government's quota for IDB issues runs out.

Many local governments still borrow or use a portion of their current or expected future tax revenues to offer incentives for the development of new businesses in their area. Unfortunately, recent research evidence suggests that most businesses decide on which states

---

[1]Some municipal bonds display characteristics of *both* GO and revenue securities. For example, a *special tax bond* is payable from the revenues generated by a special tax, such as on gasoline. Many special tax bonds are backed by the full faith, credit, and taxing power of the issuing governmental unit, giving them the character of GOs. *Special assessment bonds* are payable only from assessments against property constructed or purchased from the proceeds of the bonds issued and arise from sewer and street construction or similar projects. Special assessment issues may take on the character of GOs when backed by the taxing power of the issuer. *Authority bonds* are issued by special governmental units set up by states, cities, or counties to construct and manage certain facilities, such as airports. Authority bonds may be either GOs or revenue issues.

and localities to enter based primarily upon such features as climate, energy costs, nearness to the firms' markets, and the availability of labor with the necessary skills—factors that are often beyond a local government's control—rather than the financial incentives offered by many communities. (See, for example, Bradbury, Kodrzycki, and Tannenwald (1997).)

Innovations in Municipal Securities

The vast majority of state and local securities promise the investor a fixed rate of return. Unfortunately, this reduces the attractiveness of GOs and revenue bonds in periods of rising interest rates and inflation. In recent years, several new municipal instruments were developed to deal with this "inflexibility" problem. For example, some tax-exempt revenue bonds have been issued as *floaters.* In one case, U.S. Steel issued $48 million in government-sponsored pollution control bonds with a flexible (floating) interest rate to protect investors against future rate changes. Buyers were so attracted by this novel idea that an additional $500 million in floating-rate bonds soon came to market, promising a yield tied to changes in rates on Treasury bills and bonds.

Still another innovation is the *option bond.* Option bonds bear a fixed rate of interest but can be sold back to the issuer or the agent at par after a specific period. One example was a $43 million issue of 9 percent, single-family mortgage bonds offered by Denton County, Texas. Although these bonds do not come due until 2013, a trustee guarantees to buy back all eligible bonds. More recently, several municipal borrowers have reduced the maturities of their bonds from 30 years to the 10- to 15-year range to improve their flexibility to investors as well as to the issuer.

Lottery bonds have recently been offered in some states that have strong demands for new capital. For example, Florida recently issued these bonds, which are backed by expected lottery revenues, to finance the building of new school facilities as the state's population continues to grow rapidly. Oregon and West Virginia have also offered bonds secured by lottery revenues in recent years.

Particularly interesting is the recent development of *securitized bonds,* which pledge future government tax collections to retire a bond issue. New York City, for example, recently offered $650 million in municipal bonds tied to its anticipated future tax receipts. A few states and cities had conducted similar financings before New York City's mega-issue of securitized bonds by bundling up delinquent property tax accounts, calling them "receivables," and using them as an asset to borrow against. While this device appears to open up significant new borrowing potential for local governments, it does raise the prospect of endangering a local government's credit rating if it runs into substantial unexpected expenses and too high a proportion of its future tax revenues are already committed to paying off securitized bonds or if a weaker economy results in an unexpected fall in tax collections.

Questions *to Help You Study*

6. Please give a concise definition of each of the following state and local government securities, and explain how each is used:

Tax-anticipation notes	*Revenue-anticipation notes*
Bond-anticipation notes	*General obligation (GO) bonds*
Revenue bonds	*Special tax bonds*
Special assessment bonds	*Authority bonds*

7. *Revenue bonds* issued by state and local governments and public agencies have grown more rapidly than other types of state and local government securities in recent years. Several different kinds of revenue obligations are listed below. Please explain the principal purpose or function of each of the following financial instruments:

   SLRBs   Hospital revenue bonds

   Life-care bonds   Industrial development bonds (IDBs)

8. What are the comparative risks faced by investors in choosing between *general obligation bonds* and *revenue bonds*? What advantage(s) do revenue issues offer the investor?

KEY FEATURES OF MUNICIPAL DEBT

Tax Exemption

The unique feature of municipal securities is the **tax-exemption privilege.** The interest income from qualified municipal securities is exempt from federal income taxes; in addition, state law usually exempts municipals from income taxes levied by the state of issuance. This exemption feature was created so that federal, state, and local governments would not interfere with each other in raising funds and providing services to their citizens. It arises from a constitutional doctrine known as "reciprocity" in which various levels of government recognize each other's sovereignty in a variety of governmental functions.

Capital gains on municipal securities are *not* tax exempt, however, unless the security is issued at a discount from par. In that special case, any increase in price up to par value is considered part of the security's interest return and is tax exempt. However, if the security continues to rise in price, that portion of the gain above par is subject to taxation once the investor realizes the gain.

An Interest Subsidy to High-Income Investors

The tax-exempt feature has been a controversial issue for many years. It is a government subsidy to high tax-bracket investors. This is true because the value of the exemption privilege increases with the investor's marginal income tax rate. Exhibit 20–5 illustrates the impact of the investor's marginal income tax rate (or tax bracket) on the relative attractiveness of municipals compared to taxable securities. This exhibit compares the approximate after-tax yield on high-grade corporate bonds, which are fully taxable, with the yield on comparable quality municipal bonds, assuming that Aaa-rated corporate bonds are trading currently at a 10 percent before-tax yield and Aaa municipal bonds are trading at 7.75 percent. Because the 10 percent corporate bond yield is a before-tax rate of return, we must adjust it using the investor's marginal income tax rate to derive the after-tax rate of return. The before-tax corporate yield is multiplied by $(1 - t)$, where t is the investor's applicable federal tax rate.

Exhibit 20–5 illustrates the effect of this calculation for individual investors with marginal tax rates ranging from 0 to 39.1 percent and for corporations whose marginal tax rates range from 0 to 35 percent. For an individual investor in the top 39.1 percent tax bracket, the after-tax return on Aaa corporate bonds was 10 percent $\times (1 - 0.391)$, or 6.09 percent. Clearly, an investor in this high-income group would prefer to purchase municipal bonds yielding 7.75 percent rather than corporate bonds returning just 6.09 percent after taxes, other factors being equal. The same conclusion holds true for larger corporations and banks

EXHIBIT 20–5 The Impact of the Tax-Exemption Feature on the After-Tax Yields of Long-Term Corporate and Municipal Bonds (Tax Rates for 2001)

Investor Group	Before-Tax Yield on Seasoned AAA Corporate Bonds	Appropriate Federal Income Tax Bracket for Investor Group	After-Tax Yield on Seasoned AAA Corporate Bonds	Before-Tax and After-Tax Yield on AAA Municipal Bonds
Individuals in the highest income bracket (with surcharge)	10%	39.1%	6.09%	7.75%
Large corporate investors:				
Manufacturing and industrial corporations	10	35	6.50	7.75
Property-casualty insurance companies	10	35	6.50	7.75
Commercial banks	10	35	6.50	7.75
Individuals in middle-income tax brackets	10	27.5	7.25	7.75
Individuals and institutions in the lowest income bracket	10	10	9.00	7.75
Tax-exempt investors (governments, pension funds, charities, foundations, and credit unions)	10	0	10	7.75

confronted with the top 35 percent corporate federal tax rate.[2] Even for middle-bracket investors facing a 27.5 percent rate, municipals often are attractive in terms of after-tax return.[3]

Of course, the foregoing analysis focuses exclusively on after-tax rates of return, ignoring differences in liquidity and other features of taxable and tax-exempt securities. A corporation that needs to hold securities for liquidity purposes, for example, might well hold taxable issues, such as U.S. government securities, which can be converted into cash quickly and with little risk of loss, even though their after-tax yields may be lower than the yields on municipal bonds.

For income tax brackets below the top rung, taxable securities compare more favorably with municipals. For example, many small private investors whose applicable federal

[2]Recent federal tax laws have sharply reduced the attractiveness of municipal securities to banks and other top tax-bracket investors. Successive tax laws have lowered the top corporate tax rate, forcing the after-tax yield on municipal bonds closer to the after-tax return on taxable securities. Federal tax reform, therefore, has made municipal bonds less attractive relative to all taxable securities. Many investors, especially individuals, still find municipals attractive, however, because they are one of only a few tax shelters left after federal tax reform. Banks, on the other hand, have significantly reduced their municipal holdings relative to taxable loans and U.S. government securities because federal laws have sharply reduced or eliminated, depending upon the issuer of the municipal securities, the tax deductibility of bank borrowing costs when banks purchase municipals. Overall, these tax law changes have resulted in a shift in the municipal market toward more *retail investors*—higher-income individuals and mutual funds appealing to individuals as investors—to whom the tax exemption feature of municipals is still an important tax shelter.

[3]The Economic Growth and Tax Relief Reconciliation Act of 2001 created additional tax brackets ranging from the lowest at 10 percent to a high of 39.1 percent in the year 2001. The top U.S. federal tax rate is scheduled to be lowered gradually to 35 percent by the year 2006.

income tax rate may range from 10 to 15 percent find taxable securities more lucrative and purchase few municipals. In effect, the tax-exempt feature limits the demand for state and local government securities to high-income individuals and mutual funds that appeal to individuals as investors, to property-casualty insurers, large nonfinancial corporations, and to other higher tax-bracket investors. This limitation may represent a serious problem in future years when many local governments must raise an enormous volume of new funds to accommodate rapidly expanding populations.

The tax exemption feature is an advantage to municipal governments because it keeps their interest cost low relative to interest rates paid by other borrowers. These savings can be passed on to local citizens in the form of lower tax rates. Of course, the U.S. Treasury is able to collect less revenue from high-bracket investors as a result of the exemption privilege and must tax low-bracket taxpayers more heavily to make up the difference. Therefore, the *total* tax bill from all levels of government is probably little affected by the tax-exempt feature of municipals.

Exemption Contributes to Market Volatility

Because the market for municipal bonds is limited by the tax-exempt privilege to top-bracket investors, prices and interest rates on municipal bonds tend to be volatile. Prices of tax-exempt bonds tend to rise during periods when corporate and individual incomes are rising, because top-bracket investors have greater need to shelter their earnings from taxation at those times. However, a fall in individual or corporate earnings often leads to sharp reductions in the demand for municipal bonds. Prices of tax-exempt issues may plummet, and interest costs confronting borrowing governments may rise during those periods when corporate profits are squeezed. This makes financial planning in the state and local government sector more difficult.

A Market of "Fair Weather" Investors

Another problem that exacerbates the volatility of municipal bond prices is the limited investment horizon of many tax-exempt bond buyers. For the most part, investors active in the tax-exempt market are "fair weather" friends. Some banks and insurance companies, for example, may build up their state and local bond holdings when customer loan demand or insurance claims are low, only to sell off substantial quantities of municipals when loan demand revives or insurance claims increase. Another major group of tax-exempt investors (high-income individuals) has finite life spans, and therefore their bonds are often sold after only a short holding period. The net result is to create an active secondary market and relatively high turnover rate for better-known municipal issues.

Credit Ratings

A feature of municipal securities that makes them especially attractive to investors is their high credit rating. About 10 percent of all municipal securities are AAA-rated by Moody's Investors Service and Standard & Poor's Corporation; about half are AA- or A-rated. A relatively small proportion of all state and local government securities are rated BA or lower or carry no published rating. This means that most municipal issues are considered to be of *investment quality* rather than speculative buys.

In October 1996, Moody's Investors Service began to attach numerical modifiers to its standard A and B security ratings for municipal securities. These newer Moody's bond ratings for state and local government debt issues include the following:

Older Moody's State and Local Government Bond Rating Symbols	Newer Moody's State and Local Government Bond Rating Symbols
Aaa	Aaa
Aa1	Aa1
Aa	Aa2
	Aa3
A1	A1
A	A2
	A3
Baa1	Baa1
Baa	Baa2
	Baa3
Ba1	Ba1
Ba	Ba2
	Ba3
B1	B1
B	B2
	B3
Caa	Caa
Ca	Ca
C	C

In the above ratings, the modifier 1 means a new municipal bond issue ranks at the higher end of its rating category, 2 indicates a mid-range quality state and local security, and 3 implies the debt issue is judged to be at the low end of its rating class. Notice that the lowest-grade speculative municipal issues have *no* numerical modifiers.

Moody's went to this revised rating system because of several recent trends affecting the municipal sector, including:

1. A shift in the primary investor groups holding state and local bonds, as banks, for example, largely withdrew from heavy municipal purchases due to reduced tax incentives, while tax-exempt mutual funds and money market funds became major buyers of municipals. These latter institutions need finer grading and more accurate valuation of municipal bonds because they are frequently forced to liquidate their holdings of municipals quickly when mutual fund investors sell their shares.

2. Evidence of greater credit risk and volatility in the state and local government sector, including an increasing trend toward defaults as more and more local governments experience fiscal stress as the federal government moves to transfer more responsibilities to local governments and many local taxpayers resist new programs and higher taxes.

Factors Behind Setting Credit Ratings

In assigning credit ratings to municipals, Moody's and other rating services consider the past repayment record of the borrowing unit of government, the quality and size of its tax base, the volume of debt outstanding, local economic conditions, and future prospects for growth in the local economy. The fact that many municipal issues are backed by taxing authority or may draw on several different sources of revenue for repayment of principal and interest helps to keep the investment quality of tax-exempt municipal issues high. This is particularly important for regulated financial institutions that buy municipals. For example, regulations generally prohibit banks and other depository institutions from acquiring debt securities rated below BAA or BBB (so-called speculative issues). These restrictive rules encourage state and local governments to keep their credit ratings high in order to encourage more active participation by regulated financial institutions in bidding for new municipal securities.

Recent Credit Quality Problems

Until recently, state and local governments possessed virtually unblemished credit records. No major defaults on municipal securities had occurred for nearly half a century. However, the turbulent economic and financial environment of the 1970s, 1980s, and 1990s caused many investors to reassess the credit standing of municipals, especially the bonds and notes issued by some of the largest cities and those associated with special local government projects, such as nuclear power production.

This problem first surfaced dramatically in the financial crises experienced by New York in the 1970s and again early in the 1990s. Soaring costs for municipal services, excessive reliance on short-term debt, and high unemployment combined to threaten that city with record high interest costs and financial default. And in the wake of New York City's fiscal crisis, other northeastern cities—Chicago, Detroit, Philadelphia, and Washington, DC—also found their credit costs rising and investor resistance to buying their securities increasing. There have been relatively few actual defaults on municipal bonds in recent years (though about 6,000 local government defaults have occurred in U.S. history as a whole). However, the investors involved usually received back the principal value of their bonds (with some loss of interest). Risk premiums demanded by investors purchasing lower-grade municipal bonds have at times exceeded risk premiums on comparable quality corporate bonds, frequently setting in motion a "flight to quality" by high-tax-bracket investors, running away from lower-quality municipal bonds.

This fundamental, long-run concern about the investment quality of municipal issues was heightened in December 1978, when Cleveland became the first major U.S. city to default on its debt since the Great Depression of the 1930s. Then, early in the 1980s, the Washington Public Power Supply System (WPPSS), a nuclear power consortium, was caught in an environmental squabble, coupled with serious project delays and cost overruns on nuclear power facilities under construction. The result, in the summer of 1983, was the largest default on a local government bond issue in American history, amounting to more than $2 billion.

As the 1990s began, several states and cities had the credit ratings on their bonds either lowered or placed on a "credit watch" list. The most dramatic example was the state of California, which faced projected annual budget deficits in the $5 billion range. Several of California's small cities and other local governments appeared to be close to defaulting on their bonds due to defense cutbacks and falling real estate values that threatened future tax collections. During the summer of 1995, Orange County, California, one of the largest urban areas in the United States, declared bankruptcy with close to $800 million in unpaid obligations. The rapid growth in that county's population put its local government in a bind due to the soaring demand for public services. However, Orange County voters rejected several proposals to raise taxes. County officials then adopted an aggressive investments policy, including heavy investments in derivative securities, which lost about $2.5 billion when interest rates rose. Faced with numerous claims from creditors (including other local governments who had invested their funds with Orange County), county officials worked for nearly a year to hammer out a repayment plan to cover most of Orange County's debts.[4]

---

[4]See Chapter 8 for more discussion of the Orange County bankruptcy.

Orange County's financial collapse reminded investors in municipals that local government failures are an ever-present possibility. Government bankruptcies are more likely in areas of economic decline or in localities where growth has far outstripped the ability of cities and counties to provide government services, and citizens are unwilling to levy additional taxes or authorize the issuance of new debt. Another bankruptcy-threatening problem occurred as the new century began—power outages and rising energy costs that eroded the fiscal strength of some states (particularly California) until energy costs backed down late in 2001.

Partly as a result of recent state and local government financial problems, the Securities and Exchange Commission (SEC) amended its Rule 15c2-12 to bar security dealers from marketing new municipal security issues unless the issuers agree to provide annual financial reports and continuing disclosure of "material events" (such as delinquencies, defaults, modification of security holders' rights, credit rating changes, or sale of property backing a security issue) to designated national data banks. At almost the same time, the SEC approved a rule to severely limit the campaign ("pay to play") contributions that security dealers underwriting new municipal bond issues could make to local government officials and to those running for public office. The idea is to protect investors in municipals from the adverse consequences of political graft and corruption arising from state and local governments' borrowing money.

Insurance for Municipal Bonds

Investor concern over the quality of some municipal securities and the potential failure of some state and local government projects led to the creation of "sleep insurance" for selected municipal issues. First offered by Ambac Indemnity Corp. in the early 1970s and later by such companies as Municipal Bond Investors Assurance Corp. (MBIA), Financial Security Assurance, Inc., and Financial Guarantee Insurance Corporation, these insurance policies, which guarantee timely payment of principal and interest, now cover most top-rated state and local government bonds. Such insurance protection normally is requested and paid for by the bond issuer or the issuers' representative, not the investor purchasing the bonds. However, buyers of insured bonds usually receive lower yields compared to noninsured bonds. Therefore, issuers benefit from insurance policies because they can sell their bonds at lower interest cost. The rating agencies, such as Standard & Poor's Corporation and Moody's Investors Service, generally grant higher credit ratings to insured municipal securities. However, if the credit rating of the insurance company falls, the interest rates on municipal bonds insured by that particular company also tend to rise as investors become concerned about the insurer's ability to pay if the state or local government issuer cannot. Bond insurance has become more important in recent years as retail customers (individuals and mutual funds) have come to capture a larger share of purchases of new municipal securities.

One additional form of municipal "insurance" that has recently grown in popularity is the rise of bank credit lines and standby guarantee letters. These credit back-up contracts help to increase the salability of municipals by reassuring potential investors that a bank will provide the necessary liquidity if the issuing state or local government faces a cash shortage.

Serialization

Most municipal bonds are *serial* securities. **Serialization** refers to the splitting up of a single bond issue into several different maturities. Thus, an issue of $20 million in bonds to build a municipal auditorium might include the following securities:

Amount	Due in
$1 million	1 year
$1 million	2 years
$1 million	3 years
•	•
•	•
•	•
$1 million	20 years

Splitting a single issue of municipals into multiple maturities contrasts with the practice employed by most corporate borrowers and the federal government. Corporations, for example, generally issue *term* bonds in which all securities in the same issue come due on the same date. In effect, serialization of municipal bonds is a way of *amortizing* state and local debt.

Why is serialization so popular in the municipal field? Before serial bonds were widely adopted, state and local bonds were generally term securities. A sinking fund was created at the time of issue, and annual contributions were made to the fund until sufficient monies were accumulated to pay off the bond at maturity. However, sinking funds proved irresistible to unscrupulous politicians and to governments facing financial emergencies. Accumulated funds often disappeared, leaving virtually nothing to retire municipal debt when it came due. The serial feature seemed to offer an ideal solution to this problem.

Unfortunately, serialization has created as many problems as it has solved. For one thing, splitting a security into a number of different maturities reduces the liquidity and marketability of municipal securities. When a municipal issue is split into multiple maturities there is only a relatively small amount outstanding in any one maturity class. The potential volume of trading for particular maturities is, therefore, limited. Serialization also complicates the offering of new securities, because a number of different investor groups must be attracted into the bidding. For example, money market funds, banks, and individuals generally prefer the shorter-term (1- to 10-year) securities, and mutual funds and insurance companies often want only longer-term bonds.

HOW MUNICIPAL BONDS ARE MARKETED

Keeping up with municipal prices and interest rates is easier today due to such sites as CNN/Money at *www.cnnfm.com* and the Bond Market Association at *www.bondmarkets.com*

The selling of municipals is usually carried out through a syndicate of banks and securities dealers. These institutions underwrite municipals by purchasing them from issuing units of government and reselling the securities in the open market at a higher price. Prices paid by the underwriting firms may be determined either by competitive bidding among several syndicates or by negotiation with a single securities dealer or syndicate. Competitive bidding normally is employed in the marketing of general obligation bonds; revenue bonds more frequently are placed through private negotiation.

In competitive bidding, syndicates (which may contain from 2 to upwards of a dozen or more underwriters) interested in a particular bond issue will estimate its potential reoffer price in the open market and what their desired underwriting commission must be. Each syndicate wants to bid a price high enough to win the bid but low enough so that the securities later can be sold in the open market at a price sufficient to protect the syndicate's commission. That is,

Bid price + Underwriting commission = Market reoffer price

Salomon/Smith Barney	Lehman Brothers
Paine Webber	Morgan Stanley Dean Witter
Goldman Sachs	J.P. Morgan/Chase
Bear Stearns	First Union Capital
Merrill Lynch	Bank of America

Sources: Securities Dealers Association and Federal Reserve Board.

The winning bid carries the lowest *net interest cost* (NIC) to the issuing unit of government. The NIC is simply the sum of all interest payments that will be owed on the new issue divided by its principal amount.

Bidding for new issues of municipal bonds is a treacherous business. Prices, interest rates, and market demand for municipals change rapidly. In fact, the tax-exempt securities market is one of the most volatile of all financial markets. This is due, in part, to the key role of mutual funds, banks, insurance companies, and other financial institutions in the municipal market, whose demand for municipals fluctuates with their net earnings, loan demand, and market conditions. Legal interest rate ceilings, which prohibit some local governments from borrowing when market interest rates climb above those ceilings, also play a significant role in the volatility of municipal trading. These combined factors render the tax-exempt market highly sensitive to the business cycle, monetary policy, and a host of other factors.

The specter of high interest rates often forces postponement of hundreds of millions of dollars in new security issues, and the onset of lower interest rates may unleash a flood of new security offerings. Still another problem is the unpredictability of federal tax reform legislation, which has reduced the volume and attractiveness of many municipal securities to investors (commercial banks in particular) from time to time. The nature of this large debt market can suddenly change with serious consequences for many of its players. Still, the rewards of municipal bond underwriting can be substantial, even though only a handful of dealers make a continuous market for these securities. For example, during 1998 the largest municipal bond underwriting deal in history took place: a staggered offering amounting to almost $7 billion in bonds issued to fund New York's takeover of the Long Island Lighting Company. In this instance, the team of underwriters involved expected to receive about $40 million in underwriting fees.

PROBLEMS IN THE MUNICIPAL MARKET

Problems and Proposals Regarding Tax Exemption

The municipal market has been plagued by a number of problems over the years, some related to its unique tax-exempt character. Many observers question the social benefit of the tax-exemption privilege. Although state and local governments can borrow more cheaply as a result of tax exemption, the federal government must tax nonexempt groups more heavily to make up the lost revenue. Also, many important investor groups (such as pension funds) have little need for tax shelters and therefore display little interest in municipal bonds. Recently, commercial banks have drastically reduced their holdings of state and

Financial Developments   Devolution—The New Federalism

In recent years the federal government has been passing more and more of its former programs and activities along to the states, granting the states more power to implement federal programs and curtailing some of the old federal rules that limited what state and local governments could do. As a result, state and local government spending (net of federal aid) has recently risen to more than 10 percent of U.S. GDP, while net federal spending has fallen well below that figure. This trend is often called "devolution," with the federal government passing more of its responsibilities (such as welfare programs) to the states and their local governmental units. This movement seems more consistent with the move toward greater deregulation, decentralization, and free enterprise happening around the globe. The administration of President Clinton involved the states more proactively in rewriting federal program rules and standards, thus making it easier for many of the states to qualify for federal grants. A similar trend appears to be unfolding in the George W. Bush administration.

There is substantial concern among some state and local authorities that local governments are not well prepared to pick up the financial burdens that this "new federalism" approach will bring to them. Many states and local governments already face a lack of financial resources and growing taxpayer resistance even before adding on the burden of former federal programs tossed into their fiscal backyard. Even more worrisome, if local and regional economies weaken (as happened in the wake of the September 2001 terrorist attacks), some state and local governments may have to cut back on social services to their citizens that, in the past, when provided by the federal government, used to help them offset the impact of economic recessions and helped to stabilize their economies. The result may be an overall national shrinkage in government activity at all levels, that may benefit some states and individuals (particularly states and local areas where individuals average higher private-sector incomes) but hurt other localities not as economically well off.

Overall, the quality of government service may eventually decline in the United States, though some researchers believe devolution is still desirable because it comes closer to what the original authors of the U.S. Constitution intended regarding federal powers versus state and local government powers. Some authorities believe the ultimate long-run solution may be to take advantage of the federal government's superior ability to collect revenues while using state and local governments' superior knowledge of local and regional service needs by getting the federal government to gather most tax revenues and giving state and local authorities greater discretion in how, where, and for whom those revenues are to be spent.

local government securities due to unfavorable tax treatment following the passage of federal tax reform laws. Now banks tend to concentrate their purchases of municipals in so-called "bank qualified" issues that are issued by smaller units of government and still promise significant tax benefits for the purchasing bank.

A number of proposals have been advanced over the years for improving the depth and stability of the municipal market and eliminating the tax-exempt feature. One interesting idea calls for reimbursing state and local governments for loss of the tax-exempt privilege by paying federal subsidies. A related idea calls for paying a subsidy directly to investors who choose to buy municipal securities. A federally sponsored *Urbank* was proposed a number of years ago that would issue its own bonds and direct the proceeds of bond sales to municipal governments. One criticism of this approach is the danger of increased federal controls over state and local government activities.

The Outlook for State and Local Governments

The outlook for state and local governments as the twenty-first century dawns is more encouraging than it has been in several years. Certainly there are serious problems with which to contend—for example, growing demands for new housing, medical, and recreational facilities for the elderly; demand for more equitable funding of schools located in poorer communities versus those situated in richer communities; the huge cost of defenses against possible future terrorist attacks; and a large prison population that will continue to require large-scale expenditures for adequate correctional facilities. Added to these demands are expensive *infrastructure* problems—water and sewer systems that are wearing out; city streets and bridges long ago worn down from adverse weather and heavy usage; deteriorating public buildings and highly expensive new building codes (such as currently apply to building new jails); and developing shortages of water and electrical generating capacity.

Local government revenues will have to keep up with these demands for funds despite projected slower growth in the economy and the likelihood of less generous support from the federal government. States must plan for receiving fewer federal monies in the future; on the positive side, there are likely to be fewer federal restrictions on how local governments can spend federal money. At the same time, most states and localities are in hot pursuit of new industries to expand their economic base, which often means giving tax relief to new businesses and holding the line on the imposition of new taxes so that revenue sources are further reduced.

With slower economic growth and less federal support, more states will be under pressure to "pass the buck" to their local governments and force cities, counties, and school districts to deal with their own problems and find their own funding sources. Certainly, the need for local government services is not likely to fade, but the continued willingness of taxpayers to authorize new construction and new borrowing and the continued interest of large numbers of investors in buying state and local government debt securities (particularly through the purchase of shares in municipal-bond-oriented mutual funds) in order to support local governments' financial needs is a positive sign for the future growth of this challenging sector of the global financial marketplace.

Questions *to Help You Study*

9. What are the principal features of state and local government securities that have made them attractive to many groups of investors?

10. How has recent federal tax legislation impacted the market for municipals?

11. Describe how state and local government securities are marketed. What risks do syndicates face in this marketplace?

12. What key problems do you believe that state and local governments are likely to face in the years ahead? What factors seem to be the principal causes of these problems?

Summary of the Chapter

The borrowing and spending activities of state and local governments have proven to be one of the most rapidly growing segments of the financial system and the economy in recent years.

- State and local governments in the United States borrow billions of dollars each year to fund the construction of public facilities and to supply themselves with working capital to cover daily operations in providing government services to their citizens.

- The borrowing of these units of government are specially privileged under the U.S. Constitution and U.S. Treasury Department regulations. Their interest earnings are exempt from federal income taxation and many states also exempt the interest earnings on their own debt from state and local taxes. The tax-exemption feature makes these financial instruments (called *municipals*) uniquely attractive to investors occupying the highest tax brackets (including wealthy individuals, banks, and certain insurance firms).

- By the end of the twentieth century state and local government debt outstanding exceeded a trillion dollars, growing rapidly after World War II and especially during the 1980s and 1990s. Major factors driving local debt growth have been rapid population and income growth, the upgrading of citizen expectations, and a shifting of responsibility for funding many local services from the federal government to state and local units of government.

- Key revenue sources for state and local governments include sales and income taxes, property taxes, user fees, and funds transfers among governmental units. The largest categories of state and local government expenditures include education, social services, transportation services, health services, and construction spending.

- Inadequate revenues, rapid area growth, short-term cash needs, long-term capital investments, and advance refundings represent major motivations for state and local governments to borrow money.

- Many different types of securities are issued by states and local governments. Short-term municipals include tax-anticipation notes (TANs), revenue-anticipation notes (RANs), and bond-anticipation notes (BANs). Each of these instruments is issued in the expectation that revenues to pay them off will subsequently appear.

- Long-term security issues include *general obligation (GO) bonds* and *revenue bonds*. The latter depend for their repayment on the revenues generated by a specific municipal project, such as toll roads, toll bridges, and other revenue-generating ventures. There has been a tendency in recent years to develop many new types of state and local government securities such as floaters, securitized bonds, and lottery bonds.

- Among the many significant features of municipal securities are their *tax-exempt* feature and their *subsidization* of high-tax-bracket investors—both of which tend to create a relatively volatile market for municipal securities. State and local obligations are also usually *serialized* or broken up into a range of maturities in order to appeal to a wider variety of potential buyers and minimize the risk of misuse of public funds.

- State and local government securities are generally of high credit quality with low perceived default risk. However, over the past two decades a few notable failures have appeared, causing investors at those times to rapidly move their funds to investments of higher quality (such as U.S. Treasury securities). Recent failures have also spurred the expanded use of *municipal bond insurance* even though it slightly lowers a municipal investor's expected yield.

- Municipals are generally marketed through security dealers under competitive bidding. However, there are some signs of taxpayer resistance to the continuing issuance of a growing volume of state and local debt obligations and the higher taxes that usually follow their sale to investors in the money and capital markets.

Key Terms

Problems

1. Corporate bonds carrying an A rating are currently being priced to yield 8.62 percent. For an investor in the 27.5 percent income tax bracket, what yield must an A-rated municipal bond carry to make this investor indifferent as to the yield difference between the corporate and the municipal bond?

2. Sandoval County issued AA-rated bonds at a net interest cost of 6.85 percent. If annual interest payments promised on these bonds amount to $12.75 million, what was the principal amount of municipal bonds issued by Sandoval County?

3. Consider the case in which state and local governments across the United States collected or spent the following amounts classified as shown below (all figures in billions of dollars for the most recent fiscal year):

Property taxes	$175	Individual income taxes	$70
Education	430	Corporate income taxes	15
User fees	25	Governmental administration	49
Highways	88	Interest on debt	104
Sales & gross receipts taxes	125	Intergovernmental funds transfers	
Public safety	80	from the federal government	150
Environment and housing	78	General and miscellaneous	
Miscellaneous general revenue	200	expenditures	75

What was the total revenue and total expenditures for all state and local governments? Was the state and local government sector running an overall deficit or surplus in its combined budget? Will borrowing likely be necessary to finish out the current fiscal year?

4. Please identify the name for each of the types of state and local government securities described below:
   a. Long-term debt payable only from revenues generated by a toll road.
   b. Debt issued to support the construction of new business facilities.
   c. Short-term borrowing that will later be replaced by long-term state or local government bonds.
   d. Long-term securities issued under the Federal Housing Act to support the provision of low-income residential dwellings.
   e. State or local government debt repayable from any revenue source.
   f. Debt securities that can be sold back before maturity at face value to the issuer after a period of time has elapsed.
   g. Short-term borrowing in lieu of expected local government tax receipts.

5. Please identify each of the key terms and concepts that are described in each of the sentences and phrases presented below:
   a. Debt securities issued by states, counties, cities, school districts and other local units of government.
   b. Short-term debt obligations issued by state and local governments in order to provide financial support until tax revenues flow in.
   c. Short-term securities issued by a state or local unit of government that precede the issuance of long-term bonds.
   d. Debt obligations backed by the "full faith and credit" of the issuing unit of government.
   e. Debt obligations issued by state and local governments that are repayable only from a particular funds source.
   f. The splitting up of a single bond issue into several different maturities.
   g. The special status awarded state and local government securities under U.S. tax law.

Questions about the Web and the Money and Capital Markets

1. If you wanted to learn more about conditions today or this week in the market for municipals where on the Web could you go to get this kind of information? Which sites do you think are among the best?

2. Which state and local government security dealers appear to offer the most complete line of investor services? Whose Web site do you like the best and why?

3. Why would foreign investors be interested in municipal securities issued inside the United States?

4. The state and local government sector is changing rapidly. Where on the Web could you look to stay abreast of this rapidly changing marketplace?

Selected References

Board of Governors of the Federal Reserve System. *Federal Reserve Bulletin,* selected monthly issues.

Bradbury, Katherine L.; Yolanda Kodrzycki; and Robert Tannenwald. "The Effects of State and Local Public Policies on Economic Development: An Overview." *New England Economic Review,* Federal Reserve Bank of Boston, March–April 1997, pp. 1–47.

Rubin, Laura S. "The Fiscal Position of the State and Local Government Sector: Developments in the 1990s." *Federal Reserve Bulletin,* April 1996.

Sorensen, Bent E., and Oved Yosha. "Is State Fiscal Policy Asymmetric over the Business Cycle?" *Economic Review,* Federal Reserve Bank of Kansas City, Third Quarter 2001, pp. 43–64.

Tannenwald, Robert. "Devolution: The New Federalism—An Overview." *New England Economic Review,* Federal Reserve Bank of Boston, May–June 1998, pp. 1–83.

Part **Six**

Businesses and Consumers in the Financial Markets

The principal borrowers of funds in today's financial markets are business firms and consumers (individuals and families or households). Businesses can raise new funds in the money and capital markets through several different channels—by borrowing, by issuing shares of stock, or by selling previously accumulated assets. Consumers (households) can finance their purchases of goods and services principally by borrowing additional funds or by liquidating their savings.

In this portion of the text we explore, first of all, the various sources of funding *businesses* draw upon today, their advantages and disadvantages, the relative cost of each funding source, and the nature of the marketplace where new business capital is obtained. This part opens with two important chapters—the first (Chapter 21) dealing with business borrowing (i.e., the taking on of debt) and the second (Chapter 22) on issuing corporate stock (i.e., the expansion of equity capital). Perhaps not too surprisingly, we will find great differences between the market for business debt and the market for stock (equities). Debt and equity play similar roles in supplying new capital to fuel business growth, but each of these funding sources has its own unique features and limitations. Our goal is to understand well what these unique features and limitations mean for businesses, their owners, and the public they serve.

We also examine the *household* sector as both a lender and a borrower of funds, noting what financial services are most important to consumers and how consumer preferences for financial instruments and services have changed over time. In the last half of Part Six we explore the fundamental financial characteristics of household consumers (in Chapter 23)—how they lend funds and what alternative sources of borrowing are available to them. It is also our objective to learn about the most important consumer protection laws that have sheltered individuals and families for many years when they venture into the often treacherous financial marketplace. Part Six concludes with a look at one of the largest of all financial markets—the market for residential mortgage loans (Chapter 24). We want to know about the financial factors that consumers must consider when borrowing to purchase a new home and what types of home loans are available in the residential mortgage market.

Chapter **Twenty-One**

Business Borrowing

Learning Objectives in This Chapter

- You will examine the different ways business firms issue debt securities and negotiate loans in order to borrow loanable funds in the money and capital markets.

- You will learn about the key factors that cause businesses to increase or decrease the volume of debt funds they seek to raise within the financial markets.

- You will see the often powerful impact that business borrowing has upon market interest rates and credit conditions inside the financial system.

What's in This Chapter? Key Topics Outline

Business Borrowing from the Money and Capital Markets: Residual Funds Sources

Factors in the Decision to Borrow from the Financial Marketplace

Characteristics of Corporate Bonds and Notes

Who Buys Corporate Bonds?

Marketing Business Debt: Public Sale or Private Placement?

Volume of Business Borrowing and Mergers

Bank Lending to Business: Prime or Base Rate

Commercial Mortgages

INTRODUCTION

Business firms draw on a wide variety of sources of funds to finance their daily operations and to carry out long-term investment. In 2000, for example, nonfinancial business firms in the United States raised just over $1¼ trillion in funds to carry out long-term investments, purchase inventories of goods and raw materials, and acquire financial assets. Of this total, approximately $860 billion (about two-thirds) was supplied from the financial markets through issues of bonds, stocks, notes, and other financial instruments. In this chapter, we look at sources of borrowed (debt) funds used by businesses today. In the next chapter, we consider the advantages and disadvantages of stock (equity) as a source of business funding.

Markets on the Net

The market for borrowing by business firms is well represented on the World Wide Web. This is due not only to a rapid expansion in business borrowing in recent years, but also because growing numbers of investors have sought the higher yields on business debt compared to government securities. Thus, many private investors today like to keep up daily with the goings-on in the security markets where corporate bonds, notes, and other business IOUs are traded.

There are numerous interesting sources of information on debt issued by corporations and on the trading of corporate notes and bonds. Examples include the Bond Market Association's Investing in Bonds segment at *www.investinginbonds.com*, and an exploration of different types of corporate debt securities on Financial Pipeline at *www.finpipe.com*. Another good source, especially for keeping track of daily developments in the corporate debt market, is CBS Marketwatch at *www.cbs.marketwatch.com*.

FACTORS AFFECTING BUSINESS ACTIVITY IN THE MONEY AND CAPITAL MARKETS

The demands of businesses for funds stem from the desire of these firms to acquire new assets and to replace existing assets (such as plant and equipment) that are wearing out. Specifically, at any point in time

> *Total funding demands of business firms* = **(21–1)**
>
> *Desired increases in short-term assets* (inventories of goods and raw materials, credit (receivables) extended to customers, and holdings of marketable securities and other short-term assets) +
>
> *Desired increases in long-term assets* (plant and equipment, construction of new homes and other facilities for sale, and the start-up or acquisition of other business firms).

These total funding demands from the business sector can be met from funds generated *inside* each firm (*internal financing*) in the form of undistributed profits and depreciation reserves and from funds generated from *outside* the individual firm (*external financing*) in the money and capital markets. Specifically,

> Total business funding demands − **(21–2)**
>
> Undistributed profits and depreciation reserves from inside each firm =
>
> *Business demands for external financing from the money and capital markets.*

Many factors affect the extent to which business firms draw on the money and capital markets for external funds. One prominent factor is the *condition of the economy.* A booming economy generates rapidly growing sales, encouraging business people to borrow in order to expand inventories and to issue stocks and bonds in order to purchase new plant and equipment. In contrast, a sagging economy normally is accompanied by declining sales and a reduction in inventory purchases and long-term investment. Other factors being equal, the need for external fund-raising declines when the economy grows more slowly or heads down into a recession. In contrast, rising demand for business goods and services is usually translated into rising demand for short- and long-term capital supplied from the financial marketplace.

Credit availability and interest rates also have powerful effects on business fundraising activity in the money and capital markets. Rising interest rates that typically accompany a period of economic prosperity or inflation eventually choke off business borrowing and spending plans due to the increasing cost of carrying inventories, floating new securities, and renewing credit lines. Falling interest rates, on the other hand, can stimulate business borrowing and spending, leading to a restocking of inventories and to an expansion of long-term investment financed by bonds, stocks, and direct loans.

A third factor in influencing how heavily businesses draw on the money and capital markets for financial support is the *level and expected growth of internally generated funds* (earnings and cash flow) for each firm. The financial markets are largely a *supplemental* funds source for most businesses, drawn upon to backstop internal cash flows when credit availability and economic conditions are favorable and when internally generated cash is inadequate to cover all desired business investments. Because business firms' earnings and cash flows tend to be volatile, it should not surprise us to learn that business fund-raising activity in the financial system is also highly volatile. Heavy business borrowings in one year to fill the *funding gap* between desired business capital spending and internally generated funds often are followed by a dearth of new security offerings and significant pay-downs of outstanding loans the next year, particularly if internal funds have risen or if business expectations about the state of the economy have soured, reducing the volume of desired investment spending.

These marked fluctuations in business fund-raising in the financial markets result in wide swings in interest rates and security prices. Much of the volatility in stock and bond prices reported in the daily financial press may be attributed to the on-again, off-again character of financial market activity by the business sector. The key actors in this rapidly changing drama are, of course, the largest industrial corporations, which have the financial stature to tap both the open market and the negotiated loan markets for debt and equity funds. Skillful analysts often can read which way the wind is blowing as far as interest rates and security prices are concerned by watching what is happening to the current earnings and investment plans of major business corporations.

CHARACTERISTICS OF CORPORATE NOTES AND BONDS

If a corporation decides to use long-term funds to finance its growth, the most popular forms of long-term financing are the **corporate bond** and the **corporate note.** This is especially true for the largest corporations whose credit standing is so strong that they can avoid dealing directly with an institutional lender such as a bank, finance company, or insurance company and sell their IOUs in the open market. Small companies without the necessary standing in the eyes of security investors usually must confine their long-term financing operations to negotiated loans with an institutional lender (such as a bank), an occasional stock issue, and heavy use of internally generated cash.

Principal Features of Corporate Notes and Bonds

A distinction needs to be drawn here between notes and bonds. By convention, a *note* is a corporate debt contract whose original maturity is five years or less; a *bond* carries an original maturity of more than five years. Both securities promise the investor an amount equal to the security's par value at maturity plus interest payments at specified intervals. Because both securities have similar characteristics other than maturity, we will use the word *bond* to refer to both notes and bonds in the discussion that follows.

Corporate bonds are generally issued in units of $1,000 and earn income that, in most cases, is fully taxable to the investor. These securities are known as *registered bonds* because the owner of these instruments must register with the issuing company in order to collect interest. Each bond is accompanied by an **indenture,** a contract listing the rights and obligations of the borrower and the investor. Indentures usually contain *restrictive covenants* designed to protect bondholders against actions by a borrowing firm or its shareholders that might weaken the value of the bonds. For example, restrictive covenants in an indenture may prohibit increases in a borrowing corporation's dividend rate (which would reduce the growth of its net worth), limit additional borrowing, restrict merger agreements, or limit the sale of the borrower's assets. These and other terms in a bond indenture are enforced by a third party—the trustee (often a bank trust department)—that represents investors holding the bonds. More restrictive indentures tend to lower interest costs for a borrowing company.

Recent Trends in Original Maturities of Bonds

The maturities attached to newly issued corporate bonds have fluctuated widely with changing economic conditions and shifts in interest rate expectations and the expectations for inflation. At the beginning of the twentieth century many railroads sold bonds with 100-year-plus maturities. During the 1950s and 1960s, corporations found a ready market for 20- to 30-year bonds, and telephone companies managed to sell 40-year bonds. Such long-term debt contracts are desirable from a borrowing company's point of view because they can lock in low interest costs for many years and make financial planning much simpler. However, the 1970s and 1980s ushered in a trend toward much shorter-maturity corporate debt issues (many in the 5- to 15-year range), due in part to rapid inflation and interest rates that soared to record levels. The development of sophisticated interest rate hedging tools (such as futures, options, and swaps) aided companies moving toward shorter-maturity bonds because these tools help minimize damage from more volatile short-term interest rates. Sharply lower interest rates and subdued inflation in the 1990s and into the twenty-first century, however, set in motion a swing back to longer maturity bonds. For example, government agencies like the Resolution Trust Corporation and the Tennessee Valley Authority issued 40- to 50-year bonds, while such companies as Walt Disney and Coca-Cola brought 100-year issues to market.

Call Privileges

A considerable proportion of corporate bonds that are outstanding today carry *call privileges,* allowing early redemption (retirement) of the bonds if market conditions prove favorable. The call privilege represents a way to shorten the average maturity of corporate bonds and gives the firm greater flexibility in financing its operations but can be expensive when interest rates are high and are expected to fall. Investors realize that the bond is likely to be called if interest rates fall and therefore demand a higher yield as compensation for the risk that the bond will be retired. However, many corporate bonds are issued today *without* a call privilege attached due to the added interest cost involved and the availability of hedging instruments such as futures and options.

Sinking Fund Provisions

Certain corporate bonds are backed by *sinking funds* designed to ensure that the issuing company will be able to pay off the bonds when they come due. Periodic payments are made into the fund on a schedule usually related to the depreciation of any assets supported by the bonds. The trustee is charged with the responsibility of making sure the user places the right amount of money in the sinking fund each time a payment is due. Periodically, a portion of the bonds may be retired from monies accumulated in the sinking fund (often annually). Sinking funds tend to reduce borrowing costs.

Yields and Costs of Corporate Bonds

Yields on the highest-grade corporate bonds tend to move closely with yields on government bonds. In contrast, yields carried by lower-grade corporate bonds are more closely tied to conditions in the economy and to factors specifically affecting the risk position of each borrowing firm. Bonds issued by the largest U.S. companies are, with few exceptions, listed and traded on the New York or American stock exchanges, although the largest volume of corporate bond trading passes through dealers operating off the exchanges.

As noted in Chapter 6, there are several different ways to measure the rate of return to the investor or the cost to the firm of issuing a debt security. From the point of view of the issuing company, one widely quoted measure of the cost of a bond is its *coupon rate*—the rate of interest the company promises to pay as printed on the face of the bond. However, the coupon rate may understate or overstate the true cost of a bond to the issuing company, depending on whether the bond was issued at a discount or at a premium from its par value. A better measure of the cost of issuing a bond is to compare the *net proceeds* available for the borrowing company's use from a bond sale to the present value of the stream of cash payments the firm must make to bondholders.

For example, suppose a corporation issues \$1,000 par bonds, but flotation costs reduce the net proceeds to the company from each bond to \$950.[1] If the bonds mature in 10 years and carry a 10 percent coupon rate, the before-tax cost, k, to the issuing company is figured as follows:

$$\text{Net proceeds per bond} = \frac{\text{Interest cost in year 1}}{(1 + k)^1} + \frac{\text{Interest cost in year 2}}{(1 + k)^2} \quad \textbf{(21–3)}$$

$$+ \ldots + \frac{\text{Interest cost in year 10}}{(1 + k)^{10}}$$

$$+ \frac{\text{Principal payments in year 10}}{(1 + k)^{10}}$$

In this example:

$$\$950 = \frac{\$100}{(1 + k)^1} + \frac{\$100}{(1 + k)^2} + \ldots + \frac{\$100}{(1 + k)^{10}} + \frac{\$1,000}{(1 + k)^{10}}$$

A check of a financial calculator or of the present value tables in the appendix at the back of this book indicates that k in this example is 10.85 percent.

However, interest charges on debt are *tax deductible,* making the after-tax cost considerably less than the before-tax cost, especially for the largest and most profitable firms. For the largest corporations with annual earnings in the top tax bracket, the marginal federal income tax rate is 35 percent. Thus, a large company issuing the bond described above would incur an after-tax cost (k') of

---

[1]The major elements of flotation cost for a new bond issue are the underwriting spread of the securities dealer who agrees to sell the issue, registration fees, paper and printing charges, and legal fees.

$$k' = k(1 - t) \qquad\qquad \textbf{(21–4)}$$

where *k* is the before-tax cost and *t* is the firm's marginal tax rate. In this example,

$$k' = 10.85\%(1 - 0.35) = 7.05\%$$

Of course, if the firm were in a lower tax bracket, the after-tax cost of its debt would be higher. In the case of an unprofitable company (whose effective tax rate is zero), the after-tax cost of debt would equal its before-tax cost.

The before- and after-tax costs of debt vary not only with each firm's tax rate but also with conditions in the financial markets. During periods of rapid economic expansion, when the supply of credit is scarce relative to the demand for credit, the cost of borrowing rises. Bonds must be marketed at lower prices and higher interest rates. Conversely, in periods when the economy contracts and easier credit conditions prevail, the cost of borrowing tends to decline. The prices of bonds rise and their interest returns fall. It should not surprise us to learn that the volume of long-term corporate borrowings often increases markedly during business recessions as companies attempt to lock in the relatively low interest rates available at that time. This happened in 2000 and 2001 when market interest rates fell to 40-year lows.

The Signals That Corporate Bond Issues Send

Like the taking on of other types of debt or the issuing of new stock, firms choosing to sell corporate bonds to raise funds send "signals" to the financial markets that, in turn, can affect the value of their securities in the minds of investors. For example, the apparent *motivation* for a new bond issue can be critical. If the bond issue announcement appears to be driven by an unanticipated cash-flow shortage from the assets of the issuing company and the market is aware of this, bond and equity prices of the issuer may fall and its borrowing costs rise. On the other hand, a new bond sold to expand and/or improve a firm's capitalization, to make a timely and well-considered acquisition, or for reasons other than unexpected cash deficits seems to send a *positive* signal to the market, and bondholders of the issuing firm may receive some positive abnormal returns. Where the financial markets cannot successfully discern the motivation for a new debt issue, equity and debt investors may experience some *negative* abnormal returns due, perhaps, to the implication that the assets the issuing company holds may be of lower value than first thought.

The Most Common Types of Corporate Bonds

Debentures

There are many different types of corporate bonds issued in the financial markets. Among the most common is the **debenture,** which is not secured by any specific asset owned by the issuing corporation. Instead, the holder of a debenture is a general creditor of the company and looks to the earning power and reputation of the borrower as the source of the bond's value.

Subordinated Debentures

A related form of bond is the subordinated debenture, frequently called a *junior security.* If a company goes out of business and its assets are liquidated, holders of subordinated debentures are paid only after all nonsubordinated creditors receive the monies owed them. Thus, there is greater risk with these instruments and a higher interest cost.

Mortgage Bonds

Debt securities representing a claim against specific assets (normally plant and equipment) owned by a corporation are known as **mortgage bonds.** These bonds may be either *closed end* or *open end.* Closed-end mortgage bonds do not permit the issuance of any additional debt against the assets already pledged under the mortgage. Open-end bonds, on the other hand, allow additional debt to be issued against pledged assets, which may dilute the claims of current bondholders. For this reason, open-end mortgage bonds typically carry higher yields than closed-end bonds. Sometimes several mortgage bonds with varying priorities of claim are issued against the same assets. For example, the initial issue of bonds against a corporation's fixed assets may be designated first mortgage bonds, and later second mortgage bonds may be issued against those same assets. If the company were liquidated, holders of second mortgage bonds would receive only those funds left over after holders of the first mortgage bonds were paid off.

Income Bonds

Bonds often used in corporate reorganizations and in other situations when a company is in financial distress are known as *income bonds.* Interest on these bonds is paid only when income is actually earned, making an income bond similar to common stock. However, holders of income bonds do have a prior claim on earnings over both stockholders and holders of subordinated debentures. Some income bonds carry a cumulative feature under which unpaid interest accumulates and must be fully paid before the stockholders receive any dividends.

Equipment Trust Certificates

Resembling a lease in form, *equipment trust certificates* are used most frequently to acquire industrial equipment or rolling stock (such as railroad cars or airplanes). Title to the assets acquired is vested in a trustee (often a bank trust department), which leases these assets to the company issuing the certificates. Periodic lease payments are made to the trustee, who passes them along to certificate holders. Title to the assets passes to the borrowing company only after all lease payments are made. Both equipment trust certificates and mortgage bonds tend to post lower interest rates than other corporate bonds because they are backed by specific marketable assets.

Industrial Development Bonds

In recent years, state and local governments have become more active in aiding private corporations to meet their financial needs. One of the most controversial forms of government-aided, long-term business borrowing is the **industrial development bond (IDB).** These bonds are issued by a local government borrowing authority to provide buildings, land, or equipment to a business firm. Because governmental units can borrow more cheaply than most private companies, the lower debt costs may be passed along to the firm as an inducement to move to a new location, bringing jobs to the local economy. The business firm normally guarantees both interest and principal payments on the IDBs by renting the buildings, land, or equipment at a rental fee high enough to cover debt service costs.

New Types of Corporate Notes and Bonds

Corporate bonds are traditionally called *fixed-income* securities because most pay a fixed amount of interest each year. This creates a problem for bondholders when interest rates rise, inflation increases, or both, because then the real market value of fixed-income securities falls. In recent years, repeated bouts with inflation or reduced quality ratings on corporate bonds have spurred companies to develop *new* types of bonds whose return to the investor is sensitive to changing inflation and changing bond values. New bonds have appeared with deferred interest payments and variable coupon (promised) rates of return to investors, in an attempt to help issuing companies with near-term cash shortages. Among the most popular of these innovative securities are discount bonds, floating-rate bonds, commodity-backed bonds, and medium-term notes (MTNs).

Discount bonds are sold at a price below par and appreciate toward par as maturity approaches. Thus, the investor earns capital gains as well as interest, while the issuing corporation usually can issue discount bonds at a lower after-tax cost than conventional bonds. Some discount bonds, known as **zero coupon bonds,** pay no interest at all. First used by J.C. Penney in 1981, "zeros" pay a return based solely on their price appreciation as they approach maturity. However, the annual price increase is taxable as ordinary income, not as capital gains, under current IRS regulations.

Floating-rate bonds have their annual promised rate tied to changes in long-term or short-term interest rates. *Commodity-backed bonds* carry a face value tied to the market price of an internationally traded commodity, such as gold, silver, or oil, that presumably is sensitive to inflation.

Medium-term notes (MTNs), carrying maturities of one to 10 years, exploded onto the corporate fund-raising scene during the 1980s and 1990s. Although they were developed as long ago as the early 1970s, MTNs outstanding rose to over $100 billion during the 1990s, compared to less than $1 billion in 1980. These securities are generally noncallable, unsecured, fixed-rate obligations. One advantage of MTNs for borrowing corporations is the ability to reduce exposure to interest rate risk, because MTNs give companies more opportunities to match the maturities of the assets they wish to acquire with the maturities of their liabilities.

One of the distinguishing hallmarks of U.S. corporate debt markets is their ability to provide funds to businesses at virtually every stage of their existence—from completely *new* ventures (where venture capital funds, pension plans, and even some banks provide start-up capital), to firms going public for the first time (i.e., initial public offerings (IPOs), where venture capitalists and pension plans are often joined by insurance companies and wealthy individuals), to mature companies that have either routine long-term capital needs (often satisfied via the public sale of bonds to large numbers of investors and institutions), to companies with unusual financing needs (which may require the private sale of a new debt issue to a handful of sophisticated investing institutions). Most notable in recent years is the wider opening of corporate debt markets to small- and medium-size firms who can more easily sell lower-quality "junk" debt securities in the open (public) market than in the past, such as by getting *credit guarantees* from investment banks and other strong institutions to broaden the group of investors interested in their new debt offerings.

For more information on the European corporate debt market see especially the Bond Market Association's European Issues segment of their Web site at *www. bondmarkets. com/research*

One of the most exciting developments in the corporate bond market today is the rapid growth and development of Europe's corporate bond market, spurred on by that continent's unfolding unity into one economy and one financial system. Differences in bond yields issued from different European Community (EC) member nations have recently declined, so that European bond dealers are finding that traditional arbitrage profits—switching between the bonds of different European countries—are sharply reduced. With the decline in interest-rate spreads, European bond dealers are looking for new ways to make money, such as by increasing the size of the European junk bond market and getting bond-issuing firms more interested in asset-backed bonds. At the same time significant volumes of new Euro-denominated bonds are appearing in global financial markets in order to take advantage of public interest in the new EC international currency, the Euro. Some U.S. companies, like Citigroup, are introducing European investors to asset-backed securities, while U.S. investors are increasingly seeking out European junk bonds because American investors are more used to buying high-risk bonds than are many European investors.

Questions ***to Help You Study***

1. Please explain what is meant by the statement: "The financial markets are a supplemental funds source for business." What factors appear to affect the volume of business fund-raising from the money and capital markets?
2. What *advantages* does the issuance of debt have over other sources of funds that a business firm might pursue? How about *disadvantages?*
3. Please define each of the following terms having to do with business borrowing:

Indenture	*Sinking fund*
Call privilege	*Mortgage bond*
Subordinated debenture	*Industrial development bond (IDB)*
Income bond	*Debenture*
Trustee	*Equipment trust certificate*

4. Please explain how the *true cost* of a corporate bond may be determined.

INVESTORS IN CORPORATE BONDS

Today the investor market for corporate bonds is dominated by insurance companies, mutual funds, and pension funds (see Exhibit 21–1). Pension funds prefer buying corporate bonds in the open market; insurance companies, on the other hand, frequently purchase their corporate securities directly from the issuing company in an off-the-market transaction. The stability of cash flows experienced by pension funds and insurance companies permits them to pursue corporate bonds of long maturities and to lock in their higher yields.

One of the more dynamic investor segments in U.S. corporate bonds includes *foreign* institutions, particularly leading security dealers, banks, and insurance firms, such as Credit Suisse and Deutsche Bank. Many purchases of U.S. bonds have been associated with foreign takeovers of U.S. companies and the desire of foreign investors to pursue safer investments in the United States in order to escape political and economic turmoil abroad and

EXHIBIT 21–1
Principal Investors in Corporate and Foreign Bonds, 2000*

Source: Board of Governors of the Federal Reserve System, *Flow of Funds Accounts: Financial Assets and Liabilities,* Third Quarter 2000.

Investor Group	Amount	Percent of Total Bond Holdings
Households	$ 728.9	14.8%
Rest of the world (foreign investors)	951.9	19.4
Commercial banks	253.5	5.2
Savings institutions	107.3	2.2
Life insurance companies	1,204.4	24.5
Property-casualty insurance companies	185.1	3.8
Private pension funds	286.8	5.8
Government pension funds	324.4	6.6
Mutual funds	368.4	7.5
Security brokers and dealers	116.6	2.4
Other investors	387.6	7.9
Totals	$4,914.9	100.0%

Note: Columns may not add to totals due to rounding.
*Figures are for the third quarter of the year at annualized rates.

to take advantage of strong U.S. economic conditions relative to other parts of the globe. Then, too, the purchase of dollar-denominated assets such as corporate bonds gives foreign investors a way to store U.S. dollars at high yield until those dollars are needed either to buy U.S. goods or to purchase commodities sold in international markets that are denominated in dollars (such as oil).

Commercial banks are *not* among the heaviest investors in corporate bonds. Generally, bankers prefer to deal personally with a business customer and grant a loan specifically tailored to the borrower's needs rather than to enter the impersonal bond market. Increasingly in recent years, commercial banks have become direct competitors with the corporate bond market through the granting of *term loans*. A term loan has a maturity of more than one year. Responding to inflation and the rising cost of business equipment, bankers have gradually extended the maturity of term loans, with many falling in the 5- to 10-year maturity range. Interest rates on such loans generally exceed the interest cost on corporate debt sold in the open market, however, especially when banks also insist that the borrowing firm keep funds on deposit with the bank.

One area of concern among many corporate bond investors in recent years has been an apparent decline in the overall credit quality of corporate bonds. A substantial proportion of all corporate bonds issued over the past two decades in the United States have been "junk bonds." Significant numbers of industrial bond issuers have seen their credit ratings reduced by credit rating agencies. As the danger of default has risen, capital market investors have demanded higher promised rates of interest on newly issued corporate bonds or special covenants, allowing investors to redeem their bonds with the issuing companies at a fixed price if their credit rating is lowered or if the bondholders' position is weakened by restructuring of the issuing firm's capital.

Despite the rapid growth of bonds in the United States in recent years, bond holdings by Americans have nowhere near kept up with Americans' stock holdings. For example, the percentage of savings invested in bonds by U.S. households fell from about 26 percent in 1990 to just below 20 percent in 2000, while stock ownership rose from about 28 percent to more than 50 percent of U.S. savings over the same time period. Both individuals and institutional investors reduced their corporate bond holdings relative to stocks and other investments. In the meantime, foreign investors (especially from Europe, Japan, the Asian mainland, Canada, and Latin America) have accelerated their purchases of U.S. government and corporate bonds, whose superior yields and safety have made them particularly attractive to overseas investors worried about their own nation's economy. While the interest of foreign investors in U.S. bonds and other securities weakened somewhat after the September 2001 terrorist attacks, the U.S. bond market still looks much stronger than most overseas bond markets.

THE SECONDARY MARKET FOR CORPORATE BONDS

The resale (secondary) market for corporate bonds is relatively limited compared to the larger resale markets for common stock, municipal bonds, and other long-term securities. Trading volume is thin, even for some bonds issued by the largest companies. Part of the reason is the small number of individuals active as investors in this market. Individuals generally have limited investment time horizons (holding periods) and tend to turn over their portfolios rapidly when other attractive investments appear. In the past, secondary market trading in corporate bonds was also held back by the "buy and hold" strategy of institutional investors, especially insurance companies and pension funds. Many of these firms purchased corporate bonds exclusively for interest income and were content to purchase the longest-term issues and simply hold them to maturity. However, under the pressure of volatile interest rates and inflation, many institutions buying corporate bonds have recently shifted into a more aggressive strategy labeled *total performance.* Portfolio managers are more sensitive today to changes in bond prices and look for near-term opportunities to sell bonds and make capital gains. In fact, a number of insurance companies, pension funds, and mutual funds operate their own trading departments and keep constant tabs on developments in the corporate bond market.

Unlike the stock market, no one central exchange for bond trading dominates the market. Although corporate bonds are traded on all major exchanges, including the New York Stock Exchange (NYSE), most secondary market trading in bonds is conducted over the telephone and through electronic networks linking customers, brokers, and dealers. Dealers commit themselves to take on large blocks of bonds either from other dealers or from pension funds, insurance companies, and other clients. Due to rapid and unpredictable changes in interest rates, many dealers now try to close out positions taken in individual bonds very quickly, frequently acting only as intermediaries in trades between investors without committing their own capital.

THE MARKETING OF CORPORATE NOTES AND BONDS

New corporate bonds may be offered publicly in the open market to all interested buyers or sold privately to a limited number of investors. The first route, known as **public sale,** accounts for the largest proportion of corporate bond sales each year. Among smaller companies and those firms with unique financing requirements, however, the second route, known as a **private or direct placement,** has been popular.

The Public Sale of Bonds

The sale of new corporate bonds in the open market is handled principally by investment bankers. The term **investment banker** is somewhat misleading, because these firms have little or nothing to do with banking as we know it. In fact, the Glass-Steagall Act of 1933 prohibited U.S. commercial banks from underwriting most types of corporate securities until 1999 when the Financial Services Modernization (Gramm-Leach-Bliley) Act was passed, allowing U.S. commercial banks greater freedom to underwrite corporate bonds and stock through holding companies. Recently commercial banks in the United States and Europe have captured a growing share of the investment banking market. Among the leaders in this field today are such banking-centered firms as Citigroup, Deutsche Bank, J.P. Morgan Chase, and Bank of America. So fast has been the rise of commercial banking organizations in underwriting bonds and stock that by 2001 Citigroup Inc. had moved close to the top of Wall Street's list of underwriters.

Investment banks underwrite new issues of corporate stocks and bonds and give advice to corporations on their financing requirements. An investment banking firm may singly take on a new issue of corporate securities or band together with other underwriters to form a *syndicate.* Either way, the investment banker's game plan is to acquire new corporate securities at the lowest possible price and sell them as quickly as possible in order to turn a profit. An investment banker may purchase the securities from the issuing company directly or merely guarantee the issuer a specific price for his securities. With either approach, it is the investment banker who carries the risk of gains or losses when the securities are marked for sale in the open market.

The largest issues of corporate bonds sold in the open market are usually bid upon by several groups of underwriters. Competition among these syndicates can be intense. In-

Management Insight   Recent Top U.S. Bond Underwriters (Measured by Volume of New Issues Brought to Market)

Merrill Lynch & Co.	Credit Suisse Group
Citigroup Inc.	J.P. Morgan/Chase Bank
Morgan Stanley	Bear, Stearns, & Co., Inc.
Goldman Sachs Group Inc.	Deutsche Bank AG
Lehman Brothers	Donaldson Lufkin

Source: Security Dealers Association and the Federal Reserve Board.

vestment bankers hope to acquire a new issue at the lowest possible bid price and place the securities with investors at a higher retail price, maximizing the *spread,* or return on invested capital. Unfortunately, each new bond issue is always somewhat different from those that have traded before and may involve hundreds of millions or even billions of dollars. Moreover, a decision on what price to bid for new securities must be made *before* the bonds are released for public trading; in the interim, prices may change drastically. If the underwriter bids too high a price, the firm may not be able to resell the securities at a price high enough to recover the cost and secure an adequate spread. To cite an example, a number of years ago, IBM Corporation offered $1 billion in notes and debentures through a collection of Wall Street underwriters. Unfortunately, just as the IBM issue was coming to market, bond prices tumbled (due, in part, to an announcement by the Federal Reserve suggesting that credit conditions might be tightened to deal with inflation). The underwriters suffered a massive loss on this particular security issue.

Competition in the bidding process tends to narrow the underwriter's spread between bid and asked price. If several investment banking houses band together in a syndicate, a consensus bid price must be hammered out among the participants. Disagreements frequently arise within a syndicate due to different perceptions about the probable future direction of interest rates. Because dozens of underwriters may be included in a single syndicate, the task of reaching a compromise and placing a unified bid for a new security issue may prove impossible. The old syndicate may break apart, with those bidders still interested in the issue hurriedly piecing together a new bid.

A number of factors are considered in pricing a new corporate bond issue. Certainly the credit ratings assigned by Moody's, Standard & Poor's Corporation, or other rating agencies are a key item, because many investors rely on such agencies for assessing the risk carried by a new security.[2] Another factor is the "forward calendar" of security offerings, which lists new issues expected to come to market during the next few weeks. Obviously, if a heavy volume of new offerings is anticipated in the near term, prices will decline unless additional demand appears. Changes in government policy must be anticipated because that policy can have profound effects on security prices. Other factors considered by investment bankers include the size of the issue, how aggressive other bidders are likely to be, and the strength of the "book," which consists of indications of advance investor interest in the security being offered.

[2]See Chapter 8 for a discussion of security credit ratings.

International Focus Recent Leading Worldwide Bond Dealers

Merrill Lynch & Co.
Goldman Sachs Group Inc.
Morgan Stanley
Citigroup Inc.
Credit Commercial de France (CCF)
Bear, Stearns International Limited

Lehman Brothers
Paine Webber
UBS
Fiduciary Trust International Ltd.
J.P. Morgan/Chase Securities, Inc.
Credit Suisse Group

Once the securities are received from the issuing company, the underwriters advertise their availability at the price agreed on by all members of the syndicate. *Delay* in selling new securities is one of the investment banker's worst enemies, because additional financing must be obtained to carry the unsold securities. Also, there is the added risk of price declines as time increases. To speed the process of selling new bonds, many investment banking firms today have relationships with retail brokerage companies that maintain working agreements with large buyers, such as insurance companies and pension funds.

What happens to the market prices of securities sold by investment banking syndicates is the key determinant of the success or failure of the underwriting process. It takes only a small decline in retail price before the underwriter's profit is eliminated. Moreover, unfavorable price movements can damage the reputation of the investment banker with investors and the client companies that issue new securities. Clearly, investment banking is both risky and highly competitive.

Late in the 1990s an intense controversy began to grow about the pricing practices of dealers in the corporate bond market. Some dealer firms, for example, had been marking the prices of bonds to their customers well above the prevailing open-market price (for example, with markups of up to 5 to 10 percent and sometimes more). One problem that permitted these large markups to take place was the delays in getting up-to-date information on actual trading prices. While stocks are often traded both on organized exchanges and through dealers who post new prices almost instantaneously, bonds are traded largely over the counter through security dealers who, within the limits of competition, can quote almost any price because the buyer may not be able to easily compare the price offered against the most recent trade of the same or a similar bond.

Bond dealers often defend their markups by pointing to the risks they face when they purchase blocks of corporate bonds and then the market value of their bonds suddenly falls when interest rates rise. An added problem is the diversity in bond markets, where there are thousands of different government and private bonds trading, some of which may go several days without any current transactions, leaving the bond dealer with no current price to use as a reference point for pricing a new sale. Still, many investors would like to have a sales receipt that details all of the costs they are paying (including dealer price markups) when they purchase new bonds. Borrowers (bond issuers) sometimes report a similar information problem; often an issuer is unable to get precise price quotes on bonds sold so that the issuer can calculate the true cost he or she is paying. This price information would be of great help to a company trying to decide whether to finance itself by issuing new bonds or to explore some other financing route instead.

Private Placements of Corporate Bonds

In recent years, private placements of bonds with one or a limited group of well-informed investors have represented a significant proportion of public sales. For example, in recent years, private placements have accounted for about 20 percent of public market sales of corporate bonds. However, the ratio of private to public sales is sensitive to the changing composition of borrowing companies and to economic conditions. Usually, periods of rising interest rates and reduced credit availability bring more borrowing companies into the public market, and falling interest rates often bring a rise in private placements. For the largest corporations, public sales and private placements are *substitutes*. When interest rates are high or credit is tight in one of these markets, the largest borrowers shift to the other market. Most of the borrowers in the private market are small- and medium-sized corporations, however.

Private placements were significantly aided by a ruling of the U.S. Securities and Exchange Commission (SEC) known as Rule 144A. The SEC eliminated restrictions on the secondary trading of private placements by large institutional investors (known as QIBs, or qualified investment buyers). This step, in effect, created a secondary market for privately placed bonds, overcoming one of the historic barriers confronting investors who otherwise might be interested in privately placed securities. Revisions in Rule 144A have brought investment banks into the private placement arena to actively underwrite and distribute these securities. Privately placed bonds have become more liquid, bringing major new investors, such as mutual funds, into this market. The private-placement market has also been aided by the increasing presence of foreign investors and foreign issuers of private bonds in U.S. markets and by the growing number of corporate mergers and divestitures. Much of the divestiture activity reflects companies attempting to downsize their operations in order to trim operating costs or to raise scarce capital by selling marketable assets. Corporate mergers, in contrast, reflect the broadening of markets and the search for economies of scale in production and marketing.

Who buys privately placed bonds? Life insurance companies, finance companies, and pension funds, historically, have been the principal investors in this market. These institutions hope to secure higher yields and protection against call privileges by engaging in *direct negotiation* with borrowing corporations and by using due diligence and engaging in careful monitoring of any loans they grant. The avoidance of call privileges is of special benefit to life insurance companies and pension funds because these institutions prefer the stable income that comes from purchasing long-term bonds and holding them to maturity. In fact, institutional investors active in the private-placement market frequently impose extra fees in a sales contract containing an allowance for early retirement of a security by the issuing corporation. Investors other than life insurance companies and pension funds tend to play smaller roles in the private market due to their lack of expertise, small size, and the limited resale market for privately placed securities. In recent years, some life insurance companies have sharply curtailed their purchases of privately placed securities due to public pressure on insurers to strengthen their balance sheets and because many borrowers in the private-placement market have experienced lower credit ratings, presenting more risk to investors.

There are several advantages to the borrower from a private placement. One is the lower cost of distribution because there are no registration fees associated with the issuance of a prospectus as there would be with a public sale. Private placements are exempt from registration with the Securities and Exchange Commission (SEC). Generally, more rapid placement of bonds takes place in the private market because only a few buyers are involved and the loan is confidential. Special concessions can often be secured, such as a commitment for future borrowing. For example, a corporate borrower may negotiate a private sale of

$50 million in bonds to an insurance company but also may be granted a line of credit up to $2 million a year over the next five years. This kind of commitment is not usually possible in the impersonal public market, where bonds' features are highly standardized. Moreover, lenders in the private market try to tailor the terms of a loan to match the specific cash flow needs of borrowers. This may involve a conventional fixed-rate credit contract at the prevailing interest rate, a floating-rate loan that can be retired early if cash flows permit, or even a participating loan in which the lender charges a lower interest rate in return for a share of income from the project financed.

There is some evidence that private placements are more effective than public-sale corporate bond issues in keeping "agency conflicts" between borrowers and lenders under control (see Chapter 3). Due in part to the superior debt monitoring ability of the typical private-placement market buyer and the greater possibility of renegotiation of terms under a private sale as the conditions surrounding borrowers and lenders change, the private placement market may minimize agency conflicts between bond holders and bond issuers, helping to protect the interests of both buyers and sellers. Due to the private placement market's advantages, smaller businesses, privately held companies, and many foreign firms often prefer going the private-placement route as opposed to choosing a sale of bonds in the open market. However, predictably, private-sale borrowers usually pay higher costs for their issues than those companies (particularly very large firms) that can easily move back and forth, if they wish, between the public-sale and the private-sale markets.

One disadvantage is that interest costs generally are higher in private sales than in public sales. Moreover, private sale bonds are less liquid and often carry more risk of default. One indication of this is that privately placed debt issues tend to have more restrictive covenants in order to protect lenders. Still, the larger the size of a corporate issue, the smaller the cost differential between public and private placements tends to be.

Questions *to Help You Study*

5. Who are the *principal buyers* of corporate notes and bonds? Why are these groups of investors especially interested in acquiring these instruments?

6. Describe the important role that *investment bankers* play in the functioning of the corporate bond market.

7. What are the principal types of *risk* that investment bankers take on? What factors must an investment banker consider in *pricing* a new corporate bond issue?

8. Explain what is meant by a *private placement.* Who purchases privately placed corporate bonds and why?

9. What are the principal *advantages* to a business borrower from offering debt in the private placement market? Can you see any *disadvantages?*

THE VOLUME OF BORROWING IN THE CORPORATE BOND MARKET

The volume of borrowing through new issues of corporate bonds has grown rapidly in recent years (see Exhibit 21–2). For example, annual offerings of new corporate debt securities nearly quadrupled between 1960 and 1970, nearly doubled between 1970 and 1980, more than doubled between 1980 and 1990, and then more than quadrupled between 1990 and 2000. In 2002 GE Capital brought to market the largest U.S. dollar-denominated corporate bond issue in history at $11 billion. Much of this growth in corporate borrowing could be traced to inflation, which reduced the real cost of debt, to increased use of finan-

Financial Developments   Corporate Debt Issues Often Soar When Borrowing Is Cheap

As Finance theory teaches us, corporations and other businesses tend to accelerate their borrowings when the cost of borrowed funds falls. When it's cheaper to raise new funds by borrowing, more businesses tend to borrow and in larger amounts.

Recent history provides a dramatic example of this fundamental point. In 2001 corporate bond rates dropped to some of the lowest levels seen in decades as the economy softened and inflation appeared to be under control. For example, by the fall of 2001 high-quality, 1-to-10-year corporate notes and bonds fell to an average interest yield of only about 4.5 percent, while top-quality 10+-year corporate bonds were averaging an interest yield of only about 6.75 percent—just one and a half percentage points above the return on U.S. Treasury securities. Accordingly, several of the largest corporate debt offerings in history quickly came to market.

For example, in March 2001 France Telecom offered $16.4 billion in new corporate debt—thus far, the all-time record corporate debt offering. In June of the same year, Deutsche Telekom in Germany sold close to $15 billion in new debt, followed by a nearly $12 billion offering by WorldCom. By the third quarter of 2001, total corporate debt outstanding was close to $5 trillion, or about double its total only a decade earlier.

Does this mean that falling interest rates will always bring forth a flood of new corporate borrowings? The answer is "no, not always."

For one thing, businesses must decide what *purpose* a new borrowing will serve. For example, if a profitable investment opportunity shows up, borrowing money usually makes sense. On the other hand, if no potentially profitable investment opportunities appear, then business borrowing may not be advisable because taking on new debt increases a firm's ratio of total debt to equity capital and raises its probability of failure.

Interest rates usually drop to low levels when the economy is weak. At such times there *may* be fewer promising opportunities to make profitable investments and, therefore, fewer good reasons to borrow large amounts of funds.

cial leverage to boost returns to corporate stockholders, to the development of international capital markets, and to relatively lower long-term interest rates in the 1990s and early in the twenty-first century. This track record suggests that the corporate bond market is very sensitive to economic conditions and to changes in the cost of long-term credit.

Another factor that has spurred the private bond market's growth is a rash of corporate takeovers and merger proposals. Targets for these corporate raids have included such well-known companies as CBS, Firestone Tire, J.P. Morgan, Hilton Hotels, Uniroyal, Pennzoil, and Paine Webber to name just a few. Many of these mergers have been motivated by deregulation of key industries in recent years, including the airlines, commercial banking, and telecommunications; by more liberal antitrust rules followed by the U.S. government; and by the desire of many foreign investors to establish business operations inside U.S. territory.

EXHIBIT 21–2

The Growth of Corporate Bonds and Notes Issued by Companies in the United States ($ Millions)

Source: U.S. Department of Commerce and Board of Governors of the Federal Reserve System.

Year	New Issues of Corporate Bonds and Notes
1950	$ 4,920
1960	8,081
1970	30,321
1980	53,199
1990	114,500
2000*	809,500

*All figures in the exhibit represent gross proceeds of issues maturing in more than one year and are the principal amount or number of units multiplied by the offering price. Figures exclude secondary offerings, employee stock plans, mutual funds, intracorporate transactions, and Yankee bonds (sold by foreign corporations inside U.S. territory). Before 1987, the figures included only those issues that were underwritten.

Frequently, these proposed mergers include plans to offer billions of dollars in *junk bonds*—high-interest-cost, low-credit-rated debt securities—as well as bank loans to finance the transaction. With the expanded use of debt, the credit ratings of scores of corporations have been reduced in recent years and several major failures have occurred, led by such well-known bankrupt firms as Enron Corp., KMart, Bethlehem Steel, and Polaroid. The growth of the *junk bond market* has been spurred by corporations' desire to restructure their capital, replacing stock with debt or replacing short-term securities with long-term bonds. In fact, the volume of corporate stock retirements, replaced in most cases by debt, broke all previous records during the 1980s and 1990s. A number of these retirements were carried out to discourage "hostile" takeovers or to participate in corporate mergers and acquisitions. The federal government's antitrust policy has taken a turn toward ease in recent decades, allowing more mergers and acquisitions to take place without government challenge. Then, too, many companies not well known to investors have been able to approach the bond market for funds for the first time, thanks to the rapid expansion of the market for junk bonds and the growing use of credit enhancements that permit lower-quality borrowers to successfully tap the open market for funds. Soon, junk bond issues accounted for close to one-third of all public bond offerings in the United States, of which about two-thirds were designed for financing mergers and restructuring corporate capital.

A substantial proportion of recent corporate takeovers has been in the form of **leveraged buyouts,** in which a single investor or small group of investors (frequently including senior management of the target company) buys the publicly owned stock of a business firm by borrowing 80 to 90 percent or more of the purchase price from banks and the bond market. In many leveraged buyouts (LBOs), the assets of companies that previously were publicly owned (that is, their stock was widely dispersed among thousands of investors) were conveyed to closely held private companies and partnerships. In these instances, the takeover group is counting on faster growth and improved profitability of the target company or on selling some of its assets to pay off the huge volume of acquisition debt. Because such expectations are fraught with risk, leading analysts have expressed concern over many buyouts, fearing they may undermine public confidence in the financial system as corporate debt continues to pile higher.

Investors like to keep close track of bond market conditions in order to look for favorable trades. Several good Web sites to follow the market include *www.cnnfn.com* and *www.bondmarkets.com*

These debt-funded mergers have generated much proposed federal and state legislation to prevent "corporate raiders" from taking over some companies. Some targeted firms have developed shark repellents or poison pills, such as favorable deals for outside investors not affiliated with a corporate raider, revisions in corporate charters that make it more difficult for outsiders to take over the firm, and the taking on of heavy debt which makes the company less attractive as a takeover target. Surprisingly, research evidence shows that stockholders of companies targeted for acquisition benefit from takeover activity, even when the planned takeover is unsuccessful. Investors apparently believe that such takeovers will improve the efficiency and profitability of the target companies beyond what their existing management has been able to do and the stock of the target firm often rises in value, at least initially.

BANK LOANS TO BUSINESS FIRMS

Commercial banks are direct competitors with the corporate bond markets in making both long-term and short-term loans to business. In fact, growing numbers of corporations that once relied on banks for funds have turned instead to selling bonds in the open market, decreasing the relative importance of banks in the financial system. Still, the volume of bank credit made available to business firms remains enormous. For example, by January 2001, commercial and industrial loans extended by commercial banks operating in the United States totaled more than $1.1 trillion, or almost 30 percent of all U.S. commercial bank loans. Banks grant their loans to a wide variety of firms covering all major sectors of the business community. And bankers have come to play a key supporting role in the corporate debt market, issuing standby credit guarantees on behalf of borrowing companies to pay off their customers' debt if the borrowing companies cannot do so.

In recent years, the Federal Reserve Board has carried out periodic surveys of business lending practices by banks across the United States. These Federal Reserve surveys indicate that bank loans to business firms tend to be relatively short in maturity. For example, recent surveys suggest that short-term commercial and industrial loans average less than two months to maturity, while long-term business loans average just three to four years in maturity. The Federal Reserve surveys suggest that longer-term business loans carry *higher* average interest rates than do short-term business loans. This is due, in part, to the greater risk associated with long-term credit. In addition, yield curves have usually sloped upward in recent years, calling for higher rates on long-term loans.[3] Moreover, the larger and longer-term a business loan is, the more likely its interest rate will *float* with market conditions. Clearly, banks become more determined to protect themselves against unexpected inflation and other adverse developments through floating interest rates as the maturity and size of a business loan increase.

The Prime, or Base, Interest Rate

One of the best-known and most widely followed interest rates in the financial system is the prime bank rate, sometimes called the **base rate,** or *reference rate.*[4] The prime rate is an annual percentage rate that banks may quote to their most creditworthy customers. Most prime loans are unsecured, but the borrowers often are required to keep a deposit at the lending bank equal to a specified percentage of the loan. This *compensating balance* normally is 15 to 20 percent of the amount loaned. Even for a prime borrower, therefore, the true cost of a bank loan is normally higher than the prime rate itself. Most prime loans are short-term—one year or less—loans taken out to finance purchases of business inventory and other working capital needs or to support construction projects.

Each bank must set its own prime, or base rate, following a vote by its board of directors. Beginning in the 1930s, however, a uniform prime rate began to appear, with differences in loan rates from bank to bank quickly eliminated by competition. Split primes do occur for some periods of time, however. A bank strapped for loanable funds may keep its prime rate temporarily above rates posted by other banks in order to ration the available supply of credit. Similarly, a bank with ample funds to lend may post a prime temporarily below market to encourage its customers to borrow more frequently and in larger amounts.

---

[3]See Chapter 7 for a discussion of yield curves and the factors that shape them.
[4]*Base rate* is a more general term than prime, referring to that loan interest rate used as the basis for determining the current rate charged a borrower. Most business loan rates are scaled upward from the base rate. Many commercial loans today are tied to base rates other than prime, however. This is frequently the case for large multinational companies that have ready access to credit markets abroad. For example, the London Interbank Offer Rate (LIBOR) on short-term Eurodollar deposits is often used as a base rate for large corporate loans. In some cases, the commercial paper rate, the federal funds rate, or the secondary market rate on bank CDs is also used as a loan base rate. Smaller numbers of borrowers today remain tied to the prime rate and include less mobile customers with fewer alternatives than many of the largest corporations, which have numerous alternative sources of funds and therefore can frequently demand credit at interest rates significantly less than prime. Such large loans are often made today at contract rates only fractions of a percentage point above a bank's cost of raising funds in the money market.

Traditionally, the prime rate was set by one or more of the nation's leading banks, and other banks followed the leader. However, a major innovation in the market for prime loans occurred in 1971 when Citibank of New York (now a part of Citigroup) announced it would *float* its prime. Citibank's basic lending rate was pegged on a weekly basis at half a percentage point above the yield on 90-day commercial paper. Other leading banks soon followed, pegging their prime rates to prevailing yields on Treasury bills and other money market instruments. Linking the prime to such active money market rates as those attached to Treasury bills and commercial paper resulted in a more flexible base lending rate. The prime has come to reflect more accurately the forces of shifting credit demands, fluctuations in government policy, and inflation. A more flexible prime has enabled banks to better protect their interest margins—the difference between the return on loans and the cost of bank funds— and to make credit more readily available to customers willing to pay the price.

Many business loans today are priced at *premiums* above the prime or other base rate because only the most financially sound customers qualify for prime or below-prime loans. Nevertheless, commercial loan rates typically are tied to the base rate through a carefully worked out formula. One popular approach, *prime plus,* adds on a rate premium for default risk and often an additional premium for longer maturities (term risk). Thus, the banker may quote a commercial customer "prime plus 2," with a 1 percent premium above the base rate for default risk and another 1 percent premium for term risk. Other banks may use the *times-prime* method, which multiplies the base rate by a risk factor. For example, the business customer may be quoted a loan at 1.5 times prime. If the current prime is 10 percent, this customer pays 15 percent. If the loan carries a floating rate, then the interest rate in future periods can always be calculated by multiplying the base rate by 1.5.

Which of these formulas the banker uses often depends on his or her forecast of interest rates. In a period of falling rates, interest charges on floating-rate loans figured on a times-prime basis decline faster than those based on prime plus. When interest rates are on the rise, times-prime pricing results in more rapid increases in business loan rates. Therefore, times-prime financing is more sensitive to the changing cost of bank funds over the course of the business cycle.

COMMERCIAL MORTGAGES

The construction of office buildings, shopping centers, and other commercial structures is generally financed with an instrument known as the **commercial mortgage.** Short-term mortgage loans are used to finance the construction of commercial projects, and longer-term mortgages are employed to pay off short-term construction loans, purchase land, and cover property development costs. The majority of long-term commercial mortgage loans are made by life insurance companies, thrift institutions, finance companies, and pension funds; commercial banks are the predominant short-term commercial mortgage lender. Banks support the construction of office buildings and other commercial projects with loans secured by land and building materials. These short-term mortgage credits fall due when construction is completed, with permanent financing of the project then passing to insurance companies and other long-term lenders.

Additional information about the commercial mortgage market is available from such Web sites as REBUZ at *www.rebuz.com* and *www.bondmarkets.com/ research*

The growth of commercial mortgages has fluctuated in recent years. The dollar volume of such loans more than tripled during the 1970s. However, the market was buffeted by severe problems in the 1980s and early 1990s due to overbuilding of commercial space and weakening demand, although lower interest rates eventually stimulated a higher volume of commercial mortgage financings. By 1990, commercial mortgages had nearly tripled again from their 1980 level but then fell slightly in the mid-1990s, reflecting a more slowly growing economy and the availability of other sources of funding. These mortgages spurted upward again as the turn of the century approached, reflecting a relatively strong U.S. economy, before slowing as the twenty-first century dawned and building and office capacity rose relative to the demand for commercial space.

In the past, most commercial real estate financing was provided through *fixed-rate mortgages.* Faced with inflation and a volatile economy, however, commercial mortgage lenders began searching for new financial instruments to protect their return. Many mortgage lenders today combine both debt and equity financing in the same credit package. The best-known example is the *equity kicker,* where the lending institution grants a fixed-rate mortgage but also receives a share of any net earnings from the project. For example, a life insurance company may agree to provide $50 million to finance the construction of an office building. It agrees to accept a 15-year mortgage loan bearing a 10 percent interest rate. However, as a hedge against inflation and higher interest rates, the insurance company may also insist on receiving 10 percent of any net earnings generated from office rentals over the 15-year period.

Another device used recently in commercial mortgage financing is *indexing.* In this case, the annual interest rate on a loan may be tied to prevailing yields on high-quality government or public utility bonds. Lender and borrower may agree to renegotiate the interest rate at certain intervals, such as every three to five years. There is also a trend toward shorter maturity commercial mortgage loans—many as short as five years—with the borrower paying off the debt or refinancing the unpaid principal with the same or another lending institution.

One innovation that appeared in the commercial mortgage market during the 1990s is *securitized commercial mortgages.* Private lenders and federal agencies have sought ways to free up their lending capacity by packaging large amounts of commercial real estate loans, taking them off the balance sheet and placing them into trust accounts or with security dealers, and then issuing securities against the packaged loans. Sellers of these securities (led by such firms as Goldman Sachs and Prudential Insurance Company) frequently arrange guarantees from the security issuers, resulting in many of the commercial mortgage-backed securities being rated "investment grade," and thus attracting major financial institutions as buyers.

Questions *to Help You Study*

10. What is a *leveraged buyout?* A *junk bond?* What are the dangers associated with these financial devises and instruments?

11. Please supply a definition for each of the following terms:
    Term loan
    Floating rate
    Prime rate
    Compensating balance

12. For what purposes are *commercial mortgages* issued? What changes have occurred recently in the terms attached to these mortgage instruments?

13. What is an *equity kicker?* What are its principal advantages over a straight commercial mortgage loan?

Summary of the Chapter

This chapter focused upon businesses raising funds by borrowing in the open market and by seeking loans extended by banks and other financial institutions.

- The majority of funds drawn upon by business firms to meet their working capital and other investment needs normally come, not from the financial marketplace, but from inside the individual business firm. In most periods half or more of business capital requirements are supplied by earnings and noncash depreciation expenses (i.e., *internal cash flow*).

- Roughly a quarter to slightly less than one-half of business investment needs in recent years have been met by selling securities in the financial markets. The financial system is a backstop for the operations of business firms for those periods when internally generated cash fails to increase fast enough to support the growth of sales.

- The financial markets provide both short-term working capital to meet current expenses and long-term funds to support the purchase of buildings and equipment. The principal external sources of working capital include trade credit (accounts payable), bank loans and acceptances, short-term credits from nonbank financial institutions (such as finance companies), and sales of commercial paper in the open market.

- For businesses in need of long-term funding, the principal funds sources are the sale of bonds and notes, term loans from banks, the issuance of common and preferred stock, and commercial mortgages, with open-market business borrowing generally growing and bank borrowing declining in overall importance in recent years.

- Corporate *bonds* have original maturities of more than five years; *notes* carry maturities of five years or less. There is a trend toward shorter maturities of corporate securities due to inflation and rapid changes in technology. Indexing of corporate bond rates to broader movements in the economy has also become somewhat more common.

- A wide variety of different bond and note issues have been developed to provide investors with varying degrees of security and risk protection, including debentures, zero coupon bonds, equipment trust certificates, mortgage bonds, and industrial development bonds. Each type of bond is accompanied by an *indenture,* spelling out the rights and obligations of borrowers and investors.

- Corporate notes and bonds are purchased by a wide range of investors today, but the dominant buyers are life insurance companies, pension funds, and savings banks. New corporate bonds may be offered publicly in the *open market,* where competitive bidding takes place, or in a *private sale* to a limited group of investors. Public sales account for the largest portion of annual long-term borrowings, but the private market appeals to many smaller firms unable to tap the open market for funds and to companies with unique financing needs or lower credit ratings. Public sales offer the advantage of competition, as investment bankers bid against each other to underwrite a new security issue. The use of competitive bidding tends to result in higher security prices and lower interest costs to businesses in need of funds.

- The corporate bond market has faced competition in recent years from both domestic and foreign commercial banks making long-term business loans. These *term loans* are generally used to purchase equipment. Most such loans carry floating interest rates tied to the *prime lending rate,* or some other base rate (such as LIBOR).

- Commercial banks have always been a leading financial institution in extending both short-term and long-term loans to business firms. These loans support the construction of office buildings, shopping centers, and other commercial structures and provide working capital to support daily operations. Banks generally specialize in short-term mortgages that finance business construction, while long-term commercial mortgage financing is provided mainly by insurance companies, savings banks, and pension funds. Bankers' overall role in providing credit to the business sector has been declining in recent years as more firms turn to the open market to raise funds. Instead, banks have increasingly come to play a supporting role in guaranteeing and monitoring corporate debt.

Key Terms

Corporate bond, *592*	Industrial development bond	Investment banker, *600*
Corporate note, *592*	(IDB), *596*	Leveraged buyouts, *606*
Indenture, *593*	Zero coupon bonds, *597*	Base rate, *607*
Debenture, *595*	Public sale, *600*	Commercial mortgage, *608*
Mortgage bonds, *595*	Private or direct placement, *600*	

Problems

1. A corporation sells $5,000 par-value bonds at par in the open market, bearing an 8 percent coupon rate. Costs of marketing the issue, including dealer's commission, amounted to $200 per bond. If the bonds are due to mature in 15 years, what is their before-tax cost to the corporation? If the issuing company is in the 35 percent tax bracket, what is the bonds' after-tax cost to the firm?

2. A corporation borrows $5 million from a bank at a 12 percent prime rate. If the bank requires the company to hold 15 percent of the amount of the loan on deposit as a compensating balance, what is the effective rate of interest on the loan?

3. A bank quotes one of its corporate customers a loan at prime plus four percentage points when prime is 12 percent. Another bank, posting the same prime rate, quotes this same customer a loan at 1¼ times prime. Which loan would you recommend the corporation take? Suppose both loans carry floating rates. Prime increases to 16 percent. Which loan is the better deal? Which would be the better deal if prime rises to 18 percent? Please explain what is happening.

4. Silsbee Corporation, bearing a BB rating, is considering the public sale of $72 million in new corporate notes bearing seven-year maturities at an expected gross yield of 8.95 percent later this month. The company needs about $260 million in total but is hoping to raise the difference between its total financial need and the note offering by drawing upon other sources of funds. However, it does have an alternative offer of a private note sale to a small consortium of insurance companies at an expected gross yield of 9.04 percent. Silsbee's financial manager is trying to assess the potential advantages and disadvantages of each of these two approaches to raising medium-term capital funds. Using the information presented in this chapter, please develop a list of possible benefits and costs of a public sale versus a private sale to help Silsbee's manager weigh the two options available to the company and reach a decision.

5. Contail-Guidar Corporation is in need of a 10-year loan for the upgrading of its production processing equipment in the amount of $18 million. The company has been offered a term loan from its principal bank at LIBOR plus two percentage points (where the London Interbank rate now stands at 5.75 percent), with the stipulation that the firm

maintain 15 percent of the loan in an interest-bearing deposit at the bank, earning the prevailing LIBOR rate on this deposit balance. In contrast, Contail's investment banker has suggested as an alternative that a public bond offering be made at an estimated open market interest rate of 7.35 percent (given Contail's relatively high credit rating) with the $1,000 par value, 10-year bonds sold at a net price (after commissions and discounts) of $950 per bond. Which approach would provide the best financing alternative for this company? Please explain your answer, developing a comprehensive list of the advantages and disadvantages of each financing alternative.

6. Please identify each of the key terms and concepts that are described or defined below:

a. A debt instrument with an original maturity of more than 5 years from its date of issue.

b. A debt instrument issued by a corporation with an original maturity of 5 years or less.

c. A document describing the rights, privileges, and obligations of borrower and lender under the terms of a bond or note contract.

d. Long-term debt obligations secured only by the earning power of a corporation and not by any of the issuing corporation's specific assets.

e. Long-term corporate debt secured by a lien on specific assets of the issuing firm.

f. Debt instrument issued by a local government to aid a private company.

g. Long-term corporate debt obligations typically sold at a price below par and without any specific promised interest payments.

h. When securities are sold in the open market, usually through investment bankers.

i. Placing corporate debt securities with one or a limited number of investors.

j. A form of corporate takeover in which the management of a company or a small group of investors takes over ownership in an effort to boost earnings and pay off any debt incurred in the takeover.

k. Examples include the prime rate and LIBOR.

l. A debt instrument used to provide financing for business ventures involving the purchase of land and purchase or construction of buildings.

Questions about the Web and the Money and Capital Markets

1. If you wanted to find out more about the basic characteristics of corporate bonds and the markets in which they are traded where on the World Wide Web could you look to find such information?

2. Suppose you were to become an active investor, buying and selling corporate bonds and notes. How could you use the Web to keep track of daily corporate debt market developments? What are some of the Web information sources you could draw upon?

3. Where could you go to check up on foreign markets for corporate notes and bonds? What Web sources would you recommend and why?

Selected References

Bitler, Marianne P.; Alicia M. Robb; and John D. Wolken. "Financial Services Used by Small Businesses: Evidence from the 1998 Survey of Small Business Finances." *Federal Reserve Bulletin,* April 2001, pp. 183–205.

Booth, James. "The Persistence of the Prime Rate." *FRBSF Weekly Letter,* Federal Reserve Bank of San Francisco, May 20, 1994, pp. 1–3.

Culp, Christopher L., and Andrea M.P. Neves. "Financial Innovations in the Leveraged Commercial Loan Market." *Journal of Applied Corporate Finance* XI (Summer 1998), pp. 94–105.

Prowse, Stephen D. "A Look at America's Corporate Finance Markets." *Southwest Economy,* Federal Reserve Bank of Dallas, September–October 1997, pp. 1–11.

Chapter **Twenty-Two**

Corporate Stock

Learning Objectives in This Chapter

- You will learn about the characteristics of common and preferred corporate stock.

- You will understand how the stock market operates today and what its component parts are.

- You will be able to compare and contrast the roles and functions of the organized stock exchanges and the over-the-counter market.

- You will explore the question of *market efficiency* and examine the evidence for and against the efficiency of the stock market.

What's in This Chapter? Key Topics Outline

The Stock Market and the Economy

Features of Common and Preferred Stock

Leading Stock Market Investors

Valuing Stock, Inflation, and the Wealth Effect

Components of the Market for Corporate Stock

Exchanges and the OTC

The Third Market and Private Equity Issues

Stock Options and Index Trading

National and International Market Developments

Circuit Breakers and Crashes

Random Walk, Market Efficiency, and Fair Disclosure

INTRODUCTION

In the preceding chapters, we focused almost exclusively on debt securities and the extension of credit. In this chapter, we examine a unique security that is not debt but *equity*. It is a certificate representing *ownership* of a corporation. Unlike debt, corporate stock grants the investor no promise of return; rather, it grants only the right to share in the firm's assets and earnings, if any.

Corporate stock is unique in one other important respect. All of the securities markets we have discussed to this point are intimately bound up with the process of moving funds

The market for corporate stocks is the most widely followed of all financial markets on the World Wide Web. More than half a million Web sites related in one way or another to corporate stocks appeared in various places on the Web as the 21st century began. And perhaps this is good news for you, because if you are not an active stock investor today, the chances are pretty strong you will be involved in this market in the future (perhaps to help prepare for your retirement in future years or to start a business).

The majority of Web sites devoted to corporate stock attempt to keep up, daily and weekly, with individual stocks or groups of stocks. Among the most prominent of these daily and weekly market profile sites are Corporate Financials Online at *www.cfonews.com*, Stock Pick Performance at *www.stockpickcentral.com*, and Money Central at *www.msn.com*.

Supplementing the above sources of information on stock market movements are sites that focus upon specific issues or problems that plague the stock market from time to time. For example, there are numerous sites devoted to stock options—their advantages and disadvantages for employees and investors at large. (See, for example, *www.looksmart.com* and *www.theoptionstrader.com*.) There is also considerable discussion on the Web about insider trading and its implications for the market as a whole. A good example here that may provoke the reader's interest is found at Thomson Investors Network at *www.thomsoninvest.net*.

from ultimate savers to ultimate borrowers in order to support investment and economic growth. In the stock market, however, the bulk of trading activity involves the buying and selling of securities already issued rather than the exchange of financial claims for new capital. Thus, trading in the stock market, for the most part, is *not* closely linked to the saving and investment process in the economy unless the issue of *new* stock is involved.

A small portion of trading in corporate shares *does* involve the sale of *new* stock to support business investment. And that portion of the global stock market devoted to new stock issues is growing rapidly. Today, in nearly every nation around the world, stock is competing more vigorously with other ways of raising business capital, as thousands of new businesses are being formed and many of these are deciding to "go public" by offering new ownership shares and new debt. Moreover, the stock market continues to have a significant impact on the *expectations* of businesses when planning future investments. Therefore, stock trading indirectly affects employment, growth, and the general health of the economy.[1] In this chapter, we take a close look at the basic characteristics of corporate stock and the markets where that stock is traded.

CHARACTERISTICS OF CORPORATE STOCK

All corporate stock represents an ownership interest in a corporation, conferring on the holder a number of important rights as well as risks. In this section, we examine the two types of corporate stock issued today: common and preferred shares.

---

[1]One broad index of stock market prices—Standard & Poor's Composite Index—is considered to be a *leading indicator* of subsequent changes in economic conditions, especially of future developments in industrial production, employment, and total spending (GDP). Thus, the stock market often turns in its greatest gains in the deepest part of a recession and turns down before a boom is over. The stock market seems to provide a forecast of business capital spending plans and output, perhaps reflecting the fact that it captures the expectations of the business community.

Common Stock

The most important form of corporate stock is **common stock.** Like all forms of equity, common stock represents a *residual* claim against the assets of the issuing firm, entitling the owner to share in the net earnings of the firm when it is profitable and to share in the net market value (after all debts are paid) of the company's assets if it is liquidated. By owning common stock, the investor is subject to the full risks of ownership, which means that the business may fail or its earnings may fall to unacceptable levels. However, the risks of equity ownership are limited, because the stockholder normally is liable only for the amount of his or her investment.

If a corporation with outstanding shares of common stock is liquidated, the debts of the firm must be paid first from any assets available. The preferred stockholders then receive their share of any remaining funds. Whatever is left accrues to common stockholders on a *pro rata* basis. Common stock is generally a *registered* instrument, with the holder's name recorded on the issuing company's books.

The volume of stock a corporation may issue is limited by the terms of its charter of incorporation. Additional shares beyond those authorized by the company's charter may be issued only by amending the charter with the approval of the current stockholders. Some companies have issued large amounts of corporate shares, reflecting not only their need for large amounts of equity capital but also a desire to broaden their ownership base.

The *par value* of common stock is an arbitrarily assigned value, usually printed on each stock certificate, though some stock has no specified par value. Where present, par value is usually set low relative to the stock's current market value. Originally, par was supposed to represent the owner's initial investment per share in the firm. The only real significance of par today is that the firm cannot pay any dividends to stockholders that would reduce the company's net worth per share below the par value of its stock.

Common stockholders are granted a number of rights when they buy a share of equity in a business corporation. Stock ownership permits them to elect the company's board of directors, who, in turn, choose the officers responsible for day-to-day management of the firm. Common shareholders have a *preemptive right* (unless specifically denied by the firm's charter) which gives current shareholders the right to purchase any new voting stock, convertible bonds, or preferred stock issued by the firm in order to maintain their *pro rata* share of ownership. For example, if a stockholder holds 5 percent of all shares outstanding and 500 new shares are issued, this stockholder has the right to subscribe to 25 new shares.

Although most common stock grants each stockholder one vote per share, nonvoting common is also issued occasionally. Some companies issue Class A common, which has voting rights, and Class B common, which carries a prior claim on earnings but no voting power. The major stock exchanges do not encourage publicly held firms to issue classified stock, but classified shares are used extensively by privately held firms.

A right normally granted to all common stockholders is the right of access to the minutes of stockholder meetings and to lists of existing shareholders. This gives the stockholders some power to reorganize the company if management or the board of directors is performing poorly. Common stockholders may vote on all matters that affect the firm's property as a whole, such as a merger, liquidation, or the issuance of additional equity shares.

Preferred Stock

The other major form of stock issued today is **preferred stock.** Preferred carries a stated annual dividend expressed as a percent of the stock's par value. For example, if preferred shares carry a $100 par value with an 8 percent dividend rate, then each preferred shareholder is entitled to dividends of $8 per year on each share owned, provided the company declares a dividend. Common stockholders receive whatever dividends remain after the preferred shareholders receive their annual dividend.

Preferred stock occupies the middle ground between debt and equity securities, including advantages and disadvantages of both forms of raising long-term funds. Preferred stockholders have a prior claim over the firm's assets and earnings relative to the claims of common stockholders. However, creditors must be paid before either preferred or common stockholders. Unlike creditors of the firm, preferred stockholders cannot press for bankruptcy proceedings against a company that fails to pay them dividends. Nevertheless, preferred stock is part of a firm's equity capital and strengthens a firm's net worth, allowing it to issue more debt in the future. It also is a more flexible financing arrangement than debt because dividends may be passed if earnings are inadequate.

Generally, preferred stockholders have no voice in the selection of management unless the corporation fails to pay dividends for a stipulated period. A frequent provision in corporate charters gives preferred stockholders the right to elect some members of the board of directors if dividends are passed for a full year. Dividends on preferred stock, like those paid on common stock, are *not a* tax-deductible expense. This makes preferred shares more expensive to issue than debt for companies in the top income bracket. However, IRS regulations specify that 70 percent of the stock dividends received by corporations from unaffiliated companies are tax deductible. This deductibility feature makes preferred stock attractive to companies seeking to acquire ownership shares in other firms and sometimes allows preferred shares to be issued at a lower net interest cost than debt securities. In fact, corporations themselves are the principal buyers of preferred stock.

Most preferred stock is *cumulative,* which means that the passing of dividends results in an arrearage that must be paid in full before the common stockholders receive anything. A few preferred shares are *participating,* allowing the holder to share in the residual earnings normally accruing entirely to common stockholders. To illustrate how the participating feature might work, assume that an investor holds 8 percent participating preferred stock with a $100 par value. After the issuing company's board of directors votes to pay the stated annual dividend of $8 per share, the board also declares a $20 per share common stock dividend. If the formula for dividend participation calls for common and preferred shareholders to share *equally* in any net earnings, then each preferred shareholder will earn an additional $12 to bring her total dividend to $20 per share as well. Not all participating formulas are this generous, and most preferred issues are *nonparticipating,* because participation is detrimental to the interests of common stockholders.

Most corporations plan to retire their preferred stock, even though it usually carries no stated maturity. In fact, preferred shares usually carry call provisions. When interest rates decline, the issuing company may exercise the call privilege at the price stated in the formal agreement between the firm and its shareholders. A few preferred issues are *convertible* into shares of common stock at the investor's option. The company retires all converted preferred shares and may force conversion by simply exercising the stock's call privilege. New preferred issues are often accompanied by a sinking fund provision, whereby funds are accumulated for eventual retirement of preferred shares. A trustee is appointed to collect sinking fund payments from the company and periodically to call in preferred shares or purchase them in the open market. Although sinking fund provisions allow the issuing firm to sell preferred stock with lower dividend rates, payments into the fund drain earnings and may reduce dividend payments to common stockholders.

During the 1980s and 1990s, corporations developed new types of *variable-rate preferred stock,* carrying a floating dividend rate that makes the stock a substitute for short-term debt. Many variable-rate preferred issues allow their dividend rate to be reset several times, which may be accomplished by a marketing agent or via a special auction. Some companies have issued *Dutch-auction* preferred shares, a process by which stock buyers submit bids and the highest-priced bid becomes the price paid by all winning bidders. Frequently, the dividend rate has a ceiling rate based on a key market reference rate (such as the market yield on commercial paper). Many preferred shares issued recently have had an exchange option attached, giving the issuing company the choice of exchanging the preferred stock for debt securities. Not long ago another hybrid form of preferred stock, "MIPS" (monthly income preferred shares), appeared; MIPS are counted as equity but carry interest payments like debt. Thus, MIPS help to reduce the prominence of a company's debt and tend to lower its federal taxes. However, MIPS have recently come under attack in the wake of the failure of the huge Enron Corporation which made use of them.

Yet another form of preferred equity that appeared in the mid-1990s is *convertible preferred.* Convertible preferred shares are sometimes called "toxic" or "death" spiral convertibles. Each share can eventually be exchanged for an unspecified number of common stock shares, with the number of new common shares depending upon the common stock's market price when conversion occurs. If the issuing firm is in trouble and its common stock is plunging in value, the preferred shareholders receive a growing share of the firm's ownership.

From the standpoint of the investor, preferred stock represents an intermediate investment between bonds and common stock. Preferred shares often provide more income than bonds but also greater risk. Preferred prices fluctuate more widely than bond prices for the same change in interest rates. Compared to common stock, preferred shares generally provide less income but are, in turn, less risky.

Questions *to Help You Study*

1. In what important ways does the stock market *differ* from the other securities markets we have described in earlier parts of this book?

2. What major differences do you see between corporate stock and corporate debt obligations (discussed in the previous chapter)?

3. What are the essential characteristics of *common stock?*

4. What priority of *claim* do common stockholders have in the event a corporation is closed and liquidated? What limits the volume of shares that a company may issue and have outstanding at any point in time?

5. Discuss the nature of *preferred stock.* In what ways are preferred shares similar to corporate debt and in what ways are they similar to equity shares (especially common stock)?

STOCK MARKET INVESTORS

Corporate stock is one of the most widely held financial assets in the world. Only one other financial asset—government securities—is held by as large and diverse a group of individuals and institutions as are common and preferred stock. One important source of information on stockholders in the United States is the Federal Reserve Board's Flow of Funds Accounts.[2] Exhibit 22–1 gives the names of major investor groups and their total holdings of common and preferred stock for the years 1970, 1980, 1990, and 2000.

---

[2]See Chapter 3 for an explanation of the method of construction and types of information presented in the Flow of Funds Accounts.

EXHIBIT 22–1   Key Investors Buying Corporate Stock in the United States ($ Billions at Year-End; Market Values)

Groups of Investors	1970 Amount	1970 Percent of Total	1980 Amount	1980 Percent of Total	1990 Amount	1990 Percent of Total	2000 Amount	2000 Percent of Total
Households (individuals and families)	$728	80.3%	$1,165	71.3%	$2,008	57.3%	$ 7,447.6	39.1%
Rest of the world	27	3.0	63	3.9	228	6.5	1,691.4	8.9
Commercial banks	*	—	*	—	2	0.1	11.8	0.1
Savings banks	3	0.3	4	0.3	9	0.3	24.4	0.1
Life insurers	15	1.7	47	2.9	107	3.0	1,028.3	5.4
Property-casualty insurers	13	1.5	32	2.0	85	2.4	203.4	1.1
Pension funds:								
Private	68	7.5	231	14.1	537	15.3	2,451.2	12.9
Government	10	1.1	44	2.7	296	8.4	1,953.7	10.3
Investment companies (mutual funds)	40	4.4	42	2.6	224	6.4	3,622.4	19.0
Security brokers and dealers	2	0.2	3	0.2	9	0.3	79.0	0.4
Other investors	1	0.1	2	0.1	1	0.1	533.9	2.8
	$907	100.0%	$1,633	100.0%	$3,506	100.0%	$19,047.1	100.0%

Note: Columns may not add to totals due to rounding.
*Less than $1 billion.

Source: Flow of Funds Accounts, compiled quarterly by the Board of Governors of the Federal Reserve System.

Exhibit 22–1 makes clear that *households*—individuals and families—are the dominant holders of corporate stock in the United States. In 2000, for example, households held close to 40 percent of all corporate shares outstanding. Pension funds—both private and government—were a distant second, holding almost 25 percent of available shares. Mutual funds ranked third with about 19 percent of all stock holdings. Mutual funds—traditional institutional stock buyers on behalf of their customers—dramatically added to their stock holdings as a rising (but often volatile) market in the late 1990s captured the interest of scores of individual investors. Mutual funds have been especially attractive to middle-income investors who cannot afford to buy a large number of shares and who seek the safety of professional securities management and diversification across many different stock issues that most mutual funds provide. Foreign investors ranked fourth, with about 9 percent of the total. The deposit-type financial intermediaries—commercial and savings banks—collectively held less than 1 percent of the total. State and federal laws severely limit savings bank investment in corporate stock and prohibit most U.S. commercial banks themselves from purchasing most kinds of corporate stock for their own asset portfolios.

As Exhibit 22–2 shows, relative to most other assets held by the foregoing groups of investors, stocks have done extremely well as appreciating assets. For example, the composite value of all common stock traded on the New York Stock Exchange expanded nearly six-fold between 1985 and 2000. Much the same explosive expansion occurred in the Dow Jones Industrial Average (DJIA) of 30 leading U.S. companies and in the Standard and Poor's (S&P) Composite Index of 500 leading companies' equity shares until a slower economy and terrorist attacks damaged the market's performance early in the new century. These generally upward gains in value occurred despite the fact that companies' dividend

EXHIBIT 22–2   **Recent Movements in Common Stock Prices and Yields**

	New York Stock Exchange Indices (12/31/65 = 50)					Dow Jones Industrial Average	Standard and Poor's Composite Index (1941–43 = 100)	Common Stock Yields	
Years	Composite	Industrial	Transportation	Utilities	Finance			Dividend–Price Ratio (D/P)	Earnings–Price Ratio (E/P)
1955	21.54	—	—	—	—	442.72	40.49	4.08%	7.95%
1960	30.01	—	—	—	—	618.04	55.85	3.47	5.90
1965	47.39	—	—	—	—	910.88	88.17	3.00	5.59
1970	48.72	48.03	32.14	74.47	60.00	753.19	83.22	3.83	6.45
1975	45.73	50.52	31.10	63.00	47.14	802.49	86.16	4.31	9.15
1980	68.10	78.70	60.61	74.69	64.25	891.41	118.78	5.26	12.66
1985	108.09	123.79	104.11	113.49	114.21	1,328.23	186.84	4.25	8.12
1990	183.46	225.78	158.62	181.20	133.26	2,678.94	334.59	3.61	6.47
1995	291.15	367.34	269.41	220.30	238.45	4,493.76	541.64	2.56	6.09
2000	643.71	809.40	414.73	478.99	552.48	10,898.34*	1,427.22	1.16	3.74

Note: Index values reflect averages of daily closing prices. The NYSE figures include all stocks listed; 30 stocks make up the Dow Jones Industrial Average (DJIA); and 500 stocks are included in the S&P composite index. Dividends are aggregate cash dividend payments (annual rate) divided by the aggregate market value of the underlying shares based upon Wednesday's closing prices. Earnings-price ratios are averages of quarterly earnings-to-price ratios.
*DJIA is for May 2, 2001.

Source: Council of Economic Advisors, *Economic Report of the President,* 1998 and 2001, and the Board of Governors of the Federal Reserve System.

payments relative to the value of their stock generally fell as did their average net earnings relative to their stock prices. While many securities analysts have argued that stocks have been "overvalued" in recent years, recent research evidence suggests that, in most periods, stock prices have remained quite close to the following simple valuation model:

$$S = \sum_{t}^{\infty} \frac{E(D_t)}{[1 + (r + k)]^t} \qquad (22\text{–}1)$$

where S equals the market price per share of stock; $E(D_t)$ represents expected future dividend flows per share from the current period into the indefinite future, t (since stock is a perpetual instrument); r represents the default-free rate of interest; and k equals the premium for bearing equity risk, with the sum of these last two representing the current rate of discount applied to all expected future dividend flows by capital market investors based on their assessment of the risks involved. Stocks should not deviate very long from prevailing perceptions among capital market investors regarding their risk (k) and the cash flows they are expected to pay out over time, $E(D_t)$.

Over the last half century there have been few decades in which most stock prices did not rise, and average stock yields have usually significantly outdistanced bond yields and substantially outrun returns on bank deposits, money market fund shares, and other popular investments as shown in the accompanying Management Insight box. Not only have corporate stocks responded positively to periods of strong economic growth and moderate-to-low inflation, they have also been propelled upward in recent years by the growing urgency of many individuals to prepare for their retirement years. Thanks to significant advances in medical technology, many individuals are living much longer today. As a result, they require greater growth in their savings in order to sustain their incomes over a longer span of retirement years. For many investors, stocks have been one of the most effective investments to help savings grow faster than inflation and to offer the prospect of a decent, sustainable standard of living.

Keeping track of stock price movements on a daily basis has become easier due to the presence of several good Web sites, including WWQ Real Time Streaming Quotes at *www.quote.com* and the American Stock Exchange at *www.amex.com*

Financial Developments   Dividend Yields on Stock: Why Have They Fallen So Far Recently?

Stock prices depend upon two critical factors—the *expected stream of dividends* a share of stock will pay to its owner over time and the degree of *risk* attached to that expected dividend stream. Thus, expected earnings and earnings risk play key roles in shaping stock values.

The expected dividend stream is *positively* related to a corporation's stock price, while the risk factor is *negatively* connected to a stock's market value or price. Clearly if dividends are expected to rise or if earnings risk is expected to decline, stock prices will tend to rise. The opposite will happen if dividends are expected to fall or earnings risk is projected to climb.

One of the most remarkable developments in the stock market in recent years is a tendency for *dividend yields to decline significantly. A stock's dividend yield is determined by adding up its total per-share stockholder dividends for a year and then dividing by the current per-share price of the stock.* Since reaching a peak of close to 9 percent in the early 1950s, average stock dividend yields have generally been falling, dropping to only about one percent as the twenty-first century began. Indeed, from 1871 to 1945 average dividend yields on U.S. equities averaged about 5 percent annually, but this mean dividend yield dropped to an average of only about 4 percent between 1946 and the year 2000.

No one knows for sure *why* stock dividend yields to investors have trended downward recently. One explanation centers upon higher average stock prices coupled with a slow or even negative dividend growth trend. On average, companies have paid out a smaller share of their earnings in the form of dividends, preferring instead to plow back more funds into their business in the form of retained earnings, especially when the economy is in an uptrend. Taxation of dividends has also discouraged dividend growth.

Then, too, the past decade ushered in a wave of stock repurchases by companies, intended, in part, to prevent *dilution of ownership* as more and more employees were offered *stock options* as part of their compensation. Employee stock options are contracts that allow employees to purchase a defined number of equity shares at a specific (strike) price during a set time period. Should stock prices rise above the option's contract (strike) price, the firm's employee can purchase his or her company's stock at the contract strike price, earning a profit on each share purchased. The company involved can reduce the earnings dilution effect of employee stock options by repurchasing some of their outstanding shares.

Thus, dividend yields on stock have typically been on the decline and probably not just one factor explains this trend. Investors counting on higher stock dividend yields in the future (perhaps for retirement income) should be cautious, however, because the current trend appears to be moving against them.

Source: See especially John B. Carlson, "Why Is the Dividend Yield So Low?" *Economic Commentary,* Federal Reserve Bank of Cleveland, April 1, 2001.

One of the fascinating, yet unanswered questions about corporate stock is, What factors are stock prices most sensitive to? Two obvious candidates are *inflation* and *market interest rates.* Many investors have believed for a long time that stocks are among the best long-term hedges against inflation, though, as we saw in Chapter 7, that is not necessarily true, particularly for stocks issued by companies having contracts that cause their costs to rise faster than their revenues when inflation strikes. More rapid inflation can throw a company's stockholders into higher tax brackets and increase investors' capital gains taxes, thereby lowering their after-tax returns from stock and reducing stock prices. Stock prices would also be expected to be closely tied to movements in market interest rates because (1) interest-bearing debt securities compete with stocks for investors' money (so higher interest rates may pull money out of stocks and into bonds, for example); (2) interest rate levels affect the discount rate applied to future stock dividend streams and, thereby, should be inversely related to the level of stock prices; and (3) higher market interest rates make it more expensive for investors buying stock on margin to borrow funds and, therefore, tend to discourage the demand for those stocks not expected to be strong performers. However, a study by Golob and Bishop (1996) suggests that stock prices seem to follow inflation more closely than they do interest rates. The inflation rate measured by the consumer price index appears to explain more of the observed changes in stock earnings-price ratios than do market rates of interest.

Management Insight The Long-Run Return Premium Paid by Stocks Over Other Investments

Financial Instrument	Long-Run Average Annual Rate of Return (%)
New York Stock Exchange corporate stock returns	7.42%
Bonds issued by corporations	2.64
U.S. government notes and bonds	1.85
U.S. Treasury bills	0.60

Note: Period analyzed, 1925–2001, adjusted for inflation.

Source: New York Stock Exchange and the Federal Reserve System.

CHARACTERISTICS OF THE CORPORATE STOCK MARKET

There are two main branches of the market for trading corporate stock. One is the **organized exchanges,** which in the United States include the New York Stock Exchange (NYSE) and the American Exchange (AMEX) plus exchanges dealing in stock futures and options (such as the Chicago Board of Trade or CBOT) as well as regional exchanges scattered around the United States (including the Boston, Cincinnati, Pacific, and Philadelphia exchanges). Overseas, the Tokyo, Hong Kong, Singapore, Sydney, Paris, and London exchanges have also grown in importance as major centers for trading corporate shares worldwide, propelled in part by the privatization of many state-owned businesses and massive stock investments by U.S. investors abroad. All of the exchanges around the globe (the most important in recent years are listed in Exhibit 22–3) use similar procedures for controlling membership and regulating purchases and sales.

Trading on the exchanges is governed by regulations and formal procedures designed to ensure competitive pricing and an active market for the stock of the largest, most financially stable companies. In contrast, the second branch of the equities market—the **over-**

EXHIBIT 22–3
International Focus: Leading Stock Exchanges Active around the World in Recent Years

New York Stock Exchange	Stockholm Exchange
American Stock Exchange	Brussels Exchange
Amsterdam Exchange	Chile Exchange
Tokyo Exchange	Sydney Exchange
Osaka Exchange	Hong Kong Exchange
London Exchange	Madrid Exchange
Frankfurt Exchange (DAX)	Singapore Exchange
Zurich Exchange	Stockholm Exchange
Paris Exchange (MATIF)	Johannesburg Exchange
Manilla Exchange	Shanghai Exchange
Mexico City Exchange	Taipei Exchange
Milan Exchange	Toronto Exchange
Montreal Exchange	Wellington Exchange
New Zealand Exchange	Venezuela Exchange
Indonesia Exchange	Switzerland Exchange

Financial Developments   The Wealth Effect at Work in the Stock Market

We all know what "wealth" is—the sum of our personal holdings of cash, bank deposits, stocks, bonds, homes, automobiles, furniture, etc. A key issue in Finance recently has focused upon what happens to spending by consumers—individuals and families—when the value of their financial and nonfinancial assets changes. Economic theory suggests consumer spending depends largely upon labor income and accumulated wealth. When either income or wealth increases in amount or, if both go up, the volume of consumer spending also will rise and saving may fall.

While we might tend to jump to the conclusion that both factors—labor income and wealth—ought to be strongly related to consumer spending, there are some good arguments pulling the other way, especially for wealth measured by current stock prices. For example, in most countries only a minority of people hold significant quantities of stock. Moreover in countries like the United States a major portion of equity holdings lie in tax-sheltered retirements accounts which can't be used for immediate spending without paying tax penalties or until the owner reaches retirement. Then, too, for individuals and families wishing to build up a substantial estate for their loved ones, the tendency is not to convert wealth gains into spending, but instead to hold on to those gains as additions to accumulated saving.

Recent research suggests that wealth *does* have some impact on consumer spending and saving. However, recent studies by such research specialists as Poterba (2000), Mehra (2001), and others suggest that when stock values climb by a dollar, for example, consumer purchases increase about 3 cents. Thus, stock value gains increase consumer spending by about 3 percent of the gain. If we go further and include nonequity forms of wealth (such as homes and automobiles), the impact of a change in wealth's value on consumer purchases may be a bit larger—perhaps 4 to 6 percent of the wealth change.

In contrast, fluctuations in a family's income tend to have a far bigger impact on household spending than do wealth changes—about 10 times greater. Thus, income appears to be a lot more important to households than does wealth (including stocks) when spending decisions are on the line. Nevertheless wealth *is* a factor in shaping consumer spending and the relationship is *positive*—not huge, to be sure, but still significant statistically.

Sources: See, for example, Yash P. Mehra, "The Wealth Effect in Empirical Life Cycle Aggregate Consumption Equations," *Economic Quarterly,* Federal Reserve Bank of Richmond, Spring 2001, pp. 45–68; James M. Poterba, "Stock Market Wealth and Consumption," *Journal of Economic Perspectives,* Spring 2000, pp. 99–118; and Sydney Ludvigson and Charles Steindel, "How Important Is The Stock Market Effect on Consumption?" *Economic Policy Review,* Federal Reserve Bank of New York, July 1999, pp. 29–52.

the-counter (OTC) market—involves trading of stock through brokers operating off the major exchanges. This market is more informal and fluid than exchange trading and includes the stocks and bonds of smaller companies, financial institutions, and foreign firms (though Americans hold less than 10 percent of their stock in foreign equities).

The Major Organized Exchanges

American Exchanges

Among the best-known organized exchanges are the Big Board—The New York Stock Exchange—and the American Stock Exchange (ASE or AMEX). The NYSE and most other U.S. exchanges overlap in trading and function and are competitive markets for the most actively traded stocks. Each exchange provides a physical location for trading, and trading by member firms must be carried on at that location. On the floor of the NYSE, for example, there are several counters, each containing windows, or *trading posts*. Selected stocks are traded from each post via the auction method as prescribed by the exchange's Board of Governors. The exchanges permit the enforcement of formal trading rules in order to achieve an efficient and speedy allocation of equity shares.

To be eligible for trading on an organized exchange, the stock must be issued by a firm *listed* with the exchange. A substantial number of major U.S. corporations are listed on several different exchanges. The listing qualifications demanded by the New York Stock

Exchange are among the most comprehensive, which serves to limit NYSE trading to stocks issued by the largest companies. For example, the NYSE requires a company to have over a million shares in public trading, assets of at least $18 million, and at least 2000 stockholders. The basic intent of these listing rules is to ensure that the listed company has sufficient shares available to create an active market for its stock and discloses sufficient data so that investors can make informed decisions.

Even if a company meets all listing requirements, its stock must still be approved for admission by the exchange's board of directors, who are elected by firms with seats on the exchange. (About 2,700 firms are listed on the NYSE and close to 2,500 on the AMEX.) Corporations that are successful in listing their stock must make an annual disclosure of their financial condition, publish quarterly earnings reports, and help maintain an active public market for their shares. If trading interest in a particular firm's stock falls off significantly (as in the case of Enron in 2002), the firm may be *delisted.* Under some circumstances, a firm may be granted "unlisted trading privileges" if its stock has been listed on another exchange. Recently, foreign firms have been admitted in large numbers to most major exchanges. Foreign companies with more than $5 million in assets and at least 500 shareholders whose stock is traded in the United States must register with the Securities and Exchange Commission, unless specifically exempted.

One of the most important advantages claimed for listing on an exchange is that it improves the *liquidity* of a corporation's stock. A relatively large volume of shares can be sold without significantly depressing the price. This feature is of special concern to large institutional investors (such as mutual funds and pension funds) that have come to dominate daily trading in the equities market, because these institutions trade in large blocks rather than by a few shares at a time. Allegedly, a corporation can improve the market for its stock by becoming listed on a securities exchange.

Member firms of the exchange are the only ones that may trade listed securities on the exchange floor, either for their own account or for their customers. Most members own "seats" on the exchange and hold claims against the exchange's assets. Member firms are allowed to sell or lease their seats with the approval of the exchange's governing board. Seats on the NYSE have recently traded for about $650,000 apiece.

To learn more about the major stock exchanges go to their principal Web sites—for example, *www.nyse.com* and *www.amex.com*

Member firms fulfill a wide variety of roles on an exchange. Some act as *floor traders* that buy and sell only for their own account. Floor traders are really speculators whose portfolios turn over rapidly as they drift from post to post on the exchange floor looking for profitable trading opportunities. Other members serve as *commission brokers,* employed by member brokerage firms to represent the orders of their customers, or *floor brokers,* who are usually individual entrepreneurs carrying out buy and sell orders from other brokers not present on the exchange floor.

An interesting recent innovation on several stock exchanges are ETFs, or Exchange-Traded Funds, that are similar to index mutual funds but can be traded like ordinary stocks. See, for example, Morningstar at *www.morningstar.com* and STREETTRACKS at *www.streettracks.com*

Some traders holding exchange seats are *specialists* who oversee trading in each stock. The specialist firms operating on the New York Stock Exchange act as *both* broker and dealers, buying and selling for other brokers and for themselves when there is an imbalance between supply and demand for the stocks in which they specialize. For example, when sell orders pile up for the stocks for which a specialist firm is responsible, it moves in to buy some of the offered shares, creating a market and providing liquidity by trading for their own account. Specialists help to create orderly and continuous markets and stabilize prices by agreeing to cover unfilled customer orders and by posting firm bid and ask prices to interested investors. Finally, a few *odd-lot traders,* representing large brokerage firms dealing with the public, are also active on the exchange floor. Odd lots are buy or sell orders involving fewer than 100 shares that come primarily from individuals. The odd-lot trader purchases 100 or more shares—a *round lot*—and retains any extra shares not needed by customers in his or her portfolio.

Japanese Exchanges

The largest Japanese exchange is the Tokyo Stock Exchange (TSE), which operates in two different sections. The First Section offers exchange services for shares of the largest corporations; the Second Section deals in the shares of smaller corporations. Most investors follow changes in Japanese stock prices by consulting the Nikkei Index, which tracks the average unweighted price of 225 shares traded each day on the TSE. A broader Japanese stock price indicator is the TOPIX, which reflects the current prices of all large-company stocks traded on the Tokyo Exchange. Rivaling the growth of the Tokyo exchange has been another exchange in Osaka, about 250 miles southwest of Tokyo. Osaka trades individual shares and futures contracts linked to the Nikkei index of 225 stocks.

Contributions of Exchanges

Stock exchanges are among the oldest financial institutions. The New York Stock Exchange, for example, was set up following an agreement among 24 Wall Street brokers in May 1792. Stock exchanges were opened in Tokyo and Osaka, Japan, in 1878. Exchanges provide a continuous market centered in an established location with rigid rules to ensure fairness in trading. By bringing together buyers and sellers, the exchanges appear to make stock a more liquid investment, promote efficient pricing of securities, and make possible the placement of huge amounts of financial capital.

The Informal Over-the-Counter Market

The majority of securities bought and sold around the globe are traded over-the-counter (OTC), not on organized exchanges. There is no central trading location, but only an electronic communications network. (See Exhibit 22–4.) The customer places a buy or sell order with a broker or dealer that is relayed via telephone, wire, or computer terminal to the dealer or broker with securities to sell or an order to buy. In this system of electronically linked marketmakers, brokers and dealers seek the best possible price, and the resulting competition to find the best deal brings together traders located hundreds or thousands of miles apart. The prices of actively traded securities quickly respond to the changing forces of demand and supply, so that many security prices hover at or near competitive, market-determined levels.

For a look at the over-the-counter market explore such Web sites as *www.nasdaq.com* and *www.nasd.com*

Many traders in the OTC market act as *principals* instead of brokers as on the organized exchanges. That is, they take "positions of risk" by buying securities outright for their own portfolios as well as for customers. These dealer firms handle the same stock so that customers can shop around. All prices are determined by negotiation with dealers acquiring securities at *bid* prices and selling them at *asked* prices. The U.S. OTC market is regulated by a code of ethics established by the National Association of Security Dealers (NASD), a private organization that encourages ethical behavior among its members and that recently merged with the American Stock Exchange (AMEX). Traders who break NASD's regulations may be fined, suspended, or thrown out of the organization.

THE THIRD MARKET: TRADING IN LISTED SECURITIES OFF THE EXCHANGE

The market for securities listed on a stock exchange but traded over the counter is known as the **third market.** Broker and dealer firms not members of an organized exchange are active in this market. The original purpose of the third market was to supply large blocks of shares to institutional investors. These investors engage mainly in *block trades,* defined

EXHIBIT 22–4   **The Structure of the Market for Corporate Stock**

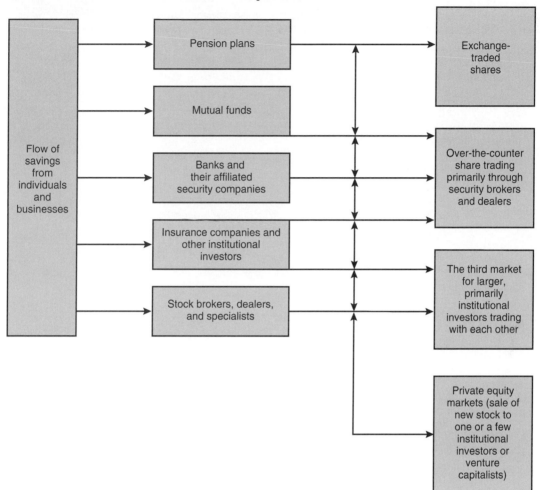

as transactions involving 1,000 shares or more. Presumably, block traders possess the technical know-how to make informed investment decisions and then carry out transactions without assistance from a stock exchange. By trading with third-market broker and dealer firms, who, in effect, compete directly with specialists on the exchanges, a large institutional investor frequently can lower transactions costs and trade securities faster.

The third market has been a catalyst in reducing brokerage fees and promoting trading efficiency, stimulating the unbundling of commissions at many U.S. broker and dealer firms in order to more accurately reflect the true cost of each security trade. Many brokerage firms offer customers an array of peripheral services, such as research on market trends, security credit, and accounting for purchases and sales; the customer may pay for these services whether or not he or she uses them. The largest institutional investors have little need for such services, however, and they seek brokers and dealers offering their services at minimum cost. Recently, numerous "discount" brokerage houses have appeared, and commissions charged institutional investors have dropped substantially, leading some institutional customers to abandon the third market and return to more traditional channels for executing their security orders.

Top Underwriters in Stocks and Bonds inside the United States

Merrill Lynch & Co.
Citigroup Inc.
Morgan Stanley
Goldman Sachs Group Inc.
Lehman Brothers
Credit Suisse Group
J. P. Morgan/Chase Bank
Bear, Stearns & Co., Inc.
Donaldson Lufkin

Top Underwriters in Non-U.S. Stocks and Bonds Worldwide

UBS Warburg
Merrill Lynch & Co.
Goldman Sachs Group Inc.
Morgan Stanley
Deutsche Bank AG
BNP Paribas
ABN AMRO
BZW/Barclays
J. P. Morgan/Chase Bank
Credit Suisse Group

Source: Federal Reserve Board.

THE PRIVATE EQUITY MARKET

Just as there is a public market for the most popular stocks, led by the organized exchanges and over-the-counter trading, so is there a *private equity market* where new businesses, privately held companies and partnerships, troubled firms, and even larger publicly traded companies can find financing for their acquisitions and other investments as well as support for out-of-the-ordinary financial transactions.

Funding a company through a private sale of stock has several distinct advantages. Privately conveyed shares are exempt from costly SEC registration requirements because the public does not become involved with these privately placed shares. Then, too, like the private corporate debt markets, firms in need of greater equity capitalization but unable to successfully reach the public market due to their small size, questionable credit ratings, complicated financing requirements, and so forth often find private equities a reasonable solution to their problems. An added factor is the recent expansion of a new type of financial-service firm almost tailor-made for the private equity markets—the so-called *limited partnership*. Limited partnerships have recently grown as an important investment vehicle for wealthy individuals and institutional stock investors, and many of these partnerships have become highly skilled in arranging private equity deals that may return substantial rewards to members of the partnership. This form of partnership allows stock market investors to turn their long-term capital funds over to a professional funds manager who accepts most of the risks of the firm and makes the key portfolio decisions that must be decided along the way.

These innovative partnership agreements can often force stock-issuing firms to put the interests of the partnership's stockholders first, unlike many publicly traded companies who have thousands of stockholders and whose managements, not the stockholders, really control the companies and may reap most of the benefits. Also, pension funds—among the very largest of all stock-buying institutions in today's global markets—have recently been allowed by regulation in many different jurisdictions to take greater positions in privately held stock. That step has also brought huge amounts of new capital into private equity markets. Certainly, the rapid rise of the private equity market has boosted the growth of new businesses. Venture capital exploded in volume over the past decade, giving tens of thousands of new firms the funds to get started and also allowing smaller companies to grow bigger by funding their buy-outs of other businesses.

Questions *to Help You Study*

6. What are the principal differences between trading in stocks *over the counter* and trading on an *organized exchange?* How would you rate these two markets in terms of their advantages for the small investor? the large investor?

7. Please explain the possible link between economic conditions and the performance of the stock market. Why do stock price movements tend to lead changes in general economic conditions?

8. Who are the principal investor groups active in the stock market? How might the investment motives of these groups differ?

9. What are the essential differences among the following segments of the market for corporate stock?

   Organized exchanges

   The third market

   Over-the-counter market

   The private equity market

THE MARKET FOR STOCK OPTIONS

Paralleling the exchange and over-the-counter markets for stock is a market for *stock options.* As we saw in Chapter 9, an option is an agreement between two parties granting one party the right (but not the obligation) to purchase an asset from or sell an asset to the other party at a set price. The price of an option is known as the *option premium*—the cost to the option buyer of insuring against an adverse change in the price of a stock. In the stock market, both *call* and *put* options are sold, each designed to manage the risk of fluctuating security prices.

Call Options

A **call option** on stock grants the buyer the right to purchase ("call away") a specified number of shares of a given stock at a specified price up to an expiration date. Call options become attractive when the investor expects the price of a given stock to rise above the price specified in the option contract (the *strike price*). Thus, an option may be available to buy 500 shares of the common stock of Caledonia Manufacturing Company at $6 per share. If the stock rises to a price of $7.50 in the open market, the holder of the option can buy $3,750 worth of stock for only $3,000. Even if the option buyer does not wish to hold the stock, he or she can resell it in the open market for a short-term gain.

Another advantage of options is the financial *leverage* they grant the investor. Less money is required to control a specified number of equity shares than would be necessary if the stock were purchased outright. However, the risk of loss is greater with options. Even small changes in the price of a stock can lead to magnified changes in the value of an option.

In 1973, the Chicago Board Options Exchange initiated trading in options for selected stocks listed on the major exchanges. Today, *listed,* or exchange-traded, options are popular, along with over-the-counter or negotiated options purchased through brokers and dealers. Holders of listed options are recorded on computerized records maintained by the Options Clearing Corporation.

Puts

The subject of stock options has become a highly controversial topic in the wake of recent company failures. See such Web sites as the Pacific Exchange at *www.pacificex.com*, Employee Stock Options at *www.nceo. org*, and Accounting for Stock Options at *www.fed.org*

The opposite of a call option is known as a **put option.** Puts grant the investor the right to *sell* a specified number of equity shares at a set price on or before the expiration date. Unlike calls, the investor in puts hopes the associated stock will *decline* in price so that he or she can sell at a price higher than currently available in the market. In this sense, puts are similar to selling a stock *short* (the sale of borrowed stock) in the hope that its price will fall. However, puts require less capital and usually result in a lower brokerage commission than short sales of stock. Also, the investor's potential loss is limited to the price of the put plus brokerage commission, regardless of what happens to the price of the underlying stock.

The Growth of Options Markets

Until 1982, only options for common stock were traded in organized markets. However, beginning in1982, new options markets appeared for *stock indexes* (such as the S&P 500, the Amex Market Value Index, the Value Line Composite Index, and the New York Stock Exchange Composite Index) and for futures contracts for the S&P 500 and the NYSE Composite Stock Index. Stock index options are based on a basket (collection) of common stocks that are thought to be representative of the whole market. The purpose of a stock index option is to permit investors to bet on which way the stock market as a whole is likely to go, while allowing risk-averse investors to protect against an adverse movement in the whole market. Options allow a risk-averse investor to shift market risk to someone else willing to bear that risk and hoping to profit from risk taking.

The Rise of Program Trading

Many analysts believe that stock markets worldwide have become more volatile due to the widespread use of computerized **program trading.** This computer-assisted investment decision-making strategy represents an attempt to shield a security investor against loss by making continuous changes in an investor's holdings as the relative prices between two or more financial instruments change.

There are several types of program trading. One of the simplest involves buying and selling stock index futures contracts (discussed earlier in Chapter 9). The most popular of such contracts is the Standard & Poor's 500 stock index contract, bought and sold on the Chicago Mercantile Exchange (CME). A *buyer* of this futures contract (who takes a *long* position in futures) promises to take delivery of the cash value of the S&P 500 index when the futures contract expires unless he or she cancels out the contract by selling a similar contract. Similarly, a *seller* of the S&P 500 index contract (who takes a *short* position in futures) promises to pay the contract buyer the cash value of the S&P index when the futures contract runs out. However, the contract seller can also cancel out his or her obligation by buying a similar contract. The clearinghouse at the futures exchange will "zero out" the sell and buy orders from the same trader, freeing him or her from the obligation to deliver or accept payment.

How can these futures contracts be used to protect against stock price declines? The investor could *sell* stock index futures that will expire on the date he or she plans to sell the stock holdings. If stock prices decline, the loss on any shares held will be offset by a gain on the stock index futures because, in a falling market, those contracts can be *bought* to "zero out" the futures position at a lower price than the original purchase price. Unfortunately, the use of pure stock index futures as just described limits profits as well as losses. For example, if stock prices rise rather than fall, the investor will suffer a loss on his or her futures position that reduces any profits earned on the stock itself.

An investor can preserve the profit potential on stock while still hedging against loss by using a *put option contract* on a stock index, such as the S&P 500 stock index. Under this arrangement, the *buyer* of a put option gains the right (but not the obligation) to *sell* units of the S&P stock index contract at a set price on the date the option contract expires. If stock prices fall below the strike price spelled out in the option contract, the put option goes up in value, offsetting the loss on the stock itself. However, if the stock itself goes up in value, the option contract will not be exercised and the investor will pocket a capital gain on selling the stock, minus only the small price paid for the put option. In this case, paying the price of the put option is equivalent to buying an insurance policy against declining stock prices. In essence, portfolio insurance of the type just described gives an investor protection against security price declines, with some reduction in potential gain.

More complicated portfolio insurance strategies have been used employing so-called "replicating" or "synthetic" security portfolios. These portfolios are built using portfolio insurance techniques—that is, *dynamic hedging* strategies that continuously adjust an investor's holdings to limit exposure to adverse market developments. Dynamic hedging programs attempt to take into account the current prices of stocks, options and futures, options and futures expiration dates, interest rates, and the volatility of stock prices. Replicating portfolios may consist of a basket of stocks that represent a major stock index (such as the S&P 500 stock index), index futures contracts, Treasury bills, or other financial instruments. If stock prices begin to fall, a common strategy is to sell off some stocks and move into other financial instruments that are safer, such as Treasury bills or stock index futures contracts. If the selloff of stocks makes them appear to be underpriced, stocks may then be purchased until once again all financial asset prices are aligned and there is no further reason for arbitrageurs to move funds from one market to another.

THE DEVELOPMENT OF A UNIFIED INTERNATIONAL MARKET FOR STOCK

The National Market System

It is clear from the foregoing discussion that the stock market is fractured into several different parts, each with its own unique collection of brokers and dealers and, in some cases, its own unique collection of customers. However, one of the most significant developments in recent decades has been a movement to weld all parts of the equities market together into a single market for all traders and investors. In 1975, the U.S. Congress passed the Securities Act Amendments, which instructed the Securities and Exchange Commission—the federal government's chief regulatory agency for the capital markets—to "facilitate the establishment of a national market system for securities" in order to further the development of widespread trading in equities and bring greater competition to the stock market.

Although the 1975 amendments did not specify what the proposed *national market system* would eventually look like as the decades went by, the intent of Congress was to ensure that all investors would have ready access to information on security prices and could transact business at the best available price. Moreover, with greater mobility of funds from one exchange to another or between the exchanges and the over-the-counter market, the resulting increase in competition in stock trading might reduce the cost to corporations of raising new capital.

Management Insight   The Great Stock Market Crash and Circuit Breakers

On October 19, 1987, the Dow Jones Industrial Average of stock values for 30 leading U.S. companies dropped by 508 points—the greatest one-day stock price fall in the history of the United States. The market's sudden "free fall" spread rapidly throughout the world, as stock prices in Western Europe, Japan, and at other exchanges around the Pacific Rim tumbled, demonstrating how intimately tied together securities markets around the globe have become.

In order to head off future market crashes, a number of "remedies" were set in place. The most highly publicized of these were the so-called **circuit breakers.** These devices would halt or slow trading during those periods when stock prices suddenly dropped. In April 1998 the Securities and Exchange Commission (SEC) and the Commodities Futures Trading Commission (CFTC) approved circuit breakers that would cause temporary trading halts if a decline of 10 percent, 20 percent, and 30 percent of the Dow Jones Industrial Average closing price occurred, when rounded to the nearest 50 points. Trading suspension points would be adjusted quarterly and their length would vary with the time of day that price declines occurred. These trading halts for the New York Stock Exchange were paralleled by a change in trading halt rules at the Chicago Mercantile Exchange (CME) for futures contracts. The CME installed "speed bumps"—30-minute trading suspensions—if futures index prices dropped 2.5 percent and 5 percent during the course of a trading day. The "speed bumps" were to be reset on a quarterly basis according to index values for the preceding month. The basic idea of these circuit breakers was to prevent panic selling, which could gather momentum like an avalanche, dragging all stock prices down with it.

Unfortunately, when trading is halted using circuit breakers, the *liquidity* of investors' stock holdings virtually disappears unless buyers can be found off the major exchanges in the over-the-counter market. When circuit breakers are tripped, investors may not be able to sell their shares even if they desperately need the cash. Equally important, circuit breakers could make financial markets even *more* volatile, accelerating trading whenever stock prices began to fall. The reason is that panicky investors may rush to sell their stock out of fear that a circuit breaker will be invoked and they won't be able to sell their shares later.

Moreover, it is not at all clear that shutting down a market for a brief period really prevents market crashes. When trading is *simultaneously* halted in stock and financial futures markets, many investors then have no efficient substitute for protecting themselves against interest rate risk. On the other hand, the tripping of circuit breakers on a stock exchange will not necessarily trigger the breakers on financial futures exchanges. The result may be that investors will rush to those markets that are still open and set off a massive selling wave there as well. Moreover, in a world with alternative trading channels for stocks and bonds, the unilateral imposition of circuit breakers and other restrictive regulations in any one nation will encourage security traders to shift their business elsewhere. If circuit breakers are to be used at all, they need to be coordinated across all exchanges in fairness to all investor groups.

Suggested references: See especially the U.S. Presidential Task Force on Market Mechanisms (1988) in the references at the end of this chapter; and Charles M. C. Lee, Mark J. Ready, and Paul J. Seguin, "Volume, Volatility, and NYSE Trading Halts," Working Paper No. 93–16, Mitsui Life Financial Research Center, The University of Michigan, May 18, 1993.

After the Securities Act Amendments became law, the New York Stock Exchange announced that it would begin reporting daily trades of NYSE-listed stocks as they occurred on the exchanges. This meant that up-to-the-minute information on the latest stock trades would be reported on a *consolidated,* or *composite, tape* regardless of which exchange handled the transaction. Although the invention of the consolidated tape was an important step in developing a national and, ultimately, international market system, it provided investors only with an indication of prevailing trends in the market. No information was provided on the best bid and asked prices available. The Securities and Exchange Commission responded to this need by asking each U.S. stock exchange to make its quotations available to brokers and dealers everywhere.

The first major step in that direction was the development of an Intermarket Trading System (ITS). Brokers and specialists could then compare bid and ask prices on all the major U.S. exchanges for about 700 different stocks through a central computer system. In effect, ITS brought major U.S. equities markets into direct price competition with one another for trades in the most popular corporate stocks. Aiding the unified market's spread was a decision by the Securities and Exchange Commission, known as Rule 19c-3. This rule stated that new stock could be traded off the exchange by exchange member firms. Previously, a broker or securities dealer with membership on a particular exchange could not trade listed stocks anywhere but on the floor of that exchange. This SEC decision brought the U.S. exchanges and OTC market into direct competition with each other for the trading of *new* stock.

NASD and Automated Price Quotations

As the 1980s began, the National Association of Security Dealers (NASD) moved to promote a broader market system by further automating price quotations on over-the-counter stock. Computer terminals with expanded capacity were set up to include a wide array of information on bid and asked prices offered by traders who might be hundreds or thousands of miles apart. At the same time, NASD and representatives of the ITS moved to link quotations and trading on the six major U.S. exchanges electronically with OTC quotations and trading through NASD's automated price quotation system (NASDAQ). NASDAQ today quotes prices for close to 5,000 financial instruments.

At about the same time, the Securities and Exchange Commission adopted new regulations aimed at improving the flow of stock price information to brokers and investors. Previously, the NASDAQ system for securities traded over the counter had carried only "representative" bid and asked prices. However, NASDAQ was soon required to display on its terminals the highest bid prices and the lowest asked prices present in the market. The new rule aided investors in determining what price brokers were actually paying to execute a customer purchase order or what the true sales price was when the customer placed his or her shares on the market. In theory, at least, the rule promoted competition among OTC brokers and made it easier for customers to negotiate low commission rates. Another SEC rule required that the consolidated tape carrying price quotations for stock listed on the major exchanges always include the *best* price available on *any* stock, regardless of which exchange is quoting that price.

Subsequently, NASD set up a so-called National Market System to shuttle information to investors immediately on completion of stock sales. NASD also set in motion a program for automated settlement of security trades, called the System of Automated Linkages for Private Offerings, Resales, and Trading (PORTAL). This system made possible purchases and sales of both unregistered domestic and foreign bonds and stocks. NASD's automated security price quotation system also set up computer telephone connections with the International Stock Exchange and the Singapore Stock Exchange, cross-listing and executing trades among a growing list of foreign securities. For example, a New York or London trader could instruct his Tokyo office to track stock prices while his home office was closed, and if stock prices reach a designated level, the overseas office would trade the securities involved according to guidelines received from the home office.

The Advent of Shelf Registration

The trend toward deregulation of the U.S. financial sector really began to exert its most potent impact on stock purchases and sales during the 1980s. On March 5, 1982, the SEC put Rule 415—the Shelf Registration Rule—into operation. This allowed many large firms selling *new* corporate stocks and bonds to register an issue with the SEC and then sell securities from that issue at any time during the next two years. *Shelf registration* substantially reduced the cost of offering new stocks and bonds and gave offering companies

Financial Developments   IPOs: Explosion and Implosion

The past decade was marked by an awesome "boom and bust" cycle in the stocks of companies "going public."

Hundreds of private businesses that had never before sold securities in the open market—many starting out as single proprietorships, partnerships, and family-owned companies—turned a corner and decided to sell their stock to the public. A substantial portion of these *initial public offerings* (IPOs) of equity shares over the past decade came from so-called "high flyers"—mainly high-technology firms that thought they had a great product idea (such as innovative new computer software). Some investment banking houses touted their new stock as "unprecedented opportunities" for quick profits. Often the market value of their shares rose sharply. Incredible gains were made by a few investors, sometimes within minutes or hours after the sale.

This situation might have gone unnoticed but for two factors—leaks of information from some firms and investors and a downturn in the stock market in 2000, followed by a downturn in the U.S. economy in 2001. A large number of the IPO firms and their new shareholders saw their stocks plummet in value. At the same time regulators began to unearth questionable transactions, including alleged kickbacks from large investors to brokers in the form of oversized commissions for the privilege of getting in on the initial sale of stock and alleged pressure on some investors to buy not only the original allocation of IPO shares but to buy additional shares at higher prices later on. Moreover, there were claims of preferential treatment for some buyers who got access to the initial sale while thousands of other investors got shut out. In order to "get in on the action" those shut out initially were compelled to pay sharply higher prices in the open market.

Targets of the hundreds of lawsuits filed and of teams of investigators were some of the largest dealer houses on Wall Street. If these charges could be proven, the violations of U.S. securities laws could result in hundreds of millions of dollars in fines. At the same time new federal rules governing future IPOs and new procedures to open up this market to a wider group of investors became more likely.

greater flexibility in selecting when to enter the financial marketplace to sell new securities. Shelf registration increased competition in the underwriting of new security issues.

Global Trading in Equities

These developments in the United States leading toward a unified national market for corporate stock were joined during the 1990s and into the new century by movement toward a true international equities market in which the sun never sets on purchases and sales of stock somewhere. The trading of both U.S. corporate stock and shares of foreign companies on exchanges in Hong Kong, Singapore, Tokyo, and Sydney began to rival exchange trading in the United States and Western Europe. Satellite, cable, and wire communications networks now girdle the globe, allowing traders in distant financial centers to search for the best prices wherever they might be. U.S. trading firms can "pass the book" to their overseas branch offices as the sun moves west to keep abreast of the international stock and debt markets. Other traders have taken to hiring "all-nighters," who remain in the home office overnight to monitor market movements overseas and execute customer orders. Recent research suggests that stock markets in Europe, Asia, and the United States are becoming cointegrated, sending shock waves to each other as price movements occur, and constantly moving toward a joint equilibrium.

As the 1990s began, the New York Stock Exchange announced plans for after-hours trading sessions via computer without fees and with minimal disclosure rules, and later, it announced plans to open its trading floor one-half hour earlier. These announcements represented an effort by the NYSE to lure back from overseas substantial numbers of pension funds, investment companies, and other large institutional investors that were trading in growing numbers away from the NYSE. Institutional trading of large blocks of stock inside the United States was given a boost recently when the U.S. Securities and Exchange Commission created Rule 144a, allowing financial institutions to trade large blocks of privately placed stocks and bonds without having to go through complicated disclosure procedures. The SEC also approved the launching of a system that made possible the trading of stocks after U.S. exchanges closed.

At about the same time, the National Association of Securities Dealers announced plans to extend the hours of operation of its automated quotations network to cover the hours when the London International Stock Exchange was open, supporting the growth of predawn stock trading inside the United States. Initially, NASDAQ International proposed to offer computer-screen trading of 400 to 500 stocks beginning at 3:30 A.M. EST in the United States. Not to be outdone, the American Stock Exchange, the Chicago Board Options Exchange, and Reuters Holdings PLC of Great Britain declared their intention to launch a system for night trading between 6:00 P.M. and 6:00 A.M. The Chicago Mercantile Exchange and Reuters announced plans for the Globex after-hours electronic order-entry and trade-maturity trading system involving purchases and sales of financial futures contracts. Globex represented an international partnership among futures exchanges in the United States and Western Europe. The Chicago Mercantile Exchange and the Singapore International Monetary Exchange also established a trading link, making it possible for identical futures contracts to be traded and closed out on either exchange. One of the areas of most rapid growth in the internationalization of the stock market is the cross-listing of stocks. For example, a U.S. corporation can request to have its stock listed on exchanges in London, Frankfurt, Tokyo, and other exchanges around the globe.

Paralleling the rapid expansion of cross-listing is global stock underwriting in which only a portion of new stock issues may be sold in their country of origin. Today many large stock issues have underwriters from more than one nation, helping a corporate customer reach the widest possible range of international buyers.

The Development of ADRs

Further evidence of the growing links between U.S. and foreign stock markets emerged in the 1980s and 1990s with the development of new international financial instruments. For example, U.S. exchanges began trading **American depository receipts (ADRs).** These are dollar-denominated claims on foreign shares of stock that are kept in safekeeping by U.S. financial institutions (usually by commercial banks and investment banking houses). In effect, ADRs are negotiable warehouse receipts for deposits of foreign stock that U.S. investors can trade without having to assume the risks of trading in foreign currencies. Among the most popular foreign firms whose ADRs are traded in the United States are Cifra and Telefonos de Mexico, British Petroleum, and Reuters Holdings in the United Kingdom.

ADRs do present some special risks of their own, however. For one thing, their underlying value is sensitive to fluctuations in foreign currency prices. A sharp decline in the value of the home country's currency, for example, can result in a significant loss of return from ADRs. Moreover, foreign stock prices tend to be more volatile than the prices of most actively traded U.S. equities. To be successful in the ADR market, U.S. investors must learn to become more aware of foreign business developments—information that often is difficult and costly to obtain, though the development of the World Wide Web has aided international investors in staying abreast of new developments around the globe. Many U.S. investors have come to prefer *sponsored* ADRs, for which the foreign firm issuing the stock hires a U.S. company (such as a bank) to serve the interests of American buyers and provide them with pertinent information about the foreign stock and its issuing company.

RANDOM WALK AND EFFICIENT MARKETS

Stock market behavior has figured prominently in the development of modern theories of what determines the market price and value of securities. One of the most popular of modern theories regarding the valuation of stocks and other securities is the *random walk hypothesis.*

Random walk is a term used in mathematics and statistics to describe a process in which successive elements in a data series are independent of each other and, therefore, are essentially random and unpredictable. The theory of random walk applied to the valuation of stocks says that the future path of individual stock prices is no more predictable than the path of a series of random numbers. Each share of stock is assumed to have an *intrinsic value* based on investor expectations of the discounted value of future cash flows generated by that stock. The market price per share is an unbiased estimator of a stock's intrinsic value and reflects the latest information available concerning the issuing company's condition and future prospects. Successive changes in the price of a stock are random fluctuations around that stock's intrinsic value, and these changes are independent of the sequence of price changes that occurred in the past. In effect, stock price changes act as though they were independent random drawings from an infinite pool of possible prices. Therefore, it is not possible to predict this week's stock price from last week's stock price, for example. Knowledge of the sequence of past price changes prior to the current time period is of little or no help in defining the probability distribution of price changes in any current or future period.

The random walk notion is not accepted by all stock market analysts. Many analysts still subscribe to chartist, or *technical analysis,* theories, which assume that the past behavior of a security's price is rich in information concerning the future behavior of that price. Patterns of past price behavior, technical analysts argue, tend to recur in the future. For this reason, careful analysis of stock price averages and the prices of individual shares reveal important data concerning future price movements. Unfortunately, empirical research evidence does not indicate any meaningful degree of dependence of future stock price movements on those occurring in the past.

Another test performed on the technical analysis theory has been to try various mechanical trading, or "filter," rules to see if the investor is better off using these rules instead of a simple "buy and hold" strategy. Filter rules usually require the investor to buy if a stock's price goes up at least Y percent and sell when the stock's price declines by X percent or more. Research studies generally favor the simple *buy and hold* strategy, especially after brokerage commissions are considered. Average earnings generated by trading rules appear to be no better than those achieved if the investor randomly selected a group of stocks representative of the market as a whole and held them for the full holding period. Trading rules do *not* appear to generate above-normal rates of return.

The Efficient Markets Hypothesis

The random walk notion has been supplemented in recent years by a broader theory of stock price movements known as the **efficient markets hypothesis (EMH).** As we saw in Chapter 3, a market is "efficient" if scarce resources are allocated to their most productive uses. In each case, buyers willing to pay the highest prices for each resource must receive the resources they require. In a perfectly efficient securities market, the prices of stocks will fluctuate randomly around their intrinsic values and are always at or near equilibrium. Any temporary deviations from equilibrium prices are quickly corrected. Information relevant to the valuation of stocks is simultaneously available to all investors at virtually no cost, and existing stock prices fully reflect the latest information available on

Financial Developments   Enron and Stock Market Efficiency

On December 2, 2001, Enron Corporation of Houston filed for bankruptcy-court protection under Chapter 11 of the U.S. bankruptcy code. An earthquake rumbled through U.S. and global stock markets as the shares of what had been one of the hottest companies around—the seventh-largest U.S. firm—dropped like a stone. By mid-January of 2002 the New York Stock Exchange had initiated steps to delist Enron from its trading floor as its shares, which only a year before had traded in excess of $80 per share, now sank below a dollar. Among the most important casualties were scores of Enron employees who not only lost their jobs, but saw their retirement savings melt away. Inquiries by government and private agencies soon revealed that at least a year before Enron's collapse several auditors and employees had warned of possible collapse from hidden debt, overvalued assets, and possible conflicts of interest involving top Enron officials and other insiders.

Could such a debacle possibly have occurred in a truly *efficient* stock market? The answer, of course, is "yes." In fact, the more efficient the financial marketplace the more likely it is that weak firms—no matter how big they are—will eventually be found and rooted out.

Moreover, recent research evidence suggests that, while most financial markets are efficient at processing and acting on *publicly available information,* they are not necessarily efficient in processing private, insider information. This is especially true if misleading accounting practices cover up internal problems which might otherwise attract public attention and cause the market to react. Even in a reasonably efficient market a "moral hazard" problem can emerge in which auditors, boards of directors, managers, and creditors of a company pursue their own self-interest at the expense of its stockholders.

Perhaps the one likely positive outcome of the Enron debacle may be actions by the Securities and Exchange Commission (SEC), the Financial Accounting Standards Board (FASB), and other key groups to improve the flow of relevant information to the public, reducing the advantages held by corporate insiders. Among possible steps for the future are new regulations on the investigatory and reporting procedures followed by outside auditors, more balanced reporting of the weaknesses as well as the strengths of publicly traded companies by security analysts and underwriters, new rules about the selection and retention of auditing firms, new guidelines for employee retirement plans that promote greater diversification in the assets held, and expanded power for government agencies (especially the SEC) to inquire into the financing and organizational structure of publicly held corporations.

the future profitability and risk of business firms. Moreover, stock prices adjust instantaneously to *new* information, and a new set of intrinsic values results, leading some investors to adjust their portfolios. All of this happens nearly instantaneously, so that market price equals intrinsic value in a state of continuous equilibrium. As a result, it is impossible in a perfectly efficient market to consistently make economic profits by trading on the information available because an efficient market is one that quickly processes *all* relevant information.

Recent Research Findings about the EMH

Research studies testing the efficient markets hypothesis (EMH) and the belief that stock prices behave as a random walk now span more than four decades. Unfortunately, the findings of literally dozens of studies are *not* uniform. There is evidence both for and against the efficient markets idea. Most scholars do seem to agree, however, that there *are* elements of efficiency present within the financial marketplace. Market efficiency is a matter of *degree.* The money and capital markets are not perfectly efficient, but probably at least partially so.

The earliest research studies focusing upon the EMH examined the correlations between stock prices over time. They asked such questions as, Are current and past stock prices positively or negatively correlated with each other? Can past stock prices be used to forecast future stock price behavior? If so the financial markets would not be efficient because investors could use data from the past to predict the future and earn excess returns simply by

Financial Developments   New SEC Disclosure Rule Takes Effect

As the twenty-first century began, the U.S. Securities and Exchange Commission put in place *Regulation FD* for "fair disclosure." This new rule prohibits a corporation's management from disclosing pertinent information about the firm only to selected market professionals (such as security brokers and mutual fund advisers) and not making this same timely information widely available to others.

The ultimate goal of Regulation FD was to give *all* investors, and not just a few market professionals, access to significant new information about a company that might well affect the value of the firm's stock and debt securities.

The new regulation was immediately attacked by security brokers and dealer firms. It was charged that Regulation FD would quickly increase the volatility of stock prices, particularly around the time corporate earnings announcements were being made. Other market professionals saw a danger that forecasts made by professional market analysts would decline in quality.

However, early research evidence found no indication that the flow of information to the financial markets had been damaged. Indeed, security prices seemed to become a bit less volatile than before (though it is probably too soon to accurately assess all the effects of the SEC's Regulation FD) when earnings news releases appeared. Time will tell whether this broadening of market information flows will bring the benefits the Securities and Exchange Commission hopes will follow.

drawing upon past information. On balance, research studies provide little evidence of statistically significant correlations between past and current stock prices or trading volumes. There seems to be no appreciable benefit from gathering mounds of historical stock market data in the hope of securing excess returns.

A challenge to the EMH emerged when some researchers uncovered evidence for so-called "market anomalies." That is, some stock prices appeared to display predictable patterns at various points in time—patterns that were persistent enough to at least offer the possibility that rational investors could make use of these patterns and score excess returns. For example, some data pointed to persistently higher or lower stock values on particular days of the week, during certain portions of a month, and at the beginning of the new year. Could a rational investor consistently generate extra returns simply by choosing to trade at special times on the calendar? If so, we would be dealing with a marketplace that was not completely efficient.

Research evidence does suggest the presence of some anomalies in stock prices related to the time of year, month, or day of the week in which trading occurs. For example, one of the most popular notions is the so-called "January effect" in which post–New Year's trading often appears to offer the prospect of unusually high returns, perhaps because the stock market was depressed the previous month by end-of-year selling for tax losses. By and large, however, the evidence that excess profits can be generated consistently by trading linked to the calendar is not strong. While market anomalies may put a small "nick" in the EMH there doesn't appear to be enough strength here to do the theory in.

Finally, we recall from Chapter 3 that some market traders possess *inside information* that the majority of market participants do not have (at least for a time). Examples include company officers, accountants, attorneys who deal with the firm involved, and friends and relatives of company officials who may know about a pending merger or imminent bankruptcy. Recognizing the profit potential inherent in inside information these individuals may move quickly to trade and reap excess returns before the marketplace sizes up what is happening. This information is special and often costly to obtain. Might there be evidence of consistent extra profits from trading on special information that is difficult or impossible for others to know?

Research evidence to date generally answers that question with a "yes." Insider trading can (and has) generated enormous profits for some. There are limits to market efficiency—which seems to hold for publicly available information open to anyone, as implied by the so-called "weak" and "semistrong" forms of the EMH that we discussed earlier in Chapter 3. You cannot consistently earn excess returns beyond those dictated by the level of risk you willingly accept if you possess only public information. However, if you trade using relevant inside information that only the few possess, the probability of earning excess profits does appear to increase substantially. Of course, if this insider information is illegally obtained or illegally used there is the risk of prosecution to consider as well!

Summary of Findings

Overall, the securities markets appear to be reasonably efficient channels for directing the flow of savings into investment. Changes in security prices do appear to conform generally to some form of random walk process in which daily price quotations cluster about a stock's intrinsic value, reflecting the latest information available. Thus, above-normal profits using publicly available information as a guide for stock trades are unlikely because that information is already included in current stock prices. A "buy and hold" strategy coupled with random selection of stocks from the *entire* market's portfolio will yield returns at least as good as those earned by professional traders, who usually turn over their portfolios rapidly. Of course, financial analysts with extraordinary (asymmetric) ability to uncover new information may be able to achieve above-average rates of return in the stock market, at least for short periods of time.

Questions *to Help You Study*

10. Please describe the different roles played by *call* and *put options* in the stock market.

11. What is *program trading?*

12. What role do *circuit breakers* play in the equities market? What are their possible advantages and disadvantages?

13. What is the *national market system? Shelf registration?*

14. Why did *ADRs* develop? Why are they important?

15. What is the *random walk* hypothesis? Does research evidence tend to support or deny the validity of this hypothesis?

16. What is an *efficient market?* What are the consequences of market efficiency for the behavior of stock prices? Does recent research support the idea that the stock market is efficient?

Summary of the Chapter

The market for corporate stock is the most widely followed of all securities markets, with millions of shares changing hands each day.

- Most stock trades involve *not* the creation of new funds—the raising of new capital—but rather the exchange of existing shares for money. Thus, most stock trading takes place in the *secondary market,* not the primary (or new issue) market.

- Trading in equity shares reveals a close correlation with *economic conditions.* Advancing stock prices appear to be a leading indicator, forecasting the growth of the economy, in part because business investment spending appears to be influenced by what is happening to stock prices.

- Corporate stock today can be divided into two major types: common stock and preferred stock. *Common stock* represents a residual claim against the assets of the issuing firm, entitling the owner to share in the net earnings of the firm when it is profitable and to share in the net market value of the company's assets if it is liquidated. *Preferred stock* carries a stated annual dividend expressed as a percent of the stock's par value.

- *Households*—individuals and families—are the dominant holders of corporate stock, followed by *pension funds* and *mutual funds.*

- Stock prices are *positively* related to the *expected stream of dividends* paid by the firm that issued the stock and *negatively* related to the *discount rate* associated with that stream of dividends (measuring *equity risk*).

- The market for corporate equity shares normally is divided into two main parts—the *organized exchanges* (such as the New York Stock Exchange) and the *over-the-counter market.* Trading on the exchanges is governed by regulations and formal procedures to promote competition and to contribute toward improved liquidity of equity shares. The over-the-counter (OTC) market is much less formal than the organized exchanges and generally involves broker-to-broker or dealer-to-dealer transactions on behalf of stock buyers and sellers.

- Other branches of the stock market have become important in recent years. These include a *third market,* in which exchange-listed stocks are traded over the counter; and a *private equity market,* where new businesses, privately held companies and partnerships, troubled firms, and even larger publicly traded companies can find financing for their long-term equity needs. The private equity market is involved in selling shares off the major exchanges with trading taking place between stock issuers and limited partnerships, venture capital companies, and other specialized investors.

- Rapid growth has occurred in the closely related market of *stock options*—an agreement between two parties granting one party the right, but not the obligation, to purchase an asset from or sell an asset to the other party at a set price. Both *put* (or selling) options and *call* (or buying) options are designed to manage the risk of fluctuating security prices.

- The stock market has become *global* in scope, rising from a series of national markets due to advances in the technology of information and funds transfer. Today the sun never sets on equity trading around the globe in an *efficient* marketplace.

Key Terms

Common stock, *615*
Preferred stock, *615*
Organized exchanges, *621*
Over-the-counter (OTC)
  market, *621*

Third market, *624*
Call options, *627*
Put options, *628*
Program trading, *628*
Circuit breakers, *630*

American depository receipts
  (ADRs), *633*
Random walk, *634*
Efficient markets hypothesis, *634*

Problems

1. A common stockholder of Milton Corporation is entitled to a *pro rata* share of any new stock issued by the company. If the firm plans to issue 500,000 new shares at a price of $3.50 per share and this particular stockholder currently holds 1.6 percent of all Milton's shares outstanding, how many new shares is this shareholder entitled to purchase? At what total cost?

2. Riter-Cal Corporation has preferred shares outstanding carrying a $35 par value and promising a 6 percent annual dividend rate. Daniel Smith holds 200 shares of R-C's preferred stock. What annual dividend can he expect to receive if the company's board of directors votes to pay the regular dividend? Suppose R-C's preferred stock consists of *participating* shares, with preferred shareholders participating equally in net earnings with the firm's common stockholders. If the company declares a $10 per share common stock dividend, how much in additional per-share dividends will each of its preferred shareholders receive?

3. Mastery Corporation expects to pay a level annual dividend of $3 per share on its common stock each year into the indefinite future. The current rate of discount applied to all expected future dividend flows by capital market investors for companies of comparable risk is 12 percent. Estimate the current per-share market price (S) of Mastery's common stock. Suppose the sum of the default-free interest rate and the premium for equity risk declines from 12 percent to 10 percent. How would your estimate of the Mastery Corporation's per-share stock price change? What if the current discount rate on comparable equity shares rises to 15 percent?

4. Please identify each of the terms and concepts listed below by matching up the definition or descriptive phrase given below with the correct term:
   a. A residual claim against the assets and earnings of a corporation.
   b. A share of ownership in a business corporation with a stated annual dividend.
   c. Formal locations where stocks, bonds, and other instruments are traded.
   d. A mechanism for trading stocks and other instruments through brokers or dealers operating away from securities exchanges.
   e. A mechanism through which stocks and other instruments listed on an exchange are traded off the exchange in the over-the-counter market.
   f. Computer-assisted decisions about security purchases and sales in order to take advantage of temporary pricing inconsistencies.
   g. Rules for trading on a securities exchange that bring a halt to trading or slow trading under certain circumstances.
   h. Dollar-denominated claims on specific foreign shares of stock held in safekeeping by U.S. financial institutions.
   i. A theory of stock price movements that contends that the future path of stock prices is no more predictable than a series of random numbers.

Questions about the Web and the Money and Capital Markets

1. If you wanted to find out more about *daily stock price movements,* where could you look on the Web? Which of the Web sources you came up with in answering this question seemed the best to you? Why?

2. Are you interested in corporate *stock options?* Many corporate employees are these days. Where on the Web could you derive further information about stock options?

3. What does the Web have to say about *insider trading* in corporate stocks? What Web site or sites would you recommend to anyone researching this particular topic?

4. Suppose you wanted to find out, not about individual stocks, but about price movements in the stock market *as a whole*. Where could you find up-to-date data on various aggregate stock market indices (like the Standard & Poor's 500 stock index or the Dow Jones Industrials)? Which source seems best to you?

5. Does there appear to be a strong or weak connection between a corporation's stock price and its recent financial performance? Use data from the Web for several leading companies (such as some of the firms represented in the S&P Market Insight Web site) to determine if there appears to be a significant relationship.

Selected References

Ashley, Lisa K. "Circuit Breakers: Back to Basics." *Chicago Fed Letter,* Federal Reserve Bank of Chicago, July 1998, pp. 1–3.

Campbell, John Y., and Robert J. Schiller. "Valuation Ratios and the Long-Run Stock Market Outlook: An Update." National Bureau of Economic Research Working Paper Series, No. 8221, April 2001.

Carlson, John B. "Why Is the Dividend Yield So Low?" *Economic Commentary,* Federal Reserve Bank of Cleveland, April 1, 2001.

Carlson, John B., and Kevin H. Sargent. "The Recent Ascent of Stock Prices: Can It Be Explained by Earnings Growth or Other Fundamentals?" *Economic Review,* Federal Reserve Bank of Cleveland, 1997, pp. 2–12.

Cochrane, John H. "Where Is the Market Going? Uncertain Facts and Novel Theories." *Economic Perspectives,* Federal Reserve Bank of Chicago, 1998, pp. 3–37.

Fama, Eugene F., and Kenneth R. French. "Disappearing Dividends: Changing Firm Characteristics or Lower Propensity to Pay." *Journal of Financial Economics* LX, No. 1 (April 2001), pp. 3–43.

Fenn, George W.; Nellie Lang; and Stephen Prowse. "The Economics of the Private Equity Market." Staff Study No. 168, Board of Governors of the Federal Reserve System, December 1995.

Golob, John E., and David G. Bishop. "Do Stock Prices Follow Interest Rates or Inflation?" Research Working Paper 96–13, Federal Reserve Bank of Kansas City, 1996, pp. 1–21.

Gou, Hui. "Why Are Stock Market Returns Correlated with Future Economic Activities?" *Review,* Federal Reserve Bank of St. Louis, March–April 2002, pp. 19–34.

Jarrell, G.; James Brickley; and G. Netter. "The Market for Corporate Control." *Journal of Economic Perspectives,* 1988, pp. 49–68.

Poterba, J., and L. Summers. "Mean Reversion in Stock Prices: Evidence and Implications." *Journal of Financial Economics,* October 1988, pp. 27–89.

Sarker, Asani, and Kai Li. "Should U.S. Investors Hold Foreign Stocks?" *Current Issues in Economics and Finance*, Federal Reserve Bank of New York, March 2002.

Shiller, Robert. *Market Volatility.* Cambridge, MA: MIT Press, 1989.

U.S. Presidential Task Force on Market Mechanisms. *Report of the Presidential Task Force on Market Mechanisms,* Washington, DC, January 1988.

Chapter **Twenty-Three**

Consumer Lending and Borrowing

Learning Objectives in This Chapter

- You will see the vital role played by *consumers*—households (individuals and families)—in supplying loanable funds through saving to the money and capital markets.

- You will learn about the important role consumers play as major *borrowers* of funds within the financial system.

- You will explore the principal characteristics and unique features of *consumer lending institutions*, including banks, credit unions, and finance companies.

- You will learn what your *rights* are under U.S. law as a consumer of financial services, including the right to know (disclosure), the right to privacy, and the right to be served without illegal discrimination.

What's in This Chapter? Key Topics Outline

Consumers as Borrowers and Lenders of Funds

Growing Menu of Consumer-Oriented Financial Services

The Democratization of Consumer Credit

Portfolio and Wealth Effects

Credit and Debit Cards: Convenience and Risk

What Determines Consumer Borrowing?

Key Consumer Lending Institutions

Factors Lenders Consider in the Consumer Loan Decision

Financial Disclosure and Credit Discrimination Laws

Consumer Bankruptcy and Proposed New Legislation

As this chapter will relate to the reader, consumers—individuals and families or households—have had a powerful impact on the money and capital markets over time, particularly with the rise of the middle class and the creation of an industrial society. With millions of households bringing home a paycheck, there are opportunities to build up and invest savings and also opportunities to borrow money, counting on future income to repay those debts.

Today individuals and families represent the main source of savings within the financial system and are among the leading groups in the economy when it comes to taking on debt. Not surprisingly, household borrowing and saving are well represented on the World Wide Web with most Web sites set up by financial institutions seeking to loan consumers money or attract their savings. However, the Web is also useful for keeping track of trends in household borrowing and saving. Examples include data on the growth of consumer debt over time—for example, at the site labeled Consumer Debt Statistics bearing the address *www.progress.org/cdebt.htm* or at the Federal Reserve data site found at *www.economagic.com*.

As more and more households have gotten into debt there has been a corresponding response by governments to pass laws to protect lenders and also to protect household borrowers from abuse. Summaries of consumer laws and consumer rights under those laws may be found at numerous Web sites, such as the Federal Reserve Board at *www.federalreserve.gov* and through various state legal agencies—for example, the Department of Justice for the State of New Hampshire at *www.state.nh.us/nhdoj*.

The recent trend toward less saving and more spending by consumers has also caught the attention of Web masters. Numerous sites have appeared dealing with the measurement of personal savings and exploring possible ways in which to encourage U.S. households to save more for the future. Two prominent examples are the Government Guide at *www.governmentguide.com* and the National Endowment for Financial Education (NEFE) at *www.nefe.org*.

INTRODUCTION

Among the most important of all financial markets are the markets providing savings instruments and credit to individuals and families (households). Many financial analysts have referred to the period since World War II as the *age of consumer finance* because individuals and families not only have become the principal source of loanable funds flowing into the financial markets today but also are one of the largest borrowing groups in the entire financial system. Moreover, the market for household financial services is the one market that *everyone*, regardless of profession or social status, will enter at one time or another during his or her lifetime. In this chapter, we examine the major characteristics of the consumer market for financial services, the principal lenders active in this market, and some important regulations applying to household borrowing and lending today.

CONSUMERS AS LENDERS OF FUNDS

Each of us is a consumer of goods and services every day of our lives. Scarcely a day passes that we do not enter the marketplace to purchase food, shelter, entertainment, and other essentials of modern living. We are also well aware, perhaps from personal experience, that consumers often borrow heavily in the financial marketplace to achieve their desired standard of living. U.S. households borrowed nearly $600 billion in 2000, for example, and by the end of that year owed more than $7 trillion to various lending institutions.

What is not nearly so well known, however, is the fact that consumers as a group are also among the most important *lenders* of funds in the economy. Loanable funds are supplied by consumers when they purchase financial assets from other units in the economy. In 2000, gross savings by U.S. households reached nearly $1 trillion, of which more than $200 billion flowed into bank deposits, bonds, stocks, and direct cash loans to others. The consuming public is among the chief sources of the raw material—loanable funds—that is exchanged in the money and capital markets.[1]

Financial Assets Purchased by Consumers

If consumers make loanable funds available to other units in the economy by purchasing financial assets, what kinds of financial assets do they buy? And what are the principal sources of borrowed funds for consumers? The Federal Reserve Board's Flow of Funds Accounts provide us with a wealth of information on the borrowing and lending habits of households. Exhibit 23–1 summarizes information contained in recent Flow of Funds reports on the kinds of financial assets acquired by households. One fact immediately evident is the wide diversity of financial assets purchased by individuals and families, ranging from those of very low risk and short maturity (such as bank deposits and government securities) to long-term, higher-risk investments (such as mortgages and corporate stock).

The single most important household financial asset today is *corporate stock* (equities), led by a dramatic rise in holdings of shares in mutual funds (investment companies). The recent growth in households' common stock investments appears to reflect continuing fears about a possible resumption of serious inflation. Then, too, many individuals and families are concerned that when they reach their retirement years, Social Security, Medicare, and other government retirement plans will simply be inadequate to cover living costs and health care expenses in their final years. Reflecting this same concern, *pension fund reserves* ranked at the top among all household assets, exceeding $10 trillion by the year 2000. Of course, many of the reserves held by pension plans are also invested in corporate stock, as are many *life insurance reserves.*

In third place among household holdings of financial assets are *deposits* in banks, savings and loan associations, credit unions, and other thrift institutions. These checkable demand deposits and time and savings deposits represented close to 10 percent of the total financial asset holdings of U.S. consumers in the year 2000. Moreover, as Exhibit 23–1 reveals, the importance of deposits in consumer financial investments generally increased until the 1980s and early 1990s, when households became concerned about a rising tide of bank and thrift institution failures. At the same time, better yields appeared to be available from investments in *corporate stock* (including mutual funds) and *government and corporate bonds.*

There has also been a significant rise in household investments in small businesses, which are often owned and operated by an individual or a family. By 2000, household investments in the equity of unincorporated business firms (included under *Other assets* in Exhibit 23–1) totaled more than $2 trillion. When jobs become more difficult to find, more individuals and families organize their own businesses. At the same time, there is a trend toward early retirement and the launching of second careers by creating new businesses.

---

[1]Portions of this chapter were originally drawn from Rose (December 1978, June 1979, and September 1979).

EXHIBIT 23–1 Principal Financial Assets Held by U.S. Households, 1960, 1970, 1980, 1990, and 2000 ($ Billions)

Financial Assets Held	1960 Amount	Percent	1970 Amount	Percent	1980 Amount	Percent	1990 Amount	Percent	2000* Amount	Percent
Demand deposits and currency	$ 70.2	7.3%	$ 118.2	4.7%	$ 270.7	4.1%	$ 514.0	3.7%	$ 325.6	0.9%
Time and savings accounts:	165.3	17.1	426.3	17.1	1,272.8	19.4	2,381.1	17.0	3,170.6	9.0
At commercial banks	62.1	6.4	—	—	—	—	—	—	—	—
At nonbank thrift institutions	103.3	10.7	—	—	—	—	—	—	—	—
Shares in money market mutual funds	—	—	—	—	64.9	1.0	438.6	3.1	909.3	2.6
U.S. government securities	73.5	7.6	102.8	4.1	246.9	3.8	841.1	6.0	729.0	2.1
State and local government securities	30.8	3.2	46.0	1.8	88.4	1.3	549.2	3.9	530.3	1.5
Open market paper	0.1	0.0	11.8	0.5	41.3	0.6	214.2	1.5	75.4	0.2
Corporate and foreign bonds	9.8	1.0	35.6	1.4	58.8	0.9	185.0	1.3	728.9	2.1
Mortgages	31.8	3.3	52.1	2.1	116.5	1.8	225.5	1.6	110.4	0.3
Corporate stock:	396.1	40.0	727.2	29.1	1,173.1	17.9	2,503.7	17.9	7,447.6	21.2
Investment companies	17.0	1.8	44.5	1.8	52.1	0.8	495.9	3.5	3,374.2	9.3
Other corporate shares	279.0	39.2	682.7	27.3	1,121.0	17.1	2,007.8	14.4	4,173.4	11.9
Life insurance reserves	85.2	8.8	130.7	5.2	216.4	3.3	373.4	2.7	821.2	2.3
Pension fund reserves	90.7	9.4	240.8	9.6	830.0	12.6	2,962.6	21.2	10,348.6	29.4
Security credit	1.1	0.1	4.4	0.2	14.8	0.2	62.4	0.4	365.3	1.0
Other assets	13.3	1.4	603.5	24.1	2,168.6	33.0	2,760.1	19.7	2,195.6	6.2
Total financial assets	$967.9	100.0%	$2,499.3	100.0%	$6,563.3	100.0%	$13,978.9	100.0%	$35,205.4	100.0%

Note: Columns may not add to totals due to rounding.
*Figures for 2000 are third quarter only (annualized).

Source: Board of Governors of the Federal Reserve System.

The Growing Menu of Savings Instruments Available to Consumers Today

One of the most important of all trends affecting consumer savings and lending today is a veritable explosion of *new financial instruments.* Banks, brokerage houses, and other financial institutions began in the 1970s to compete aggressively for consumer savings, not only by offering higher returns where the law allowed but also by proliferating new services. Like a Baskin-Robbins ice cream store, financial institutions began to offer household customers 31 or more flavors of savings and transaction accounts as well as credit plans to meet a wide variety of personal financial needs.

This trend toward financial service proliferation began with the introduction of the **NOW account** in New England in 1970. NOWs are checkbook deposits that, like any checking account, can be used to pay for purchases of goods and services. But when NOWs were first developed they broke new ground, paying *interest* on checkbook deposits which federal law prohibited for regular checking accounts. NOWs were permitted nationwide beginning in 1981 as a result of passage of the Depository Institutions Deregulation and Monetary Control Act of 1980. This law also called for the gradual phasing out of federal interest rate ceilings on all bank and thrift institution deposits so that consumers could receive competitive, market-determined interest rates on their savings.

The Depository Institutions Deregulation and Monetary Control Act of 1980 (DIDMCA) also authorized two services that compete directly with NOWs. One of these—automatic transfer services (ATS)—permits the consumer to preauthorize a bank to move funds from a savings account to a checking account to cover overdrafts. The net effect is to pay interest on transaction balances at the savings account rate. Credit unions are permitted to offer their own version of the NOW, known as the *share draft.* These checkbook plans pay among the highest interest rates on liquid funds.

In 1973, money market mutual funds first appeared, offering consumers *share accounts* with low denominations (most allowing accounts to be opened for a few hundred dollars). Like NOWs, share accounts at money funds were developed originally to get around federal deposit interest rate ceilings and give smaller savers access to competitive rates of return on their funds. Later, several prominent brokerage houses began offering *consumer cash management services,* in which funds could be held in an interest-bearing money market fund until transferred into stocks, bonds, or other securities, or accessed via check or credit card. Closely related to these services is the *wrap account,* for which a security broker assembles for the consumer a suitable portfolio of stocks, bonds, and other assets and actively manages that portfolio in return for an annual fee.

Life insurance firms began offering a related service known as *universal life insurance,* in which savings contributed by the policyholder are placed in a money market fund, with the life insurer making periodic withdrawals to pay the premiums on the life insurance policy. The consumer is offered life insurance protection plus a higher return on savings. Recently, however, universal life insurance sales appear to have slowed appreciably.

In 1981, with passage of the Economic Recovery Tax Act of 1981, wage earners and salaried individuals were granted the right to make limited contributions each year, tax free, to an *individual retirement account (IRA)* offered by banks, brokerage firms, and other financial institutions or by employers with qualified pension or profit-sharing plans. Similarly, *Keogh Plan retirement accounts* were created to help self-employed persons prepare for retirement and may be offered by the same institutions that sell IRAs. As we noted in Chapter 8, tax-favored retirement accounts were supplemented further in the late 1990s when new types of accounts—for example, *Roth* and *Education IRAs*—were created to give household investors new tax-sheltered savings vehicles to prepare for retirement and to help offset the spiraling cost of a college education. The Roth IRA proved to be particularly popular because not only could the consumer invest monies and generate tax-sheltered earnings, but for qualified accounts, withdrawals could be made tax-free (unlike the conventional IRAs and Keogh plans). Legislation in 2001 significantly expanded the amount of savings that could be placed in these tax-sheltered accounts.

Beginning in the late 1970s, flexible savings plans became popular as many consumers fought to stay ahead of inflation through savings instruments whose rates of return were sensitive to changes in the cost of living as well as to changing interest rates in the money and capital markets. *Money market certificates of deposit* were authorized by federal regulation in 1978 with interest rates that changed as market yields on U.S. government securities fluctuated. In 1982, the Garn-St Germain Depository Institutions Act allowed banks and thrift institutions to offer deposits competitive with shares offered by money market mutual funds, in the form of money market deposit accounts (MMDAs) and Super NOWs, each offering flexible interest rates but accessible via check to pay for purchases of goods and services. As the 1990s approached, several banks and savings associations, led by Chase Manhattan Bank of New York, introduced *market-index certificates of deposit,* whose return was linked to stock market performance.

Accompanying the development of more flexible-yield types of deposits, life insurance companies and pension programs began to offer new types of *life insurance policies* and *annuity accounts* that build up cash value and promise either a lump-sum payment or a stream of future income payments. The much older fixed-value insurance and annuity plans were supplanted in many markets by *variable-rate annuities* and *variable-rate insurance plans,* whose value depends on the market performance of the assets that make up these savings vehicles. With the right kinds of investments an individual or family can develop a sizeable reservoir of accumulated savings to protect their standard of living in the later stages of life.

During the 1990s and into the new century, *corporate equities,* in the form of both individual corporate stocks and pools of shares held in *mutual funds,* exploded in popularity among household savers. Many individuals and families concluded that their long-range savings were not growing fast enough for their future needs (especially in meeting the challenges of saving for retirement, inflation, and future educational costs), particularly if those savings were held in deposits at banks and thrift institutions where promised interest yields were often very low. Equities, on the other hand, seemed to offer the promise of much larger long-term returns. Moreover, the pooling of equities in mutual funds appeared to lower the consumer's risk exposure. At the same time the Securities and Exchange Commission (SEC) required mutual funds to clarify for the public their method of figuring their rates of return and required these funds to simplify their reports so that consumers could more easily understand what they were buying. The market for individual corporate stocks and shares in mutual funds sagged in 2000 and 2001 under adverse economic pressures, but appeared to be recovering as the new century moved forward.

These recent innovations have been designed to bring individuals and families into the financial markets as more active lenders of funds. The newest financial services offer the consumer greater *financial flexibility*—easier access to liquid funds for transaction purposes and the ability to move funds more easily from one type of savings instrument to another. The newest savings instruments offer the potential for higher rates of return more closely tied to changing interest rates and security prices in the open market.

One interesting feature of the consumer financial services market worth remembering is that many households do *not* make a practice of purchasing all their financial services from one source. Instead, as a Federal Reserve Board survey by Elliehausen and Wolken (1992) reveals, households tend to *bundle,* or *cluster,* their purchases of services from certain financial firms. One typical clustering centers around the purchase of a checking account. Usually, a specific depository institution will be chosen to hold a family's main checking account—in most cases, a bank, credit union, or savings and loan. Savings accounts are often placed locally as well, although increasingly households have turned to distant financial firms, such as mutual funds, to help them invest their savings at the best yields. Credit services—home mortgages, credit cards, and installment loans—frequently are purchased from a separate financial firm, such as a finance company, savings association, or bank. The financial-service firms from which households purchase credit often are *local* firms, but frequently they will search both inside and outside the local area to find a loan on the best terms, particularly if the loan is large or the consumer is seeking a new credit card. The Federal Reserve Board survey revealed that most households seem to regard checkable deposits (payments accounts), savings accounts, and credit as *separate* financial products for which they will seek out the best terms available.

Questions *to Help You Study*

1. Which sector of the economy usually provides the greatest amount of loanable funds for borrowers to draw upon? Does this sector make primarily direct loans or indirect loans to borrowers?

2. What is currently the most important *financial asset* held by U.S. households? Which financial asset is in second place in household (consumer) portfolios? Third place?

3. Define the following terms:

NOWs	Mutual funds
MMDAs	Fixed and variable-rate annuities
Roth IRAs	Share drafts
Home equity loans	Universal life insurance
ATS	Money market share accounts
IRAs	

   In what ways do the financial instruments and services listed above benefit consumers?

CONSUMERS AS BORROWERS OF FUNDS

We have noted that consumers provide most of the savings out of which financial assets are created in the money and capital markets. However, it is also true that consumers are among the most important borrowers in the financial system. Total credit market debt owed by U.S. households was more than $7.5 trillion in 2000 (see Exhibit 23–2). This was only slightly less than the total amounts owed by the federal government and all state and local governments combined.

Is Consumer Borrowing Excessive?

Are consumers too heavily in debt today? Certainly, the total volume of household debt outstanding is huge in both absolute terms and relative to most other sectors of the economy. However, to judge whether consumer borrowing is really excessive, that debt should be compared to the financial assets consumers hold. These assets, presumably, can be drawn on to meet any interest and principal payments that come due on consumer borrowings.

EXHIBIT 23–2 The Principal Debt Obligations (Liabilities) of U.S. Households, 1960, 1970, 1980, 1990, and 2000 (third quarter)

Debt (Liabilities) Outstanding	1960		1970		1980		1990		2000*	
	Amount	Percent	Amount	Percent	Amount	Percent	Amount	Percent	Amount	Percent
Home mortgages	$136.8	60.5%	$290.0	57.9%	$ 943.3	62.6%	$2,714.6	67.7%	$4,930.5	65.5%
Other mortgages	9.2	4.1	19.0	3.8	31.5	2.1	133.5	3.3	148.2	2.0
Consumer installment credit	43.0	19.0	105.5	21.1	300.4	19.9	748.3	18.7	1,495.6	19.9
Other consumer credit	13.2	5.8	37.6	7.5	74.0	4.9	60.6	`1.5	193.6	2.6
Bank loans n.e.c.**	7.2	3.2	6.9	1.4	29.5	2.0	42.4	1.1	67.5	0.9
Other loans	7.0	3.1	20.9	4.2	54.7	3.6	112.1	2.8	240.6	3.2
Security credit	5.4	2.4	10.4	2.1	27.2	1.8	38.8	1.0	270.2	3.6
Trade credit	2.3	0.9	5.3	1.1	17.2	1.1	54.6	1.4	137.7	1.8
Deferred and unpaid life insurance premiums	2.4	1.1	5.1	1.0	12.9	0.9	16.5	0.4	18.7	0.2
Other liabilities	—	—	0.2	—	16.6	1.1	86.1	2.1	18.7	0.2
Total liabilities	$226.2	100.0%	$500.0	100.0%	$1,507.3	100.0%	$4,007.5	100.0%	$7,521.3	100.0%

Note: Columns may not add to totals due to rounding.
*2000 figures are for third quarter only.
**Not elsewhere classified.

Source: Board of Governors of the Federal Reserve System.

EXHIBIT 23–3   **The Household Sector as a Net Lender of Funds to the Rest of the Economy**

Item	Amounts Outstanding at Year-End ($ Billions)					
	1950	**1960**	**1970**	**1980**	**1990**	**2000***
Total financial assets held by households	$447.5	$967.9	$2,499.3	$6,563.3	$13,978.9	$35,205.4
Total debts (financial liabilities) of households	77.4	226.2	500.9	1,507.3	4,007.5	7,521.3
Difference: Financial assets minus liabilities	$370.1	$741.7	$1,988.4	$5,056.0	$ 9,971.4	$27,684.1
Ratio of household liabilities to financial assets	17.3%	23.4%	20.0%	29.8%	28.7%	27.2%

*2000 figures are as of the third quarter.

Source: Board of Governors of the Federal Reserve System.

Exhibit 23–3 shows that, although the volume of consumer debt has increased rapidly in recent years, the volume of household financial assets has grown even faster. For example, in 2000, financial assets held by U.S. households exceeded their estimated liabilities by nearly $28 trillion. Moreover, the absolute dollar size of that financial asset cushion has increased dramatically over the past three decades (as the third row of figures in Exhibit 23–3 demonstrates).

When we measure the *ratio of consumer liabilities to financial assets,* however, the picture is not quite so optimistic. As shown in the exhibit, this liability-to-asset ratio rose from less than 20 percent in 1950 to nearly 30 percent during the 1980s and early 1990s. However, more recently, with huge household investments in retirement assets, the ratio of household debt to financial asset holdings has declined to only about 27 percent. Whether the household liability–financial asset ratio stands at an "excessive" level depends, of course, on economic conditions and the educational level of consumers. If the average consumer today is better educated and more capable of managing a larger volume of debt, a relatively high ratio of liabilities to financial assets is probably not an alarming development. Moreover, the total wealth held by consumers includes not just their financial assets but also their real assets, such as homes, automobiles, and furniture. Although we have no really reliable measure of the value of real assets held by consumers, it is obvious that the current total wealth of all individuals and families (including both real and financial assets) far exceeds their current debt, on average.

The fact that households as a group hold more financial assets than liabilities does not mean that the recent build up of consumer debt is completely innocuous, however. Recently, government policymakers have been especially concerned about a so-called *portfolio effect* that they believe might significantly slow the future growth of the U.S. economy. Consumer borrowings rose rapidly over the decade of the 1980s until, by 1990, the ratio of U.S. household debt to disposable consumer income was at an historically high 78 percent. After slackening early in the 1990s, household debt-to-income ratios rose to over 100 percent in the late 1990s and early into the new century. To the extent that U.S. households feel excessively burdened with this large debt accumulation and fearful about losing their jobs, they may cut back on their rate of consumption spending. Because consumer spending is the largest component of the nation's GDP (production and income), a slowdown of household spending

Financial Developments   The Rapid Expansion and Democratization of Consumer Credit

Emerging from the longest expansion period in the history of the American economy from 1992 through the year 2000, consumers in the United States ran up the biggest total of household debt in U.S. history. By mid-2001 total installment debt of individuals and families had reached $1.6 trillion—an all-time high.

Paralleling the rise in installment debt, home mortgage borrowings to support the purchase of new homes reached nearly $6 trillion or about three-fifths of the nation's annual income and spending (GDP) by the beginning of the twenty-first century. Moreover, American home ownership also reached an all-time high as two-thirds of U.S. households owned their own homes by the year 2001. Home equity credit—the most rapidly growing type of consumer credit—increased nearly 150 percent during the decade ending in the year 2000.

It might well be argued that as consumer debt soared, households would increase their savings as a cushion against possible loss of a job and the inability of a family to repay its debts. Quite to the contrary, however, the ratio of American households' savings compared to their personal income reached the lowest level in more than half a century. In fact, the personal savings ratio for the average American household turned *negative* in some quarters of the year as the twentieth century drew to a close.

What caused these incredible changes? Why did American household debt roughly double over the past decade, so that U.S. individual and family households owed more than a dollar in debt for each dollar of their disposable income?

We don't yet know all the answers to the foregoing questions. However, some pieces of this puzzle do now seem to fall into place. For one thing, soaring personal income during the 1990s led to expectations among many households that rapid income growth would continue into the future. Hence, there was little hesitation on the part of many consumers to take on more debt. Then, too, stock prices had risen sharply during much of the preceding decade, giving many households a shot in the arm in terms of total wealth, reducing the apparent need for current saving.

Finally, consumer borrowing in recent years increasingly has become "*democratized*"—lenders extending credit cards and other forms of credit to millions of households of low and moderate income as well as to high-income families. In the most recent period many lenders argued that they could loan money to virtually anyone, no matter the degree of risk, if they could correctly price any loan made. While in theory this might be correct, subsequent experience suggests that regulations and competition limit the pricing strategies lenders can use and they often lose more money than expected on high-risk credits, especially when the economy weakens and unemployment begins to rise. For all of the foregoing reasons American consumer debt has soared to unprecedented levels and shows little sign of retreating.

can lead directly to slower economic growth. This concept of a household "portfolio effect" argues that consumers may alter their level of spending until they once again feel comfortable with the balance between their income, financial assets, and liabilities.

Of course, pulling in the opposite direction from the so-called "portfolio effect" discussed above may be the "wealth effect." With the prices of many stocks, bonds, and other consumer-held assets rising at various times over the past decade, household net worth rose dramatically. This upsurge in consumer wealth caused many individuals and families to feel comfortable with heavier debt loads, believing they could sell off their higher-valued assets if trouble appeared on the horizon. Unfortunately, consumers may have overestimated the true value of their recent gains in wealth. If everyone tries to sell off their assets to repay debt, asset values will sink and many households will wind up poorer. Indeed, stock market declines early in the new century coupled with job layoffs did slow household spending, making some consumers feel poorer.

Categories of Consumer Borrowing

The range of consumer borrowing needs is enormous. Loans to the household sector support a more diverse group of purchases of goods and services than is true of any other sector of

Consumer borrowing
and savings activities
have captured great
interest lately and are
frequently discussed on
the Web. Two examples
are the Web sites
addressed as The
Consumer Information
Center at *www.
consumer.gov* and MSN
at *www.msn.com*

the economy. Consumers borrow *long term* to finance purchases of durable goods, such as single-family homes, automobiles, boats, and home appliances. They usually borrow *short term* to cover purchases of nondurable goods and services, such as medical care, vacations, food, and clothing. Financial analysts frequently divide the credit extended to consumers into three broad categories: (1) **residential mortgage credit,** used to support the purchase of new or existing homes; (2) **installment credit,** used primarily for long-term nonresidential purposes; and (3) **noninstallment credit,** used for short-term cash needs.

Which of these forms of consumer borrowing is most important? Exhibit 23–2 provides a clear answer. Far and away the dominant form of consumer borrowing is aimed at providing shelter for individuals and families through mortgage loans. Home mortgage indebtedness by U.S. households approached close to $6 trillion in 2000, representing about two-thirds of all household debt. Moreover, the volume of home mortgage credit flowing to households has grown rapidly in recent years with the attractiveness of home ownership as a tax shelter and with recent tax reforms that favor home-equity loans secured by the borrower's home (even though funds borrowed often go for non-housing-related expenditures).

Installment credit is the second major component of consumer debt in the United States. Installment debt consists of all consumer liabilities other than home mortgages that are retired in two or more consecutive payments, usually monthly or quarterly. Four major types of installment credit are extended by lenders in this field: automobile credit, revolving credit, mobile homes, and other installment loans. An incredibly wide variety of consumer goods and services is financed by this kind of credit, including the purchase of furniture and appliances, the payment of medical expenses, the purchase of automobiles, and the consolidation of outstanding debts. As shown in Exhibit 23–2, consumer installment debt totaled well over a trillion dollars in 2000, more than quadruple the amount in 1980.

The final major category of consumer debt is *noninstallment credit,* which is normally paid off in a lump sum. This form of consumer credit includes single-payment loans, charge accounts, and credit for services, such as medical care and utilities. The total amount of noninstallment loans outstanding is difficult to estimate because many such loans are made by one individual to another or by department stores, oil and gas companies, and professional service firms that do not report their lending activities. Commercial banks, however, make a substantial volume of noninstallment loans to consumers and are considered the leading lender in this field.

HOME EQUITY LOANS

One new form of consumer borrowing that is closely related to residential mortgage credit is the **home equity loan.** Like traditional home mortgages, a home equity loan is secured by a borrower's home. However, unlike traditional home mortgages, many home equity loans consist of a prearranged revolving credit line the borrower can draw on for purchases of any goods or services he or she wishes to buy over the life of the credit line. Thus, the consumer can literally write himself or herself a loan simply by writing a check or presenting a credit card for purchases made up to a stipulated maximum amount, known as the *borrowing base.* The borrowing base equals the difference between the appraised market value of the borrower's home and the unpaid amount of the mortgage against that home multiplied by a fraction (often 0.70, or 70 percent). Thus, a home currently valued at $100,000 with an outstanding mortgage loan against it of $40,000 would give the homeowner a base amount to borrow against of about ($100,000 − $40,000) × 0.70, or $42,000. Moreover, under current U.S. tax laws, the interest owed on a loan secured by the borrower's home that qualifies under all the rules laid down in the Internal Revenue Code represents a tax-deductible expense, encouraging consumers to substitute home equity loans for other types of credit whose interest cost is *not* tax deductible.[2]

Most home equity loan rates are linked to the bank prime interest rate (or other base interest rate, such as the U.S. government bond rate) plus an extra margin for risk (i.e., a floating loan rate). Federal law requires that a maximum (ceiling) interest rate be established for all such loans. Home equity loans cover 10 to 15 years in most cases, although a substantial proportion can be continued indefinitely. The Consumer Protection Act of 1988 prohibits a home equity lender from canceling a loan unless fraud, failure to pay, or other violations of the loan contract occur. Thus far, most home equity loans have been used to pay off other debts, make home improvements, buy automobiles, or finance an education.

Home equity credit has proved to be especially attractive to consumer lending institutions for a variety of reasons. These loans tend to have a lower rate of default because borrowers feel more responsible when their home is pledged as collateral and that collateral tends to have a more stable value. Moreover, the cost of making home equity loans when amortized over the life of each loan is usually lower than the cost of a series of short-term loans made to the same customer. In addition, these loans usually carry interest rates that adjust to the market, whereas many other consumer loans have fixed interest rates. Finally, home equity credits help the lender build a working relationship with a customer better than most other types of consumer loans, creating more opportunities for the lender to sell that customer additional services. However, if the borrower cannot make the loan payments, his or her home may be repossessed and sold to pay back the lender. Many financial experts recommend that consumers use home equity credit with caution, particularly when their future employment prospects are uncertain.

CREDIT AND DEBIT CARDS

One of the most popular forms of installment credit available to consumers today comes through the **credit card.** Through this encoded piece of plastic, the consumer has instant access to credit for any purchase up to a prespecified limit. In the language of finance, the credit card has removed the "liquidity" constraint that restricted the spending power of millions of consumers, democratizing access to credit and spending power. More recently, another piece of plastic—the **debit card**—has made instant cash available and check cashing much easier. The growth of credit and debit cards has been truly phenomenal. Current estimates suggest that there are more than one trillion credit and debit cards in use worldwide, and leading nonfinancial companies (such as General Motors and General Electric) have recently entered in large numbers as suppliers of credit-card services.

A wide array of new consumer financial services is being offered today through plastic credit- and debit-card programs. Such services include consumer revolving credit lines and preauthorized borrowing, the purchase of medical services and entertainment, and the payment of household bills using credit cards. In the future, customers will need to make fewer trips to their bank or other financial institution because transactions will be handled mainly over the telephone, through a conveniently located computer terminal, or through "smart cards" that have prepayment-encoded information (such as a credit line the card holder can use for making purchases). The hometown financial institution will lose much of its

---

[2]U.S. tax laws state that the interest paid on home equity loans may still be tax deductible even if the home mortgage is taken out for reasons other than to buy or improve the borrower's principal residence, provided the loan totals less than $100,000. There are other conditions for tax deductibility as well, so homeowners should consult IRS regulations to make sure their home loan qualifies under current tax rules.

convenience advantage for local customers. It will be nearly as convenient for the customer to maintain a checking, savings, or loan account in a city hundreds of miles away as to keep it in a local financial institution. In short, the ticket to many consumer financial services increasingly will be a plastic credit or debit card, with the capability to process financial data across great distances.

Credit Cards

Credit cards are used for very different purposes today, depending on the income and lifestyle of the user. Customers who use credit cards merely as a substitute for cash are referred to as *convenience users.* These people tend to be in upper income brackets and do not necessarily seek stores accepting their cards. Customers who maintain large outstanding credit card balances are referred to as *installment users* because they pay only a portion of their outstanding balance each month. These individuals frequently are in lower- and middle-income brackets and tend to be the most profitable credit-card customers for card-issuing firms.

One recent trend in credit cards that has benefited consumers but hurt many issuers is the heavy over-issue of credit cards. The recent mailing of millions of credit cards has resulted in increased numbers of card customers—in effect, "democratizing" the service—and many of these consumers are heavily in debt, resulting in a substantial rise in the number of delinquent accounts. Moreover, to reach out for a bigger market share, many card issuers have recently cut their loan rates. Much to the issuers' surprise, thousands of borrowers have used their ability to borrow using cheaper-rate cards in order to pay off their accumulated debts run up earlier on higher-rate cards (known as "card surfing"). The net result has been to lower the profitability of many credit-card programs. While, historically, credit-card loan rates used to be among the "stickiest" interest rates in the financial system, these rates recently have become more flexible, and competition among card issuers has intensified. Many experts in the field believe that a "shakeout" is under way, with smaller credit-card programs consolidating into larger ones and other credit-card companies simply selling off their card receivables and moving into other product lines.

For both convenience users and installment users, the principal advantage of credit cards is *convenience.* The installment loan feature of the credit card is a major attraction because it functions as a revolving line of credit, granting loans at no cost for an average of about one month by taking advantage of interest-free grace periods. In addition, the card itself serves to identify the customer and makes pertinent information available when the privilege of using the card is exercised. Most merchants know that charge cardholders tend to have higher incomes and better payment records than the general population. Recently, new cards have appeared that not only charge zero annual fees but also give customers rebates or discounts on purchases the more the card is used.

Charge-offs (bad debts) from overusage of credit-card accounts has recently been rising. Part of the explanation lies in the fact that more households (including lower-income households) now have one or more credit cards, and there has been an increase in the proportion of families actually borrowing against their cards. With heavier debt burdens, the average credit card account now appears to be somewhat riskier, resulting in growing bad debt in the credit-card field.

Debit Cards

Until recently, commercial banks were the only major financial institutions actively involved in the plastic card field. This situation changed rapidly during the 1970s and early 1980s, however, as nonbank financial institutions (principally credit unions, savings banks, and savings and loans) successfully invaded the plastic card market using debit cards and then later adding credit cards. While a credit card permits the customer to buy now and pay later, debit cards are merely a convenient way of paying *now*. A debit card enables users to make deposits and withdrawals from an automated teller machine and also to pay for purchases by direct electronic transfer of funds from their own accounts to the merchant's account. Debit cards are also used for identification and check-clearing purposes and to access remote computer terminals for information or for moving funds.

A closely related card to the debit card is a "smart card," which is encoded with the customer's account number and balance available for spending. It is a substitute for immediately spendable cash. "Smart cards" have not done particularly well in the United States due in part to the risks involved and the availability of so many other payments media. These stored-value cards have been quite successful in Europe, however, and are expected to become more important worldwide in the new century.

Debit cards appear to have gained on credit cards in recent years as the preferred method of paying for goods and services sold in stores, though credit card transactions in total today are still more than double debit card transactions. However, experts forecast a dramatic rise in the use of debit cards that eventually will lead to their dominance over credit cards in the total volume of transactions. Many consumers seem to like the discipline that debit cards bring to their lives because the money is automatically taken out of their checking account, usually the same day a purchase is made, and they have less temptation to spend more money than they have. Moreover, with debit cards the consumer has fewer checks to write.

Debit cards are profitable for the numerous small banks in the United States, who earn a fee for each transaction involving a debit card. In contrast, credit cards are profitable mainly for the largest banks. Unfortunately, debit cards may have a legal drawback, possibly protecting the customer less if the card is lost or stolen. Federal law limits consumer losses on credit cards, but a debit card can be used to drain a customer's checking account before he or she realizes what's happening. However, some depository institutions have indicated a willingness to limit losses in those cases where fraud can be verified.

Questions *to Help You Study*

4. How much money do U.S. households owe today? Do you believe consumers are too heavily in debt? Why or why not?

5. Into what broad categories is consumer borrowing normally divided? Which category is most important and why?

6. What is the difference between *credit cards* and *debit cards?*

7. Why is the distinction between *installment users* and *convenience users* of credit cards important? Which are you?

8. What advantage does a credit card grant its owner? A debit card? What are the principal disadvantages of each?

THE DETERMINANTS OF CONSUMER BORROWING

As we noted earlier, consumers represent one of the largest groups of borrowers in the financial system. Yet individual consumers differ widely in their use of credit and in their attitudes toward borrowing money. What factors appear to influence the volume of borrowing carried out by households?

Recent research points to a number of factors that bear on the consumer's decision of when and how much to borrow. Leading the list is the size of *individual or family income* and *accumulated household wealth.* Families with larger incomes and greater accumulated wealth use greater amounts of debt, both in absolute dollar amounts and relative to their income. In part, the debt-income relationship reflects the high correlation between income levels and education. Families whose principal breadwinners have made a significant investment in education are most often aware of the advantages (as well as the dangers) of using debt to supplement current income. Moreover, there is a high positive correlation between education and income-earning power of the principal breadwinners in a family.

The *stage in life* in which adult income-earning members of a family find themselves is also a major influence on household borrowing. The *life cycle hypothesis* contends that young families just starting out tend to be heavy users of debt. The purchase of a new home, automobile, appliances, and furniture follow soon after a new family is formed. As children come along, living costs rise and a larger home may be necessary, resulting in additional borrowing. Young families are willing to take on these additional debts because they expect a stream of future income throughout their working lives, which are likely to go on for many years. Later, the family's income rises, children leave home, and saving increases, while borrowing falls relative to income because older families expect a shorter future income stream before retirement arrives and, therefore, work to pay off their debts and build up their savings.

Consumer borrowing is correlated with the *business cycle.* During periods of economic expansion, the number of jobs increases, and households become more optimistic about the future. New borrowings usually outstrip repayments of outstanding loans, and the total volume of household debt rises. When an economic expansion ends and a recession begins, however, unemployment rises and many households become pessimistic about the future. Some, fearing a drop in income or loss of a job, build up savings and cut back on borrowing. Loan repayments rise relative to new borrowings, and total household debt declines.

In recent decades, *price expectations* have also influenced consumer borrowing, especially when the rate of inflation begins to accelerate. Postponing the purchase of an automobile, a new home, furniture, or appliances often means these goods may simply cost more in the future. If family incomes are not increasing as fast as consumer prices, it often pays to "buy now" through borrowing rather than to postpone purchases.

Fluctuations in *interest rates* also play a role in shaping the volume and direction of consumer borrowing. Interest rates rise as the economy expands and gathers momentum. At first, the rising rates are not high enough to offset strong consumer optimism, and household borrowing continues to increase. As the period of economic expansion reaches a peak, however, the rise in interest rates may become so significant that consumer borrowing begins to decline. The drop in borrowing leads to a decline in consumer spending, which may worsen the impending recession. Of course, as we saw earlier, interest rates are not the sole determinant of consumer borrowing. The size of debt payments and consumer income, the fate of a consumer's investments and wealth position, age, employment outlook, and a host of other impacting factors shape how much and exactly when consumers choose to borrow money.

CONSUMER LENDING INSTITUTIONS

Financial intermediaries—banks, savings and loan associations, credit unions, and finance companies—account for most of the loans made to consumers in the U.S. economy. However, as Exhibit 23–4 indicates, a growing share of consumer loans are being sold off the

EXHIBIT 23–4
Leading Consumer Lending Institutions in the United States

Source: Board of Governors of the Federal Reserve System.

Total Nonmortgage Loans at Year-End ($ Billions)

Lending Institutions	1995	1997	2000
Commercial banks	$ 502.0	$ 414.9	$ 543.7
Finance companies	152.1	160.1	193.2
Credit unions	131.9	153.7	185.3
Savings institutions	40.1	50.5	64.0
Nonfinancial businesses	85.1	78.9	82.7
Pools of securitized assets (no longer on the balance sheets of the original lenders)	211.6	311.2	500.0
Totals outstanding	$1,122.8	$1,269.3	$1,568.8

balance sheets of traditional lenders and placed in loan pools (securitizations), often under the guidance of security dealers. While many traditional consumer lenders have lost ground in terms of their share of all consumer loans outstanding, the loan pools have significantly gained market share. At the same time, the lenders pooling their loans and moving them off their balance sheets thereby gain new cash and the ability to make more loans.

Although each type of financial institution prefers to specialize in a few selected areas of consumer lending, there has been a tendency in recent years for institutions to diversify their lending operations. One important result of this diversification has been to bring *all* major consumer lenders into direct competition with each other.

Commercial Banks

The single most important consumer lending institution is the *commercial bank.* Commercial banks approach the consumer in three different ways: by direct lending, through purchases of installment paper from merchants, and by making loans to other consumer lending institutions. Roughly half of all bank loans to consumers (measured by dollar volume) consist of mortgages to support the purchase, construction, or improvement of residential dwellings; the rest consist of installment and noninstallment credit to cover purchases of goods and services. In the mortgage field, commercial banks usually prefer to provide short-term construction financing rather than to make long-term permanent loans for family housing, though most banks make both types of mortgage loans.

Banks make a wider variety of consumer loans than any other lending institution. They grant almost half of all auto loans extended by financial institutions to consumers each year. However, most bank credit in the auto field is indirect—installment paper purchased from auto dealers—rather than being made directly to the auto-buying consumer. Moreover, banking's leadership in auto lending has been challenged in recent years by finance companies and credit unions. Indeed, in many forms of consumer installment credit today, the lead of commercial banks is threatened by challenges from aggressive nonbank lenders who see the consumer market as a key growth area for the future.

Finance Companies

Finance companies have a long history of active lending in the consumer installment field, providing funds directly to the consumer through thousands of small loan offices and indirectly by purchasing installment paper from dealers. These active household lenders provide auto loans and credit for home improvements and for the purchase of appliances and furniture. Finance companies often face state-imposed legal limits on the interest rates they can charge for household loans and on loan size.

Other Consumer Lending Institutions

Other consumer installment lenders include credit unions, savings and loan associations, savings banks, and check-cashing and title loan companies. Credit unions make a wide variety of loans for such diverse purposes as purchases of automobiles; vacations; home repair; and, more recently, mortgage credit for the purchase of new homes. Only the member of a credit union may borrow from that institution, however.

Also important in the consumer loan field have been savings and loans and savings banks, which experienced dramatic growth in consumer lending in the 1970s and early 1980s but more recently have faced slower growth due to limited capital and the public's fears about the long-run soundness of some of these institutions. Although these institutions have long been dominant in residential mortgage lending, they have moved aggressively to expand their portfolios of credit card, education, home improvement, furniture, appliance, and mobile home loans over the past decade. Much of the drive for expansion in the consumer credit field is due to recent federal deregulation of the services offered by savings institutions.

Finally, small loan companies that lend primarily to distressed borrowers have mushroomed in recent years. Included here are such high-rate lenders as "check-cashing" companies, "title loan" companies, and "pawn shops." Check-cashing firms agree to accept a post-dated check from the borrowing customer which will be cashed later by the lender in return for which the lender makes an immediate loan of cash to the customer. Title loan companies agree to take control of the title to a valuable asset (such as a borrowing customer's automobile) as collateral for making a loan. If the customer fails to repay the loan the lender keeps the title to the asset. Finally, pawn shops accept assets that a customer may bring in, hold those assets, and extend the customer a loan based on a fraction of the assets' value. If the customer does not repay, the pawn shop retains the assets it has taken in and eventually sells them. The loans made by these small-loan companies are normally very short term, covering only a few days or weeks, and are designed primarily to tide families over until the next payday arrives. Unfortunately, the loan rates charged are among the highest assessed by the consumer credit industry.

FACTORS CONSIDERED IN MAKING CONSUMER LOANS

Consumer loans are considered one of the most profitable uses of funds for most financial institutions. There is evidence, however, that such loans usually carry greater risk than most other kinds of loans, and they are more costly to make per dollar of loan. On the other hand, the lender often can offset these costs by charging higher interest rates. Consumer credit markets in many communities are less competitive than the market for business loans or for marketable securities, giving the lender an advantage.

Making consumer loans is one of the most challenging aspects of modern financial management. It requires not only a thorough knowledge of household financial statements but also an ability to assess the character of the borrower. Over the years, most loan officers have developed decision "rules of thumb" as an aid to processing and evaluating consumer loan applications. For example, many consumer loan officers insist that household debt (exclusive of housing costs) should not exceed 15 to 25 percent of a family's gross income. For younger borrowers, without substantial assets to serve as collateral for a loan, a cosigner may be sought whose assets and financial standing represent more adequate security. The *duration of employment* of the borrower is often a critical factor, and many institutions deny a loan request if the customer has been employed at his present job for less than a year.

The *past payment record* of a customer usually is the key indicator of *character* and the likelihood that the loan will be repaid in timely fashion. Many lenders refuse to make loans to consumers who evidence "pyramiding of debt"—borrowing from one financial institution to pay another. Evidence of sloppy money handling, such as large balances carried on charge accounts or heavy installment payments, is regarded as a negative factor in a loan application. Loan officers are particularly alert to evidence of a lack of *credit integrity* as reflected in frequent late payments or actual default on past loans. The *character* of the borrower is the single most important issue in the decision to grant or deny a consumer loan. Regardless of the strength of the borrower's financial position, if the customer lacks the willingness to repay debt, the lender has made a bad loan.

Most lenders believe that those who own *valuable property,* such as land or marketable securities, are a better risk than those who do not own such property. For example, homeowners are usually considered better risks than those who rent. Moreover, a borrower's chance of getting a loan usually goes up if he or she does other business (such as maintain a deposit) with the lending institution. If more than one member of the family works, this is often viewed as a more favorable factor than if the family depends upon only a single breadwinner, who may become ill, die, or lose a job. Having a telephone at home is another positive factor in evaluating a loan application because the telephone gives the lender an inexpensive way to contact the borrower. One way to lower the cost of a loan is for the consumer to pledge a bank deposit or other liquid asset as security behind the loan. The disadvantage here is that such security ties up the asset pledged until the loan is repaid.

Questions *to Help You Study*

9. Please discuss the factors that influence the volume of borrowing by individuals and families. What role do you believe inflation plays in the borrowing and savings decisions of households today?

10. What factors do lending institutions usually look at when evaluating a consumer loan application? Why?

11. Who are the principal types of *consumer lending institutions* in the financial system?

12. Many lenders contend that loans to individuals and families are among the riskiest loans made within the financial system. Do you believe this is true? What kinds of risk do consumer loans present to a lender? How can lenders help combat this risk exposure?

FINANCIAL DISCLOSURE AND CONSUMER CREDIT

Important new laws have appeared in recent years designed to protect the consumer in dealings with lending institutions. One major area of emphasis is *financial disclosure:* making all relevant information available to the customer before a commitment is made. Moreover, if all important information is laid out before an agreement is reached, this may encourage the consumer to shop around to find the cheapest and most convenient terms available. However, there is considerable debate today on whether consumer protection legislation has really accomplished its goals.[3]

---

[3]It appears that many of the goals sought by recent consumer-oriented financial legislation have *not* been achieved. Many consumers do not shop for credit and appear more concerned about the affordability of monthly payments on a loan than with how one lender's interest charge compares with that quoted by another. The majority of consumers seem unaware of the rights and privileges granted them under recent federal financial legislation and see little practical benefit from these laws.

Management Insight   Financial Planning for Consumers

One of the most rapidly growing of all consumer-oriented industries is *financial planning*—rendering professional advice to the consumer on how to manage money. Although there are literally thousands of financial planners available today, each offering his or her own brand of financial advice, many financial planners seem to agree on certain principles of good money management for the consumer:

1. Use borrowing cautiously, especially when your home is pledged as collateral and your income is volatile.

2. In choosing which financial assets to acquire or how much to borrow, consider the following:

   a. Decide what your personal goals are—adequate retirement income? A vacation home? A college education?

   b. Classify your goals into short term, medium term, and long term, and estimate how much money will be required for each.

   c. Target each personal investment in assets and each borrowing to match the short-, medium-, and long-term goals you have set so that the money is there when you need it.

   d. Make sure any debt taken on is comfortably covered (both principal and interest) by your expected income plus financial investments.

   e. Diversify your investments—keep a roughly equal balance of funds invested in different stocks, bonds, deposits, mutual fund shares, and real estate to spread your risk.

3. Seek competent, unbiased professional advice, particularly where large purchases are to be made, large borrowings are contemplated, or when planning for retirement.

4. Make sure your liquid savings are at least equal to three months' living expenses in case of loss of a job or the need to move.

5. For the long-term protection of a family with dependents, establish a financial reserve equal to a multiple (usually 5 to 10 times) of the annual income of the family's principal breadwinner(s) through insurance policies and savings.

TRUTH IN LENDING

In 1968, Congress passed a watershed piece of legislation in the consumer credit field—the Consumer Credit Protection Act, more widely known as **Truth in Lending.** Shortly after the act was passed, federal regulatory agencies prepared new rules to implement and enforce the principles of Truth in Lending, such as the Federal Reserve Board's Regulation Z.

Truth in Lending simply requires banks and other lenders to provide sufficient information about a credit contract, in easily understood terms, so that the consumer can make an intelligent decision about purchasing credit. The law does not tell creditors how much to charge or to whom they may lend money. At the same time, consumers were granted certain rights. For example, they have the right to cancel or rescind a credit agreement within three business days if their home is included as part of the collateral for a loan. This *right of rescission* usually applies to the repair or remodeling of a home or the taking out of a second mortgage on an existing home. It does *not* cover an application for a first mortgage to make the initial purchase of a home, however. And the credit requested must be intended for personal or agricultural purposes and result in a debt obligation repayable in more than four installments.

The most widely known provision of Truth in Lending is the requirement that a lender must tell the customer the annual percentage rate of interest (APR) charged on a loan. Lenders must disclose the total dollar cost associated with granting a loan—known as the *finance charge*—that is the sum of all charges the customer must pay as a condition for securing the loan. These charges may include credit investigation fees, insurance to protect the lender, and points on a mortgage loan. Once the finance charge is determined, it must be converted into the APR by comparing it with the amount of the loan. The APR is really the ratio of the dollar finance charge to the declining unpaid balance of a loan, determined by the actuarial method. Because all lenders must quote the APR, computed by the same method, this makes it easier for the consumer to shop around and purchase credit from the cheapest source available.

The concept of Truth in Lending has been extended in a number of directions in recent years. One important dimension concerns *advertising*. A lender that advertises one attractive feature of a credit package to consumers must also disclose other relevant credit terms. For example, a car dealer that advertises low down payments must also disclose other aspects of the loan, such as how many payments are required, what the amount of each payment is, and how many months or years are involved before the loan is paid off.

Fair Credit Billing Act

In 1974, Congress passed the **Fair Credit Billing Act** in response to a torrent of consumer complaints about credit billing errors, especially on credit cards. Many individuals found that they were being billed for items never purchased or received, that some merchants would not respond when contacted about billing errors, and that finance charges were frequently assessed even though the consumer claimed no responsibility for charges listed on the billing statement.

The Fair Credit Billing Act requires a creditor to respond to a customer's billing inquiry within 30 days. In most cases, the dispute must be resolved within 90 days. The customer may withhold payment of any amounts in dispute, although he or she must pay any portions of a bill that are not in dispute. However, no creditor can report a customer as "delinquent" over amounts of a bill that are the subject of disagreement. A creditor who fails to respond to the customer's inquiry or makes no effort to settle the dispute may forfeit the disputed sum up to $50.

Fair Credit Reporting Act

An extension of Truth in Lending occurred when the **Fair Credit Reporting Act** was passed by Congress in 1970. This law entitles consumers to have access to their credit files, which are kept by credit bureaus active in the United States and Canada. These credit bureaus supply subscribing lenders with vital information on amounts owed and the payment records and credit ratings of individuals and families. They aid greatly in reducing the risks inherent in consumer lending. However, because the information credit bureaus supply has a substantial impact on the availability of credit to individuals and families, their activities and especially the accuracy of the information they provide have been brought under closer scrutiny in recent years.

To learn more about credit bureaus and credit ratings see especially *www.equifax.com*, *www.experian.com*, or *www.transunion.com*

Under the provisions of the Fair Credit Reporting Act, the consumer is entitled to review his or her credit file at any time. Moreover, he or she may challenge any items that appear in the file and demand an investigation. The credit bureau must respond, and if inaccuracies exist or if an item cannot be verified, it must be removed or the inaccuracies corrected. If the consumer determines that an item in the credit file is damaging and requires clarification, he or she may insert a statement of 100 words or less explaining the consumer's version of the matter. Data in the file are supposed to be shown only to properly identified individuals for approved purposes or on direct written request from the consumer. Information cannot be disclosed to anyone after a period of seven years unless the consumer is seeking a loan of $50,000 or more, purchasing life insurance, applying for a job paying $20,000 or more per year, or has declared personal bankruptcy. The consumer may sue if damaged by incorrect information in a credit file. Many financial analysts today recommend that consumers check their credit bureau report several months before applying for a major loan.

Consumer Leasing Act

In 1976, Congress passed the *Consumer Leasing Act,* which requires disclosure by leasing companies of the essential terms of any lease involving personal property, such as an automobile. The customer must be told about all charges, any insurance required, the terms under which the lease may be canceled, any penalties for late payment, and any express warranties that go with the property.

Competitive Banking Equality Act

On August 10, 1987, President Ronald Reagan signed the *Competitive Banking Equality Act* into law. It requires banks and other depository institutions to more fully disclose to customers the terms on various *deposit services* they offer. One major change was the required disclosure of how many days a depositor must wait before a check that is deposited in an account becomes available for spending. Some depository institutions had previously delayed the granting of credit for some deposits for a week or even longer. The new law stipulated that no more than one business day usually can intervene between the day of deposit of a local check and the customer receiving credit for that deposit. Nonlocal checks must be credited to the customer's account in no more than four business days.

Fair Credit and Charge Card Disclosure Act

Reflecting concern over the rapid expansion of credit card debt the *Fair Credit and Charge Card Disclosure Act* was passed in 1988. Credit-card issuers were required to notify consumers of the interest rates, fees, and other terms attached to these credit accounts, spelled out in easy-to-read format. Card customers were to be supplied with a toll-free phone number and address to help get their credit-card questions answered.

Truth in Savings Act

A further effort to make sure that consumers are adequately informed about the deposit accounts they purchase was made in November 1991 when Congress passed the *Truth in Savings Act.* This law prohibits inaccurate or misleading advertising concerning deposit accounts. Each depository institution must maintain a publicly available schedule of information for each class of accounts offered and distribute that information to both new and established account holders. If depositors would be adversely affected by a change in the terms of a deposit, notice of that adverse change must be provided to the deposit holder at least 30 days before the change becomes effective. Moreover, the customer must receive interest on the *full* amount of the principal deposited in an account, not on just the amount that a depository institution claims is available for investing in earning assets.

The Financial Services Modernization (Gramm-Leach-Bliley) Act

In an effort to protect a household's privacy in protecting its personal financial information the U.S. Congress passed the **Financial Services Modernization Act** (known also as *GLB* after its sponsors) in the fall of 1999. This new law requires financial-service firms to tell household customers, at least once a year, what their policies are in the handling of personal, nonpublic data. Consumers must be informed about any of their personal data that may be shared with other businesses (such as telemarketing firms, for example). Each consumer has to be offered the possibility to "opt out" of at least some information sharing.

However, many consumer groups have recently complained that this law is too weak in protecting consumers' personal data and have demanded new privacy laws at federal and state levels.

Very useful information about stopping identity theft is available from the Federal Trade Commission at *www.ftc.gov*. The FTC also has a downloadable pamphlet dealing with protecting your financial privacy.

The Financial Services Modernization Act's privacy rules were, in part, a response to a trend toward "identity theft" affecting thousands of consumers each year. Among the most common forms of "identity theft" are stealing a person's Social Security number and credit card accounts. In some cases the victim's credit rating and access to jobs and insurance coverage is severely damaged. Among the suggested remedies to prevent this growing form of consumer crime include periodically checking your credit bureau report for any unexpected changes, destroying any unwanted credit cards or card offers, asking mail and telephone marketers to remove your name from their lists, and restricting others access to your Social Security number.

CREDIT DISCRIMINATION LAWS

The civil rights movement has had an impact on the granting of consumer loans. Among the most important civil rights laws involving consumer credit are the *Equal Credit Opportunity Act* of 1974 and its amendments in 1976, the *Fair Housing Act* of 1968, the *Home Mortgage Disclosure Act* of 1975, and the *Community Reinvestment Act* of 1977. The fundamental purpose of these laws is to *outlaw discrimination* in the granting of credit. Today, lenders must be able to justify in terms of fairness and objectivity not only the loans that are made but also those that are not made.

Community Reinvestment Act and Financial Institutions Reform, Recovery, and Enforcement Act

One of the most important and controversial pieces of financial legislation is the **Community Reinvestment Act**, signed into law by President Jimmy Carter in 1977. Under its terms, financial institutions are required to make an "affirmative effort" to meet the credit needs of low- and middle-income customers. Each commercial and savings bank must define its own "trade territory" and describe the services it offers or is planning to offer in that local area. Once a year, each institution must prepare an updated map that delineates the trade territory it will serve, without deliberately excluding low- or moderate-income neighborhoods. Customers are entitled to make written comments, which must be available for public inspection, concerning the lender's performance in meeting the credit needs of its designated trade territory. The basic purpose of the Community Reinvestment Act is to prevent gerrymandering out low-income neighborhoods and other areas that a lender may consider undesirable.

In 1989, the *Financial Institutions Reform, Recovery, and Enforcement Act* was passed, requiring public disclosure of a bank's performance rating (known as a CRA rating) in meeting the credit needs of its local community under the Community Reinvestment Act. Moreover, the *FDIC Improvement Act* of 1991 required greater disclosure of the reasons why a depository institution received the particular community service rating that it did. The CRA ratings currently assigned to financial institutions are O (outstanding), S (satisfactory), N (needs to improve), and SN (substantial noncompliance).

Equal Credit Opportunity Act

The **Equal Credit Opportunity Act** of 1974 forbids discrimination against credit applicants on the basis of age, sex, marital status, race, color, religion, national origin, receipt of

In 1977 the U.S. Congress passed the Community Reinvestment Act, requiring banks and other covered financial institutions to fully serve their entire trade areas, advertising and supplying their services in minority neighborhoods just as they would in nonminority areas. Moreover, Congress put "teeth" in this law, stipulating that a financial-service provider must pledge to make loans and supply other financial services in minority neighborhoods and that the financial firm's record in doing so would be reviewed when that firm applied to regulators for permission to establish new offices, merge with other companies, or offer new services. Financial-service firms with poor community service records might find their applications for expansion rejected.

A good example of the enforcement of this government policy occurred in 2001 when the largest U.S. financial-service company, Citigroup, was required by the New York State Banking Department to set up "loan production centers" in minority neighborhoods inside New York City. Citigroup also agreed to wave more than $1 million in new-loan fees normally charged first-time home buyers. At the same time Citigroup was required to grant a larger volume of small loans to consumers with a minimum size of at least $3,500 each. These stipulations, resulting from Citicorp's merger with Travelers Group of San Francisco, represented the first time a U.S. financial institution had been asked to commit to projected consumer loan amounts of a fixed minimum size.

public assistance, or good-faith exercise of rights under the federal consumer credit protection laws. Women, for example, may receive credit under their own signature, based on their own personal credit record and earnings, without having their husband's joint signature. Credit applicants must be notified, in writing, of the approval or denial of a loan request within 30 days of filing a completed application. The lender may not request information on the borrower's race, color, religion, national origin, or sex, except in the case of residential mortgage loans. Under the FDIC Improvement Act of 1991, the regulatory agencies must refer loan discrimination violators to the U.S. Justice Department for possible prosecution.

Fair Housing and Home Mortgage Disclosure Act

Two other important antidiscrimination laws are the Fair Housing Act, which forbids discrimination in lending for the purchase or renovation of residential property, and the Home Mortgage Disclosure Act (HMDA). The latter requires financial institutions to disclose to the public the amount and location of their home mortgage and home improvement loans. HMDA was designed to eliminate *redlining,* in which some lenders would mark out areas of a community as unsuitable for home loans. Both HMDA and the Fair Housing Act require nondiscriminatory advertising by lenders. No longer can a consumer lending institution direct its advertisements solely to high-income neighborhoods to the exclusion of other potential customers. On written advertising, the Equal Housing symbol must be attached. Clearly, then, in advertising the availability of credit and in the actual granting of credit, the principles of civil rights and nondiscrimination apply.

Recent research evidence is mixed on the issue of whether discrimination in home mortgage lending or any other kind of financial service really exists. One study by Munnell, Tootell, Browne, and McEneany (1996) suggested that minority applicants in the city of Boston, for example, were about 40 percent more likely than white applicants to be rejected for home mortgage loans. Other recent studies question this finding because of mitigating factors and point out that minority lending has been growing faster than other forms of credit in recent years.

CONSUMER BANKRUPTCY LAWS

Over the past two decades, the number of households filing for personal bankruptcy and relief from personal debts has soared. The right to declare bankruptcy is designed to give individuals and businesses a fresh start, helping them to work themselves out from under a crippling burden of debt. Bankruptcy is mentioned specifically in the U.S. Constitution; it states that Congress shall have the power to "establish uniform laws on the subject of bankruptcy." Today, close to 1 percent of all U.S. households file for personal bankruptcy annually, which means that more than a million U.S. citizens enter some form of bankruptcy proceedings each year.

Consumers filing for bankruptcy primarily use one of two methods: Chapter 7 or Chapter 13. Filing for bankruptcy under Chapter 7 normally completely discharges all of a household's unsecured debts. The fact that a consumer has declared Chapter 7 bankruptcy can remain on the individual's credit record for as long as 10 years, however. Under the Chapter 7 method, the debtor submits a petition listing his or her assets and debts to a U.S. district court along with a filing fee. The court may decide not to free the debtor of certain debts, such as when a lender claims the debtor submitted a false financial statement, if any debts arose from illegal actions or from claims due to a drunk-driving incident, or if the petitioning debtor failed to reveal all of his or her debts when he or she borrowed money. Secured obligations—for example, home mortgage loans and auto credit—are usually still subject to being repaid by the bankrupt consumer or he or she will lose those assets because property that is used to secure debt can be repossessed by lenders under the terms of Chapter 7.

In contrast, a Chapter 13 bankruptcy filing usually sets in motion a new debt repayment plan to work gradually out of any debts owed. Such a filing normally disappears from the consumer's credit record after seven years. Under the terms of Chapter 13 the debtor asks a bankruptcy court to lift the burden on his or her earnings or property stemming from the total of all debts currently outstanding. Under this approach, the debtor pledges to make regular payments to a Chapter 13 trustee who will dispense these funds to the creditors involved. The petitioner hopes to keep all of his or her property (thus retaining more assets than under a Chapter 7 filing) but ultimately pay less than the total amount he or she owes. Filers under Chapter 13 must be in receipt of a regular source of income.

The bankrupt must agree to abide by a court-approved repayment plan. Debt used to purchase a home must be paid off on schedule, though any previously missed home mortgage payments can be rescheduled for repayment over a longer period if need be. In practice, most families using the Chapter 13 approach to bankruptcy ultimately do *not* fulfill their debt repayment plans and will not, then, be released from what they owe. Moreover, no debtor can escape via the bankruptcy code from what may be owed in child support payments, paying alimony to a former spouse, or meeting income tax obligations.

An individual can file for bankruptcy no more frequently than once every six years. As a result (and unbelievable as it may sound), lenders often seek out recently bankrupt persons, knowing they must repay any new debts they take on and cannot escape paying by declaring bankruptcy for several years into the future. The cost of filing for bankruptcy generally ranges from $500 to $2,000, but if an individual can get rid of many thousands of dollars of debt simply by filing for bankruptcy, he or she can experience a substantial net monetary return. Moreover, current bankruptcy law prohibits an employer from firing a worker merely because he or she has sought bankruptcy protection. Many experts say that if you can't see a practical way to repay most of your obligations over a five-year period, then bankruptcy *may* be a viable option for you, though the bankruptcy option should generally be considered as a "last resort" and only after receiving competent professional advice. Some bankruptcy filers experience great difficulty in getting new loans, however, and a social stigma may attach to a bankrupt individual that could last a long time. Then, too, once the bankrupt person has "gone to the well," it will be years before one can use that option again.

Recent evidence suggests that most consumer bankruptcies follow from the loss of a job, broken marriages, crippling or costly accidents (along with poor or no insurance coverage), sickness where the afflicted family has inadequate health insurance protection, family businesses that go under, the overuse of credit cards, gambling losses, and reliance on volatile or unpredictable sources of income. Added to these problems are aggressive loan advertising and lenient credit standards used by some lenders who often seem anxious to sign up new borrowers even though these customers cannot afford to take on more debt. One possibly effective long-run solution is to promote more personal financial education while people are still in school and through special community education programs for older adults. There is also a need to help families find ways of gaining access to affordable health and property/casualty insurance that will offset devastating personal losses from accidents and illnesses.

For further information about the proposed Bankruptcy Reform Act see *www. consumersunion. org*

A proposed new Bankruptcy Reform Act appeared in the U.S. Congress during 1999. This proposed new bankruptcy code would, if eventually passed, substantially restrict new bankruptcy filings and raise the cost and time involved in seeking bankruptcy protection for consumers. It would require bankrupt consumers to complete a financial education course and encourage the states to develop personal finance curricula in their elementary and high school programs. Some authorities believe that tougher bankruptcy rules, if finally passed into law, would tend to lower the cost of consumer credit for most borrowers.

Questions *to Help You Study*

13. What is *Truth in Lending?* Please describe the law's major provisions and explain why it was enacted in the first place.

14. What protections are offered to individual and family consumers under the Fair Credit Billing Act? the Consumer Leasing Act? the Fair Credit Reporting Act? the Fair Credit and Charge Card Disclosure Act? the Financial Services Modernization Act?

15. What are the principal purposes of the Community Reinvestment Act? the Equal Credit Opportunity Act? the Fair Housing Act? the Home Mortgage Disclosure Act? Please assess the benefits and costs of these laws.

16. What changes in consumer rights and required disclosure of information to the consumer occurred when the Financial Institutions Reform, Recovery, and Enforcement Act was passed? With passage of the Truth in Savings Act? the FDIC Improvement Act?

17. Why have so many consumer *bankruptcies* occurred in recent years? How might these bankruptcies be prevented?

18. Why was a *new bankruptcy law* proposed as the twentieth century drew to a close? What unique provisions does the proposed new law contain?

Summary of the Chapter

One of the most remarkable developments in the financial system over the past century is the awakening of the consumer as a borrower and lender of funds within the global financial system.

- *Households*—individuals and families—have become the principal sources of loanable funds in the money and capital markets. They are also among the leading borrowing sectors in the financial system.

- Due to intense competition in the financial-services sector new consumer-oriented financial services have appeared in profusion in recent years in an effort to attract and hold consumer accounts. Examples include NOWs, money market deposits, share accounts in money market mutual funds, universal life insurance policies, consumer cash management services, and home equity loans.

- While consumers are among the leading borrowing groups in the economy, overall their holdings of financial assets far exceed their indebtedness and the proportion of their financial-asset holdings relative to their total debt is growing, on average.

- Lenders to the household sector consider multiple factors in deciding whether or not to grant a loan, including the size and stability of a consumer's income, length of residence in current location, amount of installment debt outstanding, and any holdings of valuable assets (including stocks, bonds, and other assets of readily marketable value).

- Important federal laws have been passed in the United States over the past four decades to accomplish two major objectives: (a) *disclose the terms* of loans and other financial services so the household customer can make an informed financial decision; and (b) *prevent discrimination* in gaining access to financial services (especially access to credit). Among the key pieces of federal legislation protecting consumers are the Truth in Lending Act, the Fair Credit Billing Act, the Fair Credit Reporting Act, the Equal Credit Opportunity Act, the Community Reinvestment Act, and the Truth in Savings Act. The Truth in Lending, Fair Credit Billing, Fair Credit Reporting, and Truth in Savings acts promote greater disclosure of the terms attached to loans, savings deposits, and other financial services, while the Equal Credit Opportunity Act and the Community Reinvestment Act focus mainly on preventing discrimination against consumers seeking access to financial services.

- U.S. bankruptcy laws have been a center of controversy between consumers and lenders since the 1970s when a somewhat more liberal United States bankruptcy code was enacted and the numbers of household bankruptcies began to climb significantly. After 1995 more than a million bankruptcies a year occurred among U.S. individuals and families. Fears that debt relief rules for households might have become unbalanced in favor of the consumer, Congress debated a powerful new bankruptcy bill in the late 1990s and as the twenty-first century began. The proposed new law would raise the cost of consumer bankruptcies and demand that households seeking bankruptcy relief from their creditors receive training in the hope of avoiding future financial problems.

- The *household* has become one of the key actors in the financial system, providing the majority of savings so that borrowers and investors can find the funds they need for growth and also representing one of the largest borrowing sectors, utilizing credit to supplement current income. Innovations in financial services have brought ever growing numbers of households into the financial system as active participants. Lower-quality borrowers, in particular, have entered in much greater numbers in recent years due to increasing "democratization" of the credit-granting process. The result is growing concern about the debt burden carried by millions of families today.

Key Terms

NOW account, *645*

Residential mortgage credit, *651*

Installment credit, *651*

Noninstallment credit, *651*

Home equity loan, *651*

Credit card, *652*

Problems

1. Home equity loans to consumers are generally based on the *residual value* of a home (i.e., market value less the remaining balance on the outstanding home mortgage loan) and the fraction of that value (known as the *loan-to-value ratio*) that the lending institution is willing to lend. The customer's borrowing base is the product of these two entities. Calculate the customer's borrowing base in the situations described below:

Appraised Value of Borrower's Home	Mortgage Loan Balance Outstanding	Lender's Required Loan-to-Value Ratio
a. $173,500	$ 67,800	75%
b. 64,150	23,948	70
c. 251,400	111,556	80
d. 789,000	340,722	82

2. What consumer-oriented law or laws passed in the United States apply in each of the situations described below:

   a. Matthew Crey is discussing with a bank loan officer the terms on a loan he needs to buy a car for his family.

   b. Robert and Mary Nash believe they were discriminated against when their loan to purchase a new home was denied.

   c. Sally Ferrel was denied a loan because of an adverse report from her credit bureau, which she believes is in error.

   d. Herbert Coleman has just received his credit card bill and finds several charges were made against his account that are not legitimate.

   e. Mary Eacher leased an automobile from a dealer for three years, but the lease was abruptly canceled even though Mary was making all required payments on time.

   f. First National Bank of Arden has just announced its latest CRA rating received from federal bank examiners.

   g. Earl and Susan Tolber believe they were denied a home improvement loan because their address is in a neighborhood where the local bank does not like to make such loans.

   h. Bill Gell decides to "opt out" of letting his bank and his insurance company share information about him with other businesses.

   i. Jean Shal has just been notified by her bank that it is going to reduce the interest rate on her certificate of deposit when it is renewed.

   j   John Saral is confused about the terms of a credit card and needs additional information from the card company.

3. Which factors listed below would be regarded as *positive* and which would be regarded as *negative* by a consumer lender in evaluating an individual's request to borrow money and why?

   a. The economy's growth appears to be slowing.

   b. The borrower has held his present job about 10 months.

c. The borrower rents an apartment close to her place of work on a month-to-month basis.

d. The borrower's monthly income fluctuates significantly due to sales commissions.

e. The borrower has a ratio of current debt obligations to disposable income of about 35 percent.

f. The borrower lives near the lender's home office and has a telephone.

g. The borrower holds approximately $8,000 in shares in mutual funds and corporate bonds.

h. The borrower has a $50,000 term life insurance policy through her place of work.

i. The borrower has no health insurance plan because her employer does not offer one.

4. Please construct a balance sheet and estimate the annual take-home income of the Williams family from the information presented below:

Checking account balance	$ 2,860	Credit union deposit	$ 550
Credit card obligations	7,400	Bank loan	13,800
Department store debt	1,875	Estimated market value of	
U.S. savings bonds	3,460	Home	81,000
Unpaid life insurance premiums	625	Autos	23,780
Gas and oil credit card balances	289	Furniture and appliances	13,490
Home mortgage	68,500	Cash surrender value	3,770
Mutual fund shares	15,430	of life insurance	
Pension plan assets	47,995		
Annual take-home income—			
0.28 of the family's total assets			

Would you grant this family a loan of $10,000 to fund the purchase of new kitchen appliances and repairs to the family automobile? Why or why not?

5. Please identify each of the key terms and concepts presented in this chapter that are described or defined below.

a. An interest-bearing checking account available to individuals and nonprofit associations.

b. Liabilities of a borrowing customer (other than home mortgages) that are retired in two or more consecutive payments.

c. A loan normally paid off in a lump sum rather than in a series of installment payments.

d. Loans extended to people who pledge their homes as collateral for the loan.

e. A plastic card that allows its holder to borrow money or to pay for purchases of goods and services.

f. A plastic card which identifies the owner when he or she needs to make payments for purchases of goods and services.

g. A law passed by the United States that requires covered lenders to fully disclose the proposed terms of a loan.

h. A federal law that requires correction of billing errors and a prompt investigation of those possible billing errors.

i. Federal law that grants borrowing customers the right to view their credit record and demand that any errors in that record be corrected promptly.

j. A federal law that requires covered financial institutions to designate the trade territory they will serve and to serve fully all neighborhoods within that designated trade territory.

k. Credit discrimination is illegal when based upon gender, age, national origin, religion, or other irrelevant factors.

Questions about the Web and the Money and Capital Markets

1. How rapidly has consumer borrowing grown in recent years? Where on the World Wide Web could you go to get this kind of information?

2. Do you think American households are borrowing too much today? What indicators could you use to form an opinion about this issue? Where could you obtain data from the Web to be able to calculate the consumer debt indicators you have selected?

3. Which type of consumer debt is growing the fastest currently? Where could you find the answer on the Web? What Web sites helped you to answer this question?

4. Is consumer saving in the United States inadequate today? How could you decide whether current household saving is "adequate" or "inadequate"? Where could you look on the Web for data to back up your conclusion? After checking that data what did you conclude and why?

Selected References

Bernheim, B. Douglas; Lorenzo Forni; Jagadeesh Gokhale; and Laurence J. Kotlikoff. "How Much Should Americans Be Saving for Retirement?" *American Economic Review,* Papers and Proceedings, May 2000.

Bitler, Marianne P.; Alicia M. Robb; and John D. Wolken. "Financial Services Used by Small Businesses: Evidence from the 1998 Survey of Small Business Finances." *Federal Reserve Bulletin,* April 2001, pp.183–205.

Burke, Sarah A. "Privacy Matters: Payment Cards Center Workshop on the Right to Privacy and the Financial Services Industry." *Business Review,* Federal Reserve Bank of Philadelphia, Fourth Quarter 2001.

Canner, Glenn B.; Arthur B. Kennickell; and Charles A. Luckett. "Household Sector Borrowing and the Burden of Debt." *Federal Reserve Bulletin,* April 1995, pp. 323–338.

Elliehausen, Gregory E., and John D. Wolken. "Banking Markets and the Use of Financial Services by Households." *Federal Reserve Bulletin,* March 1992, pp. 169–181.

Emmons, William R. "Is Household Debt Too High?" *Monetary Trends.* Federal Reserve Bank of St. Louis, December 1998.

Kennickell, Arthur B.; Martha Starr-McCluer; and Annika E. Sunden. "Family Finances in the U.S.: Recent Evidence from the Survey of Consumer Finances." *Federal Reserve Bulletin,* January 1997, pp. 1–24.

Mester, Loretta J. "Is the Personal Bankruptcy System Bankrupt?" *Business Review,* Federal Reserve Bank of Philadelphia, First Quarter 2002, pp. 31–44.

Munnell, Alicia; Geoffrey Tootell; Lynn Browne; and James McEneany. "Mortgage Lending in Boston: Interpreting HMDA Data." *American Economic Review,* 86, no. 1 (March 1996), pp. 25–53.

Rose, Peter S. "Bank Cards: The Promise and the Peril." *The Canadian Banker,* December 1978, pp. 62–67.

———— . "Social Responsibility in Banking: Pressures Intensify in the U.S." *The Canadian Banker,* June 1979, pp. 70–75.

———— . "Credit Discrimination under Attack." *The Canadian Banker,* September 1979, pp. 70–75.

Chapter **Twenty-Four**

The Residential Mortgage Market

Learning Objectives in This Chapter

- You will discover how the largest of all domestic financial markets in the United States—the *residential mortgage market*—functions in order to supply credit to build and buy homes, apartments, and other dwellings.

- You will learn about the problems faced by individuals and families in finding credit to finance the purchase of their homes.

- You will come to understand the problems faced by lenders of residential mortgage money in designing new loan contracts that will protect them against inflation and other risks.

- You will discover what important jobs are performed by the federal government agencies and government-sponsored mortgage firms, such as Fannie Mae (FNMA) and Ginnie Mae (GNMA), in supporting the development of the market for mortgage loans.

What's in This Chapter? Key Topics Outline

Trends in Home Prices and Loan Terms

The Structure of the Mortgage Loan Market

Mortgage Lending Institutions and Their Preferred Market Segments

Government Reshapes the Mortgage Market: Lending, Guaranteeing, Making Markets

Mortgage-Linked Securities and Prepayment Risk

Federal Agencies and the Controversy over Fannie Mae and Freddie Mac

Innovations in Mortgage Instruments and Mortgage Lock-Ins

Refinancing Existing Loans and Home Equity Borrowing

Among the fastest growing of all financial markets today is the *residential mortgage market* where individuals and families fund their purchases of homes. This huge market—one of the largest of all the money and capital markets—answers one of the human race's most basic needs—the demand for shelter to protect people from exposure to the weather and crime. Originally a simple market that was primarily local and regional in character the residential mortgage market has become an international capital market in which home-mortgage-related instruments are bought and sold around the globe, thanks in part to heavy government support of this important marketplace.

Where on the Web can you go to learn more about mortgage loans and mortgage-related securities? Many, many places as the number of Web sites numbers in the hundreds of thousands today. Most sites were established by lending institutions seeking consumers' business. However, there are also well-crafted sites that help explain the nature of this huge market and its problems.

Examples include studies of affordable housing by City Research at *www.cityresearch.com*, as well as several sites tracking trends in mortgage market data. Examples of the latter include HSH Associates Statistical Releases at *www.hsh.com* and Wholesale Access at *www.whole saleaccess.com*. Another excellent site looks at Canada at *http://mortgagesincanada.com/residential*.

INTRODUCTION

One of the most important goals for many families is to own their own home. Besides the psychic benefits of privacy and a feeling of belonging to the local community, home ownership confers important financial and economic benefits on those families and individuals both able and willing to make the investment. The market value of single-family residences has risen substantially faster than the rate of inflation over the long run, offering individuals and families of even modest means one of the few long-term hedges against inflation. Moreover, the interest cost on home mortgages is tax deductible, reducing significantly the *after-tax* interest rate levied on residential mortgage loans.

Unfortunately for families seeking home ownership, the residential mortgage market is often treacherous, swinging quickly from low interest rates and ample credit to high and rising rates with little credit available. In this volatile market, home ownership may become an impossible dream for thousands of individuals and families, though a greater proportion of U.S. households than ever before own their own homes today. Moreover, the wide swings characteristic of the residential mortgage market send reverberations throughout the economy, contributing to the cycles of "boom" and "bust" that sometimes characterize economic activity.

RECENT TRENDS IN NEW HOME PRICES AND THE TERMS OF MORTGAGE LOANS

We can get a glimpse of the tremendous pressures buffeting the market for residential mortgages today by looking at recent trends in the prices of new homes and the cost of financing them. Exhibit 24–1 provides recent data on the average terms quoted on **conventional**

671

EXHIBIT 24–1
Prices and Yields of Conventional Home Mortgage Loans

Source: Board of Governors of the Federal Reserve System, *Federal Reserve Bulletin,* Table 1.53, various issues.

Item	1974	1980	1990	2000
Primary market: Conventional mortgages on new homes				
Purchase price ($000)	$40.10	$83.50	$153.20	$234.50
Amount of loan ($000)	29.80	59.30	112.40	177.00
Loan/price ratio (percent)	74.30	73.30	74.50	77.40
Maturity (years)	26.30	28.20	27.30	29.20
Fees and charges ("points")	1.30%	2.10%	1.93%	0.70%
Contract interest rate (percent per year)	8.71	12.25	9.68	7.41
Yield on FHA mortgages (percent per year)	9.22	13.95	10.17	7.45*

*FHA mortgage yield is for 1999.

home mortgage loans in the United States. A conventional mortgage loan is *not* guaranteed by the government but is purely a private contract between the home buyer and the lending institution. In this case, the lender of funds bears the risk that the home buyer will default on principal or interest payments associated with a mortgage loan, forcing foreclosure and resale of the home, although today most conventional loans are insured by private insurance companies. In contrast, mortgage loans issued through the Federal Housing Administration (FHA) or Veterans Administration (VA) are partially guaranteed as to principal and interest by the federal government and are primarily used to finance low-cost and moderately priced housing.

As shown in Exhibit 24–1, the average purchase price of a conventional single-family residence in the United States has nearly tripled over the past two decades. With housing prices and the demand for new homes rising, sellers and lending institutions have worked to accommodate more borrowers by increasing the average percentage of a new home's purchase price they are willing to lend, to as high as almost 80 percent in recent years. We note from Exhibit 24–1 that mortgage lenders are also willing to extend credit for longer periods. The average maturity of conventional home mortgage loans climbed to more than 29 years in 2000. Extra fees and charges ("points") levied by lenders as a condition for making home mortgage credit available have recently fallen. The average contract interest rate on conventional mortgage loans dipped to about 7 percent as the twentieth century drew to a close. By late in the year 2001 home mortgage interest rates had dropped further to the lowest levels experienced since the 1960s. These low home-loan interest rates helped to boost U.S. home ownership so that about two-thirds of American households owned their own dwelling—the highest proportion in history—as the new century began.

Unfortunately, offsetting the relatively low home-mortgage loan rates of recent years have been record-high home prices. These high prices for new and existing homes have shut out scores of families from fulfilling a long-sought-after American dream—owning your own home. Several factors account for this dramatic long-term escalation in the price of home ownership. Certainly, inflation has played a key role in driving up building costs, and this increase has been passed on to the consumer. On the demand side, a substantial rise in the number of new family formations has occurred in recent years. Added to this has been a rapid increase in individuals living alone and in single-parent households. Therefore, although the U.S. birth rate has dropped to the lowest levels in history, the increase in new families and in single-adult households dramatically increased the demand for housing, especially for low- and medium-priced homes. Overall, real home prices

Financial Developments   The Dream of Home Ownership

The dream of home ownership has been satisfied for more people today than at any other time in American history. For example, during the 1940s, the United States was mostly a nation of renters. Today, more than two-thirds of American households own their own dwellings. Many people think this is a good trend, both psychologically and financially, giving families an asset that is likely to appreciate in value and providing a borrowing base for raising funds in order to start a new business, send children to college, etc.

However, homes can be costly to maintain and difficult to sell (illiquid). Home ownership can also make it hard for a family to adequately diversify its assets, because a home often represents an individual family's largest single investment. Moreover, homes fluctuate in value with the economy and with changes in their age and condition. Many families having low or moderate income have literally "sunk" most of their wealth in a single asset whose value may plummet due to factors beyond their control. Moreover, a homeowner normally cannot buy a fraction of a home; it is a "lumpy" investment, and except for a mobile home or a house sitting on pillars, it is stuck in its initial location. In many markets today homes have become more of a psychological boost to homeowners rather than a strong financial benefit.

Homes pay out a stream of services (implicit rent) to their residents, including protection against crime and shelter from the elements, and they serve as status symbols. They *may* appreciate in value if population and incomes rise in their area and if interest rates fall. However, if housing prices rise significantly, new construction eventually may catch up to housing demand and the market value of older homes may level out or even fall. Also, houses and their surrounding neighborhoods frequently depreciate over time and, in extreme cases, may be taken over by crime and urban blight.

In the long run, however, average home prices have tended to stay up with or even outstrip inflation, though housing values have not generally performed as well as the stock market, on average, even though interest payments on home mortgage debt and property taxes do help reduce a family's taxable income. However, housing values appear to be more stable than stock prices and behave quite differently from stock (often moving in the opposite direction), helping a family to diversify its investment returns and lower its overall risk exposure. Stocks seem to do better as an investment than housing when inflation is relatively low and worse than housing when inflation is more rapid. In the future, investors may enhance the value of their investments in housing by finding unique ways to diversify their investment in a home, such as by buying shares in real estate investment trusts or by obtaining a guaranteed minimum resale price for their dwelling through the purchase of insurance.

have risen considerably faster than homeowner incomes, discouraging some potential home buyers.

THE STRUCTURE OF THE MORTGAGE MARKET

A nice summary of unfolding trends in the home mortgage industry is available through the Web site of the Mortgage Bankers Association of America at *www.mbaa.org*

Volume of Mortgage Loans

Mortgages are among the most important securities in the financial system. The total of all mortgages outstanding in the United States is now more than $7 trillion (see Exhibit 24–2). This total represents about two-thirds of the nation's gross domestic product (GDP) and makes the mortgage market the largest primary security market inside the United States.

Residential versus Nonresidential Mortgage Loans

The mortgage market can be divided into two major segments: (1) **residential mortgages,** which encompass all loans secured by single-family homes and other dwelling units, and (2) **nonresidential mortgages,** which include loans secured by business and farm properties. Which of these two sectors is more important? As Exhibit 24–3 shows, loans to finance the building and purchase of homes, apartments, and other residential units

673

EXHIBIT 24–2
Total Mortgage Debt Outstanding in the United States at Year-End ($ Billions)

Sources: Board of Governors of the Federal Reserve System, *Annual Statistical Digest,* 1971–1975, and *Federal Reserve Bulletin,* selected issues.

Year	Amount
1950	$ 72.8
1960	206.8
1970	451.7
1980	1,451.8
1990	3,807.3
2000	6,890.0
2001*	7,281.5

*Figures through second quarter of the year.

EXHIBIT 24–3
Mortgage Loans Outstanding, 2001* ($ Billions)

Source: Board of Governors of the Federal Reserve System, *Federal Reserve Bulletin,* selected issues.

Type of Property	Amount	Percent of Total
Residential properties (one- to four-family and multifamily structures)**	$5,919.3	81.3%
Nonresidential properties (commercial and farm)	1,362.2	18.7
All properties	$7,281.5	100.0%

*Figures are as of the second quarter of 2001.
**Note that not all residential loans go to just households but may include businesses and other units in the economy.

dominate the U.S. mortgage market, accounting for about four-fifths of all mortgage loans outstanding. Mortgages on commercial and farm properties accounted for less than one-fifth of all mortgages issued. Because residential mortgages dominate the market, it should not be surprising that households are the leading mortgage borrower, accounting for about four-fifths of outstanding mortgage debt. The next largest group of mortgage borrowers—business firms—runs a distant second.

Questions *to Help You Study*

1. What has happened in recent years to the prices of new homes? To interest rates and other terms on conventional home mortgage loans? What are the *causes* of these trends?

2. Residential mortgages may be classified in several different ways. Please describe the structure of the mortgage market as it relates to each of the following dimensions:

   Type of mortgage contract—conventional versus government guaranteed

   Residential versus nonresidential mortgages

   Type of mortgage borrower

3. What are the advantages and disadvantages for the consumer of home ownership?

4. How does the behavior of the home mortgage market reveal the problems that both home buyers and mortgage lenders face as they operate in this huge financial market-place?

MORTGAGE-LENDING INSTITUTIONS

In the years before World War II, mortgages were one of the most widely held securities in the financial system, comparable to stock in the great diversity of investors who chose to add these securities to their portfolios. Individuals were then the dominant mortgage

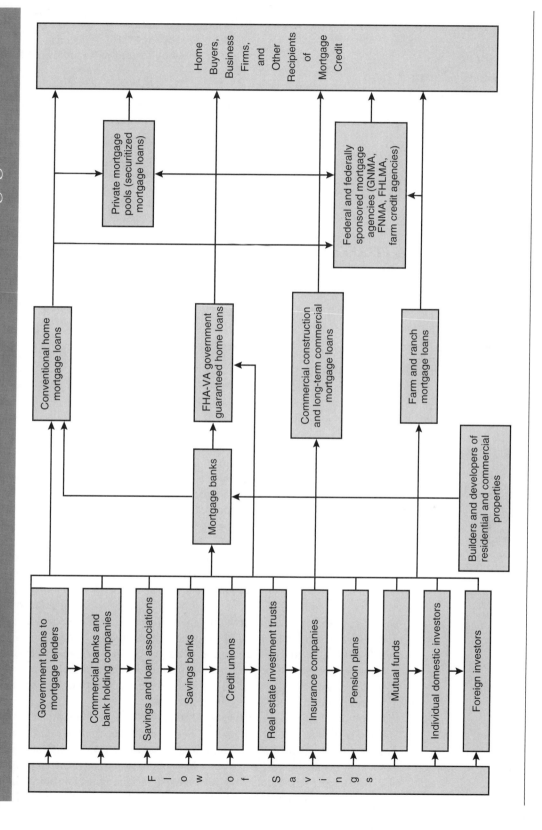

Management Insight The Structure of the Mortgage Market

EXHIBIT 24–4   **Principal Lenders in the U.S. Mortgage Market, 2001***

Lender Group	Volume of Mortgage Loans Held by Lender ($ Billions)	Percent of Total
Savings institutions (savings and loan associations and savings banks)	$ 751.6	10.3%
Commercial banks	1,727.5	23.7
Life insurance companies	237.1	3.3
Individuals and other private lenders	759.8	10.4
Mortgage pools or trusts:	3,450.2	47.4
Government National Mortgage Association	598.1	
Federal Home Loan Mortgage Corp.	873.8	
Federal National Mortgage Association	1,164.0	
Private mortgage conduits (including securitized loans)	814.4	
Federal and related agencies:	355.3	4.9
Government National Mortgage Association	0.6	
Federal Home Loan Mortgage Corporation	61.5	
Federal National Mortgage Association	159.2	
Farmers Home Administration	73.2	
Federal Land Banks	38.7	
Federal Housing and Veterans Administration	2.9	
Other agencies	19.1	
	$7,281.5	100.0%

*Figures are for second quarter of the year.

Source: Board of Governors of the Federal Reserve System, *Federal Reserve Bulletin,* selected issues.

investors, with financial institutions in second place. However, the rapid growth of commercial banks, savings institutions, insurance companies, government agencies, and mortgage pools (where groups of loans are packaged together) as major mortgage lenders during the past half century has forced individual investors into the background.

Exhibit 24–4 shows the total amounts of mortgage loans held by various lender groups in 2000. Savings and loan associations, once the principal private mortgage-lending institution in the United States, have now dropped to only about 10 percent of all mortgage loans outstanding. Commercial banks now rank number one among private lending institutions, holding nearly one-quarter of all mortgage credit outstanding. In general, the relative share of the mortgage market accounted for by traditional private mortgage-lending institutions, such as savings and loans and insurance companies, has declined, while pension funds, finance companies, and government agencies have accounted for a growing share of outstanding loans. Noteworthy in this regard has been the rapidly expanding role of *mortgage pools:* lender-packaged groups of high-quality residential mortgages insured or guaranteed by a government agency and in which investors hold shares, entitling them to a portion of any interest and principal payments generated by the pool. We will have more to say about mortgage pools later in the chapter when we discuss the expanding role of the federal government in the mortgage market.

A mortgage loan is one of the most difficult of all financial instruments for which to establish a true value. Most mortgages generate multiple potential cash-flow streams—for example: (1) the payment of origination and commitment fees when a mortgage loan is first applied for; (2) the promise of a stream of periodic loan repayments plus loan interest; (3) the added compensation to a lender for the risk that a mortgage borrower will pay off his or her loan early or perhaps, ultimately, not at all; (4) the servicing income associated with

Management Insight   Lenders' Alternative Sources of Income, Cost, and Risk in Making, Holding, or Selling Off Home Mortgage Loans

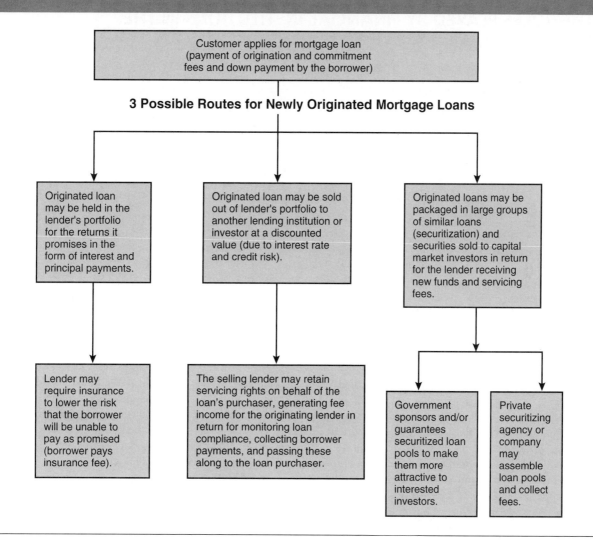

Customer applies for mortgage loan
(payment of origination and commitment
fees and down payment by the borrower)

3 Possible Routes for Newly Originated Mortgage Loans

Originated loan may be held in the lender's portfolio for the returns it promises in the form of interest and principal payments.

Originated loan may be sold out of lender's portfolio to another lending institution or investor at a discounted value (due to interest rate and credit risk).

Originated loans may be packaged in large groups of similar loans (securitization) and securities sold to capital market investors in return for the lender receiving new funds and servicing fees.

Lender may require insurance to lower the risk that the borrower will be unable to pay as promised (borrower pays insurance fee).

The selling lender may retain servicing rights on behalf of the loan's purchaser, generating fee income for the originating lender in return for monitoring loan compliance, collecting borrower payments, and passing these along to the loan purchaser.

Government sponsors and/or guarantees securitized loan pools to make them more attractive to interested investors.

Private securitizing agency or company may assemble loan pools and collect fees.

Information for buyers and sellers in the home mortgage market is available through such sites as Primary Home Mortgage Market at *www.buyersresource.com*, *www.getsmart.com*. and *www.houses4sale-online.com*

collecting and recording amounts owed and monitoring compliance with the terms of a loan; and (5) the net returns or fees from securitization that arise when a mortgage loan is packaged with other, similar mortgage loans into a pool and income-generating securities are issued as claims against that pool of home loans.

Different financial institutions operating in the mortgage market pursue one or more of the foregoing income sources. For example, many locally oriented banks, savings and loans, and other smaller depository institutions retain new mortgage loans in their asset portfolios and receive the resulting flow of borrower interest and principal payments, while other lenders may quickly sell any loans they make and instead pursue loan servicing, securitization, and other fee-generating services because of the greater geographic diversification, more predictable liquidity demands, and lower capital requirements involved with these supporting services. Each of these possible cash-flow sources from a mortgage loan has its own financial advantages and disadvantages in terms of sensitivity to default, interest rate, and liquidity risk, and possible changes in the size of cash flow expected to be received.

THE ROLES PLAYED BY FINANCIAL INSTITUTIONS IN THE MORTGAGE MARKET

Mortgage lenders tend to specialize in the types of loans they grant, and some are far more important to the residential market than to commercial mortgage lending. Moreover, even within the residential lending field, different institutional lenders will favor one type of mortgage (e.g., conventional versus government guaranteed) over another and also desire a certain range of maturities. Some lenders are organized to deal with home mortgage borrowers one at a time, while others may prefer to acquire large packages of mortgages associated with major residential building projects.

Savings and Loan Associations

Savings and loan associations (S&Ls) are predominantly local lenders, making the majority of their mortgage loans in the communities where their offices are located. Moreover, S&Ls often service the mortgage loans they make rather than turning that task over to a mortgage bank or trust company. Servicing a mortgage involves maintaining ownership and financial records on the mortgaged property, receiving installment payments from the borrower, checking on the mortgaged property to ensure that its value is maintained, and in the event of borrower default, foreclosing on the property to collect any unpaid balance on the loan.

Historically, S&Ls have preferred single-family home mortgages, which is how they began originally during the nineteenth century, lending to help families build their homes and encouraging individuals to save for the future, but they have diversified their portfolios in recent years to include many new kinds of mortgage-related assets, such as mobile home loans; mortgage credit for apartments and other multifamily housing units; and securities backed by pools of mortgage loans. The financial problems of the savings and loan industry in recent years and S&Ls' attempts to diversify and increase long-term capital relative to their assets in order to lower their risk of failure have brought about a substantial decline in S&Ls' share of the total mortgage market. Many S&Ls have been forced to sell off many of their loans, downsizing the firm just to achieve a ratio of owner's capital to total assets acceptable to industry regulators. Thus, many S&Ls have had fewer funds to devote to new mortgage loans and have lost substantial market share to other mortgage-lending institutions. Others have been purchased by bank holding companies and converted into banks with few mortgage loans or into mortgage companies that make only short-term loans in this market.

Commercial Banks

In contrast to savings and loans, *commercial banks* have expanded their market share of nearly every type of mortgage loan. Overall, they now rank first as lenders for the purchase of homes, condominiums, and apartments and in the commercial mortgage field. A large share of bank mortgage credit, however, goes for shorter-term loans to finance the *construction* of new commercial and residential projects, with other lenders usually taking on the long-term mortgage loans from these projects. Commercial banks have also shown a strong interest in financing upscale homes purchased by higher-income families in recent years—homes that command significantly higher prices and larger down payments. Finally, banks today are among the strongest supporters of the mortgage-backed securities market, devoting more than half of all their security holdings to these financial instruments which are backed by pools of mortgage loans.

Life Insurance Companies

Life insurance companies make substantial investments in commercial as well as residential mortgage properties. These companies search national and international markets for good mortgage investments instead of focusing only on local areas. They often prefer to purchase residential mortgages in large blocks rather than one at a time.

In the past, life insurers preferred government-guaranteed home mortgages. In recent years, however, the higher yields available on conventional mortgages have caused some shift of emphasis toward these more risky home loans. Despite the greater flexibility of conventional single-family home mortgages, however, life insurance companies have been gradually reducing their holdings of single-family home mortgages and emphasizing commercial and apartment mortgages. Commercial and apartment loans often carry "equity kickers" that permit the lending institution to receive a portion of project earnings as well as a guaranteed interest return.

Savings Banks

Another lender of importance in the residential mortgage market is the *savings bank,* headquartered mainly in the eastern United States. These institutions invest in both government-guaranteed and conventional mortgage loans. Although single-family homes constitute the bulk of savings bank mortgage loans, their loans supporting multifamily units (including large apartment projects) have grown in recent years. Like life insurance companies, savings banks often prefer to acquire residential mortgages in large blocks, such as a whole subdivision, rather than loan by loan. Like savings and loan associations, savings banks have lost mortgage market share to other private and government lenders.

Mortgage Bankers

Mortgage banking houses act as a channel through which builders or contractors in need of long-term funds can find permanent mortgage financing. In providing this service, mortgage bankers take on portfolios of mortgages from property developers, using mainly bank credit to carry their inventories of mortgages. Within a relatively short time span, these mortgages are placed with long-term institutional investors. Mortgage bankers supply important services to *both* institutional investors and property developers. The developers receive a commitment for permanent financing, which allows them to proceed with planned real estate projects. Institutional investors, especially life insurance companies and savings banks, receive mortgages appropriately packaged to match the timing of their cash flows and risk-return preferences. The mortgage banker often secures servicing (loan management and monitoring) fees from institutional investors who purchase the mortgages he or she packages and sells.

GOVERNMENT ACTIVITY

Adequate housing for all citizens has been a major goal of the U.S. government for many years. One of the first steps taken by Congress to achieve this goal was the establishment of the **Federal Housing Administration (FHA)** in 1934. FHA has sought to promote

FHA is a division of the Department of Health and Human Services (HUD) at *www.hud.gov*

home ownership by reducing the risk to private lenders on residential mortgage contracts, providing home loan insurance. At the same time, efforts have been made to encourage the development of an active secondary market for existing mortgage lenders in order to raise cash to make new loans and to attract new investors into the mortgage business. The combination of government guarantees and the development of a secondary market has led to greater participation in mortgage lending by *long-distance lenders,* particularly insurance companies, pension funds, and savings banks. However, government agencies today dominate the mortgage market for low- and moderately priced loans.

The Impact of the Great Depression on Government Involvement in the Mortgage Market

Any attempt to understand how the mortgage market operates today must begin with the Great Depression and the enormous impact that economic calamity had on the market for property loans, especially in the United States. The Great Depression generated massive, unprecedented unemployment; an estimated one-quarter to one-third of the U.S. civilian labor force was thrown out of work between 1929 and 1933. Few new mortgage loans were made during this period, and thousands of existing mortgages were foreclosed upon, forcing families to leave their homes. With so many forced sales, property values declined precipitously, endangering the financial solvency of thousands of mortgage lenders.

The federal government elected to tackle the mortgage market's problems by moving in several directions at once. For example, in 1932, the Federal Home Loan Bank System (FHLB) was created to supervise the activities of savings and loan associations and make loans to those S&Ls facing liquidity crises. In 1934, the National Housing Act was passed, setting up a system of federal insurance for qualified home mortgage loans. The Federal Housing Administration (FHA) was authorized to guarantee repayment of as much as 90 percent of acceptable home loans up to a ceiling amount determined by FHA, encouraging private lenders to lend more of a home's market value, accept longer terms on home mortgages, and charge lower interest rates.

The VA home loan insurance program is discussed on the Veterans Administration Web site at *www.va.gov*

Shortly before the end of World War II, the Veterans Administration (VA) was created with passage of the Servicemen's Readjustment Act (1944). The VA was designed to aid military servicemen returning to civilian life in finding adequate housing. Like FHA, VA offered to insure residential mortgages and helped reduce the required down payment on a new home.

The Creation of Fannie Mae (FNMA)

To learn more about Fannie Mae's mortgage market activities see *www.fanniemae.com*

The FHA-VA insurance program was an almost instant success, and home mortgage lending grew rapidly following its inception. Federal government efforts to create a resale (secondary) market for residential mortgages took a little longer, however. The first successful federal agency set up to buy and sell residential mortgages was Fannie Mae—the **Federal National Mortgage Association (FNMA).** Fannie Mae was established in 1938 for the purpose of buying and selling FHA-guaranteed mortgages in the secondary market. Later, in 1948, it was authorized to trade in VA-guaranteed mortgages as well. FNMA issues commitments to buy a specific dollar amount of mortgages at a predetermined yield, significantly improving the resale potential of most mortgage loans.

Fannie Mae raises money for its market-making activities primarily by selling short-term notes and longer-term debentures. In addition, in 1981, FNMA began to issue and guarantee securities backed by conventional mortgage loans purchased from lenders.

FNMA mortgage-backed securities are marketed by lenders that deal directly with FNMA or through security dealers.[1]

The Creation of Ginnie Mae (GNMA)

You can explore the programs used by Ginnie Mae to promote affordable housing at *www.ginnie-mae.gov*

Efforts by Congress to make the federal government's budget look better resulted in splitting Fannie Mae into two agencies in 1968. Fannie Mae itself became a private, shareholder-owned corporation devoted to secondary market trading. At the same time, loan programs requiring government subsidies or government credit were handed to a new corporation set up within the Department of Housing and Urban Development, known as the **Government National Mortgage Association (GNMA),** or Ginnie Mae. In one portion of its program, Ginnie Mae purchases "assistance" mortgages to finance housing for low-income families and then sells these mortgages to FNMA or to private investors.

GNMA Mortgage-Backed Securities

Far more important for the secondary market, however, is GNMA's **mortgage-backed securities** program. Backed by the full faith and credit of the U.S. government, Ginnie Mae agrees to *guarantee* principal and interest payments on securities issued by private mortgage institutions if those securities are backed by pools of government-guaranteed mortgages. These so-called **pass-throughs** are popular with institutional lenders and even individuals as safe, readily marketable securities with attractive rates of return. Mortgage lenders raise cash to make new loans by selling the pass-throughs against mortgages that they place in a mortgage pool.

The Federal Home Loan Mortgage Corporation (FHLMC)

Additional information about Freddie Mac and its activities in the home mortgage market is available at *www.freddiemac.com*

In 1970, the Emergency Home Finance Act gave birth to the **Federal Home Loan Mortgage Corporation (FHLMC),** more popularly known as *Freddie Mac.* FHLMC, like Ginnie Mae, combines the mortgages it buys into pools and issues bonds against them. Securities issued by Freddie Mac are guaranteed by that agency and have been very popular with investors, particularly savings and loan associations and banks. The creation of Freddie Mac reflected a desire by the federal government to develop a stronger secondary market for *conventional* home mortgages, of which it has purchased huge quantities.

Most recently both FNMA and FHLMC have come under sharp criticism and threats from Congress to remove their special connection to the U.S. Government. These two mortgage agencies have been aggressively expanding their market shares of both mortgage loans and mortgage-backed securities. Other private lenders soon came to resent Fannie Mae's and Freddie Mac's rapid growth which they have seen as caused primarily by the federal government's implicit support of these government-sponsored financial intermediaries.

FHLMC Mortgage-Backed Securities

To raise funds to support loan purchases, Freddie Mac sells mortgage participation certificates (PCs) and guaranteed mortgage certificates (GMCs). PCs represent an ownership interest in a pool of conventional mortgages bought and sold by Freddie Mac. FHLMC

---

[1]Fannie Mae is the world's largest mortgage bank and for a long time had a virtual monopoly in secondary market trading activities. Early in the 1970s, however, the Mortgage Guarantee Insurance Corporation (MGIC) was organized by a private group in Milwaukee, Wisconsin. Known as Maggie Mae, this corporation pledged to insure conventional home mortgage loans carrying down payments as low as 5 percent. Today, mortgage insurance, provided by a variety of private companies, is often required by lending institutions when the borrower makes a relatively small down payment on the purchase price of a home.

guarantees the investor's monthly interest and principal payments passed through from the mortgage pool. Guaranteed mortgage certificates (GMCs) are also claims against a pool of mortgages, but they are similar to corporate bonds in that interest is paid semiannually to investors.

Collateralized Mortgage Obligations (CMOs) and Real Estate Mortgage Investment Conduits (REMICs)

Another recent innovation in fund-raising by FHLMC is the **collateralized mortgage obligation (CMO)**—a bond whose value is derived from a pool of mortgages packaged together to back (collateralize) the bond. CMOs differ from other mortgage-backed securities in that they are issued in several different maturity classes (*tranches*) based on a projected schedule for repaying the mortgage loans in back of each CMO. A similar instrument that also partitions the principal cash flow from a pool of mortgages or mortgage-backed securities into maturity classes is called a **real estate mortgage investment conduit (REMIC).** Thus, CMOs and REMICs offer investors a range of different maturities from long-term to short-term and overcome at least some of the cash-flow uncertainty investors face when buying home mortgages themselves because a home owner may pay off his or her loan early—known as **prepayment risk.** More recently, some mortgage-backed securities have been issued as "strips," in which the investor can receive either principal payments from a pool of home mortgages or interest payments from the pool, depending on the individual investor's preferences for maturity and risk. During the 1990s, CMO trusts began to appear, offering even small investors a share in pools of collateralized mortgage obligations.

Impact of Securitized Mortgages

The development of the various types of **securitized mortgages**—debt securities backed by pools of outstanding mortgage loans—by Ginnie Mae, Fannie Mae, and other lending institutions have made mortgage securities more competitive with government securities and corporate stocks and bonds, allowing many mortgage lenders to invade national and international capital markets for funds. The mortgage-backed securities market has expanded tremendously, rising in volume from less than $25 billion in 1981 to more than $4 trillion in 2001. Foreign investors by the thousands have become active in providing new capital to domestic mortgage markets, for example. They have also made it much easier to get old, low-yielding mortgages off of lenders' books in order to make room for higher-yielding investments.

Further information on mortgage-backed securities is available from such sites as Speculative Bubble at *www.speculativebubble. com* and Rebuz.com at *www.rebuz.com*

On the negative side, however, these new financial instruments have increased the sensitivity of mortgage interest rates to national and international market conditions. Home mortgage rates are now more volatile than in the past. The residential mortgage market has broadened geographically, but at the price of a somewhat less predictable credit market environment.

Questions *to Help You Study*

5. Please list the principal *mortgage lending institutions* in the United States. Which is most important? In what particular areas of the market?

6. Please identify the following federal agencies and describe their roles or functions: FHA, VA, FHLB, FNMA, GNMA, and FHLMC.

7. How has the federal government's intervention in the home mortgage market over the past several decades changed the structure and operation of the home mortgage market? For what reason has all of this been done?

INNOVATIONS IN MORTGAGE INSTRUMENTS

Consumers can easily find current home mortgage interest rates and information on available homes at a wide variety of Web sites. One unique site at *www.interestratecalculator.com* shows the home buyer what his or her payments will be for a given home mortgage rate in the U.S., Canada, and Europe.

Repeatedly in recent years, interest rates have climbed upward, only to fall back during brief recessions and then move upward again. Each upward movement in interest rates forced mortgage lenders to cut back on the availability of funds for housing. In part, these cutbacks in mortgage funds were a response to the widespread use of **fixed-rate home mortgages (FRMs).** FRMs return to the lender the same annual interest income (cash flow) regardless of what is happening to inflation or to interest rates. When depository institutions are forced to pay higher rates on their deposits to attract funds, their profits tend to be squeezed because the revenues from the FRMs remain unchanged. Of course, these lending institutions are able to charge higher interest rates on *new* mortgage loans, but new loans normally are only a small fraction of an established lending institution's total loan portfolio. The bulk of that portfolio usually is in *old* mortgages, often granted during an era when interest rates were lower.

In short, the FRM amplified the normal up-and-down cycle of earnings for mortgage-lending institutions, leading to low or even negative earnings in periods of rising interest rates and to positive earnings in periods of falling rates. FRMs require the *lender* to bear the risk of interest-rate fluctuations. An alternative to the FRM was needed that both guaranteed lenders a satisfactory real rate of return on mortgage loans and made funds available to home buyers on reasonable terms.

Variable-Rate and Adjustable Mortgage Instruments

The problems created by fixed-rate mortgages led to the development of several new mortgage instruments, led by the **variable-rate mortgage (VRM),** which permits the lender to vary the contractual interest rate on a mortgage loan as market conditions change. Generally, the VRM loan rate is linked to a reference interest rate *not* determined by the lender. For example, the yield on 10-year U.S. Treasury bonds may be used as a reference rate so that, if Treasury bond yields rise, the homeowner pays a higher contractual interest rate. Alternatively, under a broader **adjustable mortgage instrument (AMI),** the maturity of the mortgage loan may be lengthened or a combination of interest rate increases and maturity changes may be made as interest rates rise. In some cases, the loan principal can be increased along with interest rate increases, reducing the growth of the homeowner's equity—a process known as *negative amortization.* VRMs and AMIs shift the *risk* of interest rate fluctuations, partially or wholly, from the lender to the borrower.

Under most state and federal laws, changes in the interest rates attached to VRMs are limited as to frequency and amount. However, AMIs, with their options of varying monthly payments, the maturity of a mortgage loan, or the loan principal amount owed as interest rates change, generally face fewer legal restrictions. Many lenders offer *teaser rates* (i.e., loan rates that are temporarily below market levels) in order to get home buyers to commit to a VRM or an AMI instead of taking out a fixed-rate mortgage which bears greater risk for the lender.

Convertible Mortgages

The volatile interest rates of recent years led to the development of a combination variable-rate, fixed-rate home mortgage loan that some home buyers find attractive. This *convertible mortgage instrument* (CMI) starts out with an adjustable interest rate, but later the home buyer can switch to a fixed-rate mortgage if interest rates look more favorable. However, some loan contracts carry a mandatory holding period before conversion to a fixed-rate loan is permitted and also prohibit switching after a certain length of time has elapsed (such as five years). CMIs have initial adjustable interest rates that are usually lower than those on new fixed-rate mortgages and the switch to a fixed-rate loan in the future typically is cheaper than refinancing an old mortgage.

Another version of the CMI is the *balloon loan.* For example, a borrower may take out a 5-year fixed-rate mortgage loan initially, but later on will probably have to refinance this 5-year loan with a new longer-term loan because the first loan pays off only a fraction of a home's total cost. Borrowers under a balloon loan often hope to sell their homes before refinancing their mortgage becomes necessary—sometimes a risky proposition if the housing resale market weakens. Both FNMA and FHLMC agreed to begin purchasing balloon loans from lenders during the 1990s.

A very recent variation on the convertible mortgage appeared as the twenty-first century began—a *hybrid mortgage,* which offers a fixed interest rate initially (say, for the first five years). Then for the remainder of the loan the mortgage interest rate can be changed periodically (often once each year). These loans can be inexpensive at first, but pose considerable borrower risk later on for those homeowners who plan to be in their homes a long time.

Reverse-Annuity Mortgages

A mortgage-financing device that may be of help to older families and retired individuals is the *reverse-annuity mortgage* (RAM). This financial instrument provides income to those who may have already paid off their mortgages but intend to keep their present home. The lender determines the current value of the home and pays the borrower a monthly annuity, amounting to a percentage of the property's value. The loan is secured by a gradually increasing mortgage on the borrower's home. Repayment of the loan occurs when the annuity holder dies, with the loan being discharged against the deceased's estate, or when the home is sold.

Epilogue on the Fixed-Rate Mortgage

It is interesting that, with all the new mortgage instruments developed in recent years, fixed-rate mortgages (FRMs) continue to hold a substantial share of the residential loan market. This is true even though FRMs usually carry a higher interest rate than adjustable mortgages, at least initially, and higher origination fees and prepayment penalties. One reason appears to be public mistrust of many of the new instruments, coupled with fear of inflation, which would push up the interest rate on a variable-rate loan. Another factor is competition. It is likely, therefore, that both FRMs and VRMs will continue to exist side by side in the home mortgage market, each serving the special needs of individual lenders and homeowners.

Mortgage Lock-Ins

For most types of home mortgages the borrower wants to know before committing to the purchase of a home: What interest rate am I going to pay? Can I afford the monthly payments that the lender will require? And what if mortgage interest rates rise after I agree to buy that new home, endangering my ability to pay for it?

This is the purpose of *mortgage lock-ins.* When a borrower "locks in" a mortgage loan rate this means the home mortgage lender agrees to extend a loan offer at the prevailing mortgage interest rate for a specified period (usually 30 to 60 days and sometimes longer). This mortgage "lock-in" device is designed to protect borrowers from an increase in mortgage loan rates before the borrower takes possession of his or her new home.

However, what if market interest rates *fall* instead of rise? Can a borrower get his or her loan revised to capture the new and cheaper loan rate? Many "lock-ins" today grant the borrower additional flexibility by including a so-called "float down" option which usually costs extra. With a "float down" clause, if interest rates fall before the closing on the new home loan occurs, the lender will make the home mortgage loan available at a lower interest rate. Otherwise, if the borrower backs out of a loan agreement because interest rates have fallen, the lender may lose a substantial amount in loan fees. Sometimes, however, even without the floating rate feature, a lender will "give a little" if market interest rates fall, knowing the customer may be more likely to run to another lending institution unless there is some flexibility in setting up a new home loan.

What happens if the loan agreement is made and the borrower takes possession of a new home, only to discover he or she can no longer afford the payments? Usually the home owner will try to sell his or her home as quickly as possible, repay the mortgage with the proceeds of the sale, and move into cheaper housing. If this doesn't happen right away and several payments are missed, the lender will *foreclose,* taking possession of the home, and selling it to recover the loaned funds.

However, in recent years a new alternative to foreclosure has become popular—a *loan modification agreement.* Loan modifications are designed to assist troubled borrowers avoid foreclosure, remain in a home, and save the lender the costs of foreclosure, repossession, and the forced sale of a home. They may also result in additional fee income for the mortgage lender.

Loan modifications usually add any missed loan payments to the remaining balance the borrower still owes on a home and a new payment schedule is worked out. Many such agreements lower the required monthly mortgage payment somewhat by stretching out the maturity of the loan. Modification agreements have noticeably slowed foreclosures recently, even during the recession of 2001 when mortgage loan defaults accelerated and thousands of families were fearful of losing their homes.

Refinancing Home Mortgages and Home Equity Loans

In recent years, many homeowners have found that it makes economic sense to convert their existing mortgage loans into *new* loans with lower interest costs because market interest rates have fallen substantially since the original loan was taken out. This happens most often to borrowers carrying a fixed-rate mortgage loan. However, many flexible-rate mortgages also allow the home buyer to convert during the early years of a home loan to a fixed-rate mortgage bearing a lower contract rate in return for a fee.

Is refinancing an existing mortgage loan a wise move for a home buyer? The answer hinges on whether the savings outweigh the costs over a designated payback period. If mortgage interest rates have dropped at least a percentage point since the borrower took out the first mortgage loan, and the borrower plans to remain in the home long enough to fully recover the costs of refinancing (normally about three years), then refinancing through a cheaper new loan is often attractive. The costs of refinancing include the loss of some of the homeowner's interest deduction on federal tax returns due to the lower interest payments on the new loan and the fees that must be paid in order to set up the new loan. Moreover, loan fees on refinanced property normally are not immediately tax deductible but must be written off gradually over the term of a new loan.

The ability of a homeowner to obtain refinancing depends critically upon a strong credit history and a significant amount of accumulated equity built up in the home to be refinanced. Increased volatility of interest rates tends to cause homeowners to postpone their plans to refinance their home mortgages. On the other hand, recent structural changes in the home mortgage market (such as greater convenience in finding lenders willing to refinance and the best terms available for getting a new loan) have made it much easier for customers to explore and possibly take advantage of refinancing opportunities.

A newer form of home mortgage refinancing that is growing rapidly today occurs when a homeowner decides to turn into usable form (liquidate) some of the built-up equity value in the home: a *home equity loan.* As discussed more fully in Chapter 23, the homeowner contracts for a new mortgage based upon his or her home's excess value over the amount of the existing home mortgage, generating extra cash for spending. Tax-reform legislation in the 1980s added special attractiveness to home-equity loans, taken out for housing and non-housing needs, because the equity loan's interest cost is usually tax deductible. About 60 percent of homeowners borrow *additional* funds when they refinanced their old home mortgages, while about 40 percent refinance purely to take advantage of lower prevailing interest rates and do not borrow more money than the amount owed on their original mortgage.

Questions *to Help You Study*

8. A number of new mortgage instruments have appeared in recent years. These new financial instruments include variable rate mortgages (VRMs), adjustable mortgage instruments (AMIs), and reverse-annuity mortgages (RAMs) in addition to the more conventional fixed-rate mortgage (FRM). Please describe how each of these home mortgage instruments works and what their advantages are.

9. What is a *mortgage lock-in?* Does it benefit the borrower or the lender? When might it not be a good idea?

10. What is a *loan modification agreement?* What is its purpose?

11. What are the advantages and disadvantages of home refinancings and home equity loans? Under what circumstances should a home owner seriously consider these financial instruments?

Summary of the Chapter

This chapter has focused on one of the most important markets in the financial system—the market for residential mortgage credit.

- *Home ownership* has grown in importance in recent years with a record number of individuals and families in the United States today (about two-thirds) owning their own homes. The value of homes as a tax-reducing investment and as a hedge against inflation has played a major role in this home ownership trend as has the drive toward more lenient borrowing terms, encouraged by government support of the home mortgage market.

- Among the leading home mortgage lending institutions today are *commercial banks, savings banks* and *savings and loan associations, life insurance companies,* and *mortgage banking firms.*

- U.S. federal government intervention in the home mortgage market began in earnest during the 1930s and 1940s with the creation of several major federal agencies, including the Federal Housing Administration (FHA), the Federal National Mortgage Association (FNMA), the Veterans Administration (VA), and the Government National Mortgage Association (GNMA). These agencies were directed to expand the supply of mortgage credit available and to make mortgages more affordable for a greater proportion of the U.S. population. This was accomplished through such devices as guaranteeing the repayment of selected home mortgages (through FHA and VA) and creating an active resale market for existing home loans (through FNMA and GNMA).

- Later the Federal Home Loan Mortgage Corporation (FHLMC) was created to assist in expanding the supply of home mortgage credit and to aid in the development of security-like mortgage instruments to broaden and deepen the market for mortgage credit.

- Among the most important of new mortgage-related securities developed in recent years to expand the depth and breadth of the residential mortgage market are mortgage-backed securities, collateralized mortgage obligations (CMOs), and real estate mortgage investment conduits (REMICs). Each is based on the notion of pooling together a group of similar home mortgage loans and issuing securities against that pool that will eventually be paid off by the cash flow (principal and interest payments) generated from the loans in the pool.

- Mortgage-loan-backed security instruments have been used to attract millions of new investors to the home mortgage market and to increase the liquidity of mortgage instruments. *Securitized* mortgage instruments have helped make the market for home mortgages a global capital market rather than a regionally isolated marketplace as it was before their invention.

- In order to encourage individuals and families to consider home ownership many new home mortgage loans and other home financing devices have been developed, some of them making mortgage credit available on more lenient and affordable terms. Examples include variable-rate mortgages (VRMs), adjustable mortgage instruments (AMIs), convertible mortgages, reverse annuity mortgages, home equity loans, and home mortgage refinancings.

- The home mortgage market today has become one of the largest markets for a single financial instrument on the planet. It has helped to make U.S. citizens among the best-housed individuals in the world and in the process has interconnected the market for home loans with those for Treasury bonds, state and local government bonds, and corporate bonds and notes. No longer are mortgage-related instruments insensitive to the broad market trends that affect the global money and capital markets today.

Key Terms

Conventional home mortgage loan, *671*

Residential mortgages, *673*

Nonresidential mortgages, *673*

Federal Housing Administration (FHA), *679*

Federal National Mortgage Association (FNMA), *680*

Government National Mortgage Association (GNMA), *681*

Mortgage-backed securities, *681*

Pass-throughs, *681*

Federal Home Loan Mortgage Corporation (FHLMC), *681*

Collateralized mortgage obligation (CMO), *682*

Real estate mortgage investment conduit (REMIC), *682*

Prepayment risk, *682*

Securitized mortgages, *682*

Fixed-rate mortgage (FRM), *683*

Variable-rate mortgage (VRM), *683*

Adjustable mortgage instrument (AMI), *683*

Problems

1. Which private mortgage-lending institutions are described in each of the profiles given below?

   a. These firms, which faced serious financial problems in the 1980s and early 1990s with numerous failures, are predominantly local lenders providing mortgage credit in the local areas where their offices are situated. These lenders began in the U.S. in the nineteenth century to enable individuals and families to save and eventually be able to afford to build or buy new homes.

    b. These firms serve as a channel for builders and contractors to ultimately obtain permanent financing by initially providing temporary financial support while construction is underway and then finding long-term lenders to take over these mortgage loans for the long haul (often for 15 to 30 years).

    c. These lending institutions make investments in both commercial and residential mortgage properties and prefer to purchase residential mortgages in large blocks rather than one at a time.

    d. Now ranking first as lenders for the construction and purchase of homes, condominiums, and apartments and in the commercial mortgage field, this mortgage-lending institution normally prefers to make shorter-term construction loans and let longer-term lenders (such as insurance companies and pension funds) provide permanent mortgage financing.

    e. A depository institution that began its history mainly in the eastern United States and prefers to acquire residential mortgages in large blocks rather than loan by loan.

2. Which federal mortgage agency is being described below?

    a. A federal agency created in 1938 to buy and sell selected residential mortgages in the secondary market.

    b. A federal agency created in 1970 to improve the resale market for predominantly conventional mortgages and to assist private lenders in securitizing pools of mortgage loans.

    c. An agency of the federal government established in 1934 to guarantee mortgage loans for low- and medium-priced homes.

    d. A federal agency aimed at providing loans through its regional banks to S&Ls and other depository mortgage lenders having significant liquidity needs.

    e. A federal government agency created in 1968 to assist the home mortgage market by purchasing mortgages to finance low-income family housing projects and guaranteeing certain mortgage loans made by private lenders.

3. Which mortgage instruments meet the definitions provided below?

    a. A home mortgage loan under which some of the terms of the loan, such as the loan rate or maturity of the loan, varies as market conditions change.

    b. A mortgage loan that begins with an adjustable loan rate that can be switched later to a fixed loan rate.

    c. Debt securities backed by pools of mortgage loans.

    d. Mortgage-backed securities issued in a range of maturity classes so that prepayment risk can be more easily selected to match an investor's particular investment goals.

    e. Home mortgage loan carrying an interest rate that varies during the term of a loan, generally depending on the movement of interest rates in the open market.

    f. Provides income to those who have already paid off their mortgage but wish to receive a cash inflow (income) based on the value of the equity in their home.

4. Please identify the key terms and concepts described or defined below:

    a. Credit funds extended to a home buyer by a private lender without a government guarantee of the home loan.

    b. Loans secured by single family homes and other dwellings.

    c. Loans secured by real property that is part of businesses and farms.

    d. Guaranteed mortgage loans for the purchase of low-priced and medium-priced homes.

e. A federal agency, now privately owned, that was originally set up during the 1930s to develop a resale market for home mortgage loans and thereby provide lenders with an additional source of mortgage funding.

f. Securities issued against a pool of mortgage loans held by a financial institution whose interest and principal payments will be passed on to security holders.

g. A federal agency created in 1970, but now privately owned, that was designed to improve the secondary market for certain types of home mortgages.

h. A type of mortgage-backed security offered in a variety of maturity classes.

i. Home mortgage loan that carries an unchanging loan rate.

j. Home mortgage loan with a loan rate that may be adjusted during the life of the loan.

Questions about the Web and the Money and Capital Markets

1. Suppose you wanted to find out how high interest rates are on home mortgages today. What Web site or sites would help you find out? Do these sites help you determine if you could afford to borrow to buy a new home? In what way?

2. Are mortgage interest rates higher or lower right now than they were a year ago? Where could you look on the World Wide Web to get an answer?

3. What is the fastest-growing segment of the mortgage loan market today? What type of mortgage loan is outpacing all the others? Which Web sites helped you answer this question?

4. With the help of the Web compare and contrast the primary and secondary markets for residential mortgages. What key differences do you observe? Why is each market important in satisfying the needs of consumers for shelter?

Selected References

Bennett, Paul; Richard Peach; and Stavros Peristiani. "Structural Change in the Mortgage Market and the Propensity to Refinance." Staff Reports no. 45, Federal Reserve Bank of New York, September 1998, pp. 1–22.

Rose, Peter S. *Commercial Bank Management,* Fifth edition. New York: McGraw-Hill, 2002.

Segal, Lewis M., and Daniel G. Sullivan. "Trends in Home Ownership: Race, Demographics, and Income." *Economic Perspectives,* Federal Reserve Bank of Chicago, 1997, pp. 53–72.

Wassermen, Mirian. "Appreciating the House: Housing as an Investment." *Regional Review.* Federal Reserve Bank of Boston, Second Quarter 1998, pp. 20–26.

Weicher, John C. "The New Structure of the Housing Finance System." *Review.* Federal Reserve Bank of St. Louis, July–August 1994, pp. 47–65.

Part **Seven**

The International Financial System

In the earliest financial systems around the world money and capital markets were largely isolated from one another. The limited technology then available for financial information transfer and storage worked to keep markets already separated by geographic barriers from melding together into broader and more extensive trading areas. However, in recent decades, the rapid and accurate transmission of financial data and financial services by satellite, microwave, fiber optic cable, and computer have resulted in the welding together of many smaller markets into truly *global* financial-service markets.

Today, no nation can view its financial system as being in complete isolation from the global money and capital markets. In the financial marketplace of the modern era trading of financial services circles the globe, 24 hours a day, with only limited impediments to the exchange of information and the flow of capital from one spot on the planet to another. As the international sector has grown, international financial institutions and the global storage and transfer of financial data have grown with it. There is greater interest today almost everywhere in promoting trade between nations. But global trade depends upon global financial services, especially the efficient transmission of payments and the rapid expansion of credit where it is most needed.

Moreover, financial-market participants in every corner of the globe closely follow daily financial developments and the monetary and fiscal policies of many nations. Lenders and borrowers, savers and investors increasingly recognize today that the value of the assets—both financial and nonfinancial—they may hold is today sensitive to happenings often several continents away. There are now few places for financial-market players to run and hide in order to escape risk and possible loss if the wrong financial decisions are made.

In Part Seven we turn to a key source of international financial information— a nation's balance of payments—and also examine the fundamental determinants of exchange rates between national currencies (such as the U.S. dollar, the Japanese yen, and the Euro). We will also explore how international banks are structured and what services they provide to their customers all over the globe. In particular, Chapter 25 explores the make-up and meaning of a country's balance of international payments and then goes on to look at the pivotal role of money within the international financial system. Chapter 26 turns our attention to the international banking firm and its critical role within that global system.

We will discover that, despite all the great technological advances that are re-shaping our world today, the international financial system faces great risks in the modern era as it has in the past. However, the make-up of that risk in all its dimensions is changing; new risks are appearing even as old risks become less of a concern.

Still, the modern global financial system also provides great benefits to businesses and consumers. Today's international financial system promotes efficient use of the world's resources—both financial and economic—and helps to insure that the public receives the goods and services it seeks from an increasingly competitive global marketplace.

Chapter Twenty-Five

International Transactions and Currency Values

Learning Objectives in This Chapter

- You will explore the functions and roles performed by the international markets within the global financial system.

- You will see how international payments for goods and services are made and how international borrowing and lending can be tracked through a nation's *balance-of-payments accounts*.

- You will come to understand how the values of *national currencies* (such as the dollar and the Euro) are determined within the modern financial system.

What's in This Chapter? Key Topics Outline

A Nation's Balance of Payments Accounts

Disequilibrium in the Balance of Payments: Consequences and Possible Remedies

U.S. Trade Deficits: The Problems They Can Cause

The Problem of Different Monetary Units

The Gold Standard and Other Monetary Rules

Managed Float and Euros on the Street

Character of the Foreign Exchange Market (FOREX)

Exchange Rate Quotations and the Forces That Shape Them

Functions of the Forward Currency Markets

Hedging and the Market for Foreign Currency Futures

Currency Swaps

Government Intervention in the Foreign Exchange Markets

INTRODUCTION

In many ways, the world we live in is rapidly shrinking. Jet planes such as the British Concorde can race across the Atlantic between New York and London in less than four hours, about the same time it takes a jetliner to travel across the United States. The Internet, fax machines, telephones, and fiber optic cable can move financial information from one spot on the globe to another in minutes or seconds. Orbiting satellites can bring news of major international significance to home television sets the moment an event takes place and make possible direct communication between those involved in international business transactions.

Accompanying these dramatic improvements in communication and transportation is enormous growth in world trade and international investment. For example, in 1965 total exports of goods and services worldwide reached $190 billion. By the twenty-first century, the estimated dollar value of world trade had climbed to more than $5 trillion, or almost as much as the U.S. gross domestic product (GDP). Moreover, the United States itself has become increasingly dependent on world trade. For example, imports into the United States represented just 4.6 percent of GDP in 1960 but had jumped to more than 15 percent of GDP in 2000; U.S. exports climbed from 6 percent to about 11 percent of GDP over the same period. Thus, more than a quarter of the value of production and spending in the U.S. economy stems from foreign trade. The international financial markets have had to grow rapidly just to keep up with the expansion in world trade.

Actually, international financial markets perform the same basic functions as domestic financial markets. They bring international lenders of funds into contact with borrowers, thereby permitting an increased flow of scarce funds toward their most productive uses. The volume of capital investment worldwide is made larger because of the workings of the global financial system. And with increased capital investment, the productivity of individual firms and nations is increased and economic growth in the international sector accelerates. The international financial markets also facilitate the flow of consumer goods and services across national boundaries, making possible an optimal allocation of resources in response to consumer demand on a global scale. With increased efficiency in resource use, the output of consumer goods and services is increased and costs of production are minimized.[1]

THE BALANCE OF PAYMENTS

One of the most widely used sources of information concerning flows of funds, goods, and services between nations is each country's **balance-of-payments (BOP) accounts**. This annual statistical report summarizes all of the economic and financial transactions between residents of one nation and the rest of the world during a specific period of time. The BOP accounts reflect *changes* in the assets and liabilities of units, such as businesses, individuals, and governments, involved in international transactions. The major transactions captured in the BOP accounts include exports and imports of goods and services; income from

---

[1]These benefits from international trade and finance are most likely to occur if each nation follows the principle of *comparative advantage*. This principle argues that each country will have a higher real standard of living if it specializes in the production of those goods and services in which it has a comparative advantage in cost and imports those goods and services where it is at a comparative cost disadvantage. In simplest terms, a country should acquire goods and services from those sources—foreign or domestic— that result in the lowest cost in terms of its own resources. The principle of comparative advantage works best in an environment of free trade that permits nations to specialize in their most efficient activities.

The international financial system performs the same roles that smaller domestic financial systems do, attracting and allocating savings and meeting the funding needs of businesses, households, and units of government. Today the global financial system is growing faster, however, as many domestic money and capital markets now are linked to each other around the globe. No longer can we say that interest rates or security prices in any one country are unaffected by what happens in other countries and on other continents.

As the global sphere of the money and capital markets has grown in importance, its position on the World Wide Web also has expanded significantly. Hundreds of Web sites touch upon the key issues raised in this chapter—trade and the balance of payments and the prices of foreign currencies. You can find a good explanation of the purpose and basic structure of the balance of payments, for example, at *www.encyclopedia.com*. Extensive data on trade and the U.S. balance of payments is provided at such key government sites as the Bureau of Economic Analysis at *www.bea.doc.gov* and the Federal Reserve Bank of St. Louis at *www.stls.frb.org*.

Trading in the world's different currencies is one of the most interesting and also one of the globe's most volatile markets, requiring great skill and in-depth knowledge if you want to be a successful currency trader. The World Wide Web can help you learn a great deal through a rapidly expanding number of educational and informative sites. Examples include The Currency Site at *www.oanda.com* and FOREX News at *www.forexnews.com*.

investments made abroad; government loans and military expenditures overseas; and private capital flows between nations.

In a statistical sense, a nation's BOP accounts are always "in balance," because double-entry bookkeeping is used. For example, every payment made for goods and services imported from abroad simultaneously creates a claim on the home country's resources or extinguishes an existing liability. Similarly, every time a domestic business firm receives payment from overseas, it either acquires a claim against resources in a foreign country, or a claim that firm held against a foreign individual or institution is erased. In practice, however, imbalances frequently show up in the BOP accounts due to unreported transactions or inconsistencies in reporting. These errors and omissions are handled through a Statistical Discrepancy account.

The U.S. Balance of International Payments

The U.S. BOP accounts are published quarterly by the Department of Commerce. The quarterly figures are then *annualized* to permit comparisons across years. The transactions recorded in the balance of payments fall into three broad groups:

1. *Transactions on current account*, which include imports and exports of goods and services and unilateral transfers (gifts).

2. *Transactions on capital account*, which include both long- and short-term investment at home and abroad and usually involve the transfer of financial assets (bonds, deposits, etc.).

3. *Official reserve transactions*, which are used by monetary authorities (the Treasury, central bank, etc.) to settle BOP deficits, usually through transferring the ownership of official reserve assets to countries with BOP surpluses.

EXHIBIT 25–1
Principal Credit and Debit Items Recorded in a Nation's Balance of Payments (BOP)

Credit Entries (Inflows of Funds, +)	Debit Entries (Outflows of Funds, −)
Exports of merchandise	Imports of merchandise
Services provided to citizens of foreign countries	Services provided to domestic citizens by foreign countries
Interest and dividends due domestic citizens from business firms abroad	Gifts of money sent abroad by domestic citizens
Remittances received from domestic citizens employed in foreign countries	Capital invested abroad by domestic citizens
Foreign purchases of securities issued by domestic firms and units of government	Dividend and interest payments to foreign countries on investments made in the domestic country
Repayments by foreigners of funds borrowed from domestic lending institutions	

Transactions that bring about an inflow of foreign currency into the home country are recorded as *credits* (+). Transactions resulting in an outflow of foreign currency from the home country are listed as *debits* (−). Thus, credit (+) items in the BOP represent an increase in a nation's buying power abroad. Debit (−) items represent decreases in a nation's buying power abroad. If a country sells goods and services or borrows abroad, these transactions are credit items because they increase external buying power. On the other hand, a purchase of goods and services abroad or a paydown of a nation's international liabilities is a debit item because that country is surrendering part of its external buying power. A summary of the major credit and debit items making up the BOP accounts is shown in Exhibit 25–1.

The actual U.S. BOP accounts for the years 1999 and 2000 (third quarter, annualized) as reported by the Department of Commerce are shown in Exhibit 25–2. We have subdivided these international accounts into the three major categories discussed above—the current account, capital account, and official reserve transactions account—to more fully understand how the BOP bookkeeping system operates.

The Current Account

One of the most publicized components of the U.S. BOP is the **current account**, which contains three elements:

1. The *merchandise trade balance*, comparing the volume of goods exported to those imported.

2. The *service balance*, comparing exports and imports of services.

3. *Unilateral transfers*, reflecting the amount of gifts made to foreigners by domestic citizens and government grants abroad.

The Merchandise Trade Balance

Prior to the 1970s, the United States reported a positive *merchandise trade balance*, with exports exceeding imports in most years due to substantial demand for U.S. agricultural products and machinery and equipment overseas. However, domestic inflation and a strong U.S. economy relative to the rest of the world, spurring U.S. citizens to buy more goods from abroad, have turned U.S. trade surpluses into substantial deficits in recent years, as shown in Exhibit 25–2. U.S. *sources* of external buying power have generally been less

EXHIBIT 25–2

The U.S. Balance of Payments in 1999 and 2000 ($ Billions)

Source: U.S. Department of Commerce, Bureau of Economic Analysis.

Credit (+) and Debit (−) Items	1999	2000*
Balance on current account	−$331.5	−$455.2
Balance on merchandise trade:	−265.0	−386.0
Exports	+956.2	+1,098.8
Imports	−1,221.2	−1,484.8
Net income	−18.5	−18.0
Investment, net	−13.1	−12.8
Direct	+62.7	+86.4
Portfolio	−75.8	−98.8
Compensation of employees	−5.4	−5.2
Unilateral current transfers, net	−48.0	−51.2
The capital account		
Changes in U.S. citizens' private assets abroad (increase, −):		
Bank-reported claims	−69.9	−45.6
Nonbank-reported claims	−92.3	+3.6
U.S. purchases of foreign securities, net	−128.6	−121.6
U.S. direct investments abroad, net	−150.9	−144.4
Private capital outflows from the United States	−441.7	−308.0
Change in foreign private assets inside the United States (increase, +):		
U.S. bank-reported liabilities	+67.4	+56.0
U.S. nonbank-reported liabilities	+34.3	+10.4
Foreign private purchases of U.S. Treasury securities, net	−20.5	−50.4
Foreign purchases of other U.S. securities, net	+331.5	+475.2
Foreign direct investments in the United States, net	+275.5	+259.6
U.S. currency flows	+22.4	+3.2
Private capital inflows into the United States	+710.7	+754.0
Total private capital flows, net (net capital inflow, +)	+269.0	+446.0
Changes in official reserve assets:		
Change in U.S. official reserve assets (increase, −):		
Gold	+0.0	+0.0
Special drawing rights (SDRs)	+0.1	−0.8
Reserve position in International Monetary Fund (IMF)	+5.5	+5.2
Foreign currencies	+3.3	−6.0
Increase (−) or decrease (+) in U.S. official reserve assets	+8.9	−1.6
Change in foreign official assets in the United States (increase, +):		
U.S. Treasury securities	+12.2	−36.0
Other U.S. government obligations	+20.4	+57.2
Other U.S. government liabilities	−3.3	−2.4
Other U.S. liabilities reported by U.S. banks	+12.7	+25.2
Other foreign official assets	+0.9	+2.4
Increase (+) or decrease (−) in foreign official reserve assets	+42.9	+46.4
Change in U.S. government assets (other than reserve assets), net (increase, −)	+2.8	+0.4
Capital amount transactions, net	−3.5	+0.8
Statistical discrepancy	+11.6	−37.6

Note: Details may not sum to column totals due to the effects of rounding error.
*2000 figures are preliminary from the third quarter of the year and are annualized.

than the nation's *uses* of external buying power. By 2000 the United States merchandise trade balance deficit approached nearly $400 billion (on an annualized basis).

The Service Balance

Because Americans typically have purchased more goods from abroad in recent years than they have sold to other countries, how has this deficit (debit balance) in the merchandise trade account been paid for? Part of the needed funds have come from the service balance—net sales of services to foreigners. Services counted in the BOP accounts include insurance policies covering foreign shipments of goods, transportation services, hotel accommodations for foreigners visiting the United States, and entertainment and medical care for foreign residents. Service income for the United States has increased significantly in recent years.

Unilateral Transfers

The third category of transaction recorded in the current account, labeled *unilateral transfers*, consists of gifts or grants from U.S. residents to foreigners. Gifts and grants are referred to as unilateral transfers because they represent a *one-way flow* of resources to the recipient; nothing is expected in return. Of course, foreigners send gifts to U.S. recipients as well, but U.S. gift-giving abroad far exceeds the return flow. For example, gifts and grants to foreigners from Americans were an estimated $51 billion larger than foreign gifts flowing into the United States in 2000 (on an annualized basis). Each gift and grant sent overseas represents the *use* of the nation's external buying power and therefore is recorded as a *debit* $(-)$ item.

The Balance on Current Account

When we put the above components—balance on merchandise trade, balance on services, and net unilateral transfers—together, we derive the *balance on current account*. The U.S. balance on current account in 2000 was an annualized debit balance estimated at more than $450 billion, though the U.S. deficit fell in 2001. The United States experienced this debit balance primarily because the rising value of the U.S. dollar in international markets for at least part of the period discouraged sales of U.S. goods abroad, while Americans bought more overseas goods due to the fact that many were lower cost than comparable domestically produced goods.

One of the most important institutions today in shaping world trading of goods and services is the World Trade Organization (WTO); see the Web site of this institution at *www.wto.org*

Persistent U.S. current account deficits tend to put upward pressure on domestic interest rates and place downward pressure on the value of the U.S. dollar in international markets. Correction of the U.S. current account deficit using the government's economic policy tools could require a slowing of domestic demand for goods and services, with resulting increases in unemployment and lower living standards.

The Capital Account

Flows of funds destined for investment abroad are recorded in the **capital account**. Investments abroad may be long term, as in the case of a U.S. automobile company building an assembly plant in Germany, or short term, such as the purchase of six-month British Treasury bills by U.S. citizens. Of course, capital investment flows both ways across national boundaries. For example, in 2000, U.S. citizens and private organizations invested more than $300 billion overseas, while foreign individuals and private institutions invested more than $750 billion (annualized) in U.S. assets. The result was a *net private capital inflow* into the United States estimated at more than $450 billion. U.S. banks, hotels, energy companies, and numerous other firms have all been acquisition targets for foreign investors. In effect, foreign capital inflows have financed a substantial portion of the U.S. merchandise trade deficit as well as supporting the creation of new U.S. businesses and jobs.

Components of the Capital Account

The capital account in the balance of payments includes three different types of international investment: (1) short-term capital flows, (2) direct investments, and (3) portfolio investments. The latter two—direct and portfolio investments—represent a long-term commitment of funds, involving the purchase of stocks, bonds, and other financial assets having a maturity of more than one year. Short-term capital flows, on the other hand, reflect purchases of financial assets with maturities of less than one year. These short-term financial assets are mainly government notes, deposits, and foreign currencies.

What is the essential difference between *direct investment* and *portfolio investment*? The key factor is *control*. Portfolio investment merely involves purchasing securities to hold in order to receive interest, dividends, or capital gains. Direct investment, on the other hand, refers to the purchase of land or the acquisition of ownership shares in an attempt to control a foreign business firm.[2]

Claims against Foreigners

In addition to direct investment and purchases of foreign securities, the capital account also records claims against foreigners reported by domestic banks and nonbanking concerns. The bulk of the claims comprise loans extended by domestic banks to firms and governments abroad. In 2000, U.S. bank claims on foreigners totaled nearly $50 billion (on an annualized basis). Privatization activities overseas have set in motion more bank lending overseas. At the same time the overall strength of the U.S. economy has generated ample funds to support overseas lending.

Official Reserve Transactions

When a nation has a deficit in its international payments accounts, it must settle up with other nations by surrendering assets or claims to foreign accounts. *Official reserve transactions*, involving transfer of the ownership of gold, convertible foreign currencies, deposits in the International Monetary Fund, and special drawing rights (SDRs), are usually the vehicle for settling net differences in international claims between nations.

Official reserve accounts are immediately available assets for making international payments. When these assets *increase*, this represents a source of external buying power by the nation experiencing the increase. On the other hand, a *decrease* in official reserve accounts represents a use of external buying power by the nation experiencing the decrease. If a nation has a surplus (credit balance) in its current and capital accounts, the balance in its official reserve accounts generally rises, indicating an excess of sales abroad over foreign purchases. Conversely, a country experiencing a deficit (debit balance) in its current and capital accounts usually finds that the balance in its official reserve accounts is falling. Such a decline can be temporarily offset, however, by official borrowing by the central bank or other government agency. In 2000, foreign governments and central banks increased their holdings of gold, currencies, and other official assets in the United States by an estimated $46 billion, net. The U.S. government lost official reserve assets in the net amount of an estimated $1.6 billion in 2000. Most U.S. BOP deficits in recent years have financed themselves primarily, not through changes in official reserve assets, but through capital inflows from abroad, particularly purchases of U.S. stocks and bonds by foreign investors, and this preference of foreign governments and foreign private investors for U.S.

---

[2]The U.S. Department of Commerce defines *direct investment* as ownership of 10 percent or more of the voting stock or the exercise of other means of control over a foreign business enterprise by an individual or corporation. Ownership of less than 10 percent of a foreign firm's stock is referred to as *portfolio investment*.

Financial Developments   U.S. Trade Deficits—
A Problem That Never Seems To Quit

When the U.S. economy teetered on the brink of a recession in 2000 and 2001, good news, at long last, seemed about to walk in the door. After years of pushing along at high levels, the American trade deficit—total U.S. exports less imports with imports in the U.S. usually outstripping its exports—began to fall. True, the trade deficit remained high—for example, in May 2001 American imports of goods and services outdistanced American exports by more than $28 billion— but the figures still looked much better than they had in earlier years.

Where has most of the persistent U.S. trade deficit come from? Mainly from trade with China, Canada, Japan, Western Europe, and Mexico. In these areas of the world the United States, since the 1950s, has been running larger and larger deficits of foreign imports relative to U.S. exports. Indeed, the U.S. trade deficit with China may grow now that China has been admitted to the World Trade Organization (WTO) and has normalized trade relations with the U.S., lowering most of the tariffs it previously faced in international markets.

These historic trade deficits appear to be caused by several factors. The huge size and leadership role of the United States have served to make the dollar the most sought-after currency in the world. The result is a huge build-up of dollar claims against U.S. assets held abroad. At the same time the long-term strength of the American economy has raised the demands of Americans for foreign goods and services, resulting in the rapid growth of U.S. imports. Among the most dramatic examples are foreign automobiles, which American families have increasingly preferred over domestic autos for their reliability and fuel efficiency.

U.S. trade deficits seem to be a virtually permanent feature of the American economy. They seem to be, in part, the consequence of economic and political leadership by the United States vis-à-vis the rest of the world. And these deficits represent a real challenge to U.S. policymakers, who must weigh them against important domestic goals, like avoidance of inflation and protecting jobs.

securities increased sharply over the past decade as the U.S. economy, despite a significant slowdown, looked strong compared to many weaker economies abroad.

Disequilibrium in the Balance of Payments

For an exploration of some of the key issues surrounding balance-of-payments deficits see, for example, The International Monetary Fund at *www.imf.org* and the Hoover Institute for Public Policy Inquiry at *www.imfsite.org*

For several years now, the United States has displayed a *disequilibrium* position in its balance of payments. This means that the nation has relied on foreign credit, foreign capital inflows into the U.S., and its stock of gold, foreign currencies, and other reserve assets to settle U.S. BOP deficits. However, the amount of these financial devices is limited—no nation can go on indefinitely accumulating BOP deficits, borrowing abroad, and using up its reserves. Moreover, relying on foreign capital inflows is dangerous, because the perceptions of foreign investors regarding the desirability of placing funds in the United States may change abruptly.

To this point, foreign central banks and foreign investors have regarded U.S. securities and dollar-denominated deposits as good investments and have been willing to extend an increasing volume of international credit to the United States. At some point, however, foreign governments and private investors *may* become satiated with dollar claims; at this point, the value of the U.S. dollar will tend to decline in international markets. U.S. purchases of goods and services abroad would also decline because of the dollar's reduced buying power. The nation's standard of living would tend to fall until equilibrium in its balance-of-payments position is restored.

One factor that gives hope for the future lies in the capital account, in which growing investment by foreigners in the United States has helped to offset outflows of capital funds from U.S. investors. In most of the years over the past several decades, capital inflows into the United States have grown faster than U.S. investments abroad, making the United States the world's largest debtor nation. A major factor boosting foreign investment in the United States is the desire to avoid U.S. import restrictions by developing production facilities inside the United States (as many foreign automobile and electronics manufacturers have recently done, for example). Even more significant is the political stability of the United States, offering an attractive haven for international investors concerned about instability abroad. If this capital inflow continues in the future, it will do much to alleviate the future international payments problems of the United States.

Questions *to Help You Study*

1. Please explain what is meant by the term *balance of payments*. Describe and list the principal components of a nation's balance-of-payments accounts.

2. Please supply a brief definition of each of the following terms associated with the balance of payments accounts:

   Current account

   Merchandise trade balance

   Service transactions

   Official reserve assets

   Capital account

3. Please describe and then discuss the major trends that have occurred in the following segments of the United States' balance-of-payments accounts in recent years:

   Merchandise trade balance

   Investments in overseas assets by U.S. residents

   Investments in United States assets by foreign residents.

4. When is a *balance-of-payments* deficit potentially a "bad" sign? In what sense can such deficits represent a "good" indicator?

THE PROBLEM OF DIFFERENT MONETARY UNITS IN INTERNATIONAL TRADE AND FINANCE

Businesses and individuals trading goods and services in international markets encounter a problem not experienced by those who buy and sell only in domestic markets. This is the problem of different monetary units used as the standard of value from country to country. Americans use the dollar as a medium of exchange and standard of value in domestic markets; the British and the European Community (EC) rely on the pound and the Euro, respectively, as their basic monetary unit. There are more than 100 different monetary units around the world. As a result, when goods and services are sold or capital flows across national boundaries, it is often necessary to sell one currency and buy another.

Unfortunately, the act of trading currencies entails substantial *risk*. Exporters and importers may be forced to purchase a foreign currency when its value is rising and the home country's currency is falling in value. Any profits earned on the sale of goods and services abroad may be outweighed by losses suffered in currency exchange. Differing monetary units also complicate government monetary policy aimed at curbing inflation and ensuring rapid economic growth. Repeatedly in recent years, massive flows of funds surged through foreign and domestic markets from speculative buying and selling of dollars, Euros, and other currencies. These speculative currency flows increased the problems associated with economic recovery and the control of inflation.

The Gold Standard

The problem of trading in different monetary units whose prices change frequently is one of the world's oldest financial problems. It has been dealt with in a wide variety of ways over the centuries. One of the most successful solutions prior to the modern era centered on *gold* as an international standard of value. During the seventeenth and eighteenth centuries, major trading nations in Western Europe made their currencies freely convertible into gold. Gold bullion could be exported and imported from one country to another without significant restriction, and each unit of currency was defined in terms of so many grains of fine gold. Nations adopting the **gold standard** agreed to exchange paper money or coins for gold bullion in unlimited amounts at predetermined prices.

One advantage of the gold standard was that it imposed a common standard of value for all national currencies. This brought a measure of stability to international trade and investment, dampened interest-rate fluctuations, and stimulated the expansion of commerce and investment abroad. A second advantage was economic discipline. Tying currencies to gold regulated the growth and stability of national economies. A nation experiencing severe inflation or excessively rapid growth in consumption of imported goods soon found itself losing gold reserves. Exports declined and unemployment rose. Eventually, the volume of imports was curtailed, and the outflow of gold slowed.

These advantages of stability and economic discipline were offset by a number of limitations inherent in the gold standard. For one thing, maintenance of that standard depended crucially on *free trade*. Nations desiring to protect their industries from foreign competition through export or import restrictions could not do so. Moreover, the growth of a nation's money supply was limited by the size of its gold stock. Problems of rising unemployment or lagging economic growth might call for rapid expansion of the domestic money supply. However, such a policy required a suspension of gold convertibility, taking the nation off the gold standard. Thus, the gold standard often conflicted with national economic goals and limited the policy alternatives open to governmental authorities.

The Gold Exchange Standard

Although government policymakers were mainly concerned about the effects of the gold standard on domestic economies, investors and commercial traders found that gold bullion was not a convenient medium of exchange. Gold is expensive to transport and risky to handle. Moreover, the world's gold supply was limited relative to the expanding volume of international trade. These problems gave rise in the nineteenth century to the **gold exchange standard**. Institutions actively engaged in international commerce began to hold stocks of convertible currencies. Each currency was freely convertible into gold at a fixed rate but also was freely convertible into other currencies at relatively stable prices. In practice, virtually all transactions took place in convertible currencies, and gold faded into the background as an international medium of exchange.

The gold exchange standard provided greater convenience for international traders and investors. However, this monetary standard possessed the same limitations as the original gold standard. National currencies were still tied to gold, and growth in world trade depended upon growth in the international gold stock. The gold exchange standard collapsed during the economic chaos of the worldwide Great Depression in the 1930s.

The Modified Exchange Standard

Dissatisfaction with international monetary systems tied exclusively to gold resulted in a search for a new payments system following World War II. In 1944, Western countries convened an international monetary conference in Bretton Woods, New Hampshire, to devise a stable money and payments system. The conference created a new mechanism for setting international payments—known as the Bretton Woods System, or **modified exchange standard**—and an agency for monitoring the exchange rate practices of member nations (known as the International Monetary Fund, or IMF, with headquarters in Washington, DC).

The IMF, which is headed by its Board of Governors with a representative from each member nation, establishes rules for settling international accounts between nations and grants short-term loans to member nations who lack sufficient international reserves to settle their BOP deficits. IMF balance-of-payments loans often are accompanied by strict requirements that a member nation receiving credit must adopt stern economic measures to curtail the growth of its imports and expand its sales abroad. The IMF's credit guarantee encourages banks and other nations to grant loans to a member nation in trouble. The funds loaned by the IMF come mainly from *quotas*, which each member nation must contribute in dollars or other reserve assets. A companion organization to the IMF, the *World Bank*, also created under the Bretton Woods Agreement, makes long-term loans to speed the economic development of member nations.

For further details on the important international services provided by the World Bank and the International Monetary Fund see *www.worldbank.org* and *www.imf.org*

The centerpiece of the Bretton Woods System was the linking of foreign currency prices to the U.S. dollar and to gold. The United States committed itself to buy and sell gold at $35 per ounce on request from foreign monetary authorities. Other IMF member nations pledged to keep their currency's price within 1 percent of its par value in terms of gold or the dollar. Central banks would use their foreign exchange reserves to buy or sell their own currency in the foreign exchange market. In practice, this usually meant that, if a foreign currency fell in value *below* par (the lower intervention point), a central bank would sell its holdings of dollars and buy that currency in the market, driving its price upward toward par. If the price of a nation's currency rose more than 1 percent *above* par (the upper intervention point), the central bank involved would sell its own currency and buy dollars, driving the currency's price down toward par. If a currency fell too far or rose too high, resulting in market disruption and threatening a massive loss of foreign exchange reserves, the country involved would simply revalue its currency, establishing a new par value relative to gold or the dollar.

Fundamentally, the success of the Bretton Woods System depended on the ability of the United States to maintain confidence in the U.S. dollar and protect its value. One of the weaknesses of the new system was that the U.S. dollar was in short supply early in the postwar period, though the system worked well at first because the dollar was the most stable monetary medium around. Later, however, the United States began to export large amounts of capital to Western Europe, Asia, and Central and South America. The result was sizable U.S. trade deficits that were dealt with by drains on the U.S. gold stock and by a buildup of dollar holdings abroad—an indication of fundamental problems developing in the U.S. economy. Foreign governments and investors began to lose confidence in the ability of U.S. policymakers to control the U.S. economy and subdue inflation.

Adoption of the Managed Floating Currency Standard

Inflation and other economic problems ultimately forced the abandonment of the Bretton Woods System during the 1970s. The first step in dismantling the old system was taken by the administration of President Richard M. Nixon in August 1971, when the U.S. dollar was devalued and the convertibility of foreign official holdings of dollars into gold suspended. Gold ceased to be an international monetary medium; it is traded today only as a commodity. Soon, the largest IMF member nations were allowing their currencies to *float* in value, responding freely to demand and supply forces in the marketplace.

In 1978, a new international payments system—the **managed floating currency standard**—was adopted by member nations of the IMF. Known as the Second Amendment to the International Monetary Fund's Articles of Agreement, the official rules under which today's international money system is supposed to operate allow *each nation to choose its own exchange rate policy, consistent with the structure of its economy and its goals*. There are, however, three principles that each member country must follow in establishing its exchange rate policy:

1. When a nation intervenes in the foreign exchange markets to protect its own currency, it must take into account the interests and welfare of other IMF member countries.

2. Government intervention in the foreign exchange markets should be carried out only to correct disorderly conditions that are essentially short term in nature.

3. No member nation should intervene in the exchange markets in order to gain an unfair competitive advantage over other nations or to prevent necessary adjustments in a nation's balance of payments (BOP) position.

Nations that attempt to keep the exchange value of their currencies within a fixed range around the value of some other currency or basket of currencies are known as *peggers*. The majority of pegging nations are developing countries that have strong commercial links with one or more industrialized trading partners. (Examples include Korea, Guatemala, Hong Kong, and Venezuela, which relate the exchange rate on their currencies to the U.S. dollar.) Frequently, when a developing country has strong trade relations with more than one industrialized nation, it uses a basket (group) of major currencies to set the value of its own monetary unit in order to "average out" fluctuations in the value of its exports and imports.

A few nations peg their currency's exchange rate to a basket of currencies assembled by the International Monetary Fund, known as **special drawing rights (SDRs)**. The SDR is an official monetary reserve unit designed to settle international claims arising from transactions between the IMF, governments of member nations, central banks, and various international agencies. SDRs are really "book entries" on the ledgers of the IMF, sometimes referred to as *paper gold*. Periodically, that organization issues new SDRs and credits them to the international reserve accounts of member nations based on each nation's IMF quota (contributions of currency and reserve assets to the IMF). To spend its SDRs, a nation requests the IMF to transfer some amount of SDRs from its own reserve account to the reserve account of another nation. In return, the country asking for the transfer gets deposit balances denominated in the currency of the nation receiving the SDRs. These deposit balances may then be used to make international payments. The value of SDRs today is based on a basket of currencies representing the five IMF member nations with the largest volume of exports. These five countries are the United States, Germany, France, Japan, and the United Kingdom. U.S. SDRs are sold by the Treasury to the Federal Reserve.

Most of the developed nations *float*, rather than peg, their currencies. This means that the value of any particular currency is determined by demand and supply forces operating in the marketplace. Usually, a **managed float** is used, in which governments intervene on occasion to stabilize the value of their home currency. The United States has officially adopted a managed float policy, but in practice it often follows a "free" floating exchange rate policy, in which the open market determines the value of the dollar, with U.S. monetary authorities intervening only in emergencies. Most recently the United States has relied heavily on the strength of its economy to achieve a strong value of the dollar.

In theory at least, a system of floating currency values should help the United States and other nations experiencing BOP deficits today. For example, if Americans are importing more goods from abroad than they are able to sell to overseas customers, an excess supply of U.S. dollars should build up abroad. The result should be a decline in the dollar's market value vis-à-vis other world currencies, making U.S. exports cheaper and foreign goods sold in the United States relatively more expensive. Ultimately, U.S. exports and imports should become more evenly balanced.

Questions *to Help You Study*

5. Please explain the meaning of *currency risk*. How does currency risk affect exporters, importers, and investors active in the international financial marketplace?

6. Why was the *gold standard* developed? What problems did it appear to solve and what problems did it create? What exactly is the difference between the gold standard and the gold exchange standard?

7. When and where was the so-called *modified exchange standard* created? Explain how this particular monetary system worked in order to stabilize the value of different foreign currencies.

8. The international monetary system we have today has often been labeled the *floating currency standard.* Briefly explain what this term means in today's world. Can you anticipate any problems that might emerge with this standard for handling currency values and currency risk?

9. What exactly are *SDRs* and what are they for?

10. Why do you think the U.S. dollar is such an important currency within the international financial system? Is the dollar's importance around the globe a matter of history, resources, economic strength, cultural values, or what?

DETERMINING FOREIGN CURRENCY VALUES IN TODAY'S MARKETS

As we saw in the preceding section, major international currencies have floated with relative freedom since the 1970s and into the twenty-first century, their values dependent primarily on demand and supply forces in the marketplace. With this newfound freedom for currency prices and the expansion of world commerce, the volume of currency trading and the number of financial institutions participating in that trading have exploded. This is especially evident in the London and New York money markets, where exchange brokers bring in trading orders from financial institutions worldwide.

However, as the international financial system has moved increasingly toward freely floating exchange rates, currency prices have become significantly more *volatile.* The risks of buying and selling currencies have increased markedly in recent years. Moreover, fluctuations in the prices of foreign currencies affect domestic economic conditions, international investment, and the success or failure of government economic policies. Governments, businesses, and individuals find that it is more important today than ever before to understand how foreign currencies are traded and what affects their relative values.

Consider the problem faced by a corporation headquartered in the United States and selling machinery overseas. This firm frequently negotiates sales contracts with a foreign importer months before the machines are shipped. In the meantime, the value of the foreign currency the U.S. company expects to receive in payment for its products may have declined precipitously, canceling out expected profits. Similarly, a U.S. importer bringing fine wines into domestic U.S. markets frequently must pay for incoming shipments in the currency demanded by a foreign exporter. The U.S. importer's profits could be significantly reduced if the value of the dollar declined relative to the values of foreign currencies used by the importer to pay for goods purchased abroad. The same problems confront investors in foreign securities who find that attractive interest rates available overseas must be protected from an erosion in value through suitable purchases and sales of foreign currencies. Knowledge of the foreign exchange markets is the *first step* toward successful international business and economic policy.

Essential Features of the Foreign Exchange Market

The **foreign exchange markets** are among the largest markets in the world, with annual trading volume in the neighborhood of $300 trillion. The purpose of the foreign exchange markets is to bring buyers and sellers of currencies together. It is an *over-the-counter market*, with no central trading location and no set hours of trading. Prices and other terms of trade are determined by negotiation using computer screens linked by electronic wire all over the world. The foreign exchange market is *informal* in its operations; there are no special requirements for market participants, and trading conforms to an unwritten code of rules.

Exchange Rate Quotations

The prices of foreign currencies expressed in terms of other currencies are called **foreign exchange rates**. There are three major markets for foreign exchange: (1) the **spot market**, which deals in currency for immediate delivery; (2) the **forward market**, which involves the future delivery of foreign currency; and (3) the **currency futures and options market**, which deals in contracts to hedge against future changes in foreign exchange rates. Immediate delivery is defined as one or two business days for most transactions. Future delivery typically means one, three, or six months from today.

Exhibit 25–3 cites some recent foreign exchange rates between the U.S. dollar and other major currencies. The exhibit shows, for example, that an American importer or investor could obtain pounds sterling (£) that could be used to buy British bonds or British goods and services at a cost of about $1.45 per pound ($1.45/£) in February 2001. Conversely, a British investor or importer seeking to make purchases in the United States would have to pay 0.6897 pounds($1/1.65 or 0.6897/$) for each dollar needed. Clearly, the exchange rate between dollars and pounds is the *reciprocal* of the exchange rate between pounds and dollars, which is true as well for any other pair of currencies. Exhibit 25–4 illustrates the commonly accepted procedures for calculating exchange rates.[3]

Dealers and brokers in foreign exchange actually post not one, but *two*, exchange rates for each pair of currencies. That is, each trader sets a *bid* (buy) price and an *asked* (sell) price. For example, the dealer department in a New York bank might post a bid price for pounds sterling of £ = $1.45US (or $1.45/£) and an asked price of £ = $1.48US (or $1.48/£). This means that the dealer is willing to buy sterling at $1.45 per pound and sell it at $1.48. These two exchange rates are sometimes referred to as "double-barreled"

---

[3]We note that in each quotation of a foreign exchange rate, one currency always serves as a unit of account (unit of value) and the other currency functions as the unit for which a price is stated. For example a quote of $1.45/£ tells us that one British pound costs $1.45. In this instance, the dollar serves as the unit of account, and the currency whose price is quoted is the pound. It is customary to place the symbol for the currency serving as the unit of account (in this case, $) in front of the stated number and the symbol of the currency whose price is being quoted (in this case, £) following the number.

EXHIBIT 25–3
Recent Foreign
Exchange Rates: The
U.S. Dollar vs. Other
Key Currencies
(Figures Are
Currency Units per
U.S. Dollar Except
as Noted)

Source: Board of Governors of
the Federal Reserve System.

Country/Currency Unit	2001 Exchange Rate with U.S. Dollars ($)*	Country/Currency Unit	2001 Exchange Rate with U.S. Dollars ($)*
Canada/dollar	1.5216	Hong Kong/dollar	7.7999
China P.R./yuan	8.2771	Japan/yen	116.23
Australian/dollar	53.38**	United Kingdom/pound	145.25**
Switzerland/franc	1.6686	European Community/Euro	0.9205

*Exchange rates are averages for February 2001.
**Exchange rate expressed in U.S. cents per currency unit.

Data on current and
forecasted foreign
exchange rates
(FOREX) may be found
in such sources as *www.
forexnewsletters.com/*
and *www.fxstreet.com*

quotations. The dealer makes a profit on the *spread* between the bid and asked price, although that spread is normally very small.[4]

Dealers in the foreign exchange market continually watch exchange rate quotations in order to take advantage of any *arbitrage* opportunities. Arbitrage in this case refers to the purchase of one currency in a certain market and the sale of that currency in another market in response to the price difference between the two markets. The force of arbitrage generally keeps foreign exchange rates from getting too far out of line in different areas around the globe.

Factors Affecting Foreign Exchange Rates

The exchange rate for any foreign currency depends on a multitude of factors reflecting economic and financial conditions in the country issuing the currency. One of the most important factors is the status of a nation's *balance-of-payments position*. When a country experiences a deficit in its balance of payments, it becomes a net demander of foreign currencies and is forced to sell substantial amounts of its own currency to pay for imports of goods and services. Therefore, balance-of-payments deficits often lead to price depreciation of a nation's currency relative to the prices of other currencies.

Exchange rates also are profoundly affected by *speculation over future currency values*. Dealers in foreign exchange monitor the currency markets daily, looking for profitable trading opportunities. A currency viewed as temporarily undervalued quickly brings forth buy orders, driving its price higher vis-à-vis other currencies. A currency considered to be overvalued is greeted by a rash of sell orders, depressing its price, as speculators move in.

The market for a national currency is also greatly influenced by *domestic political and economic conditions*. Wars, revolutions, inflation, recession, and labor strikes have all been observed to have adverse effects on the currency of a nation experiencing these problems. On the other hand, signs of rapid economic growth, rising stock and bond prices, and successful economic policies to control inflation and unemployment usually lead to a stronger currency in the exchange markets. Moreover, countries with higher real interest rates generally experience an increase in the exchange value of their currencies.

The theoretical link between each nation's currency value in the international markets and that nation's inflation rate is particularly interesting. The **purchasing power parity** theory argues that the exchange rate between two currencies will reflect differences in their countries' inflation rates. For example, if the annual inflation rate stands at 4 percent in the

[4]Dealers will usually quote the bid price first and the asked price second and, as a rule, only the last digits in the price will be quoted to the buyer or seller. Thus, the spot bid and asked rates on pounds might be quoted by a currency dealer as 95/98 because it is assumed the customer is aware of current exchange rates and knows that the bid price being quoted is $1.4595/£ and the asked price is $1.4598/£.

EXHIBIT 25–4
How to Calculate Foreign Exchange Rates

Source: Based on a similar exhibit developed originally by the Public Information Center of the Federal Reserve Bank of Chicago.

Exchange Rate Conversion

Suppose the exchange rate between the European Community's new currency unit, the Euro, and the U.S. dollar ($) is: Euro/$ = 1.5000 or Euro 1.50/$. What, then, is the $/Euro exchange rate?
Answer: 1 ÷ 1.500 = $0.6667/Euro

Exchange Rate Appreciation

Suppose the exchange rate between Euros and the U.S. dollar rises from Euro/$ = 1.000, or Euro 1.00/$, to Euro 1.50/$. How much has the U.S. dollar appreciated in percent?
Answer: 1.500 ÷ 1.000 = 0.50, or 50%

Suppose the Euro–U.S. dollar exchange rate is Euro/$ = 1.5000, or Euro 1.50/$. If the dollar appreciates by 3 percent, what is the new Euro–U.S. dollar exchange rate?
Answer: 1.5000 × 1.03 = 1.5450, or Euro 1.545/$

Exchange Rate Depreciation

Suppose the exchange rate between Euros and U.S. dollars rises from Euro/$ = 1.000 to Euro/$ = 1.500. How much has the Euro depreciated, in percent?
Answer: Note that the $/Euro exchange rate has changed from 1 ÷ 1.000 = $1.00/Euro to 1 ÷ 1.500 = $0.6667/Euro. The ratio of these two exchange rates is 0.6667 ÷ 1.000, or 0.6667. Then, 1 − 0.6667 = 0.3333. Therefore, an exchange rate depreciation of one-third has occurred.

Suppose the Euro–U.S. dollar exchange rate is Euro/$ = 1.50, or Euro 1.50/$, and thus the dollar–Euro exchange rate is $0.6667/Euro. If the Euro depreciates 5 percent, what is the new Euro–U.S. dollar exchange rate?
Answer: Because 0.6667 × 0.95 = 0.6334, the new exchange rate is 1 ÷ 0.6334 = 1.5788, or Euro $1.5788/$

Suppose, once again, the Euro–U.S. dollar exchange rate is Euro/$ = 1.5000. If the U.S. dollar depreciates 5 percent, what is the new Euro–U.S. dollar exchange rate?
Answer: 1.5000 × 0.95 = 1.4250, or Euro 1.4250/$

Cross-Exchange Rates

Suppose the Euro–U.S. dollar exchange rate is Euro/$ = 1.5000, or Euro 1.5000/$, and the Japanese yen (¥)–U.S. dollar exchange rate is 1.000, or ¥1.000/$. What, then, is the yen/Euro exchange rate?
Answer: 1.000 ÷ 1.500 = 0.6667, or ¥0.6667/Euro

Suppose the Euro–U.S. dollar exchange rate is Euro/$ = 1.500, or Euro 1.500/$, and the U.S. dollar–Japanese yen exchange rate is $/¥ = 1.000, or 1.00/¥. What, then, is the Euro/¥ exchange rate?
Answer: 1.500 ÷ (1 + 1.000) = 0.75, or Euro 0.75/¥.

United States and only 1 percent in Great Britain, the value of the U.S. dollar will fall by about 3 percent on an annual basis relative to the value of the pound, reflecting relatively cheaper British goods. Of course, other factors may intervene to upset this expected relationship.

Overshadowing the currency markets today is the ever-present possibility of *central bank intervention*. Major central banks around the world, including the Federal Reserve System in the United States, the Bank of Japan and the European Central Bank (ECB) representing the whole European Community, may decide on a given day that their national or

To learn more about the European Central Bank and the Euro see such sites as *www.ecb.int*, *www.euro.gov.uk/*, and *www.ecuactivities.be/*

regional currency is declining too rapidly in value relative to other key currencies. Thus, if the dollar falls precipitously against the Euro, support operations by the Federal Reserve System in the form of heavy sales of Euros and corresponding purchases of dollars may be employed to stabilize the currency markets. Usually, central bank intervention is temporary, designed to promote a smooth adjustment in currency values toward a new equilibrium level rather than to permanently prop up a weak currency. The reason is that, no matter how important central banks are, their resources compared to the resources of the whole foreign-exchange market are small—okay for making short-run adjustments, but not likely to be effective over a sustained period of time.

In the United States, the Treasury Department is the agency designated to pursue market intervention in order to protect the U.S. dollar in international markets. The Treasury must decide what to do about the value of the dollar, but it is usually the Federal Reserve System that carries out the buying and selling of currencies on the Treasury's behalf through the foreign exchange desk at the Federal Reserve Bank of New York. The Fed also buys large amounts of currencies for foreign central banks and government agencies abroad. We must keep in mind that central bank intervention affects not only relative currency values but also the reserves held by private banks and the money supply. This happens because the central bank generally pays for its purchases of currency by increasing the deposit balances of private banks participating in the transaction with it. Thus, a decision by a central bank to intervene in the foreign currency markets will have *both* currency market and money supply effects unless an operation known as **currency sterilization** is carried out. For example, any increase in reserves and deposits that results from a central bank currency purchase can be "sterilized" by using monetary policy tools that absorb reserves and deposits from the banking system.

Supply and Demand for Foreign Exchange

The factors influencing a currency's rate of exchange with other currencies may be expressed in terms of the market forces of demand and supply. Exhibit 25–5, for example, illustrates a demand curve and a supply curve for dollars ($) in terms of British pounds (£). Note that the demand curve for dollars is also labeled the supply curve for pounds. This is due to the fact that an individual or institution holding pounds and demanding dollars would be supplying pounds to the foreign exchange market. Similarly, the supply curve for dollars is identical to the demand curve for pounds because someone holding dollars and demanding pounds must supply dollars to the foreign currency markets in order to purchase pounds. We recall, too, that the price of dollars in terms of pounds is the reciprocal of the price of pounds in terms of dollars.

To illustrate how demand and supply forces operate in the foreign exchange markets, suppose the current exchange rate between dollars and pounds is £ = $1.65. To purchase dollars, we have to pay 0.6061 pounds per dollar; to purchase pounds costs us $1.65 per pound. This exchange rate between dollars and pounds is set in exchange markets by the interaction of the supply and demand for each currency. Exhibit 25–5 indicates that, at an exchange rate of 0.6061 pounds, the quantity of dollars supplied (*S*) is exactly equal to the quantity of dollars demanded (*D*).

If the price of dollars in terms of pounds were to fall temporarily *below* this exchange rate, more dollars would be demanded than supplied. Some buyers needing dollars would bid up the exchange rate toward the point where the demand for and supply of dollars were perfectly in balance. On the other hand, if the price of dollars were temporarily *above* 0.6061 pounds, more dollars would be supplied to the exchange markets. The price of dollars in terms of pounds would fall as suppliers of dollars willingly accepted a lower exchange rate to dispose of their excess dollar holdings. Only at that point where the

EXHIBIT 25–5
Demand and Supply of U.S. Dollars in Terms of British Pounds

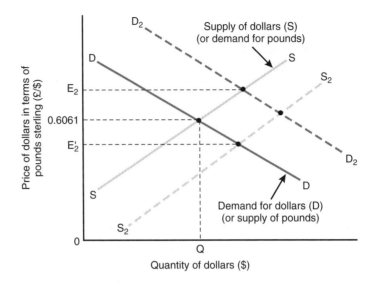

exchange rate stood at 0.6061 pounds per dollar would quantity supplied equal quantity of dollars demanded. Only at that point would there be no reason for future changes in the exchange rate between the dollar and the pound unless changes occurred in the demand for or supply of either currency.

As we noted earlier, a number of factors affect the exchange rates between currencies, including a nation's balance-of-payments position, domestic political and economic developments, and central bank intervention. Each of these factors leads to a shift in the demand for or supply of one currency vis-à-vis another, which brings about a change in their relative rates of exchange.

To illustrate the impact of shifts in currency demand and supply, suppose that consumers in Great Britain increase their demand for U.S. goods and services. As Exhibit 25–5 indicates, the demand curve for dollars would increase from D to D_2.

This is equivalent to an increase in the supply of pounds seeking dollars. The equilibrium cost of dollars in terms of pounds, therefore, will rise to E_2. British importers will be forced to surrender a greater quantity of pounds per dollar in order to satisfy the demands of British consumers for U.S. goods and services. Other things being equal, the prices of imported goods from the United States will tend to rise.

The opposite effects would occur if U.S. consumers demanded a larger quantity of British goods and services. In this case, the supply-of-dollars (demand-for-pounds) curve slides downward and to the right from S to S_2, as shown in Exhibit 25–5. Reflecting the increased demand for pounds and associated sales of dollars for pounds by U.S. importers, the dollar's price in pounds sterling falls to E'_2. The market prices of British goods and services imported into the United States tend to rise.

What happens if a central bank, such as the Bank of England, European Central Bank, or the Federal Reserve, intervenes to stabilize the dollar-pound exchange rate at some arbitrary target level? The answer depends, among other things, on which side of the market the central bank intervenes, which currency is used as the vehicle for intervention, and the particular exchange-rate target chosen. For example, suppose that increased British demand for U.S. goods and services had driven the dollar-pound exchange rate up to E_1 as shown in Exhibit 25–6. However, this upward surge in the dollar's value had sharply reduced the purchasing power of the pound for dollar-denominated goods and services and threatened to have damaging effects on British foreign trade and industrial output. The Bank of England might intervene to force the dollar-pound exchange rate down to E_2 by selling

One interesting financial institution playing a growing role in the expansion of the European Community (EC) and the Euro is the European Bank for Reconstruction and Development at *www.ebrd.com*

International Focus   Watch Out for the Tumbling Euro!

On January 1, 1999 the Euro—the single unit of currency adopted by 12 of the 15 nations forming the European Community (EC)—was introduced to the world. While Euro currency was not issued to the general public until 2002, deposits and other financial instruments denominated in Euros were traded across the European landscape before the new century began.

When the 2002 deadline for converting the old European national currencies into Euros (mainly through banks and stores) arrived, French citizens, for example, traded 6.55 francs for a Euro, while Germans paid 1.95 marks to acquire one Euro. In Italy a Euro exchanged for just over 1936 lire, while Irish citizens traded 0.78 pounds per Euro currency unit and Greeks shelled out 340 drachmas for a Euro. Exchanges of Euros to replace old national currencies also took place in Belgium, Finland, Luxembourg, the Netherlands, Portugal, and Spain in January and February of 2002. The benefits of this currency switch for businesses and households in Europe include lower prices due to greater competition, the elimination of currency risk inside Europe, and easier access to the financial markets to borrow money and merge businesses.

While many market analysts thought the Euro might trade close to one-for-one with the U.S. dollar, this guess turned out to be wrong! Many observers believed, at least initially, that the Euro would challenge the U.S. dollar for global leadership as an international reserve currency. Thus far, this has not happened. Indeed, the U.S. dollar still accounts for about three-fifths of all official currency holdings worldwide.

While the introduction of the Euro as a currency may eventually change all this, the Euro proved to be something of a disappointment to many international investors. As soon as trading began the Euro began to fall against the U.S. dollar, threatening the European community with increased inflation, higher interest rates, and a weaker economy.

Why did the value of the Euro fall against the dollar in international markets, at least during its earliest period of international trading? Several factors seem to have been at work. For example, several European economies weakened shortly after the Euro appeared, particularly Germany. Inflation began to gather momentum, worrying many international investors who sold their Euros and purchased dollars instead.

There was also some lack of confidence in the European Central Bank, the ECB, which didn't appear, at least initially, to be interested in establishing for itself a strong international leadership position. Instead, the Federal Reserve System—the U.S. central bank—has held onto its preeminent position as the leading central bank in the world. Moreover, as the Euro initially fell in value relative to the U.S. dollar, its holders experienced capital losses on many of their European assets and began to sell out, pushing the Euro's value down further.

Thus, the Euro did not experience an auspicious beginning on the world stage, though it clearly may as time unfolds and as the United States, its chief competitor, struggles to come to grips with a more slowly growing economy and recent terrorist attacks. The future may be brighter for Europe's Euro if the EC nations work to pull together and European policymakers gain greater experience in managing their combined economies. Certainly there is great potential in the EC which has a population of about 300 million people, more than in the United States.

EXHIBIT 25–6
Effects of Central Bank Intervention to Stabilize the Dollar-Pound Exchange Rate

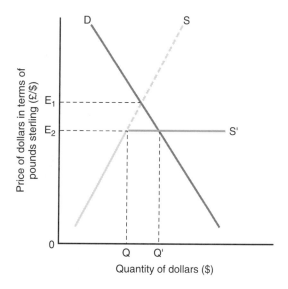

dollars out of its currency reserve and demanding pounds in the foreign exchange market. In effect, the supply-of-dollars curve would be "kinked" at the stabilization price, E_2. In order to peg the dollar-pound exchange rate at E_2, the central bank would have to spend $Q' - Q$ of its dollar reserves. Otherwise, the price of dollars would again rise toward E_1—the level dictated by demand and supply forces in the exchange markets. Conversely, if the dollar were falling to unacceptably low levels against the pound, the Bank of England or the Federal Reserve System might enter on the opposite side of the market, purchasing dollars with pounds and driving the dollar's price higher.

THE FORWARD MARKET FOR CURRENCIES

Knowledge of how the foreign exchange markets work and the ways in which currency risk can be reduced is indispensable for business managers today. Of course, the problem of fluctuating currency values is not so serious if payment for foreign goods, services, or securities must be made right away. Spot market prices of foreign currencies normally change by small amounts each day. However, if payment must be made weeks or months in the future, there is considerable uncertainty as to what the spot currency rate will be on any given future date. When substantial sums of money are involved, the rational investor or commercial trader will try to *guarantee* the future price at which currency can be purchased. This is the function of the *forward exchange market*.

Methods of Quoting Forward Exchange Rates

Trading in the spot exchange market results in agreements to deliver a specified amount of foreign currency at an agreed-upon price, usually within one or two business days and sometimes on the same day. In contrast, a **forward contract** is an agreement to deliver a specified amount of foreign currency at a set price on some future date (usually within 1, 2, 3, 6, or 12 months). The actual delivery date is referred to by traders as the *value date*. In the event customers do not know when they will need foreign currency, an *option forward contract* may be used, which gives its holder the right but not the obligation to take delivery of foreign currency in the future.

There are several different ways of measuring and quoting forward exchange rates. Suppose the spot exchange rate on Euros (€) is \$1.16US and that dealers in foreign exchange are selling forward contracts for delivery of Euros in six months at \$1.14US. We may express the *forward* exchange rate for Euros simply as \$1.14US, or \$1.14/Euro—known as the *outright* rate.

Another popular method is to express the forward rate as a premium or discount from the spot rate, known as the *swap rate*. In the example above, Euros are selling at a 2 cent *discount* in the forward market. Traders in the forward market appear to be signaling an expectation that the Euro will fall in value over the next few weeks.

We may also express forward exchange rates in terms of an annualized percentage rate above or below the current spot price. To use the example above, \$/€ spot = 1.16 and \$/€ forward = \$1.14. Then, the discount on forward Euros (€) for delivery in six months is figured as follows:

$$\frac{\text{Forward rate} - \text{Spot rate}}{\text{Spot rate}} \times \frac{12}{\text{Number of months forward}} \times 100 \qquad \textbf{(25–1)}$$

$$= \frac{1.14 - 1.16}{1.16} \times \frac{12}{6} \times 100$$

$$= -.02 \times 2 \times 100$$

$$= -4\%$$

Euros are selling at 4 percent *discount* from spot in the forward market. Because Euros are selling at a discount from their spot price, forward dollars must be selling at a *premium* over spot.

Suppose we know the current spot rate between two currencies and the forward premium or discount. We want to know the actual forward exchange rate. What formula should be used? The following will suffice:

$$\text{Spot rate} + \frac{\text{Spot rate} \times [\text{Premium} (+) \text{ or discount} (-) \text{ expressed as an annual rate}] \times \text{Number of months forward}}{100 \times \text{Number of months in a year}}$$

Suppose the \$/€ spot = 1.16 and forward Euros for delivery in three months are selling at a 4 percent premium over spot. Using the formula above, we have:

$$1.1600 + \frac{1.16 \times 4.0 \times 3}{1,200} = 1.1716\$/€ \text{ forward}$$

This means €/\$ forward is 0.8535, or €0.8535/\$.

FUNCTIONS OF THE FORWARD EXCHANGE MARKET

Contracts calling for the future delivery of currency are employed to cover a number of risks faced by investors and commercial traders. Some analysts group the functions of forward contracts into four categories: commercial covering, hedging an investment position, speculation, and covered interest arbitrage. These four uses of the forward market are discussed below.

Commercial Covering

The export or import of goods and services usually requires someone to deliver payment in a foreign currency or to receive payment in a foreign currency. Either the payor or payee, then, is subject to currency risk, because no one knows for sure what the spot price will be for a currency at the time payment must be made. The forward exchange market can be used as a buffer against currency risk.

To illustrate, suppose that a U.S. importer of cameras has agreed to pay 5,000 Euros to a German manufacturer upon receipt of a new shipment. The cameras are expected to arrive dockside in 30 days. The importer has no idea what 5,000 Euros will cost in U.S. dollars 30 days from now. To reduce the risk that the price of Euros in terms of dollars may rise significantly, the importer negotiates a forward contract with his or her bank for delivery of 5,000 Euros at \$1.16/€ in 30 days.

When payment is due, the importer takes delivery of the Euros (usually by acquiring ownership of a deposit denominated in Euros) at the agreed-upon price and pays the German manufacturer. Because the price is fixed in advance, the risk associated with fluctuations in foreign exchange rates has been eliminated. Today, export and import firms routinely cover their purchases overseas with forward currency contracts or other currency risk hedging tools (to be discussed later in this chapter).

Hedging an Investment Position

Thousands of U.S. corporations have invested in long-term capital projects overseas, building manufacturing plants, warehouse and dock facilities, and office buildings. In recent years, a large return flow of long-term investments by foreign firms in the United States has occurred due to the underlying strength of the U.S. economy and a desire to avoid U.S. tariffs. Of course, the market value of these foreign investments may change drastically as the price of a foreign currency changes over time.

To illustrate, suppose a U.S. commercial bank constructed an office building in downtown London. When completed, the office facility had an estimated market value of £2 million. The current spot rate on pounds is, let us say, $1.40/£. The bank values the new building on its consolidated financial statement, therefore, at $2.8 million. However, suppose the pound has declined rapidly in value in recent months. Some market analysts expect pounds to be selling at $1.20/£ in the near future. In the absence of a hedged position, the bank would take a loss of $400,000 on its building. This is due to the fact that, at an exchange rate of $1.20/£, the office building will have a value of only $2.4 million.

Can this loss be avoided or reduced? Yes, provided the bank can negotiate a sale of pounds *forward* at a higher price. For example, the bank may be able to arrange with a dealer for the sale of £2 million for future delivery at $1.30US ($1.30/£). When this forward contract matures, if the spot price has fallen to $1.20/£, the bank can buy pounds at this rate and deliver them to the dealer at $1.30US as agreed. The result is a profit on the foreign exchange transaction of $200,000, partially offsetting the loss on the building due to declining currency values.

Speculation on Future Currency Prices

A third use of the forward exchange market is speculative investment based on expectations concerning future movements in currency prices. Speculators will buy currency for future delivery if they believe the future spot rate will be *higher* on the delivery date than the current forward rate. They will sell currency under a forward contract if the future spot rate appears likely to be *below* the forward rate on the day of delivery. Such speculative purchases and sales carry the advantage of requiring little or no capital in advance of the delivery date. A speculator whose forecast of future spot rates turns out to be correct makes a profit on the spread between the purchase price and the sale price.

Covered Interest Arbitrage

One of the most common transactions in the international financial system arises when an investor discovers a higher interest rate available on foreign securities and invests funds abroad. When the currency risk associated with the purchase of foreign securities is reduced by using a forward contract, this transaction is often referred to as *covered interest arbitrage*.

To illustrate the interest arbitrage process, suppose that a British auto company is selling high-grade bonds with a promised annual yield of 12 percent. Comparable bonds in the United States offer a 10 percent annual return. The bonds are of good quality and there is probably little default risk, but there *is* currency risk in this transaction. The U.S. investor must purchase pounds in order to buy the British bonds. When the bonds earn interest or reach maturity, the issuing auto company will pay foreign and domestic investors in pounds sterling. Then the pounds must be converted into dollars to allow the U.S. investor to spend his or her earnings in the United States. If the spot price of sterling falls, the U.S. investor's net yield from the bonds will be reduced.

Specifically, although the investor expects a spread of 2 percent a year over U.S. interest rates by purchasing British bonds, if the spot rate on pounds declines by 2 percent (on an annual basis), the interest gain will be offset by the loss on trading pounds. Clearly, a series of forward contracts is needed to sell pounds at a guaranteed price as the bonds generate a stream of cash payments. In this case, the investor will probably purchase sterling spot in order to buy the bonds and sell sterling (pounds) forward to protect his or her expected income.

The Principle of Interest Rate Parity

The foregoing example suggests an important rule regarding international capital flows and foreign exchange rates: *The net rate of return to the investor from any foreign investment is equal to the interest earned plus or minus the forward premium or discount on the price of the foreign currency involved in the transaction.* The theory of forward exchange states that the forward discount or premium on one currency relative to another is directly related to the difference in interest rates between the two countries involved. More specifically, the currency of the nation experiencing higher interest rates normally sells at a forward *discount* in terms of the currency issued by the nation with lower interest rates. And the currency of the nation with relatively low interest rates normally sells at a *premium* forward relative to that of the high-rate country. A condition known as **interest rate parity** exists when *the interest rate differential between two nations is exactly equal to the forward discount or premium on their two currencies.* When parity exists, the currency markets are in equilibrium and capital funds do not flow from one country to another. This is due to the fact that the gain from investing abroad at higher interest rates is fully offset by the cost of covering currency risk in the forward exchange market.

To illustrate the principle of interest rate parity, suppose interest rates in a foreign country are 3 percent above those in the United States. Then the currency of that foreign nation, in equilibrium, is likely to sell at a 3 percent discount in the forward exchange market. Similarly, if interest rates are 1 percent lower abroad than in the United States, in equilibrium, the foreign currency of the nations involved is likely to sell at a 1 percent premium against the U.S. dollar. When such an equilibrium position is reached, movements of funds between nations, even with currency risk covered, do not generate excess returns relative to domestic investments of comparable risk. Capital funds tend to stay in the domestic market rather than flowing abroad.

It is when interest parity does *not* exist, even temporarily, that capital tends to flow across national boundaries in response to differences in domestic and foreign interest rates. For example, suppose that interest rates in a foreign nation are 3 percent above U.S. interest rates on securities of comparable quality and the foreign currency involved is selling at a 1 percent discount against the dollar in the forward exchange market. In this case, investing abroad with exchange risks covered yields the investor a *net* added return of 2 percent per year. Clearly, there is a positive incentive to invest overseas.

Is this situation likely to persist for a long period of time? No, because the movement of funds into a country offering higher interest rates tends to increase the forward discount on its currency and lowers the net rate of return to the investor. Other factors held constant, the flow of funds abroad will subside, and capital funds will tend to stay at home until further changes in currency prices and interest rates take place.

Questions *to Help You Study*

11. What are the principal factors affecting the value of any particular foreign currency in the international exchange markets?

12. Distinguish between the *spot* and *forward markets* for foreign currencies. Why is it necessary to have two markets rather than one?

13. Describe the principal uses of *forward exchange contracts* today. Please give an example of each use.

14. What exactly are the *advantages* of a hedged position in one or more foreign currencies? What about the *disadvantages* (if any)?

THE MARKET FOR FOREIGN CURRENCY FUTURES

Forward contracts call for the delivery of a specific currency on a specified date in the future at a set price. The intent of buyer and seller in a forward contract is to actually *deliver* the currency mentioned in the contract. In recent years, an important variation of the forward currency contract has developed—*foreign currency futures*. These, too, are contracts calling for the future delivery of a specific currency at a price agreed on today, *but there is usually no intent to actually deliver the currencies mentioned in the contracts.* Rather, *currency futures are traded in the majority of cases to reduce the risk associated with fluctuating currency prices.* Today, currency futures contracts are traded in the United States (for example, at the Chicago Mercantile Exchange) and in a number of other world financial centers on futures exchanges (unlike forward contracts, which are traded largely in an unregulated dealer market). The most popular currency futures contracts today are for the future delivery of British pounds, Japanese yen, Canadian and U.S. dollars, Eurodollars, and Euro currency units (€).

Currency futures are attractive to two groups: foreign exchange hedgers and foreign exchange speculators. The *hedgers*, who typically are banks, trading companies, and multinational corporations, seek to avoid damage to their profits from normal business transactions caused by unexpected changes in currency exchange rates. Usually, a hedging individual or institution seeks out a currency *speculator* who hopes to profit from changes in relative currency rates by taking on the risk the hedger seeks to minimize. Two basic transactions take place on currency futures exchanges: the buying hedge and the selling hedge.

The Buying Hedge

Importers of goods typically use the *buying hedge*. In this case, a domestic importer who is committed to pay in a foreign currency when goods are received from abroad fears that currency may rise in price. He therefore *purchases* a futures contract, agreeing to take delivery of pounds at a set price as near as possible to the date on which the goods must be paid for. Because the price of this contract is fixed, the importer has "locked in" the value of the imported goods, helping to protect his potential profit on the business transaction. As a final step, near the date the goods are paid for, the importer will "zero out" his futures contract purchase by *selling* a comparable currency futures contract, perhaps through a broker trading on the floor of a futures exchange. The exchange's clearinghouse, which records each transaction taking place on the exchange, will automatically cancel out the importer's obligation to take delivery of or to deliver foreign currency.

Additional information on the currency futures market is available from such Web sites as the Chicago Mercantile Exchange at *www.cme.com* and Business Jeeves at *www.businessjeeves.com*

How has the importer protected himself against loss due to currency risk? If a foreign currency rises in value during the life of a futures contract, the importer will experience reduced profits or increased losses on the imported goods themselves because the foreign currency has risen in value relative to his home currency. However, the market value of a currency futures contract also rises when the market value of the underlying currency increases. Therefore, the importer will be able to sell currency futures contracts at a higher price than the price for which they were originally purchased. The resulting profit in currency futures at least partially offsets the reduced gains or losses on the purchase of the imported goods. On the other hand, if currency values fall, potential profits on the imported goods will increase because they can be bought more cheaply, but an offsetting loss will be recorded in futures trading because the contracts must be sold at a lower price. Cash market gains (losses) offset futures market losses (gains).

The Selling Hedge

The opposite kind of hedge in currency futures is known as the *selling hedge*. This transaction is often employed by investors who purchase foreign securities and want to protect their earnings from a drop in currency values. In this instance, investors could hedge their expected earnings by *selling* futures contracts in the currency involved at the time the securities are acquired in the cash (spot) market. If contracts are sold in an amount that covers both principal and interest or dividends, investors have "locked in" their investment return regardless of which way exchange rates go. If the foreign currency involved has declined in price relative to the home currency when the security pays out cash or must be sold, a loss will be incurred in cash received, but investors will earn an offsetting futures market profit by *buying* futures contracts in an amount equivalent to those sold earlier. Conversely, if the foreign currency appreciates relative to the home currency, cash market revenues from the security will rise when the foreign currency is converted to home money, offsetting a loss from buying back futures contracts that now cost more.

OTHER INNOVATIVE METHODS FOR DEALING WITH CURRENCY RISK

The recent volatility of foreign exchange rates has given rise to an ever-widening circle of devices to deal with currency risk. For example, the *currency option* gives a buyer the right, though not the obligation, to either deliver or take delivery of a designated currency at a set price any time before the option expires. Thus, unlike the forward market, actual delivery *may* not occur, but unlike futures trading, no follow-up purchases or sales are needed to stop delivery. The advantage of the currency option is that it limits downside risk but not upside profits.

A related hedging instrument is the *option on currency futures*. *Call options* on currency futures give the buyer a way to protect against rising exchange rates by buying from another investor a currency futures contract at a fixed price, thus locking in a desired currency delivery price. On the other hand, *puts* on currency futures give a hedger protection against falling exchange rates by giving him or her the right to sell currency futures at a fixed price, regardless of how market prices change. These options carry their own market price, which rises or falls based on the probability the futures option will actually be exercised by its buyer.

Another innovative device is the **currency swap**. In straight currency swaps, a company that has borrowed a foreign currency (such as yen) for a designated length of time immediately turns around and exchanges the yen for its home currency (say, dollars) with a counterparty. The counterparty may be a bank or other business firm with an exactly opposite situation, holding dollars but needing yen. As shown in Exhibit 25–7, when the loan comes due, the borrowing company reverses the transaction with the counterparty, swapping its home currency to get back the yen needed to pay off its foreign currency loan. In this case, there is no exposure to the risk of changing yen prices. The borrower has received an inflow of dollars at the beginning of the loan and experienced a dollar outflow when the loan is paid off. The currency swap has merely facilitated the borrower's ability to borrow dollars from foreign markets without currency risk. The advantage of currency swaps is

EXHIBIT 25–7
The Currency Swap:
Converting a Foreign
Currency-
Denominated Loan
into a Domestic
Currency Loan

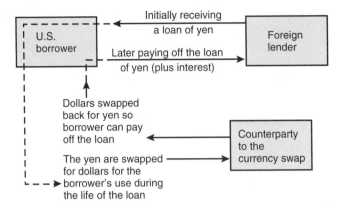

that they can be arranged with longer maturities and more suitable terms of settlement than most standard currency contracts. Central bank swaps help defend currency prices.

Innovative new approaches to currency risk continue to emerge each year, and many old methods have been resurrected lately. For example, many multinational firms have expanded their use of *local loans*—that is, securing credit inside the countries where they have sales or production operations. Others have resorted to issuing *dual-currency bonds* with principal and interest payments denominated in two different currencies. Some exporters now ship only if *prepayments* are made by a customer overseas that cover all or a substantial portion of the value of a shipment before it is made. Some companies simply *barter* (exchange) their goods or property directly so that no currency changes hands. *Selective currency pricing* is also employed, in which the seller invoices the buyer in a currency thought to be more stable or easier to hedge.

The ultimate economic response when other risk-reducing methods appear to be too costly or too risky is for a seller to use *risk-adjusted pricing* of goods and services traded across international boundaries. For example, goods sold to countries where currency risk is unacceptably high may be priced higher to compensate the seller for that added risk. Ultimately, individuals living in those countries where currency risk is unusually high will wind up paying higher prices for goods and services and, possibly, face a lower standard of living. Currency risk, like any other form of risk in the financial system, has real consequences for the economic welfare of individuals, businesses, and nations.

GOVERNMENT INTERVENTION IN THE FOREIGN EXCHANGE MARKETS

The value of a nation's currency in the international markets has long been a source of concern to governments around the world. National pride plays a significant role in this case, because a strong currency, avidly sought by traders and investors in the international marketplace, implies a vigorous and well-managed economy at home. A strong and stable currency encourages investment in the home country, stimulating its economic development. Moreover, changes in currency values affect a nation's balance-of-payments position. A weak and declining currency makes foreign imports more expensive, lowering the standard of living at home. And a nation whose currency is not well regarded in the international marketplace will have difficulty selling its goods and services abroad, giving rise to unemployment at home.

The United States has pursued an "on-again, off-again" policy of supporting the dollar in international markets over the years, sometimes supporting the dollar vigorously and at

International Focus   The Trend toward Dollarization

Seeking more stable national currencies to attract more foreign investment, spur economic growth, and avoid currency crises like those that happened in Asia during the mid-1990s several countries—including Argentina, Ecuador, El Salvador, Hong Kong, and Guatemala—recently adopted *the U.S. dollar* as legal tender for their transactions.

This new form of currency policy is called "dollarizing" or forming a "currency union." It replaces a country's national currency with dollars. However, the traditional domestic currency may still circulate on the street (as in Guatemala, for example) and may not necessarily maintain a fixed parity (exchange ratio) against the dollar. A *currency board* is usually set up to make sure sufficient U.S. dollars are held in reserve to back the dollarizing nation's currency.

There is some evidence that "dollarizing" has helped to stimulate trade in the countries involved and has more closely integrated the financial system and the economy of dollarizing nations to the United States. One possible adverse consequence centers upon giving up some control of the home nation's domestic economic policy and being forced to let the United States shape that country's economic policies.

However, as Argentina discovered after a decade of dollarizing, the dollarizing device may generate greater volatility and result in financial crises when it appears to international investors that the dollarizing country cannot sustain a particular domestic currency value relative to the dollar. In Argentina's case millions of households and businesses in 2001 and 2002 saw the value of their savings threatened and unemployment rising as that nation succumbed to bankruptcy on $132 billion in foreign debt—the largest default in history.

To discover more about currency boards and dollarization see, for example, *www.iie.com*

other times merely "signaling" its target value for the dollar with occasional intervention. When the United States has intervened in the currency markets, it has done so mainly out of concern for the condition of the U.S. economy, particularly the effects of inflation. Another factor is the key role played by the U.S. dollar in the international financial system. The dollar is a **vehicle currency** that facilitates trade and investment between many nations. For example, international shipments of crude oil, regardless of their origin or destination, are more frequently than not valued in dollars. As noted in Chapter 12, the market for dollar deposits held in banks abroad—Eurodollars—is the world's largest money market, financing commercial projects and even providing operating funds for several foreign governments. For all of these reasons, the United States, as well as foreign governments and central banks, has often intervened in the foreign exchange markets to stabilize currency values and insulate domestic economic conditions from developments abroad.

Recently, the United States and other leading industrialized nations have evidenced a strong commitment toward promoting exchange rate stability, with an eye toward preventing inflation and other serious economic problems. There seems to be more acceptance among the principal trading partners of the United States today that a strong dollar carries substantial benefits for many nations besides the United States. There seems little doubt that at least some government intervention to (1) insure smoother increases or decreases in the international market value of leading currencies and (2) coordinate more closely the economic and monetary policies of major trading nations will continue. The cost of not doing so could be extremely high. For example, a falling dollar threatens the United States with more rapid inflation because the prices of imported goods denominated in other currencies rise. Moreover, the U.S. government depends heavily on foreign investors to help finance government and business debt. A falling dollar is a sign of declining foreign investor interest in U.S. securities. U.S. policymakers could revive foreign investor interest by pushing for sharply higher interest rates, but this step would tend to slow U.S. economic growth and create more unemployment. Clearly, government intervention in world currency markets is neither an easy nor a riskless step. However, the luxury of a single nation making economic policy decisions independent of other nations affected by those decisions is today a relic of the past.

Summary of the Chapter

The international financial system performs the same roles and functions that domestic money and capital markets do around the globe. It attracts savings and allocates capital for investment purposes toward the most promising projects, stimulating the international economy to grow and provide more jobs.

- One of the most significant sources of information on world trade and the flow of savings (capital) between nations is provided to us by each country's balance-of-payments (BOP) accounts, which summarize economic and financial transactions between residents of a nation and the rest of the world. The principal components of a nation's balance of payments are the *current account* (which focuses primarily upon merchandise trade and services between nations), the *capital account* (which traces long- and short-term capital flows between nations), and *official reserve transactions* (which are mainly used by governments and central banks to aid in the settlement of balance-of-payments deficits).

- One of the most significant risks in the international financial system is *currency or foreign exchange risk*. Crossing national and regional borders with capital or merchandise usually is accompanied by transactions involving two or more different currencies whose relative values can change quickly, threatening losses on trade or in the value of capital investments.

- Reducing currency risk has been a continuing goal of nations, individuals, and businesses for centuries. Nations have resorted in the past to tying their currencies to assets (such as gold) recognized as having universal appeal and value. However, restrictions on the availability of gold and transactions costs as well as lack of flexibility in a nation's money and credit policy eventually led to a much more flexible currency standard, referred to today as the *managed floating currency standard*. Each nation chooses its own currency standard, taking into account the welfare of other nations.

- The exchange rate between one currency and another is determined by the foreign exchange (FOREX) market through the interplay of the demand and supply for each nation's currency. Currencies are traded over the counter in a relatively informal marketplace and prices are quoted as "double barrel" quotations—the price of one foreign currency expressed in terms of another.

- Foreign currency markets today are three-tiered, divided into spot, forward, and futures and options markets. While spot transactions involve immediate or nearly immediate currency exchanges, forward, futures, and options markets are designed to hedge against currency or foreign-exchange risk.

- The supply and demand forces that shape foreign currency prices are, in turn, influenced by a few powerful factors, including a nation's balance-of-payments position, speculation over future currency values, domestic economic conditions, and central bank policy.

- The forward exchange market is designed to protect against losses due to currency price fluctuations. The functions of forward currency contracts include (a) commercial covering designed primarily to affect export/import values; (b) hedging an investment position against possible loss in market values; (c) speculation about future currency values and how a trader might profit from them; and (d) covered interest arbitrage to help protect the yield on an investment instrument (such as a government bond or stock).

- The principle of *interest rate parity* prevails in international currency markets and states that the net return to the investor from any foreign investment is equal to the interest earned on the investment plus or minus the forward premium or discount on the price of any foreign currency involved in the transaction.

- Foreign *currency futures contracts* call for the future delivery of a specific currency at a price agreed upon today and are designed to transfer currency risk to another investor willing to bear that risk. Importers of goods and services typically use a *buying hedge* in currency futures while a *selling hedge* is often employed by investors who purchase foreign securities and want to protect their earnings from a drop in currency values.

- Newer and more innovative methods for dealing with currency risk include *currency swaps*, where two parties exchange payments in different currencies, the use of *local loans* to avoid currency trading, *dual currency bonds* with principal and interest payments made in at least two different currencies, the *bartering* of goods or property, and *risk-adjusted pricing* of goods and services in order to take account of foreign exchange risk.

- Government intervention in foreign exchange markets has become less common today. However, most governments will intervene to change currency values when emergency shocks occur (such as terrorist attacks, war, or a sudden plunge in the values of stock or bonds) that could damage significantly a nation's economic and financial welfare.

Key Terms

Problems

1. Please indicate whether each of the transactions below would represent a credit (+) or a debit (−) item in a nation's balance of payments.

   a. General Electric Corporation purchases electric switches from a supplier in Germany.
   b. Bell Helicopter sells new helicopters to a British oil field exploration company.
   c. Universal Studios makes the decision to begin building a new theme park in Singapore.
   d. Mr. and Mrs. Robert Alford of Indianapolis sent a check last month to a cousin living in Lebanon who was celebrating a wedding anniversary.
   e. George Elwin has just received a dividend check for the stock he holds in British Airways.
   f. Citigroup of New York agrees to provide insurance for goods shipped by the International Furniture Mart of Copenhagen to a London wholesale house.

2. Suppose the exchange rate between British pounds (£) and U.S. dollars ($) is $1.35 per pound. What is the correct way to write this pound-dollar exchange rate? The dollar-pound exchange rate?

3. Suppose the pound-dollar exchange rate is now 1.3500. Then, the U.S. dollar increases in value by 5 percent. What is the new pound-dollar exchange rate? What is the new exchange rate if the U.S. dollar appreciated by 10 percent?

4. If the pound-dollar exchange rate increased from £/$ = 1.3500 to 1.4000, by what percentage amount has the pound depreciated?

5. If the pound-dollar exchange rate is 1.4000 and the pound declines 10 percent in value, what is the new pound-dollar exchange rate?

6. Suppose the pound-dollar exchange rate is 1.4000 and the yen-dollar exchange rate is 2.3000. What is the yen-pound exchange rate?

7. In 1995 the Japanese yen was trading at 93.96 yen per dollar, and by the summer of 1998 the yen-dollar exchange rate stood at 140.79, having risen in every year of the 1995–1998 period. What economic and financial factors would likely have contributed the most to this sharp fall in the exchange value of the Japanese yen against the U.S. dollar? Using the demand and supply framework shown in Exhibit 25–5, illustrate diagramatically how the economic and financial factors you cited above would have lowered the international value of the yen vis-à-vis the American dollar. Should the Bank of Japan have intervened more aggressively during this period of erosion in the value of the yen? Why or why not?

8. Suppose the dollar-Euro (€) spot exchange rate is 0.8620 and the three-month forward exchange rate for these two currencies is 0.8315. What then is the percentage discount on Euros slated for delivery in three months?

9. You are asked to calculate the forward exchange rate on Euros (€) versus the U.S. dollar. You find out that the current dollar-Euro spot exchange rate is 0.8555 and that forward Euros scheduled for delivery in six months are selling at a 3 percent premium over the spot rate. What is the Euro-dollar forward exchange rate?

10. Please identify the key terms and concepts discussed in this chapter from the descriptions and definitions given below.

    a. A double-entry bookkeeping system for recording a nation's transactions with the rest of the world.
    b. A component of a nation's balance of payments that tracks purchases and sales of goods and services.
    c. A record of flows of short-term and long-term funds into and out of a nation.

    d. A system of payments between countries in which each nation agrees to accept paper money or coins in return for gold bullion at predetermined prices.

    e. Each nation selects its own exchange-rate policy.

    f. An official monetary reserve unit developed by the International Monetary Fund (IMF) to settle international claims between nations.

    g. A system of payments and exchange rates in which the value of any nation's currency is determined by demand and supply forces in the marketplace with governments only occasionally intervening to stabilize the value of their currencies.

    h. Channels for trading national currencies and determining relative currency prices.

    i. The prices of foreign currencies expressed in terms of other currencies.

    j. A market that makes it possible to acquire or sell foreign currencies in order to cover currency risk exposure.

    k. Actions taken by a central bank to offset the impact on bank reserves, deposits, and interest rates of government purchases and sales of currencies.

    l. An agreement to deliver a specified amount of currencies, securities, or other goods or services at a set price on a given future date.

    m. A condition prevailing in international markets where the interest-rate differential between two nations matches the forward discount or premium on their two currencies.

Questions about the Web and the Money and Capital Markets

1. What are the principal parts of the U.S. balance of payments? Where on the World Wide Web could you find an answer to this question?

2. Is the U.S. balance of trade strengthening or apparently getting weaker? At what site on the Web could you look to help you answer this question? What did you conclude and why?

3. Where can you find the latest data on the U.S. dollar-Euro exchange rate using the Web? Which of these two currencies appears to be strengthening and which is weakening? Using the Web can you suggest why this is happening?

4. Can you see a linkage between the value of the U.S. dollar and the U.S. balance-of-payments position? What Web data sources could you use to determine if there is such a linkage? After examining the data on the Web, what is your conclusion?

Selected References

Bertaut, Carol C., and Murat F. Iyigan. "The Launch of the Euro." *Federal Reserve Bulletin*, October 1999, pp. 655–66.

Hopper, Gregory P. "A Primer on Currency Derivatives." *Business Review*, Federal Reserve Bank of Philadelphia, May–June 1995, pp. 3–14.

Humpage, Owen F. "A Hitchhiker's Guide to Understanding Exchange Rates." *Economic Commentary*, Federal Reserve Bank of Cleveland, January 1, 1998.

Lambert, Michael J, and Kristin D. Stanton. "Opportunities and Challenges of the U.S. Dollar as an Increasingly Global Currency: A Federal Reserve Perspective." *Federal Reserve Bulletin*, September 2001, pp. 567–75.

Neely, Christopher J. "Technical Analysis in the Foreign Exchange Market: A Layman's Guide." *Review*, Federal Reserve Bank of St. Louis, September 1997, pp. 23–38.

Papaioannou, Stefan and Kei-Mu Yi. "The Effects of a Booming Economy on the U.S. Trade Deficit." *Current Issues in Economics and Finance*, Federal Reserve Bank of New York, February 2001, pp. 1–6.

Winnie, Mark A. "The European System of Central Banks." *Economic Review,* Federal Reserve Bank of Dallas, First Quarter 1999, pp. 2–14.

Chapter **Twenty-Six**

International Banking

Learning Objectives in This Chapter

- You will understand the important role that large *multinational banks* play in both domestic and foreign markets around the world.

- You will explore the different types of *offices* and other physical facilities that multinational banks operate around the globe and be able to identify which financial *services* each banking facility usually offers.

- You will see how and why international banking is still so closely *regulated* in many areas of the world.

What's in This Chapter? Key Topics Outline

Multinational Banking Corporations

Types of Facilities Operated by International Banking Firms

Services Offered by International Banks and Universal Banking

The Structure of the New European Central Bank

Foreign Banks Operating in the United States

Federal Regulation of Foreign Banking Activity

Regulating the Activities of U.S. Banks Abroad

The Future of International Banking: Challenges and Problems

The Risks of International Lending

Deregulation and Public Confidence in the Banking System

INTRODUCTION

No review of the international financial system would be complete without a discussion of the role of international banking institutions. Through these banking firms flow the majority of commercial and financial transactions that cross international borders. Along with British, Japanese, German, and Canadian banks, U.S. commercial banking institutions have led in the development of international banking facilities to meet the far-flung financial needs of foreign governments and multinational corporations. Until recently, the international activities of U.S. banks were concentrated principally in their foreign offices, due mainly to federal government controls over foreign lending. However, the gradual relaxation of government controls in recent decades, the high cost of maintaining a large network of foreign bank branches, political instability overseas, and improvements in communications technology have encouraged many international banks to offer more international services from their *domestic* offices.

The development of multinational banking over the past century has resulted in several benefits for international trade. One benefit to the public is greater competition in international markets, lowering the real prices of financial services. It also has tied together more effectively the various national money markets into a unified international financial system, permitting a more optimal allocation of the world's scarce resources. Funds flow relatively freely today across national boundaries in response to differences in relative interest rates and currency values. Although these developments have benefited both borrowers and investors, they also have created problems for governments trying to regulate the volume of credit, insure a stable banking system, and combat inflation.

THE SCOPE OF INTERNATIONAL BANKING ACTIVITIES

Multinational Banking Corporations

The term **multinational corporation** usually is reserved for large nonfinancial corporations with manufacturing or trading operations in several different countries. However, this term is equally applicable to the world's leading banks, most of which have their home offices in Canada, the United States, Great Britain, Germany, France, Spain, and Japan but have established offices worldwide. These giant banks have accounted for most of the growth in multinational banking in recent decades.

Types of Facilities Operated by Banks Abroad

Major banks around the world have used many vehicles to expand their international operations. All major banks have *international departments* in their home offices to provide credit, access to foreign currencies, and other services for their international customers, and many operate *full-service branch offices* in foreign markets as well. Others maintain simple

Two of the most interesting multinational banks in the world are the Hong Kong and Shanghai Banking Corp. Limited and the Deutsche Bank. See their global Web sites at *www.hsbc.com* and *www.deutschebank.com*

booking offices, known as **shell branches**, on such offshore islands as the Bahamas to attract Eurocurrency accounts while avoiding domestic banking regulations. **Representative offices** help find new customers and give local customers a point of contact with the home office, but they cannot take deposits. U.S. banks and foreign banks active in the United States have set up **Edge Act and Agreement corporations** across state lines, which are special subsidiary companies that must, under Federal Reserve regulations, devote the majority of their activities to international banking. Many banking firms have also set up **international banking facilities (IBFs)** in the United States, consisting of computerized accounts maintained for international customers and subject to minimal U.S. regulations. **Agency offices** provide specialized services, such as recordkeeping for business transactions and providing customers with liquid balances for spending as needed. In addition, multinational banks often make *direct equity investments* in foreign companies, either alone or as *joint ventures* with other financial firms.

Choosing the Right Kind of Facility to Serve Foreign Markets

Which kind of facility is adopted by a multinational bank to serve its customers depends on government regulations and the bank's size, goals, and location. Most banks begin with international departments in their home offices and then, as the volume of business grows, open up representative offices. Ultimately, full-service branches and investments in foreign businesses may be established. A recent trend toward legal liberalization of foreign trade and international lending has stimulated the growth of *home-based offices* that send officers to call on customers overseas or serve clients by satellite, the Internet, and other electronic channels. However, many multinational banks argue that successful international operations require an institution to have a stable presence overseas in the form of agencies, branches, or representative offices.

Laws and regulations play a major role in determining the nature and location of multinational banking offices. For example, in some areas of the world, such as the Middle East, fears of political upheaval or outright expropriation of foreign-owned facilities have limited the entry of multinational banks.

For several of the largest U.S. banks, international operations yield from one-third to as much as one-half of their income, and a few receive more than half their earnings from international activities. Particularly noteworthy has been U.S. bank penetration of foreign consumer banking markets, such as the "money shops" operated by Citigroup in Europe. Personal financial services represent extremely attractive opportunities in many foreign markets, and U.S. banks hold a significant share of consumer loan and deposit markets abroad, especially in Europe, but also a growing market share in Central and South America and Asia.

SERVICES OFFERED BY INTERNATIONAL BANKS

Multinational banks offer a wide variety of international financial services to customers. These services are described briefly below. Of course, the particular services offered by each bank depend on its size, location, the types of facilities it maintains overseas, and the regulations it faces.

Issuing Letters of Credit

Most banks enter the international sector initially to finance trade. In most cases, credit is needed to bridge the gap between cash expenditures and cash receipts and to reduce the risks associated with long-distance trading. In these situations, a **letter of credit** is often

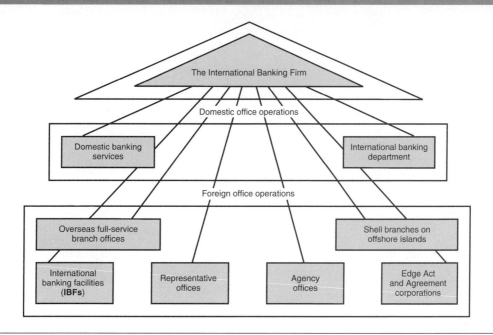

the ideal financing instrument. A letter of credit is an international bank's future promise to pay for goods stored overseas or for goods shipped between countries. Such letters may be issued to finance exports and imports or to provide a standby guarantee of payment behind IOUs issued by a corporate customer. Through a letter of credit, the bank substitutes its own promise to pay for the promise of one of its customers. By substituting its promise, the bank reduces the seller's risk, facilitating the flow of goods and services through international markets. Occasionally, the seller becomes concerned about the soundness of the bank issuing the letter of credit. The seller may then ask his or her own bank to issue a confirmation letter in which that bank guarantees against foreign bank default.

Buying and Selling Foreign Exchange (FOREX)

Trading in foreign exchange is one of the riskier activities of international banks. For an illustration see www.forexnews.com

Major multinational banks have dealer departments that specialize in trading foreign currencies (FOREX). International banks buy and sell foreign currencies on a 24-hour basis to support the import and export of goods and services, the making of investments, the giving of gifts, and the financing of tourism. They also write forward contracts for the future delivery of foreign exchange.

Accepting Eurocurrency Deposits and Making Eurocurrency Loans

International banks accept deposits denominated in currencies other than that of their home country. These **Eurocurrency deposits** are used to pay for goods shipped between countries and serve as a source of loanable funds for banks. Eurocurrency deposits may also be loaned to corporations and other large wholesale borrowers. The majority of **Eurocurrency loans** carry floating interest rates based on the London Interbank Offer Rate (LIBOR) for three-month and six-month Eurocurrency deposits. Eurocurrency credit

727

International Focus   The New European Central Banking System: Regulating and Supervising Banks in Europe and Shaping European Monetary Policy

With the formation of the European Community (EC), the regulation and supervision of international banks selling their services in Europe and the money and credit policies of the European continent will be conducted and coordinated through a new system of central banking institutions—the European System of Central Banks, or ESCB, depicted in this box.

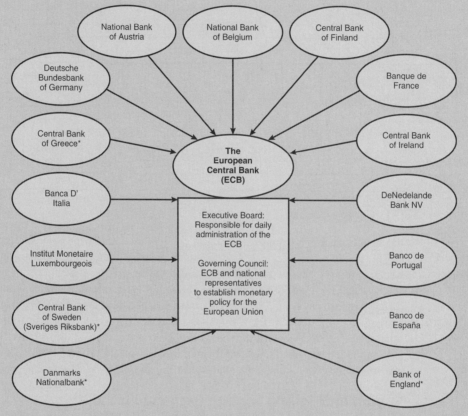

The ESCB is headed by the European Central Bank (ECB). Within the ECB itself there are two key decision-making groups—the Executive Board, which pursues daily a single monetary policy for the whole collection of European member states, and the Governing Council, which includes the Executive Board plus the governors of the central banks from each member nation. Members of the Executive Board of the ECB may serve for eight years, while Governing Council members may serve for at least five years. While the ECB is charged to lead the European continent's fight against inflation, it does not control exchange rates for the EC. That job is left to the EC's Council of Ministers. Each nation's central bank, not the ECB, will continue to examine and supervise the banks headquartered in its home country.

*These central banks from Great Britain, Greece, Denmark, and Sweden are not currently participating fully in the ESCB system, though they may participate in the future.

normally goes to borrowers with impeccable credit ratings. One important innovation in recent years is the *syndicated Eurocurrency credit*, in which one or more multinational banks will put together a loan package accompanied by an information memorandum. Other banks can then participate in the loan without direct communication with the borrower.

For more information about the European Central Bank (ECB) and European Monetary Union (EMU) see *www.ecb.in*t and *www.cepr.org*

Marketing and Underwriting of Both Domestic and Eurocurrency Bonds, Notes, and Equity Shares

For generations, leading international banks have assisted their customers in raising capital through the issuance of new securities—bonds and other forms of debt and equity shares (stock). One of the most well-known of these securities is the **Eurobond**—a debt security denominated in a currency other than that of the country or countries where most or all of the security is sold. For example, a U.S. automobile company may desire to float an issue of long-term bonds to raise capital for one of its subsidiaries operating in Greece. The company might issue bonds denominated in British pounds to be sold in Europe through an underwriting syndicate made up of banks and securities dealers. Alternatively, the borrowing company might issue bonds denominated in the *Euro,* which is now the largest corporate bond market in the world.

Multinational banks assist the Eurobond market in several ways. Major banks have established international clearing systems to expedite the delivery of Eurobonds. Banks and security brokers are the principal intermediaries through which Eurobonds find their way to the long-term investor. The borrower may contact a multinational bank and ask it to organize a syndicate to place a new Eurobond issue. At this point, a *consortium* is formed, embracing at least four or five U.S., British, Japanese, French, or German banks, and typically at least one bank located in the borrowing country as well. The consortium agrees to subscribe to the Eurobond issue at issue price minus commission and then organizes a large group of banks and securities dealers as underwriters. Sometimes more than 100 banks are included in the underwriting syndicate. Once formed, the underwriting group gives the borrower a firm offer for its bonds and, if accepted, works hard to place the issue with investors.

To further explore the market for Eurobonds see such Web sites as *www.finpipe.com* and ISI Emerging Markets at *www.securities.com*

Multinational banks also assist their corporate and governmental customers with medium-term financing through note issuance facilities (NIFs). Under a standard NIF contract, a customer is authorized to periodically issue short-term notes (usually with three-to six-month maturities) to interested investors over a designated time span (perhaps five years). The bank or banks involved agree to provide backup funding (standby credit) at a spread over prevailing Euromarket interest rates. For an underwriting fee, the bank agrees to purchase any unsold notes or advance cash to the customers until sufficient market funding is obtained.

Securitizing Loans

Over the past two decades, leading multinational banks have unfurled a new source of funds for themselves and their customers: *securitization*, or the pooling of loans having similar purposes, quality, and maturities and the selling of financial claims (securities) against the pool of loans. Good examples are New York's Citigroup and J.P. Morgan/Chase, which are among the leading packagers of consumer credit-card receivables, pooling the receivables that arise as households borrow on their credit cards and selling securities in the open market as claims against the income those receivables will ultimately bring in. International banks can earn income in several different ways from the securitization process: (1) by securitizing some of their own loans and pocketing the difference in interest earnings between the average yield on the pool of loans and the cost of issuing securities against the loan pool; (2) by agreeing to guarantee the income of investors from pools of securitized loans; (3) by retaining servicing rights on a pool of loans, collecting and recording the income received from the loans in return for a servicing fee; or (4) by acting as adviser or trustee for those customers that desire to securitize any loans or receivables they hold in order to generate new capital.

International Focus

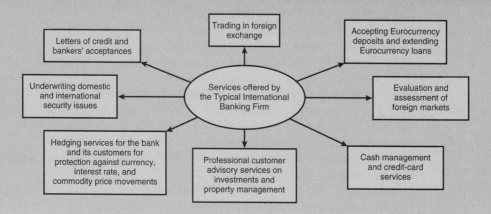

Advisory Services Provided by International Banks

In addition to the foregoing services, international banks offer extensive *advisory services* to their customers. These include analyses of foreign market conditions, evaluation of sales prospects and plant location sites, and advice on foreign regulations. International banks prepare credit reports on overseas buyers for exporters of goods and services and assist domestic firms interested in entering foreign markets.

Universal Banking Services and One-Stop Shopping

As the foregoing list of service offerings suggests, the world's largest banking firms, such as Citigroup and Deutsche Bank, are reaching out to diversify their services in many different directions, attempting to offer their customers "one-stop shopping" and becoming what European bankers have, for decades, referred to as "universal banks." Universal banking combines traditional banking, insurance, securities trading, and even real estate brokering under one corporate umbrella. Its alleged advantages include greater stability of revenues (cash flow) and profits, less risk of succumbing to market stress as declines in one service area may be offset by increased revenues from other services, and lower overall fund-raising costs.

Further information on recent developments in international banking can be found at such Web sites as *www.bankinfo.com* and *www.finance.tfp.com*

However, an international banking firm may not be able to efficiently manage all of its different service areas, resulting in lower rates of return and loss of market share. A prominent example appeared late in 2001 when Citigroup of New York, which had previously allied itself in the 1990s with Travelers Insurance Company of San Francisco to form one of the largest banking conglomerates in the world, announced plans to sell its Travelers property-casualty insurance affiliate and, at least partially, abandon its goal of becoming a "one-stop" financial supermarket. Citigroup discovered that its insurance affiliate was earning a lower rate of return than its other businesses and dragging down its overall performance relative to its competitors. Citigroup's experience suggests that international banks must proceed cautiously as they proliferate their services and avoid hasty acquisitions that may be difficult to control and reduce their competitive edge.

Questions *to Help You Study*

1. What exactly is a *multinational bank*?
2. What are the essential differences between the following types of *banking offices* or *facilities*:

International banking departments

Edge Act and Agreement corporations

Full-service branches

Representative offices

Shell branches

International banking facilities (IBFs)

3. What factors appear to influence the types of *services* an international banking firm chooses to offer its customers?

4. What are the principal *services* offered by the international banking industry? Please make a list of these services and briefly define what each is about.

FOREIGN BANKS IN THE UNITED STATES[1]

Banks owned by foreign individuals and companies have entered the United States in great numbers in recent years. The reasons behind the expansion of foreign banking activities in the United States reflect growth in international trade and investments, the opportunity for profit in the huge U.S. market, and a search for safety when overseas markets are in turmoil. Originally, foreign-based banks penetrated U.S. markets for the same reasons U.S. banks established facilities overseas: *to follow their customers who had established operations in other countries.* Once in the United States, however, foreign banks found the possibility of attracting deposits and loans from major U.S. corporations and even from U.S. households irresistible.

Recent Growth of Foreign Banks in the United States

To learn more about foreign banking in the U.S. see especially FRB: Foreign Banks in the U.S. at *www.federalreserve.gov*

The growth of foreign bank operations in the United States has been impressive indeed. Today they are strong competitors with domestic U.S. banks, particularly in the market for business loans. To illustrate, total U.S. banking assets controlled by foreign banks advanced from only about $60 billion in 1976 to more than $1.3 trillion as the 21st century began. In terms of percentages, foreign-bank holdings of U.S. banking assets climbed from just under 6 percent in 1976 to more than 19 percent in 2001. In that same year, foreign banks held about 17 percent of all bank deposits in the United States, more than 13 percent of aggregate U.S. bank loans, and better than 25 percent of all business loans extended within the U.S. banking system. Clearly foreign banks are a force to contend with inside the United States' financial marketplace.

Federal Regulation of Foreign Bank Activity

Until the 1970s, no federal laws regulated foreign bank activity within U.S. borders. However, Congress has been monitoring foreign bank operations since 1966, when IntraBank, a Lebanese institution, collapsed and several U.S. banks suffered severe losses. Passage of the Bank Holding Company Act Amendments of 1970 marked an initial step toward federal regulation of foreign banking. Under the terms of these amendments, any corporation controlling one or more domestic banks became subject to supervision by the Federal Reserve Board.

---

[1]Portions of this section are based, in part, on an earlier article by Rose (1976) in *The Canadian Banker* and are used with permission.

EXHIBIT 26–1
The Importance of
Foreign Bank
Operations in the
United States

Source: Federal Reserve Board
and the Federal Reserve Bank
of New York.

Year	Total Assets Held by Foreign Banks in the U.S. ($ Billions)	Proportion of Total U.S. Banking Assets Controlled by Foreign Banks (Percent)
1976	$ 60	5.8%
1980	201	11.9
1990	738	21.7
2001	1,300	19.3

However, with foreign banks in the United States growing more rapidly than domestic banks, the pressure on Congress for more extensive regulation of foreign banks intensified. Proponents of restrictive legislation argued that foreign banks reduced the effectiveness of domestic monetary policy and that the lack of specific regulations applying to foreign banks was unfair to domestic banks, which must conform to an elaborate system of regulations. Perhaps more important, foreign banks could branch across state lines—a privilege denied U.S. banks until the passage of the Riegle-Neal Interstate Banking and Branching Efficiency Act in 1994.

There was also a disparity between foreign and domestic banks in the services each group of institutions was permitted to offer. Until the beginning of the twenty-first century U.S. banking companies were prohibited from offering services in domestic markets not *closely related* to traditional banking services (i.e., the extension of credit and the taking of deposits). Moreover, until its repeal in the fall of 1999 the Glass-Steagall Act of 1933 prohibited U.S. banks from becoming "principally engaged" in underwriting the sale of corporate bonds and stocks. Such a prohibition did not exist for most foreign-owned banks and several foreign banking organizations moved to take advantage of this situation, taking away major corporate customers from American banks.

Responding to these pressures, Congress passed the **International Banking Act (IBA)**, which became law on September 17, 1978. Under the terms of the IBA and subsequent regulations, U.S. branches and agencies of foreign banks with worldwide assets of $1 billion or more became subject to U.S. legal reserve requirements. Foreign banks that maintain U.S. offices were required to register with the Secretary of the Treasury. Each foreign bank with an office accepting deposits from the public had to select a "home state." No foreign bank could establish a federal- or a state-chartered branch outside its home state unless granted permission by the state involved. This provision of the law limited a foreign bank's ability to accept deposits across U.S. state lines, especially consumer-type deposits.

The IBA proved to be a more lenient piece of legislation than many analysts had expected. It did not attempt to punish or discriminate against foreign banks relative to their U.S. counterparts. In fact, the act set in law the principle of *mutual nondiscrimination*, used widely as a regulatory standard. This principle permits foreign-owned banks to operate under the same conditions and to possess the same powers as domestic banks. It is a policy that avoids establishing two sets of banking regulations, one for domestic institutions and the other for foreign-owned banks.

Federal regulation of foreign banks was extended a step further in 1980 when the Depository Institutions Deregulation and Monetary Control Act was passed. (Please see Exhibit 26–2.) All foreign banking organizations offering services to U.S. residents became eligible for deposit insurance from the Federal Deposit Insurance Corporation and were required to conform to deposit reserve requirements set by the Federal Reserve Board. When a foreign bank opens an agency, branch, or loan production office in the United States, it must register as a bank holding company and conform with all holding company laws and regulations as administered by the Federal Reserve System. These new requirements even more firmly reflected Congress's intention to place all banks (foreign and domestic) on the same regulatory footing and in the same field of competition.

Finally, on the heels of the scandal involving the Bank of Credit and Commerce International (BCCI) of Luxembourg, which illegally attempted to acquire control of several U.S. banks, the Federal Reserve Board was granted even broader new powers to regulate the activities of agencies, branch offices, and subsidiaries of foreign banks inside U.S. territory. Under the terms of the Foreign Bank Supervision Enhancement Act passed by Congress in 1991, the Fed must approve any proposed bank agency, branch, or representative office to be set up in the United States. The Fed was empowered to *close* a foreign bank office if its home country fails to subject the parent bank to comprehensive supervision and regulation. Any foreign bank seeking to buy more than 5 percent of the stock of a U.S. bank or bank holding company must receive Federal Reserve Board approval. Moreover, small deposits (less than $100,000) can be accepted in the United States by foreign banks only through subsidiary companies that have FDIC insurance coverage and conform to all U.S. banking regulations.

REGULATION OF THE INTERNATIONAL BANKING ACTIVITIES OF U.S. BANKS

A far more significant problem than regulating foreign banking activities in the United States is the regulation, supervision, and control of U.S. banks offering their services overseas. What limits should be placed on U.S. banks operating overseas? Who should enforce those limits?

The *Federal Reserve Board* has been designated as the chief regulatory agency for U.S. international banking activities, especially where Fed member banks are involved. A member bank of the Federal Reserve System choosing to expand its activities abroad through the creation of foreign branches or through investments in foreign firms must secure the approval of the Federal Reserve Board. In contrast, state laws govern the foreign operations of state-chartered banks. However, most state governments have exerted only nominal control over foreign banking activities.

Of prime concern to the Federal Reserve is the protection of domestic deposits and the stability of the domestic banking system. The Fed has argued that it is difficult to separate a bank's foreign operations from its domestic activities. If a foreign subsidiary gets into trouble, the danger exists that public confidence in the soundness of the controlling domestic bank will be undermined. For this reason, the Fed, in reviewing applications of U.S. banks to expand abroad, examines closely the condition of their domestic offices to determine if their home-based operations are adequately capitalized and if the bank has sufficient management skill to support both foreign and domestic operations.

The regulatory authorities would like to develop ways to insulate the foreign activities of U.S. banks from their domestic operations. Such insulation would grant wider latitude to banking activities abroad and at the same time shield domestic banks from the hazards associated with foreign operations. Legally, one bank subsidiary is not liable for the debts of another. However, in practice, a domestic bank might feel compelled to aid its affiliates operating in foreign markets. The practical, if not legal, links between foreign and domestic subsidiaries of multinational banks force regulators to keep close tabs on the foreign operations of all banks.

Fortunately there is growing research evidence (especially from Asia and Latin America) that allowing foreign banks to enter a domestic economy tends to enhance competition, accelerate the growth of credit, and strengthen the entered nation's banking system against adversity (particularly when dealing with currency crises and severe loan losses).

EXHIBIT 26–2

Purposes and Provisions of the International Banking Act (IBA) of 1978, the Foreign Bank Supervision Act of 1991, and Other Recent U.S. Banking Laws Applying to International Banking Firms

International Banking Act of 1978

Purpose: To promote competitive equality between domestic and foreign banking institutions operating in the United States.

Provisions: Limited the interstate branching of foreign banks.

Provided for federal licensing of branches and agencies of foreign banks.

Authorized the Federal Reserve Board to impose reserve requirements on the deposits of branches and agencies of foreign banks.

Provided for foreign bank access to Federal Reserve services (such as the discount window).

Provided for federal deposit insurance for branches of foreign banks.

Granted broader powers to Edge Act corporations of U.S. banks so they could compete more effectively with branches and agencies of foreign banks.

Subjected foreign banks operating branches and agencies to the prohibitions against nonbank business ventures in the U.S. Bank Holding Company Act.

Depository Institutions Deregulation and Monetary Control Act of 1980

Purpose: To further equalize deposit regulations and services that foreign banks can offer vis-à-vis domestic banks inside the United States.

Provisions: All foreign banks selling banking services to U.S. residents were made eligible for FDIC insurance coverage on their deposits but must also hold reserve requirements behind their deposits at levels specified by the Federal Reserve Board.

International Lending and Supervision Act of 1983

Purpose: To reduce the risks to international banks and their depositors from international lending.

Provisions: U.S. banks must set aside special reserves against their foreign loans. Minimum capital requirements are imposed to protect depositors in international banks.

Foreign Bank Supervision Act of 1991

Purpose: To give U.S. authorities greater control over foreign bank activities inside the United States and to limit risk to the FDIC insurance fund from foreign banks.

Provisions: If foreign banks wish to accept deposits in the United States of less than $100,000, they must establish one or more U.S. banking subsidiaries and obtain FDIC insurance coverage for their deposits.

Uninsured branch offices of foreign banks cannot accept deposits under $100,000.

Prior approval of the Federal Reserve Board is required for the creation of new foreign bank branch, agency, or representative offices inside U.S. territory.

Foreign banks operating inside the United States must be subject to comprehensive supervision by their home country and must not violate U.S. law or engage in unsound banking practices. Their U.S. operations may be closed by the Federal Reserve Board if found to be operated in an unsafe manner.

Questions *to Help You Study*

5. Please explain why *foreign banks* have entered the United States in considerable numbers in recent years.

6. What federal government *regulations* apply to foreign banks operating in the United States today? Why did Congress pass laws to regulate foreign bank activity in the United States? What is the danger if laws of this type are made too restrictive?

7. What federal government agency is the chief *regulator* of foreign banks operating in the United States? Why do you think Congress picked this particular agency to play a leadership role in foreign bank regulation inside the United States?

8. What is meant by the principle of *mutual nondiscrimination*? What problems does this principle pose for regulators? What advantages does it have over other regulatory approaches?

THE FUTURE OF INTERNATIONAL BANKING

The future of international banking is clouded at this time due to the many cross-currents of economics and politics that pervade our world. Sluggish economic growth and high unemployment in some parts of the world (especially in Japan), trade barriers, and political struggle and terrorism threaten the flow of international commerce and make bank lending across national boundaries risky. In this section, we take a brief look at these problems and their implications for the future of international banking.

The Risks of International Lending

Political and Currency Risk

Lending funds in the international arena is riskier, on average, than is domestic lending. *Political risk*—the risk that government laws and regulations will change to the detriment of business interests—is particularly significant in international banking. Governments are frequently overthrown and confiscation of private property is a frequent occurrence in some parts of the world.[2] There is also *currency risk*—the risk associated with changing relative prices of foreign currencies. The value of property pledged behind an international loan falls if the currency of the home country is devalued, eroding the lender's collateral. Geography too works against the international lender. The large distances that frequently separate lender and borrower make it difficult for a bank loan officer to see that the terms of a loan are being followed.

The risks of international lending have become a much greater concern over the period from the 1970s to the present day because international banks have become the principal source of borrowed funds for developing countries as the United States and other heavily industrialized countries have cut back on their foreign aid programs. Unfortunately, when international commodity prices declined, as they have several times in recent years, numerous developing countries could not meet the terms of their loans. Many of these debts were rescheduled by agreement between international banks and debtor nations. Simultaneously, the International Monetary Fund and the World Bank moved to supply more funds to give

---

[2]Many financial analysts often lump political and other risks in international lending under the general term *country risk*. This is the possibility that governments borrowing money from multinational banks may be unable or unwilling to repay and that private borrowers may, because of law and regulation, be unable to make payment on their loans. For example, private borrowers may be prevented from paying due to *transfer risk*, a component of country risk in which a nation prohibits outflows of capital, dividends, or interest payments due to an internal shortage of foreign exchange. The other component of country risk—*political risk*—arises when loans cannot be repaid due to war, revolution, or changes in regulatory philosophy that adversely affect the ability of a borrower to fulfill a debt obligation.

An important government-sponsored international bank that facilitates international lending is the Export-Import Bank. See especially *www.exim.gov* and *www.tradeport.org*

these debtor nations time to adjust their domestic economies to a harsher economic climate. As the twenty-first century approached, more and more developing nations in Asia, the Americas (especially Argentina), the former Soviet Union, and Africa began to experience credit problems. Some nations periodically threatened to repudiate their international debt (as in the case of Russia) or unilaterally alter the terms of their repayment (as in the case of Argentina). At the same time, some multinational banks began to scale down their international lending operations by selling old loans at deep discounts, which limited the availability of liquidity in international markets and slowed the growth of world trade.

Some banks pioneered *debt-for-equity swaps* in which they accepted shares of stock in certain overseas projects as a substitute for holding loans. Debt-for-equity swaps also provided more flexible funding for developing countries, but most other troubled nations sought out restructuring of their existing loans. Some sought outright forgiveness of what they owed.

Geographic Distribution of International Bank Lending

Beginning in the late 1970s, U.S. bank regulators inaugurated semiannual surveys of foreign lending by U.S. banking organizations. The principal concern of these regulatory agencies was that U.S. multinational banks were overly committed to foreign loans, where the political and economic risks were unusually high. This might threaten the confidence of the public in the soundness of some of the world's largest banks. Recent surveys show that most loans extended by U.S. multinational banks are made to industrially developed nations (including Canada, Western Europe, and Japan) and to countries in Central and South America. However, close to a third of all foreign loans typically are extended to lesser-developed countries, a number of which have been in serious financial difficulty at various times as the twentieth century gave way to the twenty-first (including Argentina and Russia).

Fortunately, loans to distant nations are mainly short term (maturity of one year or less), and many are made to banks themselves. On the whole, multinational banks appear to be relatively conservative lenders, directing their credits to large bank, corporate, and governmental borrowers situated mainly in Europe, more prosperous areas in Asia, and in rapidly growing Latin American markets. The bulk of such loans is concentrated among the largest international banks.

Public Confidence and Bank Failures

A persistent problem in international banking is the preservation of *public confidence* in the banking system. Essentially, this means protecting the major multinationals against failure. To avert serious financial difficulties among the world's largest banks, regulatory authorities in the United States and elsewhere look closely at the *capital positions* of multinational banks. Regulators have often urged a slower expansion of international loans and the avoidance of excessive credit exposure in loans to any one country, especially to non-oil-producing nations of the Third World. This is coupled with an insistence on adequate levels of equity capital. One of the first steps in this direction occurred in 1983 when the United States Congress passed the **International Lending and Supervision Act**. This law ordered bank regulatory agencies to prepare new rules requiring U.S. banks to:

1. Maintain special reserves against foreign loans in those instances where the quality of a bank's assets has been impaired by protracted borrower inability to pay out loans.

2. Limit loan rescheduling fees charged troubled foreign borrowers.

3. Disclose a bank's exposure to foreign borrowers.

4. Hold minimum levels of capital as protection for an international bank's depositors.

International Focus   The Global Banking Crisis of the 1990s

In its long history, the international banking system has been subject to a series of *shocks* to its stability and growth—recurrent crises that have sometimes shaken the global banking system to its roots. A prime example occurred through much of the 1990s in Asia and in South and Central America. During that decade, the Japanese economy failed to achieve its expected recovery to the level of strength and robust growth it had enjoyed in earlier decades. The resulting decline in employment and business sales and especially the drastic loss in the value of Japanese real estate and stock prices created a major crisis for Japan's banks, whose uncollectible loans mushroomed. Bank failures multiplied rapidly. In the late 1990s, Moody's Investor Services revised downward its estimate of the quality of the Japanese sovereign debt. In April 1998, Japan's unemployment rate climbed to 4.1 percent of the civilian labor force—the highest mark since World War II.

Soon, the banking and economic crisis experienced by Japan had spread through other parts of Asia as well. For example, Thailand felt serious adverse effects from withdrawals of short-term capital by investment firms around the globe as concerns arose that Thailand's economy, particularly its real estate markets and banking system, were about to pass through a financial meltdown similar to Japan's. The International Monetary Fund (IMF), set up after World War II to aid countries experiencing international balance-of-payments problems, arranged a massive $17 billion credit package for Thailand.

Subsequently, the IMF offered an even larger rescue package, totaling about $42 billion, to Indonesia, the world's fourth most populated nation, which was beset with a seriously troubled banking system, a political leadership crisis, and social unrest.

The South Korean economy, tied closely monetarily and productionwise to Japan, began to show similar problems during the mid-1990s. The IMF felt compelled to step forward and set up a financial agreement to bolster Korea's currency unit, the *won*, and strengthen a domestic banking system beset with huge loan losses. At almost the same time, a group of U.S. and other multinational banks from Europe and Asia rescheduled their loans to Korean bank and nonbank firms.

Meanwhile, Russia began to falter again in the late 1990s after it had made significant strides toward introducing free markets in an effort to modernize its economy. Annual yields on Russian debt climbed above 80 percent as international banks and other investors began to express their concern over a developing government fiscal crisis and the need for further market-oriented reforms.

These international banking crises of the 1990s appear to be one of the best illustrations we have had in recent years of the so-called "domino effect" in international banking. One nation's banking and economic problems soon spread to other nations, largely through the damage done to international trade and to the confidence of banks and other investors in the global markets. Soon, whole regions of the global economy are mired in declining asset values, falling production and incomes, the flight of both domestic and foreign capital, and, ultimately, bank failures.

5. Conduct feasibility studies of foreign projects involving mining, metal, or mineral processing before approving a loan.

Then, as we saw earlier in Chapter 18, in 1988 representatives from the Federal Reserve System, the Bank of England, the Bank of Japan, and the central banks of eight other countries signed the Basle Agreement. This historic international contract calls on central banks to monitor the capital positions of international banks under their jurisdiction and to impose minimum capital requirements on all banks. The primary objective of this international capital standard is to ensure that banks from one nation do not have a competitive advantage over banks from other nations due to more lenient capital regulations. Beginning in 1993, all banks subject to the Basle Agreement were required to hold a ratio of core capital (mainly equity funds) to total risk-adjusted assets of at least 4 percent, and a ratio of total capital (core capital plus debt and other forms of capital) to total risk-adjusted assets of at least 8 percent. Thus, the Basle Agreement reduced permissible leverage for banks that might handicap the ability of bankers to meet some international credit needs in the future.

The Basle Agreement broke new ground in another way—each international bank's minimum capital requirement was to depend not only on the volume of its assets but also on the amount of risk it had taken on as reflected in its balance sheet and its off-balance-

Financial Developments   International Bank Mergers—The Industry's Strategic Response to Changing Competition and Risk

The high risks associated with international banking (especially the risks of international lending) have pressured multinational banks to find ways of reducing their risk exposure. At the same time the development of comprehensive trade agreements, such as the formation of the European Community and NAFTA, brought banks previously isolated from one another into close contact and increased competition, further increasing the risk of bank failure.

One of the principal ways international banks have dealt with these powerful risk factors is by *merging* into larger, more product-diversified and geographically diversified banking firms. Advances in communications technology have overcome barriers to management control and accelerated the "urge to merge." Nowhere has this merger trend been more evident than in Japan where the leading Japanese banks have engaged in dozens of recent mergers and acquisitions.

Examples include the recent combinations of Sanwa Bank with Tokai and Toyo Trust banks, the creation of Sumitomo Mitsui Bank Group from the merger of Sumitomo and Sakura banks, and the formation of the Mitsubishi Tokyo Financial Group, bringing together the Nippon Trust, Mitsubishi Trust, and the Bank of Tokyo–Mitsubishi. These great combinations created several of the largest banks on the planet. A good example is Mizuho Holdings, Inc., composed of Yasuda, Fuji,

Dai-Ichi Kangyo, and Industrial banks with about $1.3 trillion in total assets—the largest conglomerate banking firm in the world.

In Western Europe huge mergers have taken place not only between banks, but also between banks, insurance companies, and security firms. Many of these largest combinations crossed national borders in the wake of the formation of the European Community, helping to tie together the financial systems of Germany, France, Italy, and other European countries. Examples include the recent merger of giant insurer Allianz AG of Munich with Dresdner Bank AG; the acquisition by Germany's Deutsche Bank AG of Bankers Trust Company of New York; and the alliance of Verisbank Group with the Bank of Munich.

Recently the European Commission, based in Brussels, was created to review and possibly block future mergers involving European financial and nonfinancial companies. The new Commission currently reviews larger mergers for evidence of "collective dominance," indicating excessive market concentration in a handful of companies. At some point in the near future European financial-service firms may run into these competitive and regulatory barriers because banking there is much more concentrated in the hands of the very largest banks than in the United States.

---

sheet activities (such as the issuance of credit guarantees). Banks accepting greater risk must hold more capital to preserve public confidence in their long-term viability. The Basle Agreement represents only the first step in a new era of international cooperation among regulators of banks, securities dealers, and other financial firms aimed at promoting stability in international markets and at preserving the public's confidence in the global financial system and its leading banks.

The Spread of Deregulation: How Fast Should We Go?

As we saw in Chapters 15, 16, and 18, the United States began an aggressive program of *deregulating* domestic banking in the 1980s. Other nations—such as Great Britain with its Big Bang deregulation of banking and security dealer services in 1987—have also made significant strides toward lifting confining government rules and regulations, permitting their own banks as well as foreign banks operating within their borders to compete more equally. Unfortunately, the pattern of international banking deregulation has been spotty, with some nations (such as Japan) lowering regulatory barriers to competition slowly in order to protect domestic institutions. The real losers here are domestic consumers of financial services, who have fewer options and probably pay higher prices until government deregulation takes place. The key issue is how to allow government deregulation of financial services on an international scale to proceed rapidly without wholesale bank failures that destroy public confidence.

Finding the proper speed and scope for financial deregulation remains a challenging worldwide issue. Nevertheless, there is a growing trend toward relying more on the private marketplace and less on government rule-making in order to regulate global banking. Banks that have too little capital or accept greater than normal risks are likely to be punished by the private financial markets, especially when they attempt to raise new funds at reasonable cost.

An added complication was thrown into the debate over how fast and how far deregulation should go in freeing international banks from rigid government controls when the scandal involving the Bank of Credit and Commerce International (BCCI) Holdings, S.A., broke into the headlines in the early 1990s. This far-flung international bank holding company was based in Luxembourg, which, at the time, had few rules for holding company operations. Following revelations that BCCI violated U.S. holding company law by acquiring ownership interests in U.S. banks without approval of the Federal Reserve Board, further investigation uncovered possible money-laundering activities. U.S. investigators in the Department of Justice and at the Federal Reserve began to bring indictments and levy stiff fines against principals in the BCCI case. This case clearly points to a broader issue for international banking in the twenty-first century: the necessity for regulatory cooperation and for *harmonization* of banking regulations across nations so that no bank entrusted with the public's funds can find refuge from some minimum level of public scrutiny that ensures respect for the law in business dealings. This is especially important in a world that is increasingly threatened by terrorism financed and encouraged by powerful organizations in almost every corner of the globe.

PROSPECTS AND ISSUES FOR THE TWENTY-FIRST CENTURY

These recent trends suggest a somewhat different future for international banking than seemed likely in earlier years. Growth—limited by capital and the availability of experienced management—should be more gradual and loan quality more of a factor in future extensions of credit to businesses and governments abroad. However, continuing expansion of international banking activities in the United States, Western Europe, the nations that emerged from the dissolution of the former Soviet Union, Asia, and Latin America can be anticipated as long as risk exposure can be held within acceptable limits.

Certainly, a number of critical questions must be answered for international banking to prosper and grow. For example, to what extent will the regulatory authorities of different nations cooperate to control foreign banking activities? How can we *harmonize* different banking rules from one country to the next to promote competition and innovation but also public safety? What is an appropriate capital position for banks engaged in foreign lending and for those subject to significant amounts of market risk in their on-balance-sheet and off-balance-sheet activities? Where must regulation end and the free play of market forces be allowed to operate in international banking?

And, what about the rise of strong competitors in the form of nonbank firms—security dealers and underwriters, finance companies, insurance companies, and the like? These firms today are offering parallel services to those offered by international banks, supplying credit, underwriting new security offerings, securitizing loans, offering savings instruments, and managing customer cash positions, but they are usually burdened with far fewer regulations. Leading international banks have begun to respond to these new competitors. For example, Deutsche Bank of Germany is a leading underwriter of corporate securities on the European continent; France's BNP offers savers a product that looks very much like money market fund shares; and Citigroup, J.P. Morgan/Chase and Bank of America are leading securitizers of receivables emerging from credit-card loans and other forms of lending. As the opening of the twenty-first century beckons us forward into a new era, international banks must find ways to adjust to the challenges posed by this "new competition" or suffer erosion of their current share of the international financial marketplace.

These are perplexing issues that have few clear answers. However, the importance of international banking and the penetration of domestic markets by foreign banking institutions demand that effective answers be found that strengthen the global financial system and provide a basis for its future growth and development.

Questions *to Help You Study*

9. What major problems have been encountered by the international banking community in recent years? How have these problems been dealt with?

10. What is *political risk*? Why is it important in international banking?

11. What is *currency risk*? What types of currency risk exposure are of special concern to international bankers?

12. What important principle about international banking was revealed by the global banking crisis of the 1990s?

13. How did the International Lending and Supervision Act affect international banks? How about the Basle Agreement?

14. Which nonbank financial-service firms are posing a strong competitive challenge to international banking today?

Summary

International banking firms—multinational banking companies that reach across national boundaries—offer financial services around the globe today. Their growth has proceeded at a pace mirroring the growth of international trade and global capital flows as international banks typically follow their largest customers overseas.

- International banks operate many different kinds of facilities to provide services across national boundaries today. Among the best-known of these facilities are (a) international banking departments, usually located within the headquarters of a single bank: (b) shell branches in offshore island locations, designed to minimize the burden of regulation in raising funds; (c) representative offices, which funnel service requests to the banks' central facilties; (d) Edge Act and Agreement corporations, which avoid or minimize some domestic regulatory restrictions; (e) international banking facilities (IBFs) that keep computerized records of offshore transactions; (f) full-service branches that offer most of the services available from the main bank office; and (g) agency offices, which assist customers with special transactions, including record keeping and cash-management services.

- Among the leading financial services provided by international banks are (a) letters of credit to help finance international trade; (b) buying and selling of foreign currencies for the bank and its customers; (c) issuing bankers' acceptances to facilitate trade financing or the purchase of currencies; (d) accepting Eurocurrency deposits and making Eurocurrency loans; (e) marketing and underwriting security sales to help customers raise new funds; (f) securitizing loans to help the bank and its customers generate new working capital and reduce balance-sheet risk; (g) cash management services to provide liquidity for customers as spending power is needed; (h) advisory services regarding potential foreign investments and foreign markets that bank customers might be interested in; and (i) miscellaneous other financially oriented services.

- Foreign banks have come to represent a substantial share of all banking assets in the United States and account for a relatively large market share of business loans made within the American banking system. Foreign bank growth inside the United States has occurred, in part, due to foreign-bank customers entering the United States, the needs of foreign businesses to carry out security sales and other transactions within the United States in order to obtain capital and liquidity, and the continuing search of many bank customers for safety in the face of international risks. A bank that can cross national borders offers its customers the chance to enter new markets and diversify their business operations, thereby expanding potential revenues and reducing risk exposure.

- *Government regulation* of foreign bank activities has expanded considerably in recent years, subjecting foreign banks to most of the same rules and regulations that domestic banks face, including cash reserve requirements and capital requirements. In the United States recently passed federal laws have led to close supervision and regulation of foreign banks. One prime example is the Foreign Bank Supervision Enhancement Act passed in 1991. Under the terms of this law the *Federal Reserve Board* was appointed the principal supervisor of foreign bank activities in the United States and must give its approval of the expansion of foreign banking facilities inside U.S. borders. Moreover, the Federal Reserve can close a foreign-owned bank office if, in the Fed's opinion, it is not adequately supervised by its home country. The Federal Reserve is also the chief supervisor of U.S. banks' operations in overseas markets.

- The future of international banking presents significant risks today due to possible political and economic changes abroad and unanticipated movements in interest rates and currency prices. International banks also face greater lending risk because overseas loans, on average, are more risky than domestic loans due, in part, to the relative lack of information on the condition of foreign borrowers. In recent years, however, international banks have developed country risk profiles and other advanced tools to help lower the risks inherent in international lending.

- If international banks are to survive and prosper in the future, they must retain the public's confidence and control the incidence of excessive risk taking. One of the most important ways to accomplish this goal in recent years has been to impose common capital requirements on all banks in leading industrialized countries (through the Basle Agreement on Bank Capital Standards, signed by all participating industrialized nations in 1988). These common regulatory standards—a product of unique cooperation among many nations—have been changed and modified frequently in recent years to broaden the kinds of risk measurement and risk protection that international banks use.

- Today there is less emphasis in international bank regulation upon rigid standards and, instead, greater use of risk control models created by each bank to deal with its own unique risk exposures. Moreover, international banking rules are focusing today more and more on the *private marketplace* to impose discipline on bank behavior and risk taking. For example, international banks choosing to take on greater risk often find that the free market forces them to pay more for the capital they must raise in order to carry on their daily operations.

- International banking is likely to benefit in future years from greater *deregulation* as governments move to liberalize the rules limiting future bank expansion into new markets and allow private markets, rather than government dictum, to play a far greater role in shaping the services and the performance of international banking corporations.

Key Terms

Multinational corporation, *725*
Shell branches, *726*
Representative offices, *726*
Edge Act and Agreement
  corporations, *726*

International banking facilities
  (IBFs), *726*
Agency offices, *726*
Letter of credit, *726*
Eurocurrency deposits, *727*

Eurocurrency loans, *727*
Eurobond, *729*
International Banking Act, *732*
International Lending and
  Supervision Act, *736*

Problems

1. A major money center bank in the United States wishes to expand its presence in the unfolding European Community, where it currently services corporate customers but has no physical facilities. Based on the discussion in this chapter, what initial forms of facilities would you recommend to its management and why? What special problems can you anticipate given recent announcements by the European Community regarding changes in its monetary system and in its regulation of outside financial-service suppliers?

2. Which services typically offered by international banks:
   a. Involve the direct extension of credit to corporate customers?
   b. Aid customers in hedging against various forms of market risk?
   c. Assist customers in making international payments?
   d. Aid customers in restructuring their capitalization?
   e. Help customers in obtaining additional capital from the open market or from other lending institutions?

3. Should the activities of foreign banks be regulated when they enter any particular domestic economy? Why or why not? What could be gained by the nation being entered and what dangers might follow? How would you propose to deal with the dangers or risks involved? Please explain the reasons behind your recommendations.

4. If you were charged with evaluation of the *country risk* associated with the following nations, what factors would you want to examine?
   a. Brazil
   b. Korea
   c. China
   d. Japan
   e. Argentina

   Carefully explain why each factor that you specify relates to the risk exposure that an international bank making loans in each nation faces. What recent developments in each of the above nations suggest that a new assessment of country risk may be in order?

5. Please identify the key terms and concepts discussed in this chapter as described in each sentence or phrase listed below.
   a. Large, nonfinancial companies with manufacturing and trading operations in several different countries.

b. Offshore banking offices designed to collect funds and avoid regulations.

c. Facilities to aid international banking customers but these facilities cannot accept deposits or make loans.

d. Subsidiaries of U.S. banking corporations or foreign banking companies active in the United States that offer banking services to accounts overseas.

e. A domestically based set of computerized accounts recording international banking transactions.

f. Deposits in a bank denominated in a currency other than the currency of the bank's home currency.

g. Loans made by a bank in a currency other than the currency of the bank's home country.

h. A long-term debt security denominated in a foreign currency.

i. A U.S. law passed during the 1970s to bring foreign banks operating in the United States under government regulation for the first time.

j. A U.S. law passed in 1983 requiring U.S. banks to increase their capital and to pursue more prudent international loan policies.

k. An agreement among leading industrialized nations to require their banks to hold the same capital requirements and to adopt the same capital standards.

Questions about the Web and the Money and Capital Markets

1. Where are the world's leading international banks located primarily? Where on the Web can you find the answer? Which Web site did you use and what did you find?

2. After checking out the Web sites of some of the world's leading international banks (such as Citicorp, Deutsche Bank, and Barclays), can you say what key services they appear to provide their international customers? Are there differences in the international services that various banks offer? Why do you think this is so?

3. Why is the legal system of any nation important to an international banker? What differences in financial-service laws exist among various countries? Can you find some examples of these differences in banking-related laws from nation to nation on the Web?

4. If you wanted to train to be an international banker what publications that you spotted on the Web appear to be the most useful in getting you closer to that goal? Please make a list of at least 10 publications you found that appear to be helpful.

5. What did you find out about the World Bank on the Web that you didn't already know? How about the Bank for International Settlements (BIS)? The International Monetary Fund (IMF)? Why, according to the Web, are these institutions of special importance in the international financial system?

Selected References

Barth, James R.; Daniel E. Nolle; and Tara N. Rice. "Commercial Banking Structure, Regulation and Performance: An International Comparison." Economic Working Paper 97-6, Comptroller of the Currency, March 1997.

Craig, Valentine V. "Financial Deregulation in Japan." *FDIC Banking Review*, Federal Deposit Insurance Corporation, 1998, pp. 1–12.

Crystal, Jennifer S.; B. Gerald Dages; and Linda S. Goldberg. "Has Foreign Bank Entry Led to Sounder Banks in Latin America?" *Current Issues in Economics and Finance*, Federal Reserve Bank of New York, January 2002, pp. 1–6.

Curry, Timothy; Christopher Richardson; and Robin Heider. "Assessing International Risk Exposures of U.S. Banks." *FDIC Banking Review*, Federal Deposit Insurance Corporation, 1998, pp. 13–30.

Klein, Michael W. "European Monetary Union." *New England Economic Review*, Federal Reserve Bank of Boston, March–April 1998, pp. 3–12.

Rose, Peter S. *Commercial Bank Management*, 5th ed. New York: McGraw-Hill, 2002.

———— . "Foreign Banking in the United States." *The Canadian Banker*, May–June 1976, pp. 58–61.

Zarazaga, Carlos E. J. M. "Do International Financial Crises Defy Diagnosis?" *Southwestern Economy*, Federal Reserve Bank of Dallas, pp. 10–12.

Appendix

Present Value, Annuity, Compound Interest, and Annual Percentage Rate (APR) Tables

Present Value Table

Present Value of $1 to Be Received N Years in the Future

Years Hence	1%	2%	4%	6%	8%	10%	12%	14%	15%	16%	18%	20%	22%	24%	25%	26%	28%	30%	35%	40%	45%	50%
1	0.990	0.980	0.962	0.943	0.926	0.909	0.893	0.877	0.870	0.862	0.847	0.883	0.820	0.806	0.800	0.794	0.781	0.769	0.741	0.714	0.690	0.667
2	0.980	0.961	0.925	0.890	0.857	0.826	0.797	0.769	0.756	0.743	0.718	0.694	0.672	0.650	0.640	0.630	0.610	0.592	0.549	0.510	0.476	0.444
3	0.971	0.942	0.889	0.840	0.794	0.751	0.712	0.675	0.658	0.641	0.609	0.579	0.551	0.524	0.512	0.500	0.477	0.455	0.406	0.364	0.328	0.296
4	0.961	0.924	0.855	0.792	0.735	0.683	0.636	0.592	0.572	0.552	0.516	0.482	0.451	0.423	0.410	0.397	0.373	0.350	0.301	0.260	0.226	0.198
5	0.951	0.906	0.822	0.747	0.681	0.621	0.567	0.519	0.497	0.476	0.437	0.402	0.370	0.341	0.328	0.315	0.291	0.269	0.223	0.186	0.156	0.132
6	0.942	0.888	0.790	0.705	0.630	0.564	0.507	0.456	0.432	0.410	0.370	0.335	0.303	0.275	0.262	0.250	0.227	0.207	0.165	0.133	0.108	0.088
7	0.933	0.871	0.760	0.665	0.583	0.513	0.452	0.400	0.376	0.354	0.314	0.279	0.249	0.222	0.210	0.198	0.178	0.159	0.122	0.095	0.074	0.059
8	0.923	0.853	0.731	0.627	0.540	0.467	0.404	0.351	0.327	0.305	0.266	0.233	0.204	0.179	0.168	0.157	0.139	0.123	0.091	0.068	0.051	0.039
9	0.914	0.837	0.703	0.592	0.500	0.424	0.361	0.308	0.284	0.263	0.225	0.194	0.167	0.144	0.134	0.125	0.108	0.094	0.067	0.048	0.035	0.026
10	0.905	0.820	0.676	0.558	0.463	0.386	0.322	0.270	0.247	0.227	0.191	0.162	0.137	0.116	0.107	0.099	0.085	0.073	0.050	0.035	0.024	0.017
11	0.896	0.804	0.650	.0527	0.429	0.350	0.287	0.237	0.215	0.195	0.162	0.135	0.112	0.094	0.086	0.079	0.066	0.056	0.037	0.025	0.017	0.012
12	0.887	0.788	0.625	0.497	0.397	0.319	0.257	0.208	.0187	0.168	0.137	0.113	0.092	0.076	0.069	0.062	0.052	0.043	0.027	0.018	0.012	0.008
13	0.879	0.773	0.601	0.469	0.368	0.290	0.229	0.182	0.163	0.145	0.116	0.093	0.075	0.061	0.055	0.050	0.040	0.033	0.020	0.013	0.008	0.005
14	0.870	0.758	0.577	0.442	0.340	0.263	0.205	0.160	0.141	0.125	0.099	0.078	0.062	0.049	0.044	0.039	0.032	0.025	0.015	0.009	0.006	0.003
15	0.861	0.743	0.555	0.417	0.315	0.239	0.183	0.140	0.123	0.108	0.084	0.065	0.051	0.040	0.035	0.031	0.025	0.020	0.011	0.006	0.004	0.002
16	0.853	0.728	0.534	0.394	0.292	0.218	0.163	0.123	0.107	0.093	0.071	0.054	0.042	0.032	0.028	0.025	0.019	0.015	0.008	0.005	0.003	0.002
17	0.844	0.714	0.513	0.371	0.270	0.198	0.146	0.108	0.093	0.080	0.060	0.045	0.034	0.026	0.023	0.020	0.015	0.012	0.006	0.003	0.002	0.001
18	0.836	0.700	0.494	0.350	0.250	0.180	0.130	0.095	0.081	0.069	0.051	0.038	0.028	0.021	0.018	0.016	0.012	0.009	0.005	0.002	0.001	0.001
19	0.828	0.686	0.475	0.331	0.232	0.164	0.116	0.083	0.070	0.060	0.043	0.031	0.023	0.017	0.014	0.012	0.009	0.007	0.003	0.002	0.001	
20	0.820	0.673	0.456	0.312	0.215	0.149	0.104	0.073	0.061	0.051	0.037	0.026	0.019	0.014	0.012	0.010	0.007	0.005	0.002	0.001	0.001	
21	0.811	0.660	0.439	0.294	0.199	0.135	0.093	0.064	0.053	0.044	0.031	0.022	0.015	0.011	0.009	0.008	0.006	0.004	0.002	0.001		
22	0.803	0.647	0.422	0.278	0.184	0.123	0.083	0.056	0.046	0.038	0.026	0.018	0.013	0.009	0.007	0.006	0.004	0.003	0.001	0.001		
23	0.795	0.634	0.406	0.262	0.170	0.112	0.074	0.049	0.040	0.033	0.022	0.015	0.010	0.007	0.006	0.005	0.003	0.002	0.001			
24	0.788	0.622	0.390	0.247	0.158	0.102	0.066	0.043	0.035	0.028	0.019	0.013	0.008	0.006	0.005	0.004	0.003	0.002	0.001			
25	0.780	0.610	0.375	0.233	0.146	0.092	0.059	0.038	0.030	0.024	0.016	0.010	0.007	0.005	0.004	0.003	0.002	0.001				
26	0.772	0.598	0.361	0.220	0.135	0.084	0.053	0.033	0.026	0.021	0.014	0.009	0.006	0.004	0.003	0.002	0.002	0.001				
27	0.764	0.586	0.347	0.207	0.125	0.076	0.047	0.029	0.023	0.018	0.011	0.007	0.005	0.003	0.002	0.002	0.001	0.001				
28	0.757	0.574	0.333	0.196	0.116	0.069	0.042	0.026	0.020	0.016	0.010	0.006	0.004	0.002	0.002	0.002	0.001	0.001				
29	0.749	0.563	0.321	0.185	0.107	0.063	0.037	0.022	0.017	0.014	0.008	0.005	0.003	0.002	0.002	0.001	0.001	0.001				
30	0.742	0.552	0.308	0.174	0.099	0.57	0.033	0.020	0.015	0.012	0.007	0.004	0.003	0.001	0.001	0.001	0.001	0.001				
40	0.672	0.453	0.208	0.097	0.046	0.022	0.011	0.005	0.004	0.003	0.001	0.001										
50	0.608	0.372	0.141	0.054	0.021	0.009	0.003	0.001	0.001	0.001												

Source: Robert N. Anthony and James S. Reece, *Accounting Principles*, 4th ed. (Homewood, IL: Richard D. Irwin, 1979).

Annuity Table

Present Value of $1 Received Annually for N Years Running

Years (N)	1%	2%	4%	6%	8%	10%	12%	14%	15%	16%	18%	20%	22%	24%	25%	26%	28%	30%	35%	40%	45%	50%
1	0.990	0.980	0.962	0.943	0.926	0.909	0.893	0.877	0.870	0.862	0.847	0.833	0.820	0.806	0.800	0.794	0.781	0.769	0.741	0.714	0.690	0.667
2	1.970	1.942	1.886	1.833	1.783	1.736	1.690	1.647	1.626	1.605	1.566	1.528	1.492	1.457	1.440	1.424	1.392	1.361	1.289	1.224	1.165	1.111
3	2.941	2.884	2.775	2.673	2.577	2.487	2.402	2.322	2.283	2.246	2.174	2.106	2.042	1.981	1.952	1.923	1.868	1.816	1.696	1.589	1.493	1.407
4	3.902	3.808	3.630	3.465	3.312	3.170	3.037	2.914	2.855	2.798	2.690	2.589	2.494	2.404	2.362	2.320	2.241	2.166	1.997	1.849	1.720	1.605
5	4.853	4.713	4.452	4.212	3.993	3.791	3.605	3.433	3.352	3.274	3.127	2.991	2.864	2.745	2.689	2.635	2.532	2.436	2.220	2.035	1.876	1.737
6	5.795	5.601	5.242	4.917	4.623	4.355	4.111	3.889	3.784	3.685	3.498	3.326	3.167	3.020	2.951	2.885	2.759	2.643	2.385	2.168	1.983	1.824
7	6.728	6.472	6.002	5.582	5.206	4.868	4.564	4.288	4.160	4.039	3.812	3.605	3.416	3.242	3.161	3.083	2.937	2.802	2.508	2.263	2.057	1.883
8	7.652	7.325	6.733	6.210	5.747	5.335	4.968	4.639	4.487	4.344	4.078	3.837	3.619	3.421	3.329	3.241	3.076	2.925	2.598	2.331	2.108	1.922
9	8.566	8.162	7.435	6.802	6.247	5.759	5.328	4.946	4.772	4.607	4.303	4.031	3.786	3.566	3.463	3.366	3.184	3.019	2.665	2.379	2.144	1.948
10	9.471	8.983	8.111	7.360	6.710	6.145	5.650	5.216	5.019	4.833	4.494	4.192	3.923	3.682	3.571	3.465	3.269	3.092	2.715	2.414	2.168	1.965
11	10.368	9.787	8.760	7.887	7.139	6.495	5.937	5.453	5.234	5.029	4.656	4.327	4.035	3.776	3.656	3.544	3.335	3.147	2.752	2.438	2.185	1.977
12	11.255	10.575	9.385	8.384	7.536	6.814	6.194	5.660	5.421	5.197	4.793	4.439	4.127	3.851	3.725	3.606	3.387	3.190	2.779	2.456	2.196	1.985
13	12.134	11.343	9.986	8.853	7.904	7.103	6.424	5.842	5.583	5.342	4.910	4.533	4.203	3.912	3.780	3.656	3.427	3.223	2.799	2.468	2.204	1.990
14	13.004	12.106	10.563	9.295	8.244	7.367	6.628	6.002	5.724	5.468	5.008	4.611	4.265	3.962	3.824	3.695	3.459	3.249	2.814	2.477	2.210	1.993
15	13.865	12.849	11.118	9.712	8.559	7.606	6.811	6.142	5.847	5.575	5.092	4.675	4.315	4.001	3.859	3.726	3.483	3.268	2.825	2.484	2.214	1.995
16	14.718	13.578	11.652	10.106	8.851	7.824	6.974	6.265	5.954	5.669	5.162	4.730	4.357	4.033	3.887	3.751	3.503	3.283	2.834	2.489	2.216	1.997
17	15.562	14.292	12.166	10.477	9.122	8.022	7.120	6.373	6.047	5.749	5.222	4.775	4.391	4.059	3.910	3.771	3.518	3.295	2.840	2.492	2.218	1.998
18	16.398	14.992	12.659	10.828	9.372	8.201	7.250	6.467	6.128	5.818	5.273	4.812	4.419	4.080	3.928	3.786	3.529	3.304	2.844	2.494	2.219	1.999
19	17.226	15.678	13.134	11.158	9.604	8.365	7.366	6.550	6.198	5.877	5.316	4.844	4.442	4.097	3.942	3.799	3.539	3.311	2.848	2.496	2.220	1.999
20	18.046	16.351	13.590	11.470	9.818	8.514	7.469	6.623	6.259	5.929	5.353	4.870	4.460	4.110	3.954	3.808	3.546	3.316	2.850	2.497	2.221	1.999
21	18.857	17.011	14.029	11.764	10.017	8.649	7.562	6.687	6.312	5.973	5.384	4.891	4.476	4.121	3.963	3.816	3.551	3.320	2.852	2.498	2.221	2.000
22	19.660	17.658	14.451	12.042	10.201	8.772	7.645	6.743	6.359	6.011	5.410	4.909	4.488	4.130	3.970	3.822	3.556	3.323	2.853	2.498	2.222	2.000
23	20.456	18.292	14.857	12.303	10.371	8.883	7.718	6.792	6.399	6.044	5.432	4.925	4.499	4.137	3.976	3.827	3.559	3.325	2.854	2.499	2.222	2.000
24	21.243	18.914	15.247	12.550	10.529	8.985	7.784	6.835	6.434	6.073	5.451	4.937	4.507	4.143	3.981	3.831	3.562	3.327	2.855	2.499	2.222	2.000
25	22.023	19.523	15.622	12.783	10.675	9.077	7.843	6.873	6.464	6.097	5.467	4.948	4.514	4.147	3.985	3.834	3.564	3.329	2.856	2.499	2.222	2.000
26	22.795	20.121	15.983	13.003	10.810	9.161	7.896	6.906	6.491	6.118	5.480	4.956	4.520	4.151	3.988	3.837	3.566	3.330	2.856	2.500	2.222	2.000
27	23.560	20.707	16.330	13.211	10.935	9.237	7.943	6.935	6.514	6.136	5.492	4.964	4.524	4.154	3.990	3.839	3.567	3.331	2.856	2.500	2.222	2.000
28	24.316	21.281	16.663	13.406	11.051	9.307	7.984	6.961	6.534	6.152	5.502	4.970	4.528	4.157	3.992	3.840	3.568	3.331	2.857	2.500	2.222	2.000
29	25.066	21.844	16.984	13.591	11.159	9.370	8.022	6.983	6.551	6.166	5.510	4.975	4.531	4.159	3.994	3.841	3.569	3.332	2.857	2.500	2.222	2.000
30	25.808	22.396	17.292	13.765	11.258	9.427	8.055	7.003	6.566	6.177	5.517	4.979	4.534	4.160	3.995	3.842	3.569	3.332	2.857	2.500	2.222	2.000
40	32.835	27.355	19.793	15.046	11.925	9.779	8.244	7.105	6.642	6.234	5.548	4.997	4.544	4.166	3.999	3.846	3.571	3.333	2.857	2.500	2.222	2.000
50	39.196	31.424	21.482	15.762	12.234	9.915	8.304	7.133	6.661	6.246	5.554	4.999	4.545	4.167	4.000	3.846	3.571	3.333	2.857	2.500	2.222	2.000

Source: Robert N. Anthony and James S. Reece, *Accounting Principles*, 4th ed. (Homewood, IL: Richard D. Irwin, 1979).

Compound Interest Rate Table

Annual Percentage Rate

(Future Value of $1—Principal Plus Accumulated Interest)

Number of Periods	1.00%	1.50%	2.00%	2.50%	3.00%	3.50%	4.00%	4.50%	5.00%	6.00%	7.00%	8.00%	9.00%	10.00%	12.00%	14.00%	16.00%	18.00%
1	1.010	1.015	1.020	1.025	1.030	1.035	1.040	1.045	1.050	1.060	1.070	1.080	1.090	1.100	1.120	1.140	1.160	1.180
2	1.020	1.030	1.040	1.051	1.061	1.071	1.082	1.092	1.103	1.124	1.145	1.166	1.188	1.210	1.254	1.300	1.346	1.392
3	1.030	1.046	1.061	1.077	1.093	1.109	1.125	1.141	1.158	1.191	1.225	1.260	1.295	1.331	1.405	1.482	1.561	1.643
4	1.041	1.061	1.082	1.104	1.126	1.148	1.170	1.193	1.216	1.262	1.311	1.360	1.412	1.464	1.574	1.689	1.811	1.939
5	1.051	1.077	1.104	1.131	1.159	1.188	1.217	1.246	1.276	1.338	1.403	1.469	1.539	1.611	1.762	1.925	2.100	2.288
6	1.062	1.093	1.126	1.160	1.194	1.229	1.265	1.302	1.340	1.419	1.501	1.587	1.677	1.772	1.974	2.195	2.436	2.700
7	1.072	1.110	1.149	1.189	1.230	1.272	1.316	1.361	1.407	1.504	1.606	1.714	1.828	1.949	2.211	2.502	2.826	3.185
8	1.083	1.126	1.172	1.218	1.267	1.317	1.369	1.422	1.477	1.594	1.718	1.851	1.993	2.144	2.476	2.853	3.278	3.759
9	1.094	1.143	1.195	1.249	1.305	1.363	1.423	1.486	1.551	1.689	1.838	1.999	2.172	2.358	2.773	3.252	3.803	4.435
10	1.105	1.161	1.219	1.280	1.344	1.411	1.480	1.553	1.629	1.791	1.967	2.159	2.367	2.594	3.106	3.707	4.411	5.234
11	1.116	1.178	1.243	1.312	1.384	1.460	1.539	1.623	1.710	1.898	2.105	2.332	2.580	2.853	3.479	4.226	5.117	6.176
12	1.127	1.196	1.268	1.345	1.426	1.511	1.601	1.696	1.796	2.012	2.252	2.518	2.813	3.138	3.896	4.818	5.936	7.288
14	1.149	1.232	1.319	1.413	1.513	1.619	1.732	1.852	1.980	2.261	2.579	2.937	3.342	3.797	4.887	6.261	7.988	10.147
16	1.173	1.269	1.373	1.485	1.605	1.734	1.873	2.022	2.183	2.540	2.952	3.426	3.970	4.595	6.130	8.137	10.748	14.129
18	1.196	1.307	1.428	1.560	1.702	1.857	2.026	2.208	2.407	2.854	3.380	3.996	4.717	5.560	7.690	10.575	14.463	19.673

Compound Interest Rate Table (continued)

Annual Percentage Rate

(Future Value of $1—Principal Plus Accumulated Interest)

Number of Periods	1.00%	1.50%	2.00%	2.50%	3.00%	3.50%	4.00%	4.50%	5.00%	6.00%	7.00%	8.00%	9.00%	10.00%	12.00%	14.00%	16.00%	18.00%
20	1.220	1.347	1.486	1.639	1.806	1.990	2.191	2.412	2.653	3.207	3.870	4.661	5.604	6.727	9.646	13.743	19.461	27.393
22	1.245	1.388	1.546	1.722	1.916	2.132	2.370	2.634	2.925	3.604	4.430	5.437	6.659	8.140	12.100	17.861	26.186	38.142
24	1.270	1.430	1.608	1.809	2.033	2.283	2.563	2.876	3.225	4.049	5.072	6.341	7.911	9.850	15.179	23.212	35.236	53.109
26	1.295	1.473	1.673	1.900	2.157	2.446	2.772	3.141	3.556	4.549	5.807	7.396	9.399	11.918	19.040	30.167	47.414	73.949
28	1.321	1.517	1.741	1.996	2.288	2.620	2.999	3.430	3.920	5.112	6.649	8.627	11.167	14.421	23.884	39.204	63.800	102.967
30	1.348	1.563	1.811	2.098	2.427	2.807	3.243	3.745	4.322	5.743	7.612	10.063	13.268	17.449	29.960	50.950	85.850	143.371
32	1.375	1.610	1.884	2.204	2.575	3.007	3.508	4.090	4.765	6.453	8.715	11.737	15.763	21.114	37.582	66.215	115.520	199.629
34	1.403	1.659	1.961	2.315	2.732	3.221	3.794	4.466	5.253	7.251	9.978	13.690	18.728	25.548	47.143	86.053	155.443	277.964
36	1.431	1.709	2.040	2.433	2.898	3.450	4.104	4.877	5.792	8.147	11.424	15.968	22.251	30.913	59.136	111.834	209.164	387.037
38	1.460	1.761	2.122	2.556	3.075	3.696	4.439	5.326	6.385	9.154	13.079	18.625	26.437	37.404	74.180	145.340	281.452	538.910
40	1.489	1.814	2.208	2.685	3.262	3.959	4.801	5.816	7.040	10.286	14.974	21.725	31.409	45.259	93.051	188.884	378.721	750.378
42	1.519	1.869	2.297	2.821	3.461	4.241	5.193	6.352	7.762	11.557	17.144	25.339	37.318	54.764	116.723	245.473	509.607	1044.827
44	1.549	1.925	2.390	2.964	3.671	4.543	5.617	6.936	8.557	12.985	19.628	29.556	44.337	66.264	146.418	319.017	685.727	1454.817
46	1.580	1.984	2.487	3.114	3.895	4.867	6.075	7.574	9.434	14.590	22.473	34.474	52.677	80.180	183.666	414.594	922.715	2025.687
48	1.612	2.043	2.587	3.271	4.132	5.214	6.571	8.271	10.401	16.394	25.729	40.211	62.585	97.017	230.391	538.807	1241.605	2820.567
50	1.645	2.105	2.692	3.437	4.384	5.585	7.107	9.033	11.467	18.420	29.457	46.902	74.357	117.391	289.002	700.233	1670.704	3927.357
52	1.678	2.169	2.800	3.611	4.651	5.983	7.687	9.864	12.643	20.697	33.725	54.706	88.344	142.043	362.524	910.023	2248.099	5468.452
54	1.711	2.234	2.913	3.794	4.934	6.409	8.314	10.771	13.939	23.255	38.612	63.809	104.962	171.872	454.751	1182.666	3025.042	7614.272
56	1.746	2.302	3.031	3.986	5.235	6.865	8.992	11.763	15.367	26.129	44.207	74.427	124.705	207.965	570.439	1536.992	4070.497	10602.113
58	1.781	2.372	3.154	4.188	5.553	7.354	9.726	12.845	16.943	29.359	50.613	86.812	148.162	251.638	715.559	1997.475	5477.260	14762.381
60	1.817	2.443	3.281	4.400	5.892	7.878	10.520	14.027	18.679	32.988	57.946	101.257	176.031	304.482	897.597	2595.919	7370.201	20555.140

Source: Federal Reserve Bank of New York, *The Arithmetic of Interest Rates*, pp. 26–27.

Interest Rate Table for Daily Compounding (360-Day Basis Year)

Number of Years	Annual Percentage Rate					
	5.00%	**5.25%**	**5.50%**	**5.75%**	**6.00%**	**6.25%**
	(What a $1 Deposit Will Grow to in the Future)					
1	1.0520	1.0547	1.0573	1.0600	1.0627	1.0654
2	1.1067	1.1123	1.1180	1.1237	1.1294	1.1351
3	1.1642	1.1731	1.1821	1.1911	1.2002	1.2094
4	1.2248	1.2373	1.2499	1.2626	1.2755	1.2885
5	1.2885	1.3049	1.3215	1.3384	1.3555	1.3727
6	1.3555	1.3762	1.3973	1.4187	1.4405	1.4625
7	1.4259	1.4515	1.4774	1.5039	1.5308	1.5582
8	1.5001	1.5308	1.5622	1.5942	1.6268	1.6601
9	1.5781	1.6145	1.6518	1.6899	1.7288	1.7687
10	1.6602	1.7028	1.7465	1.7913	1.8373	1.8844
15	2.1391	2.2219	2.3080	2.3975	2.4904	2.5868
20	2.7561	2.8994	3.0502	3.2087	3.3756	3.5511
25	3.5512	3.7834	4.0309	4.2946	4.5755	4.8747
30	4.5756	4.9370	5.3270	5.7478	6.2019	6.6918

Number of Years	Annual Percentage Rate					
	8.25%	**8.50%**	**8.75%**	**9.00%**	**9.25%**	**9.50%**
	(What a $1 Deposit Will Grow to in the Future)					
1	1.0872	1.0900	1.0928	1.0955	1.0983	1.1011
2	1.1821	1.1881	1.1941	1.2002	1.2063	1.2124
3	1.2852	1.2950	1.3049	1.3148	1.3249	1.3350
4	1.3973	1.4115	1.4259	1.4404	1.4551	1.4699
5	1.5192	1.5386	1.5582	1.5781	1.5982	1.6186
6	1.6517	1.6770	1.7027	1.7288	1.7553	1.7822
7	1.7958	1.8279	1.8607	1.8940	1.9279	1.9624
8	1.9525	1.9924	2.0333	2.0749	2.1174	2.1607
9	2.1228	2.1718	2.2219	2.2731	2.3255	2.3792
10	2.3080	2.3672	2.4279	2.4903	2.5542	2.6197
15	3.5062	3.6421	3.7832	3.9298	4.0820	4.2402
20	5.3267	5.6036	5.8949	6.2014	6.5238	6.8629
25	8.0922	8.6215	9.1854	9.7861	10.4261	11.1080
30	12.2937	13.2648	14.3125	15.4430	16.6628	17.9790

Source: Federal Reserve Bank of New York.

Interest Rate Table for Daily Compounding (360-Day Basis Year) (continued)

Annual Percentage Rate

6.50%	6.75%	7.00%	7.25%	7.50%	7.75%	8.00%
			(What a $1 Deposit Will Grow to in the Future)			
1.0681	1.0708	1.0735	1.0763	1.0790	1.0817	1.0845
1.1409	1.1467	1.1525	1.1584	1.1642	1.1702	1.1761
1.2186	1.2279	1.2373	1.2467	1.2562	1.2658	1.2755
1.3016	1.3149	1.3282	1.3418	1.3555	1.3693	1.3832
1.3903	1.4080	1.4259	1.4441	1.4625	1.4812	1.5001
1.4850	1.5077	1.5308	1.5543	1.5781	1.6022	1.6268
1.5861	1.6145	1.6434	1.6728	1.7027	1.7332	1.7642
1.6941	1.7288	1.7642	1.8004	1.8373	1.8749	1.9133
1.8095	1.8513	1.8940	1.9377	1.9824	2.0281	2.0749
1.9328	1.9824	2.0333	2.0855	2.1390	2.1939	2.2502
2.6871	2.7912	2.8993	3.0117	3.1284	3.2496	3.3755
3.7357	3.9299	4.1343	4.3492	4.5753	4.8132	5.0634
5.1936	5.5333	5.8952	6.2807	6.6915	7.1292	7.5955
7.2204	7.7907	8.4061	9.0701	9.7866	10.5596	11.3937

Annual Percentage Rate

9.75%	10.00%	10.25%	10.50%	11.00%	12.00%	13.00%
			(What a $1 Deposit Will Grow to in the Future)			
1.1039	1.1067	1.1095	1.1123	1.1180	1.1294	1.1409
1.2186	1.2248	1.2310	1.2372	1.2498	1.2754	1.3016
1.3452	1.3554	1.3658	1.3762	1.3973	1.4404	1.4849
1.4849	1.5001	1.5153	1.5308	1.5621	1.6268	1.6941
1.6392	1.6601	1.6813	1.7027	1.7464	1.8372	1.9327
1.8095	1.8372	1.8654	1.8939	1.9524	2.0748	2.2049
1.9975	2.0332	2.0696	2.1067	2.1827	2.3432	2.5155
2.2050	2.2502	2.2962	2.3433	2.4402	2.6463	2.8698
2.4341	2.4902	2.5477	2.6064	2.7281	2.9886	3.2741
2.6870	2.7559	2.8266	2.8992	3.0499	3.3752	3.7353
4.4044	4.5751	4.7523	4.9364	5.3263	6.2009	7.2191
7.2197	7.5950	7.9899	8.4053	9.3019	11.3922	13.9522
11.8345	12.6085	13.4331	14.3116	16.2447	20.9295	26.9651
19.3990	20.9313	22.5845	24.3683	28.3697	38.4513	52.1150

Annual Percentage Rate Table for Monthly Payment Plans

Number of Payments	10.00%	10.50%	11.00%	11.50%	12.00%	12.50%	13.00%	13.50%
			Annual Percentage Rate					
			(Finance Charge Per $100 of Amount Financed)					
1	0.83	0.87	0.92	0.96	1.00	1.04	1.08	1.12
2	1.25	1.31	1.38	1.44	1.50	1.57	1.63	1.69
3	1.67	1.76	1.84	1.92	2.01	2.09	2.17	2.26
4	2.09	2.20	2.30	2.41	2.51	2.62	2.72	2.83
5	2.51	2.64	2.77	2.89	3.02	3.15	3.27	3.40
6	2.94	3.08	3.23	3.38	3.53	3.68	3.83	3.97
7	3.36	3.53	3.70	3.87	4.04	4.21	4.38	4.55
8	3.79	3.98	4.17	4.36	4.55	4.74	4.94	5.13
9	4.21	4.43	4.64	4.85	5.07	5.28	5.49	5.71
10	4.64	4.88	5.11	5.35	5.58	5.82	6.05	6.29
11	5.07	5.33	5.58	5.84	6.10	6.36	6.62	6.88
12	5.50	5.78	6.06	6.34	6.62	6.90	7.18	7.46
18	8.10	8.52	8.93	9.35	9.77	10.19	10.61	11.03
24	10.75	11.30	11.83	12.42	12.98	13.54	14.10	14.66
30	13.43	14.13	14.83	15.54	16.24	16.95	17.66	18.38
36	16.16	17.01	17.86	18.71	19.57	20.43	21.30	22.17
42	18.93	19.93	20.93	21.94	22.96	23.98	25.00	26.03
48	21.74	22.90	24.06	25.23	26.40	27.58	28.77	29.97
54	24.59	25.91	27.23	28.56	29.91	31.25	32.61	33.98
60	27.48	28.96	30.45	31.96	33.47	34.99	36.52	38.06
66	30.41	32.06	33.73	35.40	37.09	38.78	40.49	42.21
72	33.39	35.21	37.05	38.90	40.76	42.64	44.53	46.44
78	36.40	38.40	40.41	42.45	44.49	46.45	48.64	50.74
84	39.45	41.63	43.83	46.05	48.28	50.54	52.81	55.11
90	42.54	44.91	47.29	49.70	52.13	54.58	57.05	59.54
96	45.67	48.22	50.80	53.40	56.03	58.68	61.35	64.05
102	48.84	51.59	54.36	57.16	59.98	62.83	65.71	68.62
108	52.05	54.99	57.96	60.96	63.99	67.05	70.14	73.26
114	55.30	58.43	61.61	64.81	68.05	71.32	74.63	77.96
120	58.58	61.92	65.30	68.71	72.17	75.65	79.17	82.73
180	93.43	98.97	104.59	110.27	116.03	121.85	127.74	133.70
240	131.61	139.61	147.73	155.94	164.26	172.67	181.18	189.77
300	172.61	183.25	194.03	204.94	215.97	227.11	238.35	249.69
360	215.93	229.31	242.84	256.50	270.30	284.21	298.23	312.35

Source: Federal Reserve Bank of New York.

Annual Percentage Rate Table for Monthly Payment Plans (continued)

Annual Percentage Rate								
14.00%	**14.50%**	**15.00%**	**15.50%**	**16.00%**	**16.50%**	**17.00%**	**17.50%**	**18.00%**
(Finance Charge Per $100 of Amount Financed)								
1.17	1.21	1.25	1.29	1.33	1.37	1.42	1.46	1.50
1.75	1.82	1.88	1.94	2.00	2.07	2.13	2.19	2.26
2.34	2.43	2.51	2.59	2.68	2.76	2.85	2.93	3.01
2.93	3.04	3.14	3.25	3.36	3.46	3.57	3.67	3.78
3.53	3.65	3.78	3.91	4.04	4.16	4.29	4.42	4.54
4.12	4.27	4.42	4.57	4.72	4.87	5.02	5.17	5.32
4.72	4.89	5.06	5.23	5.40	5.58	5.75	5.92	6.09
5.32	5.51	5.71	5.90	6.09	6.29	6.48	6.67	6.87
5.92	6.14	6.35	6.57	6.78	7.00	7.22	7.43	7.65
6.53	6.77	7.00	7.24	7.48	7.72	7.96	8.19	8.43
7.14	7.40	7.66	7.92	8.18	8.44	8.70	8.96	9.22
7.74	8.03	8.31	8.59	8.88	9.16	9.45	9.73	10.02
11.45	11.87	12.29	12.72	13.14	13.57	13.99	14.42	14.85
15.23	15.80	16.37	16.94	17.51	18.09	18.66	19.24	19.82
19.10	19.81	20.54	21.26	21.99	22.72	23.45	24.18	24.92
23.04	23.92	24.80	25.68	26.57	27.46	28.35	29.25	30.15
27.06	28.10	29.15	30.19	31.25	32.31	33.37	34.44	35.51
31.17	32.37	33.59	34.81	36.03	37.27	38.50	39.75	41.00
35.35	36.73	38.12	39.52	40.92	42.33	43.75	45.18	46.62
39.61	41.17	42.74	44.32	45.91	47.51	49.12	50.73	52.36
43.95	45.69	47.45	49.22	51.00	52.79	54.59	56.40	58.23
48.36	50.30	52.24	54.21	56.18	58.17	60.17	62.19	64.22
52.85	54.98	57.13	59.29	61.46	63.66	65.86	68.09	70.32
57.42	59.75	62.09	64.46	66.84	69.24	71.66	74.10	76.55
62.05	64.59	67.14	69.72	72.31	74.93	77.56	80.22	82.89
66.77	69.51	72.28	75.06	77.88	80.71	83.57	86.44	89.34
71.55	74.51	77.49	80.50	83.53	86.59	89.67	92.78	95.91
76.40	79.58	82.78	86.01	89.27	92.56	95.87	99.21	102.57
81.33	84.73	88.15	91.61	95.10	98.62	102.17	105.74	109.35
86.32	89.94	93.60	97.29	101.02	104.77	108.56	112.37	116.22
139.71	145.79	151.93	158.12	164.37	170.67	177.02	183.42	189.88
198.44	207.20	216.03	224.93	233.90	242.94	252.03	261.19	270.39
216.13	272.65	284.25	295.92	307.67	319.47	331.34	343.26	355.23
326.55	340.84	355.20	369.63	384.11	398.65	413.24	427.88	442.55

Money and Capital Markets Dictionary

A

actual maturity   The number of days, months, or years between today and the date a loan or security is redeemed or retired. *(Chapter 10)*

add-on rate   A method for calculating the interest charge on a loan when the interest bill is added to the principal amount of the loan. That sum is then divided by the number of installment payments required to determine the amount of each payment needed to eventually pay off the loan. *(Chapter 6)*

adjustable mortgage instrument (AMI)   A home mortgage loan under which some of the terms of the loan, such as the loan rate or the maturity of the loan, will vary as market conditions change. *(Chapter 24)*

agency offices   Facilities operated in overseas markets by international banks in order to provide customers with selected services (such as cash management). *(Chapter 26)*

American depository receipts (ADRs)   Dollar-denominated claims on specific foreign shares of stock that are held in safekeeping by U.S. financial institutions, giving U.S. investors access to selected foreign stock without having to accept or make payments in foreign currencies. *(Chapter 22)*

annual percentage rate (APR)   The actuarially determined rate on a consumer loan that the federal Truth-in-Lending law requires lenders to communicate to borrowers. *(Chapter 6)*

annual percentage yield (APY)   The annualized rate of return on a savings account that U.S. depository institutions must report to their customers. *(Chapter 6)*

arbitrage   The purchase of a security or currency in one market and the sale of that security or currency in another market in response to differences in price or yield between the two markets. *(Chapters 1 and 25)*

asked price   The price at which a securities dealer is willing to sell securities to the public. *(Chapter 3)*

asymmetric information   The concept that different participants in the financial markets often operate with different sets of information, some possessing special or inside information that others do not possess. *(Chapter 1)*

asymmetry   The financial marketplace contains pockets of inefficiency in the availability and use of information relevant to the value *(price)* of assets. *(Chapter 3)*

auction   A method used to sell securities in which buyers file bids and the highest bidders receive securities. *(Chapter 11)*

auction method   The principal means by which U.S. Treasury securities are sold to the public. *(Chapters 11 and 19)*

B

balance-of-payments (BOP) accounts   A double-entry bookkeeping system recording a nation's transactions with other nations, including exports, imports, and capital flows. *(Chapter 25)*

bank discount method   The procedure by which yields on U.S. Treasury bills, commercial paper, and bankers' acceptances are calculated; a 360-day year is assumed, and there is no compounding of interest income. *(Chapter 11)*

bankers' acceptance   A time draft against a bank that the bank has agreed to pay unconditionally on the date the draft matures. *(Chapter 12)*

bank holding company   A corporation that owns stock in one or more commercial banks. *(Chapter 15)*

banking structure   The number, relative sizes, and types of banks in a given market or in the industry as a whole. *(Chapter 15)*

base rate   A loan rate used as the basis or foundation for determining the size of the current interest rate to be charged a borrower, such as the prime rate or LIBOR. *(Chapter 21)*

basis   The spread between the cash (spot) price of a commodity or security and its futures (forward) price at any given point in time. *(Chapter 9)*

Basle Agreement   An agreement among the central banks of leading industrialized nations, including the nations of Western Europe, Canada, the United States, and Japan, to impose common capital requirements on all their banks in order to control bank risk exposure and avoid giving one nation's banks an unfair advantage over another nation's banks. *(Chapter 18)*

bid price The price a securities dealer is willing to pay to buy securities from the public. *(Chapter 3)*

Board of Governors The chief policymaking and administrative body of the Federal Reserve System, composed of seven persons appointed by the president of the United States and confirmed by the Senate for maximum 14-year terms. *(Chapter 13)*

bond A debt obligation issued by a business firm or unit of government that covers several years, usually over five years. *(Chapter 3)*

bond anticipation notes (BANs) Short-term securities issued by a state or local government to raise funds to begin a project that eventually will be funded using long-term bonds. *(Chapter 20)*

book-entry form The method by which marketable U.S. Treasury securities are issued, with the buyer receiving only a receipt, rather than an engraved certificate, indicating that the purchase is recorded on the Treasury's books or recorded in another approved location. *(Chapter 19)*

borrowed reserves Legal reserves loaned to depository institutions through the discount windows of the Federal Reserve banks. *(Chapter 14)*

borrowing The change in liabilities outstanding reported by a sector or unit in the economy over a specified time period. *(Chapter 3)*

branch banking A type of banking organization in which services are sold through multiple offices, all owned and operated by the same corporation. *(Chapter 15)*

budget deficit A government's financial position in which current expenditures exceed current revenues. *(Chapter 19)*

budget surplus A government's financial position in which current revenues exceed current expenditures. *(Chapter 19)*

business cycle Fluctuations in economic activity, with the economy passing alternately through expansionary *(boom)* and recessionary *(depressed)* periods. *(Chapter 9)*

C

call options Grant the buyer the right to purchase a specified number of shares of a given stock or volume of debt securities at a specified price up to an expiration date. *(Chapters 9 and 22)*

call privilege The provision often found in a bond's contract (indenture) that permits the borrower to retire all or a portion of a bond issue by buying back the securities in advance of their maturity. *(Chapter 8)*

capital account A record of loans of short-term and long-term funds into and out of a nation and included in its balance-of-payments accounts. *(Chapter 25)*

capital market The institution that provides a channel for the borrowing and lending of long-term funds (over one year). *(Chapter 1)*

carry income The difference between interest income and interest cost experienced by a dealer in securities. *(Chapter 11)*

central bank An agency of government that has public policy functions such as monitoring the operation of the financial system and controlling the growth of the money supply. *(Chapter 13)*

circuit breakers Rules for trading on a securities exchange that bring a halt to trading or that slow certain kinds of trades when security prices decline beyond a prespecified limit. *(Chapter 22)*

classical theory of interest rates An explanation of the level of and changes in interest rates that relies on the interaction of the supply of savings and the demand for investment capital. *(Chapter 5)*

clearinghouse funds Money transferred by writing a check and presenting it for collection. *(Chapter 10)*

collateralized mortgage obligation (CMO) A type of mortgage-backed security offered in more than one maturity class in order to reduce prepayment risk to investors. *(Chapter 24)*

commercial mortgage A debt instrument used to provide financing for office buildings, shopping centers, and other business ventures involving the purchase or construction of land and buildings. *(Chapter 21)*

commercial paper A short-term debt security issued by a corporation that is not tied to any specific collateral but is secured only by the general earning power of the issuing corporation. *(Chapter 12)*

common stock A residual claim against the assets and earnings of the issuing corporation evidencing a share of ownership in that company. *(Chapter 22)*

Community Reinvestment Act A federal law passed in 1977 that requires depository institutions to designate the market areas they will serve and to provide services without discrimination to all neighborhoods within their designated market areas. *(Chapter 23)*

competition Rivalry between financial-services firms offering the same or similar services. *(Chapter 4)*

compound interest   The payment of additional interest earnings on previously earned interest income. *(Chapter 6)*

Comptroller of the Currency   Federal regulatory agency that charters national banks in the United States. *(Chapter 18)*

consensus forecast   A prediction of interest rates or economic conditions based on a variety of projections derived from several different forecasting methods. *(Chapter 9)*

consolidation   A trend among banks and other financial institutions in which smaller institutions are being combined through merger and acquisition into larger institutions. *(Chapter 15)*

contractual institutions   Financial institutions that attract savings from the public by offering contracts that protect the saver against risk in the future, such as insurance policies and pension plans. *(Chapter 2)*

conventional home mortgage loan   Credit funds extended to a home buyer by a private lender without a government guarantee behind the loan. *(Chapter 24)*

convertibility   A feature of some preferred stocks and bonds that entitles the holder to exchange those securities for a specific number of shares of common stock. *(Chapter 8)*

convexity   The rate of change in an asset's price or value varies according to the level of market rates of interest. *(Chapter 7)*

corporate bond   A debt contract (IOU) of a corporation whose original maturity is more than five years. *(Chapter 21)*

corporate note   A debt contract (IOU) of a corporation whose original maturity date is five years or less. *(Chapter 21)*

coupon effect   The size of a debt security's promised interest rate (coupon) influences how rapidly its price moves with changes in market interest rates. *(Chapter 7)*

coupon rate   The promised interest rate on a bond or note consisting of the ratio of the annual interest income promised by the security issuer to the security's face (par) value. *(Chapter 6)*

credit   A loan of funds in return for a promise of future payment. *(Chapter 1)*

credit card   A plastic card that allows the holder to borrow cash or to pay for goods and services with credit. *(Chapter 23)*

credit enhancements   Financial devices, such as letters of credit from a bank, that upgrade the credit rating of a borrower and allow that borrower to obtain credit at lower cost. *(Chapter 12)*

credit unions   Nonprofit associations accepting deposits from and making loans to their members. *(Chapter 16)*

cross hedge   The purchase of a futures contract for a different financial instrument than is being traded in the cash market. *(Chapter 9)*

currency-futures and options market   Agreements that allow businesses or individuals acquiring or selling foreign currencies to protect themselves against future fluctuations in currency prices by shifting currency risk to someone else willing to bear that risk. *(Chapter 25)*

currency risk   Possible losses to a borrower or lender in foreign markets or to a holder of assets in foreign markets due to adverse changes in currency prices. *(Chapter 10)*

currency sterilization   An action taken by a central bank to offset the impact from government purchases or sales of currencies on bank reserves and deposits through the use of central bank policy tools. *(Chapter 25)*

currency swap   A contract designed to reduce the risk of loss due to changes in currency prices by exchanging one nation's currency for another that is of more use to a borrower. *(Chapter 25)*

current account   A component of a nation's balance-of-payments accounts that tracks purchases and sales of goods and services (trade) and gifts made to foreigners. *(Chapter 25)*

current savings   The change in net worth recorded by a sector or unit in the economy over the current time period. *(Chapter 3)*

current yield   The ratio of a security's promised or expected annual income to its current market price. *(Chapter 6)*

D

dealer paper   Short-term commercial notes sold by borrowing corporations and issued through security dealers who contact interested investors to determine whether they will buy the notes. *(Chapter 12)*

debenture   Long-term debt instruments secured only by the earning power of the issuing corporation and not by any specific assets pledged by the issuing firm. *(Chapter 21)*

debit card   A plastic card that is used to identify the owner of the card or to make immediate payments for goods and services. *(Chapter 23)*

debt management policy   The refunding or refinancing of the federal government's debt in a way that contributes to broad national goals and minimizes the burden of the debt. *(Chapter 19)*

debt securities   Financial claims against the assets of a business firm, individual, or unit of government, represented by bonds and other contracts evidencing a loan of money. *(Chapter 2)*

default risk   The risk to the holder of debt securities that a borrower will not meet all promised payments at the times agreed upon. *(Chapters 8 and 10)*

deficit-budget unit (DBU)   An individual, business firm, or unit of government whose current expenditures exceed its current receipts of income, forcing it to become a net borrower of funds in the money and capital markets. *(Chapter 2)*

deflation   A fall in the average price level for all or a group of goods and services. *(Chapters 2 and 7)*

demand loan   A borrowing of funds (usually by a security dealer) subject to recall of those funds on demand by the lender. *(Chapter 11)*

deposit multiplier   A number that indicates how many dollars of new deposits will result from an injection of one more dollar of excess reserves into the banking system. *(Chapter 13)*

depository institutions   Financial institutions that raise loanable funds by selling deposits to the public. *(Chapter 2)*

Depository Institutions Deregulation and Monetary Control Act (DIDMCA)   Law passed in 1980 by the U.S. Congress to deregulate interest rate ceilings on deposits and grant new services to nonbank thrift institutions as well as to impose common reserve requirements on all depository institutions. *(Chapters 16 and 18)*

deregulation   The lifting or liberalization of government rules that restrict what private businesses can do to serve their customers. *(Chapters 15, 18, and 4)*

derivatives   Financial instruments (such as swaps, financial futures, and options) whose value depends upon an underlying financial instrument (such as a stock or a bond). *(Chapters 2 and 9)*

direct finance   Any financial transaction in which a borrower and a lender of funds communicate directly and mutually agree on the terms of a loan. *(Chapter 2)*

direct paper   Short-term commercial notes issued directly to investors by borrowing companies without the aid of a broker or dealer. *(Chapter 12)*

discount method   A method for calculating the interest charge on a loan that deducts the interest owed from the face amount of the loan, with the borrower receiving only the net proceeds after interest is deducted. *(Chapter 6)*

discount rate   The interest charge (in annual percentage terms) set by the Federal Reserve banks for borrowing by depository institutions from the Reserve banks. *(Chapters 11 and 14)*

discount window   The department in a Federal Reserve bank that grants credit to banks and other depository institutions in need of short-term loans of legal reserves. *(Chapters 11 and 14)*

disintermediation   The withdrawal of funds from a financial intermediary by ultimate lenders (savers) and the lending of those funds directly to ultimate borrowers. *(Chapter 2)*

duration   A weighted average measure of the maturity of a loan or security that takes into account the amount and timing of all promised interest and principal payments associated with that loan or security. *(Chapters 7 and 9)*

E

econometric models   The use of systems of equations and statistical estimation methods to explain or forecast changes in interest rates or other variables. *(Chapter 9)*

Edge Act corporations   Special subsidiaries of U.S. banking organizations authorized by federal law to offer international banking services. *(Chapter 26)*

efficient market   A competitive market in which the prices of financial instruments traded there fully reflect all the latest information available. *(Chapters 1, 3, and 22)*

efficient markets hypothesis   A theory of the financial markets that argues that security prices tend to fluctuate randomly around their intrinsic values, return quickly to equilibrium, and fully reflect the latest information available. *(Chapters 3 and 22)*

Equal Credit Opportunity Act   A federal law passed in 1974 forbidding lending institutions from discriminating in the granting of credit based on the age, race, ethnic origin, religion, or receipt of public assistance of the borrowing customer. *(Chapter 23)*

equities   Shares of common or preferred stock, with each share representing a certificate of ownership in a business corporation. *(Chapters 2 and 22)*

Eurobond   A long-term debt security denominated in a currency other than that of the country or countries where most or all of the security is sold. *(Chapter 26)*

Eurocurrency deposits   Deposits of funds in a bank denominated in a currency foreign to the bank's home country. *(Chapter 26)*

Eurocurrency loans   Loans made by a multinational bank in a currency other than that of the bank's home country. *(Chapter 26)*

Eurocurrency market   An international money market where bank deposits denominated in the world's most convertible currencies are traded. *(Chapter 12)*

Eurodollars   Deposits of U.S. dollars in foreign banks abroad or in foreign branch offices of U.S. banks or U.S. international banking facilities (IBFs). *(Chapter 12)*

event risk   The probability that changes inside a firm or other security-issuing individual or institution or external happenings will affect the value of the securities involved. *(Chapter 8)*

excess reserves   Cash and deposits at the Federal Reserve banks held by depository institutions that are in excess of their legal reserve requirements. *(Chapter 13)*

expected yield   The weighted average return on a risky security composed of all possible yields from the security multiplied by the probability that each possible yield will occur. *(Chapter 8)*

F

Fair Credit Billing Act   A federal law giving customers the right to question entries on bills sent to them for goods and services purchased on credit and giving them the right to expect that billing errors will be corrected as quickly as possible. *(Chapter 23)*

Fair Credit Reporting Act   A federal law that gives credit customers the right to view their credit record held by a credit bureau and to secure quick correction of any errors in that record. *(Chapter 23)*

federal agencies   Departments or divisional units of the federal government empowered to borrow funds in the open market in order to make loans to private businesses and individuals or otherwise subsidize private lending or borrowing. *(Chapter 12)*

Federal Deposit Insurance Corporation (FDIC)   Federal agency established in 1934 to insure the deposits of commercial banks and later expanded in 1989 to insure the deposits of savings and loan associations as well. *(Chapters 15, 16, and 18)*

Federal Deposit Insurance Corporation Improvement Act (FDICIA)   Passed by the U.S. Congress in 1991, this federal law provided additional capital and borrowing authority for the Federal Deposit Insurance Corporation (FDIC) and permitted the regulatory authorities to restrict the activities of and even close undercapitalized banks. *(Chapters 16 and 18)*

federal financing bank   A unit of the federal government created in 1973 that borrows money through the U.S. Treasury Department and channels these funds to federal agencies. *(Chapter 12)*

federal funds   Funds that can be transferred immediately from their holder to another party for immediate payment for purchases of securities, goods, or services. *(Chapters 10 and 11)*

federal funds rate   The market interest rate attached to federal funds loans and a target interest rate for Federal Reserve monetary policy. *(Chapters 11 and 14)*

Federal Home Loan Mortgage Corporation (FHLMC)   A federal agency created in 1970 to improve the resale (secondary) market for home mortgages. *(Chapter 24)*

Federal Housing Administration (FHA)   An agency of the federal government established in 1934 to guarantee mortgage loans for low-priced and medium-priced homes, thereby reducing the risks of lending by financial institutions making qualified home loans. *(Chapter 24)*

Federal National Mortgage Association (FNMA)   A federal agency created in 1938 to buy and sell selected residential mortgages in the secondary market and encourage the development of a resale market for home loans. *(Chapter 24)*

Federal Open Market Committee (FOMC)   The chief body for setting money and credit policy within the Federal Reserve System, consisting of the seven members of the Federal Reserve Board and the presidents of the 12 Federal Reserve banks, only 5 of whom may vote. *(Chapters 13 and 14)*

Federal Reserve bank   One of 12 regional banks chartered by the U.S. Congress to provide central banking services to a specific region of the nation. *(Chapter 13)*

Federal Reserve System   The central bank of the United States, created by Congress to issue currency and coin, regulate the banking system, protect the value of the dollar, and promote full employment. *(Chapters 13, 14, and 18)*

finance companies   Financial-service firms that provide both business and consumer credit. *(Chapter 17)*

financial asset A claim against the income or wealth of a business firm, household, or unit of government usually represented by a certificate, receipt, or other legal document. *(Chapter 2)*

financial disclosure The provision of relevant information to the public to aid individuals and institutions in making sound financial decisions. *(Chapters 4 and 23)*

financial futures contracts Contracts that call for the future delivery or sale of designated securities at a price agreed upon the day the contract is made. *(Chapter 9)*

financial innovation A trend in the financial system toward developing new services and new service delivery methods. *(Chapter 4)*

Financial Institutions Reform, Recovery, and Enforcement Act (FIRREA) Federal law passed in 1989 to bail out the U.S. savings and loan industry, strengthen the federal deposit insurance program, and liquidate the assets of failed thrift institutions. *(Chapters 16 and 18)*

financial intermediaries Financial-services firms that simultaneously borrow funds through the issuance of secondary securities and lend funds by accepting primary securities from borrowers. Also referred to as indirect finance. *(Chapters 2, 12, and 15–17)*

financial investment The net change in financial assets held by a sector or unit in the economy over a specified time period. *(Chapter 3)*

financial market An institutional mechanism created by society to channel savings and other financial services to those individuals and institutions willing to pay for them. *(Chapter 1)*

Financial Services Modernization (Gramm-Leach-Bliley) Act A 1999 Law of the U.S. government permitting the formation of financial holding companies that bring banks, insurance companies, and securities firms together in the same organization and allow customers to protect their financial privacy. *(Chapters 4, 15, 18, and 23)*

financial system The collection of markets, individuals, institutions, laws, regulations, and techniques through which bonds, stocks, and other securities are traded, financial services are produced and delivered, and interest rates are determined. *(Chapter 1)*

fiscal agent A role of the Federal Reserve System in which it provides services to the federal government, such as clearing and collecting checks on behalf of the U.S. Treasury and conducting auctions for the sale of new Treasury securities. *(Chapter 13)*

fiscal policy The taxing and spending programs carried out by government in order to promote high employment, price stability, and other economic goals. *(Chapter 19)*

Fisher effect The theory of inflation and interest rates that argues that nominal interest rates respond one-for-one to changes in the expected rate of inflation over the life of a loan. *(Chapter 7)*

fixed-rate mortgage (FRM) Mortgage loan that carries an unchanging loan rate. *(Chapter 24)*

Flow of Funds Accounts A system of social accounts prepared quarterly by the Board of Governors of the Federal Reserve System that reports the amount of saving and borrowing in the U.S. economy by major sectors. *(Chapter 3)*

foreign exchange markets Channels for trading national currencies and determining relative currency prices. *(Chapter 25)*

foreign exchange rates The prices of foreign currencies expressed in terms of other currencies. *(Chapter 25)*

forward contract An agreement to deliver a specified amount of currency, securities, or other goods or services at a set price on some future date. *(Chapter 25)*

forward market Channel through which currencies, securities, goods, and services are traded for future delivery to the buyer with the terms of trade set in advance of delivery. *(Chapter 25)*

G

Garn-St Germain Depository Institutions Act A law passed by the U.S. Congress in 1982 to further deregulate the depository institutions sector and to give federal deposit insurance agencies additional tools to deal with failing institutions. *(Chapters 16 and 18)*

general credit controls Monetary policy tools that affect the entire banking and financial system, such as open market operations or changes in the Federal Reserve's discount rate. *(Chapter 14)*

general obligation bonds Debt obligations issued by state and local governments and backed by the "full faith and credit" of the issuing government (i.e., may be repaid from any available revenue source). *(Chapter 20)*

Glass-Steagall Act The National Bank Act of 1933 that created the federal deposit insurance system and separated commercial from investment banking. *(Chapter 18)*

globalization The spreading of financial services and financial institutions worldwide. *(Chapter 4)*

gold exchange standard A system for making international payments in which each national currency is freely convertible into gold bullion at a fixed price and also freely convertible into other currencies at relatively stable prices. *(Chapter 25)*

gold standard A system of payments for purchases of goods and services in which nations agree to exchange paper money or coins for gold bullion at predetermined prices and allow gold to be exported or imported freely from one nation to another. *(Chapter 25)*

Government National Mortgage Association (GNMA) A federal government agency created in 1968 to assist the home mortgage market through such activities as purchasing mortgages to finance low-income family housing projects and guaranteeing principal and interest payments on securities issued by private mortgage lenders that are backed by pools of home mortgages. *(Chapter 24)*

government-sponsored agencies Insitutions originally owned by the federal government but now privately owned with the authority to borrow from and lend money to private businesses and individuals or to issue loan guarantees. *(Chapter 12)*

H

harmonization Regulatory cooperation among different nations. *(Chapters 4 and 18)*

Harrod-Keynes effect The theory of the relationship between inflation and interest rates that argues that inflation affects real rates of return but not necessarily nominal rates of return. *(Chapter 7)*

hedging The act of buying and selling financial claims or using other financial tools in order to protect against the risk of fluctuations in market prices or interest rates. *(Chapter 9)*

holding-period yield The rate of return received or expected from a loan or security over the period the investor actually holds it, including the price for which the instrument is sold to another investor. *(Chapter 6)*

home equity loan Extension of credit to individuals who own their homes in which the borrowers' homes are pledged as collateral to support the loans and the amount of the loan is based on the difference between the market value of the home and the amount of any home mortgage debt outstanding (i.e., the owner's equity in a home). *(Chapter 23)*

homogenization The tendency of different financial institutions to offer the same services. *(Chapter 4)*

I

implied rate forecast The market's expectation about future interest rates as indicated by the shape of the yield curve or by financial futures prices. *(Chapter 9)*

income effect The relationship between interest rate levels and the volume of saving in the economy that argues that the advent of higher interest rates may induce savers to save *less* because each dollar saved now earns a higher rate of return. *(Chapter 5)*

indenture A contract accompanying the issue of a bond or note by a corporation or other borrower that lists the rights, privileges, and obligations of the borrower and the investor who has purchased the bond or note. *(Chapter 21)*

indirect finance Also known as financial intermediation, in which financial transactions (especially the borrowing and lending of money) are carried on through a financial intermediary. *(Chapter 2)*

industrial development bond Debt security issued by a local government to aid a private company in the construction of a plant and/or the purchase of equipment or land. *(Chapter 21)*

inflation A rise in the average level of all prices of goods and services traded in the economy over any given period of time. *(Chapters 2 and 7)*

inflation-caused depreciation effect Changes in the expected inflation rate may not lead to equivalent increases in nominal interest rates due to the tendency of depreciation charges on existing plant and equipment to lag behind the rising cost of replacement plant and equipment, discouraging business investment and credit demand. *(Chapter 7)*

inflation-caused income effect The relationship between changes in the rate of inflation and shifts in income (including consumption and savings) that lead to changes in real and nominal interest rates. *(Chapter 7)*

inflation-caused income tax effect The presence of a progressive income tax structure tends to cause nominal interest rates to increase by more than the expected increase in inflation. *(Chapter 7)*

inflation-caused wealth effect Changes in inflation may alter the value of wealth held in financial assets by individuals and institutions, causing a change in their savings plans and leading to offsetting movements in real and nominal interest rates. *(Chapter 7)*

inflation premium   The expected rate of price inflation that, when added to the real interest rate, equals the nominal interest rate on a loan. *(Chapter 7)*

inflation risk (or purchasing power risk)   The probability that increases in the average level of prices for all goods and services sold in the economy will reduce the purchasing power of an investor's income from loans or securities. *(Chapter 10)*

insider trading   Buying or selling the securities of an issuing firm by an employee, director, or by someone under contract with the issuing firm in a fiduciary capacity who acts on the basis of private or privileged information about the issuing firm. *(Chapter 3)*

installment credit   All liabilities of a borrowing customer other than home mortgages that are retired in two or more consecutive loan payments. *(Chapter 23)*

interest rate   The price of credit, or ratio of the fees charged to secure credit from a lender to the amount borrowed, usually expressed on an annual percentage basis. *(Chapter 6)*

interest rate parity   A condition prevailing in international markets where the interest rate differential between two nations matches the forward discount or premium on their two currencies. *(Chapter 25)*

interest rate structure   The concept that the interest rate or yield attached to any loan or security consists of the risk-free (or *pure*) rate of interest plus risk premiums for the security holder's exposure to various forms of risk. *(Chapter 8)*

interest rate swap   A contract between two or more firms in which interest payments are exchanged so that each participating firm saves on interest costs and gets a better balance between its cash inflows and outflows. *(Chapter 9)*

internal financing   The use of saving by an economic unit, rather than debt, to support the acquisition of real and/or financial assets. *(Chapter 2)*

International Banking Act   A U.S. law passed in 1978 to bring foreign banks operating in the United States under regulation. *(Chapter 26)*

international banking facilities (IBFs)   A domestically based set of computerized accounts recording transactions of a U.S. bank with its foreign customers. *(Chapter 26)*

International Lending and Supervision Act   A federal law passed in 1983 requiring U.S. banks to increase their capital and to pursue more prudent international loan policies. *(Chapter 26)*

investment   Expenditures on capital goods or on inventories of goods or raw materials that are used to produce other goods and services, causing future production and income to rise. *(Chapter 1)*

investment banker   Financial institution that assists corporations and units of government in raising funds by underwriting their security offerings and rendering financial advice. *(Chapters 17 and 21)*

investment companies   Financial intermediaries that sell shares to the public to raise funds and invest the proceeds in stocks, bonds, and other securities. *(Chapter 17)*

investment institutions   Financial intermediaries selling their customers securities and other financial assets in order to build up savings for retirement or for other customer uses. *(Chapter 2)*

J

junk bonds   Corporate debt securities with low credit ratings (below investment grade). *(Chapter 8)*

L

lagged reserve accounting (LRA)   The method of determining the legal reserves a depository institution must hold behind its reservable liabilities in which the reserve computation and the reserve maintenance periods do not overlap. *(Chapter 11)*

leasing companies   Financial-service firms that provide businesses and consumers access to equipment, motor vehicles, and other assets for a stipulated period of time at an agreed-upon leasing rate. *(Chapter 17)*

legal reserves   Deposits held at the Federal Reserve banks by depository institutions plus currency and coin held in the vaults of these institutions. *(Chapters 11, 13, 14, and 15)*

letter of credit   An authorization to draft funds from a bank provided stipulated conditions are met. *(Chapter 26)*

leveraged buyouts   A form of corporate takeover in which the management of a company or other small group of investors buys the publicly owned stock of the firm, financing the transaction mainly with new debt that will be repaid from planned increases in company earnings. *(Chapter 21)*

liability management   The techniques used by banks to control the amount and composition of their borrowed funds by changing the interest rates they offer to reflect competition and the intensity of the bank's borrowing requirements. *(Chapter 11)*

life insurance companies Financial-service firms selling contracts to customers that promise to reduce the financial loss to an individual or family associated with death, disability, or old age. *(Chapter 17)*

liquidity The quality or capability of any asset to be sold quickly with little risk of loss and possessing a relatively stable price over time. *(Chapters 1, 8, and 10)*

liquidity preference theory of interest rates An explanation of the level of and change in interest rates that focuses on the interaction of the supply of and demand for money. *(Chapter 5)*

liquidity premium The added yield *(interest return)* that must be paid to investors to get them to buy and hold long-term instead of short-term securities. *(Chapter 7)*

loanable funds theory of interest rates The credit view of what determines the level of and changes in interest rates that focuses on the interaction of the demand for and the supply of loanable funds *(credit)*. *(Chapter 5)*

London Interbank Offer Rate (LIBOR) Short-term interest rate attached to Eurocurrency deposits traded between banks. *(Chapter 12)*

long hedge The purchase of futures contracts calling for the delivery of securities or commodities to a counterparty on a specific future date at a set price. *(Chapter 9)*

long position The purchase of securities outright from the seller in order to hold them until they mature or must be sold. *(Chapter 11)*

M

M1 The narrowest definition of the U.S. money supply consisting of currency outside the Treasury, Federal Reserve banks, and the vaults of banks, plus checking accounts and other checkable deposits held by the nonbank public. *(Chapter 2)*

M2 The definition of the U.S. money supply that includes M1 plus savings and small-denomination (under $100,000) time deposits, money market fund shares not held by institutions, money market deposit accounts (MMDAs), overnight Eurodollar deposits issued to U.S. residents by foreign branches of U.S. banks worldwide, and overnight and continuing-contract repurchase agreements issued by commercial banks. *(Chapter 2)*

M3 The definition of the U.S. money supply that includes M2 plus large-denomination ($100,000-plus) time deposits and term repurchase agreements issued by com-

mercial banks and thrift institutions, term Eurodollars held by U.S. residents at foreign branches of U.S. banks worldwide and at all banking offices in the United Kingdom and Canada, and institution-owned balances in money market mutual funds. *(Chapter 2)*

managed float An international monetary payments system in which the value of any currency is determined by demand and supply forces in the marketplace, but governments intervene on occasion in an effort to stabilize the value of their own currencies. *(Chapter 25)*

managed floating currency standard System of currency valuation in which each nation chooses its own currency exchange rate policy. *(Chapter 25)*

margin requirements The difference between the market value of a security and its maximum loan value as specified by a regulation enforced by the Federal Reserve Board. *(Chapter 14)*

market An institutional mechanism for trading goods and services. *(Chapter 1)*

marketability The feature of a loan or security that reflects its ability to be sold quickly to recover the purchaser's funds. *(Chapter 8)*

market broadening A tendency for financial service markets to expand geographically over time due to advances in technology and increased customer mobility. *(Chapter 4)*

market risk (or interest rate risk) The probability that the prices of securities or other assets will fall (due to rising interest rates), confronting the investor with a capital loss. *(Chapter 10)*

market segmentation argument A theory of the yield curve in which the financial markets are thought to be separated into several distinct markets by the maturity preferences of various investors so that demand and supply for loans and securities in each market determine relative interest rates on long-term versus short-term securities. *(Chapter 7)*

master note A borrowing arrangement between a corporation issuing commercial paper and an institution buying the paper in which the buying institution agrees to accept new paper each day up to a specified maximum amount. *(Chapter 12)*

maturity Length of calendar time in days, weeks, months, and years before a security or loan comes due and must be paid off. *(Chapter 7)*

member banks Banks that have joined the Federal Reserve System, consisting of all federally chartered *(national)* banks and any state-chartered U.S. banks that meet the Federal Reserve's requirements for membership. *(Chapter 13)*

modified exchange standard   A system of currency exchanges and international payments in which foreign currencies were linked to gold and the U.S. dollar, with the price of gold in terms of U.S. dollars remaining fixed. *(Chapter 25)*

monetary base   The sum of legal reserves in the banking system plus the amount of currency and coin held by the public. *(Chapter 13)*

monetary policy   The use of various tools by central banks to control the cost and availability of loanable funds in an effort to achieve national economic goals. *(Chapter 13)*

money   A financial asset that serves as a medium of exchange and standard of value for purchases of goods and services. *(Chapter 2)*

money creation   The ability of banks and other depository institutions to create a deposit, such as a checking account, that can be used as a medium of exchange (to make payments for purchases of goods and services). *(Chapter 15)*

money market   The institution set up by society to channel temporary surpluses of cash into temporary loans of funds, one year or less to maturity. *(Chapters 1 and 10)*

money market deposit accounts (MMDAs)   Deposits whose interest yields vary with market conditions and are subject to withdrawal by check. *(Chapters 15, 16, and 23)*

money market mutual fund   An investment company selling shares to the public and investing the proceeds in short-term securities, such as Treasury bills and other money market instruments. *(Chapter 16)*

money multiplier   The ratio of the size of the money supply to the total reserve base available to depository institutions. *(Chapter 13)*

money-supply expectations effect   A method for forecasting interest rates that compares actual growth of the money supply with the market's expectation for money supply growth. *(Chapter 9)*

money-supply income effect   Increases and decreases in income and spending resulting in changes in the demand for money, and leading to corresponding increases or decreases in interest rates. *(Chapter 9)*

money-supply liquidity effect   Increases or decreases in the money supply causing interest rates to move in the opposite direction (assuming money demand is unchanged). *(Chapter 9)*

moral hazard   When one party to an agreement or relationship uses their position of power or special knowledge to pursue their own self-interest and receives special benefits or rewards at the expense of the other party to the agreement or relationship. *(Chapter 3)*

moral suasion   A monetary policy tool of the central bank in which its officers and staff try to persuade bankers and the public through speeches and written communications to conform more closely to the central bank's goals. *(Chapter 14)*

mortgage-backed securities   Debt obligations issued by private mortgage-lending institutions using selected residential mortgage loans they hold as collateral; the mortgage loans generate principal and interest payments to repay holders of the mortgage-backed securities. *(Chapter 24)*

mortgage bank   A financial-service firm that works with property developers to provide real estate financing and then places the long-term loans with long-term lenders such as insurance companies and savings banks. *(Chapter 17)*

mortgage bonds   Long-term debt secured by a lien on specific assets, usually plant and equipment, held by the issuing corporation. *(Chapter 21)*

multinational corporation   A large company with manufacturing, trading, or service operations in several different countries. *(Chapter 26)*

municipals   Debt securities issued by states, counties, cities, school districts, and other local units of government. *(Chapter 20)*

mutual funds   A type of investment company that sells as many shares of interest in a pool of assets as the public demands and invests the proceeds of those sales in a wide variety of assets, particularly such financial assets as stocks and bonds. *(Chapter 17)*

mutuals   Depository institutions owned by their depositors, such as savings banks and many savings and loan associations. *(Chapter 16)*

N

national banks   U.S. banking institutions that receive their charter of incorporation from the Comptroller of the Currency, an agency of the U.S. government. *(Chapter 15)*

National Credit Union Administration (NCUA) Federal regulatory agency that oversees the activities of federally chartered credit unions. *(Chapter 18)*

National Income Accounts A system of social accounts compiled and released quarterly by the U.S. Department of Commerce that presents data on the nation's production of goods and services, income flows, spending, and saving. *(Chapter 3)*

negotiable certificate of deposit (CD) A marketable receipt issued by a bank or other depository institution to a customer acknowledging the deposit of customer funds for a designated period under a specified interest rate formula. *(Chapter 11)*

negotiated markets Institutional mechanisms set up by society to make loans and trade securities in which the terms of trade are set by direct bargaining between a lender and a borrower. *(Chapter 1)*

net wealth Total assets minus total liabilities held by an economic unit. *(Chapter 1)*

nominal contracts Agreements between contracting parties that fix prices, interest rates, or costs in terms of current (nominal) values; a theory of how inflation may influence the prices of stocks issued by corporations. *(Chapter 7)*

nominal interest rate The published rate of interest attached to a loan or security that includes both a real interest rate component and the inflation rate (inflation premium) expected over the life of the loan or security. *(Chapter 7)*

nominal value The price of assets or other purchasable items measured in terms of their current market price or face value; the price of assets or other items not adjusted for the effects of inflation. *(Chapter 2)*

nonborrowed reserves The largest component of the total legal reserves of depository institutions, consisting of all those legal reserves owned by depository institutions themselves and not borrowed from the Federal Reserve banks. *(Chapter 14)*

nondeposit funds Borrowings in the open market by banks and other institutions in order to supplement monies raised by selling deposits. *(Chapter 15)*

noninstallment credit A loan that is normally paid off in a lump sum rather than in a series of installment payments. *(Chapter 23)*

nonresidential mortgages Loans secured by business and farm properties. *(Chapter 24)*

note A shorter-term debt obligation issued by a business firm, individual, or unit of government to borrow money with a time to maturity that usually does not exceed five years. *(Chapter 3)*

NOW account An interest-bearing checking account available to individuals and nonprofit institutions from banks and other depository institutions. *(Chapters 15, 16, and 23)*

O

Office of Thrift Supervision Federal agency that charters and supervises savings and loans. *(Chapter 18)*

open market operations The buying and selling of securities by a central bank to affect the quantity and growth of the legal reserves of depository institutions and general credit conditions in order to achieve the nation's economic goals. *(Chapter 14)*

open markets Institutional mechanisms created by society to make loans and trade securities in which any individual or institution can participate. *(Chapter 1)*

option contract An agreement between contract writers and contract buyers to accept delivery of ("call") securities or place with buyers ("put") securities at a specified price on or before the date the contract expires. *(Chapters 9 and 22)*

option premium The fee that the buyer of an option contract must pay to the writer of the contract for the right to deliver or accept delivery of securities at a set price. *(Chapter 9)*

organized exchanges Locations where stocks, bonds, and other securities are traded according to the rules and regulations for trading established by members of the exchange. *(Chapter 22)*

original maturity The interval of time between the issue date of a security and the date on which the borrower promises to redeem it. *(Chapter 10)*

over-the-counter market A mechanism for trading stocks and other securities through brokers or dealers operating off the major securities exchanges. *(Chapter 22)*

P

pass-throughs Securities issued against a pool of mortgage loans held by a financial institution. *(Chapter 24)*

pension funds Financial-service firms selling retirement plans to their customers in which savings are set aside in accounts established in the customers' names and allowed to accumulate interest until those customers reach retirement age. *(Chapter 17)*

perfect market   A market in which all available information affecting the value of financial instruments is freely available to everyone, transactions costs are minimal, and all participants in the market are price takers rather than price setters. *(Chapter 1)*

political risk   The probability that changes in government laws or regulations will result in a lower rate of return to the investor or, in the extreme case, a total loss of invested capital. *(Chapters 10 and 26)*

portfolio immunization   An investment strategy that tries to protect the expected yield from a security or portfolio of securities by acquiring those securities whose duration equals the length of the investor's planned holding period. *(Chapter 7)*

preferred habitat   The theory of the yield curve that holds that investors prefer certain maturities of securities over other maturities due to differences in liquidity needs, risk, tax exposure, and other factors. *(Chapter 7)*

preferred stock   A share of ownership in a business corporation that promises a stated annual dividend. *(Chapter 22)*

prepayment risk   The probability that a loan or security (especially securities that draw their earnings from pools of loans) will be paid off ahead of schedule, lowering the investor's expected yield from the instrument. *(Chapters 8 and 24)*

price elasticity   The ratio of changes in the price of a debt security to changes in its yield. *(Chapter 7)*

price indices   A measure of the cost of a market basket of goods and services which provides an indicator of inflation or deflation in the whole economy or a sector of the economy. *(Chapter 2)*

price of credit   The rate of interest that must be paid to secure the use of borrowed funds. *(Chapter 5)*

primary dealers   Security firms that are recognized by the Federal Reserve System to buy and sell securities with the Fed. *(Chapter 11)*

primary markets   Institutional mechanisms set up by society to trade newly issued loans and securities. *(Chapter 1)*

primary reserves   Cash held in a bank's vault plus deposits held with other banks. *(Chapter 15)*

primary securities   The IOUs issued by borrowers from a financial intermediary and held by the intermediary as interest-bearing assets. *(Chapter 2)*

private (or direct) placement   Placing securities with one or a limited number of investors rather than trying to sell them in the open market. *(Chapter 21)*

program trading   Computer-assisted decisions about security purchases and sales in an effort to take advantage of temporary price differences between securities or security price indexes in different markets in order to earn above-average returns or to protect against excessive market risk. *(Chapter 22)*

property-casualty insurers   Financial-service firms selling contracts to protect their customers against losses to persons or property due to negligence, crime, adverse weather changes, fire, and other hazards. *(Chapter 17)*

public debt   The volume of debt obligations that are the responsibility of the federal government and therefore of its taxpayers. *(Chapter 19)*

public sale   When securities are sold in the open market to any individual or institution willing to pay the price, usually through investment bankers. *(Chapter 21)*

purchasing power parity   The currency value of a nation with a higher rate of inflation will tend to fall relative to the currency value of a nation with a lower rate of inflation. *(Chapter 25)*

put options   Contracts granting the buyer the right to sell a specified number of equity shares or debt securities at a set price on or before the expiration date. *(Chapters 9 and 22)*

R

random walk   A theory of security price movements that argues that the future path of individual security prices is no more predictable than is the path of a series of random numbers. *(Chapter 22)*

rate of interest   The price of acquiring credit, usually expressed as a ratio of the cost of securing credit to the total amount of credit obtained. *(Chapters 5 and 6)*

rational expectations theory of interest rates   An explanation of the level of and changes in interest rates based on changes in investor expectations regarding future security prices and returns. *(Chapter 5)*

real estate investment trusts (REITs)   Tax-exempt corporations that receive at least three-quarters of their gross income from real estate transactions and devote a high percentage of their assets to real property loans. *(Chapter 17)*

real estate mortgage investment conduit (REMIC)   A mortgage-backed security issued in a variety of maturities in an effort to reduce the purchaser's interest rate risk to an acceptable level. *(Chapter 24)*

real interest rate   The rate of return from a financial asset expressed in terms of its purchasing power (adjusted for inflation). *(Chapter 7)*

real investment   The net change in real assets held by a sector or unit in the economy over a specified period of time. *(Chapters 2 and 3)*

real value   A purchasing-power-(inflation-) adjusted price of assets, services, or other items held or available for sale. *(Chapter 2)*

regulation   Government enforcement of rules that prescribe permissible and nonpermissible activities for businesses and consumers. *(Chapter 18)*

reinvestment risk   Probability that earnings from a loan or security will have to be reinvested in lower-yielding assets in the future. *(Chapter 10)*

representative offices   Facilities established in distant markets by a bank in order to sell the bank's services and assist its clients; these offices usually cannot accept deposits or make loans. *(Chapter 26)*

repurchase agreement (RP)   A loan (usually granted to a bank or security dealer) that is collateralized by high-quality securities (usually government securities). *(Chapter 11)*

required reserves   Holdings of cash and funds on deposit with the Federal Reserve banks by depository institutions that are required by law to backstop the public's deposits held by these same institutions. *(Chapters 13 and 15)*

reserve requirements   The percentage of various liabilities (such as deposits received from the public) that must be held by depository institutions, either in vault cash or on deposit at the Federal Reserve banks. *(Chapter 14)*

residential mortgage credit   Loans provided to support the purchase of new or existing single-family homes and other permanent dwellings. *(Chapter 23)*

residential mortgages   Loans secured by single-family homes and other dwellings. *(Chapter 24)*

revenue-anticipation notes (RANs)   Short-term debt obligations issued by state and local units of government in lieu of expected future governmental revenues in order to meet near-term cash needs. *(Chapter 20)*

revenue bonds   Debt obligations issued by state and local governments that are repayable only from a particular source of funds, such as revenues generated by a toll road or toll bridge or from user fees derived by selling water or electric power. *(Chapter 20)*

risk-free rate of interest   The rate of return on a riskless security, often called the *pure rate of interest* or the *opportunity cost of money. (Chapter 5)*

risk management tools   Financial devices (such as *futures and options)* that permit a borrower or lender of funds to protect against the risks of changing prices and interest rates. *(Chapters 4 and 9)*

S

savings   The amount of funds left over out of current income after current consumption expenditures are made or, for a business firm, the current net earnings retained in the business instead of paid out to the owners. *(Chapter 1)*

savings and loan associations   A leading home mortgage lender in the United States, making predominantly local loans to finance the purchase of housing for individuals and families. *(Chapter 16)*

savings banks   Depository institutions that are owned by their depositors and can be chartered by the federal government and by some states. *(Chapter 16)*

seasonality   Patterns in the behavior of interest rates, with rate increases during certain seasons of the year and decreases during other seasons. *(Chapter 9)*

secondary markets   Institutional mechanisms set up by society to trade or exchange loans and securities that have already been issued. *(Chapter 1)*

secondary securities   Financial claims, such as deposits, issued by a financial intermediary to raise loanable funds. *(Chapter 2)*

Securities and Exchange Commission (SEC)   Regulatory body of the federal government charged with monitoring the behavior of security brokers, dealers, and investment institutions. *(Chapters 3 and 18)*

securitization   The selling of shares or certificates representing an interest in a pool of income-generating assets (such as mortgage loans) as a method for raising funds by a financial institution. *(Chapters 4 and 15)*

securitized assets   Loans packaged together in a pool and securities representing claims to the income generated by the pooled loans are sold to investors. *(Chapter 15)*

securitized mortgages   Securities issued against a pool of mortgage loans whose interest and principal payments are paid to the security holders. *(Chapter 24)*

security dealers   Financial firms that provide a conduit for buyers and sellers of marketable securities by holding a portfolio of these securities and standing ready to buy and sell these securities at an announced price. *(Chapter 17)*

selective credit controls   Monetary policy tools that affect specific groups or sectors in the financial system. *(Chapter 14)*

semidirect finance   Any financial transaction (especially the borrowing and lending of money) that is assisted by a security broker or dealer. *(Chapter 2)*

serialization   The splitting up of a single bond issue into several different maturities (used most often for state and local government bonds). *(Chapter 20)*

service proliferation   The development and spreading of new financial services so that more financial institutions offer more services. *(Chapter 4)*

share draft   Interest-bearing checking account offered by a credit union. *(Chapter 16)*

shell branches   Booking offices of multinational banks, usually set up offshore to attract deposits and avoid certain domestic banking regulations. *(Chapter 26)*

short hedge   The sale of futures contracts promising the delivery of securities or commodities to another party on a specific future date at a set price. *(Chapter 9)*

short position   Dealers and other investors promise to sell and deliver in the future securities they do not currently own, hoping security prices will fall in the interim. *(Chapter 11)*

simple interest method   A method of figuring the interest on a loan that charges interest only for the period of time the borrower actually has use of the borrowed funds. *(Chapter 6)*

social accounting   A system of record keeping that reports economic and financial activity for the whole economy and/or between the principal sectors of the economy. *(Chapter 3)*

solicitation method   A method for selling federal agency securities in which orders are taken from buyers and the securities are priced and delivered to investors after the order book is closed. *(Chapter 12)*

sources and uses of funds statements   A financial report prepared for each sector of the economy in the Federal Reserve Board's Flow of Funds Accounts that shows changes in net worth and changes in holdings of financial assets and liabilities over a specific time period. *(Chapter 3)*

special drawing rights (SDRs)   An official monetary reserve unit developed by the International Monetary Fund

to settle international claims between nations. *(Chapter 25)*

spot market   Channel through which currencies, securities, commodities, or other goods and services are traded for immediate delivery to the buyer once buyer and seller agree on the terms of trade. *(Chapters 11 and 25)*

standby credit letters   Contingent obligations issued by banks or other lending institutions promising to pay off the debt of a borrower if that borrower is unable to pay. *(Chapter 15)*

State Banking Commissions   Government boards that charter and supervise banks headquartered in a given state. *(Chapter 18)*

state-chartered banks   Banking firms whose charter of incorporation allowing them to open for business is issued by a state governmental body (such as a board or commission) in the United States. *(Chapter 15)*

stocks   Ownership shares in a corporation, giving the holder claim to any dividends distributed from current earnings. *(Chapters 2, 3, and 22)*

strike price   The price for securities specified in an option contract; also called the *exercise price. (Chapter 9)*

substitution effect   Positive relationship between rate of interest and volume of savings in the economy. *(Chapter 5)*

surplus-budget unit   An individual, business firm, or unit of government whose current income receipts exceed its current expenditures and therefore is a net lender of funds to the money and capital markets. *(Chapter 2)*

T

tax-anticipation notes (TANs)   Short-term debt obligations issued by state and local governments to provide for immediate cash needs until tax revenues come in. *(Chapter 20)*

tax-exemption privilege   A feature bestowed by law on some financial assets (such as state and local government bonds) that makes the income they generate free of taxation at federal or state and local government levels, or both. *(Chapter 20)*

tax-exempt securities   Debt securities issued by state, city, county, and other local units of government or by other qualified borrowers whose interest income is exempt from federal taxation and from most state taxes as well. *(Chapters 8 and 20)*

third-country bills Bankers' acceptances issued by banks in one country that finance the transport or storage of goods traded between two other countries. *(Chapter 12)*

third market Mechanism through which securities listed on a stock exchange are traded off the exchange in the over-the-counter market. *(Chapter 22)*

time draft A bank's promise to pay a stipulated amount of funds upon presentation of the draft on a specific future date. *(Chapter 12)*

TIPS Treasury inflation protection securities issued in order to help protect investors in U.S. government securities from lower rates of return due to inflation. *(Chapter 7)*

transaction accounts Deposits (such as a checking account or other accounts offered by financial institutions) that can be used to make payments for purchases of goods and services. *(Chapters 14 and 15)*

transparency Policy used by some central banks today to make their policy goals and actions clear enough so that the public can develop accurate forecasts of where central bank policy is headed for the future. *(Chapter 13)*

Truth in Lending A law passed by the U.S. Congress in 1968 that requires covered lenders to disclose fully all the relevant terms of a personal loan to the borrower and to report a standardized loan rate (known as the APR, or annual percentage rate). *(Chapters 6 and 23)*

U

unbiased expectations hypothesis A theory of the yield curve that contends that the curve's shape is determined exclusively by investor expectations regarding future interest rate movements. *(Chapter 7)*

U.S. Treasury bills A debt obligation, one year or less to maturity, issued by the United States government. *(Chapter 11)*

V

variable-rate mortgage (VRM) Home mortgage loans carrying an interest rate that varies during the term of the loan, generally depending on the movement of interest rates in the open market. *(Chapter 24)*

vehicle currency A monetary unit of a nation that is not only the standard of value (unit of account) for domestic transactions but is also used to express the prices of many goods and services traded between other nations as well. *(Chapter 25)*

venture capital firms Financial firms that gather funds from individual and institutional investors and direct this capital into new expanding businesses. *(Chapter 17)*

W

wealth Accumulated assets held by an economic unit as a result of saving. *(Chapter 1)*

wealth effect (of saving and interest rates) The relationship between the volume of saving and interest rates that contends that the net wealth position of savers (the balance in their portfolios between debt and financial assets) determines how their desired levels of saving will change as interest rates change. *(Chapter 5)*

Y

yield curve Relationship between short-term interest rates and long-term interest rates (that is, between yield to maturity and time to maturity of a debt security) as reflected in a smooth curve with an upward, downward, or horizontal slope. *(Chapter 7)*

yield to maturity The interest rate on a debt security that equates the purchase price of the security to the present value of all its expected annual net cash inflows (income) from now until its maturity date. *(Chapter 6)*

Index